HISTORIC SPOTS IN CALIFORNIA

Originally issued in three volumes:

The Southern Counties
Valley and Sierra Counties
Counties of the Coast Range

HISTORIC SPOTS IN CALIFORNIA

County Map
of California

HISTORIC SPOTS IN CALIFORNIA

BY

MILDRED BROOKE HOOVER

HERO EUGENE RENSCH *&* ETHEL GRACE RENSCH

REVISED BY

RUTH TEISER

WITH AN INTRODUCTION BY

ROBERT GLASS CLELAND

STANFORD UNIVERSITY PRESS

STANFORD, CALIFORNIA

STANFORD UNIVERSITY PRESS, STANFORD, CALIFORNIA
LONDON: OXFORD UNIVERSITY PRESS
COPYRIGHT 1932, 1933, 1937, AND 1948 BY THE BOARD OF TRUSTEES OF THE
LELAND STANFORD JUNIOR UNIVERSITY

Library of Congress catalog card number: 48-6969

Printed in the United States of America
First published in three volumes: *The Southern
Counties* (1932), by H. E. and E. G. Rensch; *Valley
and Sierra Counties* (1933), by H. E. and E. G.
Rensch and Mildred Brooke Hoover; *Counties of
the Coast Range* (1937), by Mildred Brooke Hoover.
This one-volume revised edition was originally pub-
lished in 1948.

Fourth printing, 1962

THIS VOLUME
IS DEDICATED TO
MRS. FRANK PHELPS TOMS
MRS. FREDERICK FRETAGEOT GUNDRUM
MRS. ELMER HORACE WHITTAKER
AND
MRS. JOSEPH TAYLOR YOUNG

PUBLISHER'S FOREWORD

The original edition of *Historic Spots in California*, sponsored by the California State Conference of the Daughters of the American Revolution, was issued by Stanford University Press in three volumes, in 1932, 1933, and 1937. Within a few years the edition was exhausted. Before a further printing could be undertaken, the war intervened and wartime paper shortages precluded reissues during that period. But the decision was made to revise the work and the Revised Edition, which combines the three volumes in one, was prepared by Ruth Teiser and issued in 1948.

In the revision certain corrections have been made and certain material has been brought up to date. Grateful acknowledgment is here expressed to county librarians and many other individuals throughout the state who helpfully responded to requests for information on their counties, and to specialists in California history who made valuable suggestions. Particular acknowledgment is due to Dr. J. N. Bowman, of Berkeley, for the use of his manuscript material on the California land grants and for data assembled by him and the late Dr. G. W. Hendry on the adobe buildings of the nine Bay counties.

ACKNOWLEDGMENTS

FROM THE PREFACES TO THE EARLIER EDITIONS

PART I. THE SOUTHERN COUNTIES

By Hero Eugene Rensch and Ethel Grace Rensch

In the concluding stages of their work, the authors are principally indebted to Carl I. Wheat, chairman of the Committee on Publications, California Historical Society, for his careful reading of the manuscript and his invaluable suggestions as to the amplification and improvement of the material, and for his unfailing interest in the work. Special appreciation is due also to Frank McKee, director of the Highway Department of the California State Chamber of Commerce, and to Francis P. Farquhar, who read the early proof and made helpful suggestions as to the treatment of the old trails and passes of the High Sierra. Specific mention should also be made of the tentative list of historic spots in California drawn up by Aubrey Drury in 1929, which, together with brief notes already collected by the D.A.R. and the list of sites marked by the Native Sons of the Golden West, supplied to the writers by Joseph R. Knowland, formed the basis for this work at its inception.

The authors have derived great satisfaction from the promptness and cordiality of the responses to their requests for co-operation in collecting and verifying data for this work, and desire to record their special indebtedness to historians in the various counties of California who have given unstinted aid in verifying and completing the material included in the present volume. Above all, we are indebted to the late Laurance L. Hill and the late Arthur Ellis, whose outstanding knowledge of and fine enthusiasm for California history and for the preservation of its historic landmarks made their co-operation invaluable.

We have been especially fortunate in receiving the co-operation of historians eminent in their various regions : George W. Beattie of the Southern California Historical Society, whose aid in checking and rendering more complete the historical data on San Bernardino and Riverside counties and also that on the old trails throughout southern California has been priceless ; W. A. Chalfant, an authority on the Death Valley, Inyo, and Mono regions ; Mrs. Winifred Davidson, historian of the San Diego Historical Society, whose generous co-operation greatly enhanced the value and interest of the San Diego material ; Marion Parks, whose intimate acquaintance with the historic landmarks and sites of Los Angeles County has added tremendously to the accuracy of that section ; E. M. Sheridan, curator of the Pioneer Museum, Ventura ; William McPherson, Orange County historian ; and Otis B. Tout, historian of Imperial County.

Particular appreciation must also be expressed for the splendid co-operation given by DeWitt V. Hutchings of Mission Inn, Riverside ; to F. I. Shepherd, Elmer W. Heald, and Leo Hetzel of Imperial County ; to Walter G. Dow of Inyo County ; to George C. Delury of Mono County ; to Elizabeth Mason and Dr. William J. Mellinger of Santa Barbara ; to Frank McCoy of Santa Maria Inn, Santa Maria ; to Mrs. Janet Gould of Corona, Mrs. Edna McCoy of Elsinore, and Mrs. Marguerite Slaughter of Perris, who have done much careful research in their respective districts in Riverside County ; to Arthur Woodward, curator of history, Los Angeles Museum ; Charles J. Prudhomme, guide of the Los Angeles City Hall Tower ; and James A. Jasper, an old resident of San Diego County.

Finally, we express our especial gratitude to Dr. Robert Glass Cleland for the lucid exposition of California's history and of its cultural and social background which introduces this volume.

H. E. R.
E. G. R.

June 15, 1932

PART II. VALLEY AND SIERRA COUNTIES

By H. E. & E. G. Rensch and Mildred Brooke Hoover

In the preparation of this volume particularly valuable and extensive services have been rendered by Owen C. Coy, Francis P. Farquhar, David Rhys Jones, F. F. Latta, and Carl I. Wheat. The authors' indebtedness to each of these individuals is hereby gratefully acknowledged and also the assistance of individuals in connection with particular counties, as follows :

Alpine, Grant P. Merrill ; *Amador,* Mrs. Elizabeth Sargent ; *Butte,* George C. Mansfield ; *Calaveras,* Judge J. A. Smith ; *Colusa,* Mrs. C. L. Schaad ; *El Dorado,* Margaret Kelley ; *Fresno,* F. F. Latta ; *Glenn,* Mrs. Rebecca T. Lambert ; *Kern,* F. F. Latta and H. A. Spindt ; *Kings,* F. F. Latta and W. L. Landsborough ; *Madera,* F. F. Latta and L. W. Sharp ; *Mariposa,* John Dexter, John Outcalt, and May Corcoran ; *Merced,* Ralph L. Milliken, F. F. Latta, and T. W. Fowler ; *Modoc,* William S. Brown and F. P. Cronemiller ; *Nevada,* W. W. Waggoner ; *Placer,* James D. Stewart and S. L. Smyth ; *Plumas,* Carl I. Wheat and Mrs. A. P. Swingle ; *Sacramento,* Harry Peterson ; *San Joaquin,* Mrs. Agnes Steiny Finkbohner ; *Shasta,* May Southern ; *Sierra,* J. M. McMahon ; *Siskiyou,* David Rhys Jones, Orlo G. Steele, and Mrs. Eileen Glidden ; *Stanislaus,* Mrs. Minerva J. MacMillan ; *Sutter,* L. A. P. Eichler ; *Tehama,* J. D. Sweeney ; *Tulare,* F. F. Latta ; *Tuolumne,* Mrs. Juliette M. Hood ; *Yuba,* Carl I. Wheat and L. A. P. Eichler.

H. E. R.
E. G. R.
M. B. H.

October 16, 1933

PART III. COUNTIES OF THE COAST RANGE

By Mildred Brooke Hoover

The method of approach to the study of material for each county has been similar. All county histories have been read, facts have been gleaned from old diaries and books of travel, data have been taken from old letters and other family documents, search has been made in various County Halls of Record, libraries in all parts of the state have been combed, much time has been spent in visiting sites, and many of the older local residents have been interviewed.

(A great deal of preliminary research for this volume was done by H. E. Rensch but was not finally checked and verified by him as was done for the *Southern Counties* and for the *Valley and Sierra Counties.*)

The entire manuscript has been read by Douglas S. Watson, chairman of the Publications Committee of the California Historical Society, to whom thanks are hereby expressed. Among others to whom gratitude is due, for information compiled or imparted or for the reading of certain parts of the manuscript, are :

Alameda, H. E. and E. G. Rensch ; *Contra Costa,* H. E. and E. G. Rensch and R. R. Veale ; *Del Norte,* H. E. and E. G. Rensch ; *Humboldt,* Owen C. Coy ; *Lake,* Mrs. Grace H. Quayle ; *Marin,* officers and members of Marin County Historical Society ; *Mendocino,* Mrs. Charles Shinn ; *Monterey,* Colonel Roger S. Fitch and Paul Parker ; *Napa,* Mrs. Elliott H. Wheeler ; *San Benito,* W. I. Hawkins ; *San Francisco,* Carl I. Wheat and Frances M. Molera ; *San Luis Obispo,* Mrs. Edith Drennan Gragg and Mrs. Erna P. Marsh ; *San Mateo,* Roscoe D. Wyatt ; *Santa Cruz,* Leon Rowland ; *Santa Clara,* John V. Young and Guy Miller ; *Solano,* William Pierce ; *Sonoma,* W. S. Borba ; *Trinity,* Judge Bartlett and Ray J. Barber.

M. B. H.

April 30, 1937

CONTENTS

ERRATA AND ADDENDA

Page 4, column 2, line 50—*for* which goes by *read* which now goes by

Page 8, column 1, line 36—*for* 276 feet *read* 279.9 feet

Page 26, column 1, line 5—*for* Robinson, William C. *read* Robinson, William W.

Page 33, column 1, line 53—*for* Borego *read* Borrego

Page 33, column 2, lines 46–47—*for* San Felipe Valley, and Warner's Pass *read* **Vallecito**, and over the Cuyamaca Mountains to San Diego Mission

Page 33, column 2, lines 47–48—*delete* From Warner's he went to San Diego via the canyon of the San Luís River.

Page 43, column 2, line 53—*for* Santa Maria *read* Santa Rosa

Page 48, column 1, line 61—*for* Foster (*twice*) *read* Forster

Page 52, column 1, lines 2–3—*for* San Felipe Valley, and Warner's Pass *read* Vallecito, and over the Cuyamaca Mountains to San Diego

Page 68, column 2, line 56—*for* June 21 *read* June 27

Page 80, column 1, line 35—*delete* is said to have

Page 112, column 1, line 21—*add* The Yosemite Valley Railroad ceased operation in 1946.

Page 159, column 2, lines 46–47—*delete* Because this was a favorite "holdup" spot in stagecoach days,

Page 264, column 1, lines 5–6—*for* Sheriff Thorne of San Andreas and H. B. Hume, *read* Sheriff Thorne of San Andreas, Detective Harry N. Thorne, and James B. Hume,

Page 264, column 1, lines 9–10—*for* Bear Mountain between Milton and Murphy's *read* Funk Hill, on the stage run between Sonora and Milton,

Page 264, column 1, line 14—*for* Sheriff Thorne *read* Detective Morse, specially hired by James B. Hume to do the job,

Page 264, column 1, line 18—*for* Charles C. Bolton *read* Charles E. Bolton

Page 265, column 2, line 4—*for* Misión San Carlos *read* Misión San Carlos Borroméo del Carmelo

Page 267, column 2, lines 31–36—*delete, and substitute*: The Custom House once belonged to the United States government, but was sold to a group of private citizens, who deeded it to the state of California. It was restored by the state and marked by the Monterey Historical and Art Association. A museum of local relics is housed in it.

Page 277, column 2, line 43—*for* calle principal *read* main street

Page 277, column 2, lines 48–49—*for* Main and Jefferson streets *read* Calle Principal and Jefferson Street

Page 278, column 1, line 7—*for* Main Street *read* Calle Principal

Page 278, column 2, lines 58–59—*for* at the junction of Alvarado, Main, and Scott streets *read* at the junction of Alvarado Street, Calle Principal, and Scott Street

Page 278, column 1, line 63—*for* four months in the spring *read* three months in the autumn

Page 282, column 1, line 47, and page 283, column 1, line 7—*for* Irwin *read* Erwin

Page 372, column 1, lines 12–13—*for* disappeared . . . in use *read* disappeared, and the dwelling was destroyed by fire in 1867

Page 374, column 1, line 15—*for* born in 1808 *read* born in 1807 according to baptismal records

Page 374, column 1, lines 33–37—*for* This house . . . in front of both *read* The house was destroyed by fire in 1867. Adjoining the site are the old barracks. Site and barracks face Spain Street along one side of the Plaza, and in front

Page 374, column 2, line 62—*for* The house *read* About four miles to the north on the road to Santa Rosa, the house

Page 377, column 1, lines 30–31—*delete* Page had been a sheriff in the Sonoma district in 1847.

INTRODUCTION

THE reign of the Emperor Charles the Fifth (1516–1556) was the period of Spain's ascendancy and splendor. In Europe no nation held so dominant a place, and in the New World the amazing energy and rashness of the Spanish adventurers were bringing about the conquest of a continent and the development of one of the greatest empires the world has ever known.

As an incident in this dramatic era of exploration and conquest, on June 27, 1542, Juan Rodríguez Cabrillo, a "navigator of great courage and honor and a thorough seaman," set sail from the tiny port of Navidad on the west coast of Mexico to explore the unknown sea which stretched into the dim mists of the northwest and to find if possible the fabled Strait of Anian which all men supposed at that time joined the waters of the "South Sea" to those of the Atlantic.

On this voyage Cabrillo and his companion, Ferrelo, in two tiny ships, the "San Salvador" and the "Victoria," sailed the full length of the California coast and for the first time made known to Europeans the characteristics and vast extent of the land which stretched away to the north above the peninsula of Lower California. Cabrillo himself did not live to return to Mexico but died from an injury he had received on the island of San Miguel, where it is supposed the body of this heroic seaman lies buried beneath the drifting sand.

But the region discovered by Cabrillo was not colonized by Spain during the reign of Charles. In 1579 a navigator even more renowned than Cabrillo appeared on the California coast. This was the Englishman, Sir Francis Drake, "master thief of the unknown world," who, having freighted the "Golden Hind" with looted treasure almost to the water's edge, sailed beyond the reach of Spanish vengeance and found refuge "in a convenient and fit harbor," supposed by most authorities to have been the present Drake's Bay, on the northern California coast. Upon leaving this port to complete his famous voyage "around the whole globe of the earth," Drake claimed the land for England, called it New Albion, and set up on the shore a "fair great poste" to which was fastened a brass plate and "a piece of sixpence current English monie" bearing the arms and picture of the Queen, as evidence of his visit and his claim.

A generation after Drake, Sebastián Vizcaíno, a man of an unusually varied and adventurous career, sailed from the port of Navidad to follow the route first taken by Cabrillo. Entering nearly all the ports of California, including that of Monterey, but missing for some mysterious reason the magnificent harbor of San Francisco, Vizcaíno carefully charted and named the prominent landmarks of the California coast. Many of these, it is true, had long before been named by Cabrillo, but, probably in ignorance of this, Vizcaíno gave no heed to the work of his heroic predecessor and today most of the names along the coast from San Diego to Monterey are those of Vizcaíno's choosing.

Following the voyage of Vizcaíno more than one hundred sixty years went by before California became again the subject of definite concern to the Spanish Crown. Then, primarily because of the fear of the advance of England to the Pacific following the Seven Years' War and the no less tangible danger of the Russian progress down the northwest coast from Alaska, the Spanish Crown awoke to the necessity of occupying Alta California or of forfeiting the control of New Spain. At that time a genuinely great king, Charles III, was on the throne and was fortunately able to find agents peculiarly fitted for the task of carrying out the colonization program. In the person of José de Gálvez, whom he appointed visitor-general of New Spain, Charles possessed an official capable of organizing and infusing with his own dynamic energy the California enterprise; and from the Franciscan Order he obtained the spiritual enthusiasm and leadership necessary for its success. Under the direction of Gálvez, four colonizing expeditions, two by sea and two by land, were sent to California in 1769. The commander-in-chief of the entire force was Don Gáspar de Portolá, a Spanish soldier of the old school, courageous, determined, jealous of his prerogatives, and unswervingly loyal to the instructions laid upon him; and in charge of the spiritual phase of the expeditions was the heroic and saintly Father Junípero Serra.

The expeditions which came by sea suffered fearfully from scurvy and many of their number died. The two overland companies reached San Diego without serious difficulty, and established there a tiny settlement, the fate of which, however, was for many months in gravest doubt. Despite this discouraging outlook, Portolá determined to carry out his instructions to open an overland route to the port of Monterey which Vizcaíno had so enthusiastically described more than a century and a half before. The members of his expedition suffered extremely from hardship, sickness, and lack of food; and, to make matters even worse, when Portolá came to the port of Monterey he failed to recognize it and continued his journey northward until his way was barred by the waters of the hitherto undiscovered San Francisco Bay. Failing utterly to appreciate the significance of this discovery, the expedition, discouraged, disheartened, and suffering continually from lack of food, retraced its steps to San Diego.

The condition of the Spanish settlement at this port was now extremely critical. Portolá, however, had no intention of abandoning the province, but on the contrary set about the organization of a second company to renew the search for Monterey; and in this determination to maintain the ground already won in California, Serra and his companions joined with even fiercer zeal. Portolá's second expedition succeeded where his first had failed, and, as a result, the long-desired settlement was founded at Monterey. With the control of this port and of San Diego definitely established, the Spanish hold on California was assured. Further explorations were carried out along the coast, other settlements were established at strategic points, and in 1774 Juan Bautista de Anza, one of the noblest figures in early California history, led a company of colonists overland from Sonora by way of the Gila River and the Colorado Desert to San Gabriel and thence to Monterey. From this time on the development of California proceeded as it had in other border provinces of New Spain. In such regions three institutions had long since proved their value in the subjugation of the wilderness and the control of the frontier; these were the presidio or military fortress, the pueblo or town, and the missions of the various monastic orders. All three of these institutions played a definite part in the development of Spanish California.

Presidios were founded at the four strategic ports of San Diego, Santa Bárbara, Monterey, and San Francisco. Pueblos, where colonists from Mexico were settled, were established at Los Angeles, Branciforte, and San José. And the Franciscan missions, which the Crown looked upon not only as a means of spreading the Faith but also as most effective agencies for civilizing and governing the Indians, were erected at more or less regular intervals, about a day's journey apart, from San Diego to Sonoma. The name most commonly spoken of in connection with the foundation and early development of these missions is that of Father Junípero Serra, whom some would almost call the patron saint of California. With Serra's name, however, should also be associated those of his companions, Palóu, Crespi, and Lasuén, men of lesser fame but no less genuine heroism and devotion.

The years which followed the settlement of California by the Spaniards constitute the romantic period in the history of the state. Life was simple, unhurried, picturesque. Almost the sole industry of the province was cattle-raising, and since a limitless empire lay at hand the landholdings, first of the missions and later of the ranchos, were of princely size. Because of the congenial nature of the climate and the fertility of the virgin soil, grass grew abundantly and the herds of cattle running wild on the ranges multiplied to an amazing degree. These herds furnished both a large part of the food supply of the population and almost their only commercial products. Some grain, however, was raised for local consumption both by the missions and to a lesser degree on the ranchos, and for the same purpose there were also gardens and orchards.

The industrial life of the province was exceedingly primitive. Handicrafts were taught at the missions, and some of these in the course of time developed into small industrial centers where the Indians were trained as blacksmiths, workers in leather, soap-makers, weavers of the coarser grades of cloth, and artisans in other lines. The women in their turn were taught to cook and sew, and even the children were trained in the simpler household tasks. The development of some such industrial life was an absolute necessity, since the province, shut off from Mexico by hundreds of miles of almost impassable mountain and desert wilderness and by an almost equally perilous ocean voyage, was thrown almost wholly on its own resources and compelled to become self-sustaining.

An event of major consequence in this period of California history was the so-called secularization of the missions in 1833–1834. This measure, which resulted in the downfall of the missions and the scattering of the Indian populations gathered about them, is scarcely defensible from the humanitarian or the economic point of view. Politically, however, it was merely in keeping with the general policy of the Spanish Crown that the missions should be disestablished as soon as the region had ceased to exhibit its frontier character; and thus, while the consequences were most unfortunate, from the standpoint both of the Indians and of the Church, the measure was not in theory at least so revolutionary as at first it might appear.

So long as Spain retained control of her provinces in the New World the political life of California ran for the most part an uneventful course. The province was governed, in accordance with the uniform policy of Spain in her control of the frontier, almost entirely by officials dependent upon the viceroy, and revolutions were practically unknown; but after the establishment of the independence of Mexico, California began to experience something of the same unrest which so continually characterized the central government. Revolutions were particularly numerous between 1835 and the outbreak of the Mexican War. In part these were a protest of the Californians against officials sent from Mexico to rule the province and in part they were merely sectional rivalries between the north and south or factional contests between the California leaders for the control of the government. In most instances these uprisings were individually of no great consequence in the life of the people or in the history of the province, but their cumulative effect was unfortunate, particularly in their influence upon the attitude of the Californians toward the sovereignty of Mexico.

It was hardly to be expected that a territory so vast and so rich in undeveloped resources as California should remain indefinitely under control of a weak and turbulent government. Mexico, torn by almost constant civil war, virtually bankrupt, and wretchedly weak from a military standpoint, was in no position to retain her hold on a province so distant, so difficult to defend, and so inviting to other nations. Indeed, very early in the nineteenth century the United States had begun to manifest an interest in the possibilities of California and a concern in her destiny. The factors which in the succeeding decades developed this interest to the point where the annexation of California became both an ambition and a necessity on the part of the United States are of definite historic significance. First came the commercial intercourse of New England, when through the activities of the "merchant adventurers" from Boston, Salem, and other New England ports a trade in the skins of the sea otter and the fur seal was carried on between the long reaches of the California coast and the Chinese Empire. Somewhat later New England whalers on their long voyages to the strange corners of the North and South Pacific frequently resorted to California ports for recuperation and fresh supplies. Through the visits of these New England seamen the people of the Atlantic seaboard thus became acquainted with the riches and defenseless condition of California and developed an interest in her destiny.

The interest aroused in California by these early American contacts was further increased and given new direction by the advent of the Russians in California and the establishment of the Russian colony at Bodega Bay, north of San Francisco, about the time of the War of 1812. This venture, which was rightly regarded by the American government not merely as an attempt at the economic control of northern California by the subjects of the Czar but also as a direct threat of political domination over the entire province, played a major role in the enunciation of the Monroe Doctrine in 1823, and directed the official attention of our government to the ultimate fate of the great bay of San Francisco and of the vast region stretching along the Pacific, west of the Rocky Mountains.

Shortly after 1820, also, the hide and tallow trade was opened between California and New England. For two decades and a half this trade constituted the chief feature of the economic life of California and in a very definite way identified still further the interests of New England with those of the distant Mexican province on the Pacific. The extent and characteristic features of this trade were afterward made familiar to the whole United States by Dana's classic, *Two Years Before the Mast.*

Another factor which led to the further development of the relation of the United States with California in these early years was the opening of the overland trails and the discovery of the routes across the mountains by the restless feet of the fur traders. These men, who played so large a part in the development of the West and whose adventurous activities shaped the whole destiny of the American nation, began to appear in California prior to 1830. The leader of the first overland expedition to California was Jedediah Strong Smith, who came with a party of fifteen ragged and semi-lawless followers from the vicinity of Salt Lake by way of the Colorado, the Mojave, and El Cajón Pass to the Mission of San Gabriel in the fall of 1826. Smith, one of the greatest explorers in the annals of Western America, an outstanding contributor to the history of California and the true pathfinder of the Sierra, was followed almost immediately by others of his adventurous kind. Space does not permit a detailed account of these fur-trading explorations, which disclosed the passes to California and made it possible for the settlers of the Missouri and Mississippi valleys to cross the mountains into California and take possession of the new land. To every student of California history, however, the names and exploits of the Patties, Joseph Walker, Ewing Young, and Kit Carson are familiar.

The coming of these fur-traders prepared the way for the advance of overland emigration from the Mississippi Valley to California during the next decade. The first of these overland trains, in which John Bidwell was the outstanding figure, followed the Platte River trail from Missouri to Salt Lake and thence crossed the unexplored desert to the Humboldt River. Eventually the party, by this time in dire extremity from fatigue and lack of provisions, found its desperate way across the Sierra through the Sonora Pass into the valley of the San Joaquin, and its members later established homes in various parts of California.

The Bidwell party was the predecessor of numerous kindred expeditions of settlers from the Mississippi Valley into California prior to the outbreak of the Mexican War. Some of these came by way of Oregon, some by way of the Humboldt and Truckee rivers, some by way of the Owens Valley, and others by way of the old Spanish trail from Santa Fé. The exploring activities of John C. Frémont also belong to this period, but lack of space prevents a detailed discussion of the genuinely great contribution this scientist-adventurer made to California history. To this period also belongs the greatest of the misfortunes of the Western trails—the tragedy of the Donner party.

With the opening of the routes to California and the advent of American explorers and settlers the people and government of the United States became definitely interested in securing this fair province on the Pacific. Conditions in California contributed also very largely to the growing feeling in the United States that the territory must become an American possession or pass into the hands of Great Britain or one of the other more powerful European nations. Mexico, as already indicated, was utterly unable to control the province, and the military defenses of California were ridiculously weak. Dissatisfaction was everywhere in evidence and revolution was resorted to on the slightest provocation. It was accordingly universally recognized that the actual control of California had all but slipped from the hands of Mexico and that the province would become either an independent state, a protectorate of one of the European nations, or a part of the United States.

At this juncture the Mexican War gave to President Polk, one of the most ardent of the expansionist presidents of the United States, an opportunity to realize his publicly expressed ambition to secure possession of California. At least two of Polk's predecessors had sought to purchase the territory from Mexico, and on one occasion, supposing that war had actually been declared between Mexico and the United States, Commodore ap Catesby Jones, an American commander, had taken possession for a few hours of the port of Monterey. The American consul and confidential agent of President Polk at Monterey, Thomas O. Larkin, had also been exceedingly active in promoting the interests of the United States in California a few years prior to the outbreak of hostilities and was deliberately setting on foot a movement among the people of California to declare their independence of Mexico and to unite with the United States. Polk himself had likewise sought to secure California by peaceful means; but these had failed, and the President, apparently convinced that California was about to pass to England, seized the opportunity of the Mexican War to establish American control over the long-desired province.

The actual military conquest of California which followed the declaration of war between Mexico and the United States must be summed up very briefly. As a prelude to the formal conquest came the highly dramatic incident of the Bear Flag Revolt. In this uprising a group of settlers in the Sacramento Valley and John C. Frémont's company of explorers sought to overthrow the California officials and set up an independent government. The movement, however, had only entered its initial stages when it was learned that the United States and Mexico were formally at war and that the American commander, Sloat, had officially taken possession of Monterey. From this beginning the sovereignty of the United States was rapidly and almost without bloodshed extended over the greater part of California. But before long, unfortunately, the smoldering hostility of the Californians flared up into armed resistance and the real struggle for the control of California thereupon began.

In this contest the most significant engagements were those of Rancho Domínguez, Natividad, San Pascual, San Gabriel River, and La Mesa. The outstanding commanders of the American forces were Kearny, Stockton, and Frémont. So far as the Californians were concerned the war was fought almost wholly by irregular mounted bands whose mobility, courage, and horsemanship to some degree made up for their lack of military equipment and regular training.

The close of hostilities came on January 13, 1847, when Andrés Pico, the leader of the last of the California detachments, entered into a formal agreement with John C. Frémont to acknowledge the sovereignty of the United States. This agreement, known as the Cahuenga Capitulations, for all practical purposes marked the close of the long period of Spanish-Mexican rule in California. The formal transfer of the territory to the United States did not take place until the Treaty of Guadalupe Hidalgo on February 2, 1848.

By a singular twist of fate, only a few days prior to the signing of this treaty a few particles of gold had been discovered by James W. Marshall in the tailrace of a sawmill which he was constructing for John A. Sutter on the South Fork of the American River in the Sierra Nevada foothills. It is no exaggeration to say that this chance discovery by a man of no more than ordinary ability or fame changed both the destiny of California and the whole course of American history as well.

With almost incredible rapidity the news of Marshall's find spread throughout the world, and within a few months the "Great Migration" was in progress. The story of the adventures, hardships, and heroism of those who joined in this rush and of the picturesque life which grew out of this mingling together of the adventurous spirits from the world's four quarters constitutes perhaps the most vivid chapter in the history of California or of any other American state.

It was hardly to be expected that the political, social, and economic institutions which function satisfactorily in a normal society could immediately adapt themselves to the unprecedented and turbulent conditions which prevailed in California in the first years of the gold rush. It is therefore a tribute to the native aptitude of the Anglo-Saxon citizen for self-government that even in the midst of such chaotic conditions he was able through his own initiative to devise ways and means of furnishing reasonable safeguards of life and property and to insure some stability for society.

In 1850, despite the obstacles imposed by the question of slavery and the long-drawn-out contest in the American Congress over the Compromise of 1850, California was formally admitted as a state of the Union. A regularly organized government then began to function, and conditions within the state gradually assumed more normal characteristics. Society, however, was as yet by no means fully stabilized, and for fully another decade "Vigilante" movements from time to time sprang up in San Francisco, Los Angeles, and other sections of the state.

By 1855 gold-mining in California had definitely declined and agriculture was coming to take its place. But to make possible the new economic development of the state it was necessary first of all to provide adequate transportation facilities. Within the state this development of transportation was at first largely by means of stagecoaches and freight wagons. Lines were opened between San Francisco, Stockton, Sacramento, Los Angeles, and other important centers. Later the great Butterfield Line was operated between St. Louis, El Paso, Los Angeles, and San Francisco. Later still came the Pony Express. But it was not until 1869 that the Central Pacific Railway, built by Stanford, Crocker, Hopkins, and Huntington, united with the Union Pacific to give California its needed transcontinental rail connection with the rest of the United States.

With the coming of the railways California entered upon its present-day development, and with the history of that development it is not necessary here to deal. Looking on toward the future one's imagination is scarcely bold enough to visualize the destiny which awaits California. Looking to the past one sees a history, fascinating, romantic, inseparably a part of the great drama of international affairs and of the development of the United States, made inspiring by the heroic figures which move across its pages, and touched everywhere by elements of true greatness. To identify and preserve the landmarks where so many of the stirring episodes of this history occurred is assuredly to render a notable service to the state. For this service we acknowledge our obligation and offer our lasting appreciation to the Daughters of the American Revolution.

ROBERT GLASS CLELAND

THE SOUTHERN COUNTIES

LOS ANGELES,
LOS ANGELES COUNTY, CAL. 1857.

Historic Spots in California

IMPERIAL COUNTY

IMPERIAL COUNTY was organized in 1907 from that part of San Diego County known as Imperial Valley. El Centro is the county seat.

A Prehistoric Wonderland

Imperial Valley is remarkable for the vast range of prehistoric and geologic relics to be found within its borders. Outlining and explaining these, as it were, is the ancient beach line extending from north to south and plainly visible for two hundred and fifty feet above the surface of the present Salton Sea. Professor William P. Blake of the Williamson survey first observed the old beach line and examined its shells while engaged in making the first governmental survey of Imperial Valley in 1853.

Extending southward from Indio in Riverside County, past the Travertine Rock at the county line and on through western Imperial County to the Fish Creek Mountains, this ancient shore line there turns east and south, skirting Superstition Mountain and crossing the U.S. 80 highway about three miles west of Dixieland. Continuing south along the West Side Canal and down into Mexico as far as Black Butte, it again turns northward, re-entering Imperial County about eight miles east of Calexico. Here the ancient water line follows the East Side Canal northward, passing east of Salton Sea into Riverside County, where the circuit is completed slightly north of Indio.

Scientists believe that this beach line indicates that the Gulf of California once extended inland as far north as San Gorgonio Pass. Along the entire length of this ancient beach, or within a short distance from its sands, may be found curious relics of bygone ages: vast coral reefs, millions of fossils and shells, and even pottery wrought by a race long since forgotten.

In view of the difficult desert trails leading to most of the places described, and also because of the excessive heat and scarcity of water, the traveller should furnish himself with detailed information as to routes and equipment before attempting any of these trips. *Touring Topics* (October 1929), in an article entitled "Fossil Hunting about Carrizo Creek" by John Edwin Hogg, gives a good idea as to the nature of some of the roads encountered.

Beginning in the north is the interesting geological upthrust known as Travertine Rock. Shared also by Riverside County, it stands near the U.S. 99 highway on the western shore of the Salton Sea. Covered by a hard crust of calcium carbonate (known as travertine), left there by receding waters at least a thousand years ago, this chalk-like surface is made even more interesting by the indelible imprint of human hands left in the Indian rock writings (petroglyphs) of a prehistoric age. About twelve miles to the south lies a petrified forest, one of two in Imperial County.

A group of prehistoric animal tracks, reached by a drive over rough roads and a short hike, are to be seen in a small canyon north of the Fish Creek Mountains. Presumably an ancient waterhole where great prehistoric animals came to drink, it is covered by hundreds of huge tracks which geolo-

gists believe to be the footprints of mastodons, solidified and preserved by succeeding geological epochs.

Mullett Island, with its museum of curious pottery and innumerable natural relics, is five miles west of Niland and eleven and one-half miles north of Calipatria. Its bubbling oxide springs and famous mudpots or geysers covering an area of twenty acres are unique and interesting.

Near the international boundary, ten miles southwest of Coyote Wells, lies the second petrified forest to be found in Imperial County. Across the Yuha wash, in a setting of many-tinted and fantastically shaped rocks, pieces of petrified wood may be found scattered over an area of ten acres.

Painted Gorge, with its rugged walls tinted in "a patchwork of colors like the design of an old-fashioned quilt," is seven miles north of the U.S. 80 highway and about thirty miles west of El Centro. At the upper end of the gorge are high coral reefs and well-preserved oyster shells. In the Coyote Mountains to the northwest, valuable pieces of Indian pottery and other relics may be found, many already having been placed in numerous valley collections.

The best and most extensive coral formations are found in Alverson Canyon (locally known as Shell Canyon) across the Coyote Mountains from Painted Gorge. These deposits are reached only by a very difficult desert road followed by three miles of hiking. Two magnificent coral canyons may also be reached from Barett Well with less difficulty: Barett Canyon in the Fish Creek Mountains to the north and Garnet Canyon in the Coyote Mountains on the south.

North and east of the petrified forest stretches the Yuha plain, with its myriad fish fossils, its beds of decaying oyster shells, and "the most amazing rock concretions ever discovered in the United States." These latter were first mentioned by Juan Bautista de Anza in 1774 and first described over one hundred and twenty-five years later by George Wharton James in his *Wonders of the Colorado Desert*. They consist of "detached rocks of various shapes and sizes, chiefly spherical . . . . and resembling petrified fruits, vegetables and flowers."

California's First Historic Spot

Probably the first white man to touch California soil was Hernando de Alarcón. On May 9, 1540, Alarcón started from Acapulco, Mexico, and sailed north until he reached the mouth of the Colorado River on August 17 or 18. On several occasions during the fall of 1540 he ascended the river, to a point probably a little beyond the site of Yuma. Joseph J. Hill says of Alarcón's visit: "It can hardly be doubted that he landed at various times on the California side of the river, probably being the first to do so." The point touched was somewhere opposite Yuma.

The next white man to walk upon California soil was Melchior Diaz, who had left Coronado's expedition near the present site of Ures, Mexico, in October 1540, with instructions to make a contact with Alarcón if possible. Diaz proceeded up the Colorado River as far as the Gila, where he crossed over on rafts, touching California soil at about the same point as Alarcón. He then traveled down the western bank, passing historic Pilot Knob on Imperial County soil.

First Passage of the Colorado Desert

A trail from Mexico to the junction of the Colorado and Gila rivers had been blazed as early as 1700 by Father Eusebio Kino, a Jesuit priest, whose purpose was to find an overland route from Sonora to the missions of Baja California.

"Francisco Eusebio Kino . . . . was the father of the cattle industry of the southwest and one of the great missionaries of New Spain." He was in Lower California from

1683 to 1685. The remainder of his life was spent in Pimería
Alta, now southern Arizona and northern Sonora, where he
founded some fifty missions and chapels. The desire to find
a way to connect the missions of Pimería Alta with those of
Lower California led to numerous exploring expeditions. In
1700 he went as far as the junction of the Colorado and Gila
rivers, and the next year descended the former nearly to its
mouth, where he crossed over on a raft. Descending the
Colorado again in 1702, Kino reached as far as the Gulf.
These explorations led him to believe that California was a
peninsula and not an island, as had previously been supposed.
Furthermore, the way had been opened to the great Colorado
Desert, a trail followed over seventy years later by Garcés
and Anza.

Fray Francisco Garcés, famous priest-explorer, was the
first white man to enter the great Colorado Desert, when in
1771, believing that he was crossing the Gila River, he
crossed the Colorado instead. During his wanderings he
skirted the Cocopah Range to its terminus at Signal Mountain near the present Calexico. To the northwest he saw two
gaps in the Sierra, which he believed could be followed into
New California without great difficulty.

On this journey, Garcés gained information which exercised a profound influence on the decision of the "junta"
which eventually recommended Anza's plan to go overland
to California. It was this journey, also, more than any
other, which helped to determine the path taken by the subsequent expedition.

In the year 1774, Juan Bautista de Anza, one of the most
heroic figures in the history of California, volunteered to find
an overland route to the coast missions in order to avoid the
perils and uncertainty of communication by sea, and to insure
the settlement of Alta California. Antonio María Bucareli,
then viceroy of Mexico, accepted Anza's offer.

Accompanied by Fray Francisco Garcés, Fray Juan Díaz,
and twenty soldiers, Anza reached the junction of the Gila
and Colorado rivers on February 7, 1774, and on the ninth
he crossed the Colorado at the ford above the Gila, camping
on the California side.

On the following day, the party went four leagues along
the river, passing Pilot Knob, which Anza named the Cerro
de San Pablo, where the river turns south. Proceeding another league, they stopped for the night at the Ranchería de
San Pablo, a Yuman Indian village at the place where the
Misión San Pedro y San Pablo was established in the autumn
of 1780.

This was just above the boundary line, and from here the
expedition continued in a southwesterly direction until they
reached a lake called by Anza, Laguna de Santa Olaya, about
twelve miles south of the boundary line and eight miles west
of the Colorado, "the end of the known land." Beyond lay
hostile Indians and league upon league of treacherous sand
dunes blocking the way into what is now southeastern Imperial County.

Undaunted, Anza set forth to cross this forbidding waste,
but, the dunes proving impassable, he was forced to retreat
to Santa Olaya, which the party reached again on February 19. Having rested for several days among the friendly
Indians at this oasis, the party resumed its journey on March
2, and finally re-entered California on March 7, camping
three or four miles southwest of the Yuha Well and about
two miles north of the international boundary line. The next
morning they reached a little group of refreshing wells,
"which, on being opened, distilled an abundant supply of most
beautiful water." Here Anza rested for a day, refreshing
both the footsore men and the famished horses. These life-
giving springs were named by Anza the Pozas de Santa
Rosa de las Lajas (the Wells of Santa Rosa of the Flat

Rocks), because of the great number of peculiar rock formations of varying forms and sizes which abounded there. How
the less poetic name of the Yuha Well later came to be attached to them is not known. They lie in a basin of the
same name about six miles southwest of Dixieland and about
two miles north of the boundary line.

The last important camp made by Anza on his first journey across the desert was reached on March 10 and was made
at the junction or sink of the San Felipe and Carrizo creeks,
called by Anza the San Sebastián, alias del Peregrino, in
honor of Sebastián Tarabal, his Indian guide, who had previously passed that way under great hardships and danger.
This place, now known as Harper's Well, was at the base of
the San Jacinto Mountains where the western wall of the
great Colorado Desert had been reached and where the expedition entered the San Jacinto Mountains by way of San
Felipe Canyon and San Carlos Pass.

On his return to Mexico in May, Anza again crossed the
desert, camping at San Sebastián on the 7th, and from there
making a short cut directly across the desert. On December
11, 1775, he again stopped at the Wells of Santa Rosa, this
time to rest and refresh the first caravan of emigrants to
enter California, the party destined to be also the first settlers
of San Francisco. This caravan, which left Tubac on October 23, 1775, was made up of two hundred and forty persons, of whom more than thirty were women and a hundred
and thirty-six were boys and girls. Only one life was lost
on the entire journey of one thousand miles, and three babies
were born en route. Over a thousand animals also began the
journey but many perished on the deserts.

On his final return to Mexico in 1776, Anza again made
a direct cut across the desert, paralleling the U.S. 99 highway
past Kane Spring as far as Westmoreland, and camping on
May 8 east of Imperial.

The Desert Trail

The old desert trail across Imperial Valley, first opened
by Anza and followed later by generations of explorers and
trappers, traders and argonauts, and finally by a long line of
homeseekers, has been variously known as the Sonora Road,
the Colorado Road, the Emigrant Trail, and the Butterfield
Stage Route. That part of the route from the San Felipe Sink
via San Carlos Pass was closed after 1782 and has never been
used since. In July 1781 the two missions established on the
Colorado River in 1780 were destroyed by Indians, and in
1781 and 1782 Pedro Fages carried dispatches to Misión San
Gabriel relative to these Indian troubles. On the first of these
trips he followed Anza's trail all the way, but on the second
he traversed it only across the desert to the San Felipe watering place, where he turned up the Carrizo Creek into the unexplored territory to the southwest, thus opening the road
which goes by way of Warner's Ranch, a trail followed by
southern emigrant trains of 1849 and the '50's, and known as
the old Emigrant Trail.

Because of the hostility of the Yuma Indians the desert
trail was probably not used again until 1826, although Santiago Argüello, while pursuing Indian horse-thieves, in 1825,
rediscovered Fages' route through the mountains. In 1826,
on the approval of Romualdo Pacheco, Lieutenant of Engineers, the Mexican government adopted the desert trail as an
official mail route and Pacheco established a small garrison
on the Colorado River that same year. From then on, the
trail was used to a small extent by traders from Sonora.

The David E. Jackson party, in 1831, followed Anza's
trail across the desert to Carrizo Creek, where they crossed
the mountains via Warner's, probably the first Americans to
pass that way. In 1834 Rafael Amador, a messenger for
President Santa Anna of Mexico, made the trip in forty-
eight days, record time, and in 1846 Stephen W. Kearny

conducted the advanced guard of the "Army of the West" across the old desert trail, and over the mountains through Warner's Pass.

The Butterfield Stage used approximately the same road from 1858 to 1861. "Winding across desert wastes, topping sand-dunes and skirting buttes, the old Butterfield trail . . . . was probably the first well-defined road across the Imperial Valley. After more than seventy years of desert cloudbursts and windstorms, portions of the road still remain like a forgotten relic of yesteryear."

The ruined walls of the old Pilot Knob station may still be seen at Araz on the U.S. 80 highway a few miles west of Yuma. Except for the station at Indian Wells (also known as Sunset Springs and by various other names), the trail through the shifting dunes from Araz westward is uncertain until Carrizo Creek is reached. It led south of the international boundary line by way of the stations at Cook's Well and Alamo Mocho (both of which have disappeared), and then northwest into the present Imperial County by way of the station at Indian Wells, halfway to the Carrizo station (San Diego County). This station was located approximately eight miles south and a little west of Seeley and about two and a half miles from Silsbee. The adobe station building continued to stand there until washed away by the flood of 1906.

Purísima and San Pedro y San Pablo

Misión Purísima Concepción and Misión San Pedro y San Pablo once stood twelve miles apart in the southeastern corner of what was destined to become Imperial County. The two were established in the autumn of 1780, by four Franciscan padres from Mexico, Fathers Díaz, Morena, Garcés, and Barreneche. The purpose of these missions was twofold: to convert the Yuma Indians living at this point along the Colorado River, and to make a way-station on the overland emigrant trail from Mexico to the California missions.

The plan followed at Purísima and at San Pedro y San Pablo was different from that followed in other parts of California. The Indians were allowed to remain on their own rancherías and the padres visited them there, ministering to their spiritual needs alone.

But this plan was not successful. The Fathers had not the means to visit the Indians often, nor had they the necessary trinkets to allure them. Moreover, the soldiers, and the few white settlers who came with them, used for themselves the scant patches of ground on which the Indians raised their melons, beans, and corn, and the white man's cattle ate up the precious pasturage which their own poor stock needed.

Naturally, the Indians soon looked upon the white people as invaders, and in July 1781 one of the most tragic occurrences in the whole history of California took place. Captain Rivera y Moncada, lieutenant-governor of Lower California, was bringing a party of settlers from Mexico to establish the proposed pueblo of Los Angeles in California. On reaching the Colorado River, the families in the train were sent ahead, while Rivera remained behind to refresh his exhausted animals. On July 17, an outbreak among the Yuma Indians came to a climax. Rivera and all of his soldiers, as well as Father Garcés and the other priests at the two missions, and all the male settlers were massacred. The women and children were made captive, being subsequently ransomed by Pedro Fages.

The missions and pueblos were not established again on the Colorado, and the route which had been opened with such great effort by Juan Bautista de Anza, in 1774 and 1775, became more dangerous to travelers than ever before.

The garrison located on the river in 1826 by Romualdo Pacheco served as a protection for government mail carriers and Sonoran traders. In the early '50's, Fort Yuma was established on the spot where Misión Purísima had stood, and American troops were stationed there for several years. It was besieged by Indians in 1851. On the same spot, in later years, an Indian School, where boys and girls were taught trades as well as reading and writing, was conducted by the Sisters of St. Joseph. The school building standing today on a high hill north of the highway on the California side of the Colorado River was built by the United States government for the education of the Indians in the Yuma reservation.

Traces of the foundations, and evidences of the building having been burned to the ground, are all that remain on the site of Misión San Pedro y San Pablo.

Early Colorado River Ferries

Several ferries were established on the Colorado below its junction with the Gila in 1849 and 1850. The first of these was built by General Alexander Anderson, from Tennessee, in order to transport his party to the California side at a point several miles south of the Gila. Anderson afterward presented his boat to the Indians with a certificate of title, the terms of which seem to have been faithfully lived up to by the latter.

Another ferry, started in September 1849 by Lieutenant Cave J. Couts at Camp Calhoun on the California side, aided gold-seekers across the river. In December Couts sold his ferry to Dr. G. W. Lincoln, reputed to have been a distant relative of Abraham Lincoln.

This ferry was destined to come to a tragic end. When John Glanton, a renegade and blackguard, purchased a half share in Lincoln's ferry the enterprise quickly degenerated. Lincoln was secretly done away with and the neighboring Indian ferry was destroyed in order to prevent opposition. The indignant natives retaliated by surprising and killing Glanton and his men and destroying their boat.

In the summer of the following year the ferry was reestablished by L. J. F. Jaeger and others, at a point several miles below the present site of Yuma near the Hall Hanlon ranch. Lumber for Jaeger's ferry was transported across the desert from San Diego by pack train. A ferry was operated at this point until the present highway bridge was erected in 1915.

Picacho, A Ghost of the Desert

On the west bank of the Colorado River, twenty-five miles north of Yuma, is the site of Picacho, an early mining camp, said to have been discovered by an Indian in 1860. It was first located by Mexican prospectors in 1862, and is said to have been one of the richest placers in California. The population was almost entirely Latin during the first few years of its existence, a bit of Old Mexico transplanted to American soil. There were arenas for bullfights, which were attended with great pomp and ceremony; and there were gay and picturesque *bailles*, accompanied by the soft music of guitars, the clatter of castanets, and the brilliant and lavish play of *cascarones* and confetti. The Americans came in later and found rich lodes in the neighboring hills, erected large stamp mills, and soon had the payroll amounting to $40,000 a month.

Near the lofty mountain from which the district is named and five miles from Picacho, the Picacho Mine was located, being connected by railroad with the mill near the river. This railroad operated for a long while, but was eventually torn up and only the old embankments are visible today.

"Deserted by her citizens, a victim of successive floods, Picacho has all but vanished. On the flank of the mountain, out of reach of lapping waters, a few buildings still remain. Of the saloons and stores, however, there is no trace; the former townsite has been almost completely reclaimed by thorny mesquite. Within a stone's throw of the former main street, the broad Colorado flows silently toward the Gulf. On either side of it rise desert mountains, boulder-strewn and chasm-riven, composing a scene in which the forbidding is blended with wild, exotic beauty."

Tumco

Tumco, discovered by a Swedish track-walker and known at first as Hedges, was a mining town of some importance thirty-five years ago. Three miles north of Ogilby Station on the Southern Pacific, it lies within a narrow desert valley hemmed in on either side by two barren mountain ranges. Once inhabited by 2,000 people, Tumco is today a ghost city of ruined adobe walls and stone foundations. Three miles northeast of Ogilby was the American Girl Mine, developed later and worked by less than 200 men.

The Rockwood Gate

At the last place where rock formation is found on the lower Colorado less than a mile above the international boundary line is located the great concrete Rockwood Gate, the portal through which flows every drop of water used by the people of Imperial Valley for irrigation and domestic purposes. It is this water from the Colorado River, conveyed through a vast system of canals and ditches to be deposited upon the rich soil of the Salton Sink, that makes Imperial Valley what it is today, a prosperous agricultural community of over sixty thousand people. It is appropriate that around this spot should cluster the memories of three pioneers of the idea of reclaiming the Colorado Desert: Dr. Oliver Meredith Wozencraft, Charles Robinson Rockwood, and George Chaffey.

Dr. Wozencraft is considered the real father of Imperial Valley, "the first man to actually plan the reclamation of the desert sink for agricultural purposes by bringing the waters of the Colorado to the arid area to the west." He came to California in the gold rush of 1849, and immediately after his arrival in San Francisco he set out on an expedition to the then little known Colorado Desert. It was there, in the year 1849, that he first conceived the idea of reclamation. The project so possessed him that he was led to devote the rest of his life to making his dream a reality.

Obtaining favorable action from the state legislature in 1859, Wozencraft was given all state rights in the Salton Sink. The next step was to get a patent from the federal government, but in spite of repeated attempts he never obtained this, chiefly because the attention of Congress was entirely taken up with the Civil War and subsequent reconstruction problems. Dr. Wozencraft died in Washington in 1887 while making a final effort to obtain Congressional action. His repeated attempts to interest capitalists in his enterprise had also been of no avail. However, an appeal made to George Chaffey for support in 1882, although not obtaining results at the time, was no doubt a factor leading to the final accomplishment of the reclamation under the latter's direction, April 1900 to February 1902.

Meanwhile, there was no one to continue the work begun by Dr. Wozencraft until Charles Robinson Rockwood, civil engineer, made a rediscovery of the agricultural possibilities of Imperial Valley in 1892. The name of Rockwood will always be associated with the early history of Imperial Valley as that of one who was pre-eminent among those entertaining the idea of turning the waters of the Colorado upon the parched soil of the Salton Sink. He never gave up hope of

success during the eight long years of toil, struggle, and disappointment through which he passed before finally locating the necessary man with capital to finance the work. This man was George Chaffey, "who was able to take hold of the project—and bring the water to the desert."

George Chaffey had begun his career of founding agricultural colonies based on irrigation, in 1881, at Etiwanda, where he originated the idea of a mutual water company and set up the first dynamo for developing hydro-electric power on the Pacific slope. The next year he laid out the Ontario Colony. In 1886 he and his brother, William, began their work of establishing colonies in the arid regions of Australia. There he learned that it was possible for white people to colonize hot and arid regions, provided sufficient water could be brought to them. With this experience as a background, Chaffey was ready, when approached by Rockwood in 1899, to undertake the very thing he had refused to do in 1882 when Wozencraft made his appeal.

Chaffey now became the chief factor in the actual reclamation of the desert. Entering into the work under his own terms, he built up the project from its very foundations, giving it credit by creating assets out of liabilities, and planning and directing the construction of vast canals and ditches. He not only established but also named Imperial Valley.

Water from the Colorado was first turned through the intake gate at Pilot Knob on May 14, 1901. This first heading was located about five hundred feet south of the present Rockwood Gate. The water arrived at the Sharpe heading, located at the international boundary line, on June 21, 1901. In February of the following year, the construction of the canals was completed.

There are now 2,500 miles of irrigation ditches and canals serving 603,840 acres of cultivated land in Imperial Valley. Within a period of thirty years, a vast desert waste had become "one of the world's most fruitful gardens," comprising 5,000 farms, the five major crops of which were, in 1930, alfalfa, lettuce, barley, canteloupe, and milo maize. From the handful of settlers who went there in 1901, the population had become 60,000 in 1930.

In the spring and summer of 1906 unusual rainfalls caused the whole flow of the Colorado River to break through the intake gates, threatening to fill the entire valley, a circumstance which had happened before in prehistoric eras. Through the almost superhuman efforts of E. H. Harriman, president of the Southern Pacific, and his agents, the flow of the river was finally turned back into its normal course February 10, 1907, thus saving the valley for the use of humanity. The runaway river had, however, left its mark in the newly formed Salton Sea, which had previously been dry land.

Rockwood Hall

There stands in Calexico, at the international boundary line a few feet south of the Southern Pacific depot, an adobe building, not so very old, but historically an important unit in the chain of Imperial Valley's metamorphosis from desert to garden. Part of this building was originally erected some time in 1905 by the California Development Company, a corporation organized by Charles R. Rockwood and his associates, April 26, 1896. As a result of the devastating flood of 1906, the California Development Company failed and the Imperial Irrigation District, organized by the people of the valley, took it over. In 1910, the little adobe was added to and remodeled as the office of the new irrigation district. In 1924 the building was abandoned by the Imperial Irrigation District and remained vacant until 1932, when it was taken over by the Veterans of Foreign Wars, and restored and

dedicated by them as Rockwood Hall. A street divides Calexico, California, from Mexicali, Mexico, being the boundary line between the two countries.

[Credit is here given for source material, and permission to quote is
hereby acknowledged]

ADAM, JOAQUIN. "Destruction of the Catholic Missions on the Rio
Colorado in 1871," in *The Historical Society of Southern Cali-
fornia Publications*, III (1893), 36–40
BANNING, CAPTAIN WILLIAM, and GEORGE HUGH BANNING. "Dust
of the 'Swift Wagon,' a Glimpse of John Butterfield and a Full
Account of the Great Southern Overland Mail," in *Touring
Topics*, XXII, No. 2 (February, 1930), 17–19
BANNING, CAPTAIN WILLIAM, and GEORGE HUGH BANNING. "Wheel
Tracks of the 'Jackass Mail,'" in *Touring Topics*, XXI, No. 11
(November, 1929), 21–25, 54
BEATTIE, GEORGE WILLIAM. *Reopening Anza's Road*. Manuscript,
1931
BLAKE, WILLIAM P. "Ancient Lake in the Colorado Desert," in
American Journal of Science; XVII (1854), No. 2, 435–438
BOLTON, HERBERT EUGENE. *Anza's California Expeditions*. 5 vols.
University of California Press, Berkeley, 1930
DAVIS, ARTHUR P. "The New Inland Sea," in *National Geographic
Magazine*, XVIII, No. 1 (January, 1907), 36–49
ELDREDGE, ZOETH SKINNER. *The Beginnings of San Francisco,
from the Expedition of Anza, 1774, to the City Charter of April
15, 1850*. 2 vols. Privately printed, San Francisco, 1912
EMORY, WILLIAM HEMSLEY. *Notes of a Military Reconnaissance
from Fort Leavenworth, Missouri, to San Diego, California*, 30th
Congress, 1st Session, Senate Executive Document No. 7, Wash-
ington, 1848
FARR, F. C. *History of Imperial County*. Elms and Franks, Berke-
ley, California, 1918
GORBY, J. S. "Steamboating on the Colorado," in *Touring Topics*,
XX, No. 7 (July, 1928), 14–18, 45
HANNA, PHIL TOWNSEND. "The Wells of Santa Rosa of the Flat
Rocks," in *Touring Topics*, XX, No. 1 (January, 1928), 18–20, 31
HILL, JOSEPH J., compiler, and DILLON LAURITZEN, painter. "A
Map of Exploration in the Spanish Southwest, 1528–1793," for
Touring Topics, XXIV, No. 1 (January, 1932), Supplement
HOGG, JOHN EDWIN. "Fossil Hunting about Carrizo Creek," in
Touring Topics, XXI, No. 10 (October, 1929), 14–17
HOWE, EDGAR F., and WILBUR J. HALL. *The Story of the First
Decade in Imperial Valley, California*. E. F. Howe & Sons, Im-
perial, 1910
JAMES, GEORGE WHARTON. *Wonders of the Colorado Desert*. Little,
Brown and Company, Boston, 1906
JOHNSTON, PHILIP. "Derelicts of the California Desert," in *Touring
Topics*, XX, No. 2 (February, 1928), 14–18, 37–42
KENNAN, GEORGE. *The Salton Sea, an Account of Harriman's Fight
with the Colorado River*. Macmillan, New York, 1917.
McKENNY, J. WILSON. "The Butterfield Trail." Reprinted from the
Calexico Chronicle
ROMER, MARGARET. "A History of Calexico, California," in *Publi-
cations, Historical Society of Southern California*, XII, Part 2
(1922), 26–66
STEWARD, JULIAN. "Words Writ on Stone," in *Touring Topics*,
XIX, No. 5 (May, 1927), 18–20, 36–38
TOUT, OTIS B. *The First Thirty Years*. Otis B. Tout, San Diego,
California, 1931

INYO COUNTY

Inyo County (according to W. A. Chalfant, the meaning
of Inyo, as given to early white settlers, is "dwelling place of
a great spirit") was organized in 1866 from territory that had
been set aside two years earlier from Mono and Tulare counties and called Coso County. However, Coso County was never
organized and Inyo took its place. Independence has been the
county seat since the organization of the county.

Inyo County contains within its borders a more varied
topography than any other equal area on this continent, probably than any other in the world. On its western boundary
stands Mt. Whitney, the highest peak in the United States
outside of Alaska, while Death Valley, the lowest spot on the
continent, is also included within its borders. The Valley
abounds in scenic as well as historic interest: Marble Canyon,
Mosaic Canyon, the Sand Dunes, Grotto Canyon, Stovepipe
Wells, Furnace Creek Ranch (a veritable oasis in the desert),
Golden Canyon, Mushroom Rock, Pluto's Salt Pools, Bad
Water, Ashford Mill, the Devil's Golf Course, Old Confidence Mill, and other places of equal interest. "While no
human being has any business there in summer, the late fall,
winter, and early spring months find the valley in a friendly
and approachable mood . . . . a favorite spot for those who
love the unique, the colorful, and the spectacular."

The Bishop Petroglyphs

Indian petroglyphs, or rock markings, may be found
throughout much of the arid West. Those of one area are
unlike those of others, and so it is thought that they were
made by different tribes. All, however, are similar in their
crudeness and simplicity of design. They are generally made
in soft tufa by chipping, and are usually found near springs
or streams on natural routes of travel, but sometimes are
discovered in secluded mountain nooks.

A few miles north of Bishop, in northern Inyo County,
the largest group of these markings in this part of the state
is found on the courses of stream beds or near ancient
springs. Among the petroglyphs found here are crude pictures of what appear to be deer, human and animal footprints,
snakes, many-legged bugs, and numerous geometrical designs.
At Deep Springs Valley, on the Midland Trail, is a great
round boulder covered with these carved pictures: sun symbols, snakes, a bird, a rabbit (possibly), and concentric circles
which may represent sweat-houses. At Little Lake, Coso
Hot Springs, and Keeler are more rocks on which animal
figures also predominate. Other hieroglyphics are found covering the granite walls at the base of the Inyo Mountains at
a point near Swansea.

Scientists, generally, do not believe that these rocks show
great antiquity, but, rather, that they were probably done by
the ancestors of the present Piutes at no far-removed period.
Probably some were made by priests or medicine men and
had a religious significance. Others acted as sign-posts to
mark water holes, trails, or other important places, and a few
may have been made to represent some important event.

Similar carvings have been found from Alaska to South
America, and scientists have sought for years to understand
their mystery. With few exceptions, however, the most penetrating study has failed to lift the veil of obscurity from their
origin. Their age is still speculative and their meaning enig-
matic.

Winnedumah

Directly east of Independence on the extreme crest of the
White Mountains stands a remarkable monolith of granite
commonly known as the Piute Monument. It is eighty feet
high, and in its position on the skyline is visible for many
miles. With it is associated the best-known of the legends of
the Owens Valley Indians, that of Winnedumah, according
to which this gigantic rock for many ages stood as an enduring symbol of faithfulness to the Indians who lived at the
base of the mountain.

The Owens Valley Emigrant Trail

Although trappers may have penetrated Owens Valley as
far south as Inyo County in the '30's, the first authentic rec-

ord we have is that of Joseph Reddeford Walker who, in 1843, led the Chiles emigrant party, the second wagon train to enter California from the east, down Owens Valley and through the pass which was later named after him. Again in 1845 Walker led the main body of John C. Frémont's second expedition into California over the same route, Frémont, himself, going by way of Donner's Pass with Kit Carson, Richard Owens, and twelve others. Frémont considered Richard Owens a very valuable man, and after the expedition had reached the San Joaquin Valley he honored him by giving his name to the Inyo river, valley, and lake which still bear it, although the man for whom they were named never saw this region.

Resting Springs

The old "Spanish Trail" into California from the northeast, opened up by William Wolfskill in 1831 and followed later by caravans from New Mexico, became the route adopted by Mormon emigrants to San Bernardino, and was used by them from 1847 until after the Mountain Meadows massacre. A branch of this trail passed by Resting Springs, Inyo County, where the Mormon caravans tarried to recuperate their livestock, on journeys across the desert.

The Resting Springs were first known as the Archilette, and to them John C. Frémont came on April 19, 1844, on his way out of California. Frémont called the place Agua de Hernández, in honor of the Mexican boy, Pablo Hernández, who had come to his camp on the Mojave River on April 24 with Andrés Fuentes, a Mexican, the two being the lone survivors of a small party of traders, victims of an Indian raid at the Archilette. More than forty years afterward an old rusty sword, of the pattern used in Frémont's day, was found at this spot, supposedly lost by one of Frémont's party.

Death Valley

Death Valley, on the southeastern border of California, is a long, sunken desert, surrounded by high mountains. It is the lowest spot in the United States, its minimum elevation as established by the latest United States Geological Survey being 276 feet below sea level. It is believed that its grim name was received from the first recorded tragedy which occurred there, that of the Lewis Manly and the Jayhawker parties, whose attempt to cross Death Valley into California, in 1849, constitutes one of the tragic episodes of California's history. Manly himself writes concerning the origin of the name:

"We took off our hats, and then overlooking the scene of so much trial, suffering, and death spoke the thought uppermost in our minds, saying: 'Goodbye, Death Valley!' . . . . Many accounts have been given to the world as to the origin of the name, but ours were the first visible footsteps, and we the party which gave it the saddest and most dreadful name that came to us first from our memories."

On Christmas Day, the Manly party entered the Valley of Burning Silence and camped beside what was later known as Furnace Creek. The following day they found a good spring at what was without doubt Bennett's Wells, on the west side of the Death Valley sink. They called this place the Last Camp, for there their situation was so critical that it was decided that the party should remain in camp while Manly and Rogers set out over the mountains to seek help. After incredible suffering and almost insurmountable difficulties, these two brave men finally reached their destination and returned to Death Valley to rescue their friends. At Last Camp it was found that only the Bennett and Arcane families remained, the others having attempted to go on alone. Some were never accounted for, but one, a Captain Culverwell, who had joined the last party out, died not far from camp. He

is the only one of the entire party known to have perished within the limits of Death Valley itself.

Of the Jayhawkers, those gay young men who set out from Galesburg, Illinois, in the spring of 1849, and other individuals associated with them, the story is even more tragic. Travelling, for the most part, by themselves, the Jayhawkers were often closely associated with the Manly-Bennett-Arcane group in their grim march across the desert, being together at some camps and apart at others. Accounts of the journey by participants in these two main parties differ, but the best authority seems to be that nine of the Jayhawkers perished to the east of Death Valley and four died after leaving it but while still in the desert. One of these, a man named Robinson, died within sight of deliverance not far from the foot of the Sierra.

Manly's route lay over the mountain barrier, through Red Rock Canyon, into the Mojave Desert, and on to the San Gabriel Mountains. There it passed through Soledad Canyon and over Newhall Pass into the San Fernando Valley.

Although the story of this trek across Death Valley is the first recorded tragedy to be associated with it, there were doubtless other lone wanderers who had met death there before. Since then, too, emigrant parties, gold seekers, and lone wayfarers, almost every element of society, have entered the valley, many of them never to return. One of the earliest expeditions from the west was a mining company headed by Dr. Darwin French, in the spring of 1860. These men discovered and named Furnace Creek, the presence of a crude furnace at the stream being the occasion for the name. It has been generally believed that this was built by Mormons but it may have been set up by Mexican miners.

The first scientific expedition was made by Dr. Owen and other members of the State Boundary Commission in 1861. It was followed in 1871 by the Wheeler expedition and in 1875 by Lieutenant Birney, who crossed the valley several times.

The ruins of the Harmony Borax Works may still be seen at the upper end of Death Valley just north of Furnace Creek. There, in 1880, large deposits of borate were discovered by Aaron Winters and his frail Spanish-American wife, Rosie, who were located at Ash Meadows, a place just eastward across the Funeral Mountains from Death Valley, 200 miles from the nearest railroad. A short while before this, Isidore Daunet, a prospector, had discovered white marshes in Death Valley a few miles north of Bennett's Wells and about twenty miles southwest of Furnace Creek. On hearing of Winters' find, Daunet opened up the Eagle Borax Works, the first borax corporation in the valley. The product, however, proved to be impure and the plant was closed, passing into oblivion. Remnants of the old works may still be seen.

The Winters deposits of borate were finally acquired by F. M. ("Borax") Smith and his partner, W. T. Coleman, who started the old Harmony Borax Works. In 1889, after the marshes had been quite thoroughly worked out, Coleman assigned his property to the Pacific Coast Borax Company and work at the old Harmony plant ceased. Smith then entered the picture in earnest, working his way to the head of the company. A deposit at the base of Monte Blanco, a thousand-foot peak southeast of Furnace Creek, proved to be in a purer state than that previously worked and so rich that even today the mountain seems to be composed of almost solid colemanite, as the deposit was called. The miles of tunnels and drifts which were made into the mountain did not begin to exhaust the supply. A picture of the twenty-mule team used to haul the borates 200 miles across the desert to Mojave became the trade-mark of the company and is used to this day, although the teams disappeared, to be replaced by the Tonopah and Tidewater Railroad in 1907. New borax deposits as rich as those of Death Valley and far more easily transported were found in Nevada, Oregon, and at Trona near Searles Lake in San Bernardino County, California. Borax is still present in Death Valley in great quantities, but the ever-present handicap of the valley itself is too great and the mines are no longer worked.

The First White Man's Dwelling

Prior to 1861 the only white population in Owens Valley was composed of transient prospectors, but in August of that year A. Van Fleet with three other men drove their cattle in and prepared to stay. A cabin of sod and stone, the first permanent white dwelling erected in this region, was built at the northern end of the valley at the big bend of Owens River about four miles northwest of Bishop.

Fort Independence

At old Fort Independence, on Oak Creek about three miles northeast of the town of Independence, a company of United States soldiers under Colonel Evans was stationed on July 4, 1862, to protect the settlers from the Indians. Troops were maintained there continuously from 1865 until its abandonment in 1877.

The town of Independence had been started in 1861 with the building of a rough stone cabin by a man named Putnam. For several years the neighborhood was known as Putnam's and the stone cabin was used as a fortress, residence, and hospital until it was torn down in 1876. Its site is southwest of the present courthouse. In 1862 gold was discovered near by, and, for several years, the place was the center of a rich mining region. On February 13, 1866, the platting of a townsite was completed, the first to be found in the county records. Upon the organization of Inyo County in 1866 it became the county seat. Independence is now an outfitting point for trips over Kearsarge Pass into the Kings River region and Mount Whitney.

The home of Mary Austin, said to have been designed and supervised by the author herself, still stands at Independence. There she wrote the *Land of Little Rain* and other books which picture the beauty of Owens Valley and Inyo desert regions.

The San Francis Ranch

Samuel A. Bishop, for whom the town of Bishop was named, came to California in 1849. He was associated with General Edward F. Beale at Rancho Tejón before coming to Inyo County and later, in 1866, became one of Kern County's first supervisors.

Bishop and his wife came to Inyo from Rancho Tejón in 1861, settling on the creek which now bears his name. Here at a place where the stream leaves the foothills and enters the valley about three miles south of west of the present town of Bishop, two small cabins of rough pine slabs were erected on August 22, and the new settlement was named the San Francis Ranch. However, Bishop did not remain here long, moving in 1864 to the abandoned fort at Tejón.

Indian Troubles

A large party of Indians threatened San Francis Ranch in the autumn of 1861, greatly alarming the settlers. Knowing that they could not withstand a siege, they agreed to hold a council with the natives. Accordingly, on January 31, 1862, the Indian chiefs met with the white settlers at the ranch and concluded a treaty which was signed by both parties.

The San Francis treaty proved to be only an episode in the Indian wars of Inyo County, for within two months the natives had started hostilities in earnest. In March, Warren Wasson, Nevada Indian agent, had asked for aid from the United States troops in order to prevent a long and bloody war. He made every effort, however, to settle the difficulty by peaceful means, but to no avail.

On April 6, between fifty and sixty pioneers under John T. Kellogg and Mayfield engaged in a pitched battle with some five hundred to a thousand Piutes who were deployed in a defiant, howling line extending from a small black butte in the valley across Bishop Creek and reaching to the foothills in the south. Three white men were killed, and after the moon had set the pioneers beat a forced retreat to Big Pine.

Troops had arrived at Owens Lake on April 2, and on the 8th they joined with the citizens in an engagement with the Indians at Mayfield canyon. Trooper Gillespie and Mayfield, a citizen, were killed. Temporary peace followed, but by May the valley was in almost undisputed possession of the Piutes and many of the white settlers left the region. On July 4, 1862, Fort Independence was established, but it was not until the fall of 1863 that settlers, believing hostilities were at an end, began coming into the valley in an ever increasing stream and new camps sprang up. Not until 1866, however, was the valley pronounced safe from Indian hostilities, and troops were maintained at the Fort until 1877.

Owensville

Notwithstanding Indian hostilities, settlements continued to be made in 1862 and 1863. Among these was Owensville on the east bank of Owens River about four miles northeast of Bishop. For a few years it held the distinction of being the chief settlement in the northern part of the valley. In its vicinity fifty or more homestead claims of a hundred and sixty acres each were taken up and in the White Mountains to the northeast were a number of mines, among them the Golden Wedge and the Yellow Jacket. By the end of 1864, however, Owensville was on the decline. Its buildings were being torn down and rafted down the river to Independence and Lone Pine. By 1871 its last inhabitant had vanished.

San Carlos

San Carlos has been for many years marked by the stone foundations of old houses, and by a lone smokestack, now fallen into ruins, showing where the old mill once stood. It was started by intrepid miners in 1862 on the east bank of Owens River near the mouth of Oak Creek and was a bustling mining camp until 1865. A letter from the district dated September 4, 1863, contains this interesting item: "Our miners, who are generally men of education, vie with each other in selecting refined names for their mines. Silver Cloud, Norma, Olympic, Golden Era, Welcome, Chrysopolis, Gem, Green Monster, Blue Bird, Red Bird, Evadne, Fleta, Bonnie Blossom, Calliope, Romelia, Lucerne, Pluto's Pet, Birousa, Proserpine, Atahualpa, and Ida are among the mines here."

Bend City

Bend City, a mining camp established in the early '60's, was named by the legislature as the seat of Coso County (which, however, was never organized). It was located near the Owens River about four miles east of the town of Independence. Nearly all of the sixty or more houses originally built at the camp were adobe. Near Kearsarge Station their ruins may be seen, one of the many "ghost towns" which still haunt California's romantic mining regions. The first county bridge across Owens River was erected at Bend City but the earthquake of 1872 changed the river's course and left the already deserted town site high and dry on the bank of an empty ravine instead of on the river.

Several ambitious mining camps farther up the river existed during the '60's and '70's, among them Galena and Riverside (alias Graham City), "now so completely buried in oblivion that even their sites cannot be learned by the enquirer." Chrysopolis, a mining camp on the east side of Owens River south of Aberdeen Station, flourished briefly in the '60's, but when the election of 1867 came, the place was found to be entirely dead and the voting precinct was abolished.

Kearsarge

Kearsarge, established in 1864 at the southern base of Kearsarge's highest crest, had developed into a considerable camp by the end of 1865. Violent storms raged about Kearsarge Peak in February 1867, and the cabins which nestled against it were almost wiped out, but in spite of this setback, the Kearsarge, Silver Sprout, Virginia, and other mines discovered on the slopes of the great mountain continued to be worked for a few years. In 1867, however, Kearsarge also was dropped from the election list.

Bell's Mill

Bell's Mill, the ruins of which may still be seen on Oak Creek near the road leading from the main highway to the Mount Whitney Trout Hatchery, was the oldest flour mill in Owens Valley and served a vast though sparsely settled territory.

Wright's Stage Station

Harry Wright's stage station on Taboose Creek, one mile north of Aberdeen and a mile west of the highway, was a popular gathering place in the '60's and '70's. Only a few locusts and black willow trees mark the site.

The Shepherd Ranch House

The Shepherd ranch house, said to be the first two-story frame dwelling erected in Owens Valley, was built in 1873 with materials which John Shepherd brought by horse-drawn wagons from San Pedro, two hundred and fifty miles away. The house stood one-half mile west of the Manzanar crossroads on the north side of the road. An earlier house, built in 1864 or 1865, of shakes made in the locality, and consisting now of one room, still stands. It was bought by Shepherd from a man named Coburn.

Lone Pine

The first cabin at Lone Pine, several miles from the mouth of Owens River, was built in the winter of 1861–1862, and a "fine settlement" was reported there two years later. Lone Pine is now an outfitting station for parties ascending Mount Whitney. On March 26, 1872, a severe earthquake rent Owens Valley, opening a great fault twelve miles long paralleling the present State Highway and running north from Lone Pine. Along this crevice, land dropped from four to twelve feet, and at Lone Pine twenty-six persons were killed. On the edge of the fault, one and one-half miles north of the present town, the victims of the disaster were buried, twenty-one of them in a single huge grave.

The White Mountain District

From the earliest coming of the white settlers to Inyo, more than one aspiring "city" was staked out in the White Mountains east of Bishop, only to be forgotten. Just over the summit of the range from Owens Valley, town plots were actually surveyed for two "would-be mining centers" which

figured in an attempted election fraud in the fall of 1861. The "Big Springs precinct," with its alleged polling place at what is now known as Deep Springs, was created less than two weeks before the election. In spite of the fact that virtually no population existed in the region, election returns showed a total of five hundred and twenty-one votes cast. Investigation finally revealed that the names had been copied from the passenger list of a steamer at San Francisco. White Mountain City, neatly laid out on Wyman Creek on the Deep Spring Slope, and its rival, Roachville on Cottonwood Creek, were still paper cities in 1864 and as such they remain today.

The Cerro Gordo Mines

About twenty miles north of east of the village of Olancha, on the ridge of the Inyo Mountains, are the famous Cerro Gordo mines, believed to have been discovered in 1865 by a Mexican named Pablo Flores, and two companions, who, later in the same year, located the Ygnacio, San Felipe, and San Francisco claims. The Cerro Gordo ("fat mountain") produced silver, lead, and zinc, and were without doubt the mines of greatest production in Inyo County. During the '70's the region had a population of several thousand. Some estimate that the mines have yielded to date approximately twenty-eight million dollars, although probably this is considerably exaggerated. Cerro Gordo mines are still producing.

Many of the mines now known in Inyo County were located within a few years after the rise of Cerro Gordo. The discovery of many of them now entirely forgotten was attended by the ever-optimistic belief that each new find was "the biggest mine in the world," "a perfect Comstock," or "a find that will surpass Cerro Gordo." Some few continue to yield a considerable harvest even today. Later discoveries include the Waucoba, discovery date unknown but worked as early as 1872 (the old road still in use for reaching properties in the vicinity); the Pigeon Springs, Log Springs, and Sylvania, 1873; Lucky Jim and Ubehebe, 1875; Beveridge District, 1877; and Poleta, 1881.

Old Panamint

"Tucked away in a remote section of a wild, unexplored range of mountains, separated from the more populous districts of the State by league upon league of hostile wilderness, Panamint was a law unto itself—a law of lead and steel. . . . . Here was a Gargantuan range of barren mountains, taking root in a shimmering desert, rising almost perpendicular for two miles, gashed and cleft with abysmal gorges, colored with bizarre tints. Death by thirst and starvation lurked in the dread valley to the east, that claimed the lives of many audacious pioneers who sought to cross it. A small edition of Death Valley bounded these weird mountains on the west, less deadly, perhaps, but holding a menace that few men cared to face. Small wonder, then, that Ishmaels of society found perfect safety within these mountains."

High on a rocky promontory southwest of the spot where Panamint later sprang up, these outlaw gangs as early as 1870 had their lookout, known as Robber's Roost. Any effort to track them to these fastnesses would have been futile and none was attempted.

In 1875, the Panamint Mining Company was organized by Senators William M. Stewart and John P. Jones. Other companies were formed, but most of them either died out or united in the Surprise Valley Mill and Mining Company. Panamint became one of the wildest camps in all the history of California, with a population of 1,500. Inability to recover the values in the ore was the chief cause of Panamint's ultimate failure. After 1877 it reverted to the wilderness.

Through Randsburg, where gold and silver are still mined, by the edge of Searles Lake with its vast deposits of potash and borax, up over the Slate Range, and down into the Panamint Valley, the road to Panamint leads past the picturesque ruins of Ballarat, a "wraith of the desert." From here the road leads on to Panamint, entering the gateway to the mighty chasm four miles from Ballarat.

Where the canyon widens to several hundred feet is the site of old Panamint, now wrecked by cloudbursts, floods, and vandals, deserted, and brooded over by the vast silence which holds undisputed sway. A tall brick chimney rises from an old smelter, and above it, on dizzy heights, hangs an aërial tram. A few skeleton houses of wood stand amid the scattered juniper and mesquite bushes, while the thick stone walls of former saloons and gambling houses cluster along the base of the cliffs. And over all hangs the deathless stillness, the awful grandeur, and the utter desolation of the wilderness.

Greenwater and Skidoo

Two later boom camps, Greenwater and Skidoo, had their start in the '80's. The former, discovered in 1884 on the eastern side of the Funeral Mountains and just over the summit from where the slope into Death Valley begins, has had few parallels in the "sudden rise, great outlays, small returns and quick decline" which have attended its brief periods of excitement. Gold, silver, and copper finds each had their day, the latter as late as 1906, when the population increased from seventy to over a thousand within a month. As many as twenty-five hundred claims were staked over a thirty-mile stretch of mountain range within four months' time, and from them the "copper kings" reaped a rich harvest. But, surrounded as they were by hundreds of miles of barren waste of mountain and desert, the inaccessibility of the place ultimately caused all claims to be abandoned. A letter written by a cheerful wag from somewhere in the locality voiced the situation in vivid terms when he said that he was employed on the "graveyard shift (miners' slang for the shift including midnight) in the Coffin Mine, Tombstone Mountains, Funeral Range, overlooking Death Valley."

Skidoo, located on the summit of the mountain on the western edge of Death Valley, was Greenwater's nearest neighbor. It had the luxury of pure mountain water piped many miles from the top of Telescope Peak. Although Skidoo never attained the fame which fell to Greenwater, it continued to produce gold and silver ores years after its sister mine was deserted. It was also above the average in the observance of law and order, and little crime occurred there. In time, however, its deposits were also apparently worked out and Skidoo was deserted.

SOURCES

[Credit is here given for source material, and permission to quote is hereby acknowledged]

CHALFANT, W. A. *The Story of Inyo.* Privately published, 1922
———. *Death Valley, The Facts.* Stanford University Press, Stanford University, California, 1930
JOHNSTON, PHILIP. "Days and Nights in Old Panamint," in *Touring Topics,* XX, No. 12 (December, 1928), 22–25, 50–51
MANLY, WILLIAM L. *Death Valley in 1849.* Privately printed, San Jose, 1894
ROSE, DAN. "The Legend of Winnedumah," in *Touring Topics,* XIX, No. 8 (August, 1927), 35, 39
STEWARD, JULIAN. "Words Writ on Stone," *Touring Topics,* XIX, No. 5 (May, 1927), 18–20, 36–38

LOS ANGELES COUNTY

Los ANGELES COUNTY (Los Angeles is Spanish for "the angels") was one of the original twenty-seven counties. Its boundaries have been changed many times. At one period the county covered an area of thirty-one thousand square miles. The city of Los Angeles has been the county seat from the beginning, and its archives contain many pre-state records in Spanish.

The Cabrillo Memorial

The Cabrillo Memorial in honor of Juan Rodríguez Cabrillo, discoverer of California, was placed in Exposition Park, Los Angeles, September 19, 1915, by the Cabrillo Chapter, D.A.R. Cabrillo first sighted the coast of Alta California at San Diego, September 28, 1542.

A replica of this tablet was also placed at Avalon, Catalina Island. Catalina had been named San Salvador by Cabrillo on October 7, 1542, but Sebastián Vizcaíno, who sighted it on November 20, 1603, St. Catherine's Day, named it Santa Catalina, the name which it still retains. Vizcaíno anchored there on November 27, 1603, en route northward in search of suitable ports for the protection of Spain's Manila galleon.

Portolá's Trail

In 1769, Gaspar de Portolá left San Diego to find a trail up the coast to the port of Monterey, where the second mission was to be established. Traveling through what are now San Diego and Orange counties, he entered Los Angeles County on July 30, making camp near the present site of Bassett on the San Gabriel River. The following day the party crossed the Lexington Wash, near El Monte, and made camp in an open space in the valley near a pass, south of the site where Misión San Gabriel was later established.

On August 2 the party reached a spot on the Los Angeles River occupied by the ancient Indian village of Yang-na, where the city of Los Angeles stands today. Camp was probably made near what is now Downey Avenue, at the juncture of the Los Angeles River and North Broadway. This site has been marked by a bronze tablet mounted on a granite boulder placed by the Daughters of the American Colonists. The hill, around which the Los Angeles River turns to the south at Elysian Park at that point where North Broadway crosses the bridge, is mentioned in the diary written by Father Crespi, the journalist of Portolá's expedition. The notation is dated Wednesday, August 2, 1769. This hill, the river, and the Arroyo Seco are the only landmarks in the present city that are described by Crespi.

Crossing the river on August 2, the Feast of Porciúncula, Crespi named it, in honor of the day, Río de Neustra Señora la Reina de los Angeles de Porciúncula. To this incident, the city of Los Angeles owes its name, Nuestra Señora la Reina de los Angeles de Porciúncula ("Our Lady, the Queen of the Angels of Porciúncula").

After leaving the Elysian Park camp site, Portolá and his party passed La Brea Pits and later camped near two springs where friendly Indians made them welcome. This spot was probably northwest of the Soldiers' Home at Sawtelle, and from there the explorers went as far as the beach west of Santa Monica.

On August 5 they entered apparently what is Sepúlveda Canyon and passed over the mountains into the San Fernando Valley, where camp was made near Encino. They camped on the seventh northwest of the site of Misión San Fernando, and on the eighth they traveled over San Fernando Pass to Newhall, pitching camp at an Indian village on the Santa Clara River near Castaic. From there, they proceeded northward by way of the Santa Clara Valley, so named by Portolá.

Misión San Gabriel Arcángel

On August 6, 1771, a party set out from San Diego, consisting of two friars, Pedro Benito Cambón and Angel Somera, and ten soldiers, to found a mission forty leagues to the north. On September 8, 1771, Misión San Gabriel Arcángel was founded.

The new mission, being on the direct overland route from Mexico to Monterey, was the first stopping-place and supply station after the desert and mountains had been crossed. This strategic location was protected with especial care by the padres, and the mission prospered, growing rich and populous. It survived the period of secularization and withstood the tide of American immigration, thus enabling it to continue its usefulness to the present time.

The original site of the mission was about five miles south of the present site, on a bluff overlooking the Río Hondo, then called the San Gabriel, about one-half mile north of the present Montebello oil district. Nothing remains of the old buildings save a few adobe tiles, which are still occasionally plowed up by the Japanese farmers, whose gay flower gardens cover the original site of California's fourth mission. A stone-mounted bronze marker has been placed on the highway near the old mission site by Walter P. Temple.

Floods from the Río Hondo eventually forced the Fathers to seek another location for their mission, and the old site was abandoned about five years after its founding. The new land chosen was higher and dryer but no less fertile, and luxuriant gardens and orchards soon flourished about the new buildings. An extensive vineyard, olive groves, and orchards of orange, fig, and pear trees covered several hundred acres of ground, and were protected from wild animals and unfriendly Indians by a high, thick cactus hedge. Remnants of this old hedge, as well as of the mission orchard, may still be seen in the fields and gardens about the town of San Gabriel. Other vineyards were planted from cuttings taken from the Mother Vineyard ("Viña Madre") at San Gabriel.

The first church building on the second mission site was dedicated in 1776. However, this was only temporary, and in 1796 the first permanent structure was erected. The present church was built after the earthquake of 1812, under the supervision of Padre José María Zalvidea. It was very solidly constructed of stone and cement as far up as the windows, and of brick above that. Its massive walls and flying buttresses, its outside stairway leading to choir and belfry, and the bell tower with its several arches quaintly built to correspond to the different sizes of the bells make it one of the most unique and harmonious of all the missions. In the yard just back of the church there are extensive ruins which include ancient soap vats, a smithy, and the kitchen, solid testimonials of that practical industrial education everywhere given the untaught natives by the zealous Franciscan Fathers.

About two miles north of Misión San Gabriel, near the site of the present Hotel Huntington, Claudio López, under supervision of Padre Zalvidea, sometime between 1810 and 1812, built the first water-operated grist mill in California. The old mill, "El Molino Viejo," was constructed of very solid masonry and still stands on the Old Mill Road in western San Marino. It has been marked by the Martin Severance Chapter, D.A.R. In 1903, H. E. Huntington bought the building and restored it to its former proportions, retaining the ancient picturesqueness of mission days. For a time after 1923 it was used as a real estate office, but it is now a private residence, a good deal altered in color and other details from its original appearance.

Anza's Route

Juan Bautista de Anza reached the Santa Ana River on March 20, 1774, crossing over it by an improvised bridge the following morning. On the twenty-first he camped in a wooded valley near San Antonio Creek a little west of the present town of Ontario. At sunset of the following day the party reached Misión San Gabriel (then located at its original site), where they were received with great rejoicing.

Anza remained at San Gabriel for nearly three weeks, awaiting necessary supplies for the journey to Monterey. On the morning of April 10 he proceeded to the Río de la Porciúncula (Los Angeles River), followed it into the San Fernando Valley, and there turned west around the point of the mountain west of Glendale. Camp was made that night near Triunfo, in what is now Ventura County.

Anza followed much the same route in 1775 with that little band of emigrants who settled San Francisco, the first settlers to come overland to California. The caravan reached the San Antonio camp site on January 2, and on the third they halted at the San Gabriel Wash, reaching Misión San Gabriel on the fourth. There they rested until February 21, when, refreshed by the welcome hospitality of the mission Fathers, they set out once more. Swinging westward to the Los Angeles River, they followed it northwest to a camp site west of Glendale. Crossing the southern edge of the San Fernando Valley on the twenty-second, the party entered the Simi Hills at Calabasas (an important stage station in the early American period, the site now being occupied by a modern garage), where they continued to the vicinity of Las Virgines Creek. There the tents were pitched for the night, and on the following day the pilgrims continued beyond the Santa Clara River, camping near El Río in Ventura County.

Where the Trails of Two Spanish Pathfinders Crossed

Early in 1772 Pedro Fages passed the site of Hughes Lake on his notable inland journey from San Diego to San Luis Obispo, while in pursuit of deserters from the Spanish army.

In April 1776 that intrepid friar Francisco Garcés crossed Fages' path at Hughes Lake. Leaving San Gabriel he "ascended San Fernando Valley, crossed over Newhall Grade to the vicinity of Castaic and swung northeast over the mountains by a trail east of the present 'Ridge Route.' Just before he entered the plains, on the edge of Antelope Valley, he mentioned a lake, evidently Hughes Lake, 'and near thereto a village where, according to the signs, Señor Capitan Faxes had been.'"

Such trailmakers as Pedro Fages and Fray Francisco Garcés "should be held in memory through monuments by the wayside," says Bolton, and he suggests that "a joint monument" be placed for both of these men at Hughes Lake. "On one face put 1772 and an arrow pointing west to commemorate Fages' discovery of Antelope Valley. On another face put 1776 and an arrow pointing north in honor of Garces' crossing of Antelope Valley to Cottonwood Creek, Tejón Canyon, and San Joaquin Valley."

Antelope Valley

Antelope Valley, geographically a part of the Mojave Desert, was the hunting paradise of Andrés Pico and other Californios, lured thither by the immense herds of antelopes which roamed through it and from which it derived its name. In the heart of this valley one of the state's most glorious poppy fields adds its flame to the gorgeous carpet of wild flowers which each spring spreads out across the valley floor at the foot of Portal Ridge from Palmdale to Del Sur.

Between Fairmont and Neenach there is a splendid forest of tree yuccas (*yucca arborescens*), with their spires of exquisite waxen lily bells. These strange denizens of the desert, more commonly known as Joshua trees, so impressed the first emigrants to California with their resemblance to the praying prophet that they bestowed his name upon them.

John C. Frémont, coming down from the north by way of Oak Creek Pass, on April 15, 1844, traversed Antelope Valley to the base of the Sierra Madre, following Fages' trail as far as Cajón Pass, where he connected with the Spanish Trail near Victorville. It is interesting to note that on this trip Frémont wrote in his diary of the "strange and singular" yucca forests and of the fields of California poppies, as well as of other shrubs and flowers in Antelope Valley.

St. Ann

Jedediah Strong Smith, the first American pathfinder to blaze an overland trail into California, camped at a spot designated by Harrison Rogers, Smith's diarist, as "St. Ann, an Indian farm house." This place, George W. Beattie assumes, was on the San Gabriel mission rancho known as San Antonio, and "at a *ciénega* formerly existing within the limits of what is now Claremont..... Emory's map in the Report of the U.S.–Mexico Boundary Commission shows nothing but San Antonio between Los Angeles and San Bernardino. Duflot de Mofras includes San Antonio among the seventeen ranchos for cattle and horses possessed by Mission San Gabriel. The Mexican grant of San José on which both Pomona and Claremont are situated was a combination of the San José and the San Antonio ranchos of Mission San Gabriel."

Ciénega

One mile south of the town of San Dimas, on Ciénega Street at its junction with Artesia, is the site of an ancient Indian camping place. In early mission days, the Indians who frequented this spot hauled logs from the neighboring San Bernardino Mountains for the building of the San Gabriel Mission. Their camp ground became the stopping-place for the Spaniards, who called it Ciénega ("a wet place"), because of the presence of natural springs which were perpetually seeping up out of the earth. Later, American pathfinders and emigrants stopped there en route from San Bernardino to San Gabriel and Los Angeles, and they called it Mud Springs.

Earlier than 1870 there was a stage station at the springs on the road from San Bernardino to Los Angeles. This station was probably located near the site of the pumping plant on the present Artesia Avenue. All that is left of the old San Bernardino road, however, is a short strip of the present highway less than one-half mile east of the springs, where Ciénega Avenue turns southeast at Grand Avenue for a short distance. Extensive orange groves now cover the path trod by the padres and American pioneers, while only a few willows and tules wave over the site of the Indians' ancient watering-place at Ciénega, the seeping springs of which have long since been pumped dry for irrigation purposes.

The Old Adobes of San Gabriel

Of the many quaint adobe homes which made the little town of San Gabriel unique and picturesque a number of years ago, only a handful remain.

In the corner of the quiet convent garden on Santa Anita Street, at the northwest extremity of the present mission grounds, is a little brown room, which, according to tradition,

was Father Serra's room. Today, the Sisters of Perpetual Adoration come there to meditate or to teach the little Mexican girls of the neighboring parochial school to sew.

Perhaps the oldest adobe in this region is the vine-clad home of Colonel Purcell, at 308 West Mission Boulevard. It is said to have been built as a home for the mission friars three years before the mission church was erected. Certainly, many indications of great age have been discovered, such as the old hand-planed doors and the original rafters blackened by the passing years. The present ceiling was originally the roof, while under three successive board floors the old tiles used for the original floor have been found. In the yard outside there are indications of other rooms having once extended beyond the present walls.

In the garden and orchard, too, are many famous old trees bearing testimony as to the age of the place. The first orange seedlings planted in California, four gnarled olive trees, two pecan trees of great size, a remarkable cocoanut palm, and a twisted lemon verbena tree are among the interesting specimens which doubtless formed a part of the old mission orchard. A bit of the cactus hedge which walled it in also remains.

It was from this hedge that the ranch received its name, Las Tunas ("the cactus"). The history of Las Tunas Ranch is still uncertain. In 1852 it was purchased by Judge Volney E. Howard from a Mr. Hildreth. It was owned earlier by Henry Dalton, when he was mission administrator. There is evidence, also, that Hugo Reid was once the owner. Reid, a Scotchman who married an Indian woman, is noted for his splendid account of the life and customs of California Indians, which has been much quoted by later writers. Present owners treasure the old house and keep its charming ancient aspect unmarred.

Just across an intervening field from the Purcell home, the ruins of one of the padres' adobes may be seen beside a bit of the tall cactus hedge.

La Casa Vieja de López, located at 330 North Santa Anita Avenue, is doubtless one of the former mission buildings, being of the type of adobe construction used during mission days. It has recently been redecorated, in keeping with its ancient quaintness, by Doña María López de Lowther, whose family has occupied the place for many years. A part of the house adjoining the López garden on the south is also of adobe, and likewise, was probably a part of one of the old mission buildings.

The "Grapevine adobe," one block west from the mission on the corner of Santa Anita Avenue and Mission Boulevard, has been altered many times and is now advertised as "Ramona's Birthplace," a title claimed by more than one southern California adobe. Many changes have taken place in the old house since it was built a century or more ago, and modern street developments have threatened its very existence. The shade of its mammoth grapevine, extending over a circumference of one hundred feet, has lured the passing generations to come in and enjoy its refreshing coolness, and modern tourists often loiter there on hot summer days.

The Vígare adobe, on South Ramona Street, is the home of Doña Luz Vigare, great-granddaughter of a soldier of the mission guard. Generously proportioned, with rather high walls, the ancient beams of the old house have been covered over by a modern roof above and a ceiling below. An old lean-to kitchen, or adobe *cocina,* in the rear, has disappeared, and the *corredor* is now a front porch.

On Twin Palms Drive stood an L-shaped adobe quaintly fashioned with a very low ceiling and narrow *corredor*. Originally, it had neither windows nor fireplace, but each of the several rooms had an outside door and there were evidences of a fire having been built in the middle of one of the rooms.

This quaint place stood on what was once Rancho Sales, granted to Francisco Sales in 1845. Local tradition says that it once sheltered Governor Alvarado. In 1866 it became the home of the Mulocks, who lived there many years. The hoary fig trees, standing in regular rows in the garden, were doubtless a part of the old mission orchard. The Sales adobe was much weakened by alterations and it has disappeared within the last decade.

At 725 West Carmelita Street is the May place, doubtless a very old adobe but thoroughly modernized. It has been identified as the residence built by John R. Evertsen in 1851. Evertsen took the first census of Los Angeles County, 1850, and his wife was among the first American woman residents of Los Angeles.

The Old and New Plazas of Los Angeles

The founding of Los Angeles has been generally placed on September 4, 1781, but this date has not yet been conclusively established by documentary evidence. The only certainty is that it was founded in 1781 some time between September 4 and the end of December. It was the second of the three pueblos to be established in Alta California. A carved wooden cross, placed on the north side of the present Plaza at the entrance to Olvera Street, commemorates the founding. An idealized bronze statue of Felipe de Neve has been erected in the Plaza in commemoration of the 150th anniversary of the founding of the city, by the California Parlor, No. 247, Native Daughters of the Golden West. It is mounted on a granite boulder rising from the center of a pool, which itself was dedicated to Felipe de Neve in 1872.

The northwest corner of the present Plaza was the southeast corner of the old Plaza, and the eastern boundary goes from this point along the east side of North Main Street to Bellevue, thence across to New High, south to Sunset, and thence back to the point of beginning.

Governor de Neve had hoped to obtain sturdy farmers for his pueblo, but, instead, only people of the lowest class came. Half-hearted, footsore, and homesick, they were not a promising beginning for a future great city. However, the settlement slowly progressed. In 1784 a Chapel was built on the Plaza, and in 1785 new settlers of good standing began to come in. By 1800, there were thirty small adobe homes clustered within the pueblo walls.

That year, floods from the Los Angeles River forced the colonists to abandon the settlement on its banks and to move to higher ground. The new Plaza, which remains today, was established, and about it the life of Los Angeles and of southern California centered during the Spanish and Mexican periods. The old Spanish aristocracy built their homes around it: the Del Valles, the Coronels and the Lugos, the Carrillos, the Avilas, and others. Gradually the village grew outward from the Plaza, but it remained the center of life even after the coming of the Americans.

The Church of Our Lady of the Angels

The Church of Nuestra Señora la Reina de los Angeles, begun in 1814 and dedicated in 1822, is the oldest building in Los Angeles. Services are still held in this church, where all Los Angeles once worshiped. It stands on the west side of the Plaza, hemmed in by ugly buildings, with a boot-black's stall crowded against it, but the historic bronze bells in the tower still chime the Angelus above the noise of the city streets, as they did above the sleepy pueblo over a century ago.

Across the way, the Plaza itself has been dressed up as a modern city square planted with trees and grass, but much of the leisurely, picturesque Mexican life may still be observed there. Swarthy-skinned men lounge on the benches, while dark-eyed girls sell their wares in the quaint shops of the Paseo, and frail little old ladies, with delicate faces half-hidden by heavy black shawls, kneel with pathetic devotion before the crucifixes in the dim old church.

The Avila Adobe

The oldest dwelling house in Los Angeles is the Avila adobe, which dates back to the year 1818. Originally twice as long as it is now and L-shaped, it still retains more of its ancient appearance than any other adobe in Los Angeles. With its high ceilings, its spacious rooms, its numerous windows, and its *corredor* facing the patio, it was a real mansion in its day, richly furnished and draped with imported satin damasks from France. However, that portion of the house which remains was the less important part in its heyday. Doña Encarnación Avila was its first mistress, and for 110 years it has been in possession of the Avila and Rimpau families. For the five days January 10–14, 1847, during the American occupation, it served as Commodore Robert F. Stockton's headquarters. It is now a local museum about which centers the Paseo de Los Angeles along Olvera Street, with its quaint Mexican shops arranged irregularly on either side or scattered picturesquely down the middle and sheltered from the summer sun by gay umbrellas. A diagonal band of brick in the paving of Olvera Street marks the line of the ancient *zanja* or "mother ditch" which furnished water to the pueblo. During La Fiesta de Los Angeles, September, 1931, the Los Angeles Chapters, D.A.R., united in placing a sundial in Olvera Street in honor of Kit Carson, the famous scout. It was unveiled by his great-granddaughter, Teresa Carson Beach.

The Lugo Adobe

The Lugo adobe, on the east side of the present Plaza on Los Angeles Street, was once one of the very few two-story houses in the pueblo. Today, it is the only two-story adobe house in the city of Los Angeles. It was probably built before 1840 by Vicente Lugo, who lived there until 1850, when he retired to Rancho San Antonio. In 1867 he donated the house on the Plaza to St. Vincent's College (now Loyola University), the first college in southern California.

The old building has undergone many changes through the years, and only a part of the upstairs balcony remains, while dormer windows and a high shingled roof have replaced the original flat roof covered with brea. A Chinese curio shop now occupies the rooms where gay caballeros and their ladies once tarried.

The Pico House

The Pico House was built by Governor Pío Pico in 1869 on the site of the old Carrillo adobe, and was the finest hotel in the Southwest at that time. It stands at 430 North Main, on the south side of the Plaza.

The Adobes of Sonora Town

None of the adobe homes which clustered about the old Plaza remain today. The original site was gradually built up with other adobes after the Plaza was moved to its present situation. This district, which came to be known as Sonora Town, still harbors a few of these historic dwellings.

One of them stands on the northeast corner of New High and Ord streets, and was probably built between 1850 and 1860. Its quaint Georgian door and window frames were brought by some "Boston ship" from far New England. But instead of the gleaming white plaster of other days, the little house annually takes on a fresh but gayly tinted coat, in which is reflected the pastoral beauty of its former environment: last year a mustard yellow, this a bright verbena pink, while another spring may see it clad in lupine blue.

La Casa Santa Cruz, at 728 North Broadway, was bought by Señora Ysabel Santa Cruz from Benito Valle in 1864. It is a typical Mexican town house without a *corredor* in front and with a secluded patio at the rear. It is distinguished by the classical design and Boston workmanship of its doorways. Doña Ysabel also purchased the adobe at 643 North Broadway from José Mascarel, it being one of the oldest houses on Buena Vista Street at that time.

Next door to this second Santa Cruz house, at 649 North Broadway, is the Gallardo adobe, tinted a gay ash-rose with bright green trimmings. Modern improvements have raised the street level three feet above the floors of these houses, which, with their already low roofs, are thus given a more distinctly quaint and diminutive appearance.

The Ybarra adobe, at 913 North Broadway, is concealed by a parking station next to the Baker Iron Works. Built over eighty years ago by Pedro Ybarra, it is still occupied by Señorita Arcadia Ybarra, who keeps store there and tends the remnant of the old garden with its two aged cypress trees.

Rancho San Rafael

One of the first grants made in Alta California was the great Rancho San Rafael granted to José María Verdugo on October 20, 1784, and on January 12, 1798, for services to the King of Spain. It was also one of the largest of all the grants, comprising 36,000 acres of fertile pasture land from the Arroyo Seco to Misión San Fernando. Many modern towns have since been established within what were once the confines of the old rancho, including Glendale, Eagle Rock, Verdugo City, and others.

Don José died in 1831, leaving the estate to his son Julio and his daughter Catalina, who, thirty years later, divided it between them. Julio took the southern portion, while his sister took the more rugged and mountainous section in the north.

Doña Catalina, who had been blind from girlhood, never married, and as she grew old she tired of living here and there with her nephews, and wished a home of her own. Accordingly, Teodoro, one of the nephews, built for her what is now the last Verdugo adobe, one of the five which were once erected by the Verdugos on Rancho San Rafael. This modest but charming little house, half-hidden under a giant rose vine and set in the midst of its historic garden of oleander, pomegranate, orange, and olive trees, is lovingly cared for and in excellent condition, being used as a clubhouse. It is located one mile from Glendale off Cañada Drive on Capistrano Avenue. Also still standing on Rancho San Rafael is the Tomas Sanchez adobe. It is now owned by the city of Glendale.

Rancho Los Nietos

Another early grant in California was made to Manuel Nieto, in 1784, just three years after the founding of the Pueblo de Los Angeles. It at first included all the land lying between the Santa Ana and San Gabriel rivers from the mountains to the sea, but this vast tract was later divided among Don Manuel's five heirs. The five ranchos thus created out of the original Rancho Los Nietos were Santa Gertrudes, Los Coyotes, Los Cerritos, Los Alamitos, and Las Bolsas, in Orange County. Old adobes still remain on Ranchos Santa Gertrudes, Los Cerritos, and Los Alamitos.

Rancho Los Alamitos

Don Abel Stearns, a native of Massachusetts and one of the first American settlers in California, helped to introduce energetic American business methods into the slow and unenterprising life of the sleepy pueblo of Los Angeles. He opened a general merchandise store, and, like everything he undertook, it prospered. Later, on the same site, he built what was known as Don Abel's Palacio. El Palacio ("the palace") was Don Abel's home, where Doña Arcadia reigned as social leader. In 1858 he built the Arcadia Block at the rear of El Palacio, fronting on Los Angeles Street. Around this, business centered for many years. The site of El Palacio is now occupied by the Baker Block on the southeast corner of Arcadia and Main streets. Dating back to about 1878, it is still a very fine building, retaining the substance of its early elegance, and itself a structure of historic interest.

Don Abel married Arcadia Bandini, the beautiful daughter of one of the haughtiest Spanish families in Alta California. By this marriage he came into possession, in 1840, of Rancho Los Alamitos, on a part of which the eastern section of the city of Long Beach now stands.

Stearns was very active in public affairs after California became a part of the United States, being a member of the first State Constitutional Convention, a city councilman, state assemblyman, and county supervisor.

In the early '70's, Don Abel's heirs sold the Rancho Los Alamitos to the Bixbys, and the Los Alamitos ranch house has remained the home of one branch of the Bixby family for over fifty years. Although it has undergone alterations and additions through the years, the old house has never lost its charm and richness and remains today an excellent example of the adobe ranch house. The spacious proportions and the simple plan of its older portion lead authorities on its history to believe that the original owners built it more than a century ago.

The Bixby ranch house, half-hidden among the fine old trees and shrubs planted by Mrs. Bixby many years ago, is located on Anaheim Road five and one-half miles east of Long Beach.

Los Cerritos

Los Cerritos, with its broad balcony stretching the full length of the front above and below, its great patio inclosed on three sides by the long wings of the house and on the fourth by a high adobe wall, is the largest and most magnificent extant adobe in southern California. A garden slopes down from the high wall of the patio to the river below, while beyond lies the valley and, in the distance, on a clear night can be seen the lights of Los Angeles. Its shaded *corredores*, its many and varied rooms, its hand-finished woodwork, and the evidences of rude fortification make a veritable castle of the old house. Recently remodeled and reoccupied, the present tile roof is misleading. The original roof was of *brea*, which was later replaced with redwood shakes.

This splendid adobe mansion was built in 1844 by Don Juan Temple, another energetic young Yankee and a native of Massachusetts, who, finding life in Alta California most agreeable and profitable, married Rafaela Cota, a descendant of Manuel Nieto. In 1840 he bought out the shares which the rest of the family held in Rancho Los Cerritos, and built his mansion about four miles north of the site of the present city of Long Beach, the main part of which stands within the confines of the old rancho. Adjoining the Virginia Country Club in the rear, Los Cerritos may be reached from Anaheim Road and San Antonio Drive.

Everything Juan Temple did was successful. Where the Federal Building now stands in Los Angeles, he opened "the first general store in the Pueblo, in front of which he planted pepper trees. . . . . The first market in the city was his; standing on the site of the new City Hall, and later becoming the Court House. The venerable landmark known as the Temple Block, lately demolished, was built by himself and brother. This was the first office building." The Temple Block was just north of the old Courthouse and was also replaced by the modern City Hall.

Rancho Santa Gertrudes

Antonio María Nieto received that part of Rancho Los Nietos designated as Rancho Santa Gertrudes, and in 1834 the Mexican government confirmed the title to his widow, Doña Josefa Cota. Later, the rancho was conveyed to Lemuel Carpenter, a Missourian, who, with his beautiful wife, María de los Angeles Domínguez de Carpenter, prospered and was happy under Mexican rule but who failed under the more difficult business methods of the Yankees. On November 14, 1859, the rancho was sold by the sheriff, John G. Downey and James P. McFarland being the fortunate bidders.

Santa Gertrudes was one of the first ranchos to be subdivided. Out of it grew the town of Downey, which was established in 1873; later, when the rich oil wells toward the eastern boundary were discovered, the town of Santa Fe Springs emerged, today "a city of derricks" and "black gold."

Governor Downey's home, on the Norwalk and Puente Mills Road about three miles north of Los Nietos, stood on the northernmost part of Rancho Santa Gertrudes. This section of the rancho had been occupied by Tomás Sánchez Colima since 1841. Don Tomás received a patent for the land from the United States government, and the estate was afterward designated as the Colima Tract of Rancho Santa Gertrudes. Tradition says that the old adobe was built at about the same time as the Mansión de Pío Pico and that it belonged to some of the Nieto grandchildren. Later , said to have been occupied by Governor Downey. Still later, it was bought by Colonel Swain, an Army officer. It was the Colonel's son who finally remodeled the old adobe, which stands today in the midst of its orchards, still retaining something of its original simple California design, with low roof, thick walls, and deep casements, but otherwise much altered.

Lemuel Carpenter and his wife, on July 14, 1855, conveyed a portion of Rancho Santa Gertrudes to José M. Ramírez. This section became known as the Ramírez Tract, and here the one-story adobe which still stands beneath a group of beautiful pepper trees was built. All about it, the great oil derricks of Santa Fe Springs loom above the fields once green with waving corn and wheat. Abandoned, yet well preserved, it is a striking witness of the change from pastoral California to the great industrial centers of today.

Rancho San Pedro and La Casa Domínguez

Only the shaded eastern *corredor* of the Domínguez adobe and the historic trees in its garden recall the atmosphere of gay rancho days long past. Arches and stucco have made the west front decidedly modern, and, where many guests once lingered to enjoy the charming hospitality of Manuel Domínguez and his lovely daughters, young novitiates now have their classrooms and dormitories.

The rich grazing lands of Rancho San Pedro covered 43,119 acres, extending from the coast at San Pedro up the estuary halfway to Los Angeles. It is one of the earliest grants in California and one of the few which have continued in the hands of descendants of the original grantee. First granted to Juan Domínguez before 1799 and again in 1822 to his heir, Sargento Cristobal Domínguez, Rancho San Pedro came into the charge of Manuel Domínguez in 1826. Don Manuel lived on the estate until his death in 1882, and his sturdy, vigorous control as well as his integrity and hospitality made the rancho famous.

In the chapel of Don Manuel's casa there is a stained-glass window bearing the inscription, "Domínguez, 1826." A few years ago, a descendant presented the old homestead as a memorial seminary to be used by the Claretian Order for the training of young priests. It stands on a low hillside to the west of Truck Boulevard, about ten miles from the town of San Pedro.

Battle of the Domínguez Rancho

Rancho San Pedro was the scene of a battle between the Californians and the Americans on October 9, 1846. After the citizens of Los Angeles had given their allegiance to the United States, Commodore Stockton (acting commander of American forces in California) and Colonel Frémont left the city early in September, 1846, leaving Captain Gillespie in charge with fifty men. But such a small garrison proved a mistake. A revolt occurred among the Californians of the city, and the garrison, forced to surrender on September 30, 1846, retreated to San Pedro. Meanwhile, Commodore Stockton had heard of the revolt and sent Captain Mervine with three hundred men from San Francisco.

Gillespie arrived in San Pedro on October 7, and was about to embark when Captain Mervine arrived on the "Savannah" with reinforcements. The two commanders then joined forces and marched toward Los Angeles. They were halted on the ninth at the Domínguez rancho, by a force of one hundred and twenty mounted Mexicans commanded by José Carrillo.

"Here began a pretty game in which the Californians used a four-pounder, known as 'The Cannon of the White Mule.' They would fire it until the Americans, charging, would almost capture it, when they would drag it away with their riatas. Mervine, worn out with charging, and discouraged by the loss of six killed and a number wounded, retired again to San Pedro."

The American dead were buried on a little island near the mouth of San Pedro Bay. Dead Man's Island, as it was christened by the burial party of the American forces, long remained a landmark in that vicinity, but it has recently been entirely removed by harbor construction work.

As a result of their victory on the Domínguez rancho, the revolt of the Californians became a temporary success, quickly spreading all over California, and the Americans were confronted with the semblance of a real war.

At this point in the game, that clever leader of the Californians, José Carrillo, played a trick on the Americans which temporarily kept them out of Los Angeles. Setting his troopefs to rounding up all the wild horses of the neighboring ranchos, he herded them back and forth across a gap in the hills where they kicked up such a dust that Stockton, watching from San Pedro harbor three miles away, took it to be a great body of mounted Californians. Knowing the daring and marvelous horsemanship of the latter, he weighed anchor and sailed for San Diego.

Misión San Fernando Rey de España

Misión San Fernando Rey de España was founded on September 8, 1797, by Padre Fermín Francisco de Lasuén. After the secularization of the missions, several thousand acres, including the lands of Misión San Fernando, were leased in December 1845 to Andrés Pico, brother of Governor Pío Pico. In order to obtain money to defend California against the Americans, the governor sold the mission lands and, among them, Rancho San Fernando was sold to Juan Celís for $14,000. When Don Juan's lease expired, in 1854, Andrés Pico bought a half-interest in the rancho from

Celís, making the old mission his country home and herding his cattle on its vast ranges. Rómolo Pico, the General's nephew, made a part of the old mission his permanent home, while Don Andrés came there in the interim of public life.

In 1851, Senator McClay and his partners, George K. and B. F. Porter of San Francisco, purchased the northern half of the rancho. The southern half had already been bought by Isaac Lankershim, and with these two purchases the era of small farms and the building up of the town of San Fernando began. The old mission days were ended forever.

The Mission Church is only a sad ruin today, but some attempts are being made to preserve it before it is altogether too late. At present the only building in a state of repair is the Convento, at the east end of which is the chapel room containing several ancient paintings and relics of mission days. The refectory, kitchens, and underground wine vats may still be seen, but only a few crumbling ruins remain of the workshops and living quarters. On the northwest side is the grass-grown graveyard where two thousand Indians lie buried.

In what is now a public park across the road from the refectory are the immense stone soap vats constructed by the Mission Fathers. There, also, are two beautiful fountains. One of them, a replica of a fountain in Cordova, Spain, was moved bodily 300 feet from its original location in the mission courtyard, in 1922. Both of them were a part of the old mission water system.

The Andrés Pico House

Andrés Pico did not sell the entire Rancho San Fernando but retained for his own use a section known as the Pico Reserve. There, in 1873, he and Rómolo Pico built a beautiful adobe mansion a quarter of a mile southwest of the old mission. The Pico house was charmingly conceived and well proportioned. Until recently it was fast falling to decay and complete ruin at the hands of vandals and the inroads of the elements. In 1929 Mr. and Mrs. M. R. Harrington (of the Southwest Museum) purchased it and restored it accurately and sympathetically and now occupy it as their home.

The López Adobe

Gerónimo López had erected an adobe home on Rancho San Fernando at an early period when the mission was the only other building for miles in any direction. It was located at some distance northwest from the mission in what is now the bed of the San Fernando Reservoir, the old house having been dynamited when the reservoir was built.

The town of San Fernando began to boom about 1873, and Don Gerónimo decided to move to town. This he did in 1878, and his son Valentino built the house which still stands at the corner of Pico and McClay streets. The López adobe has been restored somewhat elaborately, but it still retains its quaint and picturesque upper balcony and outside stairway, and an old-fashioned garden which keeps well the spirit of the past.

Across the street is a little high-roofed adobe much worn by time and weather, built in 1873. This was the first building in San Fernando and was used as the office of George K. and B. F. Porter, the first subdividers of the valley.

Rancho El Encino

Fray Juan Crespi, who, with Gaspar de Portolá and his band of explorers, first marched through the beautiful valley of San Fernando in 1769, named it El Valle de Santa Catalina de Bononia de los Encinos ("the Valley of Saint Catherine of Bononia of the Oaks"). The presence of these native trees also inspired the name for Rancho El Encino, which was provisionally granted to Alcalde Francisco Reyes of Los Angeles very early.

So desirable were the broad grazing lands of El Encino that, in 1797, Don Francisco was summarily dispossessed of them in order that they might be used by Misión San Fernando. The padres took over the adobe house which the Alcalde had built and Rancho El Encino became the first home of the mission. The rancho was later restored to private ownership, but, having been originally assigned before the mission grant was made, it was entirely surrounded by mission lands.

Rancho El Encino was granted in 1845 to the Indians, Ramón, Francisco, and Roque. In 1851 it was purchased by Don Vicente de la Osa, who erected there the long, low adobe house which still stands a few hundred yards north of the present Ventura Boulevard. The house shows evidences of having been extensively repaired and improved during the '70's or early '80's.

Rita de la Osa, on March 6, 1867, conveyed to James Thompson ("Don Santiago" of Rancho La Brea) all of her interest and that of Don Vicente in Rancho El Encino. Two years later it was purchased from Don Santiago by Eugene Garnier, a sturdy, hard-working French Basque, who made of El Encino a great sheep ranch.

The broad pool or reservoir, which may still be seen in front of the old Vicente adobe, was constructed by Garnier in 1867 or 1868, and just to the north of it he built the quaint two-story house of stone and adobe which still stands beneath magnificent eucalypti surrounded by modern highways.

In spite of his thrift and industry, Eugene Garnier was not able to hold Rancho El Encino. It passed successively to Gaston Oxarat, a Frenchman, in 1878; then to Juan Bernard; and, finally, in 1888, to Domingo Amestoy, to whose heirs the rancho still belongs. At one period the place was a stagecoach stop.

Rancho San Antonio

"No horses so fast, no cattle so fine, no land so fertile, no rancho more famous than the Rancho San Antonio. No family more prominent, no hospitality more welcome or as freely partaken, no hacienda more lovely, happy or prosperous than that of the Lugos."

Rancho San Antonio was granted to Antonio María Lugo in 1810, and for fifty years remained in the possession of the family. It consisted of 29,513 acres of land which adjoined the original pueblo grant of the city of Los Angeles on the southeast. Don Antonio and his bride lived at first in a tule house on the site of the present station of Bell. In 1819 he built an adobe dwelling in Los Angeles on what is now the east side of San Pedro Street between First and Second. Here his sons, José del Carmen, José María, and Vicente, were born.

Later, Don Vicente Lugo, sometimes called the "Beau Brummel of Los Angeles," because of his fine wardrobe, built a two-story house which was long the center of social life in the pueblo. In 1844 he erected a two-story casa in the country on what is now Baker Avenue opposite the Southern California Edison Company's power station and near the Union Plant of the Consolidated Steel Corporation. Don Antonio's original homestead no longer exists, but both of the adobes built by Vicente are in good condition today, the one on Baker Avenue being occupied by a son of Vicente Lugo.

Ultimately, the pressure of American business closed in upon the great Rancho San Antonio until, bit by bit, it was lost to its original owners. In 1927 a part of the land was sold to the Firestone Tire and Rubber Company for a factory site at seven thousand dollars an acre. On other portions of the old rancho, prosperous communities have grown up: Huntington Park, Vernon, Walnut Park, South Gate, and Lynwood.

The Blanco Adobe

Standing in the midst of an orange grove on the north side of Huntington Boulevard is an old house which, it is thought, was once the home of Michael White, alias Miguel Blanco, a sailor who came to California in 1829 and married one of the daughters of Doña Eulalia de Guillén. Blanco obtained a grant of land directly north of Misión San Gabriel and west of the Titus and Rose Ranch, where he lived from 1843, for many years.

One wing of the old Blanco house is a decrepit story-and-a-half adobe, while the later wing is a two-story frame structure of ship siding. Just west of it is "La Ramada," much remodeled and added to, once the adobe casa of the Titus Ranch.

Rancho Rincón de los Bueyes

Rancho Rincón de los Bueyes ("the corner of the oxen"), which lay northwest of Rancho La Brea, was granted to Bernardo Higuera and Camilo Lopez on December 7, 1821, a very early Mexican grant. It was confirmed by Governor Micheltorena on July 10, 1843, and in 1872 Bernardo's sons, Francisco and Secundino, were granted a patent to the land by the United States government. That same year, on November 8, 1872, Francisco Higuera conveyed all except one hundred acres of the rancho to Antonio José Rocha, the son of Antonio José I, owner of Rancho La Brea.

Since 1872, Rancho Rincón has been divided many times, but that portion on which the old home place stood has remained in possession of Antonio José Rocha's descendants until the present. La Casa de Rocha, "an ample, pleasant place, with a big square ground plan and a gringo stairway inside," erected by Don José II, has seen the broad ranges which surrounded it on all sides gradually change from country to city life. Oil derricks dot the fields which a few years ago pastured hundreds of cattle; Robertson, Wilshire, and Beverly boulevards cross and re-cross the once fertile farm lands; and the city has moved up to the very doors of the old adobe.

Abandoned for many years, La Casa de Rocha keeps its simple, pastoral charm in spite of worn plaster and loose shingles. A second story of redwood ship siding, of an early date, is superimposed on the outer adobe wall, while the roof projects from the bottom of this superstructure, forming a wide *corredor* all around the house. This quaint landmark, still showing evidences of its romantic past, is soon to become once more the home of a descendant of Antonio José Rocha.

Rancho Rincon de San Pascual

At the foot of Raymond Hill in South Pasadena is a charming adobe beautifully restored and now used as a private residence. It was the first house built on Rancho San Pascual, originally that part of the extensive lands of Misión San Gabriel granted first in 1835 to Juan Mariné, husband of Eulalia Pérez de Guíllen, reputedly the oldest white woman in California then. This land was a gift made as a recompense for Doña Eulalia's long services at the mission as nurse, overseer of spinning and tailoring, cashier, and accountant. Today, the cities of Pasadena, South Pasadena, and San Marino cover the former rancho lands.

The rancho was regranted provisionally to José Pérez, who died in 1840 before he had completed the building and stocked the rancho according to the requirements of Mexican law. The land subsequently reverted to public ownership, but was granted to Manuel Gárfias, son-in-law of Doña Encarnación Avila, in 1843.

The little casa at Raymond Hill has come to be known as the Flores Adobe because it was there that General José María Flores, provisional governor of California, took refuge in January, 1847, after the Battle of La Mesa, while Kearny and Stockton took final possession of Los Angeles and Frémont held the San Fernando Valley. General Flores and his staff held their last council within the old San Pascual rancho house on the night of January 9, while the California horsemen kept watch and guard on the hills outside. Knowing that surrender was inevitable, final plans were made, leaving Andrés Pico in command while Flores and Manuel Gárfias, both commissioned officers of the Mexican Army, fled to Mexico under cover of darkness on the night of January 11. On the thirteenth the Capitulation Treaty was signed by Frémont and Andrés Pico, and all hostilities came to an end.

A bronze tablet was placed at the Flores Adobe on September 14, 1919, by the Oneonta Park Chapter, D.A.R.

Rancho La Brea

Rancho La Brea, originally a part of the Los Angeles pueblo lands, was granted in 1828 to Antonio José Rocha and Nemicio Dominguez by Carrillo, of Los Angeles, alcalde and brother-in-law of Pío Pico. Later, the grant was confirmed by Governor Echeandía. The rancho derived its name from the La Brea Pits, where brea, or crude oil, oozed out of the ground in great quantities. Early conveyances of this land all provided that the owners were to allow the inhabitants of Los Angeles to take as much brea from the pits as they needed for the roofs of their adobe houses.

Antonio José Rocha was a Portuguese, who came to California in 1815 and became one of the most respected citizens of the pueblo of Los Angeles. He was a blacksmith by trade. He was naturalized in 1831, and in 1836 he was a resident of Santa Barbara. On November 16, 1860, José Gorge Rocha, a descendant of Antonio José Rocha, deeded Rancho La Brea to John Hancock. Parts of the estate were later conveyed to Cornelius Cole and to James Thompson, but much of it remained in the hands of the Hancocks until very recently. For years, the Hancocks extracted immense quantities of oil from the rancho lands, but the oil gradually decreased, until today the derricks of the once wealthy oil fields have been replaced by the beautiful homes of the Wilshire District, and the site of the old pits has become a public park surrounded by smooth green lawns, where only occasional pools of black asphaltum still ooze up out of the ground.

The adobe house which remains standing near the pits was very likely built by Antonio José Rocha in about 1830. It is one of several original adobes and has been restored with exceptional care by Earl C. Gilmore, oil magnate, who was born in the old house.

In the heavy crude oil, or asphaltum, which has oozed out of the ground at La Brea Pits from time immemorial, animals, once caught, were unable to free themselves. For this reason it became a mine of wealth to scientists in the early years of the twentieth century, and the specimens, numbering into thousands, of prehistoric animals which have been exhumed from these natural preserving beds and deposited in the Hancock Room of the Museum of History and Art at Exposition Park, Los Angeles, constitute one of the world's most remarkable exhibits of its kind. Bones and skeletons of many strange prehistoric animals may be seen there: the American mastodon, saber-toothed tiger, giant ground sloth, the Imperial elephant, ancient bison, and the prehistoric camel, bear, lion, and giant vulture. Scientists are still finding bones of great interest in the neighborhood.

Although Major Hancock began to uncover some of these bones during the '70's, their importance was not recognized until 1906 when Professor J. C. Merriam of the University of California investigated them. Professor Merriam and other scientists made extensive studies at the rancho. On June 23, 1913, G. Allan Hancock gave the exclusive right to excavate the beds to the city of Los Angeles, and the Hancock Room, in which the specimens were housed, was set aside as a memorial to his parents, Major Henry Hancock and Ida Hancock Ross.

Rancho Paso de Bartolo Viejo

At first a part of the lands belonging to Misión San Gabriel, Rancho Paso de Bartolo was granted to Juan Crispín Perez on June 12, 1835, the year of the secularization. Juan Perez had been alcalde auxiliar of Rancho Santa Gertrudes from 1831 to 1836, and was later mayordomo of the mission, during its declining years. Following the original grant, Paso de Bartolo Viejo was finally divided between four claimants, Juan Crispín Perez, Bernardino Guirado, Joaquina Sepúlveda, and Pío Pico. Don Pío Pico and Perez finally received their patent to 8,891 acres in 1881.

Pío Pico, last Mexican governor of California, did not inherit his wealth but obtained it by his own efforts. The vast ranchos of Las Flores and Santa Margarita were his, as well as several other extensive properties. He called the 8,000-acre rancho of Paso de Bartolo by the title "El Ranchito," both because of its diminutive size in comparison to his vaster estates and because of the affectionate regard in which he always held it. It was his favorite home place, and at the close of that pitiful struggle to compete with American business methods which finally reduced Don Pío Pico from the position of the wealthiest man in California to a pauper's grave, El Ranchito was his last possession in Los Angeles County.

It is uncertain just when La Mansión de Pío Pico was constructed, but it is unlikely that it was built in 1826, as is often asserted, and patent maps of the district, drawn in 1866, show the house of Juan Perez to have been a ruin at that time. If any portion of the old mansion was built as early as 1826, it is quite certain that it has long since disappeared.

Romance and tradition still cling about the old house, but the facts themselves are sufficiently interesting. Capacious and full of a quiet charm, the old house with its remaining seventeen rooms stands on the east bank of the San Gabriel River, which, in the flood of 1866, swept away a portion of the adobe.

In those pastoral days during which Don Pío, the governor, lived at El Ranchito, the mansion was the scene of lavish hospitality, and even in the years of his poverty, Pío Pico still entertained with gracious courtesy. In 1891 he "passed through the portals of El Ranchito for the last time," and went to Los Angeles to spend his final years in poverty. "All who came into social or business relations with the venerable ex-Governor spontaneously bear witness to the kindness of his heart, his uniform courtesy, and to his entire lack of malice or ill-will toward any human being."

Concerted efforts to preserve the Pico adobe were begun in 1906, when the Governor Pico Museum and Historical Society, of Whittier, and the Landmarks Club were formed. The house was leased from the city of Whittier and much-needed repairs were made. Later, it was turned over to the state and additional improvements made. A permanent appropriation for improvement and upkeep, however, is needed to preserve for all time this fine old historic landmark.

Rancho San José

In the beautiful valley of Pomona west of the Arroyo de San Antonio, the boundaries of the great Rancho San José were first laid out by Ygnacio Palomares and Ricardo Vejar, on May 19, the feast of San José. This was in the early '30's, and Father Zalvidea, who accompanied the party from Misión San Gabriel, performed the first Christian religious service ever held in the valley when he pronounced a benediction upon the two families about to establish their homes in the wilderness of San José. The ceremony was held under the venerable oak tree which still stands in the city of Pomona on South Kenoak Drive about two blocks from Ganesha Park. A bronze tablet commemorating this event was placed on the historic tree by the Pomona Chapter, D.A.R., in 1922.

Twenty years ago one of the old Palomares adobes still stood beneath the sheltering branches of this oak, but it has long since been torn down.

To Ygnacio Palomares was given the upper portion of Rancho San José, or San José de Arriba, while Ricardo Vejar received the lower half, known as San José de Abajo. Both the original adobe built by Don Ygnacio on the upper ranch and the one erected by Don Ricardo on the lower ranch are gone, but five other adobes remain, nestled among the orange groves of Pomona or in the foothills to the westward.

Some of the adobe bricks used in the older Palomares house were put into the construction of the later one, which Don Ygnacio built two hundred yards from it. This second Palomares adobe, built after 1837, still stands among the orange trees at 1569 North Park Avenue, Pomona. It is a place full of quaint charm and peace, where pleasant memories surge in upon one's thoughts. The low roof of the little house projects over a broad *corredor* extending down the full length of that side which faces the old-fashioned garden. A delightful outdoor stairway clambers up among the vines, which cling thickly about the eaves. Masses of oleanders, cape jasmine, peach, and orange trees diffuse their fragrance on the soft southern air and cast a grateful shade over the lilies and roses in the little garden.

About three hundred yards southwest of the second Palomares adobe, at 1475 North Park Avenue, stands the Alvarado house, once the home of Ygnacio Alvarado, the close friend of Palomares. In those days when neighbors lived many miles apart, the hospitality of Spanish settlers was proverbial, but in few other instances was it expressed in so friendly and intimate a manner as in the case of Ygnacio Palomares and Ygnacio Alvarado. At the urgent invitation of the former, Alvarado came to Rancho San José and built his home within a stone's throw of his friend, the only stipulation in the arrangement being that Alvarado should build a chapel in his house, an agreement which was accordingly fulfilled. The chapel room is still an interesting part of the old house. Both of these unique adobes are private houses today, cared for and prized by their owners.

Some time before 1850, Ygnacio Palomares built a third adobe at what is now the corner of Cucamonga Road and Orange Grove Avenue. Leaving the old homestead to his son, Francisco, Don Ygnacio made his home at the newer place on the road to Chino and San Bernardino. The little adobe became a popular stage station and tavern, where a huge fireplace welcomed many a wayfarer on chill nights. Until recently it stood among the fragrant orange groves, deserted and neglected, the *corredor* half-fallen, the walls crumbling with each winter rain, with only the untended rose vines and wisteria seeking to cover up the scars of the passing years. Now it has been restored.

On the Mountain Meadow Road above Puddingstone Dam, about two miles southeast of San Dimas, the Carrión adobe stands on the lower reaches of the hills amid a natural setting of sagebrush and schmizl, with an occasional tuna cactus and broad spreading sycamore breaking the clean and pleasant monotony of the pastoral landscape.

Here, on the old San Bernardino Road where the patient feet of the padres trod and the horses of the caballeros often passed, followed by the brave pioneers of the early American period, Saturnino Carrión built one of the most attractive of the smaller adobes in southern California. This portion of Rancho San José de Arriba was given to Saturnino Carrión by his uncle and aunt, Don Ygnacio and Doña Concepción López de Palomares, in 1843, when Saturnino was only a little boy of eleven, but it was not until 1863 (at the time of the great drought) that he finally came to San José to live.

Still in good condition, the old adobe had been used to house turkeys and chickens and as a place for the storing of grain. Neglected as it was in the midst of its exquisite pastoral setting, the little house was threatened with decay, but fortunately it has recently been restored to its former loveliness.

On Rancho San José de Abajo, Ricardo Vejar built two adobes, the first of which disappeared long ago. The second, which was built on another part of the rancho, was one of the best examples of the adobe mansion to be found in southern California. This splendid two-story ranch house, with the soft and graceful tracery of aged pepper trees flecking its mellow walls with ever changing shadows, occupies a commanding position on one of the lower slopes of the Rocky Hills, whose rugged form makes a picturesque background for the stately old house. One is glad to know that the charm of Casa Vejar has remained unmarred and that its broad *corredores*, its home-made doors, its many details of skillful and conscientious craftsmanship and fine taste, are being preserved and cared for. It is located on the Diamond Bar Ranch a few miles southwest of Pomona, far off on the right-hand side of the Valley Boulevard as one travels east.

The old house was built by Ricardo Vejar in 1850, and two years of splendid hospitality passed over its roof before the fortunes of the family changed, in 1852, when American business methods swept Vejar, along with other unhappy Mexican citizens, into poverty. But at Casa Vejar the pleasant customs, the graciousness of manners and natural hospitality, the courtesy and mirth of a picturesque and contented people, lingered, perhaps, longer than elsewhere.

Spadra

The first American settlement in Pomona Valley was at the village of Spadra, located on Rancho San José de Abajo a few miles from the Vejar adobe. Spadra, being on the Colorado Emigrant Road via Chino, was a stage station in the '50's and the '60's. Here, Rubottom, the first American settler in the valley, built a tavern in the '60's, and the place was named Spadra after his native home in Arkansas.

The old Spadra station has disappeared, but the site is still marked by two tall palms which stand on the north side of the Valley Boulevard about six hundred feet east of the present Spadra store. The stage road, which went diagonally across the present orange groves from a gap in the San José Hills, is not followed by the highway today, but has become obliterated.

About a mile east of Spadra on the south side of the highway is the two-story mansion built by Louis Phillips in the late '60's. It was the first brick house erected in Pomona Valley and is still in good condition, being occupied by a descendant of Phillips.

Ricardo Vejar, easy-going and trustful, had lost Rancho San José de Abajo to Tischler and Schlesinger by foreclosure in 1864. A year or two later, they sold it to Louis Phillips,

who proved to be an excellent manager, and in his hands and those of his descendants the great rancho prospered.

Rancho La Puente

"The arrival of the Bidwell-Bartleson company at Marsh's ranch ushered in . . . . the period of organized immigration to California. Almost contemporaneous with the coming of this party, some twenty-five immigrants, recruited partly in Missouri, and partly from American residents in New Mexico, reached Los Angeles by way of the Gila and Colorado. This company was known, from the names of its leaders, as the Workman-Rowland party; and while Bidwell and his companions, for the most part, settled along the coast north of Monterey, or in the Sacramento Valley, the immigrants who came from Santa Fe established themselves in the south. Here many of them, like Rowland and Workman, the leaders, and Benjamin D. Wilson, the [second] mayor of Los Angeles under American rule, acquired large grants of land, upon which they dwelt in entire harmony with the California authorities and became respected citizens of the province. Other parties were not slow to follow the lead of Bidwell and of Rowland."

The Workman-Rowland party arrived in Los Angeles on November 5, 1841, and almost immediately the two partners, William Workman and John Rowland, began to look for a permanent home. Both had lived in New Mexico for more than ten years and were married to New Mexican women and both had applied for Mexican citizenship in California. This entitled them to petition for grants of land, which they did in the spring of 1842 and received formally in 1845.

At first the two friends seem to have owned the great ranges of Rancho La Puente jointly, their herds mingling in the unfenced pastures and their adobe dwelling houses standing a quarter of a mile apart. Later, the land was formally divided, William Workman retaining the northern section of the rancho and John Rowland taking the southern half.

On a slight knoll overlooking the valley, with higher mountains rising in the background, the old Workman adobe still stands about a mile west of the town of Puente. Don Julian, as he was known to the Spanish, erected an adobe home similar in picturesqueness and baronial grandeur to that of Juan Temple at Los Cerritos. There he lived a quiet, industrious life, little concerned with the affairs of the world beyond the hills of his rancho.

But on September 7, 1845, a change was ushered in when Francisco P. F. Temple, younger brother of Juan Temple, became the son-in-law of William Workman. Francisco Temple, or "Templito," as the Californians called him, was greatly trusted by this proud and taciturn old Englishman whose daughter he had married. Young Templito, being ambitious and capable, brought many changes with him into the quiet pastoral life of the rancho.

After his brother's death, in 1866, Templito bought the famous Temple Block in Los Angeles, and there, between 1866 and 1870, he added the middle section, the last or northern part of which housed the bank which eventually wrecked the entire fortunes of both Templito and Julian Workman.

It was during this period that, enamored of the splendid new buildings of the Temple Block, Don Julian remodeled his simple adobe house according to the mode of the time. Much of the original U-shaped structure was torn down and replaced by additions more suitable to the fancy of the day. Although greatly altered and modernized, it retained a certain quaintness inherited from its old adobe days.

Marks of many interesting features at Rancho La Puente survive today on the remaining portion of the estate which immediately surrounded the Workman homestead. The Indian retainers of the place were allowed to keep their hereditary ranchería during Don Julian's time, and at a short distance from the ranch house the cluster of tule huts stood on the banks of San Jose Creek, the ancient course of which is still visible where it runs parallel with the hills to the southward. Just west of the village was the burial ground which treasured the dead of this simple, dark-skinned people.

On San Jose Creek, also, stood two grist mills erected by Workman and Rowland before 1850, and extensively patronized by farmers of the neighborhood in the '50's and the '60's. Some of the old millstones have been incorporated into the fountain in the patio of the modern adobe erected by Walter P. Temple just across the drive from the old homestead. Remembrance of the two mills is preserved, also, in the name of the modern highway which passes through the region, the Norwalk and Puente Mills Road.

One of the most interesting remnants of early days, however, is the tunnel, now blocked up, which started under the east wing of the rancho house and extended to the family cemetery several hundred feet to the westward. It is said that Don Julian used to send his servants on unknown errands down this underground passage-way, and tales of ghosts and witches arose among the simple-minded Indians who chanced to see these messengers emerge mysteriously from the ground. Tales of buried treasure came to be connected with this, as with many another rancho where no treasure has ever been found other than the treasures of fancy and romance.

In 1870, Francisco Temple built the third portion of the Temple Block and there, on November 23, 1871, he opened the Temple-Workman Bank. Templito was held in the highest regard by all who knew him, and his venture was backed by both his own and his father-in-law's fortunes. But the generous nature of the one and the simple trust of the other, when confronted by the financial panic which swept California after the failure of the California Bank in San Francisco in 1875, finally involved them in a net of mortgages and foreclosures. All the fortune that Don Julian and Francisco Temple together had builded was finally lost, in 1876. All, that is, except the seventy-five acres of the homestead reserve, which passed to Don Julian's grandchildren. This, too, was lost on a mortgage in the '90's, but in 1919 it was bought back again by Templito's youngest son, Walter P. Temple.

Rancho La Merced

Rancho La Merced occupied the western portion of the La Puente Grant, and Francisco P. F. Temple established a home there in 1849. The natives then, as now, called the place Misión Vieja because the first site of Misión San Gabriel had been established, in 1771, less than a mile from the spot where Francisco Temple later built his adobe home. In the same region, today, but across the river to the west, is Montebello, one of the richest oil fields in the world, and intersecting it is the San Gabriel Boulevard, which crosses the Rio Hondo bridge at this point.

The spot where the Temple adobe once stood is marked by a lonely palm tree, which lifts its green fronds beside a modern oil tank on the south side of the road. The splendid gardens and vineyards of former days have vanished and Temple's Corners is but a sad and ill-kempt settlement just across the river from the busy wells. Both the adobe and the later brick mansion erected by Templito were destroyed by fire several years ago. Francisco Temple died there on April 27, 1877, and the little home tract at Temple's Corners became the property of his widow, Doña Antonia Margarita. This portion of Rancho La Merced remained in the Temple

family until very recent years, thus escaping the grasp of "Lucky" Baldwin.

In the spring of 1912, Thomas Workman Temple, grandson of Francisco Temple, while gathering wild flowers on the hillside across the Rio Hondo from his home at Temple's Corners, discovered an outcropping of natural gas in a pool of water. This led his father, Walter P. Temple, to sell the old homestead and to purchase the 60-acre tract across the river where the oil had been discovered. Operations were begun there in April 1917 by the Standard Oil Company. Thus was the famous Montebello Oil Field established.

In this district there was an old adobe. It was built in 1869 by Jesús Andrade and Rafael Bayse and was used, first, as a store and, later, as a saloon. When Walter Temple took over the tract after the discovery of oil there, he remodeled "La Casita de Rafael Bayse," then much disfigured by the vicissitudes of the years, and made it his home. It stood lately surrounded by oil wells, with a new stucco finish covering the adobe walls without and nearly all new woodwork within. From the tract on which it stood, a wealthy oil company continues to extract a fortune in black gold. Such are the changes wrought by the passing years, both in the lives of men and in their dwelling places.

On Lincoln Boulevard, about two miles southwest of the home of Francisco Temple, Juan Matías Sánchez erected a fine adobe mansion on a pleasant hill above the Rio Hondo. Although elaborately remodeled within, the old Sánchez house still retains some of its original exterior lines and character. Juan Matías Sánchez had owned 2,200 acres of excellent land about Misión Vieja, as well as the Potrero Grande and the Potrero de Felipe Lugo. His friendship for William Workman and Francisco Temple, however, caused him to sacrifice all his possessions in a heroic effort to save the honor of his friends. His last years were spent in poverty, while rich oil wells about his adobe made later owners wealthy and preserved the old adobe house in its present lavishness.

First Discovery of Gold in California

The first discovery of gold in commercial quantities in California was made in 1842 by Don Francisco López at Placeritos Canyon. Later in the following year he found gold in San Feliciano Canyon. The story of the discovery is as follows.

Don Francisco, in March 1842, rode into the canyon with a servant boy, inspecting the stock and enjoying a day's outing. While resting in the shade of an oak tree, Don Francisco became engaged in gathering wild onions. He suddenly noticed some shining particles clinging to the roots of the plants. Plucking up more of the roots, he found more of the same kind of pebbles fastened on them. Later, in Los Angeles, he was assured that they were gold nuggets.

This discovery not only caused considerable excitement throughout the south but also brought numbers of prospectors from Sonora, Mexico. On November 22, 1842, Don Abel Stearns sent the first California gold from the mines at Placeritos to the United States Mint at Philadelphia. For many years thereafter he continued to send to Philadelphia gold dust and nuggets from this same region. Even at the present time, several small placers are being worked there, but lack of water prevents the operations from being extensive.

Placeritos Canyon is located about four miles east of Newhall in the San Fernando Hills, and about forty miles northwest of Los Angeles by way of the Newhall Tunnel. In the vicinity of the old placers on the west side of the canyon proper a boulder with a bronze plate was placed on March 9, 1930, by the Kiwanis Club and the Native Sons of the

Golden West to mark the site of the first discovery of gold in California.

Rancho Ciénega o Paso de la Tijera

There were many natural springs and marsh lands (*ciénegas*) below the hills at Rancho Ciénega, and two narrow valleys between the Baldwin Hills formed a pass, which, to the imaginative Spaniards, resembled a pair of opened scissors (*paso de la tijera*). Thus originated the double name of the great Rancho Ciénega o Paso de la Tijera, granted to Vicente Sánchez, alcalde of Los Angeles, in 1843.

Rancho Ciénega was a long day's journey into the country in those days and Don Vicente's official duties made it necessary that he live in Los Angeles. The vast ranges of his country estate were, therefore, used merely for the grazing of many cattle.

After Don Vicente's death, about 1850, his land holdings were partitioned among his heirs, and Tomás A. Sánchez, famous as sheriff of Los Angeles for nearly ten years, received Rancho Ciénega, while his sisters took the property on Nigger Alley in Los Angeles.

Don Tomás married María Sepúlveda, who received fifty acres as her portion of Rancho San Rafael after Fernando Sepúlveda's death. In 1875, Tomás Sánchez sold Rancho Ciénega and made his home on his wife's little estate, where a handsome adobe was built on the site of the original home. Near by was the famous Casa Verdugo Inn, at Glendale. However, no trace of the inn remains today except the aged trees of the garden.

E. J. ("Lucky") Baldwin finally became the owner of Rancho La Ciénega, and when the estate was settled after his death in 1909 this rancho was listed as one of the most valuable of all his extensive holdings. "Seemingly, no matter how fast this old rancho has been subdivided, the remaining unsubdivided part grows in value by leaps and bounds directly contrary to its diminishing size."

Although some of the adobes erected at La Ciénega in rancho days were in ruins when the Sunset Golf Corporation leased the estate from the Baldwin heirs, a short time ago, a number of them were still standing. Unusual restraint and appreciation were used in the restoration of these buildings, and the present clubhouse has been laid out along the lines of the original plans, as nearly as they could be ascertained. The smooth, green slopes which lie before the casa, where the herds of "Lucky" Baldwin and, before his time, those of Vicente and Tomás Sánchez once grazed, today form the broad links of a public golf course.

Rancho Aguaje de Centinela

Rancho Aguaje de Centinela was granted to Ignacio Machado in 1844. The very next year, Machado traded his new estate, which was good only for the grazing of cattle, to Bruno Abila for a small adobe house and vineyard in Los Angeles. Since the latter was considered of more value than the half-league of pasture land, Machado gave, in addition, two barrels of *aguardiente* (brandy) in exchange for the town house. Today, most of the pastures of La Centinela are covered by the thriving city of Inglewood, one of the prosperous suburbs of Los Angeles.

Rancho Centinela had a varied history. Bruno Abila finally lost it in 1857, at a sheriff's sale, when it was purchased by Hilliard P. Dorsey for about a dollar an acre. Two years later, his widow sold it for thirty-five cents an acre to Francis I. Carpenter. Meanwhile, Fernando, a Frenchman and the son-in-law of Bruno Abila, had refused to give up the land and it became the duty of Carpenter to dispossess him of it.

Joseph Lancaster Brent, a Southerner by birth, but a prominent citizen of Los Angeles for many years, and later brigadier general in the Confederate Army, next came into ownership of Rancho Centinela. He sold it in 1860, however, in order to join the Confederate Army, and his successors were Sir Robert Burnett and his wife from Crathes Castle, Scotland.

Land values in this region increased in the years following, and in 1885 the Baronet sold the rancho to Daniel Freeman, founder of Inglewood, for $140,000. During the land boom of 1886–1888, it became one of the most spectacular of the boom subdivisions, ultimately developing into the modern city of Inglewood.

The Centinela rancho house is one of the most beautifully preserved of the smaller adobes of Los Angeles County. Its simple lines, its vine-clad *corredores,* and the deeply recessed windows have remained unmarred by modern "improvements." The owners have cared for it well and no signs of deterioration mar its beauty. A portion of the rancho lands still surrounds the adobe and preserves a bit of the old-time pastoral setting even within sight and sound of the great city.

The Battle of San Gabriel

The Battle of San Gabriel occurred on January 8, 1847, ten miles south of Los Angeles at a place on the San Gabriel River near the present town of Montebello. There were quicksands at this point and a high bluff opposite the ford, making passage of the stream difficult. Here, the Californians, with five or six hundred men under command of General José Flores, held the bluff, while the Americans under Commodore Robert F. Stockton and General Stephen W. Kearny, with six hundred men, had the difficult task of fording the river with their heavy artillery under fire of the enemy. Within an hour and a half, however, the feat was successfully accomplished and the Californians were retiring toward Los Angeles.

La Mesa

On January 9 the two forces met again at La Mesa, the site of the present Union Stockyards in the great central manufacturing district of Los Angeles. A group of four granite boulders, set with bronze tablets, was placed on the spot September 9, 1926, by the Native Sons and the Native Daughters of the Golden West.

La Mesa was of slight importance in itself, merely confirming the course of events at San Gabriel. Like all the socalled "battles" of the American occupation, it amounted to little more than a skirmish. The Californians, realizing the hopelessness of resistance, soon withdrew to Rancho San Pascual, where their final decision to surrender was made. Camping that night on the outskirts of Los Angeles, Stockton and Kearny marched to the Plaza on the following day, the city having already surrendered. With this action, its control passed forever from the hands of Mexico.

Frémont's Headquarters

The site of Lieutenant Colonel John C. Frémont's headquarters in Los Angeles, in January 1847, was at the southeast corner of Aliso Street on Los Angeles Street. There he established himself in the Alexander Bell adobe, after Commodore Stockton had appointed him civil governor of the territory, January 19, an office which he held for fifty days. The old Bell adobe was torn down long ago, but the site has been marked with a bronze tablet placed by the Eschscholtzia Chapter, D.A.R.

Cahuenga

With Kearny and Stockton in control of Los Angeles and Frémont occupying the San Fernando Valley, the Californians offered no further resistance. Frémont at once sent Jesús Pico to persuade the Californians to lay down their arms, which they were eager to do. Ready to make peace if favorable terms were arranged, the two parties met on January 13, 1847, about a mile from the entrance to Cahuenga Pass, at the old Cahuenga adobe. Here, Andrés Pico and John C. Frémont signed the Cahuenga Capitulation Treaty, which ended all hostilities throughout California.

Liberal terms and common sense characterized this agreement by which the entire course of history on the Pacific slope was changed. Henceforth, Mexican laws and customs were to be replaced by those of Anglo-Saxon origin. Great cities were to arise where sleepy pueblos stood, a splendid school system was to take the place of the care-free illiteracy of the past, and the undreamed-of wealth of California's mines and forests and fertile soil was to be discovered and set free for all the world to enjoy.

The site of the old treaty adobe has been preserved by the city of Los Angeles as a memorial park called "Campo de Cahuenga." It is three miles northwest of Hollywood on Lankershim Boulevard. A bell in front of the Memorial Park marks this as having once been an outpost of Misión San Fernando. Not far from the site, below Lookout Mountain, at a place called Los Alamos, a skirmish took place on February 20–21, 1845, between a band of rebel Californians, under José Castro and Juan Bautista Alvarado, and Governor Micheltorena's Cholo army. The Governor was forced to retreat to Rancho Los Feliz, where he surrendered, and Pío Pico was made governor in his stead.

Fort Moore

When Stockton and Kearny entered Los Angeles on January 10, 1847, after the Battle of La Mesa, their troops, numbering 600 men in all, were stationed on old Fort Hill west of the Plaza. On January 11, Frémont and his men came down from Monterey, via Cahuenga Pass, and for several weeks a total of 1,000 American soldiers were quartered on the hill. At this time, work was begun by Lieutenant Emory on a temporary fort, but it was never completed. Later in the summer of 1847, Lieutenant Davidson erected another fort on this same spot overlooking the pueblo. It was dedicated on July 4 and was named Fort Moore, in honor of Captain B. D. Moore, who was killed in the Battle of San Pascual. Nothing of the old fort remains today, but the Eschscholtzia Chapter, D.A.R., placed a boulder and bronze tablet on the site on July 4, 1916, and a flagpole stands at the southeast corner of North Broadway and Fort Moore Place.

For 12 years a flag has been kept flying at this site, raised in the morning and lowered at night daily, through the efforts and at the expense of the Daughters of 1812. Each year on Flag Day, June 14, this group conducts a commemorative ceremony there.

San Pedro

On October 8, 1542, Cabrillo (according to Charles E. Chapman) discovered San Pedro Bay, calling it Bahía de los Fumos ("the Bay of Smokes"), because of the dense smoke arising from burning grass during the Indians' periodic rabbit hunts. However, the Bahía de los Fumos, or Fuegos, has also been identified as Santa Monica Bay.

Sixty years later, Vizcaíno entered the bay, and as early as 1793 San Pedro had become the port of entry for the pueblo of Los Angeles, three missions, and several ranchos. In that year, George Vancouver, the English navigator, on his second voyage to California, named the points at the two extremities of the bay Point Fermín and Point Lasuén, in honor of his friend, Father Fermín Francisco de Lasuén,

successor to Junípero Serra as Father Presidente of the missions. The names given to these two points by Vancouver are still retained on modern maps.

The first Yankee ship to anchor at San Pedro was the "Lelia Byrd" in 1805, with Captain Shaler in command, on his return voyage from the Hawaiian Islands to Boston. This was the beginning of a brisk trade between Californians and Yankee ships from New England. After this, Yankee brigs, as well as ships from other nations, called regularly at San Pedro, first in quest of otter skins and, later, of hides and tallow. This was contraband trade until 1821, when Mexico, having freed herself from Spain, made it legal. From then on, the port of San Pedro grew in importance.

The great Rancho Los Palos Verdes was given to the Sepúlveda family in 1827, and the grant was ratified to Don José Loreto and Juan Sepúlveda on June 3, 1846. It contained 31,629 acres, extending from the present city of Redondo Beach on the north to Wilmington on the south. At Sepúlveda's Landing, later called Timm's Point, a port grew up, which ultimately developed into San Pedro. The city of San Pedro is now a part of Los Angeles, and it is interesting to note that "almost the entire district was carved not out of Rancho San Pedro, as is generally understood, but out of Rancho Los Palos Verdes."

The first harbor improvement at San Pedro was begun in 1877, and in 1892 steps were taken for the creation of a deep-water port. Scarcely any of the old landmarks remain today. There is a lighthouse on Point Fermín, but Point Lasuén has been incorporated into the new harbor. Timm's Point, mentioned by Richard Dana in his *Two Years Before the Mast* as the place down which the cargoes of hides and tallow were lowered to Yankee trading ships below, is fast disappearing as harbor improvements go on. Halfway between Timm's Point and Point Fermín, on the Naval Reservation grounds, was the hide-drogher's warehouse, erected in the '20's, and long the only building at San Pedro.

El Monte

On the El Monte High School grounds, at the corner of Main and Esmeralda streets, is a bronze tablet set in a granite boulder and bearing the inscription:

This tablet commemorates the site of the oldest Protestant evangelical church in southern California, the erection of the first schoolhouse, and the end of the Santa Fe Trail. Erected by the California State Society, D.A.R., July 1930.

The "Old Spanish Trail" into California, followed by William Wolfskill in 1830–1831, has been proved "to be neither old nor strictly Spanish." The trail was first traversed by a New Mexican, Antonio Armijo, in 1829–1830, although his route, before reaching California, varied considerably from that followed by Wolfskill the following year. Later, it came to be known also as the Santa Fe Trail, and was used by many early American pioneers who came into California by the southern route. In the late '40's and early '50's, this trail, as far as Salt Lake, Utah, was also known as the Mormon Trail. For many of the covered-wagon emigrants, El Monte became the end of the trail, and here on the banks of the San Gabriel River, where natural springs made agriculture easy and where the land remained unappropriated by Spanish or Mexican grants, they made their homes. At first, El Monte was only a camping-place, but as early as 1849 Ira Thompson had established a stage station at a place called "Willow Grove," on what is now the site of the Valley Dairy and Ice Cream Factory. By 1852 the Dodson and Ryan families had arrived by ox team and Mr. Dodson had erected the first dwelling in El Monte, a crude adobe of "sticks and mud" on the spot where the Valley

Bakery now stands. Soon, however, other emigrants arrived, and permanent homes were established in this green oasis.

In 1852 the first schoolhouse was erected on a site now in the bed of the San Gabriel River, the flood of 1909 having washed out a new channel farther east. The building had previously been removed to what is now 312 Granada Street, where it still stands, remodeled and used as a private house.

John Prior, a Baptist minister, organized the first Protestant evangelical church in this old schoolhouse in 1853. The first church building, however, was not erected until the early '60's and stood on the site of the present Rialto Theater.

Additional Historic Spots

La Casa de Martín Ruiz is the last of several adobe homes built by Martín Ruiz and his sons in the Canyon del Buque (erroneously called "Bouquet Canyon" by General Beale and other early topographers). It was in this same region that Francisco, or "Chico," López, nephew of Francisco López, discoverer of gold in Placeritos Canyon, pastured his cattle during the '40's, and where Francisco Chari, one of his herdsmen, later took up land. Chari was a French sailor whom the Californians nicknamed "El Buque" (Spanish for "the ship"), because of his many tales of the sea and of the ships in which he had sailed. Ruiz sold the rancho to Battista Suraco, a Genoan, in 1874. Facing west, the surviving adobe stands a mile or two up the canyon at the point where it widens into a narrow valley. A modern road runs about ten feet from the back door. The low, rambling, one-story building has been long neglected and is rapidly crumbling under the inroads of the elements.

La Casa de Miguel Ortiz, a long, one-story adobe, stands at the left of the old stage road which came up from San Francisquito Canyon and passed by Lake Elizabeth (known to the Spaniards as La Laguna de Chico López) on its way north to Fort Tejón. It is said to have been the first building erected at the lake and was built by Miguel Ortiz, a muleteer, who was in the employ of General Beale. The land was given him by the General. This region also comprised one of the grazing lands of Chico López in the '40's, and was a haunt of Tiburcio Vásquez, the bandit, during the '70's.

The Andrada Stage Station, built of adobe, still stands where the old Fort Tejón Road entered San Francisquito Canyon, southward from Lake Elizabeth. It is only a short distance from the Ortiz adobe and is still occupied by the granddaughter of Pedro Andrada, who built it forty-five years ago.

Major Gordon's Stage Post is one old adobe still standing in San Francisquito Canyon.

La Casa del Rancho La Liebre may be seen just off the dirt road which runs between the Ridge Route and Elizabeth Lake where Antelope Valley meets "the Ridge." It stands on the floor of a small canyon known as the Cañon de las Osas (the "Canyon of the She-Bears"). This adobe, which was built by General Beale in the early '60's, was the headquarters for his Rancho La Liebre (the "Ranch of the Jack Rabbit"), a part of his vast estate composed of several ranchos and extending northward well into Kern County. It was strong and commodious, suggestive of the efficiency and thoroughness of its builder, and is said to have been his home for two or three years while he was surveyor-general. This region was another of the haunts of Tiburcio Vásquez.

Rancho Los Feliz was granted to María Ygnacio Verdugo in 1843, but was occupied by her as early as 1841. The rancho passed successively through the hands of Antonio Coronel, famous pioneer of Los Angeles; James Lick, an equally famous pioneer of San Francisco and the founder of Lick Observatory; and Colonel Griffith Jenkins Griffith,

who, in 1898, deeded 3,015 acres of the rancho to the city of Los Angeles. An old adobe still stands in this exquisitely wooded mountain park.

Frémont's Pass over the San Fernando Hills to Newhall was marked by the San Fernando Ebell Club on May 26, 1916. Frémont went this way in January, 1847, on his way from Santa Barbara to Los Angeles. The pass is directly east of the present Newhall Tunnel.

The famous Beale Cut, which was executed by General E. F. Beale and his men in 1859, went over the present Newhall Grade at Frémont's Pass. Modern engineers consider it a remarkable feat of pioneer engineering, being cut into the solid rock to a depth of from fifty to sixty feet.

The Banning mansion in Banning Park, Wilmington, was the home of General Phineas Banning, "Father of Los Angeles Transportation." He was famous, first, as an operator of stage lines, and later, as the builder of the first local railroads.

The first commercial orange grove in California was planted in 1857 by William Wolfskill on his ranch near the pueblo of Los Angeles. For a number of years it was the largest citrus grove in the United States and yielded very heavy crops. In 1885 the owners of the Wolfskill Ranch donated the ground where the Arcade depot now stands to the Southern Pacific Railroad. Soon after, the remainder of the famous orchard was sold and subdivided.

Drum Barracks, Wilmington, was the central supply station for the Union Army in southern California, during the years 1862–1868. In the early '70's Don Benito Wilson donated one of the buildings to the Southern Methodists to be used as a college. It was called Wilson College in honor of its donor and occupied the Officers' Quarters, which, still in excellent condition, stand at 1053 Cary Avenue. It is privately owned and was marked by the Native Daughters of the Golden West on October 2, 1927. The Guard House and the Powder Magazine, on the northwest corner of Lecouvreur Street, are the only other surviving buildings. Drum Barracks was named in honor of Richard C. Drum, a general of the Mexican War.

Robbers' Roost, or Vasquez Rocks, an interesting geologic formation on a high ridge between Soledad and Mint canyons about four miles northwest of the present town of Acton, was one of the hiding-places of Tiburcio Vásquez, the most feared of all the outlaws in southern California during the '60's and early '70's. He was captured in the Santa Monica foothills and executed in San Jose on March 19, 1875. The Vasquez Rocks form a part of the great San Andreas Fault, which extends from Cape Mendocino to the Colorado River in the vicinity of Yuma. The disaster of 1906 in San Francisco and other major earth shocks in California apparently follow this line. The Vasquez Rocks are composed of sandstone in which many kinds of rocks are embedded. One formation is in the shape of a huge elephant's head. Ancient Indian legends are associated with these rocks.

Lang Station, ten miles east of Saugus on the Southern Pacific Railroad, is the site of the driving of the "last spike" that united the two sections of the railroad approaching each other at this point, the one coming north from Los Angeles, and the other proceeding south from San Francisco through Tehachapi Pass. Here on September 6, 1876, with Governor Leland Stanford, Collis P. Huntington, and others officiating, the last spike was driven, thus ending the period of isolation which had hitherto kept Los Angeles a sleepy, unprogressive town, and ushered in the new era which was to make of her one of the great cities of the West.

The site of the Coronel ranch house, where Helen Hunt Jackson was hospitably entertained by Antonio Coronel, in the winter of 1881–1882, and where she conceived her novel *Ramona,* is at Seventh and Alameda streets, Los Angeles.

Rancho Santa Anita, comprising more than thirteen thousand acres, was granted to Hugo Reid in 1845. He later sold it to Henry Dalton, an Englishman, for twenty cents an acre. For a time it was in the hands of William Wolfskill, but in 1872 his son, Lewis Wolfskill, sold it to H. Newmark and Company for $85,000. In 1875 E. J. ("Lucky") Baldwin, San Francisco mining operator and "horseman *par excellence,*" purchased it for three times the amount paid by Newmark. Baldwin had made millions, it is said, in the Ophir Mines of Nevada. He soon moved from San Francisco into the large ranch house at Santa Anita. Here he continued to win fortunes not only by developing a world-famous breed of racing horses but also by acquiring and selling great landed estates.

"Lucky" Baldwin was a lover of trees as well as of horses. "He bordered every road within his rancho with trees and jealously fostered and guarded them. The towering lines of eucalyptus trees along Huntington Drive and Santa Anita Avenue through the Rancho Santa Anita" stood until recently as evidence of his planting.

The Baldwin estate, greatly diminished in size by frequent subdivision, lies to the east of Pasadena and south of the city of Sierra Madre.

La Casa de Adobe, part of the Southwest Museum, is a faithful and charming replica of an early California home, constructed of adobe and built around a patio planted exclusively with shrubs and plants grown in early California gardens. It is furnished with genuine antiques of the period, most of which were provided by Spanish and American pioneer families. It is open to the public Wednesday and Sunday afternoons.

The Pony Express Museum is "crowded with an amazingly complete assortment of 'relics' of California pioneer days, especially of the mining and Pony Express periods, and is redolent of the rough-and-ready spirit of those times. With peculiar sincerity it seems to reflect the spirit of freedom, bravado, the rough humor, the sturdiness, and at times the wildness that we associate with the Days of '49. And it is unquestionably a treasure house of mementos of quaint sort, from pantalettes and barber chairs to stage coaches and early fire engines." Privately owned by W. Parker Lyon, it is situated opposite the Santa Anita race track, and is open to the public every afternoon.

El Alisal (Spanish for "the Sycamore"), former home of Charles F. Lummis, the writer, has been the objective of more pilgrimages of famous people than any other home in southern California. "Don Carlos" Lummis wrote and lectured vividly on the Southwest, of which he was a life-long student. In 1893 he edited the *Land of Sunshine,* later the *Outwest Magazine.* He founded the Landmarks Club, which was largely responsible for the preservation of the old missions and the bettering of conditions among the mission Indians. He and others founded the Southwest Museum for the housing of the collections of the Society of the Archaeological Institute of America, which he also founded. He was Los Angeles city librarian from 1905 to 1911. At his death at El Alisal on November 26, 1928, this tribute was paid to him: "He was Southern California—he was the Great Southwest."

With his own hands, Mr. Lummis built his home around a giant sycamore in the vicinity of Sycamore Grove in northeastern Los Angeles. El Alisal now belongs to the California State Park System and is open to the public.

SOURCES

[Credit is here given for source material, and permission to quote is hereby acknowledged]

BELDERRAIN, FRANCISCA LOPEZ. "First to Gold in California," in *Touring Topics,* XXII, No. 11 (November, 1930), 32–34

BOLTON, HERBERT EUGENE. *Anza's California Expeditions.* 5 vols. University of California Press, Berkeley, 1930

———. *Fray Juan Crespi, Missionary Explorer on the Pacific Coast, 1769–1774.* University of California Press, Berkeley, California, 1927

———. "In the South San Joaquín Ahead of Garcés," in *California Historical Society Quarterly,* X, No. 3 (September, 1931), 211–219

———. "Spanish Exploration in the Southwest, 1542–1706," in *Original Narratives of Early American History,* XVII. Charles Scribner's Sons, New York, 1916

BRACKET, FRANK PARKHURST. *History of San José Rancho.* Historic Record Company, Los Angeles, 1920

CHAPIN, LON F. *Thirty Years in Pasadena, with an Historical Sketch of Previous Eras.* 2 vols. Southwest Publishing Company, Inc., 1924

CLELAND, ROBERT GLASS. *A History of California: The American Period.* The Macmillan Company, New York, 1922

CONNER, E. PALMER. *The Romance of the Ranchos.* Title Insurance and Trust Company, Los Angeles, California, 1930

DAKIN, SUSANNA BRYANT. "San Gabriel Days of Hugo Reid," in *Touring Topics,* XXIII (November, 1931), 24–26, 48

DENNIS, FREDERICK JAMES. "A Pioneer among Water Wheels," in *Touring Topics,* XXIV, No. 2 (February, 1932), 19, 36

ELDER, DAVID PAUL. *The Old Spanish Missions of California.* Paul Elder & Company, San Francisco, California, 1913

EMORY, WILLIAM H. *Notes of a Military Reconnaissance from Fort Leavenworth, Missouri, to San Diego, California,* 30th Congress, 1st Session, Senate Executive Document No. 7, Washington, D.C., 1848

ENGELHARDT, ZEPHYRIN. *The Missions and Missionaries of California.* 4 vols. First edition, The James H. Barry Company, San Francisco, California, 1913; second edition, Mission Santa Barbara, Santa Barbara, California, 1930

——— *San Fernando Rey, the Mission of the Valley.* Franciscan Herald Press, Chicago, Illinois, 1927

———. *San Gabriel Mission and the Beginnings of Los Angeles.* Mission San Gabriel, California, 1927

First of the Ranchos, the Story of Glendale. Security Trust and Savings Bank, Glendale Branch, Glendale, California, 1927

FRÉMONT, JOHN C. *The Exploring Expedition to the Rocky Mountains, Oregon and California.* Geo. H. Derby & Company, Buffalo, 1849

GUINN, JAMES MILLER. *History of the State of California and an Extended History of Its Southern Coast Counties.* Historic Record Company, Los Angeles, California, 1907

HANNA, PHIL TOWNSEND. "Our Lady in the Beginning," in *Touring Topics,* XXIII, No. 9 (September, 1931), 12–17, 40

HARRINGTON, M. R. "A House of Adobe," in *Touring Topics,* XXII, No. 11 (November, 1930), 50–51, 55

HILL, LAURANCE L. *La Reina Los Angeles in Three Centuries.* Security First National Bank, Los Angeles, 1929

———. *Six Collegiate Decades: The Growth of Higher Education in Southern California.* Security First National Bank, Los Angeles, 1929

KEAVENEY, THOMAS. "Early Days in Los Angeles County," in *Grizzly Bear Magazine,* February, March, April, 1917

NEVINS, ALLAN. *Frémont, the West's Greatest Adventurer.* 2 vols. Harper & Brothers, New York, 1928

NEWMARK, HARRIS. *Sixty Years in Southern California 1853–1913.* Edited by Maurice H. and Marco R. Newmark. The Knickerbocker Press, New York, 1916

PARKS, MARION. "In Pursuit of Vanished Days, Visits to the Extant Historic Adobe Houses of Los Angeles County," in *Annual Publications of the Historical Society of Southern California,* Vol. XIV, Parts I and II (1928–1929), pp. 7–64, 135–208

PRUDHOMME, CHARLES J. "Gold Discovery in California; Who Was the First Real Discoverer of Gold in the State?" in *Annual Publications, The Historical Society of Southern California,* Vol. XII, Part II (1922), pp. 18–25

———. "Early Days in Los Angeles," in *The Grizzly Bear,* November, 1918

———. "Old Plaza Site in Los Angeles," in *The Grizzly Bear,* January, 1919

PRUDHOMME, CHARLES J. "Reminiscences of Old Days," in *El Monte Gazette*, March 23, 1923

RIDER, FREMONT (ed.). *Rider's California; A Guide Book for Travelers*. The Macmillan Company, New York, 1925

ROBINSON, WILLIAM C. *Ranchos Become Cities*. San Pasqual Press, Pasadena, 1939

SMITH, SARAH BIXBY. *Adobe Days, Being the Truthful Narrative of the Events in the Life of a California Girl on a Sheep Ranch and in El Pueblo de Nuestra Señora de Los Angeles While It Was Yet a Small and Humble Town*. Enlarged edition, Jake Zeitlin, Los Angeles, 1931

STOCK, CHESTER. *Rancho La Brea, A Record of Pleistocene Life in California*. Los Angeles Museum, in History, Science, and Art Publication No. 1, 1930

WILLARD, CHARLES DWIGHT. *History of Los Angeles City*. Kingsley-Barnes & Neuner Company, Los Angeles, 1901

MONO COUNTY

MONO COUNTY (Mono is possibly a corruption of Monache, a name of obscure meaning but said to have been applied to the Indians of the region) was formed in 1861 of territory taken from Calaveras and Fresno counties. Its eastern boundaries were undertermined for several years, and in 1863 Aurora, the first county seat, was found to be in the state of Nevada. Bridgeport then became the seat of government and has since retained that position. From 1863 to 1870 the boundary lines of Mono County were changed four times, Alpine and Inyo counties each obtaining a portion of it in 1864 and 1870, respectively.

Rock Writings

"Among all the strange symbols inscribed on rock, up and down the globe, and especially in Southwestern America, by peoples since passed utterly out of human knowledge, it would be difficult to designate any more mysterious or fascinating than certain specimens now revealed just without our own doors."

Facing Chalfant Valley seventeen miles north of Bishop, there is a high volcanic tableland between the lofty Sierra on the west and the White Mountains on the east. Cut into the eastern escarpment of this rough ridge of rock are the remarkable petroglyphs known as the Chalfant Valley Group.

These major rock writings are so well hidden that their presence could easily lie unguessed for years, and yet they are just two miles from where the old Bishop-Benton Stage Route intersects Chidago Canyon, and about the same distance from the Mount Montgomery road running northward via Laws.

At this point, the Owens River cuts through a great plateau comprising the Piute Indian Reservation. No Indians live there today, but the region embraces most of this amazing group of ancient rock writings. A towering wall nearly half a mile in length and almost unscalable is covered with carvings (petroglyphs) and a very few paintings (pictographs). The petroglyphs are principally circular in form and are the largest, it is believed, of any of this type yet found in the United States. The most conspicuous of the group is about five and one-half feet in diameter, the other figures being carved in proportion and seemingly connected with the larger one, constituting a series more than twenty feet in length.

In the same vicinity there is a smaller group, also circular, but not drawn in proportion and arranged vertically. This entire group is three times as tall as a man and presents a weird appearance with its crisscrossings, wavy parallels, serpentine figures, and other odd shapes woven into an intricate maze, which only infinite patience and labor could have accomplished.

The "masterpiece" of this marvelous "inscriptive wall" is a mysterious carved projection which may be designated as the Sun Dial, but whether intended as sun dial, flood gauge, calendar, or simply as a landmark, no one can say. The excellence of the workmanship displayed is scarcely less cause for wonder. The projection is eight feet beyond the solid rock wall and surmountable only by a ladder. The edge is sharp and vertical, "extending eighteen feet from top to bottom and the blade cutting due east." This edge is notched its entire length with great accuracy, and, although worn by the elements, the horizontal lines on both sides are very clear, and many writings can be traced over the entire surface.

Chidago Canyon at this point is a labyrinth of carvings and paintings in many strange combinations. Many of the minor carvings represent a great variety of animal figures, bighorn sheep, bear, deer, a dragon fly, chicken or turkey tracks, lizards, snakes, and human figures, as well as geometrical designs.

Just above the Benton road, twenty miles from Bishop and six from the Chalfant Group, is one of the most unique exhibitions ever found. This is a great procession of tracks on the rock.

"For full a hundred yards along the crest, sometimes narrow, of a broken ridge .... the dramatic procession of footprints wends its precarious way, almost every individual headed northward. It conjures up a dark lost trail into another world. There are literally hundreds of tracks, prominent among others those of a giant .... the soft baby feet of a child of three years and those of a boy and girl of seven. .... Heavy marks of bears' paws, the lighter steps of dogs and coyotes, cats and indistinguishable beasts and wriggling serpents complete the queer march, which begins and ends abruptly where the stone has broken off and crumbled or been swept away by a deluge."

What pressing need caused the participants in this mysterious procession to tread so carefully along the rocky ledge? Were they fleeing from a flood or trying to evade their enemies? "The balls and toes of the feet sunk in more than half an inch and some of the heels deeper and they look perfect, but—those footprints are hand made! Close scrutiny brings to light plain proofs of chiseling. .'. . . It is marvelously done and the toil its execution entailed almost inconceivable."

But the reason for that gigantic undertaking remains a riddle. Whether the artist was attempting to tell of some unusual event or was depicting a great migration or deliverance from some impending calamity, no one can tell. Nor do the Indians of the region today have any knowledge of the meaning of these carvings. They seem to fear and evade the petroglyphs. Julian H. Steward of the Department of Anthropology, University of California, has studied the Indians of eastern California very closely, and believes that the rock pictures were made by the ancestors of living Indians, but what tribes were responsible for the work is unknown.

Indian Rock Houses

"The discovery of the principal groups of ancient stone houses or rather the foundations of brush or skin huts which they believe sheltered the rock message people" is accredited to Charles T. Forbes and Frank M. Parcher of Bishop, respectively secretary-treasurer and curator of the Eastern California Museum recently organized at Independence, Inyo County.

The largest of these rock villages "is a cluster of 150 on the barren plateau ten miles north of Chalk Bluff. Perched high above the Owens River and half a mile back upon the uninviting, wind-swept mesa is another group. At Fish Springs, near the toppled walls of the Stage Station, are forty; and two sets of former habitations comprise forty-five each, making up a total of several hundred. . . . .

"The individual 'residences' are sometimes a hundred yards apart while in other instances they adjoined and assumed communal form, thus effecting an economy in labor. They are invariably round, average twelve feet in diameter, and open on the east. Usually the natural bedrock is the floor but occasionally sand serves the purpose. The walls, in which no mortar was used, are two or three feet high where not tumbled by the elements. The prevalent tufa was employed, frequently big blocks. With the single exception of those at Fish Slough these simple dwellings are remote from water and from petroglyphs and pictographs. . . . . These were there on the arrival of the Piutes, who admit the use of the walled circles for winter camps years ago, but profess to know nothing about their origin."

It is interesting to note that these remains are similar to those of Coachella Valley, 350 miles away.

The Sonora Trail

It was in October of 1841 that the Bidwell-Bartleson party, much weakened and disheartened after many months of privation and hardship, finally ascended "the Sierras on the north side of the Walker, [and] came at last to a little stream which flowed westward instead of toward the east. This proved to be the headwaters of the Stanislaus, one of the largest tributaries of the San Joaquin. The course of the river through the mountains was too rough and precipitous to furnish an easy route of travel. The emigrants became entangled in gorges and cañons . . . . food became scarce . . . . and the emigrants, as they dragged themselves down the last weary ridge of the Sierras, were too worn with fatigue to realize that the San Joaquin Valley lay before them, and that California itself was at hand."

Nevertheless, the arrival of this, the first overland party of American settlers to enter California, "ushered in . . . . the period of organized immigration," and nine or ten years later the first faint trail left by the Bidwell-Bartleson party (varied somewhat, of course, from the original route) had become beaten down and widened into a fairly well-defined road, which led through the very heart of the Mother Lode country and was a close rival in popularity to the Truckee Road.

The Sonora Trail is thought, by some historians, to have been traversed for the first time by Jedediah Strong Smith, "Pathfinder of the Sierras." At any rate, it is certain that Smith was not only the first American to come overland to California but was also the first white man to cross the Sierra Nevada, blazing a trail through one of the high Sierran passes on his way back to the Great Salt Lake in 1827.

Harrison C. Dale, the best authority on this expedition, the record of which is very incomplete, "identifies 'Mount Joseph' with Mount Stanislaus, and tentatively fixes Smith's course along the Middle Fork of the Stanislaus River to the divide. . . . . From the eastern slope of the Sierras, Smith and his companions probably followed the course of Walker River to the vicinity of Walker Lake and then turned northeasterly toward the Great Salt Lake." Other students of Smith's travels have various explanations concerning "Mount Joseph," which is still a good deal of a mystery.

Sonora Pass lies high up in the Sierra at the converging point of what are now Mono, Alpine, and Tuolumne counties. It was one of the highest wagon roads over the Sierra Nevada.

Monoville

Monoville was the first settlement of any consequence east of the Sierra and south of Lake Tahoe, although some

mining had probably been carried on in the region from the time of Lieutenant Tredwell Moore's discovery in 1852. Continued reports that the Mormons from Nevada were washing out gold in Dogtown Creek near Mono Lake brought a number of prospectors into the region in 1857, and Dogtown quickly came into existence as a camp and trading center. After 1859 Dogtown was deserted for its more promising neighbor, Monoville, which soon boasted a population of seven hundred, made up mostly of arrivals from Tuolumne County who came in via the Sonora Pass.

Monoville was different from the majority of mining camps in that it "left no notable record of crime." Although the town soon disappeared, it is noteworthy as the starting-point from which the discoverers of other mining locations in the region set out. From it many an adventurer went forth in quest of the "lost cement mines," long the legendary "El Dorado" of the High Sierra. As late as 1864 Monoville ambitiously became a contestant for the position of county seat.

The once noted Sinnamon cut, a long, deep gash in the earth from which it is said that $90,000 in gold was washed out by a hydraulic process, is the chief landmark in the region today. By it one may locate the spot where "the once largest town of the western Great Basin lived its little day." Nothing else remains save "a forlorn, rickety windlass over a shaft sunk by a hopeful mining company."

"The Lost Cement Mines"

Three brothers, Germans (according to the accepted version of the story), on their way to California in the early '50's, finally reached the headwaters of the Owens River after many vicissitudes. While camping somewhere between Mammoth Peak and Mono Lake, one of the party found a vein of cement in which "lumps of gold were set like raisins in a pudding."

Approaching winter drove the three from the place, and only one of them survived the hardships of the journey over the Sierra. Half insane from his sufferings but still carrying some of the rich cement, he reached the settlements to the west. The story of his experiences started "the great hunt," which has persisted for more than a generation. Scarcely a summer passes by but that some prospector, even yet, sets up a camp in this region from which he starts out daily, with high hopes, seeking the long-lost treasure.

Here in the Mono country, in a region of magnificent mountain scenery in the northern section of the High Sierra, the summer vacationist with a bent for "treasure hunting" may find a place of superb enjoyment. In the neighborhood are the Minarets, Gem Lake, June Lake, Silver Lake, Shadow Creek, Rainbow Falls, Thousand Island Lake, Pond Lily Lake, and others, while, "like a tombstone in a scene of revelry," is Deadman Creek, its name reviving memories of the most gruesome incident connected with the heartless and persistent search for the "lost cement mines."

"The Bad Men from Bodie"

Bodie, "one-time metropolis of the Mono country" and one of the best preserved of the ghost towns of that region, was practically wiped out by fire on June 24, 1932. "Bodie's story dates back to the discovery of gold in that region during the '50's, but the old town's claim to fame [was] based upon the wild later years when Mono gold poured forth in millions and the 'bad men from Bodie' gained a nation-wide reputation."

Gold ore was first discovered in the Mono region in 1852 by members of Lieutenant T. Moore's detachment of the Second Infantry, U.S.A., while searching for recalcitrant Yosemite Valley Indians. This discovery led to some excitement and a party headed by Lee Vining subsequently found gold in the Leevining Canyon, through which the Tioga Road now passes.

Knowledge of the Mono diggings reached the Tuolumne mines in 1857, resulting in a rush to the new field and the blazing of the Mono Trail from Big Oak Flat in Tuolumne County through the present Yosemite National Park. In 1859, W. S. Body made a find, and the district was named "Bodie" after him.

The sensational Aurora discovery made in 1860 affected Bodie, which was twelve miles southwest, and the Mono Trail became a much-traveled highway for pack trains and miners until 1864, when the Sonora Pass wagon road was opened.

The Standard Mine, discovered in 1861, the first of Bodie's mines to become famous, is typical of the fluctuating fortunes of mining ventures. During Aurora's boom, the owners of the Standard sought to create interest in it, but with little success. In 1870, when the Aurora mines became exhausted, Bodie also suffered a relapse, and it was not until 1876 that its fortunes again cleared. The adjacent Bodie Mine, at first considered a "wild cat," also rose in value, to the great surprise of its promoters. Between the years 1876 and 1880 the town of Bodie was at the height of its success, although it continued to hold its interest until 1881. Its population during this period numbered between ten and twelve thousand people and it was known as one of the wildest mining camps in the West.

By 1883 all of the mines except the Bodie and the Standard closed down, and in 1887 these were consolidated. Of all the numerous ventures of the region, this was almost the only one which continued to uphold the fame of Bodie. Operations in recent years have been sporadic.

The neighboring camps at Mono Lake, Benton, Tioga, Lundy, and Manmouth City, in California, and Aurora and Virginia City in Nevada, have long since been deserted. Abandoned miners' cabins, picturesquely built of massive logs, still linger in Mono's mountain regions, telling tales of primitive life when "great populations" flourished there.

Little "Cities" of the High Sierra

East of Yosemite Valley high up in the mountains, many relics of early mining ventures may still be seen. One of the old camps in the region is Tioga (formerly Bennetville), a mile or two north of Tioga Pass. Here the Tioga Mine was located in 1860 as the Sheepherder Mine, and in 1874 William Brusky, a prospector, came upon the abandoned diggings and relocated the old claim under its original name.

The Tioga Mining District was organized in 1878 by the Great Sierra Mining Company, made up of men from Sonora, California. The old Sheepherder Mine was renamed the Tioga Mine and Bennetville was made the headquarters for the company. Great quantities of supplies and equipment were brought to the camp over very difficult roads from the east side of the mountain, at enormous expenditure of labor and money.

The pressing need for a good road over which to transport heavy machinery from the west side of the Sierra occasioned the expenditure of $64,000 for the construction of the Tioga Road, which was completed in 1883. However, the total expenditure of $300,000 brought about a financial collapse in 1884, and the project was abandoned before any of the ore had been milled.

The Mount Dana Summit Mine (in Tuolumne County), opened up in 1878, lay to the south of the Tioga Mine. Here a "picturesque village of long-deserted rock cabins clustered about a deep mine shaft" is all that remains of a once thriving camp. Hikers and fishermen from Yosemite Valley often come upon this interesting mountain village, which is located within Yosemite National Park.

Lundy, another deserted mining camp a few miles north of Tioga, was established in 1879. Prior to that date W. J. Lundy had a sawmill there from which he helped supply the enormous demand for lumber at Bodie. Approximately $3,000,000 were taken from the Lundy Mine and the place remained a substantial town for several years. Lundy has now been deserted for years and the building of a dam and the raising of Lundy Lake has partly submerged the townsite.

In Tuolumne County at the head of Bloody Canyon (in Mono Pass), sturdily built log cabins in various stages of decay remain as evidence of a one-time mining camp. Here in 1879 the Golden Crown silver mine was discovered by Fuller and Hayt (or Hoyt), and this as well as surrounding mines attracted considerable attention for a time. Today the entire district is deserted. It is located within the Yosemite National Park.

About twenty miles south of Tioga in the Lake District (a region of spectacular scenic grandeur), Mammoth and Pine City flourished for a very brief period. The first discoveries were made there in 1877 but the greatest activity took place in 1879–1880. A mill was erected and a trail constructed from Fresno Flats (fifty-four miles west), but the expected ore was not forthcoming. Like many other camps in which enormous capital was expended, little or nothing was produced in return, and in the winter of 1880–1881 the place was closed up. In this later day, mining men are again looking hopefully to the Mammoth region, relying on improved processes to recover the wealth in its immense ledges.

A Vacationist's Paradise

Mammoth lies in the heart of one of the most superb recreation centers in the Sierra. From it interesting short trips may be taken to the hot mineral water baths at Whitmore Tubs, the ice-cold or boiling springs of Casa Diablo, the Hot Creek Geyser, Mammoth Rock and the Old Mammoth Mill, the Devil Postpile (in Madera County), the Earthquake Fault, Minaret Pass, and Shohonk Pass. Pack trips may be taken to Shadow Lake, Thousand Island Lake, and the Upper San Joaquin, while good trails lead to splendid camping and fishing spots about the numerous lakes of the region.

The country is rough and mountainous, rising to the snowy summits of the Sierra crest on the west, while lower slopes to the east are covered with forests. Mount Dana and Mount Lyell with their splendid residual glaciers, that of the latter being the second largest in the Sierra, and Castle Peak are among the highest of the crests. In the center of the county lies Mono Lake. Having no perceptible outlet, its waters, which hold many chemical substances in solution, are apparently without life, giving rise to the appellation, the "Dead Sea of America."

Crossing a low divide several miles beyond Mammoth, the road drops down toward Mono Lake, passing the Mono Craters on the right. "A beautiful, slightly crescent-shaped range of twenty distinguishable volcanic cones," the Mono Craters have the appearance of sand dunes, the pleasing and delicate colors of their smooth pumice-stone slopes creating a picture of exceptional symmetry and beauty of form. The story of Mono's sleeping craters forms one of the fascinating chapters of California's geological epic.

Convict Lake

In the vicinity of Convict Lake and Convict Creek in southern Mono County a gun battle took place in September 1871 between some desperate fugitives from the prison at Carson City, Nevada, and a posse from Benton. On September 17, 1871, twenty-nine convicts—murderers, robbers, and horsethieves—had broken through the prison guard and made good their escape. Six of the number headed south. On their way they met William A. Poor, a mail carrier, whom they robbed and murdered.

When news of this outrage reached Aurora and Benton a posse of men from both towns was organized and sent in pursuit of the criminals. The men from Benton followed the convicts into southern Mono County, the fugitives having been sighted by Robert Morrison, a Benton merchant, who saw them making up a creek then known as Monte Diablo Creek but called henceforth Convict Creek.

On the following morning the posse followed up the canyon to the lake at its head. There, on September 24, they came upon three of the desperadoes and a gun fight ensued in which Robert Morrison (for whom Mount Morrison was afterward named) was killed. The convicts escaped toward Round Valley where they were later captured. They were taken to Bishop by irate citizens, where the two who had committed murder were hanged and the third was returned to the prison at Carson City.

SOURCES

[Credit is here given for source material, and permission to quote is hereby acknowledged]

CHALFANT, W. A. *Outposts of Civilization.* The Christopher Publishing House, Boston, 1928

CLELAND, ROBERT GLASS. *A History of California: The American Period.* The Macmillan Company, New York, 1922

FARQUHAR, FRANCIS P. *Place Names of the High Sierra.* Sierra Club, San Francisco, 1926

MILLER, H. C. "Mono's Slumbering Craters," in *Touring Topics,* XXII, No. 2, (February, 1930), 46–47, 56

RUSSELL, CARL P. "The Bodie That Was," in *Touring Topics,* XXI, No. 11, (November, 1929), 14–20

———. "Early Mining Excitements East of Yosemite," in *Sierra Club Bulletin,* XIII, No. 1 (February, 1928), 40–53

———. *One Hundred Years in Yosemite. The Romantic Story of Early Human Affairs in the Central Sierra Nevada.* Stanford University Press, Stanford University, 1932

VON BLON, JOHN L. "Rock Writings of the Owens Valley," in *Touring Topics,* XXI, No. 5, (May, 1929), 14–17, 51

WASSON, JOSEPH. *Complete Guide to the Mono County Mines.* San Francisco, 1879

ORANGE COUNTY

ORANGE COUNTY (named by the legislature after the orange groves which had made the district famous) was created in 1889 from a portion of Los Angeles County. Santa Ana has always been its county seat.

Portolá's Trail

A little company of soldiers and priests led by Gaspar de Portolá entered Orange County on July 22, 1769, on their way north to seek the port of Monterey. Passing through low, open mountain country, they made camp for the night near an Indian village in the Cristianitos Canyon north of San Onofre. Here two little Indian girls, who were very ill, were baptized by the Fathers, hence the name which the soldiers gave to the place and which it still bears, Los Cristianitos ("the little Christians").

On the following day the party "came to a very pleasant green valley, full of willows, alders, live oaks, and other trees not known to us. It has a large arroyo, which at the point where we crossed it carried a good stream of fresh and good water, which, after running a little way, formed in

pools in some large patches of tules. We halted there, calling it the valley of Santa María Magdalena."

Thus does Fray Juan Crespi describe the valley of San Juan Capistrano, in which Portolá and his men stopped, July 23, 1769. The spot chosen was a few miles above the site later selected for Mission San Juan Capistrano and is now called "Misión Vieja." At this same spot, Juan Bautista de Anza camped, January 8, 1776, on his way from Mission San Gabriel to San Diego to lend aid to Governor Rivera during the Indian uprising.

From this point, Portolá's trail lay along the foothills east of the Santa Ana Valley, and across La Puente Hills by La Habra Pass to Bassett in Los Angeles County. On July 24, camp was made on Alisos Creek, near the present site of the hamlet of El Toro, where there was a village of friendly Indians. Here the party rested for two days, moving on to the Santiago Hills east of Tustin on the twenty-sixth. Again they pitched camp "near a dry lagoon on a slope, from which [they] examined the spacious plain, the end of which [they] could not see."

On the following day, after crossing the plain, camp was again made near a stream, which to this day is called Santiago Creek. This camp site was near the hills northeast of the modern city of Orange, at a spot which the Spaniards considered suitable for the building of a city.

Skirting the mountains to the north, Portolá reached the Santa Ana River on July 28. There he pitched camp on the left bank opposite an Indian village. The site of this camp is near the village of Olive, east of Anaheim. Here Anza camped on January 7, 1776.

Crossing the swiftly flowing river with great difficulty on the twenty-ninth, the pilgrims traveled northwest until they reached "a very green little valley, which has a small pool of water, on whose bank there is a very large village of very friendly heathen." Camp was made on a hill near the pool and the place was called Santa Marta, now known as La Brea Canyon, north of Fullerton.

Descending the hill on July 30, the little band proceeded across the plain toward La Puente Hills in the west, which they crossed by way of La Habra Pass, coming into the spacious and fertile valley of the San Gabriel.

Misión San Juan Capistrano

Owing to the zeal of the Father Presidente, Junípero Serra, the founding of Misión San Juan Capistrano was first attempted as early as October 1775. Palóu writes:

"The little troop, composed of Fr. Lasuén, Lieutenant Ortega, a sergeant, and the necessary soldiers, left San Diego toward the end of October. On arriving at the site, an enramada or arbor was hastily erected, near which a large Cross was constructed, raised, blessed, and venerated by all. On an altar prepared in the arbor, Fr. Lasuén offered up the first holy Mass. This happened on October 30, 1775, the last day of the octave after the feast of San Juan Capistrano, the patron of the Mission. Formal possession was then taken of the lands and thus the beginning was made amid the rejoicings of numerous pagans who had flocked thither. They proved their satisfaction by helping to cut and bring down the timber for the chapel and the dwelling."

Hardly had the first founding of San Juan Capistrano taken place than news of the Indian uprising at San Diego forced the Fathers to give up the undertaking temporarily. It was not until October of the following year that they returned, this time in company with Father Serra himself. Palóu relates that the cross erected by Father Lasuén the year before was found to be still in place and that the two bells which had been left in hiding were disinterred, hung in position, and rung joyously to tell the Indians of the missionaries' return. An arbor was quickly erected and on November 1, 1776, the formal founding of Mission San Juan Capistrano took place.

The work of building and conversion was left in the care of Fathers Mugártegui and Amurrio, both good and efficient men, who constructed the first chapel and dwelling houses and who increased the prosperity of the mission both materially and spiritually.

It is believed by some that the first Mission Church was erected up the stream four or five miles from the present site at a place known as Misión Vieja, or La Vieja—(The Old Mission). Engelhardt, however, believes that the facts point to one location rather than to two, citing statements of Father Palóu regarding the finding of the cross and bells and the distance of the first church from the sea as evidence. "From the buildings," writes Palóu, "the ocean can be seen and the ships when they cruise there; for the beach is only about half a league [rather, a league, says Engelhardt] distant." There is no mention in any of the diaries of a change of location. Engelhardt states that Misión Vieja was only a rancho of the Mission.

San Juan Capistrano, which was planned by Father Gregorio, was nine years in the building, the first stone having been laid on March 2, 1797, and consecration taking place on September 8, 1806. On December 8, 1812, a great earthquake undid the work of years and destroyed the lives of forty neophytes. Little attempt was made to rebuild the fallen church until 1860, when some adobe restorations were made, only to be washed away by the first heavy rainstorms. In recent years, the Landmarks Club has restored the beautiful arched corridors of the patio; the old *pozolera* with its quaint chimney; and Serra's church, the long building which still stands on the east side of the patio, and said to be the oldest part of the mission, probably having been erected as early as 1777. Extensive restorations have also been carried on by the Catholic Church under the direction of Father St. John O'Sullivan.

San Juan Capistrano was perhaps the grandest and most beautiful of all the missions. Today the great stone church, which was its crowning glory, lies in magnificent ruins, the delight of artists and poets. Its exquisite carvings, done by a master mason over a period of nine years; the great dome, one of the original seven, within which was once the altar; the semi-Moorish architecture, set in its frame of green hills and purple mountains, and softened by the tenderness of the old garden still lingering within its walls, make of San Juan Capistrano an unforgettable picture, an Old World poem.

The quaint little town of San Juan Capistrano, which today clusters about the old mission's ruined towers, is described by J. Smeaton Chase as "the most interesting small town in California. The reason is that it has remained Californian in the old sense, that is to say, Spanish, Mexican, and Indian . . . . Capistrano's threescore or so of houses are mostly adobes, its stores are 'tiendas,' its meat-markets 'carnicerías,' its weekly function a 'baile,' its celebrations 'fiestas,' and the autumnal employment of its people 'pizcando nueces' in the walnut orchards."

Dana's Cove

On the coast seven and one-half miles south of Laguna, and just west of the village of Serra, a tiny cove lies tucked in behind San Juan Capistrano Point and San Juan Rock, just north of the outlet of San Juan Creek into the sea. There, in Spanish days, was the old embarcadero, which played an important part in the material life of Misión San Juan Capistrano.

This cove and the high cliff above it are described by Richard Henry Dana in *Two Years Before the Mast*, and

the cove was later named in his honor Dana's Cove. The name is also preserved in that of a modern seaside resort, Dana Point, to the north. It is easy to identify the perilous cliff from which the hides were thrown to the beach below, during the "Pilgrim's" first visit in the spring of 1835. Dana describes the loading thus:

"Down this height we pitched the hides, throwing them as far out into the air as we could; and as they were all large, stiff, and doubled, like the cover of a book, the wind took them, and they swayed and eddied about, plunging and rising in the air, like a kite when it has broken its string. As it was now low tide, there was no danger of their falling into the water; and, as fast as they came to ground, the men below picked them up, and, taking them on their heads, walked off with them to the boat. It was really a picturesque sight: the great height, the scaling of the hides, and the continual walking to and fro of the men, who looked like mites, on the beach. This was the romance of hide droghing!"

Anaheim

Anaheim, the pioneer town of Orange County and one of the oldest colony experiments in the state, was started in 1857 by some Germans, chiefly from San Francisco. The plan was to purchase a tract of land in common, lay it out in small farms, and work it under supervision of a general manager. There were fifty charter members, who purchased a part of the Rancho San Juan Cajón de Santa Ana from Don Pacífico Ontiveras, the original Mexican grantee.

This fertile tract of 1,165 acres on the north bank of the Santa Ana River, about twelve miles from the ocean, was divided into fifty twenty-acre lots for the little farms and vineyards, and fifty house lots which were to make up the nucleus of the village. Besides this, there was enough public land for school houses and public buildings. A fence made of 40,000 willow poles and 5½ miles long inclosed the entire colony. Most of the willows took root, forming a living wall about the place.

"'The colonists,' says one writer, 'were a curious mixture . . . . two or three carpenters, four blacksmiths, three watchmakers, a brewer, an engraver, a shoemaker, a poet, a miller, a bookbinder, two or three merchants, a hatter, and a musician.'

"But in spite of this medley of professions, the colony flourished almost from the beginning, and for many years its name was almost a synonym for prosperity and industry throughout the south."

For many years the town was known as the "Campo Alemán" to its Spanish neighbors, because of the continued predominance of the German element. And, in spite of the hardships and struggle of the early years while the little colony was getting established financially, only one of the fifty settlers moved away.

The Pioneer House, one of the first houses built in Anaheim Colony in 1857, has been moved from its original location and placed at the corner of West and Sycamore streets. It contains an interesting collection of relics of pioneer days, gathered in the neighborhood, and is owned and cared for by the Mother Colony Chapter, D.A.R.

Cerrito de Las Ranas

Red Hill, or Cerrito de Las Ranas ("the hill of the frogs"), as it was known to the Spaniards, was an ancient landmark followed by Indians, padres, Spanish rancheros, and early map-makers. It became the dividing line between the ranchos. Between it and the Santiago Hills near by ran the old trail. Later the stage route also followed this road, crossing the Santa Ana River near Olive and dividing north of the river, one route going through La Habra Valley via Don Pío Pico's rancho, and the other west of Anaheim, via

Rancho Coyote, north of Buena Park and the Santa Fe Springs. One of the old stage stations, a mile or two east of Red Hill, was a landmark for many years but has long since disappeared.

The old inn at Olive, which once served as a stage station, still functions as a hotel. A few hundred yards beyond Olive on the road to Irvine Park stand the stark and crumbling ruins of the old flour mill which served the early settlers for miles around. Irvine Park, Irvine Dam, and the village of Irvine (about 15 miles beyond Olive) were named for James Irvine, an early settler and large land-owner in the district.

Spanish Ranchos

Rancho Santiago de Santa Ana extended along the east bank of the Santa Ana River from the mountains to the sea. It was bounded on the east by a line extending from Red Hill to the sea and running parallel to the present Newport Boulevard one mile to the southeast. It is the only rancho in Orange County the history of which goes back to the Spanish period, some portion of it always having been in the hands of the Yorbas.

José Antonio Yorba first saw this land when he passed over it, in 1769, as a corporal in Portolá's company. Before 1800 the rancho was held jointly by Antonio Yorba and Juan Pablo Grijalva, who had accompanied Anza's expedition in 1776. In 1810 the rancho was formally granted to Don Antonio and his nephew, Pablo Peralta.

The site of the first adobe erected on Rancho Santiago is on Hoyt Hill, the most westerly point of the El Modena Hills, between El Modena and Villa Park. Another adobe site was west of Orange, and just south of Olive was an adobe designated on an old map as the "Casa de Yorba y tierras."

The most important ranch house in Orange County during the Mexican period was that of Don Bernardo Yorba, one of California's greatest landowners. It was situated on Rancho Cañon de Santa Ana on the north bank of the Santa Ana River, less than a mile above the present Yorba church. It was a large establishment dating from 1835. A spacious patio was entirely surrounded by adobe buildings, those on two sides being two stories high. The old house stood for years unoccupied and neglected. An effort to restore this fine landmark a few years ago failed, and the owner then razed its walls. Nothing is now left to show where once stood what was one of the greatest of the Mexican rancho houses in California.

On the Santa Ana River, well down toward the sea, an adobe mission *estación* belonging to Mission San Juan Capistrano was established before 1820. It is thought that the adobe still standing on the edge of the mesa between Fairview and Huntington may have been this old mission station. The Trabuco Adobe, the ruins of which still stand in Trabuco Canyon, was probably another mission station under the jurisdiction of Mission San Juan Capistrano.

Rancho San Joaquín, east of the Santa Ana River, was owned by José Sepúlveda, whose adobe home once stood at the head of Newport Bay. Later, he built another at what is now the southwest edge of Santa Ana, on Willets Street. This he called "Refugio," and there in the '50's and '60's he lived in true baronial style.

Rancho Los Alisos was owned by Juan Avila and his adobe long stood on the banks of Aliso Creek a few rods above the present state highway. As late as the early '80's, an old adobe called the "Policarpia," after a disciple of St. John, stood at the corner of Seventeenth and Bristol Streets.

On Flores Peak in Santiago Canyon, near the site of Madame Modjeska's country home, a group of bandits was captured in the winter of 1857 by a posse of men led by General Andrés Pico. Juan Flores, leader of the gang, escaped but was later captured by Andrés Pico.

The rugged canyon in the Forest of Arden was chosen by Madame Modjeska, the famous Russian tragédienne, as the home to which she retired after a long dramatic career which took her all over the world. The old home is located up the canyon about one-half mile beyond the boundary of the Cleveland National Forest, which is about where one leaves the .main road to enter the canyon. The house is entirely hidden by the forest and the estate is heavily fenced against intruders.

SOURCES

[Credit is here given for source material, and permission to quote is hereby acknowledged]

BOLTON, HERBERT EUGENE. *Fray Juan Crespi, Missionary Explorer on the Pacific Coast, 1769–1774.* University of California Press, Berkeley, 1927

CHASE, JOSEPH SMEATON. *California Coast Trails; A Horseback Ride from Mexico to Oregon.* Houghton Mifflin Company, Boston and New York, 1913

CLELAND, ROBERT GLASS. *History of California: The American Period.* The Macmillan Company, New York, 1922

DANA, RICHARD HENRY, JR. *Two Years Before the Mast; A Personal Narrative.* Harper and Brothers, New York, 1840; Houghton Mifflin Company, Boston, 1911

DAVIS, WILLIAM HEATH. *Seventy-five Years in California.* Edited by Douglas S. Watson. John Howell, San Francisco, 1929

DICKSON, LUCILE E. "The Founding and Early History of Anaheim, California," in *Annual Publications, Historical Society of Southern California,* II, Part 1 (1918)

ENGELHARDT, ZEPHYRIN. *San Juan Capistrano Mission.* The Standard Printing Company, Los Angeles, 1922

Orange County History Series, a collection of historical papers about Orange County. Orange County Historical Society, 1931–1932

SAUNDERS, CHARLES FRANCIS, and FATHER ST. JOHN O'SULLIVAN. *Capistrano Nights, Tales of a California Mission Town.* Robert M. McBride & Company, New York, 1930

STEPHENSON, TERRY E. *Caminos Viejos.* T. E. Williams, Santa Ana, California, 1930

RIVERSIDE COUNTY

RIVERSIDE COUNTY was created in 1893 from territory originally belonging to San Bernardino and San Diego counties.

Indian Rocks

Riverside County is exceptionally rich in Indian rock writings, those mysterious hieroglyphics of a people long since passed away, depicting stories of hunts, of fires, and of battles. Most of them are painted in that vivid red pigment, the secret of which has been lost. Others are in red and white, and a few in red, black, and white. Nearly always they command a spring or watering place, the camping grounds of the ancients, where these rock pictures were often left as sign boards. Modern Indian tribes do not know their origin or meaning and scientists have deciphered only a few of them. Some have traced in them the Montezuma frog and hold the theory that these people were of the same race as the Aztecs of Mexico.

There were once seven Indian villages in San Jacinto Valley: the village of Ivah; the Sobobas, near the Soboba Lithia Springs; the Jusispah, where the town of San Jacinto now is; the Ararah, in Webster's Canyon on the road to Idyll-wild; the Pahsitnah, the largest village in the valley, near Big Springs Ranch; the Corova, the most northern village, in Castle Canyon; and a fragment of the Serranos from San Bernardino, near Eden Hot Springs. It is believed that the tribes who lived here were among the most powerful of any in the Southwest, and this region about the great peaks of San Jacinto and Tahquitz remains today most replete in Indian lore. There are doubtless many carved (petroglyphs) and painted (pictographs) rocks in this region which still remain undiscovered.

One of the finest of the Riverside group of pictographs is found in Fern Valley, one of the canyons of San Jacinto. It is very accessible, being within a few moments' walk from the road by an easy trail. Painted in a vivid red on the face of a huge rock, the color is still apparently unfaded in spite of the ceaseless, age-long action of the elements upon it. The design, too, is unusual and constitutes a remarkable piece of workmanship, conforming, so scientists say, to rock paintings and designs found among the early Aztecs of Mexico. According to one theory, it tells the story of a great hunt: the long trail which the hunters follow, their encounter with a bear, the crossing of streams and the climbing of mountains, a skirmish with members of a hostile tribe, the trail again, the final kill, and the great feast.

There is a very striking petroglyph in Reinhart Canyon, three miles from the Perris-Hemet highway, carved into a massive granite boulder in the form of a huge swastika. The larger figure is made up of four smaller swastikas, the whole being about four feet in diameter. Many anthropologists from universities, from the Smithsonian institution and elsewhere, have studied it and theorized about it. Some believe that a little group of Orientals, blown in frail craft across the Pacific before the beginning of history, left their imprint upon the ancient tribes of the Southwest. There is only one other carved rock in the United States known to be like this one, and that is far in the Northwest.

"About a mile west of the Ramona Bowl, near Hemet, on the Big Springs Ranch, are many flat boulders covered with metate holes, and one object of very unusual interest. This is a table-like rock about five feet square and three feet high with slanting top surface covered with many small round depressions arranged in a series of circles, usually a central depression and five around the circumference of the circle. These depressions were not metates. They are too near together and are only deep enough to hold a small nut or stone. Whether this was for an ancient Indian game or was used as some sort of ballot box, or for something else, is unknown.

"Along the bench east and west of the Ramona Bowl, the site of the ancient village of Pahsitnah, are a number of flat granite rocks with their surface quite covered with metate grinding holes. One boulder on the property of Captain F. L. Hoffman, east of the Bowl, contains over forty metates."

There are many other Indian rocks, both pictographs and petroglyphs, scattered throughout Riverside County. In Dawson Canyon, about seven miles from Corona and a mile east of the Temescal Road, there is an interesting painted rock which has been marked by the Corona Women's Improvement Club. It is reached through the cattle gates which guard the property of the Temescal Water Company. This rock, found on the right of way of the Santa Fe Railroad, was threatened with destruction until saved by the History and Landmarks Committee of the club. Placed in a cement base by the Santa Fe Railway Company, it was unveiled on May 4, 1927, displaying a bronze tablet bearing the following legend:

In tribute to the earliest record of any people in this region, the Santa Fe Railroad has preserved this rock with ancient Indian pictographs, and the History and Landmarks Committee of the Corona Women's Improvement Club has placed this tablet, May 4, 1927.

Chief Lafio of Temecula says the painted rock was the work of the Temecula (Luiseño) Indians, perhaps telling of a three-day fiesta or a religious celebration. Again, it may have been a flood warning, as the San Jacinto River formerly flowed beside the rock and on it are four water signs similar to those found on other rocks listed in the report of the United States Bureau of Ethnography.

In this same vicinity there is also a carved rock, which is reached by the winding path leading past the old tanning vats, the aged olive trees, and the ruins of the second Serrano Adobe, to the clay pits. Here, in the midst of a great natural amphitheater, stands the rock, and near it is found the black basaltic stone which will cut the petroglyphs.

Near Norco there is an interesting community metate, a great flat boulder polished smooth by long usage, with its five holes ground deep by the pounding of meal. It lies near a spring overspread by a group of cottonwoods, undoubtedly an ancient Indian camping ground. To reach it, one goes north from Corona about two miles on Hamner Avenue, and, turning to the right, follows the road which winds along the foot of the hills to the spring and the cottonwoods.

In Mocking Bird Canyon, between Riverside and Perris, there are two groups of painted rocks near the Mockingbird Springs. One group is in the form of a cave into which one must worm one's way. Here the five basic colors used in the Indian sign language, red, blue, green, yellow, and black, have been used in the designs which cover the under side of the roof. This is probably the only instance in Riverside County where all five colors have been employed. Just east of this unusual group is another one consisting of several huge boulders painted in various simple designs in red. A sign beside the road leading to Perris indicates this spot.

In the hills about Perris many Indian relics and painted rocks have been found. Some of the best of these are located on the old Penny Ranch, two miles north of Perris, where there is also an ancient Indian council cave. Others are found on the Sill Ranch, three miles south of Perris, and on the Roberts Ranch, between Perris and Winchester. There are still others on the inland boulevard three miles south of Temecula; Rabbit Point, or Travertine Rock, at the Imperial-Riverside county line south of Oasis in the eastern end of the county; and in the mountains to the north of Lake Elsinore.

Just off the Nuevo Road a few miles east of Perris is the old red brick building at Bernasconi Hot Springs, the site of three ancient Indian battles. Back of the building are many metate holes, where corn was ground by the squaws of ancient tribesmen.

About ten miles southwest of Coachella, on the south slope of the Coachella Valley, once populated only by the Cahuilla Indians, is a remarkable group of "circular depressions among a maze of boulders just below the ancient shoreline," thought by some archaeologists to be ancient Indian fish traps. They are made in the form of circular stone walls with an opening on the ocean side so that, as the water receded with the outgoing tides, fish could be caught in the stone traps. Others say that they were foundations for ancient houses. At least, they were made by human hands a long time ago. All along the southern side of the valley the ancient shore line is plainly visible, and it has been proposed that this phenomenon be marked at the junction of the state highway and Narbonne Road, near Thermal. This ancient beach line extends down through Imperial Valley into northern Mexico.

The ancient village of Ivah once thrived in the region of the present town of San Jacinto, near Massacre Canyon, on the Relief Hot Springs Road. Many years ago a battle was fought there over a crop of chia, a grain which grew wild on nearly all of the mesa lands. The story goes that a severe drought in southern California caused the total failure of the chia crop in Temecula Valley. Now, the Temeculas, who were a tribe distinctly separate from the seven tribes at San Jacinto, and more warlike, came in search of grain. Proceeding to gather the crop belonging to the village of Ivah, a fierce battle soon raged. The Ivahs fought valiantly, but being outnumbered they were forced to flee into the narrow ravine now known as Massacre Canyon. There, with their backs against a perpendicular wall, they fought to their death. Long afterward Massacre Canyon received its name from the white settlers who heard this story from old resident Indians.

Palm Springs, now the foremost desert resort in the United States, was once the exclusive domain of the Cahuilla Indians. Two miles to the south of Palm Springs in the Palm, Murray, and Andreas canyons are magnificent groves of the native date palms, one of the grandest spectacles in all the Southwest. Here, too, in certain spring seasons after heavy rains, may be witnessed the miracle of vast wild flower gardens springing as if by magic from the dry sands of the desert.

The Pechanga Burial Ground

About four miles southeast of Temecula lies the Pechanga burial ground where, it is supposed, Alessandro, hero of Helen Hunt Jackson's *Ramona*, buried his father after the massacre at Temecula. According to the story the two hundred Indians who had been driven "from their poor homes at Temecula staggered with their dead to this little sanctuary in the hollow of the hills. Later, creeping back through the river sands to Temecula at night time, many removed their dead from the old Temecula graveyard to the security of Pechanga, which to the present day has remained undespoiled by the 'gringos.'

"The cemetery is quaint—the graves typical of the childlike people who hold them sacred. Broken bits of pottery and household utensils are placed on the graves, whether in decoration or with the thought of possible need by those buried there, is debatable. Small metates, bits of colored glass, parts of lamps, children's toys—in pitiful array, pull at the heart strings of the most callous wayfarer, who, hat in hand, steps reverently while within the sacred plot."

San Carlos Pass and Anza's Trail

San Carlos Pass, the first inland gateway to the coast of California, was discovered by Captain Juan Bautista de Anza in 1774 on the first continuous overland journey into the state. The trail and the pass have been located by Professor Herbert E. Bolton, University of California, and in 1924 the Native Sons of the Golden West marked it with a tablet bearing the following inscription:

On March 16, 1774, Juan Bautista de Anza, Indian fighter, explorer and colonizer, led through this Pass (named by him, San Carlos) the first white explorers to cross the mountains into California. The party travelled from Tubac, Arizona, to Monterey, California. On December 27, 1775, on a second expedition into California, Anza led through the Pass the party of Spaniards from Sonora who became the founders of San Francisco.

The pass was at Fred Clark's horse corral near the southern boundary of Riverside County, twenty miles west of the junction of Riverside, Imperial, and San Diego counties. Camp on the previous night, March 15, was on a flat in Nance Canyon, two hundred yards below the Royal Pass of San Carlos. Anza entered the San Jacinto Mountains from the desert via San Felipe Creek and the Borego Valley in San Diego County, and from there passed into Riverside County through Coyote Canyon.

On the 16th the travellers marched through Cahuilla Valley to Laguna Príncipe, now known as Dry Lake and located on the Contreras Ranch. Another short march on the 17th took them as far as San Patricio, at the head of Bautista Canyon. Following this canyon, the expedition descended the mountain to Río de San Joseph, now the San Jacinto River. This was on the 18th, and camp was pitched in a leafy cottonwood grove about three miles above the site of San Jacinto.

On March 19 Anza and his party passed San Jacinto Lake, now dry, camping at its western end. Turning west on the 20th, they proceeded past the site of Moreno through Alessandro Valley, and descended the ridge probably by way of Sycamore Canyon. Crossing the site of Riverside, the expedition stopped near an Indian village on the banks of the Santa Ana River about three miles south of Mount Rubidoux near the Union Pacific Railroad Bridge. Here, on the 20th a bridge of logs was thrown across the river, and on the 21st the party proceeded to pass over. On the 22d they entered San Bernardino County and on the 24th they arrived at Mission San Gabriel.

Returning from Monterey in April, 1774, Anza retraced his steps through Riverside County early in May, stopping again at some of his previous camp sites. On May 10 he was once more at Yuma.

In December, 1775, Anza again passed over this route as the leader of that remarkable band of brave and hardy pioneers who first settled San Francisco. On Christmas Eve, camp was made near the upper end of Coyote Canyon at Upper Willows, or Fig Tree Spring.

Here, shortly before midnight, a baby boy, Salvador Ignacio, was born, the third and last since leaving Tubac. The colonists, forgetting their misery for a time, spent that first Christmas Eve in California singing and dancing and partaking a little too freely, perhaps, of the aguardiente which Anza had given them against the good priest's protests. On Christmas morning, the train being held in the canyon for another day on account of little Salvador, Father Font took the opportunity to rebuke his now repentant flock by a sermon, at the close of which he wished everybody a happy Christmas.

From here on, the route was, with one variation, the same as on Anza's previous trip. After leaving Lake San Jacinto, the company went past the site of Lakeview, through Bernasconi Pass, and across Alessandro Valley by way of March Field to the old camp site on the Santa Ana River.

The route which Anza opened up at this time was used infrequently until 1782. By it came the colonists for Los Angeles, and the troops for the presidio of Santa Barbara, but after Fages' expedition in 1782 it was closed because of the hostility of the Yuma Indians.

The Old Emigrant Trail

Anza's route across the mountains was superseded by another trail opened up by Pedro Fages in 1782, who, instead of following the older path back to San Gabriel after his expedition against the Yuma Indians, blazed a new one, coming into San Diego County by way of the Carrizo Creek, San Felipe Valley, and Warner's Pass. From Warner's he went to San Diego via the canyon of the San Luís River.

Santiago Argüello, while in pursuit of Indian horsethieves, rediscovered this trail in 1825. In January, 1826, the Mexican government sent Romualdo Pacheco, Lieutenant of Engineers, to investigate it and with his approval it was adopted as an official mail route. A small garrison was established on the Colorado River to protect the road and from then on it was used occasionally by mail carriers and traders from Sonora. Probably the first Americans to come this way were David E. Jackson and his party of fur traders, who had come overland from Santa Fe in 1831. Later, it came to be known as the Emigrant Trail and formed a part of the Southern Overland Trail, a much-traveled route from the East into California during the '40's and '50's. In Riverside and San Bernardino counties there were two branches of the old Emigrant Trail. From the Colorado River to Warner's Ranch and continuing west to Aguanga there was one road. There the San Bernardino–Sonora Road branched north along the western base of the San Jacinto Mountains, while the Colorado Road went directly west and then northwest through the valley north of the Santa Ana Mountains. This section of the road through San Bernardino and Riverside counties to San Gabriel was called the Canyon Road by the mission Fathers, who opened it up immediately after Romualdo Pacheco had re-established the overland route by way of Warner's. It was by the latter route that Jackson traversed Riverside County on his way to San Gabriel, going by way of Temecula, Elsinore, Temescal Canyon, and Corona.

The San Bernardino–Sonora Road

"After reaching San Gorgonio [near the present town of Beaumont], the San Bernardino–Sonora Road turned southward and ran, via the present Lamb Canyon, to San Jacinto; thence to what is now Hemet; then through the hills, following approximately the line of the present St. John's Grade; and on until near what is now Aguanga, west of Warner's Ranch, it merged with another road from San Gabriel that was designated . . . . as the Colorado Road. From this point of junction on to the desert and Sonora, the San Bernardino–Sonora Road and the Colorado Road were one and the same.

". . . . This region had been inhabited by Indians for generations, and was traversed by well-established trails. When Sonorans and Americans began coming in to California, they naturally followed the old paths whenever possible.

"The very name of this road is intriguing. It leads back into history more than two and a quarter centuries, and recalls innumerable romances and adventures, though, up to comparatively recent times, it was but little more than a trail for horsemen and pack animals, traveled by ox carts only through the stretches that were open and fairly level. Starting in the Mexican state of Sonora, it had stretched to the northwest, over courses many of which are now almost or entirely forgotten. The name brings to mind Father Kino, the missionary who was perhaps responsible for the road's beginning; it recalls the Anzas and Pedro Fages, the adventurous soldiers and explorers; it recalls the race against time of Amador to head off the delivery of California missions to scheming colonizers; it brings to mind journeys of the 'Santa Fe Traders'; over a part of it, guided by Kit Carson, marched General Kearny and his men on their way from Santa Fe to San Diego; over it crawled thousands of Argonauts on their way to the gold fields; over long stretches of it raced Overland Mail stages on their run from St. Louis to San Francisco; over part of it Crabb and his misguided colonists — or filibusters — marched to their death; over it traveled engineers on their search for a route by which a railway could reach the Pacific. A historic road, indeed."

The Butterfield Overland Stage Route

"In 1858, the road from Los Angeles to the Colorado attained national importance when the Butterfield Company adopted it for their stages carrying mail between St. Louis and San Francisco, continuing its use until the outbreak of the Civil War. They did not travel through the San Bernardino Valley, but, after leaving Warner's Ranch, went to Los Angeles by way of Temecula, Sierra Rancho, and Chino. This latter route was the military road between California and Arizona during the Civil War, and an army post, Camp Wright, was maintained at Oak Grove [San Diego County], the first of the stage stations west of Warner's."

The ruins of one of the few extant stage stations may still be seen on the Temescal Road, near the Industrial Sands Plant on the Weisel Ranch. Horses were changed here in the stable behind the station, and, for a time, mail was delivered in the front room of the inn. A very old pepper tree formerly shaded the place, but this has disappeared. After the Civil War the Banning and Tomlinson stages passed over this road. Half-hidden among a sheltering grove of trees, the ruined walls of the old Aguanga station still stand a few hundred feet from the road which winds down the mountain from Warner's Ranch to Temecula.

One of the few intact portions of the old Butterfield Trail in the state lies in the Alberhill section of Elsinore Valley. William Collier, one of the owners of the Rancho Laguna in the early '80's, says that he went over this old trail by the following route:

"'I passed over this stage route from Coyote Wells on the desert to the Carriso stage station and through the range to San Phillipi, thence over to Warner's Ranch and across it to the base of the mountain, passing one mile from the present Warner's Hot Springs and down from the divide northerly of the Palomar mountains through Oak Grove to the Temecula stage station, at that time about two or three miles from the present town of Temecula, on the Little Temecula Ranch.

"'The stage route lay from Temecula station, as it is now known, up the valley, passing through the town-site of Murrieta, Wildomar and west, along the westerly side of the lake of Elsinore as now known and reached the Machado ranch house. From there diagonally across the northwesterly end of Laguna ranch, and after crossing the Laguna ranch line about midway of what is now known as Block "B" of Elsinore, passed through the unimproved country covered largely by chaparral, over the hills until it reached the southerly section line of Section 22, at a point across the valley to the west half of the southwest quarter of Section 22, Township 5 south, Range 5 west. It reached the level ground now occupied by the Los Angeles Pressed Brick company.

"'The line of the old stage route is still visible on the hill and going up the hill. In the valley it has been so disturbed as to be impossible to locate it.'"

The old Machado adobe, which still stands on Grand Avenue on what is now the Rippey Ranch, was used as one of the Butterfield stage stations, and the path of the old trail may still be seen near Rome Hill on the way to Temecula. There it probably skirted the chapel and the graveyard with its adobe wall, a region replete with the romance of Ramona and Alessandro.

The Serrano Memorial

On a low hill near Glen Ivy Hot Springs stands the Serrano Memorial, a granite boulder shaded by lacy pepper trees and bearing a bronze tablet which reads:

Boulder placed by residents of Temescal Valley to mark the site of the first house in Riverside County, erected by Leandro Serrano about 1824.

The spot on which this old adobe homestead once stood was located by Dolores Serrano, daughter of Don Leandro, and while the foundation for the memorial was being placed the hearthstone of the old house was unearthed. The site is in Temescal Canyon about eight miles south of Corona.

Leandro Serrano was the son of a soldier who had come to San Diego with Father Junípero Serra in 1769. He became mayordomo of Pala Chapel, and in 1818, because of his long and faithful service and his influence over the Indians, the priest at Mission San Luís Rey sent him to locate on the mission lands in Temescal Valley where many Indians were then living.

The valley was fair with groves of oak and sycamore, green *ciénegas*, and myriad wild flowers, and at the largest of the *ciénegas*, Serrano built his first adobe home in 1824. A large Indian ranchería and "sweat-house" were located near by and Serrano enlisted the natives in a drive against the bears and mountain cats of the region before bringing in his sheep and cattle.

On a small knoll about a mile from his first house, Don Leandro built a second adobe dwelling in the early '30's. The ruins may still be seen near a group of aged olive trees, said by Dolores Serrano to be 127 years old. Although a formal grant was never applied for, Leandro Serrano occupied the land at Temescal until his death in 1852.

Adjoining the second Serrano adobe, and near the bed of the San Jacinto River, are two stone tanning vats, a double one and a single one. These, according to P. Aguilar, who came to Temescal Valley in 1864, had been in use since 1819, and were, without doubt, used by the Indians of the Rancho Serrano for the tanning of hides.

The Temescal Tin Mine

The history of the Temescal Tin Mine, discovered in 1856 in the Temescal Mountains to the west, "would fill a volume." Litigation between the claimants of the mine, on the one hand, and the Serrano heirs and Abel Stearns, on the other, was long and bitter. The decision was finally made in favor of the claimants.

At the Mechanics Fair in San Francisco, in 1869, bars of tin from Temescal were exhibited. Specimens were also sent to England, where they were pronounced of the purest quality. The opinion of many investigators agreed that "here was a body of tin, unlimited in quantity and of the finest quality— the richest and, indeed, the only workable body of tin ore in the United States."

Little was done at the Temescal Mine until after the clearing of the title in 1888. English experts examined the region repeatedly and in 1890 two English companies were incorporated and more than two million dollars were invested within the two years following.

Why the mine was closed down in 1892 and has never been reopened has not been satisfactorily explained: a tariff on tin, the competition of Cornwall interests, or a mistaken estimate as to the real value of the property on the part of the English tin experts all have been offered as possible explanations of the brief heyday of tin mining at Temescal.

The Cota House

The Cota House was built by Juan Bandini (owner of the Rancho Jurupa) about 1840–1841, on what was later known as the Rancho Rincón. It was occupied by Don Juan for about three years, when Bernardo Yorba bought the house and one league of land for his daughter, who married Leonardo Cota. It was demolished about 1940.

The house, a two-story adobe, was a fine example of Spanish colonial architecture, standing on a high bluff above the Santa Ana River bottom. A magnificent view of broad rolling fields, of the bottom lands with their luxuriant cottonwood groves, and of the distant mountains made this one of the finest of all the old home sites. To reach it, one crosses the Santa Ana River near Prado, following the foothill road to Ontario. The Cota House was about a mile from the river and about two miles east of the foothill road.

Rancho Jurupa

Rancho Jurupa, a portion of which later became the Rubidoux Ranch, and on a part of which the city of Riverside now stands, was granted to Juan Bandini in 1838. Don Juan was a well-educated Peruvian gentleman of Italian descent who came to this part of California in 1828. He was a man of unusual ability. He was a member of the Terri-

torial Assembly and a delegate to Congress, and at various times held many important offices in California.

Juan Bandini was one of the first white settlers in Riverside County, and in 1839 he built his first home on the Rancho Jurupa. The site was on a high bluff along the northwest side of the Santa Ana River, about one thousand yards west of Hamner Boulevard—the road from Norco to Mira Loma. The old adobe has long since disappeared. Rancho Jurupa consisted of 31,000 acres of land which extended for about twenty miles along both sides of the Santa Ana River. The plains to the east of the river were considered worthless, being left wild and uncultivated or used for the pasturage of thousands of sheep. Today, the city of Riverside covers the old Jurupa "bench lands," and extensive orange groves have replaced the sheep ranges.

Rubidoux Ranch

Juan Bandini, on May 6, 1843, sold one and a half leagues of Rancho Jurupa to Benjamin D. Wilson, a native of Tennessee. Wilson, affectionately known as "Don Benito" among the Californians, had been a trader in New Mexico, but on coming to California he bought this ranch and settled down as a ranchero, marrying Ramona Yorba, daughter of Bernardo Yorba, his nearest neighbor. He was held in high regard by the Californians and among the American pioneers he was the most notable friend of the Indians. Robert Glass Cleland says of him: "A man of brave and adventurous spirit, who dealt justly and walked uprightly throughout the entire course of his romantic and richly varied life. B. D. Wilson might well be selected as an example of the most admirable type of manhood bred on the western border in the period immediately preceding the Mexican War. He lived through stirring times in the history of California and contributed abundantly to the making of the state."

"Santiago" Johnson seems to have become associated with Wilson and built for himself a fine adobe house, which he sold to Louis Rubidoux on March 16, 1844. By 1850, Rubidoux had purchased the remainder of the land which Bandini had sold to Wilson in 1843, obtaining a deed from Wilson on May 3, 1848, for a half-interest in his land, and a deed from Isaac Williams for the other half-interest on December 13, 1849. Louis Rubidoux, a native of St. Louis, was of French descent, his family being prominent in the early history of Missouri. His father was a pioneer merchant in St. Louis and his brother, Joseph, was the founder of the city of St. Joseph. Louis himself, as well as other members of the family, had been active in the trapping and fur trading industry in the Southwest before coming to California. Louis Rubidoux exercised considerable influence in building up his community. He served as a local judge and supervisor, fostered education, and, being a well-educated, genial, kindly man, his home became a haven for many pioneer families in southern California.

A tablet placed by the State Society, D.A.R., on the Santa Ana River bridge at the west entrance to Riverside memorializes the name of Louis Rubidoux, pioneer builder and one of the first permanent American citizens in the valley. The site of the old Rubidoux adobe (long since disappeared) is about a mile west of the bridge near the Rubidoux-Frémont Monument.

The Grist Mill

One of the first grist mills in that part of southern California was built by Rubidoux on the Rancho Jurupa in 1846–1847. Being at that time the only mill of its kind in all that region it supplied a great need. Among others to profit by it, the troops of the Mormon Battalion and Frémont's Battalion, in 1847, were the enthusiastic recipients of flour from the Jurupa Mill and beans from the rancho. One of the old millstones has been preserved in the pavement in front of Mission Inn, and some of the stone from the mill was also used in constructing the Rubidoux-Frémont Monument.

"Fort Frémont"

A United States Army post was established on Rancho Jurupa in 1852 by Captain Lovell and Colonel A. J. Smith, and a small body of troops was kept there until 1854, chiefly as a protection against the Piute and Mojave Indians. The site of the post is now called "Fort Frémont," although Frémont himself never visited this spot. It is located across the street from the old Rubidoux House. Both the fort and the house are gone, but a stone monument in honor of Louis Rubidoux and John C. Frémont stands near their sites today, about a mile west of the Santa Ana River.

Casa Loma

George W. Beattie says of Casa Loma:

"In his report to Governor Echeandía, in 1827, Fr. Antonio Peyri of Mission San Luís Rey, wrote, 'In the direction of northeast, in the sierra, at a distance of twelve leagues, the Mission has the Rancho of San Jacinto with a house of adobes for the mayordomos.'

"When José Antonio Estudillo, in 1842, applied to the Mexican Government for a grant of a portion of San Jacinto Rancho, he said:

"'The land for which I petition has upon it a dilapidated, earthen roofed house ten varas long—a menacing ruin.'

"The walls of this house were enclosed in a larger structure built by Estudillo and known as 'Casa Loma.' A year ago, Miss Pico showed me the part of their present residence represented by the old walls." Casa Loma, about five miles northwest of San Jacinto, is now the home of Miss Dolores Pico, a descendant of Governor Pío Pico.

The Judge North Memorial Park

The death of Louis Rubidoux occurred in 1868, and in 1870 the town of Riverside was founded on the eastern portion of the old Jurupa Grant by Judge J. W. North, a pioneer settler from New York.

John W. North, born in New York in 1815, and educated as a lawyer, took a prominent part in the material and cultural foundations of three American commonwealths, Minnesota, Nevada, and California. In Minnesota he was active in the territorial legislature, founded the town of Northfield, promoted the Minneapolis and Cedar Valley Railway, and helped to establish the University of Minnesota. He was active in the Republican Convention and the nomination of Abraham Lincoln in 1860, and was subsequently appointed Surveyor-General of the Territory of Nevada, and, soon after, a territorial judge. He was president of the Nevada State Constitutional Convention.

Judge North went to Knoxville, Tennessee, to open up foundries after the Civil War. While there he became interested in organizing a colony in California. Associating with him men from Massachusetts, Michigan, Iowa, and New York, he went with a committee to California over the Central Pacific Railroad, which had just been opened up. He examined sites in southern California, purchasing a portion of the Rancho Jurupa. In 1870, Riverside was founded on the old rancho. Judge North later removed to Fresno County, where he had acquired land. He died there in 1880.

The old North residence once stood on the city block now bounded on the west by the Union Pacific depot, on the east by the Santa Fe depot, on the north by Seventh Street, and on the south by Eighth Street. The site was recently set aside as a city park, and was named in honor of the founder of Riverside the Judge North Memorial Park.

The Tibbets Memorial

The Tibbets Memorial in honor of Mrs. Eliza Tibbets, the woman who raised the first navel orange trees in California, was placed by Aurantia Chapter, D.A.R., in a small park at the head of Magnolia and Arlington avenues, Riverside, in 1920. Two seedling orange trees were sent to Mrs. Tibbets from Washington, D.C., in 1873 by Professor Saunders, the husband of an old friend. Four budlings had been sent to Professor Saunders by the United States Consul at Bahia, Brazil. Two of these he sent to a friend in Florida, and two he sent to Mrs. Tibbets, in Riverside.

The two budlings sent to Florida did not survive, but, owing to Mrs. Tibbets' tender care, and in spite of somewhat adverse circumstances, the two trees intrusted to her lived. From these two little budlings grew the great navel orange industry of southern California, adding millions of dollars annually to the state's resources.

The Tibbets Memorial stands in front of one of the two trees, the other having been transplanted to the courtyard of Mission Inn by President Roosevelt at the time of his visit there in 1903.

Glenwood Mission Inn

Captain C. C. Miller came to southern California when it was first emerging from its "hacienda days." In 1873 he was made engineer of the new colony of Riverside, which had been established on the old Rancho Jurupa in 1870. As his salary, he received a block of land in the new colony, and there, in 1875, he built an adobe cottage, the first solid-walled house in town, which later became the nucleus of the famous Mission Inn.

The Miller family began to receive guests in the little adobe as early as 1876, and the name Glenwood Cottage was given to it. The old-fashioned, homely hospitality of the Millers drew an increasing number of patrons, and a small group of frame buildings grew up around Glenwood Cottage. With this growth, the name was changed to Glenwood Tavern, and later to Glenwood Hotel.

From the beginning, Frank A. Miller, son of the pioneer, was proprietor and manager at Glenwood. In 1902 he replaced the old wooden cottages by a new structure of concrete and brick, the building which now surrounds the Court of the Birds. The old adobe cottage still stands on its original site in this same court. Around these two grew the famous Glenwood Mission Inn, modeled after the old missions of California, and containing rare art treasures from all over the world. The Cloister, built in 1911, with its Music Room and Cathedral Organ; the Spanish Art Gallery, built in 1915, with the Patio of the Fountains, and the Garden of Bells, where hang bells of all shapes and sizes from all over the world, 650 in number; the Rotunda with its Galeria, St. Francis Wedding Chapel, and Oriental Court, built in 1931—these are only a few of the beautiful treasures of Mission Inn.

Mount Rubidoux

Tradition tells us that the Indians long ago held an annual sunrise service on Mount Rubidoux in honor of the sun. About the sacred sacrificial altar (now in the patio at Mission Inn), all the tribes of the valley pledged themselves to live in peace under the leadership of the Jurupas, whose name is said to have meant "peace," and whose home was at the foot of the mountain.

The mountain was named in honor of Louis Rubidoux, who owned the Rancho Jurupa, on which it was located, from 1844 until his death in 1868. In 1906 the Huntington

Park Association acquired Mount Rubidoux and developed it as a public park. On April 26, 1907, the Serra Cross was raised on the highest point of the mountain and consecrated to Fray Junípero Serra, founder of the California missions. The first annual sunrise pilgrimage to the top of Mount Rubidoux on Easter Sunday was held in 1909, and from that service have come all the subsequent Easter sunrise services of California and the United States. Every Easter morning thousands of worshippers climb Mount Rubidoux and other mountains to greet the rising sun and to pray for universal peace and brotherhood.

Wolff's Trading-Post

On the Vail Ranch about two miles north of the Pechanga burial ground and near the highway from Pechanga to Warner's Ranch, stands the old trading-post and tavern once kept by the husband of Ramona Wolff. Helen Hunt Jackson stayed there in 1879 while investigating the condition of the Temecula Indians whose tragic eviction from their homes had stirred her deeply. Mrs. Wolff, whose knowledge of the situation and whose sympathy with the red men won Mrs. Jackson's confidence and admiration, became Mrs. Hartsel of the novel, *Ramona*. Mrs. Wolff was also one of those bearing the musical name which was given to the heroine of the tale. The author had, however, heard it before and, it is said, was so impressed by it that she decided to use it in her story.

This building is now used as a store-room and as sleeping quarters for ranch laborers, but the interior of the large room which once served as a trading-post and tavern is changed but little. Visitors may gain admittance to this very interesting place on application at the office of the ranch superintendent.

Ramona's Country

Many are the old adobes in southern California posted as the "birthplace" or the "marriage place" of Ramona. Many are the homely Indian squaws advertised as "the real Ramona." In actual life, the real Ramona was a complex personality, and as one visits the various shrines of a great woman's inspiration one is able to live again the scenes which her pen pictured so faithfully and to catch the spirit of vivid romance which colored that long-ago time in which her Ramona lived.

On that historic journey which took her through Orange and Riverside counties to San Diego, gathering data which would strengthen her appeal to the United States government in behalf of the Mission Indians, Mrs. Jackson garnered and kept in memory many of the vivid scenes and incidents and appealing personalities which she later immortalized in her novel, *Ramona*. Pala Chapel, where the Indians still go to pray; Old Town, San Jacinto, where a wing of Aunt Ri's cabin, much altered, still stands; Temecula and the Pechanga burial-ground with their heart-stirring memories; the old Wolff trading-post on the Vail Ranch; these and other places used by the author in her romance are replete with vivid interest.

And each spring, one may journey to Hemet where the beautiful Ramona pageant is given at Ramona's Bowl, a rugged natural stage set in the midst of those very hills where California's most beloved romance found completion.

SOURCES
[Credit is here given for source material, and permission to quote is hereby acknowledged]

BEATTIE, GEORGE WILLIAM. "Development of Travel between Southern Arizona and Los Angeles as Related to the San Bernardino Valley," in the *Historical Society of Southern California Annual Publications*, XIII (1924–1927)

BEATTIE, GEORGE WILLIAM. *Reopening Anza's Road*. Manuscript, 1931

BOLTON, HERBERT EUGENE. *Anza's California Expeditions*. 5 vols. University of California, Berkeley, California, 1930

CLELAND, ROBERT GLASS. "Pathfinders," in the series *California*, edited by John Russell McCarthy, Powell Publishing Company, 1929

DAVIS, CARLYLE CHANNING, and WILLIAM A. ALDERSON. *The True Story of "Ramona," Its Facts and Fictions, Inspiration and Purpose*. Dodge Publishing Co., New York, 1914

ELLERBE, ROSE L. "History of Temescal Valley," in *Annual Publications, Historical Society of Southern California*, XI, Part III (1920)

GOULD, JANET WILLIAMS. *Notes on the Historical Spots of the Country around Corona*. Manuscript, 1930

HORNBECK, ROBERT. *Roubidoux's Ranch in the '70's*. Riverside, California, 1913

HUTCHINGS, DE WITT V. *Outline of Riverside County History*. Manuscript, 1930

JACKSON, HELEN HUNT. *Ramona*. Roberts Brothers, Boston, 1884; Little, Brown and Company, Boston, 1900

JAMES, GEORGE WHARTON. *Through Ramona's Country*. Little, Brown and Company, Boston, 1909

McCOY, EDNA. "The Butterfield Trail," and "Historical Background of Elsinore and Vicinity," in the *Elsinore Leader Press*, 1930

SLAUGHTER, E. MARGUERITE. *Historical Riverside County*. Manuscript, 1930

SAN BERNARDINO COUNTY

SAN BERNARDINO COUNTY (San Bernardino is Spanish for St. Bernard) was organized as a county in 1853 from territory which was at first a part of Los Angeles and San Diego counties. The city of San Bernardino has been the county seat since the county's organization.

Pueblo Settlements and Turquoise Mines

"Pueblo settlements, turquoise mines, and weapon manufactories" were discovered on the edge of the Mojave River sink, southwest of Death Valley, and about a hundred and forty miles from the Pacific Coast of California, in the winter of 1928–1929. This remarkable discovery was made by the San Diego Museum of Archaeology under the direction of Malcolm J. Rogers, field archaeologist. Pottery and other artifacts unmistakably peculiar to the Pueblo peoples were found as testimony that the Pueblo culture once spread "about two hundred miles west of the limit heretofore attached to it. . . . . Not even a guess is hazarded at the age of these recent findings . . . . but few archaeologists believe them to be less than twenty centuries old."

Dr. Rogers expressed little doubt "that what is now the Mojave River sink region once had a permanent Puebloan population. Besides the East Cronise Lake site, several other widely separated sites on the south end of the sink, produced dominant percentages of Pueblo-type pottery. . . . . On the northwest shore of East Cronise Lake is a site whose Puebloan attributes are sufficiently strong as to identify it as a permanent village of these people."

"Petroglyphs [rock carvings]," Dr. Rogers says, "are fairly common in these mountains. . . . . Some of these appear to be guide boards, and it was by following one of them that we came on the largest of the Pueblan settlements on East Cronise Lake, somewhat west of the sink of the Mojave River, and northwest from Crucero."

The line of turquoise deposits was followed by Dr. Rogers and his associates from Mineral Park, Arizona, to Granite Wells in San Bernardino County, twenty-two miles east of Johannesburg. In the Turquoise Mountains one of the largest mines was located. Here many tools of the Pueblo type were found. The most extensive digging was thirty feet long, twelve feet wide, and twelve feet deep, and from it more than a dozen smaller tunnels branched off.

Dr. Rogers said of the fifty or more ancient mines discovered: "Throughout this extensive terrain, I seldom visited an outcropping of turquoise without finding distinct evidence of the stone having been mined by the aborigines, as evidenced by ancient open cuts, pits, and stone hammers. In cases where I have failed to find such evidence, I have been assured by modern miners that the 'Indian workings' were there, but had been obliterated by the white man's methods and machinery.

"In and about the undisturbed turquoise mines of the Himalaya group," Dr. Rogers continued, "some twenty-five pieces of Pueblan pottery were found," but "of all the sites in this region, excluding the mines, the Halloran Spring site produced the most Pueblan artifacts, and, possibly, was the temporary camp of the turquoise miners."

Cajón Pass and Mojave Indian Trail

Professor Herbert Eugene Bolton says that, as early as 1772, Pedro Fages traversed the region of the Cajón Pass, while on his way north into the San Joaquin Valley in pursuit of deserters.

The first white man to cross the San Bernardino Mountains into the San Bernardino Valley was Padre Francisco Garcés, the famous Spanish priest-explorer, who came in 1776 from the Colorado River. Jedediah Strong Smith, the first American to enter California overland, traveled the same trail from the Colorado in 1826 and again in 1827.

Recent study of the diaries of the Garcés and Smith expeditions shows that the route taken by these two men did not lead directly through Cajón Pass, as has been supposed. Mojave Indians served as guides from the Colorado on both occasions, and they naturally used their ancient Indian trail, which led across the desert and up the Mojave River to its western headwaters in the San Bernardino Mountains. Crossing the range eight miles east of the present Cajón Pass, it came down into San Bernardino Valley on the ridge between Devil and Cable canyons, crossing Cajón Creek between Devore and Verdemont. From here it skirted the base of the foothills to Cucamonga, and led on to San Gabriel and the sea. The old Mojave Indian Trail is therefore extremely important historically, as it antedates the Cajón as a mountain crossing for white men.

Smith's expedition was one of the most important in all the annals of Western trail-breaking. It did for California what the expedition of Lewis and Clark did for the Pacific Northwest and what Pike's expedition did for the Southwest. It opened up the first of the great transcontinental routes to California and covered a vast stretch of country, most of which Smith was the first to explore. It "made known the valleys of the San Joaquin and Sacramento to American trappers, and, through them, to American settlers; opened a line of communication from Northern California to the Oregon country, a route the Hudson's Bay Company was quick to take advantage of; and traversed the Pacific Slope from the Mojave Desert to Puget Sound." On September 19, 1931, the San Bernardino County Historical Society placed a monument and tablet to Father Garcés and Jedediah Smith at the place where the Mojave Trail crossed the summit of the mountains.

During the years 1830-31 three pioneer pack trains from New Mexico crossed the San Bernardino Mountains into the valley beyond. The first, forerunner of the Santa Fe caravans, was led by Antonio Armijo, a New Mexican trader, who came in January 1830 by what he called the "San Bernardino Canyon," probably our present Cajón Pass. Ewing Young and his trappers came a little later in the same year,

but the trail by which he crossed the mountains is not mentioned. In the fall of 1830 William Wolfskill left Santa Fe with still another band of trappers, and, according to J. J. Warner, went through the Cajón in February 1831. Certainly the last, and possibly all three, of these parties made use of the Cajón.

Wolfskill's trip, with its course over the mountains so clearly defined, is notable. His route from Santa Fe to California was more nearly that followed later by the New Mexican caravans than was that of either Armijo or Young. It was he who established the famous pack-train route known as the "Spanish Trail," used by the Santa Fe–Los Angeles caravans for nearly two decades, until the establishment of the wagon road from Salt Lake, practically along the same line from Utah south, shoved it into the discard.

The caravan route up Cajón Canyon crossed and recrossed the wash, following the general direction taken later by the railroad and still later by the state highway. The route continued for a distance of about eight miles from the mouth of the canyon, until it reached the "Narrows," where it turned northeast. At this junction, now known as Camp Cajón, a monument has been placed by the Pioneer Society of San Bernardino commemorating the early explorers, traders, and pioneer settlers who used this trail.

Captain Jefferson Hunt of the Mormon Battalion went out of California by way of Cajón Pass in 1847. In 1851 a company of Mormons, on their way to settle San Bernardino Valley, came in by way of Cajón Canyon, and in 1857 a large number of the same settlers went out that way, when recalled to Salt Lake City by Brigham Young.

The Mormons, with their heavy wagons, could not use the "Narrows," but came out of the desert into Cajón Canyon four or five miles farther west than does the present highway. While negotiating for lands in San Bernardino Valley, they camped at Sycamore Grove, a small, verdant valley about one and one-half miles west of what is now Devore Station, near the mouth of Cajón Canyon. The Pioneer Monument erected at this spot to memorialize these sturdy emigrants was destroyed in 1938.

Lieutenant A. W. Whipple, with a part of United States topographical engineers, came through the pass in March 1854 while on a government exploring expedition.

Across the dry wash of Cajón Creek, about one-half mile from Devore on the way to Sycamore Grove, was a picturesque stone tavern, once a station on the emigrant wagon road which went along the west bank of the river at this point in the canyon. The tavern, standing in the midst of fine old trees, with a perpetual spring at its doorstep, was until its destruction a memorial to that long line of settlers, stagecoach drivers, gold-seekers, and adventurers who passed its doors in pioneer days.

Horsethief Canyon, which extends into Cajón Canyon from Summit Valley, is reminiscent of the days (1830–1860) when Indian and New Mexican horse thieves were wont to pasture their stolen animals in this region, before the long drive across the Mojave Desert. From the time of the opening up of the "Spanish Trail" by William Wolfskill, a brisk trade in California mules and horses was carried on with Santa Fe, New Mexico. Most of the mules were destined for Missouri, where there was a great demand for the superior type of animal produced in California. While a large proportion of this trade was lawful, there was also much illegitimate and clandestine traffic carried on by renegade Indians, New Mexicans, Americans, and others. Hardly a year passed that the mission Fathers and the rancheros did not lose valuable live stock, which was driven off through Cajón Pass by raiding parties of outlaws. Even after the American occupation, Indians continued these raids.

Old Trails across Euclid Avenue

Four old trails replete with historic interest once crossed what is now Euclid Avenue, that long, tree-lined drive which extends north and south through the modern towns of Ontario and Upland.

1. The first of these trails to be traversed by white men was the Anza Trail, over which Juan Bautista de Anza, in 1774, led the first overland party into California, and again, in 1775, the first overland band of settlers, the founders of San Francisco. The Boy Scouts of America and service organizations of Ontario have placed a memorial boulder in honor of Anza in a small park on Euclid Avenue one block from the Euclid School. On it a bronze tablet bears the inscription:

> To the honor and glory of Juan Bautista D'Anza, Trailmaker, and his band of intrepid followers, who, on March 21, 1774, passed near this spot on their way to San Gabriel and Monterey, the first white men to break a trail overland to California.

The San Gabriel Mission Fathers used this trail as far as the Santa Ana River in order to reach their Mission station in the San Bernardino Valley until a more direct route was cut shortly after 1822.

2. The oldest of the four trails crossing Euclid Avenue was the Mojave Indian Trail, which was well established when Father Garcés traveled it in 1776. Smith, and probably Ewing Young, followed the same route. The Spanish Trail, sometimes called the Santa Fe Trail, opened in 1831, made use of the line of the Mojave Indian Trail from the mouth of Cajón Canyon to San Gabriel, and also from "Fork of Roads" (east of Barstow) to "Lane's Crossing" (Oro Grande) along the Mojave River. This old Spanish Trail was followed by a long line of explorers, hunters, and traders; pioneer settlers of El Monte and Los Angeles who came close in the wake of these adventurers; later emigrants of covered-wagon days and the gold-seekers bound for the north; and, last of all, the daring stagecoach drivers of the '60's and the '70's, forerunners of the "iron horse" and the modern motor car. This trail followed the base of the mountains in San Bernardino Valley even more closely than does the Foothill Boulevard of today. Where it crossed the site of the modern town of Upland at Euclid Avenue, just at the beginning of "Ye Bridal Path," one of the several statues of the Pioneer Mother which mark the National Old Trails Road has been placed in honor of the mothers of covered-wagon days who passed over this part of that old road. The National Old Trails Committee of the D.A.R. has erected one of these monuments in each state through which the National Old Trails Road passed from Maryland to California.

3. The old Emigrant Trail, which followed Anza's route across the Colorado Desert as far as Carrizo Creek and crossed the mountains via Warner's Ranch, branched in two directions after leaving Aguanga: one branch, known as the San Bernardino–Sonora Road, followed north to San Gorgonio Pass and west through the San Bernardino Valley, while the other, known in mission days as the Canyon Road to the Colorado, and designated by the Los Angeles Court of Sessions, May 19, 1851, as the Colorado Road, took its course along the western mountains via Temecula, Elsinore, Temescal Canyon, Corona, and the Santa Ana River.

The San Bernardino–Sonora Road, the upper branch of the old Emigrant Trail, came from Warner's Ranch via Aguanga and passed down the San Jacinto Valley and across the hills to the site of what is now Beaumont in Riverside County. From there, it continued northwest and west through San Bernardino County via Redlands and Old San Bernardino, or Guachama, to what is now Colton. From that point the road went southwest past Slover Mountain to Agua

Mansa, where it again proceeded westward to what is now Ontario, crossing Euclid Avenue one mile north of the Southern Pacific Railroad. From there, it continued west across San Bernardino County to Los Angeles County via Ciénega (Mud Springs) near San Dimas.

The padres, after 1822 and before 1827, were the first to use this road on their way from San Gabriel to their mission outpost at Guachama. Smith took this route, in 1827, on his journey out of California, camping at Jumuba Ranchería a few miles west of the Guachama Mission Station. Here he awaited the much needed supplies which Padre Sánchez, of Mission San Gabriel, had ordered the mayordomo at Guachama to furnish him for his journey.

4. The last of the four roads crossing Euclid Avenue was the Colorado Road. This was opened up from Carrizo Creek to Warner's first by Pedro Fages in 1782 and later in 1826 by Romualdo Pacheco, leader of a government expedition seeking out an official mail route. Immediately thereafter the missionaries of San Gabriel opened up the road all the way from Warner's to San Gabriel via the canyon route. The first American to use this route was David E. Jackson in 1831, and it was used by other trappers and by those emigrants from Mexico and the East who followed the southern route via Santa Fe and the Gila River, of which the Colorado Road was a continuation. As this southern trail was the only all-year route into California from the East, it was also used by the Butterfield Stage from 1858 to 1861 for the carrying of passengers and mails.

The route of the Butterfield Stage over this section of the Colorado Road may be traced by the adobes which it passed. After crossing the Santa Ana River near the Cota House, in what is now Riverside County, the road followed the base of the hills along Chino Creek, above which the Prado Road from Chino to Santa Ana now runs. About three miles northwest of the Cota House, the stage passed the Raimundo Yorba adobe on Rancho Rincón, now in San Bernardino County. Although it was not one of the official stations along this route, doubtless stages did halt at the old adobe house, which still stands on the brow of the hill, sadly in need of care to save it from complete ruin. In 1868 Fenton M. Slaughter purchased this building from Yorba, and lived in it until his death in 1897. At Rancho Rincón, the road ran along the base of the hill, crossing the extreme southern terminus of Euclid Avenue at that point. From there it continued northwest along Chino Creek for about seven miles to Rancho Chino, where a station was maintained on the site of what is now the dairy house of the California Junior Republic.

A marker commemorating this old trail has been placed at the northwest corner of the administration building of the Republic. The inscription reads:

> "This tablet is placed by Pomona Chapter, Daughters of American Revolution, in memory of the pioneers who first broke this trail, known as the Canyon Trail, from Fort Yuma via Warners Hot Springs, Temecula, Lake Elsinore, Rancho del Chino, by this place, thence, to Mission San Gabriel. In 1858 the Butterfield stages from San Francisco to St. Louis, Missouri, traveled this way."

Rancho and Asistencia de San Bernardino

In a report on the missions issued in 1822 in connection with the transfer of California from Spain to Mexico, there is this statement from Mission San Gabriel regarding the origin of Rancho San Bernardino:

"In the year 1819, at the request of the unchristianized Indians of the place they call Guachama and which we call San Bernardino, we began the introduction of cattle raising and farming, in order to induce the natives to become Christians."

When Father Payéras visited Guachama (the "place of

plenty to eat") in 1821, he found that Mission San Gabriel had cattle grazing in the valley and that there were a number of old houses, probably for the herdsmen of the rancho, at Jumuba, a few miles west of the rancho headquarters. In 1827, Father Sánchez of Mission San Gabriel reported:

"Rancho of San Bernardino—The house is of adobe. It consists of one long building. It has an enramada or structure of boughs which serves for a chapel. It has also a building with compartments for keeping grain. The walls of this structure are of adobe."

This was the Guachama Mission Station, or the rancho headquarters, on Rancho San Bernardino, which was owned by Mission San Gabriel. The little mission station was located north of what is now Mission Road and east of where it intersects Mountain View Avenue, while the site of the Guachama Indian village was on the south side of this road. The entire region is today covered with extensive orange groves. The remains of the old adobe station were leveled in 1875, but the site is easily located by the fact that the orange trees growing where the old buildings once stood do not thrive as well as do the other trees in the same orchard. It has been marked by the State of California.

On what is now known as Barton Hill, one and one-half miles southeast of the old rancho buildings, and about two miles west of the present city of Redlands, an extensive adobe structure was begun somewhere about 1830. This was the Asistencia San Bernardino, to which Father Durán, in 1837, referred thus:

"San Gabriel founded the beautiful San Bernardino Asistencia, which has lately been given to some private individual . . . ."

From other testimonies of the times, we know that San Bernardino, like San Antonio de Pala and Santa Isabel, was to have been one of that inland mission chain which the Fathers contemplated before the decree of secularization, which ended all mission activity in California.

After secularization, all work on the Asistencia ceased and the buildings remained practically deserted until 1842, when a large section of the mission lands was granted to three sons and a nephew of Antonio María Lugo of Los Angeles. The cities of San Bernardino, Redlands, and Colton now stand on the Rancho San Bernardino of the Lugos. One of Don Antonio's sons, José del Carmen Lugo, came to live in the old Asistencia buildings, thus saving them from complete disintegration for a time.

After the Rancho San Bernardino was sold to the Mormons by the Lugo brothers, in 1851, Bishop Nathan C. Tenney, manager of agricultural operations on the lands formerly cultivated by the mission, occupied the old Asistencia buildings. Upon the withdrawal of the Mormons in 1857, Dr. Benjamin Barton, a prominent pioneer settler, and his family took over the buildings, occupying them until 1867. From this date, the old adobes, untenanted and uncared for, gradually succumbed to the inroads of the weather, until only a few mud walls remained.

The Asistencia San Bernardino has been restored by the citizens of San Bernardino County under the instructions of George W. Beattie of East Highlands. Every effort has been made to be historically accurate in the work of restoration, old court records, diaries, and mission archives having been utilized in working out the original details of construction. A native of Mexico, expert in the making of real adobe bricks, was brought to the Asistencia, where he lived. Here he molded the adobe bricks and tiles out of native clay, just as was done in the days of the mission. The whole project was extremely illuminating and fascinating, both in its picturesque and in its historical aspects, a notable example for similar projects in other parts of the state.

Mission Ranchos

Mission San Gabriel had three ranchos in the San Bernardino Valley: Rancho San Bernardino, already mentioned as the location of the mission station Guachama and later the Asistencia; Rancho Agua Caliente, on which the present city of San Bernardino is located; and Rancho Jumuba, located between the present Loma Linda and Colton. Rancho Jumuba was named after an Indian ranchería which occupied the site beside a bubbling spring of water. It was here that Jedediah S. Smith camped in 1827 while being outfitted by the generosity of the mission Fathers just before starting on his return trip to Salt Lake, via the San Joaquin Valley.

San Bernardino

"The city of San Bernardino, now making claim to 40,000 inhabitants, owes its beginning to a colony of Mormons from Salt Lake City, who arrived in June of 1851 and laid the foundation of a thriving community in the six years before they were recalled by their leader, Brigham Young."

Gradually, the lands purchased from the Lugo brothers were subdivided and sold to the individual members of the Mormon community, who established homes and farms. The town of San Bernardino was founded; in the San Bernardino Mountains, sawmills were erected; roads were constructed, the Mormons opening up the present Foothill Boulevard as far as Cucamonga; extensive agricultural activities were started; churches and schools were founded.

Adobe and log houses were soon erected on a site originally known as "Agua Caliente," but the name of the neighboring Asistencia San Bernardino was transferred to the new town. Here, because of rumored Indian uprisings, a fort and stockade inclosing eight acres of ground was erected in the form of a parallelogram, 300 feet wide and 720 feet long. The north and south ends were made of cottonwood and willow tree trunks closely fitted together and set three feet in the ground and twelve feet above, while the log houses were moved along the west side, forming a solid wall finished with logs in blockhouse fashion, with loopholes, bastions at the corners, and indentured gateways. Within this stockade about one hundred families lived; a few, however, remained outside, camping at a spot now occupied by the old cemetery.

The site of the old Mormon fort, now occupied, in part, by the new Court House, included the present Arrowhead Avenue from Third Street nearly to Fourth Street, and lands to the east, west, and south. On the Court House site, also, stood the Lugo adobe, while on the present Third and C streets was a two-story adobe built by the Mormons and used as the first court house of San Bernardino County. This was torn down in 1867.

In 1857 all this activity was halted by the decree of Brigham Young, which recalled the "faithful" to Salt Lake City because of the threatened invasion of Utah by the United States forces under General Albert Sidney Johnston. The majority of the settlers obeyed the call and left their promising homes in the beautiful valley of San Bernardino, often selling them "for a song." Their departure greatly decreased the population of the county and seriously hindered its prosperity for some time. The Mormons had been industrious, peaceable citizens with wonderful organizing ability, and they had been largely responsible for the development of the agricultural resources of the valley as well as for the substantial basis on which the city of San Bernardino was founded.

Rancho Santa Ana del Chino

Rancho Santa Ana del Chino was another of the Mission San Gabriel ranchos. Soon after the secularization of the missions it was granted to Antonio María Lugo. About three miles southwest of the modern town of Chino the Chino ranch house once stood near the site now occupied by the dairy house of the California Junior Republic. It was built by Colonel Isaac Williams (known as Don Julian to the Californians), who came to California with Ewing Young in 1832 and became one of the leading citizens of Los Angeles. He married a daughter of Antonio María Lugo, one of the finest of the old Spanish settlers, who, in 1841, deeded a half-interest in the great Rancho Santa Ana del Chino to his son-in-law. There Williams built the adobe mansion which became a refuge for every wayfarer who came into Alta California over the southern emigrant trail. Orchards and vineyards were planted; barns, shearing sheds, and adobe huts for a great army of Mexican and Indian laborers were erected; a grist mill, one of the earliest in southern California, was built; the rancho was stocked with fine cattle, horses, and imported sheep; and an extensive trade in hides and tallow was carried on. In 1851, Lugo deeded his remaining interest in this rancho to Williams.

Very soon after the death of Isaac Williams in 1856, his daughter, Francesca, married Robert Carlisle, a young southerner, and Mercedes Williams married John Rains, who had been mayordomo at Chino. John Rains and his wife moved to Rancho Cucamonga, while the Carlisles remained at Chino. Robert Carlisle was an energetic, well-educated man and a good business manager, and under his control the prosperity of Rancho del Chino continued until his death in 1865.

Francesca Williams Carlisle married again, and the Chino estate was managed by trustees. In 1881 it was sold to Richard Gird, a miner and an engineer, one of the most picturesque characters of the early American period. On Rancho del Chino, Gird lived lavishly in a fine adobe built many years before by Joseph Bridger (now occupied by the Los Serranos Country Club), and added to his estate until it contained 45,000 acres. The land boom of 1887, however, broke Richard Gird, and in 1894 the rancho was sold to Charles H. Phillips, of San Luis Obispo. In 1896 it came into the hands of English capitalists, when it was broken up into small tracts and sold.

Much of historical interest centered in the Chino adobe. During the Mexican War it was the scene of a battle between the Americans and the Californians. While Colonel Gillespie was shut up in Los Angeles, in 1846, a score of Americans, commanded by B. D. Wilson, took refuge on Rancho del Chino, which was about twenty-five miles east of Los Angeles. On September 27 the Chino house was surrounded by a force of seventy mounted Californians. During the short skirmish which followed, one of the Californians, Carlos Ballesteros, was killed and several Americans were wounded. The Californians, maddened by the death of their friend, who was very popular, set fire to the brea roof of the adobe. At this point, Isaac Williams came out with a white flag and his two little daughters, whom he insisted on placing in the hands of their uncle, Felipe Lugo, one of the attacking party, in order that he might carry them in safety to their Grandfather Lugo in Los Angeles. The leaders of the Californians, however, persuaded the Americans to surrender, promising them protection as prisoners of war. The success of the Californians in this encounter encouraged them in their attack upon Gillespie.

During the years 1858–1861, the Chino adobe assumed additional historical importance as a station on the old Butterfield Stage route, which passed its door. As before mentioned, this fact has been memorialized by the D.A.R. marker placed at the office building of the California Junior Republic.

The lands once belonging to Rancho del Chino are now occupied by the town of Chino, the California Junior Republic, and many small farms. The old adobe ranch house, so long dominated by the personality of Isaac Williams and the scene of so much of historical significance, has long since disappeared, its place being taken by the dairy house of the Republic. A monument commemorating the rancho, the Williams adobe, the battle site, and the Butterfield stage station has been proposed.

Rancho Cucamonga

Rancho Cucamonga derived its name from an Indian village which was on the land when the first white men came there. Tradition tells us that the Cucamonga Indians were unusually intelligent and industrious and that they learned much from the padres, who sometimes came down from Mission San Gabriel to visit them. Gradually, they acquired cattle and horses and raised good crops of corn and melons in the fertile hills and valleys of "Nuestra Señora del Pilar de Cucamonga," as the padres called the locality.

Tiburcio Tapia, a leading citizen of Los Angeles, petitioned for a grant to the Cucamonga lands in 1839. This grant was made on April 16, 1839, and Don Tiburcio immediately began the building of an adobe house on the crest of Cucamonga's highest hill. Its roof was covered with brea from Rancho La Brea near Los Angeles. It was as "massive as a fortress, facing south, with east and west wings and a gateway on the north side." The Tapia mansion was indeed well built for the rugged, romantic years through which it was destined to stand.

In the beginning, Don Tiburcio left his rancho largely in the care of his mayordomo, José María Valdez, who is said to have set out the "mother vineyard." This later developed into one of the large plantings of grapes in California, the first cuttings probably having been obtained at Mission San Gabriel. The history of the old rancho is closely associated with the development of its vineyard.

The Tapia adobe has long since returned to its native clay, but the site can be traced by bits of brea and other remnants of adobe days. Here, in the old hilltop "fortress," many thrilling episodes took place. The Indians, who were employed in the building operations, rebelled when they realized that the newcomers were taking their rich grazing lands from them. Retreating to the foothills and canyons, they made occasional raids upon the stock of the white men. Desert Indians, too, frequently invaded the rancho lands, and many tales are still told by old residents of raids and battles and even of attacks upon the Tapia "fortress" on "Red Hill."

Among other traditions of those hectic days at Cucamonga is that of the chest of coin which Don Tiburcio is said to have hidden when rumors of war began to herald the aggression of the United States in Alta California. It is said that this chest contained not only Señor Tapia's own money but that intrusted to him by friends as well, and also a sum collected for the building of a chapel at Cucamonga.

Not long after this, in 1845, Tiburcio Tapia died suddenly. No one knew where the chest had been hidden, save an Indian servant whom Don Tiburcio had sworn to secrecy. Nor would the Indian disclose the whereabouts of the hidden treasure, so great was his fear of the fulfillment of the terrifying oath which Señor Tiburcio had placed upon him.

A few years later, Tiburcio Tapia's daughter, María Merced, married Leon V. Prudhomme, and moved with him to the adobe on "Red Hill." Doña María, who knew the story of the hidden treasure, slept in her father's room. One night, so the story goes, she saw a mysterious light move across the chamber wall, resting upon a particular spot. The apparition was repeated a number of times, greatly disturbing the young wife. In order to prove that the vision was entirely imaginary, her husband plunged a knife into the adobe wall. To his amazement, it went through the wall, disclosing a hollow space behind. In the aperture was a purse containing some silver coins and a scrap of paper with its message faded with age. The paper was studied very carefully and much search followed. But all in vain. No treasure was ever found, though even today fresh evidences of treasure hunting may be observed in the vicinity.

In 1858, Victor Prudhomme sold Rancho Cucamonga to John Rains and his wife, Mercedes Williams. An old unpublished history of the '90's says:

"The coming of John Rains to this place marked not only a new but a progressive epoch in its history. The old Tapia residence on the hill was abandoned and a new one built at the highest point of the east bank of the arroyo, north of the vineyard. Labor and expense was not spared in its construction. . . . . The walls were built of heavy brick made of the red clay dug from the hills and roofed with thatches covered with brea mixed with tallow. . . . .

"A little to the east of the Valdez residence was built the store and nearby a blacksmith shop, stables and several dwellings. . . . . The rancho was stocked by Mr. Rains with sheep, horses and cattle, and 160 acres was set to vines. The small still and winery were proportionately enlarged and improved. The road from Los Angeles to San Bernardino by way of the Chino having been abandoned by the stage for the Arroyo San José routes to Bear Valley and the mines, this became a regular station, where the horses were changed and the traveler enabled to obtain refreshments.

"With the vaqueros in charge of the flocks and herds, the laborers in the vineyards and winery, the stable hands in charge of stage relays, mechanics at work on buildings, teamsters, the blacksmiths and a trader and postmaster, the place became not only a hive of industry, but noted as the chief trading post and assembly point for all classes and nationalities east of Los Angeles. The Rains home was a center of social life, and, attracted by the hospitality of its master, the beauty of its mistress, the sparkling wines and festivities, here frequently gathered the representative wealthy and élite of the south."

John Rains was murdered on November 17, 1862, and his widow was left with four small children and many heavy obligations to meet. In 1864 she married José C. Carrillo, and the gay life of the rancho was revived for a few years, until, in 1870, debt forced Mrs. Rains-Carrillo to sell a part of the rancho. The Hellmans and their associates finally acquired the greater part of the rancho, and Mrs. Carrillo lost all title to the estate.

The old adobe winery built by John Rains has been abandoned for many years but is still in a fair state of preservation. It has recently been restored by the present owner of the site, H. H. Thomas. Back of it is the residence long occupied by E. K. Dunlap, who had charge of the planting and building of both vineyard and winery. Splendid trees, walnut, sycamore, and eucalypti, planted in John Rains's time, still surround the place. The Rains house has been repaired and is now used as a residence. The Valdez house, "Ritchie's Store," and the blacksmith shop have all disappeared, although their sites can still be traced.

Politana

George W. Beattie summarizes the story of Politana as follows:

"From the time that the holders of Mexican land grants in the San Bernardino valley began raising stock there, raids by wild Indians were the most serious difficulty with which the rancheros had to contend. Counter attacks by the whites were made frequently, but the most effective defense of the rancheros was through the establishment of colonies of immigrants from New Mexico or of Indians that were friendly.

"From 1833 to 1848, trading caravans from Santa Fe passed through the valley twice a year, and the Santa Ana river bottoms and the adjacent damp lands afforded feed for their animals. At a point northeast of the present Colton there lived a man called Hipólito, and his house was a stopping place for the caravan people. Antonio María Lugo realized that a populated center where the caravans stopped would afford very effective protection for the stock of the region, and offered half a league (2,200 acres) near the home of Hipólito to a group of New Mexicans who were thereby induced to settle there. They occupied the land in 1843, and built adobe houses just east of the present Colton Plunge. The settlement was called Politana because Hipólito, or Polito, as he was familiarly called, lived near and had been instrumental in bringing the colonists from New Mexico. The settlement consisted largely of families that arrived in California in the winter of 1842 under the leadership of Santiago Martínez, although some had come the preceding year with the Rowland-Workman party. Many of the men had been long in the employ of the caravan traders and were experienced Indian fighters. In return for the land on which they settled, they agreed to defend the stock of the region in case of Indian raids.

"The colonists secured water from a spring northwest of the present San Bernardino Valley Junior College grounds. Vicente Lugo, however, soon established a *rodeo* center north of the colony and diverted the water of the spring. The New Mexicans became dissatisfied at this, and, in 1845, abandoned their settlement at Politana, and accepted a more favorable offer from Juan Bandini, grantee of the Jurupa Rancho, to occupy a new location on his lands south of the present cement plant at Slover Mountain. The Lugos replaced the New Mexicans with Juan Antonio and his band of Cahuilla Indians. They located their ranchería near the establishment of Vicente Lugo on Bunker Hill ridge, and the name Politana, or Apolitana, as it was more commonly termed, was transferred to their home."

Agua Mansa and San Salvador

These settlements on the "Bandini Donation" on Rancho Jurupa were composed of New Mexican colonists who, in 1845, had moved there from Politana on Rancho San Bernardino. Colonists were desirable at that time as protectors against the inroads of wild Indians; and when dissatisfaction with certain conditions at Politana arose, Juan Bandini invited the settlers to leave that place and locate on a parcel of land he donated. It lay on both sides of the Santa Ana River, and later formed part of San Salvador parish. Agua Mansa was on the north and west bank of the river, while the settlement on the south and east side was known as San Salvador. The original parish *capilla* was erected in 1852 in San Salvador, but collapsed. The *capilla* now indicated by the Auto Club marker was erected later in 1852 at Agua Mansa.

Nothing remains of Agua Mansa today save the little burial ground on the hill above the river. It is the oldest cemetery in the county, and many members of the old Spanish and Mexican families are buried there. Of Capilla San Salvador, only a mound of clay remains, but an El Camino Real Bell marks the site on the roadside about halfway between Riverside and Colton, southwest of Slover Mountain.

Spanish Town

While, as we have said, the part of the "Bandini Donation" on the south and east bank of the river was originally called San Salvador, it was known later to American pioneers as "Spanish Town." It has also been called "La Placita de

Trujillo." Like Agua Mansa, Spanish Town was a prosperous community until 1862, when both were destroyed by a flood that swept down the Santa Ana River. In both communities the settlers immediately built new adobe homes on higher ground. A remnant of Spanish Town remains today, a dreamy, peaceful spot, half-hidden among giant cottonwoods and fragrant orange groves. To reach it one may take a narrow county road north of Riverside and drive beneath the shade of the great cottonwoods along the river bottom, or one may take a more modern highway through the orange groves. Either choice will lead one out into the country where a touch of romantic, pastoral California still lingers.

Ghost Cities of the Mojave

The Calico Mountains, vivid with ever changing colors, their wild and lofty grandeur wrought by age-old volcanic action, lie in the midst of the Mojave Desert five miles north of the town of Daggett (a supply station for mines and a few ranches). At their base are the ruins of the once famous mining town of Calico, today a mere ghost·of the desert enveloped in the profound silence of the vast wastes about it. Fifty years ago the wealth of the silver mines discovered in this region brought thirty-five hundred souls to the place, and Calico became one of the most prosperous as well as one of the wildest camps of the great Southwest. A sensational drop in the price of silver was the cause of its sudden abandonment, while the pitiless fury of desert storms has wrought its final desolation.

A few roofless adobes still crouch at the foot of the gorgeous mountain looming above them. Old diggings are everywhere visible, while across the canyon in the forgotten cemetery heaps of stone guard the shallow graves of the dead in their long sleep upon the lonely hillside. Among the wooden slabs which serve as headstones is one whose painted letters stand out in startling relief, wrought by the strange erosion of many wind-driven sands. The inscription, mute with the pathos and tragedy of the great desert, reads: "In Memory of Minnie B. Whitfield, Born 1881, Died 1885."

Dale, a ghost town forty miles north of Salton Sea, in the most desolate section of the Colorado Desert, was a prosperous mining camp twenty years ago, but today its deserted cabins are reached only by roads that are faint and sometimes almost impassable. Its isolation has kept it immune from the spoliation of vandals, and its empty miners' cabins, its saloon and post office, remain much as they were when the inhabitants, discouraged by the scarcity of water and the difficulty of transportation, quitted the place.

The Spring Ranch, three miles from the modern town of Adelanto, is located on the Mojave River at a place where many cottonwoods grow. The ranch dates back to covered-wagon days, when it was the stopping-place for ox and mule trains hauling freight from Prescott, Arizona, to Los Angeles.

SOURCES

[Credit is here given for source material, and permission to quote is hereby acknowledged]

BEATTIE, GEORGE WILLIAM. "Development of Travel between Southern Arizona and Los Angeles, as Related to the San Bernardino Valley," in *Annual Publications, Historical Society of Southern California*, XIII, Part II (1925), 228–257
———. *San Bernardino Valley before the Americans Came.* Manuscript, 1931
———. *Historic Crossing Places in the San Bernardino Mountains.* Manuscript, 1931
———. "An Old Road to New Mexico," paper read before Historical Society of Southern California (1929)
———. "San Bernardino Valley in the Spanish Period," in *Annual Publications of the Historical Society of Southern California*, XII, Part III (1923), 10–28
BEATTIE, GEORGE WILLIAM. "Spanish Plans for an Inland Chain of Missions in California," in *Annual Publications of the Historical Society of Southern California*, XIX, Part II (1929), 243–264
BOLTON, HERBERT EUGENE. "In the South San Joaquin ahead of Garcés," in *California Historical Society Quarterly*, X, No. 3 (September, 1931), 211–219
CLELAND, ROBERT GLASS. *A History of California: The American Period.* The Macmillan Company, New York, 1922
———. "Pathfinders," Volume I of the series, *California*, edited by John Russell McCarthy. Powell Publishing Company, Los Angeles, 1929
COUES, ELLIOTT. *On the Trail of a Spanish Pioneer, Garcés Diary, 1775–1776.* 2 vols. Francis P. Harper, New York, 1900
CRAFTS, MRS. ELIZA PERSIS (RUSSELL) ROBBINS. *Pioneer Days in the San Bernardino Valley.* Redlands, California, 1906
DALE, HARRISON C. *The Ashley-Smith Explorations and the Discovery of a Central Route to the Pacific, 1822–1829.* The Arthur H. Clark Company, Cleveland, 1918
DUNN, H. H. "Tracing the Pueblos to the Pacific," in *Touring Topics*, XXII, No. 10 (October, 1930), 48–50, 53
ELLERBE, ROSE L. "The Mother Vineyard," in *Touring Topics*, XX, No. 11 (November, 1928), 18–20
HILL, JOSEPH J. "The Old Spanish Trail, a Study of Spanish and Mexican Trade and Exploration Northwest from New Mexico to the Great Basin and California," in *The Hispanic American Historical Review*, IV, No. 3 (August, 1921), 444–473
———. "Ewing Young in the Fur Trade of the Far Southwest, 1822–1839," in *The Quarterly of the Oregon Historical Society*, XXIV, No. 1 (March, 1923), 1–35
———. *The History of Warner's Ranch and Its Environs.* Privately printed, Los Angeles, 1927
HOUSTON, FLORA BELLE. "When the Mormons Settled San Bernardino," in *Touring Topics*, XXII, No. 4 (April, 1930), 32–34, 52
LAWRENCE, ELEANOR. "Mexican Trade between Santa Fe and Los Angeles, 1830–1848," in *Quarterly of the California Historical Society*, X, No. 1 (March, 1931), 27–39
———. "Horse Thieves on the Spanish Trail," in *Touring Topics*, XXIII, No. 1 (January, 1931), 22–25, 55
VAN DYKE, DIX. "A Modern Interpretation of the Garcés Route," in *Publications, Historical Society of Southern California*, XIII, Part IV (1927), 353–359

SAN DIEGO COUNTY

SAN DIEGO COUNTY (San Diego is Spanish for St. Didacus, a native of Spain and a Franciscan saint) was named after the harbor which Vizcaíno christened in 1602. It was one of the original twenty-seven counties, and the city of San Diego has always been its county seat. Many pre-state records of deeds and wills in Spanish are housed in the court house.

The Torrey Pines

Along the Torrey Pines grade and the plateau above, about two miles south of Del Mar, the famous Torrey Pines (*Pinus torreyana* Parry) cling to the precipitous cliffs in strangely twisted, wind-blown shapes. A distinct species, the only other place where these trees may be found is on the Santa Maria Island off the coast of southern California. Dr. Joseph L. Le Conte, in 1850, recognized them as a new species. Dr. C. C. Parry, then engaged with the Mexican Boundary Survey, was told of the find, and the two men named the aged trees after their former instructor at Columbia University, Dr. John Torrey.

The Painted Rocks of Poway

From Escondido southward to the Mexican border, and possibly beyond, a distinct and remarkable group of Indian pictographs occur. Extending over a distance of about fifty miles in the Poway Valley region, they contain not only the eleven rock paintings of the "maze" or "square" type already located by white men but, according to old resident Indians, almost a score more of like design and workmanship in the hills above Poway Valley.

The Poway pictographs are distinct from any others in

southern California, constituting a series of designs made up of squares and rectangles with occasional rows of concentric crosses. They are so uniform in "pattern, width of lines, coloring, thickness of paint, selection of sites and durability of color" that some students believe them to have all been made by one prehistoric artist.

The patterns used in these distinctive designs are of three types: "the square; the running, right-angled scroll; and the series of concentric crosses. The squares may be concentric in one pattern, and broken to fit each into the other in the next, but their lines are never crossed." The squares or the right angles of any one of these designs are so nearly of the same dimensions as to suggest the use of a measuring unit.

There is a marked similarity between these wonderful paintings in squares and rectangles in San Diego County and the more nearly perfect figures of the same type in Mitla and at San Juan de Teotihuacan, Mexico, where the temples of the Sun and Moon are located. Moreover, although the more common Indian paintings depicting many-legged bugs, birds, animals, and curious curved figures also occur in the Poway region, they never appear on the same boulders with these peculiar "maze" patterns, as they are commonly called. It would seem that these paintings were sacred to the Sun God, keeping guard over the precious water holes of that semi-desert region. Always painted with red pigment of a marvelously enduring quality, they were written on the flat surface of granite boulders facing the east, and always they overlooked the approach to a spring.

The country in which these strange manuscripts of an ancient race are found is one in which are many low hills with spurs running down from the higher elevations into Poway Valley, the basin of Lake Hodges, and other little valleys from north to south. Here, an ancient race of men of the Stone Age lived in their crude rock houses above the springs. Remains of uncemented rock walls may still be seen at some of these ancient camp sites, and there, also, many implements of crude workmanship have been found — arrowheads, stone scrapers, knives, and hammers.

Near the western end of Lake Hodges, a large camp site of this type has been located where a "granite-lined creek bed" comes down into the lake. Here, also, are two of the rock paintings belonging to this special group. One consists of the scroll design only, while the other is of a very dim pattern of concentric squares. The latter, which overlooks a perpetual spring, is about three feet wide at the base and five feet high. Facing eastward, it stands about twenty feet back from the pool and the spring, which it apparently guards.

Across the narrow canyon from this rock is the entrance to a large cave, now closed in by landslides. On the western side of this cave, facing the east, the right-angled scroll design has been placed on an overhanging wall of the cavern overlooking an arm of the lake. It is about six by three feet in size, but was probably larger originally, as much of it has been worn away by the elements.

Another perpetual spring, far up in the Poway Valley, is guarded by the crude remains of two prehistoric fortresses, crowning the summits of two low, isolated hills on either side of the spring. Ruins of uncemented stone walls still stand two or three feet high, some of them marking off small rooms. On one hill an entire room, about sixteen by sixteen feet, was built. Back of it is a cave, the entrance to which was evidently once walled in. Below this room a stone stockade reached nearly to the spring, which it was evidently built to protect, while the fortress on the opposite hill guarded that side of the spring.

At this camp a smaller series of painted squares, facing the east, overlooks the spring. Its exposed position has caused the work to be gradually erased by the action of sun and rain and blowing sands. In time it will be completely obliterated.

Other rock pictures of this unusual group are located, roughly speaking: (1) about a mile west of Escondido; (2) in Highland Valley about three miles east of the Inland Route; (3) about four miles west of the Poway Post Office and a mile west of the Inland Route near the Peñasquitos or Poway Creek; (4) about two miles east of the Lakeside-Ramona highway just northwest of San Vicente Creek, and about two miles southeast of the Earl School; (5) near El Cajón Mountain, about six miles northeast of Lakeside; (6) about two miles south of Alpine near The Willows; (7) on Sweetwater River just north of Lawson Valley and about halfway between Dehesa and the Japatul School; (8) about three miles northeast of Dulzura near Barber Mountain; and (9) about three miles southwest of Dulzura near Otay Mountain in the San Ysidro Range.

The Discovery and Naming of San Diego

The bay of San Diego was first seen on September 28, 1542, by Juan Rodríguez Cabrillo, a Portuguese navigator sent out by Antonio de Mendoza, viceroy of Mexico, to explore the coast of New Spain and to discover, if possible, the elusive strait of Anián. Cabrillo, with his chief pilot, Bartolomé Ferrelo, in the tiny vessels, the "San Salvador" and the "Victoria," anchored in that "port, closed and very good, which they named San Miguel" and which Sebastián Vizcaíno in 1602 renamed San Diego. It is believed by local historians who have made an intensive study of the topography of the region that Ballast Point was the most likely place for Cabrillo to have landed. Land (one-half acre) within the Fort Rosecrans Military Reservation on Point Loma was set aside by the government in 1913 as a National Monument to Cabrillo.

It was not until sixty years later that the bay of San Diego was again visited by white men. On May 5, 1602, Sebastián Vizcaíno with the two ships "San Diego" and "Santa Tomás," and the little frigate, "Tres Reyes," sailed northward from Acapulco. He had been sent out by the new viceroy, the Conde de Monterey, to explore the coast of Alta California for safe and convenient harbors in which the Manila galleon might stop for repairs and the recuperation of scurvy-stricken crews, and from which observations as to the whereabouts of English pirate ships might be made.

Early in November, Vizcaíno reached the port which Cabrillo had seen before him. In his diary this entry is found:

"On the twelfth of the said month, which was the day of the glorious San Diego, the general, admiral, religious, captains, ensigns, and almost all the men went on shore. A hut was built and mass was said in celebration of the feast of Señor San Diego."

Thus the naming of San Diego Bay was effected, and the first recorded house of Christian worship in Alta California (although a crude and humble one) was erected.

The Settlement of San Diego

In 1769, rumors that the Russians were planning to extend their colonies from Alaska down the Pacific Coast to Upper California, caused King Carlos III, of Spain, to put into effect what had long been contemplated. Fear that Alta California might become the possession of Russia or England finally brought about a movement to settle the land. Two hundred and twenty-seven years after the discovery of San Diego by Juan Rodríguez Cabrillo, the first colonizing project was organized by José de Gálvez, visitador general of the New World. Gaspar de Portolá, governor of Alta California, was placed in command of the entire expedition, and Padre Junípero Serra was appointed Father Presidente of the missions which were to be established in the new province. Officers, priests, soldiers, sailors, laborers, and southern Indian retainers, about one hundred men in all, made up the personnel of this, the first band of settlers in California. The primary aim of the expedition was the protection of the port of Monterey, but a base was also to be established at San Diego. The Franciscan friars were to found missions and convert the Indians, and the soldiers were to guard the country and protect the mission settlements.

The expedition was divided into four companies, two of which went by sea in the ships "San Carlos" and "San Antonio," and two by land, one under command of Portolá himself, and the other under Fernando Rivera y Moncada, his second in command. The last of the sea expeditions to leave La Paz, under command of Juan Perez, in the ship "San Antonio," was the first to arrive at San Diego, on April 11, 1769, after a voyage of fifty-five days. On April 19, the "San Carlos" with Vicente Vila in command and Pedro Fages with his twenty-five Catalonian volunteers, arrived after a voyage of terrible suffering, lasting a hundred and ten days. Rivera, accompanied by Father Crespi, the famous diarist, arrived on May 14, after a march of fifty-one days from Velicatá in Baja California. Governor Portolá and a few men of the second land expedition arrived June 29. The rest of this division, in which was Father Serra, who had made the journey while suffering from an ulcered foot and leg, arrived last, on July 1.

Already advanced in years, Father Serra entered upon experiences of the utmost hardship and privation with a cheerfulness and zeal that ignored all physical ills and dangers for the sake of that high endeavor to which he gave his life. His fiery enthusiasm for the conversion of the dusky gentiles of California was stayed by no vicissitude nor was it quenched by any amount of suffering or discouragement.

With him, in that first gathering at San Diego, were Father Crespi (the friend of his youth, with whom he had studied in the convent of Majorca, and with whom he had come to Mexico in 1749), and Fathers Vizcaíno, Parrón, and Gómez, besides Portolá and several other government officers. Immediately after the assembling of the expedition, Portolá, with Captain Rivera, and a band of soldiers, accompanied by Fathers Crespi and Gómez, and Miguel Costansó, cosmographer, engineer, and diarist, set out northward to search for the port of Monterey, where the first northern mission was to be established. Father Serra remained at San Diego to undertake the founding of the first of the Franciscan missions to be established in the wilderness of Alta California.

Misión San Diego de Alcalá, Mother of the Alta California Missions

Immediately after the departure of Portolá and his men, Padre Junípero Serra, on July 16, just fifteen days after his arrival at the port of San Diego, founded Misión San Diego de Alcalá. The ceremony was performed in the presence of twenty or thirty men, on what later came to be known as Presidio Hill. Here, overlooking the bay and the river, the first temporary chapel was erected and the first cross was raised.

The order of ceremony followed at this first founding was much the same as that subsequently used in establishing all of the twenty other missions which finally composed the chain. Helen Hunt Jackson describes the procedure thus: "The routine was the same in all cases. A cross was set up; a booth of branches built; the ground and the booth were consecrated by holy water, and christened by the name of a saint; a mass was performed; the neighboring Indians, if there were any, were roused and summoned by the ringing of bells swung on limbs of trees; presents of cloth and trinkets were given them to inspire them with trust, and thus a Mission was founded. Two monks (never, at first, more) were appointed to take charge of the cross and booth, and to win, baptize, convert, and teach all the Indians to be reached in the region. They had for guard and help a few soldiers, and sometimes a few already partly civilized and Christianized Indians; several head of cattle, some tools and seeds, and holy vessels for the church service, completed their store of weapons . . . . with which to conquer the wilderness and its savages. There needs no work of the imagination to help this picture. Taken in its sternest realism, it is vivid and thrilling; contrasting the wretched poverty of these single-handed beginnings with the final splendor and riches attained, the result seems well-nigh miraculous."

The little settlement at San Diego had, perhaps, greater hardships to endure in the beginning than any of the missions which followed. For a whole year Father Serra labored in vain among the Indians before even one child was baptized. Supplies, too, were insufficient and at the end of six months the whole enterprise was threatened with failure.

Meanwhile, Portolá and his men, under great hardships, were struggling northward on what proved to be an unsuccessful endeavor.

Portolá's Trail to Monterey

Leaving the port of San Diego on July 14, 1769, Portolá, with Fray Juan Crespi as chronicler of the expedition, had started northward on the long journey to Monterey, where the second mission was to be established.

Passing what is now called False Bay, the party came to an Indian village near the northeast point of the cove. Leaving the shore here, they passed up a narrow valley and camped not far from the present site of Ladrillo. The following day the route lay through Soledad Valley with its Indian villages, one of which was located near the site of Sorrento. Camp was again made in San Dieguito Canyon, near Del Mar, with another Indian village not far distant.

On July 16 and 17 the trail led by way of San Elijo Lagoon, Batequitos Lagoon, Agua Hedionda Creek, and Buena Vista Creek, near Carlsbad. Many Indian villages were passed along the way, all of them friendly. On July 18 the verdant valley of San Juan Capistrano, the first name given to the valley of San Luís Rey, was reached and camp made. The location was pronounced by Fray Crespi to be an excellent site for the placing of a mission, and several years later Mission San Luís Rey was indeed founded near this very spot.

From the valley of San Juan Capistrano northward Portolá passed, successively, the camp sites near Home Ranch and Las Pulgas Canyon, called by the explorers the valley of Santa Margarita and the valley of Santa Praxedis de los Rosales (because of the numerous Castilian roses and other flowers growing there). These sites are commemorated in the name of the old Spanish Rancho Santa Margarita y Las Flores, about three miles west of Mission San Luís Rey.

Passing into the region of what is now Orange County on July 22, the party continued the long journey northward seeking for the port of Monterey. Six months later, returning from their fruitless search, sick and weary, their provisions nearly gone, the little company passed over much the same route as on the earlier trip, but the homeward marches were long, and several of the old camps were passed without stopping. On January 21 camp was made apparently on

San Onofre Creek, and on January 24 the party rejoined the little group anxiously awaiting their return at the newly established Mission of San Diego.

There, Portolá found that the supply ship, which had left for San Blas six months before, had not returned and that provisions were almost exhausted. Neither Portolá nor Father Serra had any intentions of giving up the enterprise, however, and, when the hour seemed the darkest, their faith and determination were rewarded by the arrival of the "San Antonio," and the immediate settlement of Alta California was assured.

The search for the lost port of Monterey was renewed at once, Father Serra accompanying the new expedition, while Fathers Luís Jayme and Francisco Dumetz carried on the work at San Diego.

El Camino Real, the Royal Road

"It will be interesting to many to know that the original El Camino Real, or Royal Road, stretched from Guatemala to Mexico City and thence to Sonoma. The most modern section, established in the late eighteenth century by Spanish soldiers and missionary friars, is the route from San Diego to Sonoma, in California.

"In attempting to re-trace that section of the California route between San Diego and Los Angeles, it has become apparent that there was no single road, but that, in fact, there were many routes, all used at one period or another by friars, Indians, and rancheros."

The route followed by the old Camino Real "varies so slightly from the existing automobile road that the motorist who drives from San Diego to San Francisco over the King's Highway can rightfully feel that he is re-tracing the paths of the padres."

The modern Camino Real is marked by four hundred mission-bell guideposts, each one bearing a sign directing the traveler to the next mission and also to the next town. Each guidepost is surmounted by a mission bell weighing a hundred pounds or more.

The Second Mission Site

The first site of the mission at San Diego proved to be unsatisfactory because of its proximity to the Presidio, and the Fathers soon realized that it would be better for the Indian neophytes to be removed some distance from the influence of the soldiers. Furthermore, a location affording more water for agricultural purposes was desirable.

Mission buildings of wood were soon constructed six miles up the valley from the Presidio, and considerable progress had been made in the conversion of the Indians by October 1775. At that time, the number of neophytes totaled seventy-six, and sixty additional converts were baptized by the Fathers on the day before the feast of St. Francis, October 4, 1775.

The hatred of the unconverted Indians, however, finally culminated in a fierce attack upon the unprotected mission on the night of November 4, 1775. Father Jayme, who, "with the shining light of martyrdom in his eyes, and the fierce joy of fearlessness in his heart," sought to quiet the mob by walking toward them, his hand extended in blessing and with his usual salutation, "Love God, my children!" was ruthlessly slain. A stone cross has been erected to Padre Luís Jayme, California's martyr priest.

The Mission buildings were all destroyed at the time of this insurrection, but a temporary church of adobe was soon begun and was ready for use in October 1776. A more spacious and substantial building was completed in 1780. By 1800 San Diego had become the most populous as well as one of the wealthiest of all the California missions. A more elaborate church was dedicated on November 12, 1813. Within another year extensive fields and vineyards were being irrigated by water brought over an aqueduct through Mission Valley. The old Mission Dam built across San Diego River Gorge and constructed of granite and cement twelve feet thick, is still in almost perfect condition, although choked with drift. It stands as a remarkable testimony to the excellence of California's first agricultural venture.

Little of the original mission except the façade and the base of the belfry remains today, but the entire building, except the monastery wing south of the mission, was restored by the Native Sons and other organizations in 1931. Under the scholarly supervision of J. Marshall Miller, restoration was made true to the old mission in design and decorations and is exact in every detail. The five picturesque palms, planted by the mission Fathers, one of which is nearly as old as the one at Old Town, still flourish near by, and twenty-two ancient olive trees still standing near the mission were planted late in the eighteenth century, the mother orchard of all the mission olive trees in California.

The First Presidio, Birthplace of Civilization in California

Father Serra had dedicated the cross, July 16, 1769, on what later came to be known as Presidio Hill. In the shadow of this, the first cross to be raised in Alta California, the first mission was begun and the first presidio town was established. On the same spot, on July 16, 1915, one hundred and forty-six years later, a group of earnest San Diegans placed the Serra Cross, which stands on Presidio Hill today. From the heap of clay upon which it was raised, old tile from early buildings had been dug up and incorporated into the Memorial Cross. On it is a bronze tablet bearing this legend:

> Here the First Citizen, Fray Junípero Serra,
> Planted Civilization in California.
> Here he First Raised the Cross,
> Here Began the First Mission,
> Here Founded the First Town—San Diego, July 16, 1769.

Presidio Hill, being situated a little back from the river and the bay, afforded an excellent outlook over the surrounding country and made fortification easy as well. It was near the site of the ancient Indian village of Cosoy, ranchería of the Dieguefios, and here, for over sixty years, San Diego was located within the adobe walls of the Spanish garrison.

The presidio, an essential feature of Spanish colonization, was usually a fortified square, constructed, at first, of wood and, later, of brick or stone, inside of which the commander's residence and the chapel formed the central points around which the garrison for the soldiers, the officers' quarters, and adobe houses for provisions and military supplies were located.

On January 11, 1776, the presidio of San Diego became the meeting place of three men intimately associated with the beginnings of Alta California, Juan Bautista de Anza, Fernando Rivera y Moncada, and José Francisco de Ortega, who arrived there with Fathers Vicente Fuster and Pedro Font to discuss what measures should be taken to punish the Indians responsible for the burning of the mission and the death of Father Jayme.

On his way into San Diego, Anza and his men had camped on January 9 at the San Luís Rey River, then called the Arroyo de San Juan Capistrano. On the 10th they stopped in Soledad Valley, south of Del Mar about at Sorrento and some ten miles north of San Diego.

Finding that Governor Rivera expected him to remain at San Diego until danger from further Indian uprisings was past, Anza tarried until February, when word from San Gabriel informed him that there were no longer sufficient supplies for the little band of San Francisco colonists which he had left there. On February 9, in spite of storms and swollen streams, Anza left San Diego, camping that night on the Arroyo de Agua Hedionda, a creek which enters the ocean just south of Carlsbad. On February 12 he rejoined the settlers anxiously awaiting his return at San Gabriel.

San Diego passed, with the rest of California, from Spanish to Mexican control in 1822, "without much more than a ripple." Under Mexican rule it entered a little more turbulent period, when frequent revolts occurred both between the Californians and the Mexican governors and between the rival factions of the Californians themselves. José María Echeandía, the first governor sent from Mexico, established his headquarters at the presidio of San Diego, which remained the capital of Alta California during his administration, 1825–1829.

It was during this time that the second overland party of Americans to enter California came by way of San Diego County under the leadership of Sylvester Pattie and his son, James Ohio Pattie. The journal of this perilous westward trek of American trappers, written by the younger Pattie, constitutes one of the most stirring narratives of frontier history. This expedition, moreover, opened up a new overland route to the coast and added much to the knowledge of the great Southwest.

Coming down the Gila and Colorado rivers as far as the tidewaters of the Gulf of California, the party crossed the desert to the Spanish settlements on the northern coast of Baja California. At Mission Santa Catalina, they were harshly received and conducted to San Diego in Alta California under heavy guard, arriving there March 27, 1828.

Governor Echeandía was fearful and suspicious because of the recent expedition of Jedediah S. Smith, who on January 1, 1827, had come to San Diego to apply for a passport and was peremptorily refused. Consequently, the Governor treated the newcomers cruelly, thrusting them into a vile prison for several months. Under this harsh treatment, the elder Pattie, already weakened by long privation, finally succumbed to a fatal illness.

Gradually, the younger Pattie was able to soften the governor's attitude by serving as interpreter and by using his knowledge of vaccination to save the population from extermination by a smallpox epidemic. Finally, in 1830, he was given passage to Mexico City, whence he made his way back to his native Kentucky.

After Echeandía's administration the Presidio was gradually abandoned. The retired soldiers were often given grants of land and went to live on their ranchos or built homes in the village at the foot of the hill. Within a decade the old garrison was deserted and dismantled.

On December 25, 1838, earthworks were thrown up on Presidio Hill preparatory to an expected attack from José Castro, leader of the northern faction then supposedly threatening the San Diegans. Two cannon from Fort Guijarros were mounted, but the anticipated attack did not materialize.

The earthworks on Presidio Hill were never used by the Mexicans. On the coming of the Americans in 1846, they were improved by Commodore Robert F. Stockton, and United States troops, including Company B of the famous Mormon Battalion, were stationed there during the brief period of military rule before California's entrance into the Union. The old American fort, of which scarce a vestige remains, was called Fort Stockton during that period. The Native Sons of the Golden West have placed a flagstaff and bronze tablet on the site.

The Presidio has been almost completely obliterated by the inroads of the passing years—the buffeting of storms, the shock of earthquakes, and the depredations of settlers, who despoiled its structures to obtain materials for their homes. The walls of the Presidio chapel, the old Spanish garrison, and the first civilian houses long ago crumbled into shapeless mounds of earth, but in 1929 plans were culminated for the preservation of the hill and the marking and restoration of some of its ancient landmarks. Through the consistent and indefatigable efforts of George W. Marston, extending over a period of years, the land was gradually purchased and ultimately presented to the city. Thus, "the cradle of the state's civilization" was finally rescued from complete oblivion and made a public park.

Here, on July 16, 1929, the 160th anniversary of the founding of San Diego, the Junípero Serra Museum was dedicated. The museum, the Junípero Serra Cross on the site of the first mission building, the site of the old Spanish garrison, and the site of Fort Stockton are included within the park, and at the foot of the hill, also within the park, stands one of the first two date palms planted in California. These historic trees are thought to have been planted by Father Serra in 1769. Neglected and abused for many years, they were finally inclosed within a modest picket fence in 1887, and today the one remaining tree is braced by giant cables, and every care is lavished upon it. It was near this spot that the four divisions of the Sacred Expedition of Gálvez were reunited July 1, 1769, when Father Serra limped into the Spanish camp located near this spot. It is also a monument to the sixty-odd victims of scurvy who were buried there in 1769.

Misión San Luís Rey de Francia

"The stately magnificence of San Luís Rey, more typically Moorish than any other mission, is impressive today even in its ruins, and in the time of its greatest wealth and power it might easily startle and arrest the attention of the traveller." It was situated on a slight eminence in a beautiful, secluded valley four miles inland, and there, on June 13, 1798, Father Lasuén, Father Presidente of the missions after Serra's death, led the solemn ceremonies that celebrated the founding of Misión San Luís Rey de Francia.

The first substantial church building, which was completed in 1802, was planned by Father Peyri and erected under his direction. In 1811 the foundations for the present structure were laid, and on the feast of St. Francis, October 4, 1815, the completed church was dedicated. It was constructed of adobe and faced with burnt brick. Its beautifully proportioned façade, its graceful doorway and massive bell tower, its corridors and quadrangular patio filled with flowers and shrubs, long ago called forth the admiration of Duhaut-Cilly, who visited it in 1827. His description creates for us a picture of unusual splendor set in the midst of that wilderness of olden California:

"The buildings were drawn on a large and ample plan, wholly the idea of the Padre (Peyri); he directed the execution of it, in which he was assisted by a very skillful man, who had contributed also to the building of those at Santa Barbara; so, although these are much more sumptuous, at that place may be recognized the same hand. This building forms a large square of five hundred feet on each side. The main façade is a long peristyle borne on thirty-two square pillars supporting round arches. The edifice is composed, indeed, of only a ground-floor, but its elevation, of fine proportions, gives it as much grace as nobleness. It is covered with a tiled roof, flattened, around which reaches, as much without as within the square, a terrace with an elegant balustrade, which stimulates still more the height. Within is seen a large court, neat and leveled, around which pillars and arches similar to those of the peristyle support a long cloister, by which one communicates with all the dependencies of the Mission."

Under the efficient management of Father Peyri, lasting over a period of thirty years, San Luís Rey prospered and became "a model of energetic, well directed endeavor and growth." By the close of 1801 over three hundred neophytes had been enrolled. Numerous cattle, sheep, and horses grazed the surrounding fields, and large gardens supplied the inhabitants of the mission with food.

Not only was Father Peyri materially successful in his mission; the love and veneration of his Indian charges was a still greater token of his worth. It has been said that he excelled all the other missionaries in his record of achievement. "He was zealous, sensible, and energetic. He knew what he wanted and how to secure it. The Indians worked willingly for him."

When the law expelling all Spaniards from Alta California was passed in 1829, Father Peyri decided that the time had come for him to leave the scene of his long labors. Fleeing to San Diego in the night time in order to escape the sorrow of parting from his Indians, he boarded the ship, which was already weighing anchor. But his Indian friends had learned of his departure and followed him with swift ponies, hoping to bring him back. They arrived just in time to receive his farewell blessing as he stood with outstretched arms on the ship's deck, while the Indians, amid tears, begged him to remain with them.

George Wharton James says that "for many years the Indians left behind at San Luís Rey were in the habit of placing candles and flowers before the picture of Father Peyri and offering prayers to him, pleading with him to return. Even after his death this was kept up, the simple-hearted Indians preferring to pray to a Saint whose goodness they had known and felt, rather than to those of whom they knew nothing but what they were told."

After secularization, the Indians at San Luís Rey were scattered and the church property was sold. It was later returned to the church by the United States government, but it had suffered much from neglect and misuse, its garden court even having been used for numerous bullfights. United States troops used it as a military post during the Mexican War and for some time following its close.

San Luís Rey was later restored and, on May 12, 1893, it was rededicated as a Franciscan college. Something of the original simple beauty of the old mission buildings has been lost in the process of restoration.

Rancho Santa Margarita y Las Flores

For many miles round about, Mission San Luís Rey possessed great ranchos on which thousands of head of live stock grazed in mission days. Among these vast domains was Rancho Santa Margarita y Las Flores, to the north, still one of the princely estates of California.

Ruins of the stout adobe walls of the Asistencia of San Pedro, or Las Flores, built by the mission Fathers before 1823, may still be seen on a knoll overlooking the blue waters of the Pacific, at some distance from the present Las Flores ranch houses. For many years this building was the Hospice where travelers between Missions San Luís Rey and San Juan Capistrano stopped to rest.

The present Las Flores rancho house was erected by M. A. Foster, son of Don Juan Foster, who had purchased the estate of ninety thousand acres from Pío and Andrés Pico, in 1864. It is a large two-story adobe of the Monterey type, with inviting patio, verandas below and above extending across front and sides, and in the rear a low, one-story wing rambling from room to room. Set amid age-old trees, facing

the ocean, this delightful old house, with its sense of peace and tranquillity, perpetuates the traditional hospitality of the Californians, and presents a picture of early rancho life unexcelled in this state.

Asistencia de San Antonio de Pala

The most distinctive of Father Peyri's activities was the founding of the Asistencia de San Antonio de Pala, in 1816, as a branch of Mission San Luis Rey. Located in the Valley of Pala about twenty miles from the mission, a thousand Indian neophytes were soon enrolled from the rancherías of the district.

Pala Chapel is especially noted for its picturesque campanile and for its original Indian frescoes, for many years hidden by a coat of whitewash. The campanile stands apart from the main chapel building, in the old cemetery. It has been restored and is now joined to the main building by a little arched gateway. In its two graceful arches still hang the ancient bells which, for many generations, have called the Indians to prayer.

The Indian population of mission days has disappeared from Pala, but the evicted Palatinguas from Warner's Ranch who now live there, and other Indians from rancherías for many miles around still attend the services of the chapel and give freely of their labor for its restoration and preservation.

Pala Chapel stands at the base of the Palomar Mountain near Bonsall Station and Fallbrook. A modern highway up the mountain follows somewhat the same route which the old Emigrant Trail took to Warner's Ranch.

Santa Isabel

The Chapel of Santa Isabel was established by Father Fernando Martín on September 20, 1818, as an asistencia or outpost of the mission at San Diego. A permanent structure was erected later, but at what date is unknown. Until very recently, a portion of one of the walls remained, and, each spring this was used to form one end of an improvised chapel of branches and tules where mass was said for the Indians of the region. Two ancient bells hung on a rude wooden beam near-by and a tall cross made of saplings marked the consecrated spot. The appearance of the chapel has been described thus:

"When the festival time approaches, this picturesque church springs into beauty as if by magic. The walls are made of verdant boughs, interwoven with branches of green, and wild flowers are brought in to decorate the altar—a pathetic evidence of the sincerity of the worshippers of the district." Those who visit the region today will find that "nothing remains of the original buildings save the outlines of the structures, faintly visible under the pasture grass. The present chapel, a new one, is not on the site of the old structure."

Old Town

The old San Diego Presidio left an heir in the tiny town which had grown up at the foot of Presidio Hill as an overflow from the garrison. As the tide of immigration increased, the village on the lowlands grew and prospered, and there the romantic, pastoral life of Spanish San Diego was lived, leaving its imprint upon the adobe houses which still cluster about the Plaza.

The Old Town Plaza, once noisy and dusty with bullfights, Judas-hangings and other entertainments typical of its Spanish-Mexican population, today lies in a perpetual siesta amid the refreshing green of lawns and shrubbery. Above it floats the American flag, reminding one of that memorable day, July 29, 1846, when a group of men under

Lieutenant Rowan were ordered by Captain Dupont of the "Cyane" to raise the American colors (a naval emblem—not the Stars and Stripes) on the flagpole at the Old Town Plaza. Twenty minutes later, Frémont and his California Battalion arrived on the spot. Old Glory, however, was not raised until November 1846, when, according to Winifred Davidson, "amid shots from the California Rangers, young Albert B. Smith nailed up the flag to the flagpole, Señora María Antonia Machado de Silvas having boldly rushed out from her home and cut away the halyards, rescuing the Mexican flag which had been flying there for some unknown period."

The incoming practical Yankees soon saw that the old San Diego was unsuitable for a seaport town, and a New San Diego, located on San Diego Bay, at length superseded it. William Heath Davis built the first wharf there in 1850, but his venture was a financial failure and nothing more was attempted until 1867, when Alonzo E. Horton arrived and soon afterward laid out the nucleus of the present city. But something of the pastoral peace and simple charm of the past still lingers about the little Plaza at Old Town, and the lure of its quaint adobes brings many a visitor to the gates of the modern city.

Of the older adobe buildings which once stood about the Plaza, none remain today. A few of the later ones, with their low tiled roofs and cool corridors, their flower-filled patios and their many memories, still face the quiet Plaza, dreaming of yesterday: on the southeast corner, the Bandini house, recently restored by Cave J. Couts, Jr.; on the south, the Estudillo house, popularly but erroneously known as "Ramona's Marriage Place"; and on the west the Machado adobe with its romantic and colorful associations. Near by are other old buildings of equal interest: Casa de Carrillo, Casa de Pedrorena, Casa de Stewart, Casa de López, and the little Chapel of the Immaculate Conception. And, mingled with these, are places equally interesting that are associated with the coming of the Americans and the building of a new order.

Casa de Carrillo

Casa de Carrillo has been variously known as the Pear Garden House, the Fitch House, and Rose's Garden House, according to the different owners who sojourned within its walls. It is but a remnant of the earliest and one of the largest of the great casas in which the aristocratic Spanish families of the period lived. Begun as early as 1810 in the old pear orchard planted in 1807 by Francisco María Ruiz, it became the home of Joaquín Carrillo and Ignacia López de Carrillo. It was the social center of their day. From its doors, that remarkable double wedding journey set forth in the spring of 1827 for Monterey, Agustín Zamorano and Luisa Argüello, and Romualdo Pacheco and Ramona Carrillo, the principals, together with Governor Echeandía and nearly all of San Diego forming its train. Here, too, Henry Delano Fitch, the gallant New Bedford sea captain, met and wooed the beautiful Josefa Carrillo and eloped with her to South America, in 1829. The house was purchased in 1866 by Louis Rose, a pioneer business man prominent in the affairs of Old San Diego after 1850. In 1874, while occupied by Judge Benjamin Hayes, great authority on Spanish land grants, the old home was revisited by Josefa Carrillo de Fitch, nearly sixty years after her dramatic elopement.

The Estudillo Adobe

The Estudillo adobe was built about 1826 by José Antonio Estudillo. It was a center of hospitality, receiving a brilliant company of friends from San Diego to Monterey, and Don José's wife, Doña Victoria, was known as Lady Bountiful to the entire countryside.

The house was once topped by a cupola from which the family and guests could in safety watch the bullfights and other entertainments staged on the adjoining Plaza. In 1846 it "became a sanctuary" for all the women and children while Old Town was occupied by American troops and guns from Fort Stockton startled the sleepy pueblo.

The old house, with its twelve rooms and its long beamed chapel, all opening on to a spacious inner court, is well preserved, and the lovely patio garden, with its fountain and its many varieties of trees and shrubs bright with fruit and flowers, affords a vivid picture of romantic, pastoral California. For more than twenty years the late T. P. Getz cherished the place, gathering within its walls many valuable Spanish, Indian, and early American antiquities.

The Bandini House

The Bandini house, built also about 1826, was originally a one-story adobe, a second story being added when it passed into the hands of the Seeley family. Broad balconies encircle it above and below, retaining the old-time grace and charm of Spanish Californian architecture. Juan Bandini, a native of Peru, was, for nearly forty years, one of the leading citizens of Alta California. He took a prominent part in its affairs and saw it pass from Spanish to Mexican control in 1822.

Juan Bandini's daughters were noted for their beauty, and his home was a center of social gayety as well as of political affairs for nearly twenty years. Arcadia Bandini married the young pioneer Yankee, Abel Stearns, and her sister Ysidora married another American, Cave J. Couts, while Josefa married Pedro Carrillo. Juan Bandini, himself a famous dancer, introduced the waltz to Alta California society.

Don Juan was friendly to the American cause and his house was used by Robert F. Stockton as his headquarters during the period of American occupation, in 1846. His daughters there made one of the first American flags in California. Here, too, on December 9, 1846, after a harrowing three nights' journey of thirty-five miles made in bare feet over country luxuriantly covered with prickly pears and guarded by mounted Californians, the brave lad, Edward Beale, with his Indian servant and Kit Carson, the scout, delivered the message from General Stephen W. Kearny to Commodore Stockton calling for sadly needed reinforcements after the battle of San Pascual. As a result of the bravery of these men, Kearny and his soldiers, hungry and footsore, many of them wounded, arrived at Old Town, San Diego, December 12, 1846. There on the Plaza, opposite the old Bandini and Estudillo houses, the D.A.R., in 1920, placed a granite boulder bearing a bronze tablet marking the end of the Kearny trail.

The Bandini house was used as a stage station in the '60's and was then known as the Cosmopolitan Hotel. The building has recently been restored by Cave J. Couts, grandson of Juan Bandini.

Other Old Town Adobes

Casa de Pedrorena was the home of Miguel de Pedrorena, a native of Madrid and a man of high birth and excellent education. He came to San Diego in 1838, and, being courteous and polite in manner and of a gracious bearing, won the heart and hand of María Antonia Estudillo. Don Miguel was a member of the Constitutional Convention at Monterey in 1849.

Casa de Machado is one of four or five similar adobe houses built by José Manuel Machado for himself and his married daughters on the large town place where he first settled. This, one of two such homes which survive, was built for María Antonia Machado de Silvas and is almost an exact duplicate of the old Wrightington house, razed in the '90's. This historic spot, now marked only by a tall palm tree planted by Serafina Wrightington when a child, served as Colonel John C. Frémont's headquarters in 1846.

The Stewart house was built by Manuel Machado for his daughter, Rosa, who married John C. Stewart, a shipmate of Richard Henry Dana, Jr. Dana describes his visit to the house in 1859, in his book, *Two Years Before the Mast.* It was still occupied, in 1932, by "Jack" Stewart's eldest daughter, Rosa.

The López adobe was built about 1835 by Francisco López, a member of one of the older San Diegan families. The Cota house, also erected about 1835, was built by Ramón Cota, a cattle owner of the Mexican period.

Chapel of the Immaculate Conception

Perhaps the most interesting building in Old Town is the Chapel of the Immaculate Conception, "all of its adobe beauty and quaintness," as one writer puts it, "lost behind boards." There seems to be some uncertainty as to the date of construction, but Father Engelhardt says that "the Rev. John C. Holbein laid the cornerstone—September 29, 1851." This cornerstone was laid on a lot near by. The adobe chapel enclosed by clapboards was originally the home of John Brown and was sold by him to Señor Aguirre, who presented it to the Catholic congregation, after restoring and altering it to fit the needs of a church. The Chapel was the especial charge of Father Antonio D. Ubach, the last of the padres, whose ministry at the San Diego mission lasted from 1866 until his death in March 1907. Father Ubach, a native of Catalonia, was educated at Cape Girardeau, Missouri. He traveled thousands of miles as a missionary among the Indians, and came to San Diego in 1866, where he was placed in charge of the Catholic parish. He brought the first organ to San Diego, and also a football with which he played with the boys on the Plaza. He had charge of many valuable relics and records of early Spanish days, but the greater part of his work was among the Indians, by whom he was greatly beloved, and with whom he had much influence. It is said that he was the original of the "Father Gaspara" of Helen Hunt Jackson's novel *Ramona,* and he claimed intimate acquaintance with the originals of the characters in the story and with their families.

Father Ubach's death "was the sundering of the last link which connected the new day with the olden time." He had seen the final transfer of the church's activities from Old Town to new San Diego in 1875, and had lived to see the dawning of a new era and a new century.

Pioneer Americans at Old Town

One of the pioneer newspapers in California and the earliest to be published in San Diego was the *San Diego Herald,* edited by J. Judson Ames. It began in New Town, San Diego, May 29, 1851, but was moved to Old Town in 1853, where it appeared until April 7, 1860. In August 1853, while Ames made one of his frequent trips to San Francisco, he left the *Herald* in charge of George Horatio Derby ("John Phoenix"), who converted it into a humorous sheet, reversed its politics, and brought himself increased fame as a humorist. The *Herald* office occupied the second floor of a building which formerly stood on the northwest corner of the Plaza.

Closely associated with the *Herald* office, where "John Phoenix" continued to make humorous contributions to Judson Ames's paper until 1855, is the Pendleton house, now restored, in Old Town. The house was built in 1852 by Juan Bandini for his daughter Dolores, the wife of Captain Charles Johnson. Captain George Allan Pendleton, a member of the

State Constitutional Convention in 1849, purchased the place in the '60's and lived there with his wife, Concepción B. Estudillo. At that time the house was used as the office of the county recorder and the county clerk, both offices being held by the Captain himself, until his death in 1871.

But it is as the home of George Derby, author of *Phoenixiana,* that the old house has become famous. The humorist lived there during the years 1853–1855 while engineering the first turning of the San Diego River into False Bay, and, during leisure hours, writing humorous bits for the *Herald.* The "naive humor and exquisite drollery" of *Phoenixiana,* compiled and published by the author's friend, J. Judson Ames, has since become classic.

Congress Hall was originally a two-story public house built by George Dewitt Clinton Washington Robinson about 1867. It is thought that it was named after Robert F. Stockton's ship, "Congress." From this building one of the last survivors of the Pony Express rode north. During the '60's and '70's it was the meeting place for "all those colorful early transients who kept San Diego lively with their crude games, shooting affrays, etc." It has been razed.

The Whaley house, in which the San Diego County Court met for about twenty years, was the first brick building to be erected in San Diego County. The white cedar woodwork and all of the hardware used in its construction were brought around Cape Horn, but the bricks were made at Thomas Whaley's own kiln in Old Town, in 1856, and the walls were finished with plaster made from ground sea shells. Mrs. Whaley came to this house as a bride of sixteen years and the place became a center of culture, for Mr. Whaley was a man of excellent education and his wife was of pure French extraction. Five generations of the Whaley family have occupied the old home.

Other Old Town places of interest are: the site of Governor Pío Pico's early home, built in 1824; the old Catholic Cemetery, which was used from 1850–1880 and is the resting-place of some of old San Diego's most distinguished citizens, Miguel de Pedrorena, José Antonio Estudillo, Santiago Argüello and others; also the first American burial ground at San Diego, to which the bodies of the officers and men who fell in the battle of San Pascual were transferred in 1850, being later again removed to the Bennington Military Cemetery on Point Loma, the only graves remaining here in 1932 being those of Frank Ames and little Tommy Whaley; the ruins of the Cobblestone Jail, built in 1850, possibly the first instance of graft in California, having cost the taxpayers over seven thousand dollars and having housed but one prisoner, who promptly cut his way out; the Mason Street School, built about 1870, the first permanent school building erected in San Diego County; and the Altamirano house, in which the *San Diego Union* had its first office, 1868–1870.

Historic Point Loma

Remnants of old Indian trails may still be found on Point Loma. Of these the ancient Playa trail, later followed by ox-carts and carretas, horseback riders and pedestrians from the Mission, followed the curving eastern shore of the bay. It may be roughly identified today as Rosecrans Street, especially that part of it which, after crossing Canyon street in Roseville, runs through the modern La Playa and terminates beyond the Fort Rosecrans barracks.

This ancient road today leads to historic ground, for "it is within the United States Government Military Reservation of Fort Rosecrans that lie the sun-drenched, unspoiled acres where he whom we incorrectly name Juan Cabrillo in 1542 first walked in Upper California; where in 1602 Sebastián Vizcaíno built on smooth sands a temporary house of prayer; where the first Spanish graves were heaped; where in 1769 the first California coast beacon was lighted; off which early in the nineteenth century the first and only California naval battle was fought . . . . These and other beginnings . . . ." make of Loma a place of history, of adventure, and of romance. Ballast Point, Fort Guijarros, the Old "Spanish" light, and La Playa, these are some of the historic spots which witnessed those beginnings.

La Punta de Guijarros

La Punta de Guijarros ("The Point of Cobblestones"), so named by Vizcaíno in 1602, was thus designated until early in the nineteenth century when English-speaking men began to arrive at Old San Diego and La Playa. Captain George Vancouver, who anchored there in 1793, referred to it as "Punta de Guiranos." But it is the memory of long vanished Boston ships steadied on their stormy homeward voyages around Cape Horn by cargoes of cobblestones within their holds that is preserved for all time by the Yankee translation of the old Spanish name, Ballast Point.

It was on this small jutting headland that the Spanish castillo, Fort Guijarros, designed by Alberto de Cordoba, was begun about 1795, under the direction of Comandante Manuel Rodríguez. It was completed by the beginning of the nineteenth century and manned by Catalonian soldiers from the San Diego Presidio. Here occurred the so-called "Battle of San Diego" on March 22, 1803, when the American brig, "Lelia Byrd," commanded by Captain William Shaler, was fired on by the Spaniards under command of José Velásquez. The Yankees were attempting to carry on a barter in furs contrary to the Spanish law forbidding foreign trade. "El Jupiter," cast in Manila in 1783, and used at Fort Guijarros in this early Spanish-American naval engagement, is now mounted on the site of old Fort Stockton on Presidio Hill. Fort Guijarros, built of adobe bricks made by the Indians, stood at the foot of the short hill which runs down to the sea from the present Fort Rosecrans barracks. It was abandoned in 1838, and on its site the present lighthouse was erected early in the '80's.

The Old "Spanish" Light

"The actual first light on California's shores was very truly Spanish. It was a lantern hung on a pole erected at the tip of Ballast Point; and was the signal for supply ships coming northward after 1769." The first United States government beacon to be placed on this section of the California coast stood on a ridge less than half a mile from the tip of Point Loma. The Old "Spanish" Light, as it is known, although begun in 1851, was used for the first time at sunset on November 15, 1855. It is neither Spanish nor Mexican but American, and yet some very Spanish features gave it the name which still clings to it. Adobe bricks from the ruins of Fort Guijarros were incorporated into the building, and, although the keepers of Point Loma Light, No. 355, were all, with one exception, Americans, their wives were all Spanish-speaking women, "and the families that grew up on this lonely spot were more Spanish than American." Because of the heavy fogs which obscured the beacon light at this point, the station was abandoned in the '70's for a more suitable site located at the extreme southwestern tip of Point Loma.

La Playa

The canyons of Point Loma "have remained haunts of rare beauty even to this day . . . . They are secret places, the canyons . . . . Even now it is easy to understand how in them it was long ago safe for runaways to hide; for smugglers to

trade; for thieves to conceal loot; for cut-throats to rendezvous."

But not only was lonely Loma a hiding place for smugglers and bandits. "The scene of the most flourishing hidedroghing business on the Pacific Coast during the period 1824–1846 was old La Playa on Point Loma." Here a cosmopolitan town of about eight hundred men grew up about the ten or twelve great barn-like hide houses established there by the captains of Boston trading-ships and named for the vessels which they commanded. The most famous of these, the "Brookline," commanded by Captain James O. Locke, was the first to be erected and the last to disappear. It was located near the sea-wall before the south buildings of the Quarantine Station. Vessels from almost every maritime nation in the world found anchorage in the little harbor. The crude but colorful life of the day is vividly described by Richard Henry Dana, Jr., in *Two Years Before the Mast*, and by Alfred Robinson in *Life in California*. Old "Hide Park," as the Yankees called it, occupied the sandy tableland which extends from the modern La Playa through the Quarantine Station and beyond, and which reaches back to the barren ridge on the west.

The site of the old Mexican customs house maintained on Point Loma during this period is probably identified by the ruins on the property of Frank S. Jennings, 1036 Bay Street, in Roseville, just north of the modern La Playa. Don Juan Bandini was the first customs house keeper.

About halfway between the tip of Ballast Point and the present cavalry corrals, headquarters for two New England whaling companies, the Packard Brothers and the Johnson Brothers, were established during the middle of the nineteenth century. "The remains of the try-pot fires, the sand still impregnated with oil and soot," may still be seen in this locality.

Other Sites on Historic Loma

Loma's acres include other sites worthy of note: the all but forgotten "Mormon Well," that futile attempt at coal mining carried on by members of the industrious Mormon Battalion while stationed at Fort Stockton in 1847, a spot about half-way between the sea-cliffs and the crest of the promontory, now hidden and almost inaccessible because of the dense undergrowth; the Bennington Military Cemetery, established in 1852 on the crest of Point Loma, where a granite boulder from the battlefield of San Pascual marks the graves of the heroes who fell there on December 6, 1846, and where a monument marks the resting-place of those other heroes for whom the place is named, sixty sailors and marines who lost their lives on July 22, 1905, when the boilers of the U.S.S. gunboat, "Bennington," exploded while at anchor in San Diego Bay; and Fort Rosecrans, the military reservation ordered by the United States government, February 26, 1852, and taken possession of February 28, 1870, named for General William S. Rosecrans, who was in San Diego with Alonzo E. Horton in 1867.

The Old Emigrant Trail

Juan Bautista de Anza, who opened the route across the Colorado Desert into California in 1774 and 1775, entered the San Jacinto Mountains from the desert via San Felipe Creek. On March 12–13, 1774, he camped at San Gregorio at the entrance to Borrego Valley where welcome forage refreshed the half-starved animals. Passing through the valley on the 14th a halt was made at Santa Catharina at the mouth of Coyote Canyon at Reed's Springs, or Lower Willows, just above Beatty's Ranch. The following day the wayfarers entered Riverside County.

Anza's route was superseded by another trail opened up by Pedro Fages on an expedition against the Yuma Indians in 1782. Instead of taking the old path back to San Gabriel, Fages blazed a new one by way of Carrizo Creek, San Felipe Valley, and Warner's Pass. This route was rediscovered in 1825 by Santiago Argüello in pursuit of Indian horse thieves, and in January 1826 the Mexican government sent Romualdo Pacheco, Lieutenant of Engineers, to investigate it. As a result of his findings it was adopted as an official mail route and from then on it was used occasionally by mail carriers and traders from Sonora. Probably the first Americans to come this way were David E. Jackson and his fur-trading party, who came overland from Santa Fe in 1831. This road, which came to be known as the Emigrant Trail, formed a part of the Southern Overland Trail and was a much-traveled path during the '40's and '50's. From September, 1858, until the beginning of the Civil War it was also the route of the famous Butterfield Stage.

This trail, after crossing the deserts a little south of the international boundary line, entered what is now San Diego County via the Carrizo Creek and Warner's Ranch. Passing down the mountain by the old Canyon Road to Sonora, the route proceeded by way of what is now Oak Grove in San Diego County to Temecula and Elsinore in Riverside County, where it proceeded northwest to Misión San Gabriel and Los Angeles.

Another branch of the southern Emigrant Trail passed from Warner's down Palomar Mountain by the old Indian trail back of Pala Chapel to Misión San Luís Rey. Still another route, followed by General Stephen W. Kearny in 1846, led from Warner's to San Diego via Santa Isabel and San Pascual.

Warner's Ranch

When the Spaniards first visited Agua Caliente (the "hot springs"), they found an Indian ranchería there. All of the land surrounding the springs, about 49,000 acres in all, later came under the joint control of Misión San Diego and Misión San Luís Rey, remaining in their possession until the secularization and confiscation of the missions in 1836. At that time the whole valley, known as the Valle de San José, was granted to Silvestre de la Portilla, but his grant seems to have lapsed later, for when Jonathan T. Warner, a Connecticut Yankee, applied for the land in 1844 the missions still laid claim to it.

Warner, who had come to California with the David E. Jackson party in 1831, was one of the first Americans to become an extensive landholder in California. He dispensed liberal hospitality on his great estate, and Warner's Ranch became an objective for all of those early wayfarers who entered California over the old Emigrant Trail, which crossed the Colorado Desert from Yuma. It was the camping place for various divisions of the Army of the West, notably Stephen W. Kearny's regiment and the Mormon Battalion which passed that way in 1846 and 1847. Again in 1853, explorers for a Pacific railroad passed and re-passed it in their search for a suitable route.

Warner's Ranch became a stopping-place for the Butterfield Overland Stage in 1858, and remains of the old adobe stage station, one mile east of the ranch house, have been marked and are being preserved by the Native Sons of the Golden West. It stands in the midst of wide, sloping fields near a group of giant cottonwoods. Below it lie extensive meadows, perpetually green, where the famous herds of Warner's Ranch graze. The old adobe ranch house itself is still the administrative headquarters for the property.

The Butterfield Stage Route

On September 16, 1857, the Butterfield Overland Mail Company (closely affiliated with Wells Fargo Express Company) was awarded the contract for the first transcontinental mail and passenger line to California, winning over eight other bidders.

A southern route through Yuma, Arizona, was selected because it was open all the year round, and St. Louis was chosen as the central supply depot. Coaches or spring wagons were used, and they carried passengers as well as mail. Stations were erected along the entire route at twenty-mile intervals, horses being changed at every station and drivers every two or three hundred miles.

The first stage on the Butterfield line left St. Louis on September 15, 1858, and a second followed the next day. "If the chronicle of the Butterfield Stage Line could be fully told it would include stories of Indian raids, hold-ups, robberies, accidents, cloudbursts and sandstorms. . . . . Most of the relics of the days of the Butterfield stage have been swept away, but there are still standing on the southern route that crosses the Colorado desert some ruins which mark the stations of the fifties."

Butterfield Stage Stations

One of the chief remaining landmarks of the famous old Butterfield Stage route is at Vallecito ("Little Valley"). This section of the route goes northwest to Warner's Ranch and southeast through Mason Valley and Carrizo Canyon, joining the highway from San Diego to Yuma, Arizona, near Dixieland. The wagons of the Mormon Battalion, under command of Lieutenant-Colonel Cooke, in 1847, were the first vehicles to pass this way on their journey to San Diego.

Vallecito has long been deserted, a prey to vandals and earthquakes, its walls built of sod, rapidly crumbling before the elements. Near by are a number of graves, and the one gravestone in the place records the death of one "John Hart," at the age of 30 years in the year 1867."

Along this stretch of the old Butterfield route there were three other stations, one at Carrizo Creek, where little more than a heap of mud remains today; another at Palm Springs, where not even a palm is left to tell of the past; and a third at San Felipe, where Kearny and his men had camped in 1846, on their march to San Diego and the battle of San Pascual. A well-preserved station, one of the few still occupied, stands at Oak Grove, thirteen miles northwest of Warner's Ranch.

The Kearny Trail

The trail which General Stephen W. Kearny and the Army of the West followed through Imperial and San Diego counties, on their way to the fatal battle of San Pascual, has been traced by Arthur Woodward, curator of history, Los Angeles Museum, who has been over the old Kearny trail through Imperial and San Diego counties, tracing its route and locating the camp sites step by step. He describes the trail and camp sites as follows:

"On November 28, they pressed on slowly and came to the large spring near which in later days the Carrizo stage station was erected. . . . . From Carrizo, where they camped on the night of the 28th, they pushed on up the dry creek bed to Vallecito, where they camped on the night of the 29th and 30th. . . . .

"Beyond Vallecito the road winds across the valley to the base of a small rocky ridge, 4.3 miles distant. On the other side of this low ridge lies Mason Valley. Up this valley marched the troops for a distance of 4.8 miles until they came to the entrance of Box Canyon, a narrow rocky defile through the hills. . . . . Here the road emerges and swings west again and after passing over a low ridge of hills drops into San Felipe Valley. The troops marched for about twelve or thirteen miles along this route until they came to the Indian village of San Felipe, which was on the creek. They camped here on the night of December 1 and the next day pressed on up the valley, topped the divide and dropped down to Warner's Ranch. The present road to Vallecito from Warner's probably follows fairly accurately the old trail, indeed, in Box Canyon (the spot where the Mormon Battalion under Cooke had so much trouble early in 1847) it cannot have changed very much.

"The army camped a trifle south of Warner's Ranch house, ... The place upon which they camped is probably the rather level grassy flat a few hundred yards south of the house.

"Here they remained recuperating during the days of December 2 and 3. They started for Santa Isabel the morning of December 4th and, after marching for thirteen and a half miles, they camped near the old Mission station of Santa Isabel (probably in the flats southeast of the present site of the chapel on the edge of the creek).

"On the morning of the 5th, the army marched south-southwest to the ranchería of Santa María. They were delayed en route by a parley with Captain Gillespie and the naval reinforcements from San Diego, probably at Ballena, about six miles from Santa Isabel. Thence through the hills they travelled southwest, skirting the western edge of what is now the Valley of Santa Maria (in which the town of Ramona is situated) and probably camping at the head of Clevenger's Canyon. . . . . It is about nine or ten miles via the hill trail to the point where they probably emerged into the valley of San Pascual on the morning of the 6th.

"Their trail to San Pascual lay along a rolling brush covered ridge and probably emerged into San Pascual at a point just this side of the spot where the Santa Maria river empties into San Pascual Valley. . . . ."

The Battle of San Pascual

The battle of San Pascual was fought in San Pascual Valley near an Indian village of that name, nine miles east of the site of the present town of Escondido. It was the "bloodiest" of all the battles fought on California soil (aside from Indian massacres), and took place on December 6, 1846, during the period of American occupation.

A detachment of regulars under command of General Stephen W. Kearny had, after crossing the desert, reached Warner's Ranch worn and footsore. From there they marched on toward San Diego. In the narrow San Pascual valley they were met by General Andrés Pico with a superb body of horsemen, recruited mostly from the ranchos. . . . ." After severe losses, Kearny rallied his men on the top of a hill, from where Kit Carson and Lieutenant Edward F. Beale slipped out into the darkness to seek reinforcements from San Diego.

Sixteen or eighteen Americans were killed in the battle of San Pascual, and nearly a score were seriously wounded, among the latter being General Kearny and Captain Gillespie. A monument erected on the site on December 20, 1925, by the state of California memorializes the men who gave their lives in this battle. A bronze tablet was also placed, on February 22, 1924, by the Daughters of the American Revolution of California. A park under control of the State Park Commission incloses the site, the land having been donated by Colonel Edward Fletcher and other public-spirited citizens of San Diego.

The Alvarado Adobe

The Alvarado Adobe is located northeast of Sorrento Station on the Santa Fe line. It was built in 1840 by Juan Bautista Alvarado (not the Governor of the same name). It was on Rancho Peñasquitas, now locally known as the Diego Alvarado Ranch. It is mentioned in Major Emory's report of General Kearny's expedition in 1846, the welcome abundance of food which the half-starved soldiers found at this place being vividly described.

Rancho Guajome

Although erected after the Mexican period, one of the most typical of the old adobe ranch houses still standing is that on Rancho Guajome (the "Ranch of the Big Frog"), and for this reason the rancho has been proposed as a state park.

Guajome was a part of the original mission lands of San Luís Rey. In 1845 it was granted to two Indians, Andrés and José Manuel. On December 1, 1852, they sold it to Abel Stearns, who gave it as a wedding gift to his sister-in-law, Ysidora Bandini, when she married the American, Colonel Cave J. Couts. The house was built in 1852–1853.

Added historic interest attaches itself to the Guajome adobe because it was one of the several Spanish-Californian homes in which Helen Hunt Jackson was a guest while gathering material for her novel *Ramona*. Sitting with its back to the dusty highway, four miles east of Misión San Luís Rey, the house is entered through a courtyard s̩r-rounded by corrals, barns, stables, and servants' quart ̇s. Snow-white doves strut upon the red-tiled roofs or coo among the eaves. Passing through an open doorway out into the inner patio, one is greeted by the murmur of a fountain and the scent of oranges and limes mingled with that of old-fashioned flowers. Beyond are the living-room and other rooms opening on to the patio, nearly all with their individual fireplaces. In one corner is the old schoolroom with its many windows, erected by Ysidora Bandini Couts, and outside, a few feet south of the house, stands the quaint chapel, filled with quiet and with memories.

Julian, a Town That Came Back

Julian, a little alpine town nestled among forests of oak and conifer, is today the center of a modest agricultural community, where apples, pears, and honey supplant the gold of former days. Frank Gorman, a boy of thirteen years, made the first discovery of gold in the region, when, on February 22, 1870, he discovered the first mine, which was named in honor of the day, George Washington. The Julian gold stampede followed this discovery, and the Golden Chariot, Cuyamaca, Stonewall Jackson, and other locations proved to be very rich. These mines, now inactive, have produced over five million dollars.

Gold in the mines near Julian had about played out in 1880. Then came the boom at Tombstone, Arizona. "When Tombstone came up, Julian went down like a punctured tire," says an old-timer of the California town. "They loaded most of the camp on to wagons, cracked the whips, and drove off to Arizona with it. . . . ."

But Julian was not dead, and with the departure of the miners the surrounding hills and valleys were homesteaded. The region proved exceptionally suitable for fruit growing, bees, and live stock, and Julian was soon a busy trading center for the farmers. The modern motorist, too, is finding this little mountain town to be an alluring playground, with cool woods and tempered air in summer, and, in winter, a touch of snow.

SOURCES

[Credit is here given for source material, and permission to quote is hereby acknowledged]

BEATTIE, GEORGE WILLIAM. *Reopening Anza's Road*. Manuscript, 1931

BOLTON, HERBERT EUGENE. *Fray Juan Crespi, Missionary Explorer on the Pacific Coast, 1769–1774*. University of California Press, Berkeley, California, 1927

BOLTON, HERBERT EUGENE. "Spanish Exploration in the Southwest, 1542–1706," in *Original Narratives of Early American History*, Vol. XVII, Charles Scribner's Sons, New York, 1916

CLELAND, ROBERT GLASS. "Pathfinders," in the series *California*, edited by John Russell McCarthy. Powell Publishing Company, Los Angeles, 1929

DAVIDSON, WINIFRED. *Historic Spots in San Diego.* Manuscript, 1931

———. *Where California Began.* McIntyre Publishing Company, San Diego, California, 1929

DUNN, H. H. "The Prehistoric Painter of Poway," in *Touring Topics* (May, 1930), pp. 36–38, 56

ELDER, DAVID PAUL. *The Spanish Missions of California.* Paul Elder & Company, San Francisco, 1913

EMORY, WILLIAM H. *Notes of a Military Reconnaissance from Fort Leavenworth, Missouri to San Diego, California.* 30th Congress, 1st Session, Senate Executive Document No. 7, Washington, D.C., 1848

ENGELHARDT, ZEPHYRIN. *San Diego Mission.* The James H. Barry Company, San Francisco, 1920

———. *San Luis Rey Mission.* The James H. Barry Company, San Francisco, 1921

GORBY, JOHN S. "After Serra on California's Royal Road," in *Touring Topics*, XXIII, No. 8 (August, 1931), 12–17, 36

HILL, JOSEPH J. *The History of Warner's Ranch and Its Environs.* Privately published, Los Angeles, 1927

JACKSON, HELEN HUNT. *Glimpses of California and the Missions.* Little, Brown & Company, Boston, 1903

JAMES, GEORGE WHARTON. *In and Out of the Old Missions of California.* Little, Brown & Company, Boston, 1906

LOOP, A. M. "The Fight of the Paso del Mar," in *The Silver Gate*, II, No. 1 (January, 1900), edited by James A. Jasper, San Diego

SMYTHE, WILLIAM E. *History of San Diego, 1542–1908.* 2 vols. Vol. I, *Old Town.* The History Company, San Diego, California, 1908

"The Old Ames Press—A Venerable Pioneer," a letter by Edwin A. Sherman, March 22, 1873, with introductory note by Carl I. Wheat, in the *Quarterly of the California Historical Society*, IX, No. 3 (September, 1930), 193–200

"Pattie, James Ohio, A Personal Narrative of," in *Early Western Travels, 1748–1846*, edited by Reuben Gold Thwaites, Vol. XVIII. The Arthur H. Clarke Company, Cleveland, Ohio, 1905

ROBINSON, ALFRED. *Life in California During a Residence of Several Years in That Territory.* William Doxey, San Francisco, 1891

San Diego Magazine. Souvenir Number Commemorating Restoration of Old Mission. VII, No. 9 (September, 1931)

TAYLOR, BAYARD. *El Dorado, or Adventures in the Path of Empire.* H. G. Bohm, London, England, 1850; G. P. Putnam's Sons, New York, 1850 and 1864

WILCOX, HORACE FENTON. "Memories of the Gold Stampede to Julian," as told to John Edwin Hogg, in *Touring Topics*, XXIV, No. 2 (February, 1932), 16–18, 38–39

WOLCOTT, MARJORIE T. "The House near the Frog Pond," in *Touring Topics*, XX, No. 12 (December, 1928), 40–41, 53–56

WOODWARD, ARTHUR. *The Kearny Trail Through Imperial and San Diego Counties.* Manuscript. 1931

SANTA BARBARA COUNTY

SANTA BARBARA COUNTY took its name from Santa Barbara Channel, so called by Vizcaíno in honor of St. Barbara. This was one of the original twenty-seven counties of the state, and the city of Santa Barbara has been its county seat from the beginning.

Painted Cave

On the top of the mountain east of San Marcos Pass, about sixteen miles northwest of Santa Barbara, is a group of Indian pictographs, known as the Painted Cave. The cave, which is on private property, may be reached by a narrow road which branches off to the right of the San Marcos Road about half way to the summit. Conventionalized pictures of the sun, human figures, trees, snakelike creatures, and circular designs and crosses, done in red, white, yellow, and black, cover the interior of the cavern. The origin and meaning of these crudely executed designs have not been determined. The cave is protected from defacement and injury by an iron gate which will be opened by the owner of the property upon payment of a small fee.

Burton Mound

Burton Mound, located within one block north of the West Cabrillo Boulevard and about two blocks southwest from State Street, is today merely a gentle rise in the ground surrounded by city streets and dwellings. The history of the site, however, extends back into antiquity. Excavations made in 1923 by the Museum of the American Indian, Heye Foundation, of New York City, under the supervision of John P. Harrington, with David Banks Rogers, in charge of the field work, revealed the fact that three distinct Indian cultures have lived on the site.

Covering the entire surface of the knoll, the village had spread to the fringes of the surrounding marsh. Over the entire area of about five hundred and fifty feet by four hundred and twenty-five feet evidences of long occupancy were traced. The residential section had been centered about a "strong spring of sweet water" upon the eastern slope of the rise. David Banks Rogers describes the site and the artifacts thus: "A great cemetery extended southwestward from near the crest to well into the marsh. Other burial plots, smaller but highly congested with graves, existed upon the northern and western slopes. Upon the crest of the mound had probably been arranged all of the ceremonial enclosures. . . . .

"A pride in artistic accomplishment appears to have been a passion with these people," as is proved by the unusual beauty and perfection of the numerous relics unearthed. The more recent deposits showed evidence of the contact with white invaders and the loss of the old culture. In place of the "perfectly wrought sandstone bowls . . . . great pestles, as true of contour as though turned in a lathe, and striking ollas . . . . globular in form and narrow-necked," there were found "buttons from Spanish uniforms, glass beads from Venice, and all too frequently old-fashioned wine and rum bottles." The investigation also showed evidence of a more primitive people having occupied a part of the same site for a longer period of time.

Several springs of fresh sulphur water formerly existed on and about the mound. Of these the most interesting was the sulphur spring on the beach at the foot of Chapala Street. At a certain spot on the beach sulphurous fresh water is still found to issue when exposed by very low tides. Three large cold sulphur-water springs were located at the eastern end of the Potter Hotel near the base of the northern slope of the mound. For many years the only neighborhood source of good drinking water entirely free from sulphur was the Burton well, located some thirty-two feet beachward from the northeast end of the old adobe.

After long and careful study, ethnologists have compiled a partial list of the names of the numerous Indian villages which once flourished in the territory bordering the Santa Barbara Channel. Among these authorities, Kroeber, Harrington, and Bancroft have each sought to select the name of the village once located upon the site now known as the Burton Mound.

"Harrington ascribes the name of 'Siuhtun.' Kroeber gives it as 'Alpincha,' locating 'Siuhtun' farther to the north, near the present intersection of State and De la Guerra streets. This latter site was expressly described as 'Yanonalit' by Bancroft." From this Rogers concludes that a "selection of the proper Indian name for any of these moldering sites is, after this lapse of time, impossible." Indian informants, John P. Harrington says, have given the name of this village as Syujtum, meaning "where the two trails run."

The old adobe which for many years stood on the site of this ancient Indian village and which gave the present name to the mound was for nineteen years the home of Don Luís Burton, who came to California with the Wolfskill party in 1831. He became a wealthy merchant and ranchero and in 1839 married María Antonia Carrillo, daughter of Carlos Carrillo. The history of the Burton adobe, however, and the rancho on which it was built, extends back many years.

The old Puerto de Santa Bárbara, or early landing-place for the mission and presidio, was located at the foot of the present Chapala Street west of the mouth of Mission Creek and due east of and comprising the Burton Mound. During mission days this land was owned by Mission Santa Barbara and was called El Rancho de la Playa ("The Ranch of the Beach"). After secularization it became the property of the Mexican government, which granted it to James ("Santiago") Burke, who, in turn, sold it to Joseph Chapman, the young New Englander who had escaped from Bouchard's pirate ship in 1818. Chapman, it is said, erected a small adobe house on the mound, later conveying the land to Benjamin Foxen.

According to tradition, the massive adobe which for over seventy years stood on the mound, and was long the most conspicuous landmark on the Santa Barbara waterfront, was erected by Thomas Robins. For about ten years during the '40's it was the home of Captain George C. Nidever, who, it is said, planted trees and gardens and added two outbuildings to the adobe house. Nidever, in 1851, sold the place to Augustus F. Hinchman, Santa Barbara attorney and prominent citizen. In 1860 it was acquired by Lewis T. Burton, who made the old house his home until his death in 1879. At that time the tract came into the possession of the Seaside Hotel Association and plans to erect a hotel on the site were at once formulated. However, it was not until twenty years later that such a plan was realized. Meanwhile, the old house had been the home successively of various occupants, the last of whom was Max Aman, who lived there during the three years prior to the building of the hotel. In 1901–1902, under the direction of Milo M. Potter, the Potter Hotel was erected and beautiful landscape gardens soon covered the old historic Indian mound. The property again changed hands when, in 1913, it was taken over by the Ambassador Hotel Corporation. The hotel was burned in 1921 and the site was released for archaeological investigations. The place is still a vacant lot.

The Carpinteria Asphalt Pits

Lying along the beach one-quarter of a mile south of U.S. 101 highway are the picturesque asphalt pits of Carpinteria, the history of which extends back into prehistoric times. The first Spaniards who came to the coast found an extensive Indian village near these deposits, and the tar exuding from the banks along the shore was used by the natives for calking boats, baskets, and vessels for carrying liquid. The story of the naming of this village is told by Father Crespi, diarist of the Portolá expedition:

"Not very far from the town we saw some springs of asphaltum. These Indians have many canoes, and at that time were constructing one, for which reason the soldiers named this town Carpintería ('carpenter shop') but I baptized it with the name of San Roque."

The remains of Indian villages are still to be seen in this vicinity and excavations have revealed not only the fact that these locations were used for long periods by primitive peoples, but also the presence of prehistoric animals similar to those taken from the famous La Brea Pits in Los Angeles.

In the early days of Santa Barbara County, wharves were built at this asphaltum deposit and the material was taken out for shipment to San Francisco and other towns in California.

Cabrillo's Grave

Somewhere on the lonely island of San Miguel, which lies just off the coast of Santa Barbara in the Santa Barbara Channel, is the unmarked grave of Juan Rodríguez Cabrillo, discoverer of Alta California. There, in 1542, Cabrillo's ships, the "San Salvador" and the "Victoria," lay anchored for eight days in a port at San Miguel awaiting the abatement of the autumn storms which delayed their passage northward. During this time Cabrillo had a fall, breaking his arm near the shoulder.

In spite of his injury and in the face of many other misfortunes, he continued his voyage, going as far as the Northwest Cape near Fort Ross. Forced back by storms at that point, Cabrillo returned to Cuyler's Harbor on San Miguel. There, on January 3, 1543, the great discoverer passed away, his illness being a result of the injury to his arm incurred several months before.

Sebastián Vizcaíno, sixty years later, entered the Channel on December 4, 1602, the feast day of St. Barbara, whose name was accordingly bestowed upon it by Padre Asunción.

A bronze tablet mounted on a granite boulder in honor of Cabrillo was placed by the Santa Barbara Chapter, D.A.R., in 1919, in the palm garden at the intersection of State Street and Cabrillo Boulevard on the waterfront.

Point Concepción

Point Concepción, which marks a change in the direction of the coast line, was first discovered by Juan Rodríguez Cabrillo on October 18, 1542, and many other early explorers and mariners sighted it. Bolton says that, sailing up the coast from San Diego, the ships had anchored on the 14th off Carpintería, a mile west of Sand Point, on the 15th five miles west of Point Goleta off Naples, on the 16th off Cañada del Refugio, and on the 17th off Gaviota Pass. Cabrillo had difficulty in rounding the Point because of storms, and for eight days was forced to anchor his ships to the southward at San Miguel Island before finally attempting the passage. After several days of buffeting by the storms, he was driven back to anchorage off Gaviota Pass, where he remained three days, taking on wood and water. On November 6 he made a final and successful attempt to pass the Point.

The Point Concepción Light Station was established by the United States government in 1855.

Point Argüello

Point Argüello, a rocky headland located twenty miles southwest of Lompoc, forms, with Point Concepción, the corners of California where the coast line turns from an approximate north and south direction to a line running east and west. Its historic interest is largely associated with the many shipwrecks that have taken place there.

The first of these was probably that of the U.S.S. "Edith," wrecked there in 1849. The story told is that the sailors aboard the "Edith," being anxious to join the gold rush, deliberately put the ship upon the beach, where it was broken by the waves. Some of the crew and passengers stayed for a short time at Rancho Nipomo (in San Luis Obispo County), where the hospitable ranchero, Captain William G. Dana, gave them horses and money that they might continue to the mines. Afterward the ship was salvaged by Dana and the materials were used on the rancho. The smokestack on the forge in the old blacksmith shop, still standing, was among the wreckage put to good use by this thrifty Bostonian.

The most famous disaster occurring at Point Argüello took place in 1923 when seven United States destroyers southward bound in an early morning fog piled on the rocks with a loss of twenty-seven men. Remains of these vessels may still be seen just off shore. The most recent toll which the point has taken from the procession of ships which constantly pass that way was the passenger steamer "Harvard," which went aground about one and one-half miles north of Point Argüello on May 30, 1931.

The Trail of Gaspar de Portolá

On the southwest corner of the grounds of Santa Barbara's new courthouse is a boulder placed by the Santa Barbara Chapter, D.A.R., and set with a bronze tablet bearing the inscription:

In honor of Governor de Portolá, his officers and soldiers, and Fray Juan Crespi (diarist), the first white men to march through the wilderness of California. Arrived at Santa Barbara, August 18, 1769, and camped in this vicinity two days.

The land expedition from Misión San Diego to Monterey Bay, under direct command of Gaspar de Portolá, left San Diego on July 14, 1769. Traveling up the coast, the party had blazed a trail which was later the route followed approximately by El Camino Real ("the Royal Road"), along which the California mission chain was established.

On August 16 Portolá and his men made camp at an Indian village near what is now known as Rincón Point, on Rincón Creek, and on the seventeenth they reached another village where they found the natives engaged in the building of a canoe. From this incident, the place was called La Carpintería, a name still retained by the present-day town near the site.

On the eighteenth, Portolá reached a very large native town on the site of the modern city of Santa Barbara. There camp was pitched on the lagoon which lies east of the city. Proceeding up the coast along the Santa Barbara Channel, many Indian villages were passed. The natives of this region were not only numerous but were intelligent as well, being fishermen and the builders of large and well-made canoes in which they plied back and forth between the mainland and the channel islands.

In the days following, the party passed up the coast, camping successively near Mescal Island, Naples in Dos Pueblos Canyon, Tajiguas Creek, Gaviota, El Bullito Creek, Cañada del Cojo, Espada Creek, Rocky Point, Arguëllo Point, Cañada Honda, and Santa Rosalía just south of the present village of Surf. On August 30 the Santa Inez River was reached, and on the next day camp was made at San Antonio Creek. On September 1 they passed Guadalupe Lake, beyond which lay the boundaries of the present San Luis Obispo County.

The Anza Trail

Juan Bautista de Anza in 1775 followed a well-trodden path from San Gabriel to Monterey, broken first by Gaspar de Portolá and followed later a half dozen times by Pedro Fages and also by Father Junípero Serra on his way to Mexico in 1772. On his hurried trip in the spring of 1775, Anza made only three camps in Santa Barbara County: west of Goleta, April 12; east of Rocky Point, April 13; and on the south bank of the Santa Inez River near its mouth, April 14. On April 15 Anza rode all the way from the Santa Inez River to Mission San Luís Obispo, a distance of over fifty miles. On his return from Monterey, he camped on the north bank of the Santa Inez River, April 26. On the 27th he met Father Serra on his way back from the City of Mexico. At the earnest solicitation of the latter, Anza tarried for the remainder of the day recounting the story of his overland journey to the interested friar, and camping with him that night somewhere east of Point Concepción and west of Naples. On the 28th Anza continued on his way, camping at the end of the day at Dos Pueblos (Naples).

The San Francisco colonists led by Anza in 1776 made camp at the following sites: Rincón Creek, west of Rincón Point, February 24; near Carpintería Landing, at an Indian village called by Father Font, San Buenaventura, February 25; northeast of Mescal Island near the village of Mescaltitán which was west of Goleta, February 26; El Cojo Canyon, east of Point Concepción, February 27; near Surf, at the mouth of the Santa Inez River, February 28; and near the mouth of San Antonio Creek, February 29.

An Ancient Sycamore Tree

The aged sycamore tree which stands on the corner of Milpas and Quinientos streets, Santa Barbara, was used as a bearing-point for sailing vessels as early as 1800. Travelers by land also passed by the great tree, which was visible for miles on land and sea. Portolá and his band of explorers, Serra and the other mission Fathers, as they traveled up and down the coast founding missions, may, long ago, have been guided by the giant tree or have rested under its sheltering branches. It has been marked with a bronze tablet placed by the Santa Barbara Chapter, D.A.R.

The Santa Barbara Presidio

Santa Barbara, the last of the four presidial pueblos founded by the Spanish government in Alta California, was established in 1782 by Governor Felipe de Neve and Captain José Francisco Ortega and his fifty soldiers, accompanied by Fray Junípero Serra, who dedicated the site. Like the other presidial pueblos, it was, for a time, under military rule but eventually acquired its own civil government.

The outlines of the old Santa Barbara Presidio have been practically obliterated by the development of the modern city of Santa Barbara, but may still be traced by the present streets: De la Guerra, Carrillo, Anacapa, and Garden. The comandante's house, destroyed in the earthquake of 1925, formerly stood near the intersection of the present streets of Santa Barbara and Cañon Perdido ("the lost cannon," about which there is an interesting story). Where the lines of the old Presidio crossed these streets, the Native Sons of the Golden West have placed bronze markers in the sidewalks. El Cuartel, one of the small buildings in which the soldiers of the Presidio were stationed, still stands on Cañon Perdido Street, between Santa Barbara and Anacapa streets. The southeasterly boundary of the Presidio site has been marked by a boulder and tablet placed by the Santa Barbara Chapter, D.A.R.

The site of the Arellanes Adobe, also destroyed in the earthquake of 1925, was on De la Guerra Street at the northeast corner of Santa Barbara Street, at a point about fifty feet from the east corner of the old Presidio walls. Said to have been erected as early as 1795, it was probably the first house of any importance to be built outside of the Presidio inclosure.

The site of the old Presidio church, an adobe structure twenty-four by sixty feet, completed in 1797, was almost on the building line on the west side of Santa Barbara Street. Directly north, what was formerly Santa Barbara's first graveyard, the burial ground of the soldiers and early settlers until 1818, is now intersected by Carrillo Street.

The Carrillo Adobe still standing on Carrillo Street one-half block east of State Street was built about 1828 by Daniel Hill, a carpenter, mason, and "general factotum," a native of Massachusetts, who came to California in 1823, and married Rafaela Ortega. It was the home of Captain John Wilson and Doña Ramona Carrillo de Wilson, and, later, of Guillermo Carrillo. The first city council met there in 1850, and there was born the first child of American parents in Santa Barbara, Isobel, daughter of Thomas O. Larkin, first American consul in California, and Rachel (Hobson) Holmes Larkin. The building was purchased in 1928 by Major Max C. Fleischmann and later given to the Santa Barbara Foundation to be preserved as one of the historic buildings of Santa Barbara.

The Covarrubias Adobe, located at 715 Santa Barbara Street between De la Guerra and Ortega streets, was built about 1837. This house is a fine example of California architecture, and within its hospitable walls many gay social gatherings have taken place. Owing to the fact that the sunshine was permitted to enter the rooms through skylights, the building is in a remarkable state of preservation.

On the north side of Carrillo Street just east of the Carrillo Adobe is the site of the Casa de Aguirre, now occupied by the Little Town Club. Perhaps the most famous of all the old Spanish homes in its day was the Aguirre house built by Don José Antonio Aguirre. To it he brought his bride, María Estudillo, in 1842. The house of nineteen rooms was built in the form of a quadrangle, inclosing a paved court or patio. Around the latter a *corredor,* shaded by a roof supported on hand-carved posts, gave sheltered access to the house or served as an outdoor living room. An owner of ships, a man of "fine presence, affable in manner and well-liked by all . . . . and a wealthy trader"—as Bancroft characterizes him—"Don Antonio was an excellent type of the old-time Spanish merchant, keeping aloof for the most part from smuggling and politics, though often employed by the government."

Casa de la Guerra

Casa de la Guerra, which, after the mission, is perhaps the most interesting remaining landmark of old Spanish days in Santa Barbara County, was built by José Antonio Julian de la Guerra y Noriega, with the aid of Indian labor, during the years 1818 to 1826. One of the adobe bricks in the front corridor of the old house still bears the date 1826, plainly marked on it.

Don José Antonio, a native of Spain, came from Mexico to California as a lieutenant in 1806. There he married María Antonia Juliana Carrillo, and in 1815 was made comandante of the Presidio of Santa Barbara, an office which he held until 1842.. De la Guerra was a man of more than ordinary character and ability, exercising a strong political and moral influence on the history of Alta California in his day. His home was the center of social life in Santa Barbara and a stopping-place for many distinguished visitors. Among others, Richard Henry Dana, author of *Two Years Before the Mast,* visited the old adobe mansion in 1834, and again in 1859. In his book he describes the wedding of his host's daughter and gives a pleasing picture of the gayeties, the beautiful women, and the courtly gentlemen.

The patios, the shaded corridors, and the rambling rooms of the De la Guerra adobe are now occupied by studios and shops in old Spanish style. It has become not only the nucleus of an art colony, rivaling in charm and beauty the bazaars of the Old World, but also the inspiration and motif of the new Santa Barbara which has grown up since the earthquake of 1925. An architectural renaissance, imbued with the breath of old Spain, has made of Santa Barbara a vivid, colorful, distinctive city wherein unity and harmony of style form a unique and artistic ensemble. And the heart of it all is the old De la Guerra house, typifying the "cameo-sharp" outlines of the California-Spanish type of architecture and the romantic and historic charm of the past from which it survives.

El Paseo, the Street in Spain, centers about the old adobe, and there, during Santa Barbara's annual "Old Spanish Days" Fiesta, the cool shops and corridors are thronged with costumed revelers, many of them descendants of the courtly Spanish dons and doñas who came to California in the eighteenth century.

The new Santa Barbara Courthouse, the culmination of this architectural renaissance, dedicated on August 14, 1929, is one of the most beautiful adaptations of the Spanish-California architecture in the entire state and one of the most notable public buildings in America.

Misión Santa Bárbara

Misión Santa Bárbara was not founded until four years after the establishment of the Presidio. Father Serra had selected the site, but, owing to his death in 1784, the work of building the mission was carried on by his successor, Father Fermín Francisco de Lasuén, who performed the ceremonies of consecration on December 16, 1786, although the Day of St. Barbara, December 4, has always been "regarded and reported as the day of founding." (Engelhardt.)

The building of the first temporary chapel and adjoining dwellings and storehouses was begun the following year. Gradually, the establishment grew in size and prosperity until, in 1807, there were over seventeen hundred neophytes living in the Indian village of two hundred and fifty adobe huts which surrounded the mission.

In 1789 a new church of adobe roofed with tile replaced the temporary structure. In 1793 this church was replaced by a larger one, which was finished in 1794. This, in turn, was superseded by a more magnificent structure, the earthquake of 1812 having damaged the former building. The new structure, built on the same site, was dedicated on September 10, 1820. This building, mellowed by passing years, with the marks of storm and earthquake upon it, has been restored after each visitation in keeping with its ancient aspect. Its massive walls, six feet thick, its stone steps and tile floors, two of its six chapels built in the solid walls, which are of double thickness at these points, all make of it the most solidly built of any of the missions. The temblor of 1925, however, necessitated almost rebuilding the church, and Father Augustine Obrecht was tireless in seeing that the minutest detail was restored as before, only reinforcing the structure by modern methods so that the building might withstand future shocks.

In the beautiful old cemetery, inclosed by high adobe walls and shaded by lovely trees and shrubs, are the graves of four thousand Indians and five hundred white people. There, too, is a grave, said to be that of Juana María, an Indian woman reputed to have lived alone for eighteen years on San Nicolás Island off the Santa Barbara Channel. Juana María was found and brought to Santa Barbara by Captain George Nidever, in 1853. She died in 1854 and it is thought was buried in the mission garden, although no record of the burial has been found in the mission archives nor is there any document bearing testimony of her baptism and the bestowal of the Christian name, Juana María, after her rescue. However, Captain Nidever's veracity and the high regard in which he was held in Santa Barbara, where he lived for over fifty years, lends sufficient weight to the story, to which he was the chief witness, to give it credence. A bronze tablet was placed at the grave by the Santa Barbara Chapter, D.A.R., in 1928.

Before the church stands a stone fountain of simple, harmonious design, and near it is a long stone trough, once used by the Indian women for laundry purposes. Across the street about five hundred feet from the mission is a stone reservoir, a part of the irrigation system constructed and finished in 1806, to collect water for the mission orchards and gardens. This reservoir, still in perfect condition, forms a part of the water system of the city of Santa Barbara. Across Pedregoso Creek, about a mile and a half north of the mission, in what is now Mission Canyon, a dam was constructed in 1807, "at a point high enough to allow the water to flow down into the mill reservoir. This mill with its reservoir was built at the same time behind and above the larger reservoir mentioned before. . . . . The mill is in ruins and a small part of its reservoir has fallen in. The ruins may be seen just below the road that leads to the Normal School," while the dam, now much silted up, and portions of the aqueduct are still to be seen in the Blakesley Botanic Gardens and at various points in the canyon. A bronze tablet has been placed just above the dam by the La Cumbre Chapter, D.A.R.

Below the lower reservoir are ruins of the pottery kiln where utensils, adobe bricks, and tiles were made by the neophytes under the Fathers' supervision. Northeast of this reservoir is the filter, or settling tank, where the water was purified for mission use. Fairly well preserved, this interesting relic is decidedly picturesque, resembling an ornamental vault or tomb. (See Engelhardt, *Santa Barbara Mission*, p. 85, for a diagram of the mission irrigation system.)

Mission Santa Barbara has never suffered from the neglect and decay which fell to the lot of the other missions after secularization. In 1842 the bishop's residence was changed from San Diego to Santa Barbara, and, in 1853, a petition to Rome resulted in making the mission a hospice, the beginning of an apostolic college for the education of Franciscan novitiates, which is still maintained. This was the influence which saved Santa Barbara from the neglect which befell her less fortunate sister missions. Since its founding, it has been used continuously for religious observances and the light above its altar has never once gone out. It is the only one of all the missions which has remained continuously in the hands of the Franciscan Fathers since its founding.

The red-tiled corridors and twin-domed belfries of Mission Santa Barbara still stand peacefully on the high ground west of the city, facing the sea, shedding "an air of Spanish languor, of perpetual siesta, over the pleasant city." From the belfry falls the music of the ancient Spanish bells, mingling with the cooing of doves in the rafters, the singing of meadow larks in neighboring fields, and the harmonious voices of monks chanting the vesper hymn. The rich perfume of datura and orange blossoms and sweet herbs fills the soft southern air.

"The longer one stays there the more he is aware of the influence on his soul," writes Helen Hunt Jackson. "It is an inalienable benediction on the whole city."

Cieneguitas

In *Prehistoric Man of the Santa Barbara Coast*, David Banks Rogers gives the following description:

"About four miles west of the business center of the city, and nearly in front of St. Vincent's Orphanage, the highway crosses an inconspicuous ravine in which thick undergrowth and small trees form an almost impenetrable jungle as far south as Modoc Road. Throughout this tangled growth meander spring-fed rivulets that in places expand into treacherous bogs, a characteristic that early gave to the locality the name that still endures, Cieneguitas, 'the swamps.' . . . .

"The first mention of Cieneguitas that we have found in the annals is when, on the morning of August 20th, 1769, Captain Gaspar de Portolá, at the head of his little army of sixty-five leather-jacketed soldiers, and two Franciscan monks, emerged from Arroyo Burro, where they had camped the night before, and were met by a reception committee from the extensive village that clustered about the slough.

"At the time of the founding of the Mission, for some unknown reason, this village alone, of the many in the vicinity, was permitted to retain its organization. Early in 1803, the friars even went so far as to erect a substantial adobe chapel for the use of the villagers. This was located immediately to the west of the cienega, about midway between the present Modoc Road and the Coast Highway.

"About this same time, several substantial, single-roomed adobe residential huts, with tile roofs, were erected for the natives. . . . .

"All of the structures erected under the guidance of the fathers were especially sturdy. As late as 1886, a large part of the chapel was still in place. . . . ."

El Refugio

About twenty miles west of the city of Santa Barbara, the Cañada del Refugio once marked the southern boundary of the great Rancho Nuestra Señora del Refugio, which ran northward along the sea for twenty-five miles to the Cañada del Cojo. Here in this canyon the Ortega family lived for many years. José Francisco de Ortega, who had accompanied Portolá on his expedition to Monterey in 1769, was rewarded for his services by being given permission to occupy this land in 1794. After his death, it was granted to his son, José María Ortega.

The coast of El Refugio is closely linked with romance, for here on the beach Don José had his embarcadero, where he engaged in genteel smuggling, and here the pirate, Hippolyte de Bouchard, in 1818 landed and sacked and burned the adobe casa which had stood at the canyon's entrance facing the sea and El Camino Real. Here, too, the Yankee lad, Joseph John Chapman, had deserted from the pirate ship. He later married into the Ortega family and proved to be a very useful citizen.

Don José built his second adobe about three miles back in the Cañada del Refugio. Only its foundations are now traceable, and the old vineyard, one of the most famous in California, has also disappeared. The road which winds through the canyon and up the mountain leads down into the valley of Santa Inez by way of the Pass of El Refugio. Here the padres often passed on their way from Mission Santa Barbara to Mission Santa Inez beyond the mountains.

Misión La Purísima Concepción

The first site of Misión La Purísima Concepción is one-half mile south of the center of the town of Lompoc. Father Lasuén founded La Purísima on December 8, 1787. A temporary building was begun in March, 1788, but this was soon replaced by an adobe structure, roofed with tile, which was finished in 1802. This building was totally destroyed by the earthquake of 1812, and only a few bits of the ancient, ruined walls remain today. The great gash made by the earthquake may still be seen on the hillside above the ruins.

A new church, about four miles east of the present site of Lompoc, and one mile north of the Buellton-Lompoc highway, was promptly erected by Father Payéras, who did effective work in both the old and the new locations. His death, in 1823, was a great loss to the mission.

The Indian uprising that spread from Mission Santa Inez, in 1824, struck heavily at La Purísima, which was captured and held for several weeks. A force of soldiers from Monterey finally dispersed the Indians.

At one time, La Purísima was very prosperous, but the neglect which followed confiscation and the inroads of the elements caused its steady disintegration. Recently it had become a pitiful, crumbling ruin, its roof gone, its walls fallen, and its few remaining archways half-choked in wild mustard and elder bushes. Only its stately row of white pillars, standing guard with true Grecian beauty and grace, testified to past glory and charm. Across the canyon, an old stone settling tank, with a great crack threatening its existence, still stands as a picturesque reminder of the Franciscans' industry, while the mission itself has been restored.

Misión Santa Inez

Mission Santa Inez was founded in order to reach the Indians living east of the Coast Range. Father Tapis made a survey of the country in 1798, and from his report a site for the proposed mission was chosen in the beautiful valley of Calahuasá, about forty-five miles northwest of Santa Barbara via Gaviota Pass. Thirteen Indian rancherías in the vicinity, with an estimated population of over eleven hundred souls, gave promise of many converts.

After the death of Father Lasuén in 1803, Father Tapis succeeded him as Father Presidente, and in 1804 he founded the new church at Santa Inez. A simple chapel was erected at first, to be replaced, after the earthquake of 1812, by a building of brick and adobe, roofed and floored with tile. This structure, completed in 1817, still stands in the open fields with its background of rugged, purple mountains.

The Indian uprising of 1824 started at Mission Santa Inez, the occasion for discontent being the harsh treatment by the soldiers. The Indians revolted, burned a large number of the mission buildings, leaving the church unharmed, and escaped to La Purísima, where they were finally overcome by soldiers from Monterey.

Santa Inez suffered in material wealth from the effects of secularization, as did nearly all of her sister missions, and the church long remained unattended. It was in a sad state of ruin until recent years, when it was happily restored, retaining as much as possible of the old charm and grace: Indian frescoes and hand-carved doors, harmonious arcades and flower-filled patio, and a beautiful campanile, its plain wall pierced, as at Mission San Gabriel, by niches for the ancient bells which ring out their call to prayer as in days of old.

Mission Santa Inez is located in the town of Solvang, a community of thrifty Danish people who hold the mission in high regard. It is about thirty miles northwest of Santa Barbara by the San Marcos Road.

Remnants of Adobe Days

The village of Guadalupe in the northwestern corner of Santa Barbara County was named for the old Mexican rancho on which it is located. Rancho Guadalupe, of 43,681 acres, was granted on March 21, 1840, to Diego Olivera, described by Bancroft as a man who "clung to his old Spanish ways, dress and ideas to the last," and to Teodoro Arellanes, a man of "genial temper and gentlemanly manners, locally a kind of ranchero prince." The first adobes were erected at Guadalupe by Arellanes in 1840. The large one-story adobe, one of the two well-preserved mud structures, picturesque and rambling, which may still be seen at Guadalupe, was built by the Arellanes family in 1849. These adobes are now owned by the Druids, a fraternal order.

Among the several adobes remaining in northern Santa Barbara County is the Cuyama adobe built far up in the remote Cuyama Valley on the rancho of the same name. The rancho was granted to José María Rojo, April 24, 1843, and consisted of some 22,198 acres.

Several adobes still standing in the vicinity of the town of Los Alamos were built on Rancho Los Alamos, a grant of about 48,803 acres made to José Antonio Carrillo on March 9, 1839. This rancho is now owned by Edward L. Doheny, oil man. Adjoining Rancho Los Alamos was Rancho Laguna, the present street of Los Alamos being the dividing line between these two old grants.

A few fragmentary adobes exist in and about Los Alamos, most of them having been incorporated into other houses. One of these, which formerly stood on Rancho Laguna, is now owned by Dr. Shaw. To the northeast on the Todos Santos Rancho is another, now owned by the Newhalls. Little of the original adobe structure is visible in either of these houses.

Other reminders of adobe days still linger along the byways and in hidden sequestered nooks of northern Santa Barbara County. Among these are the Ontiveras adobe built in the '30's and still in a very good state of repair; the interesting but somewhat altered adobe (now owned by E. G. Marshall of Casmalia) built on Rancho Jesús María, granted to Lucas Antonio and José A. Olivera, April 8, 1837; and a very interesting adobe now owned by Eduardo de la Cuesta and situated in a beautiful spot near Buellton.

The San Marcos Pass

San Marcos Pass, about fifteen miles northwest of Santa Barbara, was one of the passes over which the early explorers and mission Fathers crossed from the coast to the inland valleys, Gaviota Pass, the most northerly of the passes, being twenty-eight miles farther up the coast from Santa Barbara.

In 1846, on his way from Monterey to reinforce Commodore Stockton in Los Angeles during the period of American occupation, John C. Frémont eluded the Spanish soldiers who were waiting for him in ambush in Gaviota Pass, by taking the route over the San Marcos grade instead. The latter route was known to very few and presented many difficulties. Guided by W. D. Foxen, the Americans succeeded in reaching the top after swinging the artillery across the intervening chasms on ropes, an all-day struggle. From the summit, Foxen's eldest son, William, led the men down the mountain and into Santa Barbara.

Beside the old trail, fifteen miles from Santa Barbara and about seven miles north of the coast highway, U.S. 101, a boulder has been placed by the Santa Barbara Chapter, D.A.R., on which is a bronze tablet bearing the legend:

In honor of Lieutenant-Colonel John C. Frémont, his soldiers and guide, W. B. Foxen, who marched over the San Marcos Pass, December 25, 1846, and took peaceable possession of Santa Barbara, while the Californians waited for them in ambush in Gaviota Pass.

Frémont's Camp in Foxen Canyon

Located in Foxen Canyon about fifteen miles northwest of Los Olivos and twenty-five miles southeast of Santa Maria is the site of the old Foxen home, of which traces are still visible. Rancho Tinaquaic, on which it was located, comprised two leagues of land and was occupied by Victor Linares by May of 1837. In 1837 and 1842, this rancho was granted to William (or Benjamin) Foxen, an Englishman who had settled in California in 1828, marrying Eduarda Osuna and becoming a citizen of Alta California.

Here in December, 1846, John C. Frémont arrived with his army of seven hundred men on their way to Santa Barbara and Los Angeles. According to Juan Francisco Dana, son of William G. Dana, in a recent account of the story, Frémont had been told by William G. Dana at Rancho Nipomo (San Luis Obispo County), where he had camped on December 18, that the Californians were waiting for him in ambush at Gaviota Pass, the main passage through the mountains, a narrow defile between towering walls of granite from which huge boulders could be rolled down upon a passing enemy. Frémont was advised to seek the services of Foxen, a man familiar with the country to the southwest where an alternate and more difficult pass might be crossed.

Proceeding to Rancho Tinaquaic, Frémont camped on December 20 in the woods near the Foxen home. There, according to Dana's account, he solicited the aid of Foxen, who, though "torn between loyalty to the Californians and the tie of English blood which bound him to the invaders," granted the request and led the little army over San Marcos Pass and into Santa Barbara unharmed. As a consequence of this kindly deed Foxen, for some time afterward, suffered at the hands of his neighbors, who, on more than one occasion, set fire to his rancho buildings.

The approximate site of Frémont's camp on the old Foxen ranch has been marked by the Pioneers Section of the Minerva Literary Club of Santa Maria. Foxen's grave is at Sisquoc, in the cemetery of the Catholic church.

First Raising of the Stars and Stripes in Santa Barbara

At the corner of State and De la Guerra streets is a bronze tablet placed by the Native Sons of the Golden West August 15, 1929, in commemoration of the first raising of the American flag in Santa Barbara by Lieutenant-Colonel John C. Frémont, December 27, 1846. Lieutenant Theodore Talbot and his small band of rangers who had occupied the town in July, 1846, participated in the ceremonies. The house over which the flag was raised and in which Frémont had his headquarters at the time was the residence of Captain Alpheus B. Thompson, later known as the St. Charles Hotel.

Stage Stations

On the old stage road running north and south between Missions Santa Barbara and San Luís Obispo, a station was maintained at the Foxen Ranch before 1876. Until that year the main stage line followed up Foxen Canyon, but after that date it went through the Los Alamos Valley instead, and a station was established at Los Alamos. From early times a station had been maintained at Los Olivos, and the old building, somewhat remodeled but very beautiful in the interior, still stands. A later building, known as Mattei's Tavern, is also standing at Los Olivos.

SOURCES

[Credit is here given for source material, and permission to quote is hereby acknowledged]

BOLTON, HERBERT EUGENE. *Anza's California Expeditions.* 5 vols. University of California Press, Berkeley, 1930
——. *Fray Juan Crespi, Missionary Explorer on the Pacific Coast, 1769–1774.* University of California Press, Berkeley, California, 1927
BRYANT, EDWIN. *What I Saw in California.* D. Appleton & Company, New York, 1848, 1849
DANA, JUAN FRANCISCO, as told by John Edwin Hogg. "Ten Decades on a California Rancho," in *Touring Topics,* XXIII, No. 11 (November, 1931), 16–19, 44
ELDER, DAVID PAUL. *The Old Spanish Missions of California.* Paul Elder & Company, San Francisco, 1913
ENGELHARDT, ZEPHYRIN. *Santa Barbara Mission.* The James H. Barry Company, San Francisco, 1923
HARDACRE, EMMA. "Eighteen Years Alone," *Scribner's Magazine,* XX, 657 (September, 1880)
HARRINGTON, JOHN P. "Exploration of the Burton Mound at Santa Barbara, California," *Forty-fourth Annual Report of the Bureau of American Ethnology,* pp. 30–168. Government Printing Office, Washington, D.C., 1928
HAWLEY, WALTER A. *Early Days in Santa Barbara.* Privately published, Santa Barbara, 1920
HILL, LAURANCE L. *Santa Barbara, Tierra Adorada.* Security First National Bank of Los Angeles, Los Angeles, 1930
JACKSON, HELEN HUNT. *Glimpses of California and the Missions.* Little, Brown & Company, Boston, 1903
ROGERS, DAVID BANKS. *Prehistoric Man of the Santa Barbara Coast.* Santa Barbara Museum of Natural History, Santa Barbara, California, 1929
SOUTHWORTH, JOHN R. *Santa Barbara and Montecito, Past and Present.* Oreña Studios, Santa Barbara, California, 1920
STORKE, YDA ADDIS, MRS. *Memorial and Biographical History of the Counties of Santa Barbara, San Luis Obispo, and Ventura, California.* The Lewis Publishing Company, Chicago, 1891

VENTURA COUNTY

VENTURA COUNTY (Ventura is a corruption of San Buenaventura, so-called after Misión San Buenaventura; the name was derived from the saint whose title, Buenaventura, meaning "good fortune," was bestowed after he was healed by Saint Francis) was organized as a county in 1872, and Ventura was made its county seat.

Cabrillo's Landing-Place

In ancient times there were numerous Indian villages along the shore of what is now Ventura County. When Cabrillo, the discoverer of California, sailed up the coast in 1542, it is thought by some historians that he came ashore on October 10 at a place where there was a large Indian village, doubtless the one to which Cabrillo gave the name El Pueblo de las Canoas ("the Town of the Canoes"), because he was so impressed by the large, finely built boats which these tribes used. The boats carried from fifteen to twenty persons, were built of boards crudely hewn by hand, and were calked with asphaltum from the neighboring hills. Their boats and their homes, their implements and utensils, as well as their mode of life, exhibited a skill in workmanship and a superiority of intelligence which placed a distinguishing mark upon the Chumash Indians of Ventura and Santa Barbara counties and of the Channel Islands. Among all the Indians of California, they were perhaps the most advanced. Being, also, the most docile, friendly, and intelligent, as well as exceedingly numerous, they proved a rich harvest for the zealous Franciscans who followed Cabrillo some two hundred years later.

Relics of this superior civilization have been found throughout the region and are preserved in the Pioneer Museum located in the Ventura County Courthouse. Water baskets lined and covered with native asphaltum, excellently wrought bowls and mortars, and finely shaped arrowheads are among the many interesting treasures displayed there. One unusual specimen is that of a crude hand-hewn board recently found in an Indian cave in the Wheeler Springs region. It seems to have served as a fleshing-board, for its sharp edge is evidence that it was used to scrape the meat side of hides in the process of tanning.

The ancient village at which Cabrillo landed may have been the one located on the seashore at the foot of what are now Figueroa and Palm streets, Ventura. In the '70's, a "kitchen midden" was still visible very near the sea on the left-hand side of Figueroa Street, on the lot now occupied by the Associated Oil Company's fire-extinguishing tanks. There is, however, some difference of opinion among historians as to the location of Pueblo de las Canoas. Many place it at Ventura, while some favor Rincón Point as the probable location. Henry R. Wagner, eminent historian and geographer, believes the site to have been Mugu Lagoon, southeast of Oxnard.

Cabrillo remained at the Pueblo de las Canoas until the thirteenth, when he sailed "six or seven leagues, passing along the shores of two large islands," anchoring off Point Rincón.

The Trail of Portolá

Leaving the camp site near Castaic in Los Angeles County on August 10, 1769, Captain Gaspar de Portolá and his men continued down the verdant valley which Fray Juan Crespi named the Santa Clara, halting for the night on the banks of an arroyo in the vicinity of Rancho Camulos very near the county line. On the three succeeding days the tents were pitched near the Indian villages in the neighborhood of Piru, Fillmore, and Santa Paula, where the friendly natives gave the strangers gifts of seeds, acorns, and baskets of pine nuts in exchange for the beads which the latter had brought. On the fourteenth the party stopped near the site of Mission San Buenaventura, where a large ranchería was located. Father Crespi, who named the village La Asunción de Nuestra Señora, expressed the hope "that such a fine site, where nothing is lacking, will become a good mission." The next night found the travelers at another native town where, the Father wrote, the villagers "disturbed us and kept us awake playing all night on some doleful pipes or whistles." The name bestowed upon this place by the soldiers has persisted in Pitas ("whistles") Point. On August 16, Rincón Point was rounded and camp was made at a native fishing village on Rincón Creek.

The Anza Trail

Juan Bautista de Anza, on April 10, 1774, traveling northward on his notable overland journey from Sonora to San Francisco, camped near Triunfo in Russell Valley west of Calabasas. "Passing among many docile heathens," the party continued their march on the eleventh, halting for the night near San Buenaventura on the San Buenaventura River. Returning from the north a little later, Anza camped on April 29 east of Camarillo at the foot of Canejo Grade, this being his only stop in Ventura County on that trip. In 1776 Anza passed this way again as leader of the first overland emigrant train to California. Retracing his former route, he made only one halt in Ventura County. This was near El Río, on February 23, 1776.

Misión San Buenaventura

In the midst of these populous native villages with their friendly, "superior" peoples, halfway between San Diego on the south and Monterey on the north, Father Junípero Serra at length planted the ninth of the missions and named it San Buenaventura. It was the last one to be dedicated by the zealous founder of the California mission chain, for his death occurred just two years later, on August 28, 1784.

From the very beginning of his work in California the Father Presidente had contemplated the founding of this halfway station in the fruitful valley of San Buenaventura. However, the Indian uprisings at San Diego and, more especially, the difficulties between the mission Fathers and the civil authorities, had long delayed the fulfilment of his wish. It was thirteen years after the founding of San Diego de Alcalá, the first of the missions, before Misión San Buenaventura was finally established on March 31, 1782. In the vicinity of the Indian village locally known as Mitz-Kana-Kan, Father Serra erected the first crude enramada for the holding of the first mass.

It was the custom, when a mission was dedicated, to erect a cross, not only as an emblem of faith, but as a beacon to guide travelers to the mission. Along the coast highway a site was usually chosen which was visible both by land and by sea. At Ventura, the place selected was a lofty hill called La Loma de la Cruz ("the Hill of the Cross"), which rises immediately back of the Mission Church in the present city of Ventura.

For nearly fifty years Serra's cross stood upon the hilltop above the mission. At last, however, wind and rain so weakened it that it fell. The old central timber was replaced by a new one, but the original scroll and cross-piece were retained. Thus it stood for another half-century, when, in 1875, it was again blown down. After that, for thirty-eight years, the hillside was without a cross. The top piece of the original cross, however, was saved and is now preserved in the Pioneer Museum. In 1913 a new cross was raised on the original hilltop site. It is made of Jeffrey pine from Santa Paula Canyon, where, it is thought, the mission Fathers obtained timber for the original cross. La Loma de la Cruz is now a city park.

Very soon after the erection of the first enramada, or chapel, the first mission church was built. According to Captain George Vancouver, this was destroyed by fire. Church records indicate that if such was the case, the disaster occurred between December 9, 1791, and June 21, 1792. "Thereupon," says Engelhardt, "buildings of a superior quality were erected" in the summer of 1792. The church built at this time, he adds, "could not have been more than a temporary structure."

The present mission church was begun as early as 1793 but was not completed until 1809. While it was in course of construction, a temporary chapel, called the Chapel of Santa Gertrudis, was erected for the Indian community, at the entrance to Casitas Pass, about seven miles north of the mission. This chapel was used intermittently for many years, even as late as 1868. After the earthquakes of 1812 and 1857, it was doubtless used for divine worship while the church was being restored.

Most of the Indians of the community soon settled about the Chapel of Santa Gertrudis, and the great numbers of their little willow-thatched houses gave the name Casitas ("Little Houses") to the entire region. The settlement was located at the present junction of the Ojai road and the road leading through Foster Park in Casitas Pass. The chapel was near what is now the gateway to Foster Park, on the property of C. J. Train. Nothing remains to indicate the thriving villages which once stood in the vicinity.

About a quarter of a mile from the Mission Church (near the southwest corner of the present Palm and Meta streets), near the ancient village of the Indians, stood the little chapel of San Miguel Arcángel. For many years, processions chanting the litanies and rosaries wended their way periodically from the church to the chapel, to the great delight of the Indians. The earthquake of 1812 damaged the building, and by 1816 it had become unserviceable and another was built on more solid ground. In 1832 it was reported that "the chapel of San Miguel, the pride of Fr. Señan, could not be saved, the floods having destroyed it entirely." The crumbling walls were still standing as late as 1873, the last vestige of the ruins being removed in the late '70's.

Even before the dedication of the present mission structure on September 10, 1809, the mission garden had become famous. In the autumn of 1793, Vancouver, on his second visit to California, wrote in his journal about the gardens of San Buenaventura, describing them as "far exceeding anything" he had seen elsewhere in California. At a later date, Richard Henry Dana spoke of them as "the finest in the whole country." Today, nothing remains of this wonderful garden save one tall palm, bending under the weight of years.

It is said that these palms were planted by the padres

when the garden was first laid out on a tract of seventeen acres on what is now the south side of Main Street. A bend in the street indicates the location of the old wall which surrounded the orchard. One of the historic palms was blown down in a windstorm in 1876. For many years the Native Daughters of the Golden West had cared for the last two, building a wall about them and bracing them with wire cables. The one remaining stands on Columbo Street a half block south of Main.

The boundaries of the old walled garden "began on what is now Main Street and extended westward to just beyond the Feraud corner, thence south to a bit beyond Meta Street, thence eastward to a point which would be in line with the east line of Columbo Street, making the Palace Hotel, at Columbo and Main, the point of beginning."

The present mission structure was not built within this walled garden but directly opposite on what is now the north side of Main Street. During the height of its prosperity it was considered one of the richest of the missions, being especially famous for its excellent horticulture. After the secularization of the missions, it suffered with the others. From 1840 to 1850 it was without a resident pastor, a priest from Santa Barbara coming down to hold occasional services. It was roofless for many years after the earthquake of 1857, and while in this condition was abandoned. For how long is not known, but we do know that the Chapel of Santa Gertrudis was being used in its stead in 1868. In 1895 the present mission structure was described by J. Torrey as a "well-preserved building, its walls still bearing traces of the rude frescoing affected by the builders of that time."

The present church was regrettably "restored" a number of years ago and much of its ancient charm obliterated. The crudely beautiful Indian frescoes were covered up by ornate scroll work and the old wooden pulpit, carved and painted by the Indians, was torn out and thrown away. Fortunately, the panels were saved by loving hands and two of them are now in the mission museum and the other is in the Pioneer Museum. It is the hope of those who treasure them that the pulpit as well as the original decorations may some day be restored to the church.

The water system built by the padres to irrigate their gardens and orchard was complete and well constructed in every way. The picturesque old settling tank and receiving reservoir, which distributed water to the mission establishment and to the homes of the Spanish families in the vicinity, still stands intact. The "horse's head," or spout, carved from sandstone by the Indians, is broken, but the massive walls of the tank itself look as if they would last forever. It was used as the early calaboose or jail of the town of Ventura. It stands at the back of the Moraga home, which fronts on Valdez Alley.

The great water ditch or stone aqueduct, which was also a part of the padres' water system and which was seven miles in length, was demolished by the floods and landslides of 1866–1867. The massive ruins may still be seen near the mouth of the Cañada Larga, eloquent testimonials of the wonderful workmanship of the mission Fathers and their Indian helpers.

The Mission Village

Standing on a slight elevation at the foot of La Loma de la Cruz, the Mission Church dominated the tiny village which grew out from it westward to the San Buenaventura River. Two irregular bridle paths formed the streets of the little settlement and along these the adobe homes were built, sometimes flat-roofed and covered with brea, again more picturesquely tiled, and, occasionally, shingled. The locations of these adobes and the names of their builders have been handed down to us through two descendants of the old families, Luís Arellanes and E. C. Ortega, and are preserved in manuscript form in the Pioneer Museum, Ventura. Only two of these old adobe homes remain in part, today, the Valdez house and the Ortega house.

Part of the Valdez adobe still stands, covered with planking. It originally belonged to the Valdez family and fronted on the present Main Street. Later, for many years, it belonged to an Italian called Pedro Constancia. Constancia conducted a stage station on his place, the stage office being in the Santa Clara Hotel from 1870 on. This hotel is now called Poinsettia Hotel and is on the south side of Main Street directly opposite the Valdez house.

Seventy years before the Ortega house was built on the east bank of the San Buenaventura River, an adobe home had been erected on the Rancho Sespe near the site of Fillmore, twenty-eight miles east of Ventura. The unknown builders of this homestead were murdered by a band of Mojave Indians, leaving the house deserted and forgotten until 1857 when it was remembered by Miguel Emigdio Ortega, who needed its sturdy timbers for his new home. Four arduous days were taken for the journey, a bodyguard of mounted horsemen accompanying the expedition as a protection against the Indians. The house was dismantled and the coveted timbers were hauled back to Ventura, where they were incorporated in the new house. In 1897, E. C. Ortega, son of the original builder, had occasion to repair the old home. The center beam, brought from the Sespe house forty years before, was found to be in perfect condition and so solid that a 20-penny spike could not penetrate it more than a quarter of an inch.

In the flood of 1866–1867, the swollen waters of the San Buenaventura swept away half of the Ortega adobe and a portion of the orchard of pear, peach, and fig trees. The remaining portion of the house is still in good condition and has been added to slightly at the eastern front end. It is owned by the city and is occupied by the Veterans of Foreign Wars.

In the beginning all of the lands about San Buenaventura belonged to the Mission. After secularization of the missions, grants were made, and the people to whom the land was given began establishing homes and building their adobe casas throughout the county. These tracts, however, were very large, over four thousand acres being included in the smaller ones. Consequently, the country homes scattered over the entire area were few, not more than a dozen all told. Of these, only a handful remain.

La Casa de la Riva still stands across the river beyond Foster Park about eight miles from Ventura. The house, set on a sloping meadow below wooded hills, is a substantial, two-story structure graced by broad Spanish balconies. On what was formerly the Lower Ojai Rancho stands the López adobe, called the "Barracks" because it once defended the lower Ojai Valley from the Matílija Indians. On the Old Creek Road to Ojai, ten miles from Ventura, stands the Santa Ana Rancho house of Don José de Arnaz.

Frémont's Camp

Don José de Arnaz was mayordomo of Ventura at the time of General Frémont's arrival at the mission in 1846. Frémont, on his way south to the reconquest of Los Angeles, wished to gain possession of Misión San Buenaventura for the United States. In order to obtain the knowledge which would enable him to carry out his plan, he arrested Arnaz and tried to get the desired information from him. Arnaz, however, claimed that he was unable to give this information and was finally released.

Until the recent publication of the memoirs of Don José

de Arnaz, the site of General Frémont's camp while at Ventura was unknown or forgotten. Arnaz writes that he "established his camp on the west side of the mission orchard." The boundary of the orchard was what is now the western boundary of the Feraud property at Main Street and what was formerly Spruce Street. This places the site of the camp about opposite the Cabrillo Hotel near Garden Street, in the vicinity of the city jail.

Arnaz's town house was on what is now West Main Street, midway between South Ventura Street and the river. In the late '50's he moved to his Santa Ana Rancho and his old home in town became the American Hotel.

Rancho San Miguel

Perhaps the best preserved of the historic adobes in the vicinity of Ventura is the Olivas house, which stands about one and one-half miles south of the state highway and three miles from the city on the northwest and from the Santa Clara River bridge on the southeast.

Don Raymundo Olivas, the original owner, was born in Los Angeles in 1801. In 1821 he came to the vicinity of Ventura. Twenty years later, on July 6, 1841, he received the grant of 4,693 acres which constituted Rancho San Miguel. The eastern half of this rancho, which formed the eastern boundary line of the present city of Ventura, was purchased later by Dixie Thompson for $1,000 cash.

The Olivas adobe was a long two-story building with balcony and veranda overlooking a walled garden below and wide fields and marsh lands beyond. There was a large family of twenty-one children and many were the gay assemblages held in the great casa, for the Olivases were famous for the fine entertainments and generous hospitality which they dispensed.

Romance and adventure still cling about the old house. Where Olivas was once surprised and robbed by Murieta and his bandits, modern sportsmen gather during the open seasons to hunt the wild ducks which come by hundreds to feed in the neighboring swamp lands. The house has been restored by its owner as a country resort for the entertainment of his friends, but the simple rural aspect of the place has been preserved, and one who visits it is rewarded by a glimpse of a real California rancho and catches an echo of the romance and adventure which held sway there in the days of long ago.

Rancho Camulos

About thirty miles east of Ventura, on the road to Los Angeles by way of Santa Paula and Newhall, is one of the most famous adobes in California. Located on Rancho Camulos, it was, until very recently, the home of the Del Valle family and famous as the setting for part of California's great novel, *Ramona,* written by Helen Hunt Jackson.

Rancho Camulos was originally a part of Rancho San Francisco, granted to Antonio del Valle in 1833 and 1839. Gradually, Don Antonio purchased 2,000 acres of the Rancho Temescal, and on this he built his home in the early '60's.

Travelers between Misión San Buenaventura and Misión San Fernando never failed to stop at Rancho Camulos to rest and to enjoy the hospitality of the Del Valles. That hospitality was famous from Spanish days well down into our own time.

The Camulos adobe is probably the best preserved and most typical of all of California's old rancho houses. From Rancho Camulos, Helen Hunt Jackson drew largely for her remarkable pictures of Spanish life in early California. There she heard the stories out of which gradually grew her

composite heroine, and there she saw the scenes which wove themselves into the opening threads of her tale. Ramona, as her creator fashioned her, was inspired, not by one real person, but by two or three, and the result was a creature of fiction and romance woven on the loom of actual life. For the stories which gave birth to this, one of the loveliest inspirations of our American literature, Helen Hunt Jackson was largely indebted to Señora del Valle, the widowed mistress of Camulos at the time of the author's visit there.

During all the years since her visit in 1881, Rancho Camulos has remained unchanged in most of its aspects. For years it was a literary and historical shrine. Recently, however, it has come into new hands and its gates are closed to visitors.

Rincón Point

About twelve miles west of Ventura, close to the sea, rise the jagged cliffs of Rincón Point, battle ground of the ancient tribes of the Chumash Indians.

It is thought by some historians that Juan Rodríguez Cabrillo may have landed at Rincón Point in 1542, but it is chiefly noted for its connection with the Battle of San Buenaventura, fought between rival factions of Californians on March 27–28, 1838, and for the dramatic poem, "The Fight of the Paso del Mar" (Spanish for "The Pass of the Sea"), written by Bayard Taylor in the early '40's.

The rival factions concerned in the Battle of San Buenaventura were led by Juan Bautista Alvarado in the north and by Andrés and Pío Pico in the south. It was a common saying among the Californians that the general who held Rincón Point could withstand any adversary with ease. Alvarado, with General Castro in command, hastened, therefore, to take the point before his opponents, under Carlos Antonio Carrillo, could do so. Castro arrived at Rincón Point to find that Carrillo did not have even a sentinel there, and so he marched down to San Buenaventura, taking it by surprise. Only a few shots were fired. Alvarado lost one man and Carrillo none, but Rincón Point became famous.

When Bayard Taylor wrote his poem, "The Fight of the Paso del Mar," in 1840, he had never seen the place of which he wrote. In 1849 he visited California for the first time and early in January 1850 saw Rincón Point. In his book, *El Dorado,* written after this visit, he said:

"We touched at Santa Barbara on the third morning out . . . . we ran astray in the channel between the Island of Santa Rosa and the mainland, making the coast about twenty-five miles south of the town. I did not regret this as it gave me an opportunity of seeing the point where the Coast Mountains come down to the sea, forming a narrow pass. . . . . It is generally known as the Rincón, or Corner. . . . . I had made it the scene of an imaginary incident, giving the name of Paso del Mar—The Pass of the Sea—to the spot. I was delighted to find so near a correspondence between its crags of black rock, its breakers and reaches of spray-wet sand, and the previous picture in my imagination."

Taylor, evidently, was geographically confused in the writing of this poem, for it seems that the story which it immortalizes was a Point Loma folk tale connected with the days of hide droghing at La Playa, when old San Diego was the shipping point for the great ranchos of the Southwest. The story, as related in full by A. M. Loop in *The Silver Gate* (January 1900), an early San Diego magazine edited by James A. Jasper, seems to have been substantiated by old residents of San Diego. But although the tragic climax of this tale was in reality set at Point Loma, Taylor himself, by his reminiscence in *El Dorado,* made it also a legend of Ventura's Rincón.

SOURCES

[Credit is here given for source material, and permission to quote is hereby acknowledged]

ARNAZ, JOSÉ. "Memoirs of a Merchant—Being the recollections of life and customs in pastoral California by José Arnaz, trader and ranchero," translated and edited by Nellie Van de Grift Sanchez, in *Touring Topics,* XX (September, October, 1928)

BOLTON, HERBERT E. *Anza's California Expeditions.* 5 vols. University of California Press, Berkeley, California, 1930

——. *Fray Juan Crespi, Missionary Explorer on the Pacific Coast, 1769–1774.* University of California Press, Berkeley, California, 1927

——. "Spanish Explorations in the Southwest, 1542–1706," in *Original Narratives of Early American History,* XVII, Charles Scribner's Sons, New York, 1916

DAVIDSON, WINIFRED. *Where California Began,* McIntyre Publishing Company, San Diego, California, 1929

ENGELHARDT, ZEPHYRIN. *San Buenaventura, the Mission by the Sea.* Mission Santa Barbara, Santa Barbara, California, 1930

JACKSON, HELEN HUNT. *Ramona.* Little, Brown and Company, Boston

JAMES, GEORGE WHARTON. *Through Ramona's Country.* Little, Brown and Company, Boston

LOOP, A. M. "The Fight of the Paso del Mar," in *The Silver Gate,* II, No. 1 (January, 1900), ed. by James A. Jasper, San Diego, California

ORTEGA, E. C. *Old Ortega Adobe, History by a Scion of the Ortega Family,* in a letter dated February 14, 1925, a copy of which is in the Pioneer Museum, Ventura, California

ROGERS, DAVID BANKS. *Prehistoric Man of the Santa Barbara Coast.* Santa Barbara Museum of Natural History, Santa Barbara, California, 1929

SHERIDAN, E. M. *Historic Spots of Ventura County,* manuscript, Pioneer Museum, Ventura, California, 1930

TAYLOR, BAYARD. *El Dorado, or Adventures in the Path of Empire.* H. G. Bohn, London, England, 1850; G. P. Putnam's Sons, New York, 1850 and 1864

VALLEY AND SIERRA COUNTIES

Historic Spots in California

ALPINE COUNTY

ALPINE COUNTY (named for its similarity to the Alpine country in Europe) was created March 16, 1864, from parts of El Dorado, Calaveras, Tuolumne, and Amador counties. The county seat was at first located at Silver Mountain but was transferred to Markleeville in 1875.

Frémont's Crossing of the Sierra

Among the few government explorers who came to the Pacific Coast before the Mexican War was John C. Frémont. In his company were French trappers familiar with the Western trails, but Kit Carson, almost as famous as his noted leader, was the chief guide.

Fired by a desire to see Klamath Lake, Mary's Lake, and the fabled Buenaventura River, Frémont left Oregon for St. Louis in November 1843. Following a circuitous route through Oregon and western Nevada, he finally reached the Carson River. By this time supplies had become greatly depleted, and with his horses and mules in no condition to negotiate the rough Rockies Frémont made the bold decision to find a pass through the Sierra into California.

Perhaps no part of the entire journey was more difficult than that which took the little company through the rugged region which is now Alpine County. The trail necessarily followed along the ridges, where the wind had cleared away a little of the snow and sometimes exposed grass and brush on which the half-starved animals could feed. Because of the difficulty of beating a path through the deep snows here encountered, the party had to make camp every few miles. On February 2 or 3 a halt was made at a spot one and one-half miles northeast of Markleeville, near the confluence of Markleeville Creek with the East Fork of the Carson River, and, on the following night, camp was made near Grover's Hot Springs, five miles farther west.

On February 6, Frémont had his first view of the great Sacramento Valley lying in the dim distance far below him. From the top of a high peak Kit Carson, who had gone to California with Ewing Young fifteen years before, recognized the low mountains of the Coast Range one hundred miles to the west. "Spots of prairie," as well as "a dark line which . . . . was imagined to be the course of the river," were vaguely distinguishable in the "snowless valley."

Again, on the 14th, in company with Charles Preuss, Frémont climbed to the summit of another peak, although Red Mountain may have been the peak in question. From this height Frémont beheld a great sheet of crystal clear water which his first map designated merely as the Mountain Lake, but which he later named Lake Bonpland, after Aimé Jacques Alexandre Bonpland (1773–1859), noted French botanist and companion of Baron von Humboldt. Early maps (1853–1862) designated it as Lake Bigler. Thousands know it today as Lake Tahoe.

At last on February 20 they reached the summit of what was later known as Kit Carson Pass, at an elevation of 8,600 feet. Here on the 21st Frémont and his companions looked out across the magnificent panorama of snowy ridges and towering peaks interspersed with deep canyons, and, far in the distance, they beheld "a shining line of water directing its course towards another, a broader and larger sheet." These water courses Frémont believed to be "the Sacramento and the Bay of San Francisco." Crossing the divide between West Carson Canyon and the American River, Kit Carson led the way through the pass which now bears his name.

At the summit a bronze memorial plate commemorates this heroic passage of the Sierra, giving especial honor to the brave scout who led the way. Placed by the Native Sons of the Golden West, August 7, 1921, it bears the inscription:

On this spot, which marks the summit of the Kit Carson Pass, stood what was known as the Kit Carson Tree on which the famous scout, Kit Carson, inscribed his name in 1844 when he guided the then Captain John C. Frémont, head of a government exploring expedition, over the Sierra Nevada. . . . . Above is a replica of the original inscription cut from the tree . . . . and now in Sutter's Fort, Sacramento.

The label on the stump in the museum states that the pine tree on which the name was carved was felled and this portion cut out on September 5, 1888, and sent to the California State Mining Bureau, which later sent it to Sutter's Fort Historical Museum.

Thus was the first passage of the Sierra in midwinter accomplished, a feat then considered well-nigh impossible. Later, the Kit Carson Emigrant Trail went by way of the Kit Carson Pass, and became one of the most popular of the routes followed by early pioneers. Today thousands of vacationists and lovers of historic and romantic places follow a modern highway over the old trail.

"Snow-Shoe" Thompson

For twenty years—from 1856 to 1876—John A. Thompson, popularly known as "Snow-Shoe" Thompson, braved the winter storms of the High Sierra to deliver the United States mail to early pioneers, in the days before railways. "Penetrating the mountains to isolated camps, rescuing the lost, and giving succor to those in need along the way," he was truly a "pioneer hero of the Sierra." On one occasion he rescued from certain death James Sisson, who had lain for twelve days in a deserted cabin in Lake Valley. When found, both Sisson's feet were frozen and he had been four days without fire, his only food being a little flour. Thompson traveled all night through deep snow in order to bring aid from Genoa, Nevada. When the rescue was at last accomplished, it was found necessary to amputate Sisson's feet, and Thompson went all the way to Sacramento and back in order to obtain the anesthetic for the operation.

"Snow-Shoe" Thompson was a "man of splendid physique. . . . . Within his breast lived and burned the spirit of the old Vikings. It was this inherited spirit of his daring ancestors that impelled him to embark on difficult and dangerous enterprises." Yet he was never reckless, and it was his knowledge of the mountains and all their ways, as well as his poise and his marvelous strength, that enabled him successfully to defy the wild storms of the Sierra winters.

Early in January 1856, while still on his ranch at Putah Creek, Thompson read in the papers of the difficulties experienced in getting the mails across the summit of the Sierra Nevada in winter. He made himself a pair of "snow skates," or skis, such as he had used in Norway when a boy, and began the arduous and heroic work which he carried on for twenty years. His first trip was made in January 1856, from Placerville, California, to Carson Valley, Nevada, a distance of ninety miles over the old Emigrant Road on which Placerville was the principal town. Not only was Thompson "the father of all the race of snowshoers in the Sierra Nevada" but he was also the forerunner of the stagecoach and the locomotive across the High Sierra. No matter how wild the mountain storms, he never failed to come through, usually on time.

During the entire period of twenty years Thompson lived in Diamond Valley on a ranch located at the head of Carson Valley, just across the line in California. This was near Woodford's, and Thompson was taken from that point to the deep snow line by sleigh or saddle horse. He had two general routes. One went from Woodford's to Placerville, following approximately the course of the present state highway along the West Carson River to a point near the mouth of Horse Thief Canyon, four and one-half miles from Woodford's. There, he bore directly west in the direction of Thompson Peak. The other route was from Woodford's to Murphy's Camp, by way of Indian Valley and sometimes by way of the Border Ruffian Pass and Blue Lakes. On a few occasions he took the trail through Ebbett's Pass, stopping at Silver Mountain. These three routes to Murphy's converged in Hermit Valley.

"Snow-Shoe" Thompson died at his ranch on May 15, 1876, and lies buried at Genoa, Nevada. A pair of skis are carved on his marble tombstone.

Alpine Highways

The entire surface of Alpine County is elevated and rugged and the view is grandly picturesque on every side. The western summit of the Sierra Nevada constitutes the western boundary of the county, which covers the eastern slope of that range as well as the outlying peak known as Silver Mountain. A road, said to have been the first surveyed route over the High Sierra, was constructed as early as 1857, from Hermit Valley to Hope Valley by way of Twin Lakes Pass. Hope Valley was named by members of the Mormon Battalion on their return to Salt Lake City in the summer of 1848. The Emigrant Trail through Ebbett's Pass to Angel's Camp was opened up in the early '50's, but no wagon road went that way until 1864, when, as a result of the opening up of the Comstock Lode in Nevada, a toll road was completed under the name of the Carson Valley and Big Tree Road. It was over this trail, in September 1861, that a little group of Bactrian camels from the Gobi Desert, Mongolia, were driven from San Francisco to Nevada, where they were used for transportation purposes in the mines.

Three branches of the present state highway system traverse Alpine County, following the general course of old roads: one from Lake Tahoe by way of Meyer's Station, Luther's Pass, Hope Valley, and Carson Canyon; a second from Jackson over the Kit Carson Pass via Silver Lake; and a third over the Big Tree or Ebbett's Pass Road from Angel's Camp through Hermit and Pacific valleys. Over these scenic highways, historic in their many associations with the past, hundreds of vacationists each year find their way into the recreation grounds of Alpine County.

Alpine "Ghost Cities"

Silver Mountain, founded in 1858 by Scandinavian miners, existed until 1886. The county seat was located there from 1864 to 1875. A "ghost" of Alpine's once thriving silver camps, its existence is marked today only by the crumbling walls of the old stone jail, the first in the county, near the site of the old courthouse. Of Silver King, located on the headwaters of the East Carson River near the new Los Angeles–Lake Tahoe Boulevard, only a little wreckage of old buildings remains to mark the site. Diamond Hill on the Ebbett's Pass state highway, Centreville, on the East Carson River at the junction of the Los Angeles–Lake Tahoe Boulevard and the highway from Angel's Camp, and Mogul, four miles north of Monitor, are only lingering memories,

little evidence aside from mining scars remaining to indicate the sites where they once stood. Monitor, flourishing from 1858 to 1886 and entirely deserted by 1893, showed some return to activity from 1898 to 1911, when it was again deserted until 1930. Today some of the old mines are being reopened, and a prospect of again reviving this small town exists.

Although silver predominates in the Alpine region, in large low-grade ledges gold is encountered in nearly every mineralized district. "Uncle Billy Rogers'" Copper Mine, situated in Hope Valley in the northwest angle of the county, is said to have been the first deposit of this ore ever opened in California or anywhere on the Pacific Coast, a considerable development here antedating the Comstock discovery by several years.

SOURCES

[Credit is here given for source material, and permission to quote is hereby acknowledged]

CLELAND, ROBERT GLASS. *Pathfinders*, of the series *California*, edited by John Russell McCarthy. Powell Publishing Company, Los Angeles, 1929

COY, OWEN COCHRAN. *The Great Trek*, of the series *California*, edited by John Russell McCarthy. Powell Publishing Company, Los Angeles, 1929

"Crossing the Sierras," in *Hutchings' Illustrated California Magazine*, I, No. 8 (February, 1857), 349–352

DELLENBAUGH, FREDERICK S. *Frémont and '49*. G. P. Putnam's Sons, New York and London, 1914

FARQUHAR, FRANCIS P., "Frémont in the Sierra Nevada," in the *Sierra Club Bulletin*, XV, No. 1 (February, 1930), 74–95

FRÉMONT, JOHN C. *The Exploring Expedition to the Rocky Mountains, Oregon and California*. George H. Derby & Company, Buffalo, 1849

FRÉMONT, BREVET CAPTAIN J. C. *Report of the Exploring Expedition to the Rocky Mountains in the Year 1842 and to Oregon and North California in the Years 1843–44*. Washington, 1845

JAMES, GEORGE WHARTON. *Heroes of California*. Little, Brown & Company, Boston, 1910

QUILLE, DAN DE (WILLIAM WRIGHT). "Snow-Shoe Thompson," in *Overland Monthly*, VIII, No. 46 (October, 1886), 419–435

TYLER, SERGEANT DANIEL. *A Concise History of the Mormon Battalion in the Mexican War, 1846–1847*. Privately published, Salt Lake City, 1881

WHITE, CHESTER LEE. "Surmounting the Sierras, the Campaign for a Wagon Road," in *Quarterly of the California Historical Society*, VII, No. 1 (March, 1928), 3–19

AMADOR COUNTY

AMADOR COUNTY (named in honor of José María Amador, a miner in that region in 1848, and previously major-domo of Mission San Jose) was created in 1854 and Jackson was made its county seat. Amador County is in the center of the Mother Lode district in the Sierra Nevada. Its southern border is the Mokelumne River, while on the north is the Cosumnes River, both linked inseparably with the days of '49.

Kit Carson Emigrant Trail

One branch of the old Kit Carson Emigrant Trail went through Jackson, its general direction being that of a later stage road to Virginia City, Nevada, and that of the present Jackson–Silver Lake highway.

On this trail, just over the line in El Dorado County, the Tragedy Springs massacre occurred on June 21, 1848, while members of the Mormon Battalion were returning to Utah.

Three scouts of the party were killed at the springs by Indians. An account of the tragedy and the names of the scouts were carved on a tree that still stands on the spot. It was marked by the Native Sons of the Golden West on their Landmarking Pilgrimage in 1921.

A second marker was placed on Odd Fellows Rock on which are carved the names of a party of early pioneers and the emblem of the Order of Odd Fellows.

Kirkwood's log stage station and inn, built in 1864 by Jack Kirkwood, still stands on the old Kit Carson Road. As sturdy as the day it was built, the place no longer serves as a hostelry ,but is used as the summer home of Mrs. Elizabeth Kirkwood, widow of the builder. The fireplace and the original floor, worn by the feet of many pioneer campers who met there for gay dancing parties, are among its interesting features. When Alpine County was formed from Amador County, the division left the barn and milk house belonging to the Kirkwoods in Alpine, while the Alpine–El Dorado line went directly through the bar room of the inn. The old emigrant road passed the house at the intersection of the three counties. The post office, known as Roundtop from the mountain near by, was also housed in the log cabin. An addition to the original cabin was made about fifty years ago.

Gold Bars of the Mokelumne

Possibly the first gold found in Amador County was discovered somewhere along the Mokelumne River, in the spring of 1848, by Captain Charles M. Weber, founder of the city of Stockton. During the summer of the same year, within two months' time, a company of eight men, headed by James P. Martin, took out several thousand dollars' worth of gold each. In the autumn Colonel J. D. Stevenson came to the river with a mining expedition composed of about one hundred of his own men recently mustered out of the army. Perhaps the first code of mining laws to be drawn up in California was made by the Colonel for the benefit of his men while encamped along the Mokelumne River bars.

Thousands of eager miners from all over the world flocked to the gulches and rivers of the Sierra in 1849, and during the first years of the '50's they continued to swarm up and down the rivers, building small cities overnight at all of the rich river bars. Within the two decades which followed, an almost unbelievable change took place. A historian writing fifty years ago described the transformation even then evident to one walking along the banks of the Mokelumne River. Hardly could one realize, he said, "that the stillness, broken only by the murmur of the water, was ever otherwise." Today, scarcely a fragment remains of the numerous cabins where, "eighty years since, the miner fried his flapjacks or dried his wet clothing after a day's toil under a broiling sun in the ice-cold water."

Of all the camps along the Mokelumne, the tide of trade and gold flowed most abundantly at Big Bar. Two of the old inns still stand, one at each end of the bridge where the present highway from Jackson to Mokelumne Hill crosses the river. On the Amador side of the river is Gardella's and on the Calaveras side is Kelton's, now in the possession of a son of the original owner. After the placers on the bars had been depleted, the center of trade moved across the river to the top of Mokelumne Hill, where the town of that name is still located. But the rushing river and the rugged canyon still recall vividly that lively era when hordes of miners thronged the alluring reaches of Big Bar.

A ferry, known as the Whale Boat Ferry, was established at Big Bar in 1850. It was superseded, in 1852 or 1853, by a toll bridge, which was swept away by the flood of 1862. Subsequently rebuilt, the bridge has been free for years,

being on the state highway and maintained by the state. There is now a fine new structure at this point.

In recent years there has been a lode mining revival at Middle Bar, two miles below Big Bar. The old homesteads, however, are all deserted, having been purchased by the East Bay Utility Company, which has built the Pardee Dam across the Mokelumne River six miles below Middle Bar. This company was formed when eleven Bay cities joined forces to secure water and power, and selected the Mokelumne River as the source of the purest and best water. Ex-Governor George Pardee was president of the company. The dam was completed in 1930. When the reservoir is filled, this region, where hundreds of busy miners with pans or cradles once washed the gold from the river, will be covered with water. The company will eventually have to buy all of the old lode mines, including the Big Tunnel or Mammoth, the Hardenburg, the Marlette, and the St. Julian or Caminetti, successors of the earlier placers and all big producers in the past.

Below Middle Bar are James and French bars, once teeming with life and activity but now entirely deserted. Miners of '49 and '50 often took out several thousand dollars a day at these places. The fragile dwellings of canvas or boards in which they sojourned for a brief time, as well as the beautiful orchards and vineyards cultivated by the industrious citizens of French Bar, have vanished.

Lancha Plana

Farther down the river, in the southwestern part of the county, many mining camps centered about Lancha Plana, among them being Poverty Bar (Calaveras County), Winter's Bar, Oregon Bar, and Put's Bar. Lancha Plana ("flatboat"), just across the river from the exceedingly rich gravels of Poverty Bar, came into existence as the mooring-place for the flatboat ferry which carried miners from the north side of the river across to Poverty Bar and the mines of Calaveras County. Lancha Plana reached the height of its prosperity after 1856, when hill and bluff mining were bringing greater returns than mining in the river ever had brought. It became a place of carousal and merrymaking, where such desperadoes as the notorious Sam Brown had a rendezvous.

A number of substantial stone buildings with iron shutters and doors erected during Lancha Plana's heyday have only recently been destroyed by dredging operations. The entire town site will soon be dredged out.

Camp Opra, at the base of the hills not far from Lancha Plana, was a lively place in 1857, outdoing its neighbor in crime; for while Lancha Plana had many substantial citizens to hold its wilder element in check, Camp Opra was especially marked as the resort of desperate whites as well as Mexicans. Among the latter, the notorious bandit Joaquín Murieta is said to have been a frequent visitor. It is also said that the graveyard near by was filled mostly by men who had been victims of whiskey.

As a result of the copper excitement in the early '60's, the ephemeral mining camps of Copper Center and Townerville (or "Hotel de Twelve") arose in the vicinity of Camp Opra.

The Boston House, a combination store and inn, once stood about four miles north of Lancha Plana on an old stage road to Jackson. A heap of stones marks the site today, but the road is still used as a short cut from Ione to Pardee Dam.

Buena Vista ("beautiful view") was the name applied to a village about six miles north of Lancha Plana, as well as to a mountain and a valley in the vicinity. The valley, located where Jackson Creek leaves the mountains, was mainly agricultural, but some mining was carried on in the surrounding hills. A historic old store, at the intersection of the Lancha Plana–Ione and the Jackson–Stockton roads, still serves the public, now made up mostly of farmers.

A "Ghost Town"

The Ginocchio Store, about two and one-half miles south of Jackson, is all that remains of what was once Butte City, a thriving mining camp in the Mother Lode country in the '50's. As early as 1854 Xavier Benoist was conducting a store and bakery in this building. For a time Butte City, located at the south side of Butte Basin, a section rich in auriferous deposits, rivaled Jackson. Today the spot is typical of the many "ghost towns" that are reminiscent of California's early mining activity: a roofless stone house standing mutely beside the highway in the midst of open fields where once a thousand miners' cabins stood; on the hill a lonely graveyard where forgotten miners lie buried. Above, Butte Peak, a high, conical mountain visible for many miles in all directions, stands sentinel.

Drytown

At Drytown, a mining camp nine miles north of Jackson, mining for gold was first begun in the spring of 1848. It was not unusual, in 1849, in the surrounding gulches to wash as much as one hundred dollars in gold from a single pan. The nomenclature of these gulches—Blood Gulch, Murderer's Gulch, Rattlesnake Gulch, and others—indicates that, although there were no doubt plenty of steady, industrious miners at Drytown, there were also desperate characters who left their mark on the vicinity. The town prospered until 1857, when fire swept the place. It never recovered from this disaster, for gold was already becoming worked out there. Two old buildings still stand in Drytown: an old store and the Town Hall. Drytown is receiving a new lease on life, however, with the reopening of most of the mines in the neighborhood, and many men are making living wages at the old diggings.

Lower Ranchería

Mining at Lower Ranchería, two miles east of Drytown, began in 1848. A mixed population, in which Mexicans and Chileans predominated, gathered there to the number of five or six hundred. Sombreros, serapes, knives, horses, and jingling spurs were strikingly in evidence at all gatherings. On the night of August 6, 1855, a series of robberies and murders were perpetrated by a gang of twelve desperate Mexican horsemen. As a result of this tragedy, the miners arose *en masse* and demanded that every Mexican be disarmed and driven from the region. Calmer counsels prevailed, but not until much injustice had been done.

Only the scars of early mining activities indicate the presence of this once busy camp. A beautiful farm covers the site and rosy, innocent children play where, three-fourths of a century since, "the very ground seemed accursed for the crimes it had witnessed."

Volcano

Volcano is located at the bottom of a deep cup in the mountains, hence its name. In the early mining days in the '50's, it claimed a population of "5,000 people," and was famous for its "many saloons, dance halls, and churches." Such is the tradition which persists there to this day.

Volcano's population has dwindled considerably since the '50's, and its isolation, together with the weirdness of the gray rocks washed out by the miners of long ago, make it a veritable "Sleepy Hollow" of the West. Almost one looks for goblins among the "ghost" rocks, or for a "headless

horseman" to come galloping down the steep wooded mountain road.

This was a very rich hydraulic mining district in early days, a million dollars in gold having been taken out of one mine alone. This particular mine was worked for over thirty years. Some gold is still found in the region, and the Lagomarsino Mine has recently run into rich gravel, causing people to believe that a revival of mining in this vicinity is imminent. Activity of another sort is evident in the region, as many summer homes are being built in the surrounding hills.

The visitor of today may see the following historic places in Volcano: the stone brewery, built in 1856; the Lavezzo Building; the old St. George Hotel building; the Masonic Temple, a two-story, stone building with a balcony, still in use; and others. Down to 1856 everyone secured his drinking water from the spring in a rock on which the Masonic hall was built. In this hall there are tintypes and daguerreotypes of pioneer members of the order, some of whom later became noted in the state. The old hostelry, which boasted three stories with broad balconies, is one of the most picturesque landmarks of the southern mining towns.

Volcano is about twelve miles northeast of Jackson, and about two miles from Pine Grove, to the left of the Jackson–Silver Lake highway. Not far away, to the north and east, are the sites of other mining towns, among them Russell's Hill, Fort John, Aqueduct City, Plattsburg, Contreras, Upper Ranchería, Ashland, Grizzly Hill, Whiskey Slide, Spanish Gulch, Hunt's Gulch, and Wheeler Springs. Fort John in 1850 rivaled Volcano in importance, the first church and school in Amador County having been established there this early. At Upper Ranchería some fine structures built of hewn lava from the surrounding hills are still standing, relics of the town's former glory.

Cosumnes Mining Camps

In the northern part of Amador County numerous mining camps were once located on the Cosumnes River and its several branches, the entire region being the setting for many animated scenes of mining life. Some of these camps have long since vanished, only scarred hills and an occasional chimney marking the spots where eager miners once toiled or where their crude cabins stood. Other camps remain today as sleepy mountain hamlets, while a few are marked only by some aging, historic building.

The richest location in the district was situated on the river bar at the main forks of the Cosumnes, and was called by the Indian name Yeomet. Several stores and a somewhat pretentious hotel were standing there in 1853, but the miners gradually took over the town, one building after another giving way to the "diggings," until nothing was left except the old toll bridge. Another bar along the river on the Amador County side was Cape Cod Bar.

On the stage road to Sacramento, four or five miles south of Yeomet, was Plymouth, where the Plymouth Consolidated Mine is located. This is still a busy town, its history largely bound up with the quartz lodes of the region. Some mining is being done there even today. Between these two camps was Enterprise, also a quartz center. At the lower end of the flat on which Plymouth is located was the hamlet of Puckerville, or Pokerville, not a trace of which is left today.

A few miles east of the site of Pokerville is the picturesque village of Fiddletown, the name of which is immortalized in Bret Harte's story "An Episode of Fiddletown." Fiddletown was first settled in 1849 by a party of Missourians. When it became necessary to name the young town, this is how the problem was settled, so the story goes: "They are always fiddling," said an old Missouri patriarch; "call it Fiddletown." And Fiddletown it was until 1878,

when the name was changed to Oleta. The change was made
by the state legislature, at the instance, it is said, of Judge
Purinton, a prominent citizen who, on frequent business trips
to Sacramento and San Francisco, had been greatly em-
barrassed at being known as "the man from Fiddletown."
Some of the old-time buildings may still be seen in the
town, one of which is the well-preserved Purinton home.
Through the efforts of the Committee on Historic Landmarks of the California Historical Society, the old name of
Fiddletown has been restored.

In the early '50's and '60's Fiddletown was the trading
center for a number of rich mining camps—American Flat
and American Hill, French Flat, Loafer Flat, Lone Hill, and
others. The entire region, including the ridge between Suck-
ertown (now Bridgeport) and Slate Creek, forms a part of
extensive ancient river deposits.

Central House, a popular stage station which still stands
on the road between Plymouth and Drytown, was built of
timbers brought around the Horn. The house is now a
private residence. Another much-frequented hostelry on this
route was at Willow Springs, a few miles west of Drytown
on the way to Sacramento. Forest Home, where a beautiful
old stone inn built in the late '50's still stands, Arkansas
Creek, and Yankee Hill were neighboring camps farther west.

The region about Fiddletown and Plymouth is now a
prosperous dry-farming community, growing grapes, walnuts, pears, and various farm products. Shenandoah Valley,
north of Plymouth, has been a rich farming section since the
early '50's, and descendants of pioneer settlers still occupy
many of the old homesteads.

Sutter Creek

Sutter Creek was named after John A. Sutter, the first
white man to come to that region in 1846, and the first to
mine the locality in 1848. There was little activity at Sutter
Creek until 1851, when quartz gold was discovered. Quartz
mining was a very hazardous occupation in the early days.
The art of timbering the shafts and tunnels was not under-
stood and many cave-ins resulted. The capital outlay, too,
was so great and the profits were so uncertain that many
men were ruined financially by the venture. Alvinza Hayward stands pre-eminent as the man who emerged victorious.
Buying out several mines, ultimately, in the face of great
odds, he made them produce millions. The Central Eureka,
discovered in 1869, and at one time part of the Hayward
holdings, is at present the best-paying mine at Sutter Creek.
In 1932 it had reached the 2,300-foot level.

In the late '50's Leland Stanford, later governor of California and founder of Stanford University, financed the
Lincoln Mine, between Sutter Creek and Amador City, for
Robert Downs, maintaining a controlling interest in it during the years from 1859 to 1872. The returns proved so rich
that Stanford, then a Sacramento business man and merchant, was greatly aided in the building of the Central Pacific
Railroad.

Sutter Creek is still a thriving mining town, with several
deep quartz mines near by. The following buildings are of
historic interest: the Masonic Hall, the John Keyes Building,
and the Alvinza Hayward Office Building. Educational and
religious activities thrived here from the beginning, making
it distinctive as a moral center in the midst of the wilder
mining camps of the region.

Amador City

Amador City, located on Amador Creek three miles north
of Sutter Creek, where it intercepts the Mother Lode ledge,
had its beginning as a mining center in 1848. But the placers
were never very rich, and, like Sutter Creek, the history of

Amador City has been connected chiefly with quartz mining.
The first quartz discovery in Amador County was made
there in February 1851 by Davidson, a Baptist preacher. As
three other ministers were associated with him, the mine was
called the "Ministers' Claim." A little later the vein was
discovered on the north side of the creek, and became known
as the "Original Amador Mine."

The present Keystone Mine at Amador is the result of
the consolidation of the Original Amador with the Spring
Hill, Granite State, and Walnut Hill mines in 1857. But the
enterprise was not a success until the discovery of the
Bonanza in 1869, when the first month's crushing paid
forty thousand dollars. This high production continued until
well into the '80's. The Keystone has been closed down for
more than a quarter of a century, but there are those who
believe that millions of dollars in gold still lie hidden within
the earth thereabouts and that Amador City may yet renew
its old-time activity. A beautiful brick building, the office
and residence of former superintendents, still stands in
good repair.

Jackson

Jackson, county seat of Amador County, is rich in old
buildings reminiscent of the mining days of the '50's. Built
largely of stone, with massive doors, iron-shuttered windows,
and balconied upper stories, they speak eloquently of the
days of Indians and robbers and gold.

The presence of these old iron-barred stores lingers like
a memory along the narrow winding street and mingles
strangely with that of the little white Greek Catholic Church
which stands at the end of town. This, and the fact that
the population is a mixture of Italian, Serbian, Slavonian,
and Mexican, with descendants of pioneer Americans, gives
the place an Old World atmosphere with echoes from the
days of '49. The National Hotel (much altered); the old
Wells Fargo Building; the George Brown House; the Native
Daughters' Room, where the Native Daughters of the Golden
West were organized in 1886; an old store at Jackson
Gate, Chichizola's since 1850; the New York Ranch near
Jackson; and the site of the Hangman's Tree on the main
street of the town—these and other historic sites and land-
marks complete the association of the present with the past.

Jackson was named by early miners in honor of Colonel
Jackson, an upstanding, energetic leader of the town during
the first few years of its history. The location had previously
been known as Botilleas Spring (Bottle Spring) because
of the large piles of bottles that had collected there as early
as 1848, travelers having been accustomed to stop and camp
on the road from Sacramento to the Mokelumne River
mines.

The diggings in the immediate vicinity of the town were
not rich, but, being the logical center for a large mining area
and a convenient stopping-place on the road from Sacramento to the southern mines, Jackson grew and prospered
in the early '50's. The richest location in the neighborhood
was below the forks of Jackson Creek, where a few prospectors took out as much as five hundred dollars a day.

The flats and gulches in the vicinity of Tunnel Hill, one
and a half miles south of Jackson, at the village of Scottsville, were also good, and the hill itself was a wealth-pro-
ducer. A number of tunnels sunk into its sides gave rise
to the name. This tremendously rich deposit was worked to
bed rock, but the scarred hills are now grass grown and
serve as pasture lands. Here, a little Indian settlement with
its group of neat homes is occupied by civilized, voting
Indians. Here, too, is the historic Scottsville store where
the pioneer proprietor, Griswold, was murdered in the early
days by eight Chinese, who robbed the safe of gold dust.

At Jackson Gate, one mile north of town, was another rich gravel digging. A deep, narrow fissure in the rocks through which the creek flows gave the place its name. Ohio Hill and Squaw Gulch near by were also very rich. During a winter's work at the former place, the operators of one mine took out from forty to fifty thousand dollars, while Madame Pantaloons, a woman dressed as a man and doing a man's work, accumulated a hundred thousand dollars and then sold her claim for twenty thousand more.

Quartz mining continued to bring prosperity to Jackson after other forms of mining had ceased to be remunerative, and in recent years has made great strides. Several deep quartz veins in the hills above the town are still being worked profitably, making Jackson a busy mining center even yet. The famous Argonaut and Kennedy mines, among the deepest in the world, are located here. The Argonaut, discovered in the early '50's, experienced many failures as well as successes, but today it continues to yield enormous profits. In 1938 its shaft went 6,300 feet below the earth's level. The total production of this mine, through 1930, was $17,391,409.

The Kennedy, about a mile in depth, was opened prior to 1870. It, too, had its ups and downs, vast sums being expended with little returns. Later, however, it became a record producer. During very recent years improvements have been made and new equipment has been installed, showing the faith of present owners in the future possibilities of the mine. A second hoist has been set up at the 4,600-foot level of its vertical shaft, now down to a depth of 4,950 feet. The shaft was to be deepened to 5,100 feet.

The Oneida, one and a half miles northeast of Jackson, was located in 1851 by a party of men from the central part of New York. The history of the mine has shown from the first an erratic production record.

North and east of Jackson, remnants of several smaller mining camps may still be found among the hills. Clinton, six miles east of Jackson, with its historic Catholic Church built in 1877 and still in good repair though unattended, and the old Robinson Hotel still standing but unoccupied, is now surrounded by small ranches. A number of miners were attracted to the vicinity in the '50's after water had been brought to the place by means of canals, but the diggings were never rich. It was a center for quartz mining as late as the '80's.

On the Clinton Road, five miles east of Jackson, Slabtown exists only as a site. Formerly a rich mining area, it is now a prosperous agricultural community known as Milligan District. The first citizens of Slabtown were too poor to build anything better than shacks of rough slabs with the bark left on, but later the place became very prosperous and a number of brick and stone structures were erected. Not a stick or stone of the old town remains today.

Irishtown, eight miles north of Jackson, has also vanished, and the story of its joyous, lively citizens is almost forgotten. The first white settlers on this spot found it a "city of wigwams" and hundreds of mortars in the rocks still testify that this was a favorite Indian camping-ground. Two miles beyond is Pine Grove, once a mining center but now rapidly building up with summer cabins scattered among the odorous pine woods. A revival of mining is, however, taking place here as elsewhere throughout the country. One of the early houses in the village and the old Clough home near Pine Grove still stand.

Ione Valley

Ione was variously known in the gold days as "Bed Bug" and "Freeze Out." But the place grew and became ambitious, and the more euphonious name of Ione, for one of the heroines of Bulwer Lytton's novel, *The Last Days of Pompeii,* replaced the old ones.

The Methodist Episcopal Church was first organized in the place in 1853. The town was so prosperous that a larger building was planned, and in 1862 a striking brick structure of Gothic architecture was erected, Bishop Simpson laying the corner stone. Ione's expectations of becoming a great city were never fulfilled, but in 1930 it was still a busy supply center with a population of 1,849. An excellent grade of potter's clay is shipped from this point, and here, also, is located the Preston School of Industry, established in 1889.

Muletown, about two miles north of Ione, was a lively camp in the '50's, and many are the stories told of the strikes in its rich foothill ravines: a native of Argentina washed out a hundred dollars a day there; a Chinaman, picking up a piece of gold weighing thirty-six ounces, was so elated that he immediately left for his home land. These and other similar tales indicate the wealth of the region. After the ravines had been worked out, the surrounding hills were attacked by hydraulic power and outdid the ravines in treasure produced. Some claims paid as high as a thousand dollars a week per man. During its palmy days Muletown claimed several hundred inhabitants, a large proportion being Irish. The pranks and adventures of these jolly citizens of Muletown would fill a book. Most of them owned horses, and, being neither skillful nor graceful riders, a Muletown crowd, riding out in quest of fun on a Sunday afternoon, could be distinguished miles away "by the flopping limbs and furious riding." Muletown and its gay riders are no more.

The Q Ranch, one and a half miles northwest of Ione, was taken up in 1850 by several men, one of whom had been a member of Company Q of the Ohio Volunteers in the Mexican War. From this fact the ranch received its name. Being on the main highway from Jackson to Sacramento, the place became a famous hostelry in the '50's and '60's. Since it was the starting- and stopping-point for the mountain stages, the drivers always aimed to reach it at mealtime. It never became a town, but accumulated quite a colony of buildings, including hotel, stables, post office, blacksmith shop, and store. It is now a fruit ranch rented out to Japanese. An old hop house and the Hangman's Tree still remind one of the past.

Adjoining the Q Ranch is "Doschville," where the old frame Dosch home and the ruins of a brick store and hop house still stand beside the road. The clay pits, in evidence throughout the Ione region, are found in close proximity to the beautiful ruined walls of the old store, a product of those same pits.

The Alabama House, five miles northwest of Ione, another old-time inn, was famous for its fine food in the early days. The house is gone and the site unmarked.

Irish Hill, situated on the north side of Dry Creek where the stream leaves the canyon, was a rich mixture of ancient river and beach deposits. Within seven months' time, four men washed out nine thousand dollars each. As late as the '80's, Stanford and Company and Alvinza Hayward mined this region by hydraulic process. Nothing remains here today.

Not even the site of Quincy is remembered today, but the fact of its existence has been preserved for us in a copy of an early newspaper published in the place. The town's main thoroughfare, a wide street called Broadway, boasted numbered houses, as well as saloons, stores, several real estate offices, and doctors' and lawyers' offices.

In memory of the many brave and self-sacrificing Wells Fargo messengers and stage drivers a tablet was placed near Ione on September 8, 1929, which contains a replica of a six-horse stagecoach, with its driver and guard. The tablet contains the following inscription:

Michael (Mike) Tovey, Wells Fargo messenger, was killed, and Dewitt Clinton Radcliff, stage driver, injured on this spot June 15, 1893, by a lone bandit who attempted to hold up the regular six-horse stage on the old Ione-Jackson stage road.

A line of stages was established in 1850, running between Sacramento and Sonora via Q ranch (near Ione), Jackson, Mokelumne Hill, Angels, and Columbia. Over $265,000,000 in gold bullion is said to have been carried in the early days over this, the main artery [from Sacramento] to the "Mother Lode" and southern mines.

In memory of these and many other brave, intrepid, self-sacrificing, and loyal Wells Fargo messengers and stage drivers of California, this tablet is dedicated.

Tablet placed by Historic Landmarks Committee, Native Sons of the Golden West, and Native Sons and Native Daughters of Amador County, September 8, 1929.

SOURCES

[Credit is here given for source material, and permission to quote is hereby acknowledged]

FARQUHAR, FRANCIS P. (editor). *Up and Down California, 1860–1864. The Journal of William H. Brewer.* Yale University Press, New Haven, 1930

MASON, J. D. *History of Amador County, California.* Thompson and West, Oakland, 1881

NATIVE SONS OF THE GOLDEN WEST. *Landmarks Committee Report, 1920–1929.* Joseph Knowland, Chairman. Tribune Building, Oakland, California

NORBOE, MAJOR P. M. *The Maiden's Grave.* Manuscript, September 26, 1916 (in State Library, Sacramento)

SARGENT, MRS. ELIZABETH ANN (editor). *Amador County History.* Amador County Federation of Women's Clubs, Jackson, California, 1927

TYLER, SERGEANT DANIEL. *A Concise History of the Mormon Battalion in the Mexican War, 1846–1847.* Privately published, Salt Lake City, 1881

BUTTE COUNTY

BUTTE COUNTY (named for the Sutter Buttes, the high hills to the south, in Sutter County) is one of the original twenty-seven counties of the state. At first the county seat was at Hamilton, but in 1853 it was moved to Bidwell Bar, and again in 1856 to Oroville.

U-I-No, the Cliff of the Giant

U-I-No, familiarly known today as Bald Rock, in the Grand Gorge of the Middle Fork of Feather River near where Fall River empties into the larger stream, was believed by ancient Indian tribes to be the home of a giant evil spirit. Even today Indians are often said to shun it. Towering sheer above the seething river for 3,600 feet, utterly devoid of vegetation, its white granite majesty resembles that of El Capitan in Yosemite Valley.

The entire region is one of spectacular beauty and so wild and rugged that the primeval Indians, early white explorers, and prospecting miners either avoided or failed to penetrate it. In 1889, Emery Oliver, later a great railroad engineer, ran a survey through the entire Middle Fork Canyon including that portion now known as Bald Rock Canyon. In 1908, two Geological Survey men also passed through it. Immense granite boulders, deep caverns, and, above all, the superb beauty of Feather Falls, one of the most imposing of Sierra waterfalls, make of this region a veritable wonderland. It is still, however, the least known of any in California. The falls drop sheer 500 feet, with an additional 200 feet of cascades, and fill the canyon with heavy mist and marvelous iridescent lights for half a mile.

Rancho Chico

General John Bidwell came to California in 1841, as one of the leaders of the first overland company of Americans to come to California with the intention of making it their home.

On his arrival, Bidwell was employed for a time by John A. Sutter at Sutter's Fort, but in the late '40's he bought Rancho Chico from William Dickey and Edward A. Farwell, the original grantees of Rancho Arroyo Chico (November 7, 1844) and of the Farwell Grant (March 29, 1844), and the first settlers of Butte County. On Rancho Chico Bidwell built the stone mansion which is now used as the Girls' Dormitory of the Chico State Teachers' College. On his ranch General Bidwell founded the town of Chico in 1860, later donating land for public schools, setting aside a plot of ground for each church organization, and designating a large section for the Normal School, now the Chico State College, established in 1889.

General Bidwell was one of the foremost builders of the commonwealth of California, being a member of the senate, serving in the state militia during the Civil War, and being also a pioneer agriculturist and horticulturist, and a man interested in humanitarian, educational, and reform movements. He has been called "a prince among California pioneers," and became "closely identified with virtually all the important movements in the development of California." He was also a nominee for United States President on the Prohibition ticket and received the largest number of votes of any one ever nominated by that party.

General Bidwell was friendly to the Indians, always treating them fairly, allowing them to occupy their ancient rancheria lands, hiring them to work on his estate, settling their disputes, and providing for them cultural as well as material advantages. He and his wife maintained a school and a church for their use, and in countless little kindly ways acted as father and mother to these dark-skinned children of the wilderness.

On the site of the Mechopa adobe, built for General Bidwell on Rancho Chico by the Indians in 1852, a marker has been placed by the Pioneer Historical Society and the Native Sons of the Golden West, assisted by the Chico chapter of the D.A.R., in honor of General Bidwell. The marker also commemorates the fact that the Oregon Emigrant Trail passed the place.

Treaty G, one of the eighteen unratified treaties of the United States Government with the California Indians, was drawn up and signed at Rancho Chico, August 1, 1851. These treaties, made by duly authorized agents of the federal government under the administration of President Fillmore, 1851–1852, were pigeonholed in the secret archives of Congress during the California gold fever and were not brought to light until 1905. They covered scattered areas throughout California.

Chico Landing, where steamers plying up the Sacramento River unloaded and from which a stage line ran north to Shasta City and the Trinity mines, was an important place in the '50's. It was located on near-by Rancho de Farwell, about five miles west of the present city of Chico. Stage service was frequent and competition keen.

Beginning as early as 1847 and continuing until his death, General Bidwell maintained an experimental orchard near his house. It contained at least one specimen of over four hundred varieties of fruit and at the time of his death included eighteen hundred acres of every species and variety adapted to the locality. He was the father of the raisin industry in that region as well as a pioneer in the manufacture of olive oil. He began wine-making in 1864 or 1865, but in 1867 the vineyard was dug up and a wine grape was never again planted on his land. In 1886 Bidwell presented almost thirty acres of his land to the state as a forestry experiment station. The gift was neglected by the State Forestry Commission and came under the care of the state university. It is now owned by the city of Chico.

The entire estate of Rancho Chico was remarkable for its splendid trees, both native and exotic. On July 10, 1905, a tract of the most desirable land along Chico Creek comprising more than nineteen hundred acres and including Oak Forest, in which may be found the Hooker Oak, Iron Canyon, and other spots of great beauty, was donated to the city of Chico by Mrs. Annie E. K. Bidwell and was named Bidwell Park by the city. On May 11, 1911, Mrs. Bidwell added 301 acres to this gift. The wooded areas along Big Chico Creek and Lindo Channel now a part of the state park system were donated to the state of California also by Mrs. Bidwell. In 1911 she gave several additional acres along Big Chico Creek to the city of Chico. The latter tract is an improved park known as the Children's Playground. Two miles southeast of the city are 240 acres owned by the United States Department of Agriculture and used as a plant introduction garden.

Just outside the Chico city limits stands the mammoth Hooker Oak, the most famous of California's valley oaks (*Quercus lobata,* the largest of all the American oaks). This magnificent tree was named in honor of the great English botanist, Sir Joseph Hooker, who visited Rancho Chico in 1877. The valley oaks were discovered in 1792 by Spanish naval officers and were often mentioned in the narratives of Vancouver, Frémont, and other early explorers. Of the many fine specimens of this oak, measurements prove the Hooker Oak to be one of the largest. Merritt B. Pratt gives the height as one hundred and ten feet and the circumference as twenty-eight feet.

Rancho Esquón

The headquarters of Rancho Esquón, granted to Samuel Neal and John A. Sutter in 1844, was located on Butte Creek seven miles south of Chico. Neal, a native of Pennsylvania, had come to California with Frémont earlier in 1844, and with the latter's permission had remained at Sutter's Fort as a blacksmith. Two years later, in April 1846, Neal entertained Frémont on Rancho Esquón, while the Captain was on his way to Oregon. The next month Neal guided Gillespie up the Sacramento Valley in an endeavor to overtake Frémont and to deliver to him certain instructions from the government at Washington.

There were other Mexican grants in Butte County: Rancho Aguas Frías (later known as the Pratt Grant), located south of the site of Durham, given to Salvador Osio in November 1844; Rancho Llano Seco (later the Parrott Grant), situated north of Rancho Aguas Frías, bestowed upon Sebastián Kayser, October 2, 1845; the Boga-Larkin Grant, occupying the southeastern part of the county, given to Charles William Flugge, February 21, 1844; and the Fernández Grant, located north of the Flugge Grant, given to Dionisio and Máximo Fernández in June 1846.

Hamilton, a "Ghost Town"

Hamilton is an extinct mining town which was situated on a bend in the Feather River, fourteen miles from Marysville. Its story is characteristic of many "ghost towns" on the Feather River and in other old mining regions. The first mining was done at this point in the early spring of 1848 by John Bidwell and others. By 1850, mining for gold in the river became active and a town grew up.

Hamilton won over Bidwell Bar in the contest for county seat in 1850, but, as mining in the latter town (twenty-five miles farther up the river) became richer and more prosperous, people left Hamilton for Bidwell Bar, and the latter became county seat in 1853.

There is nothing left of Hamilton today, but the Native Sons of the Golden West have placed a monument in the old pioneer cemetery to designate the site. Just above Hamilton was Columbus, inhabited mostly by Chinese miners.

The old stage road along the Feather River ran about one and a half miles farther east than the present highway. From Hamilton it continued north to Shasta City and the northern mines. In the middle '50's on this route there were thirteen road-houses and hotels between Marysville and Hamilton.

Bidwell Bar

Bidwell Bar was one of the many flourishing mining camps along the Feather River in the Sierra Nevada in the '50's. Gold was discovered there by John Bidwell, July 4, 1848. The camp was located on the Middle Fork of the Feather River about thirty-nine miles above the town of Marysville. In 1853 three daily stages ran to Bidwell's Bar direct from Marysville.

As the mines at Bidwell Bar became more or less exhausted, the inhabitants moved down the river to Ophir City, later called Oroville, and elsewhere.

All that is left of this camp is an old stone store on the flat below the suspension bridge, and the "Mother Orange Tree" planted there by Judge Joseph Lewis in 1856. From this tree, which still bears fruit, grew the citrus industry in northern California. It has been marked by the Native Sons of the Golden West. The site of the courthouse has been marked by the same organization and by the Butte County Supervisors. Where Bidwell Bar once flourished, a swimming resort has been developed recently for the citizens of Oroville.

The Oldest Suspension Bridge in California

At Bidwell Bar a suspension bridge spans the Middle Fork of the Feather River, ten miles east of Oroville. This is believed to be the oldest one in California, having been shipped around the Horn from Troy, New York, in 1853, and placed in service in 1856. It was operated as a toll bridge until 1889, when it was opened as a free bridge. Concerted efforts are being made to preserve this picturesque and historical landmark. At the end of the bridge, across the highway from the Mother Orange Tree, stands the old stone toll house.

Following up the South Fork of the Feather River from Bidwell's Bar, the old road led to other mining camps. Stringtown, about four miles east, received its name because its buildings were strung out in a narrow, rambling line along the canyon. Its history is brief and phenomenal. Dating from 1849, it had become very populous by 1850. In July 1856 the *Butte Record* published its obituary in the following words: "The string of Stringtown has been pulled out. It's 'gin' out."

A mile above Stringtown, on the road to Downieville, the Union Enterprise Company flumed the river in 1852, naming its camp Enterprise. About six miles beyond was Forbestown, founded in September 1850 by B. F. Forbes. It was a center of mining activities for thirty or forty years. It was a town of some cultural importance, also, with a private academy and a general assembly hall where lectures were given during the week and where large congregations gathered for services on Sunday. Today this once bustling camp is "a derelict town lost in a mountain cove where a second growth of timber is fast replacing a one-time virgin forest. Heaps of débris and old foundations mark the sites of large buildings that have collapsed or been torn down. Other structures with crumbling roofs and gaping doors are verging on dissolution. The old post office is open to the weather, its grilled window and tier of letter boxes yet intact; only the curious visitor crosses its threshold." The Masonic Hall, built in 1855, also stands. Near Forbestown was Clipper Mills, an early lumber camp.

Oroville, the City of Gold

The first miners came to the site of Oroville on the Feather River in 1849, and in 1850 they formed a mining camp there which they named, at first, Ophir City ("gold city"). By 1856 the town had been renamed Oroville and its importance had increased so considerably that it·was ambitious to be chosen as the county seat. Since Bidwell Bar, then county seat, was waning as a mining center, Oroville received the honor by popular election. The new county seat soon became a trading center for the mining towns in the surrounding hills, along Table Mountain, and up the Feather River.

Immediately east of Oroville, passengers on the Western Pacific Railroad may see a great rock wall, plainly visible from the car windows. This wall was built along one side of the Feather River for the purpose of diverting the water from its course in order that the gravel of the river's bed might be mined. This was a part of the extensive diversion operations which were carried on along the Feather River, during 1856 and 1857, by means of wing dams, coffer dams, and flumes. From Oroville to the junction of the North and Middle forks of Feather River the most extensive activities of this kind in California were carried on.

Below Oroville was Bagdad, while two miles above it was Long's Bar, founded in 1849 with the establishment of a store there by the Long brothers. The first pan of gold washed out at Long's Bar netted $400. The place became one of the principal settlements of the region during the '50's, but the old pioneer cemetery is all that remains to mark the site. Opposite Long's Bar was Adamsville (now in ruins), where hundreds of miners gathered. At the Cape Claim, in 1855, the fluming of the river is said to have netted $1,000,000 in sixty days. Lynchburg, another thriving camp with its rich surface diggings, was located on the present site of Oro Vista. It was a rival of Oroville in the contest for county seat, putting forth the claim of superior climate. Centerville, or Middletown, was a camp near the site of the Southern Pacific depot in the present city of Oroville. Thompson's Flat, first called Rich Gulch and mined as early as 1848, had so increased in population by 1854 that the town was removed to the top of the hill, which still bears the name of Thompson. Morris Ravine, near Thompson's Flat, also saw some of the earliest mining in the county. It was named for an employee of Samuel Neal, who in 1848 guided a party of Oregonians from the Neal Ranch to the Feather River diggings.

·Because of all this activity up and down the river, Oroville had become a stage center of some importance by 1856, as is indicated by an article in the *North Californian* for November of that year: "Coaches are rattling through our streets at all hours of the day and night. We have ten, semi-daily, connecting this place with different parts of the world. There are six daily stages to Marysville, three for Spanish-town, one for Shasta, one for Bidwell, one for Forbestown, one for Bangor." Numerous pack animals also traveled up and down the highways, and along the narrow trails into the higher mountains whither no wagon roads yet led.

On February 26, 1857, the "Gazelle" arrived at Oroville, the first of the river steamers to penetrate that far. For three months that spring others followed, but because of various reasons none came afterward.

Beginning in the late '50's and continuing through the '60's and '70's, hydraulic mining was the chief activity at Oroville and Cherokee, and in the surrounding country. Evidences of extensive hydraulic operations may still be seen in the form of canals, ditches, old flumes, and deeply scarred hills.

More recent years saw the development of the gold-dredging industry, which originated at Oroville and from there spread around the world. The great gravel fields about the city give some idea of the extent of the industry, which gleaned many millions in gold from the land. One dredging company offered to move the entire town of Oroville and rebuild it at the company's expense if it might be allowed to dredge beneath the town and remove the great treasure over which the city had been built. Oroville now is in the midst of a rich agricultural region. However, some mining is still carried on in neighboring towns in the hills.

Oroville's Chinatown, once said to have housed 10,000 Chinese, is one of the few typical Chinatowns remaining in California. At one time it was second only to San Francisco in the number of its Chinese inhabitants.

The Cherokee Diamond Mine

The Diamond Mine, at the old town of Cherokee, is about ten miles north of Oroville and two miles west of the Feather River. Several hundred thousand dollars in jewels, one gem alone weighing over five karats in the rough, have been taken out of a single hill. Three hundred diamonds have been found there; at no other place in North America have an equal number been discovered.

A Wells Fargo Express Station vault still stands at Cherokee. Solidly built of stone, it is a picturesque remnant of pioneer days.

Camps of the North Feather River Watershed

Scores of mining camps were once located in the hill region north of Oroville. The earlier locations on the river bars were followed by those on the flats somewhat back from the streams, and finally the ridges and hills were worked. In some instances, the names of these historic camps remain to mark their geographical locations, but often even the name has been forgotten. Throughout the Feather River district the remains of rudely constructed fireplaces, sometimes found in lonely and forgotten places, are almost the only evidence of pioneer habitation.

Among the many bars of the region, Potter's Bar, on the North Fork immediately above its junction with the Middle Fork, was first mined in the spring of 1848. Other bars of '48, '49, and the early '50's were Kanaka, Yankee, Ohio, Berry Creek, Huff's, Shore's, Lindsay, Bartee's, and Island.

Camps among the dry diggings of the surrounding hills included: Big and Little Kimshew, Wild Yankee Ranch, Deadwood, Concow, Blairtown, Chub Gulch, Jordan Hill, Hermitage, Toadtown, and Stone House.

As early as the autumn of 1848 gold-seekers from Oregon began to arrive in California, the first from the outside world. Their presence in the mining regions is evidenced by the nomenclature in many places. Oregon City and Oregon Gulch, halfway between Oroville and Cherokee, were, for some time, important mining centers in Butte County.

Perhaps the liveliest of these North Feather River camps was Spanishtown, so named because the rich diggings in the vicinity had been discovered in 1855 by a company of Chileans and Mexicans. By 1856 a town had sprung up there, twenty miles north of Oroville and one mile from Frenchtown. Near by, Yankee Hill, the successor of Rich Gulch, "fell heir to what Spanishtown and Frenchtown had to bequeath when they passed on and out."

Still farther north, twenty-five miles from Oroville, on the West Branch of the North Fork was Dogtown (now Magalia). The name had its origin, so one story goes, in the fact that an old French woman who lived at the place kept a kennel of poodles, hounds, and mastiffs that were known all over the countryside. The name Dogtown was applied not only to the town but to the entire ridge as well. Two miles east of the town a nugget was discovered in 1859 which is said to have been the largest gold nugget ever found in Butte County. It was known as the "Dogtown Nugget" and weighed fifty-four pounds in the rough and forty-nine and a half pounds when melted into a bar. It was valued at $10,690.

About five miles southwest of Dogtown, on Big Butte Creek, was Paradise, while to the west, on Chico Creek, was Helltown, with Whiskey Flat in close proximity. Some, however, would deprive us of the antithesis implied, by saying that the name Paradise had nothing to do with heavenly happiness because it was originally "Pair-o'-Dice." Northeast of Dogtown was Flea Valley, and several miles northwest was Nimshew.

Dogtown was only one of a number of mining camps and stage stations on the road from Oroville to Susanville. Twelve miles north of Oroville a Mr. Pence and four partners located the Lyon ranch in 1850, opening a store and eating-place in a tent. The place grew and became a station of some importance. By 1864 a post office, under the name of Pentz, had been established there, with Mr. Pence as postmaster.

Seven or eight miles above Dogtown another station was established in 1853 by R. P. Powell, who blazed out and constructed the road to Susanville. Powell's Ranch, with its fine orchards and vineyards, was later known as Powellton, and, being at the junction of the roads from Oroville and Chico to Susanville, became an important stage station.

Exceptionally rich diggings were found in the late '50's at Lovelock, five miles north of Dogtown, and at Inskip, seven miles above Powellton on the Susanville road.

Among the stage stations which once existed on the road from Oroville to Quincy were Hart's Mills, Berry Creek, Sinclair Hotel, Brush Creek, Mountain House, Junction House, Peavine, and the Hoad Ranch. Of these stations and many others, only the Hoad House remains today. Renovated and repainted, this picturesque landmark serves as the Elks Retreat at Camp Wilder. The ranch was noted in the early days not only for its fine fruits but also for its excellent natural hay. Today the old house, the gnarled fruit trees, and the meadow, with its luxuriant growth of wild flowers and tall grasses, present a lovely rural scene framed in a circle of dark pines. The site of Peavine is occupied by a building of later construction known as the Merrimac Hotel and Post Office. At the Junction House, the depression of the old cellar is all that is left except the aged apple and cherry trees, some of which are being crowded out by the young pines which are growing up among them. The Mountain House, too, has its old fruit trees, but the present building is not the original one. All along the highway, bits of orchard, old-fashioned wells, or portions of the original roadbed appear every mile or more, marking the path followed by the stage coaches in the '50's and the '60's, and even as late as in 1900.

"Mushroom" Towns

The year 1853 was an era of "mushroom" towns in Butte County, as elsewhere. Not only in the mining regions was this true, but in the valleys as well, and especially along the rivers. Nearly every one of the towns made enough advance to boast some kind of tavern, a blacksmith shop, and the inevitable saloon. Of those on the rivers, each claimed to be at the head of steamboat navigation on the river on which it was situated, and the usual exorbitant prices of '49 were asked and paid for lots in their precincts.

Veazie City (named after its promoter) was laid out a short distance east of the Feather River and a few miles from the southern boundary line of the county. On the same side and a few miles farther up the river was Fredonia, and nearly opposite was Yatestown. All have long since vanished. Troy, another once hopeful "metropolis," suffered a like fate, and its site is now a matter of speculation. On the Sacramento River near the mouth of Deer Creek was located Benton City, another ephemeral town. It soon vanished, however, and even its name has been forgotten by most people.

Bangor and Wyandotte

East and north of Veazie City was Bangor, one of a number of mining camps in that locality. It was settled in 1855 by the Lambert brothers from Bangor, Maine, and with the discovery of the Blue Lead mine became quite important, boasting fifty buildings—stores, saloons, hotels, gambling houses, etc. Its rival, Hylandsville, was laid out as a town in 1855, but it never attained to the importance of Bangor, its promoter being the only man who ever lived there.

Northwest of Bangor was Wyandotte, named after a company of Wyandotte Indians who mined there in 1850. It reached its greatest prosperity in 1852 and 1853. In 1857 the place boasted "a magnificent brick fireproof hotel, the only one in the county." Bangor and Wyandotte are today centers of the orange and olive industries, and the old mining ditches are being used for irrigation purposes.

Near Wyandotte is the site of the old mining camp of Evansville, first settled in 1850 by a man named Evans. By 1854 most of the place was owned by Elisha Brown. This was "one of the old towns that sprang into existence under the influence of mining, lived and flourished while mining was good, and hobbled off the theatre of life when the diggings played out" in 1870.

SOURCES

[Credit is here given for source material, and permission to quote is hereby acknowledged]

BIDWELL, GENERAL JOHN. Echoes of the Past. Chico Advertiser, Chico, California. No date

COMMONWEALTH CLUB OF CALIFORNIA. "Indians in California," in The Commonwealth, II, Part II, No. 23 (June 8, 1926)

COY, OWEN COCHRAN. Gold Days of the series California, edited by John Russell McCarthy. Powell Publishing Company, Los Angeles, 1929

FRÉMONT, JOHN C. Memoirs of My Life, Including in the Narrative Five Journeys of Western Exploration, etc. Belford, Clarke & Company, Chicago, 1887

HUNT, ROCKWELL D., and NELLIE VAN DE GRIFT SANCHEZ. A Short History of California. Thomas Y. Crowell Company, New York, 1929

HUXLEY, LEONARD. Life and Letters of Sir Joseph Dalton Hooker. Vol. II. John Murray, Albemarle Street, W., London, 1918

MANSFIELD, GEORGE C. History of Butte County, California, with Biographical Sketches. Historic Record Company, Los Angeles, 1918

———. The Feather River in '49 and the Fifties. George C. Mansfield, Oroville, California, 1924

PRATT, MERRITT B. Shade and Ornamental Trees of California. California State Board of Forestry, 1922

ROYCE, C. C. John Bidwell, Pioneer, Statesman, Philanthropist. Privately published, Chico, 1906

WELLS, HARRY LAURENZ, and W. L. CHAMBERS. History of Butte County. H. L. Wells, San Francisco, 1882

CALAVERAS COUNTY

CALAVERAS COUNTY derived its name from the river which had been named by Gabriel Moraga on his expedition of 1808. Calaveras (Spanish for "skulls") was one of the original twenty-seven counties. Pleasant Valley, on the old river road to Jenny Lind, was designated by the legislature as the first county seat, February 18, 1850, but the county government was probably never established there. Two months later Double Springs was chosen as the seat of justice, followed successively by Jackson, Mokelumne Hill, and finally, in 1866, by San Andreas.

Wayside Inns

Along the old Mokelumne Hill road from Stockton by way of Linden, many a wayside inn refreshed the wayfarers of early gold days. Just across the county line was the famous Red House, a two-story hostelry, no longer standing. Its stone corral, however, is intact today. Beyond Stone Corral, on the road to Jenny Lind, was the Pleasant Valley House, also a two-story structure, since destroyed by fire. Halfway between Jenny Lind and Valley Springs on the north side of the main road was the North America House, where the stage horses were changed; this, too, has disappeared. On the same side of the road one and one-half miles below the North America was the Tremont House, built of lumber brought around the Horn. The Spring Valley House, between Valley Springs and San Andreas, about one-half mile above Mountain Gate, was a two-story structure with barns and corrals. Both of these historic hostelries have likewise vanished.

The Kentucky House, about two miles south of San Andreas and the center of mining activities on the South Fork of the Calaveras River, was a stopping-place for the stage between Sonora and Sacramento. At present the Calaveras Cement Company has a plant there. The original Kentucky House was destroyed by fire, but a later building was erected on the same site and has been remodeled by the cement company as a clubhouse.

Double Springs, a Once Ambitious "Ghost Town"

Double Springs, one of the "ghost towns" of the Mother Lode mining region, became a thriving center after it was named county seat in 1850. Neighboring towns, however, were also growing and soon wished to hold this coveted position. One of these was Jackson (then in Calaveras County), north of the Mokelumne River. The story of the contest which arose for the position of county seat is typical of what took place in various parts of the state during the pioneer period. A few ambitious young men at Jackson drove over to Double Springs, where some of their number treated the county clerk quite liberally at the tavern bar. Meanwhile the others went to the building used as a courthouse, loaded the archives into their wagon, and hurried back across the river to Jackson. This was in July 1851. Although this high-handed action was illegal, Jackson retained its position until April 16, 1852, when by popular election Mokelumne Hill took first place. It is said that the votes cast were "out of all proportion to the number of voters." Such was the "Wild West" spirit which prevailed in those days.

In 1854 Amador County was separated from Calaveras County, and Jackson became the county seat of the new county. In 1866 San Andreas was given that honor in Calaveras County, in place of Mokelumne Hill, and it remains the county seat today.

At Double Springs, on the state highway between Valley Springs and San Andreas, only a part of the first county courthouse remains; this building, moved from its original site, was probably erected toward the end of 1849, the material having been brought from China in October of that year. It consisted of three curiously arranged clapboard structures with numerous glass-paneled doors and no windows. The section still standing, although much worn by the elements, is in use as a storehouse. The original site of the courthouse has been marked by an eight-foot shaft of native sandstone erected by the Calaveras Chamber of Commerce.

The two springs for which the town was named still bring perennial verdure to the meadow which lies between the gently sloping hills. Here, surrounded by oleanders, orange trees, and aged locusts, stands the lovely old mansion of squared sandstone built in 1860 by Alexander R. Wheat. Close by, under the shadow of a great live oak, is the little family cemetery in which he lies buried.

Angel's Camp

Romantic Angel's Camp retains many an iron-shuttered, stone building reminiscent of the early gold days. Some of the most noteworthy landmarks are: the Selkirk House, Angel's Hotel (home of the annual Jumping Frog Jubilee), the Stickle Store (1857), Scribner's Store, and the famous Utica Mine, which was originally sold for a song and which later produced millions. Ruins of an old Wells Fargo building may also be seen. The visitor to Angel's Camp wanders through streets with curious names—Finnigan Lane, Hardscrabble Street, and Raspberry Lane—vivid reminders of a lively and colorful past.

In January 1865 Mark Twain, sojourning for a time at Tryon's Hotel, which stood on the site of the present Angel's Hotel before being destroyed by fire, obtained the nucleus for his famous story, *The Celebrated Jumping Frog of Calaveras County*. The story was told him by Ben Coon, a bartender at the hotel.

The Bret Harte Country

Recent investigations, unbiased by the old popular Bret Harte "legend," have shown that it is well-nigh impossible to attach to exact sites most of the place names used by Bret Harte in his tales of California's early mining camps. That author's geography, as represented in these stories, is, for the most part, "so ridiculous as to be obviously fictitious." There is Wingdam, that illusive locale identified by some writers as Murphy's but which George R. Stewart, Jr., most recent biographer of Francis Bret Harte, characterizes as the "capital of the Bret Harte country, a place as vaguely pictured as many-towered Camelot, and as difficult to locate on any map."

Poverty Flat, and many others, "are more in the nature of figurative names than actual localities." Harte himself placed Poverty Flat contiguous to Sandy Bar on the Stanislaus River, but according to the testimony of old-timers there was no Sandy Bar with capital letters in that region. The appellative "Poverty" was prefixed to many a Sierra mining location. It was a characteristic name descriptive of the situation when thousands mined and few struck it rich. It has been suggested that Bret Harte may have borrowed the name and the "atmosphere" from the real Poverty Flat (now McDonald Flat), eight miles east of Mokelumne Hill and one mile from Whiskey Slide (now Clear View).

In spite of numerous vagaries as to individual place names and localities, the country centering about Robinson's Ferry (now Melones) on either side of the Stanislaus River, with Angel's Camp and Murphy's as its northern limit and Table Mountain (in Tuolumne County) as its southern extremity, is one of the few regions in the Sierra of which

Harte "displayed any evidence of personal familiarity" in his stories. This was the only "Bret Harte country" that really existed. He made the Stanislaus River the scene of his humorous poem "The Society upon the Stanislaus," and charming bits of description in many of his stories fit the locality. His fondness, too, for Table Mountain is shown repeatedly. In *How Santa Claus Came to Simpson's Bar*, this characteristic picture is drawn: "Simpson's Bar on the eve of Christmas Day, 1862, clung like a swallow's nest to the rocky entablature and splintered capitals of Table Mountain."

Further evidence that Harte actually sojourned in this region is found in the story of his visit to Jackass Hill (in Tuolumne County), as told to Stewart and others by William Gillis: "In December, 1855, his brother Jim was at the cabin when a very dead-beat young man came limping up. He was in city clothes, and wore patent-leather shoes which were punishing his feet. The young fellow gave his name as Harte and told a hard-luck story. . . . . Gillis offered him the ready hospitality of the mountains, and Harte stayed for a night or two. . . . . When he went on, Gillis gave him twenty dollars to see him through."

It is difficult to fasten with any finality Harte's nomenclature even to the sites along the Stanislaus River. Roaring Camp, for instance, has been placed at McLain's Bar, now a deserted spot five miles up the river from Melones, but other evidence indicates that no such name existed in this region. As to Poker Flat, the consensus of old-timers seems to be that it was the original name for Byrne's Ferry (the old crossing on the Stanislaus from Copperopolis to Mountain Pass) ; but there are others who declare that they never heard the place called by that name. Poker Flat has even been located in Sierra County, a region which Bret Harte undoubtedly never saw.

Not only was Harte's geography largely fictitious, but critics are also agreed that his stories show little intimate knowledge of mines or miners. A two months' foot journey through the southern mines looking for a school to teach, with perhaps a little amateur panning for gold (Stewart, on the testimony of Bill Gillis, favors the vicinity of Fourth Crossing as the most likely spot for the latter activity), doubtless constitutes the full measure of Francis Bret Harte's first-hand experience in the mining regions of California. The camps of his stories, moreover, are decidedly not those of '49 and the early '50's, but are those of the middle '50's or even later. "The flavor of decay hangs about his mining towns, they are just the places which he might have seen in Calaveras in 1855."

Carson Hill

Carson Hill, about four miles south of Angel's Camp, has been called "the classic mining ground of California," for it was generally considered the richest camp in all the Mother Lode. There in November 1854 a mass of gold was found at the Morgan Mine weighing one hundred and ninety-five pounds and valued at $43,534, said to have been the largest nugget ever taken out in the United States.

At Carson Hill may be seen the ruins of some of the stone and brick buildings erected there in early mining days. Between Carson Hill and Hanselman's Hill at Albany Flat is the James Romaggi adobe, built in 1852. It was located on the old road to Los Muertos, that wild camp on Arroyo de los Muertos ("creek of the dead"), where the Battle of Six Mile Creek was waged between American and Mexican miners in the autumn of 1852. Los Muertos, with its predominant Mexican and Chilean population, was a favored haunt of Joaquín Murieta and his outlaw gang.

Morgan, on the north slope of Carson Hill, rivaled Mokel-

umne Hill in population and in the richness of its gold deposits. At one time in its history, over a period of two years, quartz mines at the place yielded $3,000,000. To the east of Carson Hill is Carson Flat on Carson Creek, where gold was discovered in August 1848 by James H. Carson, for whom the region was named. He was led to the place by friendly Indians and, according to his own report, panned out one hundred and eighty ounces of gold in ten days.

On the south slope of Carson Hill on the Stanislaus River is Melones (Spanish for "melons"). It was originally called Robinson's Ferry, the name Melones (from the shape of the gold found in the vicinity by the Spanish and Mexican miners) having been borrowed recently from a former camp midway between Carson Hill and the present town of that name. In the summer of 1849, within six weeks' time, $10,000 in tolls were collected at Robinson's Ferry.

The Calaveras Skull

At Altaville (formerly Cherokee Flat, located in 1852 one mile north of Angel's Camp) are the old Prince Store and the D. D. Demarest Foundry Shop. Near Altaville is Bald Hill, on the slope of which, about halfway up, may be seen the shaft of the old Mattison Mine. Here, at a depth of one hundred and thirty feet, the famous Calaveras skull was alleged to have been found by Mr. Mattison, of Angel's Camp, in February 1866. Of the many relics of prehistoric man discovered in America, "probably none has become better known than the much-discussed Calaveras skull; certainly no other has been the occasion of such remarkably contradictory statements as have been recorded in reference to this specimen."

The general attention of the public was directed to this relic from Bald Hill by Professor J. D. Whitney, then state geologist of California, at a meeting of the California Academy of Sciences in San Francisco in July 1866. His final summary of the evidence in favor of the authenticity of Mattison's find in the Bald Hill Mine was not presented until thirteen years later. Meantime much controversy ensued among scientists over the skull, and "the unscientific public hailed the story as a huge joke on the state geologist," put over, said the press, by fun-loving citizens of Angel's Camp. Bret Harte was inspired to write a humorous poem, "To the Pliocene Skull," one of his last contributions to the *Californian*.

Scientists, however, did not dismiss the subject lightly. "Taken as a whole," says John C. Merriam, the problem "seemed . . . . to present as remarkable a case of absolutely contradictory evidence as ever appeared in science or in law. . . . . After so long a lapse of years, it will probably never be possible to trace out the history of the Calaveras skull with certainty." A paper read before the American Anthropological Association in 1903 by Professor Merriam presented the general conclusion of scientists, which is still generally accepted. The genuineness of the skull as a relic of prehistoric man was established, but its origin had been shifted from the auriferous gravels of Whitney's Pliocene man to the less remote but still ancient cave deposits found in many parts of the mining regions of the Sierra Nevada. Some suggestions as to how the skull might have reached Whitney's hands were also made, suggestions further elaborated upon by William J. Sinclair in 1908.

Five miles beyond Altaville is Fourth Crossing. Here the one surviving landmark of the gold days of that region is the old John Reddick House. Between Altaville and Fourth Crossing is the site of Hawkeye.

The Mokelumne Hill Region

Mokelumne Hill, perched on the top of a mountain above Mokelumne River, is one of the most picturesque towns in the mining region. It was the county seat from 1852 to 1866 and was the leading town in the central Mother Lode at that period.

Interesting old buildings left from mining days, many of them in ruins, entice one to linger along the crooked, hilltop road, where bandits and gold nuggets of fabulous worth are suggested by those solid houses of brick and stone with their heavy iron-barred doors and shuttered windows. Among these, the following may be named: the Leger Hotel, built in the early '50's; the United States Hotel, built by Lamphear in 1854; the old Courthouse; and the Wells Fargo Building (now used by the I.O.O.F.), built in 1854 by A. M. Sturges as a store.

Overlooking the town of Mokelumne Hill is French Hill, the scene of one of the skirmishes in the so-called "French War." Foundations of the fort erected by the Frenchmen as a barricade against the Americans may still be seen. The envy of Americans had been aroused by the good fortune of the French miners throughout the region. On the pretext that they had hoisted the French flag and defied the American government, their adversaries called upon every American to arm and drive them out. The French were cowed into submission and driven from the rich diggings which they had been working. "Although the whole countryside united to evict the original holders, none can now be found to justify the expulsion, which is looked upon as a forthright robbery."

Five miles southeast of Mokelumne Hill was Jesús María, and a mile and a half farther on was Whiskey Slide (now Clear View), where the old house built by John Noce in the early '50's still stands. Near by is McDonald Flat (formerly Poverty Flat).

A road going southwest from Mokelumne Hill leads to Campo Seco, a rich placer camp in early days, and in the '60's a copper center where the Penn Copper Mine was located. The largest cork oak (*Quercus suber*) in the state grows at Campo Seco. Stone ruins, an old two-story clap-board house, and the pioneer cemetery are reminders of the past which may be seen here. Chili Gulch, Fosteria (formerly Paloma), Chili Camp, and the quaint town of Comanche, with its several stone buildings, the heir of old Poverty Bar on the Mokelumne River, are other camps located along the same route.

At Chili Gulch a little group of Americans were driven from their claim by a superior force of Chileans in December 1849. The Americans had objected to the system by which Chilean leaders acquired many claims through their peon dependents, and had made laws against the practice. This, in turn, incensed the Chileans to such an extent that the Chilean War resulted, with the Chileans, under the leadership of one Dr. Concha, taking the aggressive. The final outcome was favorable to the Americans, but the occurrence developed considerable tension between the United States and Chile.

There are several "Rich Gulches" in Calaveras County. On the Rich Gulch which leads from Fosteria to the Mokelumne River is located the famous Gwin Mine, which was once owned and operated by Senator Gwin. Fabulous sums of gold have been taken from this Rich Gulch since early mining days.

To the east of Mokelumne Hill six miles was another Rich Gulch, a once populous camp, of which little trace is left today; while six miles beyond was Railroad Flat, once a placer and quartz-mining center, where a store and post office and a few of the old homes still remain. A near neighbor was Independence Flat; and five miles to the north was West Point, where numerous small but rich quartz ledges were once worked by Mexicans. It is now a quiet mountain hamlet.

Murphy's Camp

At Murphy's Camp may be seen an old Wells Fargo Express Office, strongly built and guarded with iron shutters and doors; the Sperry Building (Mitchler Hotel); the Travers Building; and the Jones Apothecary Shop. The Sperry Hotel, the largest building in town in 1856, was erected by J. L. Sperry to accommodate the increased travel through Murphy's, following Dowd's finding of the Big Trees of the Calaveras Grove in 1852.

"For a perfect bit of unaltered atmosphere, Murphy's has few if any equals in the entire Mother Lode district. . . . . The quaint buildings flanking its tree-lined main street have proved a delight both to the artist and to the historian. Its one surviving hotel, unchanged since it was built in the early '50's, is a splendid example of a public house of that period."

The country about Murphy's Camp was first mined in July 1848 by two brothers, Daniel and John Murphy, who came in the same company with Henry Angel and James Carson. The Murphys, like others of the group, struck out for themselves on reaching the diggings and set up camp at a site on Angel's Creek, which soon became known as Murphy's Diggings and was later called Murphy's Camp.

It is thought by some that Joaquín Murieta began his career of crime at Murphy's, and a barricade, still visible on the south shoulder of Bear Mountain, is believed to have been one of the many haunts he frequented during his years as a bandit. West of Murphy's was French Camp, now Esmeralda.

About one mile beyond Murphy's Camp are the Mercer Caves, notable limestone formations. From Murphy's the road climbs northeast up the Sierra Nevada about twenty miles to the famous Calaveras Big Trees Grove, a beautiful stand of the *Sequoia gigantea*, the larger of the two species of California sequoias. While on a scouting expedition in 1841, John Bidwell came upon one of the fallen giants of the Calaveras, the first white man known to have seen this grove. Whether he saw the North or the South Grove, however, is debatable.

Although the Big Trees had been seen by J. Marshall Wooster, Whitehead, and other miners as early as 1850, credit for their discovery has usually been given to A. T. Dowd, a hunter from Murphy's. Dowd first brought the attention of the public to the Calaveras North Grove in the spring of 1852. For many years the grove continued to attract attention, numerous tourists visiting it during the '60's and '70's. For a time it was thought to be the only stand of the *Sequoia gigantea* in existence. The hotel which was erected in the grove by James L. Sperry soon after Dowd's discovery still stands.

San Andreas

San Andreas, where the Marlette mines were located, has narrow streets and the settled air of an old town. A number of historic buildings bring memories of the rugged '50's to one's mind: the Agostino Building, the Benjamin Building, the I.O.O.F. Building (1856), the old Corcoran and Sullivan Store (1855), and the Cassinelli adobe.

East of San Andreas are Cave City; Sheep Ranch, a quartz-mining camp where George Hearst laid the foundation of his fortune; Eldoradotown; and Mountain Ranch, where some of the old adobe buildings of early days are still standing and where the first sawmill in Calaveras County was erected. Six miles southeast are Old Gulch and Calaveritas, now in ruins, and three miles beyond is Dogtown. Three miles northwest is Cottage Spring, while three miles west are North Branch and Central Hill, noted for their once rich gravel mines.

On the main road about two miles west of San Andreas on the north bank of the Calaveras River is the Old Pioneer Cemetery, the oldest known cemetery in Calaveras County. Several ancient monuments still mark the graves of early miners.

Vallecito ("Little Valley")

Vallecito, near which the famous Moaning Caves (once an Indian burial chamber) are located, is about five miles southeast of Angel's Camp. A few landmarks from mining days remain, among them the Dinkelspiel Store (now Sanguinetti's). There also is an old church bell which was brought up from San Francisco by an itinerant preacher in the early days. The bell was mounted in the large oak tree where it still hangs, and every Sunday morning scores of miners answered its vigorous summons.

To the north, between Vallecito and Murphy's, is Douglas Flat, where the so-called Central Hill Channel is located, an ancient river deposit from which vast quantities of gold have been taken.

Jenny Lind and Copperopolis

Jenny Lind, on the north bank of the Calaveras River, was once the center of most of the mining operations on the Lower Calaveras, but now only a few old stone and adobe buildings remain, vestiges of its former activity.

Prior to the discovery of the great copper deposits in the northern part of the state, Copperopolis, in the southwestern part of Calaveras County, was the principal copper-producing center in California. In 1868 it boasted a population of nearly 2,000, and had three schools, two churches, four hotels, stores, and workshops of all kinds. The village of today retains a fragment of its one-time importance in the fast-disintegrating smelters, shafts, and chutes of the old mines; in the handful of brick stores straggling along the highway; and in the pioneer Congregational Church (now the I.O.O.F. Building), a substantial brick structure with beautiful Gothic windows. Near Copperopolis, at Funk Hill, Black Bart, the "gentleman" bandit, is said to have committed his last stage robbery.

On the road from Copperopolis to Mountain Pass was Byrne's Ferry. A covered bridge now spans the river at this point, supplanting the ferry of pioneer days. The little triangular valley, hemmed in by steep and rugged mountain slopes covered with chaparral, still enfolds the ruins of this picturesque settlement. Above it, "like the ruins of a Rhineland castle," tower the lava-capped crags of Table Mountain.

SOURCES

[Credit is here given for source material, and permission to quote is hereby acknowledged]

AYRES, COLONEL JAMES J. *Gold and Sunshine: Reminiscences of Early California.* Richard G. Badger, Boston, 1922

BEASLEY, THOMAS DYKES. *A Tramp through the Bret Harte Country.* Paul Elder & Company, San Francisco, 1914

BIDWELL, GENERAL JOHN. *Echoes of the Past.* Chico Advertiser, Chico, California. No date

BROWNE, J. ROSS. *Report on the Mineral Resources of the States and Territories of the Rocky Mountains.* Government Printing Office, Washington, 1868

BUCKBEE, EDNA BRYAN. *Pioneer Days of Angel's Camp.* Calaveras Californian, Angel's Camp, California, 1932

CARSON, JAMES H. *Life in California, Together with a Description of the Great Tulare Valley.* 2d ed. San Joaquin Republican, 1852

COY, OWEN COCHRAN. *Gold Days,* of the series *California,* edited by John Russell McCarthy. Powell Publishing Company, Los Angeles, 1929

DAVIS, SHELDON. "On the Trail of Mark Twain and Bret Harte in the Mother Lode Country," in *Stockton Record,* July 16 and 23, 1921

FRY, WALTER, and JOHN R. WHITE. *Big Trees.* Stanford University Press, Stanford University, California, 1930

GILLIS, WILLIAM R. *Gold Rush Days with Mark Twain.* Boni, New York, 1930

———. *Memories of Mark Twain and Steve Gillis.* Sonora, California, 1924

JOHNSTON, PHILIP. "Legends and Landmarks of '49 along the Mother Lode," in *Touring Topics,* XXIII, No. 2 (February, 1931), 12–27, 52–53

KERR, MARK B. *Mining Resources of Calaveras County.* Golden Jubilee Mining Fair, San Francisco, 1898

MASON, J. D. *History of Amador County, California.* Thompson and West, Oakland, California, 1881

MERRIAM, JOHN C. "The True Story of the Calaveras Skull," in *Sunset,* XXIV, No. 2 (February 1910), 153–158

PAINE, ALBERT BIGELOW. *A Short Life of Mark Twain.* Garden City Publishing Company, Garden City, New York, 1920

SINCLAIR, WILLIAM J. "Recent Investigations Bearing on the Question of the Occurrence of Neocene Man in the Auriferous Gravels of the Sierra Nevada," in *University of California Publications in American Archaeology and Ethnology,* VII, No. 2 (February 1908), 107–131

STEWART, GEORGE R., JR. *Bret Harte, Argonaut and Exile.* Houghton Mifflin Company, Boston, 1931

———. "The Bret Harte Legend," in *University of California Chronicle,* XXX, No. 3 (July, 1928), 338–350

WHITNEY, J. D. *The Auriferous Gravels of the Sierra Nevada.* Cambridge, Massachusetts, 1880

WILTSEE, ERNEST A. "Double Springs, First County Seat of Calaveras County," in *California Historical Society Quarterly,* XI, No. 2 (June, 1932), 176–183

COLUSA COUNTY

COLUSA COUNTY (named for the Colus Indians, Colus being a corruption of the tribal name, Ko-ru-si) was one of the twenty-seven original counties. Colusi was the older spelling of the county name. Monroeville, now in Glenn County, was the first county seat, but was superseded by Colusa in 1854.

Ko-ru-si Indian Villages

Colusa was built on the site of the ancient Indian village Ko-rú, tribal capital of the Ko-ru-si, whence the name. In 1850, there were a thousand or more of these Indians living in villages scattered up and down the Sacramento River from Sycamore Slough in the south to the northern boundary of the present county. As early as 1846 Americans began to settle along this part of the river, and by the close of the nineteenth century only two of the ancient Indian villages remained, one, the Tat-no, four miles above the town of Colusa, on what was at that time the Colonel Hagar Ranch, and the Wy-terre on the upper end of the Rancho Jimeno.

There were at least thirteen of these villages. The Lochloch, at the head of Sycamore Slough, was about eight miles below the present site of Colusa where the town of Sycamore now stands. The Coo-coo came next, and beyond that was the Doc-doc just below Colusa. Colusa itself was built on the ruins of Ko-ru, the head village of the tribe. Opposite Colusa, on what afterward became Colonel Wilkins' farm, was Cow-peck, and about four miles above Colusa was Tat-no. Si-cope occupied the bend of the river east of the site of the old Five Mile House, while at the Seven Mile House was Cah-cheal. At the bend of the river, on the

COLUSA COUNTY

upper end of what became the Judge Hastings Ranch, was Si-ee ("view"), where there were no trees. On the upper end of Rancho Jimeno was the Wy-terre ("turn to the north"). The Cha was at the Senator Boggs Ranch and the Ket-tee was where the present town of Princeton stands at the very northeastern corner of Colusa County. Some two miles above Princeton, at the boundary line of Colusa and Glenn counties, was Tu-tu, the northernmost village of the Ko-ru-si. A remnant of the ancient tribe still lives at the Ranchería, seven and one-half miles north of Colusa.

The Larkin Grant

John Bidwell was the first recorded white explorer of Colusa County, traversing it in the years 1843–1844, while in the employ of John A. Sutter at Sutter's Fort.

On July 6, 1844, Bidwell mapped out a grant of land which extended along the west bank of the Sacramento River north of what is now the town of Colusa and into the present Glenn County. This was the first land grant made in Colusa County and was known as the Larkin Grant, having been secured for the children of Thomas O. Larkin, American consul at Monterey. John S. Williams, brother of Isaac Williams, owner of Rancho Chino in southern California, was the first white settler in Colusa County. In 1847 he was employed to look after the Larkin Grant, and on it he built the first house in the county. Senator John Boggs later bought that part of the Larkin Grant on which Williams lived, just below the present town of Princeton.

Colusa

On the spot where Ko-ru, the ancient capital of the Ko-ru-si, had been located only a few years before, Colusa was founded in 1850. The land on which the new town was laid out and two "leagues" beyond it were included in the grant made to John Bidwell in 1845. When Dr. Robert Semple, founder of Benicia, visited the country in 1847, he was so impressed with its beauty and fertility and its nearness to the great river that he thought he saw possibilities of a future city there.

Colonel Charles D. Semple, a brother of Dr. Semple, came to California in 1849. The Doctor immediately told him of this fine country to the north and Charles was most favorably impressed. He purchased the land from Bidwell the same year, and in a small home-made launch started up the river the following spring to found a new metropolis. Mistaking the site originally chosen by his brother, the Colonel "landed . . . . at a place seven miles above the Colus ranchería and afterward known as the Seven Mile House." Later that same year, when Dr. Semple arrived, the settlement was removed "seven miles lower down the river," to the location "originally designed," which was on the site of the ancient Indian village. Barges came up the river from Sacramento and trade from the northern mines was good. Thus Semple's hopes seemed justified, and the new town prospered.

In 1853 Dr. Robert Semple and his uncle, Will S. Green, purchased Rancho Alamo on Freshwater Creek, six miles west of Williams. Dr. Semple died there on October 25, 1854, and was buried in Williams Cemetery. Local funds are being raised to mark the grave with a monument and bronze tablet.

Although Colusa did not become a great city, it prospered, and in 1854 was made the county seat. Today it is the center of a thriving agricultural region.

The River Road

The old River Road, following along the west bank of the Sacramento River from Colusa to Shasta City, was the only road in Colusa County in the early '50's. Its popularity rivaled that of the river steamers, which plied as far north as Red Bluff. The volume of traffic over the road to the northern mines resulted in the building of many inns or stage stations along its course. From Wilkins' Slough in southern Colusa County to the mouth of Stony Creek in what is now Glenn County, a fringe of farms bordered the river, each with its roadhouse or inn to refresh both man and beast on the long trip to the gold fields.

The most important center along the entire route was Colusa, from which as many as fifty freight wagons often started for the north in one day. Among the several stations along the River Road were the Five Mile House, where the Maxwell Road leaves the River Road; the Seven Mile House, a few hundred feet south of where the county road crosses the railroad (the original site of the town of Colusa); the Nine Mile House, erected by S. H. Cooper; the Ten Mile House, built by L. H. Helphenstine and owned by the family for over seventy years; the Eleven Mile House, originally owned by Thomas Parton; the Sterling Ranch, or Fourteen Mile House, where John S. Williams, a representative of Thomas O. Larkin, built the first house (an adobe) in Colusa County in 1847, and where Charles B. Sterling, the second settler, succeeded him in 1849; the Sixteen Mile House, two miles above the Sterling Ranch, where Princeton now is; and the Seventeen Mile House, owned by Hiram Willits, later founder of Willits, Mendocino County.

Stone Corral

Just west of Maxwell is a hollow hemmed in on three sides by high hills, forming a natural site for a corral. As early as 1848 the place was used by Mexican vaqueros, and when John Steele came there in 1855 he found a rude brush and stone fence built about the inclosure. The advantages of the place were seen at once by Steele, who constructed a stone wall about it that year. Settlers afterward carried away many of the stones until only a remnant remained. The Old Stone Corral, as it was long known, has been restored by the Colusa Parlor, Native Sons of the Golden West.

Pierce Christian College

Pierce Christian College at College City was named after Andrew Pierce, who, at his death in 1874, left a large amount of land to the Christian church for religious and educational advancement. In 1876 a board of trustees established a college on the land and laid out a town about it. For years, this was the only school of higher rank in that part of California, and at one time most of the teachers of Colusa County had received their education in it.

In 1896 the Pierce College grounds and buildings were given to the Union High School District of College City. The college had been discontinued because the Christian church had decided to consolidate its various colleges scattered throughout the state into one adequately endowed institution, finally established at Los Angeles.

The College City Union High School still uses the Pierce College building and campus. This is what happened in many districts in northern California during the last decade of the nineteenth century when denominational and other private schools gave their lands and buildings for the use of the newly forming high schools. Pierce College, however, is the only such building still being used, as new ones have been erected on the old grounds in other cases.

SOURCES

[Credit is here given for source material, and permission to quote is hereby acknowledged]

GREEN, WILLIAM S. *Colusa County, California*. Elliott and Moore, San Francisco, 1880

McCornish, Charles Davis, and Rebecca T. Lambert. *History of Colusa and Glenn Counties, California*. Historic Record Company, Los Angeles, 1918

Radcliffe, Zoe Green. "Robert Baylor Semple, Pioneer," in *California Historical Society Quarterly*, VI, No. 2 (June, 1927), 130–158

Rogers, Justus H. *Colusa County, Its History Traced from a State of Nature through the Early Period of Settlement and Development to the Present Day*. Privately published, Orland, California, 1891

Sanchez, Nellie Van de Grift. *Spanish and Indian Place Names of California*. A. M. Robertson, San Francisco, 1922

EL DORADO COUNTY

El Dorado County was one of the original twenty-seven counties. The first county seat was Coloma, but it was superseded by Placerville in 1857.

The Spanish term *El Dorado* has the connotation of "the gilded man," or "the gilded one." The general understanding is that the name was given to this county because gold was discovered there. The legend from which the name arose is interesting and significant. "The Indians of Peru, Venezuela, and New Granada, perhaps in the hope of inducing their oppressors to move on, were constantly pointing out to the Spaniards, first in one direction, then in another, a land of fabulous riches. This land was said to have a king, who caused his body to be covered every morning with gold dust, by means of an odorous resin. Each evening he washed it off, as it incommoded his sleep, and each morning had the gilding process repeated. From this fable the white men were led to believe that the country must be rich in gold, and long, costly, and fruitless expeditions were undertaken in pursuit of this phantom of *El Dorado*. In time the phrase *El Dorado* came to be applied to regions where gold and other precious metals were thought to be plentiful."

Coloma

In the latter part of 1847, John A. Sutter, founder of "New Helvetia," later Sacramento, sent James W. Marshall to find a suitable site for a sawmill. Marshall chose a spot forty-five miles northeast of Sutter's Fort on the South Fork of the American River, where Coloma, the earliest of all the mining towns in California, was founded the following year.

Sutter's Mill was finished in January 1848, and on January 24, while deepening and enlarging the tailrace, Marshall discovered some shining particles in the running water. These were tested and found to be gold. This event proved to be one of the most important in the history of California. Its results were not only nation-wide but world-wide and have changed the whole course of history on the Pacific Coast.

Coloma is now a quiet, almost deserted mountain town, but its rugged setting remains unchanged. There are a few quaint buildings still to be found in the place which are suggestive of those wild days when thousands of gold-mad miners of many nationalities thronged the streets. On the main street are two small stone buildings with iron-shuttered windows and doors, a Chinese bank and a jail; while farther on is a wooden cabin, the lumber for which was brought around the Horn.

Half-hidden beneath gnarled locust and apple trees, several aging, weather-worn cottages still stand in a tangle of old-fashioned flowers. Snow seldom falls here, and old fig and almond trees still grow luxuriantly. During the early '80's, Chinese miners paid high prices for gravel leads running into these orchards and gardens. One man received

$800 for a tiny plot of ground on which four apple trees were growing.

On a side street is one of Coloma's historic churches, the Emmanuel Episcopal Church, which was erected in 1856. In recent years the building has been used also by the Methodists, as well as by the Presbyterians. The first Catholic Church to be built in the Sierra Nevada mining regions is also to be found here, set amidst its tiny burial ground. The building now has been taken over by bees, which refuse to be dislodged.

The Protestant cemetery on the hill is the oldest in the Sierra country and is filled with graves of members of pioneer Coloma families, some of the marble headstones dating back to the early '50's. Beautiful wrought-iron palings surround many of the plots, while fine old shade trees and shrubbery cast quiet shadows across them.

Half a mile up the hill back of Coloma is the monument erected in honor of James Wilson Marshall, whose discovery of gold at Coloma made California known to all the world. Although it is well established that Marshall was not the first to find gold in California—Bancroft, in his *Inter Pocula*, devotes two chapters to the subject of pre-Coloma gold discoveries—nevertheless his discovery exceeds "in human interest and historical significance every other episode" in California's history. The news of it brought an army of modern Argonauts to California, and in a short while a great new commonwealth had been created. James Marshall's Monument, a bronze statue on a granite base, under which he lies buried, was erected in 1890, and some distance below it on the hillside the little cabin which he built and in which he lived until about 1868 has been restored. The statue overlooks the bend in the American River where the mill stood, and the right hand of the figure points to the spot where the particles of gold were first discovered. The mill, abandoned in 1853, is gone, but the place where it stood has been marked with a monument of river stones by the California Pioneer Society. Marshall's Monument was erected by the state. The surrounding park of fourteen acres was purchased by the Native Sons of the Golden West, and presented to the state.

The Coloma Road

The earliest roads in the mining region (in reality, mere pack trails) were developed in El Dorado County. The first of these was marked out in 1847–1848 by Sutter and his men (among whom was James Marshall) as a way to his sawmill on the South Fork. Running along the south side of the river from Sacramento to where Folsom now is, this first trail followed approximately the same line as that taken later by the railroad and the modern highway. From Folsom it continued by way of Mormon Island, Green Valley (Rescue), Rose Springs, and Uniontown (Lotus) to Sutter's Mill, later Coloma—the present route of a quiet country road along which a few mementos of pioneer days still remain. The Green Valley House, still the home of a pioneer woman who came there as a young bride sixty-four years ago; the Sunrise House, with its unique design of sun rays under the east and west gables; and the Gordon House, the material for which had been brought around the Horn, still lend the charm of their quaint, old-fashioned dignity to this historic thoroughfare.

The Coloma Road evolved from a narrow pack trail into a well-beaten, crowded highway soon after Marshall's discovery of gold in 1848. Over it thousands of gold-seekers directed their eager footsteps toward that cynosure of all eyes—Coloma. Soon after the arrival of each ship at San Francisco, the Coloma Road became thronged with men afoot or on horseback, making their way to the diggings. Mexicans with long trains of pack mules loaded with freight and miners' supplies joined the procession. Oregonians, very early, brought in the first wagons. A mail business developed of such magnitude that wagon loads of letters never reached their destination and had to be sent to the dead-letter office.

Soon all available land about Coloma was staked out to claims, and newcomers were forced to seek other locations. Thus the mining area quickly expanded in all directions, numerous trails opening up fresh diggings and newer El Doradoes for the onward-moving Argonauts.

The first, and for a long time the principal, branch of the Coloma Road turned north at New York Ravine three miles east of Mormon Island. Crossing the South Fork at Salmon Falls (at first by ferry and later, in 1853, by toll bridge), this road proceeded, as it still does, to Centerville (Pilot Hill), where it branched again, one fork going through Greenwood to Georgetown. From Georgetown a road led northwest to Spanish Bar on the Middle Fork of the American River, where it crossed over into Placer County. Continuing by way of Paradise and the North Star House, this trail to Todd's Valley and Forest Hill was much traveled during the '50's and '60's. Another crossing farther up the Middle Fork at Volcano Bar led to Michigan Bluff (in Placer County).

Another branch road starting at Centerville took a more direct route from that place to Forest Hill by way of Murderer's Bar, located a few miles above the confluence of the Middle and North forks of the American River. The present Mother Lode Highway follows this road, but instead of crossing the Middle Fork at Murderer's Bar it now proceeds directly to Auburn via Lyon's Bridge.

Crossing the South Fork at Mormon Island, still another branch of the Coloma Road paralleled the North Fork, connecting the populous river-bar camps located on that stream. Along the fifteen miles of the North Fork above its confluence with the South Fork, crossings were made at Beal's, Condemned, Whiskey, Rattlesnake, and Oregon bars.

At first crude ferries plied at these points—ships' boats brought up from Sacramento or flimsy rafts, sometimes even beds of abandoned emigrant wagons serving the purpose. Soon, regular ferry boats, or scows, large enough to carry a wagon, were constructed, only to be supplanted by rough bridges, which were usually washed away by the succeeding winter's flood. Structures of a more substantial and permanent character ultimately replaced these first primitive ones. All, however, were built by private capital for profit. So great was the traffic to and from the mines that many fortunes were made from tolls collected by the owners of these pioneer ferries and bridges.

At Whiskey and Rattlesnake bars, wire-rope bridges were constructed in 1854, and in 1856 W. C. Lyon built the Condemned Bar bridge, later torn down when he moved farther up the river. Except for the one at Rattlesnake Bar, no bridge exists today at any of these former crossings, although a stone pier of the old Whiskey Bar bridge still stands on the east side of the river.

The first regular ferry in El Dorado County was operated at Coloma early in 1849. In February 1851 this was superseded by a bridge, also the first in the county. All along the South Fork numerous bridges were erected to take the place of the ferries of an earlier date. The amount of travel was tremendous and the profit reaped from tolls was correspondingly great. At the old Uniontown Bridge it was not uncommon to collect from six to eight hundred dollars monthly during the early '50's, and the Rock Bridge a few miles farther down stream was almost as well patronized.

Of the maze of roads and branch roads radiating from Coloma to the scores of camps which sprang up in all directions, less than half a dozen are being maintained by the county today: to the north the Georgetown Road through Garden Valley (formerly Johntown); the little traveled Ridge Road to Kelsey; to the south the Gold Hill Road to Cold Springs and Placerville; and the present Mother Lode Highway from Placerville via Coloma and Pilot Hill to Auburn. These few old roads, however, are rich in reminders of the historic past: scars of abandoned diggings; here and there the dark mouth of a tunnel reaching into the hillside; foundations of buildings long since vanished; crumbling walls of brick or stone standing mute and neglected by the roadside; remnants of apple orchards; a few gnarled locust trees beneath whose shade inns or farmhouses once welcomed the wayfarer; lonely hill-top cemeteries marking once thriving communities.

The Carson Emigrant Road

The main route to Coloma and the gold diggings in 1849 and the early '50's was the Carson Emigrant Road by way of the Kit Carson Pass. John C. Frémont and a few picked men led by Kit Carson himself were the first to cross the Sierra Nevada by way of this pass, in 1844, and also the first to traverse the length of what is now El Dorado County. Traveling with great difficulty down the sunny side of the Silver Fork Canyon from Silver Lake to the South Fork of the American River, they forded the latter stream and climbed the opposite wall of the canyon to the southern edge of the Georgetown Divide, down which they proceeded to the Sacramento Valley and Sutter's Fort.

Only that part of Frémont's route from the Kit Carson Pass to Silver Lake is identical with the later Carson Emigrant Road. In the summer of 1848 members of the Mormon Battalion, on their way to rejoin their coreligionists in Salt Lake City, opened up this emigrant trail over the Sierra, and again, in the spring of 1849, Jefferson Hunt, a captain in the Mormon Battalion and later founder of San Bernardino, brought the first wagon that way, thus opening the Carson Emigrant Road to the host of Argonauts who entered California by this route in 1849 and the '50's.

Winding its way over a very high pass, the Carson Emigrant Road was long and difficult, but, according to Bancroft, "the immigrants . . . . in order to avoid the sharper hills and deeper gulches of a possibly lower pass, had preferred to climb to an elevation of nine thousand feet to secure a road less broken. As they arrived at the pass late in summer when the snow was off the ground this would do very well."

The course of the old road through El Dorado County may be traced on modern maps by the names of camp sites, once important places along the divide between the Cosumnes River and the South Fork of the American River: Tragedy Springs, Leek Spring, Camp Springs, Sly Park, Pleasant Valley, Diamond Springs, Mud Springs (El Dorado), Shingle Springs, Clarksville, and White Rock Springs (in Sacramento County). From White Rock Springs to El Dorado, the Lincoln Highway follows the same route today, but from El Dorado to Silver Lake in the High Sierra no through travel goes over the old road, the Carson Emigrant Road having been superseded by the Placerville Road, now the continuation of the Lincoln Highway.

Traffic over the Carson Road was enormous during the early '50's, and a chain of wayside stations was established along its entire length between Mormon Station (later Genoa, in Nevada) and Hangtown (Placerville). Every mile had its inn or hotel. Few remnants of these early taverns remain, and even the sites of many would be difficult to determine exactly.

From the main road a number of branches diverged at various points, chiefly at Diamond Springs, where the stream of emigrants turned off to Coloma by way of Hangtown and (as new diggings were discovered) to Salmon Falls, Pilot Hill, Georgetown, Kelsey's Diggings, and numerous other camps. Two main branches led to the southern mines, one by way of Grizzly Flat to Brownsville (Mendon), Indian Diggin's, and Fiddletown (in Amador County), and another via Mud Springs to Logtown, Quartzburg (Nashville), Saratoga (Yeomet), and Drytown (in Amador County). At Clarksville still another fork of the Carson Road went to Folsom, and thence to Auburn and the river-bar camps on the North Fork of the American River. Many of these arms of the old Emigrant Road may be traversed today over good county roads, with historic reminders of a glamorous past visible on every hand.

Although the Carson Road continued to be used for twenty years or more, increased transportation needs necessitated the development of easier routes. As an all-year road, the Carson Pass route, subject as it was to the deep snows of its higher altitudes, was impossible, and a road over a lower pass became imperative. This need led to the survey and construction of the Placerville Road over Johnson's Pass and down the canyon of the South Fork of the American River to Hangtown.

The Placerville Road

Deviations from the Carson Emigrant Road began very early, gold-seekers being ever eager to reach their destination as quickly as possible, often taking great risks in trying new routes. The most popular of these shorter trails took the so-called Johnson's Cut-off, later the Placerville Road. With the construction of Bartlett's Bridge on the South Fork of the American River near the Pacific House, this route was made passable for wagons before 1854, and a large proportion of the overland emigration was early diverted to it.

In addition to the natural desire to get to the gold fields in the shortest possible time, the tremendous growth of population in California during the early '50's and a corresponding increase in overland transportation hastened the demand for improved, all-year highways to take the place of those first long and precipitous trails over the higher summits of the Sierra. After much agitation, the state legislature, on April 28, 1855, passed a bill authorizing the survey and construction of such a road, the cost of which was not to exceed $105,000. No appropriation was made for the work, however, and the expense of preliminary surveys had to be met by private subscription.

Keeping to the southern exposures of the ridges and canyons, and avoiding, as much as possible, the higher altitudes in order to chart a route that could be kept open throughout the winter, Surveyor-General H. S. Marlette and his assistant, Sherman Day, finally recommended that part of the Johnson's Cut-off route which followed the canyon of the South Fork of the American River as far as Johnson's Pass and from thence through Luther's Pass, Hope Valley, and the canyon of the West Carson River to the state line. This path avoided the steep eastern declivity over the western summit of the Sierra negotiated by the Carson and Johnson routes.

The construction of the Placerville Road was actually begun in 1858, with the appropriation of $50,000 by El Dorado, Sacramento, and Yolo counties. Before the road was graded or leveled, J. B. Crandall's Pioneer Stage Company began to operate between Placerville, California, and Genoa, Nevada, making the trip in twenty-four hours. Meanwhile, George Chorpenning had obtained a government contract to carry the weekly mails between Placerville and Salt Lake City with an annual stipend of $136,000, and the first overland mail via the central route arrived in California at 11:00 P.M., July 19, 1858. With this demonstration it was definitely proved that "a highway over the 'terrible' Sierra was both possible and practicable."

State and county governments, however, continued to be lethargic. Failing to make appropriations for further improvements or maintenance of the road, the whole enterprise, so nicely started in 1858, would have collapsed and the Placerville Road would soon have become impassable but for the timely discovery of the rich silver deposits of the Comstock Lode in Nevada. Private companies immediately obtained charters to establish toll roads, and immense sums were expended on the four or five detours routed by these companies. So great was the traffic over the Placerville turnpikes that the promoters not only cleared all expenses but made vast fortunes from the toll collections.

During the years 1859 to 1866, this "grand artery of travel" witnessed the greatest era of staging and freighting by horse-drawn vehicles ever known. By day, two continuous streams of one- to eight-span teams moved in both directions, while, at night, from four to six Concord coaches rumbled in and out of Placerville loaded with bullion, passengers, and mail. Mule-trains, filling the canyons with the music of their bells; cumbersome freight schooners, rumbling over the none-too-smooth roads; aristocratic Concord coaches, rattling at breakneck speed over that narrow, tortuous thread of road; brave Pony Express riders filling the night with the thrill of swift galloping feet—all passed over this great thoroughfare through country once traversed only by Indians.

An actual check made of this overland commerce as it passed by Swan's toll house during three months of 1864 revealed that 6,667 footmen, 833 horsemen, 3,164 stage passengers, 5,000 pack animals, 2,564 teams, and 4,649 head of cattle had gone that way. During the years 1864 and 1865, 320 tons of freight passed through Placerville daily, while the combined freight charges of 1863 could not have been less than $12,000,000. William H. Brewer, who camped at Slippery Ford in August 1863, says that 5,000 teams were then employed steadily in the Virginia City trade.

Mark Twain's humorous version of Horace Greeley's stage ride over the old Placerville Road in the summer of 1859 is one of the choice bits of *Roughing It*. His constant reiteration of the climax (put in the mouth of Hank Monk, most famous of the stage drivers on the Placerville Road), " 'Keep your seat, Horace, and I'll get you there on time!'— and you bet you he did, too, what was left of him!" is especially pointed after reading either Greeley's own description of the ride or the parallel masterpiece by Bancroft.

Markers of the Stagecoach Trail

On the present smooth-paved Placerville Road there are numerous reminders of the old thoroughfare and of the former inns along the way. The Forest Service of the El Dorado National Forest has placed a chain of "Pioneer Days" markers designating the sites of the old landmarks, most of which have long since disappeared. Merely to enumerate these historic spots is thrilling and illuminating to the sojourner with thought alert to the romance and drama of old trails. These markers indicate that the modern highway actually touches and utilizes bits of the older road from Placerville to Meyer's Station at the southern end of Lake Tahoe and beyond. Other fragments of the earlier road are plainly visible on the sides of the steep canyon walls above or below the present highway.

Leaving Placerville one may take the short by-path through Smith's Flat, with its reminders of mining days, before swinging again to the Lincoln Highway. The first "Pioneer Days" sign, designating the site of the Three Mile House, later known as the Home Ranch, marks also the beginning of the actual ascent of the high mountains. The sites of the Five Mile and Six Mile houses are passed successively, and a little later that of the Nine Mile House, now occupied by a mountain home and orchard, followed shortly by that of the Ten Mile House, where a building of a later date than that of the very first structure now serves as a residence. Beyond the Cedar Grove garage a dirt road turning east from the highway is designated as the "West end of the old Plank Road."

Passing the Snowline Auto Camp, the next point of interest is the site of the original Sportsman's Hall, one of the earliest way stations. During the middle '60's stable room for five hundred horses was maintained here. The building now standing is of a later date. A short distance beyond is the site of the Thirteen Mile House.

Coming now to a lonely stretch of road, a stone monument, erected by the Native Sons and Native Daughters of the Golden West of Placerville in honor of the brave pioneer officers of the law, stands at Bullion Bend high above the great canyon of the South Fork. At this point two coaches of the Pioneer Stage Line running between Virginia City and Sacramento were held up and robbed by a gang of fourteen men on the night of June 30, 1869. Eight sacks of bullion and a treasure chest were taken. An attempt was made to capture the bandits, resulting in an encounter at the Sommerset House (in the southern part of El Dorado County) in which one deputy sheriff, Joseph Staples, lost his life, and another, George C. Ranney, was badly wounded. Later, one of the bandits, Thomas Poole, was captured and executed at Placerville.

At Observation Point, sixteen miles from Placerville, the first glimpse is had of the South Fork of the American River, a narrow silver ribbon gleaming amid the pines more than a thousand feet below, while far to the east snow-patched Pyramid Peak stands silhouetted against the sky. Here the road begins to drop slowly into the canyon, passing Fresh Pond and the Pacific Ranger Station before reaching the Pacific House one mile beyond. Built in 1859, the Pacific House harbored many a famous wanderer in the early days. Here, legend says, Horace Greeley, Mark Twain, and Thomas Starr King all stopped on their way to Sacramento over the old emigrant trail.

Passing the old Brockliss Grade (used from 1859 to 1864 by stages only), one may see a bit of wild beauty in the Esmeralda Falls tumbling down the mountain side above the road. Riverton, a charming resort set amidst tall spires of poplar trees, an aged apple orchard, and locust trees at the very edge of the South Fork, is on the site of Moore's Station, where Baker's fast rig changed horses in toll-road days.

The site of the original White Hall watering-place and saloon a few miles up the river is now occupied by the White Hall store, post office, and resort. From here the present highway follows along the north bank of the river for several miles. On the right is the site of the old bridge which once stood at the east end of the Oglesby Grade, one of the four or five detours used between 1861 and 1864 on the Placerville Road. The west end of this grade was at the Fourteen Mile House.

The sites of Sol Perrin's Road House, the Sugar Loaf House, and Dick Yarnold's Toll House are the next points of historic interest passed. The Kyburz Hotel has succeeded the last-named, and a village of sixty-five inhabitants forms a center of trade for summer campers and tourists. Trails to the Silver Lake country here lure the modern vacationist into the magnificent scenic highlands of this region.

Narrowing to a rocky gorge, the canyon of the South Fork becomes wilder and more spectacular as the site of the old Riverside House is approached. Mother Weltie's (or the Leon Station), the Champlain House, the Georgetown Junction House (where a stone chimney still stands beside the road); Log Cabin No. 2, and the Watcheer House, once a well-patronized hotel, are passed in quick succession as one swings up the canyon.

One of the most interesting points along the entire Placerville Road is reached at Strawberry Flat, to the right of which the perpendicular walls of Lover's Leap rise more than a thousand feet above the floor of the little valley. To the left the rocky summit of Pyramid Peak towers four thousand feet above the river, Horsetail Falls gleaming white against the gray and barren crags far up the mountain side.

In the midst of a beautiful Sierra meadow which lies like an exquisite jewel within its circlet of river and canyon and mountain, stands the Strawberry House, formerly a popular teamsters' resort. The present building has supplanted the original Strawberry House, which stood below the present site not far from the river. Still owned by the original family, the old house stands with simple dignity beneath the shade of its locust trees, inviting the summer guest to tarry within its pleasant walls; to contemplate from its wide veranda the glory of overshadowing mountains; to wander from its door up numerous enticing trails; or to hear again the tales of long ago. The favorite legend of a Mr. Berry who sold hay, and of the oft-repeated salutation of his friends, "Have you any more straw, Berry?" is given here, as in other localities similarly designated, as the origin of the name which the valley bears. The Indian legend of the naming of Lover's Leap was a favorite tale, it is said, of Hank Monk's, a story duplicated in other parts of California where the same name is found.

At the base of Lover's Leap stood the Slippery Ford House, where William H. Brewer, of the Whitney Geological Survey, stopped for the night on August 19, 1863, climbing alone to the summit of Pyramid Peak on the following day. Brewer gives a realistic description of life at this typical hostelry on the Placerville Road:

"We stopped at the Slippery Ford House. Twenty wagons stopped there, driving over a hundred horses or mules—heavy wagons, enormous loads, scarcely any less than three tons. The harness is heavy, often with a steel bow over the hames, in the form of an arch over each horse, and supporting four or five bells, whose chime can be heard at all hours of the day. The wagons drew up on a small level place, the animals were chained to the tongue of the wagon, neighing or braying for their grain. . . . .

"We are at an altitude of over six thousand feet, the nights are cold, and the dirty, dusty teamsters sit about the fire in the barroom and tell tales of how this man carried so many hundredweight with so many horses, a story which the rest disbelieve—tell stories of marvelous mules, and bad roads, and dull drivers; of fights at this bad place, where someone would not turn out, etc.—until nine o'clock, when they crawl under their wagons with their blankets and sleep, to be up at early dawn to attend to their teams."

Swinging up the canyon toward Echo Summit, the highway passes Toll House Flat, the site of George Swan's Upper Toll House, where today may be seen modern summer camps half-hidden among the pines, with luxuriant wild-flower meadows on every hand. Next in succession the traveler comes to the sites of the Snow Slide House of pioneer days, and of Phillip's Station, where a modern store and camp are now located; Audrian Station and more wild-flower meadows; the beginning of the old Hawley Grade into Alpine County, over Luther's Pass, used from 1859 to 1861; and then, at last, at 7,365 feet elevation, Echo Summit, site of the old Sixty Mile House. From Echo Summit

Lodge, perched on the brow of the mountain, a magnificent panoramic view may be had of Lake Valley, the Upper Truckee River, the southern end of Lake Tahoe, and the barren mountains of Nevada rimming the horizon beyond.

From Echo Summit the highway drops quickly to the floor of Lake Valley. Upon passing the junction with the road from Woodfords (in Alpine County), a pioneer sign is seen just beyond the Echo Creek Bridge near the Liberty Bell Rock. At this spot stood the Osgood Toll House, only the cellar of which is still intact. At Meyer's (now a summer post office and inn) is the site of Yank's Station. Following around the southern end of Lake Tahoe, the old Placerville Road here continued on into Nevada by one of two routes, the Carson Valley route via Daggett's Pass, and the later road along the eastern side of the lake by way of the old Glenbrook Station in Nevada.

River Bars

In the summer of 1848, after the finding of gold by Marshall, other discoveries followed, and soon mining was being carried on along the river bars above and below Coloma. Prospectors also pushed out across the Georgetown Divide to the Middle Fork of the American River, where many stopped to pan. By 1849 thousands of newcomers were working every foot of the Middle and South forks of the American River, as well as the various branches of the Cosumnes River.

A description of a typical river-bar camp is given in an old history of Placer County:

"A rapid stream on one hand, curving around a peninsular-shaped, or rectangular, plat of land, with a sharp hilly background, down which came trails and roads, the surface of the plat being elevated but a few feet above the level of the water in the river. Next to the high ground which formed the border is the street—the main one—narrow and crowded, and upon one, or each, side are the buildings. If large enough, there may be a few square feet allotted for the plaza, near which stands the round tent where all sorts of games of hazard are played and liquors dispensed; and perhaps adjoining that is the dance-house, with squeaking violins, dark-skinned señoritas puffing cigarettes, and more liquors on sale. On the main street are found the hotels, boarding-houses, stores, bakeries, saloons, in each of which more liquors are displayed. Here are the livery stable, the butcher shop, the shoemaker, the washman, the blacksmith, all in operative order, in all sorts of structures—some stone, some shakes, some canvas, some of boards, and an occasional one of poles with brush thrown over. Pack-mules, saddle horses, donkeys, and not infrequently large freight wagons to which are hitched eight or ten mules, are seen in the street."

Practically nothing remains today to mark the exact sites of these old river camps. The bars themselves have changed location, and all of the buildings have disappeared. In El Dorado County there were scores of such camps, for the Middle Fork of the American River was generally considered to be the richest river mining region in California. At least ten thousand men worked on this Fork during the late summer and autumn of 1849, extracting something like ten million dollars' worth of gold dust from the river sands.

Above the junction of the North and the South forks on the El Dorado side of the river were the following bars: Condemned, Long, Granite, Whiskey, and Oregon. East of the confluence of the North and Middle forks were numerous other bars: Louisiana, New York, Murderer's, Wild Cat, Willow, Hoosier, Green Mountain, Maine, Poverty, Spanish, Ford's, Volcano, Big, Rocky, Sandy, Grey Eagle, Yankee Slide, Eureka, Boston, and Alabama. The most important were Murderer's Bar, Maine Bar, Spanish Bar, and Ford's Bar. Murderer's Bar, two or three miles up the Middle Fork from its junction with the North Fork, was the scene, in the spring of 1849, of the massacre of five white men by the Indians in revenge for the killing of some Indians at the place by these same men several days before. Spanish Bar, mined as early as 1848 by men who came from Coloma, was one of several bars which produced more than a million dollars.

On the South Fork were the following bars: Dutch, Kanaka, Red, Stony, Ledge, Missouri, Michigan, and Chili. Along the Cosumnes River and its branches were a dozen or more river camps, among them being Big Bar, Michigan Bar, Diving Bell Bar, Wisconsin Bar, Pittsburg Bar, and Buck's Bar.

Hangtown, or Placerville

Placerville, at first known as Old Dry Diggin's, and then as Hangtown, was founded in 1848. James Marshall stated that in the summer of 1848 he had located the Old Dry Diggin's. Usually, however, this discovery has been credited to William Daylor, owner of a ranch on the Cosumnes River not far from New Helvetia (Sacramento). Daylor did pan for gold on Hangtown Creek during that spring, in company with Perry McCoon and Jared Sheldon. With the help of a number of Indians they took out from one small ravine or gutter, "not more than a hundred yards long by four feet wide and two or three feet deep," as much as $17,000 in one week's time. Governor R. B. Mason, who had the spot pointed out to him that July, included it in his report to the federal government, mentioning Daylor and McCoon as the men who had worked it.

The Old Dry Diggin's had become quite a camp by the autumn of 1848. Practically free from crime at first, the motley society which began pouring into it by 1849 brought with it the riffraff and criminal element of all nations. Robberies and murders became prevalent, and because there was no organized government the people took matters into their own hands. Stories are told of robbers and murderers being flogged or hanged by the irate citizens of the new town, early in 1849, thus giving rise to the name Hangtown. The site of one of the hangtrees at which justice was meted out is near the corner of Main and Coloma streets where the Post Office now stands. However, by 1850, Hangtown had become a well-ordered, civilized community, and on May 13, 1854, the town was incorporated under the name of Placerville in preference to Ravine City, also suggested as a substitute for the earlier designation.

The dry diggings on Hangtown Creek fluctuated with the seasons—in winter there was "water and prosperity," in summer "dullness and departures." But with the building of the South Fork Ditch prosperity became more stabilized, and the place grew to be one of the leading mining centers of the county and one of the most populous of all the early mining camps. Its voting population in 1854 was the third largest in the state, and in 1857 it was made the county seat. As early as 1856, however, a decline had begun to set in, due to the diminution of activity in the gold fields and the occurrence of two severe fires. A revival of fortune followed the discovery of the fabulously rich Comstock Lode in Nevada and the subsequent building of the Placerville Road. From 1859 until the building of the Central Pacific Railroad, Placerville witnessed an even greater period of activity, marked by the construction of permanent church buildings, an academy, hotels, and business houses.

The picturesque quality of the Placerville of today is chiefly attributable to the fact that its streets all conform to the topography of which the town has become a part. Following the courses of the streams and gulches and the contours of surrounding hills, the earliest settlers pitched their tents or built their first log cabins along these meandering paths. Later the builders of the permanent town were content to emulate the early example set them. As the traditional cowpaths set the pattern for the streets of Boston, so the pack-mule trails of the miners as they wended their way to and from the diggings are responsible for the intriguing course of Placerville's Main Street along Hangtown Creek, as well as for the direction of the score of little side streets and alleyways which penetrate the ravines and the steep hillsides, now covered with old-fashioned homes and shaded gardens.

Placerville, with its many buildings dating back to the '60's, has an atmosphere of age. The present office of the Pacific Gas and Electric Company dates back even farther, having been erected in 1852. Built of rough native rock placed in horizontal layers (a type of construction characteristic of the early '50's), this fine relic is one of three or four which survived the fire of 1856, and the only one still in existence. It was restored recently by the Pacific Gas and Electric Company and a marker was placed on it by the Native Daughters of the Golden West and dedicated to the memory of the pioneers.

The Ivy House, a large, three-story brick hotel with wide verandas fronting the two lower floors, once served as the Placerville Academy, originally established as the Conklin Academy in the fall of 1861 by E. B. Conklin and his wife. With the cessation of travel to Virginia City and the subsequent lack of patronage, the Academy closed its doors in 1868. Three years later, Professor George P. Tyndall, from New York, purchased the buildings, and in 1881 enlarged them, also laying out a garden. The giant ivy which still grows along the front wall beneath the balcony is of a very early planting. The Academy continued its activity until 1894, when the public high school was opened in the building.

Placerville's historic churches had their beginnings in the '50's, although the present buildings all date from the early or middle '60's. The first religious organization in the town was that of the Methodists, established in April 1850, their first house of worship being erected in October 1851. The present ivy-clad, brick structure which stands near the Ivy House at the intersection of Main Street and Cedar Ravine was dedicated on September 8, 1861, during the pastorate of Adam Bland, uncle of the late Henry Meade Bland, California poet and educator.

The first record of Catholic worship in El Dorado County dates back to the spring of 1850, when Father Ingoldsby traveled on foot through the mining camps, ministering to the spiritual needs of the gold-seekers, saying Mass in miners' cabins or under the open sky, visiting the sick, and conducting the last rites for the dead. The first Mass administered in Placerville was held in a log cabin on the site of the present McCune property near Union Street. A substantial frame structure was erected in 1852 on the site of the present St. Patrick's Church, which was built in 1865. The sweet and sonorous tones of the old silver bell, a gift of the early miners, still call the people to prayer.

The Presbyterians, organized in 1853 by the Rev. James Pierpont, a missionary of the American Home Missionary Society, dedicated their first building on February 12, 1854, on the lot now occupied by the Episcopal Church. The present structure was dedicated on April 30, 1865, on the site opposite the Courthouse. Recently, the Presbyterians united with the Methodists to form the County Federated Church.

Episcopalians began their work in El Dorado County at Coloma in 1855, and the parish of St. Mary's in Placerville was organized in 1857. The greater part of the early history of this parish is associated with the ministry of the Rev.

Charles C. Pierce, lovingly called by the church at large the "modern St. Francis," because of his years of self-sacrificing devotion as a missionary in all of El Dorado County. From 1861 until his death in 1903, the influence of Father Pierce was woven into the lives of hundreds of men, women, and little children. Scattered all up and down the Mother Lode, there are those who still treasure books and cards presented by him on some christening, confirmation, or wedding day. Church records show that he conducted thirteen hundred funerals and officiated at six hundred marriages and seven hundred baptisms. "No home was so isolated nor schoolhouse so inaccessible as to be thrown beyond the radius of his ministry. When he died, all El Dorado mourned, schools closed, and business was suspended." With the coming of Rev. Pierce the name of the parish was changed to that of the Church of Our Savior, and the quaint building at 42 Coloma Street which still bears that name was erected under his leadership and dedicated by him in 1866.

There are a number of interesting historic sites in Placerville, although the buildings which originally made them famous have long since disappeared. Among these was the Cary House, built in 1857 by William Cary. Mark Twain, among other famous guests, lodged there. Horace Greeley registered there in 1859 on his overland journey to San Francisco in the interest of a transcontinental railway, and from the veranda of the hotel he delivered an address to the miners. Wells Fargo and Company had its office in this famous old hostelry, and during the Washoe silver excitement $90,000,000 in bullion is said to have passed through its doors. The present Raffles Hotel occupies the site.

Among the early settlers of Placerville was J. M. Studebaker, a wheelwright, who stuck to his trade instead of mining for gold. For five years, from 1853 to 1858, Studebaker made wheelbarrows for the miners, thus building up a nucleus for the factory which he later started with his brothers in South Bend, Indiana. There, instead of wheelbarrows, they manufactured wagons and buggies. With the advent of the automobile, the Studebakers became distributors of the car which they later bought out and manufactured for themselves under the name of Studebaker. A few years ago, J. M. Studebaker, then a very old man, revisited Placerville, the scene of his initial success. In making the visit, he kept a promise made on leaving the place that he would return at the end of fifty years. A little group of pioneers were banqueted by him on this occasion.

A marker has been placed by the Native Sons of the Golden West designating the site of the Studebaker blacksmith shop on the vacant lot next to the office of the Union Ice Company at 545 Main Street.

The old Hangtown bell, used in the early days to call out the Vigilantes as well as to ring the alarms of fire, has been removed from the Plaza, where it stood for so many years, to the lower end of Main Street near the Shell Oil Station. At the upper end of Main Street in front of the Methodist Church stands the Druid Monument, erected to commemorate the organization in 1859 of the first Grove of the United Ancient Order of Druids to be established west of the Rocky Mountains.

Hangtown's Neighbors

Almost the entire region about Placerville for miles in all directions was very rich in gold, particularly along the ravines and in the depressions of the hills. Yields here averaged an ounce per day per man during the early days of the gold rush. As a result of the incoming hordes of humanity, following the first discoveries, many smaller towns sprang up about Hangtown, or Placerville, always the central depot of supply and trade. So numerous were these little camps, which dotted the entire neighborhood with tents and cabins, that their names alone would cover several pages.

The basis of this immense supply of gold was the existence of several ancient auriferous river channels, which had drained the region in prehistoric times and which increased the wealth of later streams. The oldest of these antediluvian river channels, the Blue Channel with its cap of lava, runs in a northwesterly and southeasterly direction at a height of several hundred feet above the bed of the present Weber Creek, which cuts through it. A number of water courses called "Gray Channels," the work of a later geologic age, intersected the Blue Channel, thus adding to the accumulations of treasure-trove.

One of the richest spots in the vicinity was Diamond Springs, three miles south of Placerville. Its name was derived from the presence of crystal-clear springs located on the north side of Main Street on what is now mined-out ground. At first a camp on the old Carson Emigrant Trail and, for a time, on the later Placerville Road, Diamond Springs grew rapidly as a mining center. With a population of fifteen hundred, it rivaled Placerville and even aspired to become the county seat. No longer on the main artery of trade and travel, Diamond Springs is today a quiet town of something over eight hundred inhabitants. Nevertheless, it retains a measure of importance as a horticultural and lumbering center and on the hills near it large limekilns are still operated. The little village was once noted for its fine sandstone buildings, a few of which have survived the devastating fires which have swept the place in times past. Scars of placer diggings and remnants of early quartz mining in the outlying hills indicate the activities of other days. Among the tangled myrtle of the old graveyard just beyond the town are moss-grown obelisks bearing dates as early as 1851 and 1852.

Weber Creek, along which many evidences of early mining operations may be seen and on the banks of which there once flourished a number of thriving communities now deserted, derived its name from Captain Charles M. Weber, founder of Stockton. Weber mined along this stream in the spring of 1848, at about the same time that William Daylor discovered the rich dry diggings on Hangtown Creek. Antonio María Suñol, owner of Rancho El Valle de San José (in Alameda County), was also mining farther down stream at this time. Weber had organized the Stockton Mining Company at Tuleburg (soon to be renamed Stockton), and was working the placers at Weber Creek, assisted by a large number of Indians, twenty-five of whom had been sent by José Jesús, chief of the Stanislaus Indians and Weber's friend.

A store was established on the creek by Weber and his company in the summer of 1848, chiefly as a place where goods attractive to the Indians could be exchanged for the gold which they dug. The Stockton Company was disbanded in September 1848, Weber having determined to give his attention wholly to the building up of the city of Stockton. The Weber trading-post, however, continued to be a center for miners, and other camps soon grew up around it. The site of Weberville, two miles from Placerville, has long since reverted to wilderness.

Coon Hollow, about a mile south of Placerville, was one of the most prosperous of the early camps, no less than $5,000,000 in gold having been mined there from an area five acres in extent, the property of the Excelsior Mine. On the Placerville side of the same ridge, at Spanish Hill and Tennessee Hill, other productive mines were located on the ancient gravel channel.

Very rich surface diggings were found at Smith's Flat, about three miles east of Placerville, in 1852, and for a decade or more the camp prospered. Many tunnels were later dug into the hills in the effort to reach the old gravel beds hidden there. Originally, the town stood on the Placerville Road, but recently the course of the highway has been altered and the new road passes to one side of the village.

To the north of Smith's Flat, on the road to Mosquito Valley, another early camp, known as White Rock, also drew immense wealth from the ancient gravel beds of the vicinity, four acres alone producing $4,000,000.

Cold Springs, beyond the confluence of Hangtown and Weber creeks about five miles northwest of Placerville, was one of the liveliest of the early mining camps of El Dorado County. During its short heyday it boasted a population of two thousand souls and enjoyed a direct stage connection with Sacramento as well as with Coloma and Placerville. From the fall of 1852 to the spring of 1853 Leland Stanford (later governor of California and founder of Stanford University) with his partner, N. T. Smith, kept a store at Cold Springs; but as business began to decline, they moved to Michigan Bluff in Placer County. As mining activities slackened in the vicinity, and no new locations were found, the miners gradually left for richer fields. Stores had to close, the stage took another route, and before long the village was left isolated and deserted on an unfrequented road. The name persists today only in the designation Cold Springs School District, while the grass-grown cemetery on the hill alone bears witness to the life which once animated the now-vanished town.

On the summit of Gold Hill north of the site of Cold Springs and seven miles northwest of Placerville, ruins of the old town of Gold Hill may be seen at the crossroads. The roofless walls of two sandstone buildings, one bearing the date 1859, and the other 1861, mark the site of this one-time mining camp. Flourishing orchards and gardens have covered the scars of the diggings in the surrounding hills.

Mud Springs (El Dorado)

Mud Springs, later known as El Dorado, was an important camp on the old Carson Emigrant Trail, subsequently becoming a mining center and crossroads station for freight and stage lines. The name Mud Springs was bestowed upon the camp because the ground about the springs where the emigrants watered their stock was always muddy—a name applied likewise to a number of other old California camp sites. This was changed to El Dorado when the town was incorporated during the height of the gold fever. At that time the population was counted in thousands, and the place boasted its "full quota of saloons, hotels, and stores, and a gold-production record that gave its citizens just cause for pride."

The El Dorado of today "is little more than a wide place in the road; a frame hotel (built in 1852), one store, and a service station comprise the entire business section, with a few cottages scattered over the surrounding hills. On one side of the main street . . . . stands a block of ruined buildings, roofless, with gaping windows and doors half concealed by rank vegetation." A brush fire which encroached upon the business section of the town in 1923 left only the shell of most of the old stone and brick edifices and destroyed the little Union Church on the hill which had been erected in 1853. The roofless stores still stand just as they were left by the fire, but the church has been rebuilt along its original simple lines.

With El Dorado as its center, a rich placer-mining district spread out in 1849 and 1850 to include new diggings at Loafer's Hollow, Deadman's Hollow, Slate Creek, Empire Ravine, Dry Creek, and Missouri Flat. The latter place, about one mile to the north, was a camp of some importance during the '50's. To the north and south of El Dorado several rich Mother Lode quartz leads were also uncovered.

A number of quartz mines were developed at Logtown, two and one-half miles south of El Dorado, and at one of these mines, in 1851, a lessee put up a steam mill running eight immense stamps. Later on, others were built. One of these old mills is still standing today. At one time a continuous line of quartz mills extended southward to the crossing of the Cosumnes River at Saratoga, or Yeomet (later Huse Bridge).

Continuing south two miles on the road toward Nashville, one passes the site of King's Store on the North Fork of the Cosumnes River, an important trading-station in the early days.

About two miles farther on is Nashville, originally called Quartzburg, one of the earliest quartz-mining districts in the state. Here the first stamp mill, brought around the Horn from Cincinnati, was used at the old Tennessee Mine, later called the Nashville. The town of Quartzburg was established on the site of an ancient Indian camping-ground, and a large ranchería still existed there when the first miners arrived. Leaving the Mother Lode Highway less than a mile south of Nashville and one mile north of the Forks of the Cosumnes River, a ford crosses the North Fork to the flat where one of the eighteen unratified Indian treaties was drawn up and signed by O. M. Wozencraft, United States Indian agent, and representatives of the Cu-lu, the Yas-si, the Loc-lum-ne, and the Wo-pum-nes tribes, on September 18, 1851.

Shingle Springs

Several refreshing springs on the overland Emigrant Road and a shingle mill built in 1849 gave this historic spot the name which it bears today—Shingle Springs. A well of very cold water is still to be found beneath an aged Missouri locust beside the Shingle Spring House, the oldest building in the village. Erected in 1850 from lumber brought around the Horn, the Shingle Spring House is still sturdy and useful. Located as it is on the present Lincoln Highway, it has been restored and rechristened, and today it serves as a wayside refreshment stand.

At the foot of the hill stands the Planter's Hotel, a rambling frame structure built in 1861, now fast falling into decay through neglect and the inroads of insect pests and winter storms. Near by is the Phelps Store, which was built in the '80's and is of beautiful native stone, with deep-set, arched doorways in the lower and upper stories.

Mining at Shingle Springs began in 1850, and the gulches were soon dotted with cabins. At first the miners had to obtain their supplies at Buckeye Flat, one mile to the east, but in 1857 a store was established at Shingle Springs. Finally, in 1865, the Sacramento Valley Railroad was extended from Latrobe to Shingle Springs, and as the railroad terminus the place boomed for a year or two, becoming quite a stage and freight center. This prosperity was short-lived, however, for by 1867 the Central Pacific Railroad from Sacramento via Auburn had diverted the overland traffic from the Placerville Road, and Shingle Springs became a peaceful country hamlet.

Frenchtown, now called French Creek, was an early mining camp two miles to the southeast. It was settled largely by French and French Canadians, who later moved to Greenwood.

Clarksville, at first a way point for emigrants and later a mining camp, is marked today by a picturesque stone ruin of a building erected in the '50's, its roof and doorways gone and a sturdy locust tree growing up within it. About the countryside linger other evidences of early habitation—here an abandoned homestead with sagging roof and long-neglected garden keeping lonely watch amid the dry hills; there

the stone foundation of some former wayside inn, standing mute and nameless beside the modern highway. A deep silence, disturbed only by the faint tinkle of a cowbell across the pasture lands, enfolds these ghosts of yesteryear.

Latrobe

Latrobe, named in honor of the civil engineer who constructed the first railroad in the United States, was laid out in the southwestern part of the county in 1864 as the terminus of the Placerville–Sacramento Valley Railroad. The first store on the site had been opened the previous year by J. H. Miller. For a time Latrobe, with eight daily stages, was connected with all parts of El Dorado County and also controlled the entire trade of Amador County. From 1864 to 1865 it was an important way station for the vast stream of commerce which poured over the Placerville Road to Virginia City. During the first few years of its existence the town boasted a population of seven or eight hundred, with several stores, Masons and Odd Fellows halls, a school, and a hotel. Many of these buildings, including the Odd Fellows Hall, still stand, and the town, now numbering about two hundred inhabitants, continues to serve as an outlet for the Plymouth Mines in Amador County and as a center for cattlemen.

Pleasant Valley

Pleasant Valley, ten miles southeast of Placerville, was named by a group of Mormons who stopped to camp there en route to Salt Lake City in the summer of 1848. At the northern end of the valley a large corral was built for a portion of the cattle, and a second was placed on the South Fork of Weber Creek, one-half mile farther north. Gold was discovered during the short sojourn of the pilgrims at this spot, but even gold could not detain them from the real purpose of their journey, and after a three weeks' rest they resumed their march up the divide and over the Sierra Nevada.

When some of these same Mormons returned to California in 1849, news of their discovery at Pleasant Valley the year before spread quickly, and many miners were soon panning out the yellow dust in the vicinity of the old corrals, making an average of eight dollars a day. By July hundreds of Argonauts were pouring into California over the Carson Emigrant Trail. Coming by way of Stonebreaker Hill, the golden quest ended for some of these wayfarers at Pleasant Valley. Several villages of rude tents and cabins sprang up: Iowaville, on the low divide between the forks of Weber Creek; Dogtown, at the first of the Mormon corrals; and Newtown, one-half mile southwest of Dogtown. With the building of ditches to carry water to the mines, Newtown grew rapidly. Later on, hydraulic operations were carried on there, but in 1872 the town was destroyed by fire.

With the revival of quartz mining at Grizzly Flat in the '80's, Pleasant Valley took on new life, and the Norris Hotel became an important stage station where passengers stopped for meals and where horses were changed. The old hotel is still standing.

Tiger Lily, Hanks Exchange, and Cook's were three wayside stations on the Carson Emigrant Road between Diamond Springs and Pleasant Valley.

Old Camps on the Upper Cosumnes

Grizzly Flat is located twenty-seven miles southeast of Placerville in a wild and rugged region on the ridge between the North and Middle forks of the Cosumnes River. A company of miners who encamped here in the fall of 1850 gave the place its name, suggestive of that life of adventure common to the hardy youths of '49, and of the rough country into which the lure of golden treasure had led them. The story is typical: while preparing their evening meal over a glowing campfire, the young men were surprised by the visit of a large grizzly bear, to whom the savory odors of the coffee pot and frying pan seemed also to have been attractive.

Extensive placers were worked for miles about Grizzly Flat during the spring of 1851, and by 1852 the town had grown to such an extent that it polled six hundred votes. Hydraulic mining here was of some importance during the '70's, and a number of quartz mines were also developed— the Steely, Mount Pleasant, a very rich mine, and the Eagle, among others. Lumbering, still an important industry in this neighborhood, had its beginning in 1856, when sawmills were first erected there.

Grizzly Flat today has 110 inhabitants. A few characteristic stone buildings, with their heavy iron doors and iron-shuttered windows, date back to more prosperous days, and indelible scars of old mines mark the surrounding landscape. To the southwest, in a more remote and rugged region, ghosts of old gold camps, such as Dogtown and Cedarville, have recently found new neighbors in the mills of the Caldor Lumber Company.

Brownsville, Indian Diggin's, Fair Play, and Coyoteville, once the locale of many animated scenes, pictures in the far-flung drama of the Sierra gold regions, were also located in the Cosumnes River region, where hydraulic mining was extensively carried on. Brownsville was renamed Mendon when a post office was established (there being another Brownsville, in Yuba County), but its original name was restored after the post office was discontinued. Brownsville is distinguished as the site of the rich Volcano Claim, discovered by Henry Brown and his companions, which is said to have produced hundreds of thousands of dollars in gold up to the year 1867.

Crossing the South Fork of the Cosumnes River from Fiddletown (Amador County) in 1849, a party of prospectors located near an ancient Indian village in Telegraph Gulch. A lively camp, known as Indian Diggin's, soon grew up, becoming the center for mines on Indian Creek and in Drummond Gulch as well. A population of over fifteen hundred had gathered at Indian Diggin's by 1855, and three stage lines connected the mines with the outside world. The rich gravel beds of the region were gradually worked out by tunneling and hydraulic processes, fires swept the town in 1857 and 1860, and by 1890 only a hundred people remained in the place. Today it is a ghost village, its only importance lying in the fact that there is a Western Union Telegraph station there which serves the sparsely settled district.

Fair Play, an old camp five miles northwest of Indian Diggin's, was described as late as 1890 as "a neat little village prettily situated on a sort of table-land shelving from the slope of a large mountain to the southeast." Provisions were shipped in to Fair Play, and to Slug Gulch to the east, over steep and tortuous mountain roads. It still serves as a money-order post office for this out-of-the-way region, reached only by a rough clay road.

Coyoteville, south of Fair Play on Cedar Creek, received its name from the peculiar type of mining employed there, known as drift mining or coyoteing. Hittell explains the origin of the word "coyoteing" thus:

"Each miner had his separate hole, in which he delved. The men, while at work, were entirely out of sight of a person looking over the bar, flat, or slope in which they were operating, but the approach of night or any alarm or unusual noise would cause them to pop out of their holes; and their supposed resemblance under such circumstances to the Californian animal corresponding with the prairie wolf of the Mississippi states caused these pits, shafts, or tunnels to be

called coyote-holes and the character of mining done in them coyote-mining. . . . . While it was in vogue, many places were completely honeycombed by so-called coyote-holes."

Negro Hill

Negro Hill, first mined by Mormons in 1848, was a thriving camp located across the South Fork of the American River from Mormon Island (Sacramento County). Spaniards and Mexicans occupied ground on the south side of the hill at the mouth of Spanish Ravine, in 1849, while Negroes established the villages known as Little Negro Hill and Big Negro Hill. As white miners flocked into the place, the town of Negro Hill developed, reaching a population of twelve hundred by 1853. Repeating the experience of numerous mining camps throughout the Sierra Nevada, Negro Hill enjoyed its brief heyday of prosperity as a center of trade for outlying camps—Growler's Flat, Jenny Lind Flat, Massachusetts Flat, Chile Hill, Condemned Bar, and Long Bar. That "tide of gold and trade" has long since ceased to flow, but the deep scars of old diggings are still plainly visible among the bushes and young trees which now cover the hillsides. One or two cottages of a later date, an old-fashioned well sweep in each dooryard, stand on the site of the older village. Across the road are extensive scars surrounding the site of the later Negro settlement where the colored people, driven out of the former location by the whites, found even richer fields above the river.

Salmon Falls

At the mouth of Sweetwater Creek, near a cataract later known as Salmon Falls, where the Indians for many ages had come to catch their supplies of fish, the Mormons stopped to mine in 1848. In 1849 other white men came, and in the spring of 1850 a town, named Salmon Falls, was laid out. From the few cabins built by the Mormons, the place grew rapidly to a community of some note, with a population of over three thousand people. Many little camps in mining areas near by contributed to this flush of prosperity, among them McDowell Hill, Jayhawk, New York House, Green Springs, and Pinchem Gut or Pinchem Tight. Pinchem Tight derived its name from the fact that Ebbert, the storekeeper, not having small enough weights to measure the gold dust which the miners brought in in payment for small purchases, would loosely pinch as much of the dust as he could gather between his fingers, whereupon the miners would shout, "Pinch 'em tight."

One old frame store and a remnant of the pioneer cemetery on the slope of the hill are all that remain of Salmon Falls. Along what was once the busy main street, now a quiet country road, the passerby today may chance to meet a handsome flock of sleek Thanksgiving turkeys—in striking contrast to the scenes enacted there in pioneer gold days. At Jayhawk the only evidence of former habitation is the little pioneer cemetery lying amid the sheltering hills.

Pilot Hill

Standing up boldly above a wide expanse of hills and forested ravines, the conical promontory of Pilot Hill has served as a landmark for ages. Probably the first white men to visit the region were John C. Frémont and his men when, early in March 1844, they followed the well-defined Indian trails leading out of the High Sierra and down over the foothills into the Sacramento Valley.

Mining first began in the vicinity of Pilot Hill in the summer of 1849. During the following winter scores of prospectors from the river bars and higher mountains congregated at this point, and a town bearing the name of Pilot Hill grew up near the northern base of the mountain. Not far away, Centerville and Pittsfield developed simultaneously, but the three camps soon consolidated under the name of Centerville, a title which clung to the place even after the establishment of a post office officially designated as Pilot Hill. The sere and dusty village of today shows some signs of awakening, a few new homes appearing among the handful of old cottages scattered along the present Mother Lode Highway. A decrepit but still picturesque hotel, historic relic of 1854, serves as post office, store, and service station. On the slope above the highway one mile east of the village is a little pioneer cemetery where many graves of the '50's lie beneath the locust trees, the oldest one recording the year 1850.

Hogg's Diggings, a rich and active camp three or four miles to the north of Pilot Hill, and Goose Flat to the west not far from Rattlesnake Bridge, lived briefly during the '50's and '60's. Today they are no more than scars upon the surface of the ancient auriferous hills. South of the site of Goose Flat is the Zantgraf Quartz Mine, dating from the '50's. Worked to a distance of eight hundred feet below the river bed, its production record is estimated at $1,000,000. The old stamp mill and the village, for many years a mining center, were destroyed by fire in 1931.

North of the Pilot Hill Hotel a quarter of a mile stands that grand old relic of the early '60's, the Bayley House, erected by Alexander John Bayley, a native of Vermont, who came to California in 1849 on the "Edward Everett." From 1851 to 1861 Bayley owned the Oak Valley House at Pilot Hill. After it was destroyed by fire he built the large three-story brick structure still known by his name. Believing that the overland railroad would pass that way, Mr. Bayley expended over $20,000 in the construction of this splendid old hostelry. But the dreams he so fondly cherished on that grand opening day, May 15, 1862, were never realized. The great house beneath its aged oaks and locusts is as firm and substantial as the day it was built, but the beautiful terraced garden laid out so carefully withered long ago.

Lotus (Uniontown)

Uniontown, one and one-half miles down the river from Coloma, has enjoyed a cycle of names. In 1849 it was called Marshall, after James W. Marshall; in 1850 the name was changed to Uniontown, in honor of California's admission to the Union; and, finally, with the establishment of a post office, the town was assigned the exotic and poetic designation of Lotus, its former name having been pre-empted by Uniontown (now Arcata) in Humboldt County. Lotus it remains today.

The population of Uniontown numbered over two thousand in the '50's. It was during this peak of prosperity that A. Lohry built the sturdy brick store with iron doors which still stands on the one street of the present village. Very soon afterward, the fine old brick mansion beside it was erected. A bit of the Old World set down here in the far, rugged West is this picturesque landmark, with its gabled roof etched against a background of spreading locust trees, a quaint garden of old-time flowers at its doorway, and a little orchard of apple, peach, and pear trees tucking it in. In sharp contrast are the scars of deserted river mines furrowing the meadows which fringe the very dooryards of the scattered, sleepy village, indelible testimony of the gold-mad days when hope fashioned many a glowing dream—fairy castles which were only too often swept away like wisps of gossamer, leaving futility and emptiness to haunt the memory. The tragedy which often followed these broken dreams is told in the story of A. Lohry, a story of high hopes and subsequent losses, of brooding, and, finally, of suicide.

Passing historic ground along every mile of its course,

the Mother Lode Highway crosses the American River just east of Lotus. Here men are once more panning for gold along the old river bars, their families often camping out with them under the clear summer skies. Beyond the river the scars of countless diggings line the roadway—old claims which once boasted each its individual name, but which now are all but forgotten. Bits of old orchards still bravely fulfil their cycles of bloom and leaf and fruit, while here and there occasional stone foundations cling to some gaping, weed-grown excavation made by miners in quest of treasure.

Beside the road stands a striking stone ruin, roofless and windowless, a colorful relic of the days when hordes of miners of many nationalities fared up and down this old thoroughfare seeking a royal harvest from field and hill and gully. In those days Meyer's dance pavilion and saloon sat, not as a blind beggar in the wayside dust, but as a gay host enticing the lonely wayfarer to share the revelry and merry-making within its doors. A few miles to the northeast was Michigan Flat, now only a memory. Red Hill, Coyote Diggings, Rich Gulch—these and others lived their brief day and passed into oblivion with the old tavern.

Kelsey's Diggings

The mining area rapidly grew outward from Coloma, soon reaching across the river and up into the higher ridges. Among other rich claims was Kelsey's Diggings, located by Benjamin Kelsey, brother of Andrew Kelsey for whom Kelseyville in Lake County was named. The two brothers had come overland with the Bidwell-Bartleson party in 1841, and early in 1848 Benjamin had come to this part of El Dorado County, discovering the diggings which took his name. Within a year the place had become a large camp, its prosperity continuing into the '50's. Six hotels, twelve stores, twenty-four saloons and gambling houses, a population drawn from four continents—this was Kelsey's Diggings, a little polyglot metropolis selling its varied attractions to a wide circle of heterogeneous camps, all at one time good-sized places: Louisville, Irish Creek, Elizatown, Fleatown; and to numerous flats, such as Yankee, Chicken, Stag, American, Spanish, Union, and Columbia (later St. Lawrenceville). Spanish Flat, for many years the most important of the group, retained something of its urban appearance as late as 1883. At Louisville the store is still kept by the son of John Poor, pioneer storekeeper there.

A solitary house hidden among the hills, remnants of scattered quartz mines (a few of them still worked to a limited degree), abandoned tunnels, old roads—little else remains today to mark the sites of these old camps or to tell the oft-repeated tale of fabulous treasure and of the multitudes who came to seek for it.

Today Kelsey is only a remote hamlet of some 170 inhabitants, boasting one store, a post office, a schoolhouse, and a few scattered homesteads and farms, but with many memories vivid with the music and color of other days. Away from the beaten track, yes, but worth the climb over any of the two or three old roads leading to it, for Kelsey holds a veritable treasure. Here is the old Marshall blacksmith shop, now restored and carefully preserved inside the walls of a little fireproof building constructed by the state in June 1921. A Pioneer Museum was earlier installed therein. The truly remarkable collection which was for a time housed here has been called a cross section of the social, industrial, political, and spiritual life of the pioneers of the '50's and '60's. It has recently been acquired, in its entirety, by the State of California, and is now at the Sutter's Fort Historical Museum in Sacramento.

Among the three thousand and more relics which have been assembled, one of the most fascinating groups is that of the old books treasured in the little libraries of the pioneers and brought by them on the long journeys across the Plains—worn Bibles, family albums, primers and copybooks of Wilson's and McGuffey's day, antiquated compendiums, copies of Godey's *Ladies' Book* and of *Leslies Magazine*, an aged volume of the *Greek Trilogy*. Quaint old prints, pictures made of brushed wool and hair, a worn writing-desk, a melodeon, the first organ used in the Placerville school—these and many other items depict the cultural and spiritual background of the pioneers who planted in this new West seeds of the old East.

Among the collection are many relics which portray the life and activities of James W. Marshall. From his shop, where he wrought as a carpenter as well as a smith, many specimens of Marshall's fine workmanship have been preserved, among others, the handmade compasses with which he measured the timbers of Sutter's Mill and other buildings. The forge and anvil, the thimble-skein uprights which supported the bellows, all have been assembled just as he placed them in 1872. Back of the shop the tunnels of Marshall's old Grey Eagle Mine still reach two hundred feet into the hillside. This property is in Kelsey Ravine, one of the richest in the county.

A short distance up the road from the building, the site of the Union Hotel owned by Marshall, in which he spent his declining years, has been marked. Here the discoverer of gold at Coloma died on August 10, 1885. Next door to the Union was Siesenop's Hotel, still standing, while across the road still stands Tom Allan's saloon, the windows and doors of which were brought around the Horn. Here Marshall and his friends spent their evenings. On the hill is the little cemetery with a full quota of pioneer graves. Quartz, placer, and pocket mining are still carried on in the vicinity. The first slate quarries in the state, working a large deposit of blue-black slate, of which almost the entire mountain seems to be composed, operated there during the '90's and until 1915.

A few miles up the road from Kelsey is a pleasant ranch with an old-fashioned country house surrounded by tall locusts atop a little hill. The gateway below the house bears this sign: "Drumcarn Lands." Here, in 1851, John McClary obtained squatter's rights to the land, built a cabin, and planted an orchard at the upper end of the ravine which lies below the site of the present house. Patrick Kelley, a native of Ireland, also came to Kelsey in 1851. Three years later he brought his young bride from Massachusetts, and in 1854 he purchased McClary's orchard and surrounding lands for a home. The site of the log cabin in which the Kelleys lived until 1858 is still marked by an aged apple tree in the old orchard. The present house, which replaced a cottage built in 1860, was erected in 1887 as the fulfilment of Mrs. Kelley's long-cherished dream of a home on the hilltop. Descendants still occupy the old homestead, which they have named after their ancestral lands in Ireland.

Greenwood

John Greenwood, an old trapper, established a trading-post in Long Valley late in 1848. Soon other stores were built, and in 1850 the new town was christened Lewisville in honor of the first white child born there. When the town attained the dignity of a post office, the name was changed to Greenwood. Greenwood boasted social advantages not enjoyed by many of its neighbors, notably a well-patronized community theater. Like Placerville, the town had its hang-tree and very early purged itself of unruly elements. By 1854 Greenwood was a thriving, busy place, and, along with several other towns, aspired to be the county seat, an honor, however, which it did not attain.

Situated in the midst of an old orchard community, Greenwood is still a trading-center for a township of 385 people. A number of the old houses still stand in the village, among them the Ritchie, Desmarchais, and John Smith houses. The stone foundations of the Mulbach Brewery are intact. In the cemetery a small slab of stone bearing the initials J. A. S. and the date January 24, 1863, marks the grave of John A. Stone, a pioneer song-writer of the '50's, who lived, sang, and died at Greenwood.

Spanish Dry Diggin's, four miles north of Greenwood, received its name from the fact that its first miners were a party of Spaniards, under the leadership of General Andrés Pico, who prospected there early in 1848. During the following year a large number of Mexicans arrived at the camp. That same year a group of Germans also came to the vicinity and set up a trading-center which came to be known as Dutchtown. Yields of pay dirt were very rich throughout this region, and Spanish Dry Diggin's was soon surrounded by subsidiary camps all along the Middle Fork of the American River: Poverty Bar, Spanish Bar, El Dorado Slide, Dutch Bar, Rock-a-Chucky, and Canyon Creek, among others. The first quartz-seam diggings were discovered in this district in 1854, among them being the Grit Mine, which yielded $500,000, and the Barr Mine, totaling a production of $300,000 up to 1883.

Nothing remains at the old Spanish Dry Diggin's to indicate the wealth and glamour of its past save traces of old mines among the hills. Several quartz properties are now being reopened.

Georgetown

The first mining operations near Georgetown were carried on along Oregon Creek and Hudson's Gulch by a party of Oregonians in 1849. A company of sailors under the leadership of George Phipps followed, and in 1850 motley camps of tents and shanties grew up on the creek at the foot of what is now Main Street. Known at first as Growlersburg, it was destroyed by fire and the old site was deserted in 1852 for the present situation on the hill. The name, too, was changed to Georgetown in honor of its nautical founder.

Georgetown rivaled Placerville in the number and quality of its early social and cultural institutions. By 1855 it included in its list of attractions a school, a church, a theater, a town hall, a Sons of Temperance Hall, a Masonic Hall, and three hotels, as well as many stores. The cultural advantages of the little town, the beauty of its hill setting among the pines, oaks, and cedars of the Georgetown Divide, the mild and tonic air of its 2,650-foot elevation won for it the title "Pride of the Mountains."

The atmosphere of the early days pervades somewhat the Georgetown of today, although its population has dwindled to less than seven hundred (including the outlying districts of the township), and the only building left of those erected before the fire of 1856 is the Masonic Hall (a frame structure now restored). Wooden sidewalks lead along the broad main street beneath a double row of giant locusts. Back of these stand stores with fronts of brick and stone, an entire block of them, built in the late '50's after the fire. Many of the dim and dusty interiors are vacant, while others still make a brave showing as stores, the post office, a refreshment parlor, etc. The Graham Building, erected in 1856, with heavy iron doors and thick stone walls, fireproof and burglar-proof, is the oldest building in the business district. It was formerly used both as a general store and as a Wells Fargo Express office, but is vacant at the present time. On the corner of Main Street and the Auburn Road stands the I.O.O.F. Building, a substantial two-story brick structure formerly known as the Olmstead Hotel or Balser House, and later used as a theater. Various lodges meet in it at the present time.

Among the quaint clapboard houses of the '60's and '70's which line the village streets with their neat gardens, probably the oldest is a small cottage which stands on the bank of the irrigation ditch. On Main Street, opposite the I.O.O.F. Building, is the old Knox house, a pleasant old-fashioned country place half-hidden by gnarled apple and cherry trees. It was erected by Shannon Knox in 1864 and stands on the site of the log structure he had built about ten years earlier. The house is still owned by the Knox family.

The gardens and orchards of Georgetown were remarkable for the variety of their flowers, shrubs, and fruits, all grown from stock obtained from a pioneer nursery established by a native of Scotland in Georgetown in the '60's. Many a beautiful plant, rare today and seldom seen elsewhere, may be found in the old gardens of the town, and the cemetery is filled with them. Thrifty plants of the Scotch broom, scions of this same nursery, have grown wild all over the hills, glorifying the countryside each spring with golden bloom.

In common with many other mining districts in the Sierra Nevada, locations in the vicinity of Georgetown witnessed a revival of activity in the spring and summer of 1932. Old stamp-mill methods were superseded by new processes and improved machinery. The Beebe Mine at the edge of town, as well as four or five other properties in the neighborhood, have succeeded in making the low-grade quartz pay out under more up-to-date management. Fruit-raising and lumbering also help to maintain a considerable trade for Georgetown.

Seam mines, a formation of slate interspersed with quartz seams largely decomposed and varying in thickness from that of a knife blade to several feet, are characteristic of the Georgetown district. The Nagler or French Claim at Greenwood Valley is a seam mine that produced more than $4,000,000 from 1872 to 1885. There is another seam mine at Georgia Slide, two miles northwest of Georgetown. Here an open perpendicular bank of slate rock was found with sheets of gold-bearing quartz coursing through it. Georgia Slide, however, dates back to 1849, when a group of miners from Georgia first worked the spot for its placer gold. The camp was called Georgia Flat at first, but a big mountain slide occasioned a change in its appellation. For years it was a wild, rough place with no outside communication except by pack trail. There was but one family living there in 1933, and one frame store is all that remains of the former camp.

The ancient gravel beds of Kentucky Flat, six miles northeast of Georgetown, and of Volcanoville, three miles northwest of Kentucky Flat, once made production records. At Volcanoville, where there is a post office, a few miners still are working. Among the many old hill camps dating back to 1851 and 1852 were Mameluke, Bottle, Cement, and Jones.

Johntown, five miles south of Georgetown, was named after a sailor who discovered its gold-bearing deposits. Later, when it became more profitable to raise vegetables there than to mine, the name was changed to Garden Valley. The Empire and Manhattan creeks join at this point to form Johntown Creek. Below their confluence miners have taken out between two and three million dollars in gold.

Georgetown is situated on the old road which leads up the Georgetown Divide and thence by trail into the wild and beautiful country of the Rubicon River, now accessible only to the most hardy of out-door enthusiasts. The citizens of Georgetown, and others, still look forward to the fulfillment of a long-cherished dream—the opening up of this exceptionally fine mountain region. California's growing demand for expanding vacation lands may yet bring this to pass by the building of a through road to Lake Tahoe, as summer homes are already being built in the timbered country to the east.

SOURCES

[Credit is here given for source material, and permission to quote is hereby acknowledged]

BANCROFT, HUBERT HOWE. *California Inter Pocula, 1846–1848,* in *History of the Pacific States of North America,* Vol. XXX. The History Company, San Francisco, 1888

———. "Routes and Transportation—California," chap. iii in *Chronicles of the Builders of the Commonwealth,* V, 123–196

BEKEART, PHILIP BALDWIN. "James Wilson Marshall, Discoverer of Gold," in *Quarterly of the Society of California Pioneers,* I, No. 3 (September 30, 1924)

BOWMAN, AMOS. *Report on the Properties and Domain of the California Water Company. Situated on the Georgetown Divide.* A. L. Bancroft & Company, San Francisco, 1874

CLELAND, ROBERT GLASS. *A History of California: The American Period.* The Macmillan Company, New York, 1922

CLEMENS, SAMUEL L. *Roughing It.* Harper & Brothers, New York, 1913

COY, OWEN COCHRAN. *Gold Days,* of the series *California,* edited by John Russell McCarthy. Powell Publishing Company, Los Angeles, 1929

FARQUHAR, FRANCIS P. (editor). *Up and Down California in 1860–1864. The Journal of William H. Brewer.* Yale University Press, New Haven, 1930

FRÉMONT, JOHN C. *The Exploring Expedition to the Rocky Mountains, Oregon and California.* George H. Derby & Company, Buffalo, 1849

GREELEY, HORACE. *An Overland Journey from New York to San Francisco in the Summer of 1859.* C. M. Saxton, Barker & Company, New York, 1860

HITTELL, THEODORE H. *History of California.* In 4 vols. N. J. Stone & Company, San Francisco, 1897

HULBERT, ARCHER BUTLER. *Forty-niners. The Chronicle of the California Trail.* Little, Brown & Company, Boston, 1931

JERRETT, HERMAN DANIEL. *California's El Dorado Yesterday and Today.* Privately published, Sacramento, California, 1915

JOHNSTON, PHILIP. "Legends and Landmarks of '49 along the Mother Lode," in *Touring Topics,* XXIII, No. 2 (February, 1931), 12–27, 52–53

KELLEY, MARGARET A. "Life, Letters, and Reminiscences of James Marshall," in *The Grizzly Bear,* 1918–1919

Mountain Democrat. Seventy-fifth Anniversary Souvenir, Review Edition. Placerville, California, January 6, 1928

SANCHEZ, NELLIE VAN DE GRIFT. *Spanish and Indian Place Names of California.* A. M. Robertson, San Francisco, 1922

SIOLI, PAOLI. *Historical Souvenirs of El Dorado County, California.* Paoli Sioli, Oakland, 1883

TYLER, DANIEL. *A Concise History of the Mormon Battalion in the Mexican War, 1846–1847.* Privately published, Salt Lake City, 1881

UPTON, CHARLES ELMER. *Pioneers of El Dorado.* Privately published, Placerville, California, 1906

WHITE, CHESTER LEE. "Surmounting the Sierras, the Campaign for a Wagon Road," in *Quarterly of the California Historical Society,* VII, No. 1 (March, 1928), 3–19

FRESNO COUNTY

FRESNO COUNTY (Fresno is Spanish for "ash tree," a name first used in the region by the early Spanish explorers, who found many ash trees along the watercourses) was organized in 1856, with Millerton as its county seat. Fresno became the county seat in 1874.

The Old Los Angeles Trail (El Camino Viejo)

The oldest north and south trail to traverse the entire length of the San Joaquin Valley was known as the Los

Angeles Trail, or El Camino Viejo, and led from San Pedro to San Antonio, now east Oakland. Following a route identical with that later known as the Stockton–Los Angeles Road as far as the present Chandler Station, the road descended San Emigdio Canyon to its mouth in the extreme southwestern corner of the San Joaquin Valley. From there the trail skirted the eastern slope of the Coast Range foothills, finally passing out of the valley through Corral Hollow and Patterson Pass southwest of Tracy.

Recent investigation indicates that as early as 1800 the Spaniards drove in ox carts over this route between San Pedro and San Antonio. Many of the old water holes along its course developed into historic places: San Emigdio Mission station and pueblo in the present Kern County; Los Carneros, where there is an extremely spectacular outcropping of the famous vaqueros sandstone, which composes also Las Tres Piedras ("The Three Rocks"), Joaquín Murieta's stronghold; and Poso de Chané, six miles east of the present Coalinga.

On the site of an Indian village, Poso ("pool") de Chané, a small agricultural community made up of a dozen or so Spanish and Mexican families, was long the only Spanish settlement in this section. Later, American pioneers came in and established stores and built houses. Today nothing marks the spot where Poso de Chané stood, the pool itself having been obliterated in the flood of 1862.

Approaching Poso de Chané from the south, El Camino Viejo crossed El Arroyo de las Polvarduras ("dust clouds"); El Arroyo de las Canoas ("troughs"); El Arroyo de Zapato Chino ("Chinese shoe"); and El Arroyo de Jacelitos, "so named by the Spanish," says F. F. Latta, "because they found there many 'Indian huts' from which the inhabitants had fled in terror." Continuing north from Poso de Chané, the road passed other camp sites on Arroyo de Cantua, Arroyo de Panoche Grande ("big sugar loaf"), and Arroyo de Panochita ("little sugar loaf").

To the northeast on an eastern branch of El Camino Viejo there were two other very early settlements—the "25" Ranch, located on the Laguna de Tachi Mexican grant near the present Grant house northwest of Hub; and La Libertad, five miles east and half a mile south of the present Burrel. The latter place was occupied by Mexicans as late as 1870. Old poplar trees, which once shaded the *cantina* ("saloon"), mark the site.

Continuing northward other settlements were passed either on the main road or on laterals branching from it, among them Pueblo de las Juntas on the west bank of the San Joaquin River about three miles northeast of the present Mendota, and Rancho de los Californios on the south bank of the San Joaquin River six miles east of Fresno Slough.

Misión del Río de los Santos Reyes

Old Indians still living on the Kaweah River repeat the story told them by their parents of the visit of a pilgrim friar and of his baptizing Indian children. As a result of the preliminary visits of this friar, two attempts were made to construct missions in the San Joaquin Valley, one near the site of Laton on the Kings River, and the other at San Emigdio in the extreme southwestern corner of the valley.

The exact date of the attempted establishment of Misión del Río de los Santos Reyes (Mission of the River of the Holy Kings) near the site of Laton has not yet been determined. However, evidences that work on a large adobe building had been begun at this point were noticed by the first American settlers in the region, and as late as 1852 a huge pile of adobe bricks was seen near the bank of the river. In the '60's only a mound of earth was reported as being still visible at the site.

In the expedition which penetrated the wild San Joaquin Valley thus early for the purpose of Christianizing the Indians was Caleb Strong Merrill, a stone mason who had come to San Diego in 1831 aboard a Boston hide drogher. His services were in demand first at Mission San Diego and then at Monterey. When the decision was made to attempt to establish a mission on the Kings River, Merrill went along to help in the construction of the proposed building. From Mission San Juan Bautista the party proceeded via Pacheco Pass to the Kings River, where a temporary camp was set up. Work on the contemplated mission was pushed to the extent of making a large pile of adobes. The project, however, proved a failure, principally because of the hostile nature of the country.

"The whole valley area near Laton was described as a vast jungle and swamp. The party was never able to approach Tulare Lake. After climbing the highest trees, all they could see in all directions was more trees and a sea of tules. After about three months of unsuccessful work among the Indians . . . . the entire party returned to Monterey."

Pueblo de las Juntas

Pueblo de las Juntas, a rendezvous for adventurers, refugees, and a few pioneers from the Spanish settlements to the west, was one of the very first places in the San Joaquin Valley to be settled by Spaniards and Mexicans. The exact date when it was established will probably never be determined, although indications are that it may have been as early as 1800. "The oldest pioneers interviewed concerning the place have said that it was first an important Indian village, and that when the Indians were taken from it to the mission at San Juan Bautista some of the Spanish returned and occupied the place."

Las Juntas ("junction" or "meeting-place") was located at the confluence of the San Joaquin River and Fresno Slough, but the name may have had reference to the fact that it was a rendezvous for refugees. In the '50's and '60's it had a bad reputation of long standing. Horse-thieving, gambling, and drinking went unchecked, and murder was rife. Murieta and Vásquez and their gangs obtained supplies here where they were safe from the pursuit of American officers. In spite of its tough character a number of Spanish and Mexican families lived at Las Juntas, and in the '70's the population numbered about two hundred and fifty. The Butterfield overland stages passed this way and often stopped at the old Mexican pueblo.

Ash trees, abundant along the banks of the slough, gave the name Fresno to the locality. Two large specimens of this tree grew on the banks of the San Joaquin River at Las Juntas, and for this reason that place also was sometimes called Fresno. When Casa Blanca (now Tranquillity) was built about eighteen miles farther south at the head of Fresno Slough, it, too, was frequently called Fresno City. However, Las Juntas was the first Fresno.

Soon after the railroad was built down the west side of the San Joaquin Valley most of the inhabitants of Las Juntas moved to Firebaugh. By this time Miller and Lux had acquired the land, and the remaining settlers were forced to move.

The tule-thatched houses of brush and mud-brick at old Las Juntas have long since disappeared, and today the site is marked only by a few graves inclosed within a picket fence.

Rancho de los Californios

When things became too hot for the refugees at Las Juntas they retreated across Fresno Slough and the tule swamps to a place which became known as Rancho de los Californios. In this retreat, protected by a dense willow thicket, notorious horse-thieves found themselves secure from the pursuit of the Spanish cavalry. It continued to be a hangout for robbers, murderers, and bandits, who infested the San Joaquin Valley well into the American period. From a log stockade, which was erected about 1862, sallies into the surrounding country were made.

One of the old wooden buildings still stands at Rancho de los Californios, three miles north of the present highway between Kerman and White's Bridge. The adobes on the place were destroyed by the floods of 1862 and 1868. Traces of the old road which crossed the valley to Millerton are also visible.

Old Stage Roads

In early pioneer days the Stockton–Los Angeles Road followed along the base of the Sierra Nevada, with many laterals branching off to the mines in the foothills. The route through Fresno County passed by the sites of the present towns of Reedley, Sanger, and Friant. Today only fragments remain of the old road where pack trains traced the first dim course and where the lumbering prairie schooner later beat out a well-worn trail.

The principal streams along this road were crossed by means of privately owned bridges or ferries. Two detours, Lower and Upper, ran parallel a few miles apart. The Lower Detour crossed the Kings River at Pool's Ferry, settled as early as 1850 or 1851, and designated as one of the two voting precincts when Tulare County was organized in 1852. However, the place has been deserted since 1855. Its approximate location was three miles north of Reedley and half a mile west of the main county road.

Smith's Ferry, established by James Smith in 1855, superseded Pool's and for nineteen years was the most important crossing on Kings River. Because a crossing could be made at no other point along the river during high water, Smith's Ferry remained open to the public after all the others had ceased to operate. Only after the railroad was completed twelve miles to the west did business wane, and in 1874 Smith's Ferry likewise was abandoned. Little remains to mark the site of this once prosperous place—a bit of the old road, beginning near the water's edge on the east bank of the river and extending northeasterly toward the old hotel site, on the brow of the hill; and three ailanthus trees planted in front of the hotel in 1861.

The village of Scottsburg was established at the ferry on the Upper Detour in 1854. It was located on the "76 Ranch," and stood on a knoll in the bottom lands of the Kings River east of the present site of Sanger. Following the devastating flood during the winter of 1861–1862, when the whole town was washed away, a new site was chosen at the foot of the bluff to the northeast. Here again, in the winter of 1867, floods engulfed the settlement. Soon after, however, the town was established on the bluff and rechristened Centerville, the name which it still bears.

The old Stockton – Los Angeles Road also made two crossings of the San Joaquin River, one at Brackman's on the Lower Detour, and the other at Jones's Ferry on the Upper Detour.

The route usually followed by the Butterfield stages during the years 1858–1861 turned off from the Stockton–Los Angeles Road east of Visalia in Tulare County and, passing through Visalia, crossed the country to the Kings River Station, located on the south bank of the Kings River in Kings County. From there, the route ran through Fresno County to Firebaugh's Ferry, located on the west bank of the San Joaquin River approximately where the railroad station of Firebaugh now is. Latta says that two stations were established between Kingston's and Firebaugh's, one being known as the Elkhorn Station, one and one-half miles southeast of Burrel, and the other as Hawthorne's Station, about one mile southeast of the present village of San Joaquin. The Elkhorn Station, operated by John Barker (later a Bakersfield newspaper publisher), was opened up in 1856 and was maintained until after the Butterfield stages had stopped running. Hawthorne's Station was named after its proprietor, who was killed there by the Mason-Henry gang of outlaws in 1865. It was established by the Butterfield Company because of the great distance intervening between Elkhorn Station and Firebaugh's.

During very wet weather, when the river was too high to cross at the Kings River Station, the Butterfield stages followed the old Stockton–Los Angeles Road along the base of the hills to Smith's Ferry. From there they took the road marked out by James Smith especially for the Butterfield stages, crossing the valley fifty miles to Fresno City.

Millerton

Millerton, which started as a mining town in 1850, became the county seat in 1856 when Fresno County was organized. It was located on the south bank of the San Joaquin River in the Sierra Nevada foothills, and was near the southern border of the Mother Lode gold region. The Stockton–Los Angeles Road, sometimes called the Millerton Road, crossed the San Joaquin River at this point. In 1861–1862, floods from the river washed away half of the town, and in 1870 it was swept by fire.

When the Central Pacific Railway was constructed through the San Joaquin Valley in 1874, a new site was selected for the county seat, about twenty-five miles southwest of Millerton. The population of Millerton then moved to the new city, taking their houses with them. Fresno, thus made successor of Millerton, is the largest city in the San Joaquin Valley today. It is located in the midst of a vast agricultural belt, while Millerton lay folded in the hills, a sleeping "ghost town." It has now disappeared under the waters of the artificial lake created by Friant Dam.

Fort Miller

In 1850 the discovery of gold in the Millerton region of the Sierra Nevada foothills attracted a large number of miners, but the Indians in the surrounding hills gave so much trouble that the United States government decided to place a detachment of soldiers there in order to hold the Indians in check. The first post established was known as Camp Barbour, of which the blockhouse still remains, the oldest building in Fresno County. It was at Camp Barbour on April 29, 1851, that one of the eighteen unratified treaties with the Indians was concluded by the United States Commissioner.

In 1852 a second post was established one mile above Millerton on the left bank of the San Joaquin River. It was called Fort Miller, in honor of Major Albert S. Miller, a former officer of the Second Infantry of the United States Army. Fort Miller was evacuated on September 10, 1856, but was regarrisoned in 1863 during the Civil War. It was finally abandoned on October 1, 1864.

The first school in Fresno County was conducted in the hospital building of Fort Miller in the '50's. Almost all of the buildings of the Fort, including the hospital, officers' quarters, noncommissioned officers' quarters, commissary, guardhouse, and kitchen, are still standing—now part of a large cattle ranch. All of these will be submerged when the Friant Dam and Reservoir are constructed.

The Murieta Rocks

So much fiction has been written concerning the young bandit Joaquín Murieta, and so little has been published of an authoritative nature, that it is difficult to state the facts of his career. Francis P. Farquhar says that "to trace step by step the origin and growth of the Joaquín Murieta legend, separating fact from fancy, is perhaps at this late date impossible, even if one were disposed to attempt it. After all, what difference does it make whether he was born in Sonora or in Chile, or whether his *querida* was named Carmela or Rosita? Let us be content with Joaquín as we find him; for the story as it ultimately emerged is a good one, replete with romance, passion, color, and action. It has been novelized, dramatized, poetized; and it will bear doing over again and again, with as much embroidery as authors may choose to indulge in."

"A perusal," continues Farquhar, "of the numerous books of which Joaquín Murieta is the hero indicates that there are two principal versions of the story, distinguished by the name of the heroine. In one she is Rosita; in the other she is Carmela or Carmen . . . . The significance of this distinction is that there were two 'lives' of Murieta which gained currency not long after the bandit's death. All subsequent Murieta narratives, with the exception of Burns' recent book, appear to be derived from one or the other of these versions."

Murieta began his career as outlaw in the spring of 1851, three years after the close of the Mexican War. Mexicans throughout the state secretly flocked to him or befriended him, doubtless believing that he would some day restore their independence. He ravaged all California from the upper Sacramento Valley to the Mexican border. The Sierra Nevada mining regions were also visited on his raids. But his chief stronghold was in the Coast Range twenty miles from the old road followed later by the Butterfield stages, about forty miles northwest of Tulare Lake and sixteen miles north of the present town of Coalinga. Here, in the Arroyo de Cantua, a place of numerous caves and rocks, he lived in a tule-thatched, loopholed adobe fort at the mouth of the creek. Four massive buttes known as Tres Piedras, or Three Rocks, because only three of them are visible from the valley, surrounded the hiding-place, and from this point the lookout could see for miles in all directions across the surrounding treeless plains. From this natural fortress, Murieta and his band of outlaws swooped down upon the unsuspecting and unprotected emigrant trains, robbing and sometimes killing their victims. Retreating to their Cantuan stronghold before a counter-attack could be organized, the robbers were as safe as the birds of prey which made their homes upon the mountain's rocky ramparts.

Finally, in 1853, Murieta, at the age of twenty-one, encountered Captain Love, a ranger, at this place. Farquhar says: "It is reasonably certain . . . . that . . . . Joaquín was killed by Captain Harry Love's posse in 1853, despite rumors persisting for years afterwards that the real Joaquín still lived."

General Grant National Park

Fresno is one of the seven counties of the state in which the *Sequoia gigantea* is found. A small stand of magnificent trees is contained in the General Grant National Park on the southern boundary of the county in the High Sierra. The southern portion of this park is in northern Tulare County. The General Grant, forty feet three inches in diameter, for which the park was named, is one of the most noted of its trees. There are seven smaller sequoia groves in Fresno County, besides the Evans Grove, which contains five hundred trees.

The Converse Basin, once containing thousands of sequoias alleged by some to have been finer than those of the Giant Forest, comprises but a small part of that vast area throughout the Sierra Nevada which was ravaged by the lumber industry during the '60's and '70's. One monarch alone survives of the once glorious assemblage which filled the Converse Basin. This is the Boole Tree, a close competitor of the General Sherman as the largest of all the Big Trees. It was saved by Frank Boole, foreman, for whom it was named.

SOURCES

[Credit is here given for source material, and permission to quote is hereby acknowledged]

Burns, Walter Noble. *The Robin Hood of El Dorado*. Coward McCann, Inc., New York, 1932

Elliott, Wallace W. *History of Fresno County, California*. Wallace W. Elliott, San Francisco, 1882

Fry, Walter, and John R. White. *Big Trees*. Stanford University Press, Stanford University, California, 1930

Joaquín Murieta, the Brigand Chief of California. With Introduction and Notes by Francis P. Farquhar. The Grabhorn Press, San Francisco, 1932

Klette, Ernest. *The Crimson Trail of Joaquín Murieta*. Privately published, Los Angeles, 1928

Latta, F. F. "El Camino Viejo," in *Tulare Daily Times*, 1932

———. "Las Tres Piedras," in *Tulare Daily Times*, 1932

———. "Poso Chané," in *Tulare Daily Times*, 1932

———. "Pueblo de las Juntas," in *Tulare Daily Times*, 1932

———. "Rancho de los Californios," in *Tulare Daily Times*, 1932

———. "San Joaquin Valley Missions," in *Tulare Daily Times*, 1932

McCubbin, J. C. *The Stockton–Los Angeles Stage Road*. Manuscript, 1930.

Ridge, John Rollin. *The Life and Adventures of Joaquín Murieta, the Celebrated Bandit*. 3d ed. F. MacCrellish & Company, San Francisco, 1871

Vandor, Paul E. *History of Fresno County, with Biographical Sketches*. Privately published, Los Angeles, 1919

GLENN COUNTY

Glenn County (named in honor of Dr. Hugh James Glenn) was organized in 1891, when it was separated from Colusa County. Willows is the county seat.

The Swift Adobe

A pile of ruins on Hambright Creek, one and a half miles north of Orland, is all that remains of the adobe built by Granville P. Swift, a pioneer settler who crossed the Plains to Oregon in 1843 and entered California with the Kelsey party in 1844. He served in Sutter's campaign in 1845, participated in the Bear Flag Revolt, and in 1846–1847 served as captain in Frémont's California Battalion. Subsequently he settled at the confluence of Hambright and Stony creeks and amassed considerable wealth by working large numbers of Indians in mines on the Feather River. In 1849, in partnership with Frank Sears, he purchased from J. S. Williams the cattle and brand of the Larkin Grant. Swift soon had vast droves of cattle, herded by Indian vaqueros, and rodeos were held annually, one at the adobe on Stony Creek, and another at an adobe (no longer standing) on what later became the Murdock Ranch west of Willows. Legends of treasure buried at these places have lured the credulous many times to dig and delve there.

Swift moved to Sonoma County in 1854, but his name is perpetuated in Glenn County in Swift's Point, near Hamilton City, a place on the Sacramento River once fordable at low water. The river road from Red Bluff and Shasta City crossed here to points east of the Sacramento.

W. C. Moon and Ezekiel Merritt settled opposite the mouth of Deer Creek in 1845. Hittell says that "Merritt,

Lassen, and W. C. Moon quarried and manufactured a lot of grindstones on Stony Creek in the summer of 1845. When they were finished, they carried them twenty miles on mules to the Sacramento River and loaded them into a canoe and drifted with them down the river, selling them whenever they could."

Monroeville

Monroeville, a village at the mouth of Stony Creek in what is now northeastern Glenn County, was the county seat of Colusa County from 1851 to 1853, before Glenn was separated from Colusa. It was situated on the old Capay Rancho, a grant made to María Josefa Soto, later the wife of Dr. James Stokes of Monterey. Out of this estate Mrs. Stokes gave two leagues of land at the mouth of Stony Creek to Pierson B. Reading in return for his services in locating and mapping the land. A man named Bryant was the first to settle on the rancho lands, where in 1846 he built a house. After the discovery of gold in 1848 other settlers located there, among them being U. P. Monroe, whose ranch and hotel became a popular stopping-place on the road from Colusa to Shasta.

As in most of the Pacific and Middle Western states, county boundaries had scarcely been defined when the quarrel over the location of the county seat began. Monroe, who was an ambitious, aggressive man, determined that the county seat should be established on his land and be named for him. Colusa, with only one house and ten inhabitants, was equally anxious to attain the honor. Monroe's Ranch, therefore, became the active rival of Colusa and the scene of an adroit political conflict. Each side was vigilant and determined. Colusa, perhaps, had one advantage over its rival on Stony Creek in that it already possessed a name, but the primary question was who should first succeed in organizing the county and so capture the county seat.

Monroe at once presented a petition to Moses Bean, a judge in Butte County, requesting that the county be organized and designating Monroe's Ranch as the only polling place for the election of county officers. This procedure was high-handed and illegal, as Bean had no lawful authority to act, but it seemingly carried the day, and Monroeville assumed the rôle of first county seat of Colusa County.

No scramble for county offices followed the election and those chosen could be persuaded only with difficulty to perform their duties. The mines were too attractive and opportunity to acquire princely farm lands was too great to tempt anyone to give his time to the irksome and unremunerative task of running the government.

There was, fortunately, a notable exception, William B. Ide, primary leader of the Bear Flag Revolt in 1846. For a time, Ide performed the duties of the entire list of offices, and was judge, county clerk, auditor, treasurer, coroner, and surveyor.

The county-seat contest continued, however, and in 1853 Colusa finally won the fight. Ambitious, usurping Monroeville was soon deserted even by her founder. Projected avenues were turned into broad furrows and "bearded grain .... nodded in autumnal contentment in places where the founders of the defunct county seat had fondly visioned out church spires and courthouse dome." The name reverted to Monroe's Ranch, and the town site was eventually merged into a seven-hundred-acre farm purchased by Jubal Weston.

Nothing of Monroeville remains today except a trace of the foundation of Monroe's house, which had also served as courthouse, hotel, theater, post office, and saloon. A monument is to be erected in memory of William B. Ide in the cemetery one and a half miles from the old town site.

South of Monroeville, contemporary "paper cities," equally ambitious, arose. Among them were Placer City, about three-quarters of a mile north of Jacinto, where the first school in the county was established; and Butte City, on the east bank of the Sacramento and formerly in Butte County. A historian writing fifty years ago had this to say of the latter place in the early '50's: "Butte City had already run its race, and the spacious and only house of sheet iron and its attractive sign of 'Rest for the Weary and Storage for Trunks' were but ruins." All traces of Placer City have long since been obliterated. Butte City, however, has revived as an agricultural center for that portion of Glenn County east of the river

"The Willows"

Standing out in bold relief from a vast expanse of treeless plains, a clump of willows bordering several springs on Willow Creek, one mile east of the present town of Willows, was the only landmark in early days between the settlements on the river and those in the western foothills. Travelers from Princeton to the hills guided their course by "The Willows."

The Old Glenn Home

The old Glenn home stands in a tangle of trees and shrubbery about fifteen miles northeast of Willows at Jacinto. Dr. Hugh J. Glenn, for whom Glenn County was named, came to California from Missouri in 1849. For a time he worked in the mines and camps on the American River, but in 1853 he located temporarily in what is now Glenn County. After several trips back and forth across the continent he finally returned to settle permanently in California. In 1867 he purchased seven thousand acres of Rancho Jacinto from Isaac Sparks, and in 1868 brought his family from Missouri, establishing them on the present site of the Glenn homestead at Jacinto.

Rancho Jacinto, so named after the original grantee, Jacinto Rodríguez, who obtained the land from the Mexican government in 1844, was added to by Dr. Glenn until in 1874 it totaled fifty-five thousand acres, of which forty-one thousand were planted to wheat. Because of this Dr. Glenn was called the world's "Wheat King." His great holdings are now subdivided into small farms.

SOURCES

[Credit is here given for source material, and permission to quote is hereby acknowledged]

HITTELL, THEODORE H. *History of California.* In 4 vols. N. J. Stone & Company, San Francisco, 1897
IDE, WILLIAM BROWN. *Who Conquered California?* S. Ide, Claremont, New Hampshire, 1882
MCCORNISH, CHARLES DAVIS, and MRS. REBECCA T. LAMBERT. *History of Colusa and Glenn Counties, California.* Historic Record Company, Los Angeles, 1918
ROGERS, JUSTUS H. *Colusa County, Its History Traced from a State of Nature through the Early Period of Settlement and Development to the Present Day.* Privately published, Orland, California, 1891

KERN COUNTY

KERN COUNTY (so called after the Kern River, which Frémont named in honor of Edward M. Kern, topographer of the expedition of 1845–1846) was organized in 1866 from parts of Los Angeles and Tulare counties. Havilah was made the county seat, but it was changed to Bakersfield in 1874.

Garlock's Prehistoric Village

On Black Mountain, about five miles northwest of the village of Garlock, at the edge of the Mojave Desert, are the remains of a prehistoric Indian village, discovered in the '80's. From the nature of these ruins scientists have concluded that no recent tribe of Indians could have erected the village. On the inside of one of the doorways are stone carvings resembling those found on the famous Posten Butte near Florence, Arizona. From this evidence it is believed that the village may have been occupied centuries ago by the same race of men that built the extinct and buried cities of Arizona and Mexico.

In neighboring mountains and valleys there are many evidences of more recent tribes, among the most notable being the painted rocks (pictographs) on the Kern River near Isabella.

Grizzly Gulch

Grizzly Gulch, in northeastern Kern County, about seven miles south of the old mining village of White River (Tailholt), was noted in early days for the number of grizzly bears which infested it. Several prospectors were reported killed or crippled by the beasts, and active mining operations could not be carried on until they had been exterminated. From these circumstances the locality received its name, Grizzly Gulch.

The prevalence of fossil bones of prehistoric animals and of archaeological remains of the Yokuts Indians adds greatly to the interest of this region. South of Grizzly Gulch, and particularly in Rag Gulch and north of the Kern River, marks of an ancient shore line are plainly seen, showing that this was, in past geological ages, the eastern margin of a vast ocean. For miles, the water line may be traced by the remains of shellfish and other sea life, and at Shark Tooth Mountain, north of the Kern River, the bones and teeth of prehistoric sharks exist in great numbers.

An Indian ranchería once existed in Grizzly Gulch a little less than half a mile east of the Woody Road. Hundreds of Indian mortars, many of them deeply worn into the granite through the grinding of acorns and seeds for generations, may still be seen in the bed rock and outcropping granite surrounding the little valley. During the '90's, while prospectors were attempting to mine the flat on which the ranchería had been situated, the digging of a ditch for sluices disclosed the remains of an Indian burial ground. In 1928 three undisturbed graves of great archaeological importance were uncovered at this site.

Passes to the South

"The Tehachapi Mountains form an east and west link at about the 35th parallel, between the southern end of the Sierra Nevadas on the east and the Coast Range on the west. They mark the southern limit (head) of the San Joaquin Valley, which is walled in on three sides by these three mountain groups. South and east lie the Mojave and Colorado deserts. Lieutenant Williamson, who, under orders from the War Department, examined these Tehachapi Mountains in 1853 for purposes of finding the most practical passage for a railway, discovered six more or less available passes through them, of varying degrees of difficulty. Beginning with the most easterly, they were as follows: Walker's Pass (near Freeman); Tehachapi Pass (traversed by the railways); Oak Creek Road (Willow Springs north to Tehachapi); Tejón Pass (original pass of that name, along Cottonwood and Tejón creeks); Canyon de las Uvas (present Tejón Pass); San Emidio Pass (San Emidio Creek to Cuddy Valley).

"A seventh, Humpayamup, is only a southern branch of Walker's, debouching into the desert through Red Rock (?) Canyon. Much confusion has arisen in published accounts, due to the fact that each of three of these names, Walker's, Tehachapi, and Tejón, has been applied to two different passes in succession."

Walker's Pass

One of the pioneer trails to California followed down the Owens River valley through what is now western Inyo County, passing by Owens Lake, and thence through Walker's Pass to the South Fork of the Kern River, and down the South Fork to its junction with the North Fork at Isabella.

There the trail divided, one branch going south by way of Bodfish, Havilah, and Walker's Basin, and then west by several routes to the ferry on the Kern River (for many years called Gordon's Ferry) about five miles northeast of Bakersfield, and the other branch crossing the Kern River near Isabella, passing over the Greenhorn Mountains either to Poso Flat or to Linn's Valley (near Glennville), and then turning north to the White River and Visalia.

In 1834 Joseph Walker, captain of an exploring party, left California by the latter route, via the White River and the Greenhorn Mountains, and in 1843 he followed the same trail in while leading the Chiles emigrant party, the first wagon train to enter California from the East. In 1845 John C. Frémont, on his second expedition into California, sent his main party, led by Joseph Walker, via this route, while he and a few others crossed the Sierra at Donner's Pass. It was on this expedition that Edward Kern mapped the Kern River, which Frémont subsequently named for him.

The Tejón Passes

The pass which at present bears the name of Tejón ("badger") was first penetrated by Pedro Fages, then acting governor of Alta California, in 1772, while pursuing deserters from the Spanish Army. A recently discovered manuscript penned by Fages himself describes his inland expedition from San Diego to San Luis Obispo. Concerning the manuscript, Professor Herbert E. Bolton says that "it is a surprising story of an entirely unknown California expedition, ahead of Anza, from Imperial Valley over the mountains to San Bernardino Valley, thence through Cajón Pass, along the edge of Mojave Desert, through Antelope Valley through a pass into the southern end of San Joaquin Valley, northwest across it to Buena Vista Hills and Lake, and through the mountains to San Luis Obispo, four years before Garcés entered the Valley. . . . . It gives Captain Pedro Fages a distinctive position, hitherto unrecognized, as far-travelling trail blazer, and as pioneer · in the South San Joaquin."

The pass and canyon through which Fages blazed this trail has had various names. Fages himself called it Buena Vista ("beautiful view"). The Spaniards who came later, in their turn, designated the canyon as La Cañada de las Uvas ("the canyon of the grapes"), and it is known today as Grapevine Canyon. The route over the summit, however, is designated on modern maps as Tejón Pass. Professor Bolton suggests that a monument be placed at Castaic Lake, near the summit, in memory of Pedro Fages, the first white man to cross the Tehachapi Mountains by this pass and the first to enter the San Joaquin Valley from the south.

Leaving Grapevine Canyon, Fages traveled about thirty miles northwestward across the southwestern corner of the San Joaquin Valley to the Buena Vista Hills in the Coast

Range, perhaps taking a short cut by way of the low gap at the neck of Wheeler Ridge.

Reaching the foot of the hills on the southwestern shore of Buena Vista Lake (now used as a reservoir by the Miller and Lux interests), Fages found an Indian village, the existence of which is still attested by vast kitchen middens. Across the floor of the valley and about the lake itself Fages found a "labyrinth of lakes and tulares."

"Anyone who has stood even today on this spot and looked off to the east and south will yield ungrudging approval of the name which Fages gave to the same, but more liquid, panorama nearly one hundred and sixty years ago. The survival of Fages' place name here is most significant. Manifestly, Buena Vista Lake, the Buena Vista Hills, and the village at their foot all got their name from the same circumstance." The name has been applied to the lake ever since the earliest maps, and is the oldest Spanish place name in the San Joaquin Valley.

The second Spaniard to enter the San Joaquin Valley from the south was the Franciscan friar, Father Francisco Garcés, in 1776. Garcés left San Gabriel in April of that year and, ascending San Fernando Valley, crossed over the Newhall grade to the vicinity of the present town of Castaic, in Los Angeles County, where he swung northeast over the mountains by a trail running east of the present Ridge Route. Near Hughes Lake on the edge of Antelope Valley he crossed Fages' trail of 1772, and then proceeded north across the valley to Cottonwood Creek, up which he climbed to the pass above. From there he descended into the San Joaquin Valley by way of Tejón Creek. To this pass, fifteen miles to the east of the pass over which Fages had entered the great central valley four years before, rightly belongs the name Tejón.

Hudson's Bay Company trappers came this far south in the '30's, and in the name of the village of Lebec is preserved the memory of Peter Lebec, one of these trappers, who was killed on October 17, 1837, by a grizzly bear which he had shot and wounded near the site of Fort Tejón. The tree near which Lebec died and under which he lies buried stands at the northeast corner of the old Fort Tejón parade grounds, eight miles north of the village of Lebec.

Across the highway from Lebec lies Castaic Lake, "with its waters so blue and its fringe of snow-white salt." Old-timers tell of the massacre here of an entire Indian village by a group of "exasperated white men, of the type that modern lynchers are made of."

Rancho El Tejón

Rancho El Tejón is one of the most interesting and important of all the historic spots in the San Joaquin Valley. Here are the sites of several Indian villages which dated back to prehistoric times. They were occupied by the natives until the last quarter of the nineteenth century. Indians are yet living on Rancho Tejón who were born at one of these old rancherías.

The first historic record of the region was made by Fray Francisco Garcés, who, on his expedition in April 1776, visited and named the Indian village of San Pascual, probably the one located at the mouth of Tejón Creek, later the site of the Los Alamos Butterfield Stage Station. For many years this village was the center for the ancient Indian ceremonies described by Bishop Kip, who visited the place on October 15, 1855: ". . . . It was a wild scene as the glare of the fire fell upon the dancers and a thousand Indians gathered in a circle around them."

General Edward Beale, while Superintendent of Indian Affairs, established a government Indian reservation on Rancho Tejón in the early '50's, erecting stone buildings as headquarters for the agency on the site now occupied by the headquarters of the rancho on Arroyo del Paso. One of these buildings erected in 1856 is still in use as a store. The rancho headquarters are fifteen miles east of the Golden State Highway and are reached over a road which branches off from the main highway about three miles north of Grapevine Station.

The government reservation failed, but General Beale, as owner of Rancho Tejón, encouraged the Indians to remain on the land, employing them as vaqueros and laborers. It is said that when he finally sold the rancho he stipulated that the Indian residents should be allowed to remain and that they should be well treated. To this day many Indians live in the little adobe houses scattered up and down Arroyo del Tejón for a distance of ten miles.

Rancho El Tejón was a grant made on November 24, 1843, to José Antonio Aguirre, a Spanish Basque who was a wealthy trader, and to Ignacio del Valle. The largest Mexican grant in the San Joaquin Valley, it included 97,616 acres of land. It lay in the extreme southeastern corner of the valley, a section largely mountainous, hilly, or rolling. After the failure of the Indian reservation General Beale purchased the rancho from the original grantees and later had it surveyed under his own direction as United States Surveyor-General. The irregularity of the rancho is due to the fact that an attempt was made to include the most desirable lands in the survey.

Rancho Tejón today is but one of the several combined ranchos controlled by the *Los Angeles Times* which constitute El Tejón Ranchos, totaling nearly a quarter of a million acres of cattle range. Other old Mexican land grants, each with an interesting history, are included in this vast domain: Rancho de los Alamos y Agua Caliente, Rancho de Castaic, and Rancho de la Liebre (in Los Angeles County).

Rancho de los Alamos y Agua Caliente was first situated south of Grapevine Canyon in what is now Los Angeles County, but was later "floated" to its present location south of Rancho El Tejón by General Beale after he had purchased the estate from the Aguilar family. Watered by El Arroyo de la Pastoria ("creek of the pasture"), its verdant plateau was used as the government pasture lands during the days of the Indian reservation.

Rancho Castaic, traversed throughout nearly its entire length by the Ridge Route, extends northward from Castaic Lake, near Lebec, to a distance of two miles beyond Grapevine Station. It was granted on November 22, 1843, to José María Covarrubias, a native of France, who came to California as a teacher in 1834 and who later took a prominent part in public affairs. He served as secretary to Governor Pío Pico, and in the autumn of 1849 became a member of the first State Constitutional Convention and later of the state legislature.

The first settler at the mouth of El Arroyo de los Encinos was Samuel A. Bishop, who erected adobe corrals and an adobe house beside a large white oak. Traces of the old adobe are dimly visible today. Bishop did not at first know that he was on the old Mexican land grant, Rancho de Castaic. He later purchased the grant and in 1864 moved to Fort Tejón, thus acquiring possession of the buildings that had cost the government over half a million dollars. Here Bishop lived many years before selling to Colonel R. H. Baker of Los Angeles.

Wild-Flower Gardens

In a description of historic Rancho Tejón one cannot omit mention of the vast wild-flower gardens which each spring fling their gorgeous colors along the upland canyons and mountain meadows and marshal their flowery armies out across the broad valley floor in miles of bloom, stretching north and eastward from the mouth of Grapevine Canyon to the foot of the Tehachapi. During the rainy season, ranging from late February to the first part of May, a continuous succession of color and fragrance lures the flower lover: "the blue of lupines, the sunny yellow of baeria and desert dandelion, the tempered white of creamcups and gilias, the intense orange of poppies, each sort by itself massed acre upon acre." At Arvin, in the heart of the valley display, an annual wild-flower festival is held in March or April, depending on the season. The little hamlet of Weed-patch, "somnolent amidst the glory of her wild flowers," is another signpost to this, one of Nature's most remarkable wild gardens.

Fort Tejón

Romantic, alluring in its sylvan setting, old Fort Tejón stands amid a grove of ancient oaks and sycamores beside the winding mountain stream known on modern maps as Grapevine Creek (Arroyo de las Uvas). It was established in 1854 as a United States Army outpost to protect the region from the Indians, and became quite important in the early days of the American occupation.

In 1858 the Fort became a station on the Butterfield Overland Mail Route, when six-horse stages covered the distance between St. Louis and San Francisco in twenty-three days. Soldiers from the Fort went out to meet the stages and escorted them through the pass, where protection from Indians and bandits was needed. The post, as a military station, was abandoned on September 11, 1864, and the buildings fell into the possession of Samuel A. Bishop, who had acquired the land from the heirs of the grantee of Rancho Castaic, on which they were located.

The main walls of the old adobe fort, fairly well preserved, have been covered by an incongruous galvanized iron roof. Near by is another adobe covered by a modern wooden roof. This once served as the officers' quarters. On Armistice Day in 1923 the Bakersfield Chapter of the D.A.R. placed a bronze tablet at old Fort Tejón, which is now owned by the State of California.

The Tehachapi Passes

From Bakersfield, a road leads across the Sierra Nevada to the Mojave Desert, by way of Tehachapi Pass. Tehachapi is an Indian word, the meaning of which is uncertain, but Powers, in his Tribes of California, asserts that it was named for a now extinct tribe of Indians who once lived in the pass. Tradition gives the meaning "land of plenty of acorns and good water" to the name, and the abundance of artesian water and sturdy oaks seems to justify the interpretation.

The summit of the Sierra is reached just beyond the little town of Tehachapi, and from there the road descends into the Desert of the Mojave. The first white man to go through the Tehachapi region was Father Garcés, in 1776. On this expedition Garcés crossed the mountains from the south via Cottonwood and Tejón creeks, and penetrated into the San Joaquin Valley as far north as the White River, passing en route the present site of Bakersfield. Retracing his steps he crossed the Sierra into the Mojave Desert. His route varied considerably from that followed by the present state highway and the railroad. Instead of going up Tehachapi Creek, Garcés reached Tehachapi Valley via Rancho Tejón and Cummings Valley, where he turned south into the desert, probably by way of Oak Creek Pass.

Historians have not yet determined which of the passes through the Tehachapi Mountains Jedediah S. Smith traversed in finding his way into the San Joaquin Valley in 1827. Whether he went by way of one of the passes which have borne the name of Tejón or by one of the Tehachapi passes, no record has yet disclosed.

Other trappers and hunters went this way from time to time. John C. Frémont, on his way out of California in April 1844, went into the Mojave Desert by way of Tehachapi Creek and Oak Creek Pass, called Tehachapi Pass until the building of the railroad in 1876, when the name was transferred to the present Tehachapi Pass. Later the old trail and wagon road used by the early emigrants followed closely along the trail taken by Frémont through the original Tehachapi Pass (now Oak Creek Pass). Frémont himself called this Walker's Pass.

This became an important stage road from Los Angeles to Havilah when the Kern River mines were centers of activity during the '60's. Its importance continued during the early '70's, as it was the route between San Fernando and Caliente, which was at that time the southern terminus of the railroad under construction down the San Joaquin Valley from Stockton.

The first permanent settlers came to Tehachapi, in Tehachapi Valley, about 1854. Gold in the China Hill placers brought a large number of miners to the region, but it was not until 1870 that a post office was established there. Before this, the settlers had to get their mail from Los Angeles, about one hundred miles away, whenever they or their neighbors went there for provisions.

The original town of Tehachapi was about three and one-half miles east of the present village, which supplanted it when the railroad was built in 1876. At the first location, still known as Old Town, only a few dilapidated wooden buildings remain. The entire countryside is made fragrant each spring with the scent of millions of fruit blossoms, for in hidden nooks and upon sunny plateaus, often lying more than three thousand feet above sea-level, orchards of prize-winning apples and pears flourish.

San Emigdio

In San Emigdio Canyon there remain to this day the ruins of the San Emigdio Mission Station. Some time before 1824 an attempt was made by the Fathers of Mission Santa Barbara to establish a San Joaquin Valley outpost here. "Had the attempt been successful," says Latta, "San Emigdio would undoubtedly have developed along the lines of San Antonio de Pala," in San Diego County.

The stone foundation for a church, thirty by sixty feet, is still in evidence, but it is not definitely known whether work was ever started on the walls. Ruins of three buildings actually brought to completion still remain. The walls of the structure probably intended for the living quarters of the friars also stood as late as 1930. This latter building "was occupied as late as 1870 by Alexis Godey, noted plainsman and guide, who accompanied Frémont on several of his trips to California." Two other buildings were erected a hundred yards to the west, one being used as a blacksmith shop and the other as living quarters.

For many years these old mission adobes served as headquarters for Rancho San Emigdio, which was granted to José Antonio Dominguez in the summer of 1842. Dominguez died in 1843 or 1844 and his son, Francisco Dominguez, thereupon fell heir to the rancho. Don Francisco, however, did not occupy the rancho because of its remoteness, and he had the cattle removed to a location where they would be safer from Indian attacks. On November 29, 1851, John C. Frémont bought a half-interest in Rancho San Emigdio. Later

Alexis Godey obtained possession, probably through the influence of Frémont; at any rate Frémont's name was used to secure perfection of title for Godey.

Among the scattered boulders of Arroyo de San Emigdio, several miles from its mouth and three miles north of the ruins of the old mission station, is the site of the Mexican village of San Emigdio. Remnants of several adobe buildings still stand in this once beautiful spot, where rows of poplar and cottonwood trees shaded the homes of the Mexicans and Indians who lived there, while streams of water running in many directions irrigated their tiny vegetable gardens.

Between the pueblo site and the mission ruins are the buildings of the present headquarters of Rancho San Emigdio, now owned by the Kern County Land Company. The house erected by Godey, into which he moved in 1885, is still standing. In the orange grove back of the present superintendent's residence is a rambling structure built about an old San Emigdio schoolhouse, which was moved from the mouth of the neighboring Arroyo del Pleitito in 1904.

On the west fork of San Emigdio Creek near the head of the arroyo stands the Mill Potrero, on the site of the first steam sawmill in this part of the San Joaquin region. Here Joseph Gale milled lumber for Fort Tejón and other early neighborhood improvements, bringing the lumber down from the pine forests on the slopes of San Emigdio Peak two miles north of the mill. Joseph Gale's homestead, where he settled in 1858, was at the mouth of Grapevine Canyon, at the site of an Indian rancheria, four hundred yards north of Grapevine Station. His house and orchard have disappeared. His daughter married John Fletcher Cuddy, who came to Fort Tejón with the soldiers, and they settled in Cuddy Valley above the mouth of Uvas Creek, where their first log cabin still stands.

El Camino Viejo

The western San Joaquin Valley retains much of the atmosphere of the early Indians and Spaniards. Even today the sites of hundreds of ancient rancherías may be identified, and there are many old Spaniards still living along the dry creeks and among the oak-covered hills bordering El Camino Viejo who remember the location of every water hole along its course. The very names of those numerous arroyos and *aguajes* ("water holes") suggest a significant but little-known Spanish-Californian background.

El Camino Viejo of the Spanish period, which followed the prehistoric Indian trails and the still older paths of antelope as they wandered from *aguaje* to *aguaje* over hill and gully, through tule swamps and plains of blistering alkali, was used chiefly by Spanish and Mexican refugees. They passed over it unobserved from San Pedro to San Antonio (now east Oakland)—horse thieves and cattle rustlers, following their nefarious trade in comparative safety; bandits of the '40's and the '50's; and even the daring young lovers Ramón Solorcono and his beautiful bride, who, in 1823, fled over this path in a creaking carreta, while agents of the bride's irate father followed in a fruitless chase all the way from Chile to Fort Ross. Descendants of the Solorconos still live in Delano, Kern County.

For eight months of the year El Camino Viejo crossed a desert waste, to be traveled only when unavoidable; but in springtime it wound through one vast wild-flower garden, where every arroyo flowed with abundant, crystal-clear water. Beyond El Arroyo de San Emigdio, the old road passed a second camp site at the sink of El Arroyo de Armargosa ("bitter water"), located southwest of Buena Vista Lake at a spot occupied until the late '80's by an ancient adobe. At Pelican Island, one and a half miles from the normal shore of the lake, relics of an Indian camp and burial ground have been uncovered. Composed largely of the shells of fresh-water mussels, this island mound also contained dozens of artifacts and other materials of archaeological value. The island has been occupied by a cattle camp of the Miller and Lux Company for a number of years.

On El Camino Viejo, twenty miles to the northwest of Armargosa, was La Brea, a site now occupied by the village of Asphalto, five miles east of McKittrick. Many bones of prehistoric animals have been taken from the asphalt deposits at this point. Another three miles to the northwest was Aguaje de Santa María, while still farther on was El Arroyo de los Temblores ("earthquake"), where were found living springs said to have first issued from the canyon floor as a result of a severe earthquake. An old adobe house surrounded by giant fig trees still stands on Rancho Temblores.

Beyond the Creek of the Earthquake, El Camino Viejo crossed El Arroyo de Chico Martínez, near the mouth of which rise glistening white chalk-like bluffs and hills which may be seen for miles across the plains. The arroyo was named for Chico Martínez, a Spanish pioneer in this region, who was known as "king of the mustang-runners" because of his skill in herding wild horses into the corrals built for their capture at Aguaje Mesteño ("mustang springs") and elsewhere.

Traversing an elevated and broken country, El Camino Viejo wound along from El Arroyo de Chico Martínez to El Arroyo de los Carneros ("wether sheep"). Two chimney-like rocks rising eight hundred feet above the valley piloted travelers to this water hole. Among these rocks are caves covered with Indian pictographs. Passing successively the Aquajes de en Media ("middle water"), del Diablo ("of the Devil"), and Arroyo de Matarano, the road now ran two miles east of the Point of Rocks, known to the Spanish as Las Tinajas ("tanks") de los Indios, evidently the site of an important Indian encampment. Rock formations here acted as natural reservoirs to hold the water which collected during the winter rains. These cisterns bear evidence of having been improved by the Indians, for deeply worn steps cut into the rock lead down to the water. Indian mortars, rock writings, and other evidence that this was a prehistoric camp site have been found about the rocks.

The next water hole to be reached was at a second Aguaje de la Brea ("tar springs") near the present Paso Robles–Wasco Highway three miles southwest of the Devil's Den service station. The oil which covered the water of this spring doubtless deceived many a thirsty wayfarer, who passed it by thinking it only a pool of oil.

At Alamo Solo ("lone cottonwood"), three and a half miles north of La Brea, El Camino Viejo forked, a branch going northeast four miles to Alamo Mocho ("trimmed cottonwood") and thence on to several early Spanish settlements on the west banks of Tulare Lake, Fresno Slough, and the San Joaquin River. The main road continued northward to Poso de Chané and thence to San Antonio. At Alamo Solo, probably the most unfailing water hole on the entire west side of the valley, there was at one time an Indian encampment which covered approximately one hundred acres.

The Beale Memorial

The Beale Memorial Library was given to the city of Bakersfield by Mrs. Mary E. Beale in memory of her husband, General Edward F. Beale. It is located on the northwest corner of Chester Avenue and Seventeenth Street. A bronze tablet in the Library reads: "Edward Fitzgerald Beale, an Explorer in the West, a Founder of California, a Hero of the Mexican War."

In 1852 Edward Beale was made Superintendent of

Indian Affairs for California and Nevada. He at once initiated a policy of honest and humane dealings with the Indians. He also employed them on his ranch, where they were always kindly treated at his hands.

Edward Beale "deserves to be classed with Kit Carson and others as a pathfinder of the West." He was famous for his exploit in reaching San Diego with Kit Carson after the Battle of San Pascual, to warn Stockton of General Kearny's dangerous situation. He was the first to carry California gold to the East, after the discovery of 1848. He explored mountain passes, surveyed routes, and built roads over them, and in 1861 he was appointed Surveyor-General of California and Nevada. He also acquired the extensive Rancho El Tejón, south of Bakersfield, to which he retired after the Civil War.

Beale, who was an enthusiastic advocate of the camel as a means of transportation across the deserts of the Southwest, brought the first caravan to California, a trying journey of more than twelve hundred miles, taking from June 1857 to the following January. This feat proved beyond a doubt the great endurance of the animals. After crossing the Colorado River (where Beale proved that camels can swim), the caravan was driven to Fort Tejón, where some of the animals remained for more than a year.

The camel experiment, however, proved to be a failure, although the animals were used to a limited extent for about two years. Dislike of the animals and lack of understanding in their care and management, the Civil War, and, finally, the coming of the railroad, all combined to bring about the ultimate abandonment of the project. In 1863 the camels were sold at auction, and were soon dispersed to different parts of the country, gradually disappearing altogether. Rumors were long current that descendants of the original camel corps were occasionally encountered upon the deserts, but the only physical evidence of them today is the skeleton of one of the animals preserved in the Smithsonian Institution.

Butterfield Stage Stations

Following along the old Stockton–Los Angeles Road, the Butterfield stages rumbled back and forth through the Cañada de las Uvas and up the southern San Joaquin Valley on their periodical trips between Los Angeles and San Francisco, during the years from 1858 to 1861. Most of the stations along the way have long since disappeared, and little remains today even to indicate their sites. Through Kern County one may trace the trail by the following names: Fort Tejón, Sink or Sinks of the Tejón, Kern River Slough, Gordon's Ferry, Willow Springs, and Coyote Springs.

The Sinks of the Tejón, called Agua de los Alamos, or Los Alamitos by the Mexicans, was located at the mouth of Tejón Creek. Here, where the water of the arroyo sinks into the dry sands, there was a perpetual spring, long a gathering-place of the Indians. From 1858 to 1861 it was an important station for the Butterfield stages. Several buildings, including a barn, hostlers' quarters, and a combined general store, drug store, and post office, were erected. This site is marked today by a well, watering troughs for cattle, and a few stunted cottonwoods.

Continuing north past the substation at Kern River Slough (where horses were changed), the old stage road crossed the Kern River at Gordon's Ferry (the Kern River Station), about five miles northeast of Bakersfield near the foot of the China Grade. No remnant of the Kern River Station remains today.

According to Banning, the next station was located at Posey (Poso) Creek. To the northwest was Willow Springs. This place had a bad reputation because of several murders

which had been committed there, and weird tales developed around it—of the white ox which came to the spring to drink and then mysteriously disappeared; of the possum which hid at the watering trough disturbing the flow of water in an uncanny manner; and many others.

Six miles due north over very rough country was the station at Coyote Springs, located in a branch of the barren Grizzly Gulch where there was a good spring of water. Marks of the old stage road may yet be seen and parts of it are still in use.

William H. Brewer, April 14, 1863, described the route from Tule River to the Coyote Station thus: "The road this day was through a desolate waste. . . . . The soil was barren and, this dry year, almost destitute of vegetation. A part of the way was through low barren hills. . . . . We stopped at a miserable hut, where there is a spring, and a man keeps a few cattle." In stagecoach days a barn and a cabin served the needs of travelers at this point.

Rose Station, about four miles north of the present Grapevine Station and two miles east of the Golden State Highway, was an important stopping-place for travel between Bakersfield and Los Angeles during the late '60's and early '70's. According to Mr. Earl Rowland, Director of the San Joaquin Pioneer Museum, all that remained of the old Rose Station buildings in the summer of 1946 were a portion of a wall of the adobe station house erected in 1876 by William B. Rose, the lean-to of the barn across the road, and the old corrals.

The history of the Rose Station goes back to 1857 when the first building was erected at the sink of Arroyo del Rancho Viejo or Arroyo de los Encinos (Live Oak Creek), two hundred yards southeast of the present adobe building. The place was first known as Rancho Canoa ("trough"), and was operated by W. W. Hudson and James C. Rosemeier. William B. Rose and J. J. López purchased the station in 1872. The overland "coaches and six" often stopped at the place, the site now marked only by a mound of earth, one hundred yards south of the barn.

Keysville

Kern River, with towering granite walls, banks lined with brilliant green, and "deep-throated roar," is the gateway to one of California's most fascinating mountain regions. Here, in this stupendous natural setting, romance, comedy, and tragedy were enacted during one of California's most important gold rushes.

Robert Glass Cleland says of the discovery of gold on Kern River and of its importance to Los Angeles and southern California:

"Perhaps the most serious drawback to the material development of the south was its deplorable lack of money . . . . and under such a handicap economic progress was necessarily slow. . . . . In 1855 gold was discovered in considerable quantities on the Kern River. This at once attracted miners from the entire State, and led to a rush of no mean proportions. The southern California merchants were naturally jubilant over this event in which they saw an opportunity of reaping some of the rich harvest their San Francisco, Stockton and Sacramento rivals had previously monopolized."

The first town to spring up in this new field was known as Keysville, after Richard Keys, who had opened up a mine likewise named for him. The town was situated in a semi-circular cove of the Greenhorn Mountains at the edge of a rocky gulch, and its few stores were scattered about the middle of this flat. There were no streets and the dwelling houses went straying up the slope in a most informal way.

Keysville was the scene of gambling resorts and gunmen

as wild as in any of the larger camps in the north. The surrounding mountains, too, were wild in the extreme. In 1856 the settlers, expecting an attack from Indians who were waging war in neighboring counties, erected a rude fort on the sage-covered hill just outside of town. The Indians, however, never came and the fort was never used, but a vestige of the walls and trenches may be traced there today.

The passage of time and the depredations of vandals have well-nigh obliterated Keysville, and less than a half-dozen of the old roughly hewn board houses, with their "shake" roofs, remain. The largest of these is still occupied by descendants of its original builder, notorious gunmen, who still wage feudal war on a neighboring family, much after the manner of Kentucky mountaineers.

Quartzburg and Whiskey Flat—Rivals

In 1860, "Lovely" Rogers, a miner from Keysville, was out looking for a lost mule. In a gulch, eight miles north of home, he found his mule and also a magnificent piece of quartz where the famous Big Blue Mine was later located. That was the beginning of Quartzburg and of its rival, Whiskey Flat, later known as Kernville. The rush to the gulches and mountain sides around "Lovely's" mine soon resulted in the opening of a dozen quartz mills, and the region became the richest in the state during that period.

On a small ledge above the river the town of Quartzburg sprang up. Water from the mine pumps irrigated the trees and gardens and alfalfa patches and a homey atmosphere clung about the place from the beginning. Moreover, the influential citizens of Quartzburg believed in local option, and when an attempt was made to start a bar in town that unwelcome feature was forced to move a mile down the river to a place thereafter known as Whiskey Flat.

Kernville eventually became the most important town in the Kern River mining region, but for several years it had a rival in the little village up the river. If one tired of the quiet, orderly Quartzburg, it was but a short walk along the river bank to the bars and gambling resorts of Whiskey Flat; and, "if the iniquity of the latter town outraged him, he could find more congenial atmosphere among the devotees of prohibition in the former town."

By 1879 the Kern River region had reached its height of prosperity, and most of the mines around Quartzburg had been acquired by Senator John P. Jones, who consolidated them into the Big Blue. Soon after this, the Senator met with reverses and the mine closed down, thus shutting off the water supply for Quartzburg's houses and gardens. The former were gradually torn down and carted away, while the latter were left to run wild or die. Today, two lonely chimneys are all that remain to remind one of Quartzburg's past.

Kernville, too, "quiet, shady, somnolent," dreams of vanished glory and romance, while the great trees keep watch above the empty streets and the quaint houses, inviting the traveler to linger a while in this realm of the long ago.

Havilah, "Where There Is Gold"

Havilah, named by Asbury Harpending, a man who became involved in a Civil War plot to prey on San Francisco shipping for the benefit of the Confederate cause, was the fourth town opened up in the Kern River country. It produced a high grade of ore, which attracted miners from all over the state. Havilah was already quite a populous town when Kern County was created, April 2, 1866, and was chosen as the county seat.

Soon after 1879, however, the mines in Kern Canyon became exhausted and the population moved down from the hill regions to the valley, where railroads were already being constructed and where agriculture was taking the place of mining. Meanwhile the county seat had been changed from Havilah in the hills to Bakersfield in the valley.

Havilah has a population of about twoscore today, while Bakersfield numbers over twenty-six thousand. But, although little more than memories, these former cities of the Sierra —Keysville, Quartzburg, Kernville, and Havilah—played a tremendous rôle in the building of the greater and more enduring cities of the Southland at their doors.

Forgotten Camps of the Piute Mountains

High in the Piute Mountains above the Mojave Desert, in a land of singular charm and rest, lies isolated Kelso Valley surrounded by high peaks and primeval forests of pine and fir. This almost forgotten outpost of Kern County's feverish mining activities of the '60's, which have been replaced today by the more placid industries of small cattle ranches, "constitutes one of the few remaining frontier sections in southern California."

Eight miles north of the center of the valley is the site of Sageland, once a flourishing mining camp, now marked only by a lonely cemetery. Ascending the mountain more than three thousand feet above the floor of Kelso Valley is an old ox trail over the St. John Grade which defies all attempts of modern high-powered cars to climb it. Five miles to the south a narrow private road has been constructed up a steep and winding trail past the Dearborn Mine, terminating at the Gwynne Mine at the summit.

Descending to Landers Meadow, one reaches the site of Claraville, once the metropolis of the region and conceding a superiority of population only to Havilah and Kernville, in the lower mountains to the northwest. In all other matters Claraville had "all the concomitants of the proverbial mining camps." The dilapidated ruin of one building marks its site today.

Of all the mines in the region, the Bright Star, about six or seven miles north of Claraville, was the richest. It was owned by three brothers, who finally dissipated the vast fortune in gold taken from the mine, causing its collapse. The passing of the Bright Star "marked the beginning of a decline for the whole district. Abandoned by the hordes of miners, Piute Mountain has reverted to wilderness."

SOURCES

[Credit is here given for source material, and permission to quote is
hereby acknowledged]

ALBRIGHT, GEORGE LESLIE. "Official Explorations for Pacific Railroads, 1853–1855," in *University of California Publications in History,* Vol. XI (October 1921). University of California Press, Berkeley, 1921

BANNING, CAPTAIN WILLIAM, and GEORGE HUGH BANNING. *Six Horses.* The Century Company, New York, 1930

BOLTON, HERBERT EUGENE. "In the South San Joaquin Ahead of Garcés," in *California Historical Society Quarterly,* X, No. 3 (September 1931), 211–219

BONSAL, STEVEN. *Edward Fitzgerald Beale, A Pioneer in the Path of Empire, 1822–1903.* G. P. Putnam's Sons, New York, 1912

BREWER, WILLIAM H. *Up and Down California in 1860–1864.* Edited by Francis P. Farquhar. Yale University Press, New Haven, 1930

CLELAND, ROBERT GLASS. *A History of California: The American Period.* The Macmillan Company, New York, 1922

FRÉMONT, J. C. *The Exploring Expedition to the Rocky Mountains, Oregon and California.* 1st ed., 1847. George H. Derby & Company, Buffalo, 1849

GIFFORD, E. W., and W. EGBERT SCHENCK. "Archaeology of the Southern San Joaquin Valley, California," in *University of California Publications in American Archaeology and Ethnology,* XXIII, No. 1 (1926), 1–122

GRAY, A. A. "Camels in California," in *California Historical Society Quarterly,* IX, No. 4 (December 1930), 299–317

HARPENDING, ASBURY. *The Great Diamond Hoax.* The James H. Barry Company, San Francisco, 1913

JOHNSON, HENRY WARREN. "Where Did Frémont Cross the Tehachapi Mountains in 1844?" in *Annual Publications of the Historical Society of Southern California*, XII, Part IV (1927), 363–
373

JOHNSTON, PHILIP. "When the Kern Bore Gold," in *Touring Topics*,
XIX, No. 11 (November 1927), 26–28, 36–37

——. "Beyond the Gray Mountains," in *Touring Topics*, XX, No. 8
(August 1928), 24–26

KIP, RIGHT REV. WILLIAM INGRAHAM. *The Early Days of My Epis-
copate*. Thomas Whittaker, New York, 1892

LATTA, F. F. "San Joaquin Primeval—Archaeology," in *Tulare
Times*, 1931

——. "San Joaquin Primeval—Spanish," in *Tulare Times*, 1932

LESLEY, LEWIS B. (editor). *Uncle Sam's Camels*. Harvard University Press, Cambridge, 1929

MILLER, THELMA B. *History of Kern County, California*. 2 vols.
The S. J. Clarke Publishing Company, Chicago, 1929

MORGAN, WALLACE M. *History of Kern County*. Historic Record
Company, Los Angeles, 1914

POWERS, STEPHEN. "Tribes of California," in *Contributions to North
American Ethnology*. Vol. III. Department of the Interior, Government Printing Office, Washington, D.C., 1877

SAUNDERS, CHARLES FRANCIS. *The Southern Sierras of California*.
Houghton Mifflin Company, Boston and New York, 1923

WILLIAMSON, ROBERT S. "Report of Explorations in California for
Railroad Routes," in *Explorations and Surveys for a Railroad
Route to the Pacific*. Vol. V (1853)

KINGS COUNTY

KINGS COUNTY (named for the river which was called
El Río de los Santos Reyes, "River of the Holy Kings," in
honor of the Three Wise Men, by a Spanish explorer, probably Gabriel Moraga, in 1805) was organized in 1893 from
territory set off from Tulare County. Hanford was made its
county seat.

Tulare, a Vanished Lake

Tulare Lake was discovered in 1772 by Pedro Fages,
who called the vast marsh lands of the San Joaquin Valley
Los Tulares ("the place of rushes"). Chapman says that
as early as 1804 Father Juan Martín of Mission San Miguel
crossed the Coast Range into the San Joaquin Valley, penetrating as far as an Indian village on Lake Tulare. Again
Chapman says that "in October 1814 a fresh search for a
mission site in the tulares was made. The commander of
the expedition was a sergeant (Juan Ortega?) whose name
does not appear. The account comes from Father Juan
Cabot, who was a member of the party. They went from
San Miguel to Lake Tulare." Crossing that body of water
by way of the Alpaugh sand ridge to where there was a
large Indian village, "they got into some difficulties when
they attempted to serve as peacemakers between two war-
ring tribes. In a 'battle' with one of them the Spaniards
lost two horses and the Indians one old woman. Peace was
restored, and the party went on to the vicinity of Visalia.
On their return they crossed Kings River, and made their
way to San Miguel by a more northerly route than that by
which they had come."

Tulare Lake comprises the natural drainage area in the
valley for the Kings, the Tule, and other rivers. According
to government surveys the lowest point in the bed of Tulare
Lake is 175 feet above sea-level. During the highest water
on record the water level reached was 220 feet above sea-
level. In 1865, when its waters covered the present site of
the town of Corcoran, it was thirty-five miles wide and sixty
miles long. Its maximum depth has never been more than
forty-five feet. Sloughs fed a swamp area much larger than
the actual lake. Streams which formerly flowed into the
lake have gradually been drained for irrigation purposes, and
the entire area has been farmed and grain and cotton have
been grown on the land for the past ten years.

The Cross Creek Stage Station

A stage station known as the Head of Cross Creek was
established at Cross Creek in 1856. The site is about four
miles northwest of Goshen in Tulare County and in stagecoach days was the halfway point between Visalia and the
Kings River Station at Whitmore's Ferry. After the coming of the Butterfield stages in 1858 the station was called
Cross Creek Station. Similar to the other stations of this
section, the Cross Creek post consisted of a small board-and-
batten barn and a cabin of the same construction for the use
of the hostlers, generally two in number.

During the drought of 1864 Peter Van Valer built a
toll bridge over Cross Creek. At the time it was the only
bridge between Visalia and Stockton. Today the site of that
early structure, six and one-half miles northeast of Hanford,
is marked by a large mulberry tree beside the old stage road.
Planted about 1870, the tree stands on a spot which is now
on the extreme eastern edge of Kings County but which
was in Tulare County until 1893.

Kingston, a "Ghost City"

Kingston, a "ghost city" on the south bank of the Lower
Kings River eight and one-half miles northwest of Hanford,
was founded in 1856 at Whitmore's Ferry, which had been
put into operation in 1854 by L. A. Whitmore. After 1858
the town became a stopping-place for the Butterfield stages,
which established a regular route through the San Joaquin
Valley by way of Kingston and Whitmore's Ferry (the
Bliss Ferry in later years) after leaving the old Stockton–
Los Angeles Road at a point east of Visalia.

A toll bridge superseded the ferry in 1873, and until
quite recently its piers could still be seen near the river bank,
about a quarter of a mile below the Santa Fe railroad bridge
at Laton. On the evening of December 26, 1873, before the
toll gates of the bridge were yet in place, Tiburcio Vásquez
and his bandit gang made a bold raid on the little town of
Kingston. They bound thirty-nine men and robbed three
stores before the alarm could be spread, when they fled
across the new bridge to swift horses waiting in a corral on
the north side of the river and made good their escape. But
not before two of the bandits and a horse were mortally
wounded.

All that remains of the town today is the black walnut
trees that stood in front of the old stage barn, beside a little-
frequented dirt road one-half mile west of the Hanford–
Laton–Fresno Highway.

The Rhoads Adobe

One of the oldest houses still in use in the central San
Joaquin Valley is a long low adobe with casement windows
of Spanish design which stands beneath the shade of immense oaks and blue gums on the Rhoads Ranch two miles
north of Lemoore. It was built in 1857 by Daniel Rhoads,
who arrived in California in 1846, having come over the
Oregon Trail with the caravan of pioneers from which the
Donner party separated to take the fateful Hastings Cut-Off,
later becoming snowbound in the High Sierra. In February
1847 Dan Rhoads became a member of the first relief party,
which in the face of untold hardships and even death left
Johnson's Ranch to go to the rescue of the starving emigrants at Donner Lake. Much of the material used by Bancroft for his account of the Donner tragedy was drawn from
a manuscript prepared by Daniel Rhoads.

Carefully preserved, and containing some relics of pioneer days, the old adobe is now opened to the public at

certain stated times. Except for the roof, which is of modern construction, the house has remained unchanged since its original owners were laid to rest in the mausoleum erected by Daniel Rhoads a quarter of a mile from his home.

Many evidences of the industry and ingenuity of its builder may still be seen about the old dwelling. Picturesque remnants of footbridges across the near-by slough indicate where he obtained the clay from which the Indians, under his supervision, fashioned the eighteen-inch adobe bricks which went into the construction of the house. Of the other ranch buildings, all made of lumber which Rhoads laboriously freighted from Stockton—a trip of two weeks— only the barn, with its mangers of hand-wrought timbers, remains. The carriage shed with double hand-hewn doors, the huge millstone which once was used to grind grain into meal, the smoke-house, and the wine room, its windows stoutly barred with willow to protect its contents from the Indian dependents who once sunned themselves along the wall outside, and, not far away, an ancient Indian sweat hole, the "medicine house" of the Diggers—these are some of the reminders of that busy pioneer California homestead, telling a vivid story of its past.

Evidences of thrift and industry are also preserved in the aged trees about the place—stately Australian blue gums and tall cypress trees planted by Rhoads himself; black old olive trees and a gnarled and twisted pear; a vineyard planted from cuttings of mission grape vines—these still flourish amid the forty native oaks from which the present house derived its name of "El Adobe de los Robles."

An Adobe Trading-Post

On the west shore of Tulare Lake an adobe trading-post was established in 1870 by Cox and Clark. As it was the only building on that side of the lake at the time, it served as a landing-place for the lake boats and as a trading-center for the Indians. The site of the old post is three miles south of Kettleman City on the proposed state highway from Yosemite to Morro. About three miles north of Kettleman City is the site of another adobe known as the Vaca dugout, built in 1863 by Juan Perría and Pablo Vaca. This was a vaquero headquarters, never a boat-landing.

Both of these buildings were on the eastern branch of El Camino Viejo, which left the main road at Alamo Solo, a camp site about twenty miles to the south of the Cox and Clark adobe. Alamo Mocho ("trimmed cottonwood") was another camp site on this road and was located just south of Kettleman Hills within a hundred yards of the present Hanford–Paso Robles Highway. Here a large cottonwood stood, serving as a landmark for wayfarers. The story told of the naming of the camp site is that a traveler along the road, needing forage for his cattle, trimmed the cottonwood of all its foliage. The tree has long since disappeared and the spot where it stood is now part of an extensive cattle ranch.

At the mouth of El Arroyo de las Garzas ("herons") a camp on the western branch of El Camino Viejo was located. It was here that Dave Kettleman first settled.

The Mussel Slough Tragedy Oak

The Tragedy Oak, six and one-half miles northwest of Hanford and one-half mile east of the Grangeville–Hardwick Highway, marks the site of the old homestead built by Dick Brewer in 1872. It was here that the first shooting in the Mussel Slough Tragedy occurred, an episode during the warfare between the early settlers and the railroad agents in 1880. Five settlers and one railroad agent were killed in that encounter in less than one minute, and a second railroad agent was killed an hour later. Frank Norris, in *The Octopus,* has drawn a somewhat exaggerated picture of this warfare.

SOURCES

[Credit is here given for source material, and permission to quote is hereby acknowledged]

BANNING, CAPTAIN WILLIAM, and GEORGE HUGH BANNING. *Six Horses.* The Century Company, New York, 1930

BOLTON, HERBERT EUGENE. "In the South San Joaquin Ahead of Garcés," in *California Historical Society Quarterly,* X, No. 3 (September 1931), 211–219

BRAGG, WILLIAM F. *Old Adobe Home Built Seventy-one Years Ago, Standing at Lemoore.* Manuscript, 1928

CHAPMAN, CHARLES E. *A History of California: The Spanish Period.* The Macmillan Company, New York, 1923

HOYLE, M. F. *Crimes and Career of Tiburcio Vásquez. Evening Free Lance,* Hollister, California, 1927

LATTA, F. F. "El Camino Viejo," in *Tulare Times,* February 8 and 10, 1932

McCUBBIN, J. C. *Stockton–Los Angeles Stage Road.* Manuscript, 1930

LASSEN COUNTY

LASSEN COUNTY (named for the pioneer Peter Lassen) was organized in 1864 from parts of Plumas and Shasta counties. Susanville has been its county seat from the beginning. The eastern portion of the Lassen Volcanic National Park is in Lassen County, but the greater part of the park is in Shasta County, as is also Lassen Peak.

Noble's Pass

Noble's Road, one of the so-called northern cut-offs used by emigrants in the early '50's, passed by the site of the present town of Susanville in Lassen County. In 1851 a Mr. Noble, member of a prospecting party, saw the value of the route over the pass followed by his party and enlisted the interest of the business men of Shasta, then an important mining town on this trail. In 1852 he succeeded in raising $2,000 for surveying a wagon road over the new route, with its terminus at Shasta. Both Noble's Pass (about ten miles northwest of Lassen Peak) and Noble's Road were named in honor of the one man whose foresight and energy made this route possible.

The trail through Noble's Pass was as follows: From Humboldt River, the Applegate–Lassen Trail was followed for about sixty miles; then the newer trail turned southwest across the Smoke Creek Desert to the Susan River valley, three miles north of Honey Lake; passing the spot where the present town of Susanville stands, it continued west up the canyon of the Susan River until it reached Lassen's Trail, which it followed in a northwesterly direction as far as Poison Lake. At this point Lassen's Trail continued north, skirting the western end of Dixie Valley and following up the Pit River to Big Valley, where the present town of Bieber is located. Turning west at Poison Lake, Noble's Road reached Butte Creek, where it swerved to the south, following along the west side of the creek as far as Butte Lake. There it entered Shasta County, passing to the north of Lassen Peak and proceeding over Noble's Pass, where it continued westward as far as the city of Shasta.

At first, emigrants were persuaded with difficulty to use the new road, but, within a year or two, improvements were made and much of the travel for the northern end of the Sacramento Valley then passed over it. Noble's Road became more important than the more widely known but more dangerous Lassen's Trail.

Early in the summer of 1854, while the Roop Brothers were yet the sole occupants of Honey Lake Valley, Lieutenant E. G. Beckwith, in the interest of a transcontinental railroad, surveyed the road over Noble's Pass, one of the various Sierran passes which he explored between Goose Lake and Beckwourth's Pass.

Lassen's Monument

About five miles south of Susanville and three miles west of Janesville at the upper end of Elysian Valley, a monument was erected by the Masons on June 24, 1862, over the grave of Peter Lassen. An inscription on the tablet reads: "In memory of Peter Lassen, the Pioneer, who was killed by Indians, April 26, 1859. Aged 66 years." It was in this vicinity that Lassen mined in the summer and fall of 1855. His first cabin was located "on the south side of Lassen Creek, about one-third of a mile west of where the mountain road from Susanville to Janesville crosses that stream." This cabin was burned in 1896.

A native of Denmark, Peter Lassen came to America when twenty-nine years of age. In 1839 he journeyed overland to Oregon, and from there went down the coast by boat to Fort Ross, in 1840. One of the first white settlers in the upper Sacramento Valley, Peter Lassen settled in 1844 on what came to be known as the Lassen Ranch. In 1848 he brought a party of emigrants to California from Missouri, over the Lassen Trail, and attempted to found Benton City on his ranch in Tehama County. He was the first settler in Indian Valley, Plumas County, coming there in 1851, but in 1855 he located in Lassen County, where he played an influential part in the early history of the section.

Susanville

Susanville was named after the only daughter of Isaac Roop, the first white settler in Honey Lake Valley and the founder of Lassen County as well as of its county seat, Susanville. Roop came to Honey Lake from Shasta in 1853, in order to build a hotel on the Noble Emigrant Trail, which had been recently opened up through that region. Early in 1855 Peter Lassen discovered gold in Honey Lake Valley, and news of the find brought in a number of men from the Feather River mining region. Several land claims were staked out there at that time.

Honey Lake Valley was so isolated during the pioneer period that a local government was set up on the initiative of the people themselves. About twenty signers, all original settlers in Honey Lake Valley, met at the Roop cabin on April 26, 1856, and formed the "Territory of Nataqua," with Roop as secretary and recorder and Lassen as surveyor. With the eastern boundary of California not definitely determined, the organizers of the new territory included much of the state of Nevada in "Nataqua." However, "they made a wild shot at their location. They didn't even live in the territory they had created. It was nearly thirty-five miles from their place of meeting to the western line of Nataqua, and the settlers furthest down the lake were almost twenty miles west of it." Moreover, the citizens of the Carson, Eagle, and Washoe valleys were not even notified that they were included within the boundaries of the new political division. Actually, "Nataqua" existed for a short time only, and then merely in the minds of a few men.

Finally, in 1857, the citizens of the would-be "Nataqua" decided to cast their lot with those who were petitioning Congress for separation from Utah Territory with its Mormon dominance. While awaiting Congressional action on their petition for the formation of a new territory, the settlers met again in 1858 to set up a local government. As a result, a constitutional convention was held at Genoa, Nevada, on July 18, 1859, and in the following September Isaac Roop was chosen provisional governor of the proposed territory.

On March 2, 1861, Congress passed the bill creating Nevada Territory, but, as much of California's present territory, that is, all of the eastern slope of the Sierra Nevada, from Inyo to Modoc counties, was to be included in the new territory, California objected and attempted to assert its jurisdiction. The result was the Sagebrush or Boundary Line War waged by forty or fifty of the original settlers of Honey Lake Valley against Plumas County officers sent in to enforce allegiance to the state of California. The difficulty was finally settled by the creation of Lassen County on April 1, 1864.

Isaac Roop's old log cabin, called Fort Defiance because it was used as a fort during the Sagebrush War, still stands on the east side of Weatherlow Street in Susanville.

SOURCES

[Credit is here given for source material, and permission to quote is hereby acknowledged]

ALBRIGHT, GEORGE LESLIE. "Official Explorations for Pacific Railroads," in *University of California Publications in History*, Vol. II. University of California Press, Berkeley, 1921
BECKWITH, LIEUTENANT E. G. His report in *Pacific Railroad Reports*, Vol. II. Beverly Tucker, printer, Washington, 1855
DORNIN, MAY. *The Emigrant Trails into California.* Master's thesis in History, University of California, Berkeley, California, 1921
FAIRFIELD, ASA MERRILL. *Fairfield's History of Lassen County, California.* H. S. Crocker, San Francisco, 1916
FARISS and SMITH. *The Illustrated History of Plumas, Lassen and Sierra Counties.* Fariss & Smith, San Francisco, 1882

MADERA COUNTY

MADERA COUNTY (Madera is Spanish for "wood" or "timber") was organized from a part of Fresno County in 1893, and was given the same name as its principal town, Madera, which was made the county seat.

The Big Trees

There is but one living group of *Sequoia gigantea* within Madera County and that is the Fresno Grove, which stands about five miles south of the Mariposa Grove. Partly cut over during the years 1888–1890, it is now covered with a fine second growth. The Dead Grove, part of an ancient forest located between the Mariposa and the Fresno groves, consists of ten big trees cut many years ago and still lying where they were felled.

The Devil's Postpile

The Devil's Postpile, a spectacular mass of basaltic columns like an immense pile of posts, is located near where the Mammoth Trail from Fresno Flats (Oakhurst) to Mammoth Lakes crosses the Middle Fork of the San Joaquin River. These columns vary in size from ten to thirty inches in diameter and in some cases stand as high as sixty feet. In shape they are irregular polygons with from three to seven sides each but all closely and perfectly fitted together like a vast mosaic.

"In every scenic freak the sheep-herder recognizes the handiwork of his Satanic majesty. This formation is therefore known to local fame as the Devil's Woodpile." It was officially designated as the Devil Postpile National Monument by President Taft on July 6, 1911. It ranks with the famous Giant's Causeway in Ireland.

Old Trails

It is unlikely that the various early Spanish expeditions entered the confines of Madera County, and no Spanish settlements were ever made there. This isolation was due, first of all, to the fact that it was practically impossible to penetrate the tulares from the west or to cross the sloughs which covered the whole central portion of the San Joaquin Valley at high water. In addition to this general inaccessibility, the streams throughout the area of the county were little more than dry, sandy washes except during and immediately following a heavy rainfall. Furthermore, the water holes along the foothills of Madera County were few as compared to the broad, perennial streams to the north and south. For many years these conditions repelled both exploration and settlement. This impenetrable barrier is described by F. F. Latta:

"Between Martinez on the north and San Emigdio, two hundred and fifty miles to the south, there were only two places where the San Joaquin Valley could be crossed from east to west except at time of low water. Throughout the course of the San Joaquin River and bordering the lakes to the south was an impenetrable sea of tule, sloughs, mud flats, and water, which, until as late as 1880, was passable only at these same places. When Tulare Lake was below the extreme high water mark the sand ridge which crossed it from east to west formed a bridge over which we know the Spanish crossed. The other point at which they were able to cross during time of high water was at the head of Fresno Slough near the present town of Tranquility. . . . ."

Jedediah Strong Smith was probably the first white man to traverse what is now Madera County when he passed that way in 1827 and again in 1828. He was soon followed by Hudson's Bay Company trappers and later by Ewing Young, Kit Carson, and other Americans, who followed the trail of the beaver along the numerous streams which come down from the High Sierra on the eastern side of the valley.

The first definite record which we have of a trail across Madera County is that left by John C. Frémont on April 4–6, 1844. By means of rafts the party ferried the Bear River (in Merced County) on the 4th, and then proceeded southward, their progress being greatly impeded by the numerous sloughs of this section. Continuing up the San Joaquin River, they passed "elk . . . . running in bands over the prairie, and . . . . along the left bank . . . . immense droves of wild horses." Camp was made on the San Joaquin River on the 4th and 5th. On the 6th the party crossed the San Joaquin at Gravelly Ford, a crossing still in use.

The Millerton or Stockton–Los Angeles Road, the only north and south route which passed through Madera County during the '50's and '60's, ran along the base of the foothills, crossing the Chowchilla River at the Home Ranch a little west of where the Merced-Mariposa boundary line intersects the Madera County line. The San Joaquin River was crossed at Millerton by means of the Converse Ferry, which fell into disuse after the building of the railroad.

Most of the miners at Coarse Gold and other mining centers in Madera County migrated south from Mariposa County. Others came from Gilroy via Pacheco Pass, crossed the San Joaquin River just south of the mouth of Fresno River, and from there proceeded to the Sierra Nevada mines. Alexis Godey, famous plainsman and guide to Frémont, operated a ferry at this point for a short time during the early '50's.

In the late '70's a stage road from Madera to the Yosemite Valley was constructed, passing through Bates Station, Kelshew Corners, Coarse Gold, Fresno Flats, Fish Camp, and Clark's Station (Wawona).

An Old Indian Reservation

Living water and Indian rock writings near the headquarters of the present Adobe Ranch mark the site of an old Indian farm or reservation established at this point on the Fresno River during the early '50's. It is mentioned by J. Ross Browne among similar projects in his *California, Washoe and Crusoe Island,* and the following item in the *Mariposa Chronicle* of October 6, 1854, bears out his statement:

"We learn that Mr. Henley, the Superintendent of Indian Affairs, has leased the Adobe House and Ranch of Capt. Vinsonhaler on the Frezno, and intends locating there for the present all the Indians originally belonging in that section, many of whom have heretofore refused to remove to the Tejón."

The Savage Monument

A monument erected in honor of Major James D. Savage, hardy pioneer trader and one of the explorers of the Yosemite Valley in 1851, stands above the Fresno River sixteen miles east of Madera on the River Road. Savage was murdered on King's River in 1855; his friend and partner, Dr. Lewis Leach, marked the grave by a ten-foot shaft of granite brought from Vermont. The Native Sons of the Golden West have recently purchased a plot of ground about the monument, thus insuring its preservation.

This monument stands near the site of the fourth and last trading-post established in this region by Savage, who came to the mines early in 1848 with the Woods party, the first discoverers of gold in Tuolumne County. He later enlisted the aid of Indians in mining at Big Oak Flat (Tuolumne County) and soon developed an extensive trade with the various Indian tribes of the Sierra. His first post was at the mouth of the South Fork of the Merced River (in Mariposa County), but this was abandoned when the Yosemite Indians went on the warpath. A second post was then established at the mouth of Agua Fria Creek, near the site of Buckeye, while a branch station was started on the Fresno River near Fresno Flats. The last post of Major Savage was placed near Fresno Crossing, where the monument stands today. The adobe ruins in the vicinity which are sometimes pointed out as the old Savage trading-post are those of a structure built by Chinese and used as a store during the '80's.

A Bit of the Mother Lode

Extending from the northwest to the southeast through Madera County, the Mother Lode is marked by the shafts and tunnels of old mines and the sites of one-time mining camps. Before the quartz ledges were opened up in the '70's and '80's, however, placer mining began. As early as 1849 villages sprang up in flats and ravines and along the bars of the San Joaquin and Fresno rivers.

Among the early prosperous placer-mining camps, Coarse Gold (at first known as Texas Flat) was the largest in Madera County. There in 1849 five Texans found diggings on the creek where the sand yielded particles of gold so coarse that the stream was named Coarse Gold Creek. Many fortunes were taken from the surrounding hills and the settlement grew rapidly.

Other placer-mining centers quickly developed: Grub Gulch, six miles northwest, and Fresno Flats (now Oakhurst), seven miles northeast of Coarse Gold; Fine Gold, about six miles southeast near Mountain View Peak, Temperance Flat, on the San Joaquin River four miles east of

Fine Gold Gulch; Cassidy's Bar, also on the San Joaquin River in the vicinity of old Fort Miller; Soldier Bar; and Rootville—these made up a round of lively little camps which, during the '50's, composed a small but rich mining district. However, little trace of them is left today.

Throughout this section of the Mother Lode a number of quartz mines likewise earned records as big producers during the '70's and '80's. The old mining camp of Coarse Gold was located at the confluence of Coarse Gold Gulch and Deadwood Gulch, thirty-two miles northeast of Madera, and radiating from it in all directions were quartz mines, traces of some of which remain today: the Texas Flat Mine, one mile to the northwest, and the Topp's Mine (located in 1880), three miles north; the D'Or de Quartz, four and a half miles south, idle over fifty years; the Five Oaks, one and one-half miles southeast; the Waterloo, one and one-half miles farther on; and Last Chance, located in 1880 five miles by road from Coarse Gold.

At the Grub Gulch camp the Josephine Mine (1880) and the Gambetta (which included the Arkansas Traveler Claim) were located, while two miles to the northeast was the Enterprise Mine.

Other mines located in the Potter Ridge District east of Grub Gulch included the Flying Dutchman, the Crystal Spring, the Rattlesnake, the King's Gulch, and the Victoria. The Potter Ridge Mine was two miles southwest of Fresno Flats.

The Hildreth Mining District was named after Tom Hildreth and his brother, who operated butcher shops in various Sierra mining camps and who ranged their cattle on Madera County foothills. The district, extending ten miles or so northward from the mouth of Fine Gold Creek, which is three miles northeast of old Fort Miller, was located in the southern part of the county, with Fine Gold Gulch as the western and northern boundary line of the section. Here were the Abbey Mine, a quarter of a mile east of the small camp of Hildreth; the Morrow Mine, located in May 1881, in the same section and township as the Abbey Mine; the Hanover, the Golconda, and the Standard. One mile east of Fine Gold, too, was the Mountain View Mine, located in 1880 in the vicinity of Mountain View Peak.

During the '60's, while the copper excitement was at its height in California, a few copper mines were developed in the foothills of Madera County, notably the Daulton, located on the railroad about twelve miles southwest from Raymond, and the Daisy Bell. Productive in early days, the copper mines ceased to be worked when prices fell.

The Town of Madera

With the construction of the railroad in 1870 an increasing demand came from the East for lumber from the great sugar pine forests of the Sierra Nevada, while some trade developed also in yellow pine, fir, cedar, and other woods. Quick transit from the mountains to the railroad was accomplished by the construction of a V-shaped flume sixty inches wide and sixty-three miles in length running from the Soquel Basin. This flume, built in 1874 at a cost of half a million dollars and later extended as far as Sugar Pine, carried countless millions of feet of lumber annually from the higher mountains to the railroad. The Sugar Pine Lumber Company and the Madera Sugar Pine Company, with a monthly payroll of $140,000, employed from nine hundred to a thousand men.

A settlement grew up at the lower end of the flume where it terminated near the Central Pacific Railway on the south side of Fresno River. There in 1876 the California Lumber Company laid out the town of Madera, the Spanish word for "wood" or "timber" having been adopted as its

name. When the county was created in 1893, the same name was chosen for it, and the city of Madera became its county seat.

Borden, an Early Farm Community

The little town of Borden (originally known as the "Alabama Settlement"), located seventeen miles north of Fresno, was the center for a thriving agricultural community before Fresno and Madera even came into existence. It was the earliest farm center in this part of the valley, having been founded in 1868–1869 by families from Alabama. Borden had become quite a pretentious place by 1873–1874, boasting two hotels, two stores, and other buildings, and even aspiring to become the county seat. However, as early as 1881 it was described as already beginning to wear a deserted air.

SOURCES

[Credit is here given for source material, and permission to quote is hereby acknowledged]

BUNNELL, LAFAYETTE HOUGHTON. Discovery of the Yosemite and the Indian War of 1851. Privately published, Chicago, 1880

ELLIOTT, WALLACE W. History of Fresno County. Wallace W. Elliott, San Francisco, 1882

FARQUHAR, FRANCIS P. Place Names of the High Sierra. Sierra Club, San Francisco, 1926

FRÉMONT, JOHN C. The Exploring Expedition to the Rocky Mountains, Oregon, and California. George H. Derby & Company, Buffalo, 1849

FRY, WALTER, and JOHN R. WHITE. Big Trees. Stanford University Press, Stanford University, 1930

LATTA, F. F. Pah-Mit's Story. Tulare Daily Times, 1931

LE CONTE, J. N. "The Devil's Postpile," in Sierra Club Bulletin, VIII, No. 3 (January 1912), 170–173

MATTHES, FRANÇOIS E. "Devil's Postpile and Its Strange Setting," in Sierra Club Bulletin, XV, No. 1 (February 1930), 1–8

RUSSELL, CARL P. One Hundred Years in Yosemite. The Romantic Story of Early Human Affairs in the Central Sierra Nevada. Stanford University Press, Stanford University, 1932

VANDOR, PAUL E. History of Fresno County, with Biographical Sketches. Privately published, Los Angeles, 1919

MARIPOSA COUNTY

THE NAME MARIPOSA (Spanish for "butterfly") was first given in the plural form, Las Mariposas, to a spot in Merced County visited by the expedition of Gabriel Moraga in 1806. The old Mexican grant conferred upon Juan Bautista Alvarado in 1844 and purchased for Frémont on February 10, 1847, by his agent, Thomas O. Larkin, likewise took the plural form of the name, while the singular form, Mariposa, was bestowed first upon the creek and later upon the town and the county.

Some have erroneously thought that this place name was derived from "Mariposa Lily," the common name of the many-hued lilies (Calochortus luteus and other varieties) which in late spring and early summer give color to the hills of this region. But it is to the butterfly, which at certain seasons of the year is found here in countless numbers, that the source of this delightful place name must be traced.

Mariposa County was one of the original twenty-seven counties. Agua Fria was the first county seat, from 1850 to 1854, after which Mariposa became the seat of government.

Walker's Trail over the Sierra

Joseph Reddeford Walker, as early as 1833, came into California over the Sierra Nevada through what are now

Mono, Mariposa, and Tuolumne counties. "Reliable knowledge of the Sierra Nevada," says Francis P. Farquhar, "really begins with this expedition."

Passing down the Humboldt River valley in Nevada and thence south by Carson Lake, Walker and his men struck westward across the Sierra, probably ascending its eastern slope by one of the southern tributaries of the East Walker River. After crossing the summit of the pass, the party was lost for several days "in a maze of lakes and mountains." The description of this region, as given by Zenas Leonard, chronicler of the expedition, accords well with the character of the country in the vicinity of Virginia Canyon.

From this point, Farquhar says "they would have crossed the Tuolumne, perhaps near Conness Creek. Passing Tenaya Lake, they probably followed the general course of the present Tioga road" (mostly in Tuolumne County) down the divide between the Tuolumne and Merced rivers. On this stage of the journey the party saw either the Merced grove or the Tuolumne grove of *Sequoia gigantea,* thus being the first white men to see the Big Trees of the Sierra Nevada.

Yosemite Valley

"It is now known with reasonable certainty that Yosemite Valley was seen by the Walker party in 1833." Zenas Leonard, clerk of the expedition, recorded in his diary what is thought to be the first mention of Yosemite Valley by a white man. He writes:

"Some of these precipices appeared to us to be more than a mile high. Some of the men thought that if we could succeed in descending one of these precipices to the bottom, we might thus work our way into the valley below—but on making several attempts we found it utterly impossible for a man to descend, to say nothing of our horses."

However, "it was not until 1851 that the valley can properly be said to have been discovered and made widely known." This, the first effective discovery, was made by Major James D. Savage and Captain John Boling, who, with a strong detachment of mounted volunteers and friendly Indian guides, entered the valley in March of that year to capture the resident Indians in order to put them on the Fresno Indian Reservation. One of this party of discoverers was Dr. L. H. Bunnell, the first man to make the wonders of the Yosemite Valley known to the world.

Major Savage had come to the mines in 1848, enlisted Indian labor in his diggings in Tuolumne County, and soon developed extensive trading relations with the natives. His first post was set up at the mouth of the South Fork of the Merced River in Mariposa County, but this was abandoned when the Yosemite Indians went on the warpath against the whites in 1850.

In 1851 and 1852 a number of punitive expeditions against the Indians entered the valley, the last, led by Lieutenant Moore, finally driving the remnant of the tribe over the mountains, where they took refuge with the Monos.

The tourist history of Yosemite Valley began in 1855, when J. M. Hutchings, in company with three friends, formed the first tourist expedition to enter it. Five days of "scenic banqueting" were spent in exploring the region and sketching its wonders. "The publicity given to Hutchings' writings and to Ayers' drawings was what really called public attention to the existence of Yosemite Valley. . . . From that time on not a year passed but that tourists found their way there in ever increasing numbers." The first improved pack trail into Yosemite Valley was made in 1856 by the Mann Brothers, a livery firm in Mariposa. It led from Mariposa to the valley by way of the South Fork of the Merced River, crossing at Wawona.

Regular tourist travel to Yosemite Valley began in 1857. The first house was built there in the autumn of 1856, and the first hotel in 1859. The latter is now that part of the Sentinel Hotel establishment known as Cedar Cottage.

Nearly all of the early visitors to Yosemite Valley were Californians, mostly campers. Only a few hundreds came yearly until the completion of the Union Pacific and Central Pacific railroads. Today thousands come annually from all parts of the world. Besides the Merced–El Portal railroad, there are four main motor roads which enter the valley: the Mariposa Road, the Big Oak Flat and Coulterville routes (the latter probably obsolete), and El Portal, the all-year road from Merced.

Yosemite Valley was made a state park on June 30, 1864. A national park surrounding the valley was established in 1890, and the present Yosemite National Park was constituted in 1906, when the state of California ceded back the Yosemite Valley and the Mariposa Grove of Big Trees.

The numerous trails and roads in the valley, as well as specific points of interest such as Bridal Veil Falls, El Capitan, Cathedral Rocks, Glacier Point, Half Dome, Inspiration Point, Yosemite Falls, and many others, are thoroughly dealt with in the current government publications, as are the hotels, camps, and lodges open to visitors. A museum, established in 1921, and comprising four departments — history, ethnology, zoölogy, and botany — houses natural history exhibits and treasured relics of early days in Yosemite.

Wawona (Clark's Station)

At Wawona is the site of the log cabin built by Galen Clark in 1857, the same year in which he officially discovered the Mariposa Grove, only eight miles from his cabin and now within the Yosemite National Park. Galen Clark was a member of the first Board of Commissioners for the care of Yosemite Valley and the Mariposa Grove, and was for many years known as the "Guardian of the Valley." For more than fifty years he lived either in Yosemite or at Wawona. At the latter place his cabin was known to all travelers as Clark's Station, where kindly hospitality never failed to be extended.

Galen Clark in 1904, at the age of ninety years, published his first book, the *Indians of Yosemite,* and in 1907 another, the *Big Trees of California.* Clark finished his last book, *The Yosemite Valley,* just two weeks before his death on March 24, 1910, at the age of ninety-six years.

Historic Spots along the All-Year Highway

The All-Year Highway from Merced to the Yosemite Valley passes through one of the most interesting and romantic of California's historic regions. Many of the landmarks of mining days have been obliterated, but here and there stark ruined walls of brick or stone marking the site of some "ghost city" of the hills may be seen, or an occasional hamlet invites the passer-by to linger and picture for himself the lively scenes enacted there in the stirring heyday of its past.

Where the modern highway crosses the Merced-Mariposa county line, the route of the old Stockton–Los Angeles Road (locally known as the Millerton Road) is intersected. Following the base of the lower foothills along what is now the boundary line of the two counties, this old road (now almost lost in the grass-grown hills) avoided the winter freshets and the labyrinthine tulares then covering the floor of the valley. Along its route, at first but faintly marked and shifting, the commerce of the rich southern mines flowed in the days of pack trains and stagecoaches. This road was antedated only by the Los Angeles Trail, or El Camino Viejo, on the western side of the valley.

After traversing Cathay Valley, first settled in the early '50's and still claiming among its inhabitants descendants of the original families, the All-Year Highway passes through the lower mountains of Mariposa County. A little to the northwest is Indian Gulch, while to the northeast is Guadalupe, both flourishing mining camps at one time. At Buckeye, on the old Yosemite Highway, the road to Mount Bullion turns north, passing en route the sites of Carson and Agua Fria. The site of Carson, which is also on the new highway, is marked by two or three stone ruins, one of which is the Carson Store. One-half mile above Carson on the new highway is Arkansas Flat, where may be seen stone ruins of an old Chinese saloon and a miner's cabin. These have been taken over by modern miners, who have gleaned from ten cents to a dollar a day in the neighboring gulches.

Agua Fria

Until 1852, while mining was the main industry of the region, Mariposa County included all of what is now Merced, Madera, Fresno, Tulare, Kings, and Kern counties, and parts of Inyo and Mono counties. As agriculture developed, new counties were gradually carved out of the territory included in the original county. The first county seat of Mariposa County, from 1850 to 1854, was at Agua Fria on Agua Fria Creek. Today scarcely a trace of the place is left except a few foundation stones and abandoned diggings, but the site has been marked by the Mariposa County Chamber of Commerce.

Mariposa

Mariposa, founded on Frémont's Rancho Las Mariposas, a grant which occupied a unique position in the mining history of the state, became the county seat of Mariposa County in 1854, and was long the center of trade for the rich mining area covered by the rancho. The town of today has preserved some of the features typical of early mining camps— buildings with substantial walls of brick and stone supplemented by iron doors and shutters, with an occasional overhanging balcony; and a few old plank walks.

There are a number of sites in Mariposa of historic interest. Next door to the Red Lion gasoline station is the site of the Sullivan and Cashman store, which was opened as early as 1852 and was in operation during the time that Frémont was active in the region. The building used by Frémont as an office in the management of his grant of 44,500 acres stood in the midst of a small grove of pine trees on the site now occupied by the Mariposa Hotel. Among the several old buildings dating from early mining days the one of greatest interest is the courthouse. Lumber whipsawed from the neighboring forests was used in its construction and the timbers were fitted together with mortise and tenon and held in place by wooden pegs. Built in 1854, it is one of the oldest courthouses in California still in use. The clock in its tower has been running since the days of the Civil War. In spite of their years of service the seats and the bar in the courtroom remain unchanged. Adding to the historic interest of the building are many quaint documents and newspaper files of priceless value, which are kept within a fireproof vault.

Mormon Bar

Mormon Bar, two miles southeast of Mariposa on Mariposa Creek, was first settled in 1849 by Mormons, who stayed, however, only a short time. Their places were taken at once by other miners, while at a later period the same ground was worked over by thousands of Chinese. Ruined walls of the old adobes, half concealed by trees and giant, moss-grown boulders, still stand on the east bank of Mariposa Creek. Near by is a Chinese graveyard from which the bones of the dead have been carried by friends or relatives back to the ancestral burial grounds in China.

To the west, Buckeye (where James Savage had one of his trading-posts), Bootjack to the east, and Ben Hur to the south, all shared with Mormon Bar the prosperity of their neighbor, the town of Mariposa. The site of the present Ben Hur post office on the Quick Ranch is located about a mile southeast of the older site on the hill. Not far away is the Quick ranch house, into which has been incorporated a portion of the original house built by Morgan W. Quick, grandfather of the present owner. Quick purchased the original 160 acres of his ranch in 1859 from a man having squatter's rights to the land. The garden and orchard about the present house are still watered from the perpetual spring which attracted the first settlers to the spot, and a mammoth fig tree, planted in 1859 by Mr. Quick, almost hides the old house with its verdant, spreading branches. The four thousand acres which comprise the present ranch are fenced by a stone wall, built with infinite labor and remarkable skill by Chinese coolies in 1862. Each coolie was forced to lay a rod and a half daily or forfeit his job. For this he was paid at the rate of two "bits" a day, while the Chinese contractor received one dollar and six "bits" per rod. The old wall, which extends for five miles up hill and down, is a truly marvelous piece of workmanship, and is as perfect today as when it was laid.

At the foot of Becknell Hill, two and a half miles from Ben Hur, stands the picturesque Becknell adobe, one of the oldest original dwellings in Mariposa County. Fortunately, its present owner, who appreciates its charm and historical significance, is having the adobe repaired and restored to its original condition.

Mount Bullion

Mount Bullion, located on the mountain of that name and reached by the devious and winding Mother Lode Road, is about six miles northwest of Mariposa on a part of the former Frémont estate. The peak was named in honor of Senator Thomas H. Benton, whose nickname was "Old Bullion." Only a few buildings reminiscent of the gold days remain in the town. The most interesting of these is the Marre Store, a one-story adobe with heavy iron shutters and doors closely barred, its sturdy walls shaded by two tall cottonwood trees. It is still in the possession of the son of the original owner, who took it over soon after it was built in the '50's. Across the street is the frame store building of Frank Trabucco, still in use. The old Princeton Mine, located on Mount Bullion just south of the village was originally owned by Frémont. Its total production exceeded $3,000,000 in gold, and although long since closed down many believe that it is still capable of producing wealth.

Hornitos

Hornitos ("little ovens"), twelve miles west of Mount Bullion, derived its name from the presence of many odd Mexican graves or tombs built of stone in the shape of little square bake-ovens and set on top of the ground. On the hillside just below the Catholic Church and cemetery the ruins of two or three of these interesting relics may still be seen.

Hornitos seems to have been settled by an undesirable Mexican element driven out of the adjoining town of Quartzburg. The old plaza was the scene of many a lively fiesta. "Gamblers, girls and roughnecks . . . . they were a tough lot, the worst in the southern mines. They reverenced nothing but money, cards and wine. . . . . Blood was upon nearly every doorstep and the sand was caked with it." It is said that Joaquín Murieta, the noted bandit, on his frequent visits found friends here.

In time, however, a change came over the place. When the placers at Quartzburg (a short distance up the creek) gave out, many of its citizens came to Hornitos, where the diggings were very rich. It became the first and the only incorporated town in Mariposa County. Ordinances were passed remedying many of the old social abuses, the gambling dens became stores, and children played on the streets.

Hornitos appears today much as it was years ago—no pavements, no plate glass, and no gasoline signs to mar the subtle atmosphere of other days. The long bars are dry and deserted, and in the door casings significant bullet holes still show. A decided Mexican influence is evident in the quaint adobe and stone structures with their massive iron doors, many of them now closed. A few of the more interesting buildings remaining from mining days are the Hornitos Hotel, erected about 1860, among whose guests were many prominent men of the day, including President Grant; the Fandango Dance Hall or Campodonica Building; and the Ghirardelli Store, where a pioneer merchant "whose name has since become a household word" had an early merchandising business. The dance hall once had an underground passage—"for escape when things grew too hot"—and it is said that Joaquín Murieta found it useful on more than one occasion when he was in danger of being captured by the officers of the law. The Masonic Hall, erected in 1860, is the only one in California which has the meeting-room on the ground floor. The old Dennis house, next to the hotel, was one of the first frame dwellings to be erected in Mariposa County.

Quartzburg, once one of the populous centers of placer mining in Mariposa County, with fraternal societies and all the organizations which made up the social life of the time, consists today of two deserted houses and a few fruit and shade trees plainly showing the neglect of many years. The old Thorn house, with its tall brick chimney and its adobe walls fashioned from the dark red soil native to the vicinity, is a picturesque landmark on the present Hornitos–Bear Valley Road. It was built by Colonel Thorn in the early '50's and served as store and post office at Quartzburg. Beside it stands an old two-story frame building constructed of the resawed siding typical of the '50's and '60's.

The Mount Ophir Mint

Another "vanished" town of the Mother Lode is Mount Ophir, which was located one and a half miles northwest of Mount Bullion. Nothing remains of this once busy settlement except the ruins of a private mint, one of several such early mints in California, in which hexagonal fifty-dollar slugs were coined. Today one of these slugs, if it could be found, would probably be valued at $10,000. Near the ruins of the mint is an arched stone vault, broken and ravaged by treasure-hunters, where the raw gold is said to have been stored. Just beyond Mount Ophir, on the way to Bear Valley, walls of the Trabucco Store stand at the left of the road, "as pretty a ruin as most of the missions can show," as one traveler has described it. This old trading-post of the Mother Lode was erected by Louis Trabucco in the early '50's.

Bear Valley

The present Mariposa County includes what was once Rancho Las Mariposas, sometimes spoken of as the Frémont Grant, a vast estate constituting one of several so-called "floating grants," and located originally in what is now Merced County. After gold was discovered in the Mariposa region in the spring of 1848, Frémont "floated" his rancho up into the hills. The new location proved to be very rich in gold and for several years large operations were carried on there by Frémont.

The center of Frémont's activities was Bear Valley, thirteen miles northwest of Mariposa. At one time it was practically Frémont's own town, built by him and owned by him, and for a time was his home. Diggings were all about it, and on Saturday night hundreds of miners thronged the streets.

Along the Mother Lode Highway from Mariposa northwest to the village of Benton Mills evidences of mining activities and of Frémont's associations may still be found. In the town of Bear Valley itself can be seen remnants of past glory: a block of two-story stone and adobe structures, including saloons, stores, and public houses, some fast crumbling into decay; a huge livery stable with fallen roof; the large, jagged ruins of the old Frémont Company's store; and the Oso Hotel, a two-story wooden structure with wide upper and lower balconies which is still intact but yearly becoming more and more decrepit. It was built by Frémont in 1850, from lumber brought around the Horn, and was the main hotel of the camp as well as the headquarters for the Frémont Company. Many noted names, that of Ulysses S. Grant among others, are on its register. The Frémont residence, which stood some distance back from the main street, is gone, and the site is marked only by the old foundation stones. At Bear Valley there is also an Odd Fellows Hall, once graced by a balcony, only the iron framework of which remains. There, too, the ruined walls of old rock stores lure the photographer, and just over the rise to the south is the remnant of a typical miner's cabin, with quaint stone chimney and fireplace still intact.

Just beyond Bear Valley on the road to Coulterville stand two old Chinese adobes marking the site of Bear Valley's once thriving Chinatown. The climb up the ridge road from this point is so gradual that one is startled, on making a sudden turn, to look down a thousand feet into the heart of Hell's Hollow. It is "a sight different from all other grades, with a play of light and shadow, rolling contour upon contour until lost to sight in the long distance." When covered with a carpet of purple godetias from base to summit, the beauty of this canyon is something never to be forgotten.

Following the winding grade down into the hollow and across the bridge, the next place of historic interest is Bagby, formerly Benton Mills, the site of one of Frémont's largest mills and river dams, portions of which still remain. The entrance to the tunnel of an old mine may be seen in the mountain side just before the road crosses the bridge over the Merced River. This mine has already produced millions in gold and recently a new and promising lead was uncovered.

On the North Fork of the Merced River northeast of Benton Mills is Indian Gulch, while to the northwest, also on the river, is Horseshoe Bend, once a rich and populous mining camp. Between them is Split Rock, on the south bank of the river. To the southeast in Sherlock Gulch is one of the numerous Whiskey Flats with which the mining regions abounded.

Coulterville

The old mining town of Coulterville (called "Banderita" by the first American miners who came there because of the small red flags, or bandanas, used by the Mexican inhabitants) has suffered from several devastating fires, which have left many old stone or brick buildings roofless and in ruins. Of especial interest today are the Chinese Adobe and the Bruschi

Store. Another noteworthy feature, characteristic of the early mining days, is the Hangman Tree in the old public square.

Two miles southwest of the town are the foundations of the French Mills, built along classic lines of architecture in the early '50's. One of the tall stone chimneys still stands, bearing the date of its erection, 1852. Also in the vicinity of Coulterville are Maxwell Creek and Piñon Blanco (misspelled "Penon" on the maps), one-time flourishing mining camps.

Exchequer

Close to the bank of the Merced River, at Exchequer, stands an old stone miners' bank, where gold, panned from the streams by miners in the '50's, was placed for safekeeping before being taken to San Francisco. Many of these vaults throughout the Mother Lode region were built by the Wells Fargo Company.

Exchequer is on the railroad into Yosemite Valley, about twenty miles northwest of Mariposa. Near by is the Exchequer Dam and Reservoir, where water is impounded for generating electric power and for irrigating the farms of Merced County.

Interesting Names

In the early mining days millions of dollars in gold were washed from the gravel beds of Mariposa County's many streams. Quartz mining succeeded placer mining, and veins of fabulous wealth were located in the great Mother Lode which stretches throughout the width of the county. Numerous camps, many of them with odd or unusual names, sprang up all over the county, such as Texas Tent, Cow-and-Calf, Drunken Gulch, Red Cloud, Poison Springs, Hog Canyon, Fly Away, Boneyard, White Rock, Mariposita, Chowchilla, Sherlock's Diggings, Whitlock, Pleasant Valley, Bridgeport, and Chamisal.

Until recently, some gold mining was carried on sporadically in Mariposa County.

SOURCES

[Credit is here given for source material, and permission to quote is hereby acknowledged]

ADAMS, EDGAR H. *Private Gold Coinage of California, 1849–1855, Its History and Its Issues.* Privately published by Edgar H. Adams, Brooklyn, New York, 1912

BADÈ, FREDERIC WILLIAM. *The Life and Letters of John Muir.* 2 vols. Houghton Mifflin Company, Boston and New York, 1924

BROWNE, J. ROSS. *The Mariposa Estate.* Russell's American Steam Printing House, New York, 1868

BUNNELL, LAFAYETTE HOUGHTON. *Discovery of the Yosemite and the Indian War of 1851.* Privately published, Chicago, 1880

CLARK, GALEN. *The Yosemite Valley.* Yosemite Valley, California, 1911

CORCORAN, MAY S. *A History of the San Joaquin Valley Counties.* Manuscript, 1921

COSSLEY-BATT, JILL LILLIE EMMA. *The Last of the California Rangers.* Funk & Wagnalls Company, New York, 1928

"The Early Days in Yosemite." Reprinted from the *Mariposa Democrat* of August 5, 1856. Introduction by Ansel F. Hall, in *California Historical Society Quarterly,* I, No. 3 (January 1923), 271–285

FARQUHAR, FRANCIS P. "Exploration of the Sierra Nevada," in *California Historical Society Quarterly,* IV, No. 1 (March 1925), 2–58

HUTCHINGS, JAMES MASON. *In the Heart of the Sierras.* Pacific Press Publishing House, Oakland, California, 1886

——. *Scenes of Wonder and Curiosity in California.* Hutchings & Rosenfield, San Francisco, 1860

JOHNSTON, PHILIP. "Legends and Landmarks of '49 along the Mother Lode," in *Touring Topics,* XXIII, No. 2 (February 1931), 12–27, 52–53

LEONARD, ZENAS. *Narrative of the Adventures of Zenas Leonard....* Original edition, Clearfield, Pennsylvania, 1839. Later edition edited by W. F. Wagner, The Burrows Brothers Company, Cleveland, 1904

MUIR, JOHN. *Mountains of California.* 2 vols. Houghton Mifflin Company, Boston and New York, 1917

——. *The Yosemite.* The Century Company, New York, 1912

PETERSON, HENRY C. "Relics of Early Days to Be Seen on Sierra Landmark Expedition," in *Oakland Tribune,* May 14, 1922

RUSSELL, CARL P. *One Hundred Years in Yosemite. The Romantic Story of Early Human Affairs in the Central Sierra Nevada.* Stanford University Press, Stanford University, 1932

MERCED COUNTY

MERCED COUNTY (named from the river which Gabriel Moraga, in 1806, had called El Río de Nuestra Señora de la Merced, "The River of Our Lady of Mercy") was organized in 1855 from a part of Mariposa County. The county seat first chosen was located on the Turner and Osborn Ranch, but in 1857 it was moved to Snelling's Ranch, and in 1872 to Merced.

Ranchería Menjoulet

Elevated some forty feet above El Arroyo de los Baños just before it issues from the hills is a plateau on which the ancient Indian ranchería of Menjoulet once flourished. The smooth and regular surface of the little tableland (approximately eighty acres in extent), sheltered from the cold valley winds by a ledge of rocks and a low hill, slopes gently to the stream with its fringe of cottonwoods.

Excavations were made at the ranchería site in 1925, when the entire plateau was found to be covered with relics of the stone age. A ton or more of artifacts were removed, and the remains of some forty bodies were also taken from the cemetery. At this time well-defined outlines of six Indian houses were discovered, one of them being more than sixty-five feet across and six feet in depth. Circular basins, almost perfect in form and grouped closely together, indicated the foundations of those prehistoric tepees, in which remains of fire pits were found with blackened rocks and quantities of charcoal just as the long-forgotten occupants of the houses had left them. Near an old barn about one mile from these larger huts, four or more smaller and older basins were found filled with dust. Here, too, excavations disclosed old fire beds and fire rocks. These have been plowed up and are now only faintly visible.

The land on which this village was situated was owned for a short time in the early '70's by Anthony Pfitzer, who had purchased the possessory right of Nelson Wood, an earlier settler. Pfitzer soon sold to John Menjoulet, a French sheep man, after whom the ranch, the canyon, and the Indian village were named.

First Trails

Little was known of the great interior valleys of the San Joaquin and Sacramento until the beginning of the nineteenth century. During the second administration of Governor José Joaquín de Arrillaga, active exploration of the interior began, the motives being to check the Indians who were becoming troublesome and to establish missions for their conversion. A number of minor expeditions were made into the tulares, or swamps, of the San Joaquin in 1805 and 1806, but scant record is left of these. The first expeditions of which we have much knowledge, as well as the most important from the standpoint of accomplishments, were those made by Gabriel Moraga, the "greatest pathfinder and Indian fighter of his day."

Moraga, with twenty-five men and Father Pedro Muñoz as chaplain and diarist, left San Juan Bautista on September 21, 1806, probably entering the valley of the tules by way of San Luis Creek in Merced County. Proceeding across the San Joaquin River, they reached a slough, the haunt of numerous butterflies, which Moraga named "Las Mariposas." Father Muñoz says that here one of the soldiers was sorely afflicted by the lodging of a butterfly in his ear. The name, in the singular form, survives in Mariposa Slough, Mariposa Creek, and Mariposa County, which lay east of Moraga's march and in which the creek has its source.

Proceeding north and northwest, the party toiled for forty miles through a parched and treeless plain devoid of water. Coming suddenly upon a clear, sparkling stream, they expressed their joy and gratitude for its refreshment by naming it El Río de Nuestra Señora de la Merced, a name which was applied not only to Merced River but later to the county and to the present metropolis and county seat. The place seemed so beautiful to the tired travelers that Father Muñoz enthusiastically declared it to be an excellent site for a mission.

Moraga explored the lower course of the Merced River in the fall of 1808. He again touched the county in 1810 on his way down the west side of the San Joaquin River from the north. Turning west along San Luis Creek, he returned to San Juan Bautista by way of Pacheco Pass.

The magnitude of Moraga's achievement was never realized by himself or the mission Fathers. To them the expedition was a failure since it had discovered no sites suitable for the building of an inland mission chain.

The first American to pass through what is now Merced County, and the first white man to cross the Sierra Nevada, was Jedediah Strong Smith, the great pathfinder and trailbreaker of the West. In 1827 he and his party camped on various rivers in the San Joaquin Valley while engaged in trapping beaver. Smith called one of these the Wimmulche (Wimilche) after a tribe of Indians living there. Some historians identify this river with the present Kings River. At any rate Smith trapped there for a time and then, leaving some of his men encamped on the Wimilche, he crossed the mountains by a route as yet not definitely determined.

Following in Smith's footsteps came other adventurers, and from 1828 until the American occupation beaver skins were gathered along the rivers of Merced County by Hudson's Bay Company trappers and others, among them being Peter Skene Ogden, Michael La Framboise, and Ewing Young.

John C. Frémont, on his way out of California in 1844, proceeded southward from Sutter's Fort, passing through what is now Merced County, and reached the Merced River on April 1. On the following day a "boat" was constructed, with which the party crossed the river somewhere near its junction with the San Joaquin. Camp was made on the farther bank. On the 3d the expedition stopped on the north bank of the Bear River about five miles from its mouth, and on the 4th they ferried this stream, continuing up the San Joaquin River to Madera County.

Westside Trails

Where the foothills of the Mount Diablo Range meet the western rim of the Great Valley, El Camino Viejo, the old westside trail from San Pedro to San Antonio (now east Oakland), crossed El Arroyo de Ortigalitos ("little nettles"), a link in that long chain of arroyos and *aguajes* about which the tepees of the Red Men had clustered for ages, and along which the Spaniards later laid out their ranchos. From the life-giving water holes of Ortigalitos, El Camino Viejo pro-

ceeded northwestward to El Arroyo de los Baños de Padre Arroyo, where living water was again found.

Still farther to the north the road crossed El Arroyo de San Luís Gonzaga at Rancho Centinela, where another water hole was found fifty yards to the north. Leaving Centinela, El Camino Viejo skirted the abrupt foothills which led to El Arroyo de Romero, named after a Spanish cavalry officer who had been killed there at an early date by Indians. Finally, El Arroyo de Quinto ("fifth creek"), the last watering-place in Merced County, was reached. An adobe, probably built before 1840, stood on the plains among the cottonwoods of Quinto Creek as late as 1915.

With the coming of the Americans and the growth of transportation from Stockton to points southward, the Stockton–Visalia Road was developed parallel to El Camino Viejo. It followed along the west side of the San Joaquin River, the exact route varying according to the seasonal changes in the river country. The one-story adobe which still stands in good condition at San Luis Camp, seven miles north of Los Banos, was once an important station on this road. This adobe and other structures built in the early '40's, or even earlier, later became a part of the vast holdings of Miller and Lux. Henry Miller customarily slept in this house whenever he visited this part of his estate.

Joining the Stockton–Visalia Road eight miles northeast of Los Banos, the older Pacheco Pass stage road came in from the west. Long before the advent of the white man, Indians had worn a deep trail over the hills by way of Pacheco Pass, and Spanish explorers in search of mission sites, as well as Spanish officers in pursuit of deserting soldiers or runaway mission Indians, made use of this ancient mountain path.

A toll road was built over the Pacheco Pass in 1856–1857 by A. D. Firebaugh. Two miles west of the summit (in Santa Clara County), and a mile from where the Mountain House later stood, he built a toll station. Portions of the old rock walls of the toll house may still be seen in the narrow defile below the present highway. Along the rocky creek bed marks of the former stage road lead past the ruins and up the steep hillside, where the route is clearly marked by the remnant of a picturesque split-rail fence of the '60's. Above it is the "New Road," built in 1878 by Santa Clara and Merced counties and still in good condition, although unused. It was considered a marvelous road in its day and was traveled until 1923, when the state built the present highway.

The early stage road was used by the Butterfield overland stages from 1858 to 1861, and on it the present San Luis Station was an important stopping-place. It was eighteen miles from San Luis Ranch east to the Lone Willow Station, and from there the stages passed through a long stretch of desolate alkali wastes to Temple's Ranch and on to Firebaugh's Ferry in Fresno County. During the middle '60's the loneliness of this part of the road was relieved by the little cabin of David Mortimer Wood at Dos Palos, where a lantern was placed in the window at night to guide the drivers of the Gilroy–Visalia stages. Water for the horses was furnished here, also, and in return for these favors Wood received supplies and mail brought by the stagecoaches. That part of the old road which lay between San Luis Station and Santa Rita ran about one mile and a half north of the present highway. Along it the earliest pioneer American settlements of the Los Banos district were made. Very little remains to mark any of these places except an occasional black and gnarled tree or faint traces of the former roadbed.

A branch of the Pacheco Pass Road crossed El Camino Viejo at Rancho Centinela. From this point it continued northeast to the ford on the San Joaquin River where Hill's Ferry (Stanislaus County) was established during the gold rush.

Rancho Centinela

It is thought that Rancho Centinela was occupied in 1810, or earlier, when the father of Tiburcio Vásquez, the bandit, brought the first horses into this region. Turning the animals loose, he was never able to recapture them, owing to difficulties with the Indians. Whether or not Vásquez built the one-story adobe that stood at Centinela for so many years is not known. Basque sheep-herders, who erected a two-story adobe, occupied the rancho during the '60's and the '70's. Rumor that one of the Basques had gone insane after receiving a large sum of money in payment for some of his sheep and that he had buried his wealth only to forget the spot where he had placed it led many treasure-hunters to dig the entire yard and portions of the fields near by in a vain search for the gold. The two-story adobe house was torn down in 1890 and a frame structure was erected in its place by Miller and Lux. Somewhat dilapidated, this later house still stands across the road from the barn, which was built in 1872. Bits of the old road may be traced among the grass-grown hillocks and gullies of the open pastures stretching between Centinela and San Luís Gonzaga.

Rancho San Luís Gonzaga

José María Mejía and Juan Pérez Pacheco were granted Rancho San Luís Gonzaga on October 3, 1843. The rancho seems to have been occupied some time before that date, for the one-story adobe at San Luis Station marked by the Native Sons of the Golden West of Merced on May 3, 1931, is thought to have been built before 1835. Without doubt the structure was used as a sort of fort, as loopholes plainly visible in the walls would indicate. It is known that grants of land were often made to prominent men who in return were to help prevent the roving Tulare Indians from raiding the stock at the Coast missions. No doubt this adobe was built with such a purpose in view.

This favored spot, chosen by Don Juan for his homestead, was located on the ancient *aguaje,* or water hole, of San Luis Creek, the site of Lis-nay-yuk, a prehistoric Indian village, which had existed long before the coming of the mission Fathers. To it herds of antelope came to drink, and traveling tribes of Red Men rested by its springs on their periodical journeys over Pacheco Pass. Later came the Spanish explorers and rancheros, the stagecoach drivers of the American period, and, finally, the motorists of today. Recently the old adobe has been fitted up as a refreshment parlor, and the water hole has been cleared of drift.

Sometime in the '40's, on the site of the present San Luis House, Pacheco built a two-story adobe, only to have it destroyed by the earthquake of 1868. Later a frame structure, modeled after the original, was erected on the site. This house, which is still standing, served as a station on the Butterfield Overland Stage Line from 1858 to 1861. Near by is a barn, built in the early '70's, in which steep and winding stairs lead up to a huge hayloft, in the early days often made to serve as a ballroom. The entire rancho is still owned by direct descendants of the original grantee.

Rancho Sanjón de Santa Rita

Santa Rita, as well as San Luís Gonzaga, were place names familiar to Gabriel Moraga as early as 1806, and were mentioned in the journal of his expedition of that year. Rancho Sanjón ("deep slough") de Santa Rita was granted to Francisco Soberanes on September 7, 1841. With the coming of the Americans the grant changed hands a number of times. Nine leagues of the land were sold to Manuel Castro in 1853, and in 1858 he sold two leagues to Salisbury Haly, who in turn, in 1861, sold it to William Dumphy, the latter deeding a half-interest to Tom Hildreth. Finally, on May 22, 1863, the land of Dumphy and Hildreth came into the possession of Henry Miller, and with it the "double H" cattle brand still used by the firm of Miller and Lux. Miller thus secured his first foothold in the San Joaquin Valley.

By 1866 the remainder of Rancho Sanjón de Santa Rita had been purchased by Henry Miller. From that year the firm of Miller and Lux gradually increased their holdings in this section until, in the '80's and the '90's, they owned land extending for sixty-eight miles along the west side of the San Joaquin Valley, from Firebaugh's Ferry in Fresno County to Arroyo de Orestimba in Stanislaus County. In addition, they held thousands of acres in the Buena Vista Lake district of Kern County, two hundred thousand on the east side of the valley, as well as thousands of acres in other parts of California (including their original holdings in the Santa Clara Valley) and in Oregon and Nevada. At the time of Miller's death on October 14, 1916, it was estimated that the "Kingdom of Miller and Lux" included millions of acres.

The Miller and Lux headquarters were located at the old Rancho Santa Rita homestead, where a few of the buildings erected during Henry Miller's lifetime are still standing. A substantial two-story barn of resawed siding built in the '60's, and a group of circular cattle corrals strongly woven of willow boughs, are especially interesting. The site is on the Los Banos–Califa Highway four miles west of the San Joaquin River and thirteen miles east of Los Banos.

Henry Miller did more than acquire lands and cattle. By means of irrigation he turned desert tracts into flourishing fields. It is true he fought all who tried to forestall his seizure of waters and lands, but he also offered part of his water rights to adjacent towns and ranches for a consideration, thus making adjoining lands fertile as well as his own. In this way he built up the wealth of the entire state. The immense Miller and Lux holdings are now being divided into small farms.

Rancho Panoche de San Juan y de los Carrisolitos

Throughout the southwestern portion of Merced County ancient Indian trails may still be traced, and the remains of prehistoric Indian villages have been uncovered at various water holes. In this section, too, early in the nineteenth century, Spanish settlers evidently had sought homes, for it is said that when the survey of Rancho Panoche de San Juan (granted to Julian Ursua on February 10, 1844) was completed in 1866 adobes, already of a considerable age, stood on the rancho.

West of Rancho Panoche is the pleasant mountain valley known as Saucelitos ("little willows"). At the lower end of this valley, Vásquez and his gang of outlaws had a hang-out during the late '60's and the early '70's. Here Juan Soto, a member of that gang, was killed by Sheriff Harry Morse of Santa Clara County in 1872. The scene of the gun duel between the bandit and the sheriff was at the old adobe now used as the headquarters of the Pfeifer Cattle Company. According to one version of the story, twenty-five members of the robber band were holding a fiesta at the Alvarado adobe two miles above the Pfeifer adobe. Don Juan, who had gone to the latter place to procure onions and salt for the barbecue, was there accosted by Sheriff Morse, and the fatal shooting followed. Standing in the shadow of beautiful St. Mary's Peak, this adobe, now a part of a much larger two-story house, is still well preserved. In the adjoining meadow, kept green by a perpetual spring, Soto's grave lies about a half-mile from the house.

At the upper end of the Saucelitos Valley, three or four miles from the Pfeifer house, is a long, narrow adobe owned by the Storm family and used as headquarters for the Storm Ranch. Beside it is the spring "Lying Water," famed among early pioneers in the region and around which many legends have been woven.

El Arroyo de los Baños

Los Baños is a Spanish place name meaning "the baths," and was applied to the deep, clear pools on El Arroyo de los Baños near its source. Tradition says that here Padre Arroyo de la Cuesta was wont to refresh himself when on missionary trips to the San Joaquin Valley. The name El Arroyo de los Baños del Padre Arroyo (now Los Banos Creek) was derived from this circumstance. Padre Arroyo, who served Mission San Juan Bautista for twenty-five years, from 1808 to 1833, was an accomplished man. He invented a perpetual calendar and became familiar with as many as thirteen Indian dialects, preaching in seven different Indian tongues. He also wrote an Indian grammar and recorded many facts concerning the Indians and their manner of life.

The present town of Los Banos is located about two miles from the creek and five miles east of the site of the original settlement, which was established by Gustave Kreyenhagen after 1868. The floods of that year drove him from his trading-post at the junction of the Stockton–Visalia road and the Pacheco Pass Road three miles east of the Lone Willow Stage Station and eight miles to the northeast of Los Banos. Meanwhile Miller and Lux had fenced in the property and required teamsters to drive around it. This forced Kreyenhagen to seek a new location, which he did, locating west of the fence and two miles south of the present Volta. When a post office was established there in 1874 the place was called Los Banos. The post office was moved to the present site of Los Banos after the coming of the railroad in 1889. The town is now the center of a large dairying section and is the second city in size and importance in Merced County.

Today the firm of Miller and Lux maintains an office at Los Banos where the affairs of an estate of many thousands of acres are administered. Beginning in 1873 the headquarters of Henry Miller for the Los Banos district was at Canal Farm, just across the railroad east of the Los Banos city limits. None of the original buildings remain at Canal Farm, as many of them have been sold and the last of them were burned in 1932. The orange and olive orchards planted by Miller still flourish, oranges in this alkali region being a decided novelty. Miller had most of the orchard soil transported across Pacheco Pass from the Santa Clara Valley.

Rancho Las Mariposas

In 1847 John C. Frémont again figured briefly in Merced history when on February 14 he purchased the Rancho Las Mariposas from Juan Bautista Alvarado, who had received it from Governor Micheltorena on February 22, 1844. This grant, of ten leagues, stipulated that the land be located within the area bounded on the west by the San Joaquin River, on the east by the Sierra Nevada foothills, on the north by the Merced River, and on the south by the Chowchilla River. Alvarado never complied with the usual legal requirements by building a house on the grant and inhabiting it within a year. In fact, he never saw the land, but on account of the hostility of the Indians he did apply to the governor for a military force to enable him to take possession, and in answer to this request General José Castro was sent to the region with a company of mounted Californios. Fortifications were begun on the east bank of the

San Joaquin River about six miles south of the Merced River, at or near where the town of Dover was later located. In December 1844 the Indians stole most of the horses, and the Californios, "always averse to walking, had to return to Monterey as best they might." A final effort to take possession of the grant was made by Alvarado in August 1845, but this attempt was frustrated by the revolution against Governor Micheltorena, of which Alvarado was one of the leaders.

According to tradition, Frémont first attempted to locate his grant at the site of the present village of Stevinson, a tradition which seems to be substantiated by the name, Frémont's Ford, which still exists at this point on the San Joaquin River. More tangible evidence shows that Frémont endeavored to locate his ranch near the site of the present Le Grand on Mariposa Creek. Early surveyors' maps show a house called Frémont's Ranch south of Mariposa Creek, and it is very likely that he lived there in 1848. When gold was discovered in the foothills above this ranch, in 1849, Frémont "floated" his grant up into the hills of what is now Mariposa County. Through personal influence Frémont was able to secure confirmation of his grant as located by him in the mining regions. The precedent thus set was to cost the United States government many thousand square miles of territory claimed in other grants of a similar nature.

The First "Cattle King of Merced"

The first bona fide American settlers in Merced County were John M. Montgomery and his partner, Colonel Samuel Scott, two young Kentuckians. In the fall of 1849 they camped under one of the large water oaks on the banks of the Merced River a short distance north of the Cox Ferry Bridge on the left-hand side of the road leading from the bridge to the Hopeton–Snelling Highway and not far from the present town of Snelling.

John Montgomery became the richest man in Merced County during his time and was known as the "Land and Cattle King of Merced," the predecessor of Henry Miller and others. Before 1852 he had established a permanent home on Bear Creek, on what later became the Wolfsen Ranch, six miles east of Merced. A short distance up the river from the Exchequer gravel pits there still stands an old house known as the Montgomery House, but it is not on the original site.

The Courthouse Tree

The first county seat of Merced was located on the Turner and Osborn Ranch on Mariposa Creek, a place which afterward became known as the Givens Ranch. The Courthouse Tree, under which the first county meetings were held, stood on the bank of the old channel of Mariposa Creek, which was considerably to the south of the present channel. The spot is one and a half miles to the right of the valley highway and the Southern Pacific Railroad going south. The old course of the creek runs out a very short distance below where the tree stood. That portion of the ranch on which the tree grew is now a part of the Constance Givens property, and is about seven miles southeast of Merced. This historic tree was killed by floods in the winter of 1868–1869 and was subsequently used for firewood.

Snelling's Ranch

Early in the spring of 1851, Montgomery, Scott, and Dr. David Wallace Lewis established a house of entertainment which was the beginning of the town of Snelling. At first it was only a brush tent, but Dr. Lewis very soon built what was later known as Snelling's Hotel. In the fall of 1851 the Snelling family arrived and purchased the property.

In 1857 Snelling's Ranch replaced the Turner and Osborn Ranch as the site of the county seat, but in 1872 it was in turn superseded by the new town of Merced, located in the valley about fifteen miles to the south. By that time the mines in the mountain regions were giving out, while agriculture was steadily growing in importance. New towns sprang up in the fertile valley regions where railroads were being built, and the old hill towns soon became almost deserted.

Snelling, although not a mining town, was an overflow from the mining regions, and was of considerable importance at one time, being on the well-traveled road to the Mariposa mines. Settled largely by people from the South, it was noted for its spirit of hospitality. Today Snelling is a quiet little village, picturesquely situated, where the visitor may find a link with the past in the old Courthouse, which was erected in 1857. The lower story, part of which is now used as a women's club room, is of stone. The thick walls of that section, which was once used as a jail, are pierced by narrow windows heavily barred. A stone monument dedicated to the memory of the pioneers and commemorating the seventy-fifth anniversary of the organization of Merced County was placed in front of the Courthouse by the Native Sons of the Golden West in 1930. At the lower edge of the hamlet there is also a large brick house built in the '60's by John Montgomery.

Old River Towns

As early as 1850 settlers came to the rivers and streams of Merced County and established homes. Live stock and agricultural products were grown in the vast fertile areas along these streams, and almost invariably the ranch houses became inns on the roads which passed that way. Finally centers of trade grew up about some of them. After the advent of the railroad, however, trade deserted the old river towns and they became little more than memories.

Located on the Merced River six miles below Snelling was Hopeton, at first known as the "Forlorn Hope." It was chiefly notable for the fact that it possessed two churches before Snelling had any.

Merced Falls was one of the principal crossings on the Merced River along the route of the old Stockton–Fort Miller Road. A flour mill and a woolen mill, indicative of two of the county's most important early industries, were located there until 1893, when they were destroyed by fire. The lumber mills of the Yosemite Lumber Company are located there at present.

Dover was a landing-place on the San Joaquin River five miles above the mouth of the Merced. Freight was brought by water to this point. The first settlement at the site of Dover was made in the fall of 1844 at the time of General José Castro's attempt to build a fort at the place to facilitate the location of Alvarado's grant, Las Mariposas. Dover was occupied by Americans in 1866. Grain farming and better boat-landing facilities later led to the abandonment of the site in favor of Hill's Ferry (Stanislaus County), six miles down the San Joaquin River.

Plainsburg, first settled in 1853 and once a thriving settlement on Mariposa Creek twelve miles southeast of Merced, began to decline with the advent of the railroad in 1872.

The Old Stage Road

The numerous rivers and streams running from the Sierra Nevada down into the San Joaquin Valley made it necessary for the early roads to follow along the base of the foothills and thus avoid the tules or swamps of the lowlands. These foothill roads afforded solid foundation even in rainy seasons. Likewise, the streams were more easily forded before they spread out over the level valley floor. Population during the '50's and '60's was centered in the mines, and supplies had to be freighted into the southern Mother Lode from Stockton along the stage route at the base of the hills. At the time of the formation of Merced County, in 1855, the legislature placed the eastern boundary along this old Stockton–Fort Miller Road, which was a part of the Stockton–Los Angeles Stage Road.

At first but "a dim and shifting pack trail, as travel increased, the hoofs of the oxen and the wheels of the emigrants' covered wagons marked out a roadway that was finally worn into a deep gash by the long freight teams as they drew the big heavy prairie schooners along its meandering course. Laterals, both pack trails and wagon roads, branched off to the various mining camps in the adjacent hills."

Across the Merced River, the Stockton–Fort Miller Road had a choice of three ferries, Murray's, Young's, and Phillips', grouped within two miles or less from Merced Falls down. The smaller creeks had to be forded, a feat which would have been impossible among the tules of the valley.

After the coming of the railroad, in 1872, the bottom lands of the San Joaquin were soon converted into a rich agricultural region. Not only were the hill towns deserted but the old stage road also relapsed into a dim and forgotten trail of which only a vestige here and there is visible today. A temporary marker at the Merced-Mariposa county line indicates the intersection of the old Fort Miller Road with the present highway from Merced to Yosemite.

SOURCES

[Credit is here given for source material, and permission to quote is hereby acknowledged]

FRÉMONT, JOHN C. *The Exploring Expedition to the Rocky Mountains, Oregon and California.* George H. Derby & Company, Buffalo, 1849

LATTA, F. F. "San Joaquin Primeval—Archaeology," in *Tulare Daily Times,* 1931

———. "San Joaquin Primeval—Spanish," in *Tulare Daily Times,* 1932

McCUBBIN, J. C. *Stockton–Los Angeles Stage Road.* Manuscript, 1930

MILLIKEN, RALPH. "San Luís Gonzaga Rancho History Dates from Earliest Civilization of San Joaquin," in *The Los Banos Enterprise,* January 27, 1933

OUTCALT, JOHN. *History of Merced County.* Historic Record Company, Los Angeles, 1925

TREADWELL, EDWARD F. *The Cattle King.* Macmillan Company, New York, 1931

MODOC COUNTY

MODOC COUNTY was formed in 1874 from a part of Siskiyou County. There are different opinions as to the meaning of the name, but ethnologists generally agree that Modoc means "south people," and was probably the name given the natives of this region by the Klamaths, their kinsmen on the north.

Alturas, the first and only county seat of Modoc County, was originally called Dorris Bridge after the owner of the ranch on which it was located. The town is still bordered on the south by this ranch.

The Tule Lake Petroglyphs

At the southeastern corner of Tule Lake, in the Lava Beds National Monument, a high bluff of smooth sandstone projects into the dry bed of the lake, and a chain of Indian petroglyphs, chiseled deep into the sandstone, extends for several hundred yards along its face. The carvings of these unusual rock writings, which have been painted, are undoubtedly the work of early Indian tribes. The Indians living in the region in the early '50's disclaimed all knowledge of them, regarding them with awe and surrounding them with legends. The elements have obliterated some of the carvings, but most of them remain as clear cut, and the black and ochre colorings apparently as undimmed, as the day they were first put there by unknown hands.

Some authorities believe that these carvings were made by the last of the Rock Indians. These Indians antedated and were exterminated by the fiercer Modocs, who took possession of the lava beds with their many hiding-places and abundant water supply.

Frémont in Modoc County

A faded wooden marker east of Tule Lake, unseen from the present highway because of re-routing, commemorates Frémont's expedition through Modoc County when he traveled from Fort Sutter to Upper Klamath Lake over what was later known as the eastern branch of the California–Oregon Trail. In the vicinity of Cornell, on the J. P. Harter Ranch, the party camped May 1-4, 1846. Among the group were Kit Carson, Alexis Godey, and Richard Owens. Tule Lake is designated as Rhett Lake on Frémont's map.

The Applegate Cut-Off and Lassen's Trail

The Applegate Cut-Off from Oregon across the northeast corner of California to the Humboldt River in Nevada was opened up by Jesse and Lindsey (Lindsley) Applegate with the help of thirteen others in June and July of 1846. In the autumn of the same year ninety or a hundred wagons were piloted by the Applegates from Fort Hall into Oregon over the new road. In 1848 Peter Lassen followed this route across Nevada via High Rock Canyon and Massacre Lake and through the '49 Canyon into California by way of Surprise Valley. Passing between Upper and Middle lakes and up the west side of the valley to Fandango Pass (long known as Lassen's Pass), the old trail led down into Goose Lake Valley, where it followed the eastern shore of the lake to a narrow neck at the southern end of the basin a few miles from Sugar Loaf Hill.

Across this neck at a point on the west shore of Goose Lake the Applegate Road turned toward Oregon, passing around the north end of both Clear Lake and Tule Lake into the Klamath country. At this same point on Goose Lake the true Lassen's Trail began. Running in an almost southerly direction across the Devil's Garden and striking the Pit River near the mouth of Rattlesnake Creek four miles west of the present town of Alturas, it continued along the north side of the Pit, crossing the river near the mouth of a canyon below the site of Canby. Passing south and west, its course lay through Stone Coal Valley, where it went due west for a few miles and then turned south along the Pit River. Crossing and recrossing the stream several times or following along the sides of the hills above it, the trail finally led across the river for the last time ten miles above the site of Lookout. From there it proceeded down the east side of the Pit River to Big Valley in Lassen County. Joseph B. Chiles with a company of twelve men, among whom was Pierson B. Reading, had followed much the same route into California, by way of Goose Lake and the Pit River, in October 1843.

Tradition has it that the Pit River was so named because of the many holes or pits which had been dug in the region by Indians for trapping wild animals. Reading, who entered California by the Pit River route in 1843, makes mention in his journal of these treacherous pitfalls, into which one of his party fell. It should be noted in this connection, however, that Commodore Charles Wilkes, in his report and on his map of 1841, designated this stream as "Pitt's River" and Goose Lake as "Pitt's Lake," which indicates a different origin for the name. Hudson's Bay Company trappers had penetrated this region before 1830, a fact recorded by Peter Skene Ogden in his diary of 1829. In this record, also, we find mention of "Pitt's River" under the entries of May 21 and 28.

From 1846 on, the Applegate Cut-Off was used by emigrants from Oregon, and in August 1848 the first wagon train to enter California from the north came in over the Applegate and Lassen roads. The Oregonians, captained by Peter Burnett (afterward the first governor of California) and piloted by Thomas McKay, an old Hudson's Bay Company trapper, followed the Applegate Road to Clear Lake, where the party branched off, blazing a new road south to the Pit River. There, Burnett writes, "to our utter surprise and astonishment, we found a new wagon road. Who made this road we could not at first imagine." It was later found that this was the trail over which Peter Lassen and his party of emigrants had just passed on their way to Lassen's Ranch in Tehama County. Southeast of Lassen Peak at the headwaters of the North Fork of the Feather River, the Oregonians came upon Lassen and his party, whom they found stranded and in dire distress, their provisions almost exhausted.

The general course of Burnett's trail was followed by gold-seekers in '49 and the early '50's, and the present highway from Klamath Falls to Bieber in Lassen County follows closely the trail of the '49'ers.

The Fandango Pass Massacre

Fandango Pass, over which the Applegate Cut-Off and Lassen's Trail crossed the Warner Mountains, was the scene of an Indian massacre in the early '50's. A large emigrant train coming into California over this trail passed the summit of the mountains to the edge of the valley beyond. Below lay the shining waters of Goose Lake. Believing that this was an arm of the Pacific Ocean and that thus their long journey was at an end, the emigrants encamped near a large spring at the edge of the valley. Filled with rejoicing over their safe arrival in the new land, the party was indulging in a fandango (a lively Spanish dance) when the camp was suddenly attacked by Indians and the entire company killed. Because of this tragic occurrence the name Fandango was given to the adjoining valley, as well as to the mountain and pass. The spot where the massacre took place is now marked by a Forest Service sign.

At the head of Fandango Valley in 1866 a battle took place between a group of settlers and soldiers from Surprise Valley and a band of Piute Indians in which the Indians were badly defeated. This spot likewise is marked by a Forest Service sign.

The Massacre at Rattlesnake Ranch

Evidences of another early massacre were found on the old Lassen Trail four miles west of Alturas on what was later known as Rattlesnake Ranch. Here in 1870 the Hess family and other pioneer settlers came upon a large circle of burned wagons in a flat on the north side of the Pit River close to the present Redding–Alturas Highway. All that is known of the tragedy was gleaned from fragmentary stories told by Indians sixty or seventy years ago. Although unmarked, the site of the massacre is known to old settlers of the region.

Bloody Point

One of the most terrible of the emigrant massacres in Modoc County took place in 1850 at Bloody Point on Tule Lake near the present Dalles–Reno Highway a few miles south of the California-Oregon line. Passing over the old Oregon Trail, a band of more than ninety emigrants, men, women, and children, were attacked by the Modoc Indians at this point, and all were killed except one man, who, badly wounded, escaped to the settlements in southern Oregon with his tragic tale of disaster. Old wagon parts were still picked up at the spot twenty years ago. It is now marked by a Forest Service sign.

A second emigrant train narrowly escaped death at this point in 1851, and were rescued only by the timely intervention of Oregon Volunteers. The spot apparently was a favorite place of ambush, as several other parties were killed there by the Indians, and for many years it bore the title "The Dark and Bloody Ground of the Pacific."

The Cressler and Bonner Trading-Post

In Surprise Valley there are still standing some of the first log cabins which were built by white settlers, all loopholed for defense against the Indians. Among these is the log trading-post which was conducted by William T. Cressler and John H. Bonner. The oldest structure in Modoc County, it was built in 1865 by a man named Townsend, who, shortly afterward, was killed by Indians. Townsend's widow sold the building to Cressler and Bonner, and in it the partners set up the first mercantile establishment in the county. A thriving trade was carried on, first with emigrants en route to California and Oregon and later with the early settlers of Surprise Valley.

This interesting relic, surrounded by a magnificent grove of trees planted by the original owners, stands in a semipublic park in the center of Cedarville. The structure is marked by a Forest Service sign.

The first road from Cedarville to Alturas followed, in a very general way, the course of the present scenic highway over the Warner Mountains from Surprise Valley. John H. Bonner, in 1869, was the one who was largely instrumental in securing the construction of this road over the Bonner Grade, which was named in his honor. This route, which became an important stage and freight road to Yreka, was maintained by Bonner until 1871, when Siskiyou County took it over as a county road.

Indian Battles

The battle of Infernal Caverns, one of the most famous Indian fights in California, took place on September 26–27, 1867, between a band of Shoshones and Piutes, with a few Pits—about a hundred warriors in all—and General George Crook with sixty-five soldiers. For some time the Indians, well equipped with arms and ammunition, had been terrorizing the settlers throughout southern Idaho, western Nevada, and northeastern California, and General Crook and his men had been sent to subdue them. The Indians were finally driven into a very rough region near the site of the present village of Likely on the South Fork of the Pit River. Here, before a seemingly impregnable fortress of caves and rocks, a pitched battle took place. The Indians were eventually driven from their stronghold, leaving many of their number dead, but not before eight of Crook's command were killed and fourteen wounded.

The battleground of Infernal Caverns, where the old fortifications may still be seen, has been marked by a Forest Service sign. At the foot of the slope the graves of six of the soldiers killed in action have been marked by regulation Army headstones. Lieutenant Madigan, who was among those killed in this battle, was brevetted posthumously for conspicuous bravery. His body was secretly buried at a spot near the forks of the Pit River not far from Alturas.

One of the engagements of the Modoc War took place on December 21, 1872, on what is now the J. P. Harter Ranch, then known as Land's Ranch, at a spot located within a stone's throw of the old Frémont camp site on the Oregon Trail. Army supply wagons, escorted by a detachment of cavalrymen, had reached camp in safety, but several of the soldiers who had dropped behind were suddenly attacked by Indians in hiding among the rocks above the road. Two men were killed and several wounded.

The last of the engagements which occurred during the Modoc War was fought at daylight on May 10, 1873, when Captain Jack, leader of the Modocs, led a charge on the military camp at Dry Lake. The soldiers were aroused to a realization of their danger by the stampeding of their horses and mules. Imbued with a desire for vengeance after the long and bitter campaign of the winter and spring, they led a fierce counter-attack seldom equaled in the annals of Indian warfare. This battle resulted in a decisive defeat for the Indians and the capture of Captain Jack, thus putting an end to the Modoc War. The site of this important Indian battle is located about half a mile from the main Klamath Falls–Alturas Highway and has been marked by a Forest Service sign and by a pile of rocks placed there by veterans of the engagement.

Fort Bidwell

Fort Bidwell, at the head of Upper Lake in Surprise Valley, about thirty miles northeast of Alturas and about ten miles south of the Oregon boundary line, was named in honor of General John Bidwell. It was established in 1866, and cavalrymen were stationed there to hold in check the marauding Indians of northeastern California, southern Oregon, and western Nevada. Fort Bidwell was finally abandoned as a military outpost in 1892, but until 1930 it was used as a government school for Indians. The boarding-school was discontinued that year and the military barracks, formerly used for dormitories, were torn down. The commanding officer's quarters, however, are still standing, and near by is the old military graveyard. Modern homes have taken the place of the old hovels in which the Indians long lived, and the two hundred acres of fine bottom lands which had been used for the school farm have been given to the Indians for their use.

SOURCES

[Credit is here given for source material, and permission to quote is hereby acknowledged]

BANCROFT, HUBERT HOWE. *History of California* (Vol. V, 1846–1848), in *The Works of Hubert Howe Bancroft*. The History Company, San Francisco, 1886

BROWN, WILLIAM S. "The Land of Burned Out Fires," in *Touring Topics*, XIX, No. 8 (August 1927)

BURNETT, PETER H. *Recollections and Opinions of an Old Pioneer.* D. Appleton & Company, New York, 1880·

CLELAND, ROBERT GLASS. *Pathfinders*, of the series *California*, edited by John Russell McCarthy. Powell Publishing Company, Los Angeles, 1929

DELANO, A. *Life on the Plains and among the Diggings.* Miller, Orton & Mulligan, Auburn and Buffalo, 1854

DORNIN, MAY. *The Emigrant Trails into California.* Master's thesis in History. University of California, Berkeley, California, 1921

FRÉMONT, JOHN C. *Memoirs of My Life.* Chicago and New York, 1887

LIPPS, OSCAR H. *The Case of the California Indians.* United States Indian School Print Shop, Chemawa, Oregon, 1932

OGDEN, PETER SKENE. "Journals of Snake Expeditions, 1827–28; 1828–29, with Editorial Notes by T. C. Elliott," in *Quarterly of the Oregon Historical Society,* XI (December 1910), 355–397

READING, PIERSON B. "Journal of Pierson B. Reading, Written during His Journey from Westport, Missouri, to Monterey, California, in 1843," in *Quarterly of the Society of California Pioneers,* VII, No. 3 (September 1930), 148–198

RIDDLE, JEFF C. *The Indian History of the Modoc War.* Privately published, 1914

SANCHEZ, NELLIE VAN DE GRIFT. *Spanish and Indian Place Names in California.* A. M. Robertson, San Francisco, 1922

WILKES, CHARLES. *Narrative of the United States Exploring Expedition during the Years 1838, 1839, 1840, 1841, 1842.* 5 vols. and an atlas. Lea & Blanchard, Philadelphia, 1845

NEVADA COUNTY

NEVADA COUNTY (Nevada is Spanish for "snow-covered") was formed in 1851 from territory that had been originally a part of Yuba County. Nevada City was made its county seat. Situated in a region where the entire upper country wears a heavy mantle of snow during the winter months, the name Nevada was appropriately chosen by its citizens for the town of Nevada City. Later the same name was given to the county.

The Donner Tragedy

One of the routes into California most frequently used by the emigrants of 1849 and the '50's was known as the California Trail, or the Truckee Pass Emigrant Road, which followed up the Truckee River valley in Nevada through Donner Pass in the High Sierra.

The first overland party of emigrants to follow the California Trail was the Stevens party, which passed that way in the autumn of 1844. In 1845, John C. Frémont, with a small detachment of his company, entered California by this same trail. But the most famous group to negotiate it was the ill-fated Donner party, whose experiences in the High Sierra during the winter of 1846–1847 constitute the most heart-rending tragedy in the history of California.

In the spring of 1846 a party of emigrants, led by George and Jacob Donner and James F. Reed, was organized in Sangamon County, Illinois, and started on what proved to be the most terrible trek westward in all the annals of American history. When the party reached Independence, Missouri, the first week in May, it had grown to such proportions that between two and three hundred wagons were included in the train.

Upon arriving at Fort Bridger, the Reed-Donner party proper took the fatal step of breaking off from the larger group and following the Hastings Cut-Off, a supposed short cut which passed south of the Great Salt Lake. Instead of taking but one week as was expected, a whole month of valuable time was consumed in reaching Salt Lake. Struggling on over the great salt deserts west of the lake, where the party suffered terrible hardships, they finally reached the site of Reno, Nevada, entirely exhausted. Finding forage for their emaciated animals here, the party rested for three or four days. This delay, however, proved to be disastrous, for the storm clouds were already gathering when they reached the mountains. The little band hastened up the eastern side of the Sierra as fast as possible, but on October 28, 1846, before they could reach the summit, heavy snow began to fall—a month earlier than usual.

The emigrants, already weakened and spent, soon found it almost impossible to make progress through the rapidly deepening snow, which quickly obliterated all semblance of a trail. Several valiant attempts were made to cross the mountain barrier, but all ended in bitter defeat. With fear growing in their hearts, the party hastened to make what pitiful preparations they could for winter camp on the shores of Donner Lake. Here most of them found shelter—such as it was—in three log cabins and a few hastily constructed shacks. However, the families of George and Jacob Donner, owing to an accident which delayed them, had been forced into camp at Alder Creek, about six miles below the lake. Here their only shelters were crude huts of canvas and boughs banked with snow. With such meager protection from the elements, during what proved to be the most severe winter in thirty years, and with actual famine staring them in the face, the members of the unfortunate party would all have perished had no aid come to them.

On December 10 or, according to some authorities, on the 16th, a party of ten men and five women, who were afterward known as the "Forlorn Hope," started out in a desperate attempt to obtain help. Struggling on for thirty-two days over the snow-covered mountains and enduring almost unbelievable hardships, the five women and two of the men, William Eddy and William Foster, finally succeeded in reaching Johnson's Ranch near the present site of Wheatland, some thirty-five miles north of Sutter's Fort.

With the aid of John A. Sutter and others, four relief parties were subsequently organized to attempt the rescue of those still held prisoners in the mountains. Possessed of great stamina and courage, the men comprising these parties succeeded in carrying in provisions and in bringing out from their frightful camps of death the pitifully emaciated survivors, many of whom were children.

Of the eighty-one persons who, according to McGlashan, began the winter at Donner Lake and on Alder Creek, thirty-six perished. The suffering, black despair, and death which stalked through these camps in the mountains beggar description, but the unselfishness and enduring courage of many members of the party, especially of the women, make the story one of greatness as well as one of tragedy. Of the many acts of sacrificial heroism, none surpasses that of Tamsen Donner, wife of George Donner, who refused to leave her dying husband alone in the desolate camp. Knowing she had sealed her own fate, she watched her children go out with the third relief party. "For heroism ennobled and glorified by love and sacrifice one looks in vain in the annals of California history for a finer example than that of Tamsen Donner."

The old Emigrant Road, over which the Reed-Donner party passed, was first marked by P. M. Weddell, a San Jose high-school teacher, with signs on which the picture of a covered wagon was traced. One such sign was placed at Donner Lake, and one at the spot where the trail crossed the present highway near Donner Creek, while a third is on the pass, at the summit of which is the Donner Summit Bridge. These sites are now marked also by permanent bronze plaques. The tablet on the bridge bears the inscription, "Donner Summit Bridge dedicated to the Pioneers who blazed the Overland Trail through these mountains."

The Pioneer Monument, erected by the Native Sons of the Golden West, stands at the lower end of Donner Lake, and marks the site of the Breen cabin, one of the shelters used by the Donner party. It consists of a rock pedestal supporting a group of four figures in bronze representing a pioneer family. On the front of the pedestal is the inscription, "Virile to risk and find—Kindly withal and a ready help —Facing the brunt of fate—Indomitable—Unafraid." On the back of the pedestal are the words: "In commemoration of the Pioneers who crossed the plains to settle California. Erected under the auspices of the Native Sons of the Golden West and Native Daughters of the Golden West. Dedicated June 6, 1918."

The Breen cabin, located about a quarter of a mile below the foot of the lake, had been erected in November 1844 by Moses Schallenberger, Joseph Foster, and Allen Montgomery, and in it Schallenberger, then a lad of seventeen, spent the winter alone, guarding the goods stored there by the Elisha Stevens party, until their return March 1, 1845. The Stevens expedition had been led across the Plains in 1844 by Caleb Greenwood, trapper and mountaineer, and his two sons, Britain and John. The company had about a dozen wagons, which were the first to cross the Sierra Nevada into the valley of California.

About a mile east of the Pioneer Monument and just south of the highway stands the Donner Cross. A bronze tablet 195 feet south of the cross marks the site of the Graves cabin. Placed by the Native Sons of the Golden West, it bears the legend, "Donner Party, 1846–47. On this spot stood the Graves Cabin."

Where the Murphy cabin stood, a huge boulder, which formed the north end of the cabin's fireplace, bears a bronze tablet with the words: "Donner Party, 1846–47. The face of this rock formed the north end of the fireplace of the Murphy Cabin. General Stephen W. Kearny, on June 22, 1847, buried under the middle of the cabin the bodies found in the vicinity."

McGlashan places the site of the Donner tents at the head of Alder Creek about a mile and a half above its junction with Prosser Creek. The exact spot, however, has not been determined. Somewhere in the vicinity the body of George Donner was buried, in June 1847, by some of Kearny's men, according to Edwin Bryant, who accompanied that expedition.

The Old Emigrant Trail

One of the first permanent markers along the old Emigrant Trail was placed near Truckee. The tablet contains the following inscription:

The Emigrant Trail in the pioneer days of California came through the low pass to the north facing this monument. The trail turned west at this point for a distance of approximately twenty-six hundred feet, where a tablet describes the route then followed.
Placed by Historic Landmarks Committee, Native Sons of the Golden West, September 14, 1929.

The second tablet, mentioned in the wording of the first and placed on the same day, reads:

The Emigrant Trail in the pioneer days of California turned to the south at this point for approximately three miles, then west across the summit of the Sierras about a mile south of the present railroad. It was here that the Donner party missed the trail, owing to the early snows, resulting in tragedy.

It has been generally assumed that the Donner party and most of the other early emigrants who crossed the Sierra Nevada by way of the Truckee River and the Donner Pass traveled down the ridge north of the Bear River, entering the Sacramento Valley by that route. However, W. W. Waggoner of Nevada City presents a number of considerations which tend to show that a large proportion of the early travel followed down the San Juan Ridge between the Middle and South forks of the Yuba River and that this was the probable route of the Donner party.

Tracing the path of the "Forlorn Hope," Waggoner says that after crossing the summit the party came to the South Fork of the Yuba River. They followed the northern bank of the river on the southern exposure in order to avoid the deeper snowdrifts, and kept to the highest crest of the ridge so as to cross as few ravines as possible. The gorge down which they slid to the bottom, and out of which they climbed with so much difficulty, "must have been Canyon Creek." After regaining the top of the ridge and passing the site of Graniteville, the party proceeded over Relief Hill to Cherokee. They were now past the snow line and soon found the road. Working southward from the site of Cherokee they discovered footprints, and soon the seven survivors of the little band that over a month before had set out to seek relief for the snow-bound Donner party came in sight of an Indian village, probably at the same location as the present Indian Springs. All but dead from hunger and exposure, they were cared for by the sympathetic Indians, who later helped them secure aid from Johnson's Ranch.

In the opinion of this authority, also, the various relief parties which carried aid to the starving people at Donner Lake followed up this same ridge. The probable location of "Mule Springs" he places at the Thore Ranch near Cherokee, and that of "Bear Valley" at North Bloomfield. Relief Hill, according to some of the accounts given by pioneers, derived its name from the fact that the group of refugees brought out from the camp at Donner Lake by the first relief party were given much-needed aid at this place, when James F. Reed, leading the second relief, gave succor to Captain Reasin P. Tucker and his companions on February 27, 1847.

Other authorities, however, among them Mr. Edmund G. Kinyon, believe that the Donner refugees followed approximately the route of the Stevens party.

Whatever may be the facts regarding the route of the Reed-Donner party, there is no question that a much-traveled emigrant road came down the San Juan Ridge from Henness Pass in Sierra County. This route followed down the ridge over a soil formation and was preferable to the route over Donner Pass, which was extremely rough and rocky. During the '60's this route became one of the stage and freight roads for the mines of the famous Comstock Lode in Nevada. A few years ago the section of this road which extends above Graniteville was rebuilt and utilized in the construction of the Bowman Dam.

Toll Roads

During the '50's and '60's the rapid development of mines in the recesses of the mountains resulted in an imperative demand for the construction of roads—a demand which the county governments could not meet because of the great expense involved. Consequently, private enterprise had to be relied upon, with the result that most of the roads and bridges which replaced the former precarious pack trails were constructed and owned by individuals or by turnpike companies, and were operated for profit.

The development of a system of state and national highways following roughly the early roads and trails has in recent years almost completely eliminated the toll-road system in the state. Nevada County bought the last of her toll roads and bridges about 1890.

Among the privately owned turnpikes leading from Nevada City were the following: the Nevada–Washington; the Nevada–Little York; the Nevada–Grass Valley; and the South Yuba Road, one of the most interesting, which went from Nevada City to Lake City on the San Juan Ridge, crossing the South Fork of the Yuba at Robinson's Crossing, later known as Black's and now as Edward's Bridge. Today a fine scenic highway follows the route of this early stage road. Halfway down the rocky, mossgrown walls at Edward's Bridge is a large bald rock bearing a white triangular marking edged with black. The white is said to signify that a stage robbery occurred at this spot, while the black indicates that someone was killed during the hold-up.

Another important turnpike followed approximately the route taken by the present state highway from Nevada City to Downieville. The first ten-mile stretch of the road was known as Purdon's Grade. The bridge across the South Fork was at first known as Wall's, then as Webber's, and finally as Purdon's, before its purchase by the county. The bridge at the Middle Fork of the Yuba River was and still is known as Freeman's Crossing. Thomas Freeman, in 1854, purchased the property from Thomas Hess, who built the first bridge at this point in 1851. The winter floods carried it away and a second structure, subsequently taken over by Freeman, was erected in 1852. After the flood of 1862 Freeman built a substantial structure which he owned for some thirty years. Two of the old pilings of this bridge may still be seen in the river. That portion of the tollhouse which served as a stable also stands, and the beautiful rock walls, between which the stagecoaches passed on their way up the mountain so many years ago, are in perfect condition.

Just above the massive concrete bridge which carries the modern motorist across the river into Yuba County, Oregon Creek runs into the Middle Yuba. Here is the junction of three highways, one leading up Oregon Creek to Downieville, a second turning right across the creek through an old covered bridge to Alleghany, Forest, and the Henness Pass in Sierra County, and a third proceeding to the left by the Moon Shine Road across Moon Shine Creek to the Bullard's Bar Dam in Yuba County—modern highways of superb scenic grandeur following the routes of old historic trails and turnpike roads.

Yuba River Bars

Early in 1849 John Rose, who gave his name to Rose's Bar in Yuba County, built a cattle corral at a spot in Pleasant Valley on the lower San Juan Ridge between the sites later occupied by the Anthony House on Deer Creek (a stage station on the old turnpike up the San Juan Ridge) and Bridgeport. Apparently Rose's original purpose was to trade with the Indians of the region, but during the early summer prospectors found their way up the South and Middle forks of the Yuba River and Deer Creek, crevassing for gold and finding many rich gravel deposits on the bars along the margins of these streams. The news of these discoveries spread quickly, and by late summer and early fall of 1849 scores of miners were working the Deer Creek and Yuba River surface diggings. In order to accommodate the increasing trade, Rose established a trading-post in a small adobe which he had built. The structure has fallen into ruins but the stone and adobe fireplace is still intact.

As in practically all of the mining regions of the Sierra Nevada, the first prospecting in Nevada County was confined to the gravel bars and the beds of running streams. Scores of river-bar camps sprang up almost overnight. Typical of these mining camps was Bridgeport, on the South Fork of the Yuba, about one and a half miles from its mouth. For two years the town was exceedingly prosperous, but after river mining ceased to be profitable the camp declined. Today the name is preserved only in Bridgeport Township. A modern highway to French Corral crosses the South Fork of the Yuba at the site of Bridgeport over an old covered bridge erected in 1862.

On the Middle Fork of the Yuba additional camps were established in 1850, among them Rice's Crossing (at first known by the rather dubious title of Liar's Flat and then as Lousy Level), Frenchman's Bar, and Condemned Bar (Yuba County). On the South Fork was Jones's Bar, once famous among the river camps.

Panning for gold was, of course, the first and most primitive method of washing the precious metal from the auriferous gravel. The first machine to be employed for the purpose was the rocker, which was introduced in the summer of 1848. This was, in turn, superseded by the long-tom. Gradually the miners extended their activities to the gravel of the dry gulches, flats, and hillsides, and ground-sluicing (introduced by William Elwell at Nevada City in February or March of 1850) came into practice. With this innovation there was developed an elaborate system of ditches and sluice boxes, out of which, in time, grew the more powerful and extensive hydraulic methods of the '60's and '70's. Many old mining ditches today serve the irrigation needs of orchards and gardens in the hill country of the Sierra Nevada.

After many years, men may again be seen throughout the Sierra Nevada mining regions panning, in primitive fashion, for the gold washed by the clear waters of the mountain streams. A turn in the winding mountain highway may reveal some lone camp in a sequestered ravine, while here and there along the present bars which flank the larger streams whole families can be found encamped.

Rough and Ready

Coming up from Marysville to Grass Valley by way of Timbuctoo and Smartsville in Yuba County, the modern motorist climbs the wooded hills through a country which grows richer in historic interest with each curving vista of the highway. The many early farmhouses, tucked in among their gnarled apple trees, give to the countryside that hint of old New England found nowhere in California except in the Sierra gold regions. Touching elbows with these fast-vanishing bits of pastoral beauty are everywhere to be seen the deeply scarred gullies and gravelly hillocks which mark the abandoned diggings of the '50's and '60's.

Another turn in the road brings one to a place of green upland meadows where a tiny hamlet lies sheltered among aging shade and orchard trees. This dreamy spot, with its weatherbeaten, shake-roofed houses, belies its name—Rough and Ready—but in the feverish days of the '50's it was a busy mining town, one of the first to be established in Nevada County. A party of men calling themselves the Rough and Ready Company arrived in the vicinity on September 9, 1849, under the leadership of Captain Townsend, who had served under General Zachary Taylor ("Old Rough and Ready"), hero of the Mexican War. For several months the Rough and Readys were able to keep the richness of this region a secret, pre-empting all the land round about, but by 1850 the incoming tide of miners could not be held back and the place developed into a good-sized town.

One episode in the history of the town makes it unique. During the uncertain days of 1850, while state sovereignty was still in abeyance, E. F. Brundage conceived the idea of a separate and independent government. Issuing a high-sounding manifesto, he called a mass meeting to organize the State of Rough and Ready. For a short period he had a following of about a hundred, but the whole affair met with so much ridicule that the State of Rough and Ready soon dissolved into thin air.

On June 28, 1850, Rough and Ready had its first devastating fire. But in spite of this discouraging experience, in October it polled a thousand votes and even aspired to become the county seat of the newly organized Nevada County.

A committee to preserve law and order had been elected, a Christian Association was holding services in a little clapboard shanty, and the Masons and the Odd Fellows had joined in forming a benevolent association. The town continued to grow, and during the early '50's boasted more than three hundred substantial frame buildings.

But its decline began with the gradual exhaustion of the gold in the creeks and on the flats, and by 1870, after the fires of 1856 and 1859 had all but wiped out the place, only twenty-four houses were left in the town. A few of these are still standing. On the hill is the I.O.O.F. building, deeded by the society (now joined with the Grass Valley lodge) to the town of Rough and Ready as a community hall. The old hotel, built about 1853, serves today as post office and store, while before its door stands a gasoline pump in place of the watering trough once patronized by the thirsty stagecoach horses. A bit of local color is seen in a collection of pioneer relics preserved in a corner of the large room which formerly served as the hotel lobby and bar. Among these a shelf of old-time schoolbooks claims the visitor's special attention, as does the curious cash register with its little steel marbles with which a faithful account of each day's business was kept.

As one leaves the town, the old Fippin blacksmith shop, deserted and dilapidated, stands on the left of the road, while a little farther on to the right is the Toll House, now a private residence. Scars of old diggings are passed on either side of the road as one leaves the village behind and climbs the hills toward Grass Valley, four miles away.

In 1865–1866 during the copper-mining excitement, a boom occurred southwest of Rough and Ready, and the towns of Spenceville, Hacketville, Wilsonville, and Queen City were laid out. Only Spenceville appears on the maps of today. With a population of 150, it is the center of a small agricultural community. Three miles northeast of Rough and Ready is Newtown (formerly Sailor Flat), while west, below the mouth of Deer Creek, is Mooney Flat, both "ghost towns" of the '50's.

Grass Valley

The town of Grass Valley, replete with memories of the vivid and colorful gold-mining days, received its name from the well-watered valley in which it lies. The valley was so named by a company of emigrants who in 1849 found their way into its verdant meadows, kept green by perpetual springs, after toiling over the Truckee Pass Trail with their half-starved cattle. The poor, gaunt beasts had strayed from camp during the night and in the morning were found by their owners enjoying the abundant grass and water of this welcome meadowland.

The first white men known to have seen this valley were Claude Chana and a party of French emigrants who passed that way in 1846. Later, in the summer of 1848, David Stump and two other prospectors came from Oregon to the diggings of El Dorado County, drifting northward into Grass Valley in October. Here they crevassed for gold near the sites of the Eureka and Idaho mines until approaching winter drove them from the mountains.

In August 1849 a party of five men headed by a Dr. Saunders built a cabin on Badger Hill near the eastern edge of what is now the city of Grass Valley. The Saunders party was soon joined by others, making a colony of twenty men who spent the winter in the valley and who formed the nucleus of the present city.

Another settlement, which also became a part of the modern Grass Valley, was established in what came to be known as Boston Ravine, named after the company which arrived there on September 23, 1849, under the leadership of Rev. H. H. Cummings, its president. Four cabins were erected on the south side of the ravine, where they spent the winter. On September 28, 1849, the first Christian burial in Nevada County took place in Boston Ravine, with Rev. Cummings officiating, when an emigrant who had toiled across the Plains, only to die on the threshold of his destination, was buried on the southern slope of the ravine.

For two years Boston Ravine was the chief settlement in the vicinity, laying the foundation for the flourishing trade of the town which ultimately grew out from it. Today a number of roofless buildings of brick and stone with the customary heavy iron doors mark this once thriving community. Back of the present grocery store at the foot of a narrow dirt road the chaotic ruins of the old bake shop lie hidden in a tangle of trees and bushes. The huge brick oven is still intact, an interesting relic of a bygone era.

Among the many rich placer mines in the Grass Valley district during the '50's were the Pike and Humbug flats, Grass Valley Slide, Thode Island Ravine, Kentucky Ravine, and the Lola Montez, the Kate Hardy, and other diggings.

Beneath the pines on Gold Hill, at the southern end of the present Church Street, stands a monument bearing the following inscription:

This tablet commemorates the discovery of gold-bearing quartz and the beginning of quartz mining in California. The discovery was made on Gold Hill by George Knight, October 1850. The occurrence of gold-bearing quartz was undoubtedly noted here and elsewhere about the same time or previously, but the above discovery created the great excitement that started the development of quartz mining into a great industry. The Gold Hill Mine, 1850–1857, is credited with a total production of $4,000,000. This monument dedicated by Quartz Parlor, N.S.G.W., and Manzanita Parlor, N.D.G.W., October 20, 1929.

All about the monument is striking evidence of the extent of the old quartz diggings, the scars and mammoth accumulations of which young pines are struggling vainly to conceal.

This discovery aided the development of the city of Grass Valley, which was transformed almost overnight from a hamlet of some fifteen or twenty houses to one of the richest camps in the mining regions. Excitement became intense, and the entire hill was soon staked out. It looked as if literally a mountain of gold had been found.

The discovery of other rich veins about Grass Valley followed quickly, and soon crude mills for the reduction of the ore were built. Scores of mines with sensational production figures were opened up, some of which have continued in operation until the present. Besides the Gold Hill Mine, where the discovery was first made, there were the Massachusetts Hill; the Eureka, located in 1851 on Wolf Creek; the Allison Ranch, located in 1853 two and one-half miles south of the town and for a time one of the richest in the state; the North Star, opened in 1851 on Lafayette Hill; the Empire, located in 1850 on Ophir Hill one mile southeast of town, one of the world's major gold mines and still producing; and the Idaho, located in 1863 just across Wolf Creek from the Eureka.

About a mile from the scene of Knight's sensational discovery the hoists and stamp mills of the consolidated North Star and Empire mines (the one to the south and the other to the east of Gold Hill) stand today amid the millions of tons of tailings accumulated from operations extending over a period of more than eighty years—for these mines have produced continuously since the early '50's. From the seemingly inexhaustible lode upon which the tunnels, shafts, stopes, and winzes are situated the stupendous sum of $80,000,000 has been taken. These two mines (like others in the county) are now consolidated under one management, and with increased mechanical equipment the company is carrying on extensive exploration work. The two properties, in the spring of 1932, were turning out seven hundred tons of quartz daily. The entire project is one of staggering proportions, one vein alone extending for a distance of more than nine thousand feet—nearly two miles. The longest shaft has been sunk to an inclined depth of approximately seven thousand feet, the bottom of the shaft being four thousand feet below the earth's surface and fifteen hundred feet below sea-level.

The same evidence of recent quartz-mining development is shown in the Idaho-Maryland mine near by, which, after having been closed for twenty-seven years, reopened in 1929. The Brunswick, another old producer owned by the same company, was recently reconditioned and is now being operated with a large crew.

The atmosphere of early mining days still clings to the town of Grass Valley, which even pavements and modern stores along its narrow, irregular streets cannot entirely destroy, accented as it is by outlying aged farmsteads and by the vivid scars of diggings flanking the roadsides and bordering the very town itself.

The oldest building in Grass Valley is probably the Western Hotel. The churches of the town likewise reflect a significant historical background. Isaac Owen, the first commissioned Methodist minister in California and later the founder, at Santa Clara, of the College of the Pacific (now located at Stockton), preached his first sermon on California soil under the shade of an oak tree in Grass Valley on the north portion of Clark's Ranch in September 1849, having just come overland by ox team. In January 1852, while Owen was presiding elder of the district, a church was organized in Grass Valley in a building which had been used as a schoolhouse and a meeting-place for the Presbyterians. This building was superseded by a larger one in 1854, and by still another in 1872. The rear portion of the present edifice was used during the '50's.

Opposite the Methodist Church on Church Street is the Episcopal Church, organized in 1855. The present building, erected in 1858, has served the community all these years. A few blocks up Church Street the bells of St. Mary's still call the people to worship as they did seventy-five years ago. The Congregationalists, under the leadership of Rev. J. D. Hale, a worker from the American Home Missionary Society, erected their first building in December 1853 on the corner of Neal and Church streets, where the present edifice now stands. In the original building the first Woman's Christian Temperance Union to be organized in California was formed in 1874 by the women of the Methodist and Congregational churches.

On April 9, 1933, the Harvard Club of San Francisco dedicated a tablet in the Public Library to Josiah Royce, philosopher, historian of California, and noted Harvard professor, who was born in Grass Valley in 1855.

Lola Montez, Countess of Landsfeld, Bavaria, came to Grass Valley in 1854. A woman of marked intellectual ability, of almost angelic beauty and with regal grace, Maria Dolores Eliza Rosanna Gilbert, alias Lola Montez, had been the personal friend of George Sand, Alexander Dumas, Victor Hugo, Lamartine, and Liszt, and the favorite of kings and queens throughout Europe. "A woman of loves, marriages, divorces, adventures," the magnetic and daring Lola, while she had charmed with the grace and originality of her dancing, had also exerted a considerable political influence throughout Bavaria.

A furor was created by the appearance of this extraordinary woman in San Francisco, where her Spider Dance took the rough miners by storm. Her subsequent sojourn in the obscure mining camp of Grass Valley was of romantic significance to that community, where the charm of her personality was widely felt.

Surrounded by magnificent poplar trees, the old house in which she lived with her pet bear—at that time a one-story cottage—with its brick-lined cellar, its rose garden, and its quaint dovecote, may still be seen on Mills Street, although it is fast falling into ruins. The site was originally occupied by the first school in Grass Valley, a private institution opened in 1852 by Rosa Farrington. However, the school was soon moved to the site where the Methodist Church now stands.

Two doors from the cottage where lived the beautiful and dashing Lola stands a dwelling which once served as a boarding-house. There a small, precocious child of six shyly admired the distinguished dancer, and between the two there ultimately developed an attachment which "laid a foundation for the success of that little girl in years to come, when, as Lotta Crabtree, she endeared herself to the heart of a nation."

There are many so-called "ghost cities" of the past just east and southeast of Grass Valley, with strangely incongruous names which bespeak the rough-and-ready life of the miners who created them, among them You Bet, Red Dog, Gouge Eye, Little York, Walloupa, and Quaker Hill.

Nevada City

James W. Marshall, the discoverer of gold at Coloma, came to Deer Creek, a tributary of the Yuba River, in the summer of 1848. The first white man to pan for gold at this spot, Marshall did not suspect that the stream contained phenomenal wealth, nor did he dream that just two years later more than ten thousand miners would be at work within a radius of three miles from the spot where he had found the first shining grains of metal.

Early in September 1849 Captain John Pennington and two companions built the first cabin on Gold Run above where that stream empties into Deer Creek and just above the site of the bridge now known as the Gault Bridge. In October Dr. A. B. Caldwell erected a log cabin and set up a store on the slope of Aristocracy Hill about where the Episcopal Church now stands and where in 1854 the first public school in the city was erected. For a time the place was known as Caldwell's Upper Store (or Deer Creek Dry Diggin's), as Dr. Caldwell previously had had a store seven miles below on Deer Creek at Pleasant Flat, where the town of Deer Creek grew up. Its inhabitants later removed to Newtown, where a number of springs furnished a good water supply.

In that same month the first family, the Stampses, settled in a ravine back of the present Coyote Street. During the fall came Madam Penn, an indefatigable worker, who customarily took her turn at the rocker. In the spring of 1850 this enterprising woman built a boarding-house on a site which since has been continuously occupied by a hotel or lodging-house and on which the Union Hotel now stands.

In March 1850 the miners elected Mr. Stamps as alcalde of Caldwell's Upper Store and at the same time decided to change the name of the place. In the census of 1850 the name of the town is given as Nevada City, although in a list of post offices for the year 1851 it appears as Nevada. When a county was established in that section of the Sierra country in 1851 it was also called Nevada, and the town of that name was made its county seat. Ten years later, when the state of Nevada was formed, the citizens of the town of Nevada in California bitterly protested that they had first claim to the name. The matter was appealed to Congress, but that body refused to act. Consequently, its citizens decided that their town should henceforth be known as Nevada City.

The phenomenal growth of this region was due at first almost entirely to surface placers. So eager were the miners to find rich strikes that even the streets of the town were not secure from operations. Finally one irate storekeeper protested these liberties. Approaching a miner in the act of digging up the street, the merchant demanded that he stop. The miner refused, pleading that there was no law which prevented him from digging in the streets. "Then I'll make a law," said the indignant merchant, producing a revolver; whereupon the miner beat a hasty retreat. Thereafter the streets of Nevada City were not disturbed.

On the eastern end of Lost Hill gold was discovered early in 1850. The gravel ranges of this section proved extraordinarily rich, and news of the diggings spread rapidly, causing a "mushroom" city to spring up almost overnight. It was not uncommon for the miners to take out a quart of gold (worth $6,000) in a single day in this region. Because the peculiar method of mining called "coyoteing," or tunneling, was adopted here, the town was called Coyoteville. During the two years of its existence a total of $8,000,000 is said to have been taken from the surrounding gravel banks. The site of the old settlement constitutes the northwestern section of the present Nevada City.

Many quartz mines in the neighborhood have notable production records: the Champion, Providence, Merrifield, Wyoming, Murchie, Pittsburg, New England, Sneath and Clay, and dozens of others. Adjacent areas, too, have their quota, the Willow Valley, Blue Tent, Canada Hill, and Banner being among the most productive. There has been renewed activity in some of these mines, although the Murchie, a profitable producer after being idle for twenty-five years, is now again inactive. The Hoge holdings in the Blue Tent section are notable producers.

As the motorist of today glides down the long smooth grade from the little old mining community of Town Talk, he beholds a panorama of mountains at the foot of which nestles Nevada City, its roofs and tall church spires gleaming white through the shade trees. In spite of paved streets and busy motor cars, Nevada City is still a story-book town, a place of picturesque relics vividly depicting its historic past. Aged, steep-roofed houses, three or four stories high, cling to the precipitous walls of Deer Creek canyon. One of them, a gabled structure of substantial brick, has long been known as "The Castle."

The streets of this quaint and colorful county seat are so crooked, and go wandering across the narrow valley in such confusion, that one has cause to wonder if they were "surveyed by burro trains of prospectors, meandering from the surrounding hills." Here and there along these labyrinthine thoroughfares interesting iron-barred stores of brick and stone, erected after the first shack city had been swept by fire in the early days, suggest the stirring scenes once familiar to the Argonauts.

On Commercial Street, which led from Coyoteville to the creek where the miners washed for gold, stands the assayer's office, established in 1853 and still doing business. Through these same doors, one memorable day in 1859, a miner from across the Sierra entered with puzzling specimens from a new "strike" made near Washoe Lake in Nevada. The ore was examined, and the assayer's report carried out from this building proved to be the most sensational bit of news since the announcement of Marshall's discovery of gold at Coloma in 1848, for it heralded the fabulous wealth of the Comstock silver mines, which within a few years produced almost one billion dollars.

Next door to the assayer's office, near the Deer Creek Bridge, the Native Sons of the Golden West, together with the Wells Fargo Bank and the Union Trust Company, have placed a bronze plaque on the site of the early Wells Fargo

Express office established in 1853. Other pioneer landmarks of the town include two firehouses of the '60's, with their quaint steeples from which the old bells still clamor forth the alarms of fire.

On Commercial Street two or three brick stores are standing in the two blocks which formerly made up Old Chinatown. A shack village had stood there before an ordinance was passed requiring brick buildings as a protection against fire. The Celestials responded to this action by moving almost en masse to another site just northeast of town, where a new shack Chinatown was built—and subsequently burned. A few of the more enterprising Chinese, however, remained on the original site and erected these surviving brick structures.

"The Washington Monument Church"

The first religious services in Nevada City, as in many other mining camps throughout the Sierra, were held under the spreading branches of a tree. In the summer of 1850, at the instance of Alcalde Stamps and Mr. Lamden, a former minister, money was raised by popular subscription for the first church. This was a crude affair built of shakes, and in this humble house of worship services were held for a time by the various denominations represented in the community.

The Congregationalists, organized September 28, 1851, by Rev. James H. Warren, took over the little shake church building but replaced it in the autumn of 1855 by a frame structure. This edifice, with its fine bell, was destroyed by fire in 1856. The following year a brick church was erected, but in the conflagration of 1863 this building likewise, with a library of one thousand volumes, was lost. The present structure, now used as a mortuary parlor, was erected in 1864 during the pastorate of Rev. H. H. Cummings.

The history of this church is connected with a circumstance of state-wide significance, and illustrates the broad influence which radiated from the pioneer ministries of many of these mountain charges. W. W. Ferrier says of this event: "The movement out of which was to come the College of California [forerunner of the University of California] had its inception in May 1853, a few days after the arrival of Professor Henry Durant, in the little mountain town of Nevada City." There, on May 9, a joint session of the Congregational Association of California and the Presbytery of San Francisco (New School) was held, and on the 17th a plan was adopted for establishing an institution of learning in California.

The little pioneer shake church building in which this meeting was held is known historically as the "'Washington Monument Church'—contributions for its erection having been made by men in the mines thereabout from every state in the Union. The bell in its tower was the first to ring in the Sierra the call to worship. The pastor, James H. Warren, was a graduate of Knox College . . . . Pastor in 1853 in that little mountain town, participator in that early educational movement . . . . James H. Warren was destined as Congregational Home Missionary Superintendent . . . . to lay by his memorable service the foundations of enduring churches over all the State."

Washington and Its Neighbors

Climbing the Washington Ridge over the Ukiah–Tahoe Highway, one passes a lonely grave seven or eight miles from Nevada City. Here in 1858 an emigrant family buried their two-year-old boy, Julius Alfred Appertson. For years this grave, marked by an inscribed wooden plaque nailed to the overshadowing pine tree, was tended by unknown hands, and for the past few years it has been cared for by the

Native Sons and Daughters of the Golden West. The California State Highway Commission ignored the original specifications for the road at this point sufficiently to leave the grave of this two-year-old lad undisturbed beneath its sentinel pine.

Passing the Nevada City–Grass Valley Ski Club, the motorist suddenly comes upon a marvelous view of rugged mountain scenery dominated by the majestic Sierra Buttes, which rise above the pine-clad ridges to the north and are visible for a hundred miles in every direction. From this point a road winds down through magnificent pines to the old mining town of Washington, picturesquely situated on the bank of the South Yuba River. Seeming to belie its memories of the stirring days of '49, the quiet little village of today boasts a population of less than one hundred and fifty. Its one hotel serves also as the post office. Next to the hotel stands an old store with massive stone walls which is still occupied as a place of business. Just outside the town are immense piles of huge granite boulders carried there stone by stone by patient Chinese miners of long ago. Here a gate covered with Chinese characters leads to the homes which they once occupied.

In the vicinity of the town during the gold days were numerous mining camps located at the various wealth-producing bars and flats along the river. While many of these camps never attained to the dignity of towns, some of them developed into trading-centers of considerable activity. At the mouth of Canyon Creek about three miles up the river from Washington was Canal Bar, from which the line of camps extended down stream past Long Bar, Keno Bar, Jimmy Brown's Bar, and Boulder Bar to Rocky Bar, a prosperous village, opposite which was Grissell Bar, worked by Chinamen. Across the river from Washington was the Brass Wire Bar, which in 1880 was worked entirely by Chinese miners. Below the town the chain of camps was continued by Whiskey Bar, Brandy Flat, Jackass Flat, and Lizard Flat, opposite which was the once thriving village of Jefferson.

Two miles south of Washington was Alpha, now a "ghost town," the birthplace of the noted prima donna Emma Nevada. The Alpha mines became exhausted in 1880, but up to that time they had produced no less than $1,500,000 in gold. One mile to the east was its sister camp, Omega, where the deep pit washed out by hydraulic mining reveals the old diggings from which $2,500,000 were taken during the same period. This mine still operates during the rainy season. Across the river from Washington a road winds up the canyon to the famous Eagle Bird Mine, while from the Washington Bridge another road leads about three miles to the Spanish Mine, where Patrick Dillon first panned for gold on Poorman's Creek in 1851.

"Bring Me Men to Match My Mountains"

Along the San Juan Ridge are the gravel deposits of an ancient river channel left high and dry above the present drainage system. These accumulations, washed down in some past geologic age and containing fossil wood and nearly every kind of rock known to the Sierra region, "were partly formed from the degradation of quartz veins," the result being a richly auriferous mass. The gold, however, is disseminated unevenly throughout the whole, the lower levels being the richest. The only way in which this gold can be extracted in paying quantities is by hydraulic mining, a method prohibited by the federal Anti-Débris Act of 1883 but later allowed again with certain restrictions.

It was along the San Juan Ridge that the most spectacular hydraulic operations took place. In this gigantic search for gold, an enterprise and ingenuity were combined which "left as mementoes the great hydraulic pits that appear to be the work of a Brobdingnagian race." Three companies owned vast mines in the region, which were operated at a tremendous outlay. High up in the Sierra, six thousand feet above sea-level, reservoirs were constructed from which the water supply for hundreds of mines along the Ridge was obtained through a system of canals and flumes that, although constructed in the '50's, '60's, and '70's merely with pick and shovel and carpenter's level, are still intact, exhibiting a marvel of workmanship upon which modern engineers could scarcely improve.

These three companies were the Eureka Lake and Yuba Canal Company, with headquarters at North Columbia, which owned four reservoirs and a system of ditches two hundred miles long; the North Bloomfield Mining Company, with forty-three miles of ditches; and the Milton Mining and Water Company, with offices at French Corral, which owned eighty miles of ditches. The total expenditures of these companies for construction and equipment amounted to $5,568,000.

In order to obtain the most effective management of the ditches and flumes along the Ridge, the companies in 1878 built, co-operatively, the world's first long-distance telephone line, at a cost of $6,000. This line was sixty miles long and extended up the Ridge from French Corral through Birchville, Sweetland, North San Juan, Cherokee, North Columbia, Lake City, North Bloomfield, Moore's Flat, Graniteville, Milton, and Bowman Lake. It was managed by the Ridge Telephone Company and owned jointly by the three named mining companies. Some of the old Edison instruments manufactured in Boston in 1876 may be seen at French Corral and North Bloomfield.

"Along the route of that telephone line, one may see the results of hydraulic mining operations—hillsides washed away and gutted for gold which cradles and long-toms could never have recovered. The terrain, mountainous and extremely rugged, is traversed by roads that are narrow and tortuous; but incomparable vistas of forested heights and verdant valleys pass in a review that is never to be forgotten. .... Below the mountain rims are livid scars, where age-old formations crumbled before the onslaught of great jets of water, searching the very bowels of the earth for gold."

The largest of these colossal excavations, the Malakoff, is second in size only to the La Grange Mine near Weaverville (Trinity County). Its sheer cliffs, its multicolored pinnacles and fantastic minarets, are exquisitely molded, reminding one of those weird and spectacular formations found in the desert canyons of the arid Southwest. It is difficult to realize that this marvel is man's handiwork, and one feels that the stirring call, "Bring me men to match my mountains," has been indeed fulfilled here.

Enormous profits in gold were being washed out along San Juan Ridge when the famous Sawyer decision of January 23, 1884, finally closed all hydraulic mines of the state. A mining engineer, resident in the district many years and eminently qualified to make such a statement, has declared that $400,000,000, at the very least, remain locked in the vast storehouse of San Juan Ridge.

Certain vitalizing sections of the Caminetti Act, passed by Congress in 1893, make it possible to regulate hydraulic mining by impounding the débris under the regulations of the California Débris Commission. For many years these provisions lay dormant and unused. However, plans have been perfected which have put them into effect, and hydraulic power is again freeing the vast wealth of the Ridge—with results which are not directly destructive to the farm lands of the Sacramento Valley. With renewed activity at the mines, the towns of the San Juan Ridge have experienced some reawakening.

Many of the old dams and canals constructed so laboriously with pick and shovel for the development of placer and hydraulic mining along the San Juan Ridge have been relocated and rebuilt by the Nevada Irrigation District along larger and more massive lines. The dam at Bowman Lake, built in 1868 and raised to higher levels in 1872 and 1876, has been superseded by a new structure, a massive rock fill built of granite taken from the old dam and from quarries near by. To the credit of the builders of the original dam, the Nevada Irrigation District, after six years of careful study and survey, decided to locate the new dam on the site of the old and to use the same type of construction as in the original one. Furthermore, the Irrigation District officials attribute much of their success in carrying out the new project to the reliable and extensive records of the early mining companies.

French Corral

Equal to the wealth of her gold ridges is the inexhaustible treasure of history and romance which lies within the rugged recesses of the San Juan Ridge. Not only from the abysmal pits of its long-deserted mines and the hundreds of miles of rotting flumes and overgrown, débris-filled ditches but still more from the quaint villages which are found along the winding mountain roads may one garner the comedy and tragedy which made up one of the most thrilling periods in the great epic of California's mining era. Some of these "cities" of the past, for such they were in their heyday, claim from one to three hundred inhabitants today, while others, hidden in sequestered nooks far from the usual routes of travel, are mere "ghosts," deserted, crumbling, or entirely obliterated and unmarked except by the inevitable "diggin's," which are everywhere visible in spite of Nature's attempts to hide the scars.

Beginning at the lower tip of the Ridge the road passes through French Corral, the first of the historic mining camps to spring up along the ancient San Juan River channel. There in 1849 the first settler, a Frenchman, built a corral for his mules. Very soon it was discovered that the locality was rich in placer gold, and a town grew up on the site of the Frenchman's corral. Later, as hydraulic mining developed, French Corral became second only to North San Juan in size and importance, numbering its population in the thousands.

Now a village of only a hundred and thirty-three persons, French Corral retains a flavor of romance in its historic landmarks. The office of the Milton Mining and Water Company in which one terminus of the first long-distance telephone was located is still standing and is used today as a grocery store. The sturdy walls of the old Wells Fargo Express office, built in the '50's and equipped with iron doors and window shutters that once guarded millions of dollars of gold against possible robbers, look as though they would stand for generations to come. A hotel, built in 1851, at the lower end of town; the schoolhouse, which in the '50's was a hotel; and a number of old homes are still in use.

Beyond French Corral are Sweetland and Birchville, both of which were quite populous centers from the '50's to the '80's.

North San Juan

On the state highway from Nevada City to Downieville lies North San Juan, still the metropolis of the Ridge country, although its one block of picturesque old buildings, its scattered homes, and its three hundred and twenty inhabitants are but a remnant of the city which boasted a population of several thousand until the '80's.

San Juan Hill to the north was first mined in 1853 by Christian Kientz, who, according to tradition, was the originator of the name. The several stories purporting to explain why a Castilian name, so unusual in the northern mines, was bestowed upon this locality by a German at least indicate that the story-telling propensities of these sturdy mountaineers were not undeveloped. The most likely of the tales is that Kientz, who had been with General Scott's army in Mexico, supposedly saw a resemblance between this hill in the Sierra Nevada and the hill on which stands the old Mexican prison, San Juan de Ulloa, and named it accordingly. Later, when the whole hill had been staked out in rich claims, the name was given to the promising camp which grew up close by. By 1857 San Juan was of sufficient importance to be assigned a post office, an advance which necessitated prefixing "North" to the name in order to distinguish it from the much older San Juan in San Benito County.

This quaint hamlet retains a number of historic landmarks. An ancient frame hotel, to which "weighty presidents and secretaries" from San Francisco came "with their gold-headed canes and frock coats to seriously confer with their superintendents at the mines," burned down recently. On the shelves of the only store, established in the '50's, merchandise belonging to the nineteenth century may still be seen. Here also is found an old cash register with its curious steel balls, the twin of the one at Rough and Ready. From the ceiling hang nozzles used by the fire company which was housed next door. In the little old firehouse is an ancient hosecart, brought around the Horn in the early '50's and transported by ox-drawn wagons from San Francisco after that city had abandoned its two-wheel carts for the more up-to-date four-wheel wagons.

Across the street is an interesting brick structure labeled "Garage," to the wall of which still clings a heavy steel railing which once supported an upper veranda, reminiscent of the days when the town band gave their summer-evening concerts from the gallery. Behind the iron doors and windows of this same building there reposes a horse-drawn hearse with windows and black curtains covered with the dust of passing years. The Odd Fellows Hall, a two-story brick building dedicated in 1860, has long stood unoccupied at the end of the street.

Many houses had been built on the hill above town, but when these were found to stand on "pay gravel" they were bought by mining companies and "piped away." A high cliff forms the southern wall of the tremendous chasm washed out by hydraulic operations, along the rim of which today a road winds, while in the distance rise the magnificent snow-crested peaks of the Sierra.

Cherokee and North Columbia

Passing along the scenic Ridge Road, now through groves of pine, now above them, one comes to Cherokee, a "ghost town" of the '50's, consisting today of a little Catholic Church, a public school, and a handful of weatherworn houses which stand at the edge of the "diggin's." Just north of Cherokee is the old Badger Mine, once a famous producer.

At North Columbia, originally known as Columbia Hill, many of the old homes still stand. Here, too, is the pretentious office building formerly used as the headquarters of the Eureka Lake and Yuba Canal Company. Some of the huge nozzles and other machinery parts used in the mines lie strewn upon the ground, long neglected but still resistant to the corroding elements. Near by is the machine shop in the rear of which gold was once retorted, and across the road is the blacksmith shop where various implements and the tools used at the diggings were made. Across one of the ditches which carried the water to the mines, the superintendent's home stands, now long deserted.

North Columbia was originally built on the Pliocene gravel bed of the ancient river channel, but in 1878, when the site was found to contain rich gold deposits, the town was removed to its present location. Its neighbors, Grizzly Hill and Lake City, shared in its changing fortunes. The former is but a memory, while Lake City, three miles to the east, is now a "ghost town."

A forlorn-looking frame hotel built by the Bell Brothers in 1855, two years before the founding of Lake City, stood· at the crossroads, with lace curtains still at the dust-covered windows. An upper balcony fell to ruins, the little garden became a dense thicket, and the building was finally removed. Beyond the site the old reservoir, or "lake," is nothing more than a grass-grown depression where cattle feed. Two or three rickety houses across the way complete the picture of general dissolution.

North Bloomfield

Entering the broad, locust-lined street of North Bloomfield a feeling of remoteness comes over one. Surrounded by wild and rugged mountains, the village nestles almost at the brink of a huge hydraulic canyon, pinnacled and castellated and touched with vivid colors like a place enchanted. A few of the old homes are still occupied, and have neat gardens at their doors. The McKillian and Mobley store, which was built in 1852, was until recently used as a mercantile establishment, and housed the post office as well.

At the office of the Malakoff Mine gold used to be made into bars for transportation to the mint. The largest single bar produced there weighed five hundred and twelve pounds, more than a quarter of a ton, with a value exceeding $114,000. A model of this famous bar may be seen at the Ferry Building in San Francisco, while another is on exhibit in the courthouse at Nevada City.

Humbug, the original appellation given to North Bloomfield, was not acceptable to the Postal Department when the town applied for a post office, because of the multiplicity of Humbugs in the state. Upon the origin of the name there hangs a tale typical of those told of the various other localities to which this favorite sobriquet was applied:

"In the winter of 1851–1852 a party, composed of the incongruous elements of two Irishmen and a German, prospected along the creek, near which they discovered a rich deposit of gravel, yielding them a goodly quantity of dust. When their supplies became exhausted, one of the sons of Erin was despatched to Nevada City for provisions, being strictly enjoined to preserve due silence in regard to their good fortune . . . . After purchasing the supplies and a mule to carry them, he invested liberally in 'corn juice,' his purse strings and his tongue both becoming loosened at the same time . . . . and he boasted of his rich 'strike,' declining, however, to give the location. When he took his departure the next morning, a crowd of ravenous gold seekers tracked him to camp. Up and down the creek they wandered, panning a little here and a little there, but in no place finding the rich diggings they anticipated. Disgusted, the crowd returned to the city, calling the creek 'Humbug,' which name has always clung to it, and which it later bequeathed to the town."

North Bloomfield, with its neighboring camps at Derbec and Relief Hill, once numbered a population of about two thousand. Situated three miles to the east, Relief Hill, long a "ghost town," has now been entirely obliterated by mining operations. Reservoirs and dams have made hydraulic mining possible once more here. Farther to the northeast were three rival settlements in the '50's: Moore's Flat on the Middle Fork of the Yuba River, established as early as 1851 and named for H. H. Moore, who built the first store and house there; Orleans Flat, settled about the same time; and Woolsey's Flat. At Moore's Flat the old brick Haggerty store and two or three wooden buildings remain, but its rivals have little left but names.

Graniteville

Graniteville, a town of two hundred and six inhabitants, on the line of the old Ridge Telephone Company, lies in a beautiful forested region near the summit of the mountains twenty-six miles from Nevada City. Gold was mined in the gulches here as early as 1850 and because the diggings were shallow a number of miners were soon attracted to the spot. The original name of the place was Eureka South, to distinguish it from Eureka in Humboldt County, but when the post office was established there in 1877 the present name was adopted.

Graniteville was threatened with extinction when the surface diggings became exhausted, but during the middle '60's gold-bearing quartz was found in the vicinity and the town again became a thriving place. A severe fire swept through it in 1878, but because hydraulic-mining companies had reservoirs in the mountains above the town, Graniteville was rebuilt and until 1883 was an active distributing-point for these companies. Since that date, however, its existence has depended on quartz mining.

SOURCES

[Credit is here given for source material, and permission to quote is hereby acknowledged]

BEAN, EDWIN F. (compiler). *Bean's History and Directory of Nevada County, California.* Nevada City, California, 1867.

BRYANT, EDWIN. *What I Saw in California.* D. Appleton & Company, New York, 1848, 1849

BUCKBEE, EDNA. "Thespis in El Dorado, A Sketch and Something of a Defense of Lola Montez," in *Touring Topics,* XX, No. 10 (October 1928), 32–34, 47–48

California Mining Journal, featuring Nevada and Sierra County mines, I, No. 1 (August 1931)

FERRIER, W. W. *Origin and Development of the University of California.* The Sather Gate Book Shop, Berkeley, California, 1930

HANSON, GEORGE EMMANUEL. *The Early History of Yuba River Valley.* Master's thesis in History. University of California, Berkeley, California, August 1924

HOUGHTON, MRS. ELIZA POOR (DONNER). *The Expedition of the Donner Party and Its Tragic Fate.* A. C. McClurg & Company, Chicago, 1911

JOHNSTON, PHILIP. "Relics of the Gold-Rush among the Northern Diggin's," in *Touring Topics,* XXIV, No. 1 (January 1932), 10–25, 45–46

LARDNER, W. B., and M. J. BROCK. *History of Placer and Nevada Counties, California.* Historic Record Company, Los Angeles, 1924

McGLASHAN, C. F. *History of the Donner Party. A Tragedy of the Sierra.* A. L. Bancroft, San Francisco, 1881

The Morning Union. Commemorative Edition. Grass Valley, California, July 1, 1927

ROURKE, CONSTANCE. *Troopers of the Gold Coast, or the Rise of Lotta Crabtree.* Harcourt, Brace & Company, New York, 1928

SPENCER, MRS. DORCAS JAMES. *A History of the Woman's Christian Temperance Union of Northern and Central California.* West Coast Printing Company, Oakland, California, 1911

THOMPSON, HUGH B. *Directory of the City of Nevada and Grass Valley.* Charles F. Robbins, San Francisco, 1861

WELLS, HARRY L. *History of Nevada County, California.* Thompson & West, Oakland, California, 1880

WOLFF, J. L. *The Yuba River Canyon Country.* Manuscript, 1932

PLACER COUNTY

PLACER COUNTY was organized in 1851 from parts of Sutter and Yuba counties. Auburn was made its county seat. The name, Placer, is an old Spanish word, the origin of which has never been satisfactorily explained, but which came to be applied in Spanish countries to surface mining. At the time the name was adopted for this county, placer mining was the principal method employed there, and the placers of the region were among the richest in the state.

Lake Tahoe

Lake Tahoe, located partly in Placer and El Dorado counties, California, and partly in the state of Nevada, lies 6,225 feet above the sea. It is remarkable for its great depth, which, together with its variable bottom, seems to account for the rare and exquisite color of its waters. "It is never twice the same . . . . sometimes the blue is lapis lazuli, then it is jade, then it is purple, and when the breeze gently ruffles the surface it is silvery-gray." The exact meaning of the old Indian name Tahoe, sometimes interpreted in poetic phraseology as "Big Water" and considered by modern Indians of the region to mean "deep" and "blue," remains undetermined. The lake has also been known by other names for short periods.

Passing through Alpine County on his way into California in 1844, John C. Frémont climbed the ridge to Carson Pass. From his encampment under the shadow of the Sierra he explored, in company with Charles Preuss, the highest peak to the right, probably Stevens Peak, more than ten thousand feet above the sea, from whose lofty summit on February 14, 1844, Frémont and his companion gained the first view of Lake Tahoe ever enjoyed by a white man. In his narrative of the expedition Frémont called the newly discovered sheet of water simply the "mountain lake," but on his later map of the expedition he named it Lake Bonpland. Of this circumstance he writes: "I gave to the basin river its name of Humboldt and to the mountain lake the name of his companion traveler, Bonpland [the noted French botanist], and so put it in the map of that expedition."

Frémont's name for the exquisite body of water which he had discovered has been practically forgotten except by a few historians. The official map-maker of the new state of California, in 1853, gave to it the name of Lake Bigler, after John Bigler, the third governor of California, and people undoubtedly used this official designation for some years. An attempt to change the name to the fanciful Tula Tulia was made in 1861. A successful effort to find a more appropriate name for this most beautiful of all our lakes was made in 1862 as the culmination of the work of William Henry Knight.

Knight had come overland to California from Missouri in 1859, and it was on this journey that he had his first view of Lake Tahoe, "from a projecting cliff 1,000 feet above its surface." The scene, wrote Knight, "embraced not only the entire outline of the Lake with its charming bays and rocky headlands but also the magnificent forest of giant pines and firs in which it was embosomed, and the dozen or more lofty mountain peaks thrusting their white summits into the sky at altitudes varying from 8,000 to 11,000 feet above sea level." "No imagination," he continues, "can conceive the beauty, sublimity and inspiration of that scene, especially to one who had for weary months been traversing dusty, treeless, and barren plains. The contrast was overwhelming."

In 1861 Knight gathered data for compiling the first general map of the Pacific States, and in 1862 this map was published by the Bancroft Publishing House in San Francisco. On it the name of Lake Bigler had been changed to Lake Tahoe. Knight, who deliberately omitted the name of Bigler, urged John S. Hittell and Dr. Henry De Groot to support him in a change of names. At his request, also, Dr. De Groot had suggested "Tahoe," the Indian name for the lake, as a fit substitute. De Groot had heard the name for the first time in 1859 while on an exploring trip. Knight at once obtained the approval of the Land Office at Washington, D.C., and the new name appeared on all subsequent maps and in printed matter issued from the Department of the Interior.

Thomas Starr King, who visited the lake in 1863, used it as the inspiration for one of his famous sermons, "Living Water from Lake Tahoe." Undoubtedly this sermon helped introduce the name to the public. That it was quickly and definitely approved by the people is shown by the almost universal usage of the name from that time on, and this in spite of the fact that it is still "officially" Lake Bigler, for the state legislature, oblivious to the popular acceptance of the name of "Tahoe," legalized that of "Bigler" in 1870 and this act has never been repealed.

Mark Twain, in comparing Lake Tahoe with Lake Como, in northern Italy, wrote: "As I go back in spirit and recall that noble sea, reposing among the snow peaks 6,000 feet above the ocean, the conviction comes strong upon me again that Como would only seem a bedizened little courtier in that august presence. . . . . A sea, whose royal seclusion is guarded by a cordon of sentinel peaks that lift their frosty fronts 9,000 feet above the level world; a sea whose every aspect is impressive, whose belongings are all beautiful, whose lonely majesty types the Deity."

Very early there were those who sensed the possibilities of the Lake Tahoe region as a pleasure and health resort. With increasing frequency pioneer vacationists from Nevada and elsewhere were lured to the place by the beauty of the lake as well as by its fishing and hunting facilities. The earliest permanent settlements on the lake shore were those at the mouth of McKinney's Creek, at Ward's Creek, at Glenbrook (in Nevada), and at Tahoe City. In the summer of 1862 William Ferguson and Ward Rust built a cabin on the lake at the mouth of Ward's Creek. Two other men, John W. McKinney and Thomas Wren, had located a hay ranch on the summit near the county line in 1861, and in 1862 McKinney moved down from his ranch and settled on the shore of Lake Tahoe near the creek which bears his name. There he established a hunting and fishing resort known as Hunter's Home, or Hunter's Retreat, which as late as 1882 was patronized by tourists.

The first survey for Tahoe City was made in 1863, and the Tahoe House was erected by William Pomin the following year. While the nature-lover and tourist contributed to the early prosperity of Tahoe City, the town at first was essentially a lumbering center. After the completion of the Central Pacific Railroad as far as Truckee a wagon road was constructed from that point to the lake, resulting in the need for another hotel, which was met by A. J. Bayley, who erected the Grand Central Hotel at Tahoe City. After the decline of the lumber industry, the fame of Lake Tahoe as a summer resort increased annually.

Emigrant Gap and the Old Emigrant Trail

Emigrant Gap, an old lumbering camp and a station on the Central Pacific Railroad, established in the late '60's, derives its name from a low, grossy opening in the mountains at the head of Bear River. A branch of the old California Emigrant Trail went down into Bear Valley by way of this pass, a region of wild and magnificent scenery.

One mile east of the village, the Native Sons of the Golden West, of Auburn, have placed a marker which reads: "The true Emigrant Gap where the emigrants went into Bear Valley was on this spot." Here may be seen some of the iron spikes driven into the solid rock by these early-day emigrants to hold the rope and tackle used in lowering their wagons over the precipitous cliff.

The early California Emigrant Trail over Donner Pass skirted the present boundary line between Placer and Nevada counties, following mainly along the Nevada County side. The easier route out of the mountains led north of the Bear River, while the narrow divide between that stream and the North Fork of the American River offered no roadway without improvements such as the emigrants were unable to make.

The Dutch Flat–Donner Lake Road

It was not until the building of the Central Pacific Railroad up the divide between the Bear River and the North Fork of the American River in 1864–1866 that a wagon road was constructed along its entire length. In 1849 the head of "wagon navigation" up this ridge was at Illinoistown, and within a few years vehicles had reached as far as Dutch Flat. By 1860, after the discovery of the rich Comstock Lode in Nevada, a great demand had developed for adequate means of transportation over the mountains, and the people of Placer County became anxious to have this very profitable traffic diverted their way. Several attempts made by groups of local citizens to build roads met with failure. Finally, in the fall of 1861, the "Big Four" and others who were building the Central Pacific Railroad over the mountains organized the Dutch Flat and Donner Lake Wagon Road Company, their purpose being to attract as much of the Nevada traffic as possible. This road was completed in June 1864.

By June 1865 the railroad had been constructed as far as Clipper Gap, and in July the California Stage Company began running coaches from that point to Virginia City, Nevada. As the railroad progressed up the ridge, stations were placed at various points, while the stages and forwarding houses moved on simultaneously, making connections at the various termini. Thus the railroad company forced the stages and freight wagons over its own road. By the time Colfax had become the terminus, September 1865, the Central Pacific had acquired the greater part of the passenger and freight business between Nevada and California, most of which, up to that time, had gone largely to the Placerville road in El Dorado County.

Sicard's Ranch

The first settlement in Placer County was Sicard's Ranch, a Mexican grant on the south bank of Bear River. This grant was given to Theodore Sicard, a French sailor, in 1844, and here in 1845 he built an adobe house about one-half mile above Johnson's Crossing.

Being located on the overland emigrant trail which crossed the valley via Sinclair's Ranch to Sutter's Fort, Sicard's Ranch became of some importance as a stopping-place. One of the many emigrants to pass this way was Claude Chana (Chanay, Chané), a fellow countryman of Sicard, who arrived at the ranch in October 1846. From a few pits of dried peaches brought by an emigrant family and some almonds which Chana himself had, planted by Chana and Sicard in the fall of 1846, came the pioneer commercial orchard of the Sacramento Valley. Chana was also the discoverer of gold in Placer County, and after mining at Auburn Ravine, where the discovery was made, and, later, on the Yuba River, he purchased the Sicard Grant, and sold the products of his orchard, vegetable garden, and vineyard to the miners, at

great profit. The site of Claude Chana's pioneer orchard now lies buried beneath the débris brought down by the Bear River from the hydraulic diggings in the foothills.

Johnson's Crossing, three miles east of Wheatland, was laid out as a town on Sicard's Ranch in 1852. It received a post office in 1854, and for some years it was a lively village, being a stopping-place for many of the teams engaged in hauling freight from Sacramento to the northern mining camps. The great flood of 1862 nearly destroyed the place, but the real cause of its final desertion was the later flood of débris which poured down upon it from the hydraulic mines higher up the river.

Rogers' "Shed," a Crossroads Station

About half a mile south of the present village of Sheridan stood a very busy crossroads station during the days of stage coaches and freighters. It was situated on the Sacramento-Nevada road at a point where four other roads diverged: one running westerly to Nicolaus in Sutter County (thirteen miles); one running northwest to Marysville (fifteen miles) via Kempton's Crossing; a third going northeasterly toward Grass Valley (twenty-eight miles) via McCourtney's Crossing; and a fourth following easterly to Auburn (twenty miles) via Danetown.

At this strategic location, in 1857, a man named E. C. Rogers built a one-story house with a 150-foot shed in front. The "Shed"—"Union Shed" as it was called—soon became a place of importance. Here the long freight teams which then thronged the roads sought rest and shelter from the summer's heat or the winter's rain, and here the farmers of the surrounding country brought their hay and grain to supply the needs of these same teams.

The bustling activity about the Shed did not last long, for the building of the California Central Railroad northward from Folsom did away with staging and teaming up and down the valley. In 1861 the railroad had been built as far as Lincoln (named for the builder of the railroad, Charles Lincoln Wilson). From 1861 to 1866 Lincoln was a thriving stage and freight center; but when, in 1866, the terminus of the road was changed to Wheatland, the stage and teaming business was transferred also, and Lincoln and Rogers' Shed both lost their importance as stage centers. In 1868 the Shed, with all its buildings, was consumed by fire. Lincoln, a town of some two thousand inhabitants, is today the trading and shipping point for a thriving agricultural region, while Sheridan is still a mere village of less than two hundred people.

Manzanita Grove, situated on a wooded knoll in the midst of wide, open fields halfway between Lincoln and Sheridan, gained notoriety in early days as a stronghold for thieves. Here, hidden in the center of a thick growth of trees, was a corral where the bandits kept their stolen stock. The robbers were eventually cleared out, and by 1855 the grove had been made the cemetery for the countryside. Today there are only a few of the low-growing manzanitas left among the native oaks, which cast their shadows over the graves of the pioneers buried at this spot. The cemetery is reached over a dirt road which turns to the right from U.S. Highway 99E about four miles north of Lincoln.

About five miles northeast of Lincoln is the site of Newtown, a former mining camp established near Doty's Ravine in 1855. Many claims here paid big while others brought little. It was what was known as a "spotted" area, where "once you find it, and twice you don't." Like others of its class, Newtown has ceased to exist as a place of habitation.

River Bars

Placer County, embracing as it does several branches of the American River besides Bear River, included scores of river-bar camps. Beal's Bar was the first camp above the confluence of the North and South forks of the river. As late as 1853 it polled a vote of ninety-six, and was an active center of trade for surrounding mines. When the old bar immediately upon the river was worked out, the town was moved to a high bench adjoining, and the site of the primitive village was dug out and its gravel washed for gold.

In this vicinity John Sinclair and some fifty Indian retainers, in the spring and summer of 1848, were among the first to mine on the North Fork of 'the American River. Governor Richard B. Mason, in his report to Washington in 1848, says: "He [Sinclair] had been engaged about five weeks when I saw him, and up to that time his Indians had used simply closely-woven willow baskets. His net proceeds .... were about $16,000 worth of gold."

Following up the stream from Beal's Bar to the mouth of the Middle Fork, one encounters a strange variety of names, such as Doton's, Smith's (settled by Mormons in 1848), Horseshoe, Rattlesnake, Beaver, Milk Punch, Deadman's, Lacy's, Manhattan, and Tamaroo bars. All of these camps were at one time densely populated, and each had an interesting history of its own.

Horseshoe Bar, seven miles above Beal's, was first worked in 1849, when the entire bar was divided into claims of 20 × 30 feet. It became a trading center for adjacent bars, and as late as 1858 still claimed three hundred voters, although many of the houses had by that time been moved away. A number of permanent settlers, however, remained in the vicinity for many years and their descendants are numbered among California's most substantial citizens.

Robert E. Capson, a sea captain, came to Smith's Bar in 1848, followed seven months later by his wife and daughter, the latter a girl of fifteen. J. W. Smyth, a young Irishman, arrived in 1849. With the union of these two families, a home was established at Horseshoe Bar. This event resulted in the final preservation of that part of the old bar which remains today, for when J. W. Smyth finally patented this remnant of land and planted it to orchard he saved it from further depredations by the miners. The home of a descendant, who still lives upon the bar, perches on the very edge of the excavations. The road, once lined by the homes, stores, and hotels of the former town, now climbs the hill through an old orchard, a part of which was planted as early as 1852. A mammoth fig tree, with its myriad arms forming a green thicket, half conceals the stone foundations of an abandoned wine cellar, and the walls of an old terraced garden may still be seen among the wild growth on the hillside.

Rattlesnake Bar had become the principal town along the river by 1853, when it was moved to the flat bench known as Rattlesnake Flat, high up and back of the low bar from which it derived its name. By 1861 gardens, orchards, and vineyards had made of it a very pretty place, but after the fire of 1863 had destroyed much of the town decline began. Nevertheless, in 1865 it still had a population of more than a thousand, a post office, a Wells Fargo Express building, a theater, and the usual hotels, stores, and saloons. Like all of the river mining towns, Rattlesnake Bar is now deserted, the site being marked only by piles of rock from the diggings, by the old toll house, and by the present wire bridge, which dates back seventy years, the earlier one having been washed away in the flood of 1862. Rattlesnake Flat and surrounding lands are now covered by small fruit orchards and homes.

Beyond the junction of the Middle and North forks are the sites of numerous other bars. On the North Fork, Calf Bar comes first, followed by Kelly's, Rich, Jones', Barnes', Mineral, Pickering, and Euchre, with a score of others long since washed away or buried out of sight by the mass of débris sent down by the hydraulic mines of Gold Run and

other places. On the north bank of the Middle Fork the following camps were located: Sailor Claim, Buckner's, Rocky Point Slide, Mammoth, Texas, Quail, Brown's, Kennebec, Buckeye, American, Sardine, Yankee, Dutch, African, Drunkard's, Horseshoe (No. 2), Pleasant, American, Junction, Stony, Rector's, and a score of others, each noted at one time for its production of gold and for some interesting occurrence, comic or tragic, in the early history of the county.

Humbug Bar was located in Humbug Canyon, a tributary of the South Branch of the North Fork of the American River. The canyon, at first known as Mississippi Canyon, was rechristened Humbug early in 1850 when a group of miners became disgusted with their luck at this place. Later these same prospectors returned with others and "struck it rich," proving it to be no "humbug" after all.

The Iron Mine

On the bars of the lower American River early miners from Pennsylvania noticed that many boulders contained iron ore. In 1857 the chief center for the ore was found to be on the ranch of S. W. Lovell, near Clipper Gap, about six miles northeast of Auburn. Although tests proved the ore to be of high quality, no mining of the mineral was done until 1869, when the firm of Brown and Company began shipping ore to San Francisco. In December of that year the Iron Mountain Company was organized to develop the mine, but nothing was accomplished. The property remained undeveloped until 1880, when smelting works were erected and the town of Hotaling (named in honor of one of the owners) was founded near by. The old buildings still stand at Hotaling, although mining operations have long since ceased.

Auburn

Early in 1849, Auburn was known as Wood's or North Fork Dry Diggings. It was one of the earliest mining camps in California, gold first having been mined there in May 1848, by Claude Chana and his Indians, whom he had brought with him from Sicard's Ranch on the Bear River. The site of this discovery has been marked by the Native Sons of the Golden West, of Auburn. Chana was soon followed by Nicolaus Altgeier, who had come up from his ranch in Sutter County with his band of Indian retainers.

Hordes of prospectors and adventurers began to pour in by 1849 and camps sprang up everywhere. As a large group of the miners in the vicinity had come to California, in 1846, in Stevenson's Volunteer Regiment from Auburn, New York, the name of North Fork Dry Diggings was changed to Auburn in the summer of 1849. Records show that the early diggings here were very rich. During the peak of productiveness it was not unusual for a man to take out $1,000 to $1,500 a day. There is one instance of four cartloads of earth yielding as much as $16,000.

Auburn became the county seat of Sutter County in the spring of 1850. Its favorable location, "its preponderance of population, and the inexhaustible powers of voting possessed by its citizens and partisans, decided the contest in its favor by a majority considerably exceeding the entire population of the county." In 1851, when Placer County was created from a portion of Sutter County, Auburn was made the seat of justice of the new county. During the '60's and the '70's, Auburn became quite a cultural and social center, having a private normal school and college and enjoying a reputation as a health resort, the pure air of the lower Sierra being both mild and invigorating.

Devastating fires swept many of the mining camps several times during the early years of their history. After Auburn's first experience her citizens determined to rebuild of more substantial material. None of her very first houses remain, but in the older section there are many of those solid brick structures dating from the '50's and '60's, with the heavy iron doors and iron-shuttered windows common to that period. Contrasted with the concrete, plate-glass edifices of today, these old buildings seem like apparitions from another age, their presence scarcely less strange than would be that of the old covered wagons and ox-teams, should they suddenly reappear among the high-powered motor cars of today.

As one writer has truly said: "The Auburn of today is a city of contrasts. Entering it from the south, one descries a narrow street, flanked by old brick buildings, and overlooked by the high bell tower of a fire station. A half-mile beyond, upon the summit of a hill, is the modern portion of the community with up-to-date establishments and public buildings. It is plain to see that Auburn, like the chambered nautilus, outgrew the site upon which it was first located. But the shell that it left behind is still a part of its metropolitan area, and has changed little during the past eighty years."

Auburn, a Turnpike Center

Auburn has always been the center of extensive staging and freighting operations. In its early days a network of trails radiated from it to the numerous camps springing up in all directions, and over these trails miners' supplies were carried by pack-mule trains and their Mexican drivers. During the '50's and '60's these rough and narrow trails were gradually, and in large measure, superseded by toll roads scarcely less rude and precarious, over which daring "knights of the whip" drove the old stage coaches at reckless speed, or, with consummate skill, piloted the swaying, creaking freight wagons over those fearful mountain ways, aided by the uncanny intelligence of from six to ten horses or mules.

Even after the building of the Central Pacific Railway up the ridge, the staging and freighting business continued over the many roads reaching out from Auburn. Indeed, the advent of the railroad created a demand for additional wagon traffic into Nevada County, and, in 1866, brought about the opening of a new and more direct stage route into El Dorado County, via Lyon's Bridge, where the Mother Lode Highway now crosses the river. Today, auto stages and motor trucks still carry their quota of passengers, mail, and freight over the old mountain roads, many of them improved or reconstructed into modern highways leading to and from Auburn.

There were five main wagon roads centering in Auburn, while many laterals led out from these to all parts of Placer County. The highway from Sacramento up the ridge to Illinoistown went through Auburn, and a branch of this road was one of the main routes to Grass Valley and Nevada City, crossing Bear River at a place later known as English's Bridge, ten miles north of Auburn. A third road extended northeast to mining camps along the Forest Hill ridge, while a fourth turned west, passing down Auburn Ravine to Ophir and Virginiatown. Still another ran south along the ridge above the American River to Folsom and Sacramento, and connected with roads coming from El Dorado County. On this road six miles south of Auburn stood the Mountaineer House, on the site of which the stone mansion of J. J. Brennan has been built, over the foundations of the old stage station. Four miles beyond, the site of the Franklin House, another stage station, has been marked by the Native Sons of the Golden West.

Stupendous difficulties were encountered in transforming devious, thread-like pack-trails into roads. The turnpike from Auburn to Forest Hill furnishes an excellent example of the problems met by the builders of these old "High Ways." Leading down into the canyon of the North Fork of the American River where the traveler crossed the stream by means of a crude ferry, the Auburn–Forest Hill trail climbed another steep and meandering path up the opposite canyon wall. Only by a great expenditure of money and labor could the obstacles presented by these mighty canyons be surmounted. Since the county government was unable to raise sufficient funds for the enterprise, the work was taken up by private turnpike companies, the new routes of travel thus becoming toll roads.

The grade of the North Fork Hill Road, as it was called, was improved in 1855 at a cost of $12,000, and in the early '60's an additional sum of $50,000 was expended upon it. Over a distance of twenty miles from Auburn to Yankee Jim's—winding up the deep gorge of the North Fork or clinging to the sides of a mountain far above the stream—this road was carved out of the rocky and declivitous canyon walls only through Herculean effort.

Over this old highland thoroughfare, a continuous stream of traffic from Auburn poured into the mining camps along the Forest Hill Divide, passing a number of stations and roadhouses along the way: the Junction House, two and a half miles from Auburn; the Grizzly Bear House; Butcher's Ranch; Sheridan's; Mile Hill Toll House; Spring Garden; and others.

In the medley of humanity which passed that way, there were two types in particular which might well figure as leading characters in a dramatic epic of the road, the hero and the villain par excellence: the former, that "original and fantastic" tyrant of "the brotherhood of Jehu," the stage-driver; the latter, his equal in daring but forever his enemy, the bold, bad bandit. The stage-driver was an expert in his profession and usually possessed a steadiness of nerve, a courage, and an inherent integrity which not even his veneer of crude bravado and indifference could entirely conceal. Matched at least in daring, this sturdy jehu of the Sierra and his natural enemy, the highwayman and stage robber, often faced each other upon the lonely roads, and many a thrilling episode in the drama of gold-rush days was staged by them, a group of frightened fellow-travelers usually completing the cast.

One mile south of the Grizzly Bear House the Native Sons of the Golden West, of Auburn, have placed a marker which recalls this phase of pioneer life in the Sierra Nevada. The arrow on the sign points to Lime Rock (near Clipper Gap), at the right of which is a burner where lime was formerly made from the rock. In the early days a woman used to signal from this rock to the bandits when the stage was coming on the road. Another marker just above Butcher Ranch indicates that, even as late as 1901, robbers plied their nefarious trade along this road.

Auburn Ravine

Extending west from Auburn, down what was once the old Auburn Ravine turnpike, are a number of historic sites reminiscent of early mining activities. The present village of Ophir, three miles west of Auburn, was first known as Spanish Corral. Like the biblical Land of Ophir whence came the gold to adorn the temple of Solomon, the region about Spanish Corral was found to be fabulously rich, and the name of the settlement was changed to Ophir. In 1852 it was the most populous community in the county. Although the district about Ophir numbers not many more than two hundred inhabitants today, the village has continued to hold its own as the chief quartz-mining center in Placer County. Fruitful orchards and vineyards also abound in the surrounding hills, and the village itself is bowered in giant fig trees. A stone archway near the only store is part of a pioneer bakery built sometime in the '50's, while at the end of the street are the stone foundations of the former brewery. About a mile up the road is the site of the Oro Fino House, now occupied by the Ramona Inn. The hills are scarred with diggings, old pits and dumps, and the foundations of abandoned stamp mills. A few mines in this vicinity, especially the Paramount about two miles from Ophir, still produce.

Two miles west of Ophir was Frytown, a "mushroom city" settled in 1849. Although its palmy days were few, "'t was lively while it lasted." Gold Hill, two and one-half miles beyond, was organized as a village in April 1852, when the presidential vote numbered 444. The rich surface diggings of this earlier period were later replaced by fine orchards and vineyards, which continue to flourish today, although the little town has ceased to exist. Only a small cemetery and one large frame house with immense fig trees before it mark the site. Continuing a mile and a half along this historic road, one comes to Virginiatown, a typical "ghost city," with the abandoned shells of two iron-shuttered adobe houses standing, mute and time-scarred, beside the highway. Another mile and the traveler passes the site of the ephemeral Fort Trojan (pronounced "Troejam" by the miners), settled in 1858. When Lincoln was established three miles farther down in the valley in 1861–1862, the citizens of Fort Trojan moved to the new town.

Secret Ravine

Secret Ravine, extending southeast from Auburn, was the scene of extensive placer mining operations during the '50's and '60's, and of later granite quarrying in the '70's and '80's. Commercial orchards were planted up and down the ridges as early as 1870 and these continue to be the chief source of income in the region today. Old mining camps which flourished in the ravine during the picturesque gold-rush days were soon superseded after the coming of the railroad by other towns built along the ridge. Brick stores, in use as late as 1880, but mostly vacated by 1900, have since been torn down, and often the ground on which they stood has been plowed and planted to fruit trees.

Newcastle, at the head of Secret Ravine, is the only one of the old 1850 mining camps which thrives today, being a fruit-shipping center on the railroad with a population of 800. In the ravine to the north is a picturesque Chinatown, its balconied upper stories overshadowed by an avenue of giant cottonwoods.

Stewart's Flat, a mining town of some importance before the coming of the railroad, was located in the ravine one and a half miles east of Penryn. The Stewart's Flat Mine was worked there from 1862 to 1864. After Penryn was established in 1864, with the opening of granite quarries in the vicinity, Stewart's Flat dwindled until it was abandoned in 1867, the old graveyard being all that marks the site today.

Penryn (or Penhryn, after its patronym in Wales) was first settled in 1860, when John Kaiser and Larry Brannon built the old wine cellars, still standing intact but in disuse since 1900. The town, however, was established and named by Griffith Griffith, a Welshman, whose extensive granite quarries for a number of years supplied the building material for many structures in Stockton, San Francisco, and elsewhere, and which employed as many as 250 workmen. The quarries were closed down in 1900, but all along the line, from Penryn to Rocklin, are pits and dumps reminiscent of the days of quarry operations. A two-story building of hewn granite blocks, erected in Penryn by Griffith Griffith in 1878, is still standing in perfect condition.

About two and one-half miles southwest of the village of Penryn is Loomis, the successor of Pino. Pino had de-rived its name from the old mining camp of Pine Grove, which was established in Secret Ravine about a mile and a half from the site of Loomis, before the coming of the railroad. Mining began at Pine Grove (or Smithsville) in 1850, and a store was set up by L. G. Smith. By 1860 the place had a population of fifteen hundred people. At Pine Grove the first railroad into Placer County had its terminus, called Auburn Station. Portions of the former roadbed may still be seen in the vicinity.

Gold Run

The Gold Run region, about twenty-nine miles northeast of Auburn, on the ridge south of Dutch Flat between Bear River and the North Fork of the American River, is a good example of early hydraulic mining. A vast bed of auriferous blue gravel two miles long, half a mile wide, and two hundred and fifty feet deep, with pay dirt all the way down, it yielded immense profit until the early '80's. O. W. Hollenbeck came to the region in 1854 and mined at a place called Mountain Springs. In 1859 hydraulic mining was begun on the Gold Run claim. In 1862 Hollenbeck laid out a town on Cold Spring Mountain, calling it Mountain Springs. A post office was established in 1863 under that name, but with the coming of the railroad the name was changed to Gold Run, there being another Mountain Springs. The place developed into a mining center long after the other towns of the county, and was very flourishing during the '60's and the '70's. Squire's Canyon, Canyon Creek, Goosling Ravine, Gold Run Canyon, Potato Ravine, and Indiana Canyon all had their productive hydraulic mines. After 1883, when the courts decided against hydraulic mining, the town became almost deserted.

The original town of Gold Run is on the U.S. Highway 40 one mile south of the present Gold Run railway station. The old Union Church built by the miners, one of the pioneer stores, and the first house in the village have been preserved. Deep ravines and high cliffs in the canyon below present striking evidence of the hydraulic forces which once operated there. It is estimated that the total production of the Gold Run mines has reached $15,000,000.

Dutch Flat

Dutch Flat, quaint, colorful, somnolent, among its pine-clad mountains, lies in one of the most unique and stirring environs to be found among the old camps of Placer County. Its one street, lined by huge poplar and locust trees, climbs abruptly from the little hollow where the town had its beginning, to a narrow, sloping terrace, on which perches the village of later growth, and on up and up past the summer homes of those yearly visitors who, in ever-increasing numbers, seek the tonic air and romantic flavor of the place.

Thousands of miners, in years past, have worked the ridges and hills about Dutch Flat, until the entire region is deeply torn by hydraulic operations. Aside from its prominence as a mining center, Dutch Flat was a stage station, making it one of the largest and most important towns of the county in 1864 to 1866.

The town was named after Joseph Doranbach and his companions, Germans, who in 1851 were the first settlers in the place. The name, "Dutch," may quite naturally have been derived from the nationality of these first settlers, but why "Flat" should have been added seems quite incomprehensible to the modern visitor who looks in vain for the so-called "flat." In 1855 the citizens of the town were granted an application for the establishment of a post office under its present designation.

From the town runs the old road which from 1864 to 1866 was a much-traveled turnpike; over it the well-braced Concord coaches ran to the rich Washoe silver mines of Nevada, one branch going by way of Bear Valley, Bowman Lake, and Henness Pass, and the other via Donner Lake. The latter route, known as the Dutch Flat–Donner Lake Road, was built by the men who were at that time constructing the Central Pacific Railway. Such names as those of Governor Leland Stanford, Dr. D. W. Strong, and other promoters of the railway thus became linked with the history of this toll road and with the town. Strong, a resident of Dutch Flat, was the only one of the nine promoters of the railway who lived outside of Sacramento. He it was who, from the beginning, advocated the advantage of the Dutch Flat–Donner Pass route for the railway even when others doubted its feasibility. In the fall of 1866 after the railway had reached Cisco, about twenty miles farther up the ridge, Dutch Flat lost much of its importance as a stage center.

Just over the hill about a hundred feet north of town "lie the 'diggin's,' miles in extent, rugged man-made canyons and deep amphitheatres abounding with rocks and stones and pebbles of various shapes and colors, among them not infrequently beautiful hexagonal crystals. Gold nuggets are there also, but are rarely found." Beds of ashes, charcoal, and partly charred wood have also been discovered under a hundred feet or more of gravel in this fascinating geological hunting-ground.

During the '70's hydraulic mining operations at Dutch Flat reached their height. In 1872, the Cedar Creek Company, of London, purchased as many as thirty-two claims and worked them on a gigantic scale. Millions in gold were taken from the extensive placers of Dutch Flat, one nugget alone being worth more than $5,000. It is estimated that $30,000,000 more remain in this gravelly ridge awaiting new and less destructive hydraulic methods to release them.

The tide of gold has long since ebbed from Dutch Flat, and its citizens, "contented with what they have . . . . go their quiet peaceful way. They delight in talking of the old days when life socially was on a par with the best in California." Every building in the block that comprises the business section has a history.

There is the hotel with its long mirror, a relic of the one-time bar, and its old ledgers tabulating the ounces of gold taken from adjoining diggings. Formerly this was a quite pretentious hostelry, with some thirty rooms more than those represented in the present structure, including an annex which extended across the road. In the old Nichols Bank only a massive safe remains as a testimonial of the hundreds of thousands of dollars in dust and nuggets once stored there. On its doors is the inscription, "W. & P. Nichols, Bankers." The I.O.O.F. Building, erected in 1858, is still in use, as is also the old stone store and post office built in 1854.

Farther up the street stand the two Towle mansions built by the Towle brothers, who once owned large lumber mills in the district, and for whom the village of Towle about two miles north on the railway was named. One of these old-fashioned, high-ceilinged mansions at Dutch Flat has fallen into decay, but the other has been restored and is occupied.

In the hollow as one approaches the town a lone Chinese store stands guard. The lower half is solidly built of stone and adobe with a high superstructure of wood, and the tiny air holes which serve as windows give the structure the appearance more of a jail or a fort than of a place of trade. Adjoining the pioneer American cemetery just above the town is the Chinese burial grounds, half hidden among the pines. Most of the bodies have been removed from the graves and taken back to China, but the brick furnace in which all personal effects from the graves were burned still

stands. The old site of Chinatown, where once a thousand Celestials lived, was on the railroad one mile above Dutch Flat.

Colfax and Illinoistown

Colfax, named after Ulysses S. Grant's running mate, Schuyler Colfax, is a small town about fifteen miles northeast of Auburn in the center of a once prosperous mining region. The Central Pacific Railroad from Sacramento reached as far as Colfax in September 1865. Today, the town is an important shipping point for lumber and fruit.

Across the railroad southeast of Colfax, and now completely absorbed by it, is the site of Illinoistown, first settled early in 1849 under the name of Alder Grove. That year the town became the distributing point for supplies to neighboring camps, and quickly assumed an importance as a business and trading center second only to that of Auburn.

Goods brought in wagons to Illinoistown were there loaded on pack mules and carried to remote camps over steep and winding mountain trails, later widened into toll roads. One of the most intriguing of these old roads was the one which led from Illinoistown to Iowa Hill and was known as the Mineral Bar Bridge and Road. The cost of constructing the seven miles entering and leaving the canyon of the North Fork of the American River (which, at this point, is 1,500 feet deep) was $75,000. The scenery was magnificent—steep mountain sides seemingly ever threatening to precipitate the traveler into the abyss, where, far below, the sparkling waters of the river could be seen with the opposite canyon walls towering above them.

Iowa Hill

The site of the little old town of Iowa Hill is on the narrow neck of a high ridge between the North Fork of the American River on the north and Indian Canyon on the south. Gold was first discovered there in 1853, and in 1856 the weekly product was estimated at $100,000. The rich cement of the Blue Lead Channel running under the town has been all drifted out, while later hydraulic operations on either side of the town have all but washed the site away. The total gold production up to 1880 has been estimated at $20,000,000.

Like most of the early mining camps, Iowa Hill had its baptisms of fire. In 1857 a conflagration swept away all of the buildings "from Temperance Hall to McCall & Company's Brewery," as an old news item puts it. The last serious fire occurred in 1922, destroying most of the remaining houses in this much-stricken place.

Numerous camps flourished within a radius of five miles of Iowa Hill during the '50's and '60's. Independence Hill, Roach Hill, Bird's Flat, Stephen's Hill, Elizabethtown, Wisconsin Hill, Grizzly Flat at the head of Grizzly Canyon, Monona Flat, and Succor Flat—each lived its little day of colorful, polyglot life, only to become again a part of the great enveloping wilderness after a few short years. Hundreds of tunnels honeycomb the mountains about these old camp sites, constituting tangible evidence of the few extremely profitable claims which were once worked there: the Jamison, the pioneer of the district, producing $500,000; the North Star, $400,000; the Sailor Union, $300,000; and the Iowa Hill, $250,000.

Elizabethtown, on the south side of Indian Canyon from Iowa Hill, was the most important camp north of Shirt-tail Canyon and south of the North Fork, 1850–1854. Wisconsin Hill, separated from Elizabethtown by a deep ravine, was first settled in 1854 and soon had a population of seven hundred, but after 1856 the miners began to scatter. With the completion of a turnpike across Indian Canyon from

Iowa Hill and another across Shirt-tail Canyon from Yankee Jim's, the hopes of Wisconsin Hill's business men temporarily revived. The sad sequel of this renewal of hope was that, instead of bringing more people in, the road furnished the remaining inhabitants with an easy mode of transit to more favored localities.

Todd's Valley

Few more inviting places existed in the Sierra of Placer County than Todd's Valley before it was overrun with Argonauts, "washing away the beautiful ridges and seaming up the gently sloping vales" in their feverish quest for gold. Even the forests of pine and maple and flowering dogwood were not free from the encroachments of the early placer diggings and the tunnels and shafts of drift mining, as well as the more gigantic scars of later hydraulic action. An old brick store built by Alfred A. Pond survived the fire of 1859, and still stands on the site of the town which grew up with the coming of the first miners.

Among the few men who wintered on the Forest Hill Ridge in 1849–50 were Dr. F. W. Todd and three or four companions. Dr. Todd had established a store at his ranch in June 1849, in the valley which later bore his name. By 1850 Todd's store had become a stopping-place for miners seeking new locations on the ridges and in the canyons to the north and northeast. The old pack trail which passed by its door was an extension of the Sacramento Road to Greenwood and Georgetown via Pilot Hill in El Dorado County, crossing the Middle Fork of the American River near the Spanish Diggings. Climbing the precipitous canyon walls from this point via Paradise and the North Star House, the trail continued through Todd's Valley to the diggings at Forest Hill and camps beyond.

Forest Hill

Forest Hill, a mining and lumbering camp of some importance in the '50's and '60's, was located in a region reported by J. Ross Browne in 1868 as "the most productive cement tunnel-mining district in the state." Situated at an elevation of 3,400 feet, on the summit of the Forest Hill Divide between the Middle Fork of the American River and Shirt-tail Canyon, the town is 2,500 feet above the river. Thousands of acres of virgin pine forests surround it and the canyon scenery is superb. The auriferous gravel of the Forest Hill Diggings is a part of the Blue Lead Channel, and the early claims, limited to fifty feet each, extended along the side of the hill. The tunnels penetrated the mountain to a distance of from two hundred to five thousand feet.

Early in the spring of 1850 a great rush of miners came to the Forest Hill Ridge, lured by the news of rich diggings uncovered there. Coming from the south via Coloma and Greenwood Valley and from the west by way of Auburn, the two streams met about three miles northeast of Todd's store at the place which later became Forest Hill. The brush shanty set up at the latter site as a trading-post in 1850 was soon replaced by a substantial house and hotel. The Forest House, as it was known, became the nucleus of an important center of trade and of travel to and from the numerous camps in all directions.

The height of activity, however, began early in 1853, after the winter storms had brought down a great mass of loose gravel at the head of Jenny Lind Canyon, exposing to view many glistening chunks of gold. The Jenny Lind Mine alone later yielded $2,000 or $2,500 daily, the total yield reaching approximately $1,100,000 by 1880. The aggregate production of all the mines in the immediate vicinity of Forest Hill or within rifle-shot of the express office was estimated at $10,000,000 up to 1868. Rich mines in the region

were the Dardanelles, New Jersey, Independence, Deidesheimer, Fast and Nortwood, Rough and Ready, Gore, and Alabama.

Forest Hill had already assumed a metropolitan air in the late '50's, boasting a newspaper, fire-proof hotels and stores, banks and elegant saloons, as well as neat homes surrounded by gardens and orchards. It was still one of the larger towns of Placer County in 1880, numbering about seven hundred inhabitants at that date. Today the population is a little over four hundred. Some of the buildings along the broad main street are deserted, but two brick stores, with iron doors and shutters, are open for business, while the one hotel, a frame structure somewhat weatherworn and decrepit, still accommodates "the occasional traveler, who if he wishes may slake his thirst at the bar, or join the 'boys' at a game of cards at an old circular table."

In the tower of the old Forest Hill Church an exceptionally clear, sweet-toned bell, cast in Russia and brought around the Horn in 1860, has sounded the call to worship for many years. At times it can be heard twenty miles away through the forest.

A mile and a half northeast of Forest Hill is the site of Bath, first settled in the summer of 1850 by a merchant named John Bradford, who built a cabin and started a stock ranch. In the fall some miners came in and bought the place for a small sum. Wintering there, the party discovered gold in the dry gulches debouching into Volcano Canyon. Miners flocked to the place and the camp which sprang up that same fall took the name of Volcano. The next year the town grew rapidly after the Mint Drop and Snodgrass claims were located. Since another camp just across the Middle Fork to the south also bore the name of Volcano, the village on the Forest Hill Ridge chose to call itself Sarahsville, in honor of the first woman in the camp. When a post office was organized there in 1858, the name of Bath was finally bestowed upon the place.

The Bath claims which adjoined those of the Forest Hill district, beginning with 1852, included the San Francisco, Oro, Rip, Golden Gate, Paragon, Greek, New York, and Sebastopol claims. Bath declined after 1858, owing to the increasing importance of its neighbor, Forest Hill, but since its mines were still rich it continued to exist as a town for a number of years. A few of the old houses still stand at Bath.

Yankee Jim's and Shirt-tail Canyon

A road from Forest Hill leads north three miles to Yankee Jim's, high up on the same ridge between the North and Middle forks of the American River. A number of the old weather-worn houses at Yankee Jim's are still standing, reminders of the stirring days when it was one of the largest mining camps in Placer County. Extensive diggings lie on the outskirts of the village. Not far away is Shirt-tail Canyon, which Bayard Taylor thought should be called "Spartan Canyon"—"but we were not classical enough for the change in those days," was the comment of an old pioneer.

The origin of the name, Yankee Jim's, is one of those riddles often encountered by the student of the heterogeneous nomenclature of the mining regions. Some hold that the individual from whom the camp derived its title was, indeed, a Yankee. The majority, however, believe that he was "a son of the Emerald Isle" who, because of his luck in striking rich diggings (popularly attributed to shrewdness), had become known as "Yankee Jim."

Be this as it may, Yankee Jim (who seems to have been somewhat given to banditry) was the first to mine away from the river bars of the North Fork, and to find the rich diggings along the ridges. He sought to keep these discoveries of his a secret, but rumors spread quickly, and by 1850 miners swarmed over the entire ridge country. At the place of Yankee Jim's chief activities a town sprang up, was named for him, and became famous as a rich mining center.

Shirt-tail Canyon and its several branches—Brimstone Canyon, Brushy Canyon, Grizzly Canyon, Refuge Canyon, and Devil's Canyon—were all the scene of extensive gold excitement during the '50's. The stream bed in each of these canyons was worked and numerous tunnels were dug into the rocky walls above.

The story of how Shirt-tail Canyon got its name is typical of the refreshing unconventionality with which the hardy miners of the Sierra supplied titles to the thousands of mines, camps, creeks, and canyons in which they worked.

"Early in the summer of 1849 two men, one named Tuttle, formerly from the state of Connecticut, and the other Van Zandt, from Oregon, were prospecting upon Brushy Canyon and in that locality, and at the time supposed there was no one nearer to them than the people who were at work along the river bars. From Brushy they emerged into the valley of the larger stream into which it emptied. It was sultry and hot, and no sound but their own suppressed voices broke the silence of the gorge. A bend in the creek a short distance below them obstructed the view, and they walked down the stream to overcome it. Abruptly turning the point, they were astonished to see before them, but a little way off, a solitary individual—whether white or red they could not at first determine—engaged in primitive mining operations, with crevicing spoon, and sheath-knife and pan. The apparition was perfectly nude, with the exception of a shirt, and that was not overly lengthy. The lone miner was in the edge of the water, and, happening to look up, saw the two men who had intruded upon his domain at about the same time that they discovered him. Had this not been so . . . . they . . . . would have stepped back, made some noise, and given the man a chance to don his overalls. As it was, the eyes of both parties met, and an involuntary 'Hello' came from all three mouths. 'What in the devil's name do you call this place?' queried one of the intruders of the *sans culottes,* who proved to be an American. He glanced at his bare legs, and from them to his questioners, took in at a moment the ludicrous appearance he made, and laughingly answered: 'Don't know any name for it yet, but we might as well call it Shirt-tail as anything else,' and under that euphonious nomenclature has it since been known, and must thus go down to posterity. It is to be regretted that no record can be found of the name of the man in the shirt."

Michigan Bluff

Looking over into El Dorado County to the south, Michigan Bluff clings to the steep slope of the Forest Hill Ridge from 1,500 to 2,000 feet above the yawning gorges of the Middle Fork and the North Fork of the Middle Fork of the American River and El Dorado Canyon. Behind it old Sugar Loaf towers 250 feet or more above the main street of the village, which nestles immediately at its southern base. The first town, commonly known as Michigan City, was located about half a mile below the present site, on the stretch of comparatively level ground once existing there and later mined out. Scars of hydraulic operations may be seen all up and down the mountainside.

The first settlement on this ridge was made one mile to the west at Bird's Valley, where a party of sailors located in the summer of 1848. Later, these men reported at Sutter's Fort the rich diggings which they had worked at Rector's Bar and other places below their camp. A second company, under the leadership of J. D. Hoppe, came up from Sutter's Fort the same fall. Following the trail made by the sailors

up the mountainside, they too set up camp in Bird's Valley, crevassing for gold along the rivers in the canyons below. Seeking for the precious metal only upon and in the crevices of the bedrock, these first miners used the most primitive tools for their operations—butcher knives, iron spoons, an occasional steel bar, and a pan. As the rainy season approached, the men returned to the valley, believing it to be impossible to winter in that wild country.

In the spring of 1849, hundreds of miners trekked over the rugged mountain trails to the new diggings and a few stayed through the winter of 1849–50, among them being two men at Bird's Valley. Rich discoveries had been found in El Dorado Canyon and along the bars of the Middle Fork during the summer of '49, and with the coming of another spring a general stampede began, in February 1850. Thousands of men thronged over the trails from Hangtown, Coloma, Georgetown, Pilot Hill, and other places in El Dorado County already overrun with gold seekers. Finding it impossible to mine along the streams, the rivers still being too high, it was necessary to encamp along the ridges, and Bird's Store became an important rendezvous, with two or three thousand impatient Argonauts gathered there to await the receding of the snows and the subsiding of the waters.

A few ambitious men camped on the little flat to the east where Michigan City grew up. While grading out the mountainside for enough level ground for their cabins to stand upon, a bed of auriferous gravel was struck. Lack of water delayed the working of the find until 1853, when ditches were dug from the upper reaches of El Dorado and Volcano canyons, twelve and five miles to the north. With this year and until 1858 the town enjoyed a period of great prosperity, shipping a hundred thousand dollars worth of gold per month. The North American Mine, alone, yielded $300,000 up to 1868.

Michigan City had no sooner become established on the narrow shelf at the edge of the diggings than the shelf began to settle and to slip down the mountainside, cracking the walls of the houses and threatening to precipitate the entire village into the yawning abyss below. This was in 1858, and in 1859 the settlers moved en masse to the present site of Michigan Bluff higher up on the brow of the mountain. Hydraulic mining began in the vicinity in 1858, and during the '60's and '70's the town was one of the most prosperous centers on the Forest Hill Ridge. By 1880 the numerous smaller claims had been bought up by the owners of the Big Gun Mine, and then, in 1883, came the Anti-Débris Act and the cessation of hydraulic activities.

The decline of Michigan Bluff followed quickly, until today little of its former prosperity is apparent. Shaded by old locusts and fruit trees, the tiny hamlet still clings to the mountainside. With less than two score inhabitants, many of the old frame houses are empty and rotting on their foundations. A recent traveler has described it as "ruin—forlorn dilapidation, that speaks eloquently of decline in the gold country." Passing along the creaking boardwalks of the little main street, one sees here a decrepit wooden structure leaning "drunkenly" on its foundations, there another of stone, one whole side of which has caved outward, disclosing the interior of a one-time store and post office. Its solid iron doors and window shutters were hauled to their present location by ox-team over fearful mountain trails. The post office and store are today housed in a sturdy structure also built of native stone many years ago.

A modest clapboarded cottage just off from the main street in Michigan Bluff is still pointed out as the one-time residence of Leland Stanford, though George T. Clark gives several very conclusive reasons why it is improbable that any building still standing in Michigan Bluff belonged to the period in which Leland Stanford sojourned there, from 1853 to 1855. In the first place, Stanford himself stated that for the three years that he was in Michigan Bluff "he slept on a counter" in his store, his wife being still in the East. Moreover, Michigan Bluff then stood on its first site, and, in 1857, was swept by a fire which destroyed all of the one business block, in which Leland Stanford's store was doubtless located. Not a vestige of the original village remains today.

The claim that the building in question was Leland Stanford's home is based on the testimony of an old-time resident who is positive that he recalls "a Stanford family with children." Of course, Leland Stanford at that time had no children. On the other hand, Elijah and Lyman Stanford and their families, cousins of Leland, did live at Michigan Bluff in 1857, Lyman being listed as a merchant in the Placer County directory for 1861.

Mr. Clark concludes that it was "quite probable that the old-timers made a mistake, confusing the Stanfords and identifying as Leland's a house which probably at one time was occupied by either Lyman or Elijah, and family."

Ghost Towns of the High Sierra

If you wish to see some of the most awe-inspiring mountain scenery in California, follow up the ridge route going east from Iowa Hill past Damascus and thence to the summit into Squaw Valley. This road parallels the North Fork of the American River, which lies far below to the northward, and from it several branches lead south along narrow ridges high above deep canyons, each of them wild and rugged in the extreme, canyons long ago the scene of many a relentless quest for El Dorado, and roads which led to old camps now obliterated by the returning forest. Little travel goes this way, and for the visitor adventuring into this High Sierran realm of yesteryear, the pages of history are turned back and one may almost imagine himself a member of that hardy clan which first penetrated it.

The ridge route was constructed in 1852 by the citizens of Placer County in the hope that it would draw the tide of immigration through their territory. To some extent, emigrants did come this way for a few years, but the popularity of the road was never great, and as the people of the county did not continue to maintain it, it soon fell into disuse. During the '60's, as a result of the rush to the silver mines of Nevada, travel over the old ridge road revived. Even during this period, however, it never reached the extent of popularity enjoyed by the Placerville or the Dutch Flat–Donner Lake roads.

The old ridge road connected a chain of camps and way stations running eastward from Iowa Hill: Monona Flat (where a branch led to Succor Flat); Damascus; the Forks House (where the emigrant road from Yankee Jim's, Forest Hill, and Michigan Bluff came in from the south); Westville, beyond which a road goes south to Deadwood; the Secret Canyon station at the head of Secret Canyon; and Robertson's Flat where one road turned north past the Lost Immigrant Mine and across the North Fork of the American River to Donner Pass and another led south to Last Chance and the North Grove of Big Trees.

Damascus and Sunny South

Ten miles to the east of Iowa Hill was the village of Damascus, located on a steep mountainside more than a thousand feet above the waters of Humbug Creek. When the site was first settled, in 1852, it was known as Strong's Diggings, but with the establishment there of a post office the more dignified title of Damascus was adopted. Here the Mountain Gate, a tunnel drift mine with a 2,000-foot front-

age which pierced the mountain to a distance of 4,000 feet, was long the chief location in the district. The Damascus claim, which adjoined it, with a 500-foot frontage and a 3,000-foot tunnel, was the only other mine in that locality. For many years during the '70's and early '80's hydraulic operations in the vicinity were productive of great wealth.

Damascus, with its scattered cottages and little garden plots, its schoolhouse, and its few stores, was completely destroyed by a forest fire some years ago.

Seven miles to the south another hamlet clung to the warm, sunny slopes of the mountain in a sheltered nook which in winter seemed always to escape the heavy snows covering the surrounding country in all directions. This phenomenon gave to the place the pleasant name of Sunny South. Here the Hidden Treasure, a very rich mine during its heyday, was worked as late as the '80's. Nothing but happy memories of Sunny South and its old mine remain today.

Deadwood

At the tip of a narrow mountain spur high above the yawning chasms of El Dorado Canyon and the North Fork of the Middle Fork of the American River, is the site of Deadwood, a one-time mining camp located seven miles from Michigan Bluff by pack trail. It is twenty-five miles by the long circuitous road which winds around the head of El Dorado Canyon past the Forks House, continuing across the head of Indian Creek at Westville, and thence down the Deadwood spur.

Gold was first found at Deadwood in 1852 by a group of miners who had previously experienced very indifferent success in the prospecting game. Being greatly elated over this sudden change for the better, the party remarked to all subsequent comers that they "now assuredly had the 'deadwood' upon securing a fortune," or, in more up-to-date slang, "they had a cinch on it." Thus Deadwood got its name.

The heartening news of the Deadwood discovery soon spread far and wide and a bustling camp sprang up, composed of over five hundred miners who had toiled over fearful canyon trails to this remote Mecca of their dreams. It was a wild, austere habitat, to which only the most venturesome came. A few even built their flimsy cabins along the precipitous canyon walls on the outskirts of the village. Here they dwelt in almost constant danger of winter snows and avalanches. About these lonely domiciles cluster tales suggesting Hawthorne's *Ambitious Guest* in their tenderness of human relationships and the dramatic quality of setting and circumstances.

Deadwood's transient glory had departed by 1855, although mining with moderate returns has been carried on in the vicinity until the present time and a few of the old buildings remain at the site.

A high bench or bar in the canyon of the North Fork of the Middle Fork some two or three miles from Deadwood bears the delightfully original sobriquet of Bogus Thunder. A mile or more up the canyon from this place is a waterfall the sound of which reverberates throughout the gorge with such terrific roar that the first comers there thought it was thunder. When they finally discovered the real cause of the noise, they proclaimed the thunder bogus.

Last Chance

Even more difficult of access than Deadwood is Last Chance, overlooking the canyon of the North Fork of the Middle Fork and that great network of narrow gorges and immense canyons which runs into it from the north. Perched at the tip of an elevated promontory upon the very brink of these tremendous declivities, the visitor to Last Chance seems veritably to have arrived at the "jumping-off place."

The relentless search for treasure had led a little group of hardy prospectors into this remote region in 1850. The lure of several rich deposits discovered in the vicinity so fascinated them that they lingered until all the provisions were gone and starvation threatened. One of the company possessed a good rifle. Saying to his companions, "This is our last chance to make a grub-stake," he went into the forest, and, as luck would have it, returned with a large buck. Thus the miners were able to return to their diggings and a new camp earned its name. This at least is one of several versions of the origin of this name.

Last Chance had become a real town by 1852, and by 1859 the Masons, the Oddfellows, and the Sons of Temperance had erected halls. Forty-two of the seventy voters of the town were members of the last-named organization. Remnants of its short-lived glory are still visible at Last Chance in the old hotel and a handful of scattered homes.

Across Peavine Canyon from Last Chance and about five miles to the southward, the northernmost group of *Sequoia gigantea* in California stands in a well-watered vale on Duncan Ridge overlooking the Middle Fork of the American River. These trees, known as the North (or American River) Grove, consist of six standing trees and two large fallen ones. They are a part of the Tahoe National Forest. At the instance of the owner of the Blue Eyes Mine near by, the Placer County Chamber of Commerce in 1920 reopened the old road into this grove.

At the base of Duncan Ridge is Duncan Canyon, its story similar to that of the famous Gold Lake expedition in Plumas County. James W. Marshall is authority for the statement that the name was derived from Thomas Duncan, who came overland from Missouri with Captain Winter in 1848, entering California by way of the mountain trail which diverged from American Valley and followed down the ridge south of the North Fork.

Late in the fall of 1850, while mining in Shirt-tail Canyon, Duncan regaled his companions with tales of rich diggings, which he claimed he had found upon entering California. Taking the tale seriously, his listeners persuaded him to lead them to the favored spot. Upon arriving in the vicinity of the supposed treasure, the canyons all looked so much alike that Tom was unable to locate the right one. His followers became suspicious, threatening to shoot him unless he located the promised bonanza. Fortunately for Thomas Duncan, he did discover a fairly exciting deposit above Sailor Bar and vigilance over him was temporarily relaxed. Duncan made the best of his opportunity and escaped that night. His misguided friends never saw him again, but they named the place where they had camped Duncan's Canyon.

About a mile and a half west of the Big Tree Grove is Big Oak Flat, a park-like plateau covered with oaks. Here, in the fall of 1850 James W. Marshall and one companion dug for gold, evidences of previous diggings being found by them at that spot. Prospecting all up and down the Sierra from 1848 to 1850, Marshall was one "of that human mass who carried the advancing ripple of civilization into the canyons of the California highlands." In the summer of 1850 he had been at Antoine Canyon, just northeast of Last Chance, a location first worked earlier in the season by a half-breed Crow Indian named Antoine.

Numerous other canyons throughout this highland country were penetrated by miners in the early '50's: Lost Canyon, Secret Canyon, Dark Canyon, Black Canyon, Deep Canyon, and others, the names of which suggest the wild and mysterious character of the region.

"Donner County"

Several efforts were made to cut new counties out of the territory already belonging to Placer and other counties. The last such attempt was made in 1869–70, when it was proposed to create "Donner County" from the High Sierra regions of Placer, Nevada, and Sierra counties. The movement met with much disfavor. One opposing editor (a former resident of Placer County) expressed his opinion of the project in the following words:

"If Donner County is created, Placer County will lose several well-known places, and the glory of much of her history. 'Ground Hog's Glory,' 'Hell's Delight,' 'Miller's Defeat,' 'Ladies' Canyon,' 'Devil's Basin,' 'Hell's Half Acre,' and a few other places of like significance will be in the new county . . . . Placer County should fight the new county, in order to retain her glorious nomenclature of towns."

SOURCES

[Credit is here given for source material, and permission to quote is hereby acknowledged]

ANGEL, MYRON. *History of Placer County, California.* Thompson & West, Oakland, 1882
BROWNE, J. ROSS. *Report on the Mineral Resources of the States and Territories of the Rocky Mountains.* Government Printing Office, Washington, D.C., 1868
———. *Resources of the Pacific Slope.* H. H. Bancroft & Company, San Francisco, 1869
CLARK, GEORGE T. *Leland Stanford, War Governor of California, Railroad Builder and Founder of Stanford University.* Stanford University Press, Stanford University, 1931
FERRIER, W. W. "Berkeleyans Enjoy an Old Mining Town," in *Berkeley Daily Gazette,* July 10, 1925
FULTON, ROBERT LARDIN. *The Epic of the Overland.* A. M. Robertson, San Francisco, 1924
HEMPHILL, VIVIA. *Down the Mother Lode.* Purnell's, Sacramento, 1922
JAMES, GEORGE WHARTON. *The Lake of the Sky, Lake Tahoe.* George Wharton James, Pasadena, California, 1915
JOHNSTON, PHILIP. "Relics of the Gold-Rush among the Northern Diggin's," in *Touring Topics,* XXIV, No. 1 (January 1932), 10–25, 45, 46
LARDNER, W. B., and M. J. BROCK. *History of Placer and Nevada Counties, California.* Historic Record Company, Los Angeles, 1924
POWER, BERTHA KNIGHT. *William Henry Knight, California Pioneer.* Privately published, 1932
STEELE, R. J., JAMES P. BULL, and F. I. HOUSTON. *Directory of the County of Placer, for the Year 1861.* Charles F. Robbins, San Francisco, 1861

PLUMAS COUNTY

PLUMAS COUNTY (a name derived from El Río de las Plumas, "the river of the feathers," so named by Captain Luís A. Argüello, who led an exploring party up the valley of the Feather River in 1820, and who was impressed by the myriad feathers of wild fowl which he saw floating on the water) was organized in 1854 from a portion of Butte County. Quincy, originally known as American Ranch, has been the only county seat.

Beckwourth Pass

Beckwourth Pass over the High Sierra was discovered in 1851 by James Beckwourth, trapper, scout, and honorary chief of the Crow Indians, while on a prospecting expedition as he and his party crossed the mountains from the American River valley to the Pit River valley. This pass at the summit of the Sierra is not far from the present town of Beckwourth. Through the error of a postal clerk, the town was for many years designated by the name "Beckwith," but a recent ruling has restored the original spelling of "Beckwourth."

Jim Beckwourth subsequently proposed to interested citizens at Bidwell Bar and Marysville that a wagon road be made through this pass, across the Sierra Valley to the Middle Fork of the Feather River, and down the ridge east of the river past Bidwell Bar to Marysville. His plan was eventually adopted, and soon after the completion of the trail Beckwourth, while at Truckee in the Sierra Nevada, succeeded in persuading a passing emigrant train to try the new road. The party liked it, and others followed in their footsteps until it became a well-beaten trail. Beckwourth Pass is still in use by "present-day emigrants" who cross the Sierra on the Western Pacific Railway. .

Many emigrants came through this region in 1852. During the spring of that year Jim Beckwourth built a cabin (the first house in Beckwourth Valley), which served as trading-post and hotel. It stood on a hillside just west of the site later occupied by the residence of Alexander Kirby, and two and a half miles west of the village of Beckwourth. A second cabin was built near by, but both were burned by Indians. A third log cabin soon replaced the first two, and a part of this historic relic today serves as a milk house on the Kirby Ranch, which is now owned by Mr. Ramelli.

It was in 1852 that Ina Coolbrith, destined to become California's first poet laureate, then a child of eleven, came through Beckwourth Pass with the first covered-wagon train to enter California that way. This party had trekked across the Plains and mountains from St. Louis, Missouri, in ox-drawn schooners.

Speaking at a luncheon given in her honor in San Francisco on April 24, 1927, Ina Coolbrith said regarding this entry into California:

"Ours was the first of the covered-wagon trains to break the trail through Beckwourth Pass into California. We were guided by the famous scout, Jim Beckwourth, who was an historical figure, and to my mind one of the most beautiful creatures that ever lived. He was rather dark and wore his hair in two long braids, twisted with colored cord that gave him a picturesque appearance. He wore a leather coat and moccasins and rode a horse without a saddle.

"When we made that long journey toward the West over the deserts and the mountains, our wagon-train was driven over ground without a single mark of a wagon wheel until it was broken by ours. And when Jim Beckwourth said he would like to have my mother's little girls ride into California on his horse in front of him, I was the happiest little girl in the world.

"After two or three days of heavy riding we came at last in sight of California and there on the boundary line he stopped, and pointing forward, said:

" 'Here is California, little girls, here is your kingdom.' . . . .

"This wagon train arrived in California in September, 1852. In the Spring of that year, Jim Beckwourth, according to his own story, had established himself in Beckwourth Valley, and finally found himself transformed into a hotel keeper and chief of a trading post. His house, he said, was considered the emigrant's landing place."

By action of the United States Geographic Board a high peak, formerly known as Summit Peak, located six miles due south of Beckwourth Pass, was renamed Mount Ina Coolbrith, in honor of the late poet laureate. The peak, which rises to an elevation of eight thousand feet in Sierra County, is plainly visible from the pass through which young Ina Coolbrith rode with the famous scout. It lies near the intersection of the county lines of Plumas, Lassen, and Sierra counties, with its slopes reaching out into Plumas and Lassen counties.

The Gold Lake Excitement

The higher regions of the Sierra Nevada were the last to be prospected during the early days of the gold rush. Several hundred Argonauts in 1849 passed over the Lassen Trail through what is now northwestern Plumas County, but not one stayed to work its streams. A solitary man did, however, lead to the opening up of the country to a later influx of miners. This was J. R. Stoddard, the hero of an adventure the inception of which is so shrouded in mystery that many widely differing versions of his story have grown up. The facts of its later developments and the resulting Gold Lake migration are well known, however.

Stoddard, according to his own account, had stumbled upon a lake in the higher mountains somewhere between Downieville and Sierra Valley. The shores of this lake, he declared, were literally covered with chunks of gold. His recital of its exact location and of the circumstances attending its supposed discovery was conflicting and uncertain. The spirit of the times, however, was such as to make the wildest extravaganza seem plausible to credulous gold-seekers, and soon Stoddard found himself the leader not only of the small group originally chosen to go with him to relocate the fabled lake of gold but of several hundred others, all eager and determined to share in the imagined riches. The number increased, as rumor spread, until a thousand or more miners left their diggings on the lower reaches of the rivers to join the migration to the new El Dorado.

Gold Lake was never found, Stoddard evidently having been the victim of a disordered mind. Nevertheless, the influx of prospectors into the highlands of the upper Feather River canyons resulted in the opening up of the entire region, and many of the tributary streams were found to be very rich. The Gold Lake in Sierra County just across the line from Plumas County, and the much smaller Gold Lake just northwest of Spanish Peak in Plumas County, are reminiscent of this early excitement over the mythical lake with its gold-pebbled shores.

Intersected by the various forks of the Feather River, the land of the fabled "Gold Lake" is one of rugged scenic grandeur. The sculpturing waters have here chiseled the Sierra with canyons two thousand feet deep, flanked by lofty, forested ridges, magnificent and awe-inspiring in the extreme. Green and fertile valleys, watered by countless streams, nestle among giant hills and are made still more lovely by the mirrored beauty of numerous lakes. These valleys include Indian, American, Big Meadows, Buck's, Humbug, Mohawk, Genesee, Sierra, Beckwourth, Long, Red Clover, Round, Last Chance, Onion, and others. Near the southern boundary of the county the South Fork of the Feather River rises in the neighborhood of Pilot Peak, while the Middle Fork, a much longer stream with many tributaries, has its headwaters in Sierra Valley. The North Fork rises in the northwestern corner of the county southeast of Lassen Peak. Flowing in a nearly southerly direction through Big Meadows, now largely occupied by Lake Almanor, one of the world's largest reservoirs, it waters a considerable section of Plumas County before joining the Middle Fork of the Feather River one and a half miles west of Bidwell Bar in Butte County.

Beginning with the gold excitement of the '50's, mining, lumbering, and agriculture have played important rôles in the history of Plumas County. With an increasing horde of gold-seekers pouring into every nook and corner of the region in the early days, "mushroom" cities sprang up almost overnight. With this development came a great demand for lumber with which to erect the thousands of crude shacks and cabins which constituted these first towns. Farmers saw the need for farm and dairy products, and ranches were soon established in the fertile valleys where water and pasture lands were abundant. Although many of the old mining camps have since become "ghost towns," a few remain, forming a link in that chain of industry which reaches back into the historic past. Today, also, many of the pioneer ranches are being farmed by descendants of the original owners.

Plumas County contains scores of mineral springs located in various part of the county: in Humbug Valley, on the North Fork of the Feather River; at Soda Bar on the East Branch of the North Fork; in Indian Valley near Greenville, where there are warm bathing springs; in Mohawk Valley at the Sulphur Springs Ranch, where both hot and cold water are found; and in many other places. Numerous jets of steam and hot mud accompanied by rumbling noises suggest volcanic activities in Hot Springs Valley near the northwestern corner of the county. Since early days these places have attracted many visitors.

Onion Valley

Early in July 1850 a party of about 130 prospectors stopped in a lofty valley fifteen miles northwest of Downieville. Because of the thick growth of wild onions carpeting the place it was called Onion Valley. Here a member of the party known familiarly as "One-Eyed Moore" discovered rich diggings, and a camp was at once set up. Other discoveries were made, and soon the region was swarming with diggings: Dixon's Creek, Poorman's Creek, Nelson's Creek, Sawpit Flat, and many others. To the west, at the tip of a high ridge above the Middle Fork of the Feather River, was one of the several places in Plumas County called Last Chance.

At Onion Valley, Moore took out several thousand dollars' worth of gold and then moved on to fresher fields. However, others soon took his place, and by 1851 the camp had a population of fifteen hundred. On January 1 of that year a rich deposit was uncovered from which over $6,000 in gold was taken out in an hour and a half, including one nugget worth $1,800 and several smaller ones valued at $500 each. A few days later a large quartz boulder was turned over, and from the soil beneath it "half a man's hat full" of gold was picked up.

Just south of Onion Valley near Pilot Peak an uncommonly rich quartz vein was found sometime in the late '50's or early '60's. This extraordinary story is told of its discovery: "A Frenchman, who had gone out shooting with a Spaniard, fired at a bird but missed and struck a piece of quartz rock, which came rolling down the hill. The Spaniard picked it up and noticed that it was studded with gold. Upon going to the spot from which it had been detached, they found an outcropping of auriferous quartz, from which they broke off and carried to Pine Grove [Sierra County] a large piece that turned out to be about two-thirds solid metal." Following this discovery, a company was formed and the new vein worked. For many years it continued to yield large profits.

Nelson's Point

In the wake of the fabulous Gold Lake expedition, hundreds of miners invaded the Middle Fork of the Feather River early in the summer of 1850. Claims were soon staked out all along the tributary streams by the disappointed searchers for Gold Lake. The first of these locations was made on Nelson's Creek, a branch of the Feather River

named after one of its two discoverers. The village of Nelson's Point, at the mouth of the creek, was established soon afterward and became the trading-center for the camps along the Middle Fork, such as Hottentot Bar, Sailor Bar, Poverty Flat, Sunny Bar, English Bar, Bell's Bar, Henpeck Flat, and a score of others.

Hittell describes Nelson's Point as "one of the roughest places in California. It consisted of a few houses, piled as it were without form or shape against one another on the sides of the precipices where the spurs of three steep mountains met at the junction of Nelson's Creek. . . . As a place of carousal and wassail on Sundays for the miners of the rough and rocky regions round about, it became famous in the early times." Nelson's Point was later moved about a mile up the river to the stage road running from La Porte to Quincy. The site is marked today by a few stone foundations, remnants of an old garden, and a corral. The village, with its hotel and store kept by the Pauly family, was destroyed by a forest fire in 1924, but the land is still owned by the Paulys.

Rich Bar

Stragglers of the Gold Lake influx made one of the foremost discoveries in Plumas County, about July 1, 1850, on the East Branch of the North Fork of the Feather River at a place afterward called Rich Bar. Enormous production records were made at this point, where pans of dirt frequently yielded from one hundred to one thousand dollars. It is said that three Germans took out thirty-six thousand dollars in nuggets and gold dust during four days' time. Claims were so rich that they were limited to ten square feet. During the first two years after its discovery, Rich Bar yielded a total of from three to four million dollars in gold, thus earning its name. With the approach of the winter of 1850–1851 most of the claims at Rich Bar were deserted, although a few log cabins were erected and occupied until the spring of 1851, when a host of miners again flocked to the region.

A vivid and colorful picture of life in this old river camp in the early '50's has been preserved for us in the letters of a gifted and educated New England woman, Mrs. Louise Amelia Knapp Smith Clappe, who lived at Rich Bar from 1851 to 1852. Written to her sister Molly, in the old home at Amherst, Massachusetts, these bright and cheery epistles (playfully signed "Dame Shirley") were penned merely for the purpose of giving her sister "a true picture . . . . of mining life," with no thought of their subsequent publication. However, two years later they appeared in print, when a friend, the Rev. Ferdinand C. Ewer of San Francisco, made use of them in *The Pioneer*, a monthly magazine of which he was the publisher and in which the "Shirley Letters" appeared during the two years of its existence.

Later writers, notably Bancroft, Hittell, and Royce, have acknowledged their indebtedness to these letters. Certainly these delightful pen pictures, written on the spot, glossing nothing over, form the best first-hand account we have of life in the early gold camps. "It is easy indeed," says Carl I. Wheat, "to credit the legend that from her Bret Harte obtained many ideas, and wrought from them undying tales of California's youth. *The Luck of Roaring Camp* and *The Outcasts of Poker Flat* contain mute evidence of Harte's great debt to her."

With her husband, Dr. Fayette Clappe, "Dame Shirley" came to Rich Bar in the fall of 1851. The journey from Marysville to Bidwell Bar was made in an "excruciatingly springless wagon," with the second stage of the trip negotiated on muleback over winding mountain trails, passing, at long intervals, a rare and thrice-welcome farm house—the

Wild Yankee's (Butte County), the Buckeye Ranch, and the Pleasant Valley Ranch—where fresh butter, cream, and other luxuries might be had. The Berry Creek House (Butte County) was missed, the two pilgrims having strayed out of their way over a devious and confusing Indian trail in the mountainous region near the North Fork of the Feather River. "Who knows," Mrs. Clappe afterward wrote, "how narrowly I escaped becoming an Indian chieftainess, and feeding for the rest of my life upon roasted grasshoppers, acorns, and flower-seeds?"

Coming at length to the summit of the high ridge overlooking Rich Bar, she was enchanted with the exquisite beauty of the scene which lay before her: "shadowy nooks" and "far down valleys . . . . half a dozen blue-bosomed lagoons. . . . . It was worth the whole wearisome journey, danger from Indians, grizzly bears, sleeping under the stars, and all."

On the last stretch of her journey Mrs. Clappe had a narrow escape from death. Although warned that she should walk rather than ride down the precipitous declivity, since even the hardiest miners did so, she was determined upon the former method of transit, for, as she told her sister, "I had much more confidence in my mule's power of picking the way and keeping his footing than in my own." At one point on this fearful trail her saddle slipped and she landed on the tiniest of ledges far above the river bed. "Had the accident happened at any other part of the hill," she writes, in tearful gratitude to the good God who seemed watching over her, "I must have been dashed, a piece of shapeless nothingness, into the dim valleys beneath."

Mrs. Clappe at length found herself safely at "Barra Rica," as the Mexicans called it. The third of the series of letters describes, in vivid tone, the picture. "Imagine a tiny valley, about eight hundred yards in length and, perhaps, thirty in width . . . . apparently hemmed in by lofty hills, almost perpendicular, draperied to their very summits with beautiful fir trees, the blue-bosomed 'Plumas,' or Feather River, I suppose I must call it, undulating along their base. . . . . Through the middle of Rich Bar runs the street, thickly planted with about forty tenements, among which figure round tents, square tents, plank hovels, log cabins, etc. —the residences, varying in elegance and convenience from the palatial splendor of 'the Empire' down to a 'local habitation,' formed of pine boughs, and covered with old calico shirts."

Although numerous shanties on the Bar claimed the grandiloquent title of "Hotel," the Empire was *the* hostelry of the place, and Mrs. Clappe's portrayal of its whimsical splendor equals if not excels her other descriptions: "You first enter a long apartment, level with the street, part of which is fitted up as a bar-room, with that eternal crimson calico which flushes the whole social life of the 'Golden State' with its everlasting red—in the center of a fluted mass of which gleams a really elegant mirror, set off by a background of decanters, cigar vases, and jars of brandied fruit, the whole forming a *tout ensemble* of dazzling splendor. . . . . The entire building is lined with purple calico, alternating with a delicate blue, and the effect is really quite pretty. The floors are so uneven that you are always ascending a hill or descending into a valley." Such was "this impertinent apology for a house," a one-time gambler's palace costing its original owners more than $8,000.

On the steep hillside behind the Empire lay the lonely graveyard where Nancy Ann Bailey, "the second 'Mrs. B.,'" one of the two women who preceded Mrs. Clappe at Rich Bar, was buried a week after the latter's arrival. At the head of the Bar was the little windowless log cabin in which this pioneer mother passed away September 30, 1851 (the

date given on her headstone). Overlooking the river stands the Rich Bar Monument dedicated by the Native Sons of the Golden West on August 7, 1915, in memory of the pioneers who settled at this spot, some of whom found rest on the hillside near by, and in special honor of Nancy Ann Bailey.

Nothing of the mining period remains at Rich Bar except the decaying headstones in the tiny cemetery on the hill, the ruined foundations of the Masonic Hall and of the hotel, and the heaps of boulders along the river where miners once worked this richest of the northern "diggin's."

Indian Bar

In 1852 the Clappes moved to Indian Bar. Mrs. Clappe thus describes the river trail leading to her new home: "The crossings are formed of logs, often moss-grown. . . . . At every step gold diggers or their operations greet your vision. Sometimes in the form of a dam, sometimes in that of a river turned slightly from its channel, to aid the indefatigable gold hunters in their mining projects. . . . . As we approached Indian Bar, the path led several times fearfully near deep holes from which the laborers were gathering their yellow harvest."

A little below Indian Bar was Missouri Bar, reached by a log bridge, while half a mile beyond on the same side of the river was Smith's Bar, also reached over a bridge formed by two logs. Within a few miles were Frenchman's, Taylor's, Brown's, The Junction, Wyandotte, and Muggins' bars.

Just across from Indian Bar was Pea Soup Bar (not yet named when Mrs. Clappe wrote her letters), while opposite Rich Bar was a narrow "diggin's" later known as Poverty Bar. It was on this bar that the builders of the Feather River Highway established their camp while blasting out a roadway from the cliffs of the gorge. The road reached the point opposite Rich Bar in the autumn of 1932. The Western Pacific Railway had been constructed up the canyon in 1909.

Spanish Ranch

A quarter of a mile north of the Oroville–Quincy Highway, and about six miles west of Quincy, two Mexicans, in July 1850, set up an early camp in that part of Meadow Valley. From this circumstance the name of the camp, of the creek on the banks of which it was located, and of a neighboring mountain peak, each was prefixed with the adjective "Spanish." Miners customarily left their horses and pack mules in the care of these Mexicans, who also engaged in cattle raising and slaughtering, selling the meat at one dollar a pound.

Spanish Ranch soon became a distributing-center for surrounding camps. The first hotel, blacksmith shop, and store were erected there in 1852 by Lloyd and Snodgrass. These buildings are all still standing. A post office was established in the store in 1858, and a Wells Fargo Express office in 1868. Millions of dollars in gold dust and nuggets have passed through its doors. As late as 1881 the year's output in coin and bullion amounted to $114,076.65. Directly above the village towers Spanish Peak (7,047 feet), pierced by the tunnel of the Monte Cristo Mine at an altitude of 6,288 feet, or within 759 feet of the summit.

At the Meadow Valley Camp, two miles south of Spanish Ranch, the express office, the Phelps house, and the Dean barn, all used by W. S. Dean from 1852 to 1855, still stand. The Meadow Valley store and hotel on the old stage road from Oroville to Quincy was burned some years ago. About two and a quarter miles west of Meadow Valley is the site of Toll Gate, where tolls were collected on one of the first turnpikes in Plumas County. The buildings here, too, have all been burned.

Six miles farther southwest the road passed Buck's Ranch, which was first occupied in the fall of 1850. It later developed into another important stage station. All of the original buildings have been burned, and the site is under the waters of Buck's Reservoir, which now covers most of Buck's Valley. On a large boulder on the lake shore a bronze tablet was placed by the Native Daughters and the Native Sons of the Golden West of Plumas County on August 9, 1931. This marker designates the site of the Buck's Ranch hotel, which stood one hundred yards to the northeast at a point immediately in front of the dead pine tree which still stands in the lake. If standing, the building would be submerged by twenty feet of water when the lake is full. The Buck's Ranch hotel and store served for years as a stage station and express and post office. In the early days it was a haven for pioneers, where miners' pack trains stopped en route to the Feather River mines, while later it became an important point in the passenger, express, and mail service to and from Quincy and other towns. In the rich Gravel Range District near Buck's Ranch, miners were known to have found gold, silver, and copper all in one ledge.

Near Grizzly Creek, about three and one-half miles west of Buck's Ranch, is a meadow hemmed in by the forest. Here, not far from the road, stands an old pine tree and beside a granite monument, both marking the grave of a young pioneer who was killed by bandits and buried at this spot by his comrade in September 1852. The letters of the original carving on the tree trunk, although partly grown over, are still legible.

The site of the old Letter Box House in another pine-fringed hollow, about three miles farther on, has been marked by the Forest Service. Beyond is another site designated as Palmetto, where a miner's cabin and corral once stood. Soon after leaving this point the road enters the famous Walker's Plains or lava beds, where in pioneer days difficulty was experienced in keeping spokes in the stage-coach wheels. A good automobile road now traverses this region of interesting geological formations. The site of the Buckeye Hotel, the last stage station before entering Butte County, is passed soon after leaving the lava beds.

La Porte

La Porte, an old mining camp located on flat benches on both sides of Rabbit Creek, a tributary of Slate Creek in the southwest corner of Plumas County, was known as Rabbit Creek from 1850 to 1857. During the '60's and '70's it developed into a populous center for hydraulic mining. But after 1883, when hydraulic mining became illegal, La Porte dwindled in population, until today it is a quiet mountain hamlet with only forty-five inhabitants. The ruins of several old brick stores with their heavy iron doors lend an atmosphere of age to the place. The oldest building in La Porte is known as William's Shop, which once served as a school. The house in which Lotta Crabtree lived for a time as a child has been burned, but the foundation of the fireplace can still be found. At the west entrance to the town a granite monument was placed by the Native Daughters and the Native Sons of the Golden West of Plumas County on June 24, 1928, to mark the old Emigrant Trail and to commemorate the discovery of gold on Rabbit Creek in 1850 and the subsequent founding of La Porte.

Little Grass Valley, about four miles north of La Porte on the South Fork of the Feather River, was at the head of wagon traffic in pioneer days. Along the old stage road from Marysville to La Porte a number of inns were built, one of the most famous being the American House, the site of

which has been marked by the Forest Service. Two ancient locust trees still flourish in the adjoining meadow with its encircling evergreen forests. The Lexington House, the Winthrop House, and the Buckeye House also stood on this road.

Winter sports in the High Sierra were held annually as early as the '60's at La Porte and Onion Valley in Plumas County and at Howland's Flat in Sierra County. Thrilling ski-racing contests took place at these points, resulting in some fast speed records.

Elizabethtown, or Betsyburg

Miners flocked to the region of Betsyburg in 1852 in search of the precious yellow metal. There being only one unmarried lady in the new camp, Elizabeth Stark, the chivalrous miners named the new town in her honor. Betsyburg, or Elizabethtown as it was more decorously called, was a large camp by 1853, and in 1854 a post office was established there. However, gold in the surrounding gulches soon became exhausted, and after Quincy was made the county seat of Plumas County in 1854, and the post office was moved there in 1856, Elizabethtown began to decline. Today only a "ghost" village remains with little to indicate its former activity. Only a part of the walls of the Leavitt house may be found, almost buried under tailings from the old mines. The site of the former town was marked by a monument placed by the Native Sons and Daughters of Quincy on September 9, 1927.

American Ranch—Quincy

The American Ranch was owned by H. J. Bradley, one of the three commissioners who organized Plumas County. Owing to his influence, the seat of justice was placed by statute at the hotel on his ranch. With this as a nucleus he laid out a town, calling it Quincy after his home city in Illinois, and the people were induced to vote for Quincy as the county seat.

The oldest buildings in Quincy are the Masonic Hall, moved from Elizabethtown in 1855, the lower floor being used at first as a schoolroom; the Town Hall, erected by Billy Houck as a saloon in 1862 and purchased by the citizens of Quincy for a town hall in 1872; and the Methodist Episcopal Church, built in 1877. Several homes still standing were constructed of lumber brought from abandoned houses in Elizabethtown.

Quincy was one of the stations of Whiting and Company's Dog Express, which, in the early days, brought the mails over the snowy Sierra. For stretches of twenty miles through snow-covered mountain country, Newfoundlands or St. Bernards, driven tandem or four to a team, pulled sledges carrying loads oftentimes of over six hundred pounds. Passengers, express, and mail were all transported. Distinguished service was rendered by these faithful animals and their masters from 1858 until the invention of the horse snowshoe in 1865.

The Plumas-Eureka Mine

Operations started at the Plumas-Eureka Mine, situated on the east slope of Eureka Peak, in the summer of 1851. A company of thirty-six men was formed, but instead of setting up stamp mills at once they wisely mined with arrastras until sufficient money had been made to warrant improvements. Chili wheels superseded the arrastras, and finally, in 1856, a mill with twelve stamps was erected. Improvements continued to be made and profits were still accruing in 1870.

In the vicinity of the Plumas-Eureka other quartz mines were opened at various times. To the northeast was the

Mammoth Mine, worked by a company of eighty men with the use of arrastras until 1856, when a twelve-stamp mill was erected. Two other mines in the vicinity, the Washington and the Rough-and-Ready, were not financially successful, because their promoters spent all their profits on equipment. The Washington Mine was owned by a company of seventy-six men, who laid out an ephemeral town on Jamison Creek, calling it the City of 76.

All of these claims—the Plumas-Eureka, Mammoth, Washington, and Rough-and-Ready—were bought by John Parrott in the early '70's. Parrott, in turn, sold them to the Sierra Buttes Company, of London, and the town of Johnsville (a village of two hundred inhabitants in 1930) was laid out in 1876 on Jamison Creek one-half mile east of the Plumas-Eureka Mine. About two miles north on this same creek was Jamison, a mining camp settled in 1853. Jamison has disappeared, and its site is traced now only by old trails and piles of stones indicating the vast extent of the early mining operations carried on there. All along Jamison Creek, too, traces of early quartz mills and arrastras may still be found.

Mohawk, a hamlet of forty-five people in 1930, was once a prosperous agricultural center for surrounding mines. It is located about three miles east of the site of Jamison and one-half mile west of Blairsden, a small station on the Western Pacific Railway. All of the early buildings at Mohawk have been burned.

One mile southwest of Johnsville, at the foot of the steepest pitch on the old Marysville–Jamison City Emigrant Trail, a monument consisting of a stone taken from one of the earliest Jamison Creek arrastras was erected and dedicated by the Native Sons and Daughters of Plumas County on October 25, 1932. The modern motorist, circumventing the steep declivity over which the lumbering ox-drawn wagons of the pioneers were hauled in the early '50's, finds it difficult to believe that wagons actually negotiated that sheer bank. A few feet in front of the monument are the graves of four early-day miners who were killed in a snowslide which occurred at this point. On the flat above, the site of Eureka Hill (once numbering about five hundred inhabitants) is now overgrown with brush. Near by are the Mohawk dump, where an eighty-stamp mill used to grind out gold, and the Eureka dump, where millions of dollars in gold were produced.

At Split Rock a second marker was placed, a short distance below the first. From this rock early miners obtained material for making the arrastra stones which formed the primitive mills used to grind out the gold. The pioneer trail to Mohawk Valley passed near the site of this marker.

Other Historic Spots

At Greenville, long a center of quartz-mining activity, a bullion ledge was discovered in 1851 and first mined with profit by John W. Ellis in 1856. The Lone Star Mine was first worked there in 1857. At Round Valley, south of Greenville, John Ellis opened up the Ellis Mine in 1862, and quite a village grew up about the stamp mill. With the abandonment of the mine, the town faded out completely within a few years. Tunnels and rock piles are the only evidence of early-day activity in the locality. Southeast of Greenville at Crescent Mills quartz-mining and milling operations were carried on as late as 1926.

Two famous copper mines in the mountains east of Indian Valley have made fine production records, and continued to employ a large number of men until they were shut down. One of these was the Engle Mine (closed in 1930), fifteen miles northeast of Crescent Mills, and the other was the Walker Mine, nine miles northeast of Spring Garden.

The latter yielded $1,099,000 in copper in 1931, but was closed down in 1932.

Peter Lassen, the first pioneer to settle in Indian Valley, came there with Isadore Meyerwitz in the fall of 1850. Lassen called the spot Caché Valley, but later settlers gave it its permanent name of Indian Valley, because of the numerous natives whom they found living there. Lassen returned to the region in 1851 accompanied by a Mr. Burton. The two men built a log cabin three miles north of the site of Greenville, and developed a thriving trading-post. Vegetables were raised and sold to the miners at high prices. The site of the old Lassen cabin, which stood for many years, has been permanently marked by the Native Sons and the Native Daughters of the Golden West of Plumas County. The monument stands on the present Hannon Ranch.

Between the broad meadows of Indian Valley and the dense evergreen forests of Mount Hough lies Taylorsville, founded by Jobe T. Taylor, who settled there in 1852. A quaint charm pervades the village, with its great barns, sturdy and useful; its shady streets; a white-steepled church; its old houses, substantial and dignified; and, close against the hill in a tiny oak wood, the peaceful burial ground where sleep the pioneers. A monument here marks the grave of Jobe Taylor. Among the historic landmarks of the town is the Vernon House or Taylor Hotel, the third hostelry built by Jobe Taylor on the same site. It was erected soon after the fire of 1859 had destroyed the second structure. The Young Hotel (now called the Grange) is of later date.

SOURCES

[Credit is here given for source material, and permission to quote is hereby acknowledged]

BECKWOURTH, JAMES P. The Life and Adventures of James P. Beckwourth. Edited by T. D. Bonner. Harper & Brothers, 1856. New edition, A. A. Knopf, New York, 1931
CLAPPE, MRS. LOUISE AMELIA KNAPP (SMITH). "The Shirley Letters from California Mines, 1851–52," in The Pioneer, Vols. I–IV (January 1854–December 1855)
———. The Shirley Letters from California Mines, 1851–1852. Printed by Thomas C. Russell at his private press, San Francisco, 1922
———. California in 1851–1852. The Letters of Dame Shirley. Introduction and Notes by Carl I. Wheat. 2 vols. The Grabhorn Press, San Francisco, 1932
DORNIN, MAY. The Emigrant Trails into California. Master's thesis in History. University of California, Berkeley, California, 1921
FARISS and SMITH. Illustrated History of Plumas, Lassen, and Sierra Counties. Fariss & Smith, San Francisco, 1882
HITTELL, THEODORE H. History of California. 4 vols. N. J. Stone & Company, San Francisco, 1898
PURDY, HELEN THROOP. The Shirley Letters from California Mines, 1851–1852. A review in California Historical Society Quarterly, I, No. 3 (January 1923), 299–301
RIDER, FREMONT (editor). Rider's California: A Guide-Book for Travellers. The Macmillan Company, New York, 1925
ROURKE, CONSTANCE. Troupers of the Gold Coast, or the Rise of Lotta Crabtree. Harcourt, Brace & Company, New York, 1928
ROYCE, JOSIAH. California. Houghton Mifflin Company, Boston and New York, 1886

SACRAMENTO COUNTY

SACRAMENTO COUNTY (named for the river so called by the first Spanish explorers of that region in honor of the Holy Sacrament) was one of the original twenty-seven counties. The only changes made in its boundaries have been those necessitated by the shifting of the stream beds of the Mokelumne and Sacramento rivers. Sacramento has always been the county seat.

Old Spanish Trails

Pedro Fages, in 1772, while exploring the "Port of San Francisco" with the purpose of finding a suitable mission site, had gone up the eastern shore of the Bay as far as the San Joaquin River and had seen the great Sacramento River "from a point of vantage." Long after the mission had been founded at San Francisco, and after nineteen of the twenty-one missions had been established along the coast of Alta California, several expeditions were organized and sent into the river country of the great interior valley to search for suitable sites for new missions.

One of the most remarkable of these valley expeditions was that commanded by Gabriel Moraga in 1808. It was on this trip that the name, Sacramento, originated. On October 9 Moraga's party camped on the lower Feather River, which Moraga called the Sacramento, a name which he also gave to the great river into which it flows farther down, showing that he believed that the two composed the main stream. He considered the upper Sacramento, which he reached a little later, to be a branch of the main river and called it the Jesús María, a name which was long retained for that part of its course. It is easy to understand why Moraga reached this conclusion, for at the point where the Sacramento and the Feather come together it is the latter which makes a straight line north and south with the lower Sacramento, while the upper Sacramento flows at that point from the west.

An attempt to explore the river country by boat was made by José Antonio Sánchez in 1811, when he proceeded a little way up the Sacramento River, making the first recorded navigation of that stream. However, an undertaking of more importance in the history of Sacramento took place in 1817, under command of Luís Argüello, accompanied by Fathers Narciso Durán and Ramón Abella. Various channels which they followed, as well as a number of the places at which they camped, have been identified. At one time a fierce windstorm drove them behind the Montezuma Hills in the vicinity of the present town of Río Vista (Solano County), and, again, from a vantage point on the site of Clarksburg they had a fine view of the Sierra Nevada. Soon afterward they passed the site of what is now the city of Sacramento, probably being its discoverers.

Opening of the Sacramento Trail

The old Sacramento Trail, however, was actually opened up to trade and immigration by an American, Jedediah S. Smith, who had made the first overland journey into California in 1826. Smith came again, in 1827, to rejoin that part of his company which he had left encamped on one of the rivers of the San Joaquin Valley. Although the Mexican government had demanded his departure from the province, he did not make haste to leave the country at once by the way he had come. Instead, he opened a new route which led up the Sacramento River northward.

After several unsuccessful attempts to find a pass through the Sierra Nevada from the river, the Smith party finally left the Sacramento about the middle of April 1828. Going northwest across the Coast Range through the wild region which is now included in Trinity and Humboldt counties, Smith and his men came to the seacoast and proceeded along it to Oregon. The route thus opened by this dauntless pathfinder of the Far West was soon followed by Hudson's Bay Company hunters and traders from Vancouver by way of Oregon.

A tablet in honor of Jedediah Strong Smith, the man who first opened the doors to California from the north, has been placed by the Sacramento Chapter, D.A.R., at the west end of the bridge over the American River just out of Sacramento, on U.S. Highway 99.

New Helvetia

The first white settlement in the great central valley of California was made by John A. Sutter in 1839. Sutter, who was born in 1803 in Baden, Germany, of Swiss parents, came to America when still a young man. Eventually, he drifted to St. Louis and from there to the Pacific Coast by way of the Columbia River.

Slowly, the idea of founding a colony in California took form in the mind of this enterprising young pioneer. Sailing from Vancouver to the Sandwich Islands, he aroused the interest of a handful of Americans and native Kanakas in his project and, with this as a nucleus for the future independent state of which he dreamed, Sutter reached California early in July 1839. There he became a citizen of the province and obtained permission of Governor Alvarado to establish his settlement.

The great Sacramento Valley was, at that time, unfortified and unsettled. A few Spanish expeditions had been made into the interior to search for mission sites or runaway Indians; Jedediah Smith had traversed it in 1828; and Hudson's Bay Company trappers had hunted on its streams. The natives who inhabited the river country and the surrounding mountains were a constant problem to the scattered Coast settlements, and Sutter's proposal to establish a frontier outpost that would act as a buffer to this ever present annoyance was welcomed by the Mexican government, especially as it meant no expense on their part, other than the granting of a few leagues of wilderness land for the proposed settlement.

Thus it came about that a grant of eleven leagues of land in the great valley of the Sacramento was given to Sutter in 1841. With high hopes for the future, he embarked up the river to choose a location for his estate, landing at the site of the present city of Sacramento.

The building of a very pretentious adobe fort was begun about two miles from the embarcadero, or landing-place on the water front, 1839–1840, the outside walls not being completed until 1844. In December 1841 Sutter purchased the equipment of the Russian settlements, which were being disbanded at Bodega and Fort Ross. This purchase included, among other things, a large number of horses and cattle, a small launch, and several pieces of artillery. The cannon was set up at Sutter's Fort on the Sacramento, and armed guards and daily drill became a feature of the place, giving it a decidedly military aspect. Sutter named the little settlement New Helvetia, undoubtedly hoping one day to make of this semi-feudal barony an independent state.

Sutter's Fort

Sutter's Fort, as it soon came to be known, was not merely a fort; it was a trading post and a place of refuge as well. Cleland says that "in addition to Sutter's military activities, he displayed a vast amount of energy in more peaceful endeavors. To care for the ever growing needs of his colony, and especially to meet the pressing demands of his Russian debt, he branched out into a great variety of pursuits and tried all sorts of experiments, most of which impoverished, rather than enriched him. He planted large areas to wheat; built a flour mill; diverted water from the American River for irrigation purposes; grazed large herds of cattle and horses; sent hunters into the mountains and along the rivers for furs and elk skins; set up a distillery; began the weaving of coarse woolen blankets; ran a launch regularly for freight and passengers between his settlement and San Francisco Bay; employed nearly all foreigners who came to him for work, whether he needed them or not; trained the Indians to useful occupations; at times chastised the thieving, war-inclined tribes which the Spanish Californians could not subdue; administered justice as an official of the provincial government; and, in short, made his colony the nucleus of all activity, whether political or economic, in what was then the only settled portion of interior California.

"In addition to these varied activities, with their decided local and personal interest, Sutter contributed in a much larger way to the making of California history through his aid to American immigration. Few people today realize how large a part this hospitable, visionary, improvident land baron of the Sacramento played in the American advance to California. His fort occupied the most strategic position in all Northern California, so far as the overland trails were concerned, and became the natural objective for parties crossing the Sierras, by the central and northern routes, or coming into the province by way of Oregon.

"At Sutter's, these immigrants, exhausted and half-starved as many of them were, found shelter, food and clothing, and an opportunity to learn something of the new land and people to which they had come. More than one company [the most famous of which was the Donner party], caught in the mountain snows, was saved from destruction by a rescue party sent from Sutter's Fort. The situation of the latter also made it impossible for the California authorities, had they been so inclined, to check or turn aside the stream of overland migration. The passes and trails of the northern Sierras lay open to American frontiersmen so long as Sutter maintained his position on the Sacramento."

Sutter's Fort fell into the hands of other owners after 1850, and the buildings began to deteriorate. Final destruction was threatening when, in 1889, it was proposed to open up Twenty-seventh Street from K to L. This disaster was averted by the efforts of General James G. Martine. The Fort was restored by the state in 1891–1893, and is now used as a state museum of pioneer relics. It is located between K and L streets on the north and south and Twenty-sixth and Twenty-eighth streets on the west and east, about two and one-quarter miles from the water front.

The original adobe bricks, made by Sutter's Indians, may be seen in the Central Building, which is all that remained of the original fort when reconstruction got under way following donation of the property to the State by the Native Sons of the Golden West. This two-story building, with basement, has walls about thirty inches thick, and the original hand-hewn oaken floor joists. Other walls within the fort were reconstructed of kiln-baked bricks, as were the outer walls. The fort was reproduced in its approximate original form and dimensions, with shops, storerooms, living quarters, etc. Peter Slater's Saloon, Sutter's bedroom, office and kitchen, and an old-time print shop have been reproduced, as has the blacksmith shop. Approximately twenty-two rooms or sections are devoted to museum purposes, either for storage of reserve material, workshops, or displays of historical objects. Several cannon dating back to Sutter's time preserve the military aspect of the place. A park, beautifully landscaped, is included in the grounds, which cover two city blocks. The State Indian Museum is on the property, with an entrance on K Street.

Many an interesting object of pioneer days is housed in Sutter's Fort Historical Museum. These include an outstanding collection of Reed-Donner Party items; firearms; stagecoaches and other vehicles; mining tools; costumes; objects made or used by James W. Marshall, who is credited with the discovery of gold at Coloma; equipment used by early fire departments; household furnishings; musical instruments; maps, documents, diaries of Forty-niners, paintings, prints, and rare photographs. The Curator's office has files of information relating to California pioneers.

Labels placed on various rooms about the quadrangle of the fort give the visitor a vivid picture of the social and industrial life of the settlement. Sites of the former flour mill, granary, stores, and emigrant quarters are marked.

During the restoration of the fort some of the workmen panned dirt near the east gate and recovered a quantity of gold dust which had been dropped years before by miners, or swept from gambling rooms and stores on the premises. Doubtless this was some of the first gold mined after the discovery at Sutter's Sawmill in '48.

Owned and maintained by the State of California, Sutter's Fort Historical Museum collects, preserves, and exhibits objects used in California by the pioneers and early settlers between the years 1839, when the fort was founded, and 1869, when the Gold Spike marked the completion of the transcontinental railroad and the decline of the stagecoach era.

Sutter's Fort Historical Museum is open daily from 10 a.m. to 4 p.m. Admission is free.

Mexican Land Grants

John A. Sutter did not long remain the sole land baron in the Sacramento Valley. The beginning of the American occupation found him already surrounded by neighbors. Many of his former employees had occupied ranchos up and down the length of the Sacramento and San Joaquin valleys.

John Sinclair, a Scotchman, settled on Rancho del Paso as early as 1841. On this estate of 44,000 acres, granted to Eliab Grimes in December 1844, Sinclair built a house on the right bank of the American River two and one-half miles from Sutter's Fort. This house was, for a time, the first civilized dwelling reached by the overland emigrant trains after crossing the Sierra Nevada. Sinclair was hospitable and kindly in his treatment of those in need, and as Alcalde of the Sacramento District was especially instrumental in sending aid to the Donner party.

Rancho Río de los Americanos, extending over 35,500 acres on the south side of the American River east of New Helvetia, was granted, on October 1, 1844, to William A. Leidesdorff, vice-consul of the United States by Larkin's appointment. Leidesdorff died in 1848, leaving the rancho and other valuable property in San Francisco. Captain Joseph L. Folsom, who had come to California as assistant quartermaster of Stevenson's New York Volunteers, purchased the vast Leidesdorff estate from the heirs for a song, thus becoming one of the wealthiest men in California. He laid out the town of Folsom on his rancho in 1855 and it was named in his honor. The site of the old Leidesdorff adobe, erected in 1846, is about ten miles east of Sacramento at Routier.

One summer evening in 1840, William Daylor, an employee of Sutter, climbed a hill to the southeast of New Helvetia and saw for the first time the rich valley of the Cosumnes River, then thickly populated with Indians. Daylor decided then and there that the lands bordering the north bank of the river were to be his. On returning to the fort he talked the matter over with his friend, Jared Sheldon, also an employee of Sutter. Sheldon, a native of Vermont, had become a naturalized Mexican citizen and held claims against the Mexican government for services in building the Customs House at Monterey. The two men formed a partnership whereby Sheldon was to obtain the grant of land through W. E. P. Hartnell in liquidation of his claim, and also to supply the cattle, while Daylor was to settle upon the land and look after the stock. The first grant, made in 1841, proved to be defective, and a second was drawn up and approved on January 8, 1844, under the designation "Rancho Omochumnes."

The Delta Region

The rich delta lands of the Sacramento and San Joaquin rivers cover more than 425,000 acres of immensely productive country. It is a section suggestive of the dikes and canals of old Holland. First settled in the early '50's by gold-seekers who had failed to make a living in the mines and who had squatted on the river delta in order to raise enough food for their subsistence, the land early demonstrated its extraordinary fertility. After the completion of the Central Pacific Railroad thousands of unemployed Chinese were glad to work, for very low wages, reclaiming the delta country for agriculture. They built the first system of levees along the various islands, working laboriously with wheelbarrows. Today, 90 per cent of the world's canned asparagus comes from the delta region of the Sacramento and San Joaquin rivers.

Mining Camps of the American River

Mormon Island, in the northeast corner of Sacramento County, is the site of the second important gold discovery in California. Early in the spring of 1848 two Mormons, on their way to Sutter's Mill at Coloma, camped for the night at a bar on the South Fork near its confluence with the North Fork. One of the men remarked: "They are taking out gold above us on the river. Let us see if we can find some at this place." Panning out a little dirt in one of their cooking utensils, they revealed a fine prospect. The two Mormons returned to the fort the next day and reported their find to Samuel Brannan, leader of the Mormons in California and associated with C. C. Smith, who kept a store at New Helvetia. Brannan immediately proceeded to the place where the discovery had been made and set up a pre-emptive claim, demanding a royalty of one-third on all the gold taken out at the bar. This fee continued to be paid to Brannan as long as the Mormons were in the majority. Later, when unbelievers outnumbered those of the faith, the tithe could no longer be collected. Meanwhile, Brannan had accumulated thousands of dollars, which he invested in merchandising, becoming one of the wealthiest men in California.

By 1853 Mormon Island had become a city of over 2,500 inhabitants, but a fire in 1856 destroyed most of the town and it has never been rebuilt. A few rock cellars, the ubiquitous locust tree, and memories are all that remain to locate the site of this historic gold town. Old houses brought around the Horn have been torn down within the last ten or fifteen years, and a modern chicken ranch occupies a large portion of the former town site.

Following down the American River from Mormon Island, one passes the sites of numerous river camps, some of which were important towns in the early '50's. In quick succession came Alabama Bar, on the north bank of the river; Slate Bar, opposite the State Penitentiary, where several stores were located; and Sailor Bar. Bean's Bar was one-half mile below Alabama Bar on the opposite side of the river.

Negro Bar (later Folsom) was first mined by negroes in 1849. By 1851 it had a population of seven hundred. The town of Folsom was laid out there in 1855 by Theodore Judah, as the temporary terminus of the Sacramento Valley Railroad, the first railroad in California. This road, which began at the foot of K Street in Sacramento, where a N.S.G.W. marker indicates the site of the old depot, was completed as far as Folsom in 1856. The new town became an important center for stage and freight lines running to the northern mining camps and to Virginia City, Nevada. The greatest prosperity was enjoyed in the early '60's, when many substantial hotels and business houses were established as well as an academy and several churches. Some of these sturdy stone and brick buildings still stand along Folsom's

main street, now a part of the Lincoln Highway. Likewise reminiscent of an earlier period are its old-fashioned homes, surrounded by trees of another day.

Earlier mining methods have been replaced by the giant dredges which have piled high with boulders hundreds of acres for miles about the town. The Natoma district alone has totaled $45,000,000 since 1880, of which amount the gold dredges produced $40,000,000. Since 1922 the average annual production from gold dredging in Sacramento County has been $1,300,000.

Construction of the California Central Railroad to Marysville was begun in 1857 at Folsom, and was completed to Lincoln in 1861. That part of the line between Folsom and Roseville was abandoned in 1866, but portions of the old roadbed are still visible.

On or near Alder Creek, two miles south of Folsom, was Prairie City, a mining camp which reached the height of its prosperity in 1853, after the Natoma Water and Mining Company's ditch was completed to that point. A large quartz mill was also erected there in 1857 at a cost of $50,000. For a time, Prairie City was a city in fact as well as in name, being a center of trade for a number of other camps: Rhoads' Diggings, Alder Creek, and Willow Springs Hill Diggings. The last-named place covered about two thousand acres and yielded several million dollars' worth of the precious metal.

The history of Big Gulch, a mining camp opposite Folsom, was peculiarly colorful. The arrival of Colonel Russ at this quiet place in 1857 was quite an event, and the town was renamed Russville in his honor. Possessing a "speculative genius," Russ induced a number of San Francisco capitalists to form a company to mine the rock for the gold it never contained. Tons of quartz were crushed, but no "color" was ever produced. Russ invented a machine to plane the granite. It did not work. The company failed, and then Colonel Russ was elected justice of the peace. "He put up a small flag pole and an elevated platform about six feet high, and when a case was to be tried, up went the stars and stripes on the flag pole and the Colonel mounted the seat of justice. Law statutes were of no use to him. He dispensed his own brand of justice. Any person asking for an appeal was immediately fined for contempt. He soon became unpopular, went broke, and departed." For a time the town was called Bowlesville, but in 1860 the citizens renamed it Ashland.

Just below Big Gulch was Mississippi Bar, the name surviving today as Mississippi Township. Opposite it was Texas Hill, from which cobblestones were shipped to pave the streets of San Francisco.

Cosumnes River Mining Camps

Michigan Bar was the most prominent of all the early gold camps on the Cosumnes River in Sacramento County. Founded in 1849 by two men from Michigan, it reached a population of fifteen hundred or more in the early '50's. The original town site has since been washed out by hydraulic mining, destroying the last remaining landmarks—the old Heath Store and the Wells Fargo Express Office. The Addington Pottery Works at Michigan Bar was one of the earliest and largest in the state.

Fleeting towns developed in the vicinity of Michigan Bar during those feverish days of '49 and the '50's. Cook's Bar, founded in 1849 by Dennis Cook two miles below Michigan Bar, became quite a town in the early '50's, but by 1860 had ceased to exist. Five miles southwest of Michigan Bar on the Ione Valley Road was Sebastopol, named during the Crimean War, and a lively camp from 1854 to 1859. Katesville, near Cook's Bar, another mining center which arose in 1854, had several stores and saloons, a hotel, and a boardinghouse. By 1862 the place was deserted. Live Oak, northeast of Sebastopol, had rich returns from its diggings from 1854 to 1861. An old brick house at this point on the Sacramento-Jackson Highway still serves as the Michigan Bar postoffice, store, and service station. The McKinstry trading-post on the Cosumnes River was opened in 1849 by George McKinstry, who had been associated with John A. Sutter, Pierson B. Reading, and John Bidwell at Sutter's Fort.

Several roads to the southern mines passed through the Cosumnes River region, and ferries, succeeded by toll bridges, as well as a number of hotels, were established by enterprising men at a very early date. William Daylor and Jared Sheldon, as owners of the Omochumnes Mexican grant, were strategically situated and made great profits from mining, ranching, trading, and hotel-keeping. Sheldon, in 1850, built the Slough House on Deer Creek (a branch of the Cosumnes River) where the Jackson road crossed that stream. A later building stands on the old site, with gigantic black walnut trees bordering the highway, and an old cemetery on the knoll above the orchards. In 1930 the village of Slough House had a population of about fifty.

Daylor established himself as a trader and hotel-keeper on the Cosumnes River about a mile to the east of Slough House. This place, at first known as Daylor's Ranch, later became the Cosumne Post Office and the site is still known as Cosumne. An ancient clapboard house of the '50's, its false store front still intact, is now used as a residence, the oldest existing remnant of the former village.

Sheldon, in 1851, entered upon a mining venture which proved to be fatal. One-half mile above the site of the later McCabe's Bridge, he built a dam to impound the water for mining operations. The miners, working along the river below the dam, threatened violence, and Sheldon erected a small fort, placing a cannon there by way of warning. On July 12, 1851, the indignant miners captured the fort, and when Sheldon arrived with reinforcements two hours later a battle ensued in which he and two of his men were killed. The dam was swept away by the high water in the winter of 1851–1852.

Sutterville

Sutter laid out a town site in 1844 on his ranch about two miles below the embarcadero. Here, on high ground overlooking the river, he and his friends built a few dwellings and called the place Sutterville. The location boasted one of the few elevations above the treacherous waters of the river, and the future of the little settlement seemed promising. It flourished until 1848 as the friendly rival of the fort and the embarcadero. George Zins built a brick building there in 1847, one of the first brick structures erected in California.

The discovery of gold by James W. Marshall in the tail-race of Sutter's Mill at Coloma, in 1848, changed the course of events for Sutterville as it did for all California. Sutter's Fort became too small for the business demands which soon crowded in upon it from every side, and the old embarcadero continued to hold its own while Sutterville declined.

The site of Sutterville, across the county road from the zoo of the William Land Park, is still marked by one of its original buildings, every brick as solid as the day it was first laid, in spite of long neglect. It was built by R. H. Vance in 1853 and cost $27,000. In later years it was known as the Sutterville Brewery.

"Paper Cities"

Mushroom cities were not confined to California's mining areas. "The spirit of venture and speculation" invaded tributary regions in the valley also. Aside from Sutterville and Sacramento there were a number of other towns laid

out with the same high hope of becoming commercial centers for the mining camps. Coming up the river from the Bay region, the gold-seekers of 1849 passed the sites of several towns below Sacramento: Onisbo, opposite the mouth of Steamboat Slough; Webster, on the east bank about ten miles below the mouth of the American River; and Washington (Yolo County), on the western shore opposite Sutter's embarcadero. Just below Sacramento was Sutterville and to the north was Boston. Leaving Boston, one arrived at a second Washington City about twelve miles farther up the river. Beyond were Springfield and Vernon (Sutter County), the latter situated at the mouth of the Feather River opposite its rival, Fremont (Yolo County).

Boston, typical of these "paper cities," was described by E. G. Buffum, who visited the region in 1849. "It extends upon the banks of both rivers for several miles and is destined to become a flourishing town. . . . . [It] is situated upon a broad and well-watered plain covered with many groves of magnificent oaks, and the largest class of steamers and all vessels navigating the Sacramento River can lie and discharge directly at its banks. Boston . . . . is laid in squares . . . . subdivided each into eight building lots eighty feet by one hundred twenty feet, with large public squares and reservations for schoolhouses, churches and public buildings. . . . . Lots are selling rapidly at $200 to $1,000 each, and before many months the city of Boston on the golden banks of the Rio Sacramento will rival its New England namesake in business and importance."

A group of speculators laid out the town of Brighton in 1849 on the south bank of the American River about three miles east of Sutter's Fort, but it never came to anything and the site was abandoned in 1852. Mormons in the employ of Sutter had built a flour mill there in 1847, but with the discovery of gold at Coloma the mill was left unfinished. The frame was purchased in 1849 for $10,000. It was then moved to Sacramento, where it went into the construction of the City Hotel, Sacramento's first hotel, located on Front Street between I and J Streets. The present town of Brighton was located one mile south of the old site in 1861.

Norristown, or Hoboken, was established in 1850 on the American River two miles east of old Brighton. During the great flood of 1852 all teaming was cut off between Sacramento and the mining regions. The merchants of Sacramento, being forced to move to higher ground, established temporary branches at Norristown. Since 1853 the land has been used for farming.

Sacramento

Sacramento has more historic buildings dating from the American pioneer period than any other city in California. There are whole blocks, too, of early residences overtopped by giant elms planted many years ago.

It was around the old embarcadero at the foot of the long street leading to Sutter's Fort that the new city first grew up. A marker placed by the Native Sons of the Golden West on the Freight Building at the foot of K Street on the northwest corner of Front Street memorializes the site of the old embarcadero and later steamer landing. Sutter had become involved more and more in debt and finally, in order to evade his creditors, he turned his property over to his son John. Young Sutter laid out a new town at the embarcadero, naming it Sacramento after the river. In April 1849 the town boasted four houses. On August 1 the first town election was held. Situated as it was at the entrance to the gold regions, Sacramento profited tremendously from the mining trade, and by November 1849 its population was little short of ten thousand.

The Squatters' Riot

Many home seekers arrived at Sacramento in 1849, expecting to take up homesteads there as they had done in Oregon and the Middle West. Sacramento was being built on the Sutter Grant, but these home seekers did not see why the laws of a foreign government should have more weight than the rights of free American citizens in the assigning of land. They claimed the right to at least one free city lot each. However, those men who had been buying of Sutter hotly contested this claim, and the Squatters' Riot was the result.

A lot at the southeast corner of Second and N streets was put to the test, when Dr. Robinson, one of the outstanding leaders of the squatters, erected a shanty there, only to have it removed by the city authorities. On May 10, 1850, judgment was rendered in favor of Sutter's title, but on August 15 a body of about forty squatters contested this decision by attempting to regain possession of the lot from which Robinson had been ousted. When prevented from doing so, they retired up I Street to Third and thence to J near Fourth, where they were met by Major Bigelow with a small band of citizens. The squatters then threw a line across Fourth Street at J and fired upon the citizen group.

In the fight which followed, Major Bigelow was seriously wounded, as was Dr. Robinson, while Maloney, the leader of the squatters, and the City Assessor were killed. This so frightened the insurgents that they quickly dispersed. On August 19 a proclamation was issued calling for law and order, and the Squatters' Riot was ended. For a number of years, however, it was echoed in the city elections.

The Capitol

The state capital, after a brief career in various ambitious young cities, was finally established at Sacramento in 1854. The site of the first court house, completed on December 24, 1851, is on the north side of I Street between Sixth and Seventh, and is now occupied by the new Sacramento County Court House, erected in 1909. A tablet in the vestibule of the present building states that the first court house was offered for use as the state capitol and that the legislative sessions of 1852 and 1854 were held there. The building was destroyed by fire in 1854, but was immediately replaced by a second structure in which the state officials and the legislature were housed until the late fall of 1869.

The foundations of the state capitol buildings were laid on the present site in the fall of 1860, only to be washed away by the flood of January 10, 1861. As a protection against recurring floods, two great terraces were constructed and on this elevation the corner stone was again laid, May 15, 1861, under the auspices of the Masonic Grand Lodge of California. The unfinished structure was occupied by the government late in the fall of 1869, but the building was not finally completed until 1874. The total cost of construction with subsequent improvements is estimated at $3,400,000.

On the first floor of the rotunda of the Capitol Building is the beautiful marble statue of Queen Isabella presenting her jewels to Columbus, executed by Larkin Goldsmith Mead, an American sculptor, and presented to the state by D. O. Mills in 1883. The walls of the rotunda are decorated by twelve mural paintings done by Arthur F. Mathews and depicting four epochs in the history of California. On the second floor of the rotunda flags carried by California units in the Civil, Spanish-American, and World wars are displayed.

On the fourth floor of the building one of the finest and most complete collections of relics representing the workmanship of the prehistoric California Indian has been gathered from the ancient camp sites and burial grounds of the San Joaquin and Sacramento valleys. Arranged with scientific order and skill, it is a display that will long serve as an educational archive for scholars wishing to study the habits and handicraft of an extinct people. In this remarkable array one sees striking evidence that the California Indian was a skilled craftsman as well as an artist of rare ability: many pipes, serrated arrow points, and bowls, scores of baskets from all sections, ornaments and implements of stone, bone, and shell, all fashioned with a perfection of line and a niceness of detail that the modern artisan, with all his up-to-date tools, could not duplicate.

Surrounding the capitol buildings a park covering thirty acres of ground has been planted to more than three hundred species of trees and shrubs contributed by every continent and clime on the globe. Grecian laurels; pomegranates from Europe and Asia; the Australian bottle-brush and silk oak; camellias from Asia and the strawberry bush from Europe; pampas grass from South America and the varnish tree from Asia—these and many more seem to thrive equally well in this unusual arboretum. Fronting the building is a row of twelve fine deodars (natives of India), reputedly planted in 1869 from seeds donated by P. B. Reading. Almost as spectacular are the giant stone pines of Italy, the Norway spruce, Lawson's cypress, giant arbor vitae, cedar of Lebanon, cryptomeria from China and Japan, and a row of superb magnolias, flanking the stately white walls of the Capitol Building with dark green masses of foliage.

A semicircle of giant elm trees was planted in 1872 between Twelfth and Fourteenth streets, marking the old bridle path or exercising track for saddle and carriage horses. Near the center of the park is the Memorial Grove, composed of eastern North American trees transplanted as saplings from the most prominent battlefields of the Civil War by the women's auxiliary of the Grand Army of the Republic and dedicated by them to the state. Many varieties of such well-known Eastern trees as the walnut, ash, oak, maple, elm, tulip tree, dogwood, mulberry, and locust are represented in this interesting group.

A space of three acres at the southeast corner of the park is devoted entirely to California flora, where cacti, yuccas, and desert willows are close neighbors of ferns, azaleas, huckleberries, and tiger lilies, which thrive in the shade of sequoias and oaks and pines whose native habitat ranges from the Coast Range to the Sierra Nevada.

The work of classifying and labeling the trees and shrubs in the park was begun in July 1905 by Miss Alice Eastwood, head of the Horticultural Department of the Academy of Sciences, San Francisco. Over two hundred specimens have been tagged, each with its botanical as well as its common name and native habitat, making this grove unique in its educational value as well as in the inspiring beauty of its assembled trees.

The State Fair grounds, located on Stockton Boulevard, cover an area of 135 acres and comprise an outlay of equipment and buildings aggregating an investment of $3,000,000. The State Fair originated in 1854, when the California State Agricultural Society was organized in San Francisco. From that time it has been an annual event. For the first five years of its existence it was held in various cities, but since 1859 it has been held continuously at Sacramento. The grounds, first located at Sixth and M streets, were later moved to Fifteenth and N, and finally to the present location.

The State Library

The California State Library was created on January 24, 1850, by act of the legislature. For several years it consisted only of the one hundred volumes donated for the purpose by General John C. Frémont, there being no fund available for the purchase of books. From 1853 to 1901 all fees collected by the secretary of state were paid into the Library Fund. A monthly appropriation amounting to $5,000 is now made.

For many years the State Library occupied the semicircular central wing of the Capitol, additional rooms being assigned to it until it covered about 30 per cent of the entire floor space of the building. It is now housed in a new building of its own on M Street between Ninth and Tenth streets.

The State Library has a California department comprising a vast amount of information on the history, resources, and natural wonders, the industrial, social, and intellectual life of the state. It houses also a unique collection of early newspaper files, a newspaper index, and interesting indexed information about the old pioneers and early settlers of the state, as well as about California authors, artists, actors, and musicians, all of which is vastly interesting and important to the student of California history.

The Pioneer Memorial Congregational Church

The new Pioneer Memorial Congregational Church faces Sutter's Fort, the old site being in the present business district of Sacramento on Sixth Street between I and J, a site now occupied by the Dreamland Rink. The corner stone for the First Congregational Church in Sacramento was laid September 21, 1854, but the church had held services much earlier and is recorded as having been the first church to be organized (September 16, 1849) and to hold regular services in Sacramento. For over seventy years this historic edifice sheltered many significant gatherings, serving as a rallying point "for Christian forces through many a stormy period." Its open forum, where some of the most distinguished orators of the day spoke, satisfied the intellectual needs of the community.

The founder of this historic church was the Rev. Joseph A. Benton, who began his long and beneficent career in Sacramento in July 1849. Joseph Benton's parish, however, was boundless and his missionary journeys were often of several weeks' duration. His interests, too, were broad and included education as well as religion. He taught one of the first schools in Sacramento, and in 1849 he and Samuel Willey, with several others, were already planning for public schools and a college in California. Benton was one of the founders of the College of California (forerunner of the State University), and, later, became a professor in the Pacific Theological Seminary, Oakland (now the Pacific School of Religion, in Berkeley).

Benton's life is typical of that of many pioneer ministers of the churches of early California, Protestant as well as Catholic. Full of the earnest desire to serve and to build up a Christian civilization in a primitive land, unselfish, tireless, boundless in enthusiasm, large of vision, and great in endeavor, they were missionary heroes in every sense of the word.

The D. O. Mills Bank

The first site of the D. O. Mills bank was on the south side of J Street about sixty feet west of Third Street. It was a small one-story frame building with a stone front, erected in 1853. A picture of it was used for many years on the bank's checks. In 1865 the bank was moved to 200 J Street, at Second, and again, in 1912, to the present building at Seventh Street.

D. O. Mills came to Sacramento in 1849 and began his career as a merchant in the new, chaotic city. He was a man who was keen to see a big opportunity and quick to take it, and on October 18, 1849, he opened the first banking house on the Pacific Coast. D. O. Mills was not only a keen financier but a man of sound principles and steady, conservative judgment as well. He became a leading figure in the financial life of California, not only building up the bank at Sacramento on a sound basis, but also becoming the first president of the Bank of California, established in San Francisco in 1864. He was also interested in educational and philanthropic movements and gave much of his wealth to these activities. Later, he became a leading figure in the Bank of New York, and was famous for the three Mills Hotels which he established in New York City for the comfort of homeless men of limited means.

The Crocker Art Gallery

Judge E. B. Crocker and his wife collected many fine paintings and drawings during their travels in Europe, especially during the Franco-Prussian War, and in 1871–1873 a building was erected at the southeast corner of Second and O streets to house this private collection. In 1884, after the Judge's death, his widow donated the building and its contents to the city of Sacramento, with the California Museum Association as co-tenant and administrator. After Mrs. Crocker's death, the old Crocker home, immediately adjoining the Art Gallery at the southwest corner of Third Street, was also acquired and the two buildings thrown into one.

Other Historic Houses

Typical of the days of '49, when thousands of miners thronged the place, was the old "What Cheer House." The site of this famous hostelry is at the southeast corner of Front and K streets, diagonally opposite the Southern Pacific Freight Building.

The Western Hotel, 209–219 K Street, was established in 1854, and has continued under the same name until the present time. The rear of the building is of the original construction, but the front portion dates from 1875.

At 1023 Front Street, halfway between J and K streets, was the Booth Store, where Newton Booth, later eleventh governor of California, began business. An inscription placed over the doorway by the Native Sons of the Golden West reads: "Newton Booth Store. Erected 1853. Business started 1850. Headquarters for miners from gold diggings. Newton Booth elected as Governor of California, 1871, and U.S. Senator, 1873. Upstairs he maintained official headquarters and a magnificent ball room with capacity for 1,000 dancers. Here state functions were held during his term."

The site of the old Sacramento Theater, one of the city's earliest playhouses, which was opened in March 1853, is on Third Street between J and I streets. Ole Bull, Maurice Strakosh, Madam Anna Bishop, and the Robinson family were among the celebrities who played there. A stock company, including Edwin Booth, took it over in 1855.

The corner stone of the "Young America 6" engine house was laid on January 1, 1858, at Tenth and I streets. In 1932 this historic edifice was purchased by the Standard Oil Company of California, and on January 1, 1933, it was dedicated to the memory of the brave pioneer fire fighters. A bronze plaque presented by the Native Sons and Native Daughters of the Golden West was unveiled.

The Pony Express

The site of the Pony Express terminus, located at 1015 Second Street, between J and K streets, was marked by the Sacramento and San Francisco Bay chapters, D.A.R., in 1923.

The Pony Express was inaugurated by W. H. Russell of the firm of Russell, Majors & Waddell, in April 1860, thus preceding the telegraph and the railroad in opening up overland communication between the East and the West. Before this, mail had been carried by steamer via Panama, the official mail ship arriving at San Francisco once a month. The Butterfield Stages had begun to carry mail overland via the Southern Route in 1858, requiring from 20 to 24 days for the trip. In the same year George Chorpenning operated over the Central Route between Placerville and Salt Lake City. The Pony Express inaugurated a special semi-weekly mail service on horseback. Stations were erected about every twenty-five miles, each rider spanning three stations at the rate of about eight miles an hour. Ten days from St. Joseph, Missouri, to Sacramento, California, was the usual time required.

The little ponies with their fearless riders, who were picked with the greatest care from among the bravest and hardiest of Western men, kept the long trail open between the East and the West until November 1861, when the service was discontinued with the completion of the overland telegraph. The romance of these daring riders heroically pursuing their path regardless of snow, storm, and hostile Indians has been graphically, and except for a few minor details accurately, portrayed by Mark Twain in *Roughing It*. Although not a financial success for its promoters, the Pony Express was nevertheless a substantial aid to business and undoubtedly helped to hold California, isolated at it was, in the Union.

First Transcontinental Railway

A bronze tablet set in the wall of the Southern Pacific Freight Building, directly opposite the foot of K Street, was erected by retired employees to celebrate the semicentennial anniversary of the building of the Central Pacific Railroad. It marks the terminus of the first transcontinental railway and bears the legend:

At this point, January 8, 1863, ground was broken inaugurating the construction of the Central Pacific Railroad, the western end of the Pacific Railroad, the first Transcontinental road banding the Continent, welding the Atlantic and Pacific Coasts, and the only one built from the Pacific Coast eastward. Dedicated by retired employees, January 8, 1913.

The first General Offices of the Central Pacific Railroad, located at 220–226 K Street, still stand. From this office Leland Stanford, Collis P. Huntington, Mark Hopkins, and Charles Crocker financed and built the western end of the first transcontinental railway in California, and later controlled the political and financial affairs of California.

Actual building operations on the railroad began in Sacramento in 1863, and on May 10, 1869, the last spike was driven at a lonely spot in northern Utah, where the Union Pacific, building westward, met the Central Pacific, building eastward. "The successful completion of this great project, one of the most stupendous engineering works undertaken by man, brought to an end the frontier era of California history."

A splendid monument of granite boulders stands in front of the new Southern Pacific Depot at Sacramento. A bronze tablet on the face of the rock bears this inscription:

That the West may remember Theodore Dehone Judah, pioneer civil engineer and the tireless advocate of a great transcontinental railroad—America's first, this monument was erected by the men and women of the Southern Pacific Company, who, in 1930, were carrying on the work he began in 1860. He convinced four Sacramento merchants that his plan was practicable and enlisted their help. Ground was broken for the railroad, January 8, 1863, at the foot of K Street nearby. Judah died November 2, 1863. The road was built past the site of this monument over the lofty Sierra—along the line of Judah's survey—to a junction with the Union Pacific at Promontory, Utah, where on May 10, 1869, the "last spike" was driven.

Alexander Hamilton's Pioneer Son

William Stephen Hamilton, youngest son of Alexander Hamilton, the distinguished Revolutionary statesman, came to California in 1849. Previous to that time he had served as surveyor of public lands in Illinois; discovered the Hamilton Diggings in southwestern Wisconsin in 1827; engaged in the Black Hawk War, when, as colonel, he distinguished himself for efficiency and bravery; and was several times a member of the Territorial Legislature of Wisconsin. On coming to California, Hamilton engaged in mining for about a year, when he went to Sacramento to trade. He died in that city on October 7, 1850.

An unmarked grave in the city cemetery constituted the resting-place of William Hamilton until 1879, when friends had the body removed to a more appropriate part of the cemetery and a slab of polished Quincy granite placed over it. In 1889, at the suggestion of John O. Brown, mayor of Sacramento, the remains were again moved, this time to a new plot in the cemetery named in honor of the deceased, Hamilton Square. At this time the handsome oddly shaped monument of massive Quincy granite which still marks the grave was sent out from Massachusetts by a grand-nephew of the pioneer. On one side it bears a bronze medallion of the latter's distinguished father. A small plate below the medallion today indicates that the grave is cared for by the Sacramento Chapter, D.A.R., who thus keep in memory the worthy life of a great man's son.

SOURCES

[Credit is here given for source material, and permission to quote is hereby acknowledged]

BENTON, J. A. *The California Pilgrim: A Series of Lectures.* Solomon Alter, Sacramento; Marvin & Hitchcock, San Francisco, 1855

BIDLEMAN, H. J. *The Sacramento Directory, for the Years 1861-62.* H. S. Crocker & Company, Sacramento, 1861

BRADLEY, GLEN D. *The Story of the Pony Express.* A. C. McClurg & Company, Chicago, 1913

BRYANT, EDWIN. *What I Saw in California.* D. Appleton & Company, New York, 1848, 1849

BUFFUM, E. GOULD. *Six Months in the Gold Mines.* Lea & Blanchard, Philadelphia, 1850

CHAPMAN, ARTHUR. *The Pony Express: The Record of a Romantic Adventure in Business.* G. P. Putnam's Sons, New York, 1932

CLARK, GEORGE T. *Leland Stanford, War Governor, Railroad Builder, and Founder of Stanford University.* Stanford University Press, Stanford University, 1931

CLELAND, ROBERT GLASS. *A History of California: The American Period.* The Macmillan Company, New York, 1922

CLEMENS, SAMUEL. *Roughing It.* Harper & Brothers, New York, 1913

COLVILLE, SAMUEL. *Sacramento Directory, 1856.* Manson, Valentine & Company, San Francisco, 1856

COY, OWEN COCHRAN. *Gold Days,* of the series *California.* Edited by John Russell McCarthy, Powell Publishing Company, Los Angeles, 1929

DALE, HARRISON CLIFFORD. *The Ashley-Smith Explorations and the Discovery of a Central Route to the Pacific, 1822–1829, with the Original Journals.* The Arthur H. Clark Company, Cleveland, 1918

DAVIS, WINFIELD J. *Illustrated History of Sacramento County, California.* Lewis Publishing Company, Chicago, 1890

DELANO, ALONZO. *Life on the Plains and at the Diggings: Being Scenes and Adventures of an Overland Journey to California.* Miller, Orton, & Mulligan, Auburn and Buffalo, 1854

History of Sacramento County, California. Thompson & West, Oakland, 1880

KRYSTO, CHRISTINA. *The Romance of Sacramento.* Department Store Bulletin. Weinstock, Lubin & Company, Sacramento, California, 1923

MORSE, DR. JOHN F. "History of Sacramento" in Colville's *Sacramento Directory for the Year 1853–54.* Printed at the Union Office, Sacramento, 1853

MULDOON, SYLVAN. *Alexander Hamilton's Pioneer Son.* Aurand Press, Harrisburg, Pennsylvania, 1930

PETERSON, H. C. *List of Historic Spots in Sacramento County.* Manuscript, 1930

REED, WALTER G. *History of Sacramento County, California.* Historic Record Company, Los Angeles, 1923

Sacramento Bee. Seventy-fifth Anniversary Number, February 3, 1932

Sacramento Directory for the Year 1871. H. S. Crocker & Company, Sacramento, 1871

Sacramento Illustrated. Barber & Baker, Sacramento, 1855

WHEAT, CARL I. "A Sketch of the Life of Theodore D. Judah," *California Historical Society Quarterly,* Vol. IV, No. 3 (September 1925), 219–71

SAN JOAQUIN COUNTY

SAN JOAQUIN COUNTY (San Joaquin, Spanish for St. Joachim, was the name given by Gabriel Moraga to the river in 1813 in honor of that saint, and was later used to designate the county) was one of the original twenty-seven counties. Stockton, which is centrally located, has been its county seat from the first.

Indian Villages

More than one hundred Indian mounds, or kitchen middens, have been located in San Joaquin County, and new discoveries continue to be made from time to time. These mounds are the sites of aboriginal villages and burial places. They are found on relatively high ground along the banks of the numerous watercourses of the San Joaquin Delta region, such as the San Joaquin, Cosumnes, Mokelumne, and Calaveras rivers, and the Mormon, French Camp, and other sloughs, which furnished a well-nigh inexhaustible hunting ground for the Indians. W. Egbert Schenck says that "apparently it would be hard to exaggerate the number of water fowl that were formerly present in the marshy area of the Great Central valley. Early accounts indicate an abundance and a tameness which it is hard to conceive. . . . ."

To the inexperienced eye an Indian mound appears much the same as the land about it. The archaeologist, however, quickly perceives an appreciable difference. "Upon a mound's base," says Schenck, "there is found a mass of earth essentially the same as the base and the surrounding land, but which has been acted upon by man until in color, texture, constituents, or all of these it is readily distinguishable from the base . . . . In color the mounds are characteristically blacker than the surrounding soil . . . . Presumably this darker color is due to the greater amount of organic matter which man has accumulated upon them."

James A. Barr, for many years superintendent of schools in the city of Stockton, became interested in the archaeology of the Stockton region and during the years 1898–1901 made a large collection of specimens. His excellent field notes and carefully catalogued specimens form the main source of information on the archaeology and ethnology of the Stockton region. Of the nearly 4,000 specimens which he gathered, 1,870 came from this section.

The principal aboriginal sites explored by Barr were the Stockton Channel, Walker Slough, Ott, Pool, and Island mounds. Among others there were three on the Woods Ranch on Robert's Island; one on the Copperopolis Road; and others on Martin's Ranch and the O. R. Smith Ranch, at Brant's Ferry, on the Lewis Ranch, and on French Camp Slough.

The Stockton Channel Mound, located in Stockton between Edison and Harrison streets on the north bank of the Stockton Channel, is probably the site of the Passasimas village described by the Spanish expedition which was led by Luís Argüello and Padre Narciso Durán in 1817. It is possible, however, that this village may have been the one covered by the Walker Slough Mound. The latter, being only an eighth of a mile from the Island Mound, may be regarded as having been a part of the same settlement.

The Ott Mound (southeast of Stockton and north of French Camp Slough) and the Pool Mound (nine miles southwest of Stockton) were undoubtedly inhabited when the Spanish visited the region in 1805, in 1810, and again in 1811. One of the most interesting localities worked by Mr. Barr was that of Union Island near Bethany, where the Spanish expeditions of 1810 and 1811 found the Yokuts village of Pescadero ("fisherman"), so named because they saw Indians catching fish there. Rancho Pescadero (35,446.39 acres), which is located north of Tracy, received its name from this aboriginal settlement.

The most notable recent archaeological find in the Stockton region was made quite by accident in a field where dirt was being obtained for a bridge approach at Garwood Ferry on the San Joaquin River southwest of Stockton.

Rancho del Campo de los Franceses

French Camp, four miles south of Stockton, was first occupied about 1832 by French-Canadian hunters employed by the Hudson's Bay Company to trap beaver, mink, bear, and other fur-bearing animals then numerous along the San Joaquin River and adjoining sloughs. Evidences of beaver workmanship may still be traced along French Camp Slough. The village of French Camp was the terminus of the Oregon Trail, used by these trappers from 1832 to 1845. This trail led from the north across the county along a route later followed by the Sutter's Fort–San Jose Trail over which Frémont passed in 1844. Michael La Framboise, leader of the fur hunters, came annually to French Camp, and James Alexander Forbes, agent for the company after 1836, likewise made many trips to it. As late as 1845 the place was occupied from spring until fall by the Canadians and their families, who had constructed rude cabins of tules and willow brush, many of which were plastered with mud.

Abandoning their camp hurriedly in the summer of 1845, the trappers left their arms buried in a wood-lined hole or cache on a knoll situated one block and a half northeast of the present French Camp School and one block from the highway. Colonel P. W. Noble, who later kept a store at French Camp, told the story of the buried arms, only to be laughed at. The Reynolds brothers, Eldridge, Edward, and James, then children at the French Camp School, took the story seriously enough to dig for the hidden treasure, and uncovered forty sabers and muskets. This was in 1856 or 1857. Two of the sabers were presented to the museum at Victory Park in Stockton. Mrs. Alice B. Maloney, however, who has made a study of the weapons, believes them to be sailors' swords left by an 1846 punitive expedition.

Charles M. Weber, a native of Germany, who was later to become the founder of Stockton, stopped at French Camp in the fall of 1841 while on his way into California with the Bidwell-Bartleson party. Weber was much impressed with the fertile, oak-studded lands which bordered the San Joaquin River. Subsequently, in 1842, he settled in Pueblo de San José and soon after went into partnership with William Gulnac, a blacksmith. Gulnac came to California in 1833 (perhaps with the French-Canadian trappers) and later married a Mexican woman, after becoming a naturalized Mexican citizen. For a time the two men engaged in merchandising, manufacturing, and ranching at San Jose. In the spring of 1843 they organized a company of twelve men for the purpose of forming a colony at French Camp. On July 14 Gulnac, being a Mexican citizen, petitioned for a grant of land in the region, and on January 13, 1844, he and others received a tract of some hundred miles which included both French Camp and the site of the later Stockton. This was named Rancho del Campo de los Franceses. The company organized by Weber and Gulnac was the first colony of white settlers to take up lands in the San Joaquin Valley.

In August 1844, under the leadership of Gulnac, the first settlers arrived at Rancho del Campo de los Franceses. One of the company, Thomas Lindsay, built a tule hut on what is now Lindsay Point back of the City Hall at the west end of Lindsay Avenue in Stockton, the first dwelling to be erected by an American within the present city limits. However, in the spring of 1845, Lindsay was killed by Indians, his hut was burned, and his stock and tools were stolen.

To encourage other colonists, Gulnac proffered a square mile of land at French Camp to any prospective settler. One of the first to accept the offer was David Kelsey, who, soon after Gulnac's arrival, reached the settlement with his wife and two children from Oregon en route to Pueblo de San José. Stricken with smallpox within a few months, Kelsey died at the Lindsay cabin and was buried near the southwest corner of what are now El Dorado and Fremont streets in Stockton. Only one member of the little family did not contract the disease. This was America (a mere child at the time), whose courage and devotion in nursing her loved ones unaided places her among the pioneer heroines of California.

The task of inducing settlers to remain on Rancho del Campo de los Franceses was rather difficult in those days of hostile Indians, plagues, poor food, and primitive conditions. Before many months Gulnac became disgusted with the project, and on April 3, 1845, sold the entire estate to Weber for $60, the amount of a grocery bill he owed his partner. In order to persuade settlers to come to the region, Weber virtually gave away the major portion of his estate to those who would settle on it. The testimony and influence of dozens of these colonists ultimately forced the land commissioners to recognize Weber's claim to the grant, the whole of which would otherwise have been lost to him.

Stockton

Captain Weber, in 1847, laid out the town of Tuleburg on the south side of the Laguna, later known as the Stockton Channel. The dense tule swamps which then bordered every watercourse fully justified the name. Even the roofs of the first rude huts were thatched with tules. The head of the channel soon came to be known as the Embarcadero, the location of which was about where Weber Avenue now "approaches the water." For a time, Weber continued to make his home at Pueblo de San José, occasionally going to Tuleburg to carry supplies to his vaqueros, who lived in a tule hut on the north side of Stockton Slough. More houses and corrals were built in the spring of 1848, and wheat was planted.

After the discovery of gold at Coloma, Weber organized the Stockton Mining and Trading Company, which operated for a time on Weber Creek in El Dorado County. José Jesús, an Indian chieftain with whom Weber had made a treaty in 1844 and who remained his lifelong friend, sent many of his own tribesmen to work for Weber in the mines. Believing that it would be more profitable to devote all his time to the building of a city that would serve as an entrepôt to the southern mines, Weber dissolved his mining company in September 1848 and took up his residence in Tuleburg. In the spring of 1849 the town was resurveyed and renamed Stockton, in honor of Commodore Stockton, whom Weber

had met in Los Angeles in 1846 and admired. By the winter of 1849 Stockton had a population of approximately one thousand, and in 1850 it became the county seat of San Joaquin County, having been incorporated on August 15 of that year.

Thousands of Argonauts bound for the southern mines passed through Stockton in the early '50's. Some came up the river by boat; others traveled over the Livermore Pass from San Jose and crossed the San Joaquin River at Doak and Bonsell's Ferry, located about where U.S. Highway 48 crosses today. From Stockton this restless tide of humanity branched out over the various trails leading to the gold fields —the Mariposa, French Camp, Sonora, Mokelumne Hill, and Lockeford roads, all teeming with life and each one leading to a hoped-for El Dorado. Stockton soon became a flourishing center of trade and commerce. Freighting and staging activities developed to enormous proportions, agriculture and stock-raising in the vicinity increased, local commerce grew, and the town became a fixed settlement.

The first house built on Weber Point was of adobe. Adjacent to it Weber erected a second dwelling in 1850 or 1851. This was a two-story frame structure, the lumber for which had been brought around the Horn. To this house the Captain brought his bride, Helen Murphy, daughter of Martin Murphy, a large landowner in Santa Clara County. The Weber house, surrounded by gardens, was a notable show place during the '50's and '60's. Some time after Weber's death in 1881 it was destroyed by fire, to be replaced by a second frame house built by the family on the southeast corner of the property facing Stockton Channel. This building has since been moved to West Lane just beyond the Diversion Canal outside of Stockton, and is the home of Helen Weber Kennedy. The foundation piers which supported the first mansion and which were made of brick brought around the Horn may still be seen at the original site, while a few shrubs and century plants remain of the former garden. The Stockton Channel, which borders the old homesite, is today lined with warehouses, wharves, coal bunkers, mills, and factories, and its waters are filled with barges, ferries, and river steamers. Since the completion of the Stockton Deep Water Project, ocean-going vessels have begun to ply the river from San Francisco to the Port of Stockton.

There are not many of the early buildings left in Stockton today. At the corner of Main and Center streets is the old Weber House—the historic hostelry which later became known as the Occidental Hotel. Built with sturdy brick walls in 1853, it was fitted up with furniture brought around the Horn. The building was remodeled about twenty years ago. The Franklin School, a two-story building on the west side of Center Street between Washington and La Fayette streets, was the first brick schoolhouse in the city. It was erected in 1858 and still serves as a school building. The old " '49 Drug Store," at the corner of El Dorado and Main streets, was built in 1852 and has the distinction of being the first brick structure in San Joaquin County. On the west side of El Dorado Street between Weber Avenue and Main Street is the old I.O.O.F. Building, used by the order until about 1867. It is practically unchanged since its construction in 1853.

Even in pioneer days, although life in Stockton was full of excitement and hilarity, cultural development was not neglected. Churches and schools were established as early as 1850. Today, it is the home of the College of the Pacific, which was transferred to Stockton from Santa Clara in 1924. The Pioneer Museum and Haggin Art Galleries, in Victory Park, contain many interesting relics of San Joaquin County's early days.

The Mariposa Road

Leading from Stockton to the southern mines are various roads which were first used during the days of the gold rush. Along these thoroughfares the first settlements outside of the city were established. Every house was a wayside inn for the accommodation of travelers. The cost of a meal was usually one dollar and a half, the regular menu comprising pork and beans, with bread and coffee.

Dr. L. R. Chalmers, who settled at the site of Collegeville as early as 1850, persuaded the government teams en route to Fort Miller to pass by his ranch, thereby establishing the Mariposa Road, which became the main route to the southern mines. By 1851 the principal stopping-places along this road were Chalmers' Ranch, George Kerr's House, the Fifteen Mile House, the Lone Tree House, and Heath and Emory's Ferry, on the Stanislaus River (since 1860 in Stanislaus County). A settlement grew up at Chalmers' Ranch, and because a college was located there from 1866 to 1874 the name of Collegeville became permanently attached to the place. The college was housed in a three-story frame structure erected by members of the Cumberland Presbyterian Church at a cost of $8,000. The building was destroyed by fire in 1874, and in the following year the present Collegeville Grammar School was built on the college grounds. The children of today have their swings where the college building once stood. Of the early houses in Collegeville only the little one-story parsonage of resawed siding, built in the late '50's, remains. At the corner of the Mariposa Road and the Jack Tone Road is a remnant of the pioneer Collegeville cemetery, now grass-grown and deserted.

The Lone Tree House, built in the early '50's from lumber brought around the Horn, stood on the W. P. H. Campbell farm until about 1910. The ranch and hotel were purchased in 1854 by Campbell, whose oldest son now owns the land. The site of the hostelry, where many of the aged trees still stand, is on the Lone Tree Road just south of the Lone Tree School. In early days the road at this point branched off to the several ferries on the Stanislaus River—Burney's, Cottle's, and Heath and Emory's.

Of the many hotels and stage stations erected along the Mariposa Road during the '50's, '60's, and '70's, only one remains today. This is the two-story building about four miles from Stockton near the junction of the Sonora (now the Farmington) and Mariposa roads. Near the present highway are the sites of some of these early buildings, such as the Fifteen Mile House, marked by groups of old trees.

The French Camp Road

During flood years and always during the winter months the Mariposa Road became impassable—a veritable mire of adobe. Then it was that the stagecoaches and freighters were routed over the French Camp Road, which had a sandy loam base. This winter traffic made of French Camp an important staging and freighting center during the early '50's. Boats landed at the end of French Camp Slough, where goods destined for the mining camps were unloaded. In the summer of 1850 Major Richard P. Hammond laid out a town on the site for Charles Weber, calling it Castoria ("place of beavers"). Colonel P. W. Noble and A. Stevinson, who had come to French Camp in August 1849 and who became agents for the sale of lots in the new town, built a two-story adobe structure in 1850, using it as a hotel and trading-post. As late as 1880 the building was occupied as a home by Noble's widow. This hotel, with its broad fields for the pasturage of live stock, was thronged by travelers during the first years of its existence, but its patronage declined

when a second hotel, owned by Le Barron and Company, was erected—this hostelry likewise offering extensive pasturage facilities.

In the French Camp of today, a village of approximately 250 inhabitants, none of the early buildings are to be found. Even the cemetery has disappeared, its only identifying mark being a large oak tree which stood in one corner of the burial plot.

The principal stopping-place on the French Camp Road between French Camp and Heath and Emory's Ferry (and almost the only one in 1852) was the "Zinc House," the material for which had been brought around the Horn from New York early in 1850. The fame of the Zinc House, which stood one-half mile beyond the present Simms Station near the railroad and about a quarter of a mile south of the highway, lent color to the old road, sometimes known as the Zinc House Road. The house was a small affair, "12 × 16 out of the wet," as an old history quaintly puts it, with one room seven feet in height. The owner, E. Allen, paid "for this frontier luxury . . . . one dollar for every year that had elapsed since Christ was born; that was $1850." Here the traveler could get pie for one dollar, or the regular pork and beans, bread and coffee, for the same price. "He paid his money and took his choice." The first school in this part of the county was held in the Zinc House, and until recent years the school district retained the name of the unique old hostelry in which it had its beginning.

In October 1852 Ernest Wagner rented the Zinc House for a period of five months for $800, purchasing it soon afterward. Seven years later he erected a two-story house on the site. This served as the Wagner home until 1910, when a modern cottage took its place. Opposite the house are two sturdy brick barns, where for many years stage horses were stabled. The bricks used in their construction were fashioned on the spot and are as solid today as when they were first made.

In the course of time the number of public houses along the French Camp Road increased. Among them were the Liesy Station, a few miles east of the Zinc House, the site now marked only by a knotted fig tree, and the Minges Station, a few miles to the northwest, where the old brick barn is still standing.

The Atlanta Store, built in 1866 by Lee Wilson on a site near the present Murphy Store, was a station for the accommodation of the Fisher stages during the late '60's and '70's. William Dempsey bought the place in 1867, and in 1868 the Atlanta Post Office was established there. Since 1874 the property has been owned by the Murphy family. The store has been removed, but the site is marked by the lichen-covered locust trees which grew in front of the former tavern.

At Five Corners stands the little white Community Church built by the Methodists in 1878 and still serving the countryside, while near by is the old Protestant cemetery. A few miles to the southeast is the Catholic Church, built the same year, with its quiet churchyard dotted with the graves of pioneers.

Pioneer Farmhouses

San Joaquin County is noteworthy for the number of pioneer farmhouses dating from the '50's and '60's still owned by descendants of the original builders. Many of these houses are in excellent condition and are occupied by their owners, while others which have been replaced by more modern structures are being allowed to disintegrate. This is especially true of the frame structures built close to the ground without the protection of stone or brick foundations.

Among the historic homesteads found north of the Calaveras River, one of the most interesting is the Dodge house situated on the bank of the river and the Waterloo Road to Lockeford. A few giant oaks, all that are left of the hundreds which once flourished in the region, surround this fine old mansion. One of the oldest of the trees stands near the highway and bears a bronze tablet placed by El Toyon Chapter, D.A.R., in 1923 in commemoration of the camp made in that vicinity on March 26, 1844, by John C. Frémont. "This place is beautiful," Frémont wrote, "with open groves of oak, and a grassy sward beneath, with many plants in bloom."

Following a shady path along the levee above the stream (now drained periodically for irrigation) past the Dodge cherry orchard, one comes to a spot about half a mile from the house. Here on the levee above a dirt road a crooked apple tree marks the site of the log cabin erected by Dr. I. C. Isbel soon after he took up land there in November 1846. In 1848 Dr. Isbel sold the ranch to the Hutchinson brothers, who ten years later sold it to Jonathan A. Dodge, father of the present owners. The log house at that time was furnished with fine old mahogany pieces brought around the Horn. This furniture is still in the Dodge family. The present Dodge house is the one which was built in 1866. Slight alterations have been made on the interior, while the exterior has assumed a rather modern appearance. It is still remarkably well preserved.

The J. H. Cole house, which stands just north of the Eight Mile Road and less than a mile east of the Lockeford Road, was erected in 1863. Much of the original "fancy work" along the eaves has been removed; a front porch, over which a giant rose tree had become inextricably entwined, has been torn down; and some of the shingles have been renewed. Otherwise this fine pioneer farmhouse remains just as it was seventy years ago. Old elms and Italian cypress, which may be seen for miles across the open fields, lend a quiet dignity to the garden.

The McCall house, on the Lockeford Road about two miles north of the Dodge house, apparently stands on an ancient Indian mound, as many relics have been dug up in the garden from time to time. The original house, which was built by Samuel Martin about 1858, has been incorporated into the present structure and now serves as a bedroom. From its doors many changing scenes have been witnessed: in the winter, mud-bespattered teamsters, with eight to sixteen horses, each striving to pass the other on the miry road, gradually widened at this point to two hundred feet; in the summer, grimy stagecoaches lurching along that same lane, now deeply rutted and choked with dust; and always long lines of chattering, pig-tailed Chinamen marching single file to and from the mines, and cowboys with their lowing, stampeding herds.

A two-story brick ranch house stands on the Jack Tone Road and the north bank of the Calaveras River about eleven miles northeast of Stockton. John H. (Jack) Tone and two associates came to California as members of the Webb-Audubon party, under the leadership of Colonel Henry L. Webb and John Woodhouse Audubon, youngest son of the famous ornithologist. Most of the party were bound for the gold fields, but Audubon made the trip to gather specimens of birds and mammals. When Colonel Webb deserted his men in the Rio Grande Valley, Audubon was made leader of the party, which after many hardships reached Stockton in December 1849.

Jack Tone and his partners, in the autumn of 1850, settled on the Calaveras River, where they attempted to raise potatoes. Owing to lack of skill in irrigating, their initial experiment in California ranching resulted in failure, so the three men tried their luck at mining for a time. In

1851, however, they returned to locate permanently on the Calaveras River, where they built a one-story adobe house on the high part of the river bank about one-half mile west of the present brick house. The three partners were known thereafter as the "Dobey Boys" by the settlers who had meanwhile taken up land about them. This adobe stood for several years after the brick house was erected in 1873. The homestead is today owned and occupied by a son of Jack Tone, who treasures the stories of pioneer life on his father's ranch and is especially proud of that part of the *Audubon Journal* which mentions his father. His mother, Alice Walsh Tone, daughter of Nicholas J. Walsh, another of the original Audubon party, aided Maria R. Audubon in the biographical sketch of her father.

Another of the picturesque old San Joaquin County homesteads is the Carson house, four miles north of Stockton on the Lower Sacramento Road just across from the Lincoln School. The low, one-story structure of resawed siding, with a long ell extending in the rear, stands in a magnificent grove of oaks, almost hidden by a tangled thicket of ivy and myrtle and Trees of Paradise. The house had been built only a short time when, in 1852, William McKindre Carson, a native of Baltimore, who had come to California in 1850, purchased the ranch on which it is located. Once inviting and homelike, it is now fast falling to decay. On the north side of the grove is a more recent dwelling, built somewhat after the style of the first structure, in which the present Carson owners live in sight of the house where they and their brothers and sisters were born.

Many settlers came to the Mokelumne River in 1851 and took up homesteads along the rich river bottoms. Among these was B. F. Langford, a native of Tennessee, who became California State Senator in the '80's. This enterprising pioneer built the picturesque one-story brick house which stands in the midst of orchards and vineyards not far from the river just west of the Tretheway Road, and which today is occupied by his descendants. The bricks used in its construction were burned on the place. The house is well preserved, although changes through the years have considerably altered its original appearance. A low hip roof has replaced the former flat one, and one of the two ells which formed a patio in the rear has been torn down, since the patio feature proved to be unsatisfactory in so warm a climate. Also a long grape arbor which extended from the front door has been eliminated. Some of the trees which were planted at the time the house was built are still flourishing—a knotted pear tree, two magnificent old fig trees, and several pomegranates. Between the house and the present walnut orchard are a few ancient oaks, remnants of the splendid groves which once covered the surrounding fields. Beyond the walnut orchard on the opposite side of the river is the site of Staples' Ferry.

A number of early-day homesteads are to be found along the old Mokelumne Hill (Linden) Road. One-half mile south of the road and east of Stockton, in the district known as Sutroville, stands the Hammond house, deserted and forlorn, in a semicircle of giant fig trees. It was built in the early '50's by Alden Hammond and is still owned by his heirs.

On the Grupe ranch, at the intersection of the Linden and the Jack Tone roads eight miles northeast of Stockton, is the one-story house of resawed siding built by John Carsten Grupe in the early '50's. In spite of the passing years the house is still in good condition.

Seventeen miles east of Stockton was the "Oregon Ranch," first settled by George Theyer and David Wells, who built a tule house there in 1848. When traffic began to flow over the Sonora Road to the southern mines the partners opened the "Oregon Tent," the first stopping-place along the road, on a site in what is now Farmington. In 1852 Nathaniel Siggons Harrold, a native of Pennsylvania, who had come by ox team to Woods' Creek, Tuolumne County, in November 1849, purchased the Oregon Ranch, and in 1868 built a large brick house, now within the city limits of Farmington. Harrold, who engaged in cattle-raising, gradually increased the size of his ranch from 320 to 5,400 acres. He owned thousands of acres in other sections as well.

In 1850, about three-fourths of a mile west of the Oregon Tent, James Wasley built the Wisconsin House, which later was moved to Peters, where it was used as a boarding-house as late as 1890. The Marietta House, three miles east, and the Texas Tent, four miles west, were other taverns on the Sonora Road in the '50's. Mr. Harrold served as a cook at the latter establishment before purchasing the Oregon Ranch.

A town was laid out on the Oregon Ranch in 1858 by Dr. W. B. Stamper. It is said that he named the place Farmington because it was the center of an extensive and rich farming country.

After passing Simms, the present French Camp Road runs about one-half mile north of the course of the early-day thoroughfare. The original road can be easily traced, however, by the old-fashioned farmhouses surrounded by tall shade trees which stand out conspicuously in the wide, open fields south of the present highway. Noteworthy among these are the old homes on the ranches belonging to the Van Glahns, Sextons, and Covells. On the present highway is the J. O'Malley homestead, with its treasured locust trees planted in the '50's. The house stands today in a thick grove of orange, olive, and walnut trees. The O'Malley sisters, daughters of the original owner, tell how ranchers walked the fences all the way to Stockton during the flood of 1862 and came back in boats.

In the northwestern part of Escalon is the John Jones house, a square, two-story mansion built in 1867 of bricks fired on the place. John Wheeler Jones, a native of North Carolina, came to California with his family in 1852, and at first kept the Blue Tent Tavern on the French Camp Road one mile east of the site of Escalon. In 1855 he purchased the ranch of 160 acres on which the brick mansion was later built. By 1875 Jones had increased the size of his ranch to seven thousand acres, and in addition he owned several thousand acres in other parts of the valley. In 1894 the town of Escalon was laid out on the home ranch by James W. Jones, son of the original owner.

Mokelumne River Ferries

John C. Frémont says that on March 25, 1844, his men "halted in a beautiful bottom at the ford of the Río de los Mukelemnes," which received its name from an "Indian tribe living on the river." "The bottoms on the stream," he continued, "are broad, rich, and extremely fertile, and the uplands are shaded with oak groves." Most of these ancient woodlands have disappeared, having been supplanted by verdant orchards and vineyards. The Indian rancheria which existed at the ford when the first white settlers came has likewise vanished, but the site has been fixed on the Langford ranch some two hundred yards east of the present brick house by relics unearthed at the spot.

Among the early wayfarers and emigrants who made use of the ford mentioned by Frémont were Captain Weber, on his journeys between Sutter's Fort and Stockton, and the Murphy party, who in 1844 were the first to drive wagons along the trail and across the stream at this point. The next few years saw increased travel from Sutter's Fort

to Pueblo de San José via this route, which soon came to be known as the Sutter's Fort–San Jose Trail. Later it was designated as the Upper Sacramento Road.

Although the first to settle at the ford was Thomas Pyle in November 1846, records show that in 1849 the place was known as Laird's Ferry. That year David J. Staples, J. F. Staples, and W. H. Nichols, among others, took up their residence there. Organizing a company known as Staples, Nichols and Company, they acquired possession in February 1850 of the ferry, which was thereafter known as Staples' Ferry. In the fall of 1850 the company built a toll bridge—perhaps the first in the county—across the river west of the ferry. The first to cross on the new bridge, so the story goes, was a grizzly bear, which was given free passage without question. A post office was established at Staples' Ferry in 1852 and until 1854 all stagecoach travel to Sacramento passed that way. After that date the route by way of Woods' Ferry (Woodbridge) was used except in times of flood. Staples' Ferry, however, continued to serve travelers for many years—even as late as 1880, although by that time it was known as Miller's Ferry. The site of the old Staples' Hotel (built from lumber brought around the Horn in 1850) is on the south side of the river on the present Diederich ranch, and may be reached over the Tretheway Road. Portions of the old thoroughfare are still visible on both sides of the stream. In the former river bed (just south of the present channel) the steamboat "Pert" lies buried under twelve feet of sand.

After crossing the Calaveras River at the Isbel cabin, the Upper Sacramento Road proceeded via Staples' Ferry to Dry Creek, where in 1849 a Mr. Davis established a crossing which he operated for a few years. Turner Elder, one of the first settlers in the county, had erected a log cabin at this point in the fall of 1846. In 1852 the now extinct Liberty City was established there by C. C. Fugitt. Sixteen years later, when the Central Pacific Railroad was under construction, the town was moved one mile south in the hope that it would be made a station on the new line. This dream, however, was never realized, and before long Liberty became a "ghost city." Neither town site is definitely marked today, although the first location can be approximated from the old pioneer cemetery in the vicinity and the second by the present Liberty School.

Benedict's Ferry, about halfway between Woods' and Staples' ferries, was established in 1850 by C. L. Benedict, who had a ranch on the north side of the Mokelumne River at this point. In 1852 the government opened a post office at Benedict's Ferry and during the same year the Bramlett and Langford sawmill was built there.

Benson's Ferry, started in 1849 by Edward Stokes and A. M. Woods, was purchased by John A. Benson in 1850. After the murder of Benson in February 1859 by Green C. Palmer, an employee, and the latter's subsequent suicide, E. P. Gayetty, Benson's son-in-law, took over the operation of the ferry. The two-story Gayetty house, built in the '70's, still stands near the levee three hundred yards west of the present bridge, while not far away is the weatherbeaten shell of the old Benson house. During the flood of 1862 it was lashed to a large tree, which stood near by, and was thus saved from being washed down the river. A little to the south is a large pond which fills the pit where clay was dug for the manufacture of brick during the active days of Mokelumne City, one-half mile to the east. These historic landmarks are now on the property of G. L. Barber.

Mokelumne City was laid out at the junction of the Cosumnes and Mokelumne rivers in 1854 shortly after the Snap brothers had opened a store there. High hopes were cherished that the place might be made the head of navigation and a center of trade for the mines. For a time the town grew and prospered: boats unloaded at the landing; lots were sold; hotels, stores, shops, warehouses, and dwellings were erected. Then came the flood of 1862. The town was submerged, and as many as nineteen houses were swept away by the rushing, swirling river. Mokelumne City never fully recovered from this disaster, although there was some business activity in the place and people continued to live there until 1878, when the town site was included in the property purchased by the Barber family for a ranch. The hotel was converted into a barn and stood until replaced by the present structure sometime in the '90's. The property is now owned by E. H. Barber.

Some of the houses of Mokelumne City were removed to other localities, and a few still stand. One of these is the Jesse Thornton house, situated in a dense grove of oak trees at a beautiful spot on the Mokelumne River directly below the present bridge on the road from Thornton to Galt.

Lockeford

Dr. Dean J. Locke, a native of New Hampshire and a graduate of the Harvard Medical School, came to California in 1849 as physician for the Boston and Newton Joint-Stock Association. For a few months he engaged in mining with his brother George at Mississippi Bar on the American River, but in December 1850 they both came to the Mokelumne River, where another brother, Elmer, had already become an enthusiastic settler. The Lockes purchased 360 acres of land from D. J. Staples for one dollar an acre, and in 1851 erected a log cabin (since destroyed) on a knoll thickly sprinkled with oaks. Grizzly bears were plentiful in those days, and when night came the hired men "roosted high in the trees like turkeys," for fear of the beasts. The cabin site is now occupied by a pleasant modern farmhouse on La Lomita Ranch about half a mile northwest of Lockeford.

The village of Lockeford was laid out on the D. J. Locke ranch in 1862. Its founders envisioned the town as becoming the head of navigation on the Mokelumne River, an ambition which was strengthened when the little pioneer steamer "Pert" tied up to the Lockeford landing on April 5, 1862. Eventually the Mokelumne Steam Navigation Company was organized, and for three or four years it carried on some business. After 1865, however, the mining population gradually scattered, and the coming of the railroad ultimately put an end to all navigation on the Mokelumne.

Dr. Locke was very influential in the development of the new town, and was especially active in organizing schools, churches, and temperance societies. Even before the town was officially laid out, Locke interested himself in the cultural life of the community. On the second floor of his adobe granary, built in 1858 just west of the site of the present brick house, he fitted up a hall for public gatherings, and here the Sons of Temperance were organized. As early as November 24, 1861, the Congregationalists held services in this same hall. In 1869 the present church building was erected. The first house on the site of Lockeford was a frame structure erected in 1855, and to it Dr. Locke brought his bride that same year. This first house was outgrown in the succeeding years and in 1865 the front part of the present two-story brick dwelling was constructed on the same site.

Luther Locke, father of the Locke brothers, came to California when Dr. Locke returned with his bride. The following year he built himself a home, a frame structure, in which the first store in Lockeford was opened in 1862. Later the post office was established in this building, with Luther Locke as the first postmaster. This landmark, long known

as the "White House," stands on the main street of town and serves as the home and office of N. H. Locke, notary public, a grandson of the original owner.

One mile southwest of Lockeford where the Southern Pacific branch line to Valley Springs crosses the Victor Road is an old brick church erected by community effort in the late '50's. The building was afterward acquired by the Methodists, who still own it as well as the cemetery adjoining the Odd Fellows and Catholic cemeteries to the east. Unused since 1912, with its tall Gothic windows and doors boarded up, the old church is fast falling to decay.

Woodbridge

The first permanent settlers in the vicinity of Woodbridge were George W. Emerson and Ross C. and J. P. Sargent, all from New England. When they arrived in 1850 it is said that they found huts of rived oak left by Hudson's Bay Company trappers. In 1852 Jeremiah H. Woods and Alexander McQueen established a ferry across the Mokelumne River at this point, about where the present bridge spans the stream, with the result that before long a new road from Stockton to Sacramento was routed by way of Woods' Ferry. After 1854 the stages which had formerly traveled via Staples' Ferry on the Upper Sacramento Road adopted this more direct route. In 1858 Woods, a very energetic and enterprising man, built a bridge at the site of the ferry, which for years was known as Woods' Bridge. From it the town, which was laid out on the south side of the river in April 1859, took the name Woodbridge. For several years the place showed considerable activity, but with the death of Jeremiah Woods in 1864 Woodbridge lost its chief promoter.

Several of the early frame houses are still to be found at Woodbridge. Among these, the oldest is a small cottage, now shingled over, on the north side of Mokelumne Street. Originally it stood near the river bank west of the bridge and served first as the Jeremiah Woods store and later as the Lavinsky home. Diagonally across the road was the Woods Hotel, just recently torn down. Another old building, the Folger house, has been incorporated into the present Charles Newton home. In the Newton yard is a giant knotted old fig tree, planted years ago by Mrs. Folger. Next door is an interesting house, one of several moved up the river from the once thriving Mokelumne City. Across the street from the present grammar school is the Thomas house, a small, low structure of resawed siding, built in the '50's of lumber brought in over the rough and dusty roads by ox-team. Another of the same type and period is the old Newton house located back of the present oil station.

On the main street of Woodbridge is the I.O.O.F. Building, a two-story brick structure, the lower part of which was built in the early '60's, while the upper story dates from 1874. The older portion was at first the Lavinsky store; then later for a time it served as a school. Farther up the street are two frame buildings which have an interesting history. Originally one structure, they constituted a former hotel in old Mokelumne City ten miles down the river. After this building had been removed to Woodbridge it housed the Nevada State Insane Asylum from 1871 to 1877, when the asylum was transferred to Stockton.

The Woodbridge Academy, a two-story frame structure erected in the winter of 1878–1879 under the leadership of Professor S. L. Morehead, was taken over by the United Brethren in 1881, when it became known as the San Joaquin Valley College. As such it continued to function until the beginning of the twentieth century, when it was superseded by the public grammar school. Today a modern school building occupies the site.

The Mokelumne Hill Road

In 1850 seventeen public houses, all located within a distance of twenty-four miles from Stockton, lined the Mokelumne Hill Road (now the Linden Road). Not a vestige of these early inns can be found today, but there is one such building, erected in 1853 by Masterson and Cogswell at a cost of $8,000, which has come down to us. This is the two-story brick structure which stands a few feet from the highway about halfway between Linden and Bellota. For a time during the '60's the building housed a young ladies' seminary. Today this sturdy old landmark is unoccupied but it is carefully preserved by its owners.

The town of Linden, which was laid out in 1862, had its beginnings in the little community which grew up around the Fifteen Mile House. This tavern had been established by Dr. W. D. Treblecock in the fall of 1849. Some years later C. C. Rynerson erected a flour mill in the vicinity. Soon after, John and James Wasley, cousins of Treblecock, and later brothers-in-law to Rynerson, joined the group and were among the founders of the town. John Wasley named the new settlement, presumably after his old home at Linden, Ohio. The Rynerson flour mill was destroyed by fire in 1865 but was replaced by a second structure, which met a similar fate in 1868. A three-story brick mill, erected in 1871, now occupies the site. Other brick structures, dating from the '60's and '70's, give the present village an aspect of substantial usefulness so characteristic of its founders.

Bellota, four miles east of Linden, was originally known as Fisher's Bridge, for at this point William V. Fisher had erected a bridge and stage station on his farm, purchased in 1861. The old hotel, now a residence, stands on the present highway near the north bank of the Calaveras River. Just south of the river is a wayside store which in the early days was a community house and social hall. The old watering trough, protected from the summer heat and winter rains by a rough shed roof, is reminiscent of the days of the horse and buggy, when travel meant long arduous hours over the roads, deep with mud in the winter and choked with dust in the summer.

Before the building of Fisher's Bridge, the Mokelumne Hill Road crossed the Calaveras River a few miles east of the site of Bellota at the Davis and Atherton Ferry. The first settler in this section, David F. Douglas, took up land between Bellota and the ferry, where he built a shake house, one of the seventeen inns along the old Mokelumne Hill Road in 1850. Douglas, who had come to California from Mexico with Graham's Dragoons in 1848, became a member of the Constitutional Convention in 1849, and was Secretary of State under Governor J. Neely Johnson from 1855 to 1857.

San Joaquin and Stanislaus River Crossings

In pioneer days river crossings were important points in the San Joaquin Valley, and it was on the various watercourses that the earliest settlements were planted. Among these first attempts at colonization was New Hope, or Stanislaus City, established on the Stanislaus River in November 1846 by a party of Mormons under the leadership of Samuel Brannan. About thirty colonists came up the San Joaquin River in a schooner, landing on the east branch near the site at which Jacob Bonsell established a ferry two years later. From this point the party proceeded overland to a spot previously selected by Brannan on the north bank of the Stanislaus River one and a half miles from the river's mouth.

Soon after their arrival a log house, constructed after the Western manner and covered with oak shingles fashioned on the spot, was put up, while with a crudely improvised

sawmill boards were hewn from oak logs for the cabin floor. Elk, bear, and wild geese were so abundant that one man with a rifle could bring in enough game in three hours' time to supply the colony for a week. Wheat, farm implements, and other necessary supplies had been brought, and by the middle of January 1847 eighty acres of grain had been sown. The little settlement did, indeed, seem full of hope and promise.

But with the coming of the winter rains the whole aspect was changed. The season was so stormy that the river overflowed its banks, causing the little band of pioneers untold suffering and hardship. Then, too, serious dissension arose among the colonists. So completely disheartened did they become that gradually the group disbanded. By the summer of 1847 only one man, a Mr. Buckland, remained, and he, too, was gone by November.

An attempt to re-establish a settlement at Stanislaus City seems to have been made during the gold rush of 1849. Buffum in 1850 made the prophecy that "this point . . . . being nearer the southern mining region than Stockton, will doubtless become a great resort for miners and traders . . . ." Stanislaus City appears on a map published in 1851, which also indicates that the road from Stockton to Tuolumne City crossed the Stanislaus River at that point. Nevertheless, no substantial revival ever took place, for Henry Grissim, who took up land on the old site in May 1851, apparently was not aware that he was farming on ground occupied four years earlier by the town of Sam Brannan's "new hope"—Stanislaus City.

Various ferries along the Stanislaus River are mentioned in the journals of early travelers and in old newspapers and county records: Knight's (established in the spring of 1849), the first of the chain; George Keeler's (1849); Heath and Emory's (1849); Leitch and Cottle's; Islip's, mentioned in the *Audubon Journal*, under the date of January 6, 1850, as the "Middle Ferry"; Boland (1850); Burney's; Murphy's; Sirey's (1849); and Belcher's (1849).

After attempts to establish Stanislaus City failed, a settlement was started on the west side of the San Joaquin River a little above the mouth of the Stanislaus. Hoping to become a rival of Stockton, San Joaquin City, as it was called, persisted for a number of years. As late as 1880 it had a hotel, a warehouse, and two saloons, as well as stores and homes. Nothing marks the location today, although the name is found on some recent maps. North of the site a bridge crosses the river in the vicinity of the old Durham Ferry crossing, established by Titus and Manly in 1850, and later successively owned by Durham and Fiske.

The first ferry to be operated on the San Joaquin River was that of John Doak and Jacob Bonsell, who in 1848 began to convey passengers in a small yawl across the river at a spot located just below the present Southern Pacific Railroad Bridge, and about where U.S. Highway 48 from Oakland to Stockton crosses today. It was here that the old Sutter's Fort–San Jose Trail crossed the river. Traffic to the mines soon grew so heavy that it became necessary to have a larger and more substantial ferryboat, so Doak went to Corte Madera in Marin County where he built the new craft. With their increased carrying facilities, the partners did an enormous business, reaping equally large returns, for charges on this pioneer ferry were high—one dollar for footmen, three dollars for horsemen, and eight for horses and wagons. In 1852, however, Doak sold his share in the business to Hiram Scott, and later in the same year Bonsell died. With the subsequent marriage of Bonsell's widow to James A. Shepherd, the ferry became known as Shepherd's Ferry and was so called until 1856, when it was sold to William T Moss.

Three miles below Bonsell's Ferry was Slocum's Ferry, established in 1849, while to the north was Johnson's Ferry. In later years Frewert's and Lindstrom's ferries were put into operation still farther to the north.

Corral Hollow

Corral Hollow may be reached over the Corral Hollow Road, which branches off from U.S. Highway 48 one mile west of Tracy. Many Indian relics, including arrowheads, pestles, and beautifully shaped bowls, have been uncovered along the dry bed of the arroyo, indicating the probable existence of a former Indian encampment in the vicinity. Petrified cedar, as well as fossil leaves and shells, have been found in the arroyo and in the neighboring hills. Two miles up the canyon is Castle Rock, a vaqueros sandstone formation pierced with so-called "caves" or prospect holes, which tradition says was one of Joaquín Murieta's numerous hiding-places.

In early days the Hollow was known as El Arroyo de Buenos Ayres, through which an old Spanish trail ran. According to Bolton, Juan Bautista de Anza passed that way in April 1776. Later, Spanish and Mexican vaqueros made customary use of the trail, along which they drove their herds of cattle. Still later, during the gold days, the old trail was much traveled as a road to the southern mines.

The first white settler in the Hollow was Edward B. (Ned) Carroll, who in 1850 took up 160 acres of government land there, on which was located a fine mountain spring, still flowing today. It is believed by a descendant that the present "Corral Hollow" is a corruption of the original name, Carroll's Hollow.

Down on the arroyo among the cottonwoods, directly on the line of the old Spanish trail, Carroll and three associates, Horatio P. Wright, William Breyton, and John A. Stockholm, built a "Zinc House" about where the present pump house stands, where for several years meals were served and wayfarers were afforded shelter. Perhaps the most famous visitor to stop at the Zinc House was James Capen Adams, or "Grizzly" Adams, as he was popularly known. With his two bears, "Lady Washington" and "Ben Franklin," and his dog "Rambler," famous actors in Adams' "Mountaineer Museum" in San Francisco, he spent several days hunting in the region, his experiences afterward figuring in Hittell's biographical narrative.

In 1856 Jack O'Brien, a sea captain, who was passing through Corral Hollow, discovered an outcropping of a black mineral at the upper end of the canyon about nine miles from Carroll's Zinc House which when tested proved to be coal. The Eureka Coal Company was subsequently organized, and Captain O'Brien was given a life interest, which netted him a dollar a day until his death.

Carroll at once erected a two-story house of resawed siding to serve as a boarding house for the teamsters, who hauled coal from the mines to the San Joaquin River where it was loaded on barges at Mohr's Landing. The Mohr homestead, today owned and occupied by heirs, is near the site of the former landing on Old River near Bethany.

The old Carroll house stands at the mouth of the canyon just above the gravel pits of the Pacific Coast Aggregates, the bleakness of its surroundings softened by vividly green pepper trees and by a few magnificent old cottonwoods, all that are left of the many which flourished in the region when the first white settlers came. This historic landmark is today the home of Carroll's stepdaughter, Mrs. Mamie Burns.

When Carroll, the only surviving owner of the Eureka Coal Company, died in 1881 at the homestead in the Hollow, John and James Treadwell of the famous Bears' Nest Mine,

Alaska, purchased the Corral Hollow coal property, naming it the Tesla Mine, in honor of Nikola Tesla, the great electrical inventor. During the early '90's, under the management of the San Francisco and San Joaquin Coal Company, the yield from the Tesla Mine averaged 500 tons of coal daily. From six to ten carloads were shipped each day over a branch railroad to Stockton, where the coal was transferred to river boats bound for San Francisco.

About this time the Treadwells organized the Carnegie Brick and Pottery Company, manufacturers of white glazed brick. The plant was located in the Hollow a few miles below the coal mine at Carnegie, a town of some two thousand inhabitants, which flourished until 1906, when the earthquake and the failure of the California Safe Deposit Bank in San Francisco ruined the Treadwells financially and caused the abandonment of Carnegie.

Corral Hollow today presents a forlorn appearance. Only the wreckage of abandoned dumps and chutes marks the site of the Tesla Mine. The fine brick houses and stores which lined the streets of Carnegie have been totally wrecked, and but for the Hetch Hetchy plants at camps Thomas and Mitchell the Hollow would be almost entirely deserted. Just above Camp Thomas, a manganese mine was developed by a company of Frenchmen during the '90's. During World War I, interest again centered on this mine when about $80,000 was recovered from the tailings. The mine is no longer being worked, but pockets of the mineral still exist in the hills.

SOURCES

[Credit is here given for source material, and permission to quote is hereby acknowledged]

AUDUBON, JOHN W. *Audubon's Western Journal: 1849–1850.* The Arthur H. Clark Company, Cleveland, 1906

BOGARDUS, J. P. "A Historical Sketch of Stockton," in *Stockton City Directory for the Year 1856.* Harris, Joseph & Company, San Francisco, 1856

BUFFUM, E. GOULD. *Six Months in the Gold Mines.* Lea & Blanchard, Philadelphia, 1850

CARSON, JAMES H. *Life in California, Together with a Description of the Great Tulare Valley.* 2d ed. *San Joaquin Republican,* Stockton, 1852

DAVIS, SHELDEN. "Tesla, a Coast Range 'Ghost Town'," in *Stockton Record,* February 7, 1931, pp. 25–28

FINKBOHNER, AGNES STEINY (MRS. GEORGE). *History and Landmarks of San Joaquin County.* Manuscript, 1924

FRÉMONT, BREVET COLONEL JOHN C. *The Exploring Expedition to the Rocky Mountains, Oregon and California.* George H. Derby & Company, Buffalo, 1849

GILBERT, COLONEL F. T. *History of San Joaquin County, California.* Thompson & West, Oakland, 1879

HITTELL, THEODORE H. *The Adventures of James Capen Adams, Mountaineer and Grizzly Bear Hunter of California.* Towne & Bacon, San Francisco, 1860. New edition, Charles Scribner's Sons, 1911

Illustrated History of San Joaquin County, California. The Lewis Publishing Company, Chicago, 1890

LATTA, F. F. "San Joaquin Primeval—Spanish," in *Tulare Daily Times,* 1932

MALONEY, ALICE B. "California Rendezvous," in *Beaver,* December 1944

REYNOLDS, JAMES. Statement on French Camp, made to F. F. Latta, August 12, 1933

SCHENCK, W. EGBERT. "Historic Aboriginal Groups of the California Delta Region," in *University of California Publications in American Archaeology and Ethnology,* XXIII, No. 2 (1926), 123–146

SCHENCK, W. EGBERT, and ELMER J. DAWSON. "Archaeology of the Northern San Joaquin Valley," in *University of California Publications in American Archaeology and Ethnology,* XXV, No. 4 (1929), 289–413

TAYLOR, BAYARD. *Eldorado, or Adventures in the Path of Empire.* H. G. Bohn, London, 1850; G. P. Putnam, New York, 1850, 1864

TINKHAM, GEORGE H. *History of San Joaquin County, California.* The Historic Record Company, Los Angeles, 1923

——. *History of Stockton.* W. M. Hinton & Company, San Francisco, 1880

SHASTA COUNTY

Sʜᴀsᴛᴀ Cᴏᴜɴᴛʏ (Shasta is apparently a corruption of the name of a tribe of Indians living in the vicinity of Mount Shasta) was one of the original twenty-seven counties, and at first included within its boundaries all of the territory which later became Modoc, Lassen, and Siskiyou counties, as well as parts of the present Plumas and Tehama counties. The county seat was placed first at Reading's Ranch, but was transferred to Shasta in 1851, and, finally, on May 19, 1888, was moved to Redding, named in honor of B. B. Redding, for many years land agent for the Central Pacific Railroad Company.

Lassen Volcanic National Park

Lassen Peak (10,453 feet), the only active volcano on the North American continent outside of Alaska, was called Monte San José by the padres who accompanied Luís Argüello on an exploring expedition in 1821 to seek for mission sites. Early maps of California, however, give it as Mount St. Joseph. It was later named Lassen Buttes and, finally, Lassen Peak, after Peter Lassen, the noted pioneer of Tehama County. The Maidu Indians called it "La Lapham Yerman y'aidum," meaning "the long, high mountain that was broken." On May 30, 1914, after having been quiescent for more than two hundred years, Lassen Peak became active once more, resulting in a series of about three hundred eruptions. Since 1915 the old volcano has been relatively quiet, although quantities of smoke, at decreasing intervals, have issued from its crater.

Lassen Peak and Cinder Cone were set aside as national monuments on May 6, 1907. On August 9, 1916, the region was designated the Lassen Volcanic National Park, and in January 1929 was enlarged to its present area of 163 square miles.

The Park contains other interesting volcanic cones, such as Prospect Peak and Harkness Peak, as well as numerous fumaroles, hot springs, mud pots, and boiling lakes, as the entire region is of volcanic origin. Lying as it does at the southern end of the Cascades where they join the Sierra Nevada, the Park presents a magnificent sky line. Within the area are outstanding scenic features—multicolored lava crags of varied and fantastic forms rising to a height of over 8,500 feet above sea-level, impressive canyons, and primeval forests.

Among the most beautiful of the individual wonders included in the Park is Lake Tartarus, or Boiling Springs Lake, which lies "jade-green and ominous" amid the encircling forest. Clouds of steam arising from its surface at dawn and dusk add to the enchantment of the scene. Lake Tartarus is one of a group of volcanic phenomena lying to the south of Lassen Peak which includes the Devils Kitchen (privately owned but embraced within the boundaries of the Park), the Willow Creek Geyser, Bumpas Hell, and many other mud pots and hot springs. Through the northern gateway to the Park one may visit the Hat Creek and Lost Creek areas, which were devastated by the recent eruptions of Lassen Peak, as well as scenic Manzanita and Reflection lakes, Chaos Crags, and the Loomis Museum.

Old Trails

A number of old trails traversed the Upper Sacramento Valley in the vicinity of Redding. The earliest to be blazed, known as the Trinity Trail, was made by Jedediah Strong Smith in the spring of 1828 while on his way out of California. Smith's route led across what are now Trinity and Humboldt counties and on up the coast through the Del Norte region and thence into southern Oregon. Learning of the new pathway from Smith, a party of Hudson's Bay Company trappers, led by Alexander Roderick McLeod, almost immediately set out for California, with John Turner, a former member of Smith's expedition, acting as guide. McLeod probably reached the Upper Sacramento Valley by this trail, and for a number of years trappers no doubt continued to follow it into California.

The Trinity River was discovered and named in 1845 by Pierson B. Reading, who was trapping in the Trinity country at that time. In 1848 he found the first gold in the region. Somewhere between Kennet and Castle Crags, Reading's earliest trail into the Trinity country crossed over the stretch of steep mountains separating the Sacramento and Shasta valleys known as the "Devil's Backbone." On his way back he traversed the same mountains at a point between Castella and Delta. In 1848 he took a new route, this time over the mountains which lie at the head of the Middle Fork of Cottonwood Creek, and on his return he blazed the trail later known as the Shasta–Weaverville Road, followed by thousands of miners in 1849 and the '50's. Supplies for the mines of the Trinity, Scott, and Salmon rivers brought in by way of the town of Shasta were taken over this trail by mule back. "Between Shasta, the head of 'Whoa navigation,' and the vast mining region to the north, more than 2,000 pack mules were constantly plying." In 1861 the main section of the trail—that west from Shasta to Weaverville—was widened into a wagon road by Charles Camden. The Redding–Eureka State Highway today follows this early thoroughfare approximately.

In 1859 a through stage road to Oregon was opened up which ran from Shasta to Yreka by way of French Gulch, Carrville (Trinity County), Callahan (Siskiyou County), and Fort Jones. Today this route is no longer a main artery of travel, but during the '60's it was the principal wagon road to the north. At the junction of this road and the Shasta–Weaverville Road stands the Tower House, a landmark famous in the early days.

When Levi H. Tower and Charles Camden arrived at this spot in November 1850, they found a log cabin, occupied by a man named Schneider. Here Tower built the Tower House Hotel with lumber hewn from the surrounding forests and split by hand. Remains of the old hostelry still stand near the highway, "a gaunt framework of huge timbers from which the siding has long since been stripped. Upon those timbers appear the marks of adzes used in hewing them from tree trunks, and they are held together by hand-made nails." The residence of Charles Camden, erected some time later near the old hotel, still serves as the summer home of a daughter. In its beautiful mountain setting, Tower House and its lands was the show place of the county in early days, and it is still a magnificent estate.

The second oldest trail through the Upper Sacramento Valley may have been the east branch of the California–Oregon Trail, although no absolute proof of this has yet been found. It seems likely that McLeod took this route on his way out of the Valley in 1828. It is known that he was forced to cache his furs at the approach of winter and that on his return the following spring he found them spoiled, a circumstance which led to his discharge from the Hudson's Bay Company. At the headwaters of the North Fork of the McCloud River on Bartle's Ranch in Siskiyou County a wooden trough and some guns were uncovered in 1874. At the time it was believed that these were the remains of McLeod's cache. In any event this early trail was followed by explorers and trappers before 1829, for in Ogden's diary of that year "Pitt's River" is mentioned. In 1841 Pitt's Lake (now Goose Lake) and Pitt's River (since known as the Pit River) were quite accurately mapped by Charles Wilkes, whose source of information had been the Hudson's Bay Company, a fact which indicates that its trappers had explored the region through which the trail in question passed.

The east branch of the California–Oregon Trail, after leaving the Sacramento Valley, crossed a ruggedly mountainous country before passing out of the state between Tule and Clear lakes in the north. Traversing this difficult region, variations of the road were developed by early travelers. One such was taken by Frémont and his men in the spring of 1846. In the latter part of April they had passed up the east bank of the Sacramento River as far as its confluence with Cottonwood Creek, opposite which they turned east and then northeast across Shasta County. In Lassen County, some distance east of Fall River, Frémont's party forded the Pit River. Crossing the mountains to Big Valley (called by Frémont "Round Valley"), they spent the night of April 30 at its upper end. From there the party journeyed north over the route followed later by emigrants from Oregon.

In the fall of 1848 the first wagon train into California from Oregon followed the Applegate Road as far as Clear Lake (Modoc County). There the emigrants turned south over the trail used by Frémont, connecting with Lassen's Trail ten miles north of Lookout (Modoc County). The lure of gold brought many Oregonians into California in 1849 and the early '50's. From Big Valley, most of the Argonauts bound for Shasta and the Trinity mines climbed the mountains to the west and crossed the Pit River west of Fall River Mills. Leaving the Pit at this point, they went south for some distance and then turned west through Burney Valley and thence southwest to Shasta, the entrepôt to the Trinity region. In 1856 a road to Yreka was built by way of the Pit River crossing, and shortly thereafter the California Stage Company inaugurated a daily schedule from Sacramento to Yreka, the first through stage service to that point. Because of Indian massacres in Fall River Valley and attacks on the stage, this line was discontinued in January 1857 for a short time.

It is not known who first blazed the west branch of the California–Oregon Trail, which followed up the Sacramento River Canyon and around the west side of Mount Shasta, but it is certain that Hudson's Bay Company trappers used it annually from 1832 to 1845. Ewing Young, the trapper, making his way into Oregon to settle in 1834, followed this route, being the first to traverse the entire length of the Oregon Trail from San Bernardino in southern California to the Methodist Mission in northern Oregon. In 1837 the demand for cattle in the Willamette Valley led to Young's second expedition over the Oregon Trail, when he accomplished the arduous task of driving seven hundred head of cattle and forty horses over the Devil's Backbone. Young's party included P. L. Edwards, the diarist of the company, and twenty others, among whom were settlers bound for Oregon.

In 1841 a contingent of the Wilkes Exploring Expedition, consisting of about eighteen persons under the command of Lieutenant George F. Emmons, came down the Oregon Trail across the Siskiyou Mountains and through what are now Siskiyou and Shasta counties to New Helvetia and Yerba Buena. A number of Oregonians had joined the party, making a total of thirty-nine persons and about seventy-six animals. On his map Wilkes designated that part of the Sacramento River above its confluence with the Pit River as "Destruction River," a name which may have been given originally by Hudson's Bay Company trappers to the McLeod (now spelled "McCloud") River, on the banks of which McLeod met disaster in the winter of 1829. That part

of the Pit River which lies in Shasta County was called the Sacramento.

The largest early expedition to use the west branch of the California–Oregon Trail was led by Joseph Gale, who in May 1843, in company with forty-two settlers bound for Oregon, drove 250 head of cattle, 650 horses, and 3,000 sheep northward over this difficult path. On May 30 of the same year Lansford W. Hastings started for California with a party of discontented Oregonians. At the Rogue River they met Joseph Gale, who persuaded about two-thirds of the party to return to the Willamette Valley. With the remaining emigrants Hastings continued to California over the route just traversed by Gale. In 1845 James Clyman, with thirty-five men, one woman, and three children, also passed over this trail on the way south.

All of these parties had to cross the Devil's Backbone, and over these lofty, barren mountains they struggled with slow and painful progress. The Wilkes party, while traversing these precipitous slopes, which Clyman described as "almost too steep for brush to grow .... and in many places too narrow for a rabbit to walk over," lost their way but were guided to safety by the Indian wife of one of the company.

Late in 1848 gold-seekers from the north began using the Oregon Trail; and after the Siskiyou region was opened up in 1850, miners began pouring over it from the south. Because of the mountainous character of the route, it remained a pack trail until 1860, when a wagon road was constructed from Upper Soda Springs to Yreka. Today U.S. Highway 99 and the Shasta Route of the Southern Pacific Railway follow the old California–Oregon Trail quite closely —many of the railroad stations are on the exact line of the trail—thus making this the oldest continuously used road in northern California.

Where the California–Oregon stage road crossed the present Pacific Highway just south of the Anderson brickyard between Anderson and Redding a marker has been placed by the McCloud Parlor of the Native Sons of the Golden West of Redding. On the banks of the Sacramento River opposite this point was an early steamboat landing. This place, designated on a map of 1862 as "Reading," was the most northern point on the Sacramento reached by river boats.

On the summit of Bass Hill, fourteen miles north of Redding, a remnant of the stage road crosses the Pacific Highway and descends to the Pit River. Because this was a favorite "holdup" spot in stagecoach days, a marker has been placed there in memory of W. L. Smith, division stage agent of the California and Oregon Stage Company, and of the pioneer stage drivers along this road.

Another part of the old road in use today lies between the Pacific Highway and the McCloud River, near Briggs's Store. On a hill above the store is an ancient Indian burial ground, still used by the few remaining Indians of the region. Continuing, the road crossed the Sacramento River north of the present town of Baird at the site of the small village of Antler. About two miles above the mouth of the McCloud River, near Baird, is the Potter Creek Cave, where fossil remains of at least twenty-five distinct species, including the mastodon, elephant, giant sloth, large extinct lion, cave bear, and many other animals of a prehistoric era, have been found. Near Baird, also, is a place known as Joaquin Miller's Pass, where the poet is said to have forded the McCloud River on mule back.

On the Park Highway in the Lassen Volcanic National Park, a few hundred yards northwest of the checking station at Manzanita Lake, is a monument marking the Noble's Pass Road, followed by the pioneers of 1852. A large lava rock about five feet high, bearing a bronze plaque, stands at the junction of the two Park highways, one going down Lost Creek and Hat Creek to Burney, and the other turning west to Viola, Shingletown, and Redding. The latter was the route used by early emigrants who came over Noble's Pass. It was at this point that they caught their first glimpse of the Sacramento Valley. The summit of Noble's Pass is about three miles to the northeast.

Rancho Buena Ventura

The Reading adobe stands just south of Ball's Ferry on the west bank of the Sacramento River near its confluence with Cottonwood Creek. The original rancho consisted of a strip of land three miles wide extending for nineteen miles along the west bank of the Sacramento River from the mouth of Cottonwood Creek at the head of Bloody Island in the south to Salt Creek in the north. Later the towns of Anderson and Redding were established on the rancho.

Pierson Barton Reading, a native of New Jersey, came West with the Chiles-Walker party in 1843. He and twelve other men, among whom was Joseph B. Chiles, separated from the main party at Fort Hall, coming into California by an uncharted trail, now known as the Yellowstone Cut-Off. Passing through what is now Shasta County, Reading and his companions arrived at Sutter's Fort on November 10, 1843.

A comparison of Reading's descriptions of the trail followed by the Chiles party in 1843 with the geographical features in northern California indicates quite clearly the route traversed. Leaving Big Valley (in Lassen County) on October 25, the little band of thirteen men followed the course of the Pit River through the mountains, camping on the stream eighteen miles to the southwest. On the 26th they continued over a very mountainous country above the Pit River Canyon. "In some places," Reading writes, "the descent from the top of the bank to the water must have been 1,200 feet, the stream pitching over rocks and ledges, forming beautiful cascades, one of which had an abrupt fall of about 150 feet." This was, without doubt, Burney Falls, in the McArthur Memorial Park, whose actual drop is 128 feet.

Successive halts were made by Reading and his companions: at Goose Valley on the 28th, at the head of Hatchet Creek on the 29th, and on Cow Creek on the 31st. On the first day of November they traveled sixteen miles down Cow Creek, again pitching their tents on its banks. On the 2d, camp was made on Battle Creek, a part of the present boundary line between Shasta and Tehama counties, and on the 3d, after traveling eight miles, they passed through Iron Canyon, where they found the course of the stream "very crooked." Camp was made at the end of the day in the valley east of Red Bluff, from whence the journey was continued to Sutter's Fort.

Here Reading worked for a time in Captain Sutter's employ. In December 1844, through the latter's friendship and influence, Reading obtained a grant of 26,000 acres from Micheltorena, the most northerly grant in California, of which he took possession in August 1845. A house was built for Reading's overseer on Rancho Buena Ventura, as Reading called his new estate, and the land was stocked with cattle. This first house was burned by the Indians the following spring.

Reading participated in the Bear Flag Revolt at Sonoma in June 1846, and on July 5 or 6 he enlisted in Frémont's Battalion, serving first as lieutenant of artillery and then as paymaster with the rank of major, which office he held until May 31, 1847. In June he returned to his rancho and erected a permanent adobe house, the one which still stands four miles east of Cottonwood.

Ranch life, however, did not claim all of Reading's attention thus early. In February 1848 he was among the first to visit the scene of Marshall's momentous discovery of gold at Coloma. An examination of the soil satisfied the Major that gold must be present on his own rancho, and he returned at once to investigate. In March he and his Indians washed out the first gold to be found in Shasta County at the mouth of Clear Creek Canyon on a spot later known as Reading's Bar. In July of the same year he found the precious metal on the Trinity River. In 1849 he again mined on the Trinity, and during the summer located diggings on the site of the present town of Shasta, known for a time as Reading's Springs.

When Shasta County was established in 1850, Reading's Ranch was designated as the county seat. But with the organization of the Court of Sessions at the Major's adobe on February 10, 1851, the county seat was ordered removed to Shasta. "In the lonely stillness of the night" the court packed up the county records and carried them on horseback for a distance of twenty-five miles to the new location, perhaps "the most quiet county-seat removal on record in California." No one rejoiced more heartily over the change than did Major Reading.

In 1852 Reading was appointed United States Special Indian Agent, and for many years, without remuneration, carried on work among the Indians with splendid results. His kindliness to his charges was one of Reading's outstanding characteristics.

Going to Washington in 1855 to settle his land-grant title, Reading met Miss Fannie Wallace Washington, whom he brought with him to California as his bride. With her coming the adobe on Rancho Buena Ventura was enlarged, and became noted for its unfailing hospitality. About the great fireplace (still intact) many celebrities gathered from time to time—Bidwell, Frémont, Sutter, Lassen, and Joaquin Miller, among others. Here at his home on May 29, 1868, Pierson B. Reading died. A simple granite slab bearing a bronze memorial plate marks his grave, which lies not far from the historic adobe on a slight eminence overlooking the Sacramento River and the valley beyond. The old house, built with thick walls and high windows to protect the inmates from Indian arrows, is now falling to ruins.

Burney's Grave

The grave of Samuel Burney, a Scotchman, who was the first settler in Burney Valley, is close beside the Redding-Alturas Highway one-half mile east of the village of Burney. Numerous place names in the vicinity perpetuate the memory of this pioneer—the mountain, the valley, the falls, and the town all bear his name. Burney Falls, one of the most beautiful natural phenomena in California, is the chief attraction in the McArthur Memorial Park, a tract of 160 acres deeded to the state on May 11, 1920, by Frank McArthur as a memorial to his father and mother.

Burney came to the valley early in 1857 and built a log cabin, barn, and corral about a mile north of the present town of Burney. Although friendly with the Indians and speaking their language, he met death at their hands in March 1859.

Shasta

"Shasta, through which a stream of golden treasure once flowed, now lies in ruins. Six miles west of Redding, its crumbling [brick] structures flank the highway in serried rows. Roofs have long since caved in, and paneless windows stare vacuously into the grass-grown street. Of the old courthouse, only the walls remain standing; but the bars and grills in that portion used as a jail have stoutly resisted the elements and vandals. There is a general store at one end of the street [built by Bull, Baker and Company and still occupied] and a lone service station at the other end. The former has become rather famous as a museum of relics of the gold rush . . . ."

Called Reading's Springs by the first settlers who arrived in June 1849, the name was changed to Shasta on June 8, 1850. By that time the place had become the head of wagon transportation, from which all supplies for the outlying mines were sent on pack mules. "Measured by standards of the '50's and '60's, Shasta was indeed no mean city. She was a gateway to a large hinterland, rich in gold, that lay to the west in Trinity County." As many as a hundred freight teams have been known to stop in Shasta on a single night. Its strategic position soon made the village the commercial shipping-center of northern California, and its merchants did a thriving wholesale and retail business. It was not uncommon for the mercantile house of Bull, Baker and Company, whose brick store, erected in 1853, still stands on Main Street, to sell a consignment of goods to be taken by pack mules as far north as southern Oregon. The story is told of a member of this firm who early one morning before he had breakfasted sold a bill of goods valued at over $3,00υ.

The site of the first log house in Shasta, built by Milton McGee in October 1849, is not far from the present Stevenson residence, which stands on High Street near its intersection with Main Street. The log house was torn down in 1856. The St. Charles Hotel and the Trinity House, the first frame buildings in town, have also disappeared. Erected in the spring of 1850, they were destroyed in 1853 by the conflagration which swept Shasta's entire business section. Both stood on Main Street, the Trinity House being on the west side of Main above and adjoining High Street.

On Shurtleff Hill stands the fine old Shurtleff residence erected in the summer of 1851 by Dr. Benjamin Shurtleff, pioneer physician and Shasta's first and only alcalde. This house was used for a time by the Masons after the fire of 1853 had destroyed their original building. This Masonic lodge was the first to be established in the state, its charter having been brought to California by Peter Lassen in 1848. The lodge was first organized at Benton City on Lassen's Ranch (Tehama County), but on May 9, 1851, was moved to Shasta. The building now occupied, which has been in use since 1853, is owned and carefully preserved by Western Star Lodge, No. 2.

Shasta Mining Camps

Reading's Bar, where Major Reading in 1848 discovered the first gold in Shasta County, and where he washed out as much as fifty-two ounces daily with the aid of friendly Indians, is remembered by only a few of the old settlers. On a flat adjoining the bar a camp grew up which was known at first as Clear Creek Diggings and later as Horse Town. Three or four hundred miners had congregated at Clear Creek Diggings by October 1849, and considerable gold was taken out, although most of the miners did little more than prospect.

One of these prospectors, who had arrived in camp with one pack horse, settled there permanently and later built a hotel. As a result, so the story goes, the name of the place was changed to "One-Horse Town" in 1851. It did not remain a "one-horse" town, however, for before many years it boasted a thousand inhabitants and had two hotels, stores, shops, a Catholic Church, a newspaper (*The Northern Argus*, established in 1857), and fourteen saloons.

Horse Town was destroyed by fire in 1868 and the site has since been thoroughly dredged out. Reading's discovery of gold at this place is commemorated by a native boulder bearing a bronze tablet placed by the California Highway Commission on the Pacific Highway at the end of the Clear Creek Bridge.

In the vicinity of Horse Town were other early mining camps: Centerville to the north, Muletown to the northwest, and Piety Hill, Igo, and Ono to the west. Of the several stories told of the naming of Igo and Ono, the following is perhaps the most plausible. A Mr. McPherson, one of the first miners to build a substantial house in the place, had a small son who, whenever his father set out for the mines, would put on his own hat and say, "I go"; and always his father would answer, "Oh, no." When the appellation "Igo" became affixed to the place, a neighboring camp about six miles away became known as "Ono."

Whiskeytown, on the Eureka Highway between Shasta and Weaverville, was settled in 1849. It was a lively place, as its name might imply, where money was plentiful and freely spent. Some of its old brick and stone buildings still stand.

At French Gulch, originally called Morrowville, the diggings were very rich. In their avid search for gold, some of the miners even tore down their cabins to follow the leads extending under them. This once wild camp is today a live mining town with a population of over six hundred. Only one of the original cabins, built in 1856, remains, but there are several old brick buildings still standing which give the place something of the atmosphere of the gold days.

In October and November, 1849, hundreds of gold-seekers, many of them Missourians, camped at the mouth of Middle Creek. From this camp, which was nearly equal in size to Reading's Springs, groups of prospectors went out to all the creeks, gulches, and ravines in the surrounding country. One such company camped at or near Churn Creek, so named because a hole carved in the rocks by a waterfall in the stream resembled an old-fashioned churn. Upon being attacked by Indians the miners returned to the Middle Creek camp, bringing exaggerated reports of the rich diggings they had found. A larger company was soon organized for the purpose of making a permanent camp on the east side of the Sacramento River and of thoroughly prospecting the new site. In spite of trouble with the Indians a prosperous mining camp, which was called Churntown because of its proximity to Churn Creek, grew up there. Nothing remains of Churntown today.

In 1849 or 1850 gold was discovered on what is now known as the Vollmer Ranch, about thirty-five miles north of Redding on the Pacific Highway. At first little mining was carried on in the locality because of the hostility of the Indians in the neighborhood. By 1855, however, a thriving camp had grown up, about where the village of Delta is located today, with two or three hundred miners working the stream for its gold. During its heyday, Dog Creek, or Dogtown (as it was first called), was the largest and richest camp on the Upper Sacramento, and was the gathering-place for miners from the diggings of the entire region. Today no evidence exists to indicate the former importance of this historic spot.

Five miles north of Dog Creek was Portuguese Flat, a mining camp of the early '50's made up largely of Portuguese. This place, with its rich diggings, gained the reputation of being one of the roughest camps in the county. Today just north of Pollard's Gulch on the Pacific Highway may be seen a few old tumbledown buildings, one ancient log cabin, and some veteran apple trees—all that remains of the once prosperous Portuguese Flat.

Southern's Station

Simeon Fisher Southern arrived in Shasta in 1855, where at first he operated the Eagle Hotel, and later the St. Charles. In the autumn of 1856 he went to French Gulch, where he conducted the Empire Hotel for two years. Then, with J. S. Cameron, he became proprietor of the Dog Creek House at the mining camp of Dog Creek on the Oregon Trail. The following year Southern located forty-five miles north of Redding, at the site later known as Southern's, where he erected a cabin of shakes and hand-hewn logs. This developed into a busy trading-post for miners from Hazel Creek and the Upper Sacramento River. When stage coaches replaced pack-mule trains on the Oregon Trail in 1871, Southern's became an important station on the old road. Gradually the place took on the aspect of a summer resort, as the fame of the surrounding region spread. In 1882 a two-story extension was added to the original cabin. Eventually the old cabin was torn down and the two-story addition was considerably enlarged to care for the increasing number of summer visitors.

After the death of Southern in 1892 changes crept in, and with the sale of the property to lumber interests in 1902 the surrounding forests were cut and the old hotel disappeared, to be replaced by a modern service station and auto camp. The spot on which the hotel stood is marked only by a few old apple trees, planted in the '60's, and by a native boulder bearing a bronze tablet on which is an engraving of the original Southern cabin and its two-story addition. The names of many famous people appear on the old hotel register (still treasured by the family), among them being President R. B. Hayes, Generals W. T. Sherman and P. K. Sheridan, Robert Ingersoll, Mrs. Jay Gould, George Jay Gould, and the "Big Four"—Huntington, Hopkins, Stanford, and Crocker.

The American Ranch

Elias Anderson, one of Shasta County's first settlers, purchased the American Ranch in 1856, and on his land grew up the nucleus of what is now the town of Anderson. The ranch also was an early stopping-place for teamsters and travelers on the California–Oregon Road, and from it a trail branched off to the Trinity mines. The first buildings of the old stage station, the site of which is on the Pacific Highway across the creek from Anderson, were of adobe.

Bell's Bridge

Four miles south of Redding on the Pacific Highway a few hundred yards above the Clear Creek Bridge is the old Bell hostelry, built by J. J. Bell, who settled on the Oregon Road in May 1851. During the gold rush the place teemed with activity and thousands of men and beasts found refreshment there on their way to the Shasta, Trinity, and Siskiyou gold fields. Fabulous prices were paid for food and lodging, and with the proceeds Bell was enabled to make lavish improvements on his ranch. He also operated a toll bridge across Clear Creek at this point. The tavern now serves as a hay barn.

The Dersch Homestead

On a dirt road ten miles east of Anderson stands the Dersch homestead. The main portion of the original house, built by George Dersch in the early '60's, is a part of the Dersch family residence today. Earlier, in 1850, a Mr. Baker set up a tent hotel there, making the place an emigrant station on the Noble's Pass Road. George Dersch used Indian labor from rancherías then flourishing at Jelly's Ferry (Tehama County), Cottonwood, Reading's adobe, and Millville. Roving Indians raided the ranch in 1863, driving off the cattle, stealing the household provisions, and

leaving the family destitute. In 1866 a second raid was made, in which Mrs. Dersch was killed. The soldiers at Fort Reading were appealed to but without avail. This led to an uprising of the settlers, resulting in the extermination of most of the Indians in the surrounding rancherías.

Fort Reading

Fort Reading, named in honor of Major Pierson B. Reading, was established in May 1852 on Cow Creek on the Noble's Pass Road at a site five miles northeast of the present town of Anderson. It was abandoned in January 1867 as part of the demobilization of the Army, after the close of the Civil War. Nothing remains of the old fort itself, but the site, now in a cultivated field on the Hawes Ranch, is not far from a little country schoolhouse known as the Fort Reading School.

Millville

Fourteen miles east of Redding on the road to Lassen Park is Millville, a thriving village with a distinctive atmosphere of pioneer days. It was settled in 1853 by S. E. and N. T. Stroud, who built the first house there on the banks of Clover Creek. Millville has the distinction of having had the first grist mill in Shasta County erected there in 1856. The mill was built by D. D. Harrell and Russell Furman, who named the place Bunscombe Mills, in honor of Harrell's birthplace in North Carolina. Eventually the name was changed to Millville.

Fort Crook

About the year 1857 a fort was established by General George Crook on Fall River at the upper end of Fall River Valley to serve as a buffer against Indian attacks on the early settlers. The post consisted of twenty small log buildings placed in the form of an oblong. With the abandonment of Fort Crook in 1869 and the transfer of the soldiers to Fort Bidwell, the buildings were used for a time as a school, but were later sold and moved to Burgettville (now Glenburn). The site of the fort is now in a cultivated field on private property about seven miles northwest of Fall River Mills.

Lockhart's Fort

The first settlers in Fall River Valley were two men named Bowles and Rogers, who came there from Yreka in 1855. They brought heavy mill machinery with them by ox team and at once set to work cutting trees—many of which still lie where they fell. In the autumn other settlers joined them, among whom were the Lockhart brothers, who located on the site of Fall River Mills. Bowles, Rogers, and William Lockhart spent the winter at this place but were killed by Indians early the following spring. When Sam Lockhart returned to the valley, he was saved from a similar fate only by the timely arrival of a company of men from Yreka. The remains of "Lockhart's Fort," in which he made a gallant five-day fight for his life, may be seen today on the hill near Fall River Mills. Shortly after his arrival Sam Lockhart established a ferry where the California–Oregon stage road crossed the Pit River just below the mouth of Fall River. There, also, in the autumn of 1859 he built a bridge across the Pit River, only to have it washed away in the flood of 1862.

Castle Crags

Sharply outlined against a blue sky, the lofty gray turrets of Castle Crags afford a striking contrast to the dark green of the pine-clad mountains which surround them. This superb group rises more than 6,600 feet above sea-level and includes among its towers the Cathedral Spires, Castle Dome, Battle Rock, and others equally outstanding. Hidden high up in the recesses of Castle Crags lies Castle Lake, discovered by General Crook and his men while in pursuit of Indians.

Below this castled pile, at first known as Castle Rocks, lay historic Lower Soda Springs (called Castle Crag with the advent of the railroad in 1886) in a green meadow east of the river at the confluence of Soda Creek with the Sacramento. It was long the favorite camping-ground of the Shastas and other mountain Indian tribes. It is known that Lansford W. Hastings and sixteen companions, who had started from Rogue River, Oregon, in May 1843, camped at the Springs. An old fort of huge pine logs, known as Hastings' Barracks and said to have been built by him, once stood at the base of the hill on the north side of the little valley opposite the soda springs.

It is said that Hastings was so pleased with the magnificent location of Lower Soda Springs that he applied for a grant of land that should include both Castle Rocks and its snow-covered neighbor to the north, then known as Shasta Butte and now as Mount Shasta. The grant never materialized, as Hastings would not become a Mexican citizen and so could not receive it.

The first permanent settler in the region of Lower Soda Springs was Joe Doblondy, or "Mountain Joe," frontiersman and guide for Frémont. It is not known just when Mountain Joe came to this spot. On the Lower Soda Springs Ranch he tilled the soil, built houses, kept a sort of hotel, guided travelers up the Oregon Trail past Mount Shasta, and fought the Indians. He was also the friend of Joaquin Miller, who in 1854, when a mere boy, ran away from school in Oregon and came to live with Mountain Joe under the shadow of the Crags. "He was my ideal, my hero," wrote the poet in later years, and it was from Mountain Joe's seemingly inexhaustible mine of stories (first heard in Oregon), as well as from the majesty of the surroundings in which he lived, that Miller gained the inspiration for much of his finest poetry.

The first mining on Soda Creek was carried on in the early '50's by Bill Fox, who had escaped from the Yreka jail and had secreted himself in this isolated spot. He took out a large amount of gold, but was discovered and had to leave the country. Mountain Joe's tales of the fabulous Lost Cabin Mine and other supposedly rich diggings lured a large number of miners to Soda Creek and the Upper Sacramento River in the spring of 1855. The little valley was soon "a white sea of tents. Every bar on the Sacramento was the scene of excitement. . . . The rivers ran dark and sullen with sand and slime. The fish turned on their sides and died," or hid under the muddy clouds that obscured the deepest pools.

But the tales of wealth told by Mountain Joe proved unwarranted, and the army of angry, disgusted miners soon left the region. The results of their short sojourn, however, were not so easily removed. The fish and game on which the natives depended for their very existence had been killed or driven out, and the desire for vengeance stirred the warriors to action. One morning while Mountain Joe was absent a band of Indians, descending from Castle Rocks, plundered and burned the settlement at Lower Soda Springs. On his return, Mountain Joe and Joaquin Miller traced the flight of the marauders up the Rocks by the flour which they had unwittingly spilled along the way. With recruits from the neighboring settlements of Portuguese Flat and Dog Creek, Mountain Joe soon gathered together a company to punish the Indians. Judge R. P. Gibson, who had married the daughter of the chief of the Shastas, persuaded this tribe to join with the white settlers against the Pits and the other belligerent tribes.

The Battle of the Crags, graphically described by Joaquin Miller, youthful participant in the fight, took place on Battle Rock, the most prominent of all the spires and domes of the group. Directly under the highest crag in the northwest corner of the great castle the settlers, led by Gibson and his Shasta allies, fought face to face with their wild foes. Many on both sides were killed or wounded, and among the latter was young Miller, who afterward told how he was carried down the mountain side in a large buckskin bag tied to the back of a wrinkled old Indian squaw. Camp was made on the river bank below the site of the later Soda Springs Hotel, and there Joaquin was cared for by Mountain Joe until he recovered from his wounds. The Battle of the Crags was one of that long series of conflicts between the Indians and the white settlers of northeastern California which culminated in the Modoc War.

After passing through several hands, Lower Soda Springs came into the possession of G. W. Bailey on May 14, 1858. In order to reach his newly acquired property, he and his family were obliged to cross the river on a packer's log bridge. Bailey ranched and operated a wayside inn and summer resort at this spot until about 1887, when he sold the place to Leland Stanford for a summer home. For a short time it was called Stanford, but the name was soon changed to Castle Crag.

In 1892 the Pacific Improvement Company built the Castle Crag Tavern, the largest summer hotel ever erected in Shasta County. Its first manager was George Schoenwald, who was later manager of Hotel Del Monte at Monterey. The Castle Crag Tavern became famous, and people from all parts of the world visited it; but it was destroyed by fire in the early part of 1900 and was never rebuilt. A number of log cabins were erected in its stead and the place was operated as a summer camp until 1930, when it passed into private hands and was closed to the public—the first time in eighty-six years. It is now known as the Berry Estate. The site of the world-renowned Castle Crag Tavern is three miles south of Dunsmuir on a good dirt road one and a half miles from the Pacific Highway.

SOURCES

[Credit is here given for source material, and permission to quote is hereby acknowledged]

CAMP, CHARLES L. "James Clyman, His Diaries and Reminiscences," in *California Historical Society Quarterly*, IV, No. 2 to VI, No. 1 (June 1925–March 1927)

COX, ISAAC. *The Annals of Trinity County.* Commercial Book and Job Steam Printing Establishment, San Francisco, 1858

EDGAR, WILLIAM F. "Historical Notes of Old Land Marks in California," in *Annual Publications of the Historical Society of Southern California*, II (1893), 25–26

EDWARDS, PHILIP LEGET. *The Diary of Philip Leget Edwards.* The Grabhorn Press, San Francisco, 1932

HANNA, PHIL TOWNSEND. "Where Vulcan Works in California," in *Touring Topics*, XX, No. 7 (July 1928), 22–25, 46–47

HASTINGS, LANSFORD WARREN. *The Emigrants' Guide to California.* A facsimile of the edition of 1845 with introduction and notes by Charles H. Carey. Princeton University Press, Princeton, 1932

JOHNSTON, PHILIP. "Gold Trails of the Trinity," in *Touring Topics*, XXIV, No. 11 (November 1932), 10–17, 38

JONES, DAVID RHYS. "Pre-Pioneer Pathfinders, California–Oregon Trail, 1826–1846," in *Motor Land*, XXIX (August–November 1931)

MILLER, JOAQUIN (CINCINNATUS HEINE). "The Battle of Castle Crags," in *Leslie's Monthly* (March 1893)

———. *Life Amongst the Modocs.* Richard Bentley & Son, London, 1873

OGDEN, PETER SKENE. "Journals of Snake Expeditions, 1827–28 and 1828–29," with editorial notes by T. C. Elliott, in *Quarterly of the Oregon Historical Society*, XI (December 1910), 355–397

READING, PIERSON BARTON. "Journal of Pierson Barton Reading," in *Quarterly of the Society of California Pioneers*, VII, No. 3 (September 1930)

SHURTLEFF, DR. BENJAMIN. "Shasta," in *Overland Monthly*, XXXVI, No. 212 (August 1900), 153–158

SOUTHERN, MAY H. "The Trails of '49," in *Courier-Free Press*, Redding, California, August 1930

WILKES, CHARLES. *Narrative of the United States Exploring Expedition during the Years 1838, 1839, 1840, 1841, 1842.* 5 volumes and an atlas. Lea & Blanchard, Philadelphia, 1845

WILLIAMS, HOWEL. "Geology of the Lassen Volcanic National Park, California," in *University of California Publications. Bulletin of the Department of Geological Sciences*, XXI, No. 8 (December 1932), 195–385

SIERRA COUNTY

SIERRA (Spanish for "saw-toothed mountains") is the first part of the name, Sierra Nevada, applied to the mountain range which extends from Tehachapi Pass in the south to Lassen Peak in the north, so called because of the irregular, saw-toothed outline of the range and its heavy mantle of snow in winter, Nevada being Spanish for "snow-covered." Sierra County was organized from a part of Yuba County in 1852 and Downieville was made its county seat.

Goodyear's Bar

Superb mountain peaks look down upon the old river camp at Goodyear's Bar—Saddle Back, Monte Cristo, Fur Cap, Grizzly Peak, and others—while beneath it lie the shining, jade-green reaches of the North Fork of the Yuba River, joined at this point by the tumbling, ice-cold waters of Goodyear's Creek. The small triangular flat on which a horde of miners once lived and worked has today not more than a dozen inhabitants, with only a few scattered houses which stand almost upon the abandoned diggings.

Goodyear's Bar, settled in the summer of 1849 by Andrew and Miles Goodyear and two companions, was one of the first mining camps on the North Fork of the Yuba. By 1852 the place had become the center for a number of lively camps up and down the river as well as on the neighboring ridges. Near by were the Ranse Doddler and Hoodoo bars, with St. Joe's Bar two miles below and Woodville (at first known as Cutthroat Bar) farther up the river. On the steep slope above St. Joe's Bar was Nigger Slide.

The diggings in the vicinity yielded rich returns. At Kennedy Ranch, located at the upper end of Goodyear's Bar, Pete Yore's men "cleaned up" $2,000 in gold dust from a single wheelbarrow load of earth, a find which was kept secret from the other miners until a considerable harvest had been gathered.

Goodyear's Bar prospered through the '50's, but in the early '60's, with the gradual exhaustion of ore deposits along the river, its decline set in. This was further hastened by the devastating fire which swept through the town in 1864. The old river diggings will never again yield great wealth, but the summer vacationist is today discovering that the region offers a more lasting treasure in the joys of mountain life.

There was a Chinatown at Goodyear's Bar which covered a space of considerable size. The place was disdained by white men because the gold in its diggings could be obtained only by long hours of patient and laborious toil.

Downieville

Downieville, in one of the most rugged and elevated regions in the state, is set like a toy village in a gorgeous wooded amphitheater bounded on all sides by lofty, pine-clad mountains. No county seat in California has a more picturesque setting or a history more dramatic. At its door the North Fork of the North Fork of the Yuba River flows into the larger stream, a part of that "network of forks and tributaries which reach through deep canyons upwards into the higher altitudes of the Sierra."

Penetrating this well-nigh inaccessible mountain fastness, William Downie (usually called "Major" Downie), a Scotchman, for whom the town was later named, arrived at "The Forks" in November 1849. With him were ten Negro sailors, an Indian, an Irish lad named Michael Deverney, and Jim Crow, a Kanaka, who later became quite a notorious character in the North Yuba River country and for whom Jim Crow Canyon was named. Erecting a few log cabins, the Major and his men wintered at the flat just above the present town site. Some of the men spent their time delving into the rocky crevices under the snow, taking out as much as one hundred and two hundred dollars in gold each day.

A veritable stampede of miners into the vicinity took place the following spring, resulting in rich strikes on all the neighboring bars and flats. "The Forks" soon became the center of a wide circle of camps reaching up and down both rivers and their tributaries, and before long the name of the place was changed to Downieville, in honor of Major Downie. By 1851 the population of the town had increased to more than five thousand.

Stories told of the miners and their life on the Yuba indicate the phenomenal richness of the placers. On Durgan Flat (where the Courthouse now stands) Frank Anderson and three companions took out ore valued at $12,900 in eleven days from a claim only sixty feet square. One day's yield was valued at $4,300, while the total yield during the first six months that the location was worked brought over $80,000. Jersey Flat, just below the present town, at the spot where Downie and his party first made temporary camp, was a close second to Durgan Flat in production. According to the Major, Jim Crow killed a salmon weighing fourteen pounds here, and after the fish had been cooked for supper gold was found at the bottom of the kettle. At Zumwalt Flat each man averaged five ounces a day for three and one-half hours' labor, while at Tin Cup Diggings, opposite Zumwalt Flat, three men who worked there in 1850 were said to have made it a rule to fill a tin cup with gold before quitting work at night (hence the name), nor did they find it at all arduous to attain their goal.

But the miners were not satisfied, and in order to get out the gold that still lay in the bed rock of the river they flumed the entire Yuba between Downieville and Goodyear's Bar out of its channel. With the coming of the winter's floods, however, their means of harnessing the tremendous forces of the mountains was swept away like so much straw.

There were other diggings in the canyon country which brought vast wealth. At Gold Bluff, two miles above Downieville, in the fall of 1850 a nugget of pure gold was taken out which weighed twenty-five pounds, the largest ever found on the North Yuba. The black slate of this locale continued to produce thousands of dollars up to the time of the World War, when mining activities were discontinued. Below Slug Canyon (so called because of the coarse, slug gold found there) the Steamboat Company on Steamboat Bar took out an average of $5,000 a day for several weeks during 1851. At the head of this canyon and about three miles south of Downieville is the City of Six Quartz Mine, a famous producer in the early days. Another famous mine, Monte Cristo, is located on the south slope of Monte Cristo a thousand feet above Goodyear's Creek and three miles northwest of Downieville. It was opened in 1854 and at one time the adjoining camp had as large a population as Downieville.

To Downieville, the center of this wild region, which swarmed with all types of men, came the young Congregational minister, Rev. William C. Pond, and his wife in 1855, at a time when gambling saloons with their shining bars and roulette wheels did a thriving nightly business; when lumbering freight wagons, alias "mountain schooners," and long lines of picturesque pack mules, marshaled into town by their no less picturesque Mexican drivers, afforded the only means of travel; and when sugar sold for four dollars a pound and boots and shoes for from twenty-five to a hundred and fifty dollars a pair.

Pond preached his first sermon in a structure called the "Downieville Amphitheater" on "Piety Flat." Within a few months after his arrival a church was erected, but before services could be held in the new edifice it was destroyed by fire. The embers were barely cool when a miner reached the minister's home from his mountain cabin four miles away with the offer, "A hundred dollars, Mr. Pond, for another church." A substantial basement structure of brick and stone was built at once and in it Rev. Mr. Pond preached until 1865. In that year, however, with the marked decline of mining activity in the region, services in the Downieville church were discontinued, the building was sold, and Pond went to Petaluma to carry on his work.

Pond's influence, like that of most of the other pioneer ministers of California, reached far beyond the home parish. "Sometimes in unoccupied theaters, sometimes in the dining-rooms of the hotels or of miners' boarding houses, sometimes in miners' cabins" in outlying districts, he imparted his message. Regular services were held also at the two out-stations of Goodyear's Bar and Monte Cristo. In addition, Pond served as county superintendent of schools for three terms, making his influence still more far-reaching.

Downieville remains much as it was in the early gold days. Along the crooked main street, which is still lined by board walks, stand the same buildings, now old and quaint looking. In the shade of the huge old locusts in front of the St. Charles Hotel old-timers habitually gather today, just as others have done for seventy-five years past. In one of the trees a deep hollow has been worn by the heavy boots of these countless loungers, as they have sat tiptilted in their chairs with their feet against the tree. Along the river banks and up the mountain sides the old-fashioned houses, set amid their aged locust and fruit trees, line the shady streets and alleyways, making the residential part of Downieville one of the town's most charming features.

One of the first buildings in Downieville (thought to have been erected in 1852), a stone structure with heavy iron doors and shuttered windows, has been restored and presented to the town for use as a museum by the heirs of J. M. B. Meroux, a pioneer. The Native Daughters and Native Sons of the Golden West of Downieville dedicated it to the Pioneers of Sierra County on July 3, 1932. The walls of this building are made entirely of flat rocks laid horizontally, a very early type of construction. The nucleus of the new museum is a collection of valuable relics gathered by former Sheriff George C. Bynon, displayed until recently in the Courthouse.

In Costa's grocery store, another stone structure which has stood since 1852, one may see the $1,000 scales which were brought into Downieville by pack mule three-quarters of a century ago. These scales, made in Boston, Massachusetts, were formerly used in the bank and on them gold valued at several million dollars was weighed. They are still used for weighing the gold dust and nuggets brought in each month by river miners.

Across the river from the business section stands the little white courthouse with its shuttered square tower and its lofty-ceiled, old-fashioned courtroom. Here there are two old cannon, an arrastra wheel which was used by the pioneers to grind the gold-impregnated quartz, and at the rear of the building the gaunt old gallows. At the very edge of the courthouse lawn are the diggings—huge piles of granite boulders marking the rich river claims where miners in 1850 and 1851 averaged one or two hundred dollars daily. Here the patient Chinese came after their white brothers had ceased to consider the location worth while. Lifting the heavy stones one by one, they cleared out the bed of the North Yuba, leaving mammoth heaps as evidence of their Herculean labors.

Upon the site of the present steel bridge, where the first structure formerly stood, was enacted the closing scene of a pathetic tragedy in 1851, when Juanita, a little Mexican dance-hall girl, was hanged for the murder of Jack Cannon, an Australian, who had attempted to force himself into her room. Contemporary opinion did not condone this action of the miners' court, and much criticism was aroused in the United States and abroad.

Sierra City

Following the line of the old stage road from Downieville, a modern highway sweeps up the tortuous canyon of the North Fork of the Yuba River. Above green alpine meadows and old apple orchards, where an occasional farmhouse or miner's cabin may still be seen, the road leads past the little old village of Loganville to Sierra City (thirteen miles from Downieville), nestled at the base of the majestic Sierra Buttes, which tower almost a mile above the village.

These jagged granite peaks look down upon a region of great scenic grandeur which is redolent with historic mining lore, for in the feverish gold-rush days of '49 and the early '50's camps sprang up throughout the entire section. The tributary streams of the North Fork were panned to the very base of the Buttes, and even the almost perpendicular sides of the granite pile were climbed in the relentless search for gold.

In the spring of 1850 P. A. Haven and Joseph Zumwalt located on the site of Sierra City, in a region then thickly populated with Indians. In the same year a Mr. Murphy discovered the Sierra Buttes Quartz Ledge. Here a mine was located which has proved to be one of the state's big producers and is still in operation. By 1852 tunnels penetrated the craggy Sierra Buttes in all directions, and the miners were using as many as twenty arrastras, run by mules, to pulverize the rock. During that winter a heavy blanket of snow and avalanches from the steep mountain above crushed every house in the mining camp. In the face of this disaster it was not until 1858 that a permanent settlement was established on the town site.

Another rich quartz deposit of the Sierra Buttes was opened up at the Monumental Quartz Mine, where on August 18, 1860, an immense gold nugget, weighing 1,596 troy ounces and valued at approximately $25,500, was taken out, the second largest to be found in California.

Among the interesting historic structures still standing in Sierra City is the Busch Building, a sturdy old edifice on Main Street, erected in 1871, the lower two stories of which are of brick while the third is of wood. The building was commenced during the Fourth of July celebration and the ceremonies were conducted by the E.C.V. or E. Clampus Vitus, which had been organized in Sierra City in 1857. The letters "E.C.V." still mark the doorway in the old building through which the "Clampers" were wont to pass. The society, under the title of E. Clampus Vitus Redivivus, has recently been reorganized by a few members of the California Historical Society who are interested in preserving the lore of '49 and the '50's.

In the center of the town is a quaint old fire tower in which is housed a two-wheel hose cart, which was brought around the Horn in the early '50's. Sierra City, fortunately, has never been devastated by fire, as most early mining camps were, owing to the proximity of numerous streams which come tumbling down the mountain side. These watercourses have been harnessed to furnish power not only for the mills at the mines, as in the old days, but to generate electricity and to supply other needs of the village.

Forest City

Forest City, eight miles south of Downieville, was one of the liveliest camps in Sierra County during the middle '50's. According to Fariss and Smith, the first white men to come to the site (sometimes called Forks of Oregon Creek) were a company of sailors, who found gold there in the summer of 185?. They named their camp Brownsville in honor of one of their members. Hittell, however, cites as the probable discoverer Michael Savage, who came there in 1853.

When "the place began to look like a town," after the establishment of the first store or trading-post, it was sometimes called by the Indian name "Yomana," said to have been used by the natives to designate the high bluff, just above the village, which was their sacred hill or holy ground. The names borne by the mining camp which subsequently grew up there have given rise to some confusion as to their origin. As the champions of the musical "Yomana" and those of the plain geographical designation "Forks of Oregon" were equally divided, it was decided to name the town after the first woman who should come to reside there. Soon afterward the wife of W. S. Davis, spoken of by Hittell as "Mary" and by Wells and Bancroft as "Eliza," arrived, and the town was called after her, either "Marietta" or "Elizaville." The second woman resident was Mrs. Maria Sparks, for whom "Marietta" was also fitting. Finally, a third woman arrived upon the scene, the wife of Captain Mooney, a woman with a bent for newspaper writing. Now Mrs. Mooney's Christian name was Forest, and she invariably signed her journalistic effusions "Forest City." She also used her persuasive powers upon her fellow-citizens, with the result that the name Forest City was finally adopted instead of Marietta or Elizaville. Thus, Hittell concludes, Forest City derived its present name, not from the magnificent forest of conifers surrounding it, as is generally supposed, "but from Mrs. Forest Mooney, the newspaper correspondent."

Having worked out the streams, bars, and banks about Forest City, the miners began to tunnel into the mountain to the south. The name of one of these tunnels, the Alleghany, was given to a flourishing camp on the opposite side of the mountain, where pay dirt was struck in 1855. The town of Alleghany increased in importance so rapidly the following year that the entire population of Forest City flocked to the new camp, leaving the older place an empty shell. When a rich strike was made in the Bold Mountain district in 1870, Forest City awoke from its Rip Van Winkle sleep, only to relapse after a few years into the quiet hamlet of today. Except for the dearth of customers the old hotel and the saloon present much the same appearance as in the days when gold "dust . . . . was tendered for the drinks" at the latter place. Steep-roofed houses clinging precariously to the mountain on either side of the canyon, reached only over narrow, precipitous roads, give the village a picturesquely alpine air.

Alleghany

Alleghany may be reached either from Goodyear's Bar, about eleven miles to the north, or from North Columbia, about eighteen miles southwest, the latter road going by way of Foote's Crossing on the Middle Fork of the Yuba River.

The Goodyear's Bar approach is entirely feasible for the modern tourist, but the other road cannot be recommended except to the most fearless of drivers. That portion of the Foote's Crossing route which dips down into the Middle Fork has been described by those few venturesome motorists who have dared to negotiate it as "America's most spectacular mile of mountain road"; or, "Few roads in Switzerland are more spectacular"; or again, "It is one road for which every driver has a wholesome respect!"

This fearfully picturesque thoroughfare was built by A. D. Foote as a toll road at about the time the automobile was coming into general use. The rapid development of this means of travel, which was wholly unforeseen by Foote, caused his financial ruin. The road is a marvel of engineering skill. Cut into the very face of a stupendous precipice high above the deep gorge of the Middle Fork, it takes a narrow, thread-like course along the almost perpendicular cliffs reaching hundreds of feet above and below. A bend in the tortuous defile now and then reveals the nature of this awesome roadway and the daring and skill of its builder. The rock walls, above and below, are of the type known as dry masonry, and are "so perfectly matched and carefully laid that, after decades of winter storms, soaking water, and swelling ice, they remain in perfect condition." In places the canyon walls are so nearly perpendicular that huge iron bars had to be anchored far into the solid rock underneath the roadbed.

At the bottom of the canyon is the Foote's Crossing Bridge, where a roadhouse once sheltered the wayfarer. Recently tents have again appeared along the river banks, and men are working the bed rock of the stream (in places from thirty to forty feet below the present river bottom) for whatever gold may remain there. Beyond, the great gorge of the Middle Fork converges with that of Kanaka Creek to make one immense canyon.

Kanaka Creek was discovered in May 1850 by one of several parties of Hawaiian prospectors sent out by a certain Captain Ross, the reputed son of King Kamehameha. A general rush of miners followed. Kanaka Creek proved to be extraordinarily rich in the precious mineral and some very large nuggets were taken out.

Climbing up the north side of Kanaka Creek Canyon to Alleghany, new vistas of scenic grandeur successively unfold along the way. Evidences of one-time mining activities are visible on every hand: masses of green serpentine rock, polished and of great beauty; old "glory holes," reminding one of vanished hopes; deserted mines visible far up the wooded ravines. On nearing Alleghany the country becomes increasingly rocky, and glimpses may be had of a few of the active mines of this world-famous district: the Madden, Rainbow, Oriental, Spoohn Gold, and others, the smaller ones producing $1,500 or $2,000 each year and the larger ones millions. According to authentic record, one chunk of ore found in this region weighed 163 pounds and brought $27,000 from the mint, and from one pocket as much as $80,000 was taken. Some of these rich deposits have been lost through faulty surveys or the sudden caving-in of a tunnel and have never been relocated, as happened in the case of the old Red Star Mine, from which as much as $80,000 was taken from one shoot in 1912. Hope of recovering such leads is continually reviving, and the fascination and mystery of the quest lures the modern treasure-hunter as it did the Argonauts of old.

Alleghany is still essentially a "gold camp"—one of the few left in California—where each of the five hundred or more citizens is either directly or indirectly connected with the gold-mining industry. Clinging like a cluster of cliff swallows' nests to the side of the mountain, the houses of the village are built on a series of terraces connected by streets that approach each other at varying levels. The lowest of these narrow benches has an elevation of about one hundred feet above Kanaka Creek, while the uppermost shelf is about six hundred feet higher. In pioneer days, when the village was snowbound for weeks at a time, the people of Alleghany communicated with the citizens of Forest City on the opposite side of the mountain by means of the long tunnel which early miners had driven through in their search for gold.

Alleghany stands on the ancient channel of one of the numerous tributaries of that great antediluvian river known as the Blue Gravel or Blue Lead, which extended from near the northern boundary line of Sierra County in a south-easterly direction to the southern line of Placer County at Forest Hill. Here, as elsewhere, much of the old channel was covered by lava flows, which the miners were obliged to penetrate in order to reach the rich deposits of gold imbedded in the underlying gravel. By tunneling and drifting, and, in some places, by means of hydraulic mining, they took immense fortunes from these ancient accumulations during the '50's and the '60's and on into the '90's.

Just below Alleghany the famous Original Sixteen-to-One Mine (so called to distinguish it from the Sixteen-to-One above Washington in Nevada County) was located in 1896 by Thomas J. Bradbury. Year after year Bradbury lived at Alleghany and worked his claim on a small scale. Then in 1907 the rich Tightner Mine was discovered near by. In 1916 it was found that this location and the Original Sixteen-to-One were tapping the same vein, its apex in the backyard of the old Bradbury home. This discovery led to the consolidation of the Tightner and the Twenty-One (another adjacent property) with the Sixteen-to-One as the Original Sixteen-to-One Company. The combined claim continues to produce thousands of dollars for its owners.

Following the line of the ancient Blue Lead river channel across Kanaka Creek Canyon, auriferous gravel deposits are found on the opposite slopes at Chip's Flat, and again at what was once the mining camp of Minnesota Flat on the other side of the ridge. An outcropping of blue gravel at the latter location was discovered in July 1852 by an old English sailor, known to his fellows as "Chips," because he had previously been employed as ship's carpenter. Later "Chips" located even richer diggings on the northern slope of the same ridge, at Chip's Flat.

Gold beyond the Mountains!

Towering thousands of feet above the towns of the North Yuba River Canyon "a huge mass of mountains crowned with castellated peaks and knife-like crests forms an effective barrier to direct travel" into the old mining districts of northwestern Sierra County. In order to reach this section by automobile one must turn north above Sierra City and follow a circuitous route by way of Gold Lake, Mohawk, and Johnsville to Gibsonville, or one must retrace to Bullard's Bar in Yuba County and from there proceed northward along the Marysville–Quincy Highway via Challenge and Strawberry Valley, through La Porte in Plumas County, and thence to Gibsonville.

This remote section of Sierra County was first prospected in the spring of 1850, when gold was found along the ridge between the North Fork of the Yuba River and the South Fork of the Feather River by an old sea captain named Sears, whose name was later given to the ridge.

Returning to the Yuba, Sears prepared to lead a company of prospectors to the scene of his discovery. But the news that Sears had "struck it rich" spread, and before proceeding very far his party found that they were being followed by a group under the leadership of a man by the name of Gib-

son. When ordered to turn back, Gibson's men refused, saying that the mountains of California were as free to them as to any man, and that if there was gold beyond those mountains they were going to get their share. A compromise was at length reached and the two parties proceeded to Sears' Ridge, where operations were begun at a place afterward known as Sears' Diggings.

Before long a number of other locations were staked out in the vicinity, some of which proved to be richer than the original strike. Gibson, who was an especially enterprising and intelligent prospector, discovered very rich deposits on an adjoining ridge overlooking Little Slate Creek, a site which later developed into the large and thriving camp of Gibsonville, which even as late as 1870 was still a busy place. But with the passing years Gibsonville, in its wind-swept isolation, has grown more deserted and more ghost-like. Its dozen or more little old wooden houses straggle up and down the crazy village street like wizened dwarfs, bleached almost to the whiteness of skeletons by the action of the elements. Since the summer of 1932, however, renewed activity at the neighboring mines has instilled new life into the village and today nearly all the cabins are again occupied.

The enterprising and tight-lipped Gibson struck another rich deposit at a place which became known as Secret Ravine because he had kept the location a secret from his comrades, who charged him with playing them false. The resultant dissension among Gibson's followers and growing dissatisfaction among Sears's men caused a scattering of the two groups, resulting in new discoveries in all directions. Many new camps were established, among them being Howland's Flat, Pine Grove, Potosi, St. Louis, Queen City, Poker Flat, Craig's Flat, Deadwood, Chandlerville, Port Wine, Scales, Poverty Hill, Brandy City, Hepsidam, Whiskey Diggings (or Newark), McMahon's, Morristown, and Eureka City at the source of Goodyear's Creek. Howland's Flat, on the north side of Table Rock at an elevation of six thousand feet, reached such prominence in 1869 as a result of hydraulic operations that it was classed as one of the populous camps of the Sierra. St. Louis, staked out on the site of Sears' Diggings in the fall of 1852 by a party of Missourians, enjoyed a brief period of prosperity until it was swept by fire in 1857. Later, during the '60's, a short-lived hydraulic boom revived the place.

Like Gibsonville, these once populous towns of the High Sierra have become mere "ghost cities," marked only by weird piles of long-forgotten diggings, lonely ruins of miners' cabins, or decaying frames of former village houses.

SOURCES

[Credit is here given for source material, and permission to quote is hereby acknowledged]

California Mining Journal, featuring Nevada and Sierra County mines. I, No. 1 (August 1931)

Coy, Owen Cochran. *Gold Days*, of the series *California*, edited by John Russell McCarthy. Powell Publishing Company, Los Angeles, 1929

Downie, Major William. *Hunting for Gold*. The California Publishing Company, San Francisco, 1893

Fariss and Smith. *Illustrated History of Plumas, Lassen, and Sierra Counties*. Fariss & Smith, San Francisco, 1882

Hanson, George Emmanuel. *The Early History of Yuba River Valley*. Master's thesis, University of California, August 1924

Hittell, Theodore H. *History of California*. 4 volumes. N. J. Stone & Company, San Francisco, 1898

Johnston, Philip. "Relics of the Gold-Rush among the Northern Diggin's," in *Touring Topics*, XXIV, No. 1 (January 1932), 10–25, 45–46

Pond, William C. *Gospel Pioneering in California*. Privately printed, Oberlin, Ohio, 1921

Wolff, J. L. *Yuba River Canyon Country*. Manuscript, 1932

SISKIYOU COUNTY

SISKIYOU COUNTY (Siskiyou is an Indian name of unde-termined meaning) was created in 1852 from the northern part of Shasta County and a part of what was formerly Klamath County. Yreka has always been its county seat.

Mount Shasta

"Lonely as God, and white as a winter moon, Mount Shasta starts up sudden and solitary from the heart of the great black forests of Northern California." Thus did the indelible picture of this majestic peak imprint itself upon the mind and heart of Joaquin Miller, who spent several years of his youth within the radius of its influence. The beautiful Indian legend of how the Great Spirit "made this mountain first of all" was told him by the simple people among whom he lived, and in that story was incorporated the tradition long held by the Shasta Indians that "before the white man came they could see the fire ascending from the mountain by night and the smoke by day, every time they chose to look in that direction."

"Shasta," wrote John Muir, "is a fire-mountain, an old volcano gradually accumulated and built up into the blue deep of the sky by successive eruptions of ashes and molten lava. . . . . Periods of quiescence intervened between many distinct eruptions. . . . . Then followed a strange contrast. The glacial winter came on . . . . a down-crawling mantle of ice upon a fountain of smouldering fire, crushing and grinding its brown, flinty lavas, and thus degrading and remodeling the entire mountain. . . . . The summit is now a mass of ruins . . . considerably lowered, and the sides . . . . deeply grooved and fluted. . . . . Beneath the smooth and snowy surface the fountain fires are still aglow. The glaciers . . . . are still flowing onward . . . . sculpturing the mountain with stern, resistless energy."

Five of these glaciers—Hotlum, Bolam, Whitney, Win-tun, and Konwakiton—still scour the sides of the great mountain, principally on the north and east slopes above the 10,000-foot level. Hundreds of streams are fed by these ice rivers, which "have a habit of disappearing as you follow down their courses. The porous slopes are ever ready to absorb moisture and to allow it to flow underground un-impeded until, at the lower slopes, it gushes forth in mighty springs that give birth, full-fledged, to the McCloud and Sacramento rivers and other important streams." Big Spring, one such source of the Sacramento River, gushes from the mountain side in an ice-cold, tumultuous flood just one mile north of Mount Shasta City on the summer camp grounds of the Chico State Teachers College.

John Muir, in one of his rare word-pictures, describes the fountain-head of the McCloud. "Think of a spring giv-ing rise to a river," he wrote, "a spring fifty yards wide at the mouth, issuing from the base of a lava bluff with wild songs—not gloomily from a dark cavey mouth, but from a world of ferns and mosses gold and green."

The Mud Creek area, four miles northeast of McCloud, was devastated in August 1924 by a vast flow of mud washed down by the melting snows of the Konwakiton Glacier. Water and sediment spread out from the creek bed over the country, killing a vast extent of timber and leaving, in its stead, a desolate waste.

Shasta's snowy summit dominates the landscape for a hundred miles and is visible for almost twice that distance, but strangely enough it remained unknown until a little over a century ago. It is possible that Spanish explorers in 1817 observed it from a distance when Luís Argüello led an expedition from San Francisco by boat up the Sacramento River, reaching as far north as the mouth of the Feather. Fray Narciso Durán, diarist, made this entry in his journal on May 20: "At about ten leagues to the northwest of this place we saw the very high hill called by soldiers that went near its slope 'Jesús María.' It is entirely covered with snow." There is considerable doubt, however, that the moun-tain which these early explorers saw was Mount Shasta.

The first recorded mention of Mount Shasta was made by Peter Skene Ogden, a Hudson's Bay Company trapper, who wintered on the streams east and north of the mountain in 1826–1827, and who on February 14, 1827, wrote in his journal: "There is a mountain equal in height to Mount Hood or Vancouver I have named Mt. Sastise," and in reference to the stream he wrote: "I have named this river Sastise River." This is the first known mention of the name Shasta as applied to mountain and river.

Shasta is undoubtedly a word of Indian origin, although both derivation and meaning are uncertain. Ogden says that he derived "these names from the tribes of Indians" living there, and, according to Powers, Shas-ti-ka was the tribal name of the natives in this region. Alleged Russian or French origins for the name (tchastal, meaning "white," and chaste, meaning "pure") are now generally discredited. Its earliest known appearance (as "Shatasla") was in 1814, in the journal of Alexander Henry.

English and American explorers during the early part of the nineteenth century viewed the great mountain and placed it on their maps under a varied choice of spellings: Lieuten-ant Emmons, of the Wilkes Exploring Expedition, who saw it on October 3, 1841, mentioned it in his report and on accompanying maps as "Mount Shaste"; Frémont, who five years later saw it while on his third expedition, referred to it in his subsequent report as "Shastl" and on his map of 1848 as "Tsashtl"; Lieutenant Robert S. Williamson, of the United States Topographical Engineers, in his report of the expedition which surveyed for a railroad route from Oregon to the Sacramento Valley in 1851 and 1855, designated the mountain as "Shasta Butte," butte being a name freely used by American trappers in the West.

The first recorded ascent of Mount Shasta appears to have been that made by Captain E. D. Pearce (Pierce) in August or September of 1854. Shortly after, Pearce led a party of thirteen prominent citizens from Yreka, Humbug, and Scott valleys to the summit. Other ascents followed. Israel S. Diehl, of Yreka, climbed to the top alone on Octo-ber 11, 1855. He was followed by Anton Roman, a German, in April 1856. Joaquin Miller, who ascended the mountain several times, climbed it for the last time in 1858 when a lad of seventeen. It was his book, *Life Amongst the Modocs*, written in London in 1873 which made Mount Shasta known to the world.

In the summer of 1859 N. C. Mayhew and two com-panions spent the night at the hot spring just below the topmost crest, an experience duplicated in 1870 by Clarence King and three companions while engaged in the Survey of the Fortieth Parallel, and by John Muir and Jerome Fay on April 30, 1875. The previous November John Muir had observed the storm-clad grandeur of its summit at close range.

The first scientific ascent of the mountain was made in September 1862 by Josiah Dwight Whitney, of the Whitney State Geological Survey, William H. Brewer, his chief as-sistant, and Chester Averill, but it was not until 1870 that its glaciers were discovered by Clarence King. Captain A. F. Rodgers, of the United States Coast and Geodetic Survey, in 1875 began a series of observations from the summit. In October of that year he erected a steel monument, some fourteen feet high and capped by a nickel reflector, on the highest point of the topmost crest. This monument stood for many years. In the summer of 1877 John Muir visited Mount Shasta's forests and wild gardens with Sir Joseph Hooker, the great English botanist, and Professor Asa Gray, America's foremost botanist at that time. B. A. Colonna, of the Coast and Geodetic Survey, spent nine successive days and nights on the summit of Mount Shasta in July and August of 1878. At the end of that period he succeeded in exchanging heliograph flashes with observers posted on Mount St. Helena, 192 miles to the south.

The latest figure for the height of Mount Shasta as given by the United States Coast and Geodetic Survey is 14,162 feet. Geographically, Mount Shasta is "a connecting link between three mountain masses," although a part of none of them—"the Sierra Nevada, a hundred miles to the southeast; the Cascade Range, whose southern terminus is but fifty miles to the northeast; and the diversified ridges of the Klamath Mountains, just westward across Strawberry Valley." The Mount Shasta Recreation Area, including 29,620 acres of forest, river, and mountain vacation lands, was set aside by the national government in 1926 for the use and enjoyment of the general public.

Through the efforts of M. Hall McAllister, a stone lodge, known as the Shasta Alpine Lodge, was erected in 1922 nine miles from Mount Shasta City at Horse Camp (7,992 feet) under the auspices of the Sierra Club. Two San Franciscans made the first winter stay at the lodge when they climbed the mountain on February 22, 1924. The lodge affords a shelter to storm-bound mountaineers throughout the year, and during the summer months a record is kept by the attendant of all those making the ascent, so that rescue parties may be sent out to search for any who fail to return within a reasonable time.

The Modoc Lava Beds

For the archaeologists and the student of early Western history, as well as for lovers of unique natural formations, the Modoc Lava Beds in the Modoc National Forest (proclaimed the Lava Beds National Monument by President Coolidge in 1925) hold a distinct fascination. The old Indian name for the region is said to have meant "The land of burned-out fires," and its labyrinthine caves, seemingly bottomless fumaroles, and extinct craters testify to the fitness of that designation. This vast mesa-like formation is broken here and there by buttes or cinder cones several hundred feet high, but the harsh outlines of these frowning volcanic masses are relieved by the grateful contrast of blossoming plants and shrubs, clumps of pine or juniper, and the softening beauty of varicolored rock.

The center of the region is sixty miles due east of Yreka. The entire section is traversed by a very fair automobile road, along which one may visit the numerous caves—the prehistoric camping ground of a forgotten people, and less than a century ago the last refuge of the Indian in the West. This was the "castle" of the Modocs, their "stone house, into which no white man could come so long as they cared to defend it." Walls and entrances to many of the rooms in this gigantic castle are still decorated with aboriginal pictographs done in red, yellow, and black.

In and out among the gray and "twisted" rocks the road leads by Indian Well, where moccasined feet, in centuries long past, wore a trail which still entices the adventurous to clamber down through a worn-out crater into the vast interior of a dark cavern. An ancient Indian sign painted on the rocks near the entrance directs the way to two pools of crystal-clear ice water which seem never to diminish, even during the driest seasons, and from which present-day tourists from a public campground near by obtain water.

Near Indian Well are Labyrinth Cave, Skull Cave, Symbol Cave, and Symbol Bridge. Labyrinth Cave is a series of subterranean cells connected by a maze of tunnels running in all directions, the main gallery being almost two miles in length, with a part of the distance navigable only in a crouching position. Skull Cave, the largest cavern in the region yet explored, has three stories at its lower end. A river of ice covers the floor of the lower chamber and in it are imbedded bones of now extinct animals and even scattered human bones. From the numerous skulls of Rocky Mountain sheep, prong-horned antelope, and other animals found there the cave derived its name. On the rocks and about one of the entrances to Symbol Cave, Indian pictographs appear as clear and unfaded as the day they were placed there by the artists or medicine men of a vanished race.

Beyond Symbol Bridge and Antelope Well, with its abundant, clear, sweet water, is Bearfoot Cave, a series of rock and ice chambers connected by underground corridors. It is located on private land and guides are maintained by the summer resort located there. One of the chambers contains a river of ice that never melts, while at the opposite end of the abyss another immense cavity holds an unfailing water supply, which is used by the resort. Sentinel Cave, Crystal Cave, Chocolate Bridge, Painted Cave, Bearpaw, Jove's Thunderbolt, and "The Chimneys" (large vents projecting twenty feet or more above the ground and extending straight down into the earth to a depth so great that a rock dropped from the top is never heard to strike bottom) are among the natural phenomena most accessible to the modern tourist. The Catacombs Cavern, the most beautiful of the entire group, resembles an ancient cathedral. The roof is "buttressed by massive columns, the walls and ceilings frescoed by a delicate coral-like formation traced in a thousand fanciful designs." About 150 caves in this interesting group have been discovered and have been explored more or less thoroughly.

To the south of the Lava Beds is Glass Mountain (7,649 feet), a gigantic mass of jet-black obsidian glass which glistens and sparkles in the sunlight. At its western base lies Medicine Lake, its deep-blue waters well stocked with fish and its wide, sandy beaches bordered by dense stands of lodge-pole pine. A public camp, maintained by the Forest Service, is located on the lake shore. To the northeast rises Mount Hoffmann (7,927 feet), while to the southwest are Little Mount Hoffmann and Little Glass Mountain.

Sheep Rock and Pluto's Cave

At the foot of Shasta Pass twenty miles north of Sisson's Station (now Mount Shasta City), the first wagon road from the Sacramento Valley to Yreka led over a low divide from the eastern slopes of the mountain into Shasta Valley. There the bold and craggy summit of Sheep Rock rises 2,000 feet above the gray sagebrush and sand of the valley and 5,500 feet above the level of the sea. The rock's several square miles of comparatively level surface, dotted with bunch grass, long afforded one of the chief winter pastures of the wild mountain sheep that came down from the lofty ridges of Mount Shasta to the warm lava crags and plateaus of Sheep Rock, where the snow never lies deep. Cattlemen and sheepmen still follow the ruts of the old stage road at Sheep Rock.

John Muir draws a thrilling word-picture of the leaping or "diving" habits of the Shasta flocks that once made this place their winter rendezvous. The facts were related by a stock-raiser who lived at the foot of the rock, and who had observed the movements of the sheep each winter. On one occasion hunters had pursued the little band to a narrow bench or lava headland 150 feet and more above the floor of the valley and very nearly perpendicular. There the hunters had expected to trap the entire flock, only to find themselves eluded by the wily animals, which "made the frightful descent without evincing any extraordinary concern, hugging the rock closely, and controlling the velocity of their half-falling, half-leaping movements by striking at short intervals and holding back with their cushioned, rubber feet upon small ledges and roughened inclines until near the bottom, when they 'sailed off' into the free air and lighted on their feet, but with their bodies so nearly in a vertical position that they appeared to be diving."

Near Sheep Rock in a north–northwesterly direction from the foot of the pass is Pluto's Cave, "a long cavern sloping to the northward, nearly a mile in length, thirty or forty feet wide, and fifty or more in height, regular in form and direction like a railroad tunnel, and probably formed by the flowing away of a current of lava after the hardening of the surface." The place is not easily found, its several "mouths," caused by the falling in of portions of the roof, all being on a level with the surface of the ground. At one of these entrances, "where the light and shelter is good," says Muir, "I found many of the heads and horns of wild sheep, and the remains of campfires, no doubt those of Indian hunters who in stormy weather had camped there and feasted after the fatigues of the chase. A wild picture that must have formed on a dark night—the glow of the fire, the circle of crouching savages around it seen through the smoke, the dead game, and the weird darkness and half-darkness of the walls of the cavern, a picture of cave-dwellers at home in the stone age!" Brewer visited Pluto's Cave on October 10, 1863, shortly after its discovery.

Muir, who loved and explored Mount Shasta from summit to base, wrote with characteristic enthusiasm: "Far better than climbing the mountain is going around its warm fertile base, enjoying its bounties like a bee circling around a bank of flowers. The distance is about a hundred miles, [and] a good level road may be found all the way round, by Shasta Valley, Sheep Rock, Elk Flat, Huckleberry Valley, Squaw Valley, following for a considerable portion of the way the old Emigrant Road, which lies along the east disk of the mountain, and is deeply worn by the wagons of the early gold-seekers." Portions of this old road are still used by the Forest Service and it is possible during the summer months to circle Mount Shasta by automobile, a distance of sixty-five miles from Weed or Mount Shasta City. The road takes one through aspen thickets and forests of Shasta fir, across glacial washes, and to points where superb views may be had, all within a few miles of the snow belt.

Marble Mountain

The Marble Mountain Primitive Area in the Klamath National Forest is a region of magnificent mountains and forests covering 237,527 acres. In it lies Marble Mountain, from which the area derives its name.

Lying between the Klamath River and its tributary, Scott River, the Marble Mountain Range culminates in a castellated peak, 8,295 feet in elevation. Composed of limestone, a large proportion of which is marble of a high commercial value, the rugged grandeur and the "monumental purity" of this massive upheaval long inspired the traditions and superstitions of the Red Men, who knew the great peak as the "White Mountain."

Owing to its striking appearance, Marble Mountain served as a landmark for early pioneers, and the old Kelsey Trail, lying almost directly at its base, was one of the first paths ever blazed across these mountains into Scott Valley. Travelers over this rugged old trail almost invariably checked their mules to gaze upward with wonder and amaze-

ment at the beetling cliffs and towering domes of Marble Mountain rising above them. This route, at best a rugged and dangerous one for both man and beast, was long ago abandoned for more accessible passes through the mountains.

The California–Oregon Trail

Lying halfway between the Bay of San Francisco and the Columbia River, the Siskiyou region, first traversed by pre-pioneer trappers and settlers, was soon marked by a well-defined route of travel. This trail was the principal thoroughfare during the gold period (1850–1860), and down to the present the tide of trade and commerce has continued to flow over it. In general it has been called the California–Oregon Trail, but it should be noted that this term has been applied to several routes to and from Oregon through northern California. The first in time was the coast route, through Del Norte County, blazed by Jedediah S. Smith and followed for a time by Hudson's Bay Company trappers. In 1830 Peter Skene Ogden opened up a route by way of Klamath Lake, and in his footsteps came Michael La Framboise, the leader of trapping expeditions from the north during the years from 1830 to 1845. The central route leading up the Sacramento River Canyon was first traversed its entire length by Ewing Young in 1834. During the '50's, when gold mining was the chief industry of the Siskiyou region, two variations of the latter route developed, one of which led around the eastern base of Mount Shasta while the other crossed over Trinity and Scott Mountains into Scott Valley and thence to Yreka.

Shasta Valley, through which the central California–Oregon Trail passed, was first visited by white men early in 1827, when Ogden, with his party of Hudson's Bay Company trappers, wintered on the streams to the east and north of Mount Shasta. From his journal, written on poorly cured slabs of beaver skins, we learn that Ogden and his men left the headwaters of the Des Chutes River in the latter part of November 1826. Guided by the indomitable Thomas McKay, who, the year before, had accompanied Finnan McDonald over the same route, the party crossed the divide into the country of the "Clammitte" (Klamath), a route followed by hundreds of trappers in the interval between 1826 and 1845.

What is apparently the first recorded crossing of the Siskiyou Mountains is found in Ogden's journal for March 13 and 22, 1827. On the 13th Ogden wrote: "We left the Sasty Forks in our rear taking W.N.W. 8 miles encamped by a lofty range of mountains," and on March 22 "reached a fine large river having crossed the mtns," probably the Siskiyou divide, the stream no doubt being the Rogue River.

Ewing Young in 1834, on his way to settle in Oregon, was the first to follow the California–Oregon Trail around the western base of Mount Shasta. A scarcity of cattle in the Willamette Valley led Young to return to the San Francisco Bay region in 1837. With a drove of 700 Spanish longhorns he and about twenty other men started for Oregon. On reaching Shasta Valley Young found that they had succeeded in driving 680 of the animals over the rugged mountains of the Sacramento River Canyon. Again in 1843 the enterprising Joseph Gale, with a much larger herd of live stock, made the same difficult climb.

The old trail and the difficulties experienced by the many early travelers who passed over it are described in the journals of Philip L. Edwards, diarist of the Young party of 1837; the George Emmons report of the Wilkes Expedition in 1841; the account by Lansford W. Hastings of his trip in 1843; and the diary of James Clyman, depicting vividly a journey in 1845. By 1840 California began to attract settlers, and every year during that decade saw an increasing number of emigrants passing over the California–Oregon Trail from the Willamette Valley to the Sacramento Valley, the climax being reached during the years of the gold rush, 1848–1849 and the early '50's.

Lieutenant Emmons and his men camped on September 28, 1841, at the foot of the Boundary Range (the Siskiyou Mountains) within sight of that unique landmark known as Pilot Rock, "a singular, isolated rock, which stands like a tower on the top of the ridge, rising above the surrounding forest with a bare and apparently unbroken surface. . . . . From its top an extensive country is overlooked, and as soon as the party came in sight of it a dense column of smoke arose, which was thought to be a signal made by the Klamet Indians, to the Shaste tribe, of the approach of our party." Charles Wilkes, commander of the entire expedition, named this Emmons' Peak, in honor of the officer in charge of the California contingent of the expedition, but the name Pilot Rock has since been applied to it. Located in southern Oregon, it is visible for many miles on both sides of the mountains.

Fear of the Indians characterized the Wilkes Expedition through the Siskiyous, causing the party to avoid all intercourse with the natives and thus frustrating one of the main objects of the trip, that of making scientific observations of the Indians in their natural habitat. Ascending the Siskiyou Mountains on the 29th, the party was in constant fear of these so-called "Rogues." To the travelers the whole mountain side seemed "admirably adapted for an ambuscade." However, little difficulty was encountered except from fires set by the hostiles. At the summit the men had their first glorious view of the "Klamet Valley," and of "Mount Shaste, a high, snowy peak, of a sugar-loaf form, which rose through the distant haze."

Descending the southern slope of the Siskiyous, the expedition pitched their tents on "Otter Creek [now Camp Creek] within a mile of the Klamet River," and on October 1 they camped on the Shasta River, somewhere near the site of the present town of Montague. There they found the Indians spearing salmon, which were very plentiful. Near the present Gazelle, not far from Sheep Rock, large herds of antelope, as well as long-horned mountain sheep, were seen on the 2d. At midday the party left the Shasta Valley and encamped on a stream near the site of the present town of Edgewood (formerly Butteville). This place was the camping-ground of a tribe of Indians, which Emmons observed closely and which he pronounced "a fine-looking race," and extremely skilful in their manufacture and use of the bow and arrow. Continuing their journey on the 3d, the travelers "entered the forest on the slopes of the Shaste Range. . . . . After passing this ridge, they soon met the head waters of the Sacramento, flowing to the southward, and their camp was pitched on the banks of another stream, that came from the Shaste Peak." This was in Strawberry Valley.

Little escaped the observation of James Clyman when he climbed the Siskiyous and made his way down the Sacramento River Canyon in 1845. His diary is full of poignant descriptions revealing the rugged character of the old trail. Like other early travelers he was constantly on his guard against Indian attacks. Climbing the "Siskiew mountain" on June 23, the party neared the summit where there was "a bad thicket to pass whare nearly all the parties passing this Trail have been attacted." The Clyman company, however, met with no misadventure and soon came in sight of the vast wilderness lying to the south, "wild and awfully sublime." On the 24th, the "Clamet" (Klamath) River was crossed, a few hundred feet east of the present bridge near the site of the now extinct lumbering camp of Klamathon (1890–1900) near the mouth of Willow Creek. Following up Wil-

low Creek on the 25th, the emigrants passed over Little Shasta River, where they made camp. The unique volcanic character of Shasta Valley, with its "round conicle peaks of rock standing out in an uneven plain," appeared as striking to James Clyman as it does to the present-day tourist who looks upon its strange beauty for the first time. The valley was traversed on the 26th, and, after crossing the Shasta River, camp was set up on a site near the present town of Edgewood. From this point Clyman describes Pilot Rock, plainly visible across the Oregon border to the north. Resuming the line of march on the 28th, "the course of the trail lay through the valley west of Black Butte," later known as Wagon Valley. To the east of the pass rose the snowy peaks of Mount Shasta, while on the west stood Mount Eddy, the whole region then magnificently timbered.

This old trail, broken by explorers and trappers and followed by early emigrants in the '40's, became a well-defined pack trail in the '50's, thronged by gold-seekers in their mad rush to the mines. Pack trains transported supplies during the years of the gold rush. In 1860 a stage road from Yreka to Upper Soda Springs and from there down the Sacramento River Canyon was completed by Stone and Company, but with the coming of the winter rains floods carried away all the bridges, restricting stage travel to that section of the road between Yreka and Upper Soda Springs. From that point southward, transportation was continued by pack train to the Pit River, where stages again took up the journey. Not until 1870 did stage travel become permanently established down the entire length of the Sacramento River Canyon.

The first wagon party to cross the Siskiyou Mountains into California was led by Lindsey Applegate in June 1849. After climbing the mountains with their six wagons, the little party crossed Shasta Valley to Wagon Valley, so called because of circumstances which attended the brief stay of this party. Their feeling of remoteness and anxiety regarding the attitude of the Indians caused the emigrants to abandon their project and to return to Oregon, leaving four of the cumbersome wagons to rot in the wilderness. Governor Joseph Lane of Oregon Territory, en route to the California gold fields in 1850, also abandoned a wagon in this locality. The iron from these vehicles was salvaged and sold during the World War.

The first wagon team (1854) and the first transportation by stage and freight team (the California Stage Company, 1856) from the Sacramento Valley crossed the Pit River at Fall River Mills. Continuing in a northwesterly direction, the road passed around the eastern base of Mount Shasta, down through Sheep Rock Pass into Shasta Valley, and then in a northwesterly direction to Yreka. From there it continued in a northeasterly direction, crossing the Shasta River about five miles northwest of Montague. The Klamath River was ferried just north of its junction with Willow Creek, where the road took a route identical with the older trail followed by trappers on their way over the Siskiyou Mountains. That part of the road which passed east of Mount Shasta was used for about a year, when Indian troubles caused traffic to be transferred to the Yreka–Callahan–Shasta route, which became known as the California–Oregon Stage Road and was operated until the advent of the railroad in 1887–1888.

Henry Slicer had already opened a stage line to Callahan's in 1854. After abandoning the route around the eastern base of Mount Shasta, the California Stage Company bought out Greathouse and Slicer and began, at great expense, to complete the road to the town of Shasta (in early days sometimes called Shasta City). This road was pushed over Trinity Mountain in 1857, and in 1859 Scott Mountain was also surmounted. Meanwhile the Oregon Stage Company had completed their turnpike over the Siskiyous. Connecting with the California Stage Line at Yreka in 1860, a through route was thus staged for the first time from Portland, Oregon, to Sacramento, California. It was over this route that the first telegraph line from California to Oregon was constructed.

Four or five miles south of Callahan's a former stage station still stands on the old Mathewson Ranch at the foot of Scott Mountain.

After 1870 the route from Yreka to the Klamath River went by way of the Anderson Grade, crossing the Shasta River about four miles north of Yreka. On this road the Ten Mile House, a stage station of the '70's, still stands. Ascending the mountain over a high-line grade, the road descended to the Klamath River about six miles south of Cottonwood (Henley), where the river was ferried. The old trappers' trail over the Siskiyous continued to be used from this point on. The magnificent Pioneer Bridge on the Pacific Highway was erected over the Shasta River three miles north of Yreka in 1931 and dedicated to the memory of the early-day stage drivers who traveled this road.

Stopping-Places on the California–Oregon Trail

Along the old California–Oregon Trail many historic spots—strategic stopping-places where a long succession of travelers have rested on their arduous journeys up rugged canyons and over precipitous mountains—invite the interest of the present-day tourist. They were, at first, mere camp sites (in some cases on or in close proximity to the ancient rancherías of the Indians) where the trail-blazers and their immediate successors—the trappers and explorers of the '30's and '40's—halted on their way through the wilderness. The sites have been identified by means of diaries and journals kept by a few of these earliest travelers. Before long, the faint trails of the pathfinders were being widened by the restless feet of pre-pioneer settlers seeking new homes in Oregon or California, and they, too, have left their records of favored camp sites located on streams or by springs of clear mountain water or on the green floor of some open vale or meadow.

With the discovery of gold in California the procession down the Oregon Trail became an avalanche of excited, hurrying humanity bound for the numerous El Doradoes which California had opened to an eager world. Hotels or inns were built on the early camp grounds, and proved popular stopping-places for gold-seekers and settlers alike. With the coming of the first wagons a road was constructed, and soon the picturesque mule trains were superseded by freighters and stagecoaches. Then the wayside inns became stage stations, with villages and towns eventually growing up about them. When the Southern Pacific Railway was constructed from Redding into Oregon, in 1886–1887, its route was practically identical with that of the California–Oregon Trail and portions of the early stage road. Many of the railroad stations are either on the exact line of the first trail or very close to it.

Traveling northward, the first station located on that part of the Oregon Trail which passes through Siskiyou County was at Upper Soda Springs, a mile below Shasta Springs, where summer tourists today enjoy the beauties of mountain scenery and the tonic of pine-scented air and pure water. Once a camp ground of Hudson's Bay Company trappers and other early voyageurs, the ancient soda springs with their health-giving waters (doubtless a rendezvous of the Indians for many moons before the coming of the white man) were visited by pre-pioneer travelers up and down the old trail. During the years 1860–1870, Upper Soda Springs

was the terminus for the stage line run from Yreka by Stone and Company. From that time until the building of the railroad it continued to be a stopping-place on the through stage line to Oregon. The old stage station is still standing and is in good condition.

The next camp on the old trail, which here ran about a mile west of the present Pacific Highway, was located in Strawberry Valley, where a settlement grew up in the early '50's and where a post office was established in 1866 under the name of Berryvale. For twelve years J. H. Sisson was postmaster and hotel keeper at this point. When the railroad came through in 1887, the station, one mile east of Berryvale, was named Sisson's, and the town which soon grew up on the new site was called Sisson, a name which it bore until 1924, when it was changed to Mount Shasta City.

Sisson's Hotel at Berryvale was a favorite summer resort and outfitting point for early-day mountain climbers. From there, trails radiated in all directions to the many natural wonders and beauty spots with which the entire region abounds: Mount Shasta, with its glaciers and its panoramic vistas of northern California, southern Oregon, and western Nevada; Black Butte, that odd cinder cone which sits like a dwarf in the shadow of Mount Shasta's glowing heights; Mount Eddy, with its glorious Shasta lilies and its gem-like Castle Lake; or the simple, "flowery fringes" and wooded streams of Strawberry Valley—all these attractions, and more, lured the mountain lover to Sisson's Hotel even in pioneer days.

The route of the old stage road which passed before Sisson's door was identical with that of the present highway which goes by the State Fish Hatchery west of town, and Sisson's Hotel (since burned) stood almost at the top of the low hill just before entering the Hatchery gate. Across the road is the old post office and store kept by Mrs. S. J. Fellows, who followed Sisson as postmistress of Berryvale. It is now used as a garage at the home of Henry Ream, grandson of Mrs. Fellows. Near the road, about two miles north of the Fish Hatchery, stands the oldest house in Strawberry Valley. It was built some time in the '50's by William Sullaway and is still used as a residence.

About fifteen miles north of Berryvale the old trail passed the site of Butteville (now Edgewood), a camping ground mentioned in most of the early journals. There in 1851 William and Jackson Brown built a log cabin and in 1856 W. Starr opened a store. Starr was succeeded by Joseph Foreman and John Lennox in 1859, and in 1860 by Joseph Cavanaugh, a genial Irishman. Cavanaugh's hotel became a popular stage station on the California–Oregon Road, and he was still operating his establishment there in the '80's.

Leaving Butteville, travelers on the California–Oregon Trail next stopped where the village of Edson's (called Gazelle since 1870) later grew up. There a Mr. Brady started a station very early, and in 1853 the place was purchased by E. B. and J. R. Edson, who conducted it as a station on the stage road for many years. The Edson farm, with its beautiful home, was a very prosperous place in the '80's.

From Edson's the trail proceeded straight northward across Shasta Valley, forded the Shasta River near the site of Montague, where there was an important camp site, and continued thence to Willow Creek. After 1850 the trail, which had developed into a stage road, made a detour to Yreka, turning to the northwest eight miles north of Edson's. From Yreka this road went northeast, crossing the Shasta River five miles northwest of Montague and rejoining the old trail before it reached Willow Creek.

Near where Willow Creek runs into the Klamath River

from the south the next stopping-place on the old emigrant trail was made not far from the site of the later village of Klamathon (still a flag station on the railroad). Proceeding down stream three miles to Cottonwood Creek, which runs into the Klamath from the north, the trail followed up Cottonwood Creek Canyon and crossed the summit of the Siskiyous about where the present railroad passes over. The last camp on the trail before reaching Oregon was made in the canyon of Cottonwood Creek just before beginning the climb over the mountain.

In 1870 the stage road into Oregon was re-routed over the so-called Anderson Grade. Cottonwood (later Henley) was the place where stage coaches and freighters en route from Yreka to Oregon changed horses from 1860 to 1887, when the completion of the railroad ended stage operations.

Trails of the Northern El Dorado

The first Argonauts from Oregon passed through Siskiyou County without stopping to prospect its streams, and no mining was done there until the summer of 1850. As early as June of that year men bent on finding gold penetrated the wild and rugged fastnesses of the Salmon Mountains. Crossing the ridge from the North Fork of the Trinity River, they came upon the South Fork of the Salmon River, down which they followed to the mouth of the North Fork, where rich diggings were found. The camp established at this point came to be known as the Forks of the Salmon, and during the summer several hundred men gathered there. From this central point they spread out up the North Fork of the Salmon River and over the divide into the Scott River Valley.

Meanwhile, a party of miners had traversed the length of the Klamath River from its mouth to the Shasta River, panning for gold at every bar. "It was this group of miners," says David Rhys Jones, "that established the course of the Klamath River below the junction of the Shasta. From that time on, the river that had been variously known as the Clamitte, the Klamet, Indian Scalp River, and Smith River, has borne the name by which it was known near its source." Again Jones says that "prior to 1850 all maps delineating the Klamath River represented its source and upper course correctly—as it had been observed by trappers. The course of the river below Shasta River was unexplored, but the mouth of a large stream in southern Oregon had been crossed by Jedediah S. Smith in 1828. This was the mouth of the Rogue. So the Hudson's Bay Company map presented to Wilkes, and published as part of his travel records, shows the Klamath River turning back into Oregon through the Siskiyous, below the Shasta, and emptying into the ocean at the mouth of the Rogue."

When overtaken by the approach of winter, the miners on the Klamath left for the settlements of the Sacramento Valley, following a southerly course and passing en route the sites later occupied by Yreka and Greenhorn, where gold was discovered on the creek. A few miles to the east they came upon the Oregon Trail, where they found a fresh wagon track. Camping that night near the site of Edson's, they reached Wagon Valley the following day. There they found the abandoned wagon which Governor Joseph Lane had recently transported across the Siskiyou Mountains. Later they overtook Lane himself, bound for the gold fields.

When in San Francisco two years before, while on his way to organize the territory of Oregon, Lane had resisted the onslaught of the gold fever, but in the summer of 1850 he, too, became stricken with the malady. With the gold fields on the Sierra Nevada as his objective he crossed the border into California. The wagon with which he had

started, proving to be of considerable annoyance, was finally abandoned in Wagon Valley. At this time the Lane party did a little incidental prospecting on the Klamath River and on the Shasta River at Joe Lane's Bar near the mouth of Yreka Creek. The following year Governor Lane came to Siskiyou County at the head of a large company of men bound for Scott Bar, where they did considerable mining.

Scott Valley was first explored in 1850 by a little group of miners led by John Scott, who had crossed the Salmon Mountains from the North Fork of the Salmon River. These men panned for gold at a point on Scott River named in honor of their leader, Scott Bar. Indians soon drove them from this location. Returning to the Salmon River and crossing the mountains to the Trinity River, they spread the news of their recent discovery of gold at Scott Bar. Many parties started at once for the new location and the place was soon overcrowded with miners. As a result, prospecting parties spread out over the entire region, and many new diggings, the scene of thriving camps in 1851, were uncovered.

One such find was the chance discovery of gold on the site later occupied by Yreka. This location attracted little attention at the time, for a rich bonanza was found at Ingall's Gulch on Greenhorn Creek soon afterward. Its discoverers came to Scott Bar for provisions, where they organized as secretly as possible and returned to Ingall's Gulch. In spite of all efforts to keep the news of their good fortune from spreading, they were followed. While they lay asleep their claims were occupied by others. This was the beginning of mining on Greenhorn Creek, in January 1851.

Salmon River Camps

Coming up the Salmon River from its mouth, Somes' Bar is the first mining camp reached. Continuing up the river, one's imagination is fired by the knowledge that in the early '50's every bar, creek, and gulch along the river's course teemed with eager miners.

The Forks of the Salmon had a population of several hundred in the summer of 1850, although less than fifty spent the winter of 1850–1851 there. Before winter had passed, the report of rich diggings attracted miners from everywhere, many rushing to the spot without supplies. As a result, when late snows blocked the trails in March, thousands all up and down the Salmon River and its branches were on the verge of starvation.

Sawyer's Bar, on the North Fork of the Salmon River, is today a village of about two hundred inhabitants. Its outstanding building is the Catholic Church, built in the early days of whip-sawed lumber. South of Sawyer's Bar are a number of quartz mines, chief among them being the Black Bear Mine seven or eight miles to the southwest. The material for the mill for this mine was carried over the mountains on mule back or dragged in on sleds by oxen.

Cecilville, with its twenty Indian inhabitants, is located on the South Fork of the Salmon River in a remote section of the county. It was reached only by trail until 1926, when a road was constructed from Sawyer's Bar to Cecilville, passing near the old Black Bear Mine.

During the winter season the only means of communication which the Salmon River region had with Yreka was for many years over the snow-covered Jackson Creek Pass six thousand feet high. Until late in June, mail and supplies had to be brought in on the backs of mules shod with snowshoes. In 1926 a new road was built up the Salmon River by way of Somes' Bar. In summer this rugged Salmon River region affords a wonderful vacation land, with wooded mountains and clear trout streams to lure the lovers of beauty and adventure.

Scott Valley

Scott Valley, named after John Scott, the discoverer of gold at Scott Bar, is still the beautiful, "rich bottom, with fertile ranches, surrounded with high and very steep mountains, rough and rugged, and furrowed into very deep canyons," described by William H. Brewer, who visited the region in the autumn of 1863. Formerly famed for its rich gold production, the valley is now devoted to agriculture.

According to Brewer, "Scott's Bar . . . . was once quite an important town. Placers, rich and abundant, called together a busy and thriving population. . . . . But the placers are mostly worked out, the population has started after new mines and fresh excitements, over half the houses are empty, four-fifths of the population gone, business has decayed, and the town is dilapidated. We stopped at a rather large hotel, now desolate—its few boarders look lonely in it. . . . .

"The mines are not all exhausted, the deeper bars still pay. Deep excavations are dug below the river bed, large water wheels, turned by the swift current, pump the water out of these claims, and some are paying well. . . . . The big wheels creaked dolefully all night long, and seemed to bewail the decline of the decaying town."

The Scott Bar of 1850 was located a few hundred yards above and on the opposite bank of Scott River from the Scott Bar of 1851 and succeeding years. The old trail of the '50's zigzagged for three miles through the precipitous canyon which lay between Scott Bar and the mouth of the Scott River, the canyon proper being, in many places, at least three thousand feet deep. In the early '50's this great gorge was teeming with life. Among the bustling camps of the region were French Bar (one of the largest), Johnson's Bar, Poorman's Bar, Lytle's Bar, Slapjack Bar, Michigan Bar, and Junction Bar. Governor Lane worked Lane's Gulch on Whitney Hill near Scott Bar in 1851.

Many of the old buildings in the vicinity of Scott Bar are still intact. The Quartz Hill Mine at Scott Bar, which was operating seventy years ago and has been mined continuously for the last twenty-five years, has yielded millions, and is still a good producer.

Etna Mills (now Etna), originally known as Rough and Ready Mills, grew up around the flour mill established there in 1856 in competition with a neighboring concern known as the Etna Mills, erected in 1854. Considerable rivalry was manifested between the two communities, but the newer place finally won out as a town, when in 1863 the post office was shifted from Etna Mills to the more successful Rough and Ready. The latter, however, lost its name, there being another Rough and Ready post office in Nevada County, and the name of its rival, Etna Mills, was bestowed upon it. The present abbreviated title was legalized by the legislature in 1874.

Etna, now a town of less than four hundred inhabitants, lies in the midst of a rich agricultural district shut in by the heavily forested Salmon Mountains on the west and the Scott Mountains on the south and east.

Callahan's

Callahan's, near the junction of the East and South forks of the Scott River, was the first stopping-place after crossing Scott Mountain from the south. Here in the autumn of 1851 M. B. Callahan opened a public house and store. Soon after Callahan sold out in 1855 the place became the terminus of Greathouse and Slicer's stage line from Yreka, on which were used the two Concord coaches which Henry Slicer had brought over the Siskiyou Mountains from Oregon in 1854, the first to be seen in Siskiyou County. At Callahan's, passengers were transferred to mules for the difficult journey over Scott Mountain to the Trinity River and thence over the Trinity Mountains to French Gulch and the town of Shasta.

Callahan's old station is still on the map. Its one street, lined with an unbroken succession of bar rooms with sleeping apartments overhead, is reminiscent of early mining and stagecoach days, although the old buildings are mostly deserted. The entire township contains less than three hundred persons.

Fort Jones

The town of Wheelock (named after its founder) was started in 1851 as a hotel and stage station on the road from Yreka to Callahan's and Shasta. As the settlement grew it was variously known as Wheelock, Scottsburg, and Ottitiewa (the name of a group of Shasta Indians). In 1862 the present name of Fort Jones was adopted, that being the name of the United States Army camp which had once existed one-half mile to the south. This old military outpost, established by Major Edward H. Fitzgerald of the First United States Dragoons on October 16, 1852, served as a protection against the Indians during the '50's. The first log houses were later replaced by frame buildings, which, in turn, were sold and moved away when the post was abandoned in June 1858.

West of Fort Jones, Oro Fino, on Oro Fino Creek, and Mugginsville, in Quartz Valley, were booming gold camps in the '50's, but by 1880 Oro Fino had become depopulated. Mugginsville was the center of quartz mining in the region in the '50's and '60's. Here an eight-stamp mill was erected in 1852, and a sawmill and a grist mill on Shackleford Creek were added in 1854. The place polled three hundred votes in 1860.

Deadwood

Northeast of Fort Jones, at the junction of Deadwood and Cherry creeks, the town of Deadwood once thrived. It was there that Joaquin Miller, then a mere youth, wrote his first poem, in honor of the marriage of Deadwood's cook to a woman in Yreka. Miller recited the poem at the reception given the bride and groom on their return to Deadwood.

In 1854–1855 Deadwood ranked second to Yreka in importance, and Brewer says that it was still "a busy little mining town in 1863." The site of Deadwood may be reached by a very narrow, winding mountain road, but nothing is left today to indicate that a once thriving town existed there.

One of Deadwood's neighbors in mining days was Hardscrabble, a little settlement in Hi You Gulch, while on Indian Creek was the town of Indian Creek and on McAdams' Creek was Hooperville, both prosperous camps in the '50's.

Klamath River Camps

Among the more thriving gold bars of the Klamath River during the '50's (Mead's, Hamburg, China, Walker, Masonic, and Fort Goff), Hamburg Bar, located a few miles below the mouth of Scott River, was the most important. Above the mouth of the river, on the Klamath, were Oak and Virginia bars. All along the river picturesque water wheels were to be seen. A few dip wheels still operate on the Klamath, most of them being used to raise water for irrigation. Chinamen working on a bar five miles below the mouth of Shasta River are operating two large dip wheels, the log shafts of which are one hundred feet in length, a good example of the old-style Chinese pump and derrick boom.

Brewer, in October 1863, wrote: "We passed what was once the town of Hamburg, two years ago a bustling village

—a large cluster of miners' cabins, three hotels, three stores, two billiard saloons, and all the other accompaniments of a mining town—now all is gone. The placers were worked out, the cabins became deserted, and the floods of two years ago finished its history by carrying off all the houses, or nearly all—a camp of Klamath Indians on the river bank is the only population at present! .... Just below were some Indian graves. A little enclosure of sticks surrounded them. Each grave is a conical mound, and lying on them, or hanging on poles over them, are the worldly goods of the deceased—the baskets in which they gathered their acorns, their clothing and moccasins, arms and implements, strings of beads, and other ornaments—decaying along with their owners.

"In contrast with this was a sadder sight—a cluster of graves of the miners who had died while the town remained. Boards had once been set up at their graves, but most had rotted off and fallen—the rest will soon follow. Bushes have grown over the graves, and soon they, as well as the old town, will be forgotten. .... Alas, how many a sad history is hidden in the neglected and forgotten graves that are scattered among the wild mountains that face the Pacific!

"The population has not entirely left this portion of the river, however. Here and there may be seen a white man, and industrious Chinamen patiently ply with rockers for the yellow dust."

A revival of mining has occurred at Hamburg Bar from time to time, but today it is a quiet little village of only a hundred inhabitants or so.

About midway between Scott Bar and Happy Camp, Seiad (Sciad) Creek runs into the Klamath River from the northeast. Brewer, on his way down the river, visited the spot, describing it as "a fertile little flat of about a hundred acres, the best ranch perhaps in the entire county of Siskiyou. It is known as the Sciad Ranch. We crossed the river by a ferry to it. .... It is a delightful spot—it seems an oasis in a desert. Here lives a thriving New York farmer . . . . named Reeves, and he is making money faster than if he were mining for gold. He treated us very kindly indeed and we luxuriated on delicious apples, pears, and plums. His table groaned under the weight of well-cooked food, in pleasing contrast with the miserable taverns of the last few days . . . .

"He came here in 1854, and says that the first year he raised twenty thousand pounds of potatoes per acre, which he sold for *fifteen cents per pound!* . . . ."

Brewer and his party left the Seiad Ranch on October 26, traveling for "thirty miles over a good but rough trail." For eighteen miles down the Klamath River the way abounded "in the most picturesque views to be imagined, the mountains rising three or four thousand feet on both sides from the swift river." Many deserted cabins and houses were passed before reaching Happy Camp, one of the oldest settlements in Siskiyou County and in 1863 already on the decline. Today Happy Camp is much as it was in the early days, with a few modern houses scattered among the old buildings which date from mining days.

At Elk Creek, one and a half miles below Happy Camp, some three hundred men worked the stream in 1856, making from ten to twenty dollars per day, while north of Happy Camp between four and five hundred miners panned for gold in Indian Creek and its branches. Twelve miles up the creek was the little village of Indiantown, already "falling into piteous dilapidation" when Brewer, in 1863, stopped at the "miserable hole" which once served as a hotel.

The Klamath River country experienced a revival in mining activity in 1931. New options were taken and fresh capital invested. It is estimated that between three and four hundred placer claims were being operated along the Klamath that year.

Pick-i-a-wish Camp, on the Klamath River, just below the old mining town of Happy Camp, is the scene of a yearly Indian festival. Here, in the dark of the August moon, Indians from all the surrounding settlements and ranches gather to hold their autumn festival. With beating of drums they dance the Deerskin Dance, the Brush Dance, and the Coyote Dance. Many legends still cling about these Indian settlements and are told by their old men and women.

Cottonwood

The little town of Cottonwood, located on Cottonwood Creek just north of Hornbrook on the old Oregon Road, was the center of trade for a number of rich mining locations during the '50's. The flats and gulches near by presented a strange medley of names: Stone, Dan Davies', Dutch, Rich, Printer's, Rocky, Carruck, and Milk Cañon gulches, and Todhunter, Buffalo, Milk Ranch, and Turnip Patch flats, with John Hatch Hill, Brass Wire Channel, and Ranchería Creek added to the crude but colorful array.

"Cottonwood," said Brewer in October 1863, "is a little mining town, once busy and hustling, now mostly 'played out,' two-thirds of its houses empty, its business dull, the whole place looking as if stricken with a curse." Cottonwood was established as a post office in 1861 under the name of Henley. In 1881 it still boasted a hotel, a store, a saloon, and a blacksmith shop, but today only one or two old landmarks remain.

Yreka

In Yreka, with its streets lined with locust trees and old-fashioned houses, an atmosphere of adventure lingers, enhanced by the tales told of stagecoaches, Indians, and fabulous gold nuggets, and by the many evidences of early mining in the hills near by. Among the old buildings still standing in good condition on Oregon and Miner streets is the Odd Fellows Hall, a two-story brick structure erected in 1859. Although somewhat remodeled, the upper story of the front portion remains in its original state.

Gold was discovered in the vicinity of Yreka as early as 1850 by one of those roving bands of prospectors which pushed into the northernmost corners of California that year. In March 1851 a strike was made at Yreka Flats, an event that brought two thousand men to the spot in less than six weeks. This discovery was made by Abraham Thompson in a little ravine later known as Black Gulch. The camp which grew up there was called Thompson's Dry Diggings and was located on a knoll near some springs one-half mile northwest of the intersection of the present Oregon and Miner streets in Yreka.

Meanwhile, miners' cabins were built for three miles along Yreka Creek from Greenhorn to Hawkinsville, and business soon moved away from the Flats and nearer to the creek. A town, at first called Shasta Butte City, was laid out on the present site of Yreka in May 1851. In order to avoid confusion with the older Shasta City (in Shasta County) the name was changed to Yreka when the county was organized in 1852. That name was retained by the legislature when the place was made the county seat of Siskiyou County.

Among the stirring episodes that enlivened the early history of Yreka the Greenhorn War of 1855 was perhaps the most exciting. This was a contest over water rights waged by two mining factions, the Yreka Flats Ditch Association and the miners on Lower Greenhorn Creek. The latter precipitated the war when they cut the Yreka Flats Ditch because it was diverting water from their claims on the creek. The matter was taken before the local court, which supported the Yreka faction and enjoined against further cutting of the ditch. The injunction was disobeyed and the guilty party arrested. This was the signal for the Greenhorn miners to act. En masse they marched to the Yreka jail to obtain the release of the prisoner, an objective which was accomplished only after an encounter with the officers of the law. Nevertheless, the decision of the court stood and the Yreka Flats Association continued to use the water conveyed from Greenhorn Creek.

Many mining camps formerly existed near Yreka. Two miles to the north was Hawkinsville, where a number of very early camps were concentrated, one of them being Frogtown, the chief center of trade in 1851. Others were Long Gulch, Rich Gulch, Canal Gulch, and Rocky Gulch. To the south of Yreka was Greenhorn, a settlement of miners' cabins, while up Greenhorn Creek was Wheeler's Store.

The name Greenhorn is typical of the unique and suggestive nomenclature which grew out of the rough life of the virile Argonauts. A company of experienced miners had dug a ditch some distance back from the creek but finding their claims unprofitable had abandoned the location. A new arrival, at once dubbed a "greenhorn" by his more experienced companions, asked where he could find a good place to work. Thinking to enjoy a joke at his expense the miners directed the young fellow to the hill which they had just vacated. The "greenhorn," setting to work on the abandoned ditch, was rewarded by a rich "strike." He kept his find a secret, and as no one dreamed of his success the joke grew bigger every day. When the jokers finally learned that the "greenhorn" had been quietly working the richest ground along the creek there was an immediate rush for claims on the new lead. To perpetuate the joke, so the story goes, the creek was baptized "Greenhorn," a name which it still bears. Similar stories have been told in other sections of the mining regions in California to explain the origin of this name.

Vast piles of rock and gravel which fill the canyons and gullies with débris, in the hills to the south of Yreka, give evidence of early mining operations. These monumental relics, like the graves of some forgotten race of giants, will long disfigure the landscape with their gaunt, gray sterility, covering many spots once made beautiful with the delicate hues of wild-flower faces, the pale blue of juniper berries, and the autumn flame of the Oregon grape.

Klamath Peggy

The story of Klamath Peggy forms a romantic episode in Yreka's history. Peggy's people, the Klamaths, were on the warpath against the encroaching whites, but the horror of bloodshed touched the heart of this Indian woman, who secretly made the arduous journey of twenty miles over rough mountains to warn her white brothers and sisters of their peril. When the Klamath warriors approached the town along the devious trails of the brush-covered hills, they found it strongly guarded by sentries and were forced to retreat.

For years after this event, Klamath Peggy, fearing to associate with her kinsmen, lived among the people of Yreka, who never forgot the service which she had rendered them. When the remnants of her tribe were finally placed on the Reservation four miles to the south of town, Peggy was pensioned and cared for until her death at the advanced age of 105 years. Then all Yreka paid tribute to her memory. The humble grave of Klamath Peggy at the old Indian Reservation on Greenhorn's slopes memorializes her deed of love and self-sacrifice.

Humbug City

Ten miles northwest of Yreka, Humbug City once flourished on Humbug Creek, where gold was discovered in May 1851. The story goes that a company of men on their way to mine on the creek were met by a returning group who said it was all a humbug. Undaunted by this news, the first group continued on their way to the stream in question, where they set to work with pan and rocker. Their diligence was rewarded and they proved that the location was not a humbug after all. In deference to the opinion of their predecessors, however, they called it Humbug Creek. News of the find spread quickly, and before long the stream was thronged with miners and dotted with camps.

Two miles above Humbug City was Freetown, while on the North Fork of the Humbug was Riderville, a large camp in 1859. For a time it was known as "Plugtown," after old Dr. Nichols, who wore a "plug" hat. Two miles below the Forks was Mowry's Flat, known as Frenchtown in 1864, when a number of Frenchmen were mining there. A saloon was doing business at Frenchtown as late as 1881.

Joaquin Miller, who as a youth lived among the Indians of the Siskiyous, often joined the miners in their search for gold along the various streams. He draws a rather gloomy picture of the Humbug mining region: "It lay west of the city [Yreka], a day's ride down in a deep, densely timbered cañon, out of sight of Mount Shasta, out of sight of everything—even the sun; save here and there where a landslide had ploughed up the forest, or the miners had mown down the great evergreens about their cabins, or town sites in the camp."

It was a rough place, and wild—as wild as the mountains which hemmed it in. "A sort of Hades, a savage Eden, with many Adams walking up and down, and plucking of every tree, nothing forbidden here; for here, so far as it would seem, are neither laws of God or man." The Forks, where "three little streams joined hands, and went down from there to the Klamat together," was the common center of the region. Miller's cabin stood on the steep bank of the main stream, not far from the river. He was particularly impressed by the "Howlin' Wilderness," the principal saloon in the town. It was an immense log cabin with a huge fireplace, "where crackled and roared, day and night, a pine-log fire," the memory of which spelled enchantment to the poet for years after. The "Howlin' Wilderness" was the scene, too, of many a fight, "in this fierce little mining camp of the Forks," and the saying, "We will have a man for breakfast tomorrow," was a common one within its precincts.

The Modoc War

"In the land of great lakes, high mountains, and long shadowy mornings and evenings, may be found the 'Sacred Lands' of Modoc tradition, where it is claimed can be seen the identical sacred stone ('I-sees Jo-kol-e-kas') whereon the Son of God gave His red children His last advice. In this strange land, and among its strange people," the opening scenes in the tragic drama of the Modoc War were enacted. It was here on Lost River (in southern Oregon) that the first engagement of the war took place on November 30, 1872, climaxing a long series of troubles between the Indians and the whites which had begun in 1834 when a member of Ewing Young's party shot two Indian boys.

Alfred B. Meacham, Superintendent of Indian Affairs for the State of Oregon, 1869–1872, and chairman of the

Peace Commission, 1873, describes the circumstances and events of the war as he himself witnessed them, presenting "'the other side of the Modoc story,' with the hope that a better understanding between white and red men may be had, and that justice to both may be promoted."

"The 16th of Jan., 1873," writes Meacham, "found the Modocs in the Lava-beds, numbering one hundred and sixty-nine souls. Who shall be able to paint the anxiety, the fears, the hopes, the long councils, the great 'Ka-okes' (medicine dances), which were in reality religious meetings, in which every phase of the situation was discussed by these despised people." The same day found General Wheaton "with two hundred men encamped on the high bluff, overlooking the Lava-beds from the north, four miles distant from the Modoc camp. The remainder numbering two hundred men .... encamped about equal distance south of the Modocs." The full fighting force of the Modocs numbered fifty-three men, but the Lava-beds, with its secret dens and unknown crevices, formed an almost impregnable fortress for the little band. Day after day shells were rained upon them without effect, while the white soldiers suffered heavy losses.

Repeated attempts made by the leaders of both sides to accomplish a peaceable settlement of the war were frustrated by unfortunate events and misunderstanding. Finally, on April 11, 1873, in spite of the repeated warnings of treachery given by Wi-ne-ma, Indian wife of Frank Riddle, the four unarmed peace commissioners, General Edward R. S. Canby, the Rev. Eleazer Thomas, A. B. Meacham, and L. S. Dyar, with Wi-ne-ma and Riddle as interpreters, met Captain Jack and his men at the Peace Tent, "which stood out all alone upon the rocky plain" not far from the Modoc stronghold. The final attempt to reach an amicable agreement, made by the Indian leader and the Commissioners at this meeting, failed, with the result that treachery finally had its way. Canby and Thomas were killed, and Meacham, saved from a similar fate by Wi-ne-ma, was severely wounded. Dyar and Riddle escaped, as did Wi-ne-ma, after heroically risking her life to save her friends.

During the last engagement in the Lava-beds, when *"one thousand white* soldiers and *seventy-two* Indian allies opened the battle upon fifty-three Modocs," only one Modoc warrior was killed during the three days' conflict. "The hospital at the army camp was full of wounded soldiers," and as "the sun went behind Van Bremen's Mountain" more than one salute was fired in honor of the dead. It was during this time that Wi-ne-ma "became a Florence Nightingale in the army hospital .... bathing the burning brows, and administering nourishment prepared by her own hands. The soldiers were assured of her fidelity, and with united voice declared her to be a ministering angel. When the wounded were brought in from the battlefield, Wi-ne-ma was always among the first to reach the side of the stretcher." In later years a pension was bestowed upon Wi-ne-ma by the federal government for distinguished services, and a public school on Lost River, where she had averted bloodshed and brought about a better understanding between Captain Jack and the Americans in December 1869, recently was named for her.

Captain Jack held his position in the Lava-beds until April 18, 1873, when the Modocs finally abandoned their stronghold. After the Battle of Dry Lake, on May 10, the band broke up. Captain Jack, betrayed by members of his own tribe, was captured in Langell's Valley, Oregon, on June 1, and with his subsequent trial and execution on October 3, 1873, the closing act in that tragic drama of the last Indian war in the Far West came to an end.

For many years the spot where General Canby was killed was marked by a large wooden cross placed there by soldiers of his regiment. Recently the Native Daughters of the Golden West and other patriotic organizations erected near the spot a monument of native rock surmounted by the figure of a grizzly bear.

Captain Jack's stronghold at the southern end of Tule Lake remains almost unchanged. Rude rock forts, used by soldiers and Indians alike, are now overgrown with sage and bitterbrush, while bleached bones of horses, fragments of leather, and empty cartridge shells may still be found at the scene of conflict. The Forest Service has marked a number of sites on the battlefield. Near Canby's Cross is Guillem's Graveyard, where almost a hundred men were buried in one spot. The bodies were removed to the National Cemetery in Washington, D.C., in the early '90's, but the ruins of the rock walls surrounding the old burial place remain. Hospital Rock was a fortified position maintained by the white troops for the care of their sick and wounded soldiers. Captain Jack's Cave, where the Indian leader had his headquarters, and other interesting sites have also been marked.

SOURCES

[Credit is here given for source material, and permission to quote is hereby acknowledged]

BADÈ, FREDERIC WILLIAM. *The Life and Letters of John Muir.* 2 vols. Houghton Mifflin Company, Boston and New York, 1924

BLAND, T. A. *Life of Alfred B. Meacham, Together with His Lecture: "The Tragedy of the Lava Beds."* T. A. & M. C. Bland, Washington, D.C., 1883

BROWN, WILLIAM S. "The Land of Burned Out Fires," in *Touring Topics,* XIX, No. 8 (August 1927), 14–17, 38–39

CLYMAN, JAMES. "James Clyman, His Diaries and Reminiscences," edited by Charles L. Camp in *California Historical Society Quarterly,* IV, No. 2—VI, No. 1 (June 1925–March 1927)

EDWARDS, PHILIP L. *The Diary of Philip Leget Edwards.* The Grabhorn Press, San Francisco, 1932

FARQUHAR, FRANCIS P. (editor). *Up and Down California in 1860–64. The Journal of William H. Brewer.* Yale University Press, New Haven, 1930

FRÉMONT, JOHN CHARLES. *Geographical Memoir upon Upper California in Illustration of His Map of Oregon and California.* Government Printing Office, Washington, D.C., 1848

HALL, ANSEL F. "Mount Shasta," in *Sierra Club Bulletin,* XII, No. 3 (1926), 252–267

HASTINGS, LANSFORD W. *The Emigrants' Guide to California.* A facsimile of the edition of 1845 with introduction and notes by Charles H. Carey. Princeton University Press, Princeton, 1932

JONES, DAVID RHYS. *Early History of the Klamath.* Manuscript, 1930

———. "Pre-pioneer Pathfinders, California–Oregon Trail, 1826–1846," in *Motor Land,* XXIX (August–November, 1931)

MALONEY, ALICE B. "Shasta Was Shatasla in 1814," in *California Historical Society Quarterly,* XXIV, No. 3 (September 1945)

MEACHAM, HON. A. B. *Wigwam and Warpath; or The Royal Chief in Chains.* John P. Dale & Company, Boston, 1875

———. *Wi-ne-ma (The Woman Chief) and Her People.* American Publishing Company, Hartford, Connecticut, 1876

MILLER, JOAQUIN. *Life Amongst the Modocs: Unwritten History.* Richard Bentley & Son, London, 1873

MUIR, JOHN. *Mountains of California.* 2 vols. Houghton Mifflin Company, Boston and New York, 1917

———. *Steep Trails ....* Houghton Mifflin Company, Boston and New York, 1918

OGDEN, PETER SKENE. "The Peter Skene Ogden Journals of the Snake Expedition, 1827–28; 1828–29," with editorial notes by T. C. Elliott, in *Oregon Historical Society Quarterly,* XI (1910), 355–397

RIDDLE, JEFF C. *The Indian History of the Modoc War and the Causes That Led to It.* Marnell & Company, San Francisco, 1914

SHOW, S. B. "Primitive Areas in the National Forests of California," in *Sierra Club Bulletin,* XVIII, No. 1 (February 1933), 24–30

WELLS, HARRY L. *History of Siskiyou County, California.* Stewart & Company, Oakland, 1881

WILKES, CHARLES. *Narrative of the United States Exploring Expedition during the Years 1838, 1839, 1840, 1841, 1842.* 5 vols. and an atlas. Lea & Blanchard, Philadelphia, 1845

WILLIAMSON, ROBERT S. *Pacific Railroad Reports,* VI, Part I. Government Printing Office, Washington, D.C., 1855

STANISLAUS COUNTY

STANISLAUS COUNTY, according to differing theories, was named either for a Christianized Indian chief who was baptized by the padres under the Spanish name Estanislao, or for one of the two Polish saints, Stanislaus Kostka or Stanislaus Cracow. The county was organized in 1854 from a part of Tuolumne County, and the first county seat was placed at Adamsville. Within a few months the seat of justice was moved to Empire City; in 1856 it was transferred to La Grange; in 1862 to Knight's Ferry; and in 1872 it was finally located at Modesto. This town was first called Ralston, after an official of the Central Pacific Railroad. Being a very modest man, Mr. Ralston objected to the honor, and so the name was changed to Modesto, Spanish for "modest."

The Stanislaus

The first white man to look upon the waters of the Stanislaus, one of the most important of the wild and picturesque streams of the Sierra, was Gabriel Moraga, who discovered and named it in 1806 while on one of his several exploring expeditions through the river country of the north in search of mission sites. He explored it again on that remarkable expedition of 1808, when he crossed for the second time all the Sierra rivers as far north as the Upper Sacramento, and discovered the territory of at least ten additional counties. In 1810 he again ranged the country watered by the Stanislaus, in an unsuccessful attempt to capture runaway Indians.

The Stanislaus River was the scene of one of the most notable series of battles fought in Alta California between the Mexicans and the Indians. The encounters took place near the mouth of the river in May 1826. The leader of the Indians was Chief Estanislao, who had been educated at Mission San Jose but who had become a renegade, inciting his tribe against the Mexicans. The final contest, in which the latter were victorious, took place on May 30, with General Mariano G. Vallejo in command of the Mexican troops. To this day, farmers in that vicinity plow up relics of the Battle of the Stanislaus.

John C. Frémont, who ferried the river on March 30, 1844, and camped on the Stanislaus side, described its scenery thus: "Issuing from the woods, we rode about sixteen miles over open prairie partly covered with bunch grass, the timber reappearing on the rolling hills of the River Stanislaus, in the usual belt of evergreen oaks. The level valley was about forty feet below the upland, and the stream seventy yards broad, with the usual fertile bottom land which was covered with green grass among large oaks. We encamped on one of these bottoms, in a grove of the large white oaks previously mentioned."

The Old West Side

Recently occupied Indian camp sites existed on the arroyos along the west side of the San Joaquin Valley when the first white men came to the region. Remains of some of these ancient villages may yet be found, the most noteworthy being located on Arroyo de las Garzas, about six miles from the edge of the valley. Here the house basins, some of them measuring seventy feet across, are still intact. An old burial ground lies near by. Similar remains on arroyos de Orestimba, de la Purta, and del Hospital have been largely destroyed.

El Camino Viejo, the old refugee road of the Spanish

and Mexican periods which followed along the west side of the San Joaquin Valley, crossed arroyos many of which are known today by their early Spanish names. Among those in Stanislaus County are Arroyo de las Garzas ("the herons"), Arroyo de Orestimba ("the meeting-place," so called because the padres, when gathering the first Indians in the region, made an agreement with the remaining natives to meet them there again the following year), Arroyo Salado Grande ("big salty creek," where the pioneer known as "Salty" Smith settled in 1855), Arroyo de la Puerta ("the gate," so named because of the natural cut in the hills west of Patterson through which the creek flows during the rainy season), and Arroyo del Hospital (named from the experience of a party of Spaniards who, overcome by sickness, rested beside this stream and were healed).

Spanish settlement on the west side seems to have had an early beginning, for at least one Spaniard, a deserter from the Spanish cavalry, settled on Arroyo de las Garzas as early as 1820. A battle took place in the vicinity that year, when a detachment of Spanish cavalry came to get both the fugitive soldier and some runaway mission Indians. American pioneers in 1852 found the half-breed son of this former cavalryman living in an adobe on Arroyo de las Garzas just across the line in Merced County several miles west of the present town of Gustine. Jesse Hill (one of the owners of the ferry at Hill's Ferry on the San Joaquin River) settled on the spot in 1854, and built a house from lumber brought around the Horn and hauled to Las Garzas by ox team. The site is now occupied by the Newman sheep camp.

Above the sycamore grove on Arroyo de Orestimba a part of another adobe still stands and is occupied as a home. It was erected in 1847 as the ranch house on Rancho Orestimba y las Garzas, granted to Sebastián Nuñez on February 22, 1844.

Hill's Ferry

A ferry across the San Joaquin River at the site later known as Hill's Ferry was first operated in the autumn of 1849, when a man named Thompson carried emigrants from Mexico who were traveling to the mines via Pacheco Pass across the river at this point. Jesse Hill and John de Hart later purchased the ferry from Thompson. After Hart's death, Hill became the sole owner, until in 1865 the ferry passed into the hands of C. G. Hubner.

By this date the town of Hill's Ferry had achieved some importance as a shipping-point for grain. During the high-water season, from April to July, boats customarily came up the river this far to exchange their cargoes for grain and other farm produce. But during the balance of the year the isolation of the town was quite complete. There was no telegraph service, and the mails had to be brought in by stage from Banta, a day's journey away. Nevertheless, during its heyday, Hill's Ferry was a lively place. Its very isolation infused into it a decidedly "Wild West" spirit. Mexican horse thieves and outlaws of all nationalities found it to be a convenient crossing-place en route to their mountain hideouts. The place became noted for its tough characters, and gambling, drinking, and shooting affrays were common.

In 1886–1887, at the time the west-side railroad was being constructed, Simon Newman, who was the chief merchant at Hill's Ferry, donated some land to the railroad. When the town of Newman was laid out on this land in 1887 the people of Hill's Ferry and those living at Dutch Corners, two miles to the south, were induced to move to the new town. With this change Hill's Ferry literally ceased to exist, as most of the houses were soon carted away to other locations. Today the site of Hill's Ferry, which is on the west bank of the San Joaquin River about five miles northeast of Newman, is marked only by two small dwellings and a weather-beaten two-story structure—a one-time hotel—which stands today not far from the present highway.

Knight's Ferry

Knight's Ferry, an old mining town and trading-post on the Stanislaus River about thirty-eight miles southeast of Stockton, was founded in the spring of 1849 by William Knight, scout and fur-trader, who was reputed to have been educated as a physician. He came to California originally with the Workman-Rowland party in 1841. The following year he brought his family from New Mexico, and in 1843 they settled at Knight's Landing in Yolo County.

The first ferry to be established on the Stanislaus River was the one at Knight's Ferry, on the old Sonora Road from Stockton to the southern mines. As early as 1850 thousands of miners passed this way, when ferry receipts could scarcely have been less than $500 a day. The importance and prosperity of Knight's Ferry were further enhanced by the fact that the river bars and banks, hills and gulches, were rich in gold for miles in all directions. Above the ferry was Two Mile Bar, while below it was Keeler's Flat, where Keeler's Ferry, in the shadow of Lover's Leap, was started later in 1849.

After the death of William Knight on November 9, 1849, John and Lewis Dent came into possession of the ferry, but in 1854 it was superseded by a bridge built on the site of the present structure. During the same year Captain Dent and D. M. Locke erected a grist mill and a sawmill on the river bank some three hundred yards above the ferry. The warehouse erected by Dent and Locke still stands. In 1856 a town was laid out on the south bank of the river. This was known for a time as Dentville, but the name was later changed to Knight's Ferry. The place continued to grow and prosper and from 1862 to 1872 was the county seat of Stanislaus County.

Knight's Ferry is still one of the most picturesque of the old river towns. The approach from the south is over an old-time covered bridge, made entirely of wood, which crosses the river just above the mill. This bridge was built to replace the earlier structure erected in 1854, which was swung so close to the water that it was swept away by the flood of 1862, and along with the bridge went the grist mill near by and its flour. People living today recall the rescue of sacks of flour from a gully where the high water had deposited them, outwardly coated with a thick paste of flour and water but with the grist within perfectly dry and clean and fit for human consumption. Two old burr millwheels, once used for grinding the grain, may be seen lying on the ground near the present mill, which was erected after the flood of 1862 by David Tulloch. Not far away is a stone wall, the beginning of a woolen mill that was never finished.

Farther down the street is a little square adobe house, the former home of O Kow, who was the last remaining resident of a once populous Chinatown. Kow is gone now and only the post holes show where the quaint shops and domiciles of the Orientals once stood. Continuing down the narrow thoroughfare, one comes at length to the site of the former courthouse, erected in 1858 as the Fisher Hotel. Only the cellar and a few fragments of the brick walls remain, the building having been destroyed by fire in the '90's. Opposite the courthouse site a beautiful monument of native rock, dedicated by the Major Hugh Moss Chapter, D.A.R., Modesto, commemorates the early history of Knight's Ferry.

On the hill above the village is the Dent house, built in the early '50's and still well preserved. It was here that Ulysses S. Grant, whose wife was Julia Dent, visited his brother-in-law in 1854.

La Grange

La Grange was first known as French Bar, French miners having come to that region to prospect as early as 1852. Later the settlement was moved higher up on the bank of the Tuolumne River away from the original bar. By 1856 La Grange had become a thriving center of trade, as the bulk of the population in the county had moved up into the mining regions. The county seat was transferred from Empire City to La Grange that year, and there it remained until 1862, when another contest took it to Knight's Ferry by a majority of only twenty-nine votes.

At the height of its prosperity, La Grange had from four to five thousand inhabitants and was served daily by three or more stage lines. With the early development of agriculture on the rich bottom lands along the river, a flour mill was erected by John Talbot and Company a half mile below Branch's Ferry. The mill was washed away by the high waters of 1856, but some of the supporting timbers are still intact. During the '70's extensive hydraulic operations were carried on in the vicinity, when ditches were built at a cost of $5,000,000 to convey water to the diggings. The La Grange Dam was built in 1891–1893 and today it is one of the system of Stanislaus County reservoirs which supplies the Modesto and Turlock irrigation districts.

The tiny village of La Grange has a strikingly picturesque setting on the Tuolumne River. For several miles along the banks of the foaming, rushing river, thousands of rock mounds and pyramids stand as monuments to the Herculean efforts of early miners to harvest the golden treasure from the river's bed. Today modern dredges are at work gleaning the residue. Within the village may be seen two old stores, built of stone with heavy iron doors, which are reminiscent of the gold-rush days. Part of the old adobe post office, now board-covered, has been incorporated into a barn.

A ferry was operated at La Grange, first by Nathan McFarland and later by Anthony B. McMillan, from the early '50's until about 1880, when a bridge was built across the Tuolumne at this point. Two miles below the village, where the present bridge spans the river, is the site of Branch's Ferry, which was put into operation in 1851 by George C. Branch. After Branch sold the ferry in 1862, successive owners operated it until it finally came into the possession of Mr. Basso, who still lives on the site of the ferry landing at the north end of the present Basso's Bridge. The old moorings and heavy wire cables used in handling the ferry boats may still be seen on the river bank above Basso's cottage.

Adamsville and Empire City

When Adamsville, which was founded in 1849, was made the first county seat of Stanislaus County in 1854, there were so few buildings in the place that the initial session of court was held out of doors, under a large tree. Before many months the county government was moved to Empire City and Adamsville had lost its one claim to distinction. The town no longer exists, but its site is on the south bank of the Tuolumne River west of Paradise City.

Empire City was originally situated on the Tuolumne twenty miles from the mouth of the river and about eleven miles east of Adamsville. It was laid out on the south side of the river by John G. Marvin, a lawyer from Boston, who later became the first state superintendent of schools in California.

Because it was at the head of navigation, Empire City, in 1851, was made the Army supply station for outlying forts, including Fort Miller and Fort Tejón. Floods nearly destroyed the place in 1852, but it was rebuilt and became the county seat in 1854, after a hard political fight, only to have the seat of justice moved to La Grange two years later. Today the cemetery is all that marks the site of the first Empire City, which had ceased to exist some time before the later Empire City was laid out as a trade center for a growing farm community.

The present Empire City is approximately on the site of Crescent City, a town laid out with high hope in 1850 by Edward S. Townsend and Company of New Jersey. Its founder was enthusiastic about the location and predicted that "here will rise a city which will be world-famous for its size and importance." But his ambitious plans failed to materialize, and before many years Crescent City was nothing more than a promoter's dream.

Aspinwall, which was located on the south bank of the Tuolumne River several miles above Empire City, was another early town of which no trace remains today.

Tuolumne River Ferries

There were a number of ferries up and down the Tuolumne which served as crossings to the Mariposa mines in the '50's. Dickinson's Ferry, located one mile below the present Roberts' Bridge and about seven miles east of Waterford, was established in the early '50's by Gallant Duncan Dickinson, and developed into one of the most important stopping-places on the old Fort Miller Road. Dickinson, who came overland with his family from Missouri in 1846, was an active, energetic man who engaged in many interesting pioneer enterprises. Shortly after his arrival in California he became a member of Aram's garrison at Santa Clara, and a year later, at Monterey, he won the distinction of building the first brick house in California. The next year, 1848, saw him mining for gold at Dickinson's Gulch in Tuolumne County. From there he went to Stockton, where he operated a hotel and served as alcalde of the town in 1849. Dickinson also was a member of the first State Constitutional Convention.

In 1862 John W. Roberts, who had come from Boston in 1849, purchased the properties at Dickinson's Ferry. When the original Dickinson Hotel was destroyed by fire on February 22, 1865, Roberts immediately replaced it by the two-story brick structure which still stands near the river. A portion of the old road is discernible where it approaches the former ferry landing on the river bank a few feet above the present Roberts' Bridge.

At Horr's Ranch, near Dickinson's Ferry, an attempt was made in the '60's by Dr. B. D. Horr to found the town of Horrsville. A little pioneer cemetery located near the present highway a half mile north of the river gives the approximate site of the town.

Among other early ferries on the Tuolumne was Salter and Morley's Ferry. Calvin Salter and his partner, I. D. Morley, took up ranch land two miles east of Dickinson's Ferry (known as Roberts' Ferry after its purchase by J. W. Roberts) and four miles below Branch's Ferry. There they established a ferry, stage station, and post office. Salter's farm was on the river near the ford, while Morley's land occupied the site on which the Turlock Reservoir now stands. Two old trees on the former site of the California Nursery mark the spot where the Salter house stood.

At Waterford, formerly Bakersville, another ferry was established about 1878. The last boat used on the river at this point may still be seen near the present bridge. Five miles to the northeast was Bill Martin's hotel and stage station, a busy place on the Mariposa Road in the '50's and the '60's. The Martin Ranch, with its old family burial ground, belongs today to descendants of the original owner. Although the old ranch house is gone, the site is marked by a portion of the chimney.

Tuolumne City

Among the several towns founded with great expectations along the Tuolumne River in 1850 was Tuolumne City, located about three miles from the mouth of the river. Paxson McDowell, its promoter, dreamed of great wealth when he established the town in the spring of 1850. Lots were staked out on a plot of 160 acres and were sold at high prices. Unfortunately, when summer came it was found that the river was too low for navigation, and the place soon became deserted.

In the middle '60's Tuolumne City was revived as the center of a small farming community, and navigation on the river during high water was resumed. All was life and activity in the little river settlement until 1871, when the inhabitants moved en masse to Modesto. A few of the older houses in Modesto once stood in Tuolumne City, and some of its institutions—the *Modesto News-Herald,* among others —originated there.

The site of the old ferry at Tuolumne City is still plainly evident on the bank near the present bridge over which the Modesto–Grayson highway crosses the river. A low-water cut and a high-water cut, where the boats once moored, have been left as landmarks by the present owner of the ranch on which the town once flourished. The city extended for a half-mile along the river from this point to about where an oak tree stands in an open field, marking the site of a former hotel. Bricks are still plowed up in the fields once covered by Tuolumne City.

A rival of this town existed for a time in Paradise, laid out in 1867 by John Mitchell on his ranch in Paradise Valley five miles east of Tuolumne City. A flour mill, a warehouse, and a number of stores were erected. During the several years of prosperity which Paradise experienced, regular weekly and tri-weekly boat service from Stockton was maintained. But with the founding of Modesto, Paradise also came to an end. The site of the brick warehouse, which stood until recent years, is now occupied by the Putnam gravel bunker, located on the highway about four miles west of Modesto. Across the river from Paradise the town of Westport was established in 1868, but its existence was very short-lived.

A. J. Grayson, in 1850, established a ferry on the San Joaquin River about eight miles above the mouth of the Tuolumne, and a settlement known as Grayson grew up there. After 1852 for several years the place was practically deserted, although the ferry was still operated. In 1868, after the development of grain farming in the region, the place was surveyed and a town was laid out by J. W. Van Benschotten, who had purchased the ferry. A brisk up-river trade caused the place to flourish until the building of the west-side railroad in the middle '80's. A tiny settlement still exists at Grayson, but the streets, laid out with such high hope more than eighty years ago, are now overgrown with grass and weeds.

Burneyville and Langworth

On June 1, 1846, Alfías Basilia Thompson, of Santa Barbara, who had come to California from New England in 1825 as supercargo on the ship "Washington," was granted the Rancho del Estanislao (commonly known as the Thompson Ranch). The present towns of Riverbank and Oakdale, which date from the '70's, are situated within the confines of this old Mexican grant. Before the coming of the railroad, two other towns, Langworth and Burneyville, had been established on the same ranch. Langworth, plotted as a town in 1860 by Henry Langworthy, was located on the Mariposa Road on the hill above the ferry owned by Major James Burney, a former sheriff of Mariposa County and a member of the Yosemite Battalion under Major Savage in 1851. The Major was a gallant host, famed for his hospitality. The ferry and hotel were later purchased by a Mr. Walker, and Burney moved to the site of Burneyville on the south bank of the river near the present Burney Bridge.

At Walker's Ford the old frame hotel, with its spacious reception room and huge fireplace, still stands among the peach orchards on the rich bottom lands just south of the river about a mile north of the Modesto–Oakdale Highway. Only a two-story brick store and the cemetery mark the site of Langworth. Burneyville, where Major Burney established his second ferry, still holds its own as a separate community, although it is quite overshadowed today by the growing town of Riverbank. Near the highway not far from the Burney Bridge, which crosses the river about where the old ferry once plied, stands the Catholic Church, a building erected in 1876 by the Methodists. A few hundred feet up the river in the midst of an orange grove is the site of Burney's old home. The lower part of the tank house, which is of brick, and an ancient fig tree are all that remain from the Major's time.

SOURCES

[Credit is here given for source material, and permission to quote is hereby acknowledged]

BRANCH, L. C. History of Stanislaus County, California. Elliott & Moore, San Francisco, 1881

ELIAS, SOLOMON PHILIP. Stories of Stanislaus. A Collection of Stories on the History and Achievements of Stanislaus County. Modesto, California, 1924

FRÉMONT, JOHN C. Memoirs of My Life, Including in the Narrative Five Journeys of Western Exploration. Belford, Clarke & Company, Chicago, 1887

LATTA, F. F. "San Joaquin Primeval—Archaeology," in Tulare Daily Times, 1931

———. "San Joaquin Primeval—Spanish," in Tulare Daily Times, 1932

———. "San Joaquin Primeval—Yokuts Indians," in Tulare Daily Times, 1931

MCMILLAN, MRS. MINERVA JOSEPHINE (BROWDER). Sketches of an Early Pioneer, Anthony Bolan McMillan, of Stanislaus County, California. Manuscript, 1932.

PRATT, HELEN THROOP. "Crescent City on the Tuolumne. A Prophecy That Failed," in California Historical Society Quarterly, XI, No. 4 (December, 1932), 358–362

SANCHEZ, NELLIE VAN DE GRIFT. Spanish and Indian Place Names of California. A. M. Robertson, San Francisco, 1922

TINKHAM, GEORGE H. History of Stanislaus County, California. Historic Record Company, Los Angeles, 1921

SUTTER COUNTY

SUTTER COUNTY (named in honor of General John A. Sutter) was one of the original twenty-seven counties. During the first two years of its existence the county seat was claimed by four towns in succession: Oro, Nicolaus, Auburn, and Vernon. Auburn was later included in Placer County. The county seat was finally located at Yuba City, where it has remained.

Spanish Expeditions

Gabriel Moraga, in 1808, traversed, for a second time, the river country of the great interior valleys, searching for suitable mission sites. Proceeding farther north than he had gone on the expedition of 1806, he camped on the lower Feather River on October 9, "remarking its width and overflow plain. To this they gave the name 'Sacramento,' employing it also, henceforth, for the great river which it in fact joins farther down. In this connection it may be remarked that at the point where the Sacramento and Feather come together it is the latter which makes a straight course north and south with the lower Sacramento, whereas the upper Sacramento flows in at that point from the west.

"Moraga crossed the Feather River, presumably below Nicolaus, and went north-northwest seven leagues to 'a mountain range, in the middle of the valley'—the Marysville Buttes. Turning west he came to the upper Sacramento."

Interest in the great river country lagged for several years, but in 1817 the founding of missions in the interior was again urged by Father Presidente Mariano Payéras. As a result, in May of that year, a voyage was made by boat up the Sacramento, probably as far north as the mouth of the Feather River, or within sight of the Sutter Buttes, sometimes miscalled the Marysville Buttes. This expedition was commanded by Luís Argüello, accompanied by Fathers Narciso Durán and Ramón Abella.

The Sutter Buttes

The Sutter Buttes, a unique and picturesque series of volcanic hills rising like a miniature mountain range from the vast, level floor of the valley in northern Sutter County, bear within their rugged declivities the same marks and fossils found in the Coast Range. In the spring their slopes are clad in the rare beauty of myriad wildflowers and native shrubs. First discovered by the Spaniards, the Buttes were again seen by Jedediah S. Smith in 1828, and by the Hudson's Bay Company trapper, Michael La Framboise, and others who followed after him. In the various documents relating to Sutter's Grant, these peaks were designated simply as "los tres picos," and John C. Frémont, who camped there from May 30 to June 8, 1846, spoke of them as "the three Buttes." A monument in Frémont's honor was placed in the South Pass of the Buttes on the old stage road to Colusa, by the Bi-county Federation of Women's Clubs of Sutter and Yuba counties in 1923.

Hock Farm

One of General John A. Sutter's several ranchos was Hock Farm, named after an Indian village on the Feather River. On this rancho, which was located on the west side of the river about eight miles below Yuba City, Sutter kept agents to look after his cattle from 1841 until 1850. An adobe house was erected on the estate in the winter of 1841–1842, followed by other structures from time to time. Hock Farm became Sutter's principal stock ranch, the animals ranging freely over the entire countryside between the Feather and Sacramento rivers and south of the Buttes.

By 1850 gold-seekers had despoiled Sutter of the greater part of his lands at New Helvetia. It was at this time that he retired to a plot of ground at Hock Farm which he had reserved for a homestead. There he erected a mansion one and a half miles above the site of the adobe house. The grounds were laid out to beautiful gardens, an orchard, and a vineyard, and there Sutter kept open house to the many travelers and friends who called to pay their respects. Following the flood of 1862, débris from the mines gradually buried the best part of the gardens and orchard at Hock Farm. In 1868 Sutter left the land he so loved, and found a home among the Moravians at Lititz, Pennsylvania, where he died on June 17, 1880.

The old adobe, as well as the later mansion, has disappeared. For many years the remnant of the garden and orchard was used as a picnic grounds. Today the site is marked by one wall of the old iron fort, which stands on the Garden Highway eight miles south of Yuba City. A tablet on it reads:

This memorial is constructed of the original iron from the fort of Hock Farm, established in 1841 by John Augustus Sutter, being the first white settlement in Sutter County. The fort and farm buildings were located on the banks of the Feather River opposite this point. Erected by Sutter and Yuba Bi-county Federation of Women's Clubs, 1927.

Nicolaus

Nicolaus, the ranch and trading-post of Nicolaus Altgeier, was established on the road between New Helvetia and Hock Farm because of the need for ferry transportation at this point on the Feather River. Altgeier, a native of Germany and, for a time, a Hudson's Bay Company trapper, was employed by Sutter to help build the adobe at Hock Farm. In compensation for this work, as well as for anticipated services as ferryman, Altgeier was given a plot of land one mile square, at the crossing. Here he put up a rude hut of mud-covered tules, and in 1843 constructed a primitive ferry which he manned with Indians.

The ferry at Nicolaus was one of those numerous places in California which came into the hands of land speculators. The arrival of a United States government barque in 1849, with supplies for Camp Far West, was the signal for a broadside issued by its promoters, in August 1850, to the effect that Nicolaus was "the head of navigation," and that it was "the only port of entry that has ever been established north of Sacramento—the only town north of that city that has ever had a full-rigged seagoing vessel lying at her landing." Its advantages were already "too manifest," they said, "to be any longer denied and doubted. Furthermore, the close proximity of the town to the rich placers on the Feather and Yuba rivers, Deer, Dry, and Bear creeks, and the Forks of the American ensures its continuance as a depot for the supplies for all the northern mines."

Altgeier, who had put up an adobe house at his landing-place in 1847, built a two-story adobe hotel there in 1849. During the following year, as a result of advertising, over three hundred lots were sold, and three hotels, a dozen stores, and over one hundred dwellings were erected. For a time the little river town showed such business activity that it presented a more flourishing appearance than Marysville, twenty miles to the north.

Realization that Nicolaus was not at the head of navigation fell heavily upon that hopeful metropolis in the winter of 1849–1850. Boats could usually reach Marysville, but when the river was low they were compelled to unload at Vernon, nine miles below Nicolaus. By 1853 many of the houses had been torn down and carted away, and the town was almost deserted. Until the building of the railroad, however, the place served as a center of trade for surrounding ranches.

Nicolaus was the second county seat of Sutter County, from 1850 to 1851, but during the years 1851–1852 it lost that honor, first to Auburn and then to Vernon, after Auburn had become county seat of the newly created Placer County. The seat of justice was re-established at Nicolaus in 1852, but in 1854 it was transferred to Yuba City for a few months. Returned again to Nicolaus for a period of two years, it was permanently established at Yuba City after 1856. Nicolaus still exists as a small center for farms located in southeastern Sutter County, with a few of the old residences and one brick store as landmarks.

Oro

"A noble city of broad streets, imposing buildings, and splendid public squares—on paper—but in fact a tract of land fronting on the south bank of Bear Creek." Such was Oro, "mushroom" neighbor of Nicolaus. Thomas Jefferson Green had purchased the tract from Sutter, and as State Senator he caused his "paper city" to be declared by legislative act the county seat of Sutter County when the county was formed in 1850.

In order to win over his rivals at Auburn, Nicolaus, Vernon, and Yuba City, each better fitted for the position than Oro, Green exercised to its full extent the power of a shrewd, energetic, and imposing presence, a persuasive tongue, and a good-natured, bluff-mannered personality. The outcome was that "the active, talkative, merry-mannered" Senator won the day.

Since there was not a house in town for any purpose, much less for the holding of court, a zinc structure twenty by twenty feet was put up, "without glass or shutters for the windows, or doors for the entrances. Not a tree, or bush, or shrub grew near enough to give its shade to the building." Under a brilliant May sun the first court met in the "zinc house," but "law and equity, lawyers and litigants, jurors and witnesses, with a spontaneity of action that would astonish nothing but a salamander, rushed out of and fled that building, never again to return."

Barham's Crossing, on the river road to Marysville, was established at the site of Oro in the early '50's.

Vernon

Vernon, another of those short-lived "mushroom" cities existing along the Sacramento and Feather rivers in 1849 and 1850, enjoyed the brief illusion that it was the head of navigation and the entrepôt to the mining regions. Buffum, a contemporary writer, says:

"Vernon is situated on the east bank of the Feather River at the point of its confluence with the Sacramento, one of the most eligible positions for a town in the whole northern region of California. The banks of the river are high and not subject to overflow, and this point is said to be at the head of ship navigation on the Sacramento . . . . From the town of Vernon good and well-traveled roads diverge to the rich mineral regions of the North and Middle Forks, Bear Creek, Yuba, and Feather Rivers, rendering the distance much less than by any other route. The town is growing rapidly, and promises to become a great depot for the trade of the above-mentioned mines."

John A. Sutter in April 1849 sold a strip of land along the Sacramento and Feather rivers three miles in length and one mile back. The group of men who purchased this tract laid out a town one mile square at the junction of the rivers, "while the two miles above were designed for the country residences and elegant villas that would be the necessary accompaniments of a city such as this was designed to be."

The winter of 1849 was such a dry one that the Feather River was not navigable. Vessels were compelled to unload at Vernon, and hopes were aroused that the place would become the head of navigation. During the summer of 1849 a number of wholesale stores were erected. The prospect of a glorious future seemed bright indeed, and lots were sold rapidly at a high figure. One hotel was built entirely of mahogany from a shipment bought in Chile. Originally intended for New York, this expensive wood had been brought to California because the ship's captain desired to reach the gold fields.

The heavy rains of 1849–1850 caused the rivers to rise so that it was possible for ships to go as far as Marysville. This was a deadly blow to Vernon, as well as to most of the infant cities along the river. Erstwhile enthusiastic speculators transferred their affections to other towns farther up the river. But Vernon did not expire without a struggle.

E. O. Crosby, a property owner who was a member of the state senate, succeeded in having the county seat transferred from Auburn to Vernon in 1851. The position was lost the next year, however, and in 1853 the hotel ceased to be a public house and the post office was removed. No vestige of Vernon remains today. Only its name is preserved in Vernon Township.

The Brannan House

Samuel Brannan on May 11, 1849, bought from Sutter two square miles of land on the Feather River opposite Nicolaus. There he built a story-and-a-half dwelling of lumber brought around the Horn. In this house, with its beautiful winding stairway, its eight rooms, each with a fireplace, and its surrounding gardens, Brannan gave royal entertainment to many gay river-boat parties made up of friends and celebrities from San Francisco. The "White House," as it was often called, has been moved from its original site on the river bank to the present Garden Highway, where it serves as a modern dwelling.

Yuba City

Samuel Brannan, Pierson B. Reading, and Henry Cheever laid out Yuba City in July 1849 on the site of the Indian village found at this spot by the first white men in the region. Where the round earthen huts of the aborigines once clustered on the river bank at the foot of what is now Second Street, the levee and terraced lots of the white man now stand, and no vestige of the old mound is visible.

Until about the year 1940, at 229 B Street, Yuba City's giant walnut tree lifted a massive spread of 108 feet and extended to a height of 99.6 feet, the huge trunk measuring fifteen feet six inches in circumference at four feet above the ground. The little Lyman house and garden beneath it were completely overshadowed by the dense shade of the great tree planted there over sixty years earlier. The variety (*paradox*) was a cross between the English walnut and the California black walnut.

Camp Bethel

The site of Camp Bethel, one of the largest of the old religious camp meetings in northern California, is just east of the Buttes, two miles north of Sutter City. The land was leased to the North and South Methodist churches for ninety-nine years without cost, the donor, Gilbert Smith of East Butte, stipulating that the land revert automatically to him whenever the churches ceased to hold religious services in the grove. Rev. George Baker, pastor in charge of the Butte circuit in 1862, helped to raise a subscription fund with which to erect a board pavilion about a hundred feet square and furnished with seats. In this pavilion, situated in the midst of the beautiful oaks which then dotted the broad wooded plains at the foot of the Buttes, the Methodist camp meetings were held for three weeks each year. Families from all over the state lived in the grove in small wooden cabins, doing their own cooking or boarding with Mrs. Smith, whose husband dispensed candies and soft drinks.

Gradually, during the '70's, the meetings dwindled in attendance, and early in the '80's were discontinued altogether, the land reverting to Mr. Smith. The site is marked only by a well in the barnyard of the former Lang Ranch, while most of the oaks and the dense groves of native shrubs once carpeted with wildflowers have given way to cultivated fields and orchard lands.

The Bland Ranch

A lonely oak tree standing beside the county road about a mile south of the site of Camp Bethel once sheltered the house in which the late Henry Meade Bland, California's second Poet Laureate, spent much of his boyhood. His father, Henry James Bland, was a pastor on the Butte circuit at various times, beginning in 1868, and in 1872 he purchased the Massou Ranch of 160 acres about two miles directly south of Camp Bethel and two miles northeast of Sutter City. In the midst of changing pastorates, the Blands returned often to the beloved ranch, sometimes living there for a year or two at a time.

While in this neighborhood, Henry Meade Bland attended the Union School, a little unpainted clapboard edifice located in a thick grove of oaks near the Camp, a site now occupied by the Lang house. The second school which he attended in this district, and the one in which he first made his acquaintance with Tennyson, was on what is now the Howard place, about halfway to the Bland homesite. The spot is marked by two large oaks which stand at the corner of the road.

At "Saint's Rest," as his father called the Sutter ranch, Henry Meade Bland led a joyous, romantic life. The homely duties of the farm mingled pleasantly with long hours of delight in the woods and fields and hills about his home and daily nurtured those poetic and spiritual impulses which the poet later expressed in lyric verse.

SOURCES

[Credit is here given for source material, and permission to quote is hereby acknowledged]

BLAND, HENRY MEADE. *Autobiographical Notes*. Manuscript, 1929
BUFFUM, E. GOULD. *Six Months in the Gold Mines*. Lea & Blanchard, 1850
CHAPMAN, CHARLES E. *A History of California: The Spanish Period*. The Macmillan Company, New York, 1921
COY, OWEN COCHRAN. *Gold Days*, of the series *California*, ed. by John Russell McCarthy. Powell Publishing Company, Los Angeles, 1929
DELAY, PETER J. *History of Yuba and Sutter Counties, California*. Historic Record Company, Los Angeles, 1924
MAAS, WILLARD. "The Poet of the Pioneers," in *Overland Monthly*, LXXXV, No. 10 (October 1927), 299–300
SCHOONOVER, T. J. *The Life and Times of General John A. Sutter*. Bullock-Carpenter Printing Company, Sacramento, 1907
WELLS, HARRY L. *History of Sutter County*. Thompson & West, Oakland, 1879

TEHAMA COUNTY

TEHAMA, a word of undetermined meaning, was derived from the name of an Indian tribe. Nellie Van de Grift Sanchez says, "two definitions have been offered: 'high water,' in reference to the overflowing of the Sacramento River, and 'low land,' but these may be among those attempts to account for our names by making the name fit the circumstances . . . . All that can be positively stated is that the word is of Indian origin." Tehama County was organized in 1856 from parts of Colusa, Butte, and Shasta counties, and the county seat was located at the town of Tehama. In 1857 the seat of government was changed to Red Bluff, where it has remained.

First Trails

The first recorded expedition into Tehama County was that of the Spanish explorer Luís Argüello, who in 1821 probably pushed as far north as Cottonwood Creek. Then came the American, Jedediah Strong Smith, in 1828, and in his footsteps a stream of hunters and traders from the south. Hudson's Bay Company trappers from the north followed much the same general course during the years 1830–1845. This old Sacramento Valley route, known at first as the California–Oregon Trail and, later, as the California–Oregon Road, was soon beaten into a well-defined path by such trappers and explorers as Ewing Young, Lieutenant Emmons of the Wilkes Expedition, Joseph Gale, and many others. Sometimes traveling all the way down the western side of the river, and at other times crossing over to the east side somewhere between the sites of Red Bluff and Tehama (a variation used most frequently by the gold-seekers of '49 and the '50's), this historic road was traversed by a long succession of pack-mule trains, horsemen and footmen, herds of cattle and sheep, slow and cumbersome ox-teams and covered wagons, and finally by the stagecoach and the freighter, precursors of the modern automobile, motor truck, and "fly-by-night" busses.

In 1843 John Bidwell, accompanied by Peter Lassen and John Burheim, chased a band of horse thieves over this trail, pursuing them as far north as Red Bluff, where they overtook them and recovered the property. It was on this trip that Lassen selected the land which was later granted to him by the Mexican government.

Returning to this region the following year, Bidwell brought with him five other men who were destined to become the first settlers in the upper Sacramento Valley. Of them, Pierson B. Reading settled in what is now Shasta County, while Job. Francis Dye, William George Chard, Robert Hasty Thomes, and Albert G. Toomes followed Lassen as the earliest white settlers in Tehama County. Each of them located on Mexican grants chosen on this trip with Bidwell in 1844.

An incident of this early reconnoitering tour illustrates the charm which the vast unspoiled regions of the Great Valley held for those who first looked upon it. Going up the east side of the river, the Bidwell party crossed to the west side north of where Red Bluff now is. Continuing north perhaps as far as the site of Redding, they returned along the west side of the stream all the way. On reaching a beautiful grove of oaks south of Elder Creek, the company halted.

"Boys," said Thomes, looking up at a magnificent tree, "the land that will grow an oak like this is good enough for me. Here is where I stay." Thomes was the first of the group to go back and settle on the land of his choice.

It was on this trip, also, that Bidwell mapped the valley, giving those names to its streams which they still bear.

Bloody Island

Samuel J. Hensley, who had accompanied Reading to California in 1843, while rafting logs on the Sacramento River in the northern part of Tehama County early in 1844, had an encounter with some Indians on the island which lies in the river just below the mouth of Cottonwood Creek. It is said that Hensley named the place "Bloody Island" because of this experience. During his sojourn in the region, Hensley noted the fine land north of Cottonwood Creek (in what is now Shasta County), and later recommended it to Reading as suitable for a ranch. It was this land which the latter obtained as a grant in 1844.

Lassen's Ranch

Through the influence of General Sutter, Rancho Bosquejo, comprising 26,000 acres of excellent farming land, was granted in 1843 to Peter Lassen, a pioneer blacksmith who was a native of Denmark and who had come overland to Oregon in 1839. He set sail for California on an English ship and landed at Fort Ross. From there he went to Pueblo de San José, where he spent the winter of 1839–1840. After ranching at Santa Cruz in 1841, we find him at Sutter's Fort in 1842–1843. In December 1843 (according to some accounts) Lassen started for Rancho Bosquejo, but he did not reach his destination until the following February, as high water forced him to camp at the Sutter Buttes. Other authorities place these events one year later, in 1844–1845. Surrounded by hundreds of Indians, Lassen established a trading-post near the mouth of Deer Creek on the east side of the Sacramento River. There is no trace left of the buildings today, but the site is near Vina, about eighteen miles south of the present city of Red Bluff on the main East Side State Highway.

In 1847 Lassen laid out a town on his ranch, calling it Benton City in honor of Senator Thomas H. Benton of Missouri. That same year he returned to Missouri to induce settlers to come to his ranch in California, and to obtain a charter for a Masonic lodge which he wished to establish in the new town. This charter, granted on May 10, 1848, antedates, by six months, any other charter granted for a Masonic lodge in California.

In the summer of the same year Lassen returned to his ranch with a party of settlers, the first to come into California over the famous Lassen Trail and the first to come with the intention of settling in the upper Sacramento Valley. The party's destination was Benton City, the town which Lassen had already laid out. But the discovery of gold, in the spring of 1848, disrupted the entire plan and caused the dissolution of the proposed settlement. On May 9, 1851, the Masonic chapter was moved from Benton City to Shasta, in Shasta County. Benton City no longer exists, but the Masons of Shasta and Tehama counties have erected a monument on the site. It stands on the east side of Pacific Highway 99 E just north of Deer Creek. Near by is a marker placed by the California Trails Committee, identifying the spot as the western terminus of the Lassen Trail.

In 1848 Lassen gave to Daniel Sill, a trapper, one league of land on which the latter built an adobe and on which the town of Danville was later projected but never settled. Lassen, in 1852, conveyed his remaining lands to Henry Gerke, a German, who settled there in 1869. In 1881 Senator Leland Stanford (later founder of Stanford University) purchased from Gerke 9,000 acres of the original Lassen Grant. Subsequently Stanford purchased additional lands, all of which were included in the famous Vina Ranch of 55,000 acres which the Senator conveyed to Stanford University by the Founding Grant, November 11, 1885. The name was derived from the fact that here Senator Stanford planted a vast vineyard, one of the largest in the world. After the ranch became the property of the University plans for developing the vineyard were abandoned. In recent years much of the Vina Ranch has been subdivided and the small tracts sold to many individual owners.

Frémont at Lassen's Ranch

Frémont, coming up from New Helvetia in March 1846 on his way to Oregon, spent a month at Lassen's Ranch, from which he made a local exploring trip through what is now Tehama County. Arriving at the ranch on March 30, he noted that Lassen had a vineyard, that he was experimenting with cotton, and that his wheat crop was large.

On April 5 Frémont and his men set out up the valley, encamping that night "on a little creek on the Sacramento, where an emigrant from 'the states' was establishing himself and was already building a house." This was probably Albert Toomes on his Rancho de los Molinos. On the 6th the expedition crossed the river in canoes to another farm on the right bank, no doubt that of Toomes's friend and partner, Robert Thomes. There Frémont made camp on "a creek wooded principally with large oaks," the same oaks, perhaps, which had won the admiration of Thomes in 1844.

During the next few days the party crossed Red Bank Creek and Cottonwood Creek (later the boundary line between Tehama and Shasta counties), and on the 9th they crossed the Sacramento River to the east side, camping on Cow Creek in what is now Shasta County. On the 11th they were back at Lassen's Ranch, where they remained until April 24, when the march to Oregon was resumed. A month later, on May 24, when returning from Oregon to participate in the stirring events of the American Occupation, Frémont again stopped at Lassen's Ranch.

First Settlers

Robert Hasty Thomes, a native of Maine, came to California with the Bidwell-Bartleson party in 1841. For a time he was engaged as a carpenter and builder in San Francisco and Monterey in partnership with Albert Toomes, as is evidenced by the frequent appearance of the firm name of Thomes and Toomes in Larkin's books and other records.

In the winter of 1844, Thomes received the Mexican land grant of Rancho de los Saucos ("elder trees"), located south of Elder Creek in what is now Tehama County. Although he stocked the place in 1845, he did not settle there permanently until 1846 or 1847, when he built an adobe house on his property. This house was burned in 1858. In the late '60's or early '70's Thomes erected the frame house which still stands on what was long known as the Finnell Ranch, now the El Camino Colony. A hotel, known as the Tehama House, was erected on the site of the old adobe.

Robert Thomes was a man of character and influence in his community. He died in 1878 and lies buried in the Tehama Cemetery.

William George Chard, a native of New York, came to California from New Mexico in 1832. He was at Los Angeles until 1836 and at Santa Cruz from 1837 to 1841. During the years 1843–1845 he was in partnership with Josiah Belden in a store and boarding-house at Monterey. In 1844 Chard obtained a grant of land on the north side of Elder Creek (in Tehama County), naming it Rancho de las Flores ("the flowers"). In this same year Josiah Belden obtained Rancho de la Barranca Colorada north of Chard's grant. Chard took his cattle to Rancho de las Flores in 1845 and in 1846 erected a log cabin on the Sacramento River at a site four miles north of the present Tehama, but he did not go to his rancho to live until the following year, as he was employed at the New Almaden Mine (in Santa Clara County) from 1845 to 1847. The log house at Rancho de las Flores came to be known as the Sacramento House, and was a popular stopping-place on the road to the northern mines.

Across the river from Chard's rancho, Job Francis Dye built an adobe in 1847 on Rancho de los Berrendos ("the antelopes"). Dye, a Kentucky trapper who came from New Mexico with Ewing Young in 1831–1832, for a time engaged in hunting sea otter along the coast. Later he ran a store and distillery at Santa Cruz, where he also had a ranch. Until the '80's, Dye's adobe stood on the west bank of Antelope Creek on what later became known as the Cone Ranch. It was located on a spot not far from where the Cone Methodist Church now stands. This old adobe was long distinguished by the hospitality of its owner, who kept open house and entertained in true Southern manner the many guests who gathered there.

Albert G. Toomes, a native of Missouri who came to California with the Workman-Rowland party in 1841, was given the grant of Rancho Río de los Molinos ("river of the mills") in 1844. Toomes visited his rancho in 1845 and again in 1847, to stock it with cattle, and in 1846 he erected an adobe on the east side of the river not far from the site of the old Ellis flour mill near where the village of Los Molinos later grew up. That Toomes did not go to live permanently on the estate until 1849 is evident from the fact that the firm of Thomes and Toomes is mentioned in records at Monterey until the end of 1848.

William C. Moon, who also came to California with the Rowland-Workman party in 1841, settled on the west side of the Sacramento River opposite the mouth of Deer Creek as early as 1845, and ran a ferry at this point during the gold rush. The ferry was located about where the present Squaw Hill Bridge crosses the Sacramento River on the road from Vina to Corning. Moon lived on his ranch until his death in 1878.

Henry L. Ford, a captain in Frémont's Battalion, also settled on the Sacramento opposite Deer Creek in 1848. John Myers, thought to have been the first settler on the site of Red Bluff, is reputed to have built a hotel within the present limits of that city during the fall or winter of 1849.

The Lassen Trail

Lassen's Ranch was the end of the famous Lassen Trail across the Sierra Nevada, the first northern emigrant route into California from the East. The earliest emigrant party to come over this trail started from Missouri in the spring of 1848 under the leadership of Peter Lassen, reaching his ranch in California in the fall of the same year. A considerable number of emigrants undertook to shorten their journey overland in 1850 by using this same route. However, it never became popular, as it proved to be a long cut-off, steep, precipitous, and infested with hostile Indians.

Lassen's Trail came into California from northwestern Nevada through Surprise Valley in Modoc County. Crossing Surprise Valley south of Fort Bidwell, it bore southward around the southern end of Goose Lake at the head of Pit River. From there it swung to the west, traveling for a few miles over lava beds, then, turning southward, it struck Pit River at the mouth of Rattlesnake Creek some four miles below Alturas. Following down Pit River to the lower end of Big Valley, it crossed the river to the east side of the valley, entering Lassen County some four miles north of Bieber. From Big Valley the trail crossed over into Dixie Valley. Passing through the plain to a wooded hill, it continued some five miles until it reached Lassen's Springs. At this point, the trail passed around the western side of a big mountain to Beaver Creek, crossed over Pine Creek, and turned to the west of Feather Lake and Norval Flat. Fording Susan River, it bore a little to the southwest until it reached Robbers' Creek, which it crossed a few miles lower down. The ford at Robbers' Creek is about five miles to the north and west of the present town of Westwood in Lassen County. Soon after leaving Robbers' Creek, the trail entered Plumas County. Here it traversed Big Meadows, now covered by the waters of Lake Almanor, an artificial reservoir of great capacity. Continuing westward to Deer Creek Meadows at the head of Deer Creek in Tehama County, the trail followed along its western side through the mountains and foothills to the Sacramento Valley, striking the valley at Toomes Creek, at a point near the railroad two miles below Los Molinos and some four miles above Vina.

The William Ide Adobe

William B. Ide, a native of Rutland, Massachusetts, came with his family from New Hampshire to what is now Tehama County in 1845. He built a log cabin on the R. H. Thomes ranch and spent the winter there. In the spring of 1846 he moved to the Belden ranch, where he put up another log house in Ide's Bottom south of what was later Red Bluff. In 1847 Ide purchased, from Belden, Rancho de la Barranca Colorada ("Ranch of the Red Bluff"), so called because of an adjacent cliff on the river, fifty feet high, composed of sand and gravel of a reddish hue.

Ide took up additional land north of Rancho de la Barranca Colorada, and there built an adobe house in 1849. It was situated on the river bank about two miles north of Red Bluff. A ferry, established at this point by Ide and known for many years as the Adobe Ferry, operated in the '60's and was still running in the early '70's. When the first bridge was opened in the autumn of 1876 the ferry was abandoned.

William B. Ide was the commandant of the Bear Flag Revolt in 1846. After 1850 he resided much of the time at Monroeville, Colusa County, where he eventually held all the county offices. The William Ide adobe (now known as the George E. Sutton place and located two miles north of the present town of Red Bluff) and the old California–Oregon Road, which passed by its door in stagecoach days, have been marked.

Tehama

Robert Thomes's adobe was built on a spot later covered by Tehama, the first town in the county. It has been authentically established, however, that before Thomes settled on the site he had given to his friend, Albert Toomes, a small tract of land where Tehama now stands, thus making Toomes the founder of the town. In 1849 Tehama (then known as Hall's Ranch), located on the west side of the Sacramento River twelve miles south of Red Bluff, was an important center of trade and freighting on the Oregon Road as well as the principal ferry-crossing between Marysville and Shasta. Other ferries were soon established at Moon's Ranch, Ide's Adobe, and Red Bluff. When the "Orient" landed at the latter point in 1850, Tehama at once lost its prestige as a river town. As a stage center, however, it held its own for a number of years.

The first stage line from Colusa to Shasta was opened up by Baxter and Monroe in 1851. An opposition line from Marysville, via Hamilton, Neal's Ranch, and Bidwell's Ranch, in Butte County, was started by Hall and Crandall in 1852. The two lines converged in Tehama, creating a prosperous activity which continued until the coming of the railroad.

Tehama, with its old buildings and tree-lined streets, is today a quiet little village. The courthouse, built while the town was the county seat of the newly created Tehama County, is used as a lodge room for the Masons.

Across the river the town of Sesma once flourished. A Mr. Payne, in 1851, erected a sawmill on Mill Creek above the town, and in the '70's the Sierra Lumber Company built a mill in the neighborhood but later abandoned the site in favor of Red Bluff. A part of the cobblestone foundations of the old Ellis Flour Mill, begun near Sesma by a Dr. Crosby in the autumn of 1854, is still visible near the highway. This mill, later purchased by M. C. Ellis, was twice destroyed by fire prior to 1880 and both times rebuilt by Ellis. The stone foundations of another flour mill, built a year or so later on the Dye Ranch, may still be seen on the banks of Antelope Creek a few miles east of Red Bluff

The Washington House

Colonel B. F. Washington, great-grandson of Lawrence Washington, brother of George Washington, came overland to California from Virginia in 1849, finally settling in Tehama County. He served as agent on the "Nomee Lackee" Indian Reservation, situated in western Tehama County between Elder and Thomes creeks, a section now known as the Paskenta district. Washington, who lived here for several years, acquired title to a considerable tract of land on which his son later lived. No member of the family resides in this section today, but the old house still stands.

The "Stone House"

The Wilson home, better known as the "Stone House," still stands in excellent condition on the south side of Thomes Creek about four miles northwest of Corning. It is said to have been erected in 1859 by Henry Clay Wilson, later State Senator and a leader in local and state politics. It was substantially constructed of cobblestones picked up by Mr. Wilson's grain teamsters on their return trips from Red Bluff, the shipping-point for wheat from the ranch.

Home of John Brown's Widow

In 1864, near the close of the Civil War, the widow of John Brown, the famous abolitionist of Harper's Ferry, came to Red Bluff with her children. So great was the admiration for John Brown in that section of the country that a considerable sum of money was raised for the purpose of providing his widow and children with a home. The house was built on the west side of Main near Willow Street, not far from the southern entrance to the city, and there Mrs. Brown lived until the summer of 1870, when she and her three daughters moved to Humboldt County. The house, somewhat remodeled, is still standing and occupied.

SOURCES

[Credit is here given for source material, and permission to quote is hereby acknowledged]

DORNIN, MAY. *The Emigrant Trails into California.* Master's thesis in history, University of California, 1921
ELLIOTT AND MOORE. *Tehama County, California* . . . . Elliott & Moore, San Francisco, 1880
FRÉMONT, JOHN CHARLES. *Memoirs of My Life. Including in the Narrative Five Journeys of Western Exploration.* Vol. I. Belford, Clarke & Company, Chicago and New York, 1887
IDE, WILLIAM BROWN. *Biographical Sketch* . . . . Edited and printed by Simeon Ide, Claremont, N.H., 1880
McCOY, L. L. "Story of Early Days in Tehama County," in *River Rambler,* June 28, 1926
SANCHEZ, NELLIE VAN DE GRIFT. *Spanish and Indian Place Names of California.* A. M. Robertson, San Francisco, 1922
SCHOENFELD, GOLDA. *Some Landmarks and History of Tehama County, California.* Manuscript read before Antelope Women's Club, December 1, 1922
SHERMAN, EDWIN A. *Fifty Years of Masonry in California.* 2 vols. George Spaulding & Company, San Francisco, 1898
SWEENEY, J. D. *History and Geography of Tehama County for Use in the Public Schools.* Adopted by the County Board of Education, Red Bluff, California, 1930

TULARE COUNTY

TULARE COUNTY (Tulare is Spanish for "a place of tules, or rushes") was created in 1852 from the southern part of Mariposa County and the northern part of Los Angeles County. The first county seat was at Woods' Cabin, thenceforth known as Woodsville, but in 1853 it was moved to Visalia, where it has remained.

Sequoia National Forest and Park

Sequoia National Forest and Sequoia National Park (in which is the General Sherman Tree, the largest of all the sequoias) comprise the most extensive as well as the most remarkable group of trees in the entire Sierra Big Tree belt, numbering fifty-three individual groves in all. Within this vast assemblage some of the most magnificent of the Sierra groves are to be found, a few of the most notable being Little Boulder Grove; the General Grant Park, containing the General Grant or the Nation's Christmas Tree, one of the three largest of the Big Trees; the Muir Grove; Giant Forest, generally considered to be the largest and finest of all the Sierra Big Tree forests, where scores of separate groves merge, one into another; Redwood Canyon, another magnificent stand of over three thousand trees; Redwood Meadow; Atwell; Garfield; Dillon Wood; and Mountain Home or Balch Park.

Giant Forest, in what is now Sequoia National Park, was discovered by Hale Tharp, a stockman, who in the summer of 1856 had located in the Three Rivers district at what is now known as the Tharp Ranch, about two and one-half miles below the present village of Three Rivers. Friendly Indians told Tharp of the existence of a neighboring forest of "big trees," and in the summer of 1858, led by a desire to see for himself, as well as the need to locate a summer pasture for his cattle, made his first trip into the Giant Forest, accompanied by two of the Indians.

A huge hollow sequoia log still lying at Tharp's old camp in Log Meadow testifies to this first visit of the white man to the great forest. On this log Tharp carved his name and the year, 1858, on the day on which he arrived at the spot. The inscription is now protected by a glass placed there by park rangers. In this log Tharp built a unique home, where he spent many summers. It was fitted with a door, a window, and a stone fireplace, and contained one large room fifty-six and a half feet long. The tree itself is twenty-four feet in diameter at the base and is estimated to have been three hundred and eleven feet high when it fell. It is now carefully preserved by the National Park Service.

Tharp was not only the first white man to discover the Sequoia National Park region but he was also the first to live in the park, and his discovery led to the search for and the finding of other important groves—Kings River, Tule River, Deer Creek, and others. By the summer of 1862 all of the groves in the state had been made known.

A movement for the protection of the groves of giant sequoias in the mountains of Tulare County for purposes of permanent drainage, lumber supply, recreation, and scenic beauty was begun in 1878. A long, hard fight with the private interests which were seeking to buy up the Big Trees for commercial purposes followed. The leader in this fight was the late Colonel George W. Stewart, who, as publisher and editor of the *Visalia Delta* in 1890, was also the chief promoter of the campaign for the creation of the Sequoia and General Grant National parks.

Because of his unselfish and persistent work in pushing the cause of the giant trees, George Stewart has been justly acclaimed the "Father of the Sequoia National Park." An unnamed mountain in the Great Western Divide, rising almost thirteen thousand feet above sea-level and about five thousand feet above the Big Trees of the park, has been named in his honor, Mount George Stewart.

Mount Whitney

Mount Whitney is the highest peak in the United States and one of a group of splendid mountains of from 13,000 to 14,000 feet elevation situated in the High Sierra at the headwaters of the Kings and Kern rivers. For many years it was thought that Mount Shasta was the highest summit in California, but in 1864 the Whitney Geological Survey discovered the fact that the summit of Mount Whitney was the highest point in the Sierra. A very accurate measurement by the United States Coast and Geodetic Survey in 1928 gives an altitude of 14,496 feet.

The mountain was named in 1864 by the Brewer party, in honor of J. D. Whitney, state geologist and leader of the Geological Survey. Clarence King wrote: "For years our Chief, Professor Whitney, has made brave campaigns into the unknown realm of Nature. There stand for him two monuments: one a great report, made by his own hand; another the loftiest peak in the Union, begun for him in the planet's youth and sculptured of enduring granite by the slow hand of time."

King, attempting to climb the peak in 1871, missed it on account of obscuring storm clouds and climbed Mount Langley by mistake. Learning of his error in 1873, he hastened west to climb the real Mount Whitney on September 19. He was too late, however, for on August 18 John Lucas, A. H. Johnson, and C. D. Begole had made the first ascent of the great mountain.

Since July 1881 Mount Whitney has been the base of operations for many scientific astronomical observations, the astronomical expedition under Professor S. P. Langley that year being the first.

Approach to Mount Whitney was formerly made by way of Lone Pine in Owens Valley, up Cottonwood Creek, through Cottonwood Pass, and from there north through Whitney Meadows in Tulare County to Crabtree Meadow, which is at the base of the ascent. A more recently developed approach from the west is now available and includes the Sequoia National Park in its route, while outfitting stations are also located at Giant Forest in the park and at Mineral King. The latter, which is just outside the park, is accessible by automobile via Sequoia Park. A new trail by way of Lone Pine was opened for travel in the spring of 1931, with a base camp in Lone Pine Canyon.

The John Muir Trail

For years a ridge trail from Yosemite to the headwaters of the Kern River had been the dream of many lovers of the High Sierra. In 1914, on the annual trip of the Sierra Club, Meyer Lissner suggested that the state legislature be requested to appropriate money for the building of such a trail. While awaiting the formulation of plans, John Muir, for many years leader and president of the club, passed away. "In seeking a fitting memorial to the man who had done so much to explore and make known to the world the wonders and beauty of the High Sierra, it seemed but fitting that a trail to be constructed near the crest of his 'range of light' should bear his name."

The first appropriation of $10,000 was approved by Governor Johnson in 1915 and another $10,000 was made available in 1917. No further appropriations were secured until 1925, from which date work on the trail has been continued until the present. It is now passable, with but a few detours, throughout its entire length.

"In its course the trail passes Thousand Island Lake and the Devil's Post Pile National Monument, rounds the flanks of the loftiest and most famous mountain peaks, from Mt. Ritter and Banner Peak on the north to the Evolution Group, Mt. Goddard, the Palisades and Mt. Tyndall on the south, zigzags up a succession of the highest and most impregnable divides, and affords approach to the Tehipite Valley, Kings River Canyon and the Canyon of the Kern. It is the gateway to the best fishing, the most ambitious mountaineering, the sublimest and most diversified scenery that the High Sierra has to offer."

Walter L. Huber describes the trail thus: "The southern terminus of the trail is Mount Whitney, the highest point in the United States, exclusive of Alaska. Along the route are 148 peaks rising to elevations of more than thirteen thousand feet, including twelve of the fourteen summits in California which attain elevations of more than fourteen thousand feet. The crest of the Sierra is more than thirteen thousand feet in elevation for eight and a half miles continuously adjacent to Mt. Whitney. Even these cold statistics give an inkling of the grandeur of the region which this trail has made accessible, but not *too* accessible; for here is, I am glad to say, one of the most extensive areas in any of our Western states yet remaining practically free from automobile invasion . . . .

"With the John Muir Trail should be mentioned the 'High Sierra Trail,' now being constructed by the National Park Service in the Sequoia National Park from the Giant Forest to Mount Whitney. This trail, which is being constructed in accordance with the highest standards, will open to exploration some of the finest mountain scenery on the American continent and, with the John Muir Trail, will afford a complete loop through one of the best sections of the High Sierra. Surely the dreams of the early explorers are now being realized, if not actually exceeded. . . . ."

Indian Mounds

Within a few yards of the Golden State Highway and two miles north of the city of Tulare, there is a mound about two hundred yards long and five feet high, apparently the work of human hands. This mound, which is located on the southern portion of the old Tulare airport, extends eastward from a point near the road and is paralleled by a series of large excavations, the soil from which was evidently used in the building up of the mound.

The largest of a group of very remarkable mounds, once surrounded at flood time by the waters of Tulare Lake, is situated fifteen miles due west of Tulare City on what is now known as the old Jacobs Ranch. This mound, about a hundred and fifty yards long and six feet above the surrounding country, was composed of a solid mass of the common softshell clams of Tulare Lake, which were found in layers "as clean and as closely packed as if they had been washed and stacked by hand." Wagon loads of these thin, white shells have gradually been hauled away for chicken feed.

Locally known as the Paige Mound, remnants of one of the largest rancherías ever reported in that section of the San Joaquin Valley are still visible along an old channel of Cameron Creek about two miles east of the village of Paige. Many years ago an irrigation ditch was cut along the top of this mound, disclosing ancient burials and many Indian artifacts. Gradually over a period of years the entire southwestern portion of the mound was leveled, but some of the northeastern section still remains intact. Archaeological treasures of great value were found at this site: quantities of fired clay thought to have formed the roofs of ancient houses long since burned; the marks of small poles and tules where the houses had stood; soil repeatedly burned "until it was of the hardness, and often of the color of a brick"; the vast accumulations of fish vertebrae and other kitchen refuse; burials and artifacts.

Several miles from the eastern shore of Tulare Lake there was a long island or series of islands which remained unknown to American settlers for many years on account of the dense screen of tule swamps which stretched for miles along the lake shore in both directions. These islands always escaped the inundating waters of the winter floods. Said to

have been discovered in 1853 by a cattle man, the land was acquired soon afterward by Judge J. J. Atwell, of Visalia, who used it as a pasture for his hogs.

Atwell's Island, as it came to be known, formed at least two islands during the highest water, the one to the west being called Skull Island because the remains of Indian houses and skeletons uncovered by wave action were found there by the first white settlers to visit it.

The present town of Alpaugh is located on what was once Atwell's Island, and a little to the south and west of town may still be traced several old stream beds, along which many artifacts and remains of Indian villages have been found. Several large collections of Indian relics have been taken from the Atwell and neighboring sites within the past forty years.

The Derby Expedition, which entered the San Joaquin Valley in April 1850, a few weeks after the Woods Massacre on the Kaweah River, reported that there were two large rancherías at Outside, Cameron, and Deep creeks; and that the two hundred inhabitants of these villages had treated them with the greatest kindness and hospitality. The Broder family, which settled on Cameron Creek in the early '50's, also found several hundred Indians living in huts on what came to be known as Broder's Mound and along the ridge to the southwest. Various epidemics, however, soon reduced this number to not more than twenty.

The Broders built their first house in this region about two hundred yards from the old mound, but later a more pretentious dwelling was erected on the mound itself. This house became a refuge for neighboring white settlers during the flood of 1862, when the mound was the only unsubmerged land for miles around.

The Broder Mound property finally came into the hands of a Visalia bank in 1927, when, owing to a series of delays in leveling and building operations, local archaeologists working under the supervision of F. F. Latta succeeded in making one of the most extensive studies of ancient Indian culture in the San Joaquin Valley yet reported. Perhaps "the most remarkable example of Yokuts burial customs ever unearthed" was found at this site, yielding more than eight hundred specimens within an area of not over forty-five by sixty feet. Three distinct cultures were uncovered, including that of what was probably the first migration into the valley, as well as that of the later Indians found at the site by the first white settlers.

The Sweet Mound, located on the west bank of Elk Bayou, four and a half miles south of Waukena, was the site of one of the most extensive permanent rancherías on the east shore of Tulare Lake. This mound was found by two boys on the property of Adolph Sweet on Thanksgiving Day, 1928, and was subsequently excavated by local archaeologists. Early American settlers testified that this site was occupied by Indians as late as 1860.

The burials unearthed at the Sweet Mound appear to be extremely ancient, depicting a culture which shows no signs of contact with later Indian cultures or with the whites. Having been placed in an alkali soil, they are perfectly preserved. South and west of the cemetery, along a low ridge, marks of twenty or more Indian houses are still plainly visible, a splendid example of the general arrangement of an Indian village. Shallow, cellar-like depressions perhaps twenty feet in diameter, with a fire pit in the center and the marks of the doorway at the south side of each, show where these primitive dwellings once stood, and near the bayou remains of the community sweat house are also quite distinct.

Many ancient rock writings made by the Indians of prehistoric times may be seen along the western slope of the eastern foothills throughout Tulare County. The most re-markable of these are located north and slightly east of Visalia at Woodlake, Dillon's Point, and Kaweah Caves.

The Old Spanish Trail through Visalia

Gabriel Moraga, in 1806, went into the river country on the western side of the Great Valley to search for mission sites. On his return trip he ascended Kings River a short distance, crossing what is now Tulare County seven miles east of Visalia, at Venice Hills, known as Kaweah Hills to local Indians and early pioneers.

Another party under an unknown leader (possibly Juan Ortega) and accompanied by Father Juan Cabot, chronicler of the expedition, went into the tulares in 1814, also in search of mission sites. Again, in 1815, Juan Ortega and Father Cabot led an expedition from Mission San Miguel to hunt for runaway Indians. Proceeding up Kings River, the party crossed over to Kaweah River in Tulare County and from there went on to the vicinity of Venice Hills.

These expeditions reported favorably of the region in the vicinity of the present town of Visalia. They considered it especially suitable for mission sites, and in the biennial report for the years 1815–1816 Father Presidente Mariano Payéras renewed his recommendation to found a mission and presidio in the valley, and the district about Visalia was urged as the most suitable location. Two sites were recommended, one at Telumne, probably within the city limits of the present Visalia, and the other at Venice Hills, where the river was forded. The proposal was repeated two years later.

One other Spanish expedition crossed the Visalia Trail when, in 1819, Lieutenant José María Estudillo went into the valley in an attempt to subdue uprisings among the Indians. Estudillo was emphatic in his report that a presidio would be a necessity in connection with any mission established in that country, where the Indians were both numerous and un-friendly.

American Pathfinders

The first American to traverse the Tulare Trail was Jedediah S. Smith, who passed that way in 1826 and 1827. Skirting the Sierra foothills along the eastern side of the valley, he probably followed much the same route as that taken later by the Stockton–Los Angeles Stage Road, and now followed approximately by a modern highway through the towns of Porterville, Lindsay, Exeter, Woodlake, and others to the north. Smith was followed, in 1834, by Joseph Walker, who led the Bonneville hunters out of California over the Sierra by way of the pass which now bears his name, and which forms an outlet from the South Fork of Kern River to the eastern side of the divide.

John C. Frémont, in 1844, followed the old Tulare Trail on his way out of California. In the winter of 1845–1846, a second expedition under Frémont reached Walker's Lake in Nevada. There the company divided, Frémont himself crossing the mountains with a few men to Sutter's Fort, while the main body, under the leadership of Joseph Walker, went through Walker's Pass and down the Kern River, where they camped for three weeks early in 1846. Frémont, who had hurried south to meet his men, and who had under-stood the Kings River to be the appointed meeting-place, waited for several weeks before returning to Sutter's Fort. During this time he ascended the Kings River along its right bank to its junction with the North Fork, up which he climbed to an altitude of 10,000 feet. After waiting in vain at the Kern River camp for Frémont's arrival, Walker and his men pushed on northward through Tulare County, finally rejoining Frémont near Mission San Jose.

On these expeditions, Smith, Walker, and Frémont traveled the Tulare Trail. Others soon followed in their footsteps—explorers, hunters, pioneer settlers, and gold-seekers. A tablet placed beside the road just outside of Lindsay in 1928 by the Tierra Alta Chapter, D.A.R., commemorates the opening up of the valley route by these sturdy pioneers.

Woodsville

Under the leadership of John Woods, a party which was said to have come from the Mariposa mines settled on the southern bank of the Kaweah River either in December 1849 or early in 1850. A substantial log cabin was erected a short distance south of the Kaweah River Delta, seven miles east of the site of the present town of Visalia.

Woods and his party had been established only a few months when a group of Kaweah Indians came to their cabin and, because of earlier mistreatment at the hands of the Woods party, demanded that they leave the region within ten days. This the white men agreed to do, but were slow in making their preparations, delaying beyond the allotted time. The Indians, however, were prompt to act and all but three of the party were massacred.

Another settlement had been made at the same time as that of Woods, about a half-mile distant, by Loomis St. Johns, for whom the St. Johns River was named. Although so near the Woods cabin, the Indians left the St. Johns settlement unmolested. Also at about the same time two brothers, A. A. and C. R. Wingfield, claimed "squatter's rights" on land along the Kaweah River from the Woods cabin south. In 1851 Nathaniel and Abner Vise settled a few miles to the southwest of the Woods cabin, at a place then known as Buena Vista. A log fort was erected as a protection against the Indians, and gradually a town grew up. Later, the name was changed to Visalia, a combination, it is said, of the names of Brother Vise and Sister Salia, his wife, both members of the Christian Church.

In 1854, Abraham Hilliard and his family moved into the Woods cabin. When Tulare County was created in April 1852, the legislature provided that the seat of justice be placed at the cabin on the south side of Kaweah Creek, near the bridge built by Dr. Thomas Payne, and that it be called Woodsville.

The first election board opened its polls on July 10 under the tree which stood the farthest out in the open, now known as the "Election Tree" or "Charter Oak." The old Election Tree stands today on a quiet country road near the quarry seven miles east of Visalia, and is the property of Tulare County. A tablet on its trunk bears the legend:

> Election Tree. Under this tree on July 10th, 1852, a party under the command of Major Savage held the election by which Tulare County was organized.

The county seat remained under the "Election Tree" for some time, although the Woods cabin, a half-mile to the south, had been designated as the legal location.

The Stockton–Los Angeles Stage Road

The old Stockton–Los Angeles Stage Road crossed the Kaweah River Delta at a place long known as Four Creeks, that portion of the delta lying south of the Venice Hills. Stages and freight teams used this road, which went from Los Angeles north to Fort Miller and the mines.

The route was divided into the Upper and Lower Detours, as they were called. These detours paralleled each other as they passed along the base of the hills a few miles apart, and the southern junction of the two was near the base of the Venice Hills and a little to the southwest, near where the Southern Pacific Railroad now crosses the St. Johns River. The Lower Detour came in from the west, while the Upper Detour passed to the east of Twin Buttes and skirted the western side of the Venice Hills. Uniting at the junction on the St. Johns, the road then passed the "Election Tree" at Woodsville and followed the base of the Venice Hills about a quarter of a mile before crossing the St. Johns River. For a half-mile it continued south and then turned to the southwest for a quarter of a mile, crossing the Kaweah River a half-mile south of the "Election Tree."

Butterfield Stage Stations

During dry weather the northbound Butterfield Overland Stages, during the years 1858–1861, turned off from the old Stockton–Los Angeles route east of Visalia (where one of the main stage stations was located at what is now the southeast corner of Main and Court streets) and crossed the country to the Kings River Station (Whitmore's Ferry). When the river was too high to be crossed at Whitmore's, a route along the base of the hills was followed to Smith's Ferry in Fresno County.

Proceeding southeast from Visalia the following stations were passed: the "Pike" Lawless Ranch, one mile south of the present Outside Creek Bridge; the Tule River Station, later Porterville; Fountain Springs; and White River or Irish John's.

At the Tule River Station, Peter Goodhugh erected the first building, a shake house with a fireplace at each end and a porch on the south side. The site of this old overland station is on the present Bartlett place.

In 1859 a young man named Porter Putnam arrived at the Lawless Ranch, where he obtained a job caring for the stage horses. Soon afterward he went to the Tule River Station. Porter Putnam was an enterprising young man. He bought out Peter Goodhugh and developed the station into a popular stopping-place and hotel. His affable, hospitable nature won the hearts of his customers and associates and the place came to be known as Porter's Station. The town which grew up around it was called Portersville, later Porterville. After the coming of the railroad in the late '80's, Porterville increased in prosperity until today it is a city of over five thousand inhabitants. It is located in the heart of the "thermal belt" where high-grade oranges are produced.

Tailholt, a "Ghost" of the White River

The present hamlet of White River, for many years and in some localities still known as Tailholt, was at one time a mining camp almost as well known as Angel's, Columbia, or Sonora. Not more than a dozen people make it their home today.

First established in 1857, when placer gold was discovered on a small tributary stream in Coarse Gold Gulch about two miles east of the present village, the original settlement was called Dogtown. When the first road into Linns Valley was built, old Dogtown was left one and one-half miles to the east. A new settlement, for a short time also known as Dogtown, was established at the present site. An interesting happening gave it the curious name of Tailholt. The story, as told by F. F. Latta, is as follows:

"'Yank' Booth, the old stage driver, while en route to Visalia, stopped at Tailholt to change horses. He had with him a society lady who was returning from the Kern River Mines after having visited her husband, a mine operator at that place. This lady seriously offended the dignity of Yank by effectively 'high hatting' him. She further aroused the ire of Yank by carrying with her in the stage a pet poodle.

"As the horses were being changed at Dogtown, a large cat crossed the street ahead of them, leaving the restaurant of Mother Cummings and proceeding to the hotel of Levi Mitchell. The dog spied the cat and attempted to jump from a small window at the side of the stagecoach. The lady made one wild grab at the dog and succeeded in catching it by the tail as it was leaving the stage. Yelping at the top of its voice, the dog hung suspended from the window, and the lady screamed for help. Yank took in the situation at a glance and went ahead changing horses. Mother Cummings came to the rescue. While lifting the dog through the window she remarked, 'Well, ma'am, a tail-holt is better than no holt at all.' When Yank reached Visalia he told the postmaster and keeper of the stage station that the name of the new place on White River was Tailholt."

Two old cemeteries at Tailholt are especially interesting. One, situated on the crest of a hill to the north of the river, was reserved for respectable people, while to the other, located on "Boot Hill," south of the river, were relegated the renegades—desperate characters who died with their boots on. Five persons were buried on Boot Hill, four of them having been participants in gun battles in old Tailholt. Three of these outlaws were named Dan, while the fourth, Jack Gordon, was a member of the notorious Mason-Henry gang, exterminated at the close of the Civil War.

Traver, a "Ghost City"

"White irregular patches of alkali . . . . reaching . . . . far out among the dingy salt grass" cover the once productive and thickly settled tracts of land on which were located Traver, Vina, Scaironi, and Kitchener. Traver, once the center of the region, had a population of about one thousand in 1887. Modest homes, each with its cultivated plot of ground, adjoined the flourishing city with its warehouses, lumber yards, agricultural implement factories and mills, stores, hotels, churches, a post office, express office, and railroad depot, as well as saloons, gambling dens, and the inevitable Chinatown, which occupied two city blocks. Traver in its heyday was a typical example of the "wild and woolly" Western town. Of this once flourishing farm community a bit of the former village still remains, while scattered over the bleak fields occasional broken windmills and dilapidated barns·constitute the pathetic remnants of a hundred farmsteads.

The story of Traver's brief period of prosperity, followed by a rapid decline, has been oft repeated in mining towns but Traver is one of the few such examples in California's agricultural history. In 1882 P. Y. Baker, a civil engineer, conceived the idea of a large irrigation project which would furnish water to some hundred and thirty thousand acres of land on the south side of and adjoining Kings River in both Tulare and Fresno counties. His plan met with favor when presented to a few capitalists, and options on about thirty thousand acres of this land were secured on June 7 of the same year.

A portion of the tract was covered by the "76 Ranch," located on the Kings River bottom lands in Fresno County and owned by Senator Thomas Fowler, who turned his estate over to the newly formed company, becoming one of the original stockholders. The name of this ranch, which is still in existence and still highly productive, was given to the new corporation, "The 76 Land and Water Company."

Eventually, an immense irrigation canal was built through this territory. A portion of the tract, comprising two thousand acres, lay along the Southern Pacific Railroad near the northwest corner of Tulare County a short distance southeast of where the railroad crossed Kings River. Part of this was set aside for a town site and the remainder subdivided and sold as colony lots.

The new town reached a phenomenal prosperity in a

very short time and continued to enjoy this state until October 30, 1887, when the first of five destructive fires all but wiped it out. By this time, too, the alkali in the soil had begun to noticeably affect the crops. In spite of all efforts to counteract this blight, before long practically every tree, shrub, and plant on many of the colony lots had been killed. Utter desolation gradually ensued. This decline was further hastened after 1888 by the drawing of the population away from Traver to the new towns of Dinuba and Reedley in the heart of the fertile "76 country," and on the branch railroad line to Porterville.

But the blasted hopes and the bitter tears of disappointment which were the common experience of the members of this fated colony formed a tie which has never been broken. Each year, on or near April 8, a gay crowd gathers at the old town site to celebrate the founding of Traver and to continue the custom of earlier days when thousands of visitors from all parts of the San Joaquin Valley gathered there to participate in the festivities.

SOURCES

[Credit is here given for source material, and permission to quote is hereby acknowledged]

BOWIE, WILLIAM. "Levelling up Mount Whitney," in *Sierra Club Bulletin*, XIV, No. 1 (February 1929), 53–57

FARQUHAR, FRANCIS P. "The Story of Mt. Whitney," in *Sierra Club Bulletin*, XIV, No. 1 (February 1929), 39–52

———. "Spanish Discovery of the Sierra Nevada," in *Sierra Club Bulletin*, XIII, No. 1 (February 1928), 54–61

———. "The Topographical Reports of Lieutenant George H. Derby," with Introduction and Notes by Francis P. Farquhar, in *California Historical Society Quarterly*, XI, Nos. 2–4 (June–December 1932)

FRY, WALTER, and JOHN R. WHITE. *Big Trees.* Stanford University Press, Stanford University, California, 1930

GIFFORD, E. W., and W. EGBERT SCHENCK. "Archaeology of the Southern San Joaquin Valley, California," in *University of California Publications in American Archaeology and Ethnology*, XXIII, No. 1 (1926), 1–122

HUBER, WALTER L. "The John Muir Trail," in *Sierra Club Bulletin*, XV, No. 1 (February 1930), 37–46

KING, CLARENCE. *Mountaineering in the Sierra Nevada.* James R. Osgood & Company, Boston, 1872

LATTA, F. F. "San Joaquin Primeval—Archaeology," in *Tulare Daily Times*, 1931, 1932

——— (ed.). "San Joaquin Primeval, Uncle Jeff's Story," in *Tulare Daily Times*, Tulare, 1929

McCUBBIN, J. C. *The Stockton–Los Angeles Stage Road.* Manuscript, 1930

———. *Traver, the "Ghost City" of the Golden State Highway.* Manuscript, 1930

RIDER, FREMONT (ed.). *Rider's California, A Guide-Book for Travellers.* The Macmillan Company, New York, 1925

STEWART, GEORGE W. *Big Trees of the Giant Forest.* A. M. Robertson, San Francisco, 1930

———. "The Yokut Indians of the Kaweah Region," in *Sierra Club Bulletin*, XII, No. 4 (1927), 385–400

THOMPSON, THOMAS H. *Historical Atlas Map of Tulare County.* Privately published, Tulare, 1872

TUOLUMNE COUNTY

TUOLUMNE COUNTY was one of the original twenty-seven counties, and Sonora has been its county seat from the beginning.

Prehistoric Landmarks

Table Mountain, mentioned again and again by Bret Harte in his tales, is a conspicuous feature of the Tuolumne County landscape. For many miles its "rocky entablature and splintered capitals" dominate river gorge or spreading valley. A particularly fine view of its long, level top is obtained while crossing Rawhide Flat on the road from Tuttletown to Jamestown. In the Miocene period an andesite lava flow filled the hollows of the then existing topography. Table Mountain is a part of this huge mass of lava, a quarter of a mile wide on the average and forty miles long, that filled one of the ancient stream beds. Ages of erosion have cut away the banks that hemmed in this antediluvian river, leaving the hard andesite mountain standing out in bold relief. Deep beneath this once molten mass have been found bones of extinct animals, traces of an early flora, and implements of stone. Water-worn pebbles, gravel, and smoothly polished gold nuggets have been taken from the ancient river channel by miners, who tunneled great distances into the heart of the mountain until it was honeycombed with subterranean passageways. And, even yet, Table Mountain, once the maker of vast fortunes, holds millions of dollars in gold within its seemingly inexhaustible treasure house.

There are two groups of *Sequoia gigantea* in Tuolumne County, the South Grove of the Calaveras Big Trees and the Tuolumne Grove. The South Grove, seven miles southeast of the North Grove of the Calaveras Big Trees in Calaveras County (both of which are in the Stanislaus National Forest) is reached only by trail. It is a magnificent stand of 974 giant trees, all over twelve feet in diameter. Among them is the Louis Agassiz, one of the largest of all the Big Trees. The Tuolumne Grove on the western boundary of Yosemite National Park on the Big Oak Flat Road contains only a small number of trees.

In Pate Valley, a wooded flat in the Grand Canyon of the Tuolumne River below Muir Gorge, there are hundreds of Indian picture-writings, the first of them discovered by Harnden and McKibbie while exploring the river in 1907. These hieroglyphics, colored with red ocher, are painted on the face of a high cliff on Piute Creek a little way from its junction with the Tuolumne River. Near the middle of the precipice there is a small cave, partly natural and partly hollowed out by human hands, in which other pictographs may be seen.

The Gabriel Moraga Expedition

Gabriel Moraga, in 1806, passed and named both the Tuolumne and Stanislaus rivers. Chapman says that "the Indian village of Tualamne, visited by them, is perhaps the origin of the modern name in Tuolumne River and County, although it was located on the Stanislaus." A diary kept by Padre Pedro Muñoz contains these lines, which indicate the origin of the name:

"On the morning of this day the expedition went toward the east, along the banks of the river, and having traveled about six leagues, we came upon a village called Tautamne. This village is situated on some steep precipices, inaccessible on account of their rough rocks. The Indians live in their *sótanos* (cellars or caves)."

Tuolumne, according to Bancroft, is a corruption of the Indian word *talmalamne*, meaning "a group of stone huts or caves." Although Kroeber thinks this interpretation is unlikely, as the California Indians did not build stone houses and lived in caves only in mountain regions, the extract from the diary of Padre Muñoz is worthy of consideration. Kroeber also says that "the word Tawalimni, which perhaps was really Tawalamni or Tawalumni, would easily give rise, in either English or Spanish, to Tuolumne," and that it was the name of a tribe of Indians, "possibly Miwok, but more probably Yokuts," living in the vicinity of the lower Tuolumne and Stanislaus rivers as far up as Knight's Ferry. The river, meadows, canyon, and county now bear the name.

Sonora Pass

In the early days of California's development, the Sierra Nevada stood as an almost insurmountable barrier between the western American plains and the Pacific slope. The jagged crest on the eastern edge of Tuolumne County, which is also the eastern boundary line of parts of both Stanislaus National Forest and Yosemite National Park, was one of the most impassable stretches in the entire range. The great difficulty was not in the ascent of the eastern side, nor yet in passing the summit, but was rather in the western descent, which, though spoken of figuratively as a slope, is in reality a series of granite domes, of lakes, and of canyons with well-nigh perpendicular walls.

Sonora Pass, in the northeastern corner of Tuolumne County near its conjunction with Alpine and Mono counties, rises to an elevation of 9,624 feet. Wagons hauling supplies to the mines east of the Sierra have used this pass since 1864. It was also the route of the early passenger stage on its weekly journey from Sonora to Bodie. The Sonora–Mono Highway of today, as it winds through scenic Stanislaus Forest, over the crest, and on down to Bridgeport, 110 miles from Sonora, follows the old road approximately.

In 1841 the Bidwell-Bartleson party, the first overland group of American settlers to enter California by crossing the Sierra Nevada, used a pass located ten miles south of the present Sonora pass. By the time the party had begun the western descent the last ox had been consumed and the travelers had begun to eat crow and wildcat. In the attempt to add to their provisions, young Bidwell left the party to hunt, planning to cut across country and rejoin them later. When night overtook him he found himself in the midst of a grove of large trees. In the darkness he had particular difficulty in getting around a fallen tree, the butt of which seemed to extend some twenty or more feet into the air. In after years he visited the North Grove of the Calaveras Big Trees and found what he believed was the spot where he had been in the darkness of that night. However, since the route of the party followed down the south side of the Stanislaus, rather than the north side, it is quite likely that Bidwell discovered the South Grove rather than the North Grove.

The emigrant trails to the west of Sonora Pass were not easy to follow, and various parties became entangled in the vast labyrinth of canyons, mountains, and rivers through which it was necessary to travel. In the early '50's a party of gold-seekers were caught in a heavy snowstorm on the eastern slope of the mountains. As a result, they were forced to abandon their wagons but finally succeeded in crossing the pass and finding a comparatively sheltered spot on the western side. From this place a few members of the party pressed on for succor as far as the Jarboe ranch, about where the town of Tuolumne now is, and from that place assistance was sent back to the men in camp. It is from this episode that Relief Valley gets its name.

The first wagon trains to cross Sonora Pass were made up of the Duckwall party and the Wash Train party, named after a Cherokee Indian who was leader of the outfit. The former, consisting of W. J. Duckwall, his wife, six children, and three other men, found themselves marooned on one of the granite domes southwest of Sonora Pass, but managed to extricate themselves from this predicament by hitching one pair of oxen to the front of a wagon and three pair to the rear and slowly letting the vehicles down the precipitous granite wall. The Duckwalls arrived at Upper Relief Valley on September 27, 1853. The Wash Train party, who had lost most of their wagons in crossing the summit, reached

the valley a day later. No road has ever been built over this stretch of the old Emigrant Trail and the country has remained primitive and isolated.

From Strawberry or Pine Crest to Burst Rock (also known as Birth Rock because in the natural chamber formed by the great boulder a baby girl was born to an emigrant mother) a trail follows the old emigrant road marked by trees on which blazes made by the pioneers are still visible. Near Emigrant Lake there is a blazed tree upon which has been carved the epitaph of a traveler who perished at that spot in October 1853. Until recent months parts of ox wagons abandoned by the snow-bound emigrants were to be found at Upper Relief Valley.

Virginia Pass and Conness Pass

Long before the advent of the white man the passes of the High Sierra were used by the Indians, those living on the eastern slopes crossing over to the western side to get the venison and acorns in which that region abounded, while those whose habitat was on the western ridges passed over to harvest pine nuts on the other side or went down to Mono Lake to gather the choice larvae that are found there at certain seasons.

Two of the lesser known passes which cross the eastern border of Tuolumne County and are reached only by trail are the Virginia and the Conness, both of which lead from Yosemite National Park into the Hoover Primitive Area on the western side of Mono National Forest. The United States Forest Service has set aside here certain typical forest and mountain sections to be preserved in their primitive state and to be known as Primitive Areas. The Hoover Primitive Area contains thirty square miles at the headwaters of Green and Leevining creeks, and within it are Tioga, Conness, Excelsior, and Dunderberg peaks, as well as several glacial lakes. Two of these lakes, lying close together not far from the summit, are the Hoover Lakes, so named in honor of Theodore J. Hoover, mining engineer, who explored and mapped this region in the summers of 1904 and 1905 while in charge of the Standard Consolidated Mines at Bodie. Conness Peak was named in 1863 for John Conness, later United States Senator, in appreciation of his efforts in promoting the bill which organized the California Geological Survey. Dominating the landscape, it lifts its majestic summit 12,565 feet above the sea.

Tioga Pass

Of the several Sierra passes on the eastern border of Tuolumne County the Tioga Pass is one of the most used at the present time. Over this pass the Tioga Road crosses the summit at an elevation of 9,941 feet. The pass is dominated on the southeast by Mount Dana, 13,050 feet elevation, named in 1863 by the Whitney Survey in honor of James Dwight Dana, professor of geology at Yale University from 1850 to 1894.

Mining carried on in the Tioga district by the Great Sierra Consolidated Silver Mining Company of Sonora, incorporated in 1881, necessitated a road from Sonora to the summit. The Tioga Road, or the "Great Sierra Wagon Road," which was completed in 1883 at a cost of $61,000, was built in part over the Mono Trail, but from the point where the latter turned south toward Mono Pass the Tioga Road was continued eastward to Tioga Pass. When the mines in this rugged eastern part of Yosemite National Park were closed in July 1884, the road also was abandoned. A few of the buildings at the mines are to be found in a fair state of preservation even today.

The Tioga Road was donated to the United States Department of the Interior in 1915 and is now one of the most scenic in California. Passing south of the Hetch Hetchy Valley through the Yosemite National Park via Tuolumne Meadows and Lake Tenaya, it bisects the park from east to west. At the first ranger station west of the pass is a bronze plaque which bears the following legend:

This tablet commemorates the successful labors of Stephen T. Mather, Director of the National Service, in securing for the people the Tioga Pass Road. Dedicated to the enduring memory of a faithful public servant by the members of the Brooklyn Daily Eagle National Park Development Tour, July 20, 1924.

The Grand Canyon of the Tuolumne

One of America's most spectacular scenic canyons is the Grand Canyon of the Tuolumne, lying wholly within Tuolumne County fifteen miles due north of Yosemite Valley. Within a distance of twenty miles the Tuolumne River descends this majestic gorge from the level of Tuolumne Meadows to Hetch Hetchy Valley, a drop of almost five thousand feet, the greater part of which occurs within the two miles immediately west of the California Falls. John Muir, in one of his matchless word-pictures, describes the marvelous beauty of the canyon's superb, cascading river:

"It is the cascades of sloping falls of the main river that are the crowning glory of the Canyon. . . . . For miles the river is one wild, exulting, onrushing mass of snowy purple bloom, spreading over glacial waves of granite without any definite channel, gliding in magnificent silver plumes, dashing and foaming through huge bowlder-dams, leaping high in the air in wheel-like whirls . . . . doubling, glinting, singing in exuberance of mountain energy."

Tuolumne Meadows, one of the most beautiful of the numerous Alpine meadows found in the Sierra, lies at the junction of the Dana and Lyell forks of the Tuolumne River about fifteen miles northeast of Yosemite Valley. It is surrounded on all sides by the highest peaks of the Sierra Nevada, and many intriguing trails wind up from it into the very heart of the range. Conness, Dana, Mammoth, and Lyell peaks stand guard at the north and east. Cathedral Range, with its unique and picturesque Cathedral Peak, protects the southern boundary of the meadow. Out of the floor of the valley itself rises Lembert Dome; while at the lower end, at the entrance to the Tuolumne Grand Canyon, towers beautiful Fairview Dome.

Hetch Hetchy (originally spelled Hatchatchie), a deep valley at the lower end of Tuolumne Canyon, was discovered by Joseph Screech, in 1850, while hunting game. The valley was then occupied by Indians. John Muir is authority for the statement that the name is a Miwok Indian word for a certain grass with edible seed that grew in the vicinity. The valley was visited in 1863 by Professor J. D. Whitney and in 1871 by John Muir, who called it the "Tuolumne Yosemite." Muir explored the valley later, in 1875, with Galen Clark. The city of San Francisco, through Congressional Act in 1913, acquired rights in the Tuolumne River for a project to supply water for city use. The dam was completed and the reservoir was filled in 1923.

River Camps

Activity on the bars of the Tuolumne and Stanislaus rivers began early in 1849. Hawkins' Bar, below Jacksonville, was the site of the first river diggings on the Tuolumne. From a population of fifteen in April 1849, it increased to one of seven hundred by September. Extensive plans for damming and diverting the river were made but had to be abandoned because of an unexpected rise in the flow of the water. By 1852 Hawkins' Bar was practically deserted.

The history of Swett's Bar, where mining was begun in November 1849, is typical. A company of seventy men cut a race to divert the stream, but here, too, the sudden rise of water caused the project to be abandoned—temporarily. Characteristically enough, although misfortunes almost invariably befell the river miners, they were never disheartened. In August 1850 the work was resumed, and after fifty-nine days of hard labor the dam was completed—only to be washed away that very evening. The process was repeated a third time, with the same result. The season being then too far advanced to resume the undertaking, the work was laid aside for the year. In August 1851 the camp, although reduced in personnel to but twenty-seven men, completed a dam after a few weeks' effort, and for some time thereafter an ounce of gold per man was taken out each day.

During 1850 the river camps along the Tuolumne were among the largest in the county, thousands of miners being engaged in attempts to divert the river in order to mine its bed. Few of the camps, however, enjoyed any great prosperity, and all of them, Hawkins', Swett's, Stevens', Payne's, Hart's, Morgan's, Roger's, Signorita, York, and Texas bars, have completely disappeared. Not a vestige of former days remains to show where the cabins of busy miners once stood. Not even the bars themselves remain as they were, for the river has changed its course several times since the '50's.

Along that part of the old channel now covered by the Don Pedro Reservoir lay the bars of Don Pedro, Indian, and Red Mountain. From one claim at Don Pedro's Bar, gold valued at $100,000 was taken out before 1889, the cost of operation being only $5,000. At the time of Lincoln's election in 1860 as many as fifteen hundred votes were cast at Don Pedro's Bar. Indian Bar, the scene of eager mining activities in the '50's, continued to exist until the building of the Don Pedro Dam.

Moccasin, once a thriving camp at the mouth of Moccasin Creek, is now the site of the Moccasin Creek Power House, a unit in the Hetch Hetchy water system.

Woods' Crossing

The first discovery of gold in Tuolumne County was made in August 1848 at Woods' Crossing on Woods' Creek by a party of men led by Rev. James Woods. James Savage, J. H. Rider, and Charles Bassett were members of the party. The richness of the field proved remarkable, and for a time from $200 to $300 a day per man were taken out with pick and knife alone. Surface mining remained very good for a number of years, and a thriving camp grew up on the spot. It is said that more gold was taken from this creek than from any other stream of its size in California. Almost equally famous were two of its branches, Sullivan's Creek and Curtis Creek.

At Woods' Crossing on a slight rise above the highway a small monument of gold-bearing quartz has been erected by the Tuolumne County Chamber of Commerce commemorating the finding of gold there. The spot at which the discovery was made is located five hundred feet southeast of this marker where the old road crosses Woods' Creek.

Sonora

Very soon after the discovery of gold at Woods' Crossing, settlements were made at Jamestown and at Sonora, farther up on Woods' Creek. Located in a famous gold region of California, Sonora is one of the most picturesque and beautiful of all the old mining towns on the Mother Lode. Changing conditions have brought innovations that have somewhat marred its charm and individuality, but much of interest still remains. The trees that once interlaced their branches above Washington Street, the main thoroughfare of the town, have been removed and the street has been widened and paved to care for the motor traffic that now incessantly pours through it. Along Washington Street the heavy iron shutters of early days have been replaced by plate-glass windows, which permit the display of interesting relics of the mining era, as well as up-to-date merchandise or recently found gold nuggets. In the summer time on Saturday evenings the street is like a plaza on a fiesta day. A walk along this same route in the daytime reveals narrow, unpaved side streets that in a newer place would be called alleys, along which may be seen old stone buildings "with iron shutters, regular fortresses, the walls thick enough to stand a siege." Entering these little side passageways is like going into an Old World village. Old trees, old houses, old gardens, old stone walls covered with ivy that must have been planted in the very earliest years, lure the pedestrian this way and that.

Sonorian Camp, as it was first known, was located by a party of Mexicans who pushed up Woods' Creek beyond Woods' Crossing and were the sole occupants of this region for several months. In the spring of 1849 the first white settlers arrived, a group of nineteen men, twelve of whom were Americans. A little later they held a miners' meeting at which R. S. Ham was elected alcalde. The "inborn quality for creating order" displayed by these and other Americans held in check the degenerate characters that came in later. In July 1849 fully fifteen hundred foreigners, largely Mexicans and Chileans, poured into the camps of Tuolumne County, and by autumn there were five thousand people in Sonora. The narrow streets were constantly thronged and on Sundays were almost impassable. A tax on foreigners, which incited a bloodless war in June 1850, brought an exodus which cut the population almost in half.

In spite of frequent fires from which Sonora has suffered, some buildings reminiscent of the '50's still remain in and about the town: the City Hall, the St. James Episcopal Church, built in 1859, the Dorsey House, the Wells Fargo Building, and the Odd Fellows Hall. On Washington Street south of the center of town stands the Hotel Italia. Dr. Lewis C. Gunn, who had arrived in Jamestown in 1849, built the house and in 1851 brought his wife and family of young children from the East to live there. At that time the house, a two-story adobe, had a balcony across the entire front of the second story. The parlor at the left of the front entrance on the ground floor was used as a printing-office and the county recorder's office, Dr. Gunn having been elected county recorder in 1850. From this office was issued the *Sonora Herald*, the first number of which came out on July 4, 1850. After the removal of the Gunn family to San Francisco in 1861 the house was converted into a hospital and in 1899 was remodeled as a private residence. Only the middle part of the present structure comprises the original Dr. Gunn adobe, as both ends have been extended and a two-story colonial porch has been put across the entire front.

At the southern end of the town's business district is a monument memorializing the town's origin.

On a hill at the edge of town beyond the Grammar School building is the quiet Masonic Cemetery in which the graves of many early residents lie shadowed by oaks and cypress trees. Here stands the monument of gold-bearing quartz erected by Tuolumne Lodge No. 8 of the Masons, the Sonora Welfare Club, and the Tuolumne County Chamber of Commerce in honor of Jacob Richard Stoker, 1820–1896. The inscription reads, in part: "His heart was finer metal than any gold his shovel ever brought to light." Dick Stoker was a gallant Mexican War veteran, who came to California in 1849. He was intimately associated with Mark Twain and the Gillis brothers on Jackass Hill in the '60's, and was a member of Tuolumne Lodge No. 8, of the Masons. Just and fair, Dick settled many miners' disputes and served his community faithfully.

The Big Bonanza Mine in the heart of Sonora is the greatest "pocket" mine ever discovered. It is located on Piety Hill less than a hundred yards from the St. James Episcopal Church and within a short distance of four other churches. It was first worked in 1851 by Chileans, who took out a large amount of surface gold. In the '70's it was purchased for a pittance by three partners, who worked it for years and then one day broke into a body of almost solid gold. The next day they shipped gold valued at $160,000 to the San Francisco Mint. Within a week $500,000 worth was taken out and another half-million was mined before the property was again sold.

Among other mines in this vicinity were the San Giuseppe, located about a quarter of a mile northwest of the center of Sonora, and the Golden Gate, known all over the world for the pureness of its gold. It has been estimated that gold valued at $40,000,000 has been mined within a radius of two miles of Sonora.

Jamestown

Jamestown, frequently called "Jimtown," lies in the shadow of Table Mountain about four miles southwest of Sonora on the Mother Lode Highway. Colonel George F. James, a lawyer from San Francisco, located at this point on Woods' Creek in 1848. James fell into disfavor and after his departure the inhabitants changed the name of the settlement to American Camp. The old name, however, had more appeal to the miners and was revived.

Modern pavements cannot wholly mar the quaint charm of Jamestown's main street, with its balconied brick stores and hotels dating from the '50's. The post office is now in the building formerly occupied by the St. James Masonic Lodge. It has been partly remodeled and the original stone has been covered with stucco, but the thickness of the walls is evident at the entrance door. Two other old stone houses on the main street have been covered with a modern brick veneer. The Bellingham House, on the east side of the street, was built of adobe but was later covered by lumber brought around the Horn. The lumber is beginning to fall away and portions of the original adobe walls are again visible. The house is now used as a dwelling. The Methodist Episcopal Church, built in 1852 and still in use, the Leland Building, and the Pioneer Blacksmith Shop are among other early landmarks in Jamestown.

Three miles below Jamestown, near Mountain Pass, is a stone wall pierced by square holes and thought to be a remnant of an old fortification. Unfortunately, vandals are gradually carrying away the stones.

The Sonora Road which passes through this region was alight with campfires in 1849, and travelers needed no other guidance than the embers which marked the route of those who had pressed on ahead. Later, roadhouses sprang up as thickly and as rapidly as do oil stations today. Cloudman's, Keystone (now a post office and station on the railway about five miles west of Chinese Camp), and Crimea House were three of these old stage stations. Crimea House has been rebuilt, but the old stone corral across the way remains just as it was in pioneer days. On the Russell Ranch, near Mountain Pass School, is another stone corral, said to have been built by an industrious Chinese ranch laborer in his spare time.

At Montezuma, three miles south of Jamestown on the Mother Lode Highway, mining operations were begun in the summer and fall of 1852. Deep and extensive mines in this neighborhood produced exceptionally pure gold. Two lines of stages passed through this settlement: the line from Stockton to Sonora, and Dr. Clarke's line from Sonora and Columbia to Don Pedro's, La Grange, and other points. The old Fox Building at Montezuma has been rebuilt and is now used as a private dwelling. Remains of an old cemetery are in the corral near the building.

Yorktown, Curtisville, Sullivan's Creek, Green Springs, Campo Seco, and Hardtack were other camps in the vicinity of Jamestown.

At Quartz Mountain, south of Jamestown and east of the Mother Lode Highway, is the famous App Mine, which produced $6,500,000 in gold up to the year 1909. The mine was closed down a few years after this date and in 1927 the town of Quartz was destroyed by fire. John App and others became interested in property on this mountain as early as 1856, when they located the quartz claim on the west side. App married Leanna Donner, one of the six Donner girls orphaned by the Donner Pass tragedy. Mrs. App, who reached the age of ninety-five, lived for seventy-eight years in Tuolumne County. After the death of her husband, whom she survived many years, she continued to make her home on the old App homestead near Quartz until her death in 1930.

South of Quartz is Stent, formerly known as Poverty Hill, where an old cemetery is about all that remains of pioneer days. To the southeast stood Algerine, once a notoriously wild mining camp which boasted two streets lined with business houses. Today only a few cellars show the sites of the old stores.

Climbing Table Mountain west of Jamestown one comes to Rawhide, the location of the famous Rawhide Quartz Mine, which had a production record of over $6,000,000 up to 1909. At one time this mine, owned by Captain William Nevills, was considered one of the greatest gold mines in the world. There has been much "pocket" mining in the vicinity of Rawhide.

Jeffersonville, a thriving village in the '50's and a stage stopping-place between Rawhide and Tuttletown, was the scene of extensive tunnel mining under Table Mountain. Nothing remains to mark the site of the town but a small tree-shaded graveyard on top of a hill. West of Jeffersonville is the site of French Flat, now overgrown with chaparral. The Humbug Mine, on the east slope of the mountain a little way from the road leading from Jamestown to Rawhide, was the richest of all the tunnel mines, with a total yield of more than $4,000,000. Nuggets the size of hen's eggs were found there.

Columbia

Columbia, one of the most typical of the "Argonaut" towns still existing in the Mother Lode, is said to have been at one time a city of twenty thousand persons, probably the largest mining camp in California. From an area of three hundred acres on the outskirts of the town millions of dollars in gold were washed out, leaving a vast expanse of fantastic, ghost-like rocks partly hidden today by small trees and bushes which have grown up among them. "Truly a page from the past . . . . few if any towns like Columbia remain in California." It has recently been made a state park and is to be preserved and restored as a historic specimen of California's gold-rush days.

The rush for gold at Columbia had few parallels. On March 27, 1850, Dr. Thaddeus Hildreth, his brother George, and some other miners made camp for the night under an oak tree in the vicinity of what is now Columbia. The tree stood near the site of the bridge later built at the foot of Main Street. Rain during the night obliged the men to remain at the spot the next morning in order to dry their blankets. While there, one of the party, John Walker, found "color" in the small gulch that puts into Columbia Gulch from the east, a place afterward known as Kennebec Hill. Finding

a promising prospect the party remained and located at this point.

For a time the place was called Hildreth's Diggings but was soon named Columbia. In 1852 the town was laid out on its present site and was incorporated in May 1854, only to be almost destroyed by fire in July of the same year. The reconstructed buildings were substantial and more nearly fireproof.

In the fall of that year the Stanislaus Water Company was formed, and within two years a thirty-five-mile ditch to the South Fork was completed. The Tuolumne Water Company, organized two years earlier, also had headquarters at Columbia, and both companies supplied water for mining operations. The New England Water Company brought water from Spring Gulch to supply the town. Families soon settled at Columbia, planting gardens and cultivating ranches in the vicinity. The place was often spoken of as "Columbia, the gem of the Southern Mines," because of the great extent and rich character of its placer deposits.

In 1864 Columbia was illuminated by gas made from pitch, the lamps being set on cedar posts. Churches and public buildings were illuminated free. Large untended rosebushes are now growing where the gas tanks were located near the corner of Broadway and Washington streets. Along the main street of Columbia a number of sturdy old buildings still stand. Among these are the Town Hall; the little engine house in which is to be found one of the oldest fire-extinguishing apparatus in the state; the "Gold Dust Exchange" and bank of D. O. Mills and Company, where home-made candies have replaced the golden treasure which once poured over its counters; and the Pioneer Saloon. In one of the old corner buildings a pioneer museum and club room is maintained. The present square brick schoolhouse on the hill was opened for its first term on April 14, 1862. The old bean board, once used for learning the multiplication tables, is still exhibited.

The Wells Fargo office was established about 1852 in the American Hotel. The hotel was subsequently burned and in 1855 the present Wells Fargo Building was erected on the site next door. On it a marker has been placed by the Wells Fargo Bank and Union Trust Company of San Francisco in honor of the pioneers of California.

Across the street from the Wells Fargo Building another tablet bears this inscription:

Gold discovered 1,000 feet south, March, 1850. Population month later 5,000, finally reaching 15,000, ranking second in state. In 1853 lost movement for location of State Capital by two votes. Columbia and suburbs produced 87 millions in gold, 55 millions weighed on scales now in old Wells Fargo and Company office. St. Anne's Church southwest of here built 1856. Presbyterian church 1857, first school 1852. Largest marble quarry in state two miles northwest; worked since 1857. Erected by Tuolumne County Chamber of Commerce, 1929.

Although the story that Columbia missed being the state capital by two votes is often told, search through legislative records of the time has failed to bring forth any evidence that the town was even a candidate. The trick that kept Columbia out of the race, according to George E. Dane, was worked in this wise:

"A petition was circulated among the miners in which Columbia's claims for the honor were set forth. This petition soon grew to mammoth proportions—in fact, it had on it no less than 10,000 signatures of good citizens of the Southern Mines. This was thought sufficient to convince the legislature, and the petition was put in the safe in D. O. Mills's bank, or some such place, to await the departure of the committee that was to present it.

"Meanwhile, a murder trial had been taking place in Columbia which resulted in the conviction of the defendant, much to the chagrin of his lawyer, who, so the story goes, had never before failed to get his clients acquitted. This resourceful advocate, casting about for some means to save his own record and his client's neck, bethought himself of the 10,000 signatures on the petition to make Columbia the capital. By hook or crook he got his hands on the petition, cut off the great roll of signatures, substituted at the head a petition to the Governor to pardon his client, and took horse for 'down below.'

"By the time the loss was discovered, it was too late to circulate another petition before the vote on the capital, so Columbia lost, and the murderer won, not by the traditional two votes, but (shall we say?) by a rope length."

Marble from the Columbia Quarry is of even grain and is remarkable for its elasticity. In color it ranges from white to gray and is either banded or rose-mottled. The sidewalks laid around the Palace Hotel in San Francisco in 1878 were made of this marble.

Quaint St. Anne's Church, the Mecca of artists as well as historians, crowns a low hill overlooking the world's richest placer grounds, with the gaunt diggings encroaching to the very edge of the little cemetery. The church was erected in 1856 with funds donated for its construction by the miners. Father Daniel Slattery, leader in the work, was the first priest to officiate in the sacred edifice. The walls of this historic church were built of brick fired in a kiln which was located on the Sonora–Springfield Road, while the timbers used in its construction were obtained from Saw Mill Flat about three miles southeast of Columbia. The belfry was added in 1857. The interior decorations and altar paintings are the work of James Fallon, son of a pioneer hotel-keeper and the owner of the famous old Fallon Hotel, still in use. After having stood for half a century, the walls of the old church were considered to be unsafe and its doors were closed, but through the united efforts of the Native Sons of the Golden West and the Knights of Columbus the structure was repaired and was rededicated on June 15, 1906.

Gold Springs

In the sands of a large spring still visible about a mile and a half northwest of Columbia, a Mr. Hatch and others discovered gold in the latter part of April 1850. This spring was the source of a stream which was used for mining operations employing some three hundred miners. A camp boasting two stores, two boarding-houses, and a number of mechanics' shops, with a population of five hundred, had grown up at the spring by 1856. Its citizens were quiet, orderly, and enterprising. Several gardens and small ranches in the immediate vicinity supplied fresh fruits and vegetables to the miners at Columbia and Yankee Hill to the southeast, and to Red Dog, Dow's Flat, Heavy Tree Hill, Wayne's Bar, Simpson's Bar, and Italian Bar to the north.

Saw Mill Flat

Saw Mill Flat, so named because of the two sawmills erected there to supply mining timbers in the early '50's, was situated on a fork of Woods' Creek, three miles southeast of Columbia and one and a half miles south of Yankee Hill. At first it was a great resort for Mexicans and Peruvians, and it is said that Joaquín Murieta, at the time a monte dealer, had headquarters there in 1852, before he commenced his career of murder and robbery.

Shaw's Flat

A sign on a branch road between Tuttletown and Sonora bears the legend, "The old '49 route via Shaw's Flat." Shaw's Flat, on the eastern slope of Table Mountain, was named by Mandeville Shaw, who planted an orchard there

in 1849. A number of substantial cottages surrounded by gardens planted with fruit and ornamental trees give the place a home-like appearance today. Black walnut trees planted by Tarleton Caldwell flourish in the place known as Caldwell's Gardens, now a home. The Mississippi House, well known in early days, still attracts the passer-by and within its walls may be seen some of the old post-office equipment. On this building is a marker bearing the following inscription:

> Bret Harte Trail. When this place was alive with miners, John B. Stetson, of Holbrook, Merrill and Stetson, San Francisco, had a hardware store here. Notice the bell near the school house. It was bought by the miners so all could start and quit work at the same time. Also used as an alarm bell to call the miners to Judge Lynch's court. West of here is Rosedale Ranch where first cultivated roses were planted.

In 1855 miners sinking a shaft at Caldwell's Gardens discovered river gravel under the lava. At this point, the antediluvian stream was wide and flat and the lava coat consequently thin. Caldwell's claim is said to have yielded $250,000 in gold. Following this discovery, tunnels, some of great length, were made under Table Mountain and immense fortunes were taken out.

At the south end of Shaw's Flat stands an old chimney, the remains of an "Uncle Tom's Cabin." This "Uncle Tom" was a slave who purchased his freedom with gold which he took from the ground. In appreciation of his blessings he kept a pail of pure drinking-water outside his door for the use of thirsty wayfarers who chanced to pass that way.

Climbing over Table Mountain, the Mother Lode Highway rounds Mountain Brow, once the locale of rich placer mines and a hideout for Black Bart and other bandits. On a knoll to the left is a miner's cabin remodeled as the home of a noted Chicago photographer.

Brown's Flat and Squabbletown

Brown's Flat, located on Woods' Creek one mile above Sonora, had its beginning in 1851. Extensive hill and surface diggings independent of the creek bed were worked in the vicinity. Among these mines were the Page, the Ford, and the Sugarman, the last-named producing crystallized gold of great beauty. After 1852 steam and horse power were used in draining the many claims. At Brown's Flat the Sonora–Milton stage was frequently held up, and on January 15, 1878, over $5,000 was obtained by highwaymen.

Squabbletown, a small camp in the vicinity of Brown's Flat, has been all but effaced by the encroachment of dense undergrowth. Only the decaying remnants of old cabins show where the settlement once stood.

Tuttletown

Tuttletown, about six miles west of Sonora on the Mother Lode Highway, was named after Judge A. A. H. Tuttle, who built a log cabin there in 1848. The earliest dwellings consisted of tents and Mexican *ramadas*, or brush houses. It was a stopping-place for packers carrying miners' supplies over the old Slum-gullion Road from Angel's Camp to Sonora, and by 1849–1850 was a flourishing camp. Since that time its population has dwindled to a family or two, whose needs are supplied by a little country store built of stone, known as Swerer's, where Mark Twain once traded. On the outskirts of Tuttletown, opposite the Patterson Mine, are three old Spanish cork trees. Only one other is known to be growing in the state.

Jackass Hill

Jackass Hill, just west of Tuttletown, achieved much notoriety in '51 and '52. The diggings were rich in coarse gold and excitement was intense. Hundreds of men rushed to the scene, and many a lucky miner made his "pile" in a few hours. Some claims of a hundred square feet yielded as high as $10,000, and one quartz pocket produced from one to three hundred dollars a day for three years. Over thirty-six hundred prospect holes and shafts have been sunk on Jackass Hill during the last seventy years, and hundreds of small pocket mines have made rich yields of ore. Gradually the camp dwindled in population, but there are still prospectors scattered about over the hill and an occasional golden harvest is reported.

The hill received its name from the braying of the jackasses in the pack trains that paused overnight on their way to and from the mines. As many as two hundred of the animals are said to have been picketed on the hill at one time.

Mark Twain (Samuel Langhorne Clemens), the great American humorist, spent five months on Jackass Hill in 1864–1865 as the guest of William R. Gillis. A replica of the cabin stands on the hilltop about one mile from Tuttletown, built around the old stone fireplace, uninjured when flames destroyed the original cabin. Here, in imagination, one may see Dick Stoker, the "Dick Baker" of *Roughing It;* James Gillis, "The Sage of Jackass Hill"; and William Gillis seated with Mark Twain before a crackling wood fire on many a long winter evening.

The Landmarking Pilgrimage to the Bret Harte country, the Mark Twain Society, and other Mark Twain admirers joined at the Mark Twain Cabin on May 22, 1922, to take part in its dedication, thus making it a national event. The crowd was welcomed by Bill Gillis, Mark Twain's old-time friend. A tablet telling the story of Jackass Hill was placed near the cabin in 1929 by the Tuolumne County Chamber of Commerce.

Springfield

Springfield, a camp near the head of Mormon Creek, received its name from the fine spring there, which afforded sufficient water for the placer-mining operations of several hundred men who worked the rich auriferous claims in the vicinity. The miners often uncovered Indian mortars and pestles, showing that Indians had previously enjoyed the spring.

The town, with its stores, shops, and hotels, was well laid out about a plaza. The erection of a Methodist Church before that of a gambling house makes Springfield unique in the annals of mining towns. It was noted for the quiet orderliness and sobriety of its citizens, many of whom worked in the mines under Table Mountain near by. Today the site of the town is indicated by a stone schoolhouse, which formerly served as a church.

Chinese Camp

Some ten miles southwest of Sonora is Chinese Camp, which in 1856 had a population of about one thousand and boasted a church, several stores and hotels, a bank, an express office, and two fraternal orders, the Masonic Lodge and the Sons of Temperance. Mining there consisted principally of surface diggings on the hilltop and in the valley. Water was brought to the mines in the vicinity from Woods' Creek by means of a flume and ditch.

One of several stories told of the origin of this old place name is that the town was founded by a ship's captain who deserted his vessel in San Francisco Bay and brought his entire Chinese crew there to mine. A less dramatic version is that Chinese miners were employed there by English prospectors. A third story says that after gold became exhausted at Campo Salvado the miners, working up over the hill, ultimately joined the Chinese on the other side and named the

new location Chinese Camp, in honor of their olive-skinned brothers. It is estimated that at one time five thousand Celestials worked there, but none remain today. One may still see at Chinese Camp old stone buildings with heavy iron doors typical of the early gold days. These, interspersed with a few small modern homes, make up the present village.

Chinese Camp was the rallying-place of the first big tong war in California, three-quarters of a century ago. Two Mile Bar on the Stanislaus River was the scene of the incident that led to this war. Twelve members of the Sam-Yap Tong were working near six members of the Yan-Wo Tong when a huge stone rolled from one property to the other. Words and blows ensued. Calls from the respective tongs went out for assistance. American blacksmiths in neighboring camps were engaged to make crude weapons—pikes, daggers, and tridents—and a few firearms were supplied from San Francisco. On September 26, 1856, nine hundred members of the Yan-Wo Tong went forth from Chinese Camp to meet twelve hundred members of the opposing tong near Crimea House. The battle took place amid the beating of gongs and the reverberations of random shots from inexperienced marksmen. The casualties were four killed and four wounded. American officers of the law finally arrested two hundred and fifty of the combatants. The State Historical Museum at Sutter's Fort, Sacramento, has specimens of these locally manufactured weapons.

An old fort built by Chinese miners in 1856 may be seen near Shawmut, a mining town about two miles from Chinese Camp. At one time Shawmut boasted the longest payroll and the deepest mine shaft in the county.

Jacksonville

Jacksonville, on the Tuolumne River, was established by Colonel Alden Jackson in June 1849, and by the summer of 1851 it ranked second only to Sonora. At Jacksonville was planted the first orchard in that part of the state, known as Smart's Garden, and until a few years ago a sparse scattering of the old apple trees remained. Mining through the orchard brought about its final destruction. In the early '50's Jacksonville was the scene of extensive river operations, including the building of great dams and wing dams at high cost of labor and materials. Today the tiny hamlet is but a shadow of the once prosperous mining town. Fire and the vicissitudes of time have removed most of its early landmarks, but the old hotel that in times past sheltered a number of the prominent men of the pioneer period is still standing.

Priest's Hotel and Big Oak Flat

Priest's Hotel (named after its original owner) was on the main-traveled road to Yosemite Valley in the late '50's and '60's. A wagon road over this route was not completed to the floor of the Valley until July 17, 1874. The winding road up Priest's Grade today is one of the most picturesque in the Sierra. The original Priest's Hotel was destroyed by fire, and a later building occupies the site. From a hill in the rear a panorama of seven counties may be viewed.

About a mile from the hotel stood a famous landmark during mining days, the big oak (*Quercus lobata*) from which Big Oak Flat derived its name. This huge tree, eleven feet in diameter, was gradually killed by miners digging about its roots for gold. It was eventually felled and the stump was burned, but two small pieces have been preserved in a monument which stands on the site.

James Savage, with a retinue of Indian laborers in 1850, was the first man to mine Big Oak Flat, originally called Savage Diggings. In the vicinity, the Lumsden, Big Oak Flat, Longfellow, Cosmopolite, and Mississippi mines were notable producers. A large stone building, the I.O.O.F. Hall, still stands at Big Oak Flat.

First and Second Garotte

Groveland, formerly known as First Garotte, on the Big Oak Flat Road, is still a thriving village. On its one street stands a memento of the past, the old stone Tannehill store. About two miles above Groveland, near the edge of the Stanislaus National Forest, is Second Garotte, a tiny mountain village. Here at the edge of the road grows a huge misshapen old tree, known as the Hangman's Tree, which bears a tablet telling the story of its gruesome past. Across the road and inclosed by a fence at the rear of some newer buildings is a two-story frame house, formerly the home of Chaffee and Chamberlain, alleged to have been the originals of one of Bret Harte's stories. Mines in the vicinity of Second Garotte were the Kanaka, the Big Betsy, and the Mexican. The Big Oak Flat Road continues on through Buck Meadows, called Big Gap in the early days.

The East Lode Mines

Mining activity in the East Lode began early in the '50's. The Soulsby Quartz Mine at Soulsbyville was discovered by Benjamin Soulsby in 1856 and worked by Cornish miners. Its total production up to 1909 was over $7,000,000. Other mines in the vicinity were the Black Oak, the Live Oak, the Golden Treasure, and the Platt and Gilson. Soulsbyville has always been a place of well-kept homes, pretty gardens, and law-abiding people.

Over the lava ridge just east of Soulsbyville was Cherokee, near neighbor to Arastraville. The Confidence Mine at the village of Confidence, thirteen miles northeast of Sonora on the Sierra–Mono State Highway leading to Sonora Pass, was discovered in 1853 and is one of several good producers in this vicinity. This group of claims included the Independence, the Little Jessie, the Mary Ellen, and the Plowboy. The Excelsior Mine at Sugar Pine produced $420,000 worth of gold before the quartz vein was lost. Many attempts to relocate the vein have failed.

Tuolumne, just west of the border of the Stanislaus National Forest and the terminus of the Sierra Railway, is now a lumber center. It is less than a mile from the old mining camp of Carter's, first known as Summersville, named in honor of Mrs. Elizabeth Summers, wife of an early settler. Six miles east of Tuolumne and within the borders of the Stanislaus National Forest is located one of the largest canyon oaks in the state, measuring ten feet in diameter. Some years ago the county expended a large sum of money for its preservation.

The Buchanan Mine ten miles south of Tuolumne has yielded over $2,000,000.

SOURCES

[Credit is here given for source material, and permission to quote is hereby acknowledged]

BEASLEY, THOMAS DYKES. *A Tramp through the Bret Harte Country.* Paul Elder & Company, San Francisco, 1914
BIDWELL, GENERAL JOHN. *Echoes of the Past.* Chico Advertiser, Chico, California
CHAPMAN, CHARLES E. *A History of California: The Spanish Period.* The Macmillan Company, New York, 1921.
CLELAND, ROBERT GLASS. *Pathfinders,* of the series *California,* ed. by John Russell McCarthy. Powell Publishing Company, Los Angeles, 1929
CONLIN, THOMAS. "The Story of Columbia," in *Pacific Underwriter and Banker.* Jubilee Edition. XXXIX, No. 18, September 25, 1925

FARQUHAR, FRANCIS P. *Place Names of the High Sierra.* Sierra Club, San Francisco, 1926
GILLIS, WILLIAM R. *Gold Rush Days with Mark Twain.* Albert & Charles Boni, New York, 1930
————. *Memories of Mark Twain and Steve Gillis.* Privately published, Sonora, California, 1924
GUNN, LEWIS C., and ELIZABETH LE BRETON. *Records of a California Family.* Edited by Anna Lee Marston. Privately printed, San Diego, 1928
HECKENDORN and WILSON. *Miners' and Business Men's Directory.* Clipper Office, Columbia, 1856
HITTELL, JOHN S. *The Resources of California.* 5th Edition. A. Roman & Company, San Francisco, 1869
HOLMES, ROBERTA EVELYN. *The Southern Mines of California. Early Development of the Sonora Mining Region.* The Grabhorn Press, San Francisco, 1931
JOHNSTON, PHILIP. "Legends and Landmarks of '49 along the Mother Lode," in *Touring Topics,* XXIII, No. 2 (February 1931), 12–27, 52–53
LANG, H. O. *History of Tuolumne County.* B. F. Alley, San Francisco, 1882
MUIR, JOHN. "Hetch Hetchy Valley," in *Overland Monthly,* XI, No. 1 (July 1873), 42–43
PETERSON, H. C. "Footprints of California Argonauts," in *Oakland Tribune,* April 26, 1931
————. "Forty-Nine Tour," in *Oakland Tribune,* March 14, 1922
Reports of the State Mineralogist. State Printing Office, Sacramento, 1880–1896
SANCHEZ, NELLIE VAN DE GRIFT. *Spanish and Indian Place Names of California.* A. M. Robertson, San Francisco, 1922
SHINN, H. C. *Mining Camps. A Study in American Frontier Government.* Charles Scribner's Sons, New York, 1885
STEWART, GEORGE R., JR. *Bret Harte, Argonaut and Exile.* Houghton Mifflin Company, Boston, 1931
"Tuolumne County, California," in *The Union Democrat.* J. A. Van Harlingen Company, Sonora, 1909
WOODS, DANIEL B. *Sixteen Months at the Gold Diggings.* Sampson Low, London; Harper & Brothers, New York, 1852
YARD, ROBERT STERLING. *The National Parks Portfolio.* 6th Edition, revised by Isabelle F. Story. United States Government Printing Office, Washington, D.C., 1931

YOLO COUNTY

YOLO COUNTY (Yolo, or Yoloy, was the name of a tribe of Indians, and is said to mean "a place abounding with rushes") was one of the original twenty-seven counties. Fremont was its first county seat, from 1850 to 1851, when the honor was bestowed upon Washington (now Broderick). In 1857 another move was made, this time to Cacheville, but after four years, in 1861, Washington again became the county seat. In 1862, Woodland was finally chosen as the permanent seat of justice.

The Trail of the Fur Hunter

In the marsh lands west of the Río de Jesús María (now the Upper Sacramento River), lived the Yoloy, a tribal branch of the Suisun Indians. To the south lay fertile, unbroken plains where wild game had abounded from time immemorial. These plains were bounded on the north and south by Cache and Putah creeks, while on the east flowed the great river, and on the west lay a range of hills.

For hundreds of years, Indian hunters had roamed this region undisturbed, but in the year 1821 the first known white man crossed its primitive trails. This was Luís Argüello, in command of the last expedition of the Spanish government into the river country of the Great Valley in search of mission sites. The party crossed what are now Solano and Yolo counties before reaching the Sacramento River at a point in the present Colusa County in the vicinity of Grimes.

In 1828 the American explorer Jedediah S. Smith is thought to have hunted and trapped on the streams of Yolo County, followed by the great army of Hudson's Bay Company trappers and voyageurs, who found this a rich field for their labors. They cached their furs along the river and smaller streams, one of which became known as Cache Creek. One of their camps, known to early settlers as French Camp, was situated in a grove of oaks on the north bank of Cache Creek one mile east of the present town of Yolo (formerly Cacheville).

In the spring and summer of 1830 another band of hunters, under Ewing Young, trapped along the San Joaquin and Sacramento rivers and remained for a time on Cache Creek. Two years later, on his way to Oregon, Young again passed through Yolo County territory, camping near the mouth of Cache Creek. Following up Capay Valley past Clear Lake, the party reached the coast some seventy-five miles north of Fort Ross, where they continued north as far as the Umpqua River in Oregon.

Joseph Gale, who had come to California with Ewing Young in 1831, had a cattle rendezvous on Cache Creek in 1843. The need for more live stock in the Willamette Valley, Oregon, was the incentive to a daring project begun by Gale in 1841. Undaunted by the difficulties to be surmounted in getting the cattle to Oregon, he set to work to construct an ocean-going vessel which he proposed to take to California and there exchange for live stock. Through the intervention of Charles Wilkes, the Hudson's Bay Company equipped the vessel, and Gale, after passing a seaman's examination, was granted a seaman's license. The schooner, "Star of Oregon," was launched on May 19, 1841, and toward the end of August 1842 Gale and his crew started down the Columbia River en route to California. At San Francisco, José Y. Limantour, a Frenchman, purchased the vessel in exchange for 350 cows.

Needing more men both to help in his vast stock-driving venture over the mountains and for his Oregon settlement project, Gale waited until the spring of 1843 before starting north. Circulars had been sent out describing the advantages of the Willamette Valley for settlement, and by the middle of May forty-two men (among whom was Jacob P. Leese) had gathered at Cache Creek. From a tall cottonwood tree trimmed into the form of a flagstaff the Stars and Stripes floated for several weeks that spring. The expedition finally started northward on May 14, driving 1,250 head of cattle, 600 horses and mules, and 3,000 sheep, a mighty conclave, most of which were safely guided over the northern mountain barrier after a journey of seventy-five days.

Along the banks of historic Cache Creek the earliest settlements in the region of Yolo County were made: the Guesisosi Grant or Gordon's Ranch, Knight's Landing, Rancho Río de Jesús María, Rancho Cañada de Capay, and Hutton's Ranch or Travelers' Home, later known as Cacheville. The stream flowing out of Clear Lake in the mountains of Lake County furnishes a natural water supply for the irrigation today of thousands of acres of orchard and farm lands on the rich plains of Yolo County.

Gordon's Ranch

William Gordon, a native of Ohio, came to California with the Workman-Rowland party in 1841, and in 1842 became the first white settler in what is now Yolo County. Gordon had spent some time in New Mexico, where he had become a Mexican citizen and had married a Mexican woman. On reaching California he obtained a grant of two square leagues of land on the left bank of Cache Creek about three miles above the Stephens bridge and ten miles west of the present city of Woodland. "Uncle Billy" Gordon had been a trapper and hunter. "Rough, uneducated, honest, and hospitable," his place on Cache Creek was a "general

rendezvous for settlers and hunters" from 1843 to 1846. James Clyman, in his diary for July 12, 1845, notes that at the time of his visit Gordon was the only permanent settler on Cache Creek. Gordon moved to Cobb Valley in Lake County in 1866 and lived there until his death in 1876.

On this estate, known as the Guesisosi Grant, or Gordon's Ranch, the first wheat in Yolo County was grown, and there, in 1847, in a very primitive building one mile from the Gordon home, the first school was started with an enrolment of eight pupils. The property is still known by its historic title, Gordon's Ranch.

Knight's Landing

Dr. William Knight, a native of Indiana, who was said to have been educated as a physician, also came to California with the Workman-Rowland party in 1841. In 1843 he settled at a natural landing-place on the Sacramento River later known by his name as Knight's Landing. In 1846 he received a grant to this land, but the title to it was never confirmed.

Knight's first home on the river rancho was made of tules and willow poles fastened with rawhide and plastered with mud. It was built in 1843 on an ancient Indian mound, called by the natives the "Yodoy" mound. As this site was situated at the junction of the lower Sycamore Slough with the Sacramento River, it proved suitable for a ferry, which was established by Knight soon after his arrival, and the place became an important landing and shipping point on the Sacramento. Knight died on November 9, 1849, at Knight's Ferry in Stanislaus County. Because of a lack of business foresight his entire estate was lost to the heirs.

An attempt to start a town at Knight's was made in 1849 under the name of Baltimore, but it never materialized because of disagreements over the sale of lots. In 1853, however, Charles F. Reed laid out another town site and the place was officially named Knight's Landing. That same year, J. W. Snowball, Knight's son-in-law, and J. J. Perkins opened a general store on the Indian mound, and Captain J. H. Updegraff established a hotel business in the Yolo House. In 1860 this was superseded as the hotel by a brick structure, when the Yolo House became a private residence.

Knight's Landing, which is located about twelve miles north of Woodland, has retained the early river-town atmosphere in the older portion of the village so perfectly that it was chosen by film directors as the locale for the making of Mississippi River scenes in the film play *Showboat*. The modern town which has grown up away from the river seems detached and remote from this quaint section with its old buildings practically unchanged since the '60's, when the river, then the only highway, was a scene of lively traffic.

Rancho Río de Jesús María

The third grant made in Yolo County territory was given to Thomas M. Hardy, a Canadian, in 1843, and consisted of 26,637 acres along Cache Creek east of Gordon's Ranch, reaching as far as the Sacramento River. It was called Rancho Río de Jesús María, an early name given to the Upper Sacramento River. Hardy built a tule shack on the west bank of the Sacramento near the mouth of the Feather River, but he spent very little time there, having enlisted in military service under the Mexican government.

After Hardy's death by drowning in Suisun Bay in 1848 or 1849 his property was sold by the public administrator. Among those who purchased portions of the original rancho was James M. Harbin, who had come to this section of California in 1847. On Harbin's land the town of Fremont was afterward laid out. In 1857 Harbin moved to Lake County, where he settled at the springs which bear his name.

Rancho Cañada de Capay

Rancho Cañada de Capay (Kroeber says that Capay is from the Indian word *kapai,* meaning "stream") was located on Cache Creek and was granted to Francisco Berryessa and his brothers, Santiago and Demesio, in 1843. Their great holdings were later taken over by incoming Americans, one of whom was George Dickson Stephens. In 1850 Stephens camped on Cache Creek on what he supposed was government land, but he afterward learned that it was a part of the Berryessa grant. With his brother, John D., he acquired the property that same year and erected an adobe dwelling. This house, around which a larger frame structure was built as the needs of the family grew, is the only adobe standing in Yolo County today. The building is well preserved and is still occupied by Stephens' descendants.

The first irrigation ditch in Yolo County was constructed by James Moore in 1856. It headed on Cache Creek about eight miles above the site of Woodland and within the bounds of Gordon's Ranch. Almost simultaneously with the building of the Moore canal, another dam and ditch were begun by David Quincy Adams in 1857. The Adams canal, which was completed in 1870, was laid out by Adams on Rancho Cañada de Capay, 4,693 acres of which he had purchased with money made in the mines of the Mother Lode during the years from 1849 to 1852. Adams built his canal for the purpose of irrigating 150 acres of alfalfa and 40 acres of Chinese gardens. This alfalfa, probably the first to be grown in California, was raised from seed obtained by Adams from Chile, and nearly all of the alfalfa grown in northern California today is known as Chilean alfalfa. The Adams Dam, which was located on Cache Creek about two miles west and a little north of Capay, no longer exists, but the prior water rights on Cache Creek obtained by David Adams are now owned by the Winters Ditch Company. The old Adams ranch home, located two miles north of Esparto, stood until 1932.

Historic Capay Valley is famous for the redbud and almond blossoms which glorify the countryside each spring.

Washington

In December 1844 Rancho Nueva Flandria, consisting of three square leagues of land bordering on the west bank of the Sacramento River, was granted to John Schwartz, an eccentric German emigrant who had come to California from New Mexico with the Bidwell-Bartleson party in 1841.

In the spring of 1846 Schwartz sold six hundred acres of his rancho to James McDowell, who had come overland with his wife and daughter in 1845. McDowell built a cabin in the northwest corner of his ranch opposite the site of the present city of Sacramento, where he took his family to live. He died in 1849, and in 1850 his widow had a town site laid out on the land. This was the beginning of the little town of Washington, now known as Broderick.

When the dissolution of the town of Fremont began in 1851, Washington became the center of commerce as well as of judicial and political activity in Yolo County. From 1851 to 1857 it was the county seat, and again from 1861 to 1862. The county courthouse stood on the site now occupied by the City Hall in Broderick.

For several years most of the traffic from the northern and western sections of Yolo County passed through Washington. So great was its early promise that its citizens for a time had hopes of its becoming a great city. Later, with the transfer of growth and activity from Washington to Sacra-

mento across the river, and with the advent of the railroad, which decreased the importance of the former as a center of navigation, Washington's boom days were ended.

Fremont

On the west shore of the Sacramento River opposite the mouth of the Feather River, within the boundaries of the Harbin Ranch, Jonas Spect, a native of Pennsylvania, who had come overland to Oregon in 1847 and from there to San Francisco on the "Henry" early in 1848, established the town of Fremont in March 1849. Spect erected a temporary store of tules, willow poles, and canvas, and with the help of the Indians established a ferry across the Sacramento River. A sandbar at this point made an excellent ford across the Feather River; and the entire situation seemed to indicate that this was the head of navigation for both streams.

With a constant stream of miners, teamsters, and packers passing through it on their way to the mining regions, Fremont grew by leaps and bounds, and at the height of its prosperity claimed a population of about three thousand. But its promise was short-lived. In the winter of 1849 heavy storms washed away the sandbars and the Feather River became navigable as far as Marysville. Commerce on both rivers passed Fremont by, and it was soon superseded in importance by Washington.

The loyal citizens of Fremont did not give up their town at once, and by means of desperate "lobbying" succeeded in making it the first county seat in 1850. In July of 1851, however, the popular vote took the seat of government to Washington, and Fremont, its last hope gone, gradually disappeared. Some of its buildings were moved to Knight's Landing, some to Marysville, and others out upon newly established ranches in the vicinity. Soon empty lots were all that remained of the little river metropolis. Today the old Fremont site makes an excellent place for a day's outing for the citizens of Knight's Landing and Woodland.

Spect, who became a member of the first State Senate, lived at Fremont until 1856, when he moved to Vernon, in Sutter County.

Cacheville

In September 1849 Thomas Cochran camped on the north bank of Cache Creek about ten miles west of Fremont, on the site of the present town of Yolo, and put up a very primitive hotel for the accommodation of travelers along the west side of the Sacramento River. The place grew and became known as Cochran's Crossing. In 1853 James A. Hutton arrived and erected a large, commodious structure which he opened to the public. The hospitality of Hutton and his family became so well known that the name of the place was changed to Hutton's Ranch, or Travelers' Home. The old Hutton house is still standing. In 1857 the place became the county seat of Yolo County and was rechristened Cacheville. Later, a post office was placed there under the name of the "Yolo Postoffice."

Located in a rich farming region, Cacheville (Yolo) grew rapidly for a few years, but was outstripped by the more promising Yolo City, later known as Woodland, a few miles to the south. The Pacific Methodist (South) College was established at Cacheville in 1859 but was moved to Vacaville in 1861 and to Santa Rosa in 1871.

Woodland

The rich groves of oak trees just south of Cache Creek, where the city of Woodland now stands, were centrally located in the midst of an extensive and fertile region, which later became one of the principal agricultural belts of the county. When the final location of the county seat was voted upon, the decision was made in Woodland's favor because of its central location.

The first settlers in this region were James McClure, James McClure, Jr., and Henry Wyckoff, who came in 1853. The McClures started a blacksmith shop, and, near by, Wyckoff opened a small store on what is now Court Street. Thus was born Yolo City, which continued to grow in importance until 1859, when a post office was established there under the name of Woodland.

A pioneer experiment in agriculture was begun there as early as 1856 by the diversion of water from Cache Creek, and by 1862 Woodland had become an important agricultural center. In that year the people voted to make it the county seat in place of Washington. Today, a series of canals augments the natural outlet of Cache Creek, and about one hundred thousand acres of land are under irrigation. In the midst of this prosperous rural section Woodland has become a thriving city.

Woodland was also a center of pioneer cultural development. Schools were established in the late '50's, and in 1860 Hesperian College was located there by the Christian church. Typical of the many small denominational colleges founded throughout northern California during the '60's and the '70's, Hesperian College performed a worthy pioneer work in higher education for over thirty-five years. Modern high schools and universities began to take the place of the small colleges in the latter part of the nineteenth century, and, in 1896, the trustees of Hesperian College deeded land and buildings to the new union high-school district of Woodland. The American Legion Hall, on Bush Street between First Street and College Street, now occupies the site of the former Hesperian College.

Davisville

Where the little town of Davisville grew up in the late '60's and where the University Farm at Davis now draws hundreds of agricultural students annually, Jerome C. Davis settled in the early '50's while the entire district was yet in its primitive, unbroken condition. The State Agricultural Report of 1856 says that at that time Davis had eight thousand acres of land, one thousand of which were inclosed, and that he was irrigating a portion of the ranch by pumping water from Putah Creek with a steam engine. Even that early he had a large peach orchard and several thousand bearing grapevines, and four hundred acres of wheat and barley, as well as many horses, cattle, and sheep. By 1858 he had twenty-one miles of fences. In 1864 his ranch totaled approximately thirteen thousand acres, more than eight thousand of which were fenced.

William Dresbach leased the old Davis home in 1867 and made it into a hotel, which he called the "Yolo House." As a settlement began to grow up around the place, Dresbach named it Davisville. With the advent of the railroad the place became a thriving grain shipping-point. In 1868, however, when a branch of the Central Pacific Railroad was extended northward to Marysville, Davisville began to decline as a center of trade. Its decline was further hastened when the Vaca Valley Road was constructed to Madison in 1875. The rich farming lands which surrounded it continued to be developed, however, and in 1905 the University Farm at Davis was established by an act of the state legislature. The first buildings were erected there in 1907 and the first courses for adult farmers were given in the autumn of 1908. The following January the farm school for young men and boys was opened as a part of the College of Agriculture of the State University at Berkeley.

SOURCES

[Credit is here given for source material, and permission to quote is hereby acknowledged]

BRYANT, EDWIN. *What I Saw in California.* D. Appleton & Company, New York, 1848, 1849
BUFFUM, E. GOULD. *Six Months in the Gold Mines.* Lea & Blanchard, Philadelphia, 1850
CLYMAN, JAMES. "James Clyman, His Diaries and Reminiscences." Edited by Charles L. Camp in *California Historical Society Quarterly,* V, No. 2 (June 1926), 109–138
GILBERT, FRANK T. *The Illustrated Atlas and History of Yolo County, California.* De Pue & Company, San Francisco, 1879
GREGORY, TOM. *History of Yolo County, California, with Biographical Sketches,* etc. Historic Record Company, Los Angeles, 1913
HILL, JOSEPH J. "Ewing Young in the Fur Trade of the Far Southwest, 1822–1834," in *Oregon Historical Society Quarterly,* XXIV, No. 1 (March 1923), 1–35
JONES, DAVID RHYS. "Pre-Pioneer Pathfinders, California–Oregon Trail, 1826–1846," in *Motor Land,* XXIX, Nos. 4–5 (October–November 1931)
WARE, E. B. *History of the Disciples of Christ in California.* F. W. Cooke, Healdsburg, California, 1916
Western Shore Gazetteer and Commercial Directory for the State of California . . . . Yolo County. C. P. Sprague & H. W. Atwell, Woodland, California, 1870

YUBA COUNTY

Y UBA COUNTY (Yuba is said by some authorities to have been the name of a tribe of Maidu Indians, the Yu-ba, who lived on the banks of the Feather River) was one of the original twenty-seven counties. Marysville has been its only county seat.

Yuba Trails

Before the arrival of the white man in the territory of what is now Yuba County, its dim trails were trodden only by wild beasts and by the lowly Maidu Indians of the tribe of Yu-ba. Frémont, in his *Memoirs,* describes their villages as he saw them in 1846:

"We traveled across the valley plain, and in about sixteen miles reached Feather River, at twenty miles from its junction with the Sacramento, near the mouth of the Yuba, so called from a village of Indians who live on it. The Indians aided us across the river with canoes and small rafts. Extending along the bank in front of the village was a range of wicker cribs, about twelve feet high, partly filled with what is there the Indians' staff of life, acorns. A collection of huts, shaped like bee-hives, with naked Indians sunning themselves on the tops, and these acorn cribs, are the prominent objects in an Indian village." Powers, in his *Tribes of California,* also ascribes the name Yuba to this Indian tribe.

Perhaps the first white man to cross the plains and streams of Yuba County was Gabriel Moraga, who traversed this region in 1808, probably proceeding as far north as the present Nevada County. Some say that the name Yuba is a corruption of the Spanish word *uba,* or *uva,* meaning "grapes," and was given to the river by this expedition on account of the wild grapes which grew luxuriantly along its banks.

Hudson's Bay Company trappers occasionally crossed the region during the years 1830–1841, on hunting and trapping expeditions, and in the '40's a branch of the old California Emigrant Trail crossed the High Sierra through Donner's Pass, and followed down the mountains to Johnson's Ranch, an outpost of civilization at that time, located three miles east of where Wheatland now stands.

Marysville

A large portion of what is now Yuba County became a part of the princely domain of Captain John A. Sutter after 1841, but, as the lands included on his map covered a much larger area than the Mexican laws allowed, he resorted to the practice of subletting parts of his estate to other settlers. Some of these farms were in what are now Sutter and Placer counties, while others lay within the present boundaries of Yuba County.

The land on which the town of Marysville was later founded was located on that part of Sutter's Ranch which was leased in the fall of 1842 to Theodore Cordua, a Prussian, for a period of nineteen years. Cordua made it a stock ranch and in 1842–1843 built an adobe dwelling house, with a trading room and outhouses, at what is now the foot of D Street in Marysville.

Cordua, "a fat, jolly, whist-loving man, popular with everybody," called his settlement "New Mecklenburg," after his native land, but his neighbors called it Cordua's Ranch. It stood on the California–Oregon Trail through the Sacramento Valley, and by 1846 travel over this route from Oregon had become so extensive that Cordua's adobe became an important way station and trading-post for hunters, emigrants, and, later, for miners. The old adobe with its thick wall, seemingly built to withstand a siege, was destroyed by fire in 1851.

There was an Indian village on Cordua's Ranch at the point where the railroad now crosses the Yuba River. Cordua made friends with these Indians and utilized them in working his ranch and herding his sheep.

In 1844, Cordua obtained a grant of seven leagues of land from the Mexican government north of the Yuba River in what is now Yuba County, but not included in his former. lease from Sutter.

Charles Covillaud, a native of France and a former employee of Cordua, purchased a half-share in the ranch at Mecklenburg in 1848, and on January 1, 1849, the other half was sold to Michael C. Nye, who married Mrs. Harriet Pike, a survivor of the Donner party tragedy, and William Foster, also a member of the Donner party. For a time it was known as Nye's Ranch. Discovery of gold at Coloma in 1848 brought a period of great development to the region and a town was laid out in 1850. Covillaud's wife, formerly Mary Murphy, another member of the Donner party, received the honor of having the new town named for her, Marysville.

Marysville became the actual head of navigation on the Feather River and a center of trade for the northern mines. Its location gave it a decided superiority over all other candidates for such a position on the river, above and below. The distance to the mines, north and east, was not great, and cargoes from the river boats could be transported readily by pack-mule·trains to the outlying gold fields. These proved to be rich producers and as a result Marysville experienced a phenomenal growth from the start.

Freight and passenger boats landed at a point adjoining the old Plaza, where the freight sheds of the Western Pacific Railroad now stand, on Front between D and E streets. Today the river, held in leash by stone levees, actually flows above the city streets, but in the early days the Plaza looked down upon the stream and its rich bottom lands, originally covered with groves of cottonwood, willow, and sycamore, but which soon became dotted with the homes and orchards and vineyards of early settlers. Hydraulic mining, however, changed the face of the entire countryside, burying homes and villages beneath acres of débris, raising the bed of the river seventy feet or more, and necessitating the construction of miles of levees. On the tailings today grow thrifty peach orchards and new farm houses have replaced the old ones.

A Chinese joss house, one of the oldest in the state, still stands on Front Street near U.S. Highway 99 E, but no longer does it watch the passing of ships upon the river as it did in the stirring days of the.'50's. The balcony of this sturdy old brick temple is now about on a level with the dike which keeps the river from washing the whole structure down to the sea.

Among Marysville's many unique and interesting old houses is the Ramírez residence on Fifth between B and C streets. Of elaborate construction, with marble basement and Gothic windows, it is known locally as "The Castle."

The brick house at 630 D Street built by Stephen J. Field, young New York lawyer and son of a Connecticut minister, who came to Marysville in 1849, still serves as a private dwelling. Field worked with John A. Sutter, Charles J. Covillaud, José M. Ramírez, Theodore Cordua, Theodore Sicard, John Sampson, and others in laying out the town of Marysville and organizing the county. He purchased two hundred lots within the prospective city and named the first streets after his associates, Covillaud, Ramírez, Sicard, and Sampson. Later he became the first alcalde of the town. During Lincoln's administration Field was appointed Justice of the United States Supreme Court.

Among the public buildings of brick and stone which are of historic interest in Marysville is the County Courthouse on Sixth and D streets. Built in 1855–1856, its three towers loom up castle-like above solid brick walls. Three of Marysville's churches date from the '50's and the '60's: the Episcopal Church on Fifth and E streets, constructed of brick in Norman Gothic style; the St. Joseph's Catholic Church, Seventh and C streets, built in 1855; and the old brick Presbyterian Church, Fifth and D streets, constructed in 1860 and still using the original bell which hung in the earlier church. The old City Hall, built in 1854; the Fire House of 1857; and a score of other buildings of quaint design, sturdily constructed of brick and stone, make Marysville one of the most interesting towns dating from the early American period in California.

Among the graves of pioneers in the Marysville Cemetery is that of Mary Murphy Covillaud and that of Father Florian, the Franciscan padre. Father Florian began his work among the Californians and Indians in northern California in the gold-rush period, although he was never active in the Marysville area.

Johnson's Ranch

Pablo Gutiérrez, an employee of Captain Sutter, received a grant of five leagues of land on the north side of Bear River in 1844. Here he built an adobe house at a point later called Johnson's Crossing.

Gutiérrez was killed late in 1844, and his grant and cattle were sold at auction by Captain Sutter, magistrate of the region. The land was purchased for $150 by William Johnson and Sebastian Kyser, Johnson taking the eastern half and Kyser the western half. Just below the Crossing they built an adobe house.

This place came to be known as Johnson's Ranch, on which Wheatland was later located, and was the first settlement reached by the Argonauts who crossed the Sierra over that branch of the California Trail which went through Donner's Pass and down the San Juan Ridge or the ridge north of Bear River into Yuba County. Here many footsore emigrants rested and obtained supplies. Among these wayfarers were the seven members of the Donner party who succeeded in getting over the mountains in the winter of 1846–1847, finally reaching Johnson's Ranch, where they solicited aid for those still imprisoned in the snowbound fastnesses at Donner Lake.

Camp Far West

Camp Far West was established by the United States government in 1849 for the protection of American settlers in the Yuba region. Two companies of soldiers were stationed there under command of Captain Hannibal Day, but the post was abandoned in 1852 as it was no longer needed.

No trace of the old log fort, barracks, and officers' quarters remains today, but the site, about four miles east of Wheatland, has been marked by the Native Sons of the Golden West.

Gold Bars on the Yuba

The first prospectors in the Sierra worked along the rivers and especially on the sand bars, which were rich in gold. Like other gold-bearing streams, the Yuba River above Marysville was dotted thickly with river-bar towns by 1850, a camp to every one or two miles. According to some authorities Jonas Spect was the first to find gold in the county. His discovery was made on June 2, 1848, at a place later known as Rose's Bar, located eighteen miles east of Marysville. Almost simultaneously with Spect's discovery at Rose's Bar, Michael Nye and William Foster found pay gravel on Dry Creek near its junction with the Yuba.

In the fall of 1848 John Rose and William J. Reynolds opened a store at Rose's Bar, so called because Rose did the purchasing of goods at Sacramento. The partners also supplied the miners with fresh beef and other farm products brought up from their ranch south of Marysville. In the spring of 1849 Rose's Bar was so overcrowded with miners that at a meeting called for the purpose it was decided to limit claims to 100 feet square per man. By 1850 two thousand men were at work on this bar alone.

The floods of 1850 drove the miners away from the sand bars to higher ground, where more gold was uncovered. Gatesville, or Sucker Flat (virtually an extension of Rose's Bar away from the river), grew up at this time and had developed into a town of some importance by the time the bars along the river became depleted of their gold. Squaw Creek, another rich locality, enjoyed its brief heyday in common with such neighboring camps as Cordua, Sawmill, Lander's, and Kennebec bars. Opposite Lander's Bar near the mouth of Deer Creek was Malay Camp, worked by miners from the Malay Peninsula.

The richest of the Yuba River bars was Parks' Bar, located two or three miles west of Rose's Bar. To this location came David Parks with his wife and children on September 8, 1848. Since a man with a family was very unusual in the earliest camps, the place was named in his honor. Parks' Bar, which had become a populous camp by 1849, reached the height of its prosperity in 1852, when it rivaled Marysville for a time. When gold along the river bars became worked out, in 1855, decline set in, and Parks', as well as its neighbors, Barton's and Union bars, was soon depopulated.

Near Parks' Bar was Sicard's Bar, where Theodore Sicard was the first to find "color." The name Sicard Flat was given to the town which grew up about a mile back from the river and is still perpetuated in the Sicard Flat School District with its handful of scattered ranch houses. Other bars still farther up the river were the National, Negro, Missouri No. 1, and Horse bars.

The first mining camp of importance above Marysville was Swiss Bar, opposite Sand Flat, nine miles up the river. Little mining was done there before 1850, and the place was never the equal of Long Bar, a little farther up the river. Long Bar, in addition to being the longest bar on the Yuba, also boasted the longest period of success. It was occupied as early as October 1848, and the first organized body of

miners to come to California from the outside stopped there in November. A post office was established in 1850, and by 1851 a ferry boat was plying between Long Bar and Kennebec Bar a few miles below. Above Long Bar was Chimney Hill, and at the mouth of Dry Creek was Ousley's Bar, named after a Dr. Ousley who mined there in early days.

Hydraulic mining, after 1857, slowly destroyed the old river bars and their camps along the Yuba. They became buried "cities," lying no less than seventy feet beneath the débris washed down from the titanic diggings in the Sierra. The once famous Rose's and Parks' bars, like all their neighbors, were simply obliterated by the march of "progress" which overwhelmed them. Today the names of a few of the more important remain as school districts or townships, such as Foster's Bar Township, Rose Bar Township, Parks' Bar Township, and Long Bar Township.

Gold still lies in the bed of the Yuba River and, until recently, extensive dredging activities took out vast sums from the old tailings. In 1905 the Yuba Consolidated Goldfields began operations nine miles east of Marysville, with a capital of $12,500,000. The towns of Marigold and Hammonton (the latter named after W. P. Hammon, moving spirit of the company) grew up, direct descendants of the mining camps of the '50's. Dredging, however, is no longer very profitable and in 1932 the field was taken over by men, otherwise unemployed, who were learning to wield pan and rocker in approved pioneer style. On Parks' Bar alone, from fifty to one hundred people were mining by these primitive methods in the summer of 1932.

"Speculative Cities"

Population increased so rapidly in the fall of 1849 and in 1850 that land speculators saw possibilities of accumulating wealth by laying out cities on paper. Few mining camps had been established in the mountains before the winter of 1850, but there were a large number of flourishing towns in the foothills, settlements entirely dependent on the continuance of profitable gold diggings. In the valley, even where there was no gold, prospective cities of vaunted magnificence were laid out. Interested promoters, "with a flourish of oratorical and newspaper trumpets," proclaimed the advantages of their respective cities, both as a place of residence and as a center of business and trade. Particularly did those places tributary to the mines witness "a high degree of the spirit of venture and speculation that was so noticeable in the mining camps."

Delano says of these pioneer real estate booms: "There seemed to be a speculative mania spreading over the land, and scores of new towns were heard of which were never known, only the puffs of newspapers, the stakes which marked the size of lots, and the nicely drawn plot of the surveyor." Delano knew whereof he spoke, for he took part in some of the speculation, buying lots in Marysville and losing half of his earnings in the operation. In an effort to recoup his losses he and a friend laid out a town on the Feather River twenty miles north of Marysville, but they were unable to attract population to their town.

Yuba County boasted seven or eight of these "speculative cities": Marysville, Eliza, Linda, Oakland, El Dorado, Plumas City, Featherton, and Kearney (Kearny). Of all these aspiring towns, Marysville was the only one to survive and to become a thriving city. Nevertheless, at first, there was sufficient doubt and misgiving as to the future of Marysville to cause some capitalists to put their money into other less fortunate ventures.

Eliza, some three miles below Marysville, proved to be one of the will-o'-the-wisps followed for a time by early speculators. Several stores and houses were built there in the spring of 1850, but by summer it was evident that the place could not rival Marysville, and Eliza soon ceased to exist.

Linda, on the south bank of the Yuba River about three miles above Marysville, lasted a little longer than did Eliza, its allotted span being about two years. Arrival of the little steamer "Linda" at the site was the occasion for the establishment of the town, but the hope that Linda would become the head of navigation and a rival of Marysville was never realized. The site is now buried more than thirty feet beneath the tailings washed down from the hydraulic mines in the hills, and the only reminder of this would-be city is the name of Linda Township.

Of the other "speculative cities" in Yuba County, none of which existed but for a short time, Plumas City was situated at the mouth of Reed's Creek; El Dorado City, just across from Sutter's Hock Farm; Kearney (named in honor of General Stephen W. Kearny), on Bear River on Johnson's Ranch; Featherton, on the Feather River at the mouth of Honcut Creek; and Oakland, between Featherton and Marysville.

Smartsville

The first building at Smartsville (post office, Smartville) was a hotel built early in 1856 by a Mr. Smart. The town grew, and in 1863 the Union Church was erected. The Church of the Immaculate Conception (first organized at Rose's Bar by Father Peter Maganatta in 1852) was erected at Smartsville in 1861. This edifice was burned in 1870, but another took its place the following year. As the present-day traveler approaches the village the most conspicuous feature of the landscape is still its churches, which stand like faithful guardians among the handful of old homes half-hidden in a bower of trees. The old frame Masonic Temple, moved to Smartsville from Rose's Bar, is still in use. Remains of the rich mines developed at Smartsville in the late '50's, as well as scars of the hydraulic operations of the '60's and the '70's, may still be seen in the surrounding hills.

By 1878 the Excelsior Company at Smartsville had washed over eight million cubic yards of detritus into the Yuba River, while ten times that amount remained in the company's claims when hydraulic activities ceased in 1883.

To the north of Smartsville is a great gash in the hillside, the site of the once populous mining camp of Sucker Flat, where only one house remains today.

The Empire Ranch Station

In the early '50's, the period of stagecoaches and "six-in-hands," before the advent of railroads, the California Stage Company carried passengers from one end of the state to the other. One of the many stations used by this company was maintained on the Empire Ranch near the town of Smartsville, where meals were served and horses changed. The old Empire Ranch Station is among the very few buildings remaining of those once used by the California Stage Company. Standing near the highway, the roadhouse and the barn, with its rough hand-hewn timbers held together by wooden pegs, are as substantial as when they were placed there in 1852. Halfway up the hill, hidden among the oaks, is a neglected graveyard. Beyond it on the opposite side is another cemetery still in use.

In 1849 a Mr. Berry and his wife built a log cabin on the site of the later Empire Ranch Station, and by 1851 this location had become the rallying-point of miners for miles around. Thomas Mooney and Michael Riley bought the place that year and established a trading-post and hotel there. Sunday was a gala day at the Empire Ranch, when hundreds of miners gathered in a convivial mood for sports and other

pleasures. The ranch is still in the hands of the Mooney family.

Mooney Flat, near by, was named for Thomas Mooney. Other early-day inns in the vicinity were the Union House on the county line east of Empire Ranch, and Round Tent and Cabbage Patch on the Sacramento–Grass Valley Road by way of Spencerville. At Round Tent a circular tent was set up in 1851 by a Mr. Baker, and the name was retained when a more substantial structure was erected later.

Timbuctoo

Timbuctoo, also a neighbor of Smartsville, has only one of its original buildings left—the old Wells Fargo Express Office. Solidly built of locally manufactured brick, it retains the heavy iron doors and shutters which once protected its precious contents from fire and robbery. Several million dollars' worth of gold dust passed through its doors in the gold days. On the building is a placard, painted in 1859, and still legible, which indicates that the place served as a general merchandise store as well as an agency for Wells Fargo and Company. A bronze marker on the building reads:

Old Wells Fargo Office & Stewart Bros. Store (1855). Restored and dedicated to the memory of the pioneer men and women of Timbuctoo, May 10, 1928, by Marysville Parlour No. 6, N.S.G.W. Presented by Wells Fargo Bank and Union Trust Co., San Francisco.

A few relics of pioneer days are housed in the building. The stone foundations of other buildings long since destroyed by fire, aged fig and locust trees, as well as a few old frame dwellings, may be seen near the highway—reminders of the vanished hopes of Timbuctoo.

The first mining in this region was done as early as 1850 in the ravines near by, one of which was named Timbuctoo after a negro from Africa who was one of the first miners in the locality. The town of Timbuctoo, started in 1855, took its name from that of the ravine. During the period when hydraulic mining flourished, Timbuctoo was the largest town in the eastern part of Yuba County, with a total population at the height of its prosperity of twelve hundred. It contained a church and a theater, as well as the usual saloons, stores, and hotels.

Gold Camps on Honcut Creek

Honcut Creek and its tributaries, crowded with gold-seekers during the '50's and the '60's, are today deserted except for a few ranches and country stores. One of the many camps which once existed there was Natchez, on the Natchez branch of the Honcut, so named because of its fancied resemblance to Natchez, Mississippi. A "Major" Brown came to the locality alone in 1850, carrying with him a store of blankets and trinkets with which to win the favor of the Indians. He found the diggings in the vicinity to be very rich. These he guarded jealously, and with the aid of his Indians very soon accumulated a considerable fortune.

The story goes that a prospector from below arrived on the scene. The stranger asked Brown how far his claim extended. In reply "the Major took up his rifle and pointing it upstream calmly remarked: 'Up this way as far as she will carry a bullet,' and pointing down stream, 'down this way about the same distance.' The stranger, although he thought it was a pretty large claim, concluded not to express his opinion." It was not long, however, before "Major" Brown was surrounded by miners claiming equality with himself, and by 1851 the camp of Natchez had sprung up, reaching the height of its prosperity in 1852 and 1853. For a few years mining lagged in the district, but a revival of activities took place in 1858. This proved short-lived, and after 1860 steady decline set in.

Some of the ravines mined in the vicinity of Natchez

were Brown's, Steward's, Grub, Slug, Jackass, Jennie, Hovey, and Dicksburg.

James H. Hanson came to the site of Hansonville (now Rackerby) on Hansonville Creek, twenty-eight miles northeast of Marysville, in 1851, and within a year a town of about a thousand miners, with eight hotels and seven stores, had grown up on the spot. Scarcely a trace of the old town remains today.

Brown's Valley

On the old road to Downieville, twelve or thirteen miles northeast of Marysville, is Brown's Valley. An early settler named Brown, who came to this spot in 1850, discovered gold near a huge boulder adjoining the temporary camp which he had set up. After taking out over $12,000 in quartz, Brown "was satisfied to retire." Not long after his discovery four Frenchmen developed the famous Jefferson Mine in the vicinity, and other rich discoveries, among them the Flag, the Donnebrouge (Donnebroge), the Pennsylvania, and the Sweet Vengeance mines, followed rapidly. One of the first stamp mills to be erected in California was put up at the Sweet Vengeance Mine by a French company, which purchased the mine from Spaniards who had been milling the ore by means of an arrastra on Little Creek.

Very little mining is done at Brown's Valley today because the presence of water in the lower levels of the mines makes it a difficult and expensive operation to trace the gold veins. Ruins of some of the old mills still rise above the shafts of once prosperous mines, and within the village a sturdy stone store with iron doors is another vivid reminder of the past. It is difficult to realize that the present sleepy village once possessed five hotels, twenty-four saloons, and numerous stores. Just north of Brown's Valley was Prairie Diggings, no trace of which is left today. Mining began there in 1854, the rich surface diggings of the locality attracting many who later became residents of Marysville.

Along the old Marysville–Downieville Road the sites of many taverns and stage stations may be located. Eight miles from Marysville was Adriance's Ranch, on the north bank of the Yuba River just west of Swiss Bar. North of Brown's Valley, in rapid succession, are the sites of the Galena House (fourteen miles from Marysville), the Empire House, the Peoria House, the Sixteen Mile House, the Yuba County House, the Stanfield House, the Abbott House, the Martin House, the Phillips' House, and several others, including the Zinc House, Bowers' Place, and the Comstock Place. The Peoria House, conducted by Captain Thomas Phillips, stood on land which is still owned by the family. The name is retained in the Peoria School District and the Peoria Cemetery, in which some members of the Phillips family lie buried. The Abbott House was erected by John M. Abbott in the early '50's at the Dry Creek crossing, and was at first known as Oak Grove House. Abbott was one of the first growers of fruit in this section. The present village of Stanfield Hill stands on the site of the Stanfield House, opened up in 1852 by a man named Stanfield. The site of the Martin House is marked by an old tree.

The Oregon House

Where the Branch Turnpike to La Porte turned north from the Downieville Trail, twenty-four miles northeast of Marysville, the Oregon House was erected in 1852. It became one of the most popular of the several hostelries along that trail, and many a traveler in search of gold found rest and entertainment awaiting him within its hospitable doors. In January 1853, on the anniversary of the Battle of New Orleans, a grand party was given in the Oregon House, the first in that section of the Sierra foothills. Two hundred and fifty tickets were sold, and eighteen ladies were present, a goodly showing for those days. The original Oregon House was destroyed by fire many years ago, but the present structure stands on the old site.

The Downieville Trail continued east from the Oregon House and thence northeast to Camptonville by way of Indiana Ranch and Foster's Bar, while the Branch Turnpike went north through Frenchtown, at one time the center of trade for surrounding mines and lumber mills. One adobe store still stands on the site of Frenchtown to remind the traveler of other days. This interesting landmark, built by a Frenchman in the '50's, is well preserved and houses a small museum exhibit. The sturdy adobe walls and the thick layer of earth placed beneath the roof to serve as a protection against fire as well as against the heat of the summer sun account for the fact that this building alone escaped the fires that wiped out the rest of the town. Only a few grass-grown ruins mark the place where other buildings (among them two hotels) formerly stood.

North of Frenchtown on the west side of Dry Creek is the site of the Jefferson House, erected in 1852 by James Evans. This building disappeared many years ago.

Indiana Ranch and Greenville

The Downieville Trail and, later, the first wagon road from the Oregon House to Camptonville went by way of Foster's Bar, passing through Indiana Ranch and the town of Greenville. Beyond the Oregon House several stopping-places broke the loneliness of the old trail, among them the California House and the Keystone House, the latter a large hotel with a race track attached. Indiana Ranch, designated on many present-day maps, was at one time a thriving town. It was first settled in 1851 by the Page brothers (who came from Indiana), Peter Labadie, and John Tolles, and the settlement was called Indiana Creek or Tolles' New Diggin's. Tolles and Labadie kept the first hotels in the place. After 1860 mining declined in the vicinity, and although rich pockets have been found from time to time not one of them has proved lasting.

One and one-half miles northeast of Indiana Ranch stood the Maple Springs House, erected in 1852, and afterward sold to Peter Labadie, when it became known also as Labadie's. The Maple Springs House continued to serve as a hotel until 1860, when travel became diverted over a different route by the building of the Atchison and Rice Turnpike. Bennett's Ranch was an early settlement on the flat just below Labadie's. Additional public houses were soon established on the new road: Eich's, the New York Star, Oldfield's, and the Fountain House. The latter place, opened up in 1860 by Robert Johnston, ceased to be a public house in 1878.

Greenville, now a quiet mountain village, was originally known as Oregon Hill. Gold was first found at Oregon Hill in 1850, but the place did not become prosperous until the Nine-Horse Ditch was constructed, bringing water to the diggings. The company responsible for the building of this ditch was composed of nine members, and in order to let everyone know that it was no "one-horse" affair that they were putting in, they named it the Nine-Horse Ditch.

Halfway between Greenville and Foster's Bar was Stroud's, or the Milk Ranch, a popular stopping-place in the '50's, especially noted for its balls and gay hospitality.

Brownsville and Northeastern Yuba County

Brownsville, located on what was known in early days as the Central Turnpike to La Porte, was named after I. E. Brown, who erected a sawmill in the vicinity in 1851. For a decade or more a number of sawmills and lumbering camps, as well as mining camps, existed in the surrounding country. Among these were the Sharon Valley Mills, two miles northeast, completed in 1853 by L. T. Crane; the Challenge Mills, a mile farther northeast, erected in 1856; and the Washington (1851–1863) and Page (1852–1860) mills, located on Dry Creek, south of Challenge.

Brownsville was a "temperance town" and in 1878 became something of an educational center with the establishment there of the Knoxdale Institute by Martin Knox and his wife, with Professor E. K. Hill acting as principal. Knox, in partnership with P. E. Weeks, had purchased Brown's mill in 1852 and conducted the business until 1857. In 1855 they built a large hotel. This was subsequently burned but was replaced by another structure in 1866.

South of the Challenge Mills on the Branch Turnpike was the New York House, established by the same men who owned the New York Ranch north of Brownsville on the road to Forbestown. Continuing north and northeast from Challenge Mills to La Porte a number of stage stations were passed, all important stopping-places on the way to the gold mines of northwestern Sierra County and of Plumas County. Today some of these old houses are being used as summer resorts.

Woodville (now Woodleaf), just south of the present Butte County line, was formerly known as Barker's Ranch, or the Barker House, first settled in 1850 by Charles Barker. James Wood bought the place in 1858 and erected the beautiful two-story brick hotel, long known as the Woodville House, which still stands beside the highway.

Leaving Woodleaf behind, the motorist of today passes the site of Oroliva, a mile to the northeast in Butte County. Going through Clipper Mills one again enters Yuba County, passing the site of Barton's House before reaching Strawberry Valley. Known to the Indians as "Pomingo," the origin of the present name of Strawberry Valley is uncertain, some contending that the presence of numerous beds of wild strawberries gave rise to the name, while others say that the appellation was the combination of the names of two early settlers, Straw and Berry, both being explanations heard in other localities where this name is found.

Once in the midst of a large mining area, the Strawberry Valley district included the rich diggings on Deadwood Creek, Kentucky Gulch, Rich Gulch, and Whiskey Gulch. The town of Strawberry Valley became a lively center of trade for the surrounding mines and in the late '50's its main street was lined with stores, shops, saloons, and dwellings, the leading hostelry being the Columbus Hotel. The edifices on one side of this street were originally in Butte County while those on the opposite side were located in Yuba County, but in 1860 the legislature moved the county line a short distance northward so that all that is left of the town today (a hotel, a store, and a few dwellings) is now in Yuba County.

Proceeding up the ridge from Strawberry Valley, the early-day traveler passed in turn the Seneca House, the Union Hotel, Eagleville, and the North Star House.

Dobbins' Ranch

Located in the lovely foothill valley of Dobbins' Creek, Dobbins' Ranch was first settled in 1849 by William M. and Mark D. Dobbins. By 1850 it had become the terminus for the stage-carried express business of Langton's Pioneer Express. From that point the express had to be transported over the mountains to Downieville on mule back. Turnpikes ultimately took the place of the narrow pack trails, and in 1860 Atchison and Rice, with others, constructed a road to Downieville by way of Dobbins' Ranch, Bullard's Bar, and

Camptonville, a course followed today by a good county road.

Dobbins' Ranch exchanged hands several times from 1855 to 1862, when it came into the possession of Joseph Merriam. The pioneer store which still stands in the village of Dobbins (as it is called today) was opened in 1867 by William Slingsby and Dan Gattens, who formed an interesting partnership, maintaining a pack train on the Downieville Trail continuously for a number of years, furnishing the surrounding country with supplies, and taking an active part in community affairs.

High on the ridge halfway between Dobbins' Ranch and Bullard's Bar there stood for many years the Mountain Cottage House, built at the Five Mile Ranch by Colonel Prentice, government Indian Agent in charge of the four or five thousand Yuba Indians.

Three miles southwest of Dobbins is the site of the Kentucky Ranch. Continuing west is the site of the next stopping-place on the old stage road, the Golden Ball, two miles south of the Oregon House on the Downieville Trail. Where the road crossed Dry Creek was the Virginia Ranch, two miles south of Abbott's House, also on the Downieville Trail. The Virginia Ranch was settled in 1850 by J. A. Paxton, who built a hotel there and kept a trading-post. After Peter Rice bought the place in 1859 it ceased to be a public house.

The Gold Bars of the North Yuba River

The early miners of northeastern Yuba County had a wild and rugged country to contend with. Carl I. Wheat, in a note to the *De Long Journals*, describes this section as follows: "The map of Northeastern Yuba County gives no hint of the wildly broken nature of the terrain. The general contour of the ridges suggests an old plateau, slightly tilted to the west, greatly cut away by erosion during recent geologic times. The Yuba River and its many branches have cut deeply into this old plateau, its gorges being from five hundred to over a thousand feet in depth. Oregon Creek canyon just south of Camptonville falls away on a grand scale. The 'bars' were located along the rivers, with mountains towering up on both sides. The other towns and 'diggins' were generally located on or near the tops of the highest ridges, where the miners discovered the rich, gold-bearing gravels left by the rivers of earlier geologic ages. To one familiar with this broken terrain, De Long's active journeyings to and fro, on foot and on muleback, take on a new significance. It is a heavily wooded country, and to become lost was, and is, very easy, if one were to leave the beaten paths. . . . .

"The very names of many of the populous mining camps of these wild ridges have been lost, and in other localities only a lone cabin or an ancient apple tree remains to recall the teeming life of the early 'fifties,' for the pines have grown up even over the burying places of the dead, and Nature has hastened to take back her own."

This region, where solitude and the calm of nature now reign, was once alive with hard-working miners. It is said that in 1849 and in the early '50's miners along the Yuba River could send a message by word of mouth all the way from Downieville to Marysville, so numerous were the camps located along the river's course.

The most famous of the bars along the North Yuba River were Foster's Bar and Bullard's Bar. Early in 1849 William M. Foster, a survivor of the Donner party tragedy, mined on the west bank of the river between the mouths of Willow and Mill creeks, where he erected a store. The place soon became so crowded with gold-seekers that it was necessary to limit claims to thirty feet in width along the river bank, although a claim could extend up the hill as far as desired. Foster's Bar cast fifteen hundred votes in 1850 and was known as the roughest and toughest spot on the Yuba. The principal hotel, spoken of in the *De Long Journals* as "that Hell of bedbugs," was the El Dorado. Not even the site of Foster's Bar can be seen today, for it is covered by water backed up by the dam at Bullard's Bar to a depth of more than a hundred feet.

Bullard's Bar, three-quarters of a mile below Foster's Bar, was named after one of its pioneer miners, a Dr. Bullard, who had been shipwrecked off the coast of California while on his way from Brooklyn, New York, to the Sandwich Islands. As early as 1850 a bridge was built at Bullard's Bar, but it was washed away by the next winter's rains. Each succeeding bridge suffered a similar fate until 1858, when George Mix built a substantial structure at a cost of $7,000 which stood until carried away by the great flood of 1862. Subsequently a bridge was erected a short distance up the river, which was later purchased by John Ramm, of Ramm's Ranch. In 1875 this bridge likewise was washed away. Ramm soon built another at a cost of $15,000 which he continued to operate as a toll bridge until it was purchased by the county shortly before the beginning of the twentieth century.

Bullard's Bar and its bridges are no more. In their place is the immense Bullard's Bar Dam, which impounds 12,000 acre-feet of water to operate generators in a power house at the base of the structure.

Among the numerous camps below Bullard's Bar were the following: Kanaka Bar, first worked by Hawaiians; Winslow Bar, an important place in the '50's, named after Captain Winslow, who brought the first shipload of Chinamen to California and worked them here; English Bar, which proved unprofitable to the Englishmen who mined it but which brought $90,000 in gold to a man named Wilkins, who purchased the ground in 1851; Clingman's Point; Negro Bar; Missouri Bar; Condemned Bar; and Frenchman's Bar.

Even more numerous were the camps above Bullard's Bar. Between Bullard's Bar and Foster's Bar on the opposite side of the river was a small location called Ferry Bar, probably so named after the crude ferry used on the river at this point before bridges were built at Foster's and Bullard's bars. Above Foster's Bar was Stoney Bar, where 500 men were working in 1850 and where the principal hotel housed 250 men. Opposite Stoney was Atchison's Bar. Continuing up the river, the following bars were passed on the right bank of the stream: Long Bar No. 2, two miles above Foster's; Oregon Bar, two miles farther on; French Bar; Pittsburg Bar; Scott's Bar, at the mouth of Scott's Bar Creek; Rock Island Bar; Missouri Bar No. 2, first mined by men from Pike County, Missouri; Willow Bar; New York Bar; Mississippi Bar; Alabama Bar; Slate Range Bar; Cherokee Bar; and Cut Eye Foster's Bar near the Yuba-Sierra county line. A road crossed the river at Cherokee Bar over Wood's Bridge, later known as the Cherokee Bridge. Today the state highway from Nevada City to Downieville crosses the North Yuba near this spot.

On the left bank of the Yuba above Atchison's and Stoney bars were Texas Bar, opposite Long Bar No. 2; Elbow Bar, south of Missouri Bar No. 2; Sucker Bar, opposite Willow Bar; Fraser's and Wambo (Wambaugh's) bars, east of the mouth of Deadwood Creek; and Finley's Bar, south of Slate Range Bar.

"Today there remains no vestige of human habitation on most of these bars, and the lower portions of them are covered many feet deep with the detritus of later hydraulic washing."

Camptonville

Camptonville's present buildings are of a comparatively recent date of construction, the town having been completely destroyed by fire several times, but its citizens have wisely retained the simple New England type of architecture which influenced the earlier builders. The white steepled church, the schoolhouse on the hill, the frame hotel, home-like and hospitable and cool under its spreading elms, and the dozen or more white cottages surrounded by trees and old-fashioned flowers, all lend a delightful early American atmosphere to this quiet mountain hamlet, unspoiled by the modern highway which fortunately has passed it a little to the south.

As one enters the present village from the west, attention is arrested by a stone monument surmounted by the model of a water wheel and bearing an inscription which reads:

On this spot in 1878, Lester Allen Pelton invented the Pelton water wheel. Erected in 1929 by Gravel Range Lodge, Free & Accepted Masons.

A hotel was built on the site of Camptonville as early as 1850, when it was on the main-traveled road from Marysville and Nevada City to Downieville, and pack-mule trains stopped there daily on their way to the higher mountains. The toll road via Foster's Bar was completed to Camptonville in 1854 and the California Stage Company began running stages that far the following year. The first great boom, however, came to the town in 1852, when gold was discovered on Gold Ridge to the east. Among the new arrivals at that time was Robert Campton, a blacksmith, for whom the town was named. By 1866 Camptonville numbered fifteen hundred residents and was the center for hydraulic operations which produced one-half million dollars annually. A plank road a mile long formed the main street of the town. This was lined by more than thirty stores, numerous hotels and boarding-houses, as well as ubiquitous saloons. Most of this ground was soon washed out by the activities of giant hydraulic monitors.

Rich strikes other than that of Gold Ridge soon caused a number of settlements to spring up throughout the region. Two miles north of Camptonville a group of men from Galena, Illinois, found gold in 1852, and the camp which grew up there was known as Galena Hill. The place boasted a large hotel, two stores, and two saloons in 1856, with more than one hundred miners working the placers in the neighborhood. A single gatepost of the old hostelry is all that remains to tell the story of Galena Hill.

Young's Hill, three miles northwest, also had its beginnings in 1852, when William Young and his brother settled there. By 1856 it was a thriving center of trade with hotels, stores, saloons, blacksmith shops, and even a theater flanking its main street. This camp is mentioned frequently in the De Long diary, Charles E. De Long, the writer, having made it his home for some time.

Ramm's Ranch to the southwest was located early by John Ramm, who saw the value of the perpetual spring which existed on the spot and which he used to advantage later in his grape culture. Early settlers in the region had found an important rancheria of the Yuba Indians located there.

The first iron rails used in the Yuba mines, to convey dirt to sluice boxes, furnished the name of Railroad Hill, settled in 1852 some four miles north of Camptonville. Its neighbor, Depot Hill, was a center of hydraulic mining during the '60's and '70's.

Oak Valley, a small camp located on the headwaters of Oak Valley Creek six miles northeast of Camptonville, had a hundred miners in 1855. Three miles west of Oak Valley was Dadd's Gulch, where gold was discovered in 1851 by a man named Parsons. Weed's Point, between Oak Valley and Galena Hill on Horse Valley Creek, was first mined in 1853. Some three miles northwest of Oak Valley was Slate Range, a small but active mining community situated fifteen hundred feet above Slate Range Bar on the North Yuba River. The trail up from Slate Range Bar to Deadwood and La Porte was a back-breaking climb and for this reason the wild declivity was called Hell's Hill.

On Oregon Creek, one thousand feet below Camptonville and accessible only by trail, was Celestial Valley, where numerous Chinese mined in very early days. On a high ridge east of the Oregon Creek canyon, visible for miles in all directions, was Indian Springs, a station on the road from Camptonville to Pike City.

Camptonville Road

Camptonville, on the main-traveled road to Downieville and the center of trade for northeastern Yuba County, was located at the junction of a number of roads. The earliest trail from Marysville crossed the North Fork of the Yuba River at Foster's Bar, continuing eastward from the latter point by way of Willow Creek and Garden Valley, where the Atchison brothers had a ranch and kept a hotel. In 1854 they built a wagon road over this route as far as Camptonville. Another trail from Marysville crossed the North Yuba at Bullard's Bar, where George Mix kept the toll bridge. Mix also built the approach roads from the ridges to Bullard's Bar. By 1860 the Bullard's Bar route had superseded the one by way of Foster's Bar.

Two important hotels were located on this road—the Junction House, two miles southwest of Camptonville, and the Wisconsin House, two miles farther south. The Junction House, also known as Bogardus' Ranch, is today known as the James Ranch. At this point a branch of the Grass Valley–Forest City Road via Emory's Crossing joined the Bullard's Bar Road. At the Wisconsin House the road from Nevada City by way of North San Juan, Freeman's Crossing, and Oregon Creek likewise joined the Bullard's Bar Road. The present state highway to Downieville follows the old route up the slopes above Oregon Creek to Camptonville. Beyond Camptonville it continues to the North Yuba River and Downieville by a new route, whereas the old road turned eastward at Camptonville and followed up Gold Ridge.

This old scenic road along the backbone of Gold Ridge overlooked the heavily timbered canyons of Oregon Creek to the south and the North Yuba River to the north. A fairly good dirt road follows the same course today, passing the sites of several historic stopping-places along the way. Three miles east of Camptonville the old Sleighville House, a two-story hotel, is still standing in good condition. The original structure, built in 1849 by Peter Yore, was much smaller than the present one, for as the needs of the family increased more rooms were added from time to time. Not far from the old hostelry lies the burial ground of the Yore family. Dense evergreen forests inclose the place on all sides, and in winter the entire landscape is heavily mantled with snow. At this point, in early days, it was necessary to transfer goods from wagons to sleighs during the winter months, and from this circumstance the house took its name.

The next historic point reached on the Gold Ridge route is the site of Nigger Tent, around which centers many a thrilling tale. On this spot a negro put up a tent to serve as a wayside station on the pack trail to Downieville in 1849. Later, according to J. D. Borthwick, he replaced the tent with a cabin, on the site of which a subsequent owner erected a substantial frame hotel. In spite of changes, the original name of Nigger Tent stuck to the locality. The site is now marked by three aged poplar trees and a Forest Service sign. Beyond Nigger Tent, where the road forks, is the site of the Mountain House, where a magnificent panorama of wooded mountains and deeply chiseled canyons may be had. From here one road goes south to Forest City, while the other leads north to Goodyear's Bar and Downieville. The Mountain House was burned a few years ago and only scattered boards and the extensive cellar excavations mark the site.

SOURCES

[Credit is here given for source material, and permission to quote is hereby acknowledged]

Amy's Marysville Directory for the Year 1858. Daily News Print, Marysville, 1858

BORTHWICK, J. D. *Three Years in California.* William Blackwood & Sons, Edinburgh and London, 1857

BUFFUM, E. GOULD. *Six Months 'in the Gold Mines.* Lea & Blanchard, Philadelphia, 1850

BURNETT, PETER H. *Recollections and Opinions of an Old Pioneer.* D. Appleton & Company, New York, 1880

Colville's Marysville Directory for the Year 1855, Together with a Historical Sketch of Marysville. Monson & Valentine, San Francisco, 1855

COY, OWEN COCHRAN. *Gold Days,* of the series *California,* edited by John Russell McCarthy. Powell Publishing Company, Los Angeles, 1929

DELANO, A. *Life on the Plains and among the Diggings.* Miller, Orton & Mulligan, Auburn and Buffalo, 1854

DELAY, PETER J. *History of Yuba and Sutter Counties.* California Historic Record Company, Los Angeles, 1924

FIELD, STEPHEN J. *Personal Reminiscences of Early Days in California, with Other Sketches.* Privately printed, 1893

FRÉMONT, JOHN C. *Memoirs of My Life, Including in the Narrative Five Journeys of Western Exploration.* Belford, Clarke & Company, Chicago, 1887

HANSON, GEORGE E. *The Early History of Yuba River Valley.* Master's thesis in history, University of California, Berkeley, 1924

HITTELL, THEODORE H. *The Resources of California.* San Francisco, 1863

SANCHEZ, NELLIE VAN DE GRIFT. *Spanish and Indian Place Names of California.* A. M. Robertson, San Francisco, 1922

WELLS, HARRY L., and WILLIAM H. CHAMBERLAIN. *History of Yuba County, California.* Thompson & West, Oakland, California, 1879

WHEAT, CARL I. "'California's Bantam Cock'—The Journals of Charles E. De Long, 1854–1863," edited with an introduction by Carl I. Wheat, in *California Historical Society Quarterly,* Vols. VIII, IX, X (September 1929–December 1931)

COUNTIES OF THE COAST RANGE

SAN FRANCISCO IN 1849.

Taken from Broadway, near Kearny Street. Drawn and Engraved by Thomas Armstrong, in the Fall of 1849, and re-published by A. Rosenfield, (late of Hutchings and Rosenfield, No. 602 Montgomery Street, near Clay, San Francisco.

Historic Spots in California

ALAMEDA COUNTY

Alameda County was created in 1853 from portions of Contra Costa and Santa Clara counties. The county seat was originally at Alvarado, then called New Haven. It was removed to San Leandro in 1856, but since 1872 it has been at Oakland.

The primary meaning of the word *alameda* is "a place where poplar trees grow" and is derived from *alamo,* meaning "poplar" or "cottonwood." The county doubtless received its name from El Arroyo de la Alameda (Alameda Creek), which, when first discovered, was lined as it is now with willow and silver-barked sycamore trees, giving it the appearance of an *alameda* or road lined with trees, while the rest of the valley was treeless.

Brusha Peak

Brusha Peak is a remarkable natural formation eight miles northeast of Livermore. The front of it forms a conspicuous brush-clad eminence, rising high above the surrounding hills. Beyond lies a beautiful valley in which a group of immense rocks, now weather-beaten and full of caves wrought by the action of wind and weather, appears like an ancient ruined city. Like many another rocky outcropping situated in remote places in California, this place is said by tradition to have been one of the hide-outs of Joaquín Murieta.

The Emeryville Shell Mound

"For perhaps seventy-five years," says W. Egbert Schenck, "a number of artificial shellmounds scattered along the shoreline of San Francisco Bay have excited the curiosity of the incoming white settlers. As long as fifty years ago collections were being made of the aboriginal relics found on their surfaces or turned out by the plow."

The shell mounds of this area were first studied scientifically in the spring of 1902 by Dr. John C. Merriam and Dr. Max Uhle of the University of California. They made careful excavations on the site of the Emeryville Mound, Oakland, and published methodical considerations of the evidence obtained. N. C. Nelson completed in 1908 a survey of the entire San Francisco Bay region in which he located, numbered, and mapped nearly 425 shell heaps, analyzing them in detail and publishing a summary of his observations and conclusions. Field work was made possible by the generous support of Mrs. Phoebe A. Hearst, through the Department of Anthropology of the University of California, and was carried on by graduate students under the direct supervision of Professor Merriam.

Practically none of these ancient relics of a prehistoric people remain intact today. Encroaching tides, steam shovels leveling grounds coveted for factory sites, city streets and modern residences, the farmer's plow or his zeal for securing fertilizer, all of these and other factors have entered into the gradual but final demolition of the fascinating monuments of a vanished race. All that remain for us are one tablet of commemoration, a few monographs written by scholars, and many museum collections scattered hither and yon and some-

times widely separated from their original geographical locations.

In the Nelson Survey the site of the Emeryville Mound is designated as No. 329 and shows one large and two small "mounds" or cones "still present" and two larger ones "disappeared." Schenck explains that these several cones are not "a number of isolated 'mounds' but of a single, wide-spread, perhaps rather thin mass of mound material from which there arose a number of cones of the same material." The western cone is the one of the greatest historical interest.

"The first people who came to the site," writes Schenck, "camped just above the shoreline, possibly on little hummocks at the edge of the marsh. As shell-fish were obtained, the shells were thrown aside, and these with the by-products of daily life increased the camp ground and gradually crept out into the marsh. . . . . As the shell area increased, subsequent people utilized it because it was drier, placing camps, perhaps, over what had previously been marsh. . . . . This shell area grew until it covered some hundreds of thousands of square feet marked by several cones."

The mound was situated on the eastern shore of San Francisco Bay almost due east of the Golden Gate. It lay on the western side of the old Peralta grant, or that part of Rancho San Antonio apportioned to Vicente Peralta by his father Don Luis María Peralta. This section became known later as Emeryville, now an incorporated town lying between the cities of Oakland and Berkeley. That area once covered by the mound is bounded on the west by San Francisco Bay, on the east by the Southern Pacific Railway tracks, on the south by the bridge which once led to Shellmound Park, and on the north by the Shellmound Tower Station of the Southern Pacific lines. The last two have retained the old name. The site of the park is still bare, and in the sands numerous fragments of shell may be found

The mound is located at a point which was favorable to its use as a camping ground for prehistoric peoples. Lying on the narrow, alluvial plain which stretches from north to south along the Contra Costa between the foothills and the Bay, it was bordered on the north by open, almost treeless plains, and on the south by "a willow thicket some 20 acres in extent. . . . . Farther south . . . . the thicket merged into a marsh extending about one and a half miles along the shore and gradually increasing in width until at its southern end it was three-quarters of a mile wide." Beyond the marshes stretched a mile of rolling, oak-studded fields, the Encinal de Temescal.

Temescal Creek held a very important relation to the ancient mound in prehistoric times. The creek itself supplied fresh water to the nomadic peoples who visited its shores; the abundant shellfish beds at its mouth supplied food, while the quiet reaches of the Bay were full of sea otter, hunted perhaps in balsa rafts. Waterfowl filled the marshes, and deer were plentiful in the willow thicket and the oak grove to the southward, where were also acorns, seeds, and other vegetable foods (as is indicated by the numerous mortars found in the vicinity). The willow thickets too supplied the scantily clad natives with ample firewood.

To this favored spot groups of primitive peoples came yearly from the surrounding country, perhaps from long distances. They may have spent six months out of each year at this site, fishing and hunting, drying and pounding the shellfish for future food supplies, and taking the otter skins for clothing.

Although there may be older mounds in the Bay region and although no certainty can be attached to any estimate of when human beings first camped at the spot, scientists compute that the maximum age of the Emeryville Mound is about a thousand years. Nor is there any certain evidence as to the time when the place was last used as a rendezvous for nomadic tribes. Schenck says that it was apparently unoccupied when Fages passed that way in 1772, for no mention is made of it in the chronicles of that expedition. Anza, in 1776, and Gabriel Moraga, in the early 1800's, also failed to mention having seen Indians in the Oakland-Berkeley neighborhood, although they did note their presence both to the south and to the north. Yet even if these early explorers did not see Indians there, and even though there were no fogs concealing their whereabouts, it is very possible that the oak groves of which Father Crespi wrote, together with the willow thickets near the mouth of Temescal Creek, may have formed an effectual screen behind which the red men at the Emeryville Mound were encamped when the first white travelers passed that way.

Vicente Peralta erected his adobe dwelling not far from Temescal Creek and about one and a half miles east of the Emeryville Mound about 1836. At the mouth of the creek was the Temescal Embarcadero, and the ancient mound was a landmark familiar to travelers along the old creek road during those early days.

In 1857 the Peralta grant was surveyed and mapped by Kellesberger, and in 1859 Edward Wiard purchased that portion of it on which the mound stood. Maps of that date show buildings on both the eastern and the western cones; but in 1871 Wiard leveled a part of the eastern cone and laid out the mile race track which became noted as the Oakland Trotting Park. On the western cone in 1876 he opened the Shellmound Park, a holiday resort and picnic grounds long popular among pleasure seekers of the entire Bay region. In 1879 the park was leased to Captain Ludwig Siebe, who held the lease until the destruction of the mound in 1924. In the meantime James Mee had acquired the property from Wiard in 1887 and had passed it on to the Mee Estate in 1906.

The Emeryville Shell Mound, in the old amusement-park days, was a picturesque landmark. On its low, truncated summit were a circle of trees, some windmills, and the round dance pavilion surrounded by a high cypress hedge. An old historical atlas, dated 1878, shows this mound with the residence of J. S. Emery (at present at the corner of San Pablo Avenue and Forty-fifth Street) in the foreground.

The Emeryville Mound was leveled in 1924 in order to convert the area into a factory site. Mr. John Hubert Mee, president of the Mee Estate, made known his intentions and permitted the University of California to use the land as desired, while Captain Siebe, proprietor of the Shellmound Park, rendered every assistance possible in the work of excavation. The mound was razed by steam shovel; careful observations were made and collections were taken during the process. After the leveling operations were completed, controlled excavations of its lower levels were made by hand, excavations made possible by the generous financial patronage of Mr. P. E. Bowles of Oakland.

During the entire period extensive and intensive observations were made, and a large number of skeletal and artifact materials were collected. The pile was found to be composed principally of shells—mostly clams, mussels, and oysters, with a plentiful mixture of cockleshells. Certain other kinds, found only in rare quantities, had been treated in the manner of possessions. Beside human burials, the accumulation disclosed the skeletal remains of birds, quadrupeds, sea mammals, and fish. Many of these bone remains were placed in the Museum of Vertebrate Zoölogy at the University of California.

The Lincoln Park Shell Mound

One shell mound of the 425 mapped by Nelson in 1906-8 has been memorialized. The site of this mound, located in the city of Alameda and now covered by modern streets and residences, extended over three acres of ground bounded by what are now Central Avenue, Court Street, Johnson Avenue, and Lover's Lane, the latter a double row of trees back of the house at No. 2854 Santa Clara Avenue. The mound was removed by the city authorities in the summer of 1908, and the earth, combined with tons of mussel shells, was used for the making of roads on Bay Farm Island.

The lower levels of this ground were examined by Captain W. A. Clark, who, working the ground carefully with a hand trowel, was able to save a number of fine relics. These were placed in the Alameda Public Library, where they are still on display.

A stone monument bearing a bronze tablet was placed in Lincoln Park near the site of the old Indian mound. The inscription reads:

One thousand feet due west was a prehistoric mound, 400 feet long, 150 feet wide, 14 feet high. The remains of 450 Indians, with stone implements and shell ornaments, were found when the mound was opened in 1908. Erected by Copa de Oro Chapter, D.A.R., 1914.

Other Indian Sites

From Albany in the north to Mowry's Landing in the south, there were at least twenty shell mounds scattered along the Bay shore in Alameda County at the time they were catalogued and mapped by Nelson in 1906 to 1908. Among these there were, besides the famous Emeryville and Lincoln Park mounds, others at the mouth of El Cerrito Creek, at the mouth of Strawberry Creek, at the eastern end of the San Antonio estuary in East Oakland, at the mouth of Alameda Creek near Alvarado, at Centerville, and at Mowry's Landing west of Irvington.

"It is not to be supposed," writes Mr. N. C. Nelson in speaking of the survey of the San Francisco Bay shell mounds, "that this figure 425 exhausts the evidence of aboriginal occupation to be found within the given territorial limits, because the shellmounds are confined to a narrow belt around the open waters of the bay and grade off landwards into earth mounds of a more or less artificial character. . . . . According to reports . . . . earth mounds and 'old Indian rancherias' are situated on the banks of the Alameda Creek . . . . above the alluvial plain in the foothills; and . . . . sites of this character could be found in great numbers by following up any other minor streams. As it is, several more or less obliterated camp and village sites of late and ancient date are definitely known in the region, some of them even on the university campus in Berkeley; and the publication of news items relating to discoveries here and there of relics and skeletal material is no uncommon occurrence."

The sites mentioned on the campus of the University of California are located east of Sather Gate on the south bank of Strawberry Creek just west of the Life Science Building.

At the curve of Indian Rock Avenue where it meets the south end of San Diego Road in North Berkeley, a huge, irregular rock mass looms above the drive. From its level summit there is a commanding view of the valley and of the Bay beyond. At the base of the main boulder are a number of smaller rocks in which are deeply worn holes or mortars where the Indian women once ground the nutritious acorn for meal. Gnarled buckeyes and green bays encircle this ancient monument of a primitive people, and at the foot the city of Berkeley has planted a garden, creating of the spot a tiny public park, known as the Mortar Rock Park.

A few hundred feet lower down on Indian Rock Avenue at the head of San Mateo Road is Indian Rock Park, another prehistoric landmark set among small live oaks and tall eucalypti.

In Indian Gulch (now Trestle Glen), Oakland, there is a

level spot where an Indian village once stood. It was originally called Indian Gulch because Indians still lived there when the first white people came to that region. Nothing remains today as a reminder of the Indians; and Trestle Glen, which extends northeast from Lake Merritt, is now filled with fine residences. The narrow, winding canyon, still shaded by immense live oaks and other trees, is today made accessible by the Trestle Glen Road, which leaves Lake Shore Avenue just west of the Wesley and Lake Shore Avenue Station of the Key System Railroad.

Temescal

Temescal, a name of Aztec origin meaning "sweat house," was brought to California by the Franciscan Fathers. A. L. Kroeber describes the *temescal* thus:

"From the outside its appearance is that of a small mound. The ground has been excavated to the depth of a foot or a foot and a half, over a space of about twelve by seven or eight feet. In the center of this area two heavy posts are set up three or four feet apart. These are connected at the top by a log laid in their forks. Upon this log, and in the two forks, are laid some fifty or more logs and sticks of various dimensions, their ends sloping down to the edge of the excavation. It is probable that brush covers these timbers. The whole is thoroughly covered with earth. There is no smoke hole. The entrance is on one of the long sides, directly facing the space between the two center posts, and only a few feet from them. The fireplace is between the entrance and the posts. It is just possible to stand upright in the center of the house. In Northern California, the so-called sweathouse is of larger dimensions, and was pre-eminently a ceremonial or assembly chamber."

Dr. L. H. Bunnell, in his history of his discovery of the Yosemite Valley, notes some interesting details of the use of the sweat house. "It . . . . was used as a curative for disease, and as a convenience for cleansing the skin, when necessity demanded it. . . . . I have seen a half-dozen or more enter one of these rudely constructed sweathouses through the small aperture left for the purpose. Hot stones are taken in, the aperture is closed until suffocation would seem impending, when they would crawl out, reeking with perspiration, and with a shout, spring like acrobats into the cold waters of the stream. As a remedial agent for disease, the same course is pursued."

Through what is now a busy part of Oakland, Temescal Creek wanders down from the Piedmont Hills to San Francisco Bay. When white men first came to this section of the country, it is said that they found an old Indian sweat house on the arroyo and that because of this circumstance they named it Temescal Creek. W. E. Schenck, however, believes that the name may have arisen, not from the presence of a native Indian village and sweat house, but because the Indian retainers on the Peralta rancho doubtless set up a *temescal* on the bank of the creek near their cabins. The Vicente Peralta adobe was built about two blocks north of the point where the present Telegraph Avenue crosses the creek. Around this nucleus the Mexican village of Temescal grew up. The name first appears on the Kellesberger Survey map of 1857 as "Temesconta," which, Schenck says, "may or may not be Temescal."

Temescal Creek flowed about 450 feet southeast of the center of the Emeryville Shell Mound and discharged into the Bay some 800 feet southwest of the center of the mound. The creek seems to have been the determining physiographical feature of the region in prehistoric as well as in pioneer times, tending to focus population by its supply of fresh water as well as of food. For hundreds of years before the coming of the white man, it had been a favorite camping and

hunting ground for nomadic tribes of Indians. "Within the memory of men living nearby," wrote Schenck in 1926, "it has had salmon runs. And Mr. P. E. Bowles informs me that in the early 1880's it was a favorite resort for amateur fishermen. The marshy overflow of the stream near the bay, formed excellent coverts for game among its luxuriant plant growth."

With the coming of the Spaniards to the Contra Costa, Misión San José was settled; and the great ranchos, San Antonio, San Leandro, San Pablo, San Lorenzo, and others, were granted. Gradually embarcaderos sprang up along the eastern shore of the Bay. Among others the Temescal Landing at the mouth of Temescal Creek near the old Emeryville Shell Mound became a landing place for occasional parties from San Francisco. The path of the old Temescal Creek Road, over which the Spaniards once passed on foot or on horseback, and in creaking carretas, doubtless followed the general course of the creek as far east as Telegraph Avenue and beyond.

Land which is now covered with immense factories, paved streets, and miles of closely set homes and little gardens was still a wilderness during those early years. Only a few adobe houses stood many miles apart on the vast ranchos, and these were joined merely by horse paths or by narrow dirt roads which amounted to little more than trails through the brush. Over all that fertile plain "giants of a thousand years' growth remained undisturbed by the woodsman's axe. . . . . The songs of birds and the bellowing of the Spanish bull almost alone disturbed the air. . . . . Wild cattle roamed at large in thousands; wild oats covered the hills"; and wild mustard, each spring, colored the entire countryside with tangled, golden thickets taller than a man's head.

The Golden Age for the native Californian lasted from 1833 to 1846. This was the time when the Missions were breaking up, the presidios were well-nigh deserted, and land could be had almost for the asking. The owners of the great landed estates or ranchos lived a simple, carefree life, idyllic in many respects in spite of the crudities and hardships occasioned by frontier conditions.

During this period, visitors to the Contra Costa, landing in boats at the mouth of Temescal Creek, continued to the ranchos or to the Mission by way of the Vicente Peralta adobe one and one-half miles inland. If they called, they were sure to be hospitably entertained. Thence they would proceed close to the foothills to Antonio Peralta's adobe near what is now Fruitvale; thence to Ignacio Peralta's on the bank of San Leandro Creek. The next stop was the Estudillo rancho on the south side of the creek; and from there to Guillermo Castro's adobe at the site of the present town of Hayward. Here roads led eastward to Amador's and Livermore's ranchos and southward to Misión San José.

The old Temescal Creek Road no longer exists, and the free flow of the stream was stopped in 1866, when it was dammed up in the hills to form the reservoir still known as Temescal Lake. At that time it furnished the principal water supply for several thousand inhabitants. The course of the arroyo itself is still plainly indicated by the winding lane of native oak, willow, bay, elder, buckeye, and cottonwood trees which is apparent here and there at the rear of a long line of residences paralleling Forty-seventh and Forty-eighth streets, Claremont Avenue, and Chabot Road.

Beginning at the Bay, where the land has been filled in and occupied by factories, the stream bed is mostly invisible; but a deep, narrow ditch, often choked with rubbish, comes to view at Horton Street between Fifty-fourth and Fifty-fifth streets. Leaving San Pablo Avenue, the creek runs between Forty-eighth and Forty-seventh streets on the south and Fifty-third and Fifty-second streets on the north. Its course is marked at first by a sparse growth of willow and elderberry trees, and farther on by elms, eucalypti, acacia, and other exotics. Through this section, the arroyo forms the northern boundary of Emeryville.

East of Shattuck Avenue the pursuit becomes interesting, for there the old watercourse (sometimes entirely lost sight of and again appearing in unexpected places) proceeds through one of the busiest parts of Oakland. Now it passes under paved streets, and again houses are built directly over it. At the end of Dover Street off Fifty-first Street, Temescal's wooded banks are visible one block south of the entrance to the Children's Hospital of the East Bay, and at the end of Forty-eighth Street, off Shattuck Avenue, wild trees again mark its course. From this point, however, the channel disappears under Telegraph Avenue between Fiftieth and Fifty-first streets, where it runs beneath the Key System car barns. From there it tends eastward along a well-defined line of trees paralleled by Claremont Avenue and Chabot Road.

As one approaches the hills, the trees bordering the arroyo become thicker and larger. Especially attractive bits, in which giant oaks predominate, may be seen at the end of Arbor Avenue, off Hudson, and on Ivanhoe Road just south of Chabot Road, in one of Oakland's finest residential districts. The main branch of Temescal Creek continues south of Chabot Road to Temescal Lake, while the north branch crosses Claremont Avenue. From there it proceeds eastward, paralleling Claremont Avenue as far as Hotel Claremont. Beyond is Fish Canyon in which the north fork has its origin.

Ortega First to See the "Contra Costa"

While he was encamped on San Francisquito Creek (in Santa Clara County), after his historic discovery of the great Bay of San Francisco, Gaspar de Portolá sent a reconnoitering party under the command of José Francisco de Ortega to find, if possible, a land route to the eastern shore of the newly discovered bay to Point Reyes (in Marin County) and Cermeño's harbor, to a place which was to be called San Francisco and on which was to be founded the Mission dedicated to St. Francis.

Passing around the southern end of San Francisco Bay, Ortega and his men forded the Guadalupe River (in Santa Clara County). From there, writes Fray Juan Crespi, chronicler and chaplain to Portolá, "they went forward on the other side of the estuary eight or ten leagues, but there was still a long distance for them to go. At this distance of ten leagues, they came upon another very large stream with a very strong current, and its bed was also wooded and its course was through a great plain which was also quite well wooded." They must have gone as far north as Niles or farther, says Bolton, and the second "very large stream" with wooded arroyo was doubtless Alameda Creek, from which the county takes its name.

On the evening of November 10, 1769, "the explorers returned, very sad, and no longer believing in the reports of the heathen, which they confessed they had not understood. They said that all the territory which they had examined to the northeast and north was impassable because of the scarcity of pasture and especially because of the ferocity and ill-temper of the heathen, who received them angrily and tried to stop their passage. They said also that they had seen another estuary [San Pablo Bay] of equal magnitude and extent with the one we had in sight and with which it communicated, but that in order to go round it one would have to travel many leagues . . . . and that the mountains were rough and difficult."

The austere aspect of what the Spaniards came to call the Contra Costa ("coast opposite" San Francisco) on that November day over one hundred and sixty years ago put dismay into the hearts of Portolá's weary, half-starved soldiers. They had gone far enough north to sight the Bay of San Pablo, but the view had only made further passage seem an impossible undertaking; and, already disheartened because the long-sought port of Monterey had not been found, they voted unanimously to return to the Point of Pines (in Monterey County).

Fages, Trail Blazer of the Contra Costa

Alameda County was again penetrated by white men in the autumn of 1770, when Pedro Fages, one of Portolá's men left by him in command at Monterey, decided on his own initiative to make another attempt to reach Point Reyes by land. It was on this trip that Fages opened the first inland route from Monterey to San Jose. From there he continued over the trail opened the year before as far as Niles and on to a point "seven leagues beyond the point reached by Ortega."

During this time the party had, says Bolton, "skirted the Contra Costa for two days . . . . From the Berkeley hills they looked west through the Golden Gate and to the north they beheld San Pablo Bay cutting across their route to Point Reyes."

Fages made a second attempt in the spring of 1772 to reach Cermeño's bay. Accompanied by Fray Juan Crespi, "six Catalonian volunteers, six leather-jackets, a muleteer, and an Indian servant," he followed the trail that he had opened more than a year before. Northwest to the region of Hayward the party retraced the ground already twice covered by Ortega and Fages. To the Berkeley hills they were on Fages' old trail. Thereafter they were pathbreakers once more.

Crespi, missionary and chronicler of the expedition, wrote on Wednesday, March 25: "On this day of the Incarnation, after Mass had been said, we set out . . . . in the direction of the north–northwest. At the start we travelled about a league from the estuary at the foot of a bare mountain range, and after travelling a short distance we were three leagues from the estuary. All the land is level, black, and very well covered with good grass, mallows, and other herbs. . . . . We passed five villages of heathen, which are all on the banks of the arroyos with running water . . . . We halted on the bank of a large arroyo close to the mountains skirting the broad plain. The bed of the arroyo is very full of alders, cottonwoods, and willows . . . ."

Their route like that of the long line of travelers who were to follow in their steps, lay close to the hills, and camp was made at San Lorenzo Creek, called by Crespi, San Salvador de Horta.

Advancing as far as the site of Fruitvale on the 26th, they pitched camp near the point where Mills College is now located. During the day they had had their first view of elk, which Crespi thought were buffalo but which the soldiers called mule-deer. Five arroyos of running water had been crossed, their banks green with alders, cottonwood, live oak, and bay trees. At the end of five leagues, Fages and his men saw the Alameda peninsula, now an island, and the intervening *encinal* or live-oak groves. "The site," wrote Crespi, "is very suitable for a good settlement . . . . on account of the proximity of the forest . . . . This place was called Arroyo del Bosque"—probably Fruitvale Creek.

From here the march, as described by Bolton, traversed country now covered by crowded cities, then only a pleasant wilderness: "On the 27th they turned inland to round the estuary and the adjacent marshes, and emerged from the hills near the site of Lake Merritt. Near the Technical High School Father Crespi made his observations of the Golden Gate. The islands which he describes in the gate are Alcatraz Island, Goat Island (Yerba Buena), and Angel Island. The arroyo where they camped, a league north of the point of observation, was probably Strawberry Creek, and the camp-site near the western side of the campus of the University of California. On the 28th they continued past the sites of Berkeley and Albany to eastern Richmond" in Contra Costa County.

The first stop made in Alameda County on the return trip was made on April 1 at a place west of Pleasanton "in front of the Hacienda de las Pozas," the country home of the late Phoebe Apperson Hearst, now the Castlewood Country Club. On April 2 "they descended Arroyo de la Laguna, crossing it near Suñol. Leaving Suñol Valley [Santa Coleta] they crossed Alameda Creek, ascended Mission Pass, re-entered the valley of San Francisco Bay, and continued past the head of the bay at a point near Milpitas."

"This historic journey," says Bolton, "had more than merely exploratory significance. It was a decisive factor in determining the location of San Francisco. Cermeño's Bay on Point Reyes had been predestined for that honor . . . . but the new-found bay and its affluents stood in the way. It was now concluded that communication with Point Reyes must be maintained by water . . . . and . . . . that the proposed settlement might be planted south of the Golden Gate, in reach from Monterey by land, and on the shore of the superb new harbor. The Fages-Crespi expedition marks a distinct step forward, both in discovery and in choice of a site for San Francisco."

Anza Follows the Contra Costa Trail

After he had explored the sites for the presidio and the Mission to be established at the port of San Francisco, Captain Juan Bautista de Anza, accompanied by Lieutenant José Moraga (his second in command) and by Father Pedro Font (master chronicler and faithful chaplain of the second overland expedition from Sonora to California), passed around the southern extremity of San Francisco Bay into Alameda County. With eleven soldiers, six muleteers, and servants, Anza and his companions were on their way to "explore the Rio Grande de San Francisco, that is, Carquinez Strait and the waters above it."

On the frosty Sunday morning of March 31, 1776, after listening to Mass said by the good Father, the wayfarers left their camp on the Guadalupe and, meeting with a network of sloughs and marshes along the Coyote River, where it runs west, were forced to twist their way about for three leagues until they emerged on higher ground at the foot of the hills. From this point forward, the line of march followed "far away from the water . . . . through very level country, green and flower-covered all the way to the estuary, but with no other timber or firewood than that afforded by the trees in the arroyos which we encountered, which were five."

Font's map showed that the line of march was now close to the hills all the way, and Bolton identifies it as the route passing by way of the Arroyo de la Encarnación, probably Scott Creek, and from there "northeastward past Warm Springs, Irvington, and the Lagoon (the 'somewhat salty' lagoon mentioned by Font). The Arroyo 'about half way on the road' was apparently Alameda Creek," with its "very deep pools . . . . many sycamores, cottonwoods, and some live oaks and other trees." It was here that a band of about thirty armed but peaceful Indians ran out to greet them with the weird chorus of "AU, au, au, au, au, au, au, au, au, au, au," which seemed to Father Font "like something infernal."

Passing three arroyos and two deserted Indian villages, Anza and his men crossed the fifth stream, the San Lorenzo, near which they pitched their tents. Here they met a lone Indian, very much frightened by the sudden apparition of

strangers, the like of which he had doubtless never seen before. This is the last mention of Indians until Wildcat and San Pablo creeks were reached in Contra Costa County.

"All day," Font wrote that evening, "the commander and I have been in doubt as to whether the island at the end of the estuary which I mapped yesterday is really an island or not." "The supposed island," says Bolton, "was Coyote Hills . . . . The other long island mentioned was Richmond Peninsula, likewise not an island. With a nearer view Font's conclusion was more accurate."

Mass was said in a thick and "very damp" fog on Monday, April 1, and a small army of long-billed mosquitoes pursued the travelers as they left the Arroyo de la Harina.

Continuing along the foothills, the route was much the same as that followed by the Foothill Boulevard of today. Professor Bolton has identified and sketched the way for us:

"The arroyo where they saw the bears was San Leandro Creek. Two leagues beyond they crossed the creek at Mills College. Just beyond they climbed the hill and from there Font drew the sketch of the Oakland Estuary and oak-covered Alameda Peninsula, now Alameda Island . . . . Descending the hill they crossed Arroyo del Bosque, a stream in eastern Fruitvale. Continuing northwest they crossed the site of Oakland. It was from Berkeley that Font sighted through Lime Point and Point Bonita to determine the trend of the north shore of the Golden Gate. It was in Berkeley, too, that the elk were chased, 'at the Arroyo de la Bocana' of Crespi, a place of 'very little water' and 'a small growth of trees.' Farther down this arroyo there was 'a grove or growth of not very large timber'." This was Strawberry Creek.

Leaving the stream and its brushy coverts behind them, the explorers passed over a level plain and low hills into Contra Costa County. Following Suisun Bay as far as Antioch, they turned south on April 4. After a weary struggle with treacherous tulares and the blinding, wind-driven ash of burned tules, they at last turned southward, proceeding some six leagues "along the general course of the Old River." They were again in Alameda County; and at a point just south of Bethany, "perhaps near Lammersville School," Anza decided to give up his attempt to approach the Sierra Nevada, on account of the seemingly limitless and impassable tulares which intervened, and to return to Monterey.

Continuing south, the party entered the Lomas de las Tuzas, evidently by Midway Valley. Ascending Patterson Grade to the vicinity of the Pass, they looked down into Livermore Valley (Santa Coleta) and "descried in the distance the range of redwoods [Sierra de Pinabetes] on San Francisco Peninsula." Professor Bolton writes in this connection that "Mr. R. S. Sweet, keeper of Beacon no. 32, near the Pass, tells me that on clear days he can see the Coast Range on the San Francisco Peninsula."

"Continuing southeast along the northeastern edge of Crane Ridge for seven or eight miles, about to the San Joaquin County line, they climbed to the top of Crane Ridge, perhaps up Sulphur Springs Canyon, reaching the summit west of Eagle Mountain. Continuing south they descended to Arroyo Mocho, striking it about at Callahan Gulch, some two miles north of the Santa Clara County line."

The Founding of Misión San José de Guadalupe

"In 1794," writes Bancroft, "the eastern shores of the San Francisco Bay were almost a tierra incognita to the Spaniards . . . ." For nearly twenty years after the coming of Anza in 1776, there is no record of any exploring expedition until 1795, when Sergeant Pedro Amador visited the southern part of Alameda County some time before June. In his report, acknowledged by Governor Borica on June 2, 1795,

Amador used the name of Alameda, the first known official use of that designation. The Alameda was again visited in November 1795, when, in accordance with the governor's orders, Hermenegildo Sal and Father Antonio Danti set out from Monterey to search for suitable Mission sites.

"Having arrived at Santa Clara on the 21st," says Bancroft, "they were joined by Alferez Raimundo Carrillo, and started the next day to examine the Alameda previously explored by Amador, whose diary they had. The river of the Alameda was also called by Danti, Rio de San Clementi. The explorers continued their journey up to a point . . . . nearly or quite to the site of the modern Oakland, perhaps, and then turned backwards discovering some important salt-marshes, and finally erected a cross at the spot somewhat south of the Alameda and called San Francisco Solano, arriving at Santa Clara . . . . on the 25th of November."

And thus the preliminary explorations were made and the site was chosen for the location of Misión San José de Guadalupe. In the year 1797 Corporal Miranda and five men were detailed to act as protectors for the new adventure; and on June 9 the troops under Amador, accompanied by Father Firmen Lasuén, set out for the spot called by the natives Oroysom in the valley of San José. The following day a temporary chapel or enramada was erected, and on June 11, Trinity Sunday, the Father Presidente "raised and blessed the cross. In a shelter of boughs he celebrated holy Mass."

Five days after the founding, temporary buildings constructed of native timbers and thatched with grass were begun, and on the 28th Father Isidoro Barcenilla and Agustín Merino arrived to take charge of the new Mission. Barcenilla served until April 1802, when Father Luis Gil Taboada took his place, while Merino was replaced in 1799 by José Antonio Uria. Luis Peralta succeeded Miranda in command of the Mission guard in 1798.

Of the various Fathers who served Misión San José, Father Narciso Duran, a native of Catalonia, who came to California from Mexico in 1806, was the most prominent. He went at once to Misión San José and, with Father Buenaventura Fortuni, began in June 1806 his long ministry, which continued until 1833, when he removed to Santa Barbara. Father Fortuni left the Mission in 1825, and from then on Father Duran served alone, being also president of all the Missions during the years 1825 to 1827, and again from 1831 to 1838. After leaving San José he was *comisario* and governor of the diocese after the bishop's death in 1846. Father Duran, one of the most prominent friars in Alta California, was especially noted for his earnest and successful missionary zeal. Throughout the troublous years of secularization, he managed the affairs of the Mission with marked ability, retaining at the same time the esteem of most of his adversaries as well as the love of the people of all classes. He was also an accomplished musician. He taught the Indians how to read music and trained an orchestra of thirty Indians, with flutes, violins, trumpets, and drums.

The German explorer, Georg Heinrich von Langsdorff, who came to California on the Russian ship "Nadeshda" in 1806, visited Misión San José early in May. Coming down San Francisco Bay in an Aleut bidarka, he was the first foreigner to tread the southeastern Bay shores. He received a warm reception from Father Cueva, then in charge at the Mission, and a great Indian dance was given for his benefit. Since he was particularly interested in the manners and customs of the natives, he devoted much space to them in his narrative of the expedition.

Langsdorff also wrote enthusiastically of the orchards and gardens of Misión San José:

"The quantity of corn in the granaries far exceeded my expectations . . . . and a proportionate quantity of maize,

barley, pease, beans, and other grain. The kitchen garden is extremely well laid out, and kept in very good order; the soil is everywhere rich and fertile, and yields ample returns. . . . . A small rivulet runs through the garden, which preserves a constant moisture. . . . . The situation of the establishment is admirably chosen, and according to the universal opinion the mission will in a few years be the richest and best in New California. . . . ."

Langsdorff's prophecy was fulfilled to a large degree, for Misión San José grew and prospered throughout the years of its service, before the inevitable decadence following the secularization at last set in about 1841. Bancroft pictures this growth with the following graphic statistics:

"By the end of 1797 there were 33 converts, and in 1800 the number had increased to 286, the baptisms having been 364. . . . . Meanwhile the large stock came to number 367, and there were 1,600 sheep and goats. Crops in 1800 were about 1,500 bushels, chiefly wheat."

Ten years later the number of neophytes had increased to 545. There were 1,806 people at the Mission in 1824, when San José was excelled only by Misión San Luis Rey in population, and in the number of its baptisms the former greatly exceeded that of any other Mission. It also stood fourth on the list in regard to the number of cattle and sheep raised, as well as in the average production of grain crops.

The highest population attained at Misión San José was 1,877 people in 1831; the number fell to 1,400 in 1834, and to 580 in 1840. However, this Mission for the entire decade of the '30's maintained a remarkable record and was probably the most prosperous of all the California Missions both before and after secularization, which was effected between 1826 and 1837. Crops were good, and the livestock increased steadily. Englehardt gives the last available official report (1832) as 12,000 cattle, 13,000 sheep, and 13,000 horses.

On April 23, 1809, Father Presidente Estevan Tapis came to hold the vigil of St. Joseph and to bless the adobe just completed at the Mission. On the following day, Father Tapis delivered the sermon, while Father Arroyo de la Cuesta, from Misión San Juan Bautista, said Mass in the presence of the officers, the other priests, and many people who had come from the neighboring Pueblo de San José (in Santa Clara County).

"Three different structures," writes Halley, "have at various times been placed on the site of the present church, owing to destruction and injury by earthquakes. The last of these occurred on the 21st of October, 1868. . . . . The injured building was subsequently removed, and a wooden structure put up in its place."

When Duran left for Santa Barbara in 1833, his place at Misión San José was taken by Padre María de Jesús Gonzales Rubio, who remained to the end of the decade. San José was the last Mission but one to be secularized. In November 1836 the property was turned over to Jesús Vallejo, *comisionado,* and the transfer was completed in December. Vallejo remained in charge until April 1840, when he was succeeded by José María Amador. Temporal management of twelve Missions, including San José, was restored to the padres on March 29, 1843, but on May 5, 1846, Misión San José was finally sold by Governor Pio Pico to Andres Pico and J. B. Alvarado for $12,000.

Most of the Mission lands finally fell into the hands of strangers. The greater part of the estate of Misión San José was secured by E. L. Beard, who, according to Halley, still resided at the Mission in 1876 and who possessed one of the loveliest places in the state. The Beard homestead at Mission San Jose is still owned by descendants.

Not only was Misión San José a center for the social life of the Spanish ranchos on the east side of San Francisco Bay during the '30's and '40's, but it was also a stopping place for expeditions sent against the Indians who continually threatened the peace of the Mission. During 1849 and 1850 it provided a wayside station for those Argonauts who used the land route from San Francisco to the mines by way of Mission Pass and Livermore. At this time Henry C. Smith, a member of Frémont's California Battalion in 1846, had a trading post in the old adobe Mission building.

Of Misión San José only a part of the living quarters remain today. In 1916, the Native Sons and Daughters of the Golden West began to take measures to preserve and restore this building, and a roof was put over the whole structure in order to prevent the winter rains from washing away the adobe walls.

Beside the present steepled Catholic Church is the old cemetery, shadowy under Monterey cypress trees, where members of old Spanish families are buried. Passing through this into the garden of the Dominican Sisters' convent and orphanage, one steps into the old Mission garden. Here is a profusion of old-fashioned flowers, and in the corner to the north is a life-sized statue of St. Dominick. The cemetery of the Sisters, with its background of cypress and olive trees, is hedged in at the northwest corner of the garden. Each grave is a miniature plat decorated with a trim white cross.

About a mile west of Mission San Jose on the road to Irvington is the Ohlones burial ground. Here on a grassy knoll, surrounded on three sides by a cement wall and on the fourth by a small ravine, a granite monument marks the place where "sleep four thousand of the Ohlones tribe who helped the Padres build this Misión San José de Guadalupe."

Mission Pass, an Old Spanish Trail

Mission Pass cuts through the Mount Hamilton Range just east from Misión San José. It is the starting-point of an old Spanish and pioneer American trail (now followed approximately by the highway). Crossing over the lower hills at this point, the old trail dropped down into Suñol Valley, where it went in two directions, one branch skirting the western edge of Livermore Valley along the Arroyo de la Laguna past the present town of Dublin and up the Amador and San Ramón valleys to Concord, and from there on to the San Joaquin Valley. The other branch went straight across Livermore Valley through the hills into San Joaquin Valley. The latter was the more traveled route.

In 1772 Pedro Fages and Father Crespi came over the first of these trails by way of Concord on their return from the north, after having discovered the mouth of the San Joaquin River.

Many later expeditions went through this same pass, among them, Gabriel Moraga, on the expedition which opened up the Sacramento Valley region. Various expeditions against the Indians, made by Moraga, Vallejo, and others, started from the Mission through this pass. The first overland Argonauts from San Francisco to the mining regions also went by way of Misión San José and Mission Pass.

Jedediah Strong Smith, A Prisoner at Misión San José

In the month of May 1827, while Father Narciso Duran was in charge of Misión San José, Jedediah Strong Smith, the great American pathfinder, wrote a letter to the Padre. Duran was suspicious of the strangers. Four hundred of the neophytes had run away from the Mission on May 15 and 16, and the fur hunters were unjustly suspected of having been the instigators of the desertion.

Unsuccessful in his attempts to cross the Sierra Nevada, far from home, and well-nigh destitute of clothing, as well as of most of the necessities of life, Smith addressed to Duran a letter dated May 19 in which he made a frank statement of his purpose and condition, concluding with these appealing words: "I am, Reverend Father, your strange, but real friend and Christian brother, J. S. Smith." Father Duran did not read the letter but forwarded it to Monterey for translation.

After his historic passage of the Sierra Nevada late in October, Smith, with three of his men and some Indian guides, proceeded from his camp on the Stanislaus River to Misión San José, where he hoped to procure the supplies needed for his journey out of California. Father Duran, however, was still on the defensive, and the unwelcome strangers were put in the guardhouse.

A visit from Captain John Rogers Cooper, an influential citizen of Monterey, greatly relieved the uncertainty of the situation, since he offered to aid Smith in every way within his power. However, the Pathfinder was detained at the Mission for twelve or fourteen days before receiving a letter from the Governor and a guard to escort him to the Capital. At Monterey, on November 12, Cooper signed a bond in favor of his countryman.

Smith returned to Misión San José on November 24, and for two weeks he and his men were busy preparing for the journey out of California—rounding up their horses, drying meat, repairing their guns, and baling the goods allowed them by Governor Echeandía's orders. On holy days and Sundays they attended services at the Mission and there listened to the Father address his dark-skinned charges in Latin or in Spanish. Smith makes special note in his journal of the music, which, he says, "consisted of 12 or 15 violins, 5 base vials and one flute."

Having obtained permission from Father Duran, Smith removed his company on December 24 "to a sheep farm belonging to the Mission called St. Lorenzo [San Lorenzo], where there was plenty of grass and a pen in which I could shut up my horses and mules."

Impatient at continued delays and fearing further obstacles to an immediate departure, Smith finally "settled off with the father under pretence of moving to better grass," and on December 30, in rain and mud, the brave little band began its march northward, not by way of Bodega and Fort Ross, as officially planned, but through Mission Pass across the Livermore Valley to the Old River branch of the San Joaquin (sometimes called the Pescador by the Spanish), and from there up the Sacramento Valley as far as Tehama, where he blazed a new trail out of California through Trinity, Humboldt, and Del Norte counties.

Rancho San Antonio

The present cities of Oakland, Alameda, and Berkeley, as well as the smaller towns of Albany, Emeryville, Piedmont, and a part of San Leandro, are located on what was once Rancho San Antonio. This vast estate extended five leagues along the eastern shore of San Francisco Bay, from San Leandro Creek on the south to El Cerrito Creek, now the boundary line of Alameda and Contra Costa counties, on the north. It comprised all of the land lying between the Bay shore line on the west and the crest of the Contra Costa hills on the east, a total of ten square leagues.

Rancho San Antonio was granted to Luis María Peralta on August 3 of the year 1820, by Governor Pablo Vicente Sola. Peralta based his claim on more than forty years of military service, on valuable assistance rendered in establishing the Missions of Santa Clara, Santa Cruz, and San José, and on the number of his family. A native of Tubac, Sonora, he probably came to San Francisco with the Anza expedition as a boy in 1776. He was later in command of the guard at Misión San José, 1798–1800, and after 1807 he was *comisionado* of the Pueblo de San José. He married María Loreto Alviso, to whom were born five sons and five daughters. Don Luis never made his home on Rancho San Antonio but maintained his residence in San Jose, where his adobe dwelling still stands.

Rancho San Antonio was probably occupied by the four sons of Don Luis—Ignacio, José Domingo, Antonio María, and Vicente—before 1825, and the original adobe homestead was located in what is now the Fruitvale district of East Oakland. There, in 1821–1822, the first permanent civilized dwelling on the east side of San Francisco Bay, subsequent to the founding of Misión San José, was erected, and there for a number of years the four brothers stayed whenever they visited the rancho.

The site of this adobe is at 2511 Thirty-fourth Avenue at the northwest corner of Paxton Street and one block east of Coolidge Avenue (formerly Peralta Avenue) near the north bank of Sausal or Fruitvale Creek. This first adobe was torn down in 1897. The owner gave some of the adobe bricks to the Oakland Park Commission for the purpose of building the Scout House Memorial in Dimond Park, East Oakland. Protected by a shingle roof and overshadowed by the gigantic gnarled branches of an evergreen oak (*Quercus agrifolia*), the adobe now serves as headquarters for Troop 10, Boy Scouts of America. Some of the remaining bricks from the Peralta adobe were later used in a home at 384 Ward Street, San Leandro, where they were incorporated in that portion of the wall near the entrance to the grounds.

As early as 1829 the Peralta brothers began to build each his own adobe home on the section of the rancho later apportioned to him. To these homesteads they brought their wives, and there they reared their children. Their surroundings and mode of living were truly patriarchal. Thousands of horned cattle grazed among the oak trees where are now busy markets of trade, schools of learning, and homes of wealth and refinement. Sometimes Don Luis Peralta's former companions in arms from the Presidio de San Francisco would cross in small boats in order to participate in rodeos and to enjoy the festivities of the Contra Costa. To the north (in Contra Costa County) the Castros held Rancho San Pablo, while immediately to the south there were the Estudillos, the Higueras, the José de Jesús Vallejos, and the Guillermo Castros, all living on vast estates of their own before 1842.

The legal division of the lands of Rancho San Antonio took place in August 1842. At this time, Don Luis Peralta came up from San José to divide the estate among his four sons. As they rode over the land together, the father parceled it out among them, marking out the boundaries by natural objects. It was divided, as nearly as possible, into four equal parts, each running from the Bay to the hills. The total area was nearly 19,000 acres.

Ignacio, the oldest, was given the southern end of the grant, bordering on the north bank of San Leandro Creek. Domingo was given the northern end, where the cities of Berkeley and Albany now stand. Antonio received what is now East Oakland (where the original home house stood and the Encinal de San Antonio, now the city of Alameda). And to Vicente fell the Encinal de Temescal, that portion now occupied by Central and North Oakland, Piedmont, and Emeryville.

With his portion of the grant, Antonio Peralta received the old family homestead at Fruitvale near the north bank of Arroyo Sausal or Fruitvale Creek. To the south of the original adobe (on the present Thirty-fourth Avenue) a second adobe was built in 1840, and also an enclosure of about three acres surrounded by an eight-foot wall. Two additional structures were erected that year on the same plat, one of which was a guest house located on the southwest corner of the enclosure. Extensive additions were made to the guest house in 1851. All of these houses, except the first

one built in 1821–1822, were leveled in 1870. In that year Antonio built a frame structure on the western line of Paxton Street about halfway between Coolidge and Thirty-fourth avenues.

Only recently, Professor J. N. Bowman of Berkeley relocated the sites of Antonio Peralta's buildings, and determined the bounds of the old enclosure. The southern end of the three-acre plot is intersected by Paxton Street, and Thirty-fourth Avenue cuts across the eastern side. In 1897, Don Antonio's frame house was removed to the southwest corner of Paxton Street and Thirty-fourth Avenue, where it still stands.

Ignacio erected his first house on the north bank of San Leandro Creek about 1835, after his San Jose alcalde term. The site is at the end of South Bartlett Street, which is a continuation of One Hundred Fifth Avenue. In later years, this was called the Francisco House, because Ignacio's son, Francisco Peralta, lived there. At a short distance east of this first house, Ignacio built a second adobe in 1842. These adobes disappeared in the late '70's. The land on which they stood was occupied by commercial market gardens.

About the year 1860 Ignacio built a brick house on what is now the corner of Cherrywood and East Thirteenth Street in San Leandro, one block west of State Highway No. 17. A part of this house has been incorporated into the Alta Mira Club House. A double row of palm trees, extending across vacant lots to the highway, still marks the former drive.

The Domingo adobe was built in 1841 on the site of what is now 1304 Albina Street, just off Hopkins Street and on the south bank of Codornices ("quail") Creek, Berkeley. This adobe remained standing until the '60's. Domingo constructed a frame dwelling about 1851 on a lot, now vacant, east of 1505 Hopkins Street. This house, formerly belonging to the University of California, formed the middle portion of the building located on Sacramento Street between Rose and Cedar streets until it was razed in 1933.

The first adobe house of Vicente Peralta was erected in 1836 in that part of Oakland formerly known as Temescal. The site is east of Telegraph Avenue at the rear of 5527 Vicente Street between Fifty-fifth and Fifty-sixth streets. The second adobe (the site of which is now occupied by a modern apartment house) was built south of the first and back of 486 Fifty-fifth Street in 1847–1848. These adobes were leveled during the '80's. A frame structure, built at 5511–5522 Vicente Street in 1867, was removed in 1892 to 5275 Claremont Avenue, one block south of the adobe sites and near the north bank of Temescal Creek. The spot is now marked only by a group of black acacias, an English walnut tree, and two lone palm trees. The original site of the frame dwelling is covered by an apartment house.

The pleasant days of the '30's and the early '40's on the old Spanish ranchos of the Contra Costa were but a brief episode in the history of California. Anglo-Saxons began to visit the region as early as 1846, and the Peraltas soon found that their fertile lands were the envy of these shrewd newcomers, who saw that they could be made valuable for other than pastoral purposes. In 1850, when the greater portion of the territorial patrimony of Domingo and Vicente Peralta was sold, the first encroachment upon Rancho San Antonio was made. Don Luis Peralta, grantee of the original princely estate, died in 1851 at the advanced age of ninety-three years, having lived to realize that what he had given to his sons was one of the most valuable tracts of land in California and that it was gradually melting away before their eyes. The immense value of the grant, the claim that his daughters were entitled to a share of it, the alleged insanity of the father when he made his will, all gave rise to complicated litigation, which, says Bancroft, can hardly be regarded as ended in 1885.

The great rancho and the four Peralta homesteads are jointly commemorated by a bronze tablet set in a boulder and placed in Lakeside Park, Oakland, by eleven Bay region chapters of the Daughters of the American Revolution. The spot is just above the canoe house on the northern shore of Lake Merritt.

Rancho San Ramón

José Amador, the first white settler of Murray Township, arrived there, tradition has it, before 1830. He brought with him a rich heritage of ingenuity and industry from his father Pedro Amador, that fine old Mexican soldier who had come to California with Portolá in 1769. Don José, himself a soldier, had been born in San Francisco in 1794, had served as a private in the San Francisco Company from 1810 to 1827, during the last three years of which (1824–1827) he was stationed in the Escolta at Sonoma. He took part in the expedition of Luis Argüello to the Sacramento Valley in 1821 and went with Gabriel Moraga to Fort Ross and Bodega that same year. After his discharge in 1827 he was major-domo at Misión San José, and on January 22, 1834, and August 14, 1835, he was granted more than four square leagues of the rancho later known as San Ramón, the greater part of which lay in Contra Costa County.

The Californians were not without their native manufacturers, and they did not rely entirely upon the sale of hides and tallow. Amador was one of the first manufacturers and farmers in Alameda County, herding vast numbers of cattle over his broad, unfenced acres and making leather, soap, saddles, harness, blankets, shoes, and even wagons in the adobe workshops on his rancho with the aid of Mexican labor. At one time 300 to 400 horses, 13,000 to 14,000 head of cattle, and 3,000 to 4,000 sheep grazed on his lands. In 1848 the lure of gold drew Amador, with thousands of others, to the Mother Lode country. Assisted by a number of Indians, according to Hittell, he mined in the county which was later named for him.

The site of the two-story adobe which Amador erected at his homestead is on the northwest corner of the Stockton and Amador Valley roads at Dublin. It stood north of the spring still visible under the weeping-willow trees, and foundation stones as well as firebrick or tile are even yet found beneath the soil. Robert Livermore helped Amador to build another adobe. The latter reciprocated by assisting Livermore in the same manner at his Rancho Las Positas, located to the east.

Natural landmarks usually designated the boundary lines between the early Spanish and Mexican land grants, although the later surveys often varied from the original, less scientific ones: the first surveys which marked out the confines of Rancho San Ramón may still be identified. Later surveys vary somewhat from these. To the west, the Pita Navaga ("knife point"), a sharp knob above the summit of Bulmer Hill Grade, indicated the division line between Rancho San Ramón and Rancho San Lorenzo. It is mentioned frequently in early deeds. The southern boundary was another natural feature, a large oak tree which still flourishes in the small gulch running up the hillside opposite the old Fallon house. Old-timers in the region remember that this tree used to bear the marks of early surveyors, who used it as a landmark from which the boundary line between ranchos San Ramón and Santa Rita was drawn.

Becoming financially involved, Amador gradually sold portions of his estate to various newcomers. Michael Murray and Jeremiah Fallon, natives of Ireland, who had come west together in 1846 and who had settled temporarily at Misión San José, bought sections of the Amador holdings south of the Stockton Road, before 1852. Murray Township, organized in June 1853, was named for Michael Murray, the first county supervisor from the district.

The old Murray house, built in 1850, still stands at the rear of the present Green residence in Dublin about one hundred yards to the west of its original location. The floor and siding of this interesting landmark were of pine shipped around the Horn, while the redwood joists were cut at and shipped from Redwood City, California.

Michael Murray sold his house and lands in 1862 to John Green, a man who became prominent in local affairs and who was a leading business man of the district during the '70's and '80's. Green also was a native of Ireland and a druggist by trade. He had come west at the behest of his brother, who was then a physician at San Antonio (East Oakland). John Green did not like the drug business, however, and longed for land of his own. In 1857 he packed his goods into an ox-cart, crossed the hills east of Hayward, and stopped in the vicinity of the present Dublin schoolhouse. This well-watered, wooded spot appealed to him, and he decided to set up his tent there. No sooner had the newcomer started to unload his wagon than Michael Murray appeared on the scene, informing him that he was squatting on land already owned and occupied. The property in question was under dispute at that time, since both Murray and James Witt Dougherty claimed to have purchased it from Amador. Murray, therefore, invited Green to drive down and locate on the ranch on which he was living, and Green accepted.

During the earthquake of 1868, a deep fissure in the earth two feet wide passed just west of the original site of the old Murray house, and the wells at this location dried up. Prospecting for springs west of the fault, Green found water at the site where the house still remains and removed to that spot. The dwelling was enlarged in 1870, and in 1890 a two-story edifice was erected in front of the smaller one. The earthquake of 1906 caused the tall brick chimney of the newer house to collapse and to crash through the roof and the floor of the pioneer structure. In the process of repairing the floor, each of the old boards was found to bear the stamp of a Boston company.

A regular town plat was never laid out at Dublin. The place just grew. The old Amador Valley Road to Suñol passed just to the east of the present Green house. Deep mire during the winter rains made it almost impassable, and its course was rerouted to higher ground to the west. The decided jog in the road as it runs at present is explained by this change.

John Green led an active and useful life. He was not only storekeeper, postmaster, and supervisor for Murray Township, but also a large-scale rancher, who owned lands both at Dublin and in the Livermore mountains to the east. The village of Greenville, four miles east of Livermore at the entrance to Altamont Pass, was named for him, as he started the first store there. In spite of full days, Green spent his evenings studying law and more especially the land-tenure laws pertaining to the Spanish and Mexican land grants. He had previously learned Spanish during his apprenticeship to a New York drug firm which had trade relations with South American countries. Thus it was natural that Green became a friend and adviser to the native Californians of the Amador and Livermore valleys, and the old ranchers often drove to Dublin to discuss their increasingly complex land problems with their good Irish neighbors.

About a mile south of Dublin on the road to Pleasanton is located the Jeremiah Fallon house, also built in 1850. Its timbers were hand-hewn from the San Antonio redwoods back of Oakland, but, like the Murray house, its floor and siding were brought around the Horn. The original location of the house was on the lowlands to the east, where the road skirted the base of the hills instead of traversing the slopes, as the present highway does. A descendant of Jeremiah Fallon still resides in the old house, which has been somewhat remodeled in recent years.

During the year 1852, James Witt Dougherty, a native of Mississippi who had come to California in 1849, acquired Amador's two-story adobe when he purchased the greater portion of the rancho, the bulk of which lay north of the Stockton Road. Dougherty lived in the old Amador adobe until it was damaged by the severe earthquake of 1861. A rude dwelling of resawed siding was then put up south of the spring, and a portion of this old house, added to and altered from time to time, still stands not far from the highway.

About the Amador adobes a village gradually grew up, generally known until 1865 as Amador's or Amador Valley. The post office which was established there was called Dougherty's Station until the time that John Green was appointed postmaster. For some time before this, that portion of the village south of the Stockon Road had been called Dublin. It is said that Dougherty first bestowed the name when he was asked by a wayfarer what was the name of the community. Dougherty had replied that the post office was called Dougherty's Station, but since there were so many Irish living south of the road they might as well call that part Dublin. The name stuck, and the post office also was called Dublin.

The first business house in Dublin (then Amador's) was the two-story Amador adobe, which served as a wayside station until its destruction in the '60's. Meanwhile, the Amador Valley Hotel, built in 1858 by Tom Donlan, was becoming popular, with Pete Donlan as its proprietor. It stood on the southwest corner of the Stockton and Amador Valley roads until 1914, when it was destroyed by fire.

The oldest business house still standing in Dublin is the John Scarlett Hotel, which stands on the north side of the Stockton Highway at the head of the Pleasanton Road. It was constructed about 1860 by James W. Dougherty for a certain Granlee, then proprietor of the San Lorenzo House at San Lorenzo. John Scarlett, Granlee's bartender, purchased the hotel at Dublin in 1870, and the place afterward bore his name. Subsequent alterations have replaced the original resawed siding, except in the rear, where the older construction is still intact.

The John Green Hotel, built in 1864 on the south side of the Stockton Road, has retained its original shape, but green stucco covers the old resawed siding. A wall at the back alone retains its original covering.

The little white church and neat cemetery mark Dublin as a spot of historic interest. Set apart from the noise and hurry of the great highway which passes through the village, St. Raymond's Church still keeps the charm and dignity of other days. Built by Tom Donlan in 1859, it was the first church in the township. Its lands as well as those of the old Catholic Cemetery near by were donated by two devoted pioneers, Michael Murray and Jeremiah Fallon. The nonsectarian portion of the cemetery was given by James W. Dougherty, and descendants of Fallon and Dougherty still lavish much love and care upon the place.

Rancho Agua Caliente

Warm Springs, a hamlet near the intersection of the Foothill Boulevard and the main Oakland–San Jose highway, is located on what was once a part of Rancho Agua Caliente. This rancho was granted to Fulgencio Higuera on April 4, 1839, having been released by its earlier grantee, Antonio Suñol. About two miles south of Mission San Jose on the Foothill Boulevard is the site of the Higuera homestead. The last of its red-tiled adobes were finally demolished only a few years ago.

The hot springs at this point were first frequented by the Indians, who lived in the region long before the coming of the white man. To these springs came the Spanish señores and señoras of the '40's, bringing their linen for their Indian retainers to wash and holding their annual rodeos in the vicinity.

That portion of the rancho including the springs was purchased by Clemente Columbet in 1850, and buildings for a resort were erected. From this time on until the earthquake of 1868, Warm Springs was one of the gayest and most fashionable watering places in the state. Persons of wealth and leisure as well as invalids from many places came to enjoy the benefits of the hot sulphur water.

Columbet removed a house all the way from San José to serve as a hotel at the springs. In 1858 he leased the place to Alexander Beaty, who maintained its reputation for grand festivities. Another hotel was built in 1869 by A. A. Cohen, but it was never used as such. When Governor Leland Stanford purchased the estate in 1870 and planted it to orchards and vineyards, his brother Joshua resided there. Later, it became the home of the latter's son, Josiah Stanford. It was recently purchased by the Sisters of the Sacred Name of Jesus and Mary.

South of and adjacent to the land owned by the Sisters, there is standing today an old adobe owned for many years by Arthur Curtner, son of the pioneer Henry Curtner. Abelardo Higuera had previously lived in it. The old adobe of one story and a half with very thick walls is now used as a storehouse. Its location in the lower foothills commands a magnificent view of San Francisco Bay and the Santa Clara Valley. It is an interesting structure with arched doorways and thick partitions between the rooms. Some portions are falling, but the whole is protected by a roof.

At the base of the hills two miles south of Mission San Jose is another adobe, quite a large structure formerly owned by Fernando Higuera, son of Fulgencio Higuera. It is said to have been erected in the early 1850's. It stands in the fields west of the Foothill Boulevard on the Powers ranch. The roof has fallen in, and a few more winters may see the adobe walls washed away.

Rancho Las Positas

A young English sailor named Robert Livermore appeared in California in January of the year 1822, a deserter from the trading ship "Colonel Young." For a time, he worked at various places in California, gaining the good will of the Spanish settlers wherever he went. Soon after 1830 he came to Rancho Los Tularcitos (mostly in northeastern Santa Clara County), where he married Josefa Higuera as early as 1834.

Before 1837, the year in which Philip Leget Edwards passed through Alameda and Contra Costa counties on his way to the San Joaquin River with his herd of wild Mexican long-horned cattle, Robert Livermore had already established himself on Rancho Las Positas in what was later called for him Livermore Valley. He and William Gulnac had occupied a house on the land as early as 1835. In July of 1834, Gulnac had petitioned the governor for Rancho Las Positas, but before the grant was made he turned over his rights to Livermore and José Noriega. On April 10, 1839, Governor Juan B. Alvarado granted the land to them. It consisted of two square leagues, or about 8,800 acres. Livermore later bought Noriega's interest.

Robert Livermore became a naturalized citizen of Alta California in 1844, and about the year 1846 he purchased the Cañada de los Vaqueros, mostly in Contra Costa County but skirting the northern portion of Livermore Valley. The two ranchos were later confirmed to him, and Robert Livermore, the sailor lad, was a wealthy man. The rancho was soon well stocked with cattle, but Livermore was more interested in horticulture and viticulture than he was in cows or sheep; and after the Fathers of the Misión San José he was the first man to plant a vineyard and an orchard of pears and olives in this section of California.

An early dwelling on Rancho Las Positas was an adobe erected by Livermore as the second episode in the friendly drama which began when he helped José María Amador, his nearest white neighbor in all that great plain, to shelter his family beneath adobe walls a few years previously. For when his young English neighbor had bricks to be molded and dried and walls to be laid for a future home, Amador did not forget that Livermore had volunteered aid to him in a like situation. At times, too, Indians so harassed Livermore and his family that he had to take refuge with Amador.

This friendly old house, with its honest, hospitable host, became a popular stopping place for wayfarers on the Stockton Road. In March 1850 when Nathaniel Greene Patterson (a member of the California Battalion in 1846–1847 and a gold seeker of 1848) hired the adobe for a hotel, it became the first place of public entertainment in the valley. This house, which stood near the source of Positas Creek at a point about one and one-half miles north of the center of Livermore, was partly in ruins by 1876 and torn down later.

Livermore built a large frame dwelling near the adobe in 1849, the first wooden building in Livermore Valley. A part of the original structure, the timbers of which had been shipped around the Horn, still stands today.

The first house to be erected within the present city limits of Livermore was built by Alphonso Ladd, who came to California from New Orleans in 1850. The following year he settled with his wife near the Suñol adobe, then the only white habitation in Suñol Valley. A few years later he took up 160 acres of government land in the Livermore Extension, and in 1855 he built a hotel on the Stockton Road at the site of what was to become known as Laddville, a forerunner of Livermore.

The Ladd Hotel, a frame structure built of lumber hauled across the hills from Mowry's Landing, was very prosperous during the late '50's and the '60's and was nearly always full. It was destroyed by fire in 1876.

The tracks of the Central Pacific Railroad were laid through Livermore Valley in the summer of 1869, and in August the first train passed through, although the entire line was not yet opened up. The railroad station had been located about half a mile west of Laddville, and there William M. Mendenhall, who had come to California in 1846, had the town of Livermore surveyed on October 1, 1869. It was incorporated on April 30, 1876.

The Collegiate Institute, later called Livermore College, was founded by the Presbyterians at Livermore in 1870. The building, located about four blocks west of the present Livermore Sanatorium, was destroyed by fire a few years ago. For several years the building had been used as a sanatorium by J. W. Robertson, who sold it to John McGlinchey for use as a private residence. The new J. McGlinchey home, at 1615 College Avenue, is on the site.

Rancho San Leandro and the Town of San Leandro

José Joaquín Estudillo, the first white settler in Eden Township, petitioned for a grant of the land known as the Arroyo de San Leandro on January 8, 1837, "with the object of securing subsistence for and supporting a large family, consisting of his wife and ten children, after having been in the military service for a period of seventeen years, four months and seven days." The title was given in 1839 but lost,

and Estudillo lived on his land for "the long term of five years, five months and several days," before he again secured his grant on October 16, 1842. It was well that he did so, for Guillermo Castro, his neighbor on Rancho San Lorenzo, also desired the lands of San Leandro, but Estudillo's long period of actual tenure won the battle of possession.

José Joaquín, son of José María Estudillo and brother of José Antonio Estudillo, was a member of one of the best of the old Californian families and held several positions of honor in the military service and in the government in his own right. William Heath Davis, later a son-in-law of Estudillo, said that his father-in-law moved to San Leandro early in the year 1836, after he had first obtained a written permit from Governor Alvarado to occupy the land. He brought with him three hundred heifers, by which he increased his herd until, on his death in 1852, he left to his heirs about three thousand head of cattle. His specialty and pride was "white cattle," because he said their color enabled him "to see his stock at a great distance."

Squatters first encroached upon Rancho San Leandro in 1851, when Americans began to settle there against the wishes of the legal owner. The intruders first made their appearance on the banks of San Lorenzo Creek, at a place subsequently known as Squattersville, now San Lorenzo. They soon overran the rancho, but Estudillo, "an educated, intelligent, and up-right man," with the aid of his sons and sons-in-law consistently "opposed the evildoers in seizing the land. At times . . . . there was a tendency . . . . towards a bloody affray. But among them [that is, the squatters], there were conservative counsellors and prudent squatters, who invariably prevailed on the rougher class to avoid bloodshed." A malicious element among them, however, did much damage, shooting and wounding horses and cattle under cover of darkness, and fencing Estudillo's stock away from the creek. During "all these turbulent times [1851–1854] the members of the family were in constant fear of their personal safety."

Through the instrumentality of John B. Ward and William Heath Davis, the squatters were finally brought to terms. Some of the property was deeded to an alien, Clement Boyreau, in order to bring the case into the federal courts. Judges Hoffman and McAllister rendered a decision in favor of the Estudillo family. As a result the squatters took leases from the family pending the final decision of the United States Supreme Court, and eventually they purchased the land from the original owners.

In 1854 and 1855 the county seat was brought to San Leandro from Alvarado by popular election, and the two sons-in-law, Ward and Davis, submitted a plan to Mrs. Estudillo and her children for laying out a town for the seat of government. The family gave land for county buildings and reserved two hundred acres for the town. "The family mansion," says Davis, "was surrendered to the county for a temporary court house." This house was destroyed by fire, probably set by an incendiary who wished the county seat to be returned to Alvarado. Through some technicality of law, the center of justice did go back to the latter place in 1855, but in 1856 it was again in San Leandro, where it remained until 1872, when it was removed to Brooklyn, now East Oakland.

The first adobe dwelling, built by José Joaquín Estudillo in 1837, was located near the south bank of San Leandro Creek a little more than a mile west of the present town of San Leandro on what is now the Donovan ranch. His second residence, also an adobe, was the one used temporarily as a county courthouse and in 1855 was located on the plaza. Later, a permanent courthouse building was erected on the site now occupied by the St. Mary's Convent. This building was demolished in the earthquake of 1868.

Don José's first two adobe buildings no longer exist, but until 1929 the Estudillo House, a frame structure erected by the family in 1855 as a hotel, still stood in San Leandro at the corner of Davis Street and State Highway 17. A beautiful patio, where a mammoth grapevine, orange and lemon trees, and bright flowers grew in profusion, gave it the atmosphere and charm of long ago. Modern progress has recently removed this historic landmark; its place on the old plaza is taken by gaily painted stores. A part of the grapevine and the old garden still may be found at the rear of these buildings.

Another house built by the Estudillos is the frame structure at 1291 Carpentier Street, opposite the Convent. It took the place of a brick house built by the family and destroyed by the earthquake of 1868. This, too, is fast falling to decay, and most of its magnificent trees have disappeared.

María Jesús Estudillo married William Heath Davis at Misión Dolores in 1847. After her father's death in 1852, she inherited that portion of Rancho San Lorenzo which was located west of and adjoining the present Donovan ranch. The street which now runs west from San Leandro to the Bay and intersects what was once the Davis ranch bears the name of its former owner, Davis Road.

At San Lorenzo (the one-time Squattersville) the old San Lorenzo Hotel still stands. It was erected in 1854 by Charles Crane, one of three brothers who came to California from New York in 1850. The place was used as a stage station on the old Valley Road from San José to Oakland, and, still standing on the eastern side of State Highway 17, it is used as a private dwelling and store. Beneath the present shingles, the original resawed siding of the old house is still intact. The siding was nailed to vertical boards, making in all three layers to the walls as they stand today. The old cypress hedge is gone, and the splendid avenue of locust trees in front of the house was cut down long ago. Across the road to the north, Emerson T. Crane, a brother of Charles, also had a ranch. A son still lives on the estate. The third brother, Addison Moses Crane, was the first judge of Alameda County.

Rancho El Valle de San José

The Mission Fathers early recognized the advantages of the fertile Arroyo Valle and pastured their herds among the great sycamores there. For many years after Misión San José was secularized, Mission Indians still resided in the vicinity of Pleasanton. The original name of the locality was Alisal, from *aliso* meaning "alder tree," so called because of the numerous large trees of that species which lined the bed of the arroyo.

Rancho El Valle de San José was granted to the four relatives, Antonio María Pico, his brothers-in-law Águstín Bernal and Juan Pablo Bernal, and his sister-in-law María Dolores Bernal de Suñol, on February 23 and April 10, 1839. It was patented in 1865 to Agustín and Juan Pablo Bernal and Antonio María Suñol.

Antonio María Pico, son of José Dolores Pico, was born in Monterey in 1808. He held various public and military offices throughout his career. He was stationed at San José from 1833 to 1839 and took part in the revolt against Micheltorena in the years 1844 and 1845. After having been a member of the Constitutional Convention he was appointed by President Lincoln as register of the United States land office at Los Angeles in 1861. He was a grantee of Rancho Pescadero (San Joaquín County) in 1843 and co-purchaser of the San Rafael Mission estate in 1846. Don Antonio married Pilar Bernal and sold his fourth of Rancho El Valle de San José to Juan P. Bernal.

Antonio María Suñol, a native of Spain who had come to California as a sailor on the French ship "Bordelais," from

which he deserted in 1818, married María Dolores Bernal. He lived at the Pueblo de San José and never took up his residence on Rancho El Valle de San José. A man of "excellent reputation," he held a few public offices but was mainly a stock raiser and trader. He was owner of the Rancho Los Coches in Santa Clara County after 1837 and purchaser of San Rafael Mission in 1846 with Pico.

The son of the same name, Antonio Suñol, had an adobe on the rancho in the pleasant valley of the sycamores and alder trees, where he lived in the late '40's and the early '50's. The site of this adobe is near the Water Temple of the San Francisco water system, which stands at the intersection of three old valley roads, one from Suñol, another from Pleasanton, and a third through Mission Pass. The Suñol adobe was later owned by Charles Hadsell.

The Bernals, Agustín and Juan P., sons of Joaquín Bernal, were presidio soldiers who had served at San Francisco and San José. Agustín Bernal was in 1853 a claimant for Rancho Santa Teresa in Santa Clara County, of which his father had been grantee in 1834. In April 1850 Agustín moved to his section of Rancho El Valle de San José and erected an adobe home near the foothills at the western rim of the broad Livermore Valley. The picturesque adobe still stands in excellent condition beside the Suñol-Dublin Road on what is now the Baldwin Hereford Ranch one mile west of Pleasanton. In September 1852 Juan P. Bernal, settling near Alisal, constructed an adobe dwelling on the north bank of Arroyo Valle. A portion of this adobe has been incorporated in the present Black residence in Pleasanton, according to local tradition.

The Bernals were good business managers. Consequently, they were able to secure their large holdings from the aggressive encroachments of foreigners and to maintain possession of the original grant better than most of the native families.

The next settler in the vicinity of Pleasanton was John W. Kottinger, a native of Austria who came to California in 1849 and who married a daughter of Juan P. Bernal in 1850. Late in 1852 Kottinger went to live at Rancho El Valle de San José, and in that year he built at Alisal, later Pleasanton, an adobe and frame dwelling house on the south bank of Arroyo Valle opposite Bernal's residence. The Kottinger house was torn down only a few years ago; its owner was one of the founders of the town of Pleasanton and the first man to start a store there. Kottinger's plat lay just south of Arroyo Valle and was surveyed in 1867 and 1869.

Joshua Ayres Neal, a seaman and a native of New Hampshire who shipped to California on board a sailing vessel in March 1847, came to Livermore Valley in 1850, when he obtained the position of overseer for Robert Livermore. Afterward by marrying a daughter of Agustín Bernal, he acquired 530 acres in the immediate vicinity of Pleasanton. Neal had his portion of the town surveyed by Mr. Duerr in 1868.

Rancho Potrero de los Cerritos

The present town of Alvarado is on what was once a part of the Rancho Potrero de los Cerritos, granted to Agustín Alviso and Tomas Pacheco on March 21, 1844. Agustín Alviso, son of Ignacio Alviso, was mayordomo of Misión San José from 1840 to 1841. He was a prosperous ranchero, locally well known, who married María Antonia Pacheco in 1830. Tomas Pacheco was a soldier of the San Francisco Company from 1826 to 1832 and later held various offices at the Pueblo San José from 1834 to 1843.

The old Alviso adobe was so badly damaged in the earthquake of 1868 that Agustín Alviso would not let his wife and children live in it. A frame house was erected on the site of the adobe soon after the earthquake. In 1934, when the foundations of the building were repaired, adobe bricks were uncovered. The frame house still stands on the northeast bank of the Sanjon (Zanjon) de los Alisos, just south of the Newark-Patterson Landing Road.

The site of Tomas Pacheco's adobe was on the south bank of Alameda Creek and on the left-hand side of the Jarvis Landing Road about two and one-half miles south of Decoto.

Ex-Mission San Jose

In 1850 J. M. Horner purchased from A. Alviso 110 acres in the tract that had been the mission grazing lands. At once he plotted a town site covering the whole of his purchase; the first lots were sold on September 9, 1850. The town of Union City was a success: it drew the trade of Misión San José from the more southerly sloughs and also provided a more direct outlet for the area east of the hills.

Henry C. Smith bought 465 acres from A. Alviso and T. Pacheco on December 27, 1850. Smith had the town of New Haven laid out "at the upper embarcadero just across the boundary line from Horner's Union City . . . . The first lots were sold March 18, 1851. . . . ."

"These communities," writes J. N. Bowman, "became rivals of San Francisco. In this neighborhood, grain, vegetable and fruit ranching were proven feasible in California for Americans; flour and sugar factories were later erected, and people and investors were even attracted from San Francisco. . . . ."

Because of the success of Union City and New Haven, "two San Francisco lawyers, Strode and Jones, bought 750 acres from A. Alviso on September 30, 1852, and a new town was planned that winter," being adjacent to the two older ones to the south and west. The new town was named for the former Mexican governor, Juan Bautista Alvarado.

"In March and part of April, 1853, there were three towns." Meanwhile on March 15, "Henry C. Smith introduced his bill in the State Legislature, then meeting at Benicia, creating the new county of Alameda from parts of Contra Costa and Santa Clara Counties and designating New Haven as the county seat and Alvarado as the seat of justice. . . . . The new county officials met in the upper story of Smith's store in New Haven; but the first minutes of their meeting are dated April 11, 1853, in Alvarado," thus indicating that, "by this date, New Haven had discarded its old name and taken that of the neighboring town without taking the town itself."

The site of the New Haven embarcadero and of the building used as a county courthouse is opposite the present Alvarado Bank Building on the Oakland–San Jose highway. A service station now occupies the spot. About a half-mile due west was the Union City embarcadero.

The H. C. Smith house, built in 1852, still stands in Alvarado at the head of Vallejo Street. It is a one-story structure made of lumber brought around the Horn.

Rancho San Lorenzo

There were two divisions of Rancho San Lorenzo. That portion on which the towns of Hayward and Castro Valley are located was granted to Guillermo Castro on February 23, 1841, by Governor Juan B. Alvarado, and on October 25, 1843, by Governor Manuel Micheltorena. That portion west of Hayward and south of San Lorenzo Creek was granted to Francisco Soto, October 10, 1842, and February 20, 1844.

Guillermo Castro's adobe house was located on Castro Street between C and D streets, on the site of the present City Hall in Hayward. Its sandstone foundations were uncovered a few years ago, when excavations for the City Hall were being made. Among the buildings damaged at Hayward in the earthquake of 1868 was this old adobe. Its roof was then covered with flat tile. Soto's adobe house was located less than a half-mile to the south of Castro's on the south bank of San José Creek and on the grounds of the present Hayward Memorial Park.

Guillermo Castro married Luisa Peralta, and Francisco Soto married Barbara Castro. Since Soto died before 1852, his wife and children were claimants for the rancho that year. Castro lived for many years.

One of the first Americans to come to Rancho San Lorenzo was William Hayward from Massachusetts. In the fall of 1851 he pitched his tent in Palomares Canyon under the impression that it was government land and that he would obtain there a homestead of 160 acres. Before long, however, he was visited by Guillermo Castro, who informed him that he was a trespasser. However, an agreement was made between Castro and Hayward so that the latter remained, and the relations between the two men continued to be most friendly.

Hayward soon removed his tent to the location of the hotel that later became famous as a resort. This site is on the hill north of A Street and east of Castro Street. The hotel was destroyed by fire in 1923. The three-story annex, now shingled over, still stands on the south side of A Street. In 1854 Castro laid out the plat of the town which was given the name of Hayward in honor of his American friend.

The relations of Castro with another American, F. D. Atherton, illustrate how crafty Yankees too often took advantage of the trusting native Californians. Atherton loaned money to Castro from time to time so that he might gamble. When the latter was unable to repay, Atherton took possession of a piece of land. And so it went until Castro lost all of his vast acreage. Finally, Castro and all of his family except a daughter and one son, Luis Castro, later county surveyor of Alameda County, removed to South America.

On Castro Street there still stands the Villa Hotel, known in the '60's as the American Exchange and in the '70's as the Oakes' Hotel. Tony Oakes, the proprietor, who wrote and sang his own songs, published a little booklet of songs in 1878 called *Tony Oakes' Songster*.

The Hayward fire department possesses a very interesting old hand-drawn and hand-pumped fire engine used in Hayward during the '70's. It was in San Francisco as early as 1854 and was used in fighting fire at Stockton in the '60's.

Rancho Arroyo de la Alameda and Niles

Rancho Arroyo de la Alameda, taking its name from the stream which flows for many miles through the open plains that drain to the Bay, was granted to José de Jesús Vallejo on August 8, 1842. It consisted of 17,705.38 acres of fertile valley land. Don José, one of thirteen children of Ignacio Vallejo, a Spanish soldier of Alta California, was an elder brother of General Mariano G. Vallejo. He himself was active in military and governmental affairs from 1818 to 1847; among other things he was *comisionado* and administrator at Misión San José from 1836 to 1840 and military commander at the Pueblo de San José from 1841 to 1842. After 1852 he was postmaster at the Misión San José, where his mansion stood just west of the highway and opposite the Mission. Affairs on the rancho were left primarily in the hands of overseers, and an expensive flour mill became the most famous asset of the estate. Around the mill history centered in this section of Alameda County, after its erection about 1850.

Where the tree-lined Alameda issues from Niles Canyon and passes into the plain that slopes away to the Bay, the old village of Vallejo Mills, now known as Niles, grew up in the '50's. Historic landmarks still may be found in the neighborhood. Stone foundations of a second flour mill erected here by Vallejo in 1856, still remain one hundred feet south of the

Southern Pacific Railway tracks and just north of Niles Canyon Road. A mile up the canyon the stone aqueduct, which he built to conduct water to the mill, still parallels the road for some distance. The site of one of the several adobes built by Vallejo for his overseers is located at the entrance of the canyon.

Perhaps the most picturesque reminder of adobe days in this vicinity is the little building in the gardens of the California Nursery Company northwest of Niles. The California Nursery, founded in 1865, has played an important part in the development of the fruit industry and home beautification in California. This adobe, the first of the Vallejo adobes built in the vicinity, has been restored as a guest house.

Rancho Santa Rita

Rancho Santa Rita once skirted the western edge of the broad Livermore Valley and adjoined Rancho El Valle de San José to the east. It was granted to José Dolores Pacheco on April 10, 1839, and included more than 8,800 acres of excellent grazing land. Dolores Pacheco was often mentioned in the local annals of San José, where he held a number of public offices during the years 1838 to 1843 and again in 1846. He died in 1852.

Samuel and J. West Martin purchased about five thousand acres of Rancho Santa Rita in 1854; there were enough cattle included in the sale to provide the purchase money.

The little adobe which still stands beneath a giant oak tree on what is now the Meadow Lark Dairy was built about 1844 or 1845, possibly by Francisco S. Alviso, who came to Rancho Santa Rita as major-domo in 1844. The adobe is about 3.3 miles south of Dublin on the east side of the old Hill Road from Dublin to Suñol.

Oakland and Lake Merritt

Paradoxically, the city of Oakland is known both as a city of homes and as a great manufacturing center of the West. Its site was an untended area on the San Antonio rancho of the Peraltas until after the gold rush to California in 1848–1849.

Three men who separately had sailed around the Horn were responsible for the beginnings of the town that was incorporated as Oakland in 1852 and that changed its status from town to city two years later. These men were Edson Adams, Andrew Moon, and Horace W. Carpentier, an attorney, who after service in the California Militia was known as General Carpentier.

Edson Adams on his arrival in California went to the gold region and located a mining claim, but soon sold it and determined to settle and lay out a town on the eastern shore of San Francisco Bay. There, on May 16, 1850, he staked out a claim of 160 acres on the Peralta land as though it were public land. A line through the center of his claim passed through what is now Broadway in Oakland. On either side of him the other two men staked out similar tracts, Carpentier to the east and Moon to the west. It was long before titles to the property were cleared.

Julius Kellersberger was employed to lay out the town for these three owners. The plat included the area now bounded by First, Fourteenth, Market, and Fallon streets. Wide streets were planned, and the widest, 110 feet, was called Broadway. Sponsored by Carpentier, who had been made a member of the state legislature, a bill was approved by that body in 1852 for the incorporation of the town of Oakland.

Because adequate shipping facilities were necessary at once, the trustees of the town granted to Carpentier the right to all the water front of the town, where he was to build three wharves. Oakland Harbor now has over twenty-seven miles of deep-water frontage and about five miles of channel dredged to a depth of thirty feet in the estuary.

Lake Merritt, containing 160 acres of water, is unique in that it is a wild-fowl sanctuary in the midst of a populous city. It was named in honor of Samuel B. Merritt, a graduate from the medical department of Bowdoin College, who died in 1890. Dr. Merritt served as councilman and was chosen mayor in 1868. He furthered many projects favorable to the development of the young city. Merritt Hospital was founded by his fortune.

San Antonio Slough used to spread over a large region at the head of the San Antonio Estuary. Into it flowed salt tides from San Francisco Bay as well as several creeks carrying the fresh-water drainage from the outlying foothills of the Coast Range. Dr. Merritt was instrumental in having a dam built to impound these waters—the first step in the formation of Lake Merritt as it is today, a salt-water lake with a broad causeway and a movable floodgate. His report as mayor in 1869 includes these words: "A dam has been constructed near the Oakland bridge at a cost of at least $20,000, converting the arm of San Antonio Creek north of the bridge into a beautiful lake."

The original city of Oakland lay on one side of San Antonio Slough. On the opposite side two small settlements were made. Clinton, where the first settlers were Moses Chase and the Patton brothers, who farmed 160 acres of the Peralta land, was laid out on a tract of 480 acres in 1853. In that year a bridge was built across the slough to connect Clinton with Oakland. The area included in Clinton lay, approximately, between Eighth and Twenty-fourth streets and Lake Merritt and Fourteenth Avenue, which was then a small creek. On the other side of this small creek the town of San Antonio was surveyed on a tract of 200 acres in 1854. A flurry of excitement over a small gold discovery passed through the San Antonio region in 1856; hundreds of claims were staked out, but not enough gold was found to warrant continued enthusiasm.

By 1856 Clinton and San Antonio constituted a single town called Brooklyn. In 1870 Brooklyn was incorporated and two years later it was annexed to the city of Oakland. Clinton Square, San Antonio Park, and Brooklyn Avenue in East Oakland commemorate these early towns.

On November 8, 1869, the first train over the newly completed railroad across the continent arrived in Oakland. A salute of thirty-seven guns was fired and a grand celebration was held at which notables addressed the enthusiastic citizens. To commemorate this event, the Oakland Chapter, D.A.R., on March 12, 1931, unveiled a bronze tablet at the railway station on Seventh Street between Broadway and Washington streets.

There are many historic sites within the city. A section of the old Spanish road that led from Temescal southward to San Leandro, San Lorenzo, and Misión San José was long distinguishable near the intersection of Moss and Santa Clara avenues. When, about 1870, Edward P. Flint from Boston purchased a large tract of land in this area the ruts made by the old wheels were plainly discernible along the rear of what is now 60 Santa Clara Avenue, a piece of property still held by Flint heirs. Recent realignment of Highway 50 in connection with construction of an approach to the San Francisco–Oakland Bay Bridge here follows for a short distance the route of the old Spanish road.

The Oakland Free Library was established in 1878 with Ina Coolbrith, later California's poet laureate, as its first librarian. Other literary celebrities have lived in Oakland. Francis Bret Harte arrived in California on the "Brother Johnathan" in 1854 and came across the Bay on the ferry boat

"Clinton." He had come with his sister Margaret to live with their stepfather, Colonel Williams, who the following year became the fourth mayor of Oakland. In the stories "The Devotion of Henriquez" and "Chu-chu" later written by Harte, he refers to Oakland as "Encinal."

Jack London's father lived between Alameda and Oakland. The son lived at several different addresses in the town during his youth and early manhood. He was living at 1130 East Fifteenth Street when he entered the prize-winning manuscript, "The Typhoon off the Coast of Japan," in the contest managed by the *San Francisco Morning Call.* After his first marriage he lived in a house of the Italian-villa type, the former home of the sculptor Peano. Scenes from the windows of this house, which looked toward the bridge at Eighth Street, are described in his *Martin Eden.* In the hill region of Bayou Vista off Oakland Avenue is a recently renovated house where he lived with his family while he wrote *The Call of the Wild.*

The Heights, situated on the wooded hills overlooking San Francisco Bay and the Golden Gate, is just on the outskirts of Oakland, above Dimond Canyon and near the Skyline Boulevard. This was the estate of Joaquín Miller (Cincinnatus Heine Miller), "Poet of the Sierra," and is now a public park belonging to the city of Oakland.

Joaquín Miller spent many years of his life on this estate. He wrote most of his poems in the quaint building which he called "The Abbey." Here, too, are the house in which he lived and several unique stone monuments erected by his hands, among them the "Sanctuary to Memory," the "Funeral Pyre," the "Tower to Robert Browning," and the "Tower to General John C. Frémont." This last monument was placed on the spot where Frémont, who named the Golden Gate, is said to have stood when he first saw the San Francisco Bay opening out into the Pacific.

Joaquín Miller's first book of poetry, *Songs of the Sierras,* was published in 1871.

. In June 1888 Robert Louis Stevenson returned to California with his family after eight years' absence. He had come to prepare for the trip to the South Seas of which he had dreamed since boyhood and toward which Charles Warren Stoddard, his California author friend, had so greatly influenced him.

Dr. Samuel Merritt's schooner yacht "Casco," chartered by Stevenson, was anchored in the Oakland Estuary, about one hundred yards north of the Webster Street bridge, and Stevenson spent several weeks there fitting her out. Part of that time he berthed aboard the trim little vessel which was to carry him on his romantic voyage to the Islands of the Pacific.

The University of California

The University of California, now one of the largest and best equipped universities in the world, was established by the state legislature, March 23, 1868. Its forerunner, the College of California, began, in 1853 in Oakland, as the Contra Costa Academy. It had been founded by Rev. Henry Durant, a Yale graduate, and was sponsored by the Association of Congregational and Presbyterian Churches organized by missionaries sent to California by the American Home Missionary Society. In 1855 the Academy was incorporated as a college and regular college work was begun in 1860.

In 1867 the trustees offered to donate the campus in Berkeley and other assets, if the state would establish a university at Berkeley with a college of letters as a nucleus for other departments. Thus the State University became not merely a mechanical and agricultural school, as was

strongly advocated, but a real university formed around a liberal college. The University did not, however, get started until 1870, and the old buildings on the campus in Oakland were used until 1873, when the first new buildings were finally completed on the Berkeley campus.

The site of the old College of California, forerunner of the present University of California, covers four blocks of Oakland's present business district, and is bounded by Twelfth, Fourteenth, Franklin, and Harrison streets.

In 1874, the University moved to its present campus in Berkeley.

At the La Loma entrance to the Berkeley campus is the historic Founders' Rock. Standing on this rock, April 6, 1860, the founders of the University of California (then trustees of the College of California) dedicated it forever to learning. On Charter Day, 1896, the Class of 1896 marked it with a marble tablet.

The Hearst Memorial Mining Building, a granite structure near the La Loma entrance to the campus, was built by Mrs. Phoebe Hearst in 1907 in memory of her husband, Senator George Hearst, who came to California as a miner in 1850.

George Hearst was one of the most celebrated miners throughout the West. He had mining interests not only in California but also in Nevada, Colorado, Utah, and Idaho. Among other important projects, he developed the famous Comstock Lode in Nevada. In 1886 he became United States Senator. After his death in 1891 his wife distributed his wealth among various philanthropies, making especially large gifts to the University of California.

The Le Conte Oak stands among other large live oaks at the western side of the University campus and is dedicated to the memory of John and Joseph Le Conte, the two brothers who did so much for the upbuilding of higher education and scientific learning in California. The tree is marked with a bronze tablet.

Sather Tower was erected in honor of Peder Sather, a prominent San Francisco banker, philanthropist, and trustee of the College of California, by his widow. Sather gave much money toward the establishing and upbuilding of the State University. Sather Tower is a beautiful campanile with a carillon which is played three times daily and on special occasions. It is a landmark in the Bay region, being visible for miles in all directions.

Berkeley

Dr. Samuel H. Willey came to California in 1849 as one of the first four commissioned Protestant missionaries to California. He became a leader in pioneer religious and educational work and was one of the founders of the College of California in Oakland and also of its successor, the University of California, at Berkeley. He was also one of the founders of Berkeley, the college town. The old Willey house, located on Dwight Way above College Avenue, was built in 1865, the first town house in Berkeley. In this house the name Berkeley was first discussed as being appropriate for the new college town. Bishop Berkeley, renowned English philosopher and seer of the westward march of civilization, was the author of the poem beginning, "Westward the course of empire takes its way," which prompted the use of his name for this new educational center of the West. In the home of Dr. Willey also was formed the first city government of Berkeley. The city thus owes its existence to the College of California, and the prime promoters of the University, among whom Dr. Willey was one of the leaders, were also the builders of the town.

The site of the old Willey house is now occupied by a modern apartment house, "The Bishop Berkeley."

Mills College

Dr. Cyrus Mills and his wife conducted the Benicia Seminary in Benicia from 1865 to 1871. They then removed to what is now East Oakland, where they hoped to make their school the Mount Holyoke of the Pacific. In 1885 its name was changed to Mills College. It is now the leading girls' college west of the Mississippi and holds high rank throughout the country.

Old Washington College

The site of the old Washington College, founded in 1870, is across the Western Pacific Railroad track northeast from the Irvington depot. It was established as a non-sectarian institution by certain pioneers interested in education, E. L. Beard, Henry Curtner, and Rev. W. F. B. Lynch, among others, who intended making it a school of industrial arts for boys and girls. The pioneer missionary, Rev. S. S. Harmon, was principal of the school until 1880, when he established a school of his own in Berkeley.

In 1883 Washington College was taken over by the Christian church, and, after 1894, it ceased to exist as a college, but was used as a private school until quite recently. It is now the private home of Miss Anderson, whose father was the last one to carry on a school there. Washington College was typical of the many rural colleges of early California and was a pioneer in industrial education.

SOURCES

[Credit is here given for source material, and permission to quote is hereby acknowledged]

ADAMS, EDSON F. *Oakland's Early History*. Privately published, 1932

AKERS, TOMA ELIZABETH. *Mexican Ranchos in the Vicinity of Mission San Jose*. Master's Thesis, University of California, 1931

BANCROFT, HUBERT HOWE. "California," of the series *History of the Pacific States of North America*. Vols. 18–24. The History Company, San Francisco, 1884–1890

BOLTON, HERBERT EUGENE. *Fray Juan Crespi, Missionary Explorer on the Pacific Coast, 1769–1774*. University of California Press, Berkeley, California, 1927

——. (ed.) *Font's Complete Diary, A Chronicle of the Founding of San Francisco*. Translation from the original Spanish manuscript. University of California Press, Berkeley, California, 1933

——. *Historical Memoirs of New California by Fray Francisco Palou O. F. M.* University of California Press, Berkeley, California, 1926

BOWMAN, J. N. *The Early Peraltas of Rancho San Antonio.* Manuscript, 1932

——. *The Sites of the Peralta Dwellings on Rancho San Antonio.* Manuscript, 1932

——. "New Haven and the Two Alvarados," in *California Historical Society Quarterly*, XII, No. 2, 173–175. San Francisco, 1933

BUNNELL, LAFAYETTE HOUGHTON. *Discovery of the Yosemite*. Fleming H. Revell, Chicago, 1880

DAVIS, WILLIAM HEATH. *Seventy-five Years in California*. Edited by Douglas S. Watson. John Howell, San Francisco, 1929

DE NIER, FLORA LORETTA. *Robert Livermore and the Development of Livermore Valley to 1860*. Master's thesis in history, University of California, Berkeley, California, 1926

DE VERE, DAISY WILLIAMSON. *The Story of Rancho San Antonio.* Oakland, 1924. (Out of print at present but can be found in the Oakland Public Library and at the University of California Library at Berkeley.)

ELDER, DAVID PAUL. *The Old Spanish Missions of California*. Paul Elder & Company, San Francisco, 1913

ENGELHARDT, CHARLES ANTHONY (ZEPHYRIN). *The Missions and Missionaries of California*. 4 vols. San Francisco, 1908–1915

FARQUHAR, FRANCIS P. (ed.). *Up and Down California in 1860–1864, The Journal of William H. Brewer*. Yale University Press, New Haven, 1930

FAULKNER, WILLIAM B. *Faulkner's Handbook and Directory of Murray Township, Alameda County*. Livermore, California, 1886

FERRIER, WILLIAM WARREN. *Origin and Development of the University of California*. Sather Gate Book Shop, Berkeley, California, 1930

——. *The Story of the Naming of Berkeley*. (Pamphlet in the Berkeley City Library.)

GILLOGLY, MRS. LYDIA L. "Report" (on the Lincoln Park Shell Mound) in *Alameda Times-Star*, February 11, 1935

HALLEY, WILLIAM. *The Centennial Year Book of Alameda County, California*. William Halley, Oakland, California, 1876

Historical Atlas of Alameda County, California. Thompson & West, Oakland, California, 1878

History of Alameda County, California. M. W. Wood, Oakland, 1883

History of Washington Township, Alameda County. Compiled and published by the Country Club, the Woman's Club of Washington Township, 1904. (A copy is in the Bancroft Library, at the University of California, Berkeley.)

JONES, WILLIAM CAREY. *History of the University of California, 1868–1895*. Frank H. Dukesmith, San Francisco, 1895

KROEBER, A. L. "California Place Names of Indian Origin," in *University of California Publications in American Archaeology and Ethnology*, Vol. XII, No. 2 (1916–1917). The University Press, Berkeley

LANGSDORFF, G. H. VON. *Narrative of the Rezanoff Voyage*. T. C. Russell, San Francisco, 1927

LOUD, L. L. "The Stege Mounds at Richmond, California," in *University of California Publications in American Archaeology and Ethnology*, Vol. VII, No. 4 (1909). The University Press, Berkeley

McGINTY, RUTH MARY. *Spanish and Mexican Ranchos in the San Francisco Bay Region: San Antonio, San Pablo, and San Leandro*, Master's thesis in history, University of California, Berkeley, California, 1920

NELSON, N. C. "Shellmounds of the San Francisco Bay Region," in *University of California Publications in American Archaeology and Ethnology*, Vol. VII, No. 4, Berkeley, California, 1909

PETERSON, MARTIN S. *Joaquin Miller: Literary Frontiersman*. Stanford University Press, 1937

RIDER, FREMONT (ed.). *Rider's California; a Guide Book for Travelers*. The Macmillan Company, New York, 1925

SANCHEZ, NELLIE VAN DE GRIFT. *Spanish and Indian Place Names of California*. A. M. Robertson, San Francisco, 1922

SCHENK, WILLIAM EGBERT. "The Emeryville Shellmound," in *University of California Publications in American Archaeology and Ethnology*. Vol. XXIII, No. 3. Berkeley, California, 1926

SULLIVAN, MAURICE S. *The Travels of Jedediah Strong Smith, a Documentary Outline Including the Journal of the Great American Pathfinder*. The Fine Arts Press, Santa Ana, California, 1934

UHLE, MAX. "The Emeryville Shellmound," in *University of California Publications in American Archaeology and Ethnology*, Vol. VII, No. 1 (1907). The University Press, Berkeley

WARE, E. B. *History of the Disciples of Christ in California*. F. W. Cooke, Healdsburg, California, 1916

WILLEY, SAMUEL HOPKINS. *A History of the College of California*. Samuel Carson & Company, San Francisco, 1887

WOOD, HARRY O., ALLEN, MAXWELL W., and HECK, N. H. *Destructive and Near Destructive Earthquakes in California and Western Nevada, 1769–1933*. Coast and Geodetic Survey, Special Publication No. 191. U.S. Printing Office, Washington, 1934

WOOD, M. W. *History of Alameda County*. Oakland, 1883

CONTRA COSTA COUNTY

CONTRA COSTA COUNTY was one of the original twenty-seven counties of California, created by act of the legislature on February 18, 1850, and confirmed on April 25, 1851. Its territory included what is now Alameda County until March 23, 1853, but on that date the new county was formed from the southern portion of the original Contra Costa. The town of Martinez has always been the seat of justice of Contra Costa County.

The name Contra Costa, signifying "opposite coast," was in the beginning applied to the whole of the coast which lies due east of San Francisco. The significance of the name was destroyed when that portion directly facing San Francisco was cut off to form Alameda County.

Monte del Diablo

It is doubtful whether any other place name in California has gathered about itself so many legends as has that of Monte del Diablo ("Mountain of the Devil"). Standing out all alone on a great plain and occupying almost the exact center of Contra Costa County, this storied peak is one of the most conspicuous landmarks in the state because of its isolation. The rugged grandeur of the great mountain and the strange, fantastic natural formations with which the region abounds gave rise, in earlier days, to many legends all bordering on the marvelous or diabolical. It was regarded by the Indians of the region as the home of the Puy, or devil, and their medicine men claimed to be agents of the spirit of the mountain.

General Mariano G. Vallejo in his report to the legislature, April 16, 1850, gives the following story of the derivation of the name in its Spanish form: "In 1806 a military expedition from San Francisco marched against the tribe 'Bolgones,' who were encamped at the foot of the mount; the Indians were prepared to receive the expedition, and a hot engagement ensued in the large hollow fronting the western side of the mount. As the victory was about to be decided in favor of the Indians, an unknown personage, decorated with the most extraordinary plumage and making divers movements, suddenly appeared near the combatants. The Indians were victorious and the incognito [Puy] departed towards the mount. The defeated soldiers, on ascertaining that the spirit went through the same ceremony daily and at all hours, named the mount 'Diablo,' in allusion to its mysterious inhabitant, that continued thus to make his appearance until the tribe was subdued by the troops in command of Lieutenant Gabriel Moraga, in a second campaign of the same year. In the aboriginal tongue 'Puy' signifies 'Evil Spirit'; in Spanish it means 'Diablo,' and doubtless it signifies 'Devil' in the Anglo-American language."

General Vallejo's explanation of the origin of this intriguing place name seems the most plausible of the many thus far presented, for, as Mrs. Sanchez says, "it is quite likely that the Puy, or devil, was one of the 'medicine men' who played upon the superstitions of the Indians by pretending to be the 'spirit of the mountain.'"

An attempt was made by the legislature in 1865–1866 to change the name of Mount Diablo; this they could not do, however, for, when they undertook to rename one of California's grandest mountains they found that the people would not accept the change. The legislature might say "Coal Hill," but the people continued to say "Mount Diablo," and Diablo it has remained.

The mountain was a landmark for explorers and pioneers from the earliest days. In the spring of 1772 Pedro Fages and his trail blazers skirted the western side of the mountain, the first white men to touch its flowery slopes. During the spring of 1776, Juan Bautista de Anza also passed that way, after retracing Fages' steps as far as the junction of the Sacramento and San Joaquin rivers. Dr. John Marsh was led in 1836 by the great mountain to his rancho at its base. By it the Bidwell-Bartleson company, the first overland emigrant train to enter California by way of the Sierra Nevada, was guided in 1841 to Dr. Marsh's estate. Standing up boldly in splendid isolation from a broad, level plain without other mountains to limit its height, a view of Mount Diablo is easily recognizable from a great distance by its double summit and regular conical outline, resembling that of a volcano. The view from its highest peak, 3,849 feet above the sea, is magnificent.

A government cabin and telescope were placed on the summit of Mount Diablo in 1851. This ancient landmark was chosen in that year as the base point for United States surveys in California and was established as such by Colonel Ransome. A plaque, placed on the crest of the mountain years ago, commemorates the act. With the exception of southern California and of the Humboldt district, the locations of all lands in the state are determined by their situation with reference to the Mount Diablo "base and meridian" lines.

When the advance party of the Whitney Survey passed through Pacheco Valley in the spring of 1862 en route to Mount Diablo, the fields were studded with magnificent white oaks (*Quercus hindsu hindsii*), "their great spreading branches," writes Brewer, "often forming a head a hundred feet in diameter . . . . Across this great park the trail ran."

Camp was pitched on May 6 "in one of the loveliest localities, a pure rippling stream for water, plenty of wood, fine oaks around"; and behind it Mount Diablo rose grandly, its summit "burning with the Tyrian fire of evening." The village of Clayton—with tavern, store, etc.—stood scarce twenty rods from the camp site. The discovery of coal in the region had caused the settlement to spring up only a few months previous.

Toward evening Professor Whitney joined his men at this delightful spot. Thomas Starr King and other guests from San Francisco were with him. Here in the mild May evening, the party sat about a blazing campfire telling stories and marveling at the beauty of the majestic peak.

Very early in the morning of May 7, five of the Whitney party, with their guests, climbed the mountain. The day was one of those rare, crystal-clear days when the view from the summit stretched in unobstructed and undimmed splendor for hundreds of miles. "Probably but few views in North America," says Brewer, "are more extensive—certainly nothing in Europe . . . . I made an estimate from the map, based on the distances to known peaks, and found that the extent of land and sea embraced between the extreme limits of vision amounted to eighty thousand square miles, and that forty thousand square miles, or more, were spread out in tolerably plain view—over 300 miles from north to south, and 260 to 280 miles from east to west, between the extreme points."

The Whitney party remaining in the region until May 28, made scientific investigations and measurements both of the main crest and of the northeast peak which lies about 300 feet lower. The latter was named Mount King by the Whitney party, but the name did not persist and it is now known as Eagle Point. The two cones are separated by a wild and picturesque gap, through which "the wind roared with a violence almost terrific at times . . . . and at intervals the clouds rushed through like a torrent . . . . [It was] a peculiarly grand spot . . . . because of the surrounding rocks and the clouds which rushed among them."

The superb beauty of Mount Diablo, the loveliness of its wildflower gardens, and its profuse scattering of juniper, nut pine, oak, sycamore, and other trees very early attracted nature lovers as well as the scientific explorer to its craggy summits. Two good wagon roads were laid out in early days, one from Concord to the northwest and the other from Danville on the south side of the mountain, and two stages ran daily to the Mountain House.

This famous old hostelry was erected one mile below the summit, because the last mile was too steep for vehicles to traverse. The two roads met about three hundred feet southwest of a spring, from which a good-sized stream issued and ran down the mountainside to cross and recross the Concord road before joining the waters of Silver Creek above the head of Pine Canyon.

Travelers from many parts of the world found their way to the Mountain House and signed their names on its register. Sometimes they remained for several days or even weeks, resting in the shade of the giant oak at the doorway, admiring the magnificent views on every hand, or on foot or on horseback taking the trail which led to the summit with its never-to-be-forgotten panorama.

The government cabin burned in the early '90's, and for a time the mountain lost some of its popularity. Later, after the roads were abandoned, it was shut away from the public and the old Mountain House was burned by ranchers who did not wish visitors crossing their lands. The site is still marked by the eucalyptus tree and the century plant which grew a few feet west of the house. The glories of Mount Diablo were again made accessible to the public on April 26, 1931, when it was made a part of the state park system.

Thus Diablo, an object of worship to an ancient people, has long been a landmark for trail breakers, gold seekers, and home makers, and the mecca of nature lovers. Today, a powerful revolving beacon light on its summit guides the modern airplane in safety through the night, a fitting climax to the services of this picturesque mountain through the hundred and fifty years and more since the coming of Fages and Juan Bautista de Anza.

The Ellis Landing Shell Mound

One of the largest of the four hundred and more shell mounds or kitchen middens which existed in the San Francisco Bay region when the first white men came to its shores was located within the present city limits of Richmond at the foot of what is now Eleventh Street. As it extended across the marsh, Twelfth Street intersects the old mound site.

A large part of the Ellis Landing Shell Mound, as it was long called by Americans, was removed for grading purposes in 1907, and the final leveling took place in 1924. Like the one at Emeryville in Alameda County, this mound is of particular significance both on account of its unusual size and because of the extensive scientific explorations which were made there by the Department of Archaeology of the University of California. During the years 1906–1908, a detailed study and report of this and other mounds was made by N. C. Nelson, and for two weeks in 1907 extensive scientific excavations were made. At that time about 67,500 cubic feet of material were removed, while 265 artifacts and 126 human skeletons were uncovered.

Before civilized man began to tear down the ancient pile, it measured 460 feet in length, 250 feet in width, and about 30 feet in height, and its volume approximated 1,260,000 cubic feet. Scientists estimate that the process of accumulation extended over a period of from three to four thousand years. It consisted largely of broken shells, principally of the common clam and mussel variety mixed sparingly with oyster, cockle, and abalone shells. Many broken rocks, pebbles, ashes, artifacts, etc., were also found.

Fifteen house pits were visible upon the heap before it was leveled. These, together with the large number of human skeletons found there, indicate that the site was used both as a residence and as a burial place.

"The first inhabitants, however ancient they may have been," writes Nelson, "possessed some roughly made stone implements; they prepared vegetable foods; they knew the use of fire; and they painted and buried their dead. The last people to dwell on the mound had, besides . . . . well-made stone implements, quite a variety of bone tools as well as several forms of ornaments made of bone and shell. There is reason to believe that they tried to fashion vessels and other objects out of clay, and that they made baskets and dressed skins. They were skilled hunters by land and sea, and consequently must have had boats of some sort.

"Progress toward perfection of manufacture is generally marked; but aside from these normal changes there are no important breaks in the culture represented . . . . If more than one people have lived on the mound . . . . they were all essentially of the same type of culture, and the last occupants of the shellmound at Ellis Landing were probably Indians similar to those that have lived in middle California within historic times."

The Ellis Landing camp site seems to have afforded few of the advantages usually sought by the mound dwellers. In summer there was no fresh water for drinking, and, except for drift, there was no firewood, while at all times the location was exposed to strong winds. Since it lay on the shore edge directly north of Brooks Island with six hundred yards of marshland at its back, access to it was difficult; and at high tide on stormy winter days it became an island completely surrounded by water.

It seems reasonable to suppose that autumn was the most likely season for aboriginal hunters to visit the site, for then the thick, low growth of *Baccharis Douglasii*, which covered it, formed coverts for numerous wild fowl. It was during the autumn hunting season, too, that white men in recent times have made the place their rendezvous for the same reason.

The natural barriers about the shell heap long served to protect it from the plow, which has wrought havoc with many of these deposits. Mr. Ellis, who lived at the Landing for about forty years, stated that as late as 1890 the mound was still intact. His father ran a small canal from one of the marsh creeks up close to the mound on the landward side and began hauling away its rich and ancient soil.

Before man began its destruction, however, nature had already made telling inroads upon the mound. Because the base of the pile is from 11 to 18 feet below sea level before the leveling, the encroaching tides were yearly undermining the steep sea wall and were fast destroying the deposit itself. Since it rests upon solid gravel but is more than half buried in fine silt, Nelson estimated that "the region has sunk at least eighteen feet since the ancient inhabitants began to accumulate the refuse deposit."

The Ford Motor Company factory stands on filled land just beyond the spot where the midden for ages had faced the open waters of the Bay.

Shell Mounds at Stege

Four moderate-sized shell mounds could still be seen at Stege within the city limits of Richmond before 1915. These mounds were located on or near the Bay shore in the Harborgate Tract, the largest of the group lying within the block bounded by the present water front, Twenty-seventh, Montgomery, and Twenty-eighth streets, while the smaller mound, which measured about 240 by 160 feet, stood at the foot of Twenty-fifth Street.

A third deposit, covering an area about 350 by 250 feet, paralleled the head of a small slough which ran between the largest and the smallest mounds of the group. Across a small salt-water slough in the Owens Addition a third site was situated two or three hundred feet north of the first shell heap. This deposit was leveled before 1915.

A real estate company laid out and graded the streets in the Harborgate Tract in the autumn of 1915. At that time Llewellyn L. Loud and Leonard Outhwaite observed operations, and about 500 artifacts were secured. The tract has never been improved, and the sites of the ancient kitchen middens are easily traced. These mounds, of course, were used as burial places.

The Great Discovery

The Pedro Fages expedition continued in the latter part of March 1772 up the Contra Costa in search of a land route to Point Reyes. Leaving their camp on Strawberry Creek in Alameda County and continuing past the sites of Berkeley and Albany on the 28th, the little band turned into the Contra Costa County hills and descended past them into the arroyo which we know as Wildcat Creek. At the Indian village on its banks, the strangers were met in a most friendly manner by the natives, who expressed pleasure with their coming by presenting them with generous gifts of "cacomites, amoles, and two dead geese, dried and stuffed with grass to use as decoys." The white men reciprocated by offerings of colored beads, which were eagerly sought after by the Indians.

Four more arroyos "with running water" were passed before Fages at length halted his men on the bank of a fifth stream "at the foot of some hills." Before them "lay a large round bay, which resembles a great lake," wrote Fray Juan Crespi. This was San Pablo Bay, and in it they saw Mare Island close to the opposite shore. Camp was made at or near Pinole.

On the following day the explorers climbed the hills which come down close to the shore of San Pablo Bay, still confident that they could reach Point Reyes from this place. To their disappointment they found the passage completely shut off by Carquinez Strait. All day they trekked across the hills and gullies of the rough region above the strait, passing "five large villages of very mild heathen . . . . [where they] were well received . . . . and presented with some of their wild food." Many other villages could be made out on the opposite shore.

"According to scientists," says Mrs. Sanchez, "the name Carquinez is derived from Karkin, the name of an Indian village in that region . . . . Fray José Viader, diarist of the Moraga expedition of 1810 . . . . [and] other diarists speak of this Indian village and tribe under the name of the Carquines, making it fairly certain that the origin of the name is Indian." Crespi called it the Rio de San Francisco.

Breaking camp near Martinez on March 30, the party crossed a deep arroyo "well grown with oaks, cottonwoods, alders, and laurels," which, says Professor Bolton, was probably Pacheco Creek. After it had been left behind, the expedition entered the broad, oak-studded Concord Valley, called by Crespi, Santa Angela de Fulgino. The good Father thought that the valley seemed an excellent place for a settlement. Two native villages were seen in this neighborhood.

Leaving the valley behind them, the little cavalcade pressed eagerly forward over the western spur of Monte del Diablo. From one of the high hills of the range they gazed out across a vast new territory never before looked upon by any European. Before them lay the great Sacramento Valley, the San Joaquin and the Sacramento rivers, which converge at the head of Suisun Bay, and, far away to the southeast, "some high mountains," which doubtless were the great Sierra Nevada.

Thus the trail had been blazed through the Contra Costa; and, although the specific goal of the expedition was never attained, a discovery of far-reaching magnitude had been made. The vast inland empire of Alta California with its great intersecting watercourses had been opened to future exploration and ultimate settlement.

Camp on this eventful evening was probably pitched "westward of Antioch, near Pittsburg." "From this place," wrote Crespi, "we decided to return to . . . . Monterey, in view of the fact that our passage to Point Reyes . . . . was cut off by these rivers . . . ." Before turning back, however, the expedition "went ten leagues from Pacheco Creek, reaching the Indian village near Antioch," says Bolton.

Camp near the San Joaquin River was broken early the next morning, the range was crossed north of Mount Diablo, and Concord Valley was re-entered north of Clayton. Continuing west to Walnut Creek, the party turned southeast and

proceeded past the site of Danville through the San Ramon Valley. Camp was set just south of Danville.

Early on the first day of April, Fages and his men traveled southward through the San Ramón Valley and on into Livermore Valley, passing "many and good arroyos, and with numerous villages of very gentle and peaceful heathen . . . . It is a very suitable place," Crespi's diary records, "for a good mission, having good lands, much water, firewood and many heathen."

In the Footsteps of Pedro Fages

On April 1, 1776, Fray Pedro Font mapped, from his position east of Richmond, the Richmond Peninsula, which he took to be an island, for Juan Bautista de Anza on that epoch-making march up the Contra Costa. On the banks of Wildcat Creek (the "rather deep arroyo with a growth of trees and little water"), the party came upon an abandoned Indian village. Crossing the creek near San Pablo, they came to a second arroyo with a "very deep" bed and a "heavy growth of live oaks, sycamores, and other trees." Here they found a native village where they were greeted by some twenty-three men and seven women, who presented the travelers with a feast of roasted "cacomites" (a species of iris) in exchange for the coveted glass beads which Anza gave them.

More hills and two or three small arroyos were passed, and another village of friendly Indians greeted them. At nightfall the wayfarers came to a "high hill" from which a wide expanse of the Bay could be seen and the low murmur of waves on the shore could be heard. This, says Bolton, was evidently one of the hills at the edge of Rodeo. Camp was made at Rodeo on Rodeo Creek.

At sunrise on the morning of April 2 the camp was visited very early by a delegation of some ten Indians from a village near by. They came singing and dancing and bearing little gifts of cacomites and chuchupate roots. After Mass had been said, Anza accepted the invitation of his strange visitors to go to their village. Still singing and dancing, they led the way, the good padre now and then interrupting their demonstration by chanting the Alabado.

The village, which was soon reached, stood in a little valley on the bank of a small arroyo at about the site of the present Tormey. The Indians welcomed their guests "with an indescribable hullabaloo"; and, with the strangest of peace banners fashioned of feathers and the skins of rabbits, they led the white men to the plaza, a level spot in the center of the village, where the singers resumed the dance of welcome accompanied by "much clatter and yelling." After an exchange of gifts, Anza and his men continued their journey, apparently to the sorrow of the villagers.

The next halt was made just east of Selby and west of Carquinez Bridge. Here "at the shore of the water near to and inside the Boca del Puerto Dulce," longitudinal measurements were taken, and Father Font devoted himself to a diligent refutation of previous reports made by Fages and Crespi "that Carquinez Strait and Suisun Bay constituted a Rio Grande." At this point, too, they found Indians fishing with nets from "launches" or rafts, in which the fishermen afterward crossed to the opposite shore.

The next lap of the journey followed the line of the present highway from Selby to Martinez. Professor Bolton outlines the route thus:

"Two leagues along the top of the hills took them nearly to Port Costa, where the road forks half a mile from town. From here the highway follows a canyon for two and one-half miles and comes out at the coast opposite the Benicia ferry station, which evidently is built on the very farallon which Font describes." At this point the explorers looked across the long sweep of Suisun Bay to "an immense plain without any trees, through which the water extends for a long distance." They were looking upon the great interior rivers and valleys of the Sacramento and the San Joaquin, beyond which lies the Sierra Nevada.

Dropping down to the Martinez Valley, where the Indians from across the strait joined them, the little band continued southeast along the highway that goes to Walnut Creek (Santa Angela de Fulgino). Camp was made at about Pacheco on the edge of Concord Valley and somewhat more than a league from the Puerto Dulce. Father Crespi had thought that this pretty wooded vale should be an attractive place for a Mission if the arroyo had promised permanent water, but not enough was at hand.

April 3 "dawned very fair and warm but with a pleasant northwest wind blowing." After Mass, the cavalcade moved forward ten leagues to Antioch Bridge. "Leaving camp, they passed the site of Concord, ascended a canyon (Willow Pass) to the top of the ridge [from which they again saw the Sierra Nevada], descending on the east side, and continued to an Indian village on the site of Antioch, swung southeast a league to or beyond Oak Grove Cemetery, and then northeast a league to the bank of San Joaquin River near Antioch Bridge where camp was made." Here the tule marsh which still covers the river bank at this point caused the party to turn west about a quarter of a league to the site of an abandoned Indian village. Font's observations here further convinced him that what he saw (the San Joaquin River) was a "fresh water sea," rather than a river, as Fages and Crespi believed.

Nevertheless, the commander of the expedition determined to follow the watercourse, to cross the plain, and to explore in the direction of the Sierra Nevada. With this purpose in view, he set out on April 4 in the general direction but "to the left of the highway that runs from Antioch through Knightsen to Tracy. Just east of the starting point," continues Professor Bolton, "was the large marsh east of Antioch Bridge. Leaving the river, therefore, Anza swung southeastwardly past Oakley, keeping on the right the live oaks which continue to Knightsen, then suddenly disappear. At a point not far from Knightsen, Anza swung northeast for a league but encountered the tulares, perhaps at Rock Slough."

Escaping not without difficulty from the mire of the treacherous tules, the weary soldiers trudged through the blinding, wind-blown dust of the dry swamps eastward of Byron Hot Springs. The general course of the Old River was followed some six leagues to a point just south of Bethany (in Alameda County), where Anza finally abandoned his decision to approach the Sierra Nevada and decided to return to Monterey instead.

Rancho San Pablo and El Cerrito Adobe

Set in a sloping garden shaded by cedar and cypress trees, the venerable Castro adobe at El Cerrito still stands on the east side of San Pablo Avenue near the north bank of El Cerrito Creek, which here forms the northern boundary line of Contra Costa and Alameda counties. To the west rises El Cerrito Hill, long a landmark for early travelers and settlers along the northwest shore of the Contra Costa. This hill, round and smooth and high, cast a bold silhouette against the sky in the old days before it was planted with eucalypti and constituted one of the more substantial and permanent designations of the boundary line between Rancho San Pablo and its neighbor to the south, Rancho San Antonio.

The historic El Cerrito adobe is one of two remaining adobes built by the Castro family on Rancho San Pablo. The low southern wing, which is the older portion of the building, is thought to have been constructed by Francisco Castro, while

the two-story section, with its broad balconies sweeping across the front and rear, was erected some time in the '50's by Victor Castro, the youngest of the seven sons of Don Francisco.

The most unique addition to the old house was the little chapel at the north wing, in which the padres periodically celebrated Mass for the family, their Indian servants, and occasional guests from neighboring ranchos. In rancho days, the hacienda was enclosed by a high wall which served as a protection from wild animals or marauding Indians. Today, only a small flower shop stands between the quiet of the aged dwelling and the noise and hurry of the great modern highway at its door. A small garden patio at the rear of the adobe shelters the one-time burial plot of the Castro family.

Francisco María Castro, a native of Mexico, was a settler at San Francisco in 1800. For thirteen years he served his country as a soldier, and in 1822 was a member of the *diputación*. In June 1823 he acted as *diputado* of the exploring expedition led by Padre José Altimira north of San Francisco Bay, and in that year also he obtained the grant of Rancho San Pablo on the Contra Costa, provisionally.

As early as 1826, Francisco Castro had taken up his residence on this land, and there he lived until his death in 1831, three years before the official confirmation of the grant in 1834. The estate was left half to the widow of Don Francisco and half to his eleven children. Through years of litigation during which, says Bancroft, the whole Castro family was "kept in a state of landed poverty," the vast grant gradually dwindled to a few acres about the homesteads of El Cerrito and San Pablo.

Finally, through deaths and other circumstances, Señora Gabriela Castro received the adobe at El Cerrito with two hundred acres of land lying between Wildcat and El Cerrito creeks. Descendants of the original builder are still in possession of the adobe, one of the few old Spanish residences to retain that distinction.

The pastoral lands once occupied by the great rancho are now covered by miles of residences and paved highways, humming with the noise of commerce and of pleasure. The towns of El Cerrito and San Pablo and the city of Richmond have grown up around the old pioneer settlements, while the two aged adobes, almost alone of all the old landmarks in the vicinity, look upon the pageantry of another day and play new and strange roles in its changing scenes.

The San Pablo Adobe

Rancho San Pablo, at first called Rancho Cochiyumes, consisted of four leagues of land bordered on the west and north by the bays of San Francisco and San Pablo, and on the east by low verdant hills. There were no fences on all its vast acres and no roads; only divergent trails twisted through the wild oats which stretched like a vast sea on all sides. Here and there the tract was dotted by islands of huge oak trees. Numerous wild creatures made it their home, bears and coyotes, and herds of deer and elk.

Into this wilderness Don Francisco Castro drove the first herd of cattle north of Rancho San Antonio, and, like the herds of the Peraltas, it soon multiplied into roving bands of untamed animals which supplied the rancho with food and the Yankee traders with hides and tallow.

Here, too, the first fruit trees in the country and grape cuttings from the Mission were set out. About 1838 one of the sons of Don Francisco Castro built an adobe dwelling on the corner of what is now San Pablo Avenue and Church Street in the town of San Pablo. It is still standing. From all outward appearances, one would never suspect that a remnant of Spanish days still lingers behind those unpromising walls, for a grocery store occupies the front of the lot, and the old adobe, covered over with a wooden superstructure, is used as a storeroom.

Martina, daughter of Francisco Castro, married Governor Juan Bautista Alvarado in 1839, and through this marriage the Governor came into possession of that portion of the estate to which Martina fell heir at her father's death. This included the adobe at San Pablo, and to this spot the world-weary governor retired in 1848, remaining there until his death, July 13, 1882. Gradually, the vast acreage had been relinquished until, at the time of his death, only about fifty acres of the princely estate which once surrounded the old homestead remained.

From a contemporary description, one may still identify a few of the landscape features which once beautified the Alvarado house and garden: a portion of the old orchard, the outside staircase leading to the attic, and the patio garden with its French gateway and a remnant of tangled shrubbery.

In 1882 the house stood at the end of a "winding country road," which, wrote a historian of that day, "leads to the place, through hay-fields most of the way, and stops in front of the romantic old house. At present the house stands about thirty feet back from the road. . . .

"The house is one story in height, and is . . . . long and low, after the manner of old Californian houses. Across the outer front, about one hundred feet wide, and around the northern side and rear, is a broad porch. Over this grapevines and climbing roses trail in the wildest disorder, running up to the roof . . . . and trying to force an entrance to the low windows. The walls are about two feet thick. . . . . On the outside is a stairway which leads to the attic above. Huge roof joists of hewn timber project at both ends of the house and support the broad eaves.

"Many improvements were made by the Alvarados. The adobe walls were covered with clap-boards, and the interior was improved in many ways. The entire yard is overrun with shrubbery and flowering plants. Over the front paths and winding walks about the house are low arbors covered with grapevines [said to have been the work of a French carpenter brought from France by Governor Alvarado]. Traces of former taste and care are visible in the arrangement of the yard, but now [1882] weeds and thistles are among the flowers, and a general appearance of ruin and neglect is about the place.

"Near the house is an old orchard of many hundred bearing trees. In the rear are old sheds and yards for poultry, and nearby is the stable with tumble-down 'lean-tos' about it."

Rancho San Ramón

The vast acreage of Rancho San Ramón, granted to José María Amador by Governor Figueroa in 1834 and 1835, lay mostly within Contra Costa County, after Alameda County was separated from it in 1853. This portion of the great rancho consisted of four square leagues. Two leagues were granted to Bartolo Pacheco and Mariano Castro together on June 5, 1833, but this land soon passed into other hands. Leo Norris, a native of Kentucky who had come across the Plains to California from Missouri in 1846, filed claim for one square league which he purchased from Amador, and this was confirmed and later patented to him.

Evidently the first white settlers on Rancho San Ramón north of the county boundary line were Mariano Castro and Bartolo Pacheco. The latter was a Mexican soldier, who occupied in 1832 a tract of land by permission of Amador (according to Munro-Fraser). This land later came into the possession of Leo Norris. When Norris came to the rancho in the autumn of 1850, he found a branch of the Soto family residing in an adobe house then standing about a hundred and fifty yards from the site of his residence. Since Bancroft

states that the wife of Bartolo Pacheco was a Soto, we may therefore infer that this was the family of which Munro-Fraser speaks. However, the Pacheco-Sotos remained for only a month or two after the arrival of Norris.

Leo Norris moved to Misión San José in June 1847, remaining there until the early autumn of 1850, when he and his son William migrated to the San Ramón Valley. With them went their cousin, William Lynch, a native of New York, who had landed in San Francisco on June 28, 1849, from the pilot boat "W. A. Hackstaff." Lynch was a journeyman carpenter and practiced his trade in San Francisco before going out to the fertile valley of San Ramón, where he aided Norris in erecting his house, the first frame dwelling in the valley. It was constructed from lumber hauled from the San Antonio redwoods by the long and tedious route through Misión San José, Suñol Valley, and Amador's (now Dublin). In spite of this roundabout journey, the house was ready for occupancy before the winter. The old Norris dwelling, which stands on Norris Road at the mouth of Norris Canyon about half a mile west of the Amador Valley highway, is still the home of descendants of Leo Norris, the pioneer.

In the spring of 1851, Mr. Norris fenced the field at the rear of the Lynch house. The fence posts were willow saplings taken from the banks of the adjacent stream. The willows took root and grew, and some of these giant trees may still be seen back of the old Lynch house.

Other American pioneers purchased portions of Rancho San Ramón. Joel Harlan, a native of Indiana, came to California with his parents in the spring of 1846. After a trip to the mines, followed by his marriage in April 1849, Joel Harlan lived at different times in Napa City, Sacramento, San Francisco, San José, and San Lorenzo in Alameda County, where he was the first settler.

Finally, in 1852, Mr. Harlan purchased a tract of land on Rancho San Ramón in Contra Costa County. There he erected a dwelling, which, when the county of Alameda was carved out of the older county, was one of the points defining the boundary line between the two counties. Notwithstanding the unique, if somewhat indefinite, position of his house, Mr. Harlan always maintained that it stood on the Contra Costa side of the line. A huge oak tree standing in the corner of the original Harlan yard long served as a landmark. The spot is now marked by the iron milepost erected on the county line by Elisha Harlan and his mother, Mrs. Joel Harlan.

Approximately two thousand acres purchased from the Norris tract were added to the Harlan estate in 1856. The following year the old house at the county boundary line was removed to a site two miles south of the village of San Ramón, and there in 1858 Harlan built the fine old country mansion now known as El Nido ("The Nest"). The original dwelling was incorporated into a wing of the two-story edifice.

El Nido stands back from the highway almost completely hidden in a leafy bower of many kinds of trees and shrubs which create a vivid contrast with the gleaming white of the house and fences. Through the ornamental gateway one peers down a stately row of Italian cypress trees to the white gabled house at the end of the path. Descendants of the genial, upright, and kindly Joel Harlan still occupy and cherish the old house and its lovely garden.

Another early settler who purchased a portion of Rancho San Ramón was David Glass, a native of Pennsylvania, who had arrived with his family in California from Iowa on August 1, 1850. After a short stay in Placerville, he came direct to Contra Costa County, where he settled in November of that year in the vicinity of Walnut Creek. It was not until some nine years later that he purchased the ranch of 718 acres located three miles south of San Ramón. The original

Glass house, built on this site, stands just to the north of the later two-story residence built in the '80's and now known as the Farm House Inn.

Alamo

The village of Alamo, located on the northern portion of Rancho San Ramón two miles north of Danville, is essentially of Spanish origin. The name, which in that language signifies "poplar," was bestowed upon it because poplar trees once grew abundantly in the valley and along its streams. Giant maple trees on either side of Alamo's main street (which is also the highway) maintain the dignity and charm of the little settlement, while a few of the old houses dating from the '50's and '60's linger beneath their shadows.

On the southeast corner of the Mount Diablo Road, where it joins the highway, is the old Henry Hotel, once used by a Japanese detachment of the Salvation Army. In 1854 a portion of this structure housed the Wolf store, one of the two first stores in Alamo. At about the same time George Englemore started Alamo's other "first" store on the opposite corner of the Mount Diablo Road, and in 1854 these two establishments composed the village. They drew a large trade from the Spanish population of the neighborhood, the García's to the east, the Romero's to the west, and others who were interested in the San Ramón grant. With the coming of the Americans, this picturesque Spanish-Mexican element gradually disappeared.

An adobe was built on the site of Alamo about 1848 or 1849, and in it the first post office was located with John W. Jones as postmaster. The old Annie Humberg house now stands on the site. John Jones, a native of Kentucky, was one of those typical pioneers of the early nineteenth century who, constantly pushing westward, at last crossed the Plains with ox teams, bound for the Golden State. After a journey of six months he arrived with his family at his brother s farm in Lafayette in August or September 1853. He remained there for a year. In October 1855 Mr. Jones purchased 310 acres of land lying one mile southwest of Walnut Grove.

On the west side of the highway in Alamo, the old Foster home, built in the '50's by James Foster, still stands, although it is in very bad condition. This house was constructed of lumber shipped around the Horn from Maine, Foster's native state. Mr. Foster, a millwright by trade, came to California in 1856 via Panama. He followed his trade among the redwood forests of San Mateo County until February 1857, when he went to Placer County to build a gristmill on Bear River near Auburn. In the autumn of 1857 he came to Contra Costa County, opened a wheelwright shop in Alamo, and sent East for his wife and children.

James Foster lived in Alamo until 1881. Always an active man, he not only practiced his trade for twelve years in that place but was postmaster during most of his stay there, was justice of the peace from 1860 to 1868, served as County Assessor from 1869 to 1879, was admitted to the bar in 1872, and acted as referee at various times in important land-grant suits. Mr. Foster sold his property in Alamo in 1881 and purchased a block in Walnut Creek, where he built a fine home and became senior member of Foster and Stow, realtors. His son, Fred Lewis Foster, became one of the proprietors and junior associate editor of the *Contra Costa Gazette*. The Foster house, with its sturdy Maine origins, is worthy of preservation as a memorial to the vigor and sterling ingenuity of one of California's pioneers.

The cornerstone of an academy was laid on October 19, 1859, about one and one-half miles south of Alamo, under the auspices of the Contra Costa Educational Association. The site is on the west side of the present highway just south of and adjoining the property of Charles W. Pangburn. A marker reads: "Site of the Union Academy established 1860. Board of Trustees: Silas Stone, John M. Jones, Robert Love; Principal, David McClure."

The first master of this short-lived educational venture was the Rev. David McClure, who conducted the first services of the Presbyterian Church to be held in the San Ramón Valley in 1857. Rev. Mr. McClure later became principal of the California Military Academy in Oakland and was succeeded at the Union Academy by Professor J. H. Braly, later of the San Jose State Normal School, and, in turn, by a Rev. Mr. King. In 1868, during Mr. King's administration, the building burned. It was never rebuilt.

The García Adobe

The portion of Rancho San Ramón which lies immediately to the east of Alamo is still known as the Stone Ranch. There, in 1850, Francisco García lived in the old adobe, the crumbling ruins of which stood until about 1935 on the hill below the former Stone residence.

Albert W. Stone, a native of Pennsylvania and a blacksmith by trade, had come to California from Iowa in September 1852. After returning to Iowa the following year, he again crossed the Plains to California, this time with his family. For a while he lived in Colusa County on land later occupied by Dr. Glenn, but in January 1858 he moved to Contra Costa County, where he purchased the farm of 800 acres adjoining Alamo. The family lived temporarily in the García adobe, but very soon the one-story frame house which stands one-half mile to the east was built of redwood timbers from the Palos Colorados of San Antonio. Descendants still occupy the sturdy pioneer dwelling. The later two-story house built on the hill above the adobe has recently passed out of the hands of the family.

Limerick (San Ramón)

The northern boundary of the Norris division of Rancho San Ramón may be located by the little shoe store at the present village of San Ramón. Originally known as Lynchville, San Ramón (like Dublin to the south) long retained its Irish sobriquet of Limerick because the settlers of the vicinity were primarily of that nationality.

The first house to be erected on the site of San Ramón was put up by John White in 1852. No other was built there until 1857, when Eli Brewin constructed a smithy. Very few additions were made to the settlement until April 22, 1860, when a Catholic church was dedicated to St. Ramón. With the coming of stores and homes, the citizens secured a post office on which the name of San Ramón was bestowed, although it continued to be known popularly as Limerick for some time.

Danville

Men have said that Danville was named for Daniel Inman, the pioneer who formerly owned the land on which the village now stands. In a way it was, but the whole story, as told in the *Danville Sentinel* of 1898, reveals a happy coincidence which satisfied a personal wish and also honored a favorite son. The clipping quotes Mr. Inman's version of the story of the name as follows:

"I reached Danville, or the site where it now stands, in June, 1852. I spent the summer in the valley, but returned to the mines in the fall. In the summer of 1853 I came into the valley again and remained until 1857, when I returned to the mines. In March of the following year I came into the valley once more—this time for good—and purchased a farm, where Danville is now located, of a man named Pigmore.

"I went to farming and seeded the lands with wheat that winter. In the summer of 1859 a man named Davis came along and wanted to start a blacksmith shop where the one now stands (Close's shop), and I gave him permission to do so."

With the increased life and activity, "the people," continued Inman, "wanted a post-office. Of course it had to have a name, and quite a number were suggested. At first they thought of calling it 'Inmanville,' but my brother Andrew and I objected to that.

"Finally, 'Grandma' Young, my brother's mother-in-law, said: 'Call it Danville,' and as much or more out of respect to her, as she was born and raised near Danville, Kentucky, it took that name."

About the year 1858 H. W. Davis opened the Danville Hotel (burned in 1873). It stood at the junction of the Tassajara Road and the San Ramón Valley highway. In this same year, S. Wolf, M. Cohen, and Henry Hoffman dissolved the firm of Wolf and Company at Alamo and opened a store in Danville.

Rancho Acalanes

Rancho Acalanes, lying among the fertile little valleys west of Lafayette, was granted on August 1, 1834, to Candelario Valencia, a soldier of the San Francisco Company. The name, says Kroeber, was probably derived from "Akalan" (or something similar), the name of a Costanoan Indian village in the vicinity, which was dignified by the Spaniards into the Acalanes "tribe."

Like many another native Californian of the old Spanish and Mexican regime, Valencia eventually became indebted to a foreigner and, being unable to clear himself of entanglements, was forced to sell his land. Thus it was that Rancho Acalanes fell into the hands of William A. Leidesdorff of Yerba Buena, who put it up for sale.

Meanwhile, Elam Brown, a native of New York, had arrived in California on October 10, 1846, as captain of a company of fourteen families and sixteen wagons which apparently had crossed the mountains in company with the Boggs and Cooper parties. Mr. Brown spent his first summer in California whipsawing lumber in the San Antonio redwoods and hauling it to the old San Antonio Landing, where it was shipped across the Bay to San Francisco. Learning that Rancho Acalanes was for sale, Brown purchased it from Leidesdorff, together with three hundred cows which the latter had obtained from Vasquez at Half Moon Bay.

Brown took his family through the Moraga Valley to their new home, where they arrived on February 7, 1848. They were the second American family to settle in Contra Costa County. A rude temporary dwelling was put up that same evening. Very soon, however, a more substantial frame house was built of lumber which Brown had cut and fitted for use in the redwoods of San Antonio.

The first site of this pioneer homestead was about two miles from the present town of Lafayette, on land later owned by Thomas W. Bradley. When water failed at this point, Brown was forced to move to another site. A like circumstance occurred again before he was permanently located. The final site of Elam Brown's home in Lafayette is still pointed out by the older residents of the town and is marked by immense black walnut trees planted by the pioneer.

When Mr. Brown came to his ranch he had to make long, tedious trips on horseback or by ox team via the San Ramón Valley in order to carry his wheat and barley to Sansevain's mill in San José, where it was turned into flour. To eliminate the necessity for this trip, Brown purchased a horsepower mill at Benicia in 1849 and set it up near his house. This little mill was superseded in the summer of 1853 by the gristmill which Mr. Brown constructed near the site of the present Pat Medau house in Lafayette.

Elam Brown was fo many years a respected and prosper-ous citizen of Contra Costa County. He was a member of the Convention that framed the State Constitution in 1849 and also of the first two legislatures after its adoption.

Conveyance of one-tenth of Rancho Acalanes was made to Nathaniel Jones in the autumn of 1847, soon after Mr. Brown had acquired the property. Jones, a native of Tennessee, had started for Oregon from Missouri in April 1846 in company with fifteen or twenty other families. Circumstances diverted the immigrants to California, and Joseph Chiles induced Mr. Jones at Fort Sutter to go to Rancho Catacula in Napa County. With three or four other families the Joneses arrived in Chiles Valley on November 2, 1846. After volunteering and participating in the Battle of Santa Clara, Nathaniel Jones returned to Rancho Catacula.

Jones took his wife and small son to the San Antonio redwoods in Alameda County, and with the proceeds of the work that he did that summer he purchased a part of Rancho Acalanes from Elam Brown for $100.

Nathaniel Jones and Elam Brown moved to their new homes at about the same time, and early in 1848 Jones built his house. In the spring of the following year he began to beautify his home by setting out those fine, large black-locust trees which gave the name of Locust Farm to his homestead. The seed of these trees had been brought to California by Major Stephen Cooper in 1846 and subsequently presented to Mr. Jones. A remnant of the old farm may still be seen in Locust Grove, just east of Lafayette.

Locust Farm in 1882 contained 372 acres, part of which was cultivated and the remainder kept for grazing. Five acres were set to choice fruit trees. The comfortable eight-room house sheltered a family of five children, the eldest of whom, Robinson, had accompanied his parents across the Plains when he was only two years of age. Robinson M. Jones became a versatile and active man, being a farmer, teacher, county surveyor, newspaper man, and warehouse operator at Martinez. Nathaniel Jones himself was always interested in the affairs of his county and held such county offices as those of sheriff, public administrator, and supervisor.

Lafayette

A wayfarer passing by the Brown residence in 1852 was induced to remain. This was Benjamin Shreve, who taught school there during the winter of 1852–1853 and later opened a store and built a home. In 1853 Milo Hugh erected a hotel, which he conducted until 1855. Other settlers came, and very early a church was built and a cemetery laid out. Thus, about Elam Brown's hospitable homestead the village of Lafayette grew up.

Among the first industries to be started in Lafayette was a blacksmith shop established by Jack Elston and purchased by Peter Thomson in 1859. This shop, which sits back from the highway in the rear of a filling station, is still in use, and many of the old tools may be seen in its dingy interior. The filling station occupies the original site of the shop, and the road in front of the shop was the old race track.

Peter Thomson, an expert blacksmith of the old school, was a Canadian by birth. Having come by sailing vessel from New York, he arrived in San Francisco with two companions on June 24, 1859. After a few months in Oakland, he went to Lafayette, where he began work as a journeyman blacksmith in the shop which he later owned. This interesting shop is still owned by a son of Peter Thomson.

The original anvil used by Jack Elston is still kept in the shop. This aged relic has seen years of hard service. Besides the ordinary daily task of forging horseshoes and plowshares, it also withstood the shock of thundering forth the news of victories announced for the North in the Civil War. Broken through the waist, it has been repaired with plates fastened on both sides and firmly riveted together. For a time this historic implement was used on the old Elam Brown ranch and later found its way to Martinez, where it narrowly escaped being mounted on a pedestal in front of the courthouse. Elam, grandson of Elam Brown the pioneer, rescued it and returned it to the old shop in Lafayette.

Just outside the Elston blacksmith shop there is a millstone once used by Elam Brown in his gristmill. The marks of the sharpened hammer are still plainly visible upon it. The oldest dwelling still standing in Lafayette is the frame house of Mrs. Edward Gerow, which was erected some time in the early '50's and was originally occupied by Jack Elston.

Los Medanos

Captain Luis Antonio Argüello, accompanied by Fathers Narciso Duran and Ramón Abella, made a boat voyage up the Sacramento River in May 1817. It was on this expedition, according to Chapman, that the sand banks or dunes that lie along the Carquinez Straits between Pittsburg and Antioch were mentioned as *Los Medanos,* "the Sand-banks." The name was later applied to the ranchos Los Medanos (sometimes spelled "Meganos" but also interpreted as sand dunes), which embraced lands later known as the New York Ranch and the Marsh Estate.

During the late '30's two adjoining ranchos were granted, both of which, according to Bancroft, received the name of Los Medanos, apparently because of the presence of sand dunes lying along the left bank of the San Joaquin River in their vicinity. Later writers, however, have tried somewhat ambiguously to distinguish the two by calling the rancho originally granted to José Noriega and later purchased by Dr. John Marsh "Los Meganos" and by calling the New York Ranch "Los Medanos."

Rancho Los Medanos (Meganos), the Marsh Estate

When the ship "Natalia," bearing the Hijar and Padres colony from Acapulco, Mexico, was wrecked at Monterey in 1834, José Noriega, supercargo, was among its passengers. The following year, Noriega was made *depositario* or receiver at Misión San José and on October 13 of that year also became grantee of Rancho Los Medanos (Meganos) in Contra Costa County, where he built some corrals and a few outhouses. During 1837 Noriega sold his rancho to John Marsh, who settled upon it the same year and occupied it until his death in 1856.

"Doctor" Marsh, a native of Massachusetts, graduated from Harvard University with the degree of Bachelor of Arts, spent some time in Wisconsin, left the United States in 1835, and proceeded to New Mexico. After traversing a portion of Old Mexico, he crossed the Colorado River at the Gila and entered southern California early in January 1836. On displaying his Harvard diploma to the *ayuntamiento* of Los Angeles, it was received as a medical diploma and Marsh was given a license to practice medicine. Early in 1837 he came north and, late in December, acquired the romantic rancho under the shadow of Mount Diablo.

The Indians of the region became the Doctor's friends and helpers, and he even called his estate the Farm of Pulpones (evidently a corruption of Bolbones, or Bolgones), from the name of an Indian tribe or village in the vicinity of Mount Diablo. The Doctor was kind to his Indian neighbors—healing their sick, teaching them to trap for bear and otter, and leaving their ancient ranchería undisturbed. In return, the natives helped the "Señor Doctor" to build an adobe on the bank of the stream opposite their village. They brought grape cuttings from Misión San José and helped him to plant a vineyard and an orchard of pears, figs, and olives. They plowed his field for him and helped him to sow it to wheat.

When death finally crossed his path his dark-skinned brothers watched beside his bier and mourned his passing.

Dr. Marsh's adobe home "was a crude affair of sun-baked walls and thatched roof. Within were four large rooms and an attic.... large enough to accommodate two of his vaqueros, who always slept there and acted as his bodyguard..... The walls underneath the eaves, were perforated by loopholes. Through these the doctor and his vaqueros often drove away robbers and horse thieves....

"One room of the adobe had a fireplace.... By the light of blazing pine-knots he lay on the well-beaten floor and reflected or often read all night,—read everything that came to hand, medicine, agriculture, old newspapers and, sometimes .... he reread his Greek and Latin books until he knew long passages by heart.....

"In another room, on a shelf that ran part way around the wall, were the books he had brought with him and those he had acquired from sailing ships and men-of-war.....

"Across the entrance to his adobe, facing the mountain and an oak grove, was a portico roofed with tules, but, like the house proper, floorless. On either side of the door were rude benches, their backs against the wall. Here Marsh used to sit in the long summer twilights....."

Disappointment and tragedy experienced during his sojourn among the Indians in Wisconsin before he came to California had left their stamp upon the life and character of John Marsh. In his new environment he became a man of mystery. To all but his Indian neighbors he was notoriously parsimonious and often unkind. When the Bidwell-Bartleson party reached his rancho in 1841, the first party to cross the Sierra Nevada into California, he received them, but he made them pay well for his services. Even the Yankee traders complained about his sharp methods when he tried to beat them at their own game.

But there were those who admired the seemingly hard and tight-fisted doctor, and several Californians, among whom was General Vallejo, spoke of him in terms of warm praise. To some, indeed, he had been a ministering angel, for Dr. Marsh was the first and for several years the only man to practice medicine in the San Joaquin Valley. He often traveled many leagues to minister to the sick, his services usually being paid for in cattle. "The greater the distance," writes his biographer, "the more cows he expected, but it was generally agreed that he brought comfort and relief to the households he visited. His reputation spread. Cows or no cows, his services were in demand."

Although naturalized as a Mexican citizen in 1844, Dr. Marsh joined Sutter's forces against the Californians in 1844–1845 but took slight part in the troubles of 1846–1847. Nevertheless, he was becoming increasingly desirous of seeing California come into the possession of the United States, and almost every caravan to the East carried letters to some of his friends praising the glories and possibilities of the Golden State. The greater part of the communications were to Missourians and were published in Missouri newspapers.

These letters, written in an interesting and pleasing style by an intelligent and observing writer from first-hand knowledge, exerted a far-reaching influence on immigration to California, especially from Missouri. The influence of these letters, coupled with the practical efforts of Louis Rubidoux, probably helped the movement which resulted in the first emigrant party to California via the Rocky Mountains and the Sierra Nevada, led by Bidwell and Bartleson in 1841. The Marsh letters are still a valuable source of information on the life and times of pioneer California.

Dr. Marsh was married on June 24, 1851, to Miss Abbie Tuck of Chelmsford, Massachusetts. Abbie Tuck, the daughter of a minister, was a beautiful and accomplished young lady who had come to California in 1850 for her health. While she was living among friends in Santa Clara she was invited to take a trip through Contra Costa County. On this journey she met Dr. Marsh. A strong mutual admiration immediately grew up between the two; and after a courtship of two weeks, during which Abbie was completely swept off her feet by the fascinating and compelling personality of this mysterious man, they were married. One daughter, Alice, was born to this union.

The peak of John Marsh's happiness and prosperity passed quickly. In about a year after the birth of their child, his wife sickened and died. His Mexican neighbors were becoming increasingly irritated and vengeful over the Doctor's parsimonious acts and unkind attitude toward the rights of others. On September 24, 1856, he was murdered by four of these desperate young Californians on the lonely road between his rancho and Martinez. Ten years later one of the murderers was apprehended and sent to prison for life.

After much litigation the Marsh estate was divided between Alice and Charles, the Doctor's son by Marguerite, his common-law wife of Prairie du Chien, Wisconsin, whose death had greatly changed the tenor of the Doctor's life and brought him to California. It was largely through the efforts of the half-brother, Charles, that justice was finally obtained for the two children and the property was freed from the hands of unscrupulous persons.

The Stone House

"Soon after the wedding," writes Lyman, "the doctor took his young wife to the old adobe to live . . . . She loved the broad brook that ran, deep and still, near the kitchen door. . . . . Under the oaks and alders that fringed its bank was a favorite spot where she sat and read. Before long she had planted roses, dahlias, cinnamon pinks and peonies along its banks."

But John Marsh dreamed of greater things than the crude adobe for his beautiful wife. The stone mansion was planned with its library, its marble fireplaces, its tower, and its lovely suite of rooms for Abbie and himself. Abbie selected the site "in the portal of a pretty valley and almost directly opposite the old adobe." Abbie Marsh never lived in her castle of dreams. She died before its completion; and little Alice, helpless among strangers and in the midst of heartless litigations, was to experience poverty and hardship before coming into her inheritance.

Set in the midst of wide, open fields about four miles southwest of Brentwood, the old "Stone House" has for eighty years been one of the most striking historic landmarks of Contra Costa County. Beside the lonely Marsh Creek Road its steep English gables and solid masonry of native stone rise in picturesque solitude, reminding one of the princely acres that were Rancho Los Medanos.

A contemporary description of the mansion appeared in the *Daily Evening Bulletin*, July 19, 1856, shortly before the house was completed. Most of the details remain unchanged.

"Across the valley . . . . stretches a noble grove of oaks, through which vistas have been cut, affording glimpses of the broken country beyond, closed in by old Mount Diablo. . . . . The new and beautiful edifice, now completed, is situated in the center of the plain . . . . From a quarry which has been opened upon the estate, an abundant supply of stone for the building has been obtained. It is of the finest quality of freestone, of a beautiful drab or cream-color, slightly variegated. . . . . The architect, Thomas Boyd . . . . with a true artistic perception of the beauty of the site, and of what was wanted . . . . to make it harmonize with the surrounding scenery . . . . had adopted the old English domestic style of architecture—a pleasing and appropriate union of Manor House and Castle. The arched windows, the peaked roofs and gables, the projecting eaves, the central tower sixty-five feet in height, boldly springing from the midst and enabling the proprietor to overlook his extensive domain, must be acknowledged . . . . a most felicitous deviation from the prevailing style of rural architecture.

"The corners of the building as well as the door and window-jambs, sills and caps, are elaborately wrought, the spaces between the openings being laid with rubber-stone, giving a pleasing variety to the whole exterior. The building has a ground base of sixty by forty feet, and is three stories in height, with three gabled windows in the attic looking east, west, and south. On three sides of the building is a piazza, ten feet in width, supported by beautiful octagon pillars; over this is a walk on a level with the second floor, enclosed by an elaborately finished balustrade. The work has been performed . . . . by Messrs. Pierce and Wood . . . . with the utmost faithfulness and ability. The interior arrangements are as carefully planned as possible to subserve the purposes of convenience, comfort, and beautiful finish. The whole cost of the building . . . . will not exceed twenty thousand dollars."

Rancho El Sobrante de San Ramón

On the Stanley Dollar ranch in Tice Valley, about three miles west of Alamo, is a small stone and mud house, all that is left of a large adobe which was nearly razed in 1900. This was the homestead of Inocencio Romero *et al.*, claimants of Rancho El Sobrante de San Ramón of five leagues. This was the *sobrante* or "overplus" of land "lying between the ranchos of Moraga, Pacheco and Welch." Some six or seven years before the Romero brothers petitioned for the grant on January 18, 1844, the tract had been claimed by Francisco Soto, but it had never been used nor cultivated by him.

El Sobrante de San Ramon was never confirmed to the Romeros, because of certain legal complications and vagaries, but there is evidence that the land was occupied by the brothers, probably from 1840, but at least in 1844. Petitions for a grant made by the Romeros were favorably received by the governor, who on March 23, 1844, directed a measurement of the land to be made preparatory to the granting of the same. The measurements, however, were never made, a provisional grant was refused, and the claim was finally rejected in 1864. James M. Tice later came into the possession of the property, and the valley was named for him.

Rancho El Pinole

Rancho El Pinole, which stretched easterly from Pinole Point on San Pablo Bay to the town of Martinez at the southern end of Suisun Bay, was first given to Ignacio Martínez in 1829. It was regranted to him in 1842 and by a claim founded on the grant of the latter date was patented to his heirs in 1868.

Ignacio Martínez was born in Mexico City in 1774 and, coming to California, entered military service as cadet at Santa Barbara in 1799. He was promoted to be *alferez* of the San Diego Company in 1806 and in 1817 was again recommended for promotion, this time to go back to Santa Barbara. To his chagrin, an error in the making out of his papers sent him to San Francisco instead.

His life thereafter was spent in the central part of the state. He was retired in 1831 (three years after receiving his land), after having been comandante at San Francisco during the last four years of military service. On his retirement, he was credited with forty-one years of service, was given full pay, and was allowed the continued use of his uniform.

He lived for a time at San José, where he was alderman in 1834–1835, before settling on his land about 1836 in Contra

Costa County. In 1841 he was living on his rancho with his wife, Martina Arrelanes, and six of his daughters. Another daughter, María Antonia, had married William A. Richardson. At home Martínez threw aside the aloofness and arrogance that had marked his earlier career and became a courteous and hospitable ranchero.

The town of Pinole (Mexican word meaning "cereal meal") carried the name of his rancho, and the town of Martinez at the edge of his land is named for the family.

Rancho Las Juntas

The eastern part of the town of Martinez is on what was formerly a portion of the Rancho Las Juntas, consisting of 13,292 acres granted to William Welch, a Scotchman, in 1844. In 1849, Colonel William M. Smith, agent for the Martínez family, laid out a town there, and in 1850, this became the county seat of Contra Costa County.

Two of the old Las Juntas rancho houses may still be seen in the vicinity of Martinez. One is on what is now known as the John Muir Ranch in Franklin Canyon about two miles south of town, and the other is on the John Swett Ranch in the Alhambra Valley.

The former home of John Muir, explorer, scientist, and author, is in a little wooded valley on the Franklin Canyon Road. The large old-fashioned house where the writer lived stands on a knoll overlooking the orchards below and the hills that hem them in on all sides. At the western edge of the farm, beside the road, is one of the old Las Juntas adobes.

John Muir was born in Dunbar, Scotland, April 21, 1838. He came to the United States in 1849, and, while still a young man, he came to California. Most of his life was spent exploring, studying, and writing about the great mountains of California and Alaska, their valleys, their glaciers, and their wild life. Many of the mountain peaks and glaciers up and down the Pacific Coast were discovered and named by him. He was one of the foremost advocates of national parks, and his books, which are literary as well as scientific, have done much to cause people to know and to love the natural wonderlands of the Pacific Coast states. Perhaps the best-known and most beautiful of his writings is *The Mountains of California*, published in 1894.

John Swett has been called the "father of the California public schools" because of his untiring efforts in their behalf while he was superintendent of public instruction from 1863 to 1867. He was born in New Hampshire and came to San Francisco in 1853, where he was at once employed as a teacher. Throughout his long career as a teacher and administrator he did more to build up the public school system of California than any other one man.

The John Swett Ranch lies in the heart of the Alhambra Valley in the midst of orchards. The old house itself is hidden among the trees along a stream. Beside the big house there is a little white adobe that also once belonged to the great Rancho Las Juntas.

Walker of Walker's Pass

Joseph Reddeford Walker, trapper, trailmaker, guide, and stockbuyer of the '30's and '40's, for whom Walker's Pass is named, died in Contra Costa County and is buried in Alhambra Cemetery at Martinez.

The Pacheco Adobe

Salvio Pacheco, having held high offices in the Mexican government, was granted the Rancho del Diablo of 18,000 acres, in 1834. About ten years later he moved to it and built the adobe house still standing in the present town of Concord,

which he originally called Todos Santos. It is located on the block bounded by Concord Avenue, Salvio Avenue, and the County Road.

The Pacheco House, with its balconies, its deep casements, shuttered windows, and thick walls, is a good example of the Spanish-Californian home. Although damaged by earthquakes, it is still fairly well preserved, and has been encased in wood to protect it from the winter rains. Under the pepper trees which frame the front of the house is an old brick well; and the stone boundary posts, marked with the United States patent date, 1853, may still be seen in front of the house. By 1852 American squatters had come in large numbers to settle on this land, but in 1853 the United States government granted a patent to Pacheco, thus securing his title to the estate. The Pacheco adobe, until recently still owned by gracious descendants of the generous Don, remains in Concord as a reminder of early days.

The village of Pacheco lies five miles southeast of Martinez at the junction of the road to Concord, which lies two miles farther east.

The first house erected in this vicinity is still standing to the east of Highway 21 on a hill in the north edge of the settlement. It is easily identified by its ornamented eaves and the old trees and shrubbery that surround it. It was built by G. L. Walwrath of New York in 1853. Its timbers were hewn from the Moraga redwoods. Walwrath owned it only three years and then sold it to George P. Loucks in whose family its ownership still remains. Loucks sold his commission business in San Francisco and moved to this house in 1857, when he built a mile below his dwelling a large warehouse on Pacheco Creek, then navigable for small sternwheel steamers. He sold a piece of his land to William Hendrick, who at once erected a dwelling house and a flour mill, one of the few flour mills in the county.

In the same year, 1857, Dr. J. H. Carothers purchased a tract of land from the Pacheco family and laid out the town of Pacheco on the east bank of Pacheco Creek. Around the two enterprises of warehouse and flour mill a flourishing town grew up, attracting men who built for themselves houses similar to those of New England. The first business building, the "Long Store," was erected by Hale and Fassett. Shortly after, Elijah Hook put up a two-story brick building, which housed a general-merchandise store on its ground floor and the *Contra Costa Gazette* upstairs. In 1859 a small schoolhouse was built, followed in 1863 by a larger one of two stories that was used until 1926, when it was displaced by a modern one of cement.

A stage line with change of horses at Pacheco ran from Antioch to Martinez. A post office was early established. Mail from San Francisco was brought to Martinez by the river steamers and on to Pacheco by stage. The town was a busy one. From the Tassajara and San Ramon valleys came great four- and six-horse wagons with grain for the mill. All traffic from the southern and eastern part of the county passed through on its way to the county seat at Martinez. Traffic from the Sacramento Valley passed through, both going to the ferry at Martinez and returning from it. Conestoga wagons that had traveled far were familiar sights.

To accommodate the travelers who paused for rest and food, two hotels were built. "The Eagle," on the corner of Main and Monument streets, still stands, being now used as a family residence.

The flood of 1862 swept away much of the town. The Loucks warehouse fell a victim and was never rebuilt. Within the next six years two fires destroyed many frame buildings. In 1868 came the disastrous earthquake that leveled brick and other buildings. However, the disasters of flood, fires, and earthquake did not destroy the town, which seems to have reached the peak of its prosperity in 1870, when the Contra Costa Bank of Savings and Loan was organized.

Miscellaneous Ranchos

Other Mexican grants in this county which have received United States patents are: Boca de la Cañada del Pinole, Laguna de los Palos Colorados, Arroyo de las Nueces y Bolbones, and Cañada de los Vaqueros.

In the western part, Rancho Boca de la Cañada del Pinole, consisting of 13,316.26 acres, was granted to María Manuel Valencia and was patented to her in 1878; and the Laguna de los Palos Colorados of 13,316 acres was granted to Joaquín Moraga and J. Bernal and was long held by descendants of the first-named.

In the central part of the county is Rancho Arroyo de las Nueces y Balbones, consisting of 17,782 acres, granted to Juana Sanchez Pacheco in 1834. This rancho, located on the western flank of Mount Diablo, was patented to her heirs on April 18, 1866.

In the southeastern part of the county lies Rancho Cañada de los Vaqueros, originally granted to three Spanish Californians, and bought in 1847 by Robert Livermore.

The Gutiérrez House

On the southern bank of the Arroyo Grande, just northwest of San Pablo in the city of Richmond, stands the old Gutiérrez House, once the home of Candido Gutiérrez and his wife, Jovita Castro Gutiérrez. The Gutiérrez adobe was built about 1850. Pleasantly situated on the bank of the arroyo, where schooners came up the creek to the back door, bringing supplies and taking away products from the rancho, it was one of the finest mansions of its day. The old house is now framed in, only its form and the picturesque Spanish balcony bespeaking its true character. Beneath the balcony, María Emma, the little daughter of Candido and Jovita, lies buried, and on her tombstone is an inscription written in Spanish verse.

Pittsburg, "The New York of the Pacific"

Colonel Jonathan D. Stevenson brought the First Regiment of New York Volunteers to California by sea, arriving in three transports in March 1847 to take part in the American occupation. In 1849 he bought Rancho Los Medanos from the original Mexican grantees, José Antonio Mesa and José Miguel García.

On this ranch, Stevenson laid out the site for a city about where Pittsburg now stands. He called it "New York of the Pacific" after his home city, New York, and the rancho was called the New York Ranch. The Colonel hoped that his new city would become a large and prosperous seaport, and to that end he attempted to locate the state capital there in 1850, but the city of Vallejo won the coveted honor by popular election.

About fifty years ago, Pittsburg was a busy port for the shipment of coal from the mines discovered near Mount Diablo, and at that time was called "Black Diamond." This industry was short-lived, however, because of the poor quality of the coal, and the town has never been of real importance until within quite recent years, when it has become a manufacturing center of considerable extent. The name was changed to Pittsburg in 1909.

"Ghost Towns" of Contra Costa

North of Antioch and Pittsburg, the lingering "ghosts" of coal-mining days remind one of the brief excitements and short-lived hopes, the comedies and tragedies, of human endeavor which took place there from the middle '50's to the middle '80's. Nortonville and Somersville, Stewartsville and Empire, West Hartley and Judsonville, with their shipping counterparts at New York and Pittsburg landings, dominated the affairs of the county for a period of thirty years; and, in the case of Somersville, limited activities continued as late as 1905.

A unique and cosmopolitan population found its way into the Mount Diablo coal district from the coal fields of distant lands, especially from England and Wales. In 1882 about three hundred men and boys were employed in the mines at Nortonville, while the entire population of the place registered about nine hundred people.

Today the solitude of those deserted ravines and hillsides bears mute testimony of another episode in the mining history of the state. At Somersville a handful of windowless, weather-beaten frame cabins stand among the aged locust trees on the hillside. Below them are the "dumps," while. meandering down the deep gullies and beside the steep, rutted roadways almond trees and rows of pepper trees indicate the former paths of progress into the hills.

High up toward the west, the white headstones of the little cemetery, sentineled by five stately cypress trees, gleam against the green breast of the mountain. Many of the pioneers, including Noah Norton, were buried here. This graveyard on the side of the valley is the burial place of several Welch miners whose epitaphs are engraved in their native language.

Nortonville has one structure left of the former village, the old brick office building with its iron doors and shutters. At the head of the basin above the dump, the weathered red brick of the tall power-plant chimney blends softly with the vivid pink and violet of the cinder heaps.

There are no landmarks at Empire except the dumps and a few old trees planted by early settlers.

Bancroft states that coal was discovered in Contra Costa County as early as 1848. George W. Hawxhurst located in 1855 at the place where the town of Somersville later grew up and after prospecting for coal discovered the Union vein in March of that year. Four years later, on December 22, 1859, Francis Somers and James T. Cruikshank discovered the famous Black Diamond vein. With his associates, H. S. Hawxhurst and Samuel Adams, Somers located the lands afterward known as the Manhattan and Eureka coal mines, which comprised, with the Union and Independent, the mines forming the basin which cradled the town of Somersville. In the '80's the Pittsburg Railroad connected the district with Pittsburg Landing at the mouth of the San Joaquin River.

The Black Diamond, Cumberland, and Mount Hope mines, located about a mile west of Somersville on the same vein, were opened by Somers and another group of men. Since they were unable to finance the building of necessary roads, they never secured title to these lands. Very soon, however, Noah Norton, from whom Nortonville received its name, came upon the scene and took over the Black Diamond, while Frank Luch and others undertook to develop the Cumberland. Luch soon disposed of his share to a group of men from Martinez, who took hold of the Cumberland diggings and made a success of the enterprise and also assisted Noah Norton in getting the Black Diamond under way. Roads were opened to Clayton and New York Landing, and in the '80's a railroad connected the latter place with the Nortonville mines.

The Black Diamond and Cumberland mines, together with adjoining lands, were at first known as the Carbondale District but have since become noted as the Black Diamond coal mines. In the basin of the hills which embraces the Black Diamond, Cumberland, Mount Hope, and other lands the town of Nortonville still held its own as a mining center in the '80's.

The first house was built in Nortonville by Noah Norton in 1861; its site is now covered by one of the dumps. A second house, also built by Norton, was erected the following year, while the first hotel, known as the Black Diamond Exchange, was opened in 1863 by Atwell Pray and Charles Gwynn. In 1865 a store was opened, and in 1866 a schoolhouse was established not far from the spot where the shaft was sunk later. The building was moved to the top of the hill in 1870, and there it developed to the dignity of a seminary with four departments. This school was maintained for the most part by a charge of one per cent on all moneys paid through the office of the mine superintendent. Nothing remains of these buildings today.

Somersville's first house was probably erected some time in 1860, while a boardinghouse and hotel was opened in 1861. The place grew until the slopes and dips of the canyon were dotted with cabins, and in 1865 a schoolhouse was erected for the miners' children.

The first slump in coal mining in the Mount Diablo district occurred in 1878, when the Somersville mines were closed temporarily with the hope that they would soon reopen. Meanwhile, new locations were being made. One of these was the Empire Mine, opened near Judsonville in 1878, five miles south of Antioch and about three and one-half miles east of Somersville. A lavish outlay of capital was made, but competition demanded a cut in production cost, and this, in turn, brought the inevitable dispute between capital and labor over wages. Work was suspended early in 1880, to be continued with new men in March.

Activities speeded up in 1881, when the railroad was extended from Judsonville to the Central Mine. Fifteen new houses and a large hotel were built, and the town of Stewartsville came into existence one mile east of Somersville. Nevertheless, competition was still strangling the industry. Since the newer mines were able to pay relatively low wages for a short time and the cost of production at Nortonville was increasing, coal mining at that place was doomed by 1883.

That the industry was losing out at other points was evident when the post office was discontinued at Judsonville, "the population and business of the place having migrated to Stewartsville." One by one, men prominent in the field left for other places. As early as 1881, Mr. Pinkerton, for sixteen years superintendent of the Pittsburg mines, left for Tacoma, Washington. George Hawxhurst, who had been a resident at Somersville for almost twenty-five years, went to British Columbia in 1883 to become superintendent of a railroad and coal mine owned by a San Francisco company.

In 1885 the famous Black Diamond Mine found that it could no longer stand the heavy expense of keeping the shaft clear of water, and by March the mines were permanently closed. Nortonville ceased to have any motive for existence and became a deserted village over night. Lodges, churches, and schools were closed or moved to Martinez. Many of the houses were taken apart by their owners and moved to other places.

Activity in Mount Diablo's ancient sandstone belt has been temporarily resumed at three different times. In 1923 there was renewed life when sandstone was removed from the Clark vein by the Columbia Steel Corporation. Again in 1926 there was considerable activity about the old shafts when the coal properties were surveyed and evaluated by a group of engineers with the purpose of determining the amount of coal still available in the district. The last spurt of energy manifested among the coal beds was in 1932, when the mines at Nortonville were reopened and worked again. The coal taken out then was given to the poor and unemployed in the vicinity.

Antioch

The story of Antioch is largely the story of the devotion of two brothers, W. W. Smith and Joseph H. Smith, natives of New Hampshire. Reared and educated together, these twin brothers followed the same course in the later activities of life which led them ultimately to a new land. They both learned the carpenter's trade and pursued it in their home state as well as in California; both were married at the same time and place, in their mother's home at New Market in March 1833. Together, they were the means of organizing a Christian Church at Lynn, Massachusetts, as well as two others in the same township; and both were ordained ministers of the Christian denomination, which they had first joined as lads twelve years of age.

With the discovery of gold, the Smith brothers became fired with a desire to go to California; in company with some fifty other emigrants, they sailed on January 11, 1849, with their families from Boston harbor aboard the "Forest" en route for the Golden State, the ship "Edward Everett" sailing at the same time and in company with them. The "Forest" entered the Golden Gate on July 6, 1849, and the "Edward Everett" arrived three or four hours later.

Since carpenters were in demand, the Smith brothers agreed to go to work at a place called New York of the Pacific, located at the mouth of the San Joaquin River. Arriving with their families in the schooner "Rialto" on July 11, 1849, six months after leaving Boston, the brothers took up their work as carpenters in the embryo city.

The day following their arrival Dr. John Marsh sent an invitation extending to them the hospitality of his home. Horses were provided, and the little party took the well-beaten trail leading up the arroyo to the Doctor's adobe house, where they received a hearty welcome. As a result of this visit, the brothers took up jointly on July 19, 1849, two quarter sections of land where Antioch now stands. Here on December 24 they broke ground and set up tents. Working their lands enough to hold them, the Smiths continued their carpenter work at New York of the Pacific, often going to Smith's Landing, as it was known at first, to cut firewood for the New York House.

The Rev. Joseph Smith died at New York of the Pacific on February 5, 1850. In September of that year a shipload of settlers arrived in San Francisco aboard the "California Packet" from Maine. This group of New England frontier families had hewn their ship out of the Maine woods, and in it they had sailed to far-off California to found a colony. They brought with them all that was dearest and best in their sturdy New England culture. A school was conducted by Deacon Pulsifer of the Christian Church.

Hearing of the new arrivals and of their wish to settle in California, the Rev. W. W. Smith hastened to San Francisco to meet them. He invited them to go with him to Smith's Landing, and, although the gold mines proved too enticing for some of the company, a number of them accepted the invitation.

A street was now laid out, and to each family that wished to settle upon the land the Rev. Smith presented a lot on which to build a home. In order to keep out the animals a fence was built the following spring from the tules on the west of the town to the tules on the east. On July 4 between thirty and forty persons, men, women, and children, gathered for a basket picnic held at the home of W. W. Smith.

The all-absorbing topic of the day was "What shall we name our town?" One proposed "Minton," the name of a river boat, in the hope that it might be induced to stop at the Landing; another proposed "Paradise," which was rejected because of the uncertainty of land titles in California, a circumstance which might result in "Paradise Lost" for the holders. At length the Rev. W. W. Smith proposed that, inasmuch as the first settlers at this spot were disciples of Christ and one of them (his own brother) had died and was buried on the land, it be given a Bible name in his honor. He proposed that they adopt the name of Antioch for their town, because "at Antioch, Syria, the followers of Christ were first called Christians." By united acclamation this name was accepted.

The first house built in Antioch, the home of George W. Kimball, captain of the "California Packet," still stands on Third Street next door to Scout's Hall. It was constructed in 1851 by the Captain, who raised barley hay, hauled it to San Francisco, and with the proceeds bought Oregon pine to use in building his home.

SOURCES

[Credit is here given for source material, and permission to quote is hereby acknowledged]

BOLTON, HERBERT EUGENE. *Anza's California Expeditions.* University of California Press, Berkeley, California, 1930

———. *Fray Juan Crespi, Missionary Explorer on the Pacific Coast, 1769–1774.* University of California Press, Berkeley, California, 1927

———. *Font's Complete Diary, A Chronicle of the Founding of San Francisco.* Translated from the original Spanish Manuscript. University of California Press, Berkeley, California, 1933

BREWER, WILLIAM H. *Up and Down California in 1860–1864.* Edited by Francis P. Farquhar. Yale University Press, New Haven, Connecticut, 1930

CHAPMAN, CHARLES E. *A History of California: The Spanish Period.* The Macmillan Company, New York, 1923

CLELAND, ROBERT GLASS. *A History of California: The American Period.* The Macmillan Company, New York, 1922

HOWE, OCTAVIUS THORNDIKE. *Argonauts of '49. History and Adventures of the Emigrant Companies from Massachusetts, 1849–1850.* Harvard University Press, Cambridge, 1923

HULANISKI, F. J. *The History of Contra Costa County, California.* The Elias Publishing Company, Berkeley, California, 1917

LOUD, LLEWELLYN L. "The Stege Mounds at Richmond, California," in *University of California Publications in American Archaeology and Ethnology,* Vol. XVII, No. 6, Berkeley, California, 1924

LYMAN, GEORGE DUNLAP. *John Marsh, Pioneer.* Scribner's, New York, 1930

McGINTY, R. M. *Spanish and Mexican Ranchos in the San Francisco Bay Region.* Master's thesis in history, University of California, Berkeley, California, 1920

NELSON, N. C. "The Ellis Landing Shellmound," in *University of California Publications in American Archaeology and Ethnology,* Vol. VII, No. 4, Berkeley, California, 1910

SANCHEZ, NELLIE VAN DE GRIFT. *Spanish and Indian Place Names of California.* A. M. Robertson, San Francisco, 1914

SULLIVAN, MAURICE S. *The Travels of Jedediah Strong Smith.* The Fine Arts Press, Santa Ana, California, 1934

DEL NORTE COUNTY

DEL NORTE COUNTY (Del Norte is Spanish for "of the north," as the county is in the extreme northwestern corner of California) was organized in 1857, and Crescent City was made its county seat.

Trail Breakers

Taking "a northwest course across the Coast Range, through what is now Trinity and Humboldt counties, to the sea," Jedediah Strong Smith, trapper-explorer, in 1828, first "opened a line of communication from northern California to the Oregon country, a route the Hudson's Bay Company were quick to take advantage of." Crossing the Klamath River at the site of the former town of Klamath, south of the Humboldt–Del Norte county line on May 25, 1828, the great

pathfinder entered what is now Del Norte County on June 1. Travel during the next ten days was slow and difficult. Trails had to be blazed over steep and rugged mountains, while progress was often impeded by heavy fogs. The scarcity of wild game, which was almost their only food, added to their hardships.

A level, grassy bottom near the mouth of the Klamath River on Hunter's Creek was reached on June 5, and camp was pitched at a spot between the present Redwood Highway and Requa. At this point, where modern tourist camps are now located, the exhausted and half-starved men and animals of this first exploring party rested for three days and nights.

Unfruitful attempts to replenish their failing food supply occupied them the first two days in camp. The last dog and a horse had, finally, to be killed for meat. On June 7, ten to fifteen Indians visited camp, "bringing with them a few Muscles and Lemprey Eels and some raspberries" (thimbleberries). In the brisk trade which ensued, the white men distributed in exchange for these delicacies the glass beads which they had brought for just such occasions.

From the Hunter's Creek camp, Smith and his men crossed over to Wilson Creek on June 8. "We were weary and very hungry," wrote Smith; but again the natives came to the rescue, when several Indian lodges near the camp supplied them with a few mussels and small fish in exchange for the prized beads. They brought, also, "dried sea grass mixed with weeds and a few muscels. They were great speculators and never sold their things without dividing them into several small parcels asking more for each than the whole were worth. They also brought us some Blubber not bad tasted but dear as gold dust. But all these things served but to aggravate our hunger and having been long accustomed to living on meat and eating it in no moderate quantities nothing else could satisfy our appetites."

That afternoon Smith killed three elk, "thanks to the great Benefactor." The camp was changed from "the moody silence of hunger to the busy bustle of preparation for cooking and feasting . . . . Men could be seen in ev'ry part of the camp with raw meat and half roasted in their hands devouring it with the greatest alacrity while from their preparations and remarks you would suppose that nothing less than twentyfour hours constant eating would satisfy their appetites."

At the Wilson Creek camp, the explorers occupied the time making salt and cutting and drying their meat. The unblazed trail which they cut from June 11 to 16 through the wilderness of Del Norte County was rough and difficult in the extreme. The route of the party during this period followed, in general, that taken later by the old County road. The prairie south and east of Crescent City was reached on June 16. Although there were no mountains to be overcome on this lap of the journey, the dense redwood forest, the thick brush, and swamps still made travel difficult.

They made camp in the vicinity of Crescent City on June 17, and on June 18 Earl Lake was discovered by a reconnoitering party. On June 19 Smith himself discovered the river that was in later years honored with his name. On the north bank of Smith River tents of the brave little band were set up on June 20. On June 21 Smith pushed on northward and on June 22, 1828, crossed the California boundary into Oregon.

Alexander Roderick McLeod, at the head of the trapping expedition of the Hudson's Bay Company, entered California from the north in 1829, trying vainly to follow Smith's trail but finally coming southward via the Umpqua Valley and Klamath Lake.

The River of Mystery

A mystery to early explorers and map makers was the Klamath. Its source in the Klamath lakes and its upper course were known almost a quarter of a century before it was determined that its mouth was in the present Del Norte County. In the fall of 1826 a trapper of the Hudson's Bay Company, Peter Skene Ogden, set out from Fort Vancouver on the Columbia River for the region of the "Clamitte." His diary gives the earliest account of the visit of white men into the country north of Mount Shasta. Between 1827 and 1850, British and American trappers continued to trap for beaver on the upper Klamath and its tributaries, but not one expedition followed the river to its mouth. Thus the lower course of the river was unknown and the spot where it emptied into the sea was long a matter of conjecture. Most maps represented the Klamath as entering the ocean north of the present California-Oregon boundary line, and the lower Klamath was represented as a continuation of the present Trinity River. These two rivers, together with the South Fork of the Trinity, extended from the southeast to the northwest and on early maps were represented as one river named Smith's River.

The Klamath was the river course traversed by Jedediah Strong Smith and his party of trappers in the spring of 1828 when he blazed a northwest trail from the Sacramento Valley into Oregon. The first Indian agent, who arrived on the Klamath in 1851, was familiar with the maps of the region that indicated its chief waterway by the name of Smith's River, and he sought to locate that stream. But, by 1851, "Smith's River" had become a lost river. The true course of the Klamath had been determined late in 1850 by a party of miners who traversed its whole length from its mouth to its junction with the Shasta River, prospecting every bar for gold. Later the name "Smith's River" was given to an unnamed stream in Del Norte County also discovered by Smith.

The early miners in northwestern California had never known of a river called Smith's but were familiar with the Trinity River, first named by Major Pierson B. Reading in 1845. Reading had discovered gold in this stream, and as a consequence the upper course of the river with its tributaries was teeming with miners in 1849–1850. The approach was from the Sacramento Valley. More direct access to the sea was desirable, and soon vessels left San Francisco to explore the northern coast with the hope of finding the mouth of the Trinity River at Trinidad Bay. No river was found at Trinidad Bay, but farther north was discovered a large river (the Klamath) which many believed to be the Trinity River.

Soon all the streams of the region were being prospected for gold, and the Klamath, crossed and recrossed, was mistaken at first for the Trinity or the Salmon. Gradually, however, the true course of the Klamath was determined, and the identity of its tributaries was made known as feeders of the great stream.

Klamath City, a Dream of Yesterday

Miners came into the region in increasing numbers, and Klamath City, near the mouth of Klamath River, was established in 1851. This short-lived city arose with great expectations of becoming the port of entry for the back country, rich in gold. But, because of the shifting sand bars at the mouth of the river, navigation was uncertain, and the place was deserted soon after 1852.

Bledsoe, in his *Indian Wars of the Northwest,* describes the rise and fall of Klamath City as follows: "Klamath City was one of the ephemeral productions of the mining excitement. When the *Cameo,* driven from Trinidad Head by a storm in March 1850 reached Point St. George, she landed some of her passengers there. These, B. W. Bullet, Herman Ehrenberg, J. T. Tyson, A. Heepe, and a Mr. Gunn, walked down the coast, and about the middle of April arrived at the mouth of the Klamath, which they supposed was the Trinity.

After travelling up the stream some distance and locating homesteads near its mouth, the explorers went down to Trinidad, their stories of discovery adding fuel to the feverish excitement which already possessed the place. They and others went up to the mouth of the river and located a new town, which they called Klamath City. Here they were met by Eugene du Bertrand, sole survivor of a boat's crew of five from the *Cameo* that had come down from Point St. George and, attempting to cross the river bar in the boat, had been upset in the breakers. Bertrand, being a good swimmer, saved himself with the timely assistance of an Indian.

"Klamath City had a rapid growth and a mushroom existence. It was supposed that the river bars from the mouth up were all rich in gold, consequently, prospectors and traders flocked to the new town in large numbers. Frames of houses, ready to be put together on arrival, were shipped from San Francisco, and it is said that one iron house was imported and erected in the town," to be used by its owners as a refuge from the attacks of the Indians.

The town of Klamath City did not prosper for several reasons. Gold seekers "did not meet with the success they had anticipated and left for other localities; the river bar was too dangerous to be crossed in safety by large vessels; traders were unable to bring in their wares by sea; explorers departed for other scenes; buildings were taken down and carried away; and in a few months from its location the site of the prospective city was the same primeval solitude broken in upon by the first white explorer. Today there is not a vestige of the town to be seen, not a single visible testimonial of the busy and exciting scenes that once transpired there."

The Lost Cabin

It has been said that a great part of northwestern California and of southern Oregon was explored, prospected, and settled as a result of the spread throughout California and the Eastern states of one or another of those "Lost Cabin" stories which thrilled and fascinated the gold-mad throngs in various sections of the state during the '50's. The founding of Crescent City itself, according to an early account, was due to some wandering prospector in search of the "Lost Cabin." There were many versions of this romantic tale, but that told by Bledsoe has, perhaps, received widest currency.

"In the very earliest days of the mining excitement in California, a miner more adventurous than his fellows, armed with his rifle and supplied with necessary mining implements, crossed the Coast Range and prospected the gulches and ravines of the foot-hills near the sea-shore. One lucky day he 'struck it rich.' The rich earth yielded its yellow treasures in abundance, and the solitary miner erected a cabin in the wilderness, with the sole thought of amassing a fortune and returning to home and friends in the East. And there in the 'forest primeval' with the giant trees towering above him, the lonely gold-hunter toiled as if for life, day by day, for many weary months, adding to his store of gold until it amounted to a fabulous sum. The prowling Indians found his retreat at last, and attacking him in overwhelming numbers left him senseless on the ground, apparently dead. The treasure was too well hidden to be easily found, and failing in their search for it, the savages set fire to the cabin, burning it to ashes. When they had gone, the miner recovered consciousness, but not his reason—the light of his mind had gone out, and left a flickering flame of disconnected thought. Bereft of his reason, he wandered out of the forest and into the home of civilization. How he succeeded in finding his way back to his friends in the east the legend saith not. But (so the story goes) he did succeed in reaching home and there, after a brief period he died. Before his death his reason returned to him, and calling his friends around him he told them the story of his hidden treasure, describing minutely the locality of the cabin, and from the account he gave, it was evident that the lost cabin was situated somewhere on the northern coast of California."

Tributary Gold Camps of Southern Oregon

Mining areas along the Klamath River, of which Happy Camp (now in Siskiyou County) was the trade center, as well as the gold camps of southern Oregon, were long tributary to Crescent City in Del Norte County, although the aforesaid regions were populated and flourishing one or two years before the City itself was laid out. The Klamath section was mined and settled as early as 1851, after a party of miners, prospecting for gold on every bar, had traveled all the way up the Klamath River from its mouth. Happy Camp, Wingate Bar, Woods Bar, Indian Creek Diggings, were among the prosperous camps established as the result of the discovery of rich gold mines.

In the territory now included in southern Josephine and Jackson counties in Oregon the first location was made near Kirbyville in 1851. Another discovery made by a group of seafaring men led to the founding of Sailor Diggings, later called Waldo for a prominent California politician. Discoveries were made in Jackson Creek in 1852, and Jacksonville became the chief center of activities, while in 1853 Philip Althouse picked up gold on a creek named after himself. Soon a thousand and more eager miners rushed to the scene of these first locations and numerous mining companies sprang up. Strange names characteristic of the period were quickly appended to the sites: Democratic Gulch, Hogtown, Browntown, Butcher Gulch, Jump-off-Joe Creek, House Creek, Hungry Hill, Galiceburg, Lucky Green, Wilderville, Quartzville, Coyote Creek, Rough and Ready Creek, Murphy's Creek, Williamsburg, Webfoot Mine, Slate Creek, Canyon Creek, Yankee-Doodle Mine.

The first port of entry to all this region was Scottsburg, in Oregon, but a more direct access to the sea became desirable after the experience of high prices and famine in the winter of 1851–1852. Consequently the trail to Crescent City was opened up in the spring of 1853, and pack trains soon brought in the necessary supplies. Agitation for a wagon road was started in 1854, the surveys being made by T. P. Robinson, who in June 1854 determined the Oregon-California boundary line. Work was finally commenced in 1857 by the "Crescent City and Yreka Plank and Turnpike Company," and in 1860 the wagon road between Waldo (Sailor Diggings) and Crescent City was completed.

During the height of mining activity, southwestern Oregon was always connected more closely with California than with Oregon. Indeed, before the boundary line was determined, the miners considered themselves Californians. Regarding the boundary Bledsoe says: "The decision caused some excitement . . . . as the miners did not like to be so suddenly transported from California to Oregon. They had before both voted in California and Oregon Territory and had refused to pay taxes to either."

Of this integral relationship between southern Oregon and northern California, Walling writes: "In every respect it resembles and is identical with the history of the mining counties of California, with which state Jackson County has far closer affiliations than with the exclusively agricultural portions of Oregon. Indeed, it is a rather striking and in some sense regrettable fact that it is not a part of the former state. Settled by the same class of enterprising, fearless and progressive miners it became the abode of a population who . . . . were circumscribed precisely as those of California. The surface mining industry grew up under the same conditions, at-

tained its maximum at the same time and has declined in the same proportion . . . ."

As the surface gold was depleted, the bulk of the population departed. Hydraulic mining was introduced in the '60's and '70's, and some localities were producing as late as the '80's. The bulk of the activity had passed long before. By 1865 Althouse, one of the most prosperous towns of the '50's was said to have "nearly winked out." Waldo (Sailor Diggings), on the other hand, was still an important center in the '80's. Now it is almost extinct, being only a place on the map. The road to Crescent City was closed for many years because of the heavy cost of keeping it in repair. The revived state highway to Grants Pass avoids Waldo, so that it is necessary for the modern tourist to reach it by a side road.

Crescent City

Settlers flocked to the northwest coast of California in 1850 as a result of the discovery of gold on the Trinity. Eureka, Arcata, and Trinidad were established as trade centers, but, although a number of vessels—the "Paragon," the "Cameo," and the "Laura Virginia"—had anchored in the crescent-shaped bay as early as 1850, no settlement was made north of the mouth of the Klamath River until after 1852.

The site of Crescent City was first observed from the landward side in the spring of 1851, when searchers for the legendary "Lost Cabin," led by Captain McDermott, looked westward from the summit of French Hill toward the ocean and saw in the far distance an indentation like a bay. Reports of this discovery spread to the interior, where miners were eager to locate a short communication line to the sea. In September 1852 another party set out from Althouse Creek (now in Oregon) and after a perilous and fatiguing journey cut their way to the coast. Elk Valley, located northeast of Crescent City, was named at this time from large herds of elk seen there by the miners.

Setting up camp on the beach, the party dispatched one of their number to San Francisco to charter a vessel. In due time the schooner "Pomona" arrived with prospective settlers, and in February 1853 the town of Crescent City was laid out. By the summer of 1854, three hundred buildings had been erected and the town was the center of an increasing trade from the interior.

Crescent City, despite many ups and downs, continued to hold its own as the chief port of entry and as the supply center for the gold miners of southern Oregon, Siskiyou to the east, and a part of Trinity County, as well as for the camp in the vicinity of Crescent Bay. It was made the county seat of Klamath County in 1854, but in December of the following year lost this position to Orleans Bar.

During this period the citizens of this ambitious town, in their aspiration to make their city the capital of the state, gained the support of some members of the legislature by the offer of free lots, etc.—at least according to a story which had wide credence at the time. The following is a choice addition to that collection of tales of would-be state capitals which are continually coming to light in the annals of California's county histories:

"What a wonderful Legislature that must have been! What a number of valuable town lots must have been offered its members to induce them to propose as the capital of the state, a town in the extreme northwest corner, and at that time almost inaccessible during the winter months. What an immense amount of ignorance must have been concentrated in that legislative body of the days of '55! . . . . It excites our imaginations in contemplating the sublime ignorance of the country displayed by this early Legislature.

"Unfortunately for Crescent City, the bill removing the

state capital to that place failed to pass, and the visions of town lot speculators vanished into thin air. But the Crescentarians were buoyant with life and energy, and the news of the failure was but a passing cloud across their bright hopes and expectations. No doubt, as the principal men of the place discussed the matter over their wine and cigars, new speculations and day-dreams of future greatness served to 'solace the hopes that ended in smoke.'"

Indeed the business activity and social life of that early day in Crescent City were feverish in the extreme. Every day saw some new project for the improvement of the place. New hotels and business houses were opened continually. Soon the town was encroaching on the forest and even covered the beach. Fraternities were established and a fire department organized.

"Saloons and billiard halls flourished in close proximity to the only house of God the place supported; in fact it soon became the type of a California mining town. The streets were filled with people and presented a busy scene—the miner from the mountains jostled the farmer from the valley; the merchant and trader vied with each other in the use of cunning arguments of trade; speculators in town lots talked loudly to new comers of the advantage of this 'garden spot of God's green earth.' God bless you, sir; young men from the states, eager to join the great army who were searching for gold, bartered for animals and outfits; pack trains just in from across the mountains, passed other trains preparing to start on their trip across the Siskiyous, heavily laden with merchandise and mining implements."

By the summer of 1855, trails were completed to the gold camps of southern Oregon and to that large area to the east which drained into the Klamath River. The trail which shortened materially the way to Yreka was long known as the Kelley Trail.

Meanwhile new rich diggings were being uncovered in the hills immediately adjacent to Crescent City. In 1854 and 1855 the miners on Myrtle Creek twelve miles to the northeast were making from five to fifteen dollars per day each. New diggings were also found on the South Fork of Smith River, where individual miners were making from ten to twenty dollars per day.

Diggings were also found closer at hand. In November 1854 discoveries were made six miles from the city on a creek which emptied into Smith River at the White and Miller Ferry, later known as Peacock's Ferry. Even the beach in front of the city was staked off into mining claims. In the Bald Hills six miles to the east gold mines were found in 1856. Here, Villardville, named for a Frenchman, A. Villard, was laid out. Many another mining camp and district in the neighboring hills about Crescent Bay lived their brief day and then vanished. Some of them bore curious names: Redwood Diggings, Big Flat, Growler Gulch, Hurdy Gurdy Creek, Blacks Ferry, Altaville, Low Divide.

Altaville was a copper- and chrome-mining center during the '60's and was full of life and activity. In the '80's its glory had long departed, and it lay in the midst of indescribable peace and quiet. Black mouths of tunnels appeared on the hillsides, and heaps of bluish-colored rock showed the locality of the mines.

Indeed, by the '70's it could truly be said by any chance visitor that "the flush days of mining in Del Norte have vanished with the years, and the halcyon days when the miner with his pick and shovel could delve into the hills and streams and bring forth the golden treasure are gone forever."

Two other points of historical interest in the vicinity of Crescent City are Whale Island, where in June 1855 a company engaged in the whaling business was located; and Battery Point, where three brass cannons were placed in 1855.

They had been salvaged from the steamer "America," which was burned and wrecked on June 24, 1855. The first light, a lantern fixed on the top of a stout pole, was placed at this point before the establishment of the lighthouse by the federal government in 1856.

A Seacoast Cemetery: The Tragedy of St. George's Reef

On the bluff overlooking the sea to the west of Crescent City is a neglected pioneer cemetery, in which many of the headstones reveal the terrible tragedy of the sea which occurred in that vicinity during the summer of 1865. On July 30 of that year the "Brother Jonathan," plying off the coast west of Point St. George under the command of Captain De Wolf, was overtaken by a severe storm. The immediate thought of those in command was to seek a port of safety. There was no idea of approaching death among the hundred passengers on board the vessel. But, hidden just below the surface of the water, St. George's Reef lay directly in the path of the ill-fated vessel. "Suddenly," says Bledsoe, "she struck with tremendous power on a sunken rock, with such force that her foremast went through the hull, her foreyards resting across the rails. Instantly the deck became the scene of the wildest confusion. The crash was so sudden, so unexpected, so awful, that those on board had scarcely recovered from the shock when they saw that their doom was sealed—the ship was fast sinking in the embrace of the hungry waves, and short time was left to prepare for death." Between eighty and ninety persons, both crew and passengers, were drowned, while only one boatload was saved.

The Lighthouse of St. George's Reef

The St. George Reef Light, or the Northwest Seal Rock Light, has lighted the way by which scores of vessels have steered their course away from the treacherous, hidden reefs which lie at its base. The lighthouse is situated on a lonely, diminutive isle seven miles directly off the coast and thirteen miles from Crescent City. It was kept for a long time by Captain John Olsen and four assistants. Virtual prisoners the year round, the men could barely step out of doors, and in stormy periods even this small privilege was denied them. During moderate weather, however, they were permitted to take turns visiting shore.

The St. George Reef Lighthouse is one of the greatest structures of its kind ever erected by the United States government. Costing $750,000, it took four years to build, because work could be carried on only in fair weather. It was completed in 1891. The tower is of rock and powerfully defies both wind and wave. The rock was transported by barges to the lonely island on which it stands. The base covers 6,000 square feet, "the enclosure within which men must work and exist and have all that is necessary to their labor." Occasionally government ships visit the island, but at times supplies cannot be delivered because of storms. There are twenty fathoms of water on the east side of the islet, while on the west side the water is very deep.

Fort Terwar

Six miles from the mouth of the Klamath River, Fort Terwar was established in 1855, as an outpost to guard the Klamath River Indian Reservation.

Camp Lincoln

Camp Lincoln, four and one-half miles northeast of Crescent City, was an outpost on the old Smith River Indian Reservation, abandoned in 1868, when the Indians were removed to the Hoopa Reservation in Humboldt County. One of the old buildings of the post still stands in fair state of preservation.

Along the Redwood Highway

Del Norte long rivaled Alpine County in the High Sierra for inaccessibility, the only roads into it being by wagon and stage or by mule-back. The Redwood Highway now crosses it, passing through the beautiful redwood groves of the Klamath River region, where the trees are larger and assume more weird and grotesque shapes than elsewhere.

SOURCES

[Credit is here given for source material, and permission to quote is hereby acknowledged]

BLEDSOE, A. J. *Indian Wars of the Northwest.* San Francisco, 1885

CLELAND, ROBERT GLASS. *A History of California: The American Period.* The Macmillan Company, New York, 1922

DORNIN, MAY. *The Emigrant Trails into California.* Master's thesis in history, University of California, Berkeley, California, 1921

SULLIVAN, MAURICE S. *The Travels of Jedediah Strong Smith.* The Fine Arts Press, Santa Ana, California, 1934

WALLING, A. G. (pub.). *History of Southern Oregon, Comprising Jackson, Josephine, Douglas, Curry, and Coos Counties,* compiled from the most authentic sources .... A. G. Walling, Portland, Oregon, 1884

HUMBOLDT COUNTY

HUMBOLDT COUNTY (named, as was the Bay, for the great German scientist and traveler, Baron Alexander von Humboldt) was organized in 1853, and Union, now Arcata, was made its county seat. Before that date it had been a part of Trinity County. Eureka has been the county seat since 1856.

The "Arrow Tree"

One mile east of Korbel there is a redwood tree, now dead, around which an interesting Indian legend centers. When white men first passed by the ancient tree, they found it stuck full of arrows for thirty or forty feet above the ground. It was like a mammoth porcupine. The Indians of the region had a tradition about the "Arrow Tree" which went back to the time when it was young:

The tribes of the coast lands were at war with the tribes who dwelt in the hill country and the two met together in a great conflict. The hill tribes were defeated and peace was made at, or near, the great redwood tree, which was ever afterwards looked upon as a boundary mark between the two nations.

Both Chilulas and Wiyots passed the old tree from time to time, and, because it was sacred, they never failed to leave an arrow in its soft bark. "At first the arrows may have been real war arrows, but within the memory of living Indians, they have been merely sharpened sticks. Gradually, the original significance of the tree was partially lost sight of, and it became more and more an altar for worship and a place of prayer."

Korbel is about six miles east of Arcata.

The Rain Rock

Near the fishing place on Trinity River in Sugar-Bowl Valley and four miles from Hoopa is a boulder, not over four feet in diameter and not at all conspicuous, called by the white people the "Rain Rock" and by the Hoopa the Mi, or Thunder's Rock. By this rock, the Indians still believe, dwells a spirit who, when he is displeased, sends killing frosts, or prolongs the rains till flood time, or brings drought and famine.

When heavy frosts kill the crops or when sickness enters the village, the people believe that someone mourning the loss of a dear one has passed by on the road and displeased the Mi. Then a great feast is proclaimed which everyone in the village must attend. Fires are built here and there in the canyon until the Rain Rock is reached. There the last fire is kindled, and over it the feast is prepared. After the people have eaten, and the remnants of the feast have been burned, the priest makes a prayer for warm winds and gentle rains to melt the frost, while he sprinkles the sacred rock with water in which incense root has been mingled. Or, if heavy rains have washed away the little garden plot, the root is sprinkled on the rock dry.

Legendary lore connected with Sugar Loaf Mountain is profuse, and many other mountains, as well as rocks, trees, and rivers throughout the region, have similar legends connected with them. At many of these places Indian ceremonial dances are still held, preceded by much fasting and bathing and accompanied by chanting, singing, and wailing. The climax of the festival follows in the making of "medicine." At Weitchpec, where the Trinity River runs into the Klamath, the largest of these festivals is held annually and is attended by visitors from all over the state.

Indian Wars

The Coast Indians of the Humboldt region were generally friendly and peaceful, but the mountain dwellers were often dangerous, setting fire to grass, driving off livestock, and killing or driving out, one by one, the white settlers along the Mad River and Redwood Creek, and in the Bald Hills, until there were none left between Humboldt Bay and Trinity River.

"During the year of 1851 the trouble between the Indians and the whites became acute. The packers and miners used little caution in their treatment of the Indians, many regarding the latter as their natural enemies, to be shot down whenever opportunity offered. The Indians were unable to discriminate between these vicious white men and the more peaceful ones, and as a result when an Indian was killed some white man paid the penalty, and unfortunately it was seldom the man who had committed the wrong. Nor were the whites themselves at all times above this practice, for seldom was the effort made to apprehend the real offender among the Indians, but rather a general attack followed on the nearest ranchería."

The need of military protection for the new settlements caused the establishment of a post at old Fort Humboldt on Humboldt Heights within the present city limits of Eureka. The first troops arrived there in January 1853 under command of Brevet Lieutenant Colonel R. C. Buchanan. Ulysses S. Grant, as captain of the 4th Regiment Infantry, was stationed there in 1854. Used as an outpost against the Indians, the fort was not abandoned until the summer of 1870. The only structure now remaining is the building formerly used by the Commissary Department; this has been restored, and the plot of ground upon which it stands has been deeded to the city. A bronze tablet placed on a boulder by the Redwood Forest Chapter of the Daughters of the American Revolution, on February 7, 1925, commemorates the site.

Among the many Indian skirmishes were: Dow's Prairie (late in December 1858); Daby's Ferry (June 6, 1862) near Arcata on the Mad River; Oak Camp on Redwood Creek (April 6, 1862); Minor's house on Redwood Creek (early in 1863); the Bald Mountain Indian fort about five miles east of Angel's rancho on Redwood Creek (December 25-26, 1863); and at Chalk Mountain near Bridgeville on the Van Duzen River, one of the last battles.

The Mattole Valley, Hydesville, Yager Creek, and Van Duzen districts are rich in the history of these Indian troubles. Many military posts were scattered throughout the region, among them: Fort Baker (1862–1863), where one house still stands on the Iaqua Road at Neal's Ranch, twenty-eight miles east of Hydesville; Fort Lyons (1862), at Brehmer's Ranch on the Mad River about twenty-five miles southeast of Eureka; Fort Iaqua (1863–1866), on Yager Creek, eight miles south of Brehmer's; Martin's Ferry, on the Klamath River about three miles west of Weitchpec, where one lone house remains; Camp Grant (1863–?), on the Eel River about three miles east of Dyerville; Fort Seward (1861–1863) on the Eel River, where an old log house still stands near the railroad and the County Road about twenty miles southeast of Camp Grant; Camp Anderson (1862–1866), near Minor's Ranch, where the road to Hoopa crosses Redwood Creek; and Fawn Prairie (1863), on the Hoopa Trail. One and one-half miles north of Arcata was Camp Curtis, the headquarters of the Mountain Battalion from 1863 to 1865. The Society of Pioneers of Humboldt County marked this site, October 20, 1930.

Indian Island

In 1860 a terrible massacre of Indians who had gathered for an annual festival took place on Indian Island, now called Gunther's Island. Bret Harte, who was temporarily in charge of the *Northern Californian,* the Uniontown paper, denounced the outrage, and his attack was upheld by the majority of the community. The resentment of a "violent minority," however, was so acute that it finally caused Harte to return to San Francisco.

The massacre on Gunther's Island was only one of numerous Indian troubles which occurred in various regions throughout California during the years 1850 to 1865. For ten years after the establishment of Fort Humboldt the United States Army sought to pacify the Indians of Humboldt County, but without success. Finally, in 1863, the Mountain Battalion of the state militia, composed of six companies of volunteers, was organized. During the two years which followed this action, almost ceaseless warfare was carried on, but the winter of 1864–1865 witnessed the final establishment of reservations for the Indians and the close of the Indian hostilities.

The sites of two shell mounds are on this island.

The Hoopa Indian Reservation

The Hoopa Indian Reservation may be reached by a road from Willow Creek about fifty-six miles northeast of Eureka. Trinity River flows through the center of the reservation, affording splendid canoeing and fishing. The bulk of the surviving Klamath Indians, noted for their beautiful basketry, live here in two settlements, Hoopa in the south and Weitchpec on the northern boundary. At Weitchpec representatives of thirteen local Indian tribes, or bands, gathered in 1851 for the purpose of arranging a treaty with the United States government concerning their lands. This document, signed on October 6 of that year, is now included among the "Eighteen Unratified Treaties" on file at Washington, D.C.

A military post was established in the Hoopa Valley in 1855, and in 1864 Superintendent Wiley selected the valley and surrounding hills for an Indian reservation, for which Congress appropriated sixty thousand dollars. The first agent placed in charge was Robert Stockton.

Cape Mendocino

Cape Mendocino, the most extreme westerly point of the United States on the Pacific Ocean, has been for centuries the landmark for all mariners along the coast of northern California. Its discovery and the bestowal of its name are still shrouded in uncertainty, for, although this monumental rock may first have been seen in 1542 by Juan Rodríguez Cabrillo, the discoverer of Alta California, few writers are agreed as to the exact route of his voyage; and it is more generally believed that he went only as far as the Northwest Cape. Again, the real discoverer may have been one Arellano, a deserter from the expedition commanded by Fray Andrés de Urdaneta in 1565.

In that year, too, Urdaneta had opened up the route for the Manila galleon from Asia across the Pacific to New Spain, and in 1566 the first trading voyage of the galleon was made. For two hundred and fifty years the Spaniards followed this route, sailing across the Pacific with their holds full of rich silks, satins, and spices from the Orient, and often sighting the coast of California as far north as Cape Mendocino.

The name of the point did not appear to have been known to Ferrelo, pilot to Juan Rodríguez, in 1543, but it was mentioned by Francisco de Gali, commander of the Manila galleon of 1584, in such a casual manner as to lead one to believe that it was a name well known to him, although he, himself,. did not see it.

But many a famous voyager sighted Cape Mendocino and charted his course by it: Sir Francis Drake, in 1579, on his voyage around the world; Cermeño, in 1595, while seeking a northern port for the Manila galleon; Vizcaíno, during 1602–1603, while exploring the coast from Cape San Lucas to Cape Mendocino; and George Vancouver, sent out by England in 1792 to investigate the extent of the Spanish possessions on the Pacific Coast; all of these, and others, passed by Cape Mendocino, or turned back southward from that point.

Humboldt Bay

The first recorded discovery of Humboldt Bay was made in 1806 by Captain Jonathan Winship, an American employed by the Russian-American Fur Company to hunt seals along the coast of California. With over twoscore of small boats manned by Alieut Indians, Captain Winship in the "O'Cain" had anchored about twenty-five miles north of Eureka. While searching along the shore for sea otter, some of his men discovered the bay, and a few days later the "O'Cain" sailed through the long-hidden entrance and anchored opposite the present site of Eureka. Winship named the harbor the Bay of the Indians because of the numerous Indian villages found along its shore. To the entrance he gave the name Rezánof.

In 1827, Jedediah Smith, trapper and pathfinder, penetrated into Humboldt County, discovering Trinity River, but he did not see the bay. It remained for Dr. Josiah Gregg to rediscover the bay which Winship had seen and named forty-three years earlier. Gregg had been employed by the government to trace the Trinity River from its source to its mouth. With his companions, he started from Rich Bar, in the vicinity of Weaverville, on November 5, 1849, and reached Trinidad Head on December 7. Here the expedition turned south and on December 20 reached the bay which Dr. Gregg named Trinity Bay. In April of the following year, Lieutenant Douglass Ottinger, in command of the "Laura Virginia," anchored in the bay and named it Humboldt Bay.

Humboldt Bay lies halfway between Cape Trinidad on the north and Cape Mendocino on the south, a distance of forty-five miles. It is very capacious, being almost the only good harbor from San Francisco to Puget Sound. "It eluded discovery with even greater success than San Francisco Bay," Cabrillo, Heceta, Drake, and Vancouver all having passed it by without dreaming of its presence.

Trinidad

Trinidad is on the Redwood Highway about eighteen miles north of Eureka. It received its name from the Spanish mariners, Bodega and Heceta, who entered the bay on Trinity Sunday, June 9, 1775. In honor of the Spanish discoverers, a granite cross was placed by the women's clubs of Humboldt County near the Lighthouse on Trinidad Head.

It seems probable that Rodríguez Cermeño may have sighted Trinidad's rocky headland on November 4, 1595, when the "San Agustín," laden with silks and porcelain from the Orient, first sighted the coast of New Spain a little above 41° latitude. Trinidad was not visited again until April 1793, when Captain George Vancouver landed there and found the roughly hewn cross left by the Spaniards. He was able to read the inscription: "Carolus III Dei G Hyspaniarum Rex."

Trinidad, the oldest town along the northern California coast and the first town in Humboldt County to be settled by Americans, was founded in 1850. It was then in Klamath County (later abolished) and was the county seat from 1851 to 1854.

During the '50's, Trinidad was one of the principal ports of entry and one of the principal trading posts for the mining camps in the Klamath and Trinity River drainage area. "The mining excitement of Gold Bluffs caused a veritable boom in town lots and by February of 1851 Trinidad had a population variously estimated from 1,500 to 3,000 people." It was also one of the most important whaling stations on the California coast. This is said to be the only whaling station still operating.

The glory of Trinidad passed with the passing of mining as the chief industry. When lumbering took its place, Eureka, on the splendid Humboldt Bay, superseded all other towns in importance. Trinidad has less than one hundred inhabitants today, while Eureka has almost eighteen thousand.

Humboldt City

The first of the several towns which hoped to become the main port of entry on Humboldt Bay and the trading center for the mines was Humboldt City. On April 14, 1850, its founders entered the bay and immediately began to lay out a town opposite the entrance, just south of what later became Bucksport. The founders of the new town, the Laura Virginia Company, were certain that it would become the metropolis of the region.

"Its water front extended [on paper] for three or four miles along Humboldt Bay and the town was capable of unlimited expansion into the interior." For a time Humboldt City held its own among the rival settlements of Uniontown, Bucksport, and Eureka, all of which were founded later in the spring of 1850. Being farther from the Klamath mines (then the center of activity) than were its rivals, Humboldt City was at a disadvantage, and in 1851 the place was almost deserted in spite of the efforts of its promoters to attract settlers.

Eureka

Eureka, destined to be the metropolis of the Humboldt region, was the last of the towns to be established there. When the Mendocino Exploring Company arrived in May 1850, they found that the Union Company, located at Uniontown, already claimed the land. An agreement was made to share the establishment of the town, and lots were surveyed the same year under the supervision of James Ryan.

Advancement was at first very slow, since the new settlement was farther away from the Klamath mines than was Uniontown. When business shifted from the Klamath to

the Trinity mining district, a road was cut to the Trinity area from Eureka, and the latter's position was improved.

Gradually mining was superseded by lumbering; and, since Eureka was situated at the head of navigation not too far from the entrance of the bay (seven miles), it soon proved to be the natural shipping center and shot ahead in the race for supremacy, while Uniontown, impeded by a vast extent of mud flats, fell behind. In 1856, the final triumph of Eureka was marked by her victory in the contest for the county seat.

Arcata

Arcata, on Humboldt Bay, eight miles northeast of Eureka, was founded in 1850 by a party of thirty men from San Francisco under the leadership of L. K. Wood. Wood was one of the Josiah Gregg party, which discovered Humboldt Bay in 1849, at the point where Arcata now stands. On April 19, 1850, Wood and his party founded their town, which they called Uniontown.

When Humboldt County was organized in 1853, Uniontown became the county seat. It was the center of activity in the days of pack-trains when goods were carried to the mines over the mountain trails which began at Uniontown and followed up the Trinity and Klamath rivers. When the lumbering industry superseded that of mining, the lumber mills centered at Eureka, which was on deep water, making it the natural shipping-point of the bay. For this reason, the county seat was removed to Eureka in 1856, and Uniontown was renamed Arcata, the original Indian name for the spot.

Arcata is beautifully situated at the northern end of Humboldt Bay, surrounded by redwood forests. The Humboldt State Normal School was established there in 1913, and it became, in 1921, the Humboldt State Teachers College, the farthest west of any college in the United States. From its campus, many magnificent scenic trails lead out through the primeval redwood groves which flank the Redwood Highway in Humboldt County.

Bret Harte, California's noted short-story writer, lived at Arcata during the early part of his career, from 1857 to 1860. While there he worked on a newspaper, the *Northern Californian,* located in a building still standing. He also did tutoring at the Liscom Ranch in the suburbs of Arcata.

Bucksport

The pioneer settlement of Bucksport was first located by the Gregg party. One of the members, David A. Buck, carved his name on a tree there in December 1849 and at the same time expressed a wish to settle on the spot some day. Buck did return in the summer of 1850, but the land had already been claimed by the Union Company, with headquarters at Uniontown. Buck, not to be robbed of the fulfillment of his dream, remained in spite of protests. From that time on the place was known as Buck's Port or Bucksport.

A town was surveyed and, since it was on the main channel of the bay near its entrance, settlers were attracted to it. In 1853, the establishment of Fort Humboldt on the bluff overlooking the town gave the place added prestige. A campaign for the position of county seat of the newly formed Humboldt County was made in 1854 but was unsuccessful. Failure to secure this honor caused Bucksport to fall behind in the race. It is now within the southern limits of the city of Eureka.

Gold Bluffs

Gold Bluffs was the scene of great excitement in 1850 and 1851, when thousands of miners came there to extract gold from the beach sands. It was situated about fifteen miles south of the mouth of Klamath River, and thirty-five miles north of Trinidad. Nothing remains of the old camp today.

Orleans Bar

Orleans Bar, once a thriving mining center on the Klamath River, along which the rich mines of northern California were located, was the county seat of Klamath County from 1855 to 1875, when the county was dissolved. Its predecessors were Trinidad (1851–1854) and Crescent City (1854–1855).

Centerville Beach Memorial Cross

On January 6, 1860, the steamer "Northerner," which had left San Francisco on the 5th, struck a hidden rock off Cape Mendocino and drifted to the Centerville beach near Ferndale. Seventeen passengers and twenty-one members of the crew were lost. In 1921 Ferndale Chapter No. 93 of the Native Sons of the Golden West erected a concrete cross to honor the memory of the thirty-eight who lost their lives in this disaster.

Mail Ridge

Mail Ridge was once a part of the old mail stage route from San Francisco into the northwestern part of California before the advent of the railroad. It is about 3,500 feet above sea level with extensive views over the whole southern part of Humboldt County.

To reach the Ridge, the road leaves the Redwood Highway at Fortuna, about eighteen miles south of Eureka, and follows up the Van Duzen River to Bridgeville, thence south through high mountain country to Blocksburg, and on to Alderpoint on the main line of the railway. Crossing the railway, the route leads up hill for eight miles to the town of Harris, then turns north again and follows along Mail Ridge, the old stage road.

Redwood Groves

Along the famous Redwood Highway through Humboldt County there are many magnificent stands of primeval redwood forests (*Sequoia sempervirens*). An increasing number of these great century-old groves have been made into private or public parks to be preserved to the people for all time.

There are now approximately 22,000 acres of redwood groves in state parks in Humboldt County and also about 3,000 acres of coast-line and river areas in state parks. A few miles north of Scotia is Canyon Park, and just off the highway west of Dyerville on Bull Creek is the Bull Creek Grove on a road leading to Upper Mattole. The road south of Dyerville passes through numerous groves, many of which are memorials to noted men: the Perrot Grove, Sage Grove, Gould Grove, Mather Grove, Bolling Grove, Felton Grove, Stephens Grove, Fish Creek Grove (private), and the Franklin K. Lane Grove, a memorial to Franklin K. Lane, secretary of the interior under President Wilson and first president of the Save-the-Redwoods League. The little town of Orick lies at the lower end of the Redwood Creek Grove, and north of the town is the Humboldt Pioneer Memorial Grove, dedicated to early settlers who braved the unknown to establish their homes in the wilderness. This is also known as the Russ Grove.

SOURCES

[Credit is here given for source material, and permission to quote is hereby acknowledged]

BLEDSOE, A. J. *Indian Wars of the Northwest.* San Francisco, 1855
CARR, JOHN. *Pioneer Days in California.* Privately printed, Eureka, 1891
CHAPMAN, CHARLES E. *A History of California: The Spanish Period.* The Macmillan Company, New York, 1923
COY, OWEN C. *The Humboldt Bay Region, 1850–1875: A Study in the American Colonization of California.* The California State Historical Association, Los Angeles, 1929
————. *Pictorial History of California.* University of California Extension Division, Berkeley, California, 1925
DAVIDSON, GEORGE. "The Discovery of Humboldt Bay," in *Transactions of the Geographical Society of the Pacific,* II, No. 1. San Francisco, 1891
History of Humboldt County, California. W. W. Elliott & Company, San Francisco, 1881
HUNT, ROCKWELL D., and NELLIE VAN DE GRIFT SANCHEZ. *A Short History of California.* Thomas Y. Crowell Company, New York, 1929
KROEBER, A. L. *Handbook of the Indians of California.* Smithsonian Institution, Bureau of American Ethnology, Bulletin 78, Washington, 1925
MURDOCK, CHARLES A. *A Backward Glance at Eighty.* Paul Elder & Company, San Francisco, 1921
Publications in American Archaeology and Ethnology, University of California, Vols. I and XIV, Berkeley, California
WAGNER, HENRY R. *Spanish Voyages to the Northwest Coast of America in the Sixteenth Century.* California Historical Society, San Francisco, 1929

LAKE COUNTY

LAKE COUNTY (so named because of the presence within its confines of a large body of fresh water known as Clear Lake) was set off from Napa County on May 2, 1861, and Lakeport was made its county seat. In 1867 the courthouse and all its records were burned. Another was built in 1870, but, in the meantime, the county seat was temporarily located at Lower Lake.

Indians and Their Legends

Accessibility to a convenient food supply is the prime requisite for the habitation of a primitive people. Throughout Lake County the abundance of fish, fowl, berries, nuts, and game met this first need and attracted a large Indian population, possibly the densest in what is now California.

Tule roots grew abundantly along the shores of Tule Lake, located midway between the Blue Lakes and the upper end of Clear Lake, and here the Indians camped in great numbers during the digging season. Also of economic value were the massive bodies of obsidian found southwest of Mount Konocti and used for making spear- and arrowheads. From one of the most numerous of the game birds, the blue quail, this untutored people secured feathers for decorative purposes. George Gibbs, writing in his journal in 1851, says: "At Clear Lake the women generally wear a small round bowl-shaped basket on their heads, and this is frequently interwoven with the red feathers of the woodpecker and edged with the plume tufts of the blue quail."

Among the legends of this vicinity is one purporting to give the origin of the most notable feature of the landscape, Mount Konocti: Lupiyomi, daughter of the proud and powerful chief Konocti, was sought in marriage by a rival chieftain, Kahbel. Chief Konocti, refusing consent to the union of his beautiful daughter with this suitor, upon being challenged to battle by the latter, took up his stand on one side of the Narrows of Clear Lake, while his opponent took a position on the opposite side. The rocks hurled across the water by these warriors during the combat are the immense boulders that now cover the mountainside. The maiden's tears formed a pool—now Little Borax Lake—a lasting memorial of her grief. The lover Kahbel was killed; his blood is now seen in the red splashes on the gashed side of Red Hill, rising on the north shore. Chief Konocti, also, succumbed and, sinking back, formed the rugged mountain that now bears his name. The maiden was so distraught that she threw herself into the lake; and her unfailing tears bubble up in Omarocharbe, the Big Soda Spring, gushing out of the waters of Clear Lake at Soda Bay.

Clear Lake

Clear Lake was known to the Indians as Hok-has-ha and Ka-ba-tin, names given to it by two different tribes. It is the largest body of fresh water lying wholly in the state and is near the geographical center of the county. Ewing Young and his party of trappers crossed the Coast Range in 1832 by way of this lake on their journey from the Sacramento River to the Pacific Ocean. James Clyman, in his diary for December 1845, wrote that he camped on the outlet of Clear Lake and feasted on bear ribs and liver. Edwin Bryant, a traveler in California in the years 1846–1847, wrote: "A lake not laid down in any map and known as the Laguna among the Californians, is situated about sixty miles north of the Bay of San Francisco. It is between forty and sixty miles in length. The valleys in its vicinity are highly fertile and romantically beautiful. In the vicinity of this lake there is a mountain of pure sulphur. There are also soda springs and a great variety of the mineral waters and minerals."

Lieutenant Joseph Warren Revere, in command of the northern district for some months after the raising of the United States flag at Sonoma, made a tour to Clear Lake and wrote his experiences for publication. "Few white men have visited this magnificent Laguna." About sunset one evening, he and his men arrived at the narrowest part of Clear Lake, "opposite a pretty islet" upon which was a native village. The Indians, at first fearful because of the many raids made upon them in search of servants, were finally persuaded to ferry the travelers across on tule *balsas*. The island village, protected by this natural moat, had between two and three hundred inhabitants.

Clear Lake is divided by the Narrows and Mount Konocti into Upper Lake and Lower Lake. Mount Konocti, sometimes called "Uncle Sam Mountain," rises solitarily 2,500 feet above the level of the water, a majestic guardian of the scene. The summit of this mountain was owned in the '70's by O. S. Morford, who built the first wagon road to the top and completed it in 1878 with the intention of establishing a public summer resort far up on the mountainside. On May 1, 1878, Morford, with two companions, ascended to the pinnacle and there unfurled the Stars and Stripes. His plans for a summer resort were not carried out. Orchards now dot the slopes of the mountain, but the shores of the lake are dotted with summer settlements and at Lakeport annual water carnivals are held.

Kelseyville

General Mariano G. Vallejo founded and was placed in command of Sonoma in 1835, and in 1836 an expedition led by his brother, Salvador, and Ramón Carrillo was made into the Clear Lake country, the first white expedition to enter that region. Salvador Vallejo and his brother Antonio, as early as 1840, applied for a grant of land covering what are now known as the Big, Scotts, Upper Lake, and Bachelor valleys. It is not certain whether this grant was ever actually ceded or not, but for several years the Vallejos' cattle were herded over its fertile ranges, where they multiplied and became exceedingly wild. A log cabin and corral were built in Big Valley near the present site of Kelseyville, and a mayordomo and ten vaqueros were placed there to look after the ranch.

In 1847, Vallejo drove some of his cattle out of the valley and sold the remainder to four men, Stone, Shirley, and two Kelsey brothers, Andrew and Benjamin, who had arrived in California with the Bidwell-Bartleson party in 1841. Stone and Andrew Kelsey took possession of the ranch and employed Indians to erect an adobe house for them on the banks of Kelsey Creek where Kelseyville now stands. General Vallejo had always treated the Indians kindly and had made them his friends, but Andrew Kelsey treated them in quite a different manner and gained their ill will. In consequence of this folly on Kelsey's part, he and Stone were finally killed by the Indians in the fall of 1849.

The following spring two lieutenants, Hayes and Stoneman, arrived with soldiers to punish the offenders. They found the Indians gathered on an island at the northern end of Clear Lake. Approaching from two directions, they fired on the group and practically annihilated them; since that time the place has been called "Bloody Island," although land-reclamation projects have eliminated its water boundaries. Differing versions of this massacre are extant.

Within a few months after this slaughter, a treaty between the whites and the Indians was arranged by Henry Frederick Teschemacher, a resident of San Francisco and later claimant for Rancho Lupyomi. A grand powwow celebrated the peace-making, and the provisions of the agreement were thereafter adhered to.

The town of Kelseyville began in 1857 with Benham's store and blacksmith shop. It is now a flourishing place with a Union High School and is the center of the pear industry of the county. The graves of Stone and Kelsey are in a field on a hillside about one-fourth of a mile from the Kelseyville Cemetery south of the main Lakeport-Kelseyville highway. The grave of John Kelsey, of a later generation, with that of his wife, is in the center of a crossroads about one mile west of Kelseyville; near by is an old cemetery from which these graves were cut off by a realignment of roads.

A Lost Treaty

To meet the problem of the displacement of the native in favor of the incoming white man, a commission to negotiate treaties was appointed by President Millard Fillmore shortly after the admission of the state of California into the Union.

Commissioner Redick McKee, representing the United States government, and the chiefs and headmen of eight local Indian tribes signed a Treaty of Peace and Friendship on August 20, 1851, at Camp Lu-Pi-Yu-Mi on the south shore of Clear Lake. This treaty consisted of eight articles setting forth details of the promises on both sides, and a careful description of the lands to be given, in perpetuity, to these tribes, as well as certain benefits to be derived by them in recompense for their renunciation, as set forth in Article III of the treaty:

The said tribes, or bands, hereby jointly and severally relinquish, cede and forever quitclaim to the United States all their right, title, claim or interest of any kind, which they, or either of them hold to the lands or soil in California.

At this council a gift was made to the assembled Indians of: "Ten head of beef cattle, three sacks of bread and sundry clothing."

This treaty, along with seventeen others, was sent to the Senate by President Fillmore on June 1, 1852, for constitutional action. Never ratified, it is now referred to as one of the "Eighteen Lost Treaties."

Mexican Grants

Three grants of land were made by the Mexican government within the territory now included in Lake County.

Rancho Lupyomi, about which there was much litigation,

was originally granted to Salvador and Juan Antonio Vallejo by Governor Micheltorena on September 5, 1844. The map accompanying this grant showed the territory of Laguna de Lu-Pi-Yo-Mi as extending sixteen leagues and embracing the whole of Clear Lake. In 1854 settlers began to arrive, and by 1861 many families had located on the land, although their titles to it could not be made valid until certain claims were decided. After many delays, Judge Ogden Hoffman rendered a decision that gave satisfaction, and the potential owners met for a "jollification" at Lakeport on October 6, 1866. Soon after this, the land was surveyed and each man secured his home. Kelseyville is on a part of this grant.

Rancho Collayomi, consisting of three leagues of land in Loconoma Valley, was given to Robert T. Ridley on June 17, 1844, by Governor Micheltorena. Ridley, an English sailor, became captain of the Port of San Francisco in 1846, a position that he held but a short time. He had been naturalized as a Mexican citizen in 1844 and married to Presentación Briones. Within a few years, in 1852, the claim of Colonel A. A. Ritchie and Paul S. Forbes was confirmed to this land, and a patent was issued to them in 1863. This grant was divided in 1871 and disposed of to actual settlers.

Rancho Guenoc, containing six leagues in Coyote Valley, was ceded by Governor Pio Pico to George Rock (Roch) in 1845. Coyote Valley extends for several miles along the banks of Putah Creek. According to Bancroft, George Rock came into the valley as early as 1837. For a time he was agent there for Jacob P. Leese, who kept cattle both there and in Loconoma Valley. Rock lived in a cabin on the north side of the valley before 1850. The stone house now standing on the site of Rock's cabin was built in 1853–1854 by Captain R. Steele and Robert Sterling, the wife of the latter being the first white woman in the valley. The part of the Guenoc rancho on which this stone house stands is now the Young Ranch. Colonel Ritchie and his partner, Paul S. Forbes, who had acquired Rancho Callayomi, also received the United States patent for this grant in 1865.

A small ephemeral village, called Guenoc, was situated on the south bank of Putah Creek on the road between Middletown and Lower Lake, in 1866; but when Middletown with its superior central position with respect to roads sprang up, all activity was transferred to the new site. A plain frame building beside the highway north of Middletown bears above its one doorway the words "Guenoc Grange."

Mineral Springs

A number of medicinal springs are found in Lake County. The Harbin Springs, four miles from Middletown, were visited by A. A. Ritchie in 1852, but were known to the Indians long before that time. They were already famous when the water was examined by Dr. Winslow Anderson in 1889, and a fashionable resort grew up about them as the population of the state increased. They have been well maintained to the present time.

Seigler Springs are in Seigler Valley at the foot of Seigler Mountain. Crude bathing pools, in which the temperature of the water could be regulated, were in use by the aborigines before the place was discovered by Seigler. Among the names of prominent people connected with the development of these springs are Dr. J. T. Boone, in 1868, and Alvinza Hayward and W. Cole of San Francisco, in 1870. Long a well-kept place with attractive buildings, it has now been merged with a newer resort under a single management.

Anderson Springs, at the head of Loconoma Valley, were also notable in the early days. They were opened to the public in 1874 by Dr. Anderson and L. S. Patriquin.

Bartlett Springs, at an elevation of 2,100 feet, are renowned for the curative properties of their water. They were found in 1868 by Greene Bartlett in the Middle Fork of Cache Creek. Suffering from a severe attack of rheumatism contracted while herding sheep in Berryessa Valley, he revisited them in 1870 and found relief from his ailment by drinking the water. To this place he later led his friends, and a health resort grew up. Bartlett homesteaded the land about the springs, built a log house, and, in association with others, erected a hotel and cottages. The old log cabin was restored in later years and used as a museum in which relics of pioneer days were stored. This resort had been kept up continuously since the early days, until a fire in September 1934 practically destroyed the hotels and cottages. The log cabin also was burned, but a trunk formerly owned by Greene Bartlett was rescued from the flames.

Other springs that have been well known for many years are: Witter and Saratoga, both near Blue Lakes; Highland, six miles west of Kelseyville; and Adams, in the mountains between Kelseyville and Middletown.

Old Mills

The many streams of Lake County afforded power for two industries of great importance in a pioneer community: the grinding of grain for food, and the sawing of lumber for houses. Thomas Boyd built the first mill in the county at the foot of Cobb Mountain. It was a steam gristmill and sawmill combined and was put in operation in 1858. In 1866, H. C. Boggs purchased this mill, which from this date was known as the "Boggs' Mill," although its location was changed several times. At one time it stood on the margin of Boggs' Lake. Decaying logs and a part of the old framework mark its last location, three miles north of Harbin Springs.

Another mill, originally known as Elliot's Mill, was erected in Upper Lake Township in 1855 by William B. Elliot, who had come overland from North Carolina, arriving in California in 1845 with his wife and children. He and his sons became successful hunters of the grizzly bears then so prevalent in the mountain regions. His mill was in operation until 1867. In time it became known by the odd cognomen of "Whittle-Busy," because, since it ground very slowly, its patrons were wont to while away the time waiting by whittling.

Some of the old gristmills in Lake County are still running: the old Brown Mill (earlier called the Allison Mill) on Kelsey Creek about three miles above Kelseyville; Stoddard's Mill, west of Middletown, originally the property of Joel Stoddard and, in the '80's, known as "one of the neatest and best mills in Lake County" (this mill still uses the old-type machinery and the old method of grinding); and the Upper Lake Planing and Grist Mill, erected in 1875 with an 8½ horsepower steam engine. The proprietor at that time was "prepared for planing, grinding grain, manufacturing doors, sash, and furniture." Old-fashioned cornmeal and whole-wheat flour are still ground by the old method at this mill.

Lower Lake Flouring-Mill was built in 1869 by J. M. Evarts and William Davy on the west bank of Seigler Creek. It was run by steam and had a wide reputation in the '80's for making good flour.

Mines

Although a great variety of minerals have been discovered in the county, the quantities usually have been too small for economic development. Quicksilver, sulphur, and borax have been mined. The Great Western, a cinnabar (quicksilver) deposit, was "located" in 1850, but little work was done on it until 1856. It is four miles south of Middletown and is now producing.

The Old Sulphur Banks Mine, also quicksilver, grew out of the works of the California Borax Company in 1875. It is on the shore of Clear Lake north of the town of Lower Lake, and has been developed extensively during recent years. The Saint Anthony (or Sulphur Bank) Church, which stands not far distant in the hills, was erected about 1911 as a place of worship for workers in the mine. For many years previous to that time, the Catholic families of the vicinity had been in the habit of holding Mass in private dwellings. When it was decided to construct a church edifice, bricks, probably well impregnated with quicksilver, were obtained from the old furnaces on the Sulphur Bank property. The Catholics of the district donated the work of transporting the brick and laying the walls, assisted by local Indians. Regular services are conducted in this church of Saint Anthony, although the realignment of the highway has left it on an obscure side road.

Several other old quicksilver mines in the county are still in operation; among them are the Oat Hill, the Mirabel, and the Helen.

The town of Lower Lake lies between Big Borax Lake, discovered by Dr. J. A. Veatch in 1856, and Little Borax Lake, the first source of borax in Alta California. The California Borax Company began operation on Little Borax Lake in 1864 and worked successfully for several years. The first house in the town of Lower Lake was built by E. Mitchell in 1858. This village was a station on the stage line running from Calistoga in later years and was the county seat for two years.

Upper Lake

Dr. Josiah Gregg, scientist, explorer, and author of *The Commerce of the Prairies,* died near Upper Lake on February 25, 1850, of starvation and exposure. He was returning from an exploring trip to Humboldt Bay with a few of his men when he fell from his horse because of weakness. He was buried, "according to the custom of the prairies," in a shallow grave with a blanket for his coffin, and a pile of stones was placed over his body to protect it from prowling animals.

Two original settlements, one above and one below the town of Upper Lake, were made before 1865, when the present site near the junction of Clover, Middle, and Scott creeks was peopled. Benjamin Dewell, one of the makers of the first Bear Flag, settled on the west side of Clover Creek in 1854. His father-in-law, William B. Elliot, in whose company young Dewell had made the overland trip to California, settled on the east side of the creek in the same year. Benjamin Dewell's house, occupied by some of his descendants, still stands in the outskirts of the present thriving town. There is now no trace of the original settlement to the south, as the buildings there were removed to the present site of the town.

Lakeport

Lakeport, on the western shore of Clear Lake, was first named Forbestown. William Forbes had owned 160 acres here before the formation of the county in 1861 and gave, by deed, 40 acres as a site for the county seat in the vicinity of his previously erected house and blacksmith shop. Forbes Street now commemorates his name. The first place of business in the county was a short distance south of Lakeport, at Stony Point, where Dr. E. D. Boynton had built a store and had put in a stock of goods in 1856.

Middletown

Middletown, near the center of the Callayomi land grant and midway between Lower Lake and Calistoga (Napa County) at the junction of roads leading to several important mineral springs, was first settled in 1868. The oldest building now standing in the town was used by O. Armstrong as a

saloon in 1870. It is on the left side of the road between the High School and the bridge on the way to Lower Lake.

The site of the old Lake County House, built in the '50's, is now occupied by the Herrick Hotel. A small house built on this site by J. H. Berry in 1840 was the forerunner of the town. The first church built here was the Methodist Episcopal, which has been moved to the edge of town on the Calistoga Road and is now used as a private residence. Plans are being made to place a marker on this building.

The last years of a distinguished European scholar, Dr. James Blake, were spent in Middletown, where he died and was buried in 1893. Native of England, writer of medical books, California pioneer of 1849, one-time president of the California Academy of Science, Dr. Blake retired in 1876 to Lake County because of impaired health. He took up his residence near a large spring, where he built a cottage east of Mount St. Helena on the highway connecting Clear Lake and Calistoga (Napa County). Feeling his health vastly improved here, he erected simple buildings where others might be helped, and where he carried on his medical research until he finally moved to Middletown. The plain structures used for this sanatorium are still in existence, as is also the cottage that he occupied. They stand within the grounds of a private estate.

Clear Lake College

Clear Lake College opened its doors in Lakeport on the first Thursday in September 1876 in a two-story frame building on Twelfth Street, now a residence known as the Spencer house. Seven students matriculated on the opening day. The upholding of the classics in a frontier community met with many difficulties; nevertheless, by 1881, at the end of the fifth year, the entire classical course had been "successfully mastered by one of its students," who was granted the degree of Bachelor of Arts in June. At the same time two honorary degrees of Master of Arts and one honorary degree of Doctor of Laws were conferred. The President of the institution, Rev. John A. Kelley, said at that time: "It proves itself to be one of the permanent institutions of Lake County, and the only college in the state that places the advantages of a broad and liberal education within easy reach of all parties who may aspire to the rank of learned men."

After having been in existence about twenty years the college was forced to close its doors because it was unable to compete with the State University. Its fate was similar to that of most of the private and local colleges of California. The second and final home of Clear Lake College was a building formerly used by the Second Baptist Church on Eighth Street. This structure was later made into two flats, which are now used for residential purposes.

Lakeport Academy

In 1884, shortly before Clear Lake College ceased to function, Lakeport Academy was founded by Professor John Overholser in a discarded grammar-school building on Forbes Street between Third and Fourth. This building was destroyed after being vacated by the Academy, and a residence now occupies the site.

Moving to its own new quarters in the northwest part of the town, the Academy continued until the formation of the Clear Lake Union High School District in 1901, when the place was rented by the high school. With the erection of a new high-school building, the Academy building was vacated and was later purchased by H. S. Spillers, who made alterations which transformed it into a hospital. At that time, concrete pillars were added in the construction of a porch. The hospital was burned in 1928, but the old pillars still stand on the corner of Hartley and Eighteenth streets.

The Cache Creek Dam

A subject of great interest to the people then residing in the vicinity of Clear Lake was the construction, in 1866, of a dam across Cache Creek near the outlet of the lake by the Clear Lake Water Company. Because of this dam, the level of the water in the lake was raised to such an extent that the rich farm land, the established orchards, and the dwelling houses within a large radius were destroyed. After reasonable appeals to the Water Company had been ignored and no compensation for damage was allowed, the people set systematically to work to redress their wrongs. On Sunday morning, November 15, 1868, after being led in prayer by the Baptist minister, Rev. B. Ogle, the crowd began the demolition of the dam. The work was completed on the following Tuesday morning. Litigation ensued, but the dam was never rebuilt on this spot. Another dam on Cache Creek, below the town of Lower Lake, was completed in 1914 and is in use at the present time.

Langtry Farm

Lily Langtry, English actress in the Victorian period, who was born on the Isle of Jersey and was known as the "Jersey Lily" because of her birthplace and her great physical beauty, became joint owner of a property in the southern part of the county. "Freddy" Gebhard, wealthy clubman of New York, was the co-partner in the purchase of this 7,500-acre portion of the old Guenoc grant. At the time of the purchase, a winery was in operation and a few dwellings were on the premises.

Extensive improvements were made, and large sums were invested in fine race horses by the new owners; "Doc" Abbey, former manager at the Santa Anita ranch of "Lucky" Baldwin, was put in charge, and a one-mile race track was constructed. For some years all went well; then, in 1897, a rift in the partnership came. Barns, race track, and general operations were concentrated on the Gebhard land, and a stout fence was built to define the two holdings. Mrs. Langtry returned to England shortly thereafter.

This place, known to stock raisers of that time as the home of the Guenoc Stud, was on the County Road seven miles southeast of Middletown.

SOURCES

[Credit is here given for source material, and permission to quote is hereby acknowledged]

ANDERSON, WINSLOW, M.D. *Mineral Springs and Health Resorts of California.* Bancroft Company, San Francisco, 1892
BENSON, WILLIAM RALGANAL. "Narrative of the Stone and Kelsey Massacre," in *California Historical Society Quarterly,* XI, No. 3 (September 1932), 266–273
BRYANT, EDWIN. *What I Saw in California, Being a Journal of a Tour in the Years 1846–47.* D. Appleton Company, New York, 1849
California, State of. *Corrected Report of Spanish and Mexican Grants in California.* Complete to February 25, 1886. Prepared by State Surveyor General. Published as supplement to official *Report of 1883–84.* Sacramento, 1886
CARPENTER, AURELIUS, and PERCY H. MILLBERRY. *History of Mendocino and Lake Counties.* Historical Record Company, Los Angeles, 1914
CLYMAN, JAMES. "Diaries"; original manuscript in Huntington Library
GIBBS, GEORGE. "Journal of the Expedition of Col. Redick McKee, U.S. Indian Agent, through Northwestern California. Performed in the summer and fall of 1851." In Volume III, *History of the Indian Tribes of the United States,* by Henry R. Schoolcraft, LL.D. Lippincott, Grambo & Company, Philadelphia, 1853

HARRIS, HENRY. *California's Medical Story.* J. W. Stacey, San Francisco, 1932
History of Napa and Lake Counties, California. Slocum, Bower & Company, San Francisco, 1881
History of Northern California. Illustrated. Lewis Publishing Company, Chicago, 1891
MENEFEE, C. A. *Historical and Descriptive Sketch Book of Napa, Sonoma, Lake, and Mendocino.* Reporter Publishing House, Napa City, 1873
"Langtry Story," in *New York Times,* February 13, 1929
"Langtry Farm, The End of the." In *San Francisco Call,* August 28, 1898
QUAYLE, MRS. JAMES A. Manuscript notes
United States Congress, House of Representatives. *Indian Tribes of California.* . . . . Hearings . . . . March 23, 1920
"Visit to Lake County," in *San Francisco Post,* July 1877

MARIN COUNTY

MARIN COUNTY (Marin is thought to be a corruption of El Marinero, "the sailor," a name given to a Christian Indian who rendered excellent service as a ferryman on San Francisco Bay before 1834) was one of the original twenty-seven counties, San Rafael being its county seat. Sonoma County was a part of Marin County for the first two months.

Indian Shell Mounds

Marin County was once well populated with Indians; and the picturesque, indented shore line of its entire coast, particularly that part along San Pablo Bay (the "Round Bay" of the early Spanish explorers), San Pablo Strait, and Richardson's Bay, attracted them because of the ample supply of shellfish, one of their main foods. In this region shell mounds are numerous. These mounds, the residue of animal and vegetable matter, are sometimes found on hillsides in the vicinity of springs and small streams. The mounds made mainly of shell are nearer to the salt marshes, or even on the edge of the water, and it is from these more enduring mounds of shell that information can best be gathered regarding the primitive people who occupied these favorite village sites.

Two large mounds were near Novato; creeks between Ignacio and San Rafael are studded with smaller ones. The remains of a mound probably at one time fifteen feet high and eighty feet in diameter is at Santa Venetia, although most of it has been hauled away as fertilizer for gardens. Several good ones are being preserved in the McNear estate between Santa Venetia and China Camp; the coast line extending back from San Pedro Point in both directions and also the irregular coast of Tiburon Peninsula and Richardson's Bay show dozens more. Across the flat north of Belvedere at the edge of a hill there is still a large shell mound, through one side of which a street runs.

Shells, mortars, pestles, and bowls were found in a shell heap formerly on the site now occupied by the building at 127 Caledonia Street, Sausalito. One mound accidentally discovered at the bottom of Elk Canyon, northwest of Sausalito, and three others below Mill Valley completely covered with natural deposits are from one to three feet deep and of unknown lateral extent. A large mound at the highland edge of the marsh below Mill Valley, when measured in 1908, was 200 by 450 feet through the base, having a height of 20 feet to a truncated top 90 feet in diameter. Southeast of Kentfield and on the southeast side of the high hill along the road to Greenbrae is a notable shell mound from which hundreds of tons of material have been hauled away, leaving, however, much of the lower part showing in detail the shape and extent of the foundation. On the north side of the Redwood Highway in sight of Greenbrae and on the edge of the hill just west of the Larkspur Road and east of the Pleasant Valley Ranch house, a small house has been built at the place where a mound has evidently been leveled off for that purpose. Another good shell mound lies at the south side of the Northwestern Pacific Railroad between California Park and the east entrance of the tunnel just across the ridge from Greenbrae.

Utensils, beads, and arrowheads have been taken from various mounds in the county and placed in museums of the Bay region, and from two large mounds at Greenbrae archaeological material is said to have been sent many years ago to London. Obsidian arrow points have been found frequently near the library of Marin Junior College at Kentfield. In the recent leveling of ground on Hamilton Field, two mounds were razed, bringing to light stone and shell ornaments and conical polished stones pierced at one end and believed to be ceremonial pieces used by a "medicine man" or possibly the insignia of a chief. When the pit for the gas tank at Fourth and Irwin streets in San Rafael was dug, workmen found the skeleton of a chief decorated with strings of stone beads and ornaments made of abalone and other shells. Many small mounds have been found on the shores of Bolinas and Tomales bays—so many that the total count of mounds in this county is well over two hundred.

Drake's Bay

On November 15, 1577, sponsored by Queen Elizabeth, Francis Drake (afterward Sir Francis) set out from England in command of five sailing vessels on a voyage westward. His destination was the Orient and his mission the achievement of honor and riches for his Queen and his country. His vessel, the "Pellican," renamed in the following year the "Golden Hind," was the only one of the five to make the entire voyage and to return with acclaim to its starting point.

According to notes made by Francis Fletcher, chaplain of the expedition, all on board suffered from severe cold in the summer of 1579 as they sailed along the coast of California. Weeks of dense fog added to their discomfort and obscured their vision. He says: "We fell with a conuenient and fit harborough, and June 17 came to anchor therein where we continued till the 23 of the July following." These dates are those of the Julian Calendar; June 17 would be June 28 by today's reckoning.

In this place the vessel was reconditioned and contact was made with the native inhabitants—Indians, who were deeply impressed by their white visitors. Word of the strange arrival passed from village to village. The white men were thought to be gods. The number of natives who came down to the harbor daily increased. One day, before a week had passed, a great number of Indians came in company with their leader, whom they honored as king.

On this occasion the natives placed a crown upon the head of Drake: "inriched his neck with all their chains, and offering unto him many other things, honoured him by the name of 'Hyoh.' Adding thereunto (as it might seeme) a song and dance of triumph; because they were not onely visited of the gods (for so they still judged us to be), but the great and chiefe God was now become their God, their king and patron, and themselues the onely happie and blessed people in the world."

Some days later, Drake and many of his men made a journey up into the land and found "a goodly country and fruitfull soyle, stored with many blessings fit for the vse of man." Of the region the chaplain wrote further: "This country our Generall named *Albion,* and that for two causes; the one in respect of the white bancks and cliffes, which lie toward the sea; the other, that it might haue some affinity, euen in name also, with our own country, which was sometimes so called."

And further: "Before we went from thence, our Generall caused to be set vp a monument of our being there, as also of her maiesties and successors right and title to that kingdom; namely, a plate of brasse, fast nailed to a great and firme post; whereon is engrauen her graces name, and the day and yeare of our arriuall there, and of the free giuing vp of the prouince and kingdom, both by the king and people, into her maiesties hands: together with her highnesse picture and armes, in a piece of sixpence currant English monie, shewing itselfe by a hole made of purpose through the plate; underneath was likewise engrauen the name of our Generall, etc."

Authorities have differed as to the identity of this harbor, which, in Fletcher's narrative, is placed in Latitude 38° 30′. Drake's Bay which bears his name on our modern maps, Bodega Bay, San Francisco Bay, and other places have been mentioned as his probable landing place. On June 25, 1916, the Sir Francis Drake Association of California placed a marker upon a rocky eminence on the shore of Drake's Bay in an area which is now occupied by the United States Coast Guard.

About midsummer of 1936 chance brought to the notice of white men once again the plate described by Chaplain Fletcher. Careful study of it was made by Dr. H. E. Bolton and others before the discovery was made public at a meeting of the California Historical Society in the Sir Francis Drake Hotel, San Francisco, on April 6, 1937.

The plate is of solid brass, probably cut from a fitting on the "Golden Hind." It is five inches wide, eight inches long, and one-eighth inch thick, with holes at top and bottom to admit the nails that secured it to the post. A jagged hole near the lower right hand corner fits an Elizabethan sixpence. The words engraved upon the plate are as follows:

BEE IT KNOWNE VNTO ALL MEN BY THESE PRESENTS
IVNE 17 1579
BY THE GRACE OF GOD AND IN THE NAME OF HERR
MAIESTY QVEEN ELIZABETH OF ENGLAND AND HERR
SVCCESSORS FOREVER I TAKE POSSESSION OF THIS
KINGDOME WHOSE KING AND PEOPLE FREELY RESIGNE
THEIR RIGHT AND TITLE IN THE WHOLE LAND VNTO HERR
MAIESTIES KEEPEING NOW NAMED BY ME AN TO BEE
KNOWN VNTO ALL MEN AS NOVA ALBION.
FRANCIS DRAKE

(Hole for
silver
sixpence)

This ancient relic, presumably authentic, was picked up by Beryle Shinn, a young motorist unfamiliar with either the locality or with the Drake history, near Corte Madera, south of San Rafael and about one and one-half miles northwest of Point San Quentin. The probabilities are that the plate had been carried to this place from its original location by some human agency, and the site where the "great and firme post" originally displayed it may never be located.

The Drake plate is now the property of the University of California, where it will be kept on display.

In 1595, Sebastián Rodríguez Cermeño, a Portuguese, was sent out by the Mexican government to explore and map the California coast and sighted it first a little above 41° latitude, very near Trinidad Head. Turning southward, he entered Drake's Bay in November 1595, just sixteen years after the great Englishman had raised his country's flag upon California's shore. Here Cermeño's vessel, the "San Agustín," was wrecked by a storm and the party was forced to proceed in a launch that they had constructed there as an auxiliary boat. Before sailing, they explored inland a distance of four leagues and found several rancherías of Indians from whom acorns were obtained for food. Cermeño named the harbor the "Bay of San Francisco," a name which for many years caused great confusion among historians. Hunt and Sanchez say: "The present Drake's Bay was the place first known as 'San Francisco' to the Spaniards, and the name was not transferred to the great inland sea which now bears it until after 1769."

Rancho Olómpali

Rancho Olómpali, named for a former Coast Miwok Indian village, Olemaloke, consisted of two square leagues granted by Governor Manuel Micheltorena on October 22, 1843, to Camilo Ynitia (Ynito), who filed claim for it on February 26, 1852, and received a United States patent for it in 1862. The tract was bounded by the "Arroyo de San Antonio and the Portezuela de Novato."

Camilo Ynitia was the son of the last chief of the Olómpali Indians, who lived there as early as 1776 and for whom, according to General Mariano G. Vallejo, an adobe was constructed, the first house to be erected north of San Francisco Bay. Grateful for kindly treatment accorded to an expedition sent out from the San Francisco Presidio earlier in the year, the Spaniards gave instructions to the Indians in the making of adobe bricks and the building of this house for their chief. Near this dwelling Camilo, the son of the chief, a Christian Indian, industrious and successful, also erected an adobe. The older one is gone. When its walls fell and lay in a heap and were wetted by rains a growth of weeds covered them over.

M. Duflot de Mofras, a representative of the French government, journeyed through California in the years 1840, 1841, and 1842, and probably had reference to this place when he wrote: "On leaving San Rafael and turning away from the great salt marshes, one finds himself passing in front of the Rancho del Indio composed of some free Indians."

On June 24, 1846, a surprise skirmish occurred at this point, when Lieutenant Henry L. Ford, of the Bear Flag movement, unaware of the presence of the enemy, made a charge upon the horse corrals while a force of Californians under Joaquín de la Torre and Juan N. Padilla were at a late breakfast in the ranch house. The Californians retreated after a few shots had been exchanged, one man being killed and another badly wounded.

The greater part of this rancho was purchased in 1852 by James Black from Ynitia and his wife Suzane for the sum of $5,200. Black, originally from Scotland, was the owner of many other tracts of land. He afterward gave this one to his daughter Mary.

In 1863 the daughter and her husband, Dr. Galen Burdell, came there to live. They developed one of the earliest and finest of Marin County gardens. When Mrs. Burdell returned from a trip to the Orient in a sailing vessel, she brought with her an extensive collection of trees and shrubs, of which many choice specimens, among them camellias and Japanese maples, now flourish. The place is still owned by descendants of the Burdell family and is approached through a wooded drive off the main highway three miles north of Novato. The second adobe house (that of the son Camilo) was used by Dr. and Mrs. Burdell as their home, and three of the rooms are incorporated in the stucco house erected by their son in 1915. The former living room, now used as a storeroom, is of large dimensions with a moderately high ceiling. When the original small windows were enlarged to admit more light the workmanship was found to be excellent and the walls in the best of condition.

On the trunk of a huge oak on these grounds may be seen, although almost overgrown with bark, a deep gash in the shape of a cross, such a one as early Californians were wont to use to mark the spot where a death occurred. It is supposed that this was made to mark the one casualty in the surprise skirmish of June 1846, mentioned above. A large copper cauldron supposedly used for cooking food for Frémont's men during their encampment at this spot has remained there since that time. Another treasured relic on this old Rancho Olómpali is a bell that originally hung, according to family tradition, at the San Rafael Mission.

Misión San Rafael Arcángel

Because the mortality of the Indians at Misión Dolores had become alarming, it was suggested that a part of the neophytes should be sent across the Bay to a somewhat more equable climate. A trial move proved the wisdom of that measure, and it was determined to establish there a kind of rancho with chapel, baptistry, and cemetery. The name San Rafael Arcángel was chosen in order that "this most glorious prince who in his name expresses 'the healing of God' might care for bodies as well as souls." The Mission was founded on December 14, 1817, on a spot called by the natives "Nanaguani."

An adobe building 79 feet long, 38 feet wide, and 16 feet high was erected and divided by partitions into chapel, padre's house, and other required apartments. San Rafael was at first nothing more than an asistencia to Misión San Francisco de Assís, but by 1823 it had become self-supporting; and, although there is no record that it was raised to the position of an independent Mission, all the reports of the Fathers refer to it as such. Padre Juan Amorós, known for the zeal with which he undertook every task, served as missionary there from 1819 to his death in 1832. During this period the Mission attained its maximum strength, although Duhaut-Cilly, passing within sight of it in 1827 on his way to Sonoma, did not "deem this poor establishment worth stopping at for purposes of trade." Two years after the death of Padre Amorós came the secularization, when Ignacio Martínez, a distinguished military officer retired since 1831, was made *comisionado*. For two years he managed the affairs of San Rafael and established the boundaries of the pueblo.

The long, low adobe structure erected at San Rafael was much plainer and simpler than most of the Mission structures elsewhere. Old pictures show that the bells, which are now scattered, were hung in a wooden frame placed outside the chapel entrance. After the secularization the uncared-for walls soon melted away, and no sign of them now remains. On the site of the chapel stands the present Catholic Church. A map of 1852, found among Marin County records, shows the extreme southerly point of the Mission at the corner of Fifth and A streets, with one side of the building paralleling the present De Heiry Street. The Mission garden extended from the present Courthouse to the Lincoln Highway.

The Misión San Rafael rancho, consisting of sixteen square leagues, was sold by Governor Pío Pico on June 8, 1846, to Antonio Suñol, a Spanish member of the San José Council, and Antonio María Pico for $8,000, but they failed to get possession and their title was later decided to be invalid. In 1859 Bishop J. S. Alemany obtained patent for something over six acres of this land for the church.

The Mission Embarcadero and the City of San Rafael

The farthest inland meanderings of Estero San Rafael de Aguanni are now lost beneath the pavements and buildings of the city of San Rafael. On A Street, at Third, is the probable landing place used by the padres, the Mission embarcadero. This was the scene of a most unfortunate episode in the Bear Flag Rebellion. Frémont and his men had just arrived for a week's sojourn at the dismantled buildings of Misión San Rafael on June 28, 1846, when a boat was seen approaching the shore from the direction of San Pablo, where two divisions of Castro's army were stationed. It was assumed that the passengers were carrying messages to Castro's aides. When the three occupants of the boat stepped on land, before any words were spoken or their errand ascertained, they were shot down by Kit Carson and his two companions, who had been sent to intercept the travelers. The men killed were Francisco and Ramón, twin sons of Don Francisco de Haro (former alcalde of San Francisco), and their uncle, Don José de los Reyes Berryessa, owner of Rancho San Vicente near Santa Clara. Several different reasons have been given for this seemingly cold-blooded murder, but even the greatest admirers of Frémont and Carson have to agree that it was an ill-advised and unnecessary act.

On C and D streets between First and Second, bridges span the old channel of San Rafael Creek. A post to which small craft had formerly tied stood as a landmark near the intersection of E and First streets for many years after canoes and small rafts had ceased to come up so far. At the corner of C and Second streets freight was received in 1850.

The oldest part of the city of San Rafael lies west of a line drawn between the site of the Mission and that of the Mission embarcadero. The adobe residence of Don Timoteo Murphy, started in 1839, two years after he assumed charge of the Mission estate and the Indians thereon, stood on the site now occupied by the Bank of America at Fourth and C streets. It was the most pretentious building in the county at the time and the center of social activities. In 1844, it was occupied by Don Antonio María Osio, grantee of Angel Island, a man who held important positions in different parts of California previous to the American conquest.

The alcaldes transacted the business of their offices in the old Mission building up to 1850. In 1851 a hall, which was called the Juzgado, was set aside for the holding of the sessions of the newly established County Court. In 1853, the year of the death of Don Timoteo, the seat of justice was removed to his house and there remained until the completion, in 1873, of the present Courthouse. The road leading from this adobe house to the freight landing of the '50's became C Street; and on the east side of this road, between what are now Third and Fourth streets, a general merchandise store was opened in 1850 by Davis and Taylor, whose building still remains in this location.

On April 14, 1871, a corporation known as the Mechanics Institute was organized for the purpose of conducting a library and reading room "for literary, beneficial, moral, and educational purposes unconnected with other Societies, religious denominations, or political parties." For this, a one-story frame building was erected, almost covering the 30 × 50 foot lot which the corporation had purchased. This library existed but a short time; the building, however, now altered for a residence, is still standing at 1016 C Street. One of the sponsors of the Mechanics Institute was William T. Coleman, chosen leader of the San Francisco Vigilantes of 1856. In addition to his San Francisco interests, he owned a vast tract of land in Marin County, and his home at 950 Mission Street was one of the first frame buildings of San Rafael. It had been erected by Walter Skidmore; and Mr. Coleman, after purchasing it, took great pains to preserve it intact while making additions suitable for his own use.

In 1853 Paul de Heiry bought a tract of land just back of the old Mission and sent to his native France for seeds, fruit trees, roses, and grapes that even down to the present

are enriching the gardens of San Rafael. A street in the vicinity now bears his name. In 1863 the de Heiry property passed on to Henry Wilkins, who fashioned a swimming pool, using redwood planks to confine the water flowing from the old Mission spring. This spring is now in the park ground donated by Mr. Robert Dollar to the city of San Rafael.

Several houses now standing in San Rafael were erected by convict labor in the years 1859 and 1860, at which period prisoners were hired under contract to a firm known as Sims and McCauley. Two of these houses were on the public square: one, used as a pharmacy in 1859 by Dr. Taliaferro, is now standing in the middle of the block on Fourth Street between B and C streets; and the other, the old Central Hotel, a brick building quite famous in the early days, is now the Dubois property. A third house was built for an official of the prison on the block bounded by Second and Third streets between B and C and is now an apartment house.

Mill Valley, Larkspur, and Rancho Corte de Madera del Presidio

Rancho Corte de Madera del Presidio, consisting of one square league, was granted by Governor José Figueroa to Juan (John) Read (Reed, Reid) on October 2, 1834. It lies on the peninsula northwest of Raccoon Straits and extends inland between the Punta de Quentín and Saucelito ranchos. On December 23, 1852, his widow, Hilaria Sánchez de Read, and her four children, Juan, Hilaria, Inéz, and Picardo, filed petition for it, amending the petition on June 13, 1854, when it was confirmed to them.

Read was an Irish sailor who was in the vicinity of Sausalito in 1832, where, as opportunity arose, he ran a boat for hire to Yerba Buena antedating the regular ferry services by many years. He was naturalized as a Mexican citizen in September 1834, one month before he received the grant of his rancho. For the interim of about five months between the Martínez and the Murphy administrations of the affairs of the secularized San Rafael Mission, he filled that position which he undertook on November 30, 1836. His first house was a temporary structure near the beach, but he later erected an adobe dwelling on a knoll one-quarter of a mile off the highway running from Mill Valley Junction to the town of Mill Valley. The ruins of this adobe were removed in 1918, and the site is now occupied by a modern cottage not far from which some of the old pear trees stand. Many years after Juan Read died and was buried in the Catholic Cemetery in San Rafael, Hilaria Sánchez lived on.

The timbers of Read's old sawmill, after which Mill Valley was named, stand on Old Mill Plaza at the entrance to Ferny Cascade in the town of Mill Valley. This mill, built at an uncertain date during the ten years previous to Read's death in 1843, has been marked by the Outdoor Art Club of Mill Valley.

One of the early settlements in this vicinity was Blithedale. This sunny place, through which ran the Arroyo del Corte de Madera del Presidio, was chosen in 1873 by Dr. John Cushing and his wife for the location of a sanatorium. The idealistic agricultural community portrayed by Hawthorne in his Blithedale Romance, written twenty years earlier, inspired Dr. Cushing to give the name Blithedale to this place. Because of difficulty in obtaining title to the property, Dr. Cushing did not succeed in actually establishing the sanatorium before his death in 1879, but his wife and son remained on the property and managed it as a summer resort for years afterward. The extensive cement walks that were then made on the place now surround a private home on the site. The original Blithedale Glen, between Eldridge and Cottage avenues, has been subdivided and built up as a part of the town of Mill Valley.

The town of Larkspur is located in the northwest corner of Rancho Corte de Madera del Presidio. Here an Indian shell mound formed a knoll practically surrounded by marshes upon which Captain Frémont and some of his soldiers are said to have camped for a time in the summer of 1846. On this knoll, just northwest of the Larkspur Nurseries, the first dwelling in Larkspur was erected of brick in 1852—by convict labor, so tradition says. In 1850 a steamboat, plying by way of Corte Madera Creek between what is now Larkspur and San Francisco, made three or four trips a week to carry away lumber, hides, beef, and other produce from the country and to return with goods purchased in the city.

Rancho Saucelito and the Town of Sausalito

Rancho Saucelito, according to legend granted in 1835 to José Antonio Galindo, afterward a corporal in the San Francisco militia, was granted on February 11, 1838, to Guillermo Antonio Richardson (William A.), by Governor Alvarado.

Richardson, arriving in San Francisco as first mate on the whaling vessel "Orion" sixteen years earlier, had procured papers allowing him to remain on land, and thereafter became active in the region of San Francisco Bay, spending some time also at San Gabriel, Sonoma, and Monterey. In 1823, when twenty-seven years of age, he was baptized at the Mission in San Francisco. In 1825 he married María Antonia, daughter of Ignacio Martínez, at that time comandante of the Presidio. In 1830 he obtained naturalization as a citizen, his name being placed on record as pilot and shipbuilder with a knowledge of the Spanish language. In 1837 he was appointed Captain of the Port of San Francisco by Vallejo, and after 1841 he made his home at Rancho Saucelito, filing his petition as claimant for it with the Land Commission on March 16, 1852. The final patent for 19,571.92 acres was issued August 7, 1879. His private business was the collection of country produce by means of a launch which visited the various embarcaderos about the Bay. The shore of his own rancho was washed by the waters of Richardson's Bay, thus named at the time of his land ownership there.

Fine hillside springs on Rancho Saucelito gave life to the *sausal* or willows, from which the name is derived; and in 1850 Captain Richardson piped water from these springs to a great cistern thirty feet square and fifteen feet deep which he had dug for the purpose. From this cistern (still extant on Richardson Avenue, Hurricane Gulch, Sausalito) pipes were run on a trestle to the water front and thence to a boat, the "Water Nixie," equipped with tanks and casks for transporting the water to Meiggs' Wharf, San Francisco. From this point Marin County spring water was distributed to dwellers in the growing city by means of horse- and mule-drawn carts for the price of fifty cents per bucket. Even today Marin County water in large bottles is delivered by motor truck in the Peninsula region. The mooring place of the old "Water Nixie" is on Richardson Street, between Water and Front streets near the place of the first settlement of the town of Sausalito, where in 1862 there were a half-dozen houses.

For many years the Sausalito water front was widely known as an anchorage and supply station for whaling vessels and men-of-war. Captain Beechey, in 1826, saw "seven whalers" anchored there; and Sir George Simpson, governor-in-chief of the Hudson's Bay Company territories in North America, on entering San Francisco Bay in December 1841, wrote: "We saw on our left in a deep bay known as 'Whaler's Harbor,' two vessels, the Government schooner California and the Russian brig Constantine, now bound to Sitka with the last remnants of Bodega and Ross on board, ... about a hundred souls, men, women, and children, all patriotically

delighted to exchange the lovely climate of California for the uncongenial skies of Sitka, and that, too, at the expense of making a long voyage in an old, crazy, clumsy tub at the stormiest season of the year."

Captain Richardson in 1855 sold a piece of property near Sausalito to S. R. Throckmorton, who in turn sold it to the Sausalito Land and Ferry Company. This company built wharves, filled in marshy places, and put on a reliable boat for frequent rapid transit across the Bay to San Francisco. Their first boat, the "Princess," made four round trips daily. It is in the vicinity of this wharf that the newer part of Sausalito has grown up. On the opening of the line of the North Pacific Railway in 1875, the franchise of the ferry company was leased to the railway company.

The Golden Gate Bridge has in effect brought Saucelito closer to San Francisco. The town has spread far up the hills above the landing; and from the homes located on the steep, curving streets, magnificent views of islands and Bay are obtained—views undreamed of by the motorists speeding up the Redwood Highway.

On Bulkeley Avenue, near Harrison Avenue, on the drive above the wharf, a crescent-shaped cement seat has been placed honoring the memory of a poet who had a retreat in these hills: Daniel O'Connell, grandnephew of the Irish patriot of the same name. He came to California after resigning from the British Navy and was a teacher in Santa Clara College in 1868; later he taught Greek in St. Ignatius College in San Francisco before devoting his entire time to newspaper and other writing. He was one of the early members of the Bohemian Club in San Francisco. His published poetical works, *Lyrics* and *Sweethearts and Wives,* hold high rank in the literary world. He lived in Wildwood Glen with his family in "the little house on the hill." This site, the house now remodeled and modernized, is 261 Cazeneau Street. The memorial seat, on the back of which are inscribed three stanzas of the poem "The Castle of Silence," written ten days before his death, rests upon a tiled platform shaded by pepper trees overlooking the Bay from Bulkeley Avenue.

Rancho Punta de los Reyes

When on December 28, 1841, the "Cowlitz" lay becalmed offshore at Drake's Bay after coming from the inhospitable climate of the northern region, its passengers "began sensibly to feel the influence of a more congenial climate. The sails flapped listlessly against the mast, the vessel heaved reluctantly on the sluggish waters." Sir George Simpson, one of the passengers, continues: "During the whole of the 29th we lay in this state of inactivity about five miles from shore which presented a level sward of about a mile in depth, backed by a high ridge of grassy slopes—the whole pastured by numerous herds of cattle and horses, which, without a keeper and without a fold, were growing and fattening, whether their owners waked or slept, in the very middle of winter, and in the coldest nook of the province. Here, on the very threshold of the country, was California in a nutshell, Nature doing everything and man doing nothing—a text on which our whole sojourn proved to be little but a running commentary. While we lay like a log in the sea, we were glad to be surrounded by large flights of birds—ducks, pelicans, cormorants, gulls, etc."

The land so described is that of Rancho Punta de los Reyes Sobrante, which after the advent of the American settlers became the first great dairy center of the state.

The names of several outstanding men have been connected with this great rancho on the western slope of Marin County. James Richard Berry, an Irish gentleman who in his travels had spent much time in Spanish countries, received on St. Patrick's Day in 1836 (he arrived that year) a grant of land in the vicinity of Inverness from Governor Nicolas Gutiérrez. He was known to be in Sonoma in 1844, but in the meantime he had sold this rancho to Joseph Francis Snook, who received a grant of it from Governor Juan B. Alvarado on June 8, 1839. In about 1837, the grantee had built a house of logs and mud on this land. Snook, an English shipping master, whose boats plied up and down the California coast, married María Antonia, daughter of Governor Alvarado. He retired from his active service to spend the last years of his life with his family on a rancho near San Diego, granted to him in 1842. His death came suddenly in 1847.

In 1843 Rancho Punta de los Reyes, Sobrante, was granted to Antonio María Osio, a public official under Mexican authority, who held it for but a few years and who probably never lived upon it. In 1844, the fourth year of his position as justice, Osio occupied the dwelling of Don Timoteo Murphy near the San Rafael Mission, while the owner of the house lived at the Mission itself. Two years later, in 1846, he escaped the Bear Flag disturbance by taking his family to Honolulu. On his return he moved to his former home in Lower California and wrote *Historia de California*, a book of some value.

Early in the '50's, Rancho Punta de los Reyes and Rancho Punta de los Reyes Sobrante ("surplus") were acquired by Andrew Randall, and on March 2, 1853, he filed a petition for them, basing his claim on the grant of eleven Spanish leagues formerly made to Osio. Randall had arrived on the West Coast as a gunner on the U.S.S. "Portsmouth," and was reputed to be a doctor and a scientist. He received patents for the two pieces of land, a total of 57,066.98 acres, on June 4, 1860.

From Randall these two grants passed into the hands of three men who were notable in the early development of the state: Justice Oscar L. Shafter, of the State Supreme Court; his brother, Judge James McMillan Shafter; and Charles Webb Howard, president of the Spring Valley Water Company. To their large holding was later added Rancho Tomales y Baulenes, which had been granted in 1836 by Governor Nicolás Gutiérrez to Rafael García. The combined property stretched from the coast north of Point Reyes southward and eastward until it included the top of Mount Tamalpais.

Judge James McMillan Shafter, after a distinguished career in the East, arrived in California in 1853. He became State Senator and was a member of the Constitutional Convention of 1878. He was a regent of the University of California and at the time of the founding of Leland Stanford Junior University delivered the dedicatory address and became a trustee of the new institution. His house, "The Oaks," located on this extensive holding, was built of lumber ferried out of the Golden Gate and into Tomales Bay, then hauled by oxen to the site two miles south of Olema. The rough timbers for the buildings on the many farms into which his land was divided were sawed by his own mill on the place.

Dairying became the major business in this part of Marin County. Almost the entire area of this rancho was leased out by the grantees to dairy farmers, and houses were built for them near clear-flowing springs, of which there were a considerable number. The butter made was shipped to San Francisco by schooner to supply the needs of that city. Judge Shafter was greatly interested in blooded stock, horses as well as cattle, and frequently entertained his friends at his private race track, where his fine horses were trained and shown. After his death many of the customs of the family were continued, for the son, Payne Jewett Shafter, "Squire" Shafter as he was generally known, was likewise deeply interested in agriculture and country life. A daughter of "Squire"

Shafter, Mary Shafter, also inherited a love of similar activity, pursuing courses at the State University to that end. Her book *American Indian and Other Folk Dances* reveals a historical interest in the native peoples who inhabited the grass-covered hills up to the time the white man came.

The three ranchos that were combined into the one vast property are now divided into many parts: some passed down to descendants of Charles W. Howard and the Shafters, and others have been purchased by newer residents. Judge Shafter's town house at 951 Chestnut Street, San Francisco, still stands, as does his country home, "The Oaks," surrounded by old trees. The latter residence is still owned by the family.

Rancho Punta de Quentín

The name of this rancho is derived from a point off its coast which received its name from an episode that occurred on an island at the mouth of the Estero de San Rafael. A hostile Indian chief, Marín, and his companion in flight, Quentín, both sought by Spanish soldiery under Lieutenants Ignacio Martínez and José Sánchez, were captured in their hiding place on this small island and taken to San Francisco as prisoners. A good sailor, Quentín was there employed by the Fathers at Dolores as skipper of one of the lighters trading in the Bay. Fifteen years later he was employed by General Vallejo for making trips between Sonoma and Yerba Buena. General Vallejo is the authority for this explanation of the origin of the name "Punta San Quentín." The island on which the fugitives hid was named Marín for the chief.

Rancho Punta de Quentín consisted of two square leagues, extending westerly from the shore of the Bay into the mountains lying north of Mount Tamalpais. Larkspur is near its southern line, and San Anselmo its northern. It was granted in 1840 to Juan Bautista Roger Cooper, who received at various times other ranchos in the state and does not seem to have held this one for very long. A claim for the confirmation of ownership of this rancho was filed by Benjamin R. Buckelew in 1853, basing his action on a grant made to him by Governor Alvarado on September 24, 1844. He received the confirmation in 1855, and the patent for 8,877.64 acres was issued to his heirs on April 10, 1866. One-time publisher and editor of *The Californian* during the brief existence of that newspaper, Buckelew died in 1859 at the early age of thirty-seven.

On the eastern part of this rancho stands San Quentin prison, begun in 1853. Before its erection the state's convicted criminals were confined on hulks of ships anchored off Angel Island. It stands on the site of the projected but never built Marion City. In its vicinity were found beds of a medium quality clay. In 1888, the State Mineralogist reported: "At San Quentin there are manufactured from clay on the prison ground 500,000 common and 80,000 pressed brick, annually." This industry ended after a few years because of the exhaustion of the clay deposit.

Rancho San Pedro, Santa Margarita y las Gallinas

This rancho, extending northwesterly from Point San Pedro and the Gallinas canal and consisting of five square leagues, was granted on February 14, 1844, by Governor Manuel Micheltorena to Timoteo Murphy. The grantee was a tall blue-eyed man from Ireland, good natured and generous, who after some commercial experience had come to California in 1828 to supervise the packing and exporting of beef for Hartnell and Company at Monterey. He brought with him letters to the Spanish authorities. From 1833 to 1835 he was engaged in otter hunting; and shortly afterward, having made the acquaintance of the Vallejo family, this Irishman of commanding presence was chosen by General Vallejo to be the husband of one of his attractive sisters. He also gave him a certain amount of property and established him as administrator of the Mission at San Rafael. The sister, however, did not acquiesce in the arrangement and married Jacob P. Leese—if Sir George Simpson, a visitor to both Don Timoteo and the Vallejo family in 1841, was correctly informed.

From 1837 to 1842, Timoteo held the position at the Mission and was a faithful guardian of the neophytes, who were otherwise abandoned to their own devices after the secularization of the Mission and who were in need of wise supervision. In 1839, while in charge of affairs of the Mission, he became naturalized. Before receiving this grant in 1844, he began building an adobe house, probably the first dwelling outside of the Mission that was built on the site of the present town of San Rafael. Here he dispensed hospitality, his house being widely known. Lieutenant W. T. Sherman and party, on their way to Sutter's Fort in June 1848, spent one night with him. The house is said to have been Frémont's headquarters for a time, possibly when he marched with 130 men to the Mission on June 26, 1846, and made a stay of a few days. After Don Timoteo's death in 1853 the adobe was used as a place of justice until the erection of the present Courthouse in 1873, when a piece of adobe from the Murphy house was sealed within the cornerstone of the new building.

In 1850 Don Timoteo gave funds to the Sisters of Charity of St. Vincent de Paul for the foundation of what is now St. Vincent's Orphanage for Boys. The approach to this establishment is through a long eucalyptus-lined drive after one turns off the Redwood Highway about six miles north of San Rafael. His estate was left to his nephews, John Lucas and the sons of Matthew Murphy.

Rancho Cañada de Herrera

Rancho Cañada de Herrera, or La Providencia, or Vale of the Blacksmith, was granted by Manuel Jimeno, acting governor, to Domingo Sais (Saez) in 1839 at the end of the latter's two-year term as elector and *regidor* of San Francisco. The Sais heirs received United States patent for 6,658 acres in 1876.

Dr. A. W. Taliaferro, a skillful surgeon and physician who had come to Marin County in 1849 with a group of young men from Virginia, while wandering one day up San Anselmo Valley "came upon a tract of park-like land, shaded by ancient trees with a sparkling stream of water running through it." He at once began negotiations for its purchase. When Don Domingo learned that he wanted only forty acres he said: "It is worth forty acres to us to have a good neighbor. Select your forty acres, we give it to you thankfully." The Doctor fenced in his land and erected a commodious house on the bank of the "sparkling stream," cleared a considerable area of brush, built appropriate outbuildings, and settled down to the life of a gentleman, as his forebears had done in Virginia. The abundance of wild game in this part and his unstinted hospitality at once made the place popular with his sportsman friends.

Among his visitors in 1856 were Charles S. Fairfax and his wife. Fairfax was a lineal descendant of the barons of that name in England; and his wife, famous alike for her wit and beauty, was niece of Senator John C. Calhoun. Both of these visitors became fascinated with the place; some sort of a deed of gift was made: they took over the property, and Dr. Taliaferro remained as their permanent guest. Fairfax, in later years always called "Lord Fairfax" on account of his known line of descent, had come in 1849 as a youth of twenty from the county of Fairfax in Virginia and had spent his first winter in a cabin near Grass Valley. A young man of good education and pleasing address, he became a member of the House of Representatives from Yuba County in 1853 and in 1854 was elected clerk of the Superior Court, which position he held for five years.

The Fairfax home was located not far from the present railroad stations of Fairfax and Manor. Presided over by the gracious southern lady, it became one of the centers of the social life of that period where notables óf the state and nation were entertained. Here a luncheon party, tense and unusual, gathered on May 21, 1861, the day following the close of the state legislature, where hot political debate had resulted in a challenge to a duel. At the moment of the challenge the prompt action of an official had prevented the duel from taking place on a site selected at that time; and the principals, their seconds, and the surgeon had gone to the house of "Lord Fairfax," where their host attempted a reconciliation. The antagonists, Daniel Showalter of Kentucky and Charles W. Piercy of Illinois, had crossed the continent in the same small company some years before but on arriving in California had gone their separate ways. They had met again as members of the legislature in opposing factions of one of the political parties—the Breckinridge and Douglas factions of the Democrats. After the luncheon, when all hope of preventing the conflict was abandoned, the hour of three o'clock was set for the duel. Following the first shots, in which neither had been injured, Fairfax again attempted to pacify the hot-tempered men, but to no avail. On resuming their positions and firing, Piercy was instantly killed. Showalter, immediately filled with remorse, pleaded with the surgeon to save his opponent. He was killed not long afterward in ambush by Apaches as he journeyed through a wild part of Texas on his way to join the Confederate Army.

In May 1868 the heirs of Domingo Sais deeded this 40-acre tract to the Fairfaxes. In that year Charles Fairfax was made chairman of the California delegation to the Democratic National Convention in New York. He attended the Convention, but died in the following year at Baltimore. After his death his Marin County home became the restaurant of Madame Pastori, who, on the decline of her career in Italian opera, came here with her husband, a former master of stagecraft. Attracted by the lovable Adele and the epicurean viands produced by her husband, the artists of San Francisco soon made this their rendezvous.

Since the passing of the Pastoris, this sylvan retreat has been taken over by the Emporium-Capwell Corporation and is now operated by them as a country club. Although the original buildings used by Dr. Taliaferro and "Lord and Lady" Fairfax are no longer there, the houses erected by the Pastoris still stand and are distinguishable from the newer buildings of the Country Club by their shingled roofs.

Rancho San José

Don Ignacio Pacheco, whose father of the same name was a Mexican soldier in San Francisco in 1790, was born in San José in 1808. When he was nineteen years of age, he became likewise a soldier in the San Francisco Company, where he was a sergeant ten years later. At the expiration of his military service in 1838 he settled on a tract of land bordering San Pablo Bay south of the Feliz grant of Rancho de Novato, and on October 3, 1840, the tract was granted to him by Governor Alvarado. A year or so later he began erection of an adobe house of one story like those of old Mexico, using Indians from Mendocino County as laborers.

Don Ignacio was married three times: first to Josephine Higuera, a pious woman, who named the rancho for her patron saint; second to Guadalupe Duarte; and third to

María Loreto Duarte. In 1846, as alcalde at San Rafael, he held his court in the large hall of the Mission, and he is remembered as a man who used his influence for the best interest of town, county, and state. At one time during the Mexican War, he was taken prisoner by Frémont to compel the relinquishment of all his horses to the Bear Flag troops, but was released speedily on acceding to the demand. He received United States patent for his rancho of 6,659.25 acres on May 14, 1861, and, dying in 1864, left it to his five sons and his daughter Catalina. To the latter, child of his third wife, he gave the family home and 600 acres of land. The sons—Salvador, Gumesindo, Augustin F., Juan F., and Benjamin—divided their property, each having his separate part. Catalina married a Valencia, and the four-room adobe home of her parents became known as the Valencia adobe. It stood protected by a wooden sheathing until destroyed by fire on May 23, 1916; its foundations remained for many years beside the main highway north of San Rafael and not far from Ignacio, the village founded by the original grantee and named for him. The site is now a wayside resort.

Hamilton Field, United States Army air base, has been established on a part of Rancho San José, while descendants of Don Ignacio still reside on other parts. Pacheco Point on the San Pablo Bay is the easternmost extent of the grant.

Rancho Nicasio

Attempts were made to give three grants in the county to Christian Indians: Rancho Olómpali was successfully patented to Camilo Ynitia; but the other two, ranchos Nicasio and Tenicasia, were not confirmed. The former, twenty square leagues of Nicasio, had been granted to Teodosio Quilajuequi and others of his tribe in 1835 by Governor Figueroa, but it was rejected by the Land Commission in 1855. The latter, Tenicasia, given by General M. G. Vallejo to the San Rafael Mission Indians in 1841, was rejected by the Commission in 1854 because of "failure of prosecution." Vallejo was a valiant friend of the neophytes, but he alone could not carry through the plan of placing them upon farms of their own where they could put into practice the agricultural knowledge obtained under former instruction at the Mission. Timoteo Murphy, his friend and co-worker who held the confidence of the Indians and was furthering their interests, had died the year before the matter was settled; and no one else remained to intercede in behalf of the native claimants.

In 1844, another part of Rancho Nicasio, containing ten square leagues, was granted by Governor Micheltorena to Pablo de la Guerra and Juan Cooper, men important politically and commercially, who seem to have parted with the land before 1852. In that year a claim for it was filed by H. W. Halleck and James Black; and a supplementary claim was filed the following year by Benjamin R. Buckelew, Daniel Frink, and William Reynolds. The long and comparatively narrow stretch of this rancho reached from Keyes Creek, flowing into Tomales Bay, to the western boundary of Murphy's Rancho San Pedro, Santa Margarita y las Gallinas. It was surveyed in the autumn of 1859 and found to contain 56,621.04 acres, for which patent, signed by President Abraham Lincoln, was issued to all five claimants on November 1, 1861.

The extreme northwestern and northeastern ends were claimed by and patented to Henry Wager Halleck, a graduate of West Point, who had come in 1847 with a company of United States artillery to inspect Pacific Coast fortifications. He resigned his commission, was an active and influential member of the Constitutional Convention of 1849, acted as inspector of lighthouses on the Coast, became leading member of a law firm in San Francisco, prepared a report on Cali-

fornia land titles, and was the author of law books of standard value. Halleck resumed his military career and was Lincoln's chief reliance as a general during much of the Civil War. The southeastern corner of this large grant was patented to Benjamin R. Buckelew, who was also the owner of Punta de Quentín. The two middle tracts, along the eastern shore of Tomales Bay, were patented to the other three claimants: Frink and Reynolds, owning the northern piece; and James Black, who also had Rancho Olómpali, the southern.

Other Mexican Grants

The official map of Marin County, published in 1892, shows several old ranchos about which little material is available. The northern line of the county runs through the southern part of two grants, Blucher and Laguna de San Antonio, lying partly in Sonoma County to the north. From the angle between these two extends the Bolsa de Tomales, of 22,193 acres, westerly to the shore from Keyes Creek to the Estero de San Antonio, a property formerly granted to Juan Padilla, who was in command of a party of Californians north of the Bay of San Francisco at the time of the raising of the Bear Flag.

Rancho Soulajule, south of Rancho Laguna de San Antonio, was granted in 1844 by Governor Micheltorena to Ramón Mesa, a former soldier in the San Francisco Company. In 1879 the patent to this rancho was issued to five men: G. N. Cornwall, L. D. Watkins, Pedro J. Vásquez, J. S. Brackett, and M. F. Gormley.

Rancho de Novato extends northwest from Black Point to San Pablo Bay. It was granted in 1839 by Governor Alvarado to Fernando Felis (Feliz) and afterward owned jointly by Frederick Billings, James R. Bolton, and Henry W. Halleck, assignees of Bezar Simmons, who died in 1850. Archibald Peachy purchased the rancho from these assignees, one of whom, Billings, was a brother-in-law of Simmons.

Rancho Corte de Madera de Novato, of two square leagues, granted October 16, 1839, by Governor Alvarado to John Martin, to whom 8,878.82 acres were patented on May 23, 1863, lies to the east of Soulajule.

Rancho Los Baulenes, granted in November 1845 by Governor Pio Pico to Gregorio Briones, extends around Bolinas Bay. Don Gregorio's house stood on the west shore of the bay near an embarcadero. The house of Pablo Briones, undoubtedly his son, stood near the northeast boundary line of the rancho.

Rancho Tomales y Baulenes was owned by two men to whom patents were issued. The northern part was claimed by Rafael García, to whom Nicolás Gutiérrez, political chief of Upper California, granted two square leagues on March 18, 1836. It was surveyed in October 1865, and a final patent was issued to García on October 15, 1883, for 9,467.77 acres. At the time the survey was made a number of houses stood along his eastern line, which lay along Gerónimo Creek. He and his wife, María Loretto, raised eight children to maturity. The southern portion of Rancho Tomales y Baulenes was claimed by Bethuel Phelps; 12,000 acres of this was afterward owned by Shafter and Howard.

Rancho San Gerónimo, lying west of Cañada de Herrera, was granted to Rafael Cacho by Governor Micheltorena in 1844 and patented to Joseph Warren Revere in 1860. Revere, a native of Massachusetts and grandson of Paul Revere, came to California in 1846 as a lieutenant of the United States Navy and was commander of the northern district for several months. In his *Tour of Duty*, published in 1849, he wrote of his adventures and observations in California. Becoming colonel of a New Jersey regiment, he lived in Morristown after his return to the East.

Islands of Marin County

The western boundary line of Marin County runs from Petaluma Point in San Pablo Bay south into San Francisco Bay far enough to include Angel Island. Within the water area lie small islands of some interest. The Sisters lie a little to the northwest of Point San Pedro. The Marin Islands, upon which Chief Marín hid when escaping from his white pursuers, lie midway between San Pedro Point and San Quentin Point. Just south of the mouth of San Rafael Creek is San Rafael Rock. Directly to the northwest of California Point is Red Rock, called on some maps "Golden Rock," an uninhabited area of one or two acres through which the boundary lines of three counties, Marin, San Francisco, and Contra Costa, are traced and about which cling traditions of buried treasure. The largest of all, Angel Island, opposite Tiburon Point, is separated from the mainland by Raccoon Strait.

On August 2, 1775, Lieutenant Ayala reached an island in San Francisco Bay to which he gave the name of Nuestra Señora de los Angeles—today known as Angel Island. Ayala's mission at that time was to explore in the interest of Spain the estuaries of San Francisco Bay and to discover whether or not a strait connected Drake's Bay and San Francisco Bay. Finding good anchorage and plenty of wood and water, these explorers remained on the island forty days while making careful surveys of the surrounding topography. The chaplain of the expedition, Santa María, and some of the officers landed several times upon the Marin shore, where they visited a hospitable ranchería, undoubtedly that of the Olómpali.

"The grants of this and other islands were made by the express direction of the Superior Government of Mexico and the governor [of Alta California] was enjoined to grant the islands to Mexicans in order to prevent their occupation by foreigners who might injure the commerce and the fisheries of the Republic, and who, especially the Russians, might acquire otherwise a permanent foothold upon them." This Island of Los Angeles, or Angel Island, was granted Feb. 19, 1838, by Governor Juan B. Alvarado to Antonio María Osio, who used it for the raising of horses and cattle. He did not live upon it himself; but he subdivided it, built four houses, made a dam for the conservation of water for his stock, and put a part of the land under cultivation. His claim was recognized at the time but later rejected by the courts.

According to Bancroft, Angel Island was ceded by the state of California to the federal government as early as 1852 or 1853. Osio, then living in Mexico, whither he had gone when the Mexican authority ceased in Alta California, put in a claim for it in 1855, but the claim was adjusted. The Detention Station for immigrants entering the United States through the Port of San Francisco was on Angel Island until 1940.

Old Lime Kilns

An outcrop of limestone on Olema Creek was worked in the early '50's by two men who held a lease on the property and shipped lime to San Francisco via Sausalito. This lease is on file in the book of mining claims in the County Recorder's Office.

The mossy, fern-bedecked masonry of an old kiln is situated on one side of a ravine four hundred yards west of State Highway 1 about four and one-half miles south of the village of Olema. The stone façade is about 39 feet long and 15 feet high. Its arches show the skill of master craftsmen. A ledge of limestone appears near by.

Pits for three fires extend some feet into the earth below the façade. In one of these pits a Douglas fir seed has sprouted and grown into a tree with a diameter of twenty-four inches. Above the pits tower two almost intact chimneys built against a cut in the hillside and standing adjacent to each other with a common wall between them. In a crevice at the very top of the common wall another Douglas fir seed long ago took lodgment. The trunk of this tree had grown to a diameter of 42 inches when, in 1935, borings were made to its center by the County Agricultural Commission and its age was estimated to be 128 years.

Either these chimneys were not used by the lessees of the '50's or the computed age of the tree is incorrect. Divergent opinions are held by persons interested in the history of the region: some believe that the kilns were originally worked during the Spanish period; others that the Russians may have found and used this outcrop; while still others contend that those ideas are fantastic and that the development occurred after Americans reached the scene.

Bolinas and the Lighter Wharf

Otter hunting, the first occupation engaged in by settlers in the vicinity of the town of Bolinas, was followed by lumbering and shipbuilding in the '50's, when many sawmills were operating in the tree-filled canyons back from the shore. No evidence of the former industry remains, and the only reminder of the latter are the few piles that mark the site of the Lighter Wharf beside the road leading from Bolinas to Olema.

From the mills the product was hauled to the wharf by ox-drawn wagons, which creaked their way along the uneven roads on wooden wheels made from sawn sections of huge trees. The loads were transferred at the wharfs to flat-bottomed boats, or lighters, that carried the cargo to seaworthy vessels offshore. These vessels, in turn, transported the lumber and fuel to the growing city of San Francisco. It is estimated that 13,000,000 feet of lumber were shipped to that city for building purposes from the Lighter Wharf at the end of Bolinas Bay before the supply was exhausted. After the trees suitable for lumber had been worked up, the smaller trees were felled for domestic fuel and sent to the same market.

On the afternoon of April 9, 1853, a schooner starting with its load of lumber was hailed by Lieutenant William T. Sherman, who was on his way to summon assistance for the stranded steamer "Lewis," sailing from San Juan del Sur. A fog had carried the "Lewis" past the Port of San Francisco and had grounded it on "Ducksworth Reef" a few miles from Bolinas Bay. Lieutenant Sherman had been one of the passengers; and, when all had safely reached a bleak beach by means of small boats, he and a young companion had set out for assistance. By walking about three miles, they reached a board shanty, where lumbermen told them of this schooner soon to start. They hastened to it and were accommodated on top of the lumber. But before this vessel had reached its destination, it too was submerged because of a heavy ebb tide and a strong wind. The remainder of the journey to San Francisco was made in a little rowboat that appeared on the scene of the second disaster.

Nothing in the topography of the west shore of Bolinas Bay softened the force of ocean gales for the little settlement of Bolinas. Cypress hedges, some of them now ten feet across, had to be planted as windbreaks before the informal cottage gardens of the pioneers could grow successfully. In some parts of the village the roses, fuchsias, and lemon verbenas of the early days have now attained tree-like proportions.

Tomales

"Tomales" is a word in the Coast Miwok Indian dialect meaning "bay." When Lieutenant Juan Francisco de Bodega y Cuadra, commander of the schooner "Sonora," discovered by chance on October 3, 1775, the bay which he then named "Bodega," he thought that the body of water to the southward, now called Tomales Bay, would be found to afford a waterway to San Pablo Bay. However, for lack of time, he did not investigate, nor did he land on the shore, where he saw many natives, but proceeded southward toward San Francisco, the port that was then his destination.

This part of Marin County has never been thickly populated by white people, although the vicinity of the bay is a favorite vacation retreat, particularly toward its southern end. The town of Tomales, originally located at the head of Keyes Creek, which flows from the northeast into this bay, had its beginning in a store located there in 1852. The site of its old steamer landing is now covered with pasture land. The North Pacific Coast Railroad, in which Governor Latham was financially interested, ran its first freight train from a warehouse there on December 3, 1874, with a load of three hundred sacks of potatoes shipped by James Fallon. This was the forerunner of many trainloads of produce raised in the vicinity and shipped over this line to Sausalito and thence to San Francisco. The railroad has now been discontinued.

The Clark School, not far from Tomales, is in possession of one of the old bells of the San Rafael Mission. Before being presented to the school, the bell had been used by a parochial school in the county.

Ross and Kentfield

Ross is a station on the Northwestern Pacific Railroad within driving distance of beautiful country homes and of the grounds of the Katharine Branson School, a preparatory school for Bryn Mawr College. It received its name from James Ross, who settled on this part of Rancho Punta de Quentín in 1859, the year of the death of the former owner of the rancho, Benjamin R. Buckelew. There was an old house standing on the property which was thought to have been "built by convict labor from the old leg-irons found in the cellar." This was renovated and enlarged for the uses of the family.

In 1869 the name of James Ross is listed among directors of the local railroad, a line of three and one-half miles between San Rafael and San Quentin, afterward incorporated in the system managed by Peter Donahue. After Ross's death, the family home was burned, and his widow moved to the site which is now a park opposite Ross Station.

Kentfield is on land that passed from the estate of James Ross to Albert Emmet Kent when the latter came to California in search of health in 1871. It was called Ross Landing in earlier days, when steamers came up above the present state highway bridge to load the thousands of cords of wood which they carried to San Francisco. The original commodious colonial house built by the Kents faced due east and had an old-fashioned formal garden on the south with a fountain in the middle and numerous box-edged flower beds; vineyards and orchards were at a little distance. On these grounds in the autumn the annual Grape Festival for the benefit of the Protestant Orphanage at San Anselmo is held.

A canyon on the Kentfield Estate is called Baltimore Gulch, and a station on the railway is called Baltimore Park. Both names are reminiscent of the group of young men from Maryland, sponsored by the Baltimore and Frederick Trading Company, who came to Marin County in 1849 and erected a sawmill on Rancho Corte de Madera. Their venture, made in high hope, was not a financial success and was of short duration; but such stable citizens as Judge Barney, Daniel Taylor, David Clingan, and S. S. and Harry S. Baechtal were of this group and remained in the county to settle in different

parts. Judge Barney founded the *Marin Journal* in 1861. His one-story-with-attic house, built two and one-half miles northeast of San Rafael on the Santa Venetia Road, although weatherworn, still stands and is occupied as a residence.

Tennessee Cove

Tennessee Cove at the foot of Elk Valley and just outside the outer limits of the Golden Gate received its name after the disaster of March 6, 1853, when the steamer "Tennessee," plying between Panama and San Francisco, went ashore. At that date no lighthouse had been erected on the Pacific Coast; in trying to enter the Golden Gate, this boat, with six hundred passengers, struck the beach about two and a half miles north of Bonita Point. No lives were lost. The place since that time has borne the name of the vessel. The first light station on the Coast was erected at Alcatraz in the following year.

Bonita Point Light Station

The southwestern extremity of Marin County and the outer north headland of the Golden Gate is Bonita Point, where a much-needed light station was established by the United States government in 1855. When it was first placed, great difficulty was experienced in keeping this isolated, fog-ridden station manned; at the end of the first nine months' period, seven different keepers had been employed, none having found the place to his liking.

Here, also, was established in the same year the first fog signal on the Pacific Coast: an iron cannon transferred from the Benicia Arsenal. Sergeant Maloney, placed in charge at the Point with instructions to "fire the gun every half hour during fogs," reported two months later that as there was almost continual fog and no one to relieve him "for even five minutes" he had been unable to get the "two hours' sleep necessary out of the twenty-four." This gun remained in use for two years before its expense and ineffectiveness caused its abandonment in favor of another type of fog signal. However, it remained on the Point until the Panama Pacific Exposition of 1915, when it was displayed in San Francisco and afterward stored, along with its wheels and a part of its framework, in the Lighthouse Service storehouse on Yerba Buena Island.

The Pioneer Paper Mill

Samuel Penfield Taylor erected a paper mill in 1856 on Daniels Creek, afterward known as Paper Mill Creek. It is supposed to have been the first paper mill built west of the Mississippi River and was run by water carried by a flume from a dam in the creek one-half mile above. The warehouse was situated at the end of Tomales Bay, where Point Reyes village now is.

Rags to supply this mill were gathered by Chinese in San Francisco, made into great bales, and shipped by schooner to the head of Tomales Bay. They were then loaded on a scow and floated on the tide to Taylor's warehouse, whence a team of oxen completed the transportation to the factory. The finished paper was conveyed in reverse manner to San Francisco, where the product found a ready sale and was sent to all parts of the Pacific Coast. The undertaking was prosperous from the beginning and was especially so during the Civil War period. By 1884 the demand for paper had become so great that a larger mill was built at a cost of $165,000 and employment there furnished a livelihood for about one hundred families. Steam power was added, and the mill did a flourishing business until the depression of 1893.

After lying idle for several years, the red-painted building with windows and doors outlined in white was mysteriously burned. Now only the damaged foundations remain; the columns that acted as supports for the water wheel are still standing and crumbling brick walls outline the space where the boiler was located. These ruins are about two miles above Camp Taylor on the road from San Rafael to Olema.

Another mill, the Pacific Powder Mill, built for a different purpose, was erected in 1866 about three miles upstream from the paper mill. These buildings were vacant in 1880, and even the exact site is now lost.

Dominican College

The convent grounds on which stand the Dominican College and its preparatory schools occupy a large and beautiful tract in the outskirts of San Rafael. While the establishment of the convent in this locality is of recent date, its beginnings are to be found in the earliest days of the state.

The Dominican Sisters, originally from Paris, located on the West Coast first in Monterey in 1851. From Monterey they moved to Benicia in Solano County and from Benicia removed to San Rafael, where they have acquired by gift and purchase property that belonged to families prominent in early days. Forest Meadows, the outdoor auditorium, is on land which was owned by William T. Coleman; Meadowlands, the dormitory on Palm Avenue, was the country home of the M. H. de Young family of San Francisco. On the same avenue is the home formerly owned by William Babcock, also of San Francisco. His widow gave this completely furnished house to the convent.

Presbyterian Theological Seminary

When William Anderson Scott, D.D., a native of Tennessee, first sailed through the Golden Gate in 1854, he resolved to establish a school which should be a training center on the Coast for the ministry somewhere on the land surrounding the harbor. The realization of his ideal took years of endeavor and saw several changes of location.

The seminary was started in two rooms of the City College in San Francisco, but was moved twice later. For its third location, a building, still standing at 121 Haight Street, was erected in 1877 by the Trustees. Here the seminary remained until its removal to the permanent site in San Anselmo in 1891. The piece of land upon which it is now situated was the gift of a generous citizen of San Rafael, A. W. Foster. The small hill upon which the substantial buildings have been placed overlooks the town. The Montgomery Memorial Chapel, built at the foot of the hill, was the gift of the chief benefactor of the institution, Alexander Montgomery, whose remains were interred there.

Mount Tamalpais and Tamalpais Park

Two Indian words—*tamal* (bay) and *pais* (mountain or country)—form the name of the heavily wooded elevation that dominates the landscape on the north side of San Francisco Bay. In the '60's it was occasionally called Table Mountain, but that unsatisfactory appellation has been forgotten in the general use of the more musical name of Indian derivation. Its three peaks, East, West, and Middle, are all over 2,500 feet high, the highest being the West Peak 2,608 feet above sea level.

Pedestrian trails, some of which were made originally by red men and others blazed by white men in the early years, are still used by hiking parties. These pathways begin at different places around the base of the mountain; a favorite one starts beneath the shadows of the trees back of the old mill at Mill Valley. In 1896 the eight-mile Mill Valley and Tamalpais Scenic Railroad was laid out, and after its completion a train drawn by a steam engine carried passengers over a road bed "the crookedest in the world." About halfway to the top, at Mesa, the track described a double bowknot to accomplish a 100-foot rise within a distance of 1,000 feet. The railway is now a thing of the past, but a motor road now makes it possible for people to enjoy the extensive panorama displayed at every turn.

From the broad trail that encircles the summit one may see close at hand bays, islands, cities, and the two new bridges, one spanning the Golden Gate, and the other connecting San Francisco and Oakland, with a firm foundation between the two cities on Yerba Buena Island. With good atmospheric conditions, are visible to the north Mount Saint Helena and Mount Shasta; on the east Mount Diablo with the snow-capped Sierra Nevada in the distance; to the south Mount Hamilton and Loma Prieta; and toward the west the limitless Pacific.

Tamalpais State Park, a wooded area of 725 acres with unusually comprehensive flora, includes the West Peak. Below Rock Spring lies the natural amphitheater where plays, legendary and historical in character, are enacted annually in May. Steep Ravine in this park, a gift of the Honorable William Kent shortly before his death in 1928, is an abrupt descent where grow redwoods, firs, and thickets of underbrush.

Muir Woods

Adjoining Tamalpais State Park on the south is a stand of Coast redwoods (*Sequoia sempervirens*) that has been growing in this sheltered canyon on the lower western slope of Mount Tamalpais for centuries. Some of these majestic trees, whose ages are estimated at from one to three thousand years, have attained a diameter of 12 feet and a height of 240 feet.

This forest area was made a National Monument by presidential proclamation on January 9, 1908, a gift to the nation from William Kent, a member of the 62nd Congress, and his wife, Elizabeth Thacher Kent of Kentfield. Although President Theodore Roosevelt expressed his desire in accepting the gift to name it for the donors, they insisted upon its being named for John Muir, California's noted naturalist, explorer, and writer, who had labored many years in the cause of forest conservation. One of the pioneer proponents of the preservation of the sequoias, John Muir was at that time seventy years of age. He lived for six years to enjoy the honor conferred upon him in the naming of Muir Woods. The original gift has been supplemented until the area is now 426 acres, a memorial to John Muir in name but a monument, as well, to its donors.

SOURCES

[Credit is here given for source material, and permission to quote is hereby acknowledged]

BANCROFT, HUBERT HOWE. *History of California*. A. L. Bancroft Company, San Francisco, 1884

BARBER, ROGER. "Mill Valley Yesterdays," in *Mill Valley Record*, XXXV, No. 47 (February 16, 1934), 1. Mill Valley, California

BINGHAM, HELEN. *In Tamal Land*. Calkins Publishing House, San Francisco, 1906

BOLTON, HERBERT EUGENE. "Francis Drake's Plate of Brass," in *California Historical Society Quarterly*, XVI, No. 1, Part 2 (March 1937), San Francisco, 1–16

———. "Spanish Explorations in the Southwest, 1542–1706," in *Original Narratives of Early American History*, XVII. Charles Scribner's Sons, New York, 1916

BOYD, MARGARET KITTLE. *Reminiscences of Early Marin County Gardens*. Privately printed, 1934

BROWN, BELLE C. *Findings of Marin County Historical Landmarks Committee*. Manuscript, 1935

CALIFORNIA STATE MINERALOGIST. *Report*. State Printing Office, Sacramento, 1888

DAVIDSON, GEORGE M. *Identification of Sir Francis Drake's Anchorage on the Coast of California in the Year 1579.* California State Historical Society Publication, San Francisco, 1890 (Maps)

DODGE, GEORGE M. *Official Map of Marin County.* Schmidt Label and Lithograph Company, 1892

DRAKE, SIR FRANCIS. *The World Encompassed.* Hakluyt Society, London, 1854

DUFLOT DE MOFRAS, EUGÈNE. *Exploration du territoire de l'Orégon, des Californies et de la mer Vermeille, exécutée pendant les années 1840, 1841 et 1842.* A. Bertrand, Paris, 1844 (2 vols. and atlas)

ECKEL, EDWIN C. "Limestone Deposits of the San Francisco Region," in California State Mineralogist, *Report,* XXIX. State Printing Office, Sacramento, 1934

EDWARDS, PHILIP LEGET. *Diary.* "The Great Cattle Drive from California to Oregon in 1837." Grabhorn Press, San Francisco, 1932

ELDER, DAVID PAUL. *The Old Spanish Missions of California.* Paul Elder & Company, San Francisco, 1913

FRÉMONT, JOHN CHARLES. *Memoirs of My Life.* Bedford Clarke & Company, Chicago and New York, 1887

GREENE, CLAY M. "Life and Death of Daniel O'Connell, 1899," in the Annals of the Bohemian Club, IV. Recorder Printing and Publishing Company, San Francisco, 1930

GUINN, PROFESSOR J. M. *History of the State of California, Memorial and Biographical Record of Coast Counties of California.* Chapman Publishing Company, Chicago, 1904

HARPENDING, ASBURY. *The Great Diamond Hoax and Other Stirring Incidents.* The James H. Barry Company, San Francisco, 1913

History of Northern California, Memorial and Biographical. Lewis Publishing Company, Chicago, 1891

JAMES, GEORGE WHARTON. *In and Out of the Missions of California.* Little, Brown & Company, Boston, 1906

Land Grants, Book of Patents. Manuscript. Marin County Hall of Records

MUNRO-FRASER, J. P. *History of Marin County.* Illustrated. Alley, Bowen & Company, San Francisco, 1880

NELSON, N. C. "Shellmounds of the San Francisco Bay Region," in *University of California Publications in American Archaeology and Ethnology,* XVII, No. 4. The University Press, Berkeley, 1909

NEVINS, ALLAN. *Frémont, the West's Greatest Adventurer.* Harper & Brothers, New York and London, 1928

ROYCE, JOSIAH. *California from the Conquest in 1846 to the Second Vigilance Committee in San Francisco.* Houghton, Mifflin Company, Boston and New York, 1917

SHAFTER, PAYNE J. *Reminiscences.* Manuscript

SHERMAN, W. T. *Memoirs.* D. Appleton & Company, New York, 1875

SIMPSON, SIR GEORGE. *Narrative of a Journey round the World during the Years 1841–42.* 2 vols. Henry Colburn, London, 1847

WAGNER, HENRY R. *Sir Francis Drake's Voyage around the World, Its Aims and Achievements.* John Howell, San Francisco, 1926

WILKINS, JAMES H. "The Story of Fairfax," in *Marin County Leader,* I, No. 2 (March 6, 1926)

———. "The Duel at Fairfax," in *Marin County Leader,* I, No. 2 (March 6, 1926)

WINN, W. B. *Souvenir of Marin County.* Published by *Marin County Journal,* San Rafael, 1893

MENDOCINO COUNTY

MENDOCINO COUNTY (Mendocino was first applied to Cape Mendocino, so named in honor of Antonio de Mendoza, the first viceroy of New Spain) was one of the original twenty-seven counties, but until 1859 the government was administered by Sonoma County officials. Ukiah has always been its county seat.

Point Arena

Point Arena, or Punta de Arenas (Sandy Point), is a prominent headland on the coast in the southwestern part of the county. Offshore at this point Captain George Vancouver spent the night of Friday, November 10, 1792, in his ship "Discovery," while on his way from Nootka to San Francisco. Captain Vancouver called the place "Punta Barro de Arena."

The land stretching back from this point was included in an unnamed and unconfirmed grant made in 1844 to Rafael García, an early soldier of the San Francisco Company and already owner of two grants in what is now Marin County, who stocked the land with cattle. The Garcia River flowing through the tract bears his name. This grantee and Antonio Castro were reported to have been the leaders of a party of white men who raided the Indians in the vicinity of Ross in 1845 in search of laborers.

Although a store was built and goods were sold on the site in 1859, the town of Point Arena was not incorporated until 1908. It is said that when the lumbering industry was at its height Point Arena was the busiest town between San Francisco and Eureka. Asphalt, which exuded from an ocean bluff near by in quantities insufficient for commercial exploitation, as was proved during the oil excitement of 1865, is used on the streets of the town and makes a satisfactory road surface.

In 1870 a light station was erected well out on the point. The tower, built of brick, was destroyed in the earthquake of 1906; another, of reinforced concrete, was built subsequently a little distance back from the point. The present tower is 115 feet high, one of the two highest on the coast of California, and supports a light of 380,000 candle power. Previous to the establishment of this light many vessels were lost in the vicinity. The night of November 20, 1865, is memorable as that of a most disastrous storm in which ten vessels went ashore within a few miles of the point.

The Sanel Grant, Sanel, and Hopland

Fernando Felix (Feliz), a former *regidor* at the Pueblo de San José and already owner of Rancho Novato, received in 1844 a large tract of land in Sanel Valley lying along the Russian River. He erected an adobe house, 30 by 50 feet, and lived with his family just south of where Hopland now stands. He had lived there for seven years when in 1860 he received the United States patent for the 17,754 acres comprised in his estate.

The village that grew up around the Felix home was known as Sanel in 1859 and later, until, with the building of a toll road down the east side of the river which rerouted all the traffic that way, the town gradually moved over to the road, leaving only one building, a brick store, behind. The new site was called Hopland. Later the building of a railroad drew business back to the original site; and eventually the two places consolidated as Hopland, being now called by the residents Old Hopland and New Hopland.

A populous Indian village once existed just south of Old Hopland on the south bank of McDowell Creek. It was called "Sanel," and from this village the grant, the township, and the town preceding Hopland all inherited the name Sanel.

The first hops grown in this now famous center of hop raising were planted by Stephen Warren Knowles, who settled in Sanel Township in 1858, after arriving in San Francisco on the steamer "Northern Light" a few years earlier. He sold his first crop, dried in the loft of his barn, in Petaluma for thirty cents a pound. The Hermitage post office of early days was on the Knowles's place.

The Yokaya Grant and Ukiah

The Indian word *yokaya* means "south valley." This rancho of eleven square leagues lay in the fertile valley of the Russian River. It was given by Governor Pio Pico in 1845 to Cayetano Juarez, a native Californian who was a captain of militia and had engaged in many Indian expeditions. Captain Juarez was also the grantee of Rancho Tulucay in the

Napa Valley four years earlier. He had built an adobe there for a permanent home, where he died in 1885 at the age of seventy-five. He distinguished himself somewhat at the time of the capture of General Vallejo by his offer (which was rejected) to rescue that officer. The message to Vallejo regarding his release was carried by a brother of Captain Juarez disguised as a woman. Patent to this land was received by Juarez from the United States in 1867. Later owners (Hastings, Curry, and Carpenter) surveyed the property and sold it in tracts to suit purchasers.

The town of Ukiah, within the boundary of the grant and taking its name phonetically, had its origin in the '50's. The first settler on the site, S. Lowry, had established himself there by 1856. Three years later, when Sonoma County officials were relieved of the administration of county affairs, the village was chosen as the county seat. At that time only one hundred people were dwelling in the Russian River Valley. Ukiah is easily accessible today by means of the scenic Redwood Highway, which each year brings thousands of tourists through the town.

Three institutions of interest to scientists in the divisions of biology, geodesy, and botany have been established in or near Ukiah. The first one, biological, brought there in 1893, is the Fish Hatchery. Through the joint efforts of the Northwestern Pacific Railway and Mendocino County, this scientific exhibit had been placed in the Midwinter Fair in San Francisco. After the close of the Fair, it was brought to Ukiah and maintained at the expense of the railway company until eventually it was taken over by the State Fish and Game Commission and moved to a more suitable location eight miles out of town. The second of these scientific institutions, a geodetical one, was established in Ukiah in 1898. It is the International Latitude Observatory, one of four established by the International Geodetic Association. The third, which is botanical, is the pioneer project, started in 1900, for the preservation and propagation of native Western wild flowers, bulbs, shrubs, and trees. The originator of this interesting venture, Carl A. Purdy, arrived with his parents in the Ukiah Valley in 1870. In 1878, while still on the home farm, chance gave him the opportunity to gather native bulbs and plants for an Eastern firm. The interest thus stimulated in the youth led to the development of those now internationally known gardens, The Terraces, eight miles east of Ukiah.

Early Sawmills

A vessel carrying a cargo of silk and tea to San Francisco in 1851 encountered a severe storm and was driven ashore at the mouth of Noyo River. A party sent from Bodega to salvage the freight saw the timber along this part of the Coast, with its readily available lumber supply, and carried the information to Alderman Harry Meiggs of San Francisco. Meiggs, in addition to his political interests, was a mill owner and lumberman, with his main depot at North Beach in San Francisco. Finding his equipment inadequate for handling such large logs, he immediately ordered more substantial machinery from the East, procuring an engine and boiler from Norwich, Connecticut, and other parts from Painted Post, New York. When the ordered goods arrived in San Francisco, he chartered the brig "Ontario" and with the new outfit entered the mouth of Big River, or Booldam, as the Indians had named it, on July 19, 1852. Finding that William Kasten, one of those who had been driven ashore by the foul weather, claimed the water front, he purchased Kasten's claim, giving him some of the first product of his mill as part payment. With this lumber, Kasten built a dwelling house on what is now Kasten Street in Mendocino City, the first house of sawed lumber in the town. The house was occupied for many years by William Heeser, a pioneer.

The California Lumber Company was immediately formed, with Harry Meiggs the most active member of the firm, and J. B. Ford, who had arrived with eight yoke of oxen ten days before the brig, one of its important employees.

During the height of the lumber industry, a number of towns grew up along the Coast, each one a shipping point. Twenty mills, including some for making shingles only, were erected in Beaver Township before 1880. In almost every mile, along some creek or gulch or river, could be found a mill with its narrow-gauge railway built up the canyon a few miles for the purpose of bringing lumber or logs from the mountains down to the landing places. Ox teams dragged the logs from where they were felled to the railways. Most of these mills along the Coast were operated with no loading facilities other than chutes from the cliffs down which the lumber was slipped to the vessels lying at anchor below.

From north to south these coast towns and hamlets were: Usal, Rockport, Hardy Creek, Westport, Cleone, Fort Bragg, Noyo, Caspar, Mendocino City, Little River, Albion, Navarro, Greenwood, Elk River, and, on the very southern edge of the county, Gualala. With the decline of lumbering many of the old villages, with their railways and their wharves, have been abandoned, and the latter are fast falling to decay.

Such an abandoned place is Rockport. Hardy Creek, with its score or two of cottages scattered along a deep canyon opening into a "triangle of bluest sea," has become a "ghost" town, as has Caspar, a village of two hundred persons, invitingly situated beside a millpond with wooded canyon walls rising in the background. Noyo, however, lying on a neck of land between Noyo and Hare creeks not far from Fort Bragg, is making a name for itself again, this time by its fishing industry. Plants for the canning and drying of fish are now located there. Its deep-water harbor is also used for the export of lumber.

Mendocino City, "with its red and white houses, schools, and churches ranged on a long promontory above the bay at the mouth of Big River," remains a thriving community with a population of about a thousand. Here is an interesting old Masonic temple with carved wood figures. The cliffs at the harbor hide deep caves around which legends of disappearing ships are woven. The lumbering operations which were started there in 1853 by the California Lumber Company are now controlled by the Union Lumber Company, with a main plant at Fort Bragg.

South of Mendocino City is Little River, "a pretty, straggling village of high-gabled houses with quaint dormer windows, and red roses clambering all about." Between it and Albion, the Coast is cut by wooded headlands, fiords, and islets.

Albion today is a quiet town, no lumbering operations being carried on. It was there that the second mill in the county was erected during the winter of 1852–1853, on contract with Captain William Richardson of Marin County. In 1845 Captain Richardson had applied for a grant of land covering this area which extended from the Albion River to the Garcia River. This estate, known as the Albion Grant, was never confirmed by the United States.

Navarro, set in a deep valley at the mouth of a broad, winding river, is today the "deserted village of gray and withered houses" described by J. Smeaton Chase. "Most of the buildings were out of plumb; the church leaned at an alarming angle; and a loon, swimming leisurely in the middle of the stream, seemed to certify the solitude of the place." Greenwood, too, is deserted. But Elk River, a small town of four hundred inhabitants two miles south, retains some of its old-time milling activity. Gualala, at the mouth of the picturesque Gualala River, had its lumbering heyday in the '60's and '70's.

Spy Rock

About two miles south of Twin Rocks and thirty-three miles north of Willits a road branches east from the Redwood Highway. About eight miles distant along this road is Spy Rock, an isolated peak in the Eel River Canyon, where Indians in early days built their smoke signal fires.

Round Valley

East of Spy Rock and north of the town of Covelo is Round Valley, so named because it has about the same diameter (seven miles) in any direction. Here is the Round Valley Indian Reservation, where in 1856, early in the administration of Thomas J. Henley, superintendent of Indian affairs, a farm called the Nome Cult Station (*Nomcult* being a Wintun word meaning "West Tribe") was established by the government, principally as a breeding and fattening station for beef to supply the Reservation at Fort Bragg on the Coast. It was declared a Reservation in 1858. In 1863 a military post was established there with seventy soldiers under the command of Captain Douglas. Soon afterward a company of cavalry came as reinforcement. This post was maintained until the Reservation was turned over to the care of the Methodist Episcopal Church, in pursuance of the policy of General U. S. Grant toward the Indians.

The Round Valley Indian Reservation is now under the jurisdiction of the Sacramento Indian Agency. In 1932 representatives of fifteen different tribes resided there.

Fort Bragg

Lieutenant Horatio Gates Gibson was ordered in June 1857 to establish a military post on the Mendocino Indian Reservation. The post was placed one and one-half miles north of the mouth of the Noyo River and was named Fort Bragg in honor of General Braxton Bragg of Mexican War fame. Lieutenant Gibson, who afterward attained the rank of brigadier general, remained there for one year. For some years before his death in his nineties he had the distinction of being the oldest living graduate of West Point.

A thriving town grew up at Fort Bragg. It is still the largest city in the county and the only one on the Coast to have a rail connection. This railway route, one of the most scenic in the state, passes along the Noyo River through magnificent redwood forests. The town is a shipping point for fish, farm and dairy products, and lumber. Located there is the nursery which was started by the Union Lumber Company in 1922 to raise seedling trees for reforestation work, giving the nursery the distinction of conducting the first private venture of this kind in the state. From it a systematic planting of cutover land is carried on.

From Fort Bragg the coast road runs north through several miles of sand dunes. At Ten Mile River the shore becomes rugged with high cliffs and surf-beaten rocks honeycombed with caves.

Willits

The town of Willits, now a railway junction twenty-five miles east of Fort Bragg, lies on the Redwood Highway between Ukiah and Eureka. It had its origin in a store opened in 1865 by Kirk Brier from Petaluma, whose venture was followed by a blacksmith shop and saloon. Hiram Willits, who had come to the county in 1857, purchased the store; and the town, incorporated in 1888, was called by his name.

Mineral Springs

Ukiah Vichy Springs, known and used by the Indians before the arrival of the white man, are three miles east of Ukiah. These waters are said to be similar to the Vichy Waters of France, noted since Roman times. Anderson's

report of 1888 mentions these springs as the "Doolan Ukiah Vichy" and says: "Bathing in the vichy renders the skin soft and clear and very soon heals up any skin irritation." The place was developed into a summer resort and continued popular until the buildings were destroyed by fire.

Orr's Hot Sulphur Springs, equipped with a small hotel and a number of cabins, are located on the edge of the redwood belt fourteen miles west of Ukiah. At Duncan Springs, on a hillside south of Hopland, also are a summer hotel and cottages with mineral-water baths.

Redwood Groves

The humid coast belt in which this county lies is the natural habitat of the Coast redwood (*Sequoia sempervirens*). The rugged shore line, famous for its vistas of the Pacific Ocean, is cut by wooded canyons formed by numerous mountain streams flowing seaward through fine stands of these and other native trees. Fortunately, some of these forests escaped the axe and saw of the pioneer lumberman.

In the interior, also, are many timbered areas either publicly or privately owned. Among these are the Coolidge Redwood Park; the Devoy, or Tuomey, Grove; Hickey Memorial Grove; Hartsook's Grove; and Lane's Redwood Flat, containing very beautifully placed trees on a bluff above Eel River. Just west of Ukiah, on the Orr's Springs Road, is the Montgomery Redwood Grove, a stand of virgin timber. The Paul Dimmick Memorial Grove of 11.80 acres of second-growth redwood on a part of the old Albion Grant, "logged off" half a century ago, lies on the MacDonald-to-the-Sea Highway.

On the Coast is the Russian Gulch Redwood Park, containing 1,103 acres, and near by is the Van Damme Park, a sandy beach tract, willed to the state by the late C. G. Van Damme. Certain areas east of Fort Bragg and Albion are famous for their magnificent display of wild rhododendrons in the spring.

The southern part of Mendocino National Forest is in this county. It extends into the adjacent counties of Humboldt and Trinity. Formerly known as the California National Forest, to avoid confusion the name was changed on July 12, 1932, by executive order from Washington.

A Bandit's Rock

A huge boulder near Willits, known as the Black Bart Rock, was once the hiding-place of Black Bart, the bandit, who robbed the mail stage there in pioneer days. More intriguing than Sherlock Holmes is the story of Black Bart, who, between the years 1875 and 1883, became "a synonym for elusiveness and mystery." During that time he robbed twenty-seven coaches, traveling on foot for thousands of miles through rough mountain country from the Sierra to the Coast Range. Calaveras, Sierra, Plumas, Yuba, Butte, Shasta, Sonoma, Mendocino and Trinity, all knew the terror of this lone highwayman in the linen duster and mask who had eluded years of diligent search on the part of detectives. His endurance seemed uncanny, for, although he always traveled on foot, he was known to have robbed two coaches sixty miles apart in a rough mountain region within twenty-four hours.

Black Bart was never vicious and seemed averse to taking human life. He was immaculate in dress and extremely polite, a man of refinement and education. Because he was such a quiet, respectable, delicate-looking individual, he lived in San Francisco for years under the very eyes of the detectives without once being suspected. He even frequented the favorite restaurant of the police headquarters staff, a bakery on Kearny Street, sometimes eating at the same table with the officers. Black Bart seemed thoroughly to enjoy his own cleverness and notoriety, and a decided sense of humor often expressed itself in facetious rhymes left on empty mail or express boxes for the baffled officers to read.

The mystery of Black Bart's identity was finally unraveled through the combined efforts of Sheriff Thorne of San Andreas and H. B. Hume, special agent of the Wells Fargo Company, whose iron-bound boxes were so frequently rifled in transit. The bandit's propensity for cleanliness finally proved his undoing, for on November 3, 1883, at Bear Mountain between Milton and Murphy's in Calaveras County, not far from the scene of the first robbery of his career, he dropped a handkerchief while he was busily engaged in opening an express box containing $4,100 in coin. The mark "F.X.0.7" on this piece of linen led Sheriff Thorne after a most careful search to a laundry on Bush Street in San Francisco to which the fastidious Black Bart had for years carried his little bundle. He had lived in San Francisco all that time under the name of Charles C. Bolton, ostensibly a mining man, who made periodic trips to the mines. He was lodged in jail at San Andreas and was shortly sentenced to San Quentin, where he entered upon his term November 21, 1883, and was released January 23, 1888. His whereabouts after that date are unknown.

SOURCES

[Credit is here given for source material, and permission to quote is hereby acknowledged]

ANDERSON, WINSLOW (M.D.). *Mineral Springs and Health Resorts of California.* The Bancroft Company, San Francisco, 1892
AYERS, ROBERT W., and HUTCHINSON, WALLACE. *National Forests of California.* U.S. Department of Agriculture, Circular No. 94, Washington, D.C. No date
BELLEW, TOM. "Laundry Mark Ends Career of Black Bart, Gentleman Stage Robber," in *San Francisco Chronicle*, Sunday, May 20, 1934
California, State of. *Corrected Report of Spanish and Mexican Grants in California, Complete to February 25, 1886.* Prepared by State Surveyor-General. Published as supplement to *Official Report of 1883-1884.* Sacramento, 1886
California State Mineralogist. *Report, 1887-1888, 1889-1890.* Sacramento
CARPENTER, A. O., and MILLBERRY, P. H. *History of Mendocino and Lake Counties.* Historic Record Company, Los Angeles, 1914
CHASE, J. SMEATON. *California Coast Trails.* Houghton Mifflin Company, Boston and New York, 1913
DANE, EZRA and BEATRICE. *New Strikes in Old Diggins.* Manuscript, 1932
GIBSON, HORATIO GATES (Brigadier General, U.S.A.). "Letter to the Mayor of Fort Bragg," in *Fort Bragg News*, March 2, 1923
History of Northern California. Illustrated. Lewis Publishing Company, Chicago, 1891
JOHNSTON, PHILLIPS. "Gentleman Black Bart," in *Touring Topics*, October, 1929
LANE, D. R. "State Parks, a Heritage for All," in *Motor Land*, XXXII, No. 6 (June, 1933), 3-5
MENEFEE, C. A. *Historical and Descriptive Sketch Book of Napa, Sonoma, Lake, and Mendocino.* Reporter Publishing House, Napa, 1873
MUNRO-FRASER, J. P. *History of Mendocino County.* Illustrated. Alley, Bowen & Company, San Francisco, 1880
PURDY, CARL A. Notes. Manuscript, 1934
PUTNAM, GEORGE R. *Lights and Lightships of the United States.* Houghton Mifflin Company, Boston and New York; Riverside Press, Cambridge, 1917
RUSSELL, CARL PARCHER. *One Hundred Years in Yosemite.* Stanford University Press, 1931
SANCHEZ, NELLIE VAN DE GRIFT. *Spanish and Indian Place Names of California.* A. M. Robertson, San Francisco, 1922
Union Lumber Company. *Historical Files.* San Francisco, 1934
WOODS, RUTH KEDZIE. *The Tourist's California.* Dodd, Mead Company, 1914

MONTEREY COUNTY

MONTEREY COUNTY (Monterey is Spanish for "hill or wood of the king," so named in honor of Gáspar de Zúñiga, Count of Monterey, viceroy of Mexico) was one of the original twenty-seven counties. Monterey was the original county seat, but in 1873 the honor was given to Salinas. The county archives contain many pre-state records in Spanish.

The Discovery of Monterey Bay

Juan Rodríguez Cabrillo, in command of the "San Salvador" and the frigate "Victoria," discovered California in 1542 and sailed up the coast as far as the Northwest Cape. On his return voyage, his chronicle records that, on November 18, "they ran along the coast, and at night found themselves off Cape San Martín [Point Pinos]." This entry would indicate that, although Juan Rodríguez may have seen what we know as Point Pinos, the southern headland of Monterey Bay, he did not actually see the bay itself.

The Pacific Grove Lighthouse was established on Point Pinos in 1872, and a marker has been placed there by the Pacific Grove Chapter, D.A.R., in honor of Cabrillo, the first European to see the coast of California at Pacific Grove.

Probably the first white man to see Monterey Bay itself was Sebastián Rodríguez Cermeño, a Portuguese in command of the Spanish galleon "San Agustín," in 1595. Cermeño had been sent out to discover a northern port on the California coast where the Manila ships might find protection and supplies and receive warning of enemies. On November 30, the "San Agustín" was wrecked at Drake's Bay, but Rodríguez continued his voyage in the "San Buenaventura," a little launch, or open sailboat, which he had constructed In this frail craft he saw Monterey Bay on December 10, 1595, seven years before it was seen by Vizcaíno, the so-called discoverer. Cermeño called it San Pedro Bay.

The Vizcaíno-Serra Oak

Sebastián Vizcaíno was a merchant trader who had had much experience on the Spanish galleon route, and who had also been a shipmate of Rodríguez Cermeño on his voyage of discovery in 1595. In the flagship "San Diego," Vizcaíno entered Monterey Bay on December 15, 1602, the second European to enter its waters, and the first to make a landing there.

Even more important than his landing was Vizcaíno's description of the bay as he saw it, for he was so enchanted with its beauty that "he wrote almost too enthusiastically to his Majesty concerning it." He spoke of it as a harbor "sheltered from all winds," and a legend grew up concerning the port of Monterey, which became "one of the moving factors for a century and a half in Spanish expansion to the northwest." It explains, too, the difficulty which later Spanish explorers had in finding it again.

The entrance into Monterey Bay and the act of taking possession of it were the principal events of Vizcaíno's voyage. The ceremony was performed under a live oak very close to the shore, the same oak under which Padre Junípero Serra performed a similar ceremony in 1770, when the Mission and Presidio of Monterey were founded.

The Vizcaíno-Serra Oak died in 1905, but the trunk was removed to the San Carlos Church, where it is preserved in the courtyard. The site of the tree and of the landing-place is marked by the Junípero Serra Cross, on the south side of the main gateway to the Monterey Presidio. On Presidio Hill, overlooking the bay, is the Junípero Serra Monument erected by Mrs. Jane L. Stanford in 1891.

Portolá's Trail through Monterey

Starting from San Diego on July 14, 1769, Gáspar de Portolá started north with his men to search for the Bay of Monterey, described in such glowing terms by Vizcaíno in 1602. Traveling up the coast by way of Gaviota Pass, the expedition entered the confines of what is now Monterey County and camped, September 21–24, on the banks of the Nacimiento River, near its source. The high ridges of the Coast Range had just been traversed with great difficulty, and the men were much in need of rest.

After they had somewhat recuperated, the party pushed on and reached the San Antonio River at a point near Jolón, where they camped on September 24. On the twenty-fifth they camped again in the upper Jolón Valley, and on September 26 they descended Kent Canyon, reaching the Salinas River near King City.

During the days following they camped successively near Metz, Camphora, Chualar, and on September 30, below what is now Old Hill Town, near the mouth of the Salinas River. From October 1 to October 6 they camped near Blanco (former site), and from this point explored the Monterey Bay region and saw the river and bay at Carmel.

During all this week the party did not recognize Vizcaíno's wonderful harbor "sheltered from all winds" and described in Cabrero Bueno's sailing directions as a bay "round like an O" for which they sought. It was doubtless shrouded in gray fog, and not until a year later did they know what they had missed.

Leaving a cross planted upon the beach, near Monterey, the party continued the journey northward, camping on October 7 near Del Monte Junction and then proceeding across Pajaro River and camping near the present site of Watsonville, in Santa Cruz County.

Misión San Carlos Borroméo (El Carmelo)

The settlement of Monterey was at the point farthest north in the original plan for the colonization of California, and there the Presidio and the Mission were to be established. Portolá's party had failed to find the bay in 1769, but a second expedition was organized the following year, Portolá and Father Crespi going by land and Father Serra, who was ill, proceeding by boat.

Portolá reached the Bay of Monterey for the second time on May 24, 1770, to find the cross which he had erected there the year before still standing near the beach, but curiously decorated ". . . . with arrows stuck in the ground and sticks with many feathers, which the gentiles had placed there; suspended from a pole beside the cross was a string of small fish, all fairly fresh, while pieces of meat were deposited at the foot of the cross and a pile of mussels." The Indians later told the padres how, at night, the cross had become wonderfully illuminated, reaching far up into the heavens, and they were afraid and brought peace offerings to the foreigners' God. The day being calm and clear, the entire sweep of the bay was visible, and Crespi and Fages exclaimed: "Why, this is the Port of Monterey, for it is as Sebastián Vizcaíno tells, to the very letter!"

Father Serra arrived in the "San Antonio" seven days later, and, on June 3, 1770, under the same oak where Vizcaíno had held services one hundred and sixty-eight years before, the Misión San Carlos Borroméo and the Presidio of Monterey were dedicated.

The first Mission building was erected at the Presidio on the site where the San Carlos Parish Church stands today. But the presence of the soldiers and the lack of good agricultural land caused Father Serra to look about for a more suitable location. This was found five miles to the south in a fertile valley watered by the Río Carmelo (so named for the Carmelite Fathers who accompanied Vizcaíno), which empties into the ocean at this point, and the formal transfer of the Mission site was made in December 1771. Misión San Carlos became the favorite of Father Serra, and there he sleeps within the sanctuary today.

The present building at Carmel was begun in 1793 and dedicated in September 1797. Being beautifully situated and prosperous, it became the headquarters for the Father Presidentes of all the missions in California. After 1836, it quickly fell into ruins, until 1882, when, through the efforts of Father Casanova, the graves of the Presidentes, Serra and Lasuén, and Fathers Crespi and López were discovered within the church. Public interest was then aroused and funds were raised for the restoration, which was accomplished and the church rededicated in 1884.

Robert Louis Stevenson in "The Old Pacific Capital," written shortly before the restoration of San Carlos, calls the valley drained by the Carmel River "a true Californian valley, bare, dotted with chaparral, overlooked by quaint, unfinished hills. The Carmel runs by many pleasant farms, a clear and shallow river, loved by wading kine; and at last, as it is falling towards a quicksand and the great Pacific, passes a ruined Mission on a hill. From the Mission church the eye embraces a great field of ocean, and the ear is filled with a continuous sound of distant breakers on the shore. The roof has fallen; the ground-squirrel scampers on the grass; the holy bell of St. Charles is long dismounted; yet one day in every year the church awakes from silence, and the Indians return to worship in the church of their converted fathers. I have seen them trooping thither, young and old, in their clean print dresses, with those strange, handsome, melancholy features, which seem predestined to a national calamity; the Mission church is in ruins; the ranchería, they tell me, encroached upon by Yankee newcomers; the little age of gold is over for the Indian; but he has had a breathing-space in Carmel Valley before he goes down to the dust with his red fathers."

The Presidio of Monterey

The Presidio of Monterey and Misión San Carlos were founded on the same day, June 3, 1770, when Gáspar de Portolá took possession of the land in the name of King Carlos III of Spain. A fort of rude palisades and a few huts were erected at once and the second presidio in Alta California was instituted.

Late in the eighteenth century, Spain erected a fort on the hill overlooking Monterey Bay, where the present presidio grounds are located. Count de la Pérouse, who visited Monterey in September 1786, says that the guns of the Castillo greeted him; and in 1793, when George Vancouver sailed into the harbor, he also noted the battery on the hill. Vancouver's party was long and gratefully remembered by residents of the Monterey vicinity (who numbered less than five hundred by 1800), for they "left fruit stones, or seeds of trees . . . . extending their generosity by leaving likewise different grains of the best quality," which, planted and tended, added greatly to the variety of foods available in after years.

During the Spanish and Mexican periods, Monterey held first place as the military and social capital of Alta California where the élite of society made their home. It was also the port of entry where "Boston ships" and whaling vessels came with their tempting inducements to trade with the colonists, finally breaking down the barriers placed by the reluctant Spanish government against foreign trade.

The little port, set like a jewel within its pine-clad hills beside the bluest of blue bays, is charmingly described by

Richard Henry Dana, Jr., in his *Two Years before the Mast.* When Dana sailed into the harbor on the brig "Pilgrim," in the year 1834, ". . . . the town lay directly before" him, "making a very pretty appearance; its houses being of white-washed adobe. . . . . The red tiles, too, on the roofs, contrasted well with the white sides and with the extreme greenness of the lawn upon which the houses—about a hundred in number—were dotted about, here and there, irregularly. . . . . This, as they are of one story, and of the cottage form, gives them a pretty effect when seen from a little distance. . . . .

"In the centre of it is an open square, surrounded by four lines of one-story buildings, with half a dozen cannon in the centre. . . . . This is the Presidio, or fort."

In 1822 the Mexican government built a fort on the present Presidio grounds on the hill overlooking Monterey Bay. In 1846, after the American occupation, a blockhouse was erected there and ship guns were mounted. It was named Fort Stockton at first, but later in the same year the name was changed to Fort Mervine in honor of the officer in charge. The old fort is no longer there, but the place where it stood has been marked.

The Sloat Monument, erected in honor of Commodore John Drake Sloat, U.S.N., commemorates the act of taking possession of California for the United States, July 7, 1846, and the raising of the United States flag over the Custom House at Monterey. The base of the monument was erected by the people of California through popular subscription, and the superstructure was added by the United States government. It was dedicated and unveiled on the hilltop on the present Presidio grounds, June 14, 1910.

Fort Halleck was built at the present Presidio in 1847 and named in honor of Lieutenant H. W. Halleck of the corps of engineers which laid out the fort. Halleck later became secretary of state in California during Governor Riley's military rule, and was a prominent general in the Civil War. He was a man of considerable influence during the period of transition from Mexican to American rule, interpreting the Spanish and Mexican law for the Americans, and thus helping to prevent much confusion and disorder. In the early '50's he was a prominent lawyer in San Francisco. Fort Halleck no longer exists, but the site has been marked.

Misión San Antonio de Padua

Father Junípero Serra, as soon as he had explored the Río Carmelo and had set his people to work building the Misión San Carlos on the new site, set out for the Santa Lucía Mountains to found the third of the missions in Alta California. At length he came to the beautiful valley covered with oaks which was named Los Robles, and which Portolá, in 1769, had called La Hoya de la Sierra de Santa Lucía.

Close by the little river, which Father Serra named the San Antonio, the bells were hung from the branch of a live oak. Grasping the rope and ringing the bells loud and long, the venerable Father cried: "Hear, O Gentiles! Come! Oh come to the holy Church of God! Come, Oh come, and receive the Faith of Christ!" And to his companion's plea that it was useless to ring the bells he replied: "Let me give vent to my heart's desires; for I would that these bells were heard all over the world, or at least by all the pagan people who live in this sierra."

And, as though a miracle had been wrought, after the rustic enramada had been raised and the simple altar placed, one dark native hesitatingly approached to witness the celebration of the Mass. This was the first instance of a native being present at the founding of a Mission. By 1805 there were 1,296 neophytes from the neighboring rancherías.

Misión San Antonio was founded July 14, 1771, at a site one and one-half miles from the present church, which was begun in 1810. It is said to have been not only one of the largest but also one of the most picturesque and interesting of all the Missions, unsurpassed in its artistic arrangement and the loveliness of its rural setting. The beautiful brick *fachada* withstood the neglect of years and the encroachments of both storm and earthquake, even after the body of the main building and the roof of the long corridors had crumbled.

Standing in a well-watered valley through which the San Antonio flows in a southeasterly direction to join the Salinas River, the Mission became famous for its excellent wheat and its fine horses. A stone mill for the grinding of the wheat was constructed and operated by water brought for many miles through a stone-walled ditch, or *zanja*. Remains of this marvelous, if primitive, engineering feat still exist in the valley a few hundred yards from the Mission, in what was once the garden, or orchard.

After the death of the Reverend Doroteó Ambris, the last resident priest at San Antonio, the Mission structures were deserted and from year to year became a more complete ruin. Finally, in 1903, the Historic Landmarks Committee, Native Sons of the Golden West, made a plea for restoration, and in September of that year it was begun. Except for the year 1906, when much of their efforts were destroyed by the earthquake, the work has steadily progressed up to the present time. A yearly pageant is given in June to help create interest in this work, and it is hoped that complete restoration will soon be accomplished.

Misión San Antonio is twenty miles southwest of King City and about six miles north of the village of Jolón. Services are held and presided over every two weeks by a visiting priest from San Lucas.

Anza's March through Monterey

Anza and his little band of settlers crossed the Río del Nacimiento on March 5, 1776, and proceeded another mile to El Primo Vado (the First Ford) of the Río de San Antonio, near King Well in what is now Monterey County. Here they camped for the night, continuing up the river valley the following day to Misión San Antonio de Padua, where Anza had made a brief stop on his previous journey in 1774 and where they now remained two days. The Fathers welcomed them as royally as their brothers at San Gabriel and San Luis Obispo had done.

On the morning of the 8th, the expedition once more resumed its march, following up Sulphur Spring Canyon northeast to Upper Milpitas Road, east to the Jolón Road, northeast over the ridge, and down Kent Canyon to the valley of what was then known as the Río de Monterey and which is now called the Salinas River Valley. Camp was made northwest of the site of King City at Los Ositos (the "little bears"), where Anza had stopped on April 17, 1774. On the 9th they rested at Los Correos north of the Somavia School and on the 10th, in a pouring rain, reached the Presidio of Monterey.

Father Junípero Serra welcomed the travelers and escorted them to Misión San Carlos del Carmelo, where Anza was very ill. Before recovering fully he insisted on fulfilling his mission and proceeded north to explore and to map out the site for the new settlement to be established at San Francisco, leaving his people at Monterey until arrangements could be made for their final migration to the new presidio.

On his way north, Anza followed along to the left of what is now the highway to Salinas and San Juan Bautista. He made his final camp in Monterey County on March 23, at a place called La Natividad, near Sugar Loaf Mountain. A village and a rancho of that name are in the vicinity today.

Having finished his work at San Francisco, Anza returned to Monterey on April 8. Greatly disappointed not to be able to settle his people at the new presidio site (owing to Governor Rivera's jealousy), Anza finally set out on his return march to Mexico on April 14, after bidding a sad farewell to the people who had learned to love him on their long and perilous journey from Sonora and who wept bitterly at his departure.

Misión Nuestra Señora Dolorosísima de la Soledad

Misión Soledad was founded by Father Lasuén on October 9, 1791, thirty miles south of Monterey and about a mile west of the Salinas River, with thousands of acres of bare, brown plains stretching away on every side. Although very nearly limitless in acreage, soil and pasturage were only fairly good, and the growth in the number of neophytes was very slow.

Gradually, however, the faithful labors of the Fathers surmounted these handicaps until Soledad was quite prosperous, and its occupants lived quiet, peaceful lives for about forty years. Governor Arrillaga died at Soledad in 1814 and was buried under the center of the church, and in 1818 the Mission became a refuge for the coast missions during the appearance of the pirate Bouchard. After the decree of secularization, Soledad fell into a state of abject poverty, and Father Sarría, who refused to forsake his little flock of Indians, died there, destitute and enfeebled by age.

The first temporary adobe structure at Soledad was erected in 1797, and a new church was begun in 1808. Today, only forlorn-looking mud walls stand in mute desolation beside the roadway. Great haystacks tower above them and roaming cattle pasture there. Wrapped in solitude and loneliness, the pitiful remnants of the old church bring sadness to the hearts of those who know and love its story of sacrifice and devotion.

San Carlos Parish Church

After the removal of the Mission to Carmel, the old Mission building at the Presidio in Monterey became the Presidio Chapel. The present building was erected in 1794 and was then called the Royal Chapel because the King's representative worshiped there. At the time of the secularization of the Mission at Carmel, in 1836, the chapel at Monterey became the Parish Church.

The San Carlos Parish Church is well preserved and in regular use today. In 1836 many of the furnishings from the old Mission at Carmel were brought to the Parish Church, where they are still treasured.

The Custom House

The old Custom House in Monterey occupies a prominent place in California's history. The flags of three nations have floated over this building: that of Spain until 1822; that of Mexico from 1822 to 1846; and that of the United States from 1846 on. Robert Glass Cleland says that "California history is vastly more significant because of its national and international aspects than for any local interest it may possess. From this standpoint, the event of primary importance in the history of California is its transformation from a Mexican province into an American state. To this event, as Dr. Chapman shows, the Spanish period looks forward; from this event, dates the California of today and the greater California of tomorrow."

The Custom House at Monterey was the most important in the province of Alta California, and all trading vessels were compelled to enter their cargo on its records. Here came the intrepid sealers and hunters of sea otter, the pioneers of trade on the Pacific Coast, and, following closely in their wake, the battered whaling vessels put in to the quiet harbor of Monterey to be reconditioned after perilous voyages in far northern seas; while, most important of all, the "Boston ships" from New England came early seeking hides and tallow, and with their coming a new era on the coast of Alta California was foreshadowed.

The American flag was raised over the Custom House, temporarily, on October 19, 1842, by Commodore Thomas ap Catesby Jones, owing to misapprehension of the seriousness of affairs between the United States and Mexico and of the much feared invasion of England. However, he took it down again the following day and apologized for his mistake. But on July 7, 1846, the American flag was raised permanently by Commodore John Drake Sloat, signalizing, by that act, the passing of California from Mexican rule.

The Custom House is a picturesque structure of stone and adobe begun by the Spanish and added to, at different times, by the Mexican and American governments. Statements as to the dates of construction differ. Some authorities say that the low central portion was begun first, the foundations being laid in 1814 by the Spanish and the walls and roof being completed by the Mexicans after 1822, while the two square, balconied towers, one at the north end and one at the south, were erected during the Mexican and American periods, the north tower having been built first. Gertrude Atherton has used the Custom House and the rocks in front of its veranda as the setting for a dramatic incident in *The Pearls of Loretto*.

The Custom House now belongs to the United States government and is well conditioned, having been restored by the state of California. It was marked by the Native Sons and Daughters of the Golden West, who have their local headquarters in the building. A museum of local relics is also housed in it.

Land Grants

In 1773 the Spanish Viceroy Bucareli, in preparation for the establishment of future pueblos, authorized Captain Rivera to distribute lands to worthy persons, either native or Spanish, who would devote themselves to farming and stock raising. Among those considered to be worthy persons were Spaniards who had married baptized Indian girls.

Such a man was Manuel Butron, a soldier, who married Margarita María of the San Carlos Mission and to whom Rivera gave a plot of land 140 varas square near the Mission in 1775. This was the first grant of land made by the Spanish in Alta California. The grantee, however, abandoned it later and was living in the Pueblo de San José in 1786.

After the Butron grant, pueblo lots were given to settlers, and by 1784 other tracts of larger dimensions were temporarily granted to individuals by Fages. By 1786 grants of land up to three square leagues were authorized, provided that they did not overlap the boundaries of already established missions, pueblos, or rancherías. By 1793 a few had been granted provisionally to *inválido* soldiers and other settlers on the Salinas River.

By January 1795 a half-dozen provisional ranchos were held in the Monterey district, none of which seem to have been made permanent at any later date. They were: Buena Vista, five leagues, near Monterey, held by José Soberanes and Joaquín Castro; Salinas, four leagues, held by Antonio Aceves and Antonio Romero; Bajada a Huerta Viega, one-half league, by Antonio Montano; Cañada de Huerta, three-quarters league, by Antonio Buelna; Mesa de la Polvora, "a musket shot," by Eugenio Rosalio; and Chupadero, "1 mile," by Bernardo Heredia and Juan Padilla.

Rancho Bolsa de San Cayetano

Don Ignacio Vicente Ferrer Vallejo, a Spanish native of Jalisco, Mexico, came to Alta California in 1774 with Lieutenant Ortega and became the progenitor of the Vallejo family in the state. He had a brother, Juan José, who was a priest, but he himself inclined to a military rather than an ecclesiastical life and enlisted in that service. Records show that he was praised for his bravery on many occasions. After the termination of his enlistment he was employed at San Carlos, where he directed agriculture and irrigation. He re-enlisted in military service in the Monterey Company and held positions at Soledad, San José, and Branciforte. In 1824 he was at San Luis Obispo for the purpose of preventing an Indian revolt and while there received the grant of Rancho Bolsa de San Cayetano. The northerly limit of this tract was the Pajaro River; its westerly, Monterey Bay; its easterly, Rancho Vega del Río del Pájaro; and its southerly, an estuary separating it from the Carneros Rancho. Because it was the first land owned by the Vallejo family within the boundary of California, the original house built on it has been termed the "Casa Materna of the Vallejo's" ("mother house").

Another name by which the adobe was known is the "Glass House," because of the many glass windows that formerly enclosed its upper porch. Built on a hill overlooking the Pajaro Valley, supposedly about 1824, the old structure is still standing, although all its windows are gone and it is fast falling to ruin. It is plainly visible from the Salinas-Watsonville highway in an open field to the north of, and opposite to, the Watsonville Golf Club. The house was occupied up to 1870 or perhaps later, but now the main building is used for the storage of hay, and the rough two-story addition serves as a cow barn.

The structure is 44 feet long, and the outer walls are 20 inches thick. The joists, 4 by 6 inches, and the window frames are of hewn redwood still in good condition; a shingle roof, upheld by a 6- by 8-inch beam extending the whole length of the building, covers the structure. Two large rooms with floors of hard earth make up the first floor; the upper story is without partitions and forms one large room with a floor of hewn boards. All the original openings for doors and windows are boarded over, but a hole through the outer wall indicates the location of a fireplace.

Two versions of the placing of the windows have become traditions: one story is to the effect that the glass, which is said to have come from Spain, was intended for use in the house of General Vallejo at Sonoma but proved unsuitable for that purpose. The other story relates that the owner of this adobe ordered one dozen glass windows but found, when the shipment arrived, that twelve dozen had been consigned to him. He refused them at first, but finally accepted them and not only placed them in his window frames but glassed in the whole of his upper veranda as well. An extensive view is obtained from the spot.

The wife of Don Ignacio, whom he married in 1790, was María Antonia, daughter of Francisco Lugo. Their family consisted of five sons and eight daughters. Five of the daughters married men of more than ordinary position in the country: Mariano Soberanes, José Amesti, J. B. R. Cooper, J. P. Leese, and Juan Alvarado, all of whom received large grants of government land. Four of the five sons survived the father, who died at Monterey in 1831 at the age of eighty-three. The most distinguished of the sons was Mariano, a leading figure in the annals of California.

José de Jesús, probably the eldest son in the family, as his birth date is ten years before that of Mariano, lived on his father's rancho and became the owner of it by grant from José Figueroa, then political chief or governor of Alta Cali-

fornia. It was confirmed to him as executor of his father's estate, and he received final patent to it in 1865. That this son had been interested in the land for many years is proved by a petition which he signed on October 27, 1826, in which he asks for two *sitios* at San Cayetano. He states in this document that his father and Dolores Pico had earlier received a grant for the property and that his father had used it for a cattle range but that Don Dolores had not fulfilled the conditions essential to its possession and had therefore forfeited his right, which the petitioner now desired and had need of. He apparently lived upon this rancho only a few years after settling the estate, as he became the grantee of Rancho Arroyo de la Alameda in 1842. He spent the last years of his life at Misión San José, where he died in 1882 at the age of eighty-four years.

In 1847 another son, Juan Antonio, was still living on the rancho, for in the spring of that year Lieutenant Sherman, who claimed him as a friend, attempted to call upon him at the breakfast hour. At this time Lieutenant Sherman was accompanying Governor Mason to Monterey. Sherman states that by "nine o'clock we had reached the ranch. It was on a high point of the plateau, overlooking the plain of the Pajaro, on which were grazing numbers of horses and cattle. The house was of adobe, with a long range of adobe-huts occupied by semi-civilized Indians, who at that time did all the labor of a ranch, the herding and marking of cattle, the breaking of horses, and cultivating the little patches of wheat and vegetables which constituted all the farming of that day. Everything about the house looked deserted, and, seeing a small Indian boy leaning up against a post, I approached him and asked him in Spanish, 'Where is the master?' 'Góne to the Presidio' [Monterey]. 'Is anybody in the house?' 'No.' 'Is it locked up?' 'Yes.' 'Is no one about who can get in?' 'No.' 'Have you any meat?' 'No.' 'Any flour or grain?' 'No.' 'Any chickens?' 'No.' 'Any eggs?' 'No.' 'What do you live on?' '*Nada*' ['nothing'].'' As a result, the travelers went a short distance to a pond and made a slim breakfast from the contents of their knapsacks.

An adobe house of two stories, sometimes called the Hipilito Adobe and sometimes the Pope Adobe, originally constructed four miles from Watsonville on this rancho, was badly wrecked in the 1906 earthquake, but its material afterward was used in the construction of a small one-story cottage on Blackburn Street in the town of Watsonville, where it is now used as a Girl Scout House. When in use on the rancho, the structure housed a grist mill in its northwest corner with millstones on the second floor turned by ox power from the ground floor.

It is not definitely known how many adobes were built on this rancho in early days. Two Vallejo houses are indicated on the map of the 1859 survey: that of A. Vallejo, situated near the Watsonville Road; and that of José de Jesús Vallejo, situated a little south of the center of the property. Whether or not General Vallejo lived on the rancho after he became famous is not definitely known, although it is said that a black and white sign on the "Glass House" once bore the name "General Vallejo."

Rancho El Alisal and El Colegio de San José

Rancho El Alisal, consisting of one and one-third square leagues, was granted by Governor Figueroa to Feliciano and Mariano Soberanes on June 26, 1834. Through this tract runs Alisal Creek, on the bank of which W. E. P. Hartnell had established a school of higher learning a few months earlier.

Mr. Hartnell, an Englishman who had married Teresa de la Guerra in 1825, obtained a grant of land in this vicinity in 1834 for the purpose of building a summer home to be called El Patrocinto de San José. Seeing the need of education for the youth of the country, he decided to establish at his home a place where certain studies might be pursued and on December 10, 1833, sent out a prospectus inviting a limited number of students to attend. One young man who availed himself of this opportunity was Pablo de la Guerra, later a member of the Constitutional Convention and after that a state senator and chairman of the committee on counties and their boundaries.

The school, called El Colegio de San José, opened on January 1, 1834, with fifteen pupils enrolled, and continued for a few years. Two adobe buildings used in this undertaking are still standing: the smaller one (its roof is now gone) was the dormitory, dining-room, and kitchen and contained a fireplace, deep and broad, where the cooking may have been done; the larger, oblong structure served as the family residence and housed Mr. Hartnell's private library and the classrooms. Both were of two stories with roofs made of shingles split by Indians under the instruction of the Mission Fathers. Both, now vacant, stand in unkept grounds with no trace of the flower gardens, orchards, and vineyards that once beautified the site. Not far away has been built a modern frame bungalow, in which the present owners of the property live.

The genial Mr. Hartnell established picnic grounds a few hundred yards distant to which his invited guests from far and near came to partake of his hospitality. El Colegio was the scene of many gay social festivities given by its host for the entertainment of his many friends. The grounds were known as the Alisal Picnic Grounds and were a favorite gathering place. They were kept open by later owners until the privilege, too often abused, had to be withdrawn. The grounds and the two adobes are now a part of a private stock ranch five miles east of Salinas on the Natividad-Gonzales Road. The rancho, consisting of 2,971 acres, was patented to M. T. de la Hartnell on February 2, 1882, and afterward passed from the Hartnell heirs to the Spreckels Sugar Company, which has since disposed of the property.

Frémont, on March 3, 1846, camped on the rancho. He approached it over the Salinas Plain, where "the wild oats were three feet high and well headed." It was while here that he received the peremptory order from Castro to "return with your people out of the limits of this territory," an order which he refused to obey. He fortified himself in the Gabilan (Gavilan) Mountains and raised the American flag.

A part of Rancho El Alisal was purchased by the Bernal family, who owned Rancho Santa Teresa in Santa Clara County. Bruno Bernal, son of Don Joaquín, filed his claim for 5,941.26 acres of it in 1853. For this tract patent was issued to him in 1866. The house in which he lived, a long, low adobe from which the traditional Bernal hospitality was dispensed, is in ruins. The walls may be seen from the Natividad-Gonzales Road in a field lying to the east of that thoroughfare. It is not far from the Hartnell adobes, although the latter cannot be seen from the road.

The house of the original grantees, the Soberanes, is in the same vicinity but to the west of the road. Hidden by trees, fences, and farm buildings, it is approached by a pathway lined with fruit trees in a fenced garden. The path leads to a sheltered ell corner where grow fuchsias and citrus trees between the two-story part of the house and a one-story extension. Roofed by the original tiles, the place is still used as a family residence.

Rancho Sausal

Although a large part of the city of Salinas lies on Rancho Nacional, the northern part lies on the adjoining Rancho Sausal, which extends north and east of the city. Over this area the Natividad and Gabilan creeks find their way into some of the sloughs that abound in this part of Monterey County.

The American pioneer Jacob P. Leese, who was a landholder in several parts of the state, acquired this property. He filed claim for a confirmation of his right on February 5, 1853, and two amendatory petitions on July 12 and August 4, 1854. He founded his claim on two Mexican grants: the first, made August 2, 1834, by Governor José Figueroa; and the second, August 10, 1845, by Governor Pio Pico. He received a patent for 10,241.19 acres in September 1859.

Earlier mention of this rancho goes back to 1823; in which year a certain Soberanes was its occupant. In 1828 it was used, along with Alisal and Cañada de Natividad, by Manuel Butron and Nicolas Alviso as a range for their cattle.

Although the grant was made to José Tiburcio Castro in 1834, he seems to have resided there much earlier, for his house, still standing, is said to have been built in 1823. The old residence is in excellent condition, with leather thongs still binding the hand-hewn rafters. It is located two miles from the Salinas Rodeo Field.

Bolsa Nueva y Moro Cojo

According to *Spanish and Indian Place Names in California* by Sanchez, the name Moro Cojo literally means "lame Moor"; but, as the Spaniards used *moro* to mean anything black, tradition says that a lame black horse gave the name to this particular tract of land.

This rancho of eight square leagues was granted to Simeon Castro in three parts: the first, called Moro Cojo, was granted February 14, 1825, by Governor Luis Arguello; the second, Bolsa Nueva, May 14, 1836, by Governor Chico; and the third by Alvarado November 20, 1837. The last one, according to Bancroft, had been given first to John Milligan, an Irishman who taught weaving at San Juan Mission. The whole was revalidated to the heirs of Castro by Governor Micheltorena on September 26, 1844. Irregular in shape, it reached from the swamp near Monterey Bay to rolling, timbered hills. Its southeastern corner is Lagunita, a lake on which three other ranchos touched: Bolsa de las Escarpinas, La Natividad, and Los Vergeles.

The widow, Doña María Antonia Pico de Castro, and her nine children filed claim for this land in 1853. In December 1872 a survey was made, and a patent was thereafter issued to these claimants for 30,901.34 acres.

The northwestern corner of this grant is near the Elkhorn Slough and the railway station of Elkhorn. The town of Castroville, founded in 1864 by Juan Castro, son of the grantee, is situated within the bounds of this old grant.

Rancho Los Gatos, or Santa Rita

José Trinidad Espinosa had received a provisional grant to Rancho Los Gatos, or Santa Rita, many years before September 30, 1837, the date on which the land was formally made his by act of Governor Alvarado. Its location may be identified approximately by the town of Santa Rita, which is in the eastern part of the old rancho, and by Lake Espinosa, which lies on the northwest border.

The Espinosa adobe, of which nothing now remains, was erected on the brow of a hill between Lake Espinosa and the "Tembladera" (quaking bog). Don José married Jacinta Archuleta; and their daughter, Fermina, married Domingo Pérez, who is mentioned in records as having lived on Rancho Nacional in 1836 when he was twenty-seven years of age.

The date of the death of José Trinidad Espinosa lies between the year 1845, when he took part in the battle of Cahuenga, and January 29, 1853, when his daughter filed her petition with the Land Commission as claimant for the rancho. Doña Fermina's death occurred before the confirmation of her claim. The final papers of ownership to the 4,424.46 acres were made out to the surviving husband, Domingo Pérez and the children, Fermina, María Trinidad, Mateo Ascunción, Pedro, José Manuela, and Crysonogo. Patent was issued to these claimants on April 4, 1870.

Rancho La Natividad

Rancho La Natividad consisted of two square leagues of land south of a stretch of Gabilan Creek. The tract was granted to Manuel Butron and Nicolas Alviso by Governor Alvarado on November 16, 1837, and their ownership was confirmed by the United States in 1853.

A site on this land near the village of Natividad was leased in 1836 to "Ysaac Graham, Enrique Nale y Guillermo Dockey" for the erection of a plant for manufacturing *aguardiente*. The signing of this lease by Manuel Butron proves that he, at least, was considered owner of the tract before his formal receipt of the grant from the governor.

In 1853 the children of Butron and of Alviso filed claim for this rancho. A patent for 8,641.21 acres was issued to them by the United States in that same year.

The village of Natividad, six miles east of Salinas, became a flourishing station on the Coast Line Stage in the '50's. Since the discontinuance of the line and the routing of the main traffic between the northern and southern parts of California through Salinas, it has become nothing more than a deserted crossroads where a few vacant frame buildings are fast falling to ruin.

Rancho El Sur

In March 1852 Juan Bautista Roger Cooper, then harbor master at Monterey, filed claim to two ranchos in Monterey County: Bolsa del Potrero y Moro Cojo in the vicinity of Salinas, and Rancho El Sur on the seacoast south of the town of Monterey. To the former he received patent in 1859; and to the latter, in 1866.

Rancho El Sur had been granted to Juan B. Alvarado, Cooper's brother-in-law, July 30, 1834, by Governor José Figueroa and thereafter was approved by the Territorial *Diputación*. The grantee was the son of Sergeant José F. Alvarado and his wife, María Josefa Vallejo. He was born on February 14, 1809. His official life began in his twentieth year, when he became secretary of the *Diputación*—the first step toward the central position in California history which he eventually held. At the age of twenty-five he was elected a member of the *Diputación* and two years later became president of that body. In 1839 he married Martina, daughter of Francisco Castro. It is said of him that he never used his political position to enrich himself.

Before 1852 Juan Bautista Roger Cooper, the owner of other ranchos, became the owner of this one also. Cooper Point on the coast is the most southerly extension of this tract, and the mouth of the Little Sur River is the most northerly limit. The son, John Baptist Henry Cooper, later relieved his father of a great part of the burden of managing his property and eventually inherited it. The headquarters of this rancho were in a frame house (which is still standing), constructed of timbers brought around the Horn.

Rancho Milpitas

Rancho Milpitas, the grant extending for many miles along the San Antonio River, has its comparatively narrow northwest boundary within the Santa Barbara National Forest. In the fertile level areas along the river and along some of its tributaries were probably located those small plots, cultivated by the natives in a crude manner, that gave rise to the name Milpitas—"little gardens."

Mission Creek was the name given to one of these tributary streams after the establishment of the San Antonio Mission near its bank. From it a supply of water was obtained.

The southeast corner of the rancho is at Jolon (said to be an Indian word for "valley of dead oaks"), once an Indian settlement and later a settlement of white people served by early stagecoaches. Here now stands the larger part of the two-story adobe hotel then kept by Dutton, an American. The barroom at one end of the building has been torn down, leaving a large brick fireplace standing alone in the open air about twenty feet from the main building. An ancient grapevine spreads its leaves over the upper balcony that extends across the entire front. For the protection of the adobe walls, a coat of cement plaster marked out in squares to simulate stone covers the long front of the building next the road. The end from which the barroom has been torn is protected by building paper.

Ygnacio Pastor, a neophyte of the San Antonio Mission, received the grant of Rancho Milpitas from Governor Alvarado on May 5, 1838. He filed claim for it with the United States Land Commission in August 1852, and the patent for 43,280.90 acres was issued to him on February 18, 1875. A few acres, 33.19, in the immediate vicinity of the Mission, were patented to the Catholic Bishop J. S. Alemany in 1862 during the administration of President Abraham Lincoln.

For many years the lack of a definite understanding concerning the boundaries of this grant led to considerable squatter trouble. Faxon D. Atherton, whose home was on a subdivision of Rancho de las Pulgas (San Mateo County), became the owner, and evictions of undesired tenants became general. Many families of the dispossessed sought refuge temporarily at San Antonio Mission.

Atherton sent his son George to be manager of the rancho. George and his wife, the novelist Gertrude Atherton, their small son and a Chinese servant took up residence for a time in an adobe vacated by a squatter and whitewashed for their use: "an adobe mansion with three rooms, an attic, and a lean-to that served as kitchen." Mrs. Atherton's *Los Cerritos* drew its local color from the period spent on this rancho.

This rancho is now a part of the holdings of William Randolph Hearst, whose elaborate Milpitas ranch house on the hill overlooks the ruins of the San Antonio Mission.

Rancho Los Ojitos

Rancho Los Ojitos (the meaning of which in free translation is "ranch of little springs"), adjoining the southern tip of Rancho Las Milpitas, is a long narrow strip of land lying along the San Antonio River. A few hills and canyons are in its south central part, but in the main it is composed of bottom land. A part of the herds belonging to the San Antonio Mission were pastured there; and it is recorded that in 1823 an adobe house of two rooms was built and roofed with tiles, supposedly for the use of neophyte herders. This building still remains, as does another larger one, near the San Antonio River. The date of their construction is conjectured to be before 1825.

Both of these houses came into the hands of Mariano Soberanes on April 5, 1842, when, after the secularization of the Mission, the grant of Los Ojitos was given to him by Governor Alvarado.

Because the grantee had been active against the American invaders, the place was pillaged by Frémont's men on their way to Los Angeles in 1846. Don Mariano later put in a claim for $40,000 damages, of which he finally received by court decree a mere pittance. In 1871 patent for 8,900.17 acres was issued to him. Previous to that time (in the '60's), the Roth family became the owners of a part of the rancho, and that part is still held by descendants of that family.

The two old houses are today in excellent repair. Certain

changes have been made and certain parts have been replaced at various times; for instance, the upper verandas and outside stairways have been removed and the original tiles, which were taken away to restore other adobe structures elsewhere, have been replaced by the present corrugated iron roofs. Interesting features of the construction of these houses are the upper floors. They are fashioned of logs and poles laced together with rawhide. On top of this rude frame was placed a layer of cornstalks, which in turn was covered with mud and thoroughly tamped to make a hard, smooth surface. Such floors were used in the earliest construction of the Missions.

Rancho Pleyto

Early Spanish travelers through the San Antonio River Valley remarked upon the groups of natives frequently seen engaged in earnest conversation there. To all appearances, they were endeavoring to settle disagreements that had arisen among themselves, and this valley seemed to be a customary meeting place for that purpose. The Spanish word *pleito* means "lawsuit," and from it the name of Rancho Pleyto is supposed to have been derived.

The grant of this land was made on July 18, 1845, by Governor Pico to Antonio Chavez (Chavis), who two years previously had received Rancho Cienaga del Gabilán.

A claim founded on this grant was filed with the Land Commission in 1853 by W. S. Johnson and Preston K. Woodside. The two were both members of the regiment of New York Volunteers brought to California by Colonel Stevenson in 1847. Their claim, first rejected, was settled upon appeal in their favor, and 13,299.27 acres were confirmed to them in 1872.

Through the long narrow valley which comprises this rancho ran the trail between Misión San Antonio and Misión San Miguel; and when the days of the stagecoach arrived it was still the main line of travel between these two points. At the village of Pleyto lived J. T. Betts, who was for many years responsible for keeping the horses on the line properly shod. His duty was to go to the various points on the route and to shoe the horses resting there. His children grew up in the little town, and his sister kept the hotel there.

A part of this rancho was sold to a Mr. Pinkerton, whose children were all born in an adobe ranch house a little way from the village. A school in this region bears the name of Pinkerton. The old adobe is still standing, but the village of Pleyto has disappeared.

Ranchos along the Salinas River

Of the thirty-two private land grants in the Salinas Valley, twenty-six lie adjacent to the Salinas River for a greater or less distance. The fertile acres in this region early attracted the Spaniard, Mexican, and American as severally they journeyed over the level terrain in adventurous quest.

Near the mouth of the Salinas River is Rancho Rincon de las Salinas ("corner of the salt marshes"), extending from Twin Bridges to the ocean. This was granted by Governor Figueroa to Cristina Delgado on June 13 of 1833; and Rafael Estrada, having occupied it in 1853, received United States patent for it in 1881. The ranch house, situated on the hillside about half a mile southeast of the Neponset Railway Station, fell to ruin, but its foundations were visible until recently.

Across the river from the Rincon de las Salinas was the Bolsa del Potrero y Moro Cojo, or La Sagrada Familia, originally granted to José Joaquín de la Torre, who had arrived in Alta California in 1801. He thereafter had served long and well in the Monterey Company, much of the time as secretary to the governor. In a petition to Governor Pablo Vicente de Sola, dated June 20, 1822, Don José Joaquín stated that he had served his nation for twenty-one years as cadet and corporal and that, as his pay was inadequate for the proper support of his wife and seven children, the eldest of whom was then sixteen years of age, he desired "most humbly" a piece of land that he might call his own and that he might pass on to his descendants. He further stated that he owned horses and cattle and that, having been allowed to pasture them on the Bolsa del Potrero y Moro Cojo, he would be pleased to receive a grant of that particular piece of land in order that he might build houses and fences. Having been afflicted with a paralysis on his left side, he was fearful that his life might be cut short or that he might become entirely disabled. Furthermore it was his belief that the land in question belonged to the government and that no one else had claim upon it. Such apparently was the case, for within two days after the signing of the petition the grant was made to him by the governor.

The tract was almost surrounded by water, lying as it did between the Salinas River and the "Tembladera" (quaking bog), with branching sloughs meandering through it. In 1829 Don José Joaquín sold the entire property, consisting of nearly 7,000 acres, to Juan Bautista Roger Cooper, the older half-brother of Thomas O. Larkin. After Cooper had filed claim for it on March 30, 1852, a survey was made. Cooper's house stood about a mile up from the Cooper Switch.

Southeast of Don Joaquín de la Torre's Rancho La Sagrada Familia lay the Rinconada del Sanjon (*zanjon,* "deep ditch") of 2,229.70 acres. Its boundary line on the south and southwest was made up of the curves of the Salinas River and the adjacent sloughs. At the Cooper Switch, about one and one-half miles northwest of Salinas, the northbound trains leaving the town of Salinas enter this rancho and traverse it for three miles.

The grant of this property was given by Governor Alvarado to José Eusebio Boronda on February 1, 1840. After being confirmed by the United States government in 1854, the grant was surveyed in December 1858 and patented in July 1860. At the time of the survey five different houses were standing across the Salinas River from the southwest boundary of the grant.

Don José Eusebio was thirty years of age when he received this rancho; four years earlier he had been majordomo of Rancho Vergeles, that lay along the road from Monterey to San José. He married Josefa Buelna. Their home, built on a hill, was so situated that it could be seen for miles over the Salinas Plain. Horsemen traveling through the rank growth of wild mustard, by standing on their saddles, could see the red tiles of the Boronda adobe over the yellow blossoms, as Lieutenant W. T. Sherman did in 1846 after crossing the Salinas River on his way from Monterey. Cultivation of the land has now largely eliminated the wild mustard, and the little that remains is less luxuriant. The house no longer stands, but a second house erected by Don Eusebio in a more protected location may be seen less than three miles northwest of the city of Salinas. It is reached by traversing the Salinas-Castroville Road and turning due north opposite the Catholic Cemetery.

Rancho El Tucho, a part of which was patented to David Jacks in 1867, had been granted to José Joaquín Gomez in December 1843. It was in the heart of the Blanco country, where the Portolá expedition of 1769 had maintained a base camp during the first week of October, while scouts were endeavoring to find the Port of Monterey. Another part was granted in 1841 to Simeon Castro.

Antonio Aceves and Antonio Romero had held a four-league grant, called Las Salinas, before 1795. But, as was frequently the case with grants given at that period when the whole domain was unpeopled except by roving bands of Indians, its value was not appreciated, and the grantees made little effort to hold their lands.

On April 15, 1836, Governor Nicolas Gutiérrez gave one square league out of this area to Gabriel Espinosa. The most westerly point of his rancho reached almost to the Bay of Monterey southwest of the station of Bardin, and the rancho stretched in the opposite direction to the Salinas opposite Blanco. Lucinda E. Pogue and the heirs of Don Gabriel filed claim for this property on February 9, 1853, and the patent was issued in 1867. Lucinda E. Pogue received an undivided two-sevenths, and the children of Gabriel Espinosa—José María, María Jesús, Barbara Lucille, Juan José Jesús, and José Manuel—each received an undivided one-seventh.

To the south of Rancho Las Salinas lay a part of the City Lands of Monterey, the vast tract extending from the Bay of Monterey to the Salinas, with title dating back to 1830. Divided from these City Lands of Monterey by the Pilarcitos Canyon was Rancho El Chamisal, granted by Governor Castro to Felipe Vasquez on November 15, 1835. Nicanor Lugo, widow of Don Felipe, and his three children, Pedro, Dionisio, and Manuel, filed their claim on January 31, 1853, and received patent for 2,737.44 acres in 1877.

Lying parallel with El Chamisal and on the same side of the Salinas River was Rancho El Toro, lengthwise of which ran Toro Creek. Old Hilltown is near the northwestern corner of this tract. The rancho was granted to José Ramón Estrada on October 17, 1835, by Governor Castro. The grantee had attended school at Monterey for the five years ending in 1820. Don José Ramón married María Castro and was administrator at Santa Clara for two years after receiving this grant. In 1852 Charles Walters filed claim to the grant and in 1862 received patent for 5,668.41 acres.

Rancho Nacional lay northeast of, and across the river from, the narrow ends of the two last-mentioned grants. Its corner was at Old Hilltown, and it extended from the river into Salinas City, the county seat. Here were once pastured the herds of cattle, the bands of horses, and the flocks of sheep belonging to Carmel Mission and the Presidio of Monterey. It was one of the *ranchos del rey,* land belonging to the King of Spain to be used as directed by the government. The grazing here was particularly good because of the rich bottom land and the moisture from the many streams and sloughs. At the time of the threat of the Argentine pirate Bouchard, in 1818, not only the flocks and herds but the people themselves sought refuge in this interior haven.

On April 4, 1839, Governor Alvarado granted two square leagues of this domain called Rancho Nacional to Vicente Cantua. United States patent was obtained by the grantee on April 7, 1866, for 6,633.29 acres.

Up the river from Old Hilltown (near which there used to be a ford called Paso del Quinto) stretched two ranchos belonging to the Estrada family—Buena Vista and Llano de Buena Vista. The walls of the ranch house on Buena Vista still stand, guarded by two pear trees. Llano de Buena Vista was granted to José Mariano Estrada in 1823. Don José Mariano had come to Alta California in 1797 and was at once made *alferez* of the Monterey Company, a position which he held for twelve years. He was rewarded for his service in 1818 against Bouchard by being made brevet lieutenant and, in 1824, was made full lieutenant for his services in suppressing Indian uprisings. He retired from military services in 1829 and the following year was made executor of the Luis Argüello estate. His daughter Adelaide married David Spence, to whom this rancho, consisting of 8,446.23 acres, was patented in 1860. On this grant is the station of Spreckels.

Rancho Buena Vista was granted to José Santiago Estrada and his father José Mariano Estrada by Governor Pablo Vicente de Sola on May 28, 1822. It consisted of two square leagues. José Santiago and his brothers filed claim for this rancho in April 1852, and through the offices of their attorney, Mariano Malarin, received patent in 1869.

Southeast of Llano de Buena Vista was Rancho Encinal y Buena Esperanza, also bordering on the roving Salinas River. It was granted to the son-in-law of Don José Mariano Estrada, David Spence, by Governor Figueroa on November 29, 1834. At this date the governor stipulated that "within a year at latest he shall build a house thereon and it must be habitable." It was also provided that, when the property should be confirmed the corners should be marked not only by boundary stones but by planting some fruit trees, "either wild or tame, of some utility." Any violation of these and other conditions would cause him to forfeit his right to the land, which could then be given to another. Another square league was granted on April 15, 1839, by Juan B. Alvarado, governor ad interim. Both of these grants were approved in due time, and a patent for 13,351.64 acres was issued on May 23, 1862.

A conservative and much-respected man was David Spence from Scotland. After living in Peru for a few years he had come to California, where he spent the remainder of his life until his death in 1875. Debarking at Monterey in 1824 from the "Pizzaro," he superintended meat packing for Begg and Company for three years. At the end of that time he went into business for himself and was successful from the first. In 1828 he was baptized at Santa Cruz as David Estevan Spence and the following year married Señorita Adelaide Estrada. After nearly forty years of life together, they died within one month of each other. Since their son David, who had been educated in Honolulu, had died seven years previously, their large estate was left to the three grandsons and a granddaughter. The station of Spence on the Southern Pacific Railway is in the northwestern part of this rancho.

South of Don David's property were Ranchos Chualar and Zanjones, both of which finally came into the possession of Don Juan Malarin. On the western bank of the river along this stretch lies the land once contained in Rancho Guadalupe y Lanitos de los Correos, granted to Don Juan between 1831 and 1835. Total acreage contained in the three grants was 24,469.61.

Juan Malarin, the grantee, was a native of Peru. He came to California as master of the "Señoriana" in 1820 and came again in 1824 as master of the "Apolonia." In 1825 he was chosen by Governor Argüello to take the prizes, "Asia" and "Constante," to Acapulco; and for this service, which he performed for the government, he was made a lieutenant in the Mexican Navy. He thereafter made Monterey his home between his sea voyages and married Josefa Estrada before receiving any grants of land. The fine character of Don Juan and his unobtrusive manner made him an influential citizen and he became president of the Monterey Council. Dying at the age of sixty, he left a large family of children. His eldest son, Mariano, who had been sent to Peru to be educated, was made executor of the estate. The son succeeded in obtaining patents for all three of the ranchos, for Zanjones in 1866, Guadalupe in 1869, and Chualar in 1872.

The village of Chualar with its pepper trees stretches along State Highway 101 for a quarter of a mile near the western boundary of Rancho Chualar. The next rancho to the south was Zanjones.

The Malarin house stood on Rancho Guadalupe, the first grant made to Don Juan. In the settlement of property, Josefa Estrada, the widow, received one-half of the whole property. The remainder went to the ten children: Mariano, Ysabel,

Concepción, Ramona, Urbano, María, Refugio, Josefa, Cristino, and Ignacio.

Along the river southeast of the Malarin estate was Rancho Rincón de la Puente del Monte of four square leagues, granted by Governor Gutiérrez to Teodoro Gonzales on September 20, 1836. A patent for 15,218.62 acres was given to him in 1866. Don Teodoro, a Mexican otter hunter, became a man of good standing and wealth and at one time served as *alcalde* in Monterey. His widow and sons later resided in San Francisco. The town of Gonzales, named for this family, lies within the bounds of this irregularly shaped rancho.

Southwest and across the river from the Gonzales property was Rancho Paraje de Sanchez. El Camino Real ran through this grant between Misión Soledad and the Missions to the north. The 6,584.32 acres in this rancho were patented to C. Lugo and others in 1866.

The Salinas River curves in and out of the southwestern line of Rancho San Vicente. The town of Soledad is in the southern part of this nearly 20,000-acre grant made to Francisco Soto, Francisco Figueroa, and Estevan Munras [Munraz]. On April 1, 1852, when the seven children and heirs of Estevan Munras, deceased, filed their claim, it was stated that "possession had been had and enjoyed" under the grant.

Estevan Munras was an early Spanish trader at Monterey. His wife was Catalina Manzanelli of Tepic, Mexico, under whose name Ranchos Laguna Seca and San Francisquito were held. Don Estevan, unlike many of his compatriots, was prominent in aiding foreigners and quite ready for a change from Mexican political intrigues.

Across the river from Soledad and Rancho San Vicente lay the lands of Misión Soledad. In behalf of the church, Bishop J. S. Alemany was given patent in 1859 to 34.47 acres, containing orchards, vineyards, and springs. Feliciano Soberanes purchased 8,899.82 acres of the Mission lands in June 1846, and his title to them was confirmed. The purchase price was reputedly $800. It was reported at the time that the Mission was in ruins and that the traveling public who stopped there to rest were grossly overcharged.

Three adobes which were occupied by members of the Soberanes family and which were located along the old thoroughfare El Camino Real are still standing. Although the largest residence was almost destroyed by fire on January 5, 1935, three of the original eleven rooms are left standing and can be used. This remnant is hidden from view by a modern cottage that has been erected on the site of the burned building. Two large cypress trees still stand guard. Between this site and the ruins of the Mission farther down the road stands another Soberanes adobe, apparently unused.

On Rancho Los Coches ("the pigs"), southeast of the Mission beyond a turn of the road, was an adobe structure which is in good condition today, considering its use and age. It stands directly on the corner of the north-and-south highway between Soledad and King City at the junction of the road leading up Arroyo Seco. This one-and-one-half-story building, in front of which is a row of black locusts, faces the branch road and is not protected by a fence. A porch extends along the entire front directly on the roadside. This structure has had different uses: a family residence, a post office, a stage station, and now a house used by tenant farmers. Bancroft says the grant of Los Coches was made in 1841 to Josefa, daughter of Feliciano Soberanes.

Rancho Arroyo Seco, which adjoined Los Coches on the south, consisted of 16,523.35 acres. Its northwest corner is near Paraiso Springs School. For this property Joaquín de la Torre filed a claim founded on a grant of four square leagues made to himself by Governor Alvarado on December 30, 1840. Don Joaquín was a Mexican patriot of energy and courage, active against incoming foreigners. Greenfield

has grown up on the southeast boundary of this rancho. Southeast of Arroyo Seco was Rancho Poza de los Ositos, which was granted to Carlos Cayetano Espinosa by Governor Alvarado on April 16, 1839. This tract, consisting of 16,938.98 acres of rolling land lying on the west side of the Salinas River, was patented to the grantee on June 29, 1865.

Across the river from Arroyo Seco and Poza de los Ositos was Rancho San Lorenzo, stretching southerly along the river as far as San Lorenzo Creek. King City is located on the southern part. This grant of 21,884.38 acres, made by Governor Alvarado to Feliciano Soberanes in 1841, was in addition to Rancho Alisal already held by the grantee, who later purchased some of the land which formerly belonged to Misión Soledad.

South of King City lay Rancho San Bernabe. Through it flowed the Salinas River. From its banks the rancho lands extended back to the hills on both sides. Two old grants made by Governor Alvarado were consolidated in this one rancho. The first grant was made to José Molina on March 10, 1841, and the second to Petronelo Rios on April 6, 1842. Don Petronelo was a Mexican sergeant of artillery in San Francisco from 1827 to 1840. His wife was Caterina Avila.

From the westernmost point of this rancho, a trail led up Pine Canyon and through the forest down to Rancho Milpitas. Somewhere along that trail near the summit is an immense pile of jagged rocks and within them a cave frequently used by early travelers as a night shelter. On top of these rocks, unseen until the perilous ascent is made, is a flat piece of ground several acres in extent. This is said to be the hidden pasture where the bandit Vasquez concealed his stolen horses.

The King City–Jolon Road passes through this rancho. At the left, two miles after crossing the river bridge at King City, may be seen the thick adobe walls of an abandoned ranch house originally covered by a shingle roof. In this building lived David Leese, son of Jacob P., as manager of the ranch. During his residence there with his family, the place was struck by lightning and burned to such an extent that it has not been repaired.

San Bernabe, consisting of 13,296.38 acres, was confirmed in 1855 to Henry Cocks, a famous justice of the peace in the county, and was patented to him in 1873. Before the destruction of the adobe, the land had been purchased by J. B. R. Cooper. David Leese, to whom the management of the ranch had been given, was the nephew of Cooper's wife.

South of the San Bernabe lay Rancho San Benito, extending on both sides of the river. The station of San Lucas on the Southern Pacific Railway is situated in its southeastern corner. Here, one and one-half square leagues were granted to Francisco García by Governor Alvarado on March 11, 1842. The patent for 6,671.08 acres was given in 1869 in the name of James Watson, deceased claimant. Watson was an Englishman engaged in trading in Monterey who had married Mariana Escamilla and whose descendants still live in the county. The original grantee, Francisco García, built an adobe house of eight rooms with a tile roof on the bank of the Salinas River about two miles northwest from San Lucas. The river has so changed its course since that time that it no longer flows near the house, the ruins of which stand on an embankment in an open field about one mile west of Highway 101. One wall of the house was so constructed as to leave apertures through which prowling enemies could be shot. A twenty-year-old son of the family was ambushed by Indians and killed on his return journey from Monterey, where he had gone with an ox-team load of hides to be sold. The house was occupied by the patentee until the year before his death in 1865.

The southernmost rancho in the Salinas River region was

San Bernardo, composed of 13,345.65 acres of rich bottom lands which reached up the river to Sargent's Canyon. It was founded on a grant made by Governor Alvarado to Mariano and Juan Soberanes on June 16, 1841. At its northern line it adjoined Rancho San Lucas. San Ardo, a station on the Southern Pacific Railway, is about midway of the long narrow tract. The property was owned by M. Brandenstein at the time of the purchase of the rights of way for the road, and as a result of stipulations made by him every train that is flagged must stop at this small village.

Rancho San Lucas

The group of buildings which composes the headquarters of Rancho San Lucas lies about six miles south and west of the railway station of San Lucas. The grant of this land was made to Rafael Estrada in 1842, and the ranch house, still standing, was built near the northern line of the rancho west of the Salinas River.

James McKinley, a Scotch sailor who deserted his ship at Monterey in 1824, became patentee of 8,874.72 acres here on February 23, 1872. Alberto Trescony, who came to California from Italy in 1842, eventually became the owner of the land and moved there with his family. He added adjoining properties to his holdings until he possessed many thousand acres over which his herds of cattle ranged. The patent for the branding iron used in his "roundups" was issued by the last Mexican governor of Alta California. The iron is a treasured relic of those early years. Descendants of Señor Alberto who still own a large part of the estate now give their attention to sheep raising.

Approaching this rancho by the road from San Lucas station, the group of some five adobe structures comes into view after rounding a bend. The buildings lie in a pocket valley protected by hills and trees. The main dwelling house consists of one story only. It has thick walls and is nearly surrounded by porches. The barn is of two stories, both made of adobe bricks. At least one of the farm structures is roofed with handmade tiles.

Ranchos El Pescadero and Punta de Pinos

The land contained in these two grants occupies the greater part of the area of the Monterey Peninsula, and through both of them runs the scenic Seventeen-Mile Drive.

Rancho Punta de Pinos was the more northerly of the two. For this tract three men, Jacob P. Leese, Milton Little, and Santiago Gleason, as joint claimants, petitioned the Land Commission on September 2, 1852, their claim being founded upon a grant made by Governor Figueroa to José María Armenta on May 13, 1833. Later other names were substituted for these claimants: Henry de Graw, for Leese; Charles Brown, for James H. Gleason. Finally Milton Little's interest, in addition to that of Leese, was absorbed by de Graw. The courts approved the claim, and patent for 2,666.51 acres was issued on November 19, 1880. Point Pinos, southwesterly headland of Monterey Bay, early and present site of the Light Station, is the northernmost limit of the rancho.

The whole shore line of Rancho El Pescadero, extending from near Seal Rocks to Carmel-by-the-Sea, is threaded by the Seventeen-Mile Drive, of which Cypress Point is the most westerly limit and the most famous spot on the route. At this point on the rugged shore line are found the picturesque Monterey cypress trees, whose branches have been grotesquely bent and gnarled through long exposure to ocean winds. Few species of cypress—trees of ancient origin—are found in the state, and *Cupressus macrocarpa Hartweg* (commonly known as the Monterey cypress) has a restricted habitat and is found only on the coast adjacent to the mouth of the Carmel River.

Because of early fishing activities carried on at the water's edge on the southern part of Monterey Peninsula, the name Pescadero ("place where fishing is done") was given to the rocks off the shore in Carmel Bay, to a point to the west of them, and to the rancho itself.

The grant, containing one league, was made by Nicolas Gutiérrez to Fabian Barreto February 29, 1836. Other names associated with its ownership were: John Frederick Romie, who came to California in 1841 and bought the rancho before he died in 1848; John C. Gore, who filed a claim for it on February 9, 1853, which was rejected by the court; and David Jacks, whose name was substituted for that of Gore and to whom a patent for 4,426.46 acres was given in 1868. The grantee, Fabian Barreto, a Mexican who came to Monterey in 1827, became a permanent resident of the place and married Carmen García, who outlived him. As an aftermath of the Bear Flag depredations the widow filed a claim for $2,582.

That Gore actually lived on the land is proved by the map made by the survey of 1864, which shows the location of his house somewhere in the vicinity of the modern Pebble Beach. A cistern, which is remembered to have been filled about 1926, was in an open space among the trees in the vicinity and was supposedly an adjunct to the Gore home.

Both of these ranchos, Punta de Pinos and El Pescadero, became a part of the large holdings of David Jacks, who owned, as well, Rancho Aguajito adjoining El Pescadero on the east. Mr. Jacks developed in the '70's a tent city in the cove on the bay shore northwest of the city of Monterey. He patterned it after one on the Atlantic Coast and named it Pacific Grove. Instead of remaining a tent city, it has grown to be a city of broad paved streets lined with business houses and good homes.

Standing two miles southeast from the Custom House on Rancho Aguajito in the suburbs of Monterey is the old Castro adobe, now restored by the Jacks family.

Ranchos along the Río Carmelo

The novelist Mary Austin has used this region as the setting for *Ysidro,* an idyl of Mission days in the quiet Carmel Valley. The land grants in this vicinity which were finally recognized and patented by the United States were six in number.

Los Tularcitos, the great triangular tract of 26,581.34 acres covering the Buckeye Ridge and Burnt Mountain, has a short stretch of the upper part of the Carmel River. As it flows through the southwestern corner of the rancho, the river receives the drainage from Los Tularcitos Creek. This rancho was granted by Governor Figueroa to Rafael Gomez on December 1, 1834; and in April 1852 his widow, Josefa Antonia Gomez de Walters, and his children filed claim for the property and received a patent in 1866.

Rancho Los Tularcitos has been kept intact to a large extent, and the present owners hold about 20,000 acres. The frame ranch house is near Tularcitos Creek, some two or three miles above its confluence with Carmel River.

There were two ranchos Los Laurelles along the river: the larger one, through which the river flows, joined Los Tularcitos on the west; the smaller rancho lay to the west of the Boronda grant. The former, granted to José Manuel Boronda and Vicente Blas Martínez by Manuel Jimeno on September 19, 1839, contained one and one-half square leagues, which were patented to Don José Manuel and his son, Juan de Mata, on August 9, 1866. The original adobe home, with later additions, is still standing between the road and the river to the east of Los Laurelles Grade Junction. The old part of it is of unusual architectural interest. It is

64 feet long and 19 feet wide. The thick-walled rooms are well preserved; roughly squared beams of the simple ceilings are carefully fitted. The ceiling of one room shows an interesting example of veneering done in soft wood.

The smaller Laurelles rancho lay wholly north of the river. It was given by Governor Micheltorena to José Agricio on March 4, 1844, and its 718.23 acres were patented to Leander Ransom on April 18, 1871.

Also on the north side of the river, beyond the oblong tract granted to James Meadows, an Englishman who married a native Indian woman, was Rancho Cañada de la Segunda, which reached westerly to Carmel-by-the-Sea. It originally consisted of one league given by the prefect Castro to Lazaro Soto in 1839. The eastern end lies in the Cañada de la Segunda. Patent for this was issued to Fletcher M. Haight in 1859, after the death of Andrew Randall, who had filed a claim for it on February 5, 1853.

On the south bank of the river was Rancho Potrero de San Carlos, granted by Governor Alvarado to Fructuoso del Real on December 12, 1839. In 1852 claim to this was filed with the Land Commission by Joaquín Gutiérrez and María Estefana, daughter of the original grantee, to whom patent for 4,306.98 acres was issued on June 9, 1862. This property was purchased by Bradley V. Sargent in 1858. Back from the river this land becomes hilly. Potrero Canyon, stretching down from the mountains, opens out upon a place that was once an Indian ranchería composed of a cluster of small and very plain adobe structures, one of which still stands. One of the native inhabitants of that settlement, its last member in the region, now owns a small piece of land across the river in the Meadows' tract.

The adobe house in which the owners of the rancho lived, formerly standing a half-mile farther up the canyon, has fallen to decay. It was a symmetrical, five-room dwelling with the usual wooden kitchen addition in which Indian servants prepared food for the household.

Bradley Sargent purchased other lands adjoining Rancho Potrero San Carlos. One of his purchases was Rancho San José y Sur Chiquito, located on the western boundary of Rancho Potrero San Carlos and stretching from the lower reaches of the Carmel River along the coast southward. This rancho had been granted on April 16, 1839, to Marcelino Escobar, and for it José Castro filed claim on February 2, 1853. After lengthy legal vicissitudes this tract was finally patented May 4, 1888, to J. S. Emery and N. W. Spaulding as administrators for the will of Abner Bassett and his widow, successors in interest to the deceased José Castro. In the northern part of this rancho near the river stood the "Las Virgenes" adobe, so called because tradition says that local Indians saw there, from time to time, apparitions of the Virgin.

Bradley V. Sargent purchased also Rancho San Francisquito, lying to the southeast of Rancho Potrero de San Carlos. Rancho San Francisquito, two square leagues, had been granted by Governor Castro to Doña Catalina Manzanelli, wife of Estevan Munras, on November 7, 1835. For this land, a joint petition had been filed by José Abrego, for himself; and by Milton Little, for the minor heirs of William R. Garner. To these claimants patent was given in 1862 for 8,813.50 acres.

The San Francisquito ranch house is mentioned in the writings of Robert Louis Stevenson as the place where he, an invalid, was visited by Captain Wright. A frame house now stands upon the site of the adobe formerly there, and an old stone threshing floor may still be seen on the property.

Ranchos on the Eastern Boundary of the County

Following the boundary line between Monterey and San Benito counties from north to south, one locates Ranchos Vega del Río del Pájaro, Cañada de la Carpinteria, Los Carneros, Los Vergeles, and Cienaga del Gabilán.

Vega del Río del Pájaro ("a meadow along the Pajaro River") covered the level plain along the river and stretched to the south into the hills, none of which reach an altitude much higher than 500 feet. It was granted to Antonio María Castro on April 17, 1820, by Don Vicente de Sola under the Spanish régime and was recognized and confirmed by Don José Figueroa, political chief under the Mexican rule, on June 14, 1833. The grantee was probably the first permanent settler in the now productive Pajaro Valley. He had been a soldier but retired from his military life in 1809, and about the time of receiving this land from the Spanish authorities was one of the alternates for the five electors of the province.

Thirty years after the Spanish grant, Juan Miguel Anzar filed a petition on June 28, 1852, as claimant for this rancho but died before his title was clear. His widow married Frederick A. McDougal. She too died, leaving as heirs her husband and her four children, to whom the 4,310.29 acres of the rancho were patented on January 18, 1864. Not far from the river, the highway and railway now run a parallel course across the rancho, the name of which is perpetuated in the Vega School.

Adjoining the southwestern corner of Rancho Vega del Río del Pájaro lay Rancho Cañada de la Carpinteria, a tract of hilly and mountainous land granted by Governor José Castro to Joaquín Soto, September 25, 1835. The patent for 2,236.13 acres was given to the heirs of the grantee in 1873. A small town near the center of this area is Dunbarton.

The next rancho to the south, Los Carneros, extended a little way across the present county line. This, like Vega del Río del Pájaro, was finally patented to Frederick A. McDougal and his stepchildren after the death of his wife, who was the claimant.

To the southeast of Los Carneros was Rancho Los Vergeles with its eastern boundary across the county line. This rancho was founded upon two grants to José J. Gomez, one made on August 2, 1834, by Governor Figueroa; the other on August 28 of the following year, by Governor Castro. The original name of the two combined was "Cañada en Medio y la Cañada de Ceboda." José Joaquín Gómez was a Mexican trader, who after coming to California in 1830 on the "Leonor" became a customs officer in Monterey and thereafter held many different positions of trust. His adobe, located on the direct route between Monterey and San José, was a favorite stopping place for travelers on that route. It stood about six miles from Salinas at the bottom of the San Juan Grade.

Consul Thomas O. Larkin, on his way from Monterey to Yerba Buena, whither he had sent his family for safety during the troublous months of the Bear Flag Rebellion, stopped at Los Vergeles for the night of November 15, 1846. When his whereabouts became known to the Californians encamped in the Salinas Valley, one of their number, José Antonio Chavez, determined to capture him. About midnight the consul was awakened from his sleep and compelled to accompany his captor to Castro's camp, where he was treated kindly but detained as a hostage.

Another visitor at Don Joaquín's home was William T. Sherman, who relates the circumstances in his memoirs. In the course of duty Sherman was in Monterey for a short time in the winter of 1847. Wishing to see something of the country back from the coast, he set out on February 1 with one companion. "In the morning we crossed the Salinas Plain, about fifteen miles of level ground, taking a shot occasionally at wild-geese, which abounded there, and entering the well-wooded valley that comes out from the floor of the Gavilano. We had cruised about all day, and it was almost dark when we reached the house of a Señor Gomez, father of those who at Monterey [the evening before at an entertainment] had performed the parts of Adam and Eve. His house was a two-story adobe, and had a fence in front. It was situated well up among the foothills of the Gavillano, and could not be seen until within a few yards. We hitched our horses to the fence and went in just as Gomez was about to sit down to a tempting supper of stewed hare and tortillas. We were officers and *caballeros* and could not be ignored. After turning our horses to grass, at his invitation we joined him at supper. The allowance, though ample for one, was rather short for three, and I thought the Spanish grandiloquent politeness of Gomez, who was fat and old, was not over-cordial. However, down we sat, and I was helped to a dish of rabbit, with what I thought to be an abundant sauce of tomato. Taking a good mouthful, I felt as though I had taken liquid fire; the tomato was *chili colorado,* or red pepper, of the purest kind. It nearly killed me, and I saw Gomez's eyes twinkle for he saw that his share of supper was increased. I contented myself with bits of meat, and an abundant supply of tortillas. Ord was better case-hardened and, stood it better. We staid at Gomez's that night, sleeping, as all did, on the ground, and the next morning we crossed the hill by the bridle-path to the old Mission of San Juan Bautista."

South of Los Vergeles and lying between Gabilan Creek and Gabilan Peak, which rises to an elevation of 3,169 feet on the eastern line of the grant, was the Cienaga del Gabilán (Cienaga meaning "swamp or morass" and Gabilán meaning "hawk"), with its southern end extending into the Salinas Valley. This rancho was granted on October 26, 1843, by Governor Micheltorena to Antonio Chavez, who three years after this date captured Thomas O. Larkin at the neighboring Rancho Los Vergeles as above related.

José Antonio Chavez had been brought to California from Mexico by Figueroa. In 1843, the year of receiving the grant, he was tax collector at Monterey and in 1846 a lieutenant under Castro. He was wounded in the battle of Natividad but, befriended by prominent Californians, he escaped being taken by the enemy by remaining in hiding. In 1848 he left the state and was afterward with Castro in Lower California. José Y. Limantour filed claim for this rancho in 1853, but Thomas O. Larkin received confirmation of it and afterward turned it over to Jesse D. Carr, who received patent to 48,780.72 acres in the '60's.

Farther to the southeast, not extending to the county line but embracing the upper end of Peach Tree Valley, was Rancho San Lorenzo patented to the heirs of Andrew Randall in 1870. The original five-league grant had been made to Francisco Rico in 1842.

Miscellaneous Ranchos

One square league of land called Rancho Noche Buena, lying near the bay northeast of the town of Monterey, was granted to Juan Antonio Munoz on November 15, 1835, by Governor Castro. At that date, the grantee was thirty-five years of age, a captain in the Mexican artillery with a wife, Manuela Cruz, and three children. The year following, he was exiled with Gutiérrez. In March 1853 José Monomany and Jaime de Rinz Monomany filed a claim for the property; and in 1854 five-sixths of it was confirmed to them. The other sixth was held for José Munoz, infant heir of the original grantee. Both the railway and the highway which leads into Monterey from the north traverse the entire length of this rancho. Gigling is a point on the railway near its northern line.

Governor José Figueroa granted the one square league of Rancho Saucito to Graciano Manjares on May 22, 1833; and

for it John Wilson, Josiah H. Swain, and George C. Harris filed claim on February 23, 1853. This land was surveyed in October 1858 and found to contain 2,211.65 acres, which were patented to the men mentioned on October 7, 1862.

Little is known of Don Graciano, the original grantee, except that he married Maximiana Gongora and that, in 1836, their family consisted of five children. In 1842 he was *jeuz auxiliar.* The Saucito ranch house stands, in the Canyon del Rey east of Monterey, on the northern part of the rancho close to the remains of a pear orchard said to have been planted in the '80's. The Monterey–San Juan Road runs through the property from west to east.

East of Rancho Saucito lay Rancho Laguna Seca, granted to Doña Catalina Manzanelli in 1833 and 1834. Doña Catalina was the wife of Estevan Munras, grantee of San Vicente. She received patent for Rancho Laguno Seca, 2,179.50 acres, on November 24, 1865. The Laguna Seca ("dry lake") lies in the northeastern corner and the Canyon del Rey runs through the middle of the grant.

Two ranchos given out by Governor Alvarado lay along the Nacimiento River: the San Miguelito, to José Rafael Gonzales on July 21, 1841; and El Piojo, to Joaquín Soto on August 20, 1842. After José Rafael Gonzales filed his claim to San Miguelito the court found that he had divested himself of all rights by a deed to his son Mauricio Gonzales; and, therefore, a patent for the 22,135.91 acres in question was issued to the latter in 1867. Stony Creek, rising in the Santa Barbara National Forest, threads the mountainous northern part of this rancho and empties into the Nacimiento River, which lies along the southwestern line. The patentee had also another tract of land, Rancho Cholame, in the southern edge of the county, about one-half of the grant lying across the boundary in San Luis Obispo County. It had been given to him in 1844 by Governor Micheltorena; and in 1852 Ellen, widow of Charles White, filed claim upon it. The ranch house was on the Monterey County end of the grant south of Gold Hill.

Rancho El Piojo, lying adjacent to both San Miguelito and Los Ojitos, has a stretch of the Nacimiento River in its southwestern corner. The San Carpojo Trail enters the rancho from the west, crosses the river, and continues its almost due east course the entire length of the rancho. El Piojo ("louse") Creek, a tributary of the Nacimiento, makes its way from the middle of the rancho to its southeastern corner.

Salvador Espinosa filed petition for Rancho Bolsa de las Escarpinas on September 22, 1852, basing his claim on a grant received by himself on October 7, 1837. This tract lay north of Rancho Los Gatos, or Santa Rita, which was granted the same year to José Trinidad Espinosa. The line dividing the two runs through Espinosa Lake.

There were two ranchos Los Carneros in Monterey County: one was in a hilly part near the eastern boundary, the other just east of the Elkhorn Slough. The latter consisted of 4,482.33 acres granted to David Littlejohn in 1834 and patented to his heirs in 1866.

Rancho Corral de Tierra lay south of Rancho El Torro and adjoined the northern boundary of Los Laurelles. It was patented in 1876 to Henry McCobb, whose claim was founded on a grant made by Nicolas Gutiérrez to Francisco Figueroa for his daughter Guadalupe.

Three grants named San Lorenzo were given in the county, one on the Salinas River, one on the San Benito County boundary line, and one in the upper part of the San Lorenzo Canyon. The last-named, 22,264.47 acres, covered Peach Tree Valley and extended from both sides of it into rough broken hills. It was granted to Francisco Rico on November 16, 1842, and was patented to the heirs of Andrew Randall on June 4, 1870.

The Battle of Natividad

The battle of Natividad took place on November 16, 1846, about twenty miles northeast of Monterey and five miles from the present town of Salinas. The village of Natividad now marks the site, at the foot of the old San Juan Grade, over which the stagecoach traveled from Monterey to Misión San Juan Bautista in the '50's.

There was nothing decisive about the battle of Natividad, its chief significance being that it was the only severe engagement which took place in the north during the revolt of the Californians against the military occupation of the Americans under Commodore Stockton. It was different from the southern engagements, in that no regular United States troops took part in it, the participants being an American recruiting and foraging party under Captain Burroughs and a small band of Californian patriots.

Burroughs, with seventy-five men, was on his way to Monterey to join Frémont, who was preparing to go to Los Angeles to reinforce Stockton. On hearing of this, a group of native Californians under Manuel Castro determined to hamper Frémont. Making a night march from Monterey toward San Juan, Castro and his men met Burroughs at Natividad. In the skirmish which followed, four Americans were killed and as many wounded, while the Californians sustained a somewhat greater loss.

Colton Hall

Colton Hall was erected by Rev. Walter Colton, chaplain of the United States frigate "Congress" and named alcalde of Monterey by Commodore Stockton. On August 15, 1846, in company with Robert Semple, he established the *Californian,* the first newspaper to be published in California. His journal, *Three Years in California,* published in New York in 1850, is one of the most fascinating books on the early American period in California and is a mine of information for the historian.

Colton Hall "was for many years the most useful building in the city, having been used as a constitutional hall, a schoolhouse, a courthouse, a public assembly hall and a place of religious worship." California's first Constitutional Convention met at the Hall, September 1 to October 13, 1849. The forty-eight delegates held their sessions on the upper floor, which ran the length of the main building. Robert Semple was chairman and William G. Marcy, secretary. While Monterey was county seat of Monterey County, from 1850 to 1878, Colton Hall was used as the county courthouse. One of the first schools in California was held in this building, in 1849, by Rev. Samuel H. Willey, later prominent in the founding of the College of California and its successor, the University of California.

Unlike most of Monterey's early buildings, Colton Hall was distinctly of the old New England academy style. Rev. Mr. Willey, who was one of the chaplains of the Constitutional Convention, says in his reminiscences that when he landed from the steamship "California,"·on February 3, 1849, he was struck by the contrast between the architecture of this plain white building and the many Spanish adobe cottages and mansions by which it was surrounded. "It might have dropped down from a New England village," was his comment.

The building itself is a two-story structure of stone and remains today in excellent condition. The state of California made provisions in 1903 for its preservation, protection, and improvement, and it is now owned by the city of Monterey. It was permanently marked by a bronze tablet placed by the Native Sons of the Golden West on June 3, 1931.

California's First Convent School

The first convent school in California was established at Monterey in the spring of 1851 by three Dominican Sisters who had arrived in California in 1850. The old adobe building in which the school was held proved to be in very bad condition, and, as population in Monterey was diminishing while that around San Francisco Bay was rapidly increasing, the Sisters, in 1854, decided to move to Benicia, then a more central location.

Concepción Argüello, the story of whose life is closely associated with San Francisco and Benicia, was the first novitiate to enter the Convent of St. Catherine at Monterey, and when the school was moved to its new location she became its Mother Superior, continuing in that capacity until her death.

After the removal of the convent to Benicia, the old building at Monterey was used as a chapel and parish house for a time. Later, it was rented to private parties and rapidly fell into decay. Soon after 1885 it was torn down. The site where it stood is on the northwest corner of Main and Franklin streets and is now occupied by the San Carlos Hotel.

The Moss Landing Whaling Station

One of the most important whaling stations on the coast of California in early days was at Moss Landing, about fifteen miles northeast of Monterey. The whale fishery, one of the chief industries on the coast for a period of nearly thirty-five years, was finally abandoned in 1888. The old Moss Landing station remains as one of the few landmarks of this adventurous calling of the sea and may be seen from the coast highway. This landing was named for Charles Moss, who had a farm near the Five-Mile House on the Santa Cruz–Watsonville Road. He and a partner, Beadle, after starting a line of schooners at the landing in 1865, constructed a wharf to facilitate the loading of freight. Within a year, Moss moved his family from the ranch to a house near the landing and later removed to Texas.

The Adobes of Old Monterey

At the western entrance to Old Monterey stands one of the earliest of its historic dwellings, the Munraz House, one of the first homes to be built outside the original Presidio grounds. It was erected by Esteban Munraz, who came to California as a merchant. Considerably remodeled but still occupied by descendants of the original owner, the Munraz adobe stands at 656 Munraz Street, opposite what was once the southwest corner of the old Presidio grounds.

Alvarado Street is the *calle principal* of Monterey, where the old and the new mingle and into which run other streets replete with memories of Spanish California. From the water front it leads up the hill to a group of dwellings rich in historic interest, centering about the Larkin House.

The Larkin House, located on the corner of Main and Jefferson streets, is typical of the Spanish-Californian type of architecture which prevailed throughout Alta California: softly tinted adobe walls, cool veranda and picturesque upper balcony, iron-barred windows, and walled gardens bowered in roses and fig trees. It was built by Thomas O. Larkin, who had come to Monterey as a merchant in 1832 and was appointed American consul in 1843. Being thoroughly acquainted with conditions in the province, he rendered important services as consul and confidential agent; and his sane, intelligent policies helped to prepare the way for a peaceful annexation of California. The old house is now in the possession of the Larkin family, who have preserved it with great care and in keeping with its original appearance.

The House of the Four Winds, also built by Thomas O.

Larkin in 1834, still stands on Main Street. It was used as a residence for many years, but in 1846 the first Hall of Records in the state of California was housed there, and the first recorder in Monterey had his home as well as his office in the building. Now the Monterey Civic Club use it. Its picturesque name was derived from the fact that it boasted a weathervane, the first in Monterey.

Between the Larkin House and the House of the Four Winds is a small one-room adobe built by Larkin in 1834 and known as Sherman's Headquarters. It is an integral part of the architecture of the old Larkin garden, with its redwoods and palms and fig trees, and may be reached through the walled patio of the big house. Here, in 1847, Lieutenant Sherman of Civil War fame had his civil and military headquarters.

The Cooper House, located at 508 Munraz Street, formerly California Street, is one of the largest extant adobes in northern California. It was built in 1826 by Captain J. B. R. Cooper, who was a native of Alderney Island, England, and a pioneer in California in 1823. His mother, by a second marriage, became the mother of Thomas O. Larkin, whom Cooper had influenced to come to California and to establish himself at Monterey as a merchant. Cooper himself married Encarnación Vallejo, a sister of Mariano G. Vallejo. In 1864 he moved to San Francisco, taking up his residence at 821 Bush Street. The Cooper adobe is now more generally known as the Molera House.

A quaint adobe gift shop facing on Polk Street, with a delightful garden opening at the side on Hartnell Street, was originally the "First Federal Court Building in California," according to the inscription on the house. The Cooper House and barn are near neighbors on the northeast at Munraz Street, while across the way on the north side of Polk is the Amesti House, a two-story, balconied adobe built before 1835 by José Amesti. Don José was a Catalonian, who had come to California in 1822 and who, in 1824 had married Mariano G. Vallejo's sister, Prudenciana.

On the northwest corner of Webster and Abrego streets is the one-story Abrego Adobe, built by José Abrego, a Mexican, before 1835. Bayard Taylor, in his *El Dorado,* describes an evening party which he attended in this house in 1849 and also comments that José Abrego was the most industrious Californian he had seen in the country, having amassed a large and substantial fortune within a few years.

The Pacheco House, later known as the Malarin House, is a picturesque two-story adobe located on the southwest corner of Abrego and Webster streets opposite the Abrego House. It was used for a time as a hospital but is now a family residence. It was built in 1840 by Francisco Perez Pacheco, a wealthy landowner who came from Mexico in 1819.

On the corner of Pearl and Tyler streets is a little stone and adobe house neatly whitewashed and bearing a craftsman's placard, "Shuttle de Oro." On the Pearl Street entrance is the smithy, now the workshop of mastercraftsmen, where handwrought ironwork is executed in the ancient manner over a glowing forge. This was once the home of General José Castro and originally faced the old Plaza of Monterey, the scene of many a bullfight in Mexican days. The house itself later became a saloon and gambling resort.

Just around the corner on Houston Street between Pearl and Webster is the Robert Louis Stevenson House, where the beloved Scotch poet and author of *Treasure Island* lived for nearly four months in the spring of 1879. His attachment for Mrs. Fannie Van de Grift Osbourne, whom he had met in France, brought Stevenson to California. This proved to be one of the most decisive and vital steps he had ever taken, for both his character and the entire trend of his life were influenced by this sojourn in the West. In Monterey some of

his greatest friendships were matured; among them were those of Fannie Osbourne, who became his wife; her sister, Nellie Sanchez, his amanuensis; and Jules Simoneau, his lifelong friend.

Stevenson occupied two airy rooms in the ell of Simoneau's house, with five sunny windows opening on the balcony to the west. Two San Francisco clubwomen recently purchased the place for the purpose of preserving it. The building is in good condition, the lower floor being used as an antique shop and the upper story as a lodging for artists.

Directly back of Colton Hall is one of Monterey's most picturesque adobes, set in an old-fashioned garden amid a bower of trees. Now a private home, it was once the reputed abode of Tiburcio Vasquez, California's most ruthless bandit, who terrorized the old stage roads up and down the state in the '70's and the '80's. The Vasquez Adobe is situated on a cozy little alleyway with other pretty adobe cottages to keep it company.

On the northwest corner of Alvarado and Pearl streets is a two-story adobe now used for stores. Here, it is said, lived Juan Bautista Alvarado, provisional governor of California under Mexican rule from 1836 to 1842 and known to his contemporaries as the "silver-tongued" orator because of his brilliant eloquence and great personal magnetism. This Alvarado House is only one of several in various parts of the state in which Don Juan is said to have lived.

On Monterey's quaint and picturesque water front is the old Whaling Station with its vivid memories of high adventure on many seas. It was built in 1855 by the Monterey Whaling Company soon after its organization. Today it is a private home. The sidewalk in front of the house, which faces Decatur Street, is still paved with whalebones, placed there by gallant sea captains many years ago. A stone wall, crowned with red tile, encloses an old-fashioned flower garden at the rear, while a balcony in front looks out from the second story over the encircling harbor with its multitude of gay yachts and fishing boats.

One door to the west, at 351 Decatur Street, stands the first brick house in California. It was built for Duncan Dickenson, son of a Virginia planter and a survivor of the Donner party. The main part of the house was erected in 1848, but the wings were never completed, as the gold rush took the owner away to the mines. It is now a Spanish restaurant.

California's first American theater, a long rectangular adobe built by a Jack Swan in 1843, was originally a sailors' boardinghouse and was first used for amateur dramatics by members of Colonel J. D. Stevenson's regiment of New York Volunteers. That part of the original structure which was used for the theater is now a local museum, and the part once occupied by a saloon houses a quaint tea and gift shop. The building, which was restored in 1917, now belongs to the state and stands at the corner of Pacific and Scott streets about one block northwest of the Pacific Building. However, the first theater in California was not American but Spanish, and was erected in the early '40's. At present, the building serves as a store at 517 Polk Street.

The Pacific House, at the junction of Alvarado, Main, and Scott streets, was originally a hotel built in 1847 by James McKinley, a Scotchman who had come to California in 1822. For many years, the Presbyterian Church held its services in this building; the second story is now used by the Salvation Army, while the lower floor is occupied by the Army and Navy Y.M.C.A. At the rear, a beautiful patio, bright with flowers and trees and musical with the murmur of a fountain, breathes the spirit of old Spain.

The House of the Sherman Rose was the setting for a legendary romance linking the names of General W. T.

Sherman and the pretty Señorita Bonifacio, or Dona Nachita, as she was sometimes called. The gallant young American, then a lieutenant, called several times at the rose-bowered casa where the señorita lived. On one of these visits, so the story goes, he unpinned a rose from his uniform and planted it in her garden, saying that if it took root and grew their love would endure. The flower did grow into a marvelous rose tree which almost covered the little adobe cottage and which was, for years, the admiration of hundreds of tourists. But because Sherman never returned and Señorita Bonifacio never married, the legendary threads of romance were gradually woven about the old house. A modern bank building now stands in its place on Alvarado Street between Pearl and Frémont. The adobe bricks from the little cottage were removed to the Mesa district and incorporated into the home of the artist Percy Gray, and a part of the original rose tree was transplanted to the Municipal Rose Garden.

The House of the Sherman Rose, however, has a more real association with the name of Robert Louis Stevenson, for it was here that his fiancée, Mrs. Fannie Van de Grift Osbourne, and her sister, Nellie Sanchez, lived with Señorita Bonifacio. Stevenson was a frequent visitor at the place and there he began *The Amateur Emigrant,* gathered notes for *The Old Pacific Capital,* and wrote *The Pavilion on the Links,* as well as the unfinished work, "A Vendetta of the West."

In addition to the adobe structures mentioned above, the following are still standing: On Van Buren Street at No. 456 is located Simoneau's House; and two blocks down the street toward the Presidio is the Doud House at No. 177. Pierce Street has the Gordon House at No. 526, the Casa de la Torre at 502, and the Casa de Soto at 460. On Pacific Street one finds the Casa Soberanes at No. 336, the Merritt House at 386, and the Casa Serrano at 412. And 200 Olivier Street (a short street one block from Pacific) is the location of the House of Gold. At right angles to Olivier Street in Decatur Street, on which stands the Stoddard House at No. 303. The Casa Gutiérrez is at 590 Main Street, very close to the Stokes House at 500 Hartnell and to Frémont's Headquarters at 539 Hartnell Street. On the corner of Hartnell and Polk (599 Polk Street) is a second Casa de la Torre. Madison Street, continuing from Hartnell, is the location of the Brown Adobe. Alvarado Street contains the first Post Office at No. 497, the Casa Sanchez at 412, and the Casa Osio at 378. On the street next to Alvarado and in the same block with the old Post Office is the Mission Inn, at 456 Tyler Street, standing on the site of the Estrada House; and not far distant is the Casa Abrego at 592 Abrego Street.

These are only a few of the many adobes built in Monterey during the time that it flourished. As late as the 1890's, Pacific and Main streets were lined with adobe buildings, most of which have been demolished to give way to more modern structures, and now not a half-dozen can be found on either of these thoroughfares.

The Pear Orchard

Since its name is given on few maps, the location of the Pear Orchard on Dutra Creek is known principally to persons residing in the coast area south of Monterey Bay. Only one pear tree, with a diameter of forty inches, now remains to give reason for the name, but it has as companions perhaps a dozen old olive trees. Smeaton Chase, in his classic ramble on horseback along the California coast trails, turned aside to visit this pear orchard. He found the pear tree to be oak-like in its dimensions, "the Nestor of mortal pears"; and in comparing the olive trees with those at the Missions he decided that they could be little less than a century old.

The origin of the place is given by tradition to the period of the first Missions. It is said that the priests maintained there a station and residential quarters for the workers in a silver mine farther up Dutra Creek, the northwest fork of San Carpojo Creek, which enters the Pacific in San Luis Obispo County.

This mine is locally called the "Priest Mine." It is said that the natives procured silver from the place before the advent of the Spaniard and that, afterward, under the direction of the Fathers, it was mined more systematically and the ore carried over the trail to the San Antonio Mission. Aged Indians have described the location of the mineral deposit as being north of the Pear Orchard, where the trail passes a pine tree. At this point, a distant view of the ocean is obtained.

Prospectors of a later day have found evidence of a small amount of excavation but have discovered no silver thereabouts. The region is accessible only by rough trails.

Los Burros Gold Mines

The Los Burros Mining District in the Santa Lucia Range was organized in 1876. Traditions of gold being mined there by the Spaniards prior to that date were rife in Indian lore, but there is nothing definitely known of such old workings. Placer mining had been carried on for years in the surface gravels of the Jolon vicinity, where at one time over one hundred Chinese were engaged in gold mining. It is difficult to form an estimate of the amount of gold procured there, but Dutton and Tidball, who owned a store at Jolon patronized by these Orientals, took in $2,500 in gold dust in 1877–1878. After the land upon which the washing was done was proved to be a part of Rancho Milpitas and the title to it was cleared, placer mining by the public was forbidden.

In 1887 W. D. Cruikshank, prospecting in Alder Creek over the summit of the range, found gold ore. Here he established Alder Creek Camp and developed the mine which he called the "Last Chance." Other mines opened later in the vicinity, to name but a few, were: Mars, Manchester, Queen, King, and Grizzly. All supplies of food and implements had to be brought from Jolon by pack train over the trail that led to the summit at an altitude of 3,600 feet and down the western slope to the camp at Alder Creek at an altitude of 2,800 feet. Mining of ore that ran under $12 to the ton was not sufficiently profitable to warrant such an expense to take it out of the ground. There is now little activity in this region.

Tassajara Hot Springs

From early records and folklore it appears that Tassajara (probably a corruption of "tasajera," a place where jerked meat is hung up to cure) has long been a gathering place for many peoples: first, the Indians, who made annual pilgrimages thither to receive the benefit of its waters; later, pioneer white men, who built a rough log cabin and baths; and today, the modern vacationist, who seeks the Tassajara Springs for his summer's outing.

The Tassajara Hot Springs are in the heart of the Monterey National Forest, forty-five miles south of Salinas. Somewhere in the wilderness to the south the California redwood (*Sequoia sempervirens*) finds its most southerly native habitat.

SOURCES

[Credit is here given for source material, and permission to quote is hereby acknowledged]

ANDRESEN, ANNA GEIL. *Historic Landmarks of Monterey, California.* Privately printed, Salinas, California, 1917

BLAND, HENRY MEADE. *Stevenson's California*. The Pacific Short Story Club, San Jose, California, 1924

BOLTON, HERBERT EUGENE. *Anza's California Expedition*. 5 vols. University of California Press, Berkeley, California, 1930

——. *Fray Juan Crespi, Missionary Explorer on the Pacific Coast, 1769–1774*. University of California Press, Berkeley, California, 1927

——. "Spanish Explorations in the Southwest, 1542–1706," in *Original Narratives of Early American History*, XVII. Charles Scribner's Sons, New York, 1916

CHAPMAN, CHARLES E. *A History of California: The Spanish Period*. The Macmillan Company, New York, 1921

CHASE, J. SMEATON. *California Coast Trails*. Houghton Mifflin Company, Boston and New York, 1913

CLELAND, ROBERT GLASS. *A History of California: The American Period*. The Macmillan Company, New York, 1922

COLTON, WALTER. *Three Years in California*. A. S. Barnes & Company, New York, 1850

DANA, RICHARD HENRY, *Two Years before the Mast, a Personal Narrative*. Houghton Mifflin Company, Boston and New York, 1911; first edition, 1840

DAVIS, WILLIAM HEATH. *Seventy-five Years in California* (a reissue and enlarged, illustrated edition of *Sixty Years in California*). Edited by Douglas S. Watson. John Howell, San Francisco, 1929

ELDREDGE, ZOETH SKINNER. *The Beginnings of San Francisco from the Expedition of Anza, 1774, to the City Charter of April 15, 1850*. Privately printed, San Francisco, 1912

ELDER, DAVID PAUL. *The Old Spanish Missions of California*. Paul Elder & Company, San Francisco, 1913

ENGELHARDT, ZEPHYRIN. *Mission Nuestra Señora de la Soledad*. Mission Santa Barbara, Santa Barbara, California, 1929

——. *San Antonio de Padua, the Mission in the Sierra*. Mission Santa Barbara, Santa Barbara, California, 1929

GUINN, JAMES MILLER. *History and Biographical Record of Monterey and San Benito Counties*. Historic Record Company, Los Angeles, 1910

HUNT, ROCKWELL D., and NELLIE VAN DE GRIFT SANCHEZ. *A Short History of California*. Thomas Y. Crowell Company, New York, 1929

JAMES, GEORGE WHARTON. *In and Out of the Old Missions of California*. Little, Brown and Company, Boston, 1916

JOCHMUS, A. C. *The City of Monterey, Its People, Its Connection with the World, Anecdotes, Legends, Romances, Achievements, 1542–1930*. Privately published, Pacific Grove, 1930

OSBOURNE, KATHARINE D. *Robert Louis Stevenson in California*. A. C. McClurg & Company, Chicago, 1911

PALÓU, FRANCISCO. *Historical Memoirs of New California*. Translated into English from the manuscript in the archives of Mexico; edited by Herbert Eugene Bolton. University of California Press, Berkeley, 1926

PEIXOTTO, ERNEST CLIFFORD. *Romantic California*. Charles Scribner's Sons, New York, 1910

(ROBINSON, ALFRED). *Life in California*. (H. G. Collins, Paternoster Row, London, 1846); Wiley & Putnam, New York, 1846; republished in part by W. Doxey, San Francisco, 1891

ROBINSON, W. W. "Mellow Monterey," in *Touring Topics*, August, 1927

SMITH, FRANCES RAND. *The Mission of San Antonio de Padua*. Stanford University Press, Stanford University, California, 1932

STEVENSON, ROBERT LOUIS. "The Pacific Capital," in *Across the Plains*. Charles Scribner's Sons, New York, 1905

TAYLOR, BAYARD. *El Dorado, or Adventures in the Path of Empire; Compromising a Voyage to California, Via Panama; Life in San Francisco and Monterey*. H. G. Bohn, London, England, 1850; G. P. Putnam, New York, 1850 and 1864

WAGNER, HENRY R. *Spanish Voyages to the Northwest Coast of America in the Sixteenth Century*. California Historical Society, San Francisco, 1929

WILLEY, SAMUEL HOPKINS. Manuscript of reminiscences in possession of Native Sons of the Golden West Landmarking Committee, Joseph Knowland, Chairman, Tribune Building, Oakland, California

NAPA COUNTY

NAPA COUNTY (Napa, accented as Napá in old documents, was the name of a tribe of Indians who once occupied the valley and were said to have been the bravest of all the California tribes, but who were almost completely annihilated by smallpox in 1838) was one of the original twenty-seven counties. The city of Napa has always been its county seat.

The first courthouse was a two-story frame building erected in 1850, material for which is said to have been brought around the Horn from the East.

The First Trail

The first recorded expedition into what is now Napa County was made in 1823, when a party led by Francisco Castro, and accompanied by José Sánchez and Father José Altimira, made explorations north of San Francisco Bay preliminary to the founding of Misión San Francisco Solano.

The party left San Francisco in a launch, on June 25, and went north to Misión San Rafael. From that point they explored the valley from Petaluma to Sonoma, Napa, and Suisun. Sites at Petaluma, Sonoma, and Napa were favorably considered, but Sonoma was finally chosen for the mission, while Petaluma and Napa were to be used as mission cattle ranches.

Ranchos Caymus and La Jota

George C. Yount, "representative American pioneer, soldier, hunter, trapper, overlander and frontiersman," and a native of North Carolina, came to California from New Mexico with the Wolfskill party in 1831. After he had traveled almost the entire breadth of the continent, his name was linked with many early events in the history of the American occupation of the West. Soon after his arrival in California, he was engaged (1831–1833) in hunting sea otter on the Santa Barbara Channel Islands and along the coast of the mainland. While at Santa Barbara in 1833 he made for Captain A. B. Thompson probably the first shingles that were fashioned in California. During the same year, Yount trapped beaver in San Francisco Bay and along the San Joaquin River. Toward the end of the year he proceeded to the Missions at San Rafael and Sonoma, where his all-round usefulness and ingenuity appealed to the padres, who engaged him to repair the Mission buildings and where General Vallejo had him make shingles for his house in Sonoma.

Mission life pleased Yount, and he lingered at San Rafael and Sonoma for almost three years. In 1835, when he was baptized into the Catholic faith at Misión San Rafael, his name, as was the custom in Alta California on such occasions, was rendered in the Spanish as Jorge Concepción Yount.

It was during this eventful year of Yount's career that he penetrated the Napa Valley with the purpose of making it his home. Here this hardy pioneer lived for many years practically alone with his Indian neighbors. From the nearest tribe was derived the name "Caymus" which he bestowed upon his estate. Within a territory one hundred miles long and twenty miles wide, there were six distinct aboriginal nations: the Napa, whose villages were situated near the site of the present city of Napa; the Ulucas, on Rancho Tulucay; the Caymus, near Yount's house two miles north of the site of Yountville; the Mayacomas, with their villages located near the hot mineral springs of Calistoga; the Calajomanas, at the Bale ranch; and the Suscols, on Suscol Creek and Rancho Suscol (in Solano County).

Through the influence of Father José L. Guigas of Misión San Francisco Solano at Sonoma and of General M. G.

Vallejo, Yount obtained the princely grant of Rancho Caymus on March 23, 1836. It consisted of 11,814 acres, lying in the heart of Napa Valley and including within its southern boundary a bit of what was later to become the northern edge of the town named in his honor, Yountville. Rancho Caymus was the first grant made in Napa County, and Yount's first dwelling was, at the time it was built in 1835 or 1836, the first white habitation inland between Sonoma and the settlements on the Columbia River.

A second grant, known as Rancho de la Jota, was made to Yount on October 23, 1843, and comprised 4,543 acres of timber land lying on Howell Mountain north of his first estate. The Seventh-Day Adventists founded their Pacific Union College high up on the western slope of the mountain. About four miles west of this thriving institution is the St. Helena Sanitarium, located on the lower slopes of the mountain overlooking Napa Valley.

Some of the mission Indians accompanied Yount to Rancho Caymus, where they helped him to build his first dwelling, a Kentucky blockhouse (probably the only one of its kind ever erected in California), as well as subsequent buildings. During his first years on the rancho, this blockhouse apparently served as a fort. It consisted of an upper room twenty-two feet square used as living quarters and a lower one eighteen feet square fitted with portholes through which Yount could defend himself and his friendly Indians against any wild tribes which might come down the mountains.

The blockhouse, well stocked with food and other supplies, could have withstood a siege. Yount, however, found it unnecessary to use his fort except on rare occasions. His long experience with the Indians, his fearlessness, together with his tact in forming alliances with the strongest rancherías, made it possible for him to dwell in peace among them; and his kindly treatment soon made them his friends.

In 1837 the blockhouse was superseded by a low, narrow building, its massive adobe walls, about one hundred feet long, pierced by portholes. This so-called adobe "fort" antedated that of Sutter by two years. It is said that the "fort" was torn down in 1870, but a map of that year shows it standing just below the point where the old road to Chiles Valley crossed Napa River. Charles L. Camp of the University of California, who has made a study of some of California's earliest pioneers, says that "after Yount moved into his new adobe house, built on the spot which the Napa State Farm buildings now occupy, his daughter, Mrs. Vines, lived in the old fort."

The warm red tiles of this old adobe long remained a vivid memory to Mary E. Bucknall, Yount's granddaughter, who speaks of the place tenderly as the scene of pleasant childhood days: Before the broad veranda a little stream flowed with liquid melody. A tall hedge of sweet-scented Castilian roses enclosed the garden plot, while a clump of weeping willows afforded welcome shade on warm summer days.

James Clyman, adventurous surveyor-trapper from Virginia, visited Yount's homestead at three different times. The first date recorded was July 14, 1845, when he wrote in his diary he had "passed a low range of hills and arrived at Mr. Younts ranch or farm on a small stream running a saw and grist mill here we sat down to a Breakfast of good mutton and coffee having rode 60 miles without food and mostly without water."

Clyman remained with his hospitable host three days, resting his animals and watching the threshing activities of the Indians, who used half-wild horses, in the old Mexican manner. Leaving the ranch, Clyman "took a northern direction up the valley of the creek of which Mr. Younts mills are located."

The hunter again stopped at the Yount homestead in

August; and again in March of the following year, he "finally lift on the 31 the head of Napa valley and proceeded down 18 miles to Mr. Yount . . . . [who] has a Flouring and saw mill in opperation . . . . as far as I could learn this [is] the only Flouring mill in the province . . . ."

Although these references to Yount's mills are vague as to location, they prove beyond a doubt that he had both a flour mill and a sawmill on his property as early as 1845. Bancroft's statement that Yount had built a sawmill on Rancho de la Jota soon after 1843 seems to harmonize with the tradition that he brought pine and redwood timbers from Howell Mountain for rebuilding his flour mill in 1854–1855. Run by water power with a wide overshot wheel, this mill had a capacity of thirty bushels per day.

The platform of Yount's flour mill, fast falling to decay, may still be seen on the creek back of the barns located on the present Cook ranch two miles north of Yountville. Some of the old hand-hewn timbers have been used to form the pergola in the garden, and four of the millstones fashioned by William Gordon have been placed in the walk. A few of the aged pear trees planted by Yount are still growing south of the stream in the vicinity of the first adobe site.

Fred Ellis, Yount's miller, leased the mill from 1865 to 1870, and later purchased it from the Yount heirs. The property was bought from the widow of Mr. Ellis by the present owners in 1915.

Rancho Carne Humana

In the year 1837 a young English surgeon, Edward Turner Bale, landed at Monterey, where he practiced medicine for five or six years and where for part of that time (1840–1843) he was surgeon of the California forces by appointment of General Vallejo. Dr. Bale married María Ignacia Soberanes, a niece of the General, and in 1841 he became a naturalized citizen of Alta California. He subsequently received the grant of Rancho Carne Humana in Napa County, to which he went in 1843. By the time of his death in 1849 or 1850, the success of his struggles against the odds of Nature in a new land had gained for him a rich estate, which he left to his widow, two sons, and four daughters.

Dr. Bale was a man of good education, hardy, bold, and adventurous. Unfortunately, "his debts and personal quarrels," says Bancroft, got him into many difficulties. One such complication arose between himself and Salvador Vallejo, the reckless, hot-tempered brother of the General and uncle of Bale's wife. The story goes that in 1844 Don Salvador paid the Doctor and his wife a visit. "It seemed to Dr. Bale that the captain and the charming Señora . . . . greeted each other too heartily. Their close family relationship and the fact that Salvador had just returned from dangerous Indian fighting did not seem sufficient reason for the warmth of those Latin embraces.

"The irate doctor quarrelled with Vallejo and challenged him to a duel. Well might the soldier smile: he was the best swordsman in the land.

"The duel was a farce. Vallejo skillfully twisted his cumbersome opponent into ridiculous knots. Then sardonically, he beat the Englishman with his sword as though it were a whip. In a rage, Bale drew a revolver and fired.

"Luckily, the attempted Murder was a failure. The intention, however, was counted more important than the deed. The doctor found himself in jail."

It was rumored that the Kelseys and other foreigners planned to rescue Bale, and there was much excitement on foot for a time. Narrowly escaping with his life, Bale was finally released.

Rancho Carne Humana, within the confines of which the

towns of St. Helena and Calistoga grew up in the '50's, comprised the whole of that part of Napa Valley lying north of Rancho Caymus. It consisted of two leagues of fertile land skirted on the west and east by wooded hills and overshadowed on the north by the purple, castled crags of Mount St. Helena.

An idyllic spot on the west side of Napa Valley beside a small stream was chosen for the Bale adobe. The site is on a country road two miles south of St. Helena and one mile west of the highway. In the background a low, round hill covered with native woods once sheltered numerous wild creatures, among which the grizzly bear was the most formidable. To the south and east of the house site is an aged pear orchard, still gay with bloom each spring. To the west, beyond a huge, twisted oak tree, the half-obliterated roadway leads to the ford, beyond which lie the woods and the protecting hill. Between the hill and the stream is a second orchard, its gnarled apple and pear trees gray with lichens and Spanish moss.

The Bale adobe is mentioned in the diary of James Clyman, who passed that way on July 16, 1845, while en route to hunt wild game in Lake County. The orchards and cultivated fields which resulted later from Dr. Bale's efforts were not at all in evidence on that blistering hot summer day, if we are to judge from the hunter's rather disgusted account:

"Passed the farm house of Dr. Bales this hous looked desolate Enough standing on a dry plane near a dry black volcanis mountain allmost destitute [of] vegitation no fields garden of any kind of cultivation to be seen and about 10 or 12 Indians lying naked in the scorching sun finished the scenery of this rural domain."

The old adobe collapsed in 1931, and the ruins were subsequently cleared away.

The enterprising doctor had two mills on his land, a sawmill and a gristmill. The former, long since disappeared, was constructed for Bale by Ralph L. Kilburn in 1846. This mill, according to Palmer, was located north of St. Helena on the Napa River just a little northeast of Krug's wine cellar. As payment for its construction and subsequent operation, Bale gave Kilburn three-fourths of a league of land. During the winter of 1847, lumber for six buildings was cut and framed at this mill and shipped to Benicia and San Francisco. It also supplied the lumber for the first frame structure put up in the city of Napa. John York, who came to the valley in 1845, cut the first logs for Bale's sawmill.

The gristmill, that picturesque landmark which stands beside the highway three miles northwest of St. Helena, was constructed between 1840 and 1842 by Irwin Kellogg, who also was paid for his services in land. Fred W. Ellis, who afterward operated George Yount's mill on Rancho Caymus, worked at the Bale mill during the early '60's.

While the Forty-niners were eagerly searching for gold in the hills and ravines of the Sierra Nevada, the great water wheel of Bale's mill was daily grinding the golden grain of the Upper Napa Valley into flour for the settlers, who, for a period of over twenty-five years, brought their grist here to be ground. The construction of this mill is interesting to the student of pioneer days. The lumber which went into the building (ultimately of three stories with a false store front) was cut from neighboring forests. The millstones were taken from the hill back of the mill, while the cogs in the great wheel, which made such a clatter when in operation, were all made of wood.

This mill, together with surrounding land, was at length given to the Native Sons of the Golden West by the widow of W. W. Lyman, owner of the mill for many years. It was restored through the efforts of the combined parlors of the Native Sons in Napa County under the leadership of Past Grand President Bismarck Bruch, a grandson of Dr. Bale,

and of the Historic Landmarks Committee of the Native Sons. The restored mill was dedicated on June 21, 1925, and a large native boulder surmounted by a bronze plaque was placed at the site.

A number of American pioneers settled on Bale's rancho in the middle '40's. In the year 1845 came John York, William and David Hudson, William Elliot and sons, the William Fowlers—father and son, Henry Fowler, William Hargrave, and Benjamin Dewell. They found Benjamin Kelsey already living on what was soon to become the Kilburn place, owned in later years by Peter Teal and located one mile south of Calistoga. Ralph Kilburn came to Napa Valley in 1844. After Kilburn became established on the tract of land which he had received from Dr. Bale, Peter Storm, a Norwegian sailor, lived with him.

The incoming settlers of 1845 also found Samuel Kelsey living near Bale's mill with his wife and two or three children, while Elias Barnett already had a log cabin on what later became the George Tucker place. The old Tucker house still stands across the highway from Paradise Park.

During the winter of 1845–1846 John York built a log cabin for himself within the present city limits of Calistoga. This cabin, remodeled and incorporated in a larger house, stood until recently on the highway on the site now occupied by a Standard Oil filling station. York had the distinction of planting the first wheat crop in this section of Napa County.

It is interesting to note the number of women and children mentioned in the records of the pioneers. The hardihood of these wives and mothers, as well as the strenuousness of the training to which their young people were subjected, was remarkable. The experience of one pioneer mother and grandmother, who came thus early to the valley, is typical. She was the wife of William B. Elliot, and with her came several grown children and grandchildren. For a time the family lived in a cloth tent, a frail protection, indeed, not only against the elements but also against the marauding animals of that untamed wilderness. The entire family had to spend the nights on a platform built in the forks of a mammoth oak tree, often watching helplessly while their uninvited guests below plundered the tent of all edibles. During the day the men frequently went on hunting expeditions; and in their absence Mrs. Elliot and the smaller children often had to take refuge in the trees to get away from prowling bears. Mrs. Elliot, however, was herself an excellent shot and of no mean prowess as a bear hunter.

At the head of the valley one and one-half miles northwest of Calistoga on the road to Knight's Valley was the log cabin of Enoch Cyrus, who came to California with his wife and six children in 1846. Next in order were the Fowlers, who lived with William Hargrave in a log house at the foot of the Mayacamas Range west of Calistoga. Calvin Musgrove and his wife also lived on the Fowler ranch. Wells and Ralph Kilburn lived with their families one mile south of Calistoga.

In 1849 the Owsley family—husband, wife, and eight children—erected a log cabin, and during the same year they set out an orchard and put up a frame house two miles south of Calistoga. One-half mile farther south was the home of William Nash, who had come with his wife and fourteen children to California in 1846. Purchasing 330 acres of land from R. L. Kilburn in 1847, Nash settled on his ranch on November 26, 1848, naming it Walnut Grove. There he put up a house of boards cut at Bale's mill, and in January of the following year planted an orchard from seedlings brought by Elias Barnett from Kentucky. Nash was among the first to inaugurate new and better methods of agriculture in California, practicing, among other things, deep plowing and cultivation. He sold Walnut Grove in 1868 and moved to his Magnolia Farm five and one-half miles north of the city of Napa.

The chain of pioneer homesteads continued southward to the log house of M. D. Ritchie, who lived with his wife and five children across the road from Reason Tucker. The latter had a split-redwood house for his wife and three or four boys. Irwin Kellogg had a frame house one-half mile beyond. Having arrived in the valley in 1846 with a wife and seven children, he had obtained this land for services rendered in building Dr. Bale's gristmill.

Up in the hills David Hudson built a temporary cabin of round logs chinked with mud, but later he fashioned a split-redwood house on the north side of Hudson Creek, where he lived with his wife and boy. On the south side of the creek, but higher up in the hills, John York took his wife and three boys, putting up a little split-redwood cabin 10 by 15 feet. Not far to the south was Dr. Bale's adobe *casa*.

In this vicinity none of the original log cabins or split-redwood houses remain, but a few of the later dwellings still stand.

Rancho Yajome

On an elevated shelf of land above the Napa River where a splendid view of the valley stretches westward, the mellow buff walls of the old Salvador Vallejo adobe stand amid the orchards and gardens of the present Longwood ranch. This was the third of three adobes built by Don Salvador, the other two (no longer in existence) having been located on Rancho Napa. In excellent condition today, the adobe is an outstanding example of an early Californian rancho house. The first floor comprises the original structure, with its thick walls and its deeply recessed doors and windows, while the second story, added at a later date, is of wood. On the east veranda, overlooking the garden, one may see the old hand-hewn redwood pillars with the round redwood beams overhead. Indian mortars, dug from the soil about the house, attest the presence of a native ranchería at the site before the white man took it for his own.

This adobe was built by Don Salvador on Rancho Yajome, an estate of some 6,652 acres of fertile land lying on either side of the Napa River north of Rancho Tulucay. The grant was made to Damaso Antonio Rodríguez, a soldier, on March 13, 1841. It appears, however, that Rodríguez never lived on the land, and claim to it was filed by Salvador Vallejo on April 20, 1852, and confirmed to him on February 21, 1853.

That part of the grant now contained in the Longwood farm was purchased by the present owner from William Watt, who had lived on it for twenty-five years. In the early '60's the long row of native trees, which still border the river below the house, gave the estate its present name.

Rancho Napa

On March 2, 1853, Don Salvador Vallejo and his wife, María de la Cruz Carrillo, filed a claim for about 3,000 acres of the much larger Rancho Napa originally granted to them on September 21, 1838, by Governor Alvarado. From time to time they had sold parts of their land that lay some distance back from the Napa River.

The part retained and for which confirmation was now asked was called "Trancas and Jalapa," which may be translated to mean "Sticks and Morning-glories" (*trancas* means "sticks," and *jalapa* is the name of a Mexican trailing plant in appearance like a wild morning-glory). A Mexican village lay in the south end of this area between the road and the river. South of this village was Pueblo de Salvador, a piece of the original grant, where James Clyman purchased a piece of land in 1850 shortly after his marriage to Hannah McComb, a member of the party that he had guided across the plains and mountains in the autumn of 1848.

Rancho Tulucay

A Napa County historian lamented in 1881 the disappearance of California's historic landmarks, saying: "And so the old landmarks are passing away, and the links which bind the present, or American regime to the Spanish-Mexican or past, are disappearing one by one .... The few relics of that people will, in another half century, be matters of legend and history."

More than fifty years have now passed since those words were written, and the prophecy has been almost fulfilled in many sections of California. In the Napa Valley only four of the many adobes which once stood there are extant today. Of these remaining adobes, two were built in the '40's, both by Cayetano Juárez. They stand near the highway one mile southeast of the city of Napa on what was once known as Rancho Tulucay.

Rancho Tulucay, comprising two square leagues of land just east of the city of Napa, was granted to Cayetano Juárez on October 26, 1841. He had stocked the land as early as 1837 and became a permanent settler there before 1840, having built a small adobe house, no longer extant, and brought his family out from Sonoma. About 1847 he built a second and larger adobe house, which stands today.

Juárez, a native of California and a military man of some importance, had been a soldier of the San Francisco Company during the years 1828–1831, had been promoted to the rank of corporal in 1832, and apparently had served as sergeant from 1833. He had engaged in many Indian expeditions, was made mayordomo at Solano in 1836, and later served as captain of the militia. In 1845 he was appointed alcalde at Sonoma, the same year in which he received the grant of Rancho Yokaya (Ukiah, in Mendocino County). He distinguished himself somewhat in 1846 by his plans to rescue the Bear Flag prisoners and by a famous swim of nine miles which he made to escape capture. Juárez, who died in Napa in 1883, lies buried in Tulucay Cemetery, for which he had donated the land to the city as early as 1859. The cemetery is east of the city and is surrounded by a high wall of exceptionally fine native stone.

One and one-half miles south of the city of Napa, the imposing towers of the Napa State Asylum for the Insane dominate the entire landscape, which once lay within the confines of Rancho Tulucay. This institution was initiated by the legislature in 1869–1870, when a commission was appointed to visit asylums throughout the United States and Europe and to report on management, modes of treatment, etc. Dr. E. T. Wilkins was appointed to head the commission. A second commission was appointed in March 1872 for the purpose of selecting a site for the building. Napa was chosen on August 2 of that year, and in March 1873 the cornerstone was laid, while the first patient was admitted on November 15, 1875.

Other Land Grants

Nicolás Higuera, a soldier in San Francisco from 1819 to 1823 and afterward alcalde on the frontier, received two grants from Governor Mariano Chico on May 9, 1836. One was Rancho Entre Napa, which lay to the west of Napa Creek. The northeast section of this was bought by Nathan Coombs in 1848 and later patented to him; here he laid out plans for the present city of Napa. The other was Rancho Rincon de los Carneros, a tract of 2,557.68 acres lying to the north and west of the confluence of Carneros Creek and the Napa River. This afterward passed into the possession of

Julius Martin, who received United States patent for it on April 3, 1858.

Rancho Las Putas, on Putas Creek, covering most of the Berryessa Valley, consisted of eight square leagues. It was granted by Governor Micheltorena in October of 1843, to two men, probably brothers, who had served as soldiers at San Francisco in the '30's. The grantees were José de Jesús and Sixto (Sisto) Berryessa, whose wives, probably sisters, were María Anastasia and María Nicolasa Higuera. With the consent of their husbands, the wives filed claim for this tract on May 21, 1852, and received confirmation of their rights to 35,515.82 acres in January 1863.

Joseph B. Chiles, who came to California first alone in 1841 and for the third time in 1848, bringing family and friends, received a grant of Rancho Catacula in November 1844. The grant covered 8,877 acres along the Arroyo de Napa east of Yount's Rancho La Jota. Near the arroyo, Chiles built a house and a gristmill, which is still standing. The place has remained to the present time in the possession of the Chiles family.

In 1841 Manuel Jimeno granted Rancho Locoallomi, consisting of 8,872 acres, to Julian Pope and Rancho Huichica, of two square leagues, to Jacob P. Leese. Leese received an extension of his property three years later, when Governor Micheltorena gave him another three and a half leagues. The Huichita grant lay southeast of Pueblo de Sonoma and the Buena Vista tract of Colonel Haraszthy. Carneros Creek formed its northeastern boundary, with Ranchos Napa and Rincon de los Carneros as neighbors across the stream.

William Gordon and Nathan Coombs filed claim for the four square leagues of Rancho Chimiles, granted to José Ignacio Berryessa on May 2, 1846. In 1859 the route of the county road between Suisun and the Berryessa Valley lay along the creek.

Vineyards and Wineries

On the wooded hillsides in Napa County, famous for its 15,000 acres of vineyards, stand picturesque structures of stone and brick similar to those built long ago in Germany and France. These wineries, however, date back only to the '60's, when certain citizens of the state began to be aware that the climate and soil in this region were favorable to the culture of the vine and the care of its yield.

Samuel Brannan, active in several parts of California, purchased a tract of land in the region around Calistoga Springs in 1858, with the intention of establishing a popular summer resort there. He built a hotel and twenty cottages near the springs, coined the word Calistoga from "California" and "Saratoga" (an Eastern watering place) as a name for his resort, and then turned his attention to the adjacent hillsides. Encouraged by the example of Colonel Agaston Haraszthy in Sonoma County and by a few growers near Napa, he planted the slopes with cuttings of superior wine and table grapes.

Both the Spanish and early American settlers had made wine from Napa County vineyards. A notable year, however, was 1858, when Brannan planted his hillside. That autumn Charles Krug made about 1,200 gallons for a Mr. Patchett at Napa. In the year following, he went to the Bale Mill place north of St. Helena and made wine for Louis Bruck and, in 1860, made 5,000 gallons at Mr. Yount's place at Yountville. His reputation now established, Krug began in 1868 to build a stone wine cellar immediately south of St. Helena on the floor of the valley. Additions were made periodically to this winery until it was finally completed in 1884. Standing amid plantings of shrubbery in a large grove of oaks, it is in splendid condition today and is still in operation, although not under the original ownership. Not far away

is "Larkmead," the winery of the late Mrs. Howard Coit, better-known in San Francisco as Lillie Hitchcock—the friend of the firemen.

The wine industry of the county is centered at St. Helena, where, in its infancy, the custom of a vintage festival was established. About six miles north of St. Helena, Jacob Schram planted in 1862 vineyards in the western hills of Napa Valley. His winery was a series of tunnels built into the hill. Only two of these tunnels are to be seen at the present time.

In 1869 Charles Wheeler purchased property two miles south of St. Helena at Pine Station, later known as Bell Station and now as Zinfandel, and here a stone winery was built by W. P. Weeks and J. Weinburger. Mr. Wheeler's son, John W., was secretary of the State Board of Viticulture in 1861 and its executive head in 1888. During this time another son, Rollo, was associated with his father in the management of the Wheeler Winery. In 1889 John W. took his brother's place with the father. This winery is now in operation near the highway about two miles south of St. Helena.

In 1870 Seneca Ewer came to live at St. Helena. In 1882 he and a partner, Atkinson, built a stone winery near Rutherford. The son, Fred S. Ewer, afterward carried on his father's business and about 1915 sold the wine cellar to Georges de Latour, who enlarged the original stone building by an addition built of cement. In recent years much attention has been given to the surrounding gardens. Sacramental wines made here have received the approval of the Church. This, now called the Beaulieu Winery, stands on the main highway at Rutherford.

In the foothills directly west of Rutherford is the beautifully designed Inglenook Winery. The land for this vineyard, formerly the property of a sanatorium, was purchased by Gustave Niebaum in 1880 and planted with cuttings of the finest kinds of wine grapes brought from Europe. The winery, built of stone quarried on the estate, was completed in 1887. It is a three-story structure of chateau type, its walls now festooned with trailing greenery. The tap room contains a rare collection of tankards, pewter and pottery mugs, and valuable old glass.

An interesting winery stands upon the site selected in 1875 by Jacob L. Beringer, who had been foreman of the Charles Krug cellar. This stands on the north side of St. Helena and is built into the west hills, where the limestone formation is peculiarly adapted to the storing and aging of wines. The winery and 800 feet of cellars are cut through the stone. The tunnels running 250 feet directly into the hill are connected by several laterals, honeycombing the entire hill. This underground storage space is filled with old oak casks, each with a capacity of about 500 gallons. At the entrance to the cellar is a large oval cask, with a capacity of 2,700 gallons, built in the early '80's by a San Francisco cooper and decorated by a wood carver from Germany. The management of this business has always remained in the Beringer family.

The Montelena Winery, about three miles north of Calistoga at the foot of Mount St. Helena, was built of wood in 1880. In 1881 the owner, A. L. Tubbs, had the stone cellar built, copying the Chateau Lafitte of France. This huge cellar is built into the hill and is filled with large oak ovals for the storing of wines. In 1897 the son, William B. Tubbs, succeeded his father in the management and, in turn, passed the control on to a later generation.

The Greystone Winery, situated a mile north of St. Helena and a few hundred feet away from the main highway on the western side of the hill, is one of the largest stone wineries in the world. It was built in 1889 by W. B. Brown and Everett Wise. The ownership changed in 1894, 1896, 1925, and again in 1943. It is a magnificent building 400 feet long with tunnels into the hills at the rear.

Stevenson's Silverado

In the spring of 1880, Robert Louis Stevenson brought his bride to Silverado. There, in the woody canyon filled with the scent of sweet bay trees and wild azaleas, he lived from May 19 until July. That delightful collection of descriptive and narrative essays, *Silverado Squatters,* completed in France, came from the memories of that dreamful, health-giving summer on the heights of St. Helena.

From Calistoga, with its geysers and hot springs and orchards, it is a scant nine miles to the old Toll House, nestled in a little glen high on the mountain's breast. A steep and winding stage road, vestiges of which still remain, climbed the mountain in Stevenson's day, and the coach, driven by the reckless Foss, bumped perilously over the zig-zag trail, to come at last to a halt before the Toll House Hotel, "dozing in sun and dust and silence, like a place enchanted." They say that the old gray inn is much the same today, as it sleeps behind the green thicket which isolates it from the modern highway leisurely circling the mountain grades.

The old mining camp of Silverado had already, in Stevenson's day, "been carted from the scene; one of the houses was now the schoolhouse far down the road; one was gone here, one there, but all were gone away. It was now a sylvan solitude."

A quarter of a mile along the rutted, sinuous road through the forest, one comes to the canyon, where "a rusty iron chute on wooden legs came flying, like a monstrous gargoyle, across the parapet" down which the precious ore was once poured.

Proceeding another quarter-mile, one reaches the "triangular platform, filling up the whole glen, and shut in on either hand by bold projections of the mountain. Only in front the place was open like the proscenium of a theatre," and one looks forth, as Stevenson did, "into a great realm of air, and down upon treetops and hilltops, and far and near on wild and varied country."

Here Stevenson took possession of a deserted miner's cabin with its sashless windows "chocked with the green and sweetly smelling foliage of a bay," and its three rooms "so plastered against the hill, that one room was right atop of another." The old cabin is gone, its place being marked by the Stevenson Monument carved from polished granite in the form of an open book, on a base of ore taken from the Silverado Mine.

One hundred yards from the cabin site, the trail leads abruptly up the mountain side and around a sharp bend to the cavernous tunnel of the Silverado Mine, going down into the bowels of the mountain from which "a cold, wet draught tempestuously blew." Abandoned ore cars and a narrow-gauge railroad testify to recent activities, for there have been sporadic and not highly profitable mining efforts at Silverado since the early '70's.

Here in this deeply wooded glen filled with its thousand mountain fragrances and lifted high above the valley fogs, Robert Louis Stevenson spent his honeymoon with Fannie Van de Grift Osbourne, and then returned to France with rich memories and recuperated health.

SOURCES

[Credit is here given for source material, and permission to quote is hereby acknowledged]

BUCKNALL, MARY E. *Early Days.* Pamphlet, privately printed (no date)
CHAPMAN, CHARLES E. *A History of California: The Spanish Period.* The Macmillan Company, New York, 1921
CLYMAN, JAMES. *James Clyman, American Frontiersman, 1792–1881.* California Historical Society, San Francisco, 1928
History of Napa and Lake Counties. Slocum, Bower & Company, San Francisco, 1881
HYATT, T. HART. *Handbook of Grape Culture.* H. H. Bancroft & Company, San Francisco, 1867
KANAGA, TILLIE. *History of Napa County.* Privately printed, Oakland, 1901
STEVENSON, ROBERT LOUIS. *The Silverado Squatters.* Charles Scribner's Sons, New York, 1904
TUOMEY, HONORIA, and LOUISA VALLEJO EMPARAN. *History of the Mission, Presidio, and Pueblo of Sonoma.* Press-Democrat, Santa Rosa, California, 1923
WHEELER, MRS. ELLIOTT H. Manuscript notes

SAN BENITO COUNTY

SAN BENITO COUNTY (San Benito is Spanish for St. Benedict) derived its name from San Benito Creek, which was named by Father Crespi in 1772. The county was formed in 1874 from a part of Monterey County, and the county seat was placed at Hollister. By act of the state legislature in 1887 the area of the county was increased by additions from the adjoining counties of Fresno and Merced.

Misión San Juan Bautista

Following the expressed wish of the viceroy, establishments were made as fast as possible to fill gaps in the chain of Missions from San Diego to San Francisco. Soon after the dedication of Misión San José, Father Lasuén proceeded to the San Benito Valley, where on St. John's Day, June 24, 1797, Misión San Juan Bautista was founded. The Father had chosen this spot from others suggested to him because this location "promised the most abundant harvest of souls."

Assisting in the ceremonies attendant upon this dedication were Father Majín de Catalá from Misión Santa Clara and Father Manuel Martiarena, who was to be left in charge of the new establishment. The rites took place before a large assemblage of gentiles, consisting principally of the Indians who lived on the plain in the vicinity. These were peaceful Indians, but there were other Indians who inhabited the mountains to the east, including the warlike Ausaymus tribe, who gave much annoyance for several years.

The temporary building constructed for use as a church had a "mud roof." It was not until June 13, 1803, that the cornerstone of the new church was laid. Within this stone were placed coins and a sealed bottle containing a narrative of the proceedings at the celebration.

The new building, when it was finished, was "about one hundred ninety feet long from the entrance door in front to the altar at the rear, thirty feet wide and forty feet high from floor to ceiling, having the chancel separated from the nave by a railing, over which was sprung an arch spanning the full width of the church. The nave was subdivided on either side into seven sections by as many arches. The church and adjacent buildings, which as usual throughout the country were of adobe, occupied two sides of a court-yard which was completed by a wall; and in front, next the church, there was a corridor of twenty arches, resting on pillars of brick."

The new group of buildings was completed in 1812, and Father Estevan Tapis, who had succeeded to the office of Father Presidente on the death of Father Lasuén, officiated at the dedication on June 25 of that year. Later in the year, at the end of his term as Father Presidente, Father Estevan

Tapis went to live at San Juan, remaining there until his death in 1825 at the age of seventy-one. He was an excellent man for his position. He was familiar with several Indian dialects, was noted for his habit of studying the traits of the individual neophytes, and was fond of teaching the boys to read and write. After his death, it was said of him that he had been remarkably wise in his dealings with the superior officers and the civil governors who also lived at San Juan. As a result of this ability to get along with people, "all friars, military, civilians, and Indians loved him." Two years before his death, in 1823, population figures at the Mission reached their highest point.

In 1831, the Mission was visited by Captain Alfred Robinson, who wrote: "It is conveniently located in the center of a large valley, with an abundance of rich land and large stocks of cattle. Padre Felipe Arroyo was the missionary, whose infirm state of health kept him confined closely to his chamber. For amusement, when tired of study, he called in the children of the place and set them to dancing and playing their games. In his eccentric taste he had given them the names of all the renowned personages of antiquity, and Ciceros, Platos, and Alexanders were to be found in abundance."

In 1835, when Misión San Juan Bautista was secularized, José Tiburcio Castro, grantee of Rancho Sausal not far away, was made mayordomo. Sixty-three families of Indians were secularized at the time, and payments were made to them amounting to over $8,000. The value of the remaining Mission property was estimated to be $138,973, with a debt of only $250 standing against it.

The mayordomo had some trouble with the Indians and some with the padres; but, on the whole, he settled the Mission affairs promptly and well. He gave his final report in 1836. There were at that date 900 head of cattle and 4,000 sheep belonging to the Mission and an account of $1,300 against the property.

The Mission, sadly neglected for many years, was restored in 1884. Only one of the original nine bells remains. The long, arched corridors, extending the entire length of the building, still give grace and charm to the ancient chapel, which is now used as the parish church for the village of San Juan.

San Juan

In 1825 José Castro, ad interim governor of California ten years later, built a two-story adobe house on the south side of the plaza opposite the Mission church in San Juan. In 1836 he and Juan B. Alvarado made this house their headquarters in the revolt which resulted in the exile of Governor Gutiérrez and in the election of Alvarado in his stead.

From 1837, after the affairs of the Mission had been settled, continual depredations of savages with ex-neophyte allies contributed to the ruin of that establishment. However, a small group of civilized people, Spanish and Mexican, still remained in the vicinity of the Mission. Others came, until by 1846 probably fifty persons were living in San Juan de Castro, as the place was called for a time.

Having completed his period of governorship, Don José Castro petitioned on April 4, 1839, for land on which to place his livestock: "being the owner of a considerable quantity of cattle and horses without possessing any land of my own whereon to place them to increase and prosper I have become acquainted with a suitable place in the neighborhood of this pueblo known by the name of San Justo which does not belong to any owner and is entirely unoccupied." The land requested was granted to him. On July 6, 1844, Castro conveyed that property to Francisco Perez Pacheco.

In 1846, while ad interim comandante general, Castro

again organized forces at San Juan; this time he wished to expel Frémont from his temporary stronghold on Gabilan Peak, where the American captain of topographical engineers maintained his forces from March 6 to March 10. On July 17, 1846, Frémont raised the United States flag on the plaza at San Juan and drilled there his ten companies of volunteer troops before starting for Los Angeles to support Commodore Stockton in suppressing the revolt of General Flores.

Castro's house in the pueblo of San Juan was deeded to Patrick Breen on February 7, 1849, three years after Mexican rule had ceased in California. Breen and his family, the first English-speaking settlers in San Juan, were among the members of the Donner party who survived the tragic winter at Donner Lake. Breen purchased some of the Mission property in addition to the Castro house and established an inn which became famous as a stopping place for travelers between Monterey and the mines in 1849–1850. In it, years later, Helen Hunt Jackson was a guest. There she began to write *Ramona* and might have staged her story on one of the ranchos near by had not an ardent Catholic house manager for the Breens discovered that she was not a Catholic and thereupon ejected her.

In the '50's and '60's San Juan was the site of an exchange station on the route between San Francisco and Los Angeles. At one time eleven lines made it a stopping place. During the Civil War the United States established military headquarters in the National Hotel in the town. At that time the place was called Camp Low in honor of California's governor.

A few adobes stand today along the streets of the old town. Chief among them is the old Castro adobe. This building is included in the San Juan Bautista State Monument, which was dedicated on September 29, 1935, by the State Park Commission and the San Juan Preservation League.

The Pacheco Ranchos

Francisco Pérez Pacheco was a Mexican carriage-maker, who came to California in 1819 with the artillery detachment under Ramírez. His bravery and success in quelling Indian revolts won his promotion to *brevet-alférez* in 1824. Afterward, he was commander of the Custom House guard and then of the military post at Monterey.

Since the Mission Fathers at San Juan Bautista had no need for all the land set aside for Mission use, they allowed Pacheco to settle upon a part of it before 1833. This part was apparently the Bolsa de San Felipe, which came by the name Bolsa ("pocket") because it was nearly enclosed by a swamp, a willow grove, and a ravine called Sanjón de Tesquisquite. The family of the mayordomo of the Mission and some of the Mission Indians who were living upon it were allowed by Pacheco to remain.

The formalities that attended the legal taking possession of land at that period included: pulling up grass, cutting a few tree branches, throwing a few stones, and taking up a handful of earth. After taking possession, Pacheco built a stone house, where he and José María Sánchez, owner of the adjoining Rancho Llano del Tesquisquite, lived together for a time.

On petition to Governor Figueroa for adjoining property, the Ausaymus tract of two leagues was granted to Pacheco on November 21, 1833. In 1836 he petitioned for another two leagues, which he called Guadalaxarita but which the padres called San Felipe, and this tract was probably included in the grant of six leagues made by Governor Gutiérrez on April 1, 1836. With a good start of stock the first year, his herds gradually increased, although they were troubled by Indians, who made a raid in 1838. Pacheco became an extensive landowner, eventually having in his possession the San Justo, conveyed to him by José Castro on July 26, 1844; the Bolsa de San Felipe, in the vicinity of Hollister; the Ausaymus de San Felipe, extending into Santa Clara County; and the San Luis Gonzaga, lying in the counties of Santa Clara and Merced, on which are the Pacheco Pass and several miles of the Pacheco Pass Road. All of these ranchos were patented to him by the United States in after years.

In 1844 Don Francisco Pacheco was captain of *defensores* and in 1846 tithe collector. Testimony given in 1852 states that he was then the owner of a house valued at between $15,000 and $20,000, ten cabins for laborers, and thousands of horses, cattle, and hogs with pens and corrals for them, and that enough of his land was in cultivation to provide for all living upon it.

Pacheco's large house stood near the creek crossed by the present highway seven miles north of Hollister. The foundations, sometimes called the remains of an old fort, could be seen within recent years enclosed within a modern packing shed which has been built on the site.

The only child surviving Don Francisco was a daughter, who married Mariano Malarín.

The lands passed through the ownership of Máximo Taboas, who sold them on May 14, 1859, to Isadora Pacheco.

Rancho San Justo, through which runs the San Benito River, was afterward sold to W. W. Hollister and Flint, Bixby and Company, men who brought a flock of sheep from the East and turned the place into a sheep ranch.

Rancho Llano del Tesquisquite

José María Sánchez, who came from Mexico in 1824, received the grant of this land situated in San Benito and Santa Clara counties from Governor Castro on October 10, 1835. With Thomas O. Larkin the grantee instituted an early soapmaking enterprise near the northern end of his grant. A rough frame building was erected by them on the edge of Soap (now San Felipe) Lake into which the Tesquisquita Slough drains. The kettle used for boiling the soap was a cauldron from an old whaling vessel enlarged by placing slabs of wood to extend upward from its edges until its capacity was increased many times. These slabs of wood were held in place by hoop iron, and the whole was made stationary by adobe built up around it. The soap works, superintended by an Englishman, were remunerative until 1848, when they were deserted in the rush to the gold region.

Don José María was still living in 1852, when he filed claim with the Land Commission for this rancho and for Rancho Las Animas in Santa Clara County. He and his wife, Encarnación Ortega, died before 1871, for in that year patents for both of these tracts were issued to their children—Vicente, Refugio, Candelaria, Gregorio, and Guadalupe. The last-named daughter married into the Roche family and lived until 1935. Don José is supposed to have buried a fortune on his estate, but no treasure has been found, although his rancho has been cut up into many small farms and has been long cultivated.

Rancho Santa Ana y Quien Sabe

Rancho Santa Ana y Quien Sabe, consisting of over 48,000 acres, covered the Santa Ana and the Quien Sabe valleys. Quien Sabe had been granted Francisco J. C. Negrete, one of the Hijar colonists of 1834, who petitioned for this land in December of that year. He received the grant of six leagues in April 1836, after serving as secretary of the *ayuntamiento* at Monterey. Some time later that same year, as secretary to Governor Chico, he went to Mexico. As he did not return to Alta California, his land was granted on April 8, 1839, to two other men, who held it in a sort of partnership for a number of years.

One of these partners was Juan Miguel Anzar, brother of Father José Antonio Anzar. This partner did not live on the land but furnished 800 head of cattle and paid Manuel Larios, the other partner, to oversee the property. Manuel Larios was a native of San José who had spent his early years as a soldier and, like his father, Don José Larios, was a famous bear hunter. He was married three times: first to María A. Pacheco, and the second time to Guadalupe Castro, both of whom died. He then married Rosario Arnas, who bore him twenty-two children, four of whom were born on this rancho.

Larios furnished 300 head of cattle in the partnership and cultivated a certain amount of ground for garden crops, but no orchard was planted because of lack of water. His adobe house was built beside the road leading to San Juan Bautista, where he was *juez* in 1840. Work of various kinds was carried on under his supervision. Cheese was made, and in shops erected for the purpose a primitive sort of manufacturing was done. Weavers, shoemakers, saddlers, silversmiths, and blacksmiths had each a place. Consequently, a guard had to be kept to prevent depredations by hostile Indians; even so, loss was suffered because of their raids.

A chapel was built on the rancho in the early '40's. After its completion, the celebration of Santa Ana's Day on July 26 became an annual event. On those occasions Mass was said in the chapel, followed by out-of-door festivities common to that period: bull-and-bear fighting, horse-racing, feasting, and dancing.

The other owner, Miguel Anzar, had but three children. Although he did not live on the rancho, some of his employees were placed in a house in the northern part. In the late '40's the two men divided their joint grant: Larios, who died in 1865, took Santa Ana; and Anzar, who owned also Ranchos Carneros and Real de Aguillas, took Quien Sabe.

No trace of any of the old buildings remains on either part of the property. A modern barn in which relics of Mexican days were stored was destroyed by fire on May 2, 1933. Among the heirlooms lost at that time were Spanish worked leather bridles, bronze-studded harness, carriages, and other vehicles.

Rancho Cienaga de los Paicines

Rancho Cienaga de los Paicines was granted by Governor Alvarado to Angel Castro and José Antonio Rodríguez on October 5, 1842. Rodríguez died before 1853, when a claim to the property was filed by Angel Castro and Hilario Castro de Rodríguez, widow of the co-grantee, and her three children. A patent for 8,917.52 acres was issued to these claimants on September 23, 1869.

This grant covered the land extending from Tres Pinos Creek on the east to the Cienaga Valley at the foot of the Gabilan Mountains on the west. Through it runs a stretch of the San Benito River and its tributary, Pescadero Creek. The southeastern boundary of the rancho is near Paicines School, which is located on a road running south from the little settlement of Paicines.

Before receiving the grant of this land, Angel Castro, a native Californian, had married Isabel Butron. In 1835 he had been sub-mayordomo of Misión San Juan Bautista and at the time of receiving this grant was the commander of a militia company at San José and Branciforte.

Castro's house, a two-story adobe, was built about two miles south of the village of Paicines. The large living room in this house was reproduced and used as the setting for the ballroom scene in Belasco's production of *The Rose of the Rancho*, in which a daughter, one of the eight children of Angel Castro, was the heroine. In 1916 the adobe, no longer used as a family residence, had been reduced to the position of bunkhouse for farm laborers.

Rancho Cienaga de los Paicines has passed through several ownerships since the day of Angel Castro. The present owner purchased it from Dr. Macomber, who in turn had purchased it from Alexander B. Grogan. A good part of it is now planted to prune orchards and farm crops.

Other Ranchos

Two other ranchos in this county that received recognition from the United States in the form of patents were: Lomerias Muertas, along the Pajaro River, consisting of one and one-half square leagues granted to José Antonio Castro in 1842 and patented in 1866 to the heirs of José María Sánchez, who was the claimant in 1842; and Rancho San Joaquín, or Rosa Morada, 7,424 acres lying northeast of Hollister and granted by Governor Gutiérrez to Cruz Cervantes in 1836. The grant followed Cervantes' petition of the previous year. At the end of ten years Cervantes had horses, cattle, and sheep, with corrals for them, on his land. He had also four or five acres under cultivation.

Ranchos lying on the boundary line and extending far into Monterey County were: Los Vergeles, Cienaga del Gabilán, and San Lorenzo.

Gabilan Peak

The highest peak in the Gabilan range of mountains on the border between the counties of San Benito and Monterey is sometimes called Gavilan ("sparrow hawk") Peak and sometimes Hawk's Peak, as well as by the name by which it is locally known, Gabilan Peak. It was to this spot that Frémont took his little band of followers, after having been ordered by Mexican officials to leave the country.

Taking possession of the peak, he erected a log fort there on March 6, 1846. The United States flag was raised over the fort, and Frémont held possession for three days. Meanwhile, General José Castro was making preparations to dislodge the Americans, and, since Castro's force outnumbered his, five to one, Frémont slowly retreated northward to Sutter's Fort.

Hunt and Sanchez have this to say concerning the outcome of the Gabilan episode: "The affair of Hawk's Peak amounted to but little in itself, but the results were unfortunate, both in stirring up antipathy on the part of the Americans toward the Californians and in outraging the feelings of the Californians and giving color to the persistent rumor that the Mexican Government had purposed expelling all foreign residents from the province. In the light of subsequent events, the episode may be regarded as a direct cause of the Bear Flag revolt."

A memorial flagstaff of iron was erected in 1908 on Gabilan Peak. There are no traces of the old fort left.

The New Idria Mines

The New Idria Quicksilver Mine, where work began in the '50's, lies on the slope below San Carlos Peak. The date of the discovery of this ore deposit is unknown, but tradition says that the Mission Fathers, before the coming of the Americans, made assays of it and determined it to be cinnabar. Bret Harte, in his *Story of a Mine*, attributes the accidental discovery of the first quicksilver in the region to a group of prospectors who were burning specimens of rock to test it for silver and were surprised to find a pool of "liquid silver" in the ashes of their improvised furnace.

With actual records that go back to 1854, it ranks among the most famous quicksilver mines of the world. The name, New Idria, was copied from the Idria Mine in Austria. The same square type of furnace used in that country was also used here at first, but was supplanted long ago by a more effective type.

In 1861 William Brewer of the Whitney Geologic Survey kept a record of the findings of that party on a visit paid to this region. They visited three mines, the New Idria, the San Carlos, and the Aurora, all within a radius of a few miles. They found the square furnaces of the New Idria at an approximate elevation of 2,500 feet and the excavation of the San Carlos at almost double that elevation. The two mines, not then under the same management, were later consolidated into one company. Ore from the higher mine, however, was treated at the New Idria works even at that early time, when it was hauled down the mountain side by means of ox teams. In later years iron buckets suspended from a cable have lowered the ore to be treated.

By July 1861 many miles of tunnels had been driven into the mountain side, among them the 700-foot Sleeman tunnel in 1859 and the Day and Myers tunnel. Through these dark passages Brewer and his party wandered "mole-like" for six hours; a part of this time they were "a thousand feet from daylight."

In the '50's and '60's the town nearest to the mine was San Juan, sixty-eight miles away. The stage route between them became a well-traveled road livened with the jangle of bells worn by the freight teams. From six to twelve horses or mules constituted one of these teams. The driver sat on a wheel horse and guided the team by means of a jerk line fastened to the bit of one of the lead horses.

The road from the mine followed San Carlos Creek down to Griswold Creek, named for a rancher who somehow eked out an existence in the region that is still called Griswolds. It passed several adobe houses, a few of which stand vacant beside the route today, and also certain cabins constructed of rough lumber (also vacant today). Next it came to Panoche Creek and ran through the Panoche Valley, famous for cattle pasture, until it reached Tres Pinos Creek, which it crossed and recrossed by means of fords. That part of the road has long been called the "wiggletail." The roadbed of today has been somewhat improved and, for a part of the distance, is now cut out of the canyon side at a higher level. However, few bridges have been built, and it is still necessary to ford the stream at many places. Finally the village that was then called Tres Pinos, now called Paicines, was reached, and the remainder of the journey to San Juan was on a more even grade.

At the time of Brewer's visit a force of between two and three hundred men was employed at the New Idria mines. The crew has since varied below or above that number, but work has continued practically all these years. The mines were sold in 1898 to a company of men who formed the New Idria Quicksilver Mining Company, the name under which it carries on business today. During the World War the place was policed by a company of soldiers.

Needed supplies are now received by motor truck from San Francisco. Many of the old cabins are vacant, but those that are occupied are furnished with electricity. Descendants of some of the very early miners live and work here. On the top of a hill approached over paths red with cinnabar stands the neatly painted schoolhouse, above the door of which appears the name "New Idria."

Eight miles from New Idria are the Picacho mines, which were discovered in 1858. The huge red peaks in their vicinity rise out of a wild and picturesque country, seventy-five miles south of Hollister, where grizzly bears were once numerous. The town of Picacho once existed but had disappeared by 1880.

Tres Pinos; Paicines

The settlement, little more than a post office and general store, that is known as Paicines stands at the junction of the

Pinnacles Road and the Hollister–New Idria Road. This spot used to be called Tres Pinos, named for three stunted pine trees that grew near there on the bank of Tres Pinos Creek. It was known as Tres Pinos when Vásquez made his last robbery at Snyder's store that used to stand near this junction. The robbery occurred in August 1873. Three men were killed by the bandit at that time: one a deaf man, who did not hear the peremptory orders given by the bandit; one a Portuguese, who did not understand the language in which the orders were given; and the third, the hotel keeper across the street, who refused to open his door and was felled by a bullet sent through it. The residents of the county became so incensed at the callous crime that Vásquez and his gang sought safety in the south. Trailed by sheriffs, they were brought back to Hollister in May 1874; and, after trial in San José, Vásquez was executed there on March 19, 1875.

When the railroad was built out from Hollister to a point west of the original settlement of Tres Pinos, a town grew up at the station and it also was called Tres Pinos. After a time the older settlement came to be called Paicines, for Rancho Cienaga de los Paicines in its vicinity. The word itself is supposed to be the name of a tribe of Indians that once lived in the region. The main activity of the new Tres Pinos was the handling of freight for the New Idria mines. Although hauling by railroad has been largely superseded by modern motor-truck service, the village still seems to be prosperous.

Hollister

In the autumn of 1868 the San Justo Homestead Association was formed by a group of fifty farmers, who held in it one share each. They purchased from Colonel W. W. Hollister the eastern part of Rancho San Justo, containing 21,000 acres, for the sum of $400,000 and divided the best part of the land into fifty homestead lots—one for each member. One hundred acres in the middle was reserved for a town site and was laid out in blocks, lots, and streets. This one hundred acres is now the center of Hollister.

A man very prominent in the formation of the Association and the town was T. S. Hawkins, who came to California from Missouri in 1860. He settled first in Santa Clara County but came to what is now San Benito County in 1867, renting 1,000 acres of virgin soil and planting it to grain. He hauled seed for this planting from Gilroy over a robber-infested road. The produce of his planting was hauled by wagon to Alviso, whence it was carried by boat to San Francisco. In the following year, Mr. Hawkins helped to form the San Justo Homestead Association, of which he was made secretary and general manager in 1870. At that time he gave up farming and turned his attention wholly to the advancement of the town.

Because it seemed a waste of time to go all the way to the Coast to transact legal business at the county seat at Monterey, the suggestion of forming a new county met with approval. Agitation of the subject resulted in the organization of San Benito County on February 12, 1874, with the new town of Hollister as the county seat.

The Hazel Hawkins Memorial Hospital, completed in Hollister in 1907, was erected by Mr. Hawkins as a tribute to his granddaughter, who had died in 1902.

The Pinnacles

On November 19, 1794, Vancouver, who had been ill for some time in Monterey, had sufficiently recovered to go on an exploring expedition. With a small party on horseback, he set out across the Salinas Valley and reached the southern termination of the Gabilan Range, where he "was gratified with the sight of the most extraordinary mountains" that he had ever beheld. One side "presented the appearance of a sumptuous edifice fallen into decay; the columns, which looked as if they had been raised with much labor and industry, were of great magnitude, seemed to be of an excellent form, and seemed to be composed of . . . . cream coloured stone." Vancouver is apparently the only early traveler who left a record of a visit to this region. The curious rocks that he saw have occasionally been called "Vancouver's Pinnacles" since that time.

In *The Days of a Man,* Dr. David Starr Jordan has written: "From 1904 to 1908 it was my pleasure to assist an ardent mountain lover, Mr. C. S. Hain of Tres Pinos, in securing for the people as a Government Forest Reserve, a singular district known as the 'Pinnacles' lying in the Gavilan Range on the line between San Benito and Monterey counties. There the mountain range of yellow Miocene sandstone has been scored into deep gulches by the long action of small streams unaided by frost or ice. The cuts are very narrow and regular scarcely widened even at the top, and the cliffs assume varied fantastic and picturesque forms. The forests are of little consequence, being of scant oak and digger pines, but many rare flowers are found in the tract, and some of the precipitous walls bear nests of the great California Condor—Gymogyps—a majestic vulture with wing spread of from nine to ten feet."

This area was set aside as a National Monument by proclamation of President Theodore Roosevelt on January 16, 1908. By grants made in 1923 and 1924, the area was increased to 2,980 acres. In 1931 the county of San Benito purchased land from private owners that increased the total acreage to 4,609 acres, and by the further acquisition of the Chalone Peak in July 1933 the monument now covers nearly 10,000 acres. The spire-like formations of the Pinnacles rise to a height of from 600 to 1,000 feet, and beneath them are caves and subterranean passages. An amphitheatre enclosed by smaller pinnacles has been named in honor of Dr. Jordan.

Mortars, pestles, and other relics have been found within the reserve, and a museum for their preservation is planned. The Pinnacles National Monument lies, except for a very small corner, in San Benito County and is entered about thirty-five miles south of Hollister.

SOURCES

[Credit is here given for source material, and permission to quote is hereby acknowledged]

ELDER, DAVID PAUL. *The Old Spanish Missions of California.* Paul Elder & Company, San Francisco, 1913

GOODWIN, CARDINAL. *John Charles Frémont: An Explanation of His Career.* Stanford University Press, Stanford University, 1930

HARTE, BRET. *The Story of a Mine.* Houghton Mifflin Company, New York, no date

HITTELL, THEODORE H. *History of California.* 4 vols. Pacific Press Publishing House and Occidental Publishing Company, San Francisco, 1885

HOYLE, M. F. *Crimes and Career of Tiburcio Vasques, the Bandit of San Benito County and Notorious Early California Outlaw.* Evening Free Lance, Hollister, California, 1927

HUNT, ROCKWELL D., and NELLIE VAN DE GRIFT SANCHEZ. *A Short History of California.* Thomas Y. Crowell Company, New York, 1929

JORDAN, DAVID STARR. *The Days of a Man.* 2 vols. World Book Company, Yonkers on Hudson, New York, 1922

NEVINS, ALLAN. *Frémont, the West's Greatest Adventurer.* 2 vols. Harper & Brothers, New York, 1928

(ROBINSON, ALFRED). *Life in California.* H. G. Collins, Paternoster Row, London, 1845

SMITH, SARAH BIXBY. *Adobe Days, Being the Truthful Narrative of the Events in the Life of a California Girl on a Sheep Ranch and in El Pueblo de Nuestra Señora de Los Angeles While It Was Yet a Small and Humble Town.* Enlarged edition, Jake Zeitlin, Los Angeles, 1931

SAN FRANCISCO COUNTY

San Francisco County (San Francisco is Spanish for St. Francis) derived its name from Misión San Francisco de Asís, established within the present boundary lines of the city in 1776. San Francisco County was one of the original twenty-seven counties. Until 1856 the county included what is now San Mateo County, and the city of San Francisco was the county seat of the entire section. After that date, the government was consolidated, operating as the City and County of San Francisco. At the time of the fire, following the earthquake of 1906, the bulk of the city records were destroyed. Fortunately, however, many of the pre-state records in Spanish were saved.

Discovery of the Golden Gate

The entrance to San Francisco Bay, La Boca del Puerto de San Francisco, was discovered November 1, 1769, by Sergeant José de Ortega, pathfinder of Gaspar de Portolá's expedition and the first white man to see San Francisco Bay.

The expedition was searching for the lost bay of Monterey and had proceeded up the coast as far as San Pedro Valley. From this point, Portolá had commissioned Ortega to explore as far north as Point Reyes, which he had seen from the summit of the Montara Mountains just east of Point San Pedro. The channel of the Golden Gate, however, prevented Ortega and his party from reaching their objective. They were obliged to return without reaching Point Reyes; but, unknowingly, they had discovered the greatest harbor on the Pacific Coast.

Ortega's trail had covered the coast from San Pedro to Point Lobos, but when his way was blocked by the deep waters of the Golden Gate, he proceeded along the south shore of the channel and climbed La Loma Alta (later called Telegraph Hill). From this vantage point, he could see the whole expanse of the Bay, its islands, and the Contra Costa Hills beyond.

Having made his observations, Ortega returned to camp to report. Portolá, however, did not realize the tremendous importance of his discovery. He was looking for the bay of Monterey.

The Spaniards had called the gateway to the newly discovered bay "La Boca del Puerto de San Francisco," but an American gave it the name of "Golden Gate." In his *Memoirs* General John Charles Frémont says: "To this gate I gave the name of Chrysopylae, or Golden Gate; for the same reason that the harbor of Byzantium [afterward Constantinople] was called Chrysoceras, or Golden Horn." In a footnote he appends: "The form of the entrance into the bay of San Francisco and its advantages for commerce, Asiatic included, suggested to me the name which I gave to this entrance and which I put upon the map that accompanied a geographical Memoir addressed to the Senate of the United States in June 1848."

Juan Manuel de Ayala, in the historic ship "San Carlos," and José Cañizares, his subordinate, were the first white men to enter San Francisco Bay. In the spring of 1769 the "San Carlos" had carried supplies and colonists for the new pueblo to be founded in San Diego. Again, in 1775, with Manuel de Ayala in command, it sailed with the fleet sent from Mexico to explore San Francisco Bay. On August 4 the entrance to the Bay was reached. Ayala, suffering from a wound accidentally incurred on the voyage, sent Cañizares ahead to find anchorage. The latter did not return all that day, the currents and tides of the Golden Gate being too strong for the little launch in which he made the reconnoiter-

ing expedition. On the evening of August 5, therefore, Ayala, in the little "San Carlos," passed through the Golden Gate and into the great port of the West. Cañizares and Ayala had thus jointly gained the honor of making the first recorded entrance into San Francisco Bay by way of the Golden Gate. Ayala and his men remained in the Bay for forty-four days, exploring every arm and inlet and going as far as the mouth of the San Joaquin River, at the same time taking soundings and making a map. Two of the names given at this time are in use today in slightly different forms. One is that of the island just inside the strait, which was called Nuestra Señora de los Angeles, "Our Lady of the Angels," and is known today as Angel Island. In a sheltered cove of this island, the "San Carlos" remained during most of its stay in the Bay. Another island was named Isla de los Alcatraces, the "Island of the Pelicans," and we have the name today in Alcatraz Island. The first lighthouse to be put to use on the coast of California by the United States Light Service was placed on Alcatraz Island in 1854.

It was Ayala's exploration of San Francisco Bay that established the suitability of its shores for a settlement, and the location at San Francisco of the mission and presidio was largely influenced by this expedition.

The Founding of San Francisco

Juan Bautista de Anza, "one of the most remarkable men who ever appeared on the field of California history . . . . , was a member of the presidial aristocracy of the frontier provinces of New Spain." He early distinguished himself, not only as a valiant Indian fighter, but as an officer of unusual abilities and irreproachable character.

Anza's lifelong ambition to find a practicable overland route to California began in early boyhood, but it was realized only after meeting and overcoming many delays and difficulties. The great need for a land route for carrying supplies to the struggling colonies in Alta California and the inadequacy of the route by way of Baja California were clearly pointed out by Padre Junípero Serra. This, together with the growing menace of foreign aggression in California, finally influenced Bucareli, viceroy of New Spain, to push Anza's proposed expedition.

Anza successfully accomplished his first journey overland to California in 1774. Although the jealousy of Governor Rivera prevented him from proceeding as far as San Francisco at this time, the route had been opened and the way paved to the real colonization of California and the founding of San Francisco.

The success of Anza's expedition in 1774 caused Bucareli to do everything in his power to strengthen Alta California, both within itself and against any possible attacks from without, and to utilize the new route to the fullest extent possible. All plans finally culminated in the project to settle San Francisco and the region round about what was known to the Spaniards as the Río Grande de San Francisco (now known as the mouth of the Sacramento and the San Joaquin rivers). These settlements were to serve not only as buffers against possible outside enemies, but as a base for further settlements to the north.

Accordingly, a second expedition was planned on which Anza was to take settlers and supplies with him to found a presidio and mission at San Francisco. After fearful hardships encountered in desert and mountains, and needless delays caused by the jealousy of Rivera, this remarkable undertaking was accomplished.

Anza himself reached San Francisco on March 27, 1776, but Rivera's dilatory movements made it necessary for him to leave his settlers temporarily at Monterey. The final lap of the journey had led along the hills, by way of Ingleside, with a "good-sized lake of fresh water," clearly what is now called Lake Merced, lying to the westward. From this point the little company marched through what is now Golden Gate Park to the southern edge of the Presidio's military reservation, a mile and a half south of Fort Point. His camp at San Francisco was made at what is now known as Mountain Lake, later called by the Spaniards Laguna del Presidio. The creek, which Anza called Arroyo del Puerto, is now known as Lobos Creek and forms the southern boundary of the Presidio reservation. Anza made a thorough survey of the region, marking out the sites for the presidio and mission. For the presidio fort he chose a location which the Spaniards called Cantil Blanco ("White Cliff"), but which is today known as Fort Point, where old Fort Scott now stands. Here Anza planted a cross "on the extreme point of the white cliff" to mark the place where the fort should be built. He selected a place for the mission near a little rivulet which he named Dolores. The mesa, or table-land between the Laguna del Presidio and the Cantil Blanco, he designated as the spot where the presidio town was to be.

After exploring the Bay and the River of San Francisco to the junction of the San Joaquin and Sacramento rivers, Anza returned to Monterey. He was greatly disappointed not to be able to settle his colonists in San Francisco, but since he could not do so without the aid of Rivera, he left Monterey amid "the tears and lamentations of the settlers, who had learned to revere and love him in the course of their long march from Sonora."

The final settling of the colonists at San Francisco was accomplished by José Joaquín Moraga, Anza's faithful and capable lieutenant, in the summer of 1776. The Presidio was dedicated on September 17, and on October 9 the Misión San Francisco de Asís was founded.

"Thus had the great port been occupied, and the vitally needed settlers, with their equally needed herds of domestic animals, were now in Alta California to stay. For the first time it was possible to say that the province had been placed upon a permanent basis. There was no longer any likelihood that it would be abandoned and left open for another power."

Anza never returned to the land of his boyhood dreams, but his work there had "an enduring importance beyond anything that had ever happened in the history of the Californias." Back of his work, too, stood that other great figure, Antonio Bucareli, viceroy of Mexico, who had aided, encouraged, and pushed the enterprise in every way within his power from the beginning to the end.

The Presidio of San Francisco

The site of the Presidio of San Francisco was selected by Juan Bautista de Anza on March 28, 1776. On June 27, 1776, Lieutenant Moraga and the little band of settlers, which had traveled all the way from Sonora to Monterey with Anza, made temporary camp on the Laguna de Manantial, now Eighteenth and Dolores streets. There they stayed throughout the summer while the Presidio was being built. On September 17 the Presidio was dedicated and Moraga took formal possession in the name of the King of Spain.

The Spanish and Mexican governments never supported the Presidio of San Francisco adequately, and, consequently, it was never well garrisoned. After 1835 regular troops were no longer stationed there, and by 1840 it was in ruins. Since the American occupation on July 9, 1846, it has been one of the principal United States Army reservations on the Pacific Coast.

The sites of the old Spanish Presidio buildings have been marked. A bronze tablet set in a granite block was placed by the California Chapter, D.A.R., in 1928 at the southwest corner of the original Presidio building, and the other three corners were also located and marked by concrete posts bearing bronze inscriptions. The only building left from the Spanish period is the adobe comandante's headquarters on the south side of the parade ground. This was the officers' quarters under Spanish, Mexican, and American rule, and is now used as the Officers' Club House. Four old Spanish cannon, dated as early as 1673, stand in front of this building.

Misión San Francisco de Asís (Dolores)

The first plans of the Visitador of Mexico, José de Gálvez, did not call for a mission dedicated to St. Francis, founder of the Franciscan Order. The Father Presidente, Junípero Serra, protested this omission, but Gálvez replied, "If Saint Francis wishes a mission, let him show you a good port, and then let it bear his name."

Accordingly, when Portolá's party discovered San Francisco Bay, the Franciscan chroniclers in the party exclaimed, "This is the port to which the Visitador referred and to which the Saint has led us."

But it was not until seven years later, on October 9, 1776, that Misión San Francisco de Asís was dedicated. Juan Bautista de Anza had selected the site of the Mission in the spring of 1776, and the place which he designated was never changed. This was on the bank of the little lake which Anza called Laguna de Manantial, now filled in. The stream which flowed into it he called "Arroyo de los Dolores," because it was on the Friday of Sorrows (Viernes de los Dolores) that he examined it. The name of the Mission itself in after years became popularized to "Mission Dolores." Laguna de Manantial covered roughly the city blocks bounded by Fifteenth, Twenty-third, Guerrero, and Harrison streets at one time. They are now filled with residences.

The present Mission church was begun on April 25, 1782, when the first stone was put in place, and finished by 1791. Mission Dolores, with its simple yet massive façade, its bells, and its overhanging roof (all well preserved), has a quaint individuality which sets it quite apart from its more elaborate sister Missions. It has none of the usual arches, arcades, and towers which adorned the latter, but its massive simplicity makes it none the less impressive.

In the baptistry, which has remained at the Mission from the beginning, the infant María de la Concepción Marcella Argüello, daughter of José Darío Argüello, was christened on February 26, 1791. Her story is told in our section on Solano County, her burial place.

The shadow of a redwood cross in the enclosed cemetery beside the Mission falls athwart old graves. Here lies the dust of Don José Joaquín Moraga, follower of Anza and founder of the San Francisco Presidio, who died in 1785. Here, too, lie the remains of Don Luis Antonio Argüello, governor of Alta California from November 1822 to November 1825, who was laid here with religious rites after his death in 1830. Other marked graves are here. In memory of forgotten dead stands the Grotto of Our Lady of Lourdes.

Today, Mission Dolores stands in the shadow of a modern parish church. Only in Lent are services held in the old chapel, but in its quiet aisles and its peaceful graveyard are rich memories of San Francisco's picturesque and romantic beginnings.

Castillo de San Joaquín

Castillo de San Joaquín was a Spanish fort located on Fort Point near the old Presidio but separate from it. It was completed and dedicated on December 9, 1794. Castillo de San Joaquín would never have withstood a siege for "the structure rested mainly on sand; the brick-faced walls crumbled at the shock whenever a salute was fired; the guns were badly mounted, and, for the most part, worn out." The fort, built principally of adobe in the form of an immense horseshoe, gradually became a ruin, and after 1835 no troops were stationed there.

On July 1, 1846, as an aftermath of the Bear Flag Revolt, Frémont and twelve of his men crossed over from Sausalito in the launch "Moscow," and spiked the guns of the Castillo de San Joaquín. In telling of this affair in his *Memoirs,* Frémont says that the guns he spiked were large handsome pieces but he fails to add that they were dismounted and lying on the ground.

During the years 1854 to 1860 the old site of the Castillo was dug down to sea level and an American fort, Fort Winfield Scott, now useless and out of date, was built on the leveled site. It stands within the present Presidio reservation.

Yerba Buena Cove

The first Englishman to sail into San Francisco Bay was Captain George Vancouver, who came on the night of November 14, 1792, in the sloop-of-war "Discovery," dropping anchor "about a league below the Presidio in a place they called Yerba Buena." Eldredge says that this "is the first reference we have to the little cove where, forty-three years later, Richardson's tent marked the beginning of the modern city. Vancouver's map . . . . shows the anchorage in Yerba Buena Cove, in other words, off the foot of Market Street."

Vancouver was received hospitably by the priest of the Mission, Father Antonio Danti, and by the comandante of the Presidio, Hermenegildo Sal. He has left an interesting description of the country, the Bay, the Presidio, and of his trip to Misión Santa Clara.

When Vancouver came again the next year, he was not received so warmly, for Don Hermenegildo had been reprimanded for letting an Englishman see the defenseless condition of the Spanish possessions on the Bay.

The Russians in San Francisco

Count Nikolai Rezánof came to San Francisco in 1806. The colonists in Russia's Alaska settlements were starving and could no longer survive unless a permanent source of food supply could be found. With this purpose in mind, Rezánof sailed south to seek negotiations with the Spanish officials of San Francisco, well knowing that trade with foreigners was forbidden and that entry into San Francisco Bay was against Spanish law. He was desperate, however, for his voyage was a race with death, and on April 5, 1806, he sailed past the Presidio fort and entered the harbor.

José Darío Argüello, a very influential man and the best friend of Governor Arrillaga, was comandante of San Francisco at this time. His daughter, Concepción, or Concha, as she was affectionately called by her family, was reputed to be the most beautiful woman in Alta California. Count Rezánof was entertained in the Argüello household during his entire stay in San Francisco. While there he not only was captivated by the lovely Concepción but also won her heart.

Meanwhile, by gifts and a display of the eagerly sought Russian wares, he had won the favor of the settlers, and especially of the Mission Fathers. With such powerful allies to aid him, Rezánof at length overcame Governor Arrillaga's reluctance to grant the exchange of goods which he sought.

On May 21, six weeks after his coming, Rezánof sailed away to succor his starving people in Alaska and to obtain permission from the Czar of Russia and the Pope to return to California and claim his Spanish bride. The mission in

Alaska was accomplished, but Rezánof's untimely death on the steppes of Siberia frustrated all further plans. Concha's lover never returned to her.

The beautiful aftermath of this romance rightfully belongs to Benicia, Solano County, the place where Concepción spent the closing years of her life and where she lies buried. Its political significance concerns the Russian settlements at Bodega and Fort Ross.

The Farallones

In 1543 the Farallon Islands were discovered by the Cabrillo-Ferrelo expedition, and in 1579 Sir Francis Drake landed there to secure a supply of seal meat. Drake named them the Islands of St. James, but in 1775 Bodega named them the Farallones de los Frailes, in honor of the Franciscan friars.

During 1809 to 1812, these islands developed as a station for the Russian-American Fur Company, and a Russian settlement was made there. San Francisco Bay was full of sea otter, and the Russians entered the harbor in their canoes, hunting under the very guns of the Spanish fort.

The Farallones have always been a natural rookery. In 1849, when food soared to fabulous prices in San Francisco, it became a profitable source of supply for the egg hunters. This traffic continued for forty years, until the quarrels of rival egg companies caused the United States marshals to interfere. Bird lovers were later aided by Admiral Dewey in their efforts to have the islands declared a bird sanctuary. It is now one of the four in the state.

In 1855 a lighthouse was erected on the Farallon Islands. The place has a long disastrous record of shipwrecks, its bays and inlets bearing the names of many lost steamers and sailing vessels.

Yerba Buena, the Forerunner of San Francisco

Captain William A. Richardson was the founder of Yerba Buena ("good herb," Spanish for wild mint), which became the nucleus of the modern city of San Francisco. Richardson, an Englishman by birth, came to San Francisco in 1822, when the Mexican flag was floating over the Presidio, and Governor Solá, the last Spanish ruler, was just leaving California. From Solá, Richardson had gained permission to settle permanently at San Francisco, and in return for this privilege he was to teach the young Spaniards the arts of navigation and carpentering, two things of which the inhabitants were sorely in need.

Richardson was a master mariner, and not only taught the Spaniards and Indians at the San Francisco Presidio the trades of carpenter and shipwright, as well as navigation, but was also the first to develop extensively trade and communication by water on San Francisco Bay. For three years he was manager of the transporters which traded between San Francisco and the embarcadero at Misión San José. He piloted vessels in and out of the Bay, and later became Captain of the Port and Bay of San Francisco under the direction of General Vallejo, comandante general.

It was Richardson's plan to found a port town on San Francisco Bay at the best possible anchoring place. For this purpose he chose Yerba Buena Cove. Governor Figueroa, California's most enlightened Mexican governor, acted upon these plans and made Richardson San Francisco's first harbor master.

In 1835 Richardson moved to Yerba Buena with his family, living in a tent for three months. "This tent was the first habitation ever erected in Yerba Buena. At the time, Richardson's only neighbors were bears, coyotes and wolves. The nearest people lived either at the Presidio or at Mission

Dolores." In October 1835 he replaced the tent by a board house. He was the "solitary settler" described by Richard Henry Dana, Jr., in his *Two Years before the Mast*. This region is now in the heart of Chinatown, and the site where Richardson's tent stood is now on Grant Avenue (formerly Dupont) between Clay and Washington streets.

In 1836 he built a more elaborate dwelling, an adobe house, "which contained a parlor, commodious bedrooms, and a sitting and dining room which was used at times as a ballroom. The walls were thick with blinds or massive shutters closing the windows on the inside." This was the "Casa Grande" of the village until 1848, it being the largest and most pretentious building there. It withstood several devastating fires, but was taken down in 1852 and replaced by the Adelphi Theater.

The settlement at Yerba Buena Cove was, from the first, predominantly Anglo-Saxon and American, a group of foreigners surrounded by Spanish, Mexicans, and Indians.

The next settler there was Jacob Primer Leese, an American trader, who erected a second substantial frame house in the settlement in 1836. The site of the Jacob Leese house is "in Grant on the west side, mostly in the intersection of Grant and Clay," according to J. N. Bowman. The first Fourth of July celebration in San Francisco was held at this house in 1836. Many notable families about the Bay attended the festivities, among them being the Estudillo, Martínez, Castro, Guerrero, and de Haro families. General Vallejo himself was present, and several ships, anchored in the Cove, took part in the celebration.

This house, which was built of redwood, was the center for a large trading business which Leese and his partners, Spear and Hinckley, carried on with the ranchos bordering San Francisco Bay. To commemorate this house, the Tamalpais Chapter, D.A.R., placed a tablet October 3, 1931.

Mexican Land Grants

Within the original boundary of San Francisco County lay private ranchos obtained through Mexican governors. When the county was divided in 1856, by far the greater part of the land thus granted was given to San Mateo County. The diminished county of San Francisco occupied the tip of the peninsula, where lands had been reserved for Mission and Presidio use and where little had been granted to private individuals. The line drawn to separate the two counties passed due west from a point on San Francisco Bay a little east of Visitacion Valley to the Pacific Ocean and cut the southern end of Lake Merced.

Two of the old ranchos were cut by this line. Rancho Laguna de la Merced, consisting of one-half a square league, was one of these. It was granted in 1835 to José Antonio Galindo, a corporal in the San Francisco militia. After holding it for two years, he sold it on May 12, 1837, to Francisco de Haro for one hundred cows and $25 in goods.

The purchaser, Francisco de Haro, had arrived in California with Governor Argüello in 1819, as a sublieutenant in the San Blas Infantry. In 1824 he was one of the leaders in the suppression of a revolt among Indian neophytes. In that year, too, he married Josefa, daughter of José Sánchez, and thereafter lived in what is now San Francisco, where they reared a family of interesting children. In 1838, within a year after purchasing the rancho, he was made alcalde of the village and in that office was responsible for the guardianship of persons arrested for offenses against law and order. A problem arose when Galindo, former owner of the rancho, was taken into custody for the murder of José Peralta. Lack of a jail compelled Alcalde de Haro to order his fellow townsmen to act as guards. After holding the prisoner under trying circumstances for three months, he finally appealed to

Governor Alvarado on February 27, 1839, for permission to send Galindo to San José, where prison facilities were available.

Francisco de Haro held many important positions under the Mexican regime and is frequently mentioned in the annals of San Francisco. He died at a comparatively early age in 1849, his death being hastened by grief over the tragic deaths of his twin sons at the San Rafael Mission embarcadero across the Bay.

The second rancho cut by the new county boundary line was the Cañada de Guadalupe la Visitación y Rodeo Viejo, only a small portion of which was left in San Francisco County. It consisted of two leagues and was granted by Governor Alvarado in 1841 to the well-known early resident of San Francisco, Jacob Primer Leese. As the grantee had a house in Yerba Buena, forerunner of San Francisco, he and his family resided for only a short time upon the rancho property, which he afterward sold. The United States patent for the tract was issued in 1865 to Henry R. Payson and William Pierce; the former possessed the larger part, 5,473 acres, the latter, 942 acres.

A tract of 12,643.44 acres of Pueblo land was patented to the City of San Francisco in June 1884.

Other grants of land in the San Francisco area recognized by the United States government were few in number and small in extent. One of these was the Ojo de Agua de Figueroa, 100 varas, granted to Apolinario Miranda in 1833. Miranda was a soldier in the San Francisco Company from 1819 to 1836. He constructed an adobe house to replace an earlier temporary structure in 1834. His wife was Juana Briones. It is recorded that in her house in the North Beach section, the only dwelling between Yerba Buena and the Presidio, she ministered to distressed sailors who required aid. The house is known to have stood about where Filbert and Powell streets intersect. Her husband was at one time brought before the alcalde for ill-treating his wife. She long outlived her husband, who was buried at Mission Dolores, ending her days in Santa Clara County.

Among the other small grants were: Las Camaritas, 18.57 acres, patented to Ferdinand Vassault; two lots in the Pueblo land patented to J. P. Leese in 1858; Mission Dolores, 8.54 acres, patented to Bishop J. S. Alemany in 1858; and a few others, varying from half an acre to 25 acres, given to various persons.

The Old Custom House

The building of a Custom House at San Francisco was authorized by the Mexican governor in 1844. Work was begun that summer and completed in September 1845. It was a one-story, four-room adobe with veranda and tile roof and was erected mostly by Indian labor. It fronted the northwest corner of the Plaza (now Portsmouth Square), while its north end faced what is now Washington Street.

During the American occupation, the Custom House was used as a barrack, and in front stood the flagpole on which Captain Montgomery raised the American flag on July 9, 1846. The alcalde and revenue officers used it later, and in 1850 it was occupied by a bank and law offices. It was destroyed by fire in 1851.

The Plaza Called Portsmouth Square

Captain John B. Montgomery, of the "Portsmouth," received orders from Commodore Sloat, on July 8, 1846, to take possession of Yerba Buena and the northern frontier. On the morning of July 9, Montgomery and his men landed at what is now the corner of Clay and Leidesdorff streets.

Montgomery Street was named after Captain Montgomery, and the Plaza, where the first American flag was raised in San Francisco, was afterward called Portsmouth Square in honor of the United States sloop-of-war "Portsmouth," which had conveyed Montgomery and his men into the harbor. A marker placed by the San Francisco chapters of the D.A.R. in 1924 commemorates this, the first raising of the American flag in San Francisco.

A tablet at the corner of Clay and Montgomery streets was placed by the Native Sons of the Golden West in 1916. This tablet not only commemorates the historical event referred to but also brings to the attention of all who view it the fact that the water of San Francisco Bay once came up to the foot of Clay Street almost as far as Montgomery Street.

Portsmouth Square, which thus superseded the Plaza, became, in 1849 and the '50's, the place where the principal gambling houses were situated. "Neither tree, shrub, nor grass adorned it, but it contained a rude platform for public speaking, a tall flag staff, and a cow pen enclosed by rough board."

Today, Portsmouth Square is planted with trees and grass. The fantastic pagoda roofs of Chinatown look down upon it, and Chinese mothers sun their plump babies on its green slope. As in the days of Stevenson and Jack London, men of all nations still seek its hospitable benches, where they may let the wheels of progress roll by unheeded for a few brief, restful moments.

"Portsmouth Square is now the chief center of Stevenson associations in the city; for it was here Robert Louis went to observe at close range and to talk to the flotsam and jetsam of humanity drifting in from the mighty Pacific Ocean. Who knows but he found here Long John Silver and Blind Pew? The monument in Portsmouth Square, planned and executed by Bruce Porter and Willis Polk, is the perpetual memorial of San Francisco to Stevenson." This is the first monument to be erected anywhere to him, and, of all the landmarks in San Francisco, is the one most nearly connected with Stevenson. It stands in the midst of that part of the city which he found most interesting and which he portrayed in *The Wrecker*.

Much of the work which Stevenson began in Monterey was finished in San Francisco, notably *Across the Plains* and *The Amateur Emigrant*. Some of his dearest friendships, too, were formed there, among them those with Virgil Williams, painter and founder of the California School of Art, and his wife; Judge Rearden and Judge John Boalt; and Charles Warren Stoddard, professor and author. Stoddard was influential in centering Stevenson's interest in the South Seas, where he spent the latter part of his life.

"No other Stevenson land-mark remains in the city. The old Carson House (608 Bush Street) was torn down long before the great fire and a new building erected, and this, with all that section, was eventually burned. The house at No. 7 Montgomery Street, in which he lived a few days after his marriage, is gone, as well as Donadieu's (the restaurant on Bush Street, between Kearny and Dupont—now Grant) and the Sixth Street Coffee House (near Market)— all gone! And the Stoddard Studio on Rincon Hill where Stevenson visited the author of the 'South Sea Idylls'— this has been swallowed up by ravenous time too. No other building was frequented by Robert Louis in his San Francisco sojourn, which in truth was doubtless not more than five months," from December 1879 to May 1880.

San Francisco's First Schools

Soon after the American occupation, in 1846, the need of a school for the children of the rapidly growing town began to be agitated. In April 1847 the first private school in San Francisco was opened by J. D. Marston in a shanty on the west side of Grant Avenue between Broadway and Pacific. This was also San Francisco's first school and was attended by some twenty or thirty children, but it lasted only a few months.

The site of what has been called San Francisco's first public school is on the southwest corner of Portsmouth Square. In the autumn of 1847 a committee met to plan the building, and on April 3, 1848, school was opened by Thomas Douglas, a graduate of Yale. The gold excitement took Douglas away to the mines six weeks later, but the school was resumed in April 1849 by Rev. Albert Williams, a Presbyterian minister.

This small shanty of a schoolhouse was used for various purposes, "town hall, court house, people's court for trial of culprits by the first vigilance committee, school, church, and finally, jail. Owing to the range and variety of its uses, the building was dignified by the name of Public Institute." The Public Institute School, however (like others in that early period), was not a public school in the modern sense, for it was obliged to charge some tuition and was not under complete governmental control.

In October 1849, John Cotter Pelton, a young New England schoolteacher and a layman of the Baptist church, came to California to establish free public schools. On December 26, 1849, he opened a school in the First Baptist Church on Washington Street east of Stockton. There were only three children present the first day, but within a few days the number had increased to fifty. In spite of financial discouragements, Pelton would accept no tuition in his school and worked indefatigably to arouse public interest and action in behalf of the free public school as an established institution.

As a result of Pelton's efforts, his school was adopted by the city in March 1850, and the first public school in California became a reality. On April 8, 1850, the first school ordinance in the state was passed. This site has been marked with a bronze tablet placed by the Northern California Baptist Convention.

The First Churches

The Mormons, under Sam Brannan, held religious services in Captain Richardson's "Casa Grande" on Dupont Street soon after their arrival, and a Sunday school was organized by a Methodist missionary, Rev. James H. Wilbur, May 16, 1847. The former organization did not hold together long, and the Sunday school was soon disrupted by the gold stampede. But other organizations at once took the place of these.

On July 25, 1847, Chaplain Chester Newell, of the United States frigate "Independence," preached in the C. L. Ross store, on the northwest corner of Washington and Montgomery streets. Although there were probably other services held by ships' chaplains, this is the first recorded Protestant divine service in San Francisco.

The first record of a sermon preached after the opening of the mines was that of Rev. Elihu Anthony, a Methodist from New York. It was delivered in the Public Institute on September 3, 1848. Other services were held in this building that month, and in October Rev. Timothy Dwight Hunt, a native of New York, who had just returned from missionary work in the Sandwich Islands, was appointed chaplain of the town for one year. Services were held in the Institute, this being the only organized institution for Protestant worship in the city until the spring of 1849. It was patronized by members of every religious persuasion.

The first ships landing at San Francisco in the year 1849 brought not only feverish Argonauts seeking for the golden fleece but several missionary preachers as well. These men, together with the teachers and some of the merchants, such as C. L. Ross, W. D. M. Howard, Nathan Spear, and C. E. Wetmore, were the real builders and founders of San Francisco. They were the molders of the spiritual life of the city, working quietly in the midst of the rough, mad turmoil of the gold days to plant the finest traditions of the American nation in this new and chaotic commonwealth. In many cases these missionaries and their successors were both preachers and teachers and played a considerable part in the government as well.

In August 1849 the following Protestant organizations were holding services in the city: (1) The Chaplaincy, Rev. T. D. Hunt, Public Institute; (2) First Presbyterian, Rev. Albert Williams, in a large tent on Dupont Street, near Pacific; (3) First Baptist, Rev. O. C. Wheeler, church on Washington Street, near Stockton; (4) Protestant Episcopal, Rev. Flavil S. Mines, in the house of J. H. Merrill. It is interesting, also, to learn that "on the 8th of October, a Methodist Episcopal Church, shipped from Oregon and set up on a Powell Street lot, was dedicated by the missionary minister, the Rev. William Taylor, assisted by the Rev. Mr. Hunt, Rev. Albert Williams, and Rev. O. C. Wheeler."

On McAllister and Leavenworth streets, near the Civic Center, stands a structure named in honor of San Francisco's pioneer Methodist preacher, William Taylor, whose "unique career as street preacher earned for him the nickname 'California Taylor'." This building was erected as the William Taylor Church and Hotel by the united efforts of the Methodist churches of San Francisco and their friends, at a cost of over $3,000,000. Taylor and the Rev. Isaac Owens did much to establish religious and educational institutions in California, in the years between 1849 and 1856.

The present St. Francis Church on Vallejo Street is, after the Mission Dolores, the oldest parish in San Francisco. The present building is dated 1859. Its interior was destroyed by the great fire of 1906, but the walls remained intact, and it is now fully restored.

The Native Sons' Monument

On Market Street, at its junction with Turk and Mason streets, stands the Native Sons' Monument given to the city by James D. Phelan to commemorate the admission of California into the Union, It was unveiled on Admission Day, September 9, 1897, and was dedicated to the Native Sons of the Golden West. It is in the form of a drinking fountain surmounted by the bronze figure of an angel holding aloft an open book on which is inscribed the date of California's admission into the Union. At the base of the shaft stands a miner with a pick in his right hand, while in his left he holds high an American flag, with California's new star in the field.

Happy Valley

"The space from California Street to the line of Market Street was a region of high sand-hills covered with a scattering growth of brush and scrub oak; but following the curving shore of the cove to the south, one came to a little valley protected on the west by the sand-hills of Market Street. Here, sheltered from the harsh winds, tents had been set up and the place named Happy Valley. This was between First, Second, Market, and Mission streets. It was supplied with a good spring of water and contained, in the winter of 1849–50, about one thousand tents. . . . . In Happy Valley, W. D. M. Howard put up a number of cottages that he had made in Boston, in one of which he lived."

In 1850 a school was opened in this district, which, through the efforts of those interested, became very flourishing. One of its founders was Rev. Samuel H. Willey, pastor of the Howard Presbyterian Church in Happy Valley, and,

later, one of the founders of the College of California in Oakland. W. D. M. Howard, a prominent merchant, and Thomas J. Nevins greatly aided Willey in building up this school, which became known as the Happy Valley Public School. In November 1851 it became the first school opened under the city public school system.

The San Francisco Post Office

"The establishment of the San Francisco Post Office became effective November 9, 1848, when William Van Vorheis was commissioned Assistant Postmaster General for California, by President Polk, and Samuel York, at Lee, was appointed first Postmaster. For some reason, York never entered upon the discharge of his duties, and Stephen J. Dallas was appointed, November 21, 1848, serving for the brief period of two months only. General John W. Geary, for whom Geary Street was named, became Postmaster on January 22, 1849, and served for less than three months, when he was chosen First Alcalde of San Francisco. He was succeeded by Jacob B. Moore, who was appointed April 17, 1849. Mr. Moore was the real Organizer of the Postal Service in San Francisco.

"The first post office was located at the northeast corner of Stockton and Washington streets. The office consisted of one room only, in which there were two clerks. It remained there but a short time, when it was moved to the corner of Clay and Pike streets, the latter now called Waverly Place. There it remained for a few years and was the scene of many memorable events in San Francisco's postal history. From Clay and Pike streets it was moved to a location on Clay Street just above Kearny facing Portsmouth Square. It remained in this location until 1857, when it was transferred to the ground floor of the Custom House building, and from that place it was moved to its present location at Seventh and Mission, in 1905."

During the days when mails arrived only at long intervals, the Post Office was still located on the Waverly Place site. It was then "a place of popular interest not only for San Francisco but for all the mining district. When leaving home for the mines the only known address to give was San Francisco. So, notwithstanding the fact that the man might be two hundred miles away, his mail came to the San Francisco Post Office. The building was small and could accommodate but few clerks within. Outside there was little space for standing room. The mail arrived once a month. The task of sorting the mail kept the clerks busy for many hours. Meanwhile the anxious were awaiting their letters. Often they would hold their place in line all night in the rain in order to reach the window early in the morning. The lines often extended many blocks even out into the brush-covered sandhills. Many desirous of adding to their funds, would secure good positions only to be able to sell them to others with more money than time. Ten to twenty dollars are said to have been paid for positions near the delivery window. Express carriers from the mines gathered up letters for their patrons and delivered them at one dollar each. The Postmaster at San Francisco was given twenty-five cents of this amount for permitting the sorting of the mail."

The Old Shore-Line Markers

The location of the shore line on Market Street as it was at the time of the discovery of gold at Coloma, in 1848, was marked by two bronze tablets on April 16, 1921, by the Landmarks Committee of the Native Sons of the Golden West.

One of the tablets was placed on the corner of Market and First streets and reads as follows:

The Shore-line of San Francisco reached a point twenty-five feet northeasterly from this spot at the time gold was discovered by James W. Marshall at Coloma, California, January 24, 1848.

The other tablet was placed across the street at the base of what is known as the Donohue Monument, where Battery and Bush streets run into Market Street. On this tablet is reproduced a map of the old shore line, that is, the water line from Howard Street to Pacific Street.

The Tide Lands of Yerba Buena Cove

Eldredge says that "San Francisco began to improve immediately after the American occupation and its future greatness as the metropolis of the Pacific was clearly foreseen. The people recognized the necessity for wharves to deep water and for filling in and building upon the mud flats lying before the town."

On February 15, 1847, a petition was made to the Governor asking that the tide lands of Yerba Buena Cove be granted to the town. On March 10, 1847, General Kearny released to the town all government claims of title to the beach and water lots between what was formerly Clark's Point and the Rincon, except the claims to a few lots reserved for government use. Although it was thought that General Kearny did not have the right to make such a grant, the state, in 1851, ceded this section "to the city for a period of ninety-nine years and confirmed previous sales."

The First Wharves

A little pier for the landing of small boats at high tide was built at the foot of Clay Street in 1846. The principal landing place, however, was at the Punta del Embarcadero, or Clark's Point, now the corner of Broadway and Battery streets. A small wharf was built there in 1847 by William S. Clark, replacing the town's first permanent wharf built there in the year 1839. Clark's Point was at first known as the Punta de la Loma Alta. In 1839 this land was granted to Jacob Primer Leese and Salvador Vallejo, who later transferred his interest to Leese. The grant was bounded by what are now Vallejo, Front, Pacific, and Davis streets.

In 1848 William S. Clark came to Yerba Buena and occupied this same land. Years of litigation, which resulted unfavorably to Leese, followed this action, while Clark enjoyed the rich proceeds of the property. Bordering as it did on the new city's best water front where deep-sea vessels could discharge, its value became very great. Today, it is covered by extensive warehouses and receives the bulk of storage merchandise from ships.

All of San Francisco's present streets below Montgomery between California and Broadway were originally wharves.

In the spring of 1848 the old Central, or Long, Wharf was built "from the bank in the middle of the block between Sacramento and Clay streets, where Leidesdorff Street now is, eight hundred feet into the Bay." After 1850 it was. extended 2,000 feet, and the Pacific Mail steamers and other large vessels anchored there. At the shore end of Leidesdorff Street was the office of the Pacific Mail Steamship Company.

Central Wharf, or Long Wharf, as it was called, soon "became the favorite promenade. Buildings perched on piles sprang up quickly on either side, and commission houses, groceries, saloons, mock auctions, cheap-John shops, and peddlers did a thriving business. Central Wharf is now Commercial Street."

The success of Central Wharf caused others to be built until the whole area was covered with wharves and alleyways. Gradually the entire cove was filled in, mostly with sand from the great dunes stretching behind Yerba Buena.

As population increased on both sides of the Bay, the question of convenient trans-bay travel arose. Ferry lines increased in number as did also the docks along the Embarcadero, the name given to the street at the water's edge.

On the Embarcadero at the foot of Market Street, where a shed had been erected in 1877, the Ferry Building of Colusa sandstone, located about midway between Black Point and Mission Rock, was under construction from 1896 to 1903. Through it have poured the morning and evening throngs of local commuters as well as overland passengers from and for the transcontinental trains at their Oakland terminal. This building is flanked by wharves and docks for the use of vessels of all descriptions — from the ferryboats that still cross the Bay at irregular intervals to ocean liners flying flags of foreign nations.

San Francisco Bay, long crossed only by boats, is now crossed by means of five bridges that are located between its entrance and its southernmost tip. The most southerly bridge, completed in 1911 by the Southern Pacific Railroad Company, is used mainly for freight trains. Completed respectively in 1927 and 1929, the Dumbarton Bridge and the San Mateo Bay Bridge, connecting the counties of Alameda and San Mateo, are designed for motor traffic.

Two bridges have now been built across the Bay to meet the demands of modern travel between San Francisco and the regions to the north and east. These are the San Francisco–Oakland Bridge and the Golden Gate Bridge.

The San Francisco–Oakland Bridge was opened to traffic by a gala celebration on November 15, 1936. This giant structure of steel and concrete is approached at its western end by ramps that lead over certain downtown streets in San Francisco to the first span over the water near Pier 26 at the Embarcadero. A land link of this bridge is constructed on Yerba Buena Island, midway between the two cities and just within the boundary of San Francisco County.

The Golden Gate Bridge crosses the channel between old Fort Point (the site now occupied by Fort Winfield Scott) in San Francisco and Lime Point on the Marin County side. Its construction was begun in January 1933 and the last rivet was ceremoniously driven on April 27, 1937. Converging roadways at either end lead to the single suspension span, which is 4,200 feet long and at its center is 230 feet above the water.

Niantic Hotel

The site of the old Niantic Hotel is on the northwest corner of Clay and Sansome streets. Early in the spring of 1849 the ship "Niantic" was anchored on this spot, after it had brought 250 emigrants from Panama at $150 per head. As it was impossible to obtain a crew for the return voyage, because of the lure of the gold mines, it was necessary to leave the ship where it was.

Storeroom and lodging accommodations were very meager in San Francisco at that time, and any sort of space covered with a roof brought enormous rents. Thus, it was not long before the old ship was leased out to various occupants, who used it as stores and offices. The hull was used as a warehouse. This ship was connected with the land by the Clay Street Wharf, which, before long, was lined with structures built on piles.

On May 4, 1851, the ship "Niantic" was burned to the water's edge in one of the great fires that devastated San Francisco in the early '50's. On the hulk of the ship was erected the Niantic Hotel, which gave place in 1872 to the Niantic Block.

On September 8, 1919, the Native Sons of the Golden West placed a marker on the building now standing on the site of the old emigrant ship "Niantic." The legend reads as follows:

The emigrant ship, "Niantic," stood on this spot in the early days, "when the water came up to Montgomery Street." Converted to other uses, it was covered with a shingle roof, with offices and stores on deck, at the level of which was constructed a wide balcony surmounted by a veranda. The hull was divided into warehouses, entered by doorways on the side.

Sites of Abandoned Ships

Many other ships were abandoned in Yerba Buena Cove in 1849. Although some of them were unseaworthy, even sound ships often had to remain where they had been anchored, owing to the inability of their owners to obtain a crew for the return voyage.

Ships other than the "Niantic" were the "General Harrison" (northwest corner of Clay and Battery streets), the "Apollo" (northwest corner of Sacramento and Battery streets), the "Georgian" (between Washington and Jackson streets, west of Battery Street), and the "Euphemia" (near Battery and Sacramento). Most of them were used as warehouses until the fire of May 1851, when they were burned. Before 1851 the "Euphemia" was purchased by the city government and used as a prison.

Pioneer Buildings

Several pioneer buildings known to be standing in San Francisco at the present time are in the vicinity of Montgomery Street.

On the southeast corner of Montgomery and Jackson is one of the very oldest; opposite, on the northeast corner, is the bank building owned by W. T. Sherman in 1853. The oldest brick building now standing—the old Bolton and Barron Building, erected in 1849—is at the northwest corner of Montgomery and Merchant. At 724 Montgomery is the building opened as a variety theater on December 15, 1857. On Montgomery near Washington is a store, erected in 1849, still displaying its old sign. On the northwest corner of Montgomery and Commercial stands a building the lower story of which was erected in 1851.

The Montgomery Block, first known as the Washington Block, stands on Montgomery Street with sides on Washington and Merchant streets. It was begun in July 1853 and was opened in December of that year. The architect was Gordon C. Cummings. It was a four-story-and-basement brick structure with iron shutters at the windows and a doorway flanked by cut-stone pillars. The chief features of the building were cast-iron keystones with portrait heads. Above the heavy doors of the main entrance on Montgomery Street was carved the head of George Washington. While the building was new, the owners, the law firm of Halleck, Peachy and Billings, had their offices on the second floor. Among the tenants were other law firms and financiers. For thirty years a part of the Sutro Library was housed there. The tenants today are mainly persons engaged in some aesthetic craft. The old redwood foundations have been replaced by concrete and the exterior has been modernized.

The Olympic Theater, built in 1853 and known until October of that year as Armory Hall, stands at the northwest corner of Washington and Sansome streets.

The Humphrey house, a private residence built in 1852, stands at the northeast corner of Hyde and Chestnut streets. It is the oldest continually inhabited dwelling in the city.

Sites of other buildings, not standing but mentioned in old writings, are interesting.

Under the rule of Spain, and later of Mexico, business had been transacted mainly through barter; for a time after the American occupancy, and the discovery of gold in quantity, payment was made with gold dust, which led to the coining of that metal. Between 1849 and 1850 there were fifteen different institutions making coins of various kinds in California. One of these establishments was situated on the south side of Portsmouth Square. O. P. Dutton was its director and F. D. Kohler the assayer. Coins made here were stamped with the name of the Pacific Company and dated 1849.

An act passed by the United States Congress on July 3, 1852, directed the establishment of a government branch mint in San Francisco. Private coins were, however, legal tender until 1856. The building of the first United States Branch Mint in San Francisco stood at 608 Commercial Street on the north side between Montgomery and Kearny. It was opened April 9, 1854. Bret Harte was employed at this place as bookkeeper for a time. The Mint, recently vacated (1936), was erected in the early '70's, survived the fire of 1906, and still stands, a dignified edifice, on the corner of Fifth and Mission streets. A new Mint has been erected at Buchanan and Duboce streets.

In the early '40's the Hudson's Bay Company had an establishment on Montgomery Street between Clay and Sacramento streets. William Glen Rae was sent to San Francisco as agent for the company, with Robert Birnie as a clerk. The lot was bought from Jacob P. Leese, the purchase price being $4,600, of which half was paid in money and the other half in goods. The building already standing upon the site occupied a space of about 30 by 80 feet and was divided in the middle by a hall into store and dwelling. The Hudson's Bay Company business was carried on there until 1846, when the San Francisco office was abandoned and the property was sold to Mellus and Howard. The building was afterward the United States Hotel.

The office of the first newspaper published in San Francisco, *The Star,* was on Brenham Place and the southwest corner of Washington, back of the house of its publisher, Sam Brannan. Elbert P. Jones was the editor, and the first number was issued January 9, 1847. The name of this paper was twice changed. From 1849 until it was discontinued in the late '80's it was called the *Alta California.*

On the south side of Clay Street, between Kearny and Montgomery, is the site of the Portsmouth House opened as California's first hotel in 1846.

The El Dorado and the Parker House, once on the east side of the Plaza, or Portsmouth Square, were among the most famous of the saloons and gambling resorts clustered about the center of the city's activity, in 1849 and the early '50's. The Parker House was destroyed by fire three times and as many times rebuilt. Later it was incorporated into the Jenny Lind Theater, which, after two fires, became the City Hall in 1852. This was finally taken down, in 1895, to make way for the Hall of Justice. This in turn was destroyed by the fire of 1906 but has since been rebuilt. The four-story El Dorado, also destroyed by fires and rebuilt, was eventually incorporated into the old City Hall as the Hall of Records.

Another hotel, the What Cheer House, stood between Montgomery and Leidesdorff streets on the south side of Sacramento Street; the Oriental Hotel (1854) stood on the southwest corner of Battery and Bush streets; the Tehama House (1851), frequented by the elite of the town, stood at the northwest corner of California and Sansome streets where now the Bank of California is located.

The International Hotel (1854) stood on the north side of Jackson Street east of Kearny. The Russ Building on Montgomery Street today occupies the site of the Russ home and hotel owned by J. C. Christian Russ, who came to California with Company C, New York Volunteers, in 1847.

The American Theater was built on the northeast corner of Sansome and Halleck in 1851. Maguire's Opera House was built in 1852 on Washington Street between Montgomery and Kearny.

The site of the old California Theater is at 444 Bush Street. It was built by a syndicate headed by William C. Ralston, William Sharon, C. N. Felton, and H. P. Wakelee. The architect, S. C. Bugbee, was ordered to construct a building seating sixteen hundred and guaranteed to withstand earthquake and fire. Its grand opening was on January 15, 1869, under the direction of the actor-managers Lawrence Barrett and John McCullough, who presented Lytton's comedy *Money* with a distinguished cast. A tablet installed by the Commonwealth Club at the suggestion of the last surviving member of the cast, Emily Melville, marks the site.

The first bridge erected in San Francisco was placed over the tidal inlet to a salt-water lagoon on the east side of Montgomery Street at Jackson by Alcalde William S. Hinckley. This site is marked by a tablet placed on an old building now at that corner by the National Society of Colonial Dames on November 12, 1936.

The site of the first Mechanics Fair, 1857, is on the west side of Montgomery Street between Post and Sutter. The site of the first Pioneer Hall, built in 1863, is at the corner of Montgomery and Gold streets.

The main entrance to Woodward's Gardens, a pioneer amusement resort still fresh in the memory of a few, was on the west side of Mission Street between Duboce Avenue and Fourteenth Street. R. B. Woodward built here his private home about 1866 and filled it with objects of art. Finding that his collections would be appreciated by the public at large, he opened his grounds for that reason and added attractions suitable for the purpose. He built an octagonal pavilion with a seating capacity of more than five thousand, to be used for plays, dances, and skating. He added a zoölogical department across Fourteenth Street, where he placed live wild animals and an aquarium. A tunnel beneath the street connected the two parts.

"Fort Gunnybags"

The site of old "Fort Gunnybags," or Fort Vigilance, the headquarters of the San Francisco Vigilance Committee of the year 1856, is located at 243 Sacramento Street. The city at that time was given over to a reign of terror, the officials themselves being corrupt and in league with the lower elements, so that crime remained unpunished.

The occasion for the formation of the Vigilance Committee of 1856 was the murder of James King of William, free-lance editor of the *Bulletin,* by James P. Casey, whom King had denounced in his paper because of his political corruption.

The people of San Francisco demanded immediate punishment of the murderer, and since the regularly elected officials could not be depended upon, a committee of prominent citizens undertook to see that justice was meted out. William T. Coleman, organizer and leader of this Vigilance Committee, was made chairman, and thousands of citizens gave him their support. The Committee not only brought Casey to justice, but it made a general clean-up of the city and many notorious criminals were banished.

Hubert Howe Bancroft has called the work of the Committee "one of the grandest moral revolutions the world has ever witnessed."

The Vigilance Committee was succeeded by the reform People's party, which governed San Francisco so well that, for years, it was one of the best regulated cities of the country.

The site of "Fort Gunnybags" was first marked on March 21, 1903, by the California Landmarks League. In the fire of 1906 the old building was destroyed, and when the tablet was replaced on June 1, 1918, by the Native Sons of the Golden West almost all who had taken part in the work of 1856 had

passed beyond. At the top of the tablet is a representation of the all-seeing eye that adorned all official documents issued by the Committee.

Starr King's Church

Thomas Starr King, beloved Unitarian preacher and "apostle of the Union cause, toured the State in a remarkably effective campaign to arouse the spirit of loyalty" throughout California. He "threw himself with his marvelous talent into the breach to champion his country's cause with an irresistible eloquence. . . . . It was the eloquence of Starr King that saved the [Sanitary] Commission's work from financial ruin." His portrait was hung in the state Capitol and bears the inscription: "The man whose matchless oratory saved California to the Union."

Starr King came to San Francisco from Boston in 1860, a young man already winning fame. Until his death in 1864 he served as pastor of the First Unitarian Church, the first site of which was on Stockton Street near Sacramento. Since the town was growing southward, a new church was built on Geary, near Stockton, soon after King's arrival. In this church he preached and there he was buried. Later, the city's growth necessitated the removal of the church to its present site on Geary and Franklin streets. Here the body of Starr King lies before the door of the church. A bronze statue was erected in Golden Gate Park as an expression of San Francisco's appreciation of his life and services. A statue of him done by Haig Patigian has been placed, along with one of Father Junípero Serra done by Ettore Cadorin, to represent California in Statuary Hall in Washington, D.C.

Hills of San Francisco

The hills upon which San Francisco is built separated three original settlements now lying within the one great city. These settlements were: the Presidio, where soldiers were stationed for the protection of the interests of Spain; the Mission, where the Spanish Fathers carried on the work of civilizing and Christianizing the native Indians; and Yerba Buena, where persons of several nationalities who were mainly interested in commercial pursuits made early headquarters. The last named, Yerba Buena, was the youngest and soon became the strongest. It grew and spread, up and over the hills, so that today's streets ascend and descend all those moderate heights. Former steep declivities have been somewhat lessened by grading for the pavements that now cover them; yet visitors frequently view them with surprise.

Telegraph Hill, called by the Spaniard "Loma Alta" (high hill), with an elevation of 275 feet, is first in historic interest. It stands at the extreme northeast corner of the San Francisco Peninsula and extends back and upward from the Clark's Point of early days. From its top, on October 29, 1850, a fire signal was given to announce the news, brought by the steamer "Oregon," of the admission of California as the thirty-first state of the Union.

The area considered a part of this hill up to 1850 was bounded by a line that runs, roughly, from the intersection of Broadway and Battery streets north and then westward to Powell and Francisco streets, thence to the corner of Broadway and Kearny, and along Broadway to the point of beginning at Battery. A battery built in 1846 under the direction of Captain Montgomery on the east side of Telegraph Hill gave the name to Battery Street.

Many people of position in the San Francisco of early days had homes near the southern base of the hill and in after years smaller homes clustered about its top. The language spoken in these small houses was more often Italian, Spanish, Portuguese, or French than English, which fact gave rise to this section being called the "Latin Quarter." The part between Kearny and Montgomery and Green and Greenwich streets housed what was called the "Artist Colony" in the '90's.

As early as 1849, Loma Alta was used as a station from which to observe incoming vessels and was sometimes called "Signal Hill." In September 1849 a two-story house, 25 by 18 feet, was erected on the top by Sweeney and Baugh. Within this house lived the observers who transmitted the character of the approaching vessel—whether side-wheel steamer, sailing vessel, or other craft—to the people in the city below. Upon the top of this house stood a sort of semaphore by which an elaborate system of signals could be given. The place was known as the Inner Signal Station. The Outer Signal Station was established near Point Lobos, where incoming craft could first be seen and reported to the Inner Station. In 1853 the Inner Station was abandoned when telegraph connection was made from the Merchant's Exchange directly to Point Lobos. In this year the North Point Docks were constructed below the hill and Sansome Street was cut through it. The old house that had stood on the top of the hill since 1849 blew down in a storm of 1870 and was not replaced.

Among the writers who have lived on Telegraph Hill are: Mark Twain; Joaquin Miller; Frank Norris; Ambrose Bierce, "cynical poet and philosopher of old San Francisco"; and Bret Harte, who complained that goats browsed on the geraniums in his second-story windows and tramped over the roof at night "like heavy hailstones." His story "The Secret of Telegraph Hill" is associated with this historic landmark. Charles Warren Stoddard was wont to call the goats that wandered here the "mascots of the hill," and Robert Louis Stevenson called the summit the "Peak of the Wind."

Actors likewise chose to live upon this hill. Among them perhaps the most famous was Edwin Booth.

"At 31 Alta Street is a little house built about 1852, with red brick foundation and frame superstructure, and narrow balcony with spindle railing . . . . At 228 Filbert Street opening on the terraced staircase of the hill is a very old and interesting house of slate-gray color, with several balconies and railings painted blue. The location, the ornamentation over the windows, the architectural ornaments at the gable and eaves make it quite unusual . . . . At the corner of Montgomery and Union streets, on Telegraph Hill, is a square, flat-roofed house called 'the old Spanish House.' It has very thick walls, no window mouldings, deep window embrasures. The local inhabitants say it is the oldest house on Telegraph Hill, and that the modern pink stucco covers a foundation of red brick."

In 1876 a group of leading citizens donated to San Francisco a tract 275 feet square between Kearny, Greenwich, and Filbert streets, extending almost to Montgomery Street, as a park; later the city purchased an area of about the same size to extend the park to the summit. In the '80's a "castle" stood on the top and a funicular railway ran up Greenwich Street. In the early 1900's the top of the hill was cleared and the area named Pioneer Park.

On March 15, 1929, a ceremony attended the placing of a marker on this summit. The Sequoia Chapter, D.A.R., presented to the city a bronze tablet memorializing the Inner Signal Station and the first Western Telegraph Station. The tablet at that time was placed out of doors upon a wall but, at the erection of the Coit Tower upon the top of Telegraph Hill, it was placed within that structure near the entrance.

The Coit Tower, about 180 feet in height, was constructed with funds left by Mrs. Lillie Hitchcock Coit for the beautification of the city. Lillie, daughter of Dr. Hitchcock, arrived in San Francisco in 1851—a child of eight years. In her girlhood she was made an honorary member of one of the fire companies, the Knickerbocker Number Five, and maintained her interest in the city until her death in July 1929. The view from the tower, or even from the ample parking space below it, is magnificent.

Russian Hill, so named because of an early unenclosed Russian graveyard upon its summit, is now a favored residential section. The growth of scrub oaks and chaparral that used to flourish on the lower western side of Telegraph Hill continued to the top of Russian Hill, not far beyond, where a few of the oaks may still be seen.

An elevation of 360 feet is reached at the summit, where wonderful sunset views may be obtained. An observatory which stood there as early as 1863 was reached by means of a spiral staircase.

Among writers who have resided on this hill was Helen Hunt Jackson, who died there in 1886. Near her home on the eastern brow a mast was erected for use in the early days of wireless telegraphy.

Gallows for the first official execution in San Francisco were erected one hundred feet west of the summit of Russian Hill, and there a Spaniard who had committed a murder in Happy Valley—now the vicinity of Mission Street between First and Third streets—was hanged.

Rincon Hill, which, along with Telegraph Hill, was recommended by Robert Louis Stevenson to the city dilettante, rose from Rincon ("corner") Point shown on old maps of San Francisco. On the sheltered southern side of this point was a wooded area favored for picnic outings, and in that region George Gordon laid out South Park, patterning it somewhat after the squares in London. Each man who purchased a lot there was required to erect a fireproof house of brick. The center of the place was planted to grass and trees and was protected by an oval curbing that still remains. In this South Park lived many people of education and social position.

Higher up on Rincon Hill grander homes were built, among others those of the Ralstons, the Milton Lathams, and General and Mrs. Halleck. In 1854 the United States Marine Hospital was built on the eastern extremity. In 1866 Rincon Hill was cut at Second Street, after which the social prestige of the place declined, the fine homes disappeared, and the region was given over entirely to commercial enterprises. In *The Wrecker* Stevenson tells of seeing it in 1879. A row of clapboard houses painted yellow remained on Harrison Street. They faced to the south and were surrounded by little gardens that gave some relief from the constant view of the scarred hillside. In one of these small houses, almost overhanging the cut, lived Charles Warren Stoddard.

The western anchorage and ramps of the San Francisco–Oakland Bridge have necessitated the almost complete leveling of Rincon Hill.

West of Kearny Street is the elevation originally called Fern Hill, now called either California Street Hill or Nob Hill. Not until the perfection of the cable car was it possible to make this ascent in comfort and, safety. A. S. Hallidee, English builder of aerial cables for use in Western mines, invented an arrangement whereby heavy cables could be laid underground to draw cars up hill. The first car thus equipped ran from Kearny Street to Leavenworth on Clay Street in August 1873, and soon thereafter such lines were in general use. For many years cable cars have served this region by plying up and down California, Sacramento, Clay, and Powell streets.

Pretentious homes erected on this hill by early financiers whose fortunes had been carved out of Western enterprises gave rise to the name "Nob Hill." Some of these homes were too lavish to be in good taste; others were beautiful. Most of them were destroyed in the fire of 1906. After the fire the pillars of the Grecian doorway of the A. N. Towne residence were left standing among the ruins. (These "Portals of the Past" have been placed in Golden Gate Park on the banks of Lloyd Lake near the main drive.) On the hill stood the homes of three of the builders of the Central Pacific Railroads the mansion of Governor Leland Stanford, where now are the Stanford Court Apartments; that of Mark Hopkins, where stands the Mark Hopkins Hotel; and that of Charles Crocker, on whose property Grace Cathedral, the crowning edifice of the hill, is now nearing completion.

Among other notable residents on the hill were the Fair and Flood families. On the Fair property has risen the Fairmont Hotel. Upon its top the time ball, placed there in 1909, daily descends to mark the hour of noon. The time ball was originally placed on the top of Telegraph Hill, then on the Ferry Building until 1909. The Flood residence is the only one of the great houses remaining. This brownstone structure is now the home of the Pacific Union Club.

Lone Mountain rises to an elevation of 468 feet between Golden Gate Park and the Presidio. For years it was surmounted by a cross recently removed to make room for the building of the San Francisco College for Women, a Catholic institution, while at its base lay four old cemeteries: to the north, Laurel Hill; to the east, Calvary; to the south, the Masonic; and to the west, the Odd Fellows.

Laurel Hill Cemetery was laid out in 1854 when earlier burial places in the city were abandoned. Two earlier ones had been on Telegraph Hill, one on the southern slope near the corner of the present Sansome and Vallejo streets and one on the North Beach slope in an area bounded by Powell, Dupont, Chestnut, and Francisco streets. Another small one had been near the top of Russian Hill and still another in an area near the location of the present Civic Center. The oldest of these early cemeteries was the Catholic one at the Mission, still intact.

Until recently, the only burials permitted within the city were at the National Cemetery, now superseded. Laurel Hill Cemetery, where many of the most distinguished figures of California's early days were buried, has been removed to make way for city dwellings.

Twin Peaks has, as its name implies, two distinct elevations at its top: a north one of 903 feet and a south one of 910 feet. These were early called the "Mission Peaks" and, sometimes, "Los Pechos de la Choca" (the breasts of an Indian maiden). Here an extensive view repays a pleasant drive over a winding roadway to the top. From this vantage point may be seen: Mount Hamilton and the Lick Observatory; Loma Prieta, stretching from Santa Clara County into Santa Cruz County; Mount Diablo in Contra Costa County; Mount Tamalpais and Point Reyes in Marin County; and the Farallones, off the coast.

Mount Davidson, with an elevation of 938 feet, is the highest peak in San Francisco. It was surveyed in 1852 by the United States Geodetic Survey under George Davidson and was named "Blue Mountain." It was included in Rancho San Miguel, afterward purchased by Adolph Sutro, outstanding citizen of San Francisco, who began the planting of the trees that now form Sutro Forest. Mount Sutro, with an elevation of 920 feet, is also in this forest.

By 1911 the saplings, earlier planted, had grown into trees and the highest peak was renamed Mount Davidson in honor of its original surveyor. In 1923 a cross was erected upon its summit and the first Easter Sunrise Services held there, a service now held annually.

Sponsored by the City and County Federation of Women's Clubs, twenty-six acres of land on the mountain were acquired by the city of San Francisco. This area was dedicated and named Mount Davidson Park on December 20, 1929, the dedication being a part of the celebration of the eighty-third birthday of John McLaren, creator of Golden Gate Park and superintendent of the city's parks until his death in 1943.

The first two crosses erected upon this site were destroyed by fires that swept over them. A third cross, 103 feet in height, made of concrete to be fireproof, was set up in March 1934.

Among other hills of less historical importance than the seven mentioned are Strawberry Hill, with an elevation of 426 feet in Golden Gate Park, and Hyde Street Hill, on the slope of which is a sheltered park dedicated to the memory of the poet George Sterling, the latter part of whose life was spent in San Francisco.

Old Cisterns

In the early days of San Francisco many sunken water tanks or cisterns were constructed in the town. One of these, elliptical in form and having a capacity of 32,000 gallons, is located at the corner of California and Montgomery streets. Made originally of tar-drenched plank in 1852, it was rebuilt with brick four years later. Another, known as the Plaza cistern, at Kearny and Merchant streets, with a capacity of 36,000 gallons, has a similar history, having been built and rebuilt of similar materials at approximately the same dates.

Thirty-six such cisterns were in use by 1856. Most of them were square or oblong in shape and not more than fifteen feet in depth. They were first filled with water hauled in carts from springs on the hillsides of regions near by. In later years they have been filled from the city water mains.

When, in April 1906, the great earthquake broke the modern water pipes supplying San Francisco, water from these old underground receptacles was brought into use to assist in quenching the fire that eventually consumed a great part of the city. Since that date modern cisterns have been constructed beneath street pavements in all parts of the city.

Chinatown

From the vicinity of its intersection with Sacramento Street, Grant Avenue leads into one of the largest colonies of Chinese outside of China itself. This colony originated on Sacramento Street west of Kearny and by 1885 it had expanded to cover about ten blocks, "closely packed," says Bancroft, "with some 25,000 souls." The same authority states that the first Chinese to enter California under American rule were two men and one woman who came on the clipper bark "Eagle" in 1848.

On April 1, 1848, the *California Star* published in San Francisco said, in an editorial: "We have received information from a very reliable source, that a large immigration from China may be expected here. We already have two or three of the 'Celestials' among us who have found ready employment."

By about 1876 labor troubles were precipitated, in the mining districts and elsewhere, by the presence of the 116,000 Chinese who had come and were scattered about over the state. These troubles arose partly on account of race prejudice and partly because of the low scale of wages accepted by these immigrants. At length drastic laws governing the entry of these aliens were enacted, laws revoked in 1943.

A word picture of the Chinatown of the late '70's comes from Benjamin F. Taylor, a visitor from the Eastern part of the United States: "Fancy yourself walking along the gay streets of San Francisco in the edge of the evening—streets bright with light, pleasant with familiar forms, musical with

English speech, and feeling all the while, that under the patriotic flight of July flags as thick as pigeons and as gay as redbirds, you were still at home though thousands of miles away—fancy this, and then at the turn of a corner and the breadth of a street, think of dropping with the abruptness of a shifting dream into China, beneath the standard of Hoang-ti who sits upon the dragon throne . . . .

"A strange chatter as of foreign birds in an aviary confuses the air. A surf of blue and black shirts and inky heads with tails to them is rolling along the sidewalks. Colored lanterns begin to twinkle. Black-lettered red signs all length and no breadth, the gnarled and crooked characters heaped one above another like a pile of ebony chair-frames, catch the eye. You halt at a building tinseled into cheap magnificence, and hung with gaudy paper glims . . . .

"The creak of a Chinese fiddle shaped a little like a barometer all bulb and no body, scrapes through a crack in the door . . . . Lights stream up from cellar stairs . . . .

"You enter the restaurant. It is the 'Banquet Saloon' of Yune Fong. And there is Yune Fong himself, a benign, double-chinned old boy who is of a bigness from end to end. He sits by a counter . . . . Under his hand is a well-thumbed arithmeticon, a family of boys' marbles strung like beads upon parallel wires and set in a frame, wherewith Fong ciphers out your indebtedness and his profits . . . . The lights are feeble, as if there were nothing worth their while to shine on.

"You climb stairs into an improved edition of the ground floor. The furniture is faintly tidier and better, the tableware costlier . . . . One more lift and you are in large and elegant apartments with partitions of glass . . . . The furniture is of Chinese wood dark as mahogany at a hundred years old . . . . Lacquered boxes and curious cabinets abound."

After partaking of tea in the restaurant, Taylor and his friends, returning to the street, set out to see the Joss House: "Up a few steps, down a few steps, round a corner, up a whole flight, along a gallery as dumb as a tomb," they reach the "Joss-House, one of eleven heathen temples in San Francisco. It is never closed and we enter . . . . In the great shrines are rows of sinister gods with trailing black beard and moustache . . . . the god of War . . . . the deity of Medicine . . . . the god of Fortune . . . ."

Then on to an opium den and afterward to the Chinese theater, whose orchestra consisted of "ticks and clucks and jingles and squeaks, and tinkles of bells, and a frog and locust interlude, and emaciated fiddles," followed by a roar of gongs and a clash of cymbals. "The music and the acting were alike—a marvelous jumble. It was as if a medley had swallowed itself."

Much of the labyrinth of old Chinatown was destroyed by the fire of 1906; yet a large part has been rebuilt, under more sanitary regulations, and interest in this section is not lacking today.

The pedestrian, wandering along Grant Avenue northward, suddenly finds that he has reached Chinatown. The windows are filled with curios and beads and jewelry; shops with young English-speaking Chinese attendants display silks and wearing apparel from the Orient. Strange foods with their unusual odors are in some of the doorways leading to similarly filled interiors.

Both sides of the streets in this section are lined with shops, some large, some small. A few Chinese costumes are worn by the older men and women met on the street. A few old men with queues appear. The bones of most of the wearers of queues in the old Chinatown are probably now in their native land, where all Chinese hope to secure a final resting place. The younger generation are usually clothed in modern American dress.

SOURCES

[Credit is here given for source material, and permission to quote is hereby acknowledged]

Annals of San Francisco. Frank Soulé, John H. Gihon, and James Nisbet (comp.). D. Appleton & Company, New York, 1855; Authors and Newspapers Association, New York and London, 1906

BLAND, HENRY MEADE. *Stevenson's California.* The Pacific Short Story Club, San Jose, California, 1924

BOLTON, HERBERT EUGENE. *Anza's California Expeditions.* 5 vols. University of California Press, Berkeley, 1930

California Historical Society Quarterly, San Francisco, 1922–1936

CHAPMAN, CHARLES E. *A History of California: The Spanish Period.* The Macmillan Company, New York, 1921

CLELAND, ROBERT GLASS. *A History of Califorma: The American Period.* The Macmillan Company, New York, 1922

COY, OWEN C. *Pictorial History of California.* University of California Extension Division, Berkeley, 1925

DAVIS, WILLIAM HEATH. *Seventy-five Years in California.* (A reissue and enlarged illustrated edition of *Sixty Years in California.*) Edited by Douglas S. Watson. John Howell, San Francisco, 1929

DEERING, MARGARET PERKINS. *The Hills of San Francisco.* Privately printed, San Francisco, 1936

ELDER, DAVID PAUL. *The Old Spanish Missions of California.* Paul Elder & Company, San Francisco, 1913

ELDREDGE, ZOETH SKINNER. *The Beginnings of San Francisco from the Expedition of Anza, 1774, to the City Charter of April 15, 1850.* 2 vols. Privately printed, San Francisco, 1912

ENGELHARDT, ZEPHYRIN. *San Francisco, or Mission Dolores.* Franciscan Herald Press, Chicago, 1924

FRÉMONT, JOHN CHARLES. *Memoirs of My Life.* Bedford Clarke & Company, Chicago and New York, 1887

HITTELL, JOHN S. *A History of the City of San Francisco, and Incidentally of the State of California.* A. L. Bancroft & Company, San Francisco, 1878

HUNT, ROCKWELL D., and NELLIE VAN DE GRIFT SANCHEZ. *A Short History of California.* Thomas Y. Crowell Company, New York, 1929

KELLY, D. O. *History of the Diocese of California from 1849 to 1914.* San Francisco, 1915

NATIVE SONS OF THE GOLDEN WEST. Landmarks Committee Report, 1920–1929, Joseph Knowland, Chairman, Tribune Building, Oakland

PALÓU, FRANCISCO. *Life and Apostolic Labors of the Venerable Father Junípero Serra, Founder of the Franciscan Missions of California.* With an Introduction and Notes by George Wharton James; English translation by C. Scott Williams. Pasadena, California, 1913

PURDY, HELEN THROOP. *San Francisco, as It Was, as It Is, and How to See It.* Paul Elder & Company, San Francisco, 1912

RENSCH, HERO EUGENE. *Educational Activities of the Protestant Churches in California, 1849–1860.* Master's thesis in history, Stanford University, 1929

STEVENSON, ROBERT LOUIS. *The Wrecker.* Charles Scribner's Sons, New York, 1898

———. *Across the Plains, Essays and Reviews.* Vol. IX of his *Works,* ed. de luxe. The Davos Press, New York, 1906

TAYLOR, BENJAMIN F. *Between the Gates.* Ninth ed. S. C. Griggs & Company, Chicago, 1882

TAYLOR, WILLIAM. *California Life Illustrated.* English edition, Jackson, Walford & Hodder, London, 1867

TODD, HARRY L. Manuscript on "The San Francisco Post Office"

WATKINS, ELEANOR PRESTON. *The Builders of San Francisco.* Privately printed, San Francisco, 1935

SAN LUIS OBISPO COUNTY

SAN LUIS OBISPO COUNTY (named for the Mission) was one of the original twenty-seven counties of the state. San Luis Obispo has been its county seat continuously.

The Carrizo Plain and the Painted Rock

A singular geologic formation in the southeastern part of the county is the elevated plateau, or basin, over sixteen hundred feet above sea level. Off the beaten trail, it can be reached by taking the road that runs east from Santa Margarita and by passing through the little villages of Pozo (cup, well) and La Panza to a point beyond. This highway passes through the plain, which extends to the east and to the south.

The plateau is about fifty miles long and from eight to twenty miles wide. The drainage appears to be entirely to the center, where an area of four square miles is a swamp in the winter and a salt bed in the summer season. Farmers and stock men of the vicinity used to get their supply of salt from this place. General Parkes, in his report of the Pacific Railroad survey in 1853 and 1854, says: "The hills on either side supply it with water, small in quantity, which collects in lagoons or ponds in the center of the plain, which is uninhabited by man, and occupied by only herds of deer, antelope, and wild horses, with which it abounds." However, by 1890, the plain had become private property with many prosperous settlements upon it.

In the southwestern part of the plain is an isolated butte, covering an area of about five miles and rising to a height of 140 feet. It is of conical formation, like the crater of a volcano, but has a narrow opening toward the east on a level with the plain. The opening is twenty-four feet in width and leads to a vast oval cavity two hundred and twenty-five feet in its greatest and one hundred and twenty feet in its least diameter, the walls rising to a height of one hundred and thirty-two feet at the highest point. The rock is of coarse sandstone, and the walls are irregular and overhang in places, making the inner space like a cave. In these recesses, covering a space twelve feet in height and sixty feet in length, are a great number of paintings, representing in rude form men, suns, birds, and other designs not easily described, probably hieroglyphics or writings of meaning to the prehistoric people who made them. When and by whom these were made is unknown, as the oldest inhabitant says that when discovered by the pioneer Spanish missionaries they were as they are at the present time. The aborigines knew nothing of their origin, but regarded them with mysterious awe.

The paintings are in three lines of red, white, and black; the colors are remarkably bright and distinct but now much defaced by unthinking curious visitors. This supposed temple of the ancient pagan has been used as a cattle corral and has had no care exercised for its preservation. The rock, called La Piedra Pintada (The Painted Rock) by the early Spanish settlers, is located about five miles from the foot of the Diablos in the Carrizo Plain.

The Portolá Trail

The present Oso Flaco (Lean Bear) Lake, situated near the coast in southwestern San Luis Obispo County, was so named by the soldiers of Gaspar de Portolá's expedition on September 3, 1769, when a very lean bear was killed near their camp on the shore of the lake. On the 4th, a halt was made in Price Canyon, north of Pismo, and on the 5th, one in San Luis Canyon, where the party rested on the 6th. Again the tents were pitched on the 7th, this time on the banks of Chorro Creek, where the soldiers spent the day replenishing their food supply with bear meat. This was the occasion for naming the valley La Cañada de los Osos (The Canyon of the Bears), a name which it retains today.

On a hill overlooking the waters of Morro Bay opposite majestic Morro Rock, camp was made at the mouth of Morro Creek on September 8. Again the expedition was halted on the 9th, on this date at Ellysly's Creek just east of Point

Estero. Continuing up Ellysly's Creek and over Dawson Grade, the band stopped on the 10th at Santa Rosa Creek near Cambria; and on the 11th, at Little Pico Creek east of San Simeon Point. The following day the party ascended Arroyo Laguna to Arroyo de la Cruz. Reaching Ragged Point on San Carpojoro Creek (now shortened to San Carpojo) on the 13th, Portolá found that further progress up the coast was barred by steep mountain precipices. The 14th and 15th were spent in preparing a trail over a most difficult pass by way of San Carpojoro Creek to its junction with Chris Flood Creek, where camp was made on the 16th. On the 17th the march was resumed over very rough country to Wagner Creek, within the present confines of Monterey County.

The Anza Trail

As far as the site of Misión San Luis Obispo, Juan Bautista de Anza passed over practically the same trail in San Luis Obispo County as Portolá had before him in 1769. The Southern Pacific Railroad follows much the same route today. From the Mission, Anza crossed the Santa Lucía Range through Cuesta Pass over the present state highway route. Continuing along its course to Paso Robles, he turned his trail northwest over the hills along Oak Flat Road (Paso de los Robles) to San Marcos Creek. There the road went almost due north to Nacimiento River about at Rancho Nacimiento and thence proceeded to the first crossing of the San Antonio River, about at King Well, now in Monterey County.

On Anza's first trip, in 1775, two stops were made in San Luis Obispo County, one at the Mission on April 15, and a second at the Nacimiento River on April 16. On his second trip, in 1776, as leader of the San Francisco colonists, camps were made at the following places: at the Indian Village, El Buchon, in Price Canyon two miles north of Pismo on March 1; at Misión San Luis Obispo on March 2 and 3; and at La Asunción, a short distance beyond Atascadero, on March 4.

Cave Landing

Cave Landing is situated about two miles northwest of the San Luis Obispo highway and one-half mile east of the tiny seaport town of Avila. The padres used this landing-place for shipping tallow and grain. "The boat came as close in shore as it could and the freight was let down from the cliff by means of a rude crane. Later, along in the sixties, when settlers began coming into the county, the schooners and sailing vessels stopped at Cave Landing and the pioneers climbed rope ladders to the top of the cliff after being brought ashore in little rowboats. Sometimes the surf and spray dashed far up the side of the cliff.

"A path leads down the side of the cliff to a pretty curving beach. From the beach you can see the great Arch Rock and the mouth of Robbers' Cave. This cave was the hiding place for many a bandit's loot. It is said there is much treasure still buried there and often do the treasure seekers dig and delve for it." Between Arch Rock and Robbers' Cave lies tiny Moonstone Beach, which derives its name from the presence of moonstones among the pebbles and shells washed up by the waves.

From the white sands of Moonstone Beach one clambers over the rocks, sometimes stooping to pass through a short tunnel made by the sea, and at last, rounding a corner, one comes suddenly upon an immense level rock which juts out for 150 feet into deep water. This is Cave Landing, an excellent natural pier beneath which the tide swirls and from which deep-sea fishing may be done. Here, where the Indian had fished for hundreds of years before the white man and where he buried his dead in crude graves along the rugged cliffs facing the east, smugglers and bandits, priests and sea captains, came later.

About seventy years ago David Mallagh, an Irish sea captain, erected a warehouse on the cliffs above the sea, with a long wooden chute leading down to the water. Huge iron spikes, with immense rings of iron fastened to them, were driven into the solid rock at the top of the cliff. To these rings, the great ship cables were fastened. For a decade, Captain Mallagh handled all of the shipping at the cove and hauled passengers and freight to San Luis Obispo. After his death and the advent of the railroad a mile farther down the coast, Cave Landing was abandoned and gradually fell into decay. Only the rusted iron rings and spikes and the great post holes remain to tell the tale of adventure, of pirates, and of lost treasure in that long ago.

Misión San Luis Obispo de Tolosa

Misión San Luis Obispo de Tolosa was founded by Padre Junípero Serra, September 1, 1772, while on his notable journey from Monterey to Mexico. As no other priest was available at the time, Father Cavaller was left in sole charge of the new post, contrary to the rule that two priests must be stationed at each Mission. He continued to serve there until his death in 1789.

The first attempt to manufacture tile in California was made at San Luis Obispo, after the buildings had been three times badly damaged by fire, because of the ease with which the tule thatching ignited. The first of these disasters occurred in November 1776, when hostile Indians shot burning arrows into the roofs. After the success of this first experiment in tile-making, that method of roofing was adopted by all of the Missions from about 1784 afterward. At San Luis Obispo an adobe church, completed in 1793, replaced the original chapel.

Helen Hunt Jackson in her novel *Ramona* gives a pleasing picture of Father Luis Martínez, who began his long services at the Mission in 1798. The story tells how, when he wished to entertain General Moreno and his bride, he "caused to be driven past the corridors, for their inspection, all the poultry belonging to the Mission. The procession took an hour to pass. The Indians had been hard at work all night capturing, sorting, and guarding the rank and file of their novel pageant. It would be safe to say that a droller sight never was seen, and never will be, on the Pacific Coast or any other. Before it was done with, the General and his bride had nearly died with laughter." Father Martínez was one of the best known of the friars to serve at San Luis Obispo. "Portly of figure and gruff of speech," he was very jovial and much beloved by Indians and Spaniards alike.

The Mission is now the active parish church of the city of San Luis Obispo. Alterations and make-shift restorations made during the passing years included the boarding over of crumbling walls and the erection of a steeple entirely out of place on such an edifice. Efforts are now being made to restore the whole establishment to its original appearance. The steeple has been removed and red tiles again cover the roof of the old church. As funds are available, the work of restoration is proceeding with adjoining buildings, and the garden at the rear, where great old grapevines have survived long neglect, is receiving attention and will be fittingly enclosed as it was in earlier years.

Misión San Miguel Arcángel

Misión San Miguel Arcángel was founded July 25, 1797, by Father Lasuén, assisted by Father Buenaventura Sitjar. It was located on a beautiful spot on the Salinas River where

there was plenty of water for irrigation. Many of the ancient canals and dams built by the Fathers for irrigating their orchards and crops may still be seen in the vicinity of the Mission.

The first temporary wooden buildings were gradually replaced, from 1799 to 1804, by adobe structures. Fire almost destroyed the entire establishment in 1806, and plans were made for reconstruction on a more spacious scale. The church building which was begun in 1816 and completed in 1818 still stands. Secularization took place in 1836, followed by confiscation and neglect. In later years, the building was restored, and services are now held there by Franciscan Fathers.

San Miguel remains more unspoiled by restoration than any of the other Missions, and contains perhaps the finest examples of the original decorations done by the Indians under supervision of the padres. Crude they are, but plainly a work of love and devotion.

Great rafters and corbels hewn from solid trees which the faithful Indians had brought forty miles from the mountains support the ceiling, and all are colored in light green, pink, blue, and white. The walls are designed to represent fluted pillars tinted in blue, while between these are conventionalized designs of leaves and carved figures. A frieze in reddish brown represents a gallery with railings and pillars. The ancient pulpit, also decorated and colored by the Indians, the confessional built into the adobe wall, the floor of burnt brick laid in alternate rows of squares and oblongs, all these features remain as they were when first completed with such loving care by the padres and their charges. The monastery with its beautiful low-arched corridor, which extends from the side, is unique in the fact that its arches are of different sizes, the two central ones being larger than the others and elliptical in form, balanced by four smaller, semicircular arches set off by one still smaller on each side. Further restoration of this Mission is now in progress.

The Asistencia of Santa Margarita

The Asistencia of Santa Margarita, belonging to Misión San Luis Obispo, was an outpost, or chapel and storehouse, located fourteen miles north of the Mission. It was built on a knoll near the Santa Margarita River, where lived a large Indian population, whom the padres hoped to enroll as converts.

A visitor to this place in 1831, while the building was still intact, was Alfred Robinson. He wrote: "We reached 'El Rancho de Santa Rita' a place used for the cultivation of grain, where, on an eminence that overlooked the grounds, an extensive building was erected. It was divided into store rooms for different kinds of grain, and apartments for the accommodation of the mayordomo, servants, and wayfarers. At one end was a chapel, and snug lodging-rooms for the priest, who, I was informed, frequently came and passed some weeks at the place during the time of harvest; and the holy friars of the two missions occasionally met there to acknowledge to each other their sins."

Of special interest today are the massive stone doorway, several windows with arched tops in almost perfect condition, and the side and end walls which still stand. A ranch barn has been constructed with the nave as the main part of the building. Here hay is stored and is fed through the window openings to cattle and horses having stalls and mangers beneath a shed that extends the whole length of the building.

Ranchos of San Miguel

In compliance with the decree of Governor José M. Echeandia of October 7, 1827, that the missionaries make a detailed report on the lands of their respective Missions, Father

Juan Cabot reported on November 26, 1827, for Misión San Miguel, in part, as follows:

"Towards the south the lands of Mission San Luis Obispo are recognized to extend to the Rancho de la Asuncion, distant from here seven leagues.

"Toward the north, the Mission claims the land to the Rancho de San Bartolomé, or Pleyto, distant' about seven leagues to the boundary of Mission San Antonio.

"From the Mission to the beach the land consists almost entirely of mountain ridges, devoid of permanent water. For this reason that region is not occupied until one reaches the coast where the Mission has a house of adobe. Here it may cultivate some clear land for planting grain in summertime but it is entirely dependent upon rain, since there is no irrigated land there. In the same district eight hundred cattle, some tame horses and breeding mares are kept at said Rancho, which is called San Simeon.

"In the direction toward the south, all the land is occupied, for the Mission there maintains all its sheep, besides the horses of the guards. It is there it has the Rancho de Santa Isabel, where there is a small vineyard. Other ranchos of the Mission in that direction are San Antonio, where barley is planted; Rancho del Paso de Robles, where the wheat is sown; and the Rancho de la Asuncion. In these last two named ranchos there is an adobe building, roofed with tiles, for keeping the seed grain. However, all is dependent upon rain, because there is no means to irrigate the land, save at Asuncion, where there is a little spring with sufficient water for a garden; and at Santa Isabel, which has a little more in summer."

Ranchos of Senator Hearst

The ranchos of Piedra Blanca, San Simeon, and Santa Rosa became the property of George W. Hearst. The three stretch along the Pacific from the mouth of San Carpojoro Creek southeasterly to the mouth of Villa Creek and extend far back into the hills.

Rancho Piedra Blanca is the northernmost of the three. It was granted, in 1840, to José de Jesús Pico, one of the thirteen children of Don José Dolores Pico. He was a former soldier at Monterey and shortly after receiving this grant was administrator of San Miguel Mission. Although at one time he was arrested by Frémont and condemned to death, he was pardoned at the intercession of his wife and children and afterward became a devoted friend of that leader and assisted him in bringing about the treaty of Cahuenga. In 1848 and again in 1849 he made successful trips to the gold mines but later spent his time on his rancho.

Mariano Pacheco purchased a portion of Rancho Piedra Blanca from Pico, and until the '70's his family lived in the adobe house overlooking the ocean and located three miles north of the town of San Simeon. Don Mariano was buried in the vicinity. After the departure of the Pacheco family, the extensive two-story adobe was used by tenants until about 1906. Its ruins, marked by a few old cypress trees, are hidden in a tangle of weeds on a hill in a cattle pasture.

The village of San Simeon, which lies on this rancho, was for many years the center of an extensive whaling industry. As early as 1864 Captain Joseph Clark, still active in the '80's, here engaged in whaling, using a fleet of five boats outfitted for that purpose. Not many years ago a fire wiped out a large part of the buildings of the little village. A warehouse built in 1878 is still standing; and a store, a post office, and a few other frame buildings are in use. New residences, a little farther from the wharf, have been built and are attractive with their red-tiled, stucco exteriors.

Up the road back of the town is the large frame ranch house of Senator George Hearst. On a commanding height overlooking San Simeon Bay, William Randolph Hearst, son of Senator George W. and Phoebe Hearst, has built a stately country residence in which he has placed treasures from far lands.

Southeast of Rancho Piedra Blanca lies Rancho San Simeon through which flows San Simeon Creek. This was a grant of one square league made to José Ramón Estrada, son of José M. Estrada, and patented to J. M. Gomez in 1865. The San Simeon adobe, gone long ago, was on San Simeon Creek back from the beach about three-quarters of a mile.

The farthest south of the three is Rancho Santa Rosa, a three-league grant made to Julián Estrada, son of José Ramón Estrada, and patented to him in 1865. The Estrada adobe stood on the road north of Swallow Rock at an elevation of 130 feet. Nothing now remains to indicate the site. The town of Cambria, first called Rosaville, was located on the property. It originated during the copper excitement of 1863 and was aided in its growth by the quicksilver prospecting of 1871 and by the activities of lumbermen.

When the last-named rancho was purchased by Senator Hearst, Pancho Estrada, son of Don Julián, an expert horseman from early childhood, entered the employ of the new owner and continued in the service of that family until his death, at the age of eighty-three, on July 26, 1936. Don Pancho, as he was generally called, had great pride in the sleek horses under his care. He was a colorful figure, when, clad in Spanish vaquero costume, on fiesta days he headed the gay procession.

Rancho Moro y Cayucos

Cayuco is a nautical term applied to a small fishing boat, which is like a canoe and often made of skins. A point on the coast of California that was early found to make a possible port came by that name, because the schooners, pausing off shore from the mouth of a small stream, had commerce with the land by means of these small boats. The creek, the little settlement that grew up near its mouth, and, eventually, the land in the vicinity were all known by that designation.

In 1842, Rancho Moro y Cayucos was granted to Martin Olivera, from Rancho Sauzal in Monterey County, and to Vicente Feliz, former mayordomo of another rancho. It was later owned by James McKinley, a Scotch sailor, who married Carmen Amesti, daughter of José Amesti of Rancho Corralitos. McKinley sold it in smaller tracts for dairy farms.

In 1867 this coastal region was served by a weekly stage running from San Luis Obispo to San Simeon. In this year James Cass came to the vicinity of Cayucos Landing and lived first in the hills just back of the settlement, but soon he built a large house that now stands vacant near Cayucos Creek in the town of Cayucos. Because of his well-directed efforts the settlement began to increase. He built a wharf in 1870 and soon afterward a store and warehouse. In 1875 the broad streets of the town were laid out, and in the early '80's a stage bringing passengers from San Miguel and way stations made connections with a weekly boat at Cayucos.

For many years considerable shipping was done from this place, but finally a storm destroyed a large part of the pier and motor transportation eliminated the need of steamer calls. Only a small pleasure wharf is now on the site of the wharf built by Captain Cass.

Rancho San Bernardo

Vicente Cané, a Spanish sailor, settled in Alta California before 1828. On February 11, 1840, he received a grant of one square league of land lying between San Bernardo and Morro creeks, both of which empty into Morro Bay. The following year Don Vicente was *juez* at Misión San Luis Obispo. His rancho home was built about that time on a hill above San Bernardo Creek two miles east of Morro Rock. An idealized picture of the old adobe in which it is described as a "castle" or a "great mansion," whereas it was in reality only a story-and-a-half house, is here given, because it conveys something of the spirit of that time.

To this country the Don came, in those days of romance, to seek "a place of great beauty where he might build his castle, gather about him his friends, his flocks and herds, and live the ideal life of a Spanish gentleman of the new world. He had chanced to hear of the famous Morro Rock from a sea-faring friend and hither he came and was fascinated by what he beheld.

"The great red cone rising majestically from the limpid blue of the sea, ... the long sandbar that was a barrier to the rough waters of the ocean protecting the bay, the golden sunshine, the balmy breezes, and near at hand all sorts of wild game, ... No farther would Don Canet seek, for here was Elysia.

"He sought the skilled labor of the Indians from the two great missions of San Luis de Tolosa and San Miguel the Arcángel. Some made adobe bricks for the walls of the castle while others hewed out the great oak timbers and bore them to the site of the castle. On a gently sloping knoll, beside the San Lusita, with the mountains rising behind it, the great mansion was erected. . . . .

"The Don spent over $40,000 for labor and materials for the castle. It was plastered with crushed gypsum from the nearby hills and the flooring was brought around the Horn in sailing vessels. The wings contained sleeping rooms and servants' quarters. In one wing was a chapel with a raised altar. Here in great grandeur lived Don Canet. Many a fiesta, many a bear and bull-fight, many a wild horse race broke the monotony of life, if monotony could ever be in a land so fair and favored. . . . .

"It is said that long after master and horse were dust, his steed could be heard champing and neighing in the courtyard on moonlight nights and then madly galloping down to the bay. Those watching saw a misty form enter a phantom skiff and row away towards the rock."

Today this interesting house may be seen from the San Luis Obispo–Morro Bay highway as it stands above the road not far from a bridge two miles east of Morro Bay. It is well preserved but is not adequately maintained. One side is board-covered, and two others have been plastered with cement. Tar paper has replaced the tiles of the original roof. Its once impressive front door is flanked by deep-set windows, which are protected by perpendicular iron bars. Cypress and eucalyptus trees, now grown to great size, obscure the view oceanward. At the rear of the house is a patio, open on one side, around which extends a veranda with grapevines clambering over its top. These vines, the trunks of which are a yard in circumference, are probably of the same age as the building. An adobe house, now board-covered, built by a son of the grantee faces the patio and forms one of its walls.

Lands of Captain John Wilson

John Wilson, Scotch shipmaster and captain of the "Ayacucho," who had engaged in trading for years on the coast, settled in California in April 1848. Within the next ten years, he married Ramona Carillo de Pacheco, a widow with two sons, one of whom, Romualdo, afterward held many high offices in the state and became acting governor in. 1875. About 1839 Captain Wilson and James Scott, another native of Scotland, had entered into a business partnership, which continued until 1847.

Rancho Cañada del Chorro, on the southwest of the Santa Lucía Range, consisting of 3,166.90 acres, was granted to them; but as James Scott died in 1851 and Captain Wilson in 1860, the patent to it was issued to the heirs of the latter in 1861.

The Cañada de los Osos, so named by Portolá's men in 1769 because here they killed bears to replenish their meager food supply, was a part of Rancho Cañada de los Osos y Peche y Islay. This rancho was granted to Captain Wilson and James Scott, after having been previously granted to Francisco Badillo, a convict who came from Mexico in 1825; and Victor Linares, a soldier at San Diego in 1826, who came to San Luis Obispo before 1839. The whole of this became the property of Captain Wilson.

Between Rancho El Chorro and Rancho Cañada de los Osos, an Indian named Romualdo cultivated a bit of level land at the base of Cerro Romualdo. This tract, consisting of 117 acres, was purchased by Captain Wilson and called Huerta (vegetable garden) de Romualdo.

Captain Wilson built a house in the Cañada de los Osos and lived there from 1845 until his death. After the death of her husband, his widow continued to live there with her children. Her eldest son, who had now gained an enviable position in governmental affairs, resided with her. The property afterward passed to her daughter. The house still stands, two miles north of Port San Luis and eight miles west of San Luis Obispo.

Rancho San Miguelito

Rancho San Miguelito lay along the shore of San Luis Obispo Bay with a further shore line extending northwesterly along the ocean almost to Pecho Creek. On this rancho an asistencia to Misión San Luis Obispo was maintained for a time, and along the valley of the San Luis Obispo River the padres raised fields of corn and beans. The asistencia stood near the town of Avila, where now only a mound of melted clay marks its site.

Miguel Avila, born in Santa Barbara and educated in San Francisco, was a soldier and copyist at Monterey and in 1824 a corporal of the guard at Misión San Luis Obispo. One day at the Mission he took issue with Padre Martínez because the latter had harshly reproved him in the presence of a group of Indians for talking with an Indian at the ranchería. Both padre and corporal were men of spirit, and both apparently became angry. The padre called the corporal a perjurer and a traitor; and the soldier, in trying to induce the Father to go with him and settle the matter quietly, touched the robe of the holy man. This gave rise to curses and threat of excommunication. The corporal called the soldiers, and the padre rang a bell for all of his assistants and neophytes to come at once. "The two forces faced each other in battle array, armed on one side with guns and lances, and on the other with book, holy water, and cross. Martínez began to read and Avila seized the book, thinking thus to escape damnation; but the padre went on, finished the rite in bad Latin from memory, and retired in triumph to the church." The matter, later sent to the comandante, was compromised and the excommunication of the corporal annulled.

In 1826, two years after the trouble with the padre, Miguel Avila married María Inocenta, daughter of Dolores Pico, who was then in charge of Rancho Nacional. He lived in Monterey with his increasing family.

In 1839 Don Miguel obtained the grant of San Miguelito, and in 1845 he obtained the use of another part of the Mission lands, Rancho Laguna, patented to Bishop J. S. Alemany in 1859. In 1849, Don Miguel was alcalde at San Luis Obispo. In his later years he became interested in the preservation of documents, and the large collection, which he kept in his house, was lost when that building was destroyed by fire. His original house on the rancho, located at Avila (a town later named in his honor), is gone; but three other adobes built on his property are standing. On the state highway, one adobe, erected by David Castro (a son-in-law), is well preserved; another, formerly the home of Pancho Avila, lies off the east of the highway; while on the Marre Ranch, originally a part of San Miguelito, is an adobe built by Bertola Zúñiga about 1862.

The Ranchos of Francis Ziba Branch

Francis Ziba Branch, a native of New York, arrived in California with the Wolfskill party in 1831. For a few years he made his home at Santa Barbara, where he kept a store and boardinghouse, going away occasionally to hunt otter. In 1835 he married Manuela, daughter of Serefino Carlon, a soldier of the Santa Barbara Company. In 1837 he received a grant of over 16,000 acres of land lying to the north of Santa Barbara and named it Rancho Santa Manuela.

When Mr. Branch moved to his rancho, which was situated in the Arroyo Grande Valley, Misión San Luis Obispo about thirteen miles to the north was almost the only community in the entire region which was inhabited by white people. The valley which lay in front of his home was an impenetrable swamp—a thicket of willow and cottonwood trees where wild cats, lions, and grizzly bears made their homes. His stock was often attacked by these wild animals and by the Tulare Indians from the east. Edwin Bryant, in his *What I Saw in California*, describes the old Branch adobe and the usual life of that district. In contrast with the wild life out of doors, the domestic life of the fireside furnished comforts and luxuries unexpected at that time on the Pacific Coast.

Two years after Francis Ziba Branch received his rancho, his father-in-law, Don Serefino, obtained an adjoining grant of one square league named the Arroyo Grande but frequently called the Ranchita. It lay along the head waters of the Arroyo Grande, and in after years it was patented to the son-in-law.

At the lower end of the Arroyo Grande Valley was Rancho Pismo of two leagues granted to José Ortega in 1840. This was purchased by Isaac Sparks, who resold it, one half to Mr. Branch and one half to John M. Price. To further add to his possessions, Mr. Branch bought a part of Rancho Bolsa de Chamisal adjoining the Pismo on the south and a tract of land, Rancho Huer Huero, lying several miles to the east of his earlier holdings.

The town of Arroyo Grande lies in the Arroyo Grande Valley on the boundary line between Ranchos Manuela and Pismo. Near the town, on the present Jones Ranch, are the remains of a floor and the crumbling foundations of an old adobe believed by some to have been erected by Misión San Luis Obispo as one of the buildings of an asistencia. It is known that agricultural operations were carried on by the Mission Fathers on the rich bottom lands of the Arroyo Grande as early as 1780. There yet remains one room of an adobe where the Indians were instructed, its walls decorated with pictures drawn by the neophytes.

The house erected by Branch on Rancho Arroyo Grande was for many years the most noted one in the county. It is now gone, but a frame house in which his son Fred lived stands near the site. Three adobes built for other sons of Francis Ziba Branch are standing: the Ramón Branch adobe, the Santa Manuela, and the Ranchita. The Santa Manuela on the road to Huasna was a magnificent structure. It now has a coat of stucco and a corrugated iron roof.

John M. Price, who held the half of the Pismo grant not purchased by Mr. Branch, built an adobe home on the land which is well preserved. An unusual feature of it was its three distinct gables. John Price also built an adobe schoolhouse that is still standing.

The town of Pismo lies on the coast about midway of the shore line of the grant.

Rancho Nipomo

One of the famous old ranchos of California was the vast domain of almost 38,000 acres which constituted Rancho Nipomo (an Indian word said to mean "foot of the mountain"), for many years the first stopping place on El Camino Real south of Misión San Luis Obispo. Nearly all of the early books on California, as well as government reports and orders, frequently mentioned Captain Dana, the owner of this rancho, his pleasant home at Nipomo, and his never-failing and unstinted hospitality. The venerable casa, which stands beneath huge eucalyptus trees on an elevation commanding an extensive view, is a conspicuous landmark, a monument to the historic past of the county—second only to the old Missions. In ranchero days when the great land-holders of Alta California were the lords of the country, Rancho Nipomo was the headquarters for the region, and Casa de Dana was the stopping place for all travelers. Lieutenant Colonel John C. Frémont, Edwin Bryant, author of *What I Saw in California,* and General Henry W. Halleck were among the distinguished visitors who were entertained there.

William Goodwin Dana, a cousin of Richard Henry Dana, Jr., the author of *Two Years before the Mast,* was born in Boston on May 5, 1797, and there he received his education. When eighteen years of age, he went to Canton, China, and later to India in the service of an uncle, a Boston merchant. Returning to Boston after three years, he soon re-embarked, possibly on the "Waverley," as we find him captain of that vessel a few years later. In this capacity he engaged for several years in trade between China, the Hawaiian Islands, California, and Boston.

In 1825 Captain Dana established his business in Santa Barbara, where he soon after settled permanently. He became quite a prominent citizen, holding a number of important offices at different times. In 1828 he married María Josefa Carrillo, daughter of Carlos Antonio Carrillo, a resident of Santa Barbara and for a short time provisional governor of California in 1835, and about this time Dana applied for Rancho Nipomo. The grant, however, was not confirmed until April 6, 1837. In 1839 the Captain moved on to his rancho and built the large adobe house of thirteen rooms which still stands and was, until recently, the home of one of Captain Dana's sons, Juan Francisco Dana, who lived to be ninety-two years of age.

John C. Frémont, in December 1846 on his way from Monterey to Los Angeles, camped on Rancho Nipomo with his battalion of four hundred and thirty hungry and footsore soldiers, soaked to the skin by the rains through which they had tramped on the long, weary march from the north. The camp site was located in an oak grove at a point known as The Summit, not far from Casa de Dana.

Rancho El Paso de los Robles

Rancho El Paso de los Robles received its name from the presence of numerous large white oaks which dotted the valley, and the name has survived in the modern town and the famous resort located there. Known to the Indians from time immemorial, the hot springs on this rancho were also noticed by the Franciscan friars, who, possibly as early as 1797, placed a rude wall of logs about the edge of the main spring forming a pool of water. Alfred Robinson, who visited San Miguel in 1830, says that Father Juan Cabot "had erected a small house over the spot for the purpose of shelter and convenience for bathing, and it was resorted to by many persons . . . ." Even the grizzly bears of the region are said to have sought the warm waters of the spring and the pleasures of the bath. The following story from an old history is told of one such visitor:

"There was formerly a large cottonwood tree growing on the bank of the spring, with a limb extending low over the water. A huge grizzly was in the habit of making nocturnal visits to the spring, plunge into the pool, and, with his fore paws grasping the limb, swing himself up and down in the water, evidently enjoying his bath, his swing, and the pleasant sensations of his dips in warm water."

At first an outpost of Misión San Miguel, Rancho El Paso de los Robles was granted to Pedro Narváez on May 12, 1844, and later confirmed to Petronillo Rios. It was purchased in 1857 by Daniel D. and James H. Blackburn and Lazare Godchaux, and improvements were begun at once. James Blackburn built a frame house near the old adobe, said to have been erected by the Mission Fathers, and used the adobe for servants' quarters. Both stood on the west side of the road six and one-half miles south of Paso Robles, the site marked now only by a grassy mound near the entrance gate to the Crescent Dairy.

Drury James, a brother-in-law of James and Daniel Blackburn, purchased the hot springs tract along the west bank of the river where now the town of Paso Robles is situated and built the first substantial house on the site—a duplicate of the James Blackburn house south of town. The site of the original hot springs and the first bathhouse built for it is the northeast corner at Tenth and Spring streets, where a filling station now stands and across the street from the Paso Robles Hotel property.

An early Protestant church in the region was built of adobe through the co-operation of church members of several denominations, in 1877–1878. This structure, badly in need of repair, stands near the likewise uncared-for cemetery about five miles northeast of the town on the Estrella Plain.

Ranchos Atascadero and Asunción

Rancho Atascadero, granted to Triphon García on May 6, 1842, and Rancho Asunción, granted to Pedro Estrada on June 18, 1845, both of which lie between Ranchos Paso de Robles and Santa Margarita, became parts of the large Murphy estate, with its headquarters at the last-named rancho. An adobe, demolished years ago, stood on Rancho Atascadero near the spot now occupied by the Community Building in the town of Atascadero.

The adobe house in which Pedro Estrada lived on Rancho Asunción is still standing about two miles out from Atascadero on Traffic Way, a section of the old El Camino Real that was left out in the construction of Highway 101. This building, consisting of one story only, is very close to the road. The round-pole rafters of its roof sag with the weight of old tiles. Possibly it is a part of one of the large houses mentioned by Alfred Robinson in his tour of 1830. He wrote: "We afterwards stopped at the sheep farm belonging to the Mission of San Miguel where were two large houses and a number of straw huts. Gardens were attached to them, in which a variety of vegetables were cultivated by the Indians who were there as keepers of eight or ten thousand sheep."

A spring furnishing a copious supply of water and now called the Estrada Spring is on the hillside above this adobe. The quantity and quality of this water has not varied within the memory of man.

Rancho Santa Margarita

After secularization, Rancho Santa Margarita passed from the control of Misión San Luis Obispo and was granted to Joaquín Estrada, brother of Pedro. Comprising more than 17,000 acres, the rancho extended seven or eight miles along the rich bottom lands of the Salinas River Valley on which the Mission Fathers had raised beans, corn, and vegetables. Estrada neglected horticulture and devoted his attention to the raising of vast herds of long-horned Mexican cattle, his estate becoming famed as the queen of cattle ranches.

After giving up the ownership of this place, Don Joaquín removed with his family to the place now known as Estrada Gardens on the east side of Highway 101 two miles north of Mission San Luis Obispo. Here he planted fruit and ornamental trees and had a small vineyard. At his death he was buried on the hill above the house. His adobe home still stands. The tiles of its roof rise above the frame additions that have been built adjoining the original structure. A frame barn and other outbuildings are near by, while at the foot of a slope at the rear may be seen the darkened trunks of ancient grapevines and a picnic pavilion where merrymakers gather in the summer season. An inconspicuous gateway carries in faded letters across its top the words "Estrada Gardens."

Descendants of both Joaquín Estrada and his brother Pedro still live in the vicinity of the village of Santa Margarita.

Many tales of gay fiestas and extensive hospitality are told of the early days at Rancho Santa Margarita, and it is said that at one time the feasting was prolonged for thirty days. The rodeos here were festivals celebrated by people of leisure from all parts of the country, and during such times a great camp was formed, with every day a picnic and every night a round of revelry.

In 1860 Martin Murphy, Jr., who lived at Rancho Pastoria de las Borregas (Santa Clara County), came into possession of Rancho Santa Margarita, which, together with Ranchos Atascadero and Asunción and others that he also owned, made up a magnificent landed estate totaling 70,000 acres. Martin Murphy's son Patrick took charge of the entire domain, making Santa Margarita his home and business headquarters. As late as the '80's, thousands of head of beef cattle were pastured upon this huge territory.

Three adobe buildings, aside from the ruins of the old Santa Margarita Asistencia, remain today. The two-story residence which faced that large building stood in front of a row of low-roofed rooms used for the purpose of preparing and serving food and also as quarters for employees. These two parts are now connected by a wooden structure which makes of the whole a commodious and comfortable country home. The tiles on the roof became insecure and were replaced by shingles during the Murphy ownership. The reception rooms, entered from the long, broad veranda, are high of ceiling, thick of wall, and generous of floor space, while the entire residence, in its setting of old trees and ornamental shrubs and vines, calls to mind the gracious living of some of the families of the last century.

Standing some two or three hundred feet from the front of the main residence and a little to its left is another adobe building now called the hacienda. It consists of perhaps two rooms and was formerly used as a post office and store in the days when stagecoaches stopped in passing. It is now merely a storehouse on the rancho. A still smaller adobe structure, of uncertain former use, is now a pump house. All of these buildings are within a few hundred yards of the ruins of the old Asistencia with its little chapel room in one end.

The property passed from Patrick Murphy to the Reis Estate, which now holds it.

Miscellaneous Ranchos

Other grants of land in the county made by the Mexican government and recognized by the United States were the following:

Rancho Huasna, containing five square leagues, was granted to the hunter and trapper Isaac Sparks in 1843. On this rancho an old adobe house stands about twelve miles east of Arroyo Grande.

Rancho Corral de Piedra, seven leagues, was granted in 1841 and 1846 to José María Villavicencio. An adobe built about 1846, near the town of Edna, was demolished in about 1937. Another adobe built about 1851 by Rodríguez, son-in-law of the grantee, is still standing and is used as a residence. Rancho Corral de Piedra was one of the tracts purchased by the Steele brothers for the great dairy industry which, already established along the coast in Marin and San Mateo counties, spread to this county in the late '60's.

Rancho Bolsa de Chamisal, lying on the coast near the southwest corner of the county, was granted to Francisco Quijada in 1837, was later owned by Lewis T. Burton, and was sold by him for a part of the Steele dairy lands.

Potrero de San Luis Obispo was granted to María Concepción Boronda. In 1878 her father, José Cantua Boronda, was living on the rancho with her.

Rancho San Luisito, west of Rancho El Chorro, was granted by Governor Alvarado to Guadalupe Cantua in 1841. The wife of Guadalupe was Carmen Castro.

Rancho San Gerónimo, consisting of two leagues lying on the coast northwest of Cayucos, was granted to Rafael Villavicencio in 1842. An adobe house, originally 120 feet long, stood here. Little if any of it now remains.

Rancho Santa Ysabel is a tract lying across the Salinas River from Rancho Paso de Robles. It consisted of four leagues and was granted to Francisco Arce in 1844. He was at one time employed to collect debts due to the Missions and at different times in his life held different clerical positions.

Grants of land lying partially across the boundary lines of the county were: the Cholame, stretching a little way over into Monterey County, and Ranchos Guadalupe, Sisquoc, Suey, and Tepusquite, extending over into Santa Barbara County. The Cholame land figures prominently in early history as a stopping place for early travelers. Across it ran a road leading to San Luis Obispo and a branch road leading to the Visalia region. It consisted of six leagues granted to Mauricio Gonzales by Governor Micheltorena on February 5, 1844. It was named after the Cholam tribe of Indians who lived in that section.

SOURCES

[Credit is here given for source material, and permission to quote is hereby acknowledged]

ANGEL, MYRON. "Carrisa Plains," in *Report of State Mineralogist*, State Office, Sacramento, 1890

———. *History of San Luis Obispo County*. Thompson & West, Oakland, 1883

BOLTON, HERBERT EUGENE. *Anza's California Expeditions*. 5 vols. University of California Press, Berkeley, 1930

———. *Fray Juan Crespi, Missionary Explorer on the Pacific Coast, 1769–1774*

BRYANT, EDWIN. *What I Saw in California*. D. Appleton & Company, Philadelphia, 1849

COY, OWEN C. *Pictorial History of California*. University of California Extension Division, Berkeley, California, 1925

DANA, JUAN FRANCISCO. "Ten Decades on a California Rancho," as told to John Edwin Hogg, in *Touring Topics*, XXIII, No. 11 (November, 1931), 16–19

DARLING, VELVA G. "Cove Landing, A San Luis Obispo County Scenic Spot," in *Touring Topics*, March, 1926

ELDER, DAVID PAUL. *The Old Spanish Missions of California*. Paul Elder & Company, San Francisco, 1913

ENGELHARDT, ZEPHYRIN. *San Miguel Arcángel, the Mission on the Highway*. Mission Santa Barbara, 1929

JACKSON, HELEN HUNT. *Ramona*. Little, Brown & Company, Boston, 1919

(ROBINSON, ALFRED). *Life in California*. Published anonymously. (H. G. Collins, Paternoster Row, London, 1845)

SAN MATEO COUNTY

SAN MATEO COUNTY (San Mateo is Spanish for St. Matthew) was organized in 1856, being formed from the southern portion of San Francisco County. The county seat, located at Belmont in May 1856, within a year was changed to Redwood City, at which place it has remained, although the question of its removal came up in 1861, 1873, and 1874.

In 1868, by an act of the state legislature, the southern boundary, which had been a line running due west from the source of the south branch of San Francisquito Creek, became an irregular line running southwest to the coast below Point Año Nuevo. This change transferred a large tract from Santa Cruz County to San Mateo County.

Indian Mounds

Indian villages were widely scattered along the shores of both Ocean and Bay where sea food was easily obtained. Near Point Año Nuevo, the most southerly corner of the county, are acres of shifting dunes, where the moving sands have revealed from time to time such evidences of Indian occupation as are usually found in "kitchen middens" (the refuse heaps of the native tribes): broken shells, arrow points, bones of wild animals that have been used for food, and human skeletons that were buried near tribal dwellings. Farther north on the coast at Half Moon Bay are several mounds, the largest of which lies just inside Pillar Point out on the marsh and extends below sea level.

Perhaps the largest mounds in the county were in the vicinity of South San Francisco on the shore of San Francisco Bay, where remnants of them may still be found.

At San Mateo Point, one mile northeast of the city of San Mateo on the edge of the Bay, are the remains of a "kitchen midden." This and other mounds thereabouts are composed largely of the shells of the succulent native oyster used extensively by the Indians for food. On and near the banks of San Mateo Creek, once a favorite haunt of native tribes, have been found many indications of early human habitation. In excavating for house foundations on Baywood Avenue to the west of Highway Alternate 101, as many as six skeletons have been taken out of one small area. The ground in this vicinity is largely impregnated with broken shell. Across the highway where the creek, for a little distance, is held within proper bounds by concrete walls, larger shell mounds are found. The creek first passes south of Mills Memorial Hospital and the San Mateo Junior College, separating those two institutions from the Public Library and the San Mateo Civic Center. At the corner of San Mateo Drive and Baldwin Avenue it is completely lost to sight as it turns sharply around the base of the mound upon which the school is located and flows beneath the pavement down one edge of Baldwin Avenue. Large oaks have grown upon this mound since its abandonment by the red men. About two feet of surface shell, in which a few relics such as mortars were found, were removed before the erection of the school buildings. It was probably from this village that the helpful visitors, mentioned by Anza, came to his camp on San Mateo Creek in March 1776.

Farther down the creek is another mound site, now leveled and crossed by Cypress Avenue between El Dorado and Grant streets. To the north of the mouth of the creek were other mounds near the Bay shore; one still stands at the end of Mount Diablo Avenue between the Bay and the Bayshore Highway. West of the Bayshore Highway between Poplar and Peninsula avenues, and North Humboldt and North Delaware streets, is the site of the largest of all the mounds in or near the city of San Mateo. The dimensions of this heap through the base were 150 by 225 feet, and the height may have been as much as 15 feet. Made up largely of oyster shells, its material has been screened and put to various uses. The High School building and football field are upon this site.

In Redwood City the part of Main Street that runs between El Camino Real and the railroad track, formerly Mound Street, traverses the site of another Indian village.

La Punta del Año Nuevo

Sebastián Vizcaíno set sail from Mexico on May 5, 1602, to survey the California coasts for a good harbor to be used by the Spanish galleons on their trips to and from the Philippines. He found a harbor that pleased him at Monterey and remained there at anchor for a few days. When he resumed the voyage on January 3, 1603, the first conspicuous point he sighted was a low headland to which the name La Punta del Año Nuevo (New Year's Point) was given—the name that the extreme southwestern point of San Mateo County still bears. It was the point that mariners following Vizcaíno described as the northwestern extremity of Monterey Bay.

The Mexican grant of land made in this vicinity in 1842 perpetuated the name, and there is a local tradition that at the time the grant was made it was possible to walk from the mainland out to the point, a feat no longer possible on account of the shallow strait that now makes an island of the extreme tip of land. This island is frequented by numerous sea lions. The United States Light Service maintains a station here.

The Portolá Trail

On Monday, October 23, 1769, Gaspar de Portolá and the members of his party, including Father Crespi and Miguel Costansó, diarists of the expedition, having rested over Sunday in the Cañada de la Salud in what is now Santa Cruz County, resumed their march in search of the bay of Monterey. Traveling two leagues that day, they entered the region now included in San Mateo County, passed La Punta del Año Nuevo, and camped for the night at the mouth of Gazos Creek near an Indian village called, in the diary of Costansó, "La Casa Grande."

During the following days they continued their journey north, crossing Pescadero Creek and the little lake which, though now dammed up for irrigation purposes, still lies at Arroyo de los Frijoles halfway between Bolsa Point and Pescadero Point. They stopped and made camp at San Gregorio Creek about half a league from its mouth, remaining there for two days for the benefit of some of the tired and sick soldiers. The location of an Indian village near the beach so impressed Father Crespi that he proposed the place for a Mission site.

On October 27 they halted on the south bank of Purisima Creek, and on the 28th they crossed the "Plain of Wild Geese" and pitched camp at the mouth of Pilarcitos Creek, just north of the town of Half Moon Bay. Pillar Point, first seen by the navigator Francisco de Gali in 1585, could be discerned from this place, lying to the north-northwest. Here a halt was made over Sunday, October 29, as Portolá himself was ill. On October 30, a stop was made on the bank

of Martini's Creek one and one-half miles north of Montara Light. Here the way was blocked by the Montara Mountain, and Sergeant Ortega was sent to break a trail over the barrier.

From there the party ascended the mountain and looked down upon the Gulf of the Farallones and also Point Reyes forty miles to the north. A base camp was established, October 31, on a lagoon near the mouth of San Pedro Creek. From this point Sergeant Ortega made an extended exploring trip, discovering on November 1, not the long-sought bay of Monterey, but the bay of San Francisco instead. A hunting party, which left camp on November 2 and returned at nightfall with news of an inland valley and sea, was the first to report the discovery of the bay, as Ortega did not return until the night of November 3. However, the explorers were interested only in the news which Ortega brought of a report from the Indians of "a port and a ship therein" only two days distant from their camp.

Their strength having been revived by the plentiful feast of mussels afforded by San Pedro Cove, Portolá and his men proceeded over Sweeney Ridge into the valley to the east by way of Cañada de San Andreas. Down this they traveled about one mile and pitched camp beside a lagoon, a spot now covered by the waters of San Andreas Lake. The trail followed on November 5 is today covered by the Crystal Springs Lakes, and camp was made at a large lagoon now included in the upper lake about two miles south of the dam over which the Skyline Boulevard passes. Here the mountains on the right were covered with oak, redwood, and madroña trees, and the party saw many herds of deer. This section is today the San Francisco Game Refuge, where numerous deer may often be seen grazing.

On November 6, a base camp was again established, this time on the north bank of San Francisquito Creek near the Southern Pacific Railway bridge and opposite the huge old redwood known as the "Palo Alto." From this point Ortega explored the east side of San Francisco Bay, possibly as far as Niles. On November 10, he returned with the discouraging news that hostile Indians and another great arm of the sea barred further progress. After conference with the other members of the party, Portolá decided to discontinue the search for the harbor of Monterey.

Retracing its steps, the little company returned to the unrecognized Monterey Bay over the route by which they had come, camping on the 11th at the south end of the Cañada de Raymundo near Woodside, on the 12th near San Andreas Lake, and on the 13th at San Pedro Creek. Bolton says that from there they proceeded down the coast, stopping successively at Martini's Creek, Half Moon Bay, Tunitas Creek, Pescadero Creek, and Año Nuevo, and entering Santa Cruz County once more on November 20. On the 27th they were back at the harbor of Monterey, which they again failed to recognize.

Rivera's Trail in 1774

The Spanish Viceroy in Mexico, Don Antonio María Buchareli, desirous of establishing a Mission at the Port of San Francisco, ordered Don Fernando de Rivera y Moncada, a member of the expedition led by Governor Gaspar de Portolá, which had discovered that port, to go to that place to look for a suitable site.

Setting out from Monterey on November 23, 1774, the party reached San Francisquito Creek at the southern boundary line of San Mateo County on November 28. Accompanying Captain Rivera on this journey were nineteen individuals, the most important one of them being Fray Francisco Palóu. Their camping place at the creek seemed to them suitable for a Mission, since it met the requirements of wood, water, and native peopl to be Christianized. Therefore a cross made of

two beams was erected to mark the spot for future consideration.

On the next day's march northward, they turned into the
hills near the present town of Belmont, where they found
affable Indians whom Fray Palóu, in his religious zeal, embraced and to many of whom he made gifts of beads, hoping
to hold their friendship by this means until the time for gathering them into the fold of the Mission. As the day wore on,
more and more natives joined the travelers, pressing them to
enter their villages, which were numerous along the route
both in the hills and down nearer the shore of the bay.

On November 30, the day of the feast of St. Andrew,
Rivera and his party came to a pleasant valley which since
that day has borne the name they gave—San Andres or Andreas. On that day, too, friendly Indians enjoyed the company
and the food of these strange white men, and again Fray
Palóu interested them by intimating that he would return and
would bring seeds for planting so that they could grow similar food for themselves.

Just before noon of December 4, the party halted upon
the hills above a lake which they called Merced, although it
appears to have been south of the lake now called by that
name; and for the next few days they explored in the territory now embraced in San Francisco County. Then, deciding
not to retrace their steps but to follow down the coast of the
ocean as the earlier Portolá expedition had done, they reached
San Pedro Valley, where they spent an afternoon and a night;
and the next day crossed San Pedro Mountain, where they
found a temporary camp of Indians. Misty and rainy weather
delayed progress. But, on December 8, the morning sun arose
in a clear sky, and they proceeded to the Arroyo Domingo,
now called San Gregorio Creek, and passed on the way a
large village to which they were cordially invited by a long-
bearded native, not stopping, however, because accepting the
invitation would have taken the travelers from their course.
Then on through the valleys of Pescadero Creek and Arroyo
de los Frijoles, they went on December 9 past the Ranchería
Casa Grande, visited by the Portolá expedition, thence southward over the present border line of Santa Cruz County on
December 10.

Anza's Trail in 1776

Juan Bautista de Anza, on his way from Monterey to the
Port of San Francisco with a party of thirteen (among whom
were Lieutenant Don Joseph Joaquín Moraga and the Rev.
Father Fray Pedro Font), entered the border of what is now
San Mateo County by crossing the San Francisquito Creek
in the vicinity of the "Palo Alto" tree on Tuesday, March 26,
1776. An Indian village of about twenty huts was near the
creek, and on the north bank stood the cross erected by Father
Palóu when he had passed the place with Captain Rivera two
years previous to this time. Font's diary gives the information that along this arroyo were various trees: laurel, ash, and
a beautiful cypress called redwood.

After making gifts of beads to the women in this village,
they proceeded through a plain of oaks, and near where
Atherton now is they were met by a group of shouting natives
whose long-haired chief was recognized by Corporal Robles
as being one of a group whom his companions of a former
journey had called the "Shouters." Approaching the place
where Redwood City now stands, they came to another village,
where they saw a large heap of mussel shells. During the
day's march, they passed four Indian villages. The last one
was located on San Mateo Creek shortly before they made
their camp for the night—on El Camino Real where Burlingame Avenue now intersects it in the city of Burlingame.
Along the arroyos passed this day grew many scented trees
which they called laurel.

Arising early the next morning, they were on their way
before seven o'clock, after Mass had been said by Father
Font. This day, March 27, the line of travel led past Millbrae
(whence, off to the left, they saw the Buri Buri Ridge called
by them "Pinabetes"), past San Bruno, the cemeteries and
Colma, toward the Port of San Francisco. Two days later
half of the party with the camp equipment returned along
this same route to await the commander at San Mateo Creek.
Anza, accompanied by his Father Chaplain and five soldiers,
spent the day exploring and making various detours. Coming
down the San Andres Valley, they saw extensive groves of
trees suitable for timber and a long narrow lake, the San Andres, which has since been utilized as one of the reservoirs
for the water supply of the city of San Francisco. In the
course of the afternoon, Corporal Robles shot an immense
bear which appeared out of the woods near Crystal Springs
Lake. The skin of this animal was preserved as a gift for
the Viceroy.

On reaching camp at the site of El Camino Real and
Third Avenue in the city of San Mateo, they found most of
the men from the neighboring Indian village congregated
there—"a poor-looking lot" but inclined to be helpful. After
a heavy rain during the night, they set out in the morning in a
southeasterly direction. When San Francisquito Creek was
reached, Father Pedro Font set the graphometer 36 varas
from the foot of the great redwood tree there and found its
height something over 50 varas, a vara being a measure of
2.78 feet. The Indians of the vicinity watched this proceeding in quiet wonder.

From this point the party passed on into Santa Clara
County. Within a short time the route thus established was
again traversed, this time by Anza's great company of settlers
which, bound for San Francisco from Mexico, had rested for
a time in Monterey while their leader went ahead.

Old Land Grants

The northern boundary line of the county runs through
the Mexican grant of Rancho Laguna de la Merced, only a
small portion of which extends from San Francisco County
south into San Mateo County. South of this, on the ocean
side of the Peninsula, of which this county forms so large a
part, are the lands of eight ranchos each having one boundary line at the low-tide mark on the beach and having their
inland limit defined by some natural configuration such as a
stream, a canyon, or a ridge. These eight ranchos occupy all
of this stretch of coast line down to the border of the adjoining county of Santa Cruz.

Rancho San Pedro

Rancho San Pedro, reaching east to the crest of the
hills and south to the crest of the Montara, was granted by
the Mexican authorities in 1839 to Francisco Sánchez and
patented to him by the United States government in November 1870. On this stretch of coast are located Salada Beach
and San Pedro Point. In San Pedro Valley, a little way back
from the point, is an old adobe reached by going a quarter
of a mile east on a narrow road that leads from State Highway 1 at the base of the San Pedro Mountain grade. Legend
has it that a house built on this site was repaired in 1817 with
materials salvaged from a ship wrecked on San Pedro Point
and carried ashore by the waves. The adobe now standing was
built about the year 1837, according to J. N. Bowman, by Don
Francisco Sánchez and is called "El Viejo de Sánchez." It
is in fair condition, has a balcony across its front, and is still
used as a residence.

Francisco, son of José Antonio Sánchez who owned
Rancho Buri Buri, was a native of San Francisco and a highly
respected citizen. As a member of the San Francisco Company,

he attained the rank of captain and finally that of acting commander. In 1846, while he was holding the latter position, he became so annoyed by the depredations of Americans that he headed the short-lived revolt in which Alcalde Bartlett was captured and held hostage. His wife was Teodora Higuera; and his four children were Luisa, Luis, Dolores, and Pedro. Kind-hearted and genial, he was living in Misión Dolores in 1855, and it is probable that his earlier duties in the San Francisco Company and his later position at the Mission prevented him from spending much time on his rancho.

Rancho El Corral de Tierra

This rancho, extending from the south face of San Pedro Mountain to Half Moon Bay, included the coast from north of Point Montara to Pilarcitos Creek and contained one and three-quarters leagues granted in two parts by Manuel Jimeno and Micheltorena.

The northern and larger part was given on October 16, 1839, to Francisco Guerrero Palomares, whose widow, Josefa Haro de Guerrero, filed her claim in 1852 and received the patent for the land in 1866.

The ranch home, since known as the Guerrero Adobe, stood on a hillside near a creek about one mile northeast of the present town of Princeton and was in fair condition until the earthquake of 1906. It contained four rooms on the ground floor, with an attic above. This adobe, with a porch across its entire front, faced south looking on a garden of flowers and vegetables where still stands an old magnolia tree.

The village of Princeton, where now are two wharves, was formerly known as Old Landing. Produce from the country thereabouts was shipped by schooner to San Francisco.

The southern end of Rancho Corral de Tierra, granted to Tiburcio Vásquez, was separated from the land of Palomares by the Arroyo de en Medio. Vásquez's tract extended from this stream southerly along the coast to Pilarcitos Creek. It was granted to him on October 5, 1839. His claim was filed with the Land Commission in 1853, but the patent was not issued until 1873.

The Vásquez adobe home of five rooms was built on the north bank of Pilarcitos Creek a little way northwest of the bridge now at the northern edge of Half Moon Bay. A small flower garden was near the house. The family of Don Tiburcio consisted of his wife, Alvira Hernández, and his ten children. The youngest son, after spending some years of service at Misión Dolores, built a frame house near his father's home and engaged in business in Spanishtown, now Half Moon Bay. His name is still visible in faded letters on a wooden structure near the bridge—"Pilarcitos Livery Stable, Pablo Vasquez, Proprietor."

Above the gateway of a well-enclosed cemetery a few hundred yards north of this bridge may be read—"Pilarcitos Cemetery 1820–1923." Many of the graves within are of pioneers who were born in Spain and whose presence in this settlement helped to give to it the name of Spanishtown.

The bridge, originally built of "preserved wood," over Pilarcitos Creek near the Vásquez livery stable, was considered at the time of its erection to be the finest wagon bridge in the country. It was a part of the construction of the turnpike from San Andreas Valley to the sea, and a toll gate stood two miles up Pilarcitos Canyon. The present motor road running from Crystal Springs Lakes to Half Moon Bay crosses the summit in approximately the same place as did the old turnpike. Motor stages from San Mateo to Santa Cruz have displaced those drawn by horses. Descending the mountain at the head of the canyon, the road has been realigned to eliminate the former steep grades. The roadbed of the lower stretch remains in about the same place as in former years. The "preserved wood" bridge has been replaced by one of concrete.

Rancho Miramontes

This rancho, known also as Arroyo de los Pilarcitos and occasionally as San Benito, was granted to Candelario Miramontes by Governor Alvarado in 1841; according to Bancroft, it was a re-grant of land given to Don Candelario before 1830.

Grain had been raised there and sold to Russian traders before 1820; hides and tallow were shipped from there. Probably this is the "grazing ground twenty-five miles southeast of San Francisco" mentioned by Philip Leget Edwards in his journal as the place where he and Ewing Young obtained two hundred head of cattle for the herd which they drove to Oregon in 1837.

When the first member of the Miramontes family, the son Rudolfo, took up his residence there in 1840, grizzly bears and other predatory animals native to the country had not been subdued and proved destructive to his roaming herds of cattle. The Miramontes house was built on the south bank of Pilarcitos Creek east of the present highway, not far from the bridge, and opposite the Vásquez adobe. A one-story house with an attic, immaculate in its exterior coat of white, it had a large reception room, two large bedrooms, and a kitchen built of adobe bricks. A porch extended in front where doves clambered, and a woodshed was at the rear. The door leading to the attic storeroom was in the ceiling of the reception room, and access to it was by a removable ladder. Winter stores of beans, corn, and squash were kept there. The rosebush in front was so large that a child could hide beneath it at the approach of strangers. The daughter Carmelita, who married Francisco Gonzales, a vaquero from Santa Cruz, lived in this adobe after her marriage, and all of her children were born there. On the site of this adobe on the first street on the east side of the highway south of the Pilarcitos Creek bridge stands a small modern home erected after the removal of the adobe. Between it and the highway is a colorful flower plot owned and cared for by the descendants of Don Candelario.

The two families, Vásquez and Miramontes, afforded each other company and protection. Around these houses the settlement called Spanishtown grew up. The low-roofed adobe homes built by these families, characteristic landmarks until fairly recent years, were still occupied when early American settlers began to arrive. One of these settlers was Henry Bidwell, nephew of John Bidwell, who not only started the first place of public amusement in Spanishtown but was also its first postmaster. The town was platted in 1863 in the southwest angle formed by the confluence of Arroyo León and Pilarcitos Creek and continued to be called Spanishtown for forty years or more, although its post office was called Half Moon Bay—the name of the town today.

The grant of Rancho Miramontes contained one and one-half square leagues lying between Pilarcitos Creek and Purisima Creek, as described in the petition filed by Don Candelario in 1852; but the patent issued in 1882 was for only one league and made the southern boundary at Arroyo Verde.

The one-half league that had been in dispute lies between Arroyo Verde and Purisima Creek. In this area through which the Coast Road south of Half Moon Bay now runs are a few small houses within sight of the road. Well located on sloping grounds, having in its isolation a certain dignity, each one looks out from vacant windows between the trees, now old, that were young when the houses were new.

The once flourishing, but no longer extant, town of Purisima stood on the hill above Purisima Creek. It was a lively village in the '60's with Richard Dougherty's good hotel (burned in the '70's) as its center. Repair shops for wagons and farm machinery were maintained there, and its post office was served by the stage running from San Mateo to Santa Cruz. Before 1860 one of the first schools on the west side of the mountains was established on land donated by a large landowner for the purpose. In 1866, the Purisima district had 115 pupils and in that year was divided into three districts. The original schoolhouse, built of hand-sawed lumber, stood until 1875, when an imposing two-story building took its place. This large structure has now been torn down, and from its material a smaller one has been constructed.

In 1868 Henry Dobbel, of Alameda, purchased 907 acres of land in the immediate vicinity of Purisima and erected the finest house in the settlement. In 1878, it is reported, he planted 900 acres of potatoes, a venture that proved unfortunate. His home, long a landmark, has been dismantled. But the trees that he planted, now tall and dark around the site, stand to the west of the road at the turn down the hill after the road passes what remains of the small shops and houses of the today deserted hamlet. In the Protestant cemetery opposite the school several members of the Dobbel family are buried.

Rancho Cañada Verde y Arroyo de la Purísima

This grant was made provisionally on March 26 of 1838 to José María Alviso, a military officer in San José in 1837, who had formerly held important posts in San Francisco and who was in command of troops with Arce in 1846. This property was surveyed in 1860, and United States patent was issued to José Antonio Alviso in 1864 for 8,905.58 acres lying between Purisima and Tunitas creeks.

On the south bank of the winding Purisima Creek at the northern edge of the rancho is a large old frame house with an old-fashioned, two-story balcony across its entire front. This was the well-kept ranch home of John Butts, a German, who owned 543 acres here in the '70's. His barns are still standing across the road from the house.

Just before crossing Tunitas Creek by the long bridge at the southern border of this rancho, one sees a high bank on which are a group of weather-worn farm buildings amid an old planting of cypress and pines. The road from King's Mountain, crossing the Coast Road near this point, leads on toward the beach, where stand the few remnants of Tunitas Glen, the terminal of the defunct Ocean Shore Railroad from San Francisco. Plans had been made by a group of San Francisco men to connect that city and Santa Cruz by trains running through this scenic and productive coastal region; but the trains never ran beyond this point. A stage service completed the journey. The railroad was discontinued in 1920, and the timbers of an unfinished bridge still form a network across the deep gulch of Tunitas Creek just south of Tunitas Glen.

An elaborate chute and extensive warehouses on the coast near this point antedated the railway by several years. Occupying the spot known as Gordon's Landing, it was constructed in 1873 by Horace Templeton and Alexander Gordon. Produce from the farms of the region was lowered to boats on the water below by a movable apron. It long remained a landmark of this coast area.

A flurry of excitement about oil deposits found in the canyons of the two creeks bordering this rancho ran through the countryside in 1888. Developments were carried on by C. M. Cook, who obtained a lease to properties on Tunitas and Purisima creeks, but the yield of oil has been trifling.

Rancho San Gregorio

Rancho San Gregorio, consisting of four square leagues, was granted April 16, 1839, by Governor Alvarado to Antonio Buelna; and the grant was approved by the Departmental Assembly in 1840. The northern line of this rancho was Tunitas Creek, from the mouth of which it extended southward to the mouth of Pomponio Creek, a region which included practically the whole of the San Gregorio Valley and watershed. Buelna conveyed one square league lying toward the sources of San Gregorio Creek to Salvador Castro, one-time member of the San José Council, who filed petition for the United States patent in 1860.

At the time of receiving the grant of this rancho, Don Antonio Buelna was in command of an expedition against Indians and foreigners; and his adobe home was on his San Francisquito rancho now within the confines of Santa Clara County. Among Indians formerly sought by the Mexican authorities was Chief Pomponio, renegade from a Mission, captured at Monterey in 1824. Pomponio's mountain fastness had been at the headwaters of Pomponio Creek, a short stretch of which formed the southern line of Buelna's Rancho San Gregorio.

Don Antonio died in 1842, and in 1853 a petition "on behalf of Encarnación Buelna, widow of Don Antonio Buelna now married to Chino Rodríguez," was filed. A patent was issued to her in 1861 for 13,344.15 acres. This property passed from the hands of the family at a very early date. The survey map, made in 1860 for the issuance of the patent, shows a fence belonging to Hugh Hamilton, an early American settler. His large frame house, now torn down, long stood on the north bank of San Gregorio Creek and was visible from the junction of the La Honda and the Half Moon Bay roads in the village of San Gregorio.

The settlement of San Gregorio is an old one. The original part of it lay just south of the bridge at the base of the hill where the store building (in which the old post office also had a place) is still standing, although vacant. On the flat plot of ground near that store were at one time a number of shacks inhabited by Chinese, who were employed to cut brush on the hillsides. Here, too, was one of the old-time "washhouses," where Orientals did the laundry work for lumbermen and others. Eventually these shacks floated off toward the sea during a period of heavy rains and high water. A frame hotel, called the San Gregorio House, stood on the hill above the creek. It was at one time a popular vacation resort for families who lived on the other side of the mountains, and names of distinguished visitors appeared in its register. Horses were kept for hire; the sands of the beach where the children might play were not far distant; both salt- and fresh-water fishing were good; and great quantities of quail and deer afforded sport for the hunter. San Gregorio House has changed ownership many times. A part of it stands vacant without much change in its construction, but the rear has been remodeled and is used as a residence by descendants of former owners.

Rancho San Antonio

Rancho San Antonio, or El Pescadero, was granted in 1833 by Governor José Figueroa to Juan José Gonzales, a soldier of the San Francisco Company, and was patented to him by the United States government in June 1866. It consisted of 3,282.32 acres in the vicinity of the town of Pescadero on Pescadero Creek.

In 1852 Gonzales erected a small adobe on the north bank of the creek one block east of the bridge over that stream at the north end of town. The Bartlett V. Weeks family, natives of Maine who came to California in 1859 via Nicaragua, purchased in 1860 the 157-acre tract upon which this adobe stood. No vestige of it now remains; and its site, remembered by the older local residents, is now surrounded by farm buildings.

The first American to take up residence in this vicinity

was Alexander Moore, who after traveling across the Plains by covered wagon reached California in 1847 with his father, Eli, and other members of the family. They camped for the night of November 15 of that year on the plaza by the Santa Cruz Mission. The father remained in Santa Cruz until his death in 1859. Alexander built a house where the Santa Cruz Light House now stands, and settling his family there he went to the mines on the Tuolumne River for six months. In 1853, attracted to the Pescadero region by the rank growth of mustard which proved to him the fertility of the soil, he erected a large L-shaped house north of Pescadero Creek, using lumber hauled by ox team from Santa Cruz. This house, occupied by his descendants, still stands about a half-mile east of the Pescadero High School. On the mantel of the living room of this comfortable home is a large clock which still keeps accurate time in spite of its long journey, nearly a hundred years ago, across the Plains in the top of a covered wagon. Alexander's wife, Adeline Spainhower, was a pioneer woman of sterling worth whose activity extended beyond her own family to her neighbors. Since no practicing physician was available nearer than San Mateo and the fee asked for coming that distance was from fifty to five hundred dollars, Mrs. Moore, as emergency doctor, would go long distances on horseback to relieve suffering.

Alexander and Adeline Moore had a family of six children: Eli, Joseph, William, Ida, David, and Walter; and for their benefit their father employed a teacher and started the first school in the vicinity.

When the property was divided after the deaths of the parents, the portion on which the family house stood was given to Ida, the only daughter, then married to Charles Steele, a son of the owner of the ranch lying to the southeast. To Ida also went the old clock. Other portions of the land went to the sons, and to William went the muzzle-loading gun that had done duty on the long overland journey. Many of the original land holdings of Alexander Moore are still held by his descendants.

Rancho Butano

Rancho Butano, consisting of one square league lying along the Pacific Ocean between Butano Creek and the Arroyo de Frijoles, was given to Ramona Sánchez on February 19, 1838. It was the first grant made by Governor Alvarado, and it was confirmed by Governor Micheltorena six years later. Doña Ramona held and occupied it until 1852, when she sold it to Manuel Rodríguez, who received the United States patent for it in 1866.

This rancho was afterward purchased by Loren Coburn, a native of Vermont, who arrived by steamer in San Francisco in 1851 and who, after spending a time in mining on the American River, returned to San Francisco and engaged in business there for many years. Becoming interested in lands in this part of the county, he moved to this region in 1872 and spent the later years of his life in its development.

On the coast a little to the south of the mouth of Butano Creek is a deposit of varicolored, water-worn pebbles. They lie several feet deep over an area of approximately two acres; agate, chalcedony, jasper, moonstones, and sardonyx are found among them. On this beach Loren Coburn erected a large three-story hotel, expecting to have it filled by people who, attracted to the resort, could reach it easily by means of the railroad then being planned to run south from San Francisco. He spent money lavishly on its construction, and the town of Pescadero near by profited by the pay checks that he gave to these imported workmen. In 1906 when the disaster of the earthquake and fire in San Francisco definitely ended the further construction of the Ocean Shore Railroad, because the funds of its promoters were needed elsewhere, the hotel was

permanently closed. In 1934 this solitary, red-roofed landmark was partially removed, and the unprotected rooms of the part now standing are exposed to wind and weather. The members of the Coburn family are all gone, and their white-painted residence, with the emblem of the rising sun in a gable-end, stood unoccupied facing the main street in Pescadero for many years until it was destroyed by fire.

Rancho Punta del Año Nuevo

Rancho Punta del Año Nuevo, as granted May 27, 1842, by Governor Alvarado to Simeon Castro (already the owner of two ranches in Monterey County), covered that vast tract of 17,753.15 acres in the extreme southwestern part of San Mateo County and stretched from Butano Creek to the Año Nuevo Light Station. In 1857 after the death of Don Simeon, his widow, María Antonia Pico, and his family received the United States patent for the property.

However, in 1866 the part of this ranch that lay to the north between Butano Creek and Arroyo de los Frijoles was patented to Manuel Rodríguez as Rancho Butano. Apparently another part was also called in·question when Isaac Graham deposited for record a patent held by himself. On the survey map of 1857 the site of Isaac Graham's house is shown on an unnamed creek north of Point Año Nuevo. There he lived for a time with his family, after his milling operations on Zayante Creek, on land which his descendants call his "cattle range." Graham's house, said to have been brought around the Horn, is still used as a residence. A two-story, frame dwelling with interior walls plastered, it originally stood nearer White House Creek than it now does, because the old house was moved about a hundred feet to allow for the erection of a larger house for later owners. But for several years it had the distinction of being the finest dwelling in the region; and the story is told that, before trees grew up to hide it from the view of passing boats, mariners reckoned the distance to the Port of San Francisco by sighting this lone white house.

The greater part of the original rancho of Simeon Castro came once again into the hands of one man. Loren Coburn, after purchasing the smaller, boot-shaped Rancho Butano, eventually became the owner of Rancho Punta del Año Nuevo, which he leased out for dairy farms.

In 1862, 7,060 acres of Coburn's land was rented to a small group of men who took their several allocations and carried on an extensive dairying business. In this group were Horace Gushell, Charles Wilson, and three men of the Steele family: Rensaeler E., Isaac C., and Edgar W. The Steeles were natives of Delaware County, New York, who, coming across the Isthmus, arrived in California in 1857. They located first north of San Francisco Bay, where they commenced to make butter and cheese of the highest quality and to ship it to San Francisco. After removing to Rancho Punta del Año Nuevo in 1862, they continued the same line of work. A brother of Isaac was General Frederick Steele of the Army of the Potomac in the Civil War. In 1864, as a donation to the Sanitary Fund (the forerunner of the Red Cross of today), the Steeles of this rancho made a two-ton cheese for display at the Mechanics' Fair at San Francisco. After the Fair ended, slices of the cheese were sent to President Lincoln, General Grant, and General Steele and the remainder was sold for one dollar a pound. The total amount realized and sent to the Sanitary Fund was $2,820.

Isaac Steele was keenly interested in matters tending to the upbuilding of business enterprise; he helped to establish the Grangers Bank in San Francisco and was a director of the Grangers' Business Association. When, at the termination of the lease held by the Steeles, they purchased the land, all three built good homes that are still standing. E. W. built a few miles east of the Coast Road in the Cloverdale region and lived there for a time before he moved to San Luis Obispo County. The other two made their homes nearer the coast; Rensaeler built on Cascade Creek, and Isaac on Green Oaks Creek. Both of the latter planted long rows of Monterey cypress to break the force of the wind from the Pacific Ocean, and many fine specimens of these trees have now attained immense size. Both of the latter continued to reside on this rancho during the remainder of their lives and left the property to their children at their deaths. Most of the original land purchased by the Steele men still remains in the possession of their descendants.

Along the shore line of this rancho are certain spots of interest. The old lumber wharf at Point Año Nuevo attracted a small settlement around a fresh-water spring near the beach. Horace Steele erected there a small frame building as a dwelling and a place for the sale of food and drink. After business at the wharf came to an end, this building was moved about a quarter of a mile and now is used as a garage and general storage place near one of the Steele residences. The piles of the old wharf may still be seen at low tide.

Pigeon Point, where a Light Station was established in 1872, received the name because there the clipper ship "Carrier Pigeon" was wrecked on May 6, 1853. A chute for the loading of lumber was located there before 1866, and timber products have been shipped from this place until the last ten years. Other names have been applied to Pigeon Point: during the Spanish regime, Herrera called it "Cabo de·Fortunas," or Cape of Adventure, and when a Portuguese company had a whaling station there it was called "Punta Ballena."

A point less noticeable than either Point Año Nuevo or Pigeon Point lies between them and is called Franklin Point, so named from the wreck of the schooner "Sir John Franklin." On the top of a wind-swept sand dune on this beach lies a fallen marble tombstone, inscribed "To the memory of Edward B. Church of Baltimore Maryland, and ten other seamen lost on the ship, Sir John Franklin, January 17, 1865." A long heavy plank upon which the name "Sir John Franklin" was cut was found on the beach after the wreck and carried to the farm buildings near the old Isaac Graham house on White House Creek, where it still remains (1934) nailed above the wide doors of a large barn.

Rancho Feliz

Three of the old land grants later recognized by the United States government lay entirely in the interior of this county with no border on tidewater: Ranchos Feliz, Raymundo, and El Corte de Madera.

The northernmost rancho of this group of three inland ones, Rancho Feliz, was granted April 30, 1844, by Governor Manuel Micheltorena to Domingo Feliz (Felis, Felix), to whom 4,448.27 acres were confirmed by United States patent in 1873. Don Domingo built a house situated, according to a grant-map of 1856, on the southern edge of his property west of a slough. Near it passed the road leading from San Mateo to the coast, converging near the location of his house with the one leading from Belmont to the coast. The Skyline Boulevard coincides with the old San Mateo Road where it crosses between Upper and Lower Crystal Springs Lakes on an earthen causeway.

In this Rancho Feliz lie the upper lakes of the San Andres Valley that have been made by damming the sloughs and lagoons to form reservoirs for the San Francisco water system. Lower Crystal Springs Lake now covers the site of the house of Don Domingo and the settlement of Crystal Springs. This settlement included the hotel mentioned in one of the pivotal scenes in Bret Harte's *A First Family of the Tasajara,* and also the San Felix Station, of which M. Carey was pro-

prietor in 1877, when the San Mateo–Half Moon Bay stages were accustomed to stop there with passengers, mail, and freight. Byrnes's Store, a little farther on up the hill, was another stage stop at the point where the modern Mountain House stands on the Skyline Boulevard.

In the vicinity of Crystal Springs an early planting of wine grapes (other than the Mission variety) was made by Colonel Agaston Haraszthy in 1852, when he set out a half-dozen varieties imported from Europe. Colonel Haraszthy, a nobleman from Hungary, whose name is mentioned whenever the story of California's wine industry is told, was a naturalized American citizen before he came to the West Coast and, in the early years of California's statehood, a member of the Assembly. After a sufficient test of his thirty-acre vineyard had proved that the fruit would not ripen properly in this location, he sold his property and removed the vines to Sonoma County, where soil and climate were fitted to grape culture and where he established the Buena Vista Vineyard.

Rancho Cañada de Raymundo

Rancho Cañada de Raymundo (Raimundo), granted August 4, 1840, by Governor Alvarado to John Copinger, "a man of ability and learning," once a British naval officer and later, in California, a lieutenant under Isaac Graham, consisted of 12,545 acres. It lay to the northeast of the Sierra Morena and had boundary lines in common with Rancho Feliz on the north near the causeway between Upper and Lower Crystal Springs Lakes, with El Corte de Madera on the south at Arroyo Alambique, and with Rancho de las Pulgas on the northeast.

After John Copinger's death this property was patented to his heirs in 1859. The heirs were the widow, María Luisa, daughter of Rafael Soto, who had at that time remarried and was the wife of Captain Greer; and Manuela Copinger, a daughter, who afterward married Antonio Miramontes and lived in the large white house with green shutters that now stands north of the Woodside school and opposite the present site of a filling station. Miramontes Road in this vicinity is named for this family.

The original Copinger residence was built at the corner of La Honda Road and King's Mountain Road. The first house of shakes was followed by one of adobe that stood until the earthquake of 1906. Both of these are now gone, but the old storehouse, built in 1854 and later used by the Greers, remains standing under a large oak tree. With a pleasant porch added on the front, it is now a comfortable-looking family dwelling.

On a map of the rancho made in 1856, several houses are shown, and a tavern is indicated near the Whipple Mill–Embarcadero Road. The part of the Whipple Road used today extends from the Cañada Road to Redwood City, but in former years it continued southwestward from the Cañada Road at the place where the octagonal stone wall has been placed.

The Mountain Home Ranch, on the Portola Road just below the junction with the La Honda Road, is a part of Rancho de Raymundo sold by John Copinger to Charles Brown, a man from New York who had deserted a whaling vessel in San Francisco in 1833. Brown had lived at various locations prior to this purchase. Upon coming to this region, he built an adobe house, probably about 1842, and a sawmill in 1847 near the stream southwest of the house. The small adobe, now standing on the grounds of the Hooper residence, formerly the Burr place, is supposed to be a part of the one erected by Charles Brown. A thoroughfare not far from Searsville Lake takes its name, Mountain Home Road, from this ranch. The property has changed ownership several times, and has been subdivided, and now a number of luxurious homes stand within the confines of the Charles Brown holdings.

The site of one of the several wineries that have from time to time operated in San Mateo County is on the Cañada de Raymundo tract. The brick building, later used as a sheep shelter, stood on the hillside southwest of the Cañada Road until 1936, when it was removed. This structure had been erected by C. Scalmanini, who owned in 1882 over a thousand acres here and whose name is given in the *Winegrowers Register* of 1889 as the owner of 82 acres of wine grapes from which he made three kinds of wine: Zinfandel, Burgundy, and Malvoisie.

East of this grant, on Rancho de las Pulgas, at the cross now towering above Emerald Lake Bowl is held an annual sunrise Easter service; and every night during the preceding week the lighted cross can be seen for many miles.

Rancho El Corte de Madera

This rancho, which lay above the confluence of Los Trancos and San Francisquito creeks, covered a large tract between these streams. The Portola Road runs across it; and Searsville, Coon, and Felt lakes, which are named for men who held property near them, are within the boundaries of the old rancho.

Governor Figueroa gave one square league of land there to Domingo Peralta and Maximo Martínez in 1833. Peralta, who had also Rancho San Ramón and a share of his father's great San Antonio rancho across the Bay, kept his part of the grant for only a short time and divided it on May 19, 1834, between his co-grantee, Martínez, and Cipriano Thurn. On June 13, 1882, a part of El Corte de Madera was patented to Thurn and H. W. Carpentier. This part contained 3,565.91 acres.

More land appears to have been granted to Martínez on June 11, 1834, and Governor Micheltorena made a grant to him on May 1, 1844. The whole tract of 22,979.66 acres, of which a part extended across Los Trancos Creek, was confirmed in his name on September 10, 1855. Of this area, the United States patent was given him on July 14, 1858, for 13,316.05 acres.

Maximo Martínez had been a soldier in the San Francisco Company from 1819 to 1827 and at the time of receiving the first grant was *regidor* at San José, where the parents of his co-grantee, Peralta, were living. The wife of Don Maximo was Damiana Padilla; and in 1841, when his age was given as fifty-one, their family consisted of seven children.

As the children grew up, they established homes of their own on the land. The son Nicholas lived in the adobe that stood where the present Ormondale Ranch home now stands. Whether or not the adobe was built by his father is not known. Nicholas and his family lived in it until after the death of his wife. He sold the place in 1868 and moved with his young children to Half Moon Bay, where some of his descendants still live. Grandchildren of Don Maximo and Doña Damiana are scattered. One branch of the family treasures the sword carried by Maximo when he was a Mexican soldier.

A very large tract of Rancho El Corte de Madera passed through the hands of Nicholas Larco, who lost it through non-paying ventures in silkworm growing and silver mining. The next owner was a man named Barriolet. Since before 1895, when it was purchased from him by W. O. B. McDonough, the place has been noted for the fine stock raised there. In the late '90's, Ormond, winner of the English Derby in 1886, was purchased for this ranch. This animal had been unbeaten during his racing career in England and when sold by his English owner commanded the highest price given for a horse

up to that date. After his death some years later, his bones were returned to England. One of Ormond's sons was called Ormondale, and for this reason the ranch has been named "Ormondale."

The Martínez adobe continued to be used as a family residence until 1901, when the present stucco house was built. It was composed of three rooms with a tile roof. A kitchen and a bedroom of frame construction gave additional space. The plan of incorporating the adobe rooms in the new house had to be abandoned for some reason, and the old structure was entirely demolished.

The present luxurious home of the owners of Ormondale Ranch occupies the commanding position of the earlier building. It is built in a style commemorative of Mission days, with courts, pools, and spacious terraces. Old pepper trees survived until the unusual frost of 1934. Large eucalyptus trees are flourishing near the patio.

Rancho Cañada de Guadalupe la Visitación y Rodeo Viejo

Of all the old land grants in the county those bordering on San Francisco Bay have become most widely known and most thickly settled, because there ran the El Camino Real of Spanish days and there today run the great highways that lead southward from San Francisco.

The northernmost of these ranchos was Rancho Cañada de Guadalupe la Visitación y Rodeo Viejo consisting of two square leagues given in 1841 by Governor Alvarado to Jacob P. Leese. The grantee appears frequently in the early history of California because he engaged in commercial ventures in Monterey and San Francisco and because he married Rosalia, sister of General Mariano Vallejo. When in 1856 San Mateo County was formed by the division of San Francisco County, the dividing line ran through this rancho, placing most of its area in the new county.

Rancho Buri Buri

Rancho Buri Buri, which, according to Bancroft, had been granted to José Sánchez in 1827, was granted to him by José Castro on September 18, 1835. Although the petition for patent was based on the grant of 1835, probably Sánchez had tentatively received it as early as 1827, because it was not unusual for a man to be given land which he had occupied for a longer or shorter period. The petition for confirmation was made in 1852 by the heirs of José Sánchez; and patent was given to José de la Cruz Sánchez and others of the family, in 1872, for 14,639.19 acres extending from the salt marshes on the Bay to the Spring Valley lakes and from the Colma cemeteries to the middle of Burlingame.

Extending through this long bayshore rancho ran the main trail down toward the Santa Clara Valley—a trail used by all travelers of that day who had reason to go south by land from San Francisco (meaning, by San Francisco, the Presidio, Yerba Buena, and Misión Dolores). This trail, El Camino Real, is now followed approximately by U.S. Highway Alternate 101. Before this land was given to Don José Sánchez, it was used as a government cattle ranch. In 1797 Governor Borica had sent 265 head of cattle to it to provide meat for the Presidio at San Francisco. Some idea of the place just before Don José settled upon it may be found in the journal of Captain William Frederick Beechey of the British Navy, whose ship, the "Blossom," anchored in San Francisco Bay for a short while on the long voyage (1825–1828) on which he had been sent. Since he was unable to obtain in San Francisco certain supplies necessary for the continuance of the expedition, the captain dispatched his surgeon, his purser, and his interpreter to Monterey, where he hoped the things needed might be found.

These men set out with horses and proper escort, and "about noon they reached a small cottage named Buri Buri, about twelve miles from San Francisco, being unused to traveling, especially upon Californian saddles, which are by no means constructed for comfort, they determined to rest, until the baggage that they had left in the rear should overtake them. The house in which they lodged was a small miserable cottage full of holes, which, however, afforded them some repose and some new milk. Its inhabitants had been engaged in tanning, in which process they used a liquid extracted from oak bark, contained in a hide suspended by the corners. They had also collected in great quantities a very useful root called in that country *amoles,* which seems to answer all the purposes of soap."

When the survey of this rancho was made in 1864, a preliminary to the granting of the patent, several houses were found along the road that skirted the salt marshes. Near Laguna San Bruno on the north line of the rancho, the map of this survey shows the Corral de Madera, where stables were maintained by the stage company. Along the road southward were houses of Manuel Sánchez, Wilson, a grocery store, a Spanish house at the embarcadero, "charcoal Shanties," Frenchman's, San Bruno House, and two designated as "Irish house." The house of José Sánchez is shown a little to the west of the road. And on an earlier map in 1857 the house of Chino Sánchez is indicated on the southeast corner of the rancho between a small lagoon and the shore of the Bay. In recent years indications of the foundations of an adobe house, possibly that of José Sánchez, have been found halfway between Millbrae Dairy and the station of Millbrae.

On Rancho Buri Buri are now located the towns of South San Francisco, San Bruno, Millbrae, and a part of Burlingame. Millbrae received its name because of the home there of Darius Ogden Mills, a native of New York and a man of influence in both the East and the West, who became the owner of the greater part of this rancho. In 1866 he erected a large house which is still standing and is one of the few fine houses of that period now remaining on the Peninsula. It was used during the second World War as a Merchant Marine convalescent home. In 1872, by employing a large group of Chinese as laborers to drain the marshland, Mr. Mills reclaimed thousands of acres which he used as pasturage for his fine dairy herd. About this time he, with other fanciers of fine stock on the Peninsula, imported by way of Boston eleven Alderney cows from the Alderney Islands. In his later years he made his home in New York and spent only his summers at Millbrae. After his death, his daughter, then the widow of Whitelaw Reid, former United States Ambassador to the Court of St. James, erected the Mills Memorial Hospital in San Mateo as a tribute to her father.

Rancho San Mateo

Rancho San Mateo was given in 1846 by Governor Pio Pico to his secretary, Cayetano Arenas, as a reward for military service. The one and one-half leagues was taken from Rancho del Rey, where the Mission cattle had grazed, and was the last parcel of land to be granted in San Mateo County by the Mexican government. It lay along San Francisco Bay between Rancho Buri Buri on the north and San Mateo Creek on the south and was bounded on the west by Rancho Feliz along the course of the San Andres Creek, which is now covered by Crystal Springs Lakes.

In November 1827, when some of the officers of the British ship "Blossom" passed through this region on their way to Monterey, they were impressed by its strong resemblance to "a nobleman's park; herds of cattle and horses were grazing upon the rich pasture, and numerous fallow deer, startled at the approach of strangers bounded off to seek protection among the hills. The resemblance, however, could not be traced farther. Instead of a noble mansion in character with so fine a country, the party arrived at a miserable hut dwelling before the door of which a number of half naked Indians were basking in the sun." The litter scattered about the building "sadly disgraced the park-like scenery. This spot is named San Matheo, and belongs to the mission." This hut called by some a mission station, stood on San Mateo Creek near where today Baywood Avenue joins El Camino Real. Its ruined state is mentioned in *Eldorado* by Bayard Taylor, who saw it in 1849. The earthquake of 1868 completely wrecked the walls, and in 1869 all that remained of them was leveled to the ground. Some of the tiles in the roof were preserved and have been used in the railroad station at Burlingame. Today there is only a vacant lot at the site of the old adobe opposite the Mills Memorial Hospital.

Before 1854 this rancho had passed into the hands of William Davis Merry Howard, for which it was said he paid $25,000. On the map of the rancho made in 1857 following the death of Howard in 1856 and preliminary to the confirmation of the tract to the executors, a bridge is shown where El Camino Real crossed San Mateo Creek. The present-day bridge is probably on the same site. The Howard house was also shown a little way upstream.

W. D. M. Howard, a native of Boston, had first come to California as cabin boy of a hide-drogher and had afterward with Henry Mellus purchased the abandoned office buildings of the Hudson's Bay Company in San Francisco, where they carried on mercantile pursuits. Wishing to have property in whatever city might prove to be the metropolis of the new state, Howard bought large tracts of land in the towns of San Francisco, Sacramento, and Vallejo. Because of his renown, for his philanthropic and commercial activities, Howard Street in San Francisco was named in his honor, and a memorial to him stands in St. Matthew's Church in the city of San Mateo, situated in one corner of his vast holdings.

That part of the city of San Mateo north of San Mateo Creek and the towns of Hillsborough and Burlingame lie within the confines of Rancho San Mateo. Anson Burlingame was one of the purchasers of a part of the Howard property. He was then U.S. Minister to China and was influential in having the doors of the Chinese Empire opened to foreign commerce, and it is in his honor that the town of Burlingame was named.

Rancho de las Pulgas

The name Argüello stands for much that is the best in the annals of the settlement of the Spanish in Alta California, and the history of Rancho de las Pulgas is traced through children and grandchildren of the pioneer father and mother of this family.

Don José Darío Argüello, one of the finest characters of that early period, arrived at San Gabriel with his bride in 1781 after having traveled overland from Mexico as ensign in the company that Rivera had formed for the Santa Barbara presidio, which was soon to be established. He remained at San Gabriel for a few months, and there his first child was born and christened, before the company moved on to its destination. In June 1787 he was promoted to the position of lieutenant in the San Francisco Company, where he served as comandante until March 1791 and again for a ten-year period beginning in 1796. He was holding a like position at Santa Barbara in 1814, when, at the death of Governor Arrillaga, he was made acting governor of Alta California. He continued to live at Santa Barbara during the year that he held the two offices simultaneously. Receiving a commission as governor of Baja California in October 1815, he traveled overland to that place with his wife and some of his children. He never again returned to Alta California, although he much desired to do so. During his thirty-four years of residence in the northern territory, he had filled positions of trust continuously and was held in high esteem. His gentle wife, Ignacia Moraga, niece of Lieutenant José Moraga—first comandante of San Francisco—made both arduous overland journeys with him in those days when riding a horse or traveling in a creaking carreta were the only alternatives to walking. Their daughter Concepción, awaiting word from her long-unheard-from lover, Rezánof, was one of the children who accompanied the parents to Baja California, where she stayed for a time before returning to Alta California to spend the rest of her life.

The nine children of Don José and Doña Ignacio were all born in California, and all received a careful home education. The eldest son, José Ignacio Maximo, was sent to Mexico to be trained for the priesthood and in after years came back to California to officiate on especial occasions. Francisco Rafael, Toribio de Jesús, Ana Paula (who married a man named Obregon in Guadalajara), and Gertrudis Rudesinda were four of whom little is known. Gervasio, of some military importance, married Encarnación Bernal during the year that his father was acting governor at Santa Barbara and spent his last years in Mexico.

The best-known is the faithful María de la Concepción Marcella, whose romance with the Russian Rezánof has been immortalized by the pen of Bret Harte and others. Santiago, one year younger than his sister Concepción and a cadet at the San Francisco Presidio when the Russian visitor, Rezánof, made the acquaintance of the family, married Pilar, daughter of Francisco Ortega of Santa Barbara, when he was very young and became the father of twenty-two children. He became grantee of several tracts of land, held many important military positions, and left an honorable record in all parts of the state when he died in 1862 at his Tia Juana rancho at the age of seventy-one. The most prominent among the children of Don José was Luis, one of the older ones, born in San Francisco in 1784. Having been elected acting governor of California in 1822, a position which he held until 1825, he had the distinction of being the first native-born governor of the territory. He was frequently involved in controversies and, although he had the welfare of his country at heart, he did not win universal approval as his father had done.

Two tracts of land appear to have been granted to Don José before the year 1800. One, called "El Pilar," was given in 1797 "in consideration of his large family." Of this, little is known: according to Hittell, it was an indefinite tract on the coast between Point San Pedro and Point Año Nuevo, and the grant was never confirmed. The other, granted two years previously and known at that time as "Cachinetas" but afterward known as "Las Pulgas" (the fleas), contained about twelve square leagues and was situated on San Francisco Bay between San Mateo Creek on the north and San Francisquito Creek on the south. The remaining boundary line of this tract was the cause of much litigation.

The history of Rancho de las Pulgas was brought to light after a petition for settlement of title was filed on January 21, 1852, by the claimants, Doña María de la Soledad Ortega de Argüello (widow of Don Luis), and her two sons, José Ramón and Luis Antonio, and a third party, S. M. Mezes, who had purchased a part of the land from one of the heirs. A transcript of the ensuing court proceedings before the Land Commission was filed on July 26, 1854, and this document states that from an "early period in the settlement of Alta California the Argüello family held this property by a lawful and sufficient title. That as far back as 1795 Don José Darío

Argüello .... was the owner of said tract of land at that time called Rancho 'Cachinetac' by a title or license derived from Don Diego Borica, then governor and by virtue of his said office authorized and empowered to grant lands, which said Rancho soon after obtained the name of Las Pulgas, and which by name and as the property and inheritance of said family it has since been known. That for many years Alta California was disturbed by political commotions and that from the comparatively small value of lands but little attention was paid to the preservation of title, that the said José Darío Argüello being long since dead the history of their early title is only in traditions and the memory of the old inhabitants in the county. That in 1820 or 1821, Don Pablo Vicente de Sola .... made a new title to said Rancho or tract of land to Don Luis Argüello, a son of the said Don José Argüello, and that said Don Luis Argüello died about 1830 leaving his widow the petitioner Doña Soledad and the following named children, to wit:—Francisco, a child by a former marriage and who died without issue in 1832 and was never married; María Concepción, María Josefa, and the petitioners José Ramón and Luis Antonio, all children of his second wife Doña Soledad. That said María died in 1845 unmarried and without issue, and that said Doña Josefa is married to Don Eulogio de Celis and that her interest in said property has passed to the claimants by purchase . . . ."

Don Luis had "died in full possession and enjoyment" of this rancho, and the widow and her children continued to live on it. The site of their home is believed by descendants now living to be at the corner of Cedar near Magnolia Avenue in San Carlos, where now stands a small frame house of modern construction. This location agrees with that described by Captain Alfred Robinson, who visited the rancho on one of his journeys down the Peninsula before 1840: "El Rancho de Las Pulgas was the next place of any importance in our route, and is situated a little retired from the road at the foot of a small rising ground. It is the property of Donna Soledad Ortega, widow of Don Luis Argüello, formerly governor of California. I found her a beautiful woman, and the mother of three or four fine children. She was very lady-like in her manner and treated us with the utmost courtesy. After dinner we bade her adieu and proceeded on our way."

This rancho consisted of very rich and accessible land, and there was much misunderstanding in regard to ownership. The western boundary "back to the sierra or range of mountains," long in dispute, was finally settled; and a patent was issued for 35,240.47 acres in 1856. Doña Soledad and her two sons and S. M. Mezes were then able to dispose of their respective parts as they saw fit. The widow received one-half; the son José Ramón, one-fourth; the son Luis Antonio, one-tenth; and S. M. Mezes, three-twentieths. Since this time the vast grant has been cut into uncounted portions of varying sizes, and the land that comprised this old rancho is now well populated. El Camino Real, on whose borders the towns of San Mateo, Belmont, San Carlos, Redwood City, Atherton, and Menlo Park have clustered, runs from the northern border of the grant to San Francisquito Creek on the southern boundary. The close proximity of the towns makes the road for the entire distance like a city street. To carry the congested traffic the parallel Bayshore Highway has been constructed, but already the towns have stretched some of their streets over to the new road. A railroad bridge and the Dumbarton Toll Bridge span the Bay a short distance above the lower end of the rancho. South of these bridges, in the very southeastern corner of the grant, the now almost forgotten town of Ravenswood was platted. The Steinburger property at this point was purchased in 1853 by men named I. C. Woods, William Row, Hackett, and Judah, who laid out the town. A long wharf was built to deep water to facilitate the shipping of lumber that was hauled from the mills in the mountains, lots were sold, a few houses were erected, and a store was opened by William Paul. Hope was later entertained by the promoters of the town that the Central Pacific Railroad Company would choose this spot for the end of a bridge across the Bay. But when that plan did not materialize, the village was abandoned, and the temporary structures that had been erected soon disappeared.

Lester Phillip Cooley, a Vermont man who had come overland to California and had at first spent some time in the mining regions, later purchased property contiguous to Ravenswood for a ranch and constructed a home for his family from lumber brought around the Horn. A part of this old homestead stands today among fine old trees about one-half mile from the Bayshore Highway. Perhaps a half-mile from the house in a northeasterly direction stands a sandstone monument, one of many erected by the United States Coast Survey. This monument is six feet high and thirty-one inches square at the base tapering to twenty-two inches at the top. It bears the inscription: "East end of the Pulgas base. Alexander Dallas Bache, U.S. Coast Survey. Measured in July and August, 1853."

The site of the old Ravenswood wharf, for many years known as Cooley's Landing, is now identified by old piles and a decaying platform. The immediate vicinity is used as a rubbish dump. Not far away is a large pit where clay was taken for the Hunter, Shackleford and Company brick-making plant established there in 1874. Its products were shipped to San Francisco and San Jose for building purposes. The bricks for the original Palace Hotel in San Francisco were made here.

In 1873 Clark's Landing at the mouth of San Francisquito Creek, the extreme southeastern point of the rancho, was established and five years later was operating under lease to W. C. Wilson, who there erected a large and commodious warehouse.

Woodside, San Mateo's First Settlement

At the time of the American occupation in 1846, there had been a settlement at Woodside for some ten years or more. As early as 1834, William Smith, an American, came to the Santa Clara Valley to saw lumber for the Mission Fathers at Santa Clara. He became so skilful with the saw that he was known as "Bill the Sawyer."

Four years later another settler arrived at Woodside, James Peace, who had deserted from a British ship anchored at Yerba Buena. Peace and Smith became partners, teaching the Mission Indians to saw lumber and to make carretas and agricultural implements for the Fathers at Santa Clara.

Soon after 1846 lumber mills were erected at Woodside, Searsville, and neighboring sections of the valley where the redwoods grew. Lumber was supplied to the incoming settlers of Santa Clara Valley, and by 1850 it was also shipped to San Francisco. Today, the lumber camps of Woodside and Searsville are scarcely a memory. Dim roads into the hills, a few blackened stumps where thick green groves of young redwoods have partly covered the scars of former years, and stories of the village buried beneath the waters of Searsville Lake, these are all that remain.

The old Tripp Store, the first store opened between San Francisco and Santa Clara, is the one surviving landmark of pioneer days in Woodside. The present structure was built in 1854 by Dr. R. O. Tripp ("Doc Tripp"), a dentist, who had opened a store at Woodside as early as 1849. With his two partners he engaged in cutting shingles, and in 1850 he built a barge in which he made the first lumber shipment to San Francisco. He soon gave up the lumber business for merchandising. For almost fifty years Tripp kept his little store on the Woodside–King's Mountain Road, one and one-half miles from the present town of Woodside. A tablet placed upon the building by the Department of Natural Resources records the fact that it was the center of redwood-lumbering operations. There were fifteen sawmills within a radius of five miles. "Here, at times, more than one thousand lumberjacks found their mail, food supplies, and liquid refreshments." On this byroad is also the old "Temperance Hall," standing on an elevation above the road; its weather-beaten clapboards give little evidence that it was once the social gathering place for young and old.

The commercial part of Woodside of the present day has moved from the Tripp Store nearer to the vicinity known in the old days as "Whiskey Hill," because the three saloons there (two of these buildings are still standing) dominated the settlement. The only other structures were a blacksmith shop and two hotels; both of the latter are still in existence. One is still a country hotel, and the other has been moved back from the road to give place to a general merchandise store. Roads in four directions from this present Woodside lead to large country estates. The settlement of Greersburg, originally named in honor of the Greer family, who owned Rancho Raymundo on which these several settlements are located, is included in the modern Woodside, but the school district retains the name of Greersburg. When the modern Woodside schoolhouse was built on the site of the original Greersburg School near the end of Miramontes Road, the little old schoolhouse was removed to the rear and used as an annex.

Bear Creek

Bear Creek, which comes down the mountain and flows under a bridge on the road running from the base of the La Honda Grade to Woodside, was so named in the '50's because of the encounter between "Grizzly" Ryder and one of the numerous grizzly bears that infested the region at that period.

Ryder was a partner of Dr. R. O. Tripp, with whom he had journeyed from San Francisco on horseback for the purpose of establishing a lumber camp in the forest. Arriving at the spot that became Woodside, they began lumber operations, using oxen for hauling the fallen trees. One evening, while returning alone after an unsuccessful day's tramp in the Portola Valley looking for his strayed oxen, Ryder was attacked by a mother bear as he rose from drinking at a pool in the stream. Having no weapon other than a knife, he suffered a severe mauling; but, after he had made a pretense of being dead, the bear left him in a fainting condition with one ear torn off. Found in a short time by searchers, he was carried back over the trail to the adobe on the Mountain Home Ranch, where he had called earlier in the evening. His bleeding wounds were closed by a sailor, who used a sail needle and some string; there followed treatment with poultices of native herbs gathered and steeped by an Indian woman. These primitive methods proved efficacious, for he recovered after some weeks. The pool where the attack occurred is near the modern barns of the "Why Worry Farm" one mile west of the Woodside Inn.

Searsville and La Honda

Searsville Lake, at the junction of the Portola and Sand Hill roads, covers a part of the site of the old town of Searsville. John L. Sears, who came from New York state via Cape Horn in 1849, built in this vicinity a house later used as a hotel and known as the "Sears House." A town grew up about this house, because the location was a convenient stopping place for drivers of mule and ox teams hauling lumber from the mills east of the La Honda ridge for loading on schooners at the Embarcadero at Redwood City.

The little village was the scene of considerable activity on Sundays, when ox-pulling, horse racing, and cockfighting were popular amusements. A hotel built by August Eikenkotter stood on what is now the crossroads at the entrance to the Searsville Lake grounds. This hotel was pulled down when the building of the dam forming the lake necessitated realignment of the roads. At the same time a large pine tree, used for years as a target for men whiling away their time on the porch of the hotel, was cut down. It was so full of leaden slugs that saws could not be used in working it up into firewood.

The Searsville schoolhouse, abandoned after the spring term of 1893, stood on the hill between the end of the Sand Hill Road and the present lake. Nothing remains to show where the building stood or where the dwellings that lined the street leading to it were except the short avenue of pine trees that still grow on this slight eminence. The lake formed by the dam now supplies irrigation water for the Stanford University campus and provides, as well, a place for swimming and boating.

At about the time of the excitement over the Comstock mine in Nevada a trace of silver was found in this vicinity. In 1875 John Murray, a resident of Searsville who owned land on the west edge of the ridge to the east of the settlement, sold his mineral rights to a group of six men from Redwood City. A tunnel was driven into the hill a short distance south of the Searsville dam, but the occurrence of the ore was too erratic for profitable development. This old tunnel is now below the level of the lake.

About one-half mile northeast of Searsville on the Sand Hill Road at the bridge across San Francisquito Creek, there stood for many years a broad and tall wooden barn built originally for the stabling of oxen used in lumber hauling. No vestige of the structure remains—only the leveled ground of its site.

John L. Sears removed from Searsville in the winter of 1861–1862 and settled seventeen miles from Redwood City in the mountains. To this place he gave the name La Honda. Here he built a store that is still in use and sometimes called the "Bandit-Built Store," because he employed in its construction two newcomers to the vicinity, Jim and Bob Younger, who afterward were proved to be members of the "James Boys Gang," outlaws in the Midwest, where the pair were jailed soon after they left California. The frame residence built by Sears (its site was in front of the present La Honda Hotel) has been destroyed by fire, but his farm of perhaps three hundred acres extending back of the mountain village is still held by the family.

St. Denis Church and Cemetery

One of the tragic developments attendant upon the confused situation of boundary lines between some of the grants of land was the hardship inflicted upon the purchaser of a tract on the north bank of San Francisquito Creek while California was still under the Mexican government. Dennis Martin, who came to the state in 1844 with the Murphy-Stevens party (the first wagon train to cross the Sierra) and who heroically retraced his track into the mountains in the following year to succor Moses Schallenberger, who had stayed behind to guard a stock of valuable merchandise, settled on San Francisquito Creek and became one of the first and most extensive lumbermen in the Woodside area. He purchased land then supposed to be in the lower part of Rancho Cañada de Raymundo, the deed for the tract from Juan Coppinger to him being signed in the Pueblo de San José de Guadalupe on March 15, 1846.

Immediately after making the purchase, he took possession of the land with his family, erected his house near the creek, built barns and corrals for his horses and cattle, planted a large fruit orchard, and fenced a goodly portion of his domain. He also purchased a piece of the neighboring Rancho Corte de Madera, making his holdings in all 1,250 acres. He built two mills, called the Upper and Lower, on Dennis Martin Creek in the timber region of his property and eight more houses for his workmen.

As there was no church nearer than Misión Dolores to the north and Santa Clara to the south and as he was a man of deep religious sentiment, he built a place of worship near his home for his family, his employees, and his scattered neighbors who might care to participate. In this simple frame structure he placed costly candlesticks and insignia suitable for the use to which they were consecrated. A churchyard large enough for all usual religious purposes was enclosed by a fence; and another enclosure, a little farther up the hill, became the little cemetery. Archbishop Alemany, who officiated at the dedication service in 1852, named the church St. Denis in honor of the donor.

In the year of the dedication of the church, the question of the boundary line between the Las Pulgas and the Cañada de Raymundo ranchos came to the fore, and a petition for its settlement was filed by heirs and claimants. Four years later, the United States courts decided that the line of Las Pulgas extended along San Francisquito Creek and included the Dennis Martin property. As his land had been purchased from the owner of the adjoining Cañada de Raymundo, the decision had the effect of dispossessing him, and he was obliged to give over his improvements, including a young orchard then bearing fruit. At his death in San Francisco on June 16, 1890, his body was brought back to the place and interred near the graves of other members of his family.

The site of the Dennis Martin house and the church lies about one-half mile off the Sand Hill Road toward San Francisquito Creek. A gate on the bridle path opposite the end of the Walsh Road leads into a pasture where some large cypress trees overshadow the grounds of the little cemetery that is still enclosed by a fence (1934).

When the Las Pulgas grant was broken up and sold to various owners and when Leland Stanford acquired a part of what had been the Martin property, it was his wish that the graves remain undisturbed. But the buildings were long ago removed, and many of the bodies in the enclosure have been transferred to newer cemeteries. Little remains to commemorate the worthy pioneer endeavors of Dennis Martin.

Belmont

The wooded hills where the town of Belmont nestles today made a strong appeal to Captain George Vancouver, who stopped there for a brief rest on November 20, 1792, on his way from Misión Dolores to Misión Santa Clara. The noon meal was spread in an open place beside a stream, enclosed on all sides by hills so entrancing that Vancouver says that the entire party left them with reluctance. "In short, a spot more delightful, they all agreed, could hardly be met with on the whole globe." Captain Vancouver had just brought into San Francisco Bay the first vessel other than Spanish to pass through the entrance that was later named the "Golden Gate." On his land journey down the Peninsula, he and his cortege were accompanied by a sergeant from the Presidio and "six, stout, active soldiers."

In 1850, the year that saw the beginning of a settlement where the town of Belmont now is, a hotel was built. This hotel housed the first county court in 1856, since Belmont had been chosen the first county seat.

Back of the village lies the Cañada del Diablo, chosen by

S. M. Mezes, one of the patentees of the Pulgas rancho, for his home. There, too, lived Lussetti Cipriani, Italian patriot, in a small villa set on the hillside. Count Cipriani's villa was the beginning of the mansion built there by William C. Ralston after his purchase of an acreage in this location in the early '60's. With discriminating taste, Mr. Ralston made his large estate a place of unusual charm, where he entertained people of world-wide distinction during the '60's and '70's.

William Chapman Ralston, a native of Ohio, who had already gained valuable experience in the shipping world before his arrival in San Francisco on September 1, 1854, became a powerful Western financier. He maintained both a city home and a country home, and upon the latter he spent lavishly of his wealth. From the modest villa of Count Cipriani he evolved a residence of faultless architecture and furnishings. Here were great glass doors, crystal chandeliers, parquetry floors, and everything else of corresponding elegance and taste. Assisted by his wife, the home-loving and gracious Elizabeth Fry, he became the perfect host, giving delightful week-end parties, banquets, and balls. From his stone-built, mahogany-stalled stables, he was able to provide mounts for a score of guests.

For the illumination of his country seat he erected costly gas works that benefited also the village of Belmont; for his own use, primarily, he built a wharf on the Bay shore but generously shared it with the public. He built a great dam and reservoir in the hills on his estate to provide irrigation for the plantings that have now grown to park-like proportions. Rows of pines and other trees that he placed for wind-breaks are now proving their value.

After his tragic death by drowning in August 1875, the marvelously developed estate was taken over by his former business associate, William Sharon, of Comstock Lode fame.

Following its occupancy by Senator Sharon, the house at Belmont was used for a private school kept by the widow of Alpheus Bull, a business associate of both Ralston and Sharon. Later, the house was turned into a hospital by Dr. Gardiner.

In 1923 the place was taken over by the Sisters of Notre Dame, who removed to it their convent and college established in San José in 1851. As a memento to their pioneer efforts, they brought to this new location, section by section, the simple wooden structure in which their labors had begun, and re-erected it within the spacious new grounds.

The Ralston mansion is now Berchman's Hall, named in honor of one of the founding Sisters. The former banqueting room is now the college dining-room, the former ballroom now the chapel. All that remains of the former magnificence of buildings and grounds is guarded and appreciated.

San Mateo

An early settler in what is now the city of San Mateo was John S. Cooper, a native of Suffolk, England, who had deserted as steward from a British man-of-war in 1833. In 1851 he made a brush booth around a large oak tree on his ranch on San Mateo Creek beside El Camino Real. There he lived with his wife, a native woman, and their children while he built a better home. His wife died two years later, leaving him with a family of small children.

In 1863, after the railroad had been built down the Peninsula from San Francisco, a town was platted there by C. B. Polhemus; and this station became the northern terminus of the San Mateo, Pescadero, and Santa Cruz Stage Company lines owned by Taft and Garretson, who ran tri-weekly stages to the southern terminus at Santa Cruz. Outlying places thus afforded communication with the railroad were: Crystal Springs, San Felix, Byrnes's Store, Eureka Gardens, Spanishtown, Purisima, Lobitos, San Gregorio, Pesca-

dero, Pigeon Point, Seaside, Davenport, and Santa Cruz—the last three lying south of the present county line.

The town was eventually hedged around on three sides by large properties: that of W. D. M. Howard, who had purchased Rancho San Mateo on the north; that of Frederick Macondray, one of the first great merchants of San Francisco, who chose in 1854 for a country home land just south of San Mateo Creek; and that of Alvinza Hayward, retired mine operator and financier, on the southeast. The Macondray home was purchased by John Parrot, a man originally from Virginia, who was United States consul at Mazatlán during the year 1845–1846 and who remained identified with shipping and financial interests along the Pacific Coast until 1859. The home that he developed there was called Baywood; and in it he lived the last thirty years of his life, an influential citizen whose counsel was widely sought. This property remained in the hands of the Parrot family until 1927, since which time it has been made into a residential subdivision called Baywood. The site of the original house near San Mateo Creek west of El Camino Real is now occupied by a large apartment house.

The property of Alvinza Hayward is a residential section south of San Mateo. His home, afterward used as a hotel, stood near the tall palms on what is now called Hayward Avenue. His handsomely built stable, afterward a garage, stands now quite vacant and deserted but in full view of the passing railway trains between Rosewood Drive and South B Street, near Ninth Street. The stable as originally built had rosewood and mahogany stalls for the carefully groomed horses which were their owner's pride. Its white-painted exterior remains as it was except that the word "Garage" above the entrance doors on both streets indicates the interior changes. In this vicinity Mr. Hayward had a large enclosed area for deer; both the stables and the deer park were show places where visitors were welcome. Nothing is left of the park except the magnificent oaks under which the animals browsed. Hayward established as a private enterprise a system of waterworks whereby the town of San Mateo was supplied with pure spring water before the date of its incorporation. The name of the station for the residential district into which the Hayward property has been portioned, formerly called Leslie, is now Hayward Park.

St. Matthew's Episcopal Church

The first services that led to the eventual establishment of this church were conducted by the Rev. G. A. Easton of San Francisco, who spent the spring and summer of 1864 in the town. They were held in the newly completed reception room of Miss Buckmaster's San Mateo Young Ladies Institute, afterward a school called "Laurel Hall." In the autumn of 1864 the Rev. A. L. Brewer was sent out from Detroit, Michigan, under the auspices of the Episcopal Board of Domestic Missions; and in February he conducted services in the public schoolhouse.

In July of the same year the family of George H. Howard donated a lot of two acres from their rancho and headed the list of subscriptions for a building with a substantial contribution. In October the church was organized; and on the 12th of that month the cornerstone was laid on the north side of San Mateo Creek and east of the county road where the building still stands. The church was constructed of stone taken from a quarry on the Crystal Springs Road on the Howard property. A memorial to W. D. M. Howard, the pioneer member of the family in this vicinity, has been placed within the edifice.

San Carlos

Two spots of historic interest are near the station of San Carlos: the site of the Argüello adobe on the west side of El

Camino Real at the corner of Cedar and Magnolia streets, and the house of Timothy Guy Phelps east of Highway Alternate 101.

T. G. Phelps, as his name usually appears, was born in New York, arrived in San Francisco in 1849, and went at once to the mines in Tuolumne County. He later purchased 3,500 acres of land around San Carlos, and the large white-painted frame building erected by him for his home now stands on the east side of El Camino Real in the midst of trees that screen it from view from the highway. He was elected to the state legislature in 1856 on the first Republican ticket in California, and there introduced a bill to correct mistakes made in the organization of San Mateo County the previous year. This bill was passed and became a law on April 18, 1857. He served as representative in Congress from 1861 to 1863, ably maintaining the cause of ranch owners in their struggle for rightful title to land.

Embarcadero de las Pulgas, Redwood City

A little creek, running through Rancho de las Pulgas where Redwood City, the county seat, now stands and emptying into a slough or arm of the Bay, formed a natural shipping point, or embarcadero, used in the Spanish and Mexican era.

With the coming of Americans, lumbering became an important industry wherever the redwoods grew, and there were many of these trees in the mountains within a few miles of this place. In 1850 the shipment of lumber from the Woodside and Searsville mills began, and the old Embarcadero became a busy wharf. Ships were built there, and a number of schooners were launched that year. Wagonmaking and blacksmithing were important adjuncts to the business of hauling the product of the mills to the Embarcadero and were early established there. This was the nucleus around which the present Redwood City developed. Redwood Creek flows under the city today, and Redwood Slough is filled in. On the spot where the vessels were launched in the '50's, a bronze tablet was placed in 1926 by the history and civics classes of the Sequoia Union High School to commemorate the pioneer industry which created Redwood City. The marker stands in front of the Public Library on the southwest corner of Broadway and Washington Street.

William Carey Jones, who had come to the West Coast in 1849 as a special government agent to investigate the condition of land titles in California, acquired 1,021 acres near Redwood City from Argüello in 1851 and called it Redwood Farm. It extended from Finger Creek to Woodside Road and from Highway Alternate 101 to the brow of the hill. This property was put up for sheriff's sale on January 2, 1858, when it was purchased by Horace Hawes, a native of New York who had been appointed consul for the Society and other South Sea islands by President Polk in 1847. By an unanticipated routing of the vessel on which he took passage, he arrived in San Francisco, where a few years later he became prefect. He resided in San Francisco and at his country home in the foothills near Redwood City from 1850 to the date of his death in 1871. He was a staunch supporter of the Union side during the Civil War. Western Redwood City is now on this land, as are Redwood Highlands, Wellesley, Edgewood, and Dingee parks. If the original plans of the owner had been carried through, a seat of learning called "Mount Eagle University" would have been located in this area.

The first Protestant church in the county was organized in Redwood City in 1862. Land was purchased at the corner of Webster and Jefferson streets on which to erect a building for the First Congregational Church group, which had been meeting in the courthouse for some months. The second Protestant church was the St. Peter's Episcopal. Its members held their first meetings in the schoolhouse, then in the court-

house, and afterward in a small building of their own. This congregation worships today in a new building on Clinton Street between Brewster and Broadway.

Captain Morgan and the Oyster Industry

On the tidelands of the Bay from San Bruno Point southward as far as San Francisquito Creek, native oysters had flourished for untold centuries. After the building of the transcontinental railroad in 1869, Eastern oysters were imported and planted along the Bay shore off San Mateo County. Several companies engaged in this pursuit, most of them being finally consolidated into the Morgan Oyster Company. This company owned several houses built by ship joiners on piles above the water. Like cottages in a garden enclosed by a picket fence, these oyster houses stood within a water area surrounded by partially submerged wickets that insured the safety of the bivalves growing in their salty beds.

John Stillwell Morgan, a frugal, industrious man and a native of New York, was made captain of the schooner "Telegraph" then (1846) plying the sea in the oyster business. Sailing in 1849 for California in the bark "Magdella," he arrived in San Francisco and thoroughly prospected the Bay for oysters without success. He then went to the mines and afterward to Oregon, where he again engaged in the oyster business.

The Morgan Oyster Company was formed in 1887 when Morgan took in four partners. With the formation of the new company, the transplanting of the bivalves from Shoalwaters Bay, Washington Territory, to the vicinity of Mission Creek, south of San Francisco, was begun

The business did not come up to expectations. In the course of time, the oyster industry ceased, and the Morgan holdings were purchased by the Pacific Cement Company, which now dredges the Bay for shells which it uses in making cement. The office building of this company on the wharf at Redwood City is one of the old oyster houses that has been moved from the piles on which it was originally built south of Dumbarton Bridge, where the piles remain. The wreck of another of these houses is directly opposite the discharge of Westpoint Slough into Redwood Creek, on what is now known as Grecco Island. The only one of the Morgan oyster houses still in use for its original purpose stands two miles out in the tidewater opposite Millbrae and Burlingame. This station was established in 1874, and its location was one of the most valuable.

The house in which the Captain lived while directing his company was located at the junction of Steinburger and Corkscrew creeks. Legislators, met by the Captain in his launch at San Francisco or Oakland, were once taken for a tour of the Bay and afterward entertained by him in the spacious dining room of his house before being returned to their respective duties, which included the making of suitable laws to cover industrial ownership of tidewaters. His house, moved from its piles in the water, now stands at the corner of Chestnut and Spring streets in Redwood City. A two-story, nearly square building, its exterior is covered with a coat of stucco, but its interior appears much as it did when owned by Captain Morgan.

Menlo Park and Atherton

The adjoining areas of Menlo Park and Atherton lie near the southern part of the county along El Camino Real. Their common boundaries are so irregular that it is difficult to distinguish the territory of the earlier-named Menlo Park from its more widely spread neighbor.

Dennis J. Oliver and his brother-in-law, D. C. McGlyn, became owners of a 1,700-acre tract on the Pulgas rancho and erected in 1851, just south of where Santa Cruz Avenue now enters El Camino Real, a gate with a wooden arch across its top. They called their place "Menlo Park" in memory of the "most beautiful spot in the world"—their former home in Menlo Park, Ireland.

This Menlo Park gate became weatherworn, but it was preserved during the occupancy of its immediate vicinity by Camp Frémont, used for the concentration of troops during World War I. It stood until July 7, 1922, when it was destroyed in a motor accident.

Upon the building of the San Francisco–San José Railroad down the Peninsula in 1863, a station called Menlo Park was placed a short distance from this old gate; and men successful in statesmanship, finance, and industry chose this locality for the luxurious country homes which they built on ample estates at convenient driving distances from the railroad station. A village of small houses, hotels, and stores grew up near the station, and in 1873 the first church in the town was organized by a group of Presbyterian residents. In the following year a house of worship was erected upon land donated for that purpose, and in it Protestant families of the town and the surrounding countryside attended services. In this frame structure, still standing on its original location on Santa Cruz Avenue a little way west of State Highway 101, regular services continue to be held. On March 23, 1874, the year in which the church was built, the town was incorporated; but the incorporation was allowed to lapse and was not renewed until November 15, 1927.

Not far from the station a fine residence was built by Milton S. Latham, a man from Ohio who had arrived in California in 1850 and had purchased land from John T. Doyle on December 18, 1871. He eventually bought several other small tracts adjoining his original purchase. He was elected governor of the state nine years after his arrival, only to renounce that honor to fill the unexpired term of United States Senator David C. Broderick, who had been slain in a duel that took place within the county. Mr. Latham entertained extensively in this country home. This house, with its stately pillars, its costly interior, its elaborate fountains placed in well-landscaped grounds among large native oaks, became the property of Mary Hopkins, the widow of Mark Hopkins, one of the pioneers of the state who had arrived from New York in 1849 and had been one of the "Big Four" who put through the building of the Central Pacific Railroad. After her remarriage in 1888, the great house passed to their adopted son, Timothy, who followed in the footsteps of Mark Hopkins by becoming treasurer of the Central Pacific Railroad Company. The mansion was badly wrecked in the earthquake of 1906 and has since been unfit for occupancy, although its damaged form still stands at the end of a once well-kept drive far back in the grounds entered at the keeper's gate on Ravenswood Avenue. On the property still stand also the elaborate stables and carriage houses, now unused.

Across Ravenswood Avenue from the Hopkins estate stands the fine old home maintained with so much pride during the life of its first owner, Edgar Mills, whose brother D. O. Mills lived at Millbrae at that same period. The house passed from the ownership of the family years ago and has had various occupants since that time. It now houses the Park Military School.

Beside the wealthy residents who came to the region of Menlo Park for rest and recreation on their large estates were also permanent residents who gained their livelihood there. One such family was established by John and Margaret Murray, who came around the Horn from New York in 1854. They purchased various lands within the confines of the present county and lived in a wood-framed adobe, a part of which is still standing near Ringwood Road in Menlo Oaks. From this place they shipped milk to San Francisco by stage, and in this house twin sons were born to them. In later years Margaret, the mother, divided twenty-eight acres of land which she held on San Francisquito Creek among her four children. A son, John Jarvis, was given the part nearest the creek and on it erected a house and barn about the year 1885. To this son also fell the possession of a copper kettle brought around the Horn by his parents, and to his son James eventually passed both the land and the kettle. In 1930 the land was acquired by the Allied Arts Guild of California; and at the place where the old kettle was treasured for its sentimental value many objects are now exhibited for their artistic value. The old house and barn of the Murrays have been utilized as a part of this attractive and philanthropic venture on Arbor Road and Creek Drive.

Atherton, incorporated in 1923, extends in its longest direction from that portion of the Bay Road lying between Ringwood Road and Marsh Road across Middlefield Road, the railway, El Camino Real, and to a little distance west of the Alameda de las Pulgas. Within this area are many stately modern homes and the sites of older ones no longer standing.

Faxon Dean Atherton, originally from Massachusetts, later, while a member of a firm engaged in the hide-and-tallow trade, a resident of Chile, first visited California in 1836. On September 29, 1860, he acquired a tract of five hundred acres from the Pulgas rancho and built a country mansion among the native oaks growing there. He named his estate "Valparaiso Park," from the city of Valparaiso in South America where his wife had been born and where he had spent his early manhood. Life in this house is depicted by the daughter-in-law, Gertrude Atherton, in her *Adventures of a Novelist*, written of the period when the country was sparsely settled and quiet afternoons on a comfortable veranda had few interruptions.

After the Atherton family was gone from the place it was used as a school for boys kept by Ira G. Hoyt, a former state superintendent of public instruction, and during the occupancy of this school the mansion was destroyed by fire. The location, two miles south of Redwood City, near the intersection of Elena and Isabella avenues (names of the Atherton daughters) is now owned by the Menlo Circus Club, which was organized primarily for the purpose of raising funds for the Stanford Home for Convalescent Children. Valparaiso Avenue, not far distant, carries the name of the old house; and the name of the former Fair Oaks station where a post office was established in 1867 has been superseded by the name Atherton in honor of that family.

A five-hundred-acre tract, adjoining that of Faxon D. Atherton, was purchased by Thomas H. Selby, a pioneer industrialist of the West Coast. Mr. Selby was born in New York City, landed in San Francisco in 1849, and originated the Selby Silver and Lead Smelting Works, where a vast quantity of the bullion from the mines of the state has been handled. The home which he established there was a "model of rural attractiveness and high cultivation" and was his favorite resort after office hours in San Francisco. The house has since been destroyed by fire; but Selby Lane, a road running along two sides of the old estate, identifies the place whereon he specialized in the raising of grains and fine fruits. The smelting firm that he organized still carries his name in San Francisco and elsewhere.

John T. Doyle, a "scholar of rare culture and refinement" and one of the foremost lawyers of his day, in 1856 purchased land in the vicinity from Horace P. Jones and gradually added to the acreage until he owned a large tract. One of his accomplishments for the welfare of the new state was the final disentangling of the affairs of the Missions at the request of Archbishop Alemany. In the course of his duties to that end, he traversed the ill-kept roads between the Missions time and again, always receiving a hearty welcome from the resident Fathers. The highways, little more than trails then, were all but obscured by the rank-growing mustard; and yet his approach was always noted by a "look-out" so that when he reached the door a room with all possible comforts, even luxuries, was ready for his immediate occupancy.

General William Tecumseh Sherman was one of the honored and frequent visitors at the Doyle home, a palatial frame house still occupied by descendants, approached through a driveway flanked by tall palms leading off from Ringwood Road. The ample veranda is shaded by a wisteria now grown to huge proportions. The library built to contain Mr. Doyle's valuable books is a large and friendly room today, although most of his volumes have found place elsewhere.

Not far from the Doyle house is the Joseph A. Donohue residence on Middlefield Road, still occupied by members of that famous banking family. And the Frank Fielding Moulton house, that grew from its original size of five rooms to eighteen rooms before the family built a residence elsewhere within the Atherton region, stands about three miles from El Camino Real beyond Selby Lane Extension.

Another man who had one of the early houses in the Menlo-Atherton vicinity was Charles N. Felton, who entertained there extensively. Originally a New York man, he became sub-treasurer at San Francisco and also served from March 1891 to March 1893 as United States Senator. He built his house in 1870 and lived in it until his death in 1913. The mansion is no longer standing; but the property, which stood near Encinal Avenue and the Southern Pacific Railway track, is now a residential subdivision called "Felton Gables."

James Clair Flood, who arrived in San Francisco in 1849 on the boat "Elizabeth Ellen" and became one of the "Bonanza Kings" of the Comstock Lode days, bought a tract of land along Middlefield Road in 1876 and two years later began the erection of "a great white mansion" upon it. The house was called "Linden Towers" and was placed well back from the road and surrounded by lawn and fine trees. After Mr. Flood's death in Heidelberg during a world tour, the place passed by will to his daughter, who gave it to the University of California. After this institution found the property to be non-income-producing, it was sold to the son, James L. Flood, who purchased neighboring land as well and enclosed the estate by placing a brick wall along the entire frontage on Middlefield Road and by erecting massive iron gateways. The death of this son occurred in 1926. The brick wall, the gate, and the lodge still stand, but "Linden Towers" was torn down after the public auction of its contents in 1934.

Amesport

A wharf erected in 1867 by Ames, Byrnes, and Harlow on the ocean side of the county was called Amesport Landing. It was located near the mouth of Arroyo Medio, a small stream dividing the property of the two owners of Rancho Corral de Tierra. Warehouses used for the shipping of grain from this fertile region were built just south of the mouth of the creek.

J. P. Ames, the leader in the activity, was a native of England who had lived east of the Mississippi for some time before starting west as a member of Stephenson's Regiment. The men of this regiment had been chosen for qualities that would serve them well in a pioneer settlement after military duties should be ended. Ames was honorably discharged at Monterey in 1848 and, coming to this vicinity in 1856, became county treasurer in 1862. He was appointed by Governor Booth to settle the Yosemite claims and was a member of the state legislature in 1876–1877.

Amesport Landing was afterward acquired by the Pacific Steamship Company, which disposed in 1917 of the site of the old warehouses to the present owner of a small hotel erected

there. The settlement is now called Miramar, where the wave-beaten piles of an old wharf may be seen near the hotel.

The Hermit Mine

Within the old Corte de Madera grant on the ridge southeast of Searsville Lake is a mining property on which were dug about the year 1875 two vertical shafts, one of seventy-five feet, the other of two hundred feet; and with them is identified Domenico Grosso, the hermit.

Grosso came to San Francisco about 1869 from Genoa, Italy. Little is known of his early life, but he told friends that he had served under the great Italian patriot Garibaldi. After living in San Francisco for a time and being unfortunate in financial ventures there, he came to this vicinity and entered the employment of Nicholas Larco, first as cook and later as ranch foreman on land now a stock farm adjoining Stanford University property. While there employed, he discovered silver on the Dennis Martin ranch southeast from Searsville and persuaded Larco to buy the mineral rights from Martin. After Larco became insolvent through his ventures in ranching, mining, and mulberry-tree growing for the culture of silkworms, the mineral rights came to Grosso. With the lumber from miners' bunkhouses, he constructed a home for himself in a canyon near by.

He built a cabin, a barn, and a shop; he planted grapevines, roses, and fruit trees; he made hillside terraces and an ornamental pool for trout into which the waters of a spring trickled over an arrangement of serpentine rocks. This home he called the "Palace Hotel" and seemed pleased with occasional visitors, whom he honored by hoisting the American and the Italian flags and by bringing out wine and small bread cakes, while chatting in a friendly way. Sometimes he mentioned the name of "Julia," but in such a vague way that who Julia was and where he had known her were not divulged.

At length the deep shaft, called the Portola shaft, in which he had so much confidence, became filled with water, and he could do nothing with it. Since his death after years of proud isolation, some twenty or more "prospects" that had apparently been dug by him have been found. Although he had one or two rich specimens of ore to show, neither he nor anyone else has realized any profit from these mines other than the experience gained there by Stanford University mining students, who have at times been permitted to work in them.

The Broderick-Terry Duel

An aftermath of the bitter political campaign of 1859 in California was a duel that reverberated throughout the nation because of the prominence of the participants and the death of one of them; both men were pioneers of 1849 and members of the same political party, although they had espoused opposite factions.

David C. Broderick, born in Ireland in 1820, had lived in New York as a lad and had come from there to California, where he became a power in the Democratic party. He was acting lieutenant-governor in 1851 and became United States Senator in 1857.

David S. Terry, born in Kentucky in 1823, had seen military service in Texas and Mexico before coming to the Coast in 1849. He became Chief Justice of the California Supreme Court and was active in politics, first as a Whig, afterward as a leader in the "American" or "Know-Nothing" party; and in the campaign of 1859 he allied himself with the "Chivalry" faction of the Democratic party. Incensed by certain statements made by Senator Broderick of the "Tammany" faction in his campaign speeches, Terry challenged him to a duel, in which Senator Broderick was fatally wounded.

The site of the famous Broderick-Terry duel was definitely located and marked in 1917 by the Landmarks Committee of the Native Sons of the Golden West as being just south of the San Francisco–San Mateo county line, near Lake Merced. Two granite shafts were later erected on the spot where the two principals stood. On one appears the name "Broderick," in bronze letters, and on the other, "Terry." On the eminence near by, where spectators witnessed this duel, there is a bronze tablet upon a foundation of granite, stating the historic facts of the event. The words are as follows:

U.S. Senator, David C. Broderick, and Chief Justice of the Supreme Court, David S. Terry, met here in the early morning of September 13, 1859, Senator Broderick receiving a mortal wound. This was the last of the great duels fought in California. With the exception of the Burr-Hamilton affair, no duel has taken place in the history of the United States where the principals were as well known or occupied as high official positions.

This event did not end Terry's stormy career. After the termination of the Civil War, in which he had been made a brigadier general in the Confederate Army, he returned to California and settled in Stockton, casting his influence with the "Sand-lotters" or Workingman's party. His fiery temper embroiled him in many an altercation; and he was finally shot in the railway station at Lathrop by United States Marshal David Naglee, bodyguard of United States Supreme Court Justice Stephen J. Field, whom he had threatened.

SOURCES

[Credit is here given for source material, and permission to quote is hereby acknowledged]

ATHERTON, GERTRUDE. *Adventures of a Novelist.* Liveright, Inc., New York, 1932

BANCROFT, HUBERT HOWE. "Pioneer Register" in *History of California*, Vols. II–VI. History Company, San Francisco, 1886

BEECHEY, FREDERICK WILLIAM. *Narrative of a Voyage to the Pacific and Beering's Strait, in the years 1825, 26, 27, 28.* 2 vols. Henry Colburn and Richard Bentley, New Burlington St., London, 1831

BOLTON, HERBERT EUGENE. *Anza's California Expeditions.* 5 vols. University of California Press, Berkeley, California, 1930

———. *Fray Juan Crespi, Missionary Explorer on the Pacific Coast, 1769–1774.* University of California Press, Berkeley, California, 1927

BONESTELL, CUTLER L. *A Woodside Reminiscence as told by Grizzly Ryder.* Privately printed, San Francisco, 1920

CLOUD, ROY W. *History of San Mateo County, California.* 2 vols. The S. J. Clarke Publishing Company, Chicago, 1928

COSTANSO, MIGUEL. *Diary of the Portolá Expedition, 1769–1770.* Edited by Frederick J. Teggart. Publications of the Academy of Pacific Coast History, University of California, 1911

DAVIDSON, GEORGE. "Voyages of Discovery and Exploration on the Northwest Coast of America from 1539 to 1603," in *United States Coast and Geodetic Survey, 1886,* Washington, D.C., 1887

EDWARDS, PHILIP LEGET. *Diary of: The Great Cattle Drive from California to Oregon in 1837.* Grabhorn Press, San Francisco, 1932

EVANS, COLONEL ALBERT S. *A la California, Sketches of Life in the Golden State.* A. L. Bancroft Company, San Francisco, 1873

GWINN, PROFESSOR J. M. *History of the State of California and Biographical Record of Coast Counties.* Chapman Publishing Company, Chicago, 1904

HARTE, BRET. *A First Family of the Tasajara.* Argonaut Edition. P. F. Collier & Son, New York, 1891

History of San Mateo County, California. B. F. Alley, San Francisco, 1883

History of San Mateo County. Illustrated. Moore and DePue, Publishers (no address), 1878

HUBBARD, ELBERT. *A Little Journey to San Mateo County.* Roycroft Shop, East Aurora, New York, 1915

MILLARD, BAILEY. *History of the San Francisco Bay Region.* 3 vols. American Historical Society, Inc., Chicago, San Francisco, 1924

MILLER, GUY C. Manuscript notes. Palo Alto, 1901–1934

NELSON, N. C. "Shellmounds of the San Francisco Bay Region," in *University of California Publications in American Archaeology and Ethnology,* Vol. VII, No. 4. University of California Press, Berkeley, California, 1909

NEUMAN, J. V. Unpublished research, map, 1907–1918, by the Surveyor San Mateo County

PALÓU, FRAY FRANCISCO. *Historical Memoirs of New California.* Edited by H. E. Bolton. University of California Press, Berkeley, California, 1926

REPASS, MERLE M. *The Hermit Mine.* Thesis, Stanford University, 1923

[ROBINSON, CAPTAIN ALFRED.] *Life in California.* [H. G. Collins, Paternoster Row, London, 1845]

WAIT (COLBURN), FRONA EUNICE. *Wines and Vines of California.* The Bancroft Company, San Francisco, 1889

WATTS, W. L. "San Mateo County," in *Report of the State Mineralogist,* October 1890. State Printing Office, Sacramento, 1890

WEYMOUTH, ALICE JENKINS. *The Palo Alto Tree.* Stanford University Press, Stanford University, California, 1930

WYATT, ROSCOE D. Unpublished research

SANTA CLARA COUNTY

SANTA CLARA COUNTY (named after Misión Santa Clara, which was established in that region in 1777) was one of the original twenty-seven counties. San Jose has been its county seat from the beginning. Many pre-state records written in Spanish are filed in the courthouse.

Indian Mounds

Indians in considerable numbers dwelt in the region of Santa Clara County when the first white explorers came this way. Portolá's party reported in 1769 "many and large villages" of generous and affable heathen at the lower end of San Francisco Bay. Anza, in 1775, saw three large rancherías with many residents on the Guadalupe River and another about two miles to the north, possibly near the lower end of Moffett Field, where Chief Ynigo later had his ranch.

Even after homes had been established by the Spanish, some of the old Indian villages were occupied at times, for the wife of Don Secundino Robles said that three groups of natives were within a short distance of their house, which had been built between the present town of Mayfield and Castro Station. One of these was undoubtedly the place known as the Castro Indian Mound. It lies beyond the end of San Antonio Avenue near Castro Station and is the largest mound in the lower Bay region. Spreading out to a width of 290 feet, it has a length of 450 feet and a height at the present time of ten feet or more. It is easily overlooked, as its grass-covered slopes are within a pasture field and appear from a little distance as a gentle, natural rise of ground. Excavations have been made in this mound in past years by scientists from the State University at Berkeley and from Stanford University, both of which institutions have museum specimens from the place.

The skeletons found there were from two to four feet below the surface of the ground and lay facing in differing directions, showing no particular system of burial. Certain peculiarities were noted in the skulls.

The main artifacts discovered were mortars, pestles, bone strigils, awls, needles, chains of small beads, and an occasional bowl of a soapstone pipe very evidently obtained through barter. The few obsidian implements found must also have been carried in from elsewhere. The height of the mound has been reduced by means of scrapers, and much of the soil has been hauled away for fertilizer. This "kitchen midden," unlike those farther north along the Bay shore, shows a scarcity of certain ordinary species of shell and a preponderance of a small species less satisfactory for food but common in all the Bay district. The appearance of this small species of shell and no other throughout the depth of the mound seems to prove that the salt marsh along the Bay has been an effective barrier to more desirable species of edible shellfish from the time of the earliest habitation of the mound.

Today at various places where excavations, or even mere cultivation of field crops, is carried on, artifacts and human remains are sometimes unearthed. Such was the case a few years ago on the Peck property just south of Los Altos, where mortars and pestles were found. Skeletons have been discovered along the banks of Coyote Creek, and it is surmised by ethnologists and antiquarians that careful search would reveal the sites of old Indian encampments on many of the lesser streams.

On the northeast side of Middlefield Road, south of Marion Avenue in Palo Alto, is the site of an Indian village. Many oaks formerly grew on the spot where now only one remains. The ground at this place is only a trifle higher than the surrounding land.

On the Adams School grounds five miles west of Gilroy may be seen stationary mortars in large flat boulders. Arrowheads and stone implements have been plowed up in several fields in the vicinity.

Old Trails of Santa Clara

In 1769, Gaspar de Portolá was sent by José de Gálvez, visitador general of Spain, to take possession of and fortify the ports of San Diego and Monterey in Alta California. Portolá failed to find Monterey on this expedition but discovered instead the Bay of San Francisco.

Leaving their camp on San Pedro Creek on November 5, Portolá's party passed down into the Santa Clara Valley, probably by way of what are now the Spring Valley Lakes and Woodside, to the lone redwood tree beside the San Francisquito Creek at Palo Alto. Fray Crespi, chronicler of the expedition, says:

"We pitched camp in a plain some six leagues long, grown with good oaks and live oaks, and with much other timber in the neighborhood. This plain has two good arroyos with a good flow of water, and at the southern end of the estuary there is a good river, with plenty of water, which passes through the plain mentioned, well wooded on its banks [Guadalupe River] . . . . This entire port is surrounded by many and large villages of barbarous heathen who are very affable, mild, and docile, and very generous . . . ."

The site of the camp under the redwood tree at Palo Alto has been marked by a boulder, on which is a bronze tablet carrying the following inscription:

Under this giant redwood, The Palo Alto, November 6–11, 1769, camped Portolá and his men on the expedition that discovered San Francisco Bay. This was the assembling point for their reconnoitering parties. Here in 1774, Padre Palóu erected a Cross to mark the site of a proposed mission. The celebrated Pedro Font topographical map, of 1776, contained the drawing of the original double-trunked tree, making The Palo Alto the first official living California landmark. Placed by the Historic Landmarks Committee, N.S.G.W., November 7, 1926.

This tree was long a landmark for the Indians and, later, for the Spanish explorers and the missionaries and soldiers traveling up and down the Peninsula between San Francisco and the Missions of Santa Clara and San José. The Spaniards called it the Palo Alto ("high tree"), and the name passed on to the modern city which grew up beside it, the college town of Stanford University.

From this central camp at the Palo Alto Tree, José Francisco de Ortega went up the eastern shore of the Bay, and it is thought that he explored as far as Alameda Creek, near Niles. On their return journey to Monterey, Portolá's party retraced its former trail through San Mateo, Santa Cruz, and Monterey counties.

Pedro Fages was the first white man to go inland from Monterey Bay to San Francisco Bay. His first expedition was made in 1770. In 1772 he made a second trip which was recorded by Fray Juan Crespi, diarist of both the Portolá and Fages expeditions. Fages left Monterey on March 20, 1772, and, passing over the Salinas River and through the valley which bears its name, he climbed the Gabilan Mountains, dropping down into the valley on the other side, where, in 1797, Misión San Juan Bautista was to be established.

From there, continuing north, he entered the Santa Clara Valley north of Hudner, passed Tequisquita Slough and San Felipe Lake, traversed the broad valley which he named San Bernardino de Seña, and, on March 22, pitched camp on Llagas Creek a little north of Gilroy.

The next day the party followed along the west side of the Santa Clara Valley and climbed the low hills which extend eastward into the valley near San Martin. Camp that night was made near Coyote Creek, on the shores of a lake named by Crespi, San Benvenuto (erroneously called Benito). On the 25th the party passed along the edge of the eastern foothills and camped at San Lorenzo Creek in Alameda County.

After discovering the Sacramento Valley, Fages re-entered the Santa Clara Valley by way of Mission Pass, continuing around the head of San Francisco Bay to a point near Milpitas. "Retracing their old course, on April 3, camp was made at the spur of hills near San Martin. Near there is the watershed between Coyote Creek and Pájaro River, hence 'the hills which separate the valley of the arroyo of the live oaks of the bay from that of San Bernardino' (Gilroy)." On April 4 the camp was pitched near the site of San Juan.

Juan Bautista de Anza, in 1776, made his second expedition from Sonora, Mexico, to San Francisco. After stopping a few days at Monterey, he proceeded northward March 23, by way of the Salinas River and the Gavilan Mountains to the San Bernardino Valley, the southern end of what is now the Santa Clara Valley. There he camped at Llagas Creek. On March 24 he passed through the low hills to the Coyote River, and entered the Llano de los Robles del Puerto de San Francisco ("Plain of the Oaks of the Port of San Francisco"), now called the Santa Clara Valley. The party kept to the western side of the valley along the foothills, camping on the Arroyo de San José Cupertino on March 25, from where they had a broad view of San Francisco Bay.

When, on March 26, the little band reached the tall redwood tree on the banks of San Francisquito Creek, they found the cross which Palóu had placed there on November 28, 1774, just five years after Portolá first passed that way. From this point, Anza proceeded up the Peninsula, where he explored and located the sites for the Presidio and Mission of San Francisco.

Over this old trail up the Santa Clara Valley, marked out by Pedro Fages, the Mission Fathers came later. El Camino Real, it was called, the "Royal Road" between the Missions to the south, at Santa Clara, San Juan, and Monterey, and Misión San Francisco de Asís, at the northern end of the Peninsula.

Misión Santa Clara de Asís

The founding of Misión Santa Clara de Asís took place on January 12, 1777, with Father Tomás de la Peña, from Misión San Francisco de Asís, officiating, and José Joaquín Moraga and his soldiers from the Presidio of San Francisco also present at the ceremonies. The site chosen for the new Mission was on the banks of Río Guadalupe, the chief camping and fishing grounds of the Indians of the region. They called it So-co-is-u-ka, meaning "laurel-wood." Here the Mission cross was planted on the banks of the stream on a spot now forming a part of the Laurelwood Farm. The exact location of the original Mission is in some doubt. The probable site is marked by a cross near where the Bayshore Highway crosses Guadalupe River.

Twice within the next two years, the river, swollen by the winter rains, flooded the church, and in 1780 the Fathers sought a site on higher ground. This site was on what is now the corner of Franklin and Campbell streets, one block west of the Santa Clara station on the Southern Pacific Railway, and two blocks from the present Santa Clara Mission Church. Some of the old adobe inclosure still remains today, and the site is marked by a cross. The building erected on this spot is said to have been one of the most elaborate and beautiful of all the Mission structures in California. It was begun November 19, 1781, and was dedicated by Father Serra on May 15, 1784. Its site was called, by the Indians, Gerguensun ("the Valley of the Oaks"). The third Santa Clara Mission building was begun by 1818 and dedicated August 11, 1822.

The earthquakes of 1812 and 1818, however, had caused serious damage to the buildings, and the Fathers were obliged to move again. The third and last site was chosen where the Santa Clara Mission Church of the University of Santa Clara now stands. After the secularization of the California Missions, in 1836, its lands were confiscated and the buildings became sadly neglected. In 1850, however, the Rt. Rev. Joseph S. Alemany, bishop of the diocese, invited the Society of Jesus to Santa Clara to restore the church and to build up a college. Accordingly, on March 19, 1851, Santa Clara College was established in the old Mission buildings by Rev. John Nobili, who adapted what was left of the old adobe buildings to the requirements of a school. Changes necessitated by the growth of the school finally altered the Mission buildings until little of the original remained. By 1855 frame structures had replaced many of the former adobes.

In 1855 the state granted a university charter to the College of Santa Clara, but it was fifty-seven years before it attained real university rank. On April 29, 1912, Santa Clara College became the University of Santa Clara, and since that date many fine new buildings have grown up around the site of the old Mission. On October 25, 1926, the adobe church which, started by 1822, was completed in 1825, was destroyed by fire. In its place a concrete structure was built in 1928, as nearly as possible like the adobe church which was dedicated on the same site by the padres earlier. Many relics, dating from the beginning of its history, were rescued and preserved, and in the garden at the rear some of the adobe walls of the original cloisters still stand, shaded by aged olive trees planted by the padres of old.

El Pueblo San José de Guadalupe

Because the Spanish government found difficulty in supplying provisions for the religious and military establishments in Alta California, Governor Felipe de Neve, during his journey in 1777, under orders of the Viceroy Antonio María Bucarelli, selected certain locations for the placing of agricultural settlements. One of those chosen was near the newly established Misión Santa Clara in what has since become, under proper cultivation, the fertile Santa Clara Valley.

Here the first of these contemplated pueblo towns was established, the Governor appointing in that same year Lieutenant José de Moraga to found a settlement on the Guadalupe River two and one-quarter miles from the Santa Clara Mission. He was to take with him nine soldiers of "known" skill in agriculture, two settlers, and three laborers.

On November 29, 1777, the new town was founded on the margin of the small river from which it derived its name, El Pueblo San José de Guadalupe. It was about one and one-half miles from the center of the present city of San Jose, on a spot "where a bridge spanned a little stream on the road to Alviso." The traditional site is marked by a bronze tablet in the Jefferson School grounds on Hobson Street, adjoining the grounds of the old Hotel Vendome, now torn down.

The floods of March 1778 inundated the marshy land on which this first settlement had been started during the previous dry season and washed away the nearly completed dam built for irrigation purposes. In July a new dam was constructed farther upstream; and the handful of *pobladores,* or first settlers, removed to higher ground. This move caused a change in land titles; and Don José Moraga, who had directed the first settlement, was instructed in 1782 by Governor Pedro Fages to untangle the land lines, to make the allotments uniform and regular, and to designate the common lands and the vacant lands. The first houses, hastily constructed, were gradually replaced by more permanent adobe ones made from the local soil by admixture of a certain amount of cut grass and weeds and dried in brick form.

The site on the Guadalupe River proved unsatisfactory for a town because of the yearly winter floods. In about the year 1785 the town was moved to higher levels, and the center of the new location laid near what is now the corner of Market and San Fernando streets.

San José de Guadalupe was visited by Captain George Vancouver in 1792, when the beauty and fertility of the valley in which it was situated won his enthusiastic praise. He was especially impressed by its broad, oak-studded fields, of which he said: "For almost twenty miles it could be compared to a park which had originally been planted with true old English oak."

In 1803 the Mission Fathers built a small adobe church on the new plaza, opposite the present Post Office. It was improved in 1835 and was later encased in brick, but was finally destroyed by fire. In 1887 the present stone structure, known as St. Joseph's Church, was completed. It stands on the site of the old adobe chapel. The park in front of the City Hall is a part of what was San José's second plaza.

El Embarcadero de Santa Clara (Alviso)

Just as Misión San José had its embarcadero on the east shore of San Francisco Bay during the Spanish and Mexican periods, so Misión Santa Clara also had its embarcadero, or landing-place. It was at the head of the navigable slough which extends southward from San Francisco Bay, and which is known today as the Alviso Slough. In early Mission days it was called the Embarcadero de Santa Clara de Asís, and played a very important part in the life of the settlers at Misión Santa Clara and the Pueblo of San José.

Yankee ship captains, from 1835 to 1850, opened up an extensive trade with the dons who owned the vast ranchos bordering on San Francisco Bay. Every rancho had its embarcadero. Among them, the Embarcadero de Santa Clara was one of the foremost. Richard Henry Dana, Jr., in *Two Years before the Mast,* says:

"The Mission of Dolores, near the anchorage, has no trade at all; but those of San José, Santa Clara, and others situated on the large creeks or rivers which run into the bay, ... do a greater business in hides than any in California. Large boats, or launches, manned by Indians . . . . are attached to the missions, and sent down to the vessels with hides, to bring away goods in return."

Ignacio Alviso settled at the Embarcadero de Santa Clara in 1840. He had been granted, in 1838, Rancho Rincón de los Esteros. Alviso was mayordomo at the Mission and was engaged in construction work there at about the time the building was moved to its last site. About this time the name of the old embarcadero was changed to Alviso.

The development of the quicksilver mines at New Almaden, in 1845 and for many years after, played a large part in Alviso's shipping industry. Then came the discovery of gold at Coloma in 1848. Trade increased so substantially that a steamer was run from San Francisco to Alviso, and the first warehouse was built there in 1849–50. It was during this period that the state capitol was located at San José. It is rather astonishing to note that during those years the fare one way on that old steamer was $35 per passenger as far as Alviso and $10 from there on the stage to San José by way of Santa Clara and the Alameda.

From 1850 to 1861, Alviso enjoyed its greatest period of development. In 1865 the railroads began to divert trade from the embarcaderos on the Bay, and Alviso, like many similar pioneer ports, became practically deserted. There was a slight revival of activity in 1876, when a branch railroad was built through the town. Today there seem to be new signs of life in the little faded village. The Alviso Salt Works, the old Bayside Canning Company, two large California oil companies, and quite an extensive shell business, all show signs of reviving the dreams of the past. Transportation boats dock at the wharves, and the gay boats of the South Bay Yacht Club sometimes gather to the number of twenty in the little cove.

Alviso still has aspirations, but it is chiefly as the scene of Spanish embarcadero days that the seeker of historic spots finds it interesting.

The Alameda

The tree-lined avenue known as the Alameda was first planted by the padres for the benefit of wayfarers between Misión Santa Clara and the Pueblo de San José. The planting of the trees was begun in 1799 by Father Majín de Catalá, who employed two hundred Indians to transplant common black willows from the river bank and to water and protect the young grove until the trees should be large enough to withstand the presence of roving herds of cattle that pastured in this unfenced territory. Bordering one side of this grove was a three-mile ditch, or *acequia,* detouring water from the Guadalupe to irrigate the Mission garden and other land. Three rows of willows grew there in the early days, and they served as shade from the hot summer sun and as protection from the wild cattle that resented the presence of pedestrians.

Captain Alfred Robinson, who visited this locality on several occasions before 1841, says of this road: "It is frequented generally on the Sabbath or feast days when all the town repair to the church at Santa Clara. On a Sunday may be seen hundreds of persons of both sexes, gaily attired in silks and satins, mounted on their finest horses, and proceeding leisurely up the road. No carriages are used, and, of course, the scene is devested of all the pomp and splendor which accompanies church-going in the larger places of the republic, yet in one respect it excells them all, that is, in the display of female beauty. No part of Mexico can show so large a share of bright eyes, fine teeth, fair proportions, and beautiful complexions."

For nearly three-quarters of a century the grove remained undespoiled. As the region was opened up and traffic grew heavier over this highway, it became evident that a more solid roadbed would be necessary. Although the most important and the best road in the region, winter rains made havoc with it. In the winter of 1852 it became impassable, and all traffic was compelled to use a route to the west, making the journey from the Mission to the town much longer. In 1856

Crandall Brothers established an omnibus line to carry passengers along the Alameda, but the roadbed was still far from satisfactory. In order to secure maintenance, a franchise to collect tolls was granted to the Alameda Turnpike Company in 1862 in return for making and maintaining a good road. When this franchise terminated in 1868, a railroad with horse-drawn cars began operations. Two years later, the means of locomotion was changed to steam and the line was extended some miles at the southern end.

When electrification of the line came in 1887, public opinion finally consented to the destruction of the center line of trees. One of the county papers on November 24, 1887, announced: "The last of the beautiful grove of trees which has stood for a century in the Alameda, San Jose's lovely drive, has been cut down to make room for the electric road to Santa Clara." Tradition has it that two willows planted in 1799 are living. These stand on the east side of the Alameda near the University of Santa Clara.

On this stretch of El Camino Real that has seen the heyday of all modes of travel, automobiles now predominate; and the well-paved United States Highway 101, stretching from the southern to the northern boundaries of the state, has utilized the three miles of the old "Alameda."

Adobes in San Jose

A bronze tablet to commemorate the original Pueblo San José de Guadalupe, founded November 29, 1777, is attached to a large tree in the grounds of Jefferson School on Hobson Street in the modern city of San Jose.

Many buildings in the pueblo were constructed of abobe and travelers writing of them as late as 1850, when a few frame houses were being built among them, had little to say in their favor. One by one they have been replaced by better structures. A part of one of those early dwellings stands at the rear of a small cottage at 184 San Augustine Street. This was the residence of Luis Peralta, *comisionado* of the pueblo for the years immediately following 1807. It was probably built about 1808. The main part was torn down in 1918. The two rooms that remain are enclosed in walls about 18 by 40 feet and are used as storerooms. The building is almost entirely covered with boards and has a tin roof.

All of Don Luis' children were born in this house, which along with fourteen acres was left to his two maiden daughters, Josefa and Guadalupe.

Another adobe relic stands at the rear of the large residence at 243 South Market Street. A stretch of wall about twenty-five feet long and one story high is exposed between two frame additions made at either end. An interior wall divides this structure into two rooms. It was occupied in the late 1830's by José Felíz.

At 770 Lincoln Avenue, toward the Willow Glen section of San Jose, stands an adobe and frame house; a porch across its front supports an upper balustrade. At the rear of the building, built in the early 1840's, are fig trees of the Black Mission variety. One of these trees is especially large, although from its trunk many large branches have been cut. A part of the tree lies across a trellis. It bears a never failing crop of figs.

Adobes in Santa Clara

At 1067 Grant Street, on Highway 101 between Franklin and Benton streets, is a one-story adobe building that was part of José Peña's house. It is being preserved by the Santa Clara Women's Club and is used by this group as a clubhouse. It stands well back from the street in a garden where grow pears, apricots, and flowering shrubs.

In the grounds of the University of Santa Clara may be seen an adobe remnant of the old Mission, a room now used for storage, and a few adobe arches along a corridor.

At 401 Jefferson Street stands a modest family residence of two stories called the Fernández adobe. A narrow porch runs along the front; at one side is a wooden stairway leading to the one room upstairs, or attic. A lusty grapevine clambers over the back door; a rear window is protected by vertical iron bars; and a large olive tree shades the front corner of the building.

Off Scott Lane, at a point east of the scene of the Battle of Santa Clara and across the State Highway from the town of Santa Clara, stands a large frame house that was beautifully kept in the days of the early American settlers. It was then the residence of John Grandon Bray. At the rear of this house is a low, oblong building, one adobe room of which was built perhaps in the middle 1850's. All four rooms were used during Mr. Bray's ownership, one for storing fruit and nuts, one for keeping cured meats, one as a milk room, and the fourth as quarters for the Chinese cook. Concrete now paves the stretch of a few feet between the two buildings, an area formerly laid over with red bricks that became uneven through use.

Hall of Justice

The Courthouse now standing on First Street opposite St. James Square in San Jose was preceded by buildings of lesser dignity in various parts of the city. These buildings served as places for the administration of justice and the care of records.

The first tribunal of the region, the *juzgado*, was built in 1783 within the original Pueblo de San José. After removal of the pueblo to higher ground a second *juzgado* was erected in 1798 (the date is debatable) in Market Street at the intersection of Post Street. That second adobe structure, before it was torn down in 1850 and the bricks removed for use elsewhere, saw the growth of the Spanish pueblo into an American village. It was a low building with sloping tiled roof, and in front of it Thomas Fallon hoisted the United States flag on July 13, 1846.

Before the admission of California to statehood in the Union on September 9, 1850, the first county court had been organized. It convened in March 1850 in the adobe building on the west side of North First Street opposite the passageway then known as Archer Alley (now Fountain Alley). This remained the site of the hall of justice until the latter part of 1851, when it was moved into the "Bella Union" building on the north side of West Santa Clara Street. It remained there less than a year, when it was moved to the former "State House," which was purchased by the county from the city. From there it was forced to move again by a fire which destroyed the building in the spring of 1853. A temporary location was found in Lightston's adobe building on the west side of Lightston Alley, where the *Mercury Herald* pressroom now stands.

For the next seven years, 1853 to 1860, the seat of justice was at the southeast corner of Second and San Fernando streets. The next move was to the San Jose city hall on the west side of North Market Street, where the firehouse now stands. It remained there until 1862 and was then changed to the two-story building just erected by Martin Murphy. The structure is the only one of the number thus far named that is still standing. From this place, the hall of justice went on January 1, 1868, to its permanent location on North Market Street opposite St. James Square. This fine building had been carefully constructed and it stood until the fire of May 18, 1931, ruined the interior and left only the staunchly built outer walls intact. About eighteen months later the present courthouse of three stories was ready for occupancy on the same site and within the exterior walls of the building erected in 1868 and burned in 1931.

Rancho Los Tularcitos

Rancho Los Tularcitos lay in the northern part of Santa Clara County near the lower end of San Francisco Bay. It extended from the confluence of Calera and Penitencia creeks southerly along the latter stream to the Calaveras Road in the town of Milpitas and easterly to include the mountains at the heads of Calera Creek and the Arroyo de los Coches. The southeastern point is marked by a live oak tree, which also denotes the northeastern point of the outlying lands of the Pueblo de San José.

This rancho was granted by Pablo Vicente de Sola, the last of the Spanish governors of Alta California, to José Higuera on October 4, 1821. The grant was renewed by the Mexican governor, Juan B. Alvarado, on February 18, 1839; and patent for 4,394.35 acres was issued by the United States government to the heirs on July 8, 1870. This land was afterward purchased by Henry Curtner, a native of Vermont, and remains in the possession of his family.

Two of the old José Higuera adobes, built on Rancho Tularcitos by José Higuera, may still be seen on the banks of the Calera Creek a few hundred yards from the Curtner house. The first story of the older building was constructed about 1828, and the upper added some time later, in the 1860's. The later building has been almost completely destroyed by fire, but the broken, crumbling walls still remain, and the doorways, hearth, and partitions may also be distinguished.

A marker on the early building, placed by the Landmarks Committee of the Native Sons of the Golden West in 1928, commemorates the historic "Higuera Adobe Home Erected by José Higuera." This was the larger of the two buildings and was about two hundred feet farther north along the stream. It is protected by a wooden superstructure, much warped by earthquakes, erected about eighty years ago by a Frenchman named Columbet, who owned that part of the rancho before Curtner purchased it of him.

Near the stream there may also be seen a part of the ancient cactus hedge and a little of the adobe wall which inclosed the house and gardens over a hundred years ago. There, also, is an ancient fig tree, gnarled with age but still prolific. Near the larger Higuera house, old fig and pear and olive trees still bear fruit.

The Curtner house itself is built on the site of an Indian temescal ("sweat-house"). Stone implements, bowls and pestles, and hundreds of melted stones used in the sweathouse ceremonies, as well as several Indian skeletons, have been found during the process of building and gardenmaking. Beads and arrowheads have also been found in neighboring hills and canyons.

This rancho had its part in the stirring times of 1846, for, on the day after Christmas of that year, Sánchez brought his troops to a halt near the house of Don José Higuera and rested there for two days before moving on toward San José. Sánchez had with him on this occasion six American prisoners, one of them Lieutenant Washington A. Bartlett, then acting alcalde of San Francisco. He had captured all six near the Sixteen-Mile House south of San Francisco, while they were on a foraging expedition for meat for the United States forces.

Of all the merrymakings at the Higuera home with its numerous progeny, the one longest remembered in the countryside was the marriage feast of the granddaughter Margarita. She was very beautiful; and at the time that she became the wife of Nicolas Chavarri, the fiesta continued for three days and was attended by friends from far and near. Some of her descendants still live on a bit of the old grant.

Valentín, the father of Margarita, sold his portion of land to Clemente Columbet and received $3,000 for it. Columbet, who had a hotel in San José in 1849, attempted to conduct a country hostelry in this old adobe. He divided the upstairs into several bedrooms and arranged a huge reception room on the ground floor. He ran a stage to connect with other conveyances at Alviso and Milpitas. But a short trial convinced him that the resort would yield no profit, and he therefore closed its doors.

These old adobes are about one mile east from the San Jose–Oakland highway on a private road which turns from the highway one and three-quarters miles north of the center of Milpitas.

Rancho Rinconada de los Gatos

Rancho Rinconada de los Gatos, consisting of one and one-half square leagues, was granted by Governor Alvarado on May 21, 1840, to Sebastian Peralta and José Hernández, who had made application for it as early as 1824. The Arroyo San Tomás Aquino formed its western boundary and separated it from Rancho Quito. This rancho extended a little way south of the town of Los Gatos into the broad lower end of the canyon; thence by various turns to north, northwest, and east the boundary line reached the easily identified spot called Austin Corners, which is a corner of the western part of the rancho.

The location of the rancho at the mouth of a canyon in the Santa Cruz Mountains is described by John C. Frémont in his *Memoirs* as being a valley "openly wooded with groves of oak, free from underbrush, and after the spring rains covered with grass. On the west it is protected from the chilling influence of the northwest winds by the Cuesta de los Gatos [Wild-cat Ridge], which separates it from the coast."

It is said that a fight took place there in 1831 between the Indians of the region and soldiers from Santa Clara Mission. Several legends, too, are connected with the naming of the place, all having to do with the number of large native cats. These seem to have been both plentiful and fierce, as these legends tell of several encounters with them. The ridge was known by the name Los Gatos as early as 1831, and the rancho and the modern city of Los Gatos adopted the name from the ridge.

Sebastian Peralta, a former *regidor* (alderman) at San José, had led certain expeditions against troublesome Indians during his term of office. His adobe house on this grant is no longer standing, but its site is about one hundred yards from Roberts Road near the bridge across Los Gatos Creek. It was a long one-story building with a sloping roof extending over an ell at one end.

About one and one-half miles by airline from this Peralta home was the adobe house of the other grantee, José Hernández, a house of which a part still stands incorporated into the country home of the present owner. The entrance to this residence on an elevation near a bend in the Arroyo de San Tomás Aquino is one-half mile from Austin Corners. It was a structure of two stories with small, square, deep-recessed windows both upstairs and down. Surrounding it is a pergola upon which are old-fashioned banksia and other kinds of roses that are still flourishing on their huge old trunks. Additions to the old house to fit it for comfortable, modern living have been carried out with great care in order to retain the original character of the place. A commemorative bronze

tablet was affixed to the outer wall of the old part by the Colonial Dames of America in 1927.

New Almaden

From time immemorial the Indians of the Santa Clara Valley visited the hill of red earth (cinnabar) above the poplar-lined stream which the Spaniards later called the Arroyo de los Alamitos ("the Little River of the Poplar Trees"). The red earth made excellent pigment with which the proud Indian loved to adorn himself.

As early as 1824 the Spanish settlers of the valley knew about the red hill and its strange pigments. In that year an attempt was made by the Robles brothers, Secundino and Teodoro, and by Don Antonio Suñol, a member of the San José Council, to find silver or gold in the deposit; and in time the excavation was called "La Mina Santa Clara."

In the year 1842 Governor Alvarado made grants of land in this vicinity to two men: on August 1 he gave Rancho San Vicente to José Reyes Berryessa and on June 16, Cañada de los Capitancillos to Justo Larios. Three years later actual interest in the mineral deposits therein contained arose.

Andres Castillero had made several trips between Mexico and Alta California in the decade previous to 1845, the year in which he was shown a sample of ore from La Mina Santa Clara. His presence in the north at this time as a deputy of the Mexican government was occasioned by a plan for moving troops from Mexico to aid in the control of foreigners who were invading California in considerable numbers. By some chance, upon this visit, he was told of this earlier identified but forgotten ore.

On November 22, 1845, Andres Castillero filed with Alcalde Pedro Chaboya in San José a document wherein he claimed discovery of "silver with a ley of gold" on the rancho of José Reyes Berryessa. In conformity with the mining ordinances he asked that notices of his discovery and of his intention for its development be affixed in public places. After making certain crude tests he filed a second document in the following month reporting the discovery of "liquid quicksilver" in the deposit, and shortly thereafter went back to Mexico.

Soon there began the long-drawn-out litigation over the ownership of the mine—a litigation finally injected into affairs at Washington. The New Almaden Company, Barron, Forbes and Company of Mexico, and the Quicksilver Mining Company of Pennsylvania and New York were all involved.

In 1846, Barron, Forbes and Company of Tepic, Mexico, owned the controlling interest in the project, and, after the discovery of gold at Coloma in 1848, there was a tremendous increase in the demand for quicksilver. New Almaden became the most famous and one of the most productive quicksilver mines in the world, and, at one time, there was a thriving town centered about it. In 1864 the mine and all the improvements were sold to the Quicksilver Mining Company of New York and Pennsylvania for $1,700,000.

Recently the mine has been worked only intermittently. Abandoned shafts and flumes are today visible on the steep hillside topped by tall brick chimneys, like the ruins of an ancient castle. The upper Arroyo de los Alamitos is choked with "tailings," from which a little quicksilver is still taken.

A small plateau beyond the St. George Shaft, one of the many shafts that are still evident, was called Bull Run, and here were held the outdoor games and holiday festivities.

The oblong building, the mine office of the '50's, is still standing near the road that leads from the hacienda to the site of the old settlements on the hill. By following the curving road and "rounding Cape Horn," one reaches English town. An old schoolhouse stands here. Still farther up is the Chilian camp, and to the left is Spanish town. The whole place is dotted with mine shafts.

Three cemeteries were used at Almaden, two of them in the vicinity of Spanish town, where the graves are marked by wooden slabs with epitaphs in Spanish. In recent years these isolated burial places have been desecrated by vandals. The third, and oldest, cemetery is near Alamitos Creek, back of the hacienda. Here the graves are marked with slabs of stone.

The drowsy village, which has slept there for a quarter of a century, remains little changed today. Its one street follows the bank of the stream, where poplars still grow undisturbed as in days long gone by. At the head of the long row of tiny, low-roofed frame and adobe houses with their half-deserted gardens, stands a great mansion, the "Casa Grande" of the village. It is thought that it was erected on the site of the adobe built there by the Spanish in 1827.

This was truly one of the grandest mansions in all California in its day, being staunchly built with walls almost two feet thick and with magnificent fireplaces, hand-carved and inlaid, material for which was brought around the Horn. It contains twenty rooms today and has wide balconies running clear around the lower story.

The little sleepy town awoke to new life in 1927 when it was restored as a week-end and summer resort. Happily, much of the picturesque aspect of the place has been preserved and the romance of old California still gathers about its quaint adobe domiciles.

The men to whom the grants of these lands were given by Governor Alvarado in 1842 are of some interest. José Reyes Berryessa, who received Rancho San Vicente, in which the mine works were established and where the mouth of the tunnel was dug, was the son of Nicolás and Gertrudis Peralta de Berryessa, who were among the earliest settlers in San Francisco. Don José had served his time in the militia of San Francisco and was a teacher there during the latter part of this military period. His wife was María Z. Bernal, a daughter of the owner of the neighboring Rancho Santa Teresa. In 1846, less than four years after receiving his land, Don José, then well on in years, was killed at the embarcadero of Misión San Rafael in Marin County. Patent to this rancho, consisting of 4,438 acres, was given to the widow on June 24, 1868.

Justo Larios, grantee of Rancho Capitancillos, on which was the peak of the Almaden mine hill, was the son of José M. Larios, and was thirty-four years of age when he received his grant in 1842. He was a militia artilleryman and a soapmaker and was one of those unfortunate ranchers whose horses were appropriated by Frémont's men. His wife was Cecelia, daughter of Joaquín Castro. After giving possession of his rancho to the quicksilver interests he went to the Mother Lode region, where he made a small fortune in the gold mines in 1849–1850. He soon lost much of his wealth, however, and spent his later years in Gilroy. A part of his land through which Los Capitancillos Creek flows was patented as Rancho Capitancillos (3,360.48 acres) to Charles Fossat on February 3, 1865. A lesser part, Cañada de los Capitancillos, containing 1,109.67 acres, was patented to the Guadalupe Mining Company on September 20, 1871. This company developed the Guadalupe mine two miles beyond the New Almaden; while it has not had the spectacular career of the latter, the Guadalupe has been a heavy producer.

Rancho Quito

In the fertile country between the town of Saratoga and State Highway 101 lies Rancho Quito, or "Tito" as it was sometimes called, granted by Governor Alvarado in 1841 to José Noriega and José Zenon Fernández. It is well watered, as both Campbell and Calabasas creeks flow through it and along its eastern boundary flows the Arroyo San Tomás Aquino.

Both of the grantees were Hijar colonists who reached California under the spell of enthusiasm kindled by José María Padres and his associate José María Hijar. Noriega came as supercargo on the vessel bringing this group, and Fernández was one of the six teachers in the party; both lived in San José after their arrival, and both became members of the council in that pueblo. Don José Fernández taught for a time at Santa Clara. In 1839 he was secretary of the *ayuntamiento* (municipal government) and in 1840–1841, at the time of receiving this grant, was secretary of the *junta* (council). He continued to hold important offices up to the time of his death three years later. Both owners transferred the property to Manuel Alviso, under date of July 8, 1844. Noriega continued to live in the vicinity. The land, comprising 13,309.85 acres, was patented on May 14, 1866, to Alviso jointly with the heirs of Fernández—the widow, Petra Enriques de Fernández, and her children, Manuel Loreto, Francisco Máximo, and Dionesa.

Manuel Alviso sold his interest in Rancho Quito on March 9, 1859, to José Ramón Argüello, Octavius F. Cipriani, and S. M. Mezes for "a valuable and considerable consideration." Two deeds bearing the signatures of him and his wife, Doña María Luisa Peralta de Alviso, were executed.

Don José Ramón Argüello, one of the purchasers of Alviso's land, was the grandson of Don José Darío Argüello and son of Don Luis. After the death of Don Luis, the family had continued to reside on the Pulgas rancho in their adobe house at San Carlos, but after José Ramón became the owner of this property the widowed mother came to live with him. She died in 1874, and he in 1876. Their place there was about eight miles from San Jose, at the junction of Saratoga Avenue and the Quito Road, and is called the Quito Farm. He planted olive trees, a fruit orchard, and a small vineyard, which passed in 1882 into the possession of Edward E. Goodrich, who further developed the property by building a winery, an oil mill, and houses for his employees.

The town of Saratoga lies at the southwest corner of Rancho Quito near Campbell Creek. The old settlement of Gubserville was on the road from Santa Clara that stretches through this rancho. This little settlement, remembered by few today, was the first place on this stage route out of Santa Clara at which the driver paused to leave mail.

Before the boundary lines of Rancho Quito were definitely known several industrious families made homes in the region east of Cupertino on land then supposed to be public land. When it was suspected that this area might belong to the old grant, the farmers banded together and engaged an attorney to represent them. The court decided against the rights of these men, and many of them gave up their homes and moved away. Those who elected to remain were allowed a term of five years in which to make payments ranging from twenty to thirty dollars an acre; at the end of this period they became the owners of their chosen locations.

Robert Glendenning was one of the group that remained. From their native Scotland, he and his wife arrived in San Francisco via Australia in 1850. In 1851 they took up 160 acres northeast of Cupertino, living at first in a tent with a board shed as a storage place where food and other goods that might prove tempting to wild animals or roving Indians would be safe. The family prospered, built a good home, purchased adjoining land, and was an asset to the community. Descendants of Robert Glendenning have remained on the property to the present time. Their home is on Glendenning Avenue, a private road leading south from Homestead Road.

Rancho San Antonio and Los Altos

South of Los Altos on a hill overlooking a wide terrain long stood the crumbling ruins of an adobe building, called by many a fort but which in truth was the home erected there by Prado Mesa, owner of Rancho San Antonio, who died about 1845.

Juan Prado Mesa, a soldier in the San Francisco Company from 1828 and a corporal in the Santa Clara Escolta (guard) beginning in 1832, was promoted to sergeant and acting *alferez* in 1837. Later in the same year he was made full *alferez* in charge of the San Francisco garrison. In 1841 he is mentioned by the British Simpson as "Captain" Prado with a corporal's guard in the square huts that then made up the Presidio at San Francisco back from a dismantled fort "fast crumbling into the undermining tide beneath."

Don Prado married into the Higuera family (according to a grandson, the name of the grandmother was Miciali Higuera) and had seven children: Agustín, Antonio, Concepción, Mejín, Francisco, Ramón, and Nicandro. According to J. N. Bowman, the adobe house was built in 1844, although local tradition places the date earlier. On March 24, 1839, he had received a grant, extending from San Antonio Creek to Stevens Creek, from Governor Alvarado. Rancho San Antonio was an oblong strip of land stretching from San Antonio Creek to Stevens, or Cupertino, Creek, and was divided near its center by Permanente Creek.

The square construction of the house and its corrals gave rise to the tradition of its having been a fort—a conclusion which is perhaps warranted by the fact that any house in those days was built to withstand attacks of unfriendly natives. Don Prado also owned a lot in San Francisco, as did Juana Briones de Miranda, whose Rancho Purísima Concepción was separated from Rancho San Antonio by San Antonio Creek and two of whose daughters, Manuela and Refugia, married Don Prado's sons Agustín and Ramón.

William A. Dana purchased the southern part of this rancho at executor's sale. He filed claim in 1853 for 3,541.80 acres of it lying along Permanente Creek and received patent for it on December 19, 1857. Several other claimants to certain parts of the rancho appeared: James W. Weeks, H. C. Curtis, William W. White, Mary S. Bennett, and Henry F. Dana. Patent, however, was given August 6, 1866, to Encarnación Mesa and other heirs for the remaining 4,440.31 acres.

The town of Los Altos with its surrounding country homes is on this Rancho San Antonio. The site of the original adobe house of Don Juan Prado Mesa on a hill near El Monte Station is now occupied by a modern stucco residence.

Rancho La Purísima Concepción

Rancho La Purísima Concepción was granted June 30, 1840, to the Indians José Gregorio (Gorgonio) and José Ramón by Governor Alvarado. Little is known of these grantees other than that they occupied the land for some years before it was formally granted to them and that they continued to reside there until it was sold to Juana Briones de Miranda. This sale is reported to have taken place in 1844; but the deed, as recorded, bears the date of November 6, 1850, at which time José Ramón signed by making his mark.

According to family tradition, the elder Briones, the parents of Juana, came with Father Majín de Catalá, the much beloved Franciscan friar, to Monterey and on to Santa Clara Mission, when he was sent there in 1794. The children in the family were: Guadalupe, who married Ramón de Miramontes of Half Moon Bay; María la Luce, who died unmarried at an advanced age; Juana, born at Carmel or Monterey, who married Apolinario Miranda; another sister,

who married into the Martínez family and lived in the town of Martinez; and one son, Gregorio, who became a doctor and lived in Bolinas, near which some of his descendants still live.

The home of the pioneer Briones family was apparently broken up before all of the children were grown, as Juana lived with her elder sister Guadalupe and moved with her to Misión Dolores. In San Francisco Juana married Apolinario Miranda, a soldier in that place from 1819 to 1836 and grantee of Rancho Ojo de Agua de Figueroa. In 1843 he was sent before the subprefect for not living harmoniously with his wife. He was buried in the cemetery at Misión Dolores.

Juana had a house, built of adobe, in the North Beach region of San Francisco, where she was kind to sick and deserting sailors. She seemed to possess ability similar to that of her brother and frequently went out on cases where she acted as doctor, nurse, or midwife, not only in San Francisco but also after moving to her rancho in Santa Clara County.

A three-day trip by oxcart brought her and her seven children to Rancho La Purísima Concepción, a rather hilly tract of land in which rise several small streams that, uniting, form a creek. This creek, early known under the names of Yeguas and Adobe and now called San Antonio, carries the drainage waters to the San Francisco Bay. The adobe house in which they lived is still standing on the top of a hill not far from the junction of Junipero Serra Boulevard and the Page Mill Road. This property was duly confirmed to her in 1856, the final patent being given August 15, 1871.

When the Briones de Miranda family lived on this hill, a shopping trip to San Francisco required a full week, three days going and three days returning and one day for the necessary errands in the city. The carreta, drawn by a team of oxen and piled with hides to be sold, got an early morning start and, jolting over the uneven road, reached the first night's destination at the Argüello rancho, where accommodation for man and beast was obtained. On the morrow, the oxen of the first day's journey being left there to rest, a fresh team was supplied for the second lap of the journey, which ended on the second night at the Sánchez rancho. There another exchange of oxen took place on the third morning and Misión Dolores was reached that night. The fourth day was the one in which the travelers greeted old friends and took the hides to Davis or to Leidesdorf, the two most successful merchant-shipowners of the time, exchanging them for needed supplies. The return journey, made in reverse order, saw all the oxen returned to their home corrals; and the family, or those members of it who had been permitted to take the journey, reached home with their own animals on the night of the seventh day.

After the children were married and gone, with the exception of José de Jesús and José Dolores who never married, Juana continued to reside there; and each year, as long as she lived, the family gathered at the home place for a barbecue festivity, lasting for several days. The family reunion included: Presentación and her English husband, Robert T. Ridley; Tomás and his wife, Bjorques; Narcisa and her husband, Jesús García; Refugia and her husband, Ramón Prado, son of Prado Mesa of the neighboring Rancho San Antonio; and Manuela and her husband, Agustín, also a son of the neighbor Prado Mesa. All of the grandchildren came too, and in addition Juana's sister Guadalupe from Half Moon Bay with her musical family, which within its own circle formed a whole brass band and added much to the gaiety of the occasion.

Small tracts of this rancho nearest the original home were apportioned to the children, but the greater acreage early passed into the possession of outsiders. The daughter Manuela continued to live at her mother's place for some time after her marriage; and her elder children were born in this adobe before she moved to a house located where Alta Mesa Cemetery now is. In 1873 she moved to the neighboring village itself so that her children might attend the Mayfield School (a smaller schoolhouse than the present one located on the same site). Manuela lived for a year in a rented house on what was then Washington Street, now changed to Page Mill Road, and the next year she built a frame house on Sheridan Street.

Another daughter also lived in Mayfield; and finally the mother Juana, crippled by rheumatism, left the adobe on the hill and moved to a little house in the village near the two daughters, where she was cared for until her death in 1890 at a ripe old age. The house in which she spent her last years (still a small house although enlarged since she lived in it) is at the corner of Second Street and the Page Mill Road.

María la Luce survived her sister for two months. The family burials are in Holy Cross Cemetery at Menlo Park and at Dolores in San Francisco. The daughter Manuela died in 1901; and her house, containing several family documents, was afterward destroyed by fire. The lot on which it stood is now vacant. Two of Manuela's sons live in the vicinity, and the children of her brother and sisters are scattered in three counties of the state.

The Juana Briones de Miranda adobe has since known other owners. Dr. Charles Palmer Nott, a botanist at Stanford University, purchased the place and made many improvements to both the house and the grounds. The adobe, originally long and narrow and found falling into decay, was preserved by being covered with boards. As Dr. Nott's family grew in number, he added rooms, first two frame ells to the adobe so that an attractive court was formed around the old well. In this protected spot he and his wife planned pathways and cared for little flower borders. Later a stairway was built, leading through the former dining room, and a second story was added. The whole was done in such a way that the place did not lose its original charm, although it became a more comfortable domicile. Ornamental shrubs and vines, planted on the hillside by this owner, are now thriving. A later owner was Dr. Eaton of San Francisco. Since his death the property has remained in his family.

Rancho Santa Teresa

Rancho Santa Teresa originally consisted of about 9,647 acres granted to Joaquín Bernal, a native of Spain educated at Barcelona and sent by King Carlos to investigate the mineral wealth of Mexico and California in 1795. As a reward for his services, he was allowed to choose land for himself, and the land chosen lies in the Santa Clara Valley immediately south of San Jose and bounded on the east by the Coyote River. On the other sides were the following ranchos: San Felipe and Las Animas on the east, Laguna Seca on the south, and San Juan Bautista and San Vicente on the west. The exact date of his taking possession is not known. But in July 1834, when he (at the age of ninety-four) petitioned Governor Figueroa for the property, he had lived on the place for some years, had built four adobe houses, and had large flocks and herds and a progeny of seventy-eight children and grandchildren. The grant was made to him within the month.

A large framed picture on the wall of a modern house on the ranch shows the place as it appeared in the year 1835: a spacious and well-built two-story adobe house with a balcony across the front; a tile-topped adobe wall enclosing perhaps an acre of ground into which the back of the house projects; a fenced kitchen garden at one side; a pool for swimming in a roofless enclosure; a sturdily built fence with heavy gate

surrounding an arena for the "bull and grizzly" fights to which settlers from the whole countryside came on days of celebration, and on the hillside some one hundred and fifty yards away the Santa Teresa Spring. This picture and family portraits of Don Joaquín and the gracious Josepha Sánchez, his wife, preserve the true feeling of early Spanish life as it existed in this hacienda eight miles south of San Jose.

Don Joaquín died at the age of eighty-seven, and his wife, at the age of one hundred and ten. Their home was on the site of the present frame house in which the fourth generation was born. The never failing spring supplies water, which flows through lead pipes as it did for the adobes a century ago. A statue of Santa Teresa, brought from Rome by Father Seraphina, was presented to Jesusita, wife of Ygnacio Bernal, grandson of the original grantee. Pedro Bernal, Jesusita's son, placed the statue of the patron saint in a glass-enclosed niche on a boulder beside the Santa Teresa Spring.

Near the spring, on slightly lower ground, is the stone work of an old vat where a French saddle maker, Changara, was allowed to tan hides from some of the cattle slaughtered on the place. He was given a small adobe for living quarters and there made saddles much esteemed by the horsemen of the period. When an extra supply accumulated, he journeyed up and down the state to dispose of them. On his return it was his custom to bury the proceeds in the vicinity of his works. On one of his journeys he was murdered, probably for the money on his person. Diligent search was instituted for the old cache in the ground near his vat, but as far as known no treasure has ever been found there.

Relics of Indian and of Spanish life are found from time to time by workers in field or orchard. An earring of onyx, perhaps once worn by an Indian princess; mortars and pestles for grinding grain by and for the Indians; two huge, hard millstones that ground flour for the Spanish; and a sweet-toned bell worn by the herd mare of a past generation: these are among the articles found and treasured by the family. Three hundred acres are now held by descendants of the original grantee. On these acres are large orchards and a commercially developed marl deposit.

Rancho El Potrero de Santa Clara

One of the very earliest boundary markers in California was placed somewhere between Misión Santa Clara and the Pueblo de San José to fix the extent of the Mission pastures. In 1797 serious question of its exact position arose; and on July 29 of that year a parley was held between Don Alberto de Córdoba, engineer extraordinary and envoy of the governor, and the three founders of the pueblo: Manuel Gonzales, Tiburcio Vásquez, and Ignacio Archoleta. Don Alberto questioned each of the three founders separately, and all three pointed out the same spot as the one designated when the line was originally laid out by José Joaquín Moraga. But the Fathers of the Mission were not convinced. As it was of vital importance to know just where the Mission lands ended and the pueblo lands began, most of the civil and religious authorities took part in the controversy before it was finally settled with the Guadalupe River as the dividing line.

After the secularization of the Missions, this land reverted to the Mexican government; and in 1844 Governor Manuel Micheltorena granted El Potrero de Santa Clara (the pasture lands of Santa Clara), consisting of one square league, to James Alexander Forbes, a native of Scotland, who had arrived in Alta California in 1830 or 1831.

Mr. Forbes had been naturalized as a Mexican citizen ten years previous to receiving this rancho and in 1834 had married Ana María, daughter of Juan Crisostomo Galindo, claimant of Mission lands near Milpitas. According to some authorities, El Potrero de Santa Clara was given as a marriage dower to the bride. In 1842 James Alexander Forbes, well educated and speaking Spanish with a Scotch accent, was appointed British vice-consul and assumed the office in October of the following year. He attended to his duties for some years, although he did not change his residence to Monterey, the capital. After holding his rancho a few years, he sold it to Commodore Stockton, to whom it was twice confirmed: in 1853 by the Land Commission, and in 1855 by the District Court. It was known for a long time as the Stockton Ranch.

Commodore Robert Field Stockton, U.S.N., born in 1795, was one of the earliest notable Americans connected with the history of California. He served in the War of 1812; was sent West in command of a squadron in 1845; with Frémont conquered California in 1846–1847; was made military governor of the state by proclamation at Los Angeles on August 17, 1846, and organized the government in the newly acquired land; and appointed Colonel John Frémont to take the governorship in January 1847 before he started home on June 20, 1847, across the Rockies with his small and heterogeneous collection of men.

The rancho which he purchased from James Alexander Forbes lay in the angle formed by the Alameda and the Guadalupe River and was well watered by ditches dug from that stream to the vicinity of Misión Santa Clara. Three business ventures in California are credited to the Commodore, who resigned from the Navy in 1850: a nursery for the propagation of fruit trees, a residential subdivision called Alameda Gardens, and the importation of houses from the East around the Horn. All of these projects arose from the one idea of the establishment of pleasant living conditions for families in this new part of the United States. Although he had returned to California in 1848, the carrying out of his ideas must have been delegated to responsible agents, as he himself was United States Senator serving in Washington for his native state of New Jersey for the term of 1851–1853.

Nursery stock, consisting of apples, pears, plums, peaches nectarines, and strawberry plants, was ordered from Hovey's Nursery in Massachusetts in 1852. When the stock arrived, two men, Fox and Egan, came in charge of it, and James F. Kennedy, a salesman, came also. The nursery was well established by 1853. It is said that in this shipment came the first strawberry plants to be received in the Santa Clara Valley, where they are now so abundant. Stockton also imported bees from Italy—one queen bee and seven other bees as a start.

For the Alameda Garden subdivision the Commodore ordered houses to be made in New England ready to be erected in California after being shipped around the Horn. Misfortune befell the first shipment; but, undaunted, he ordered another though smaller lot. Eventually the ten houses of the second shipment came and were put up. Few, perhaps only one, of these are now standing; one, a two-story-and-attic structure with a cupola on the top, stands at the corner of Newhall and Spring streets on the edge of the city of San Jose. Formerly called the "White House," it was occupied by James F. Kennedy, a native of Pennsylvania, who came from the East in 1852 to manage the large rancho property for the Commodore, bringing his family with him. He lived in it prior to 1853, for family tradition gives the birth of his daughter Clara there on January 1, 1853. During his occupancy a pergola extended along one side of the house and out to the stables, which stood at some distance from the house. An iron fence ran completely around the property. The house has a balcony on three sides of its first and second stories and a similar one completely around the cupola, within which appears to be a fair-sized room with sufficient doors and windows to make

a comfortable place for observation of the landscape in all directions. Mr. Kennedy, who served as adjutant general for California during the Civil War, later purchased a large ranch near Los Gatos.

The border line of this rancho facing on the Alameda is entirely built up. Originally these buildings were all private homes, but lately business houses are creeping in along the "Willow Way" of early Mission days.

Among the hospitable homes well known a generation ago and still standing is that of the late Judge and Mrs. F. S. Leib, who found it necessary to annex a neighboring house in order to accommodate their family and their many guests. A passageway between the two buildings was constructed on the upstairs level; and by means of this connecting link the house is still identified. Judge Leib, although then a mere youth, served his country during the last year of the Civil War. After finishing his law course at the University of Michigan, he settled in San José in 1869, began the practice of law, was appointed judge of the Superior Court, and became, in addition, a successful orchardist owning other property in the county beside that on which he resided. He and his wife, Lida Campbell Grissim, who outlived him many years, enjoyed to the full extent the extensive and colorful gardens which had been nurtured around the double house that was their home for so many years. On the grounds, still owned by the family, are long pergolas wide enough to admit the passage of a modern motor car.

Rancho Los Coches

By the treaty between Mexico and the United States which was signed at the cessation of hostilities for the possession of California, all bona fide titles to land existing prior to that date were recognized by the conquering Americans. Claims to the ownership of land were immediately forthcoming, and it became an urgent matter to settle those claims in order that life in the newly acquired territory might proceed lawfully. The appointment on March 3, 1851, of a Federal Land Commission was secured by the first Senators sent from the new state to Washington: John C. Frémont and William M. Gwin. This Commission proceeded to San Francisco, where it sat for the hearing of the cases brought before it.

The first case decided for property in Santa Clara County was that of Rancho Los Coches, consisting of one-half square league lying southwest of the Alameda and 309 feet along the Guadalupe River and, from the angle this formed, extending thence southwest to certain sycamores along the Arroyo de los Gatos. This rancho had been given by Governor Micheltorena on March 12, 1844, to Roberto, a Christianized Indian of Misión Santa Clara who had been living on this land with his wife and children before that date. The question in this case was concerned with the legality of a grant to an Indian and further with his right to dispose of the property. This question being decided in the affirmative by the Commission, a claim, based on Roberto's ownership, was filed in 1852 by Antonio Suñol, Paula Suñol de Sansevain, and Henry M. Naglee; and the patent to the rancho was given on December 31, 1857, to the claimants.

Antonio María Suñol, a Spaniard in the French naval service, had lived in California since 1817, when he had deserted from the "Bordelais" in San Francisco harbor. He settled in San José, where he kept a shop and about 1824 married María Dolores Bernal. He was postmaster from 1826 to 1829, *sindico* (receiver) from 1839 to 1840, and sub-prefect from 1841 to 1844. During his ranch activities, he sold cattle to Captain Sutter on credit and had difficulty in obtaining payment. Duflot du Mofras, as he journeyed through the state in 1841, found him to be sympathetic to

France. Several children were born to Don Antonio and Doña María Dolores, one of the daughters, Paula, being named as one of the three patentees of this rancho.

Henry M. Naglee, a distinguished officer in the Civil War and one of the three joint patentees of Rancho Los Coches, long held a portion of it in his name. Naglee Park, extending from Eleventh Street to the Coyote River in the city of San Jose, was once his property, and here on a 140-acre tract stood his residence, reached by a driveway one and one-half miles long. Now remodeled as the Naglee Apartments, the building stands at the northwest corner of San Fernando and Fourteenth streets. The redwood trees and the stately palms remaining from his planting, that line some of the streets in this vicinity, give some idea of the extent and beauty of the grounds laid out around his home in 1865.

Rancho Las Animas

The first census of San José, taken in 1778, lists José Mariano Castro, thirteen years of age, eldest son of Joaquín Castro and his wife, Maria Botiller, both of whom came to California in 1776 with the Anza colonists. This boy, grown to manhood and married to Josefa Romera, journeyed back to Mexico in 1801 and obtained the grant of Rancho La Brea. The document, directly from the Spanish Viceroy Marquina, was dated August 17, 1802. In later years some difficulty regarding the title was encountered; but in August 1835 the matter was adjusted by the granting of Las Animas by the Mexican governor, José Figueroa, to the widow of José, Doña Josefa.

In some way this rancho passed into the possession of José María Sánchez. The 26,518.68 acres patented to his heirs in 1873 extend from the border line of San Benito County near Sawyer Station northwesterly across State Highway 101 south of Gilroy (incorporated in 1868) to Mount Madonna County Park in the Santa Cruz Mountains. On this rancho, the Carnadero Creek flows for miles through a series of rolling hills, after it leaves the higher region in the vicinity of Mount Madonna. Wonderful pasture lands are on these hills; and here around Miller's Station was the celebrated Bloomfield Farm of Henry Miller, the German boy who climbed to success through his ability to grow and market cattle and sheep.

Henry Kreiser was the name of this young German in his native land, but in his journey from New York via Havana he had used a ticket purchased from a chance acquaintance named Henry Miller. On March 30, 1858, eight years after he had reached California, he changed his name by legal procedure to Henry Miller. In that year he made the acquaintance of and formed a partnership with Charles Lux—a partnership which lasted until the death of Mr. Lux twenty-five years later. As time passed, the firm of Miller and Lux became familiar throughout the West. Henry Miller seemed to succeed in all that he undertook; his ability to foresee the outcome of his plans was remarkable. The lands and herds of this firm stretched well over the state; in several counties large feeding grounds and fields for cultivation were acquired. More than a dozen of the old ranchos were owned in whole or in part by them, and the number of their employees was legion. When their animals were driven to market in San Francisco, no matter how long the journey, feeding and resting places on their own property were always convenient.

On Mount Madonna, which has an elevation of 1,897 feet in the mountains on the northwest part of this rancho, Henry Miller built an elaborate country home overlooking the broad valley below. There he rested with his family and entertained his friends. Since his death, the house, which was purchased for erection elsewhere, has been removed, piece by piece; and

the fountains, terraces, and choice trees and shrubs that graced the grounds not many years ago are now untended.

Rancho San Francisco de las Llagas

The name Las Llagas de Nuestro Padre San Francisco (Stigmata of Our Father St. Francis), bestowed on March 22, 1772, by Don Pedro Fages on his stopping place beside a stream north of the village of San Martin, has clung to the place ever since. It was a convenient and suitable camp site for the parties of explorers and colonists who trod the same path later. Anza spent the night there in March 1776; and the colonists of his party under the leadership of Lieutenant Commander Moraga rested there for a day, about June 23, in the summer of the same year, as they proceeded from Monterey to the Port of San Francisco. The expedition consisted of Fray Francisco Palóu, Fray Pedro Benito Cambón, the leather-jacketed soldiers, the colonists and their families equipped with utensils and provisions, as well as the herdsmen and muleteers driving plodding livestock for use in the permanent settlement. As they traveled along the dusty trail, they had seen herds of large animals which, on capture, proved to be elk with wide-spread horns and which they found most palatable for food. They had seen, as well, on this broad plain herds of fleet antelope that sped away before them frightened by this strange cavalcade.

The rancho granted by Governor José Figueroa to Carlos Castro on February 3, 1834, lay in this region and covered a long stretch of Las Llagas Creek. Don Carlos was probably Carlos Antonio, who as a child of three years had come with his parents to California with the Anza party in 1776. He had held important official positions at Santa Cruz and San José before receiving this rancho, to which he retired in 1836 at the age of sixty. He is described by Bancroft as an eccentric host whose hospitality was shown by affecting the abuse of his guests. The northern line of the tract is at Tennant Station on the railway which passes through the level lands of the central part of the grant.

The property, however, soon passed out of his hands, for in the '40's it is mentioned as belonging to Bernard and Daniel Murphy, and it was patented to James and Martin Murphy on March 19, 1868. It was bordered on the north by the land of Martin Murphy, Sr., who built a chapel in about the center of this rancho and called it San Martín in honor of his patron saint. About this chapel has grown up the quiet village of San Martin (the only settlement of importance in the area), through which passes State Highway 101 between Gilroy and Morgan Hill, bisecting the area originally contained in the 22,283-acre Rancho San Francisco de las Llagas.

Rancho La Laguna Seca

J. C. Frémont in his *Memoirs* says: "By the middle of February [1846] we were all re-united in the Valley of San Jose, about 13 miles south of the village of that name on the main road leading to Monterey which was about 60 miles distant . . . . The Place which I had selected for rest and re-fitting was a vacant rancho called the Laguna, belonging to Mr. Fisher. I remained here until February, in the most delightful spring season of a most delightful climate. The time was occupied in purchasing horses, obtaining supplies, and thoroughly re-fitting the party."

The rancho of four square leagues had been granted on July 22, 1834, by Governor José Figueroa to Juan Alvírez, former alcalde of San José (1812–1813), and was confirmed to Liberata Ceseña Bull and other heirs of William Fisher, to whom it was also patented in 1865.

William Fisher was a sea captain from Boston, who came to California and purchased this rancho in 1845. The Fisher family had not yet arrived at their new home at the time of Frémont's February visit. In addition to managing the rancho, Captain Fisher conducted in San José a mercantile business which he sold on account of ill health in 1849, one year before his death, to Josiah Belden.

The Twelve-Mile House, Coyote Station, and the Fifteen-Mile House, Perry's Station, south of San Jose were on this grant, as was also Madrone Station. The Coyote River flows through this grant, entering it from the hilly region near the southeast corner and flowing westward past Coyote Station. The Southern Pacific Railway runs from north to south through the grant near the middle. Miller and Lux, holders of vast tracts of land, later purchased the southern part of this rancho adjoining Rancho San Felipe de las Animas, and it became a part of the chain of ranches owned by this firm.

Rancho San Ysidro

John Gilroy, the first foreign settler in California, arrived, ill of scurvy, at Monterey in 1814 on the "Isaac Todd," which he there deserted. Of Scotch parentage, his rightful name was John Cameron, but he assumed the name of Gilroy to avoid being found and returned to the ship. In the September after his arrival he was baptized at Misión San Carlos as Juan Bautista María Gilroy. In 1821 he was married at Misión San Juan Bautista to María Clará de la Ascunción, daughter of Ygnacio Ortega, the owner of Rancho San Ysidro.

Rancho San Ysidro seems to have been the home of Don Ygnacio for many years previous to this time. Bancroft says that this rancho, one of the finest in the district; was granted in 1810 to Ygnacio, son of Captain José F. Ortega, who probably came with his father from Mexico between 1769 and 1773. Don Ygnacio, whose wife was Gertrudis Arce, was a *"soldado distinguido"* of the San Diego Company in 1792.

Governor Figueroa granted this rancho to the heirs of Don Ygnacio, on June 3 and 19, 1833, following his death. In later years it was divided approximately equally between Quentín and his sister's husband, John Gilroy. The line dividing the rancho into two parts ran along the old road from Gilroy to Pacheco Pass, according to notes of the 1850 survey of the property, crossed "the former site of an oven between two adobe houses." The houses of these two younger men were about fifty yards apart, that of John lying in the sharp angle of the Y formed by the present Pacheco Pass Road and the Frasier Lake Road, and that of Quentín on the opposite side of the latter road. On the site of Gilroy's three-room adobe, a blacksmith shop was later placed. The lot is now vacant, and back of it is a little flower plot beside a country store on the highway. Quentín's adobe, probably the home of his father before him, was larger and was a landmark for years. Its arches of hewn logs stood long after the adobe house itself was gone. Cultivation of the fields that cover the site has now removed every trace. W. T. Sherman relates in his *Memoirs* that, on a certain occasion, he and his men camped by a stream near three or four adobe huts known as Gilroy's Ranch.

John Gilroy, a man of fine physique and pleasant manners, though possessed of little education, had much natural ability and became influential in his locality. When he became a naturalized Mexican citizen in 1833 he produced certificates to show that he was a soapmaker and a millwright of good character, with a wife and four children, and had also some livestock on Rancho San Ysidro. Two millstones remained on the property until a few years ago. As the years passed, he lost his Scotch thrift, lost all his property, and toward the end of his life became dependent on charity. He died in 1869, aged about seventy-five years. The little village of San Ysidro, over which he was alcalde for a time, stretched along the Pacheco Pass Road. It is now known as Old Gilroy, and old settlers living there point out sites of many adobes that have fallen.

Across the Pacheco Pass Road from the site of Gilroy's adobe is a place called the "old soap-factory site." Upon it now stands a weather-beaten frame cottage known to have been the home of the mother of the bandit Tiburcio Vásquez. Originally a building of six small rooms, partitions have been removed to make it suitable for the storage of prune crops. Within it is the little old brick fireplace, crumbling to pieces. The mother continued to reside there after the execution of her son in San José.

While John Gilroy was still living, the first American to locate permanently in the vicinity came upon the scene. This was Julius Martin, who, born in North Carolina in 1804, had come overland from his former home in Missouri with his wife and daughters and arrived at San Ysidro on December 26, 1843. For a part of the overland journey this family had been with a larger group, most of whom proceeded to Oregon. Near Fort Laramie they had met Joseph Reddeford Walker, who, returning to California as leader of the smaller group, brought them across Walker Pass. During the ensuing years Walker was a frequent visitor at the Martin home, where he was always welcome however long he might prolong his stay there.

Julius Martin settled in San Ysidro, where he constructed a small horsepower mill with a capacity of twenty bushels a day. He became a captain of the American Scouts under Frémont and saw the Bear Flag raised in Sonoma. When Charles Bennett, Sutter's messenger, paused in San Ysidro on his way to report the discovery of gold at government headquarters at Monterey, his story so intrigued the settlers that most of them left for the diggings. Julius Martin was among the number who went; and after he returned in 1850 he was able to pay cash for 1,220 acres of Rancho San Ysidro which he purchased from John Gilroy. The deed, signed by John Gilroy and his wife, was dated January 8, 1852. This property Martin held until his death in 1891, and a part of it still belongs to his heirs. Although blind for the last thirty years of his life, he was able to come out victorious in litigation which threatened to deprive him of his land. He was a man of good education and had a marvelous memory. To his reminiscences, told to interviewers during his last years, are due many of the details of the early history not only of the immediate vicinity but also of other parts of the state. He built three houses on this property, one of which still stands in the eastern limits of the new town of Gilroy; Odd Fellows Avenue, formerly Martin's Lane, leads directly to it.

Rancho Milpitas

The right to the lands of Rancho Milpitas (*milpa,* "maize field") was claimed by two men: Nicolas Berryessa, who considered it his by a decree issued by Alcalde Pedro Chaboya on May 6, 1834; and José María Alviso, to whom it was granted by Alvarado on September 23 and October 2, 1835.

These men were both sons of Spanish pioneers in Alta California; both soldiers of the military company in San Francisco, where they served together eight years, from 1819 to 1827. Both were leading men in the Pueblo de San José, the latter being alcalde in 1836, at which time the former was *regidor;* and both were residing in San José in 1841.

Berryessa was married to Gracia Padilla, and Alviso's wife was Juana, whose father was José de Jesús Galindo, a man who lived to the reputed age of one hundred and six years and died in Milpitas in 1877.

Beginning at the time of the Bear Flag activities, Nicolas Berryessa's years were full of misfortune: his cattle were plundered by Frémont's battalion; his brother, José de Reyes, was killed by Frémont's men; squatters settled on his land; and, as the last straw, his claim for Rancho Milpitas was rejected by the Land Commission when it finally reported on October 16, 1855. He died insane in 1863. His name Berryessa, however, is carried by a creek which flows through a part of the contested property, by the school and the village on adjoining pueblo lands, and by the road that leads from this village toward San Jose. It was in the town of Berryessa that Sierra Nevada Smith, a covered-wagon baby of 1853, lived. Born in Utah, she came here and in her later years lived in a house located on the spot where a Methodist church was burned in the '60's.

On March 3, 1856, the year following the rejection of Berryessa's claim, the Land Commission decreed the confirmation of Alviso's claim; and on June 30, 1871, a patent for 4,457 acres was issued to him.

José María Alviso was the son of Ygnacio Alviso, a juvenile member of the Anza expedition. In 1841 he was living in San José with his wife and six children. His home on this rancho stood about two miles from the town of Milpitas and east of the Oakland–San Jose highway, near the corner of Piedmont and Calaveras roads. The only remaining building of the original group of four adobes comprising the hacienda was built probably in the middle 1830's. The second story of this adobe above the upper veranda is covered with modern weatherboarding to afford adequate protection to the original material. The house, painted white with gray trimming, stands in a colorful flower garden in the midst of fruitful orchards. It is occupied, and the remnant of the old rancho on which it stands is still farmed.

Near the western boundary of Rancho Milpitas, running parallel to the main direction of Penitencia Creek, are the railroad tracks and State Highway 101, both of which pass through the town of Milpitas. The town was originally called Penitencia by the Spanish, but after the American settlers became numerous it was changed. The vicinity was once a part of the outlying land of the Pueblo de San José, and along this creek were the gardens where corn, peppers, and squashes were grown by residents of the pueblo. In these gardens were held the harvest-time merrymakings. The creek itself came by the name Penitencia because, according to tradition, at the place where it curves around a bank, once stood a house of penitence, a small adobe building where priests from the Missions came at stated intervals to hear confessions. The structure was about twenty feet square. It was demolished about 1900, and a tree east of the highway now grows near the site.

Rancho Rincón de los Esteros

Rancho Rincón de los Esteros, lying between Penitencia Creek and the Guadalupe River and traversed lengthwise by Coyote Creek, was granted February 10, 1838, by Governor Alvarado to Ygnacio Alviso. As a lad, he had been one of the three children who accompanied their Spanish mother on the overland journey of the Anza colonists from Mexico to San Francisco. He was born in Sonora in 1772, both of his parents being Spanish. When he became eighteen years of age, he enlisted as a soldier in the San Francisco Company, where he served for twenty-nine years and retired in 1819 as sergeant on half pay by request of the King of Spain.

At the age of twenty-four he married Margarita Bernal in San Francisco. From 1840 to 1843 he was administrator of the Santa Clara Mission properties. He died in 1848, leaving eight children: Agustín, José Antonio, Gabriel, Anastasio, José María (grantee of Rancho Milpitas), Domingo, Concepción, and Dolores.

After the death of Don Ygnacio the rancho was divided into three parts. The 2,308.17 acres lying between Peniten-

cia Creek and Coyote Creek were confirmed to Ellen E. White on December 28, 1857, and were patented to her in 1862. The lower part of her land, near the slough into which both streams flowed, was inundated with water much of the time. Ellen E. White and her husband Charles E., whom she survived, were owners of several other pieces of land in this and other counties.

A second part of Rancho Rincón de los Esteros, which contained 1,844.54 acres, was confirmed to Francisco Berryessa on the same day that Ellen E. White received confirmation of her part. The Berryessa land reached from Coyote Creek to the town of Alviso, for which tract the heirs received a patent in 1873.

The tract of 2,200.19 acres retained by the Alviso family lay south of the other two and extended from the Guadalupe River across Coyote Creek to Penitencia Creek. It was confirmed to Rafael Alviso and other heirs on December 24, 1857, and was patented to them on July 29, 1872.

Rancho Ulistac

Rancho Ulistac lay between the Guadalupe River and Campbell Creek, beginning at their confluence near Alviso, and contained about one-half square league granted by Governor Pío Pico, May 19, 1845, to three Indians, Marcelo, Cristoval, and Pío. On March 2, 1857, this was confirmed to the claimant Jacob D. Hoppe, to whose heirs a patent for 2,217.09 acres was given on October 12, 1868.

Jacob D. Hoppe, a native of Maryland and later a resident of Kentucky and Missouri, reached California in 1846 at the age of thirty-three. A year after his arrival on the West Coast, he became interested in the establishment of a weekly newspaper. The printing materials that he had were afterward turned over to the proprietors of the *Alta California*. He lived in San José, except for a visit to the mines lasting a few months, and was a delegate to the Constitutional Convention before finally becoming one of the unfortunate victims of the steamer "Jenny Lind" explosion in San Francisco Bay on April 11, 1853.

Through the entire length of Rancho Ulistac ran the old narrow-gauge railroad from Alviso to San José, and paralleling the railroad was the old stage road between the two places.

About midway between the ends of this ranch, William Hannibal and his son-in-law, Edward Burrell, who both came overland from the East with their families in 1854, purchased 132 acres of land, which stretched from this road to the Guadalupe River and which they named Bay Tree Farm. In the central part of their tract was a house which Mr. Hannibal chose for his home; the daughter and her husband owned the lands on either side of it, on one of which they built an adobe house. On this grant was also the Laurelwood Farm belonging to Peter Donahue; and the Riverside Farm, adjoining it, belonging to W. W. Montague, for whom the Montague Road, separating it from the James Lick property, is named.

Rancho Posolmi

On the Bay side of the Bayshore Highway between Moffett Field, home of the ill-fated dirigible "Macon" that sank off Point Sur in 1935, and the junction of that highway with the Mountain View–Alviso Road, there used to be seen a picket fence enclosing a small plot of ground wherein lay the dust of the original grantee of Rancho Posolmi. The neglected fence in the midst of the pasture land was finally knocked down by cattle, and later cultivation of field crops on the site has obliterated all surface trace of the spot now remembered by only a few descendants of the pioneers of that locality.

From an early period a band of Indians had occupied this

region near the lower end of San Francisco Bay; and on February 15, 1844, Governor Micheltorena gave to their chieftain, López Ynigo, a formal grant of a tract shown on old maps as the Ynigo Reservation. It consisted of 1,696.90 acres of level land, about square in outline, partially a salt marsh before its subsequent reclamation for farming purposes. The apex of one right angle of this square jutted into Rancho Pastoria de las Borregas at the junction of the Mountain View–Alviso Road with the Bayshore Highway. The United States patent to this land was given to Chief Ynigo and two others on January 18, 1881.

Before the date of the patent, the land had been sold, and the homes of five white men had been established within its confines: D. Frink, J. Bailey, E. Jenkins, W. Gallimore, and Robert Walkinshaw. The last-named, Robert Walkinshaw, a native of Scotland and long a resident of Mexico, arrived in California in 1847 as supercargo on the "William" and assumed charge of the New Almaden Mines. He built his home not near the mines but on Rancho Posolmi, where he owned the largest of the five tracts and, in addition, had purchased an adjoining piece of land stretching to the Guadalupe Slough. His house, a part of which is still standing within half a mile of the junction of the Alviso Road with the Bayshore Highway, was an elaborate frame structure of U-shape, and here he entertained lavishly, living the life of a British country squire and riding to hounds with his daughters. He returned to Scotland in 1858 and died there in the following year. The greater part of his land was purchased by an American pioneer, Henry Curtner, the owner of much property in Santa Clara and Alameda counties.

Rancho Pastoria de las Borregas

Rancho Pastoria de las Borregas, also called Rancho Refugio, adjoined Rancho Rincón de San Francisquito to the northwest, Rancho San Antonio of Don Prado Mesa and Rancho La Purísima Concepción on the west and southwest, and extended in the direction of the Bay of San Francisco around two sides of the land given to the Indian Ynigo—a tract along the Bayshore Highway south of the Sunnyvale Air Base.

On March 3, 1852, Martin Murphy, Sr., filed a claim with the Land Commission for a part of this area founded on a grant made January 15, 1842, by Governor Alvarado to Francisco Estrada, and in the same year Mariano Castro, father-in-law of the original grantee, also filed claim to a part of it. Confirmations of the rights of these two men are dated October 17, 1856, and November 23, 1859, respectively, and are followed by patents to Martin Murphy, Jr., September 15, 1865, for 4,894.35 acres and to Mariano Castro on September 17, 1881, for 4,172.13 acres. Permanente Creek was to be the dividing line between the two holdings.

Francisco Estrada had married Inez, daughter of Don Mariano Castro, who had assisted the young couple to acquire the land. When both of the young people died, leaving no progeny, Don Mariano became claimant for the property, part of which he sold to Martin Murphy, Sr.

Don Mariano was the only child of Ignacio Castro and his wife Barbara Pacheco. After this rancho came into his hands, he and his wife, Trinidad Peralta, lived for a time upon it in an adobe house the site of which was on the northwest corner of Rengstorff Avenue and the road running parallel with the railroad near the Castro Station. When right of way was given for the building of the railroad across his property, an agreement was made whereby a flag stop would be maintained near the house. A small shelter was built, and residents of this sparsely settled community are still able to board the passing trains. The adobe house and all its surrounding garden are gone; and a vacant, bleak-looking, two-story house

stands naked to view on the site. Across Rengstorff Avenue from the site is a well-cultivated orchard (put in later) on land that formerly belonged to the Castros. While it was still in their possession the family awoke one morning to see a rough board shanty standing in what is now the orchard. So noiselessly had neighbors erected the little domicile and moved into it that no one had been wakened by their activities. This was typical of the "squatter" period, when land titles were uncertain and when only recourse to expensive litigation, lasting sometimes for years, proved the rightful owner.

The stucco house of Crisanto Castro, son of Don Mariano, stands on the opposite side of the railroad track from this orchard and east of Rengstorff Avenue near the flag station of Castro. The present dwelling was built upon the site of the former frame house in which the children of Crisanto were born, and is surrounded by the trees and shrubs of the older house. It was built after the death of the wife, Francisca Armijo, a daughter of the grantee of the Armijo rancho in Solano County. Don Crisanto lived in the new structure about one year before he too died in 1912, leaving the house with a few acres to his descendants, who still own and occupy it.

Martin Murphy, Sr., purchased the part of Rancho Pastoria de las Borregas lying south of Permanente Creek. To this place came his eldest son, Martin, Jr., who had made the trek from Ireland via Canada and Missouri either following or accompanying his father. The son had married in Canada and remained there for some time after his father departed for the United States. Finally taking his family and his goods by boat on the devious lakes and rivers between Quebec, Canada, and St. Joseph, Missouri, he joined his father in Missouri.

Arriving in California with his father's party in 1844, he first settled on the Cosumnes River, whence in 1849 he came to Rancho Pastoria de las Borregas. The house of Martin Murphy, Jr., in the suburbs of Sunnyvale, on Sunnyvale Avenue near California Street, is probably the only house in California that was framed in Boston, brought around the Horn in 1849, and occupied continuously to the present day by members of the same family. It is in excellent condition, having been regularly painted and cared for by a thrifty, intelligent family. It is of two stories, with the stairs leading to the upper floor in the hall that runs through the center of the house from front to back, with doors opening into the garden at both ends. When the house was put in place, the travel up and down the Peninsula passed on its Bay side; passenger boats, plying between Alviso and San Francisco, could be seen from the door, and El Camino Real passed between the house and the Bay. With the coming of the railroad the activities of travel changed to the opposite side of the dwelling, on which side now passes the main highway between San Francisco and San Jose.

The ample white house stands in attractive grounds in which immense fig trees grown from Mission cuttings still flourish. Within the house are family portraits, done in oil by various artists, of several generations of fine men and gracious women. To this house walked the priests from Misión Santa Clara to celebrate Mass at regular intervals. A room with an altar and a consecrated altar-stone was set aside for the purpose, and here marriage and christening ceremonies took place as well. Mary Bulger, whom Martin, Jr., had married in Canada, kept one of the rooms in the house always ready for the comfort of the Bishop should he stop for a night's rest on his way between the Missions.

At the time of their golden wedding, Mr. and Mrs. Murphy issued a general invitation to their acquaintances to attend, with a request that no gifts be offered. A large platform was erected in an oak grove near the railroad, and special trains were engaged by the host for the transportation of the guests. Many came in their own carriages or on horseback. Thousands voiced their congratulations on that day, July 18, 1881. The material used for the great platform was afterward donated by Mr. Murphy to the priests, who constructed from it the first chapel erected in Mountain View.

The mantle of his kindly and capable father, Martin, Sr., fell upon the son, Martin, Jr. Among the achievements in which he had a vital part was the establishment of the College of Santa Clara, from which his sons were graduated, and the Convent of Notre Dame, where his daughters obtained their education. He lived three years after the golden wedding, his wife long outliving him.

Rancho Rincón de San Francisquito

The person most closely identified with Rancho Rincón de San Francisquito, or Rancho Santa Rita, was the tall, blue-eyed Castilian, Secundino Robles, remembered still by some who had seen him genially conversing at his home near El Camino Real or capably driving a span of spirited horses over the country roadways. The rancho on which he lived had once been a part of the outlying land of Misión Santa Clara.

At an early date, José Peña, artilleryman at San Francisco and a teacher at that place in 1822, obtained permission to occupy two square leagues of the Mission cattle range lying between the Bay of San Francisco and the low hills between San Francisquito and San Antonio creeks. In 1841, at the age of sixty-four, while teaching at Santa Clara, he received a formal grant of the piece and built thereon a small adobe house.

Secundino Robles, born in Santa Cruz in 1811 (or 1813?), and married in 1835 at Misión Santa Clara by Father Picos to María Antonio García, also a native of Santa Cruz, was mayordomo at the Mission in 1841, and was commander of some of Sánchez' troops in 1846, when he was taken prisoner and distinguished himself by breaking his sword in twain before surrendering it to his captors. Some years before his marriage he had discovered the location of an outcrop of cinnabar on Almaden Creek—the secret source of the red paint so long prized by the Indians for the decoration of their bodies. Afterward, when the cinnabar deposit proved to be rich in quicksilver, he and his brother Teodoro received a payment of $13,000 in cash, besides a certain interest in the company which was formed for the development of the mine.

The brothers traded their interest in the mine to José Peña for his rancho and the buildings upon it, "orchard, corrals, and all property he may have on said land." The deed was drawn up in the presence of the *"juez de paz,"* Ygnacio Alviso, September 10, 1847. Secundino took immediate possession with his wife and four children, enlarging the small Peña adobe for their better accommodation. He gave the contract for the carpentering to a Mexican named Meña and that for adobe work to Jesús Ramos, paying the two together, it is said, the $13,000 cash received from the mining company. Jesús Ramos continued for some years in the employ of Don Secundino, living in Mayfield with his family.

On the flat roof of the enlarged adobe a dancing floor open to the sky was laid. The hospitality of the family was unbounded, and the Robles adobe became widely known as a stage station between San Francisco and San José. Twenty-five children were born to Secundino and his wife María Antonia after they took up their residence in this house, making twenty-nine in all. As the family increased and more space became necessary, a shingle roof was put over the dancing floor and the upstairs was divided into three rooms similar to the three on the lower floor. From the middle and larger room on each floor doors opened front and back to the verandas, six and a quarter feet wide, extending the full length of the house. The kitchen of the establishment was separate from the main building, except that a small wooden stairway ran at the rear of the house from the kitchen to the balcony.

Three attractions drew visitors to this place: the liquid refreshments so genially dispensed by the host; the bear and bull fights held in the arena in front of the house; and the game conveniently near—bear, mountain lion, and deer in the forested hills and quail, ducks, geese, and snipe in the lowlands near by. It became a rendezvous of hunters.

Not satisfied with the entertainments which he had at his own door, Don Secundino was an ardent patron of the traveling circus. On one occasion, finding himself short of funds, he borrowed $75 so that he might attend a circus at San José, for which sum he gave 50.6 acres of his fertile soil in repayment. In later years he sat more quietly at home in the shade of his grape arbor and conversed with visitors. His death occurred on January 10, 1890, his wife outliving him by several years.

The house, long unoccupied, stood about three and one-half miles south of Mayfield on the private road across the railroad track at the end of San Antonio Road. The three lower rooms had redwood ceilings; in the main room, which was a little over seventeen feet square, a middle beam across the ceiling was painted with bacchanalian scenes. The walls, twenty-nine inches thick, were composed of four-inch clay-and-gravel blocks and a one-inch layer of adobe. Sand-finish plaster covered the interior, white plaster laid upon a half-inch coating of clay and straw, the exterior. The separate kitchen was fifteen by thirty-three feet, inside measurement, with a brick chimney at the west corner.

The steeply pitched roof of the main building had a middle height of six feet. The present owner, a truck gardener, purchased the twenty acres of land on which the adobe was standing shortly before the earthquake of April 18, 1906, when the structure collapsed. The shingle roof was salvaged by being supported on strong posts, while the underlying debris was removed and spread about on the adjacent garden patch. A barn has since been built under the old roof on the identical adobe site. This roof and a weather-beaten black maple tree planted by the Robles family are all that now remains of this old home.

The rancho, when confirmed by the United States to Teodoro E. and Secundino Robles, contained 4,418.21 acres of the larger tract that was asked for originally by José Peña, and for that number of acres the brothers received patent on February 19, 1868. Jeremiah Clarke, of San Francisco, purchased a part of it from María Rosalia Robles, former wife of José Teodoro, giving "all her right, title, and interest" on June 8, 1859; and gradually, from that time on, the vast property dwindled. The Encino Farm, bordering on San Antonio Creek, was the portion of one of Secundino's daughters; a very small part of this is yet owned by descendants. The plot of ground on which "Dinah's Shack" on the highway now stands is the most recently sold piece of the original property.

Jeremiah Clarke held a considerable piece of land in the vicinity; he had a boat landing on Mayfield Slough and built a private road from it to Mayfield. He built a two-story house, a barn, and a granary on Matadero Creek east of Middlefield Road, and this house was his headquarters during his stay on his frequent trips from San Francisco. Although the road has been obliterated and the house is now gone, the granary and two oak trees near its site still stand. He sold his farm to the Spokane Land Company, which graded new roads and planned an extensive settlement. A hammer factory built and equipped during that period (its machinery has been long since removed) stands vacant on Matadero Creek on the Bay side of Middlefield Road. Colorado and Louis streets, south of the Seale place, are on this old tract.

Rancho Ojo de Agua de la Coche

An epic of the Western movement might be written using as a theme the Martin Murphy family.

Martin Murphy, Sr., nearing the age of sixty years, arrived in 1844 in California with his sons and daughters and several grandchildren, having come across the plains from Missouri. At a point on the Missouri River the Murphy and the Stevens parties had joined forces for mutual protection and aid; in the long westward journey Captain Elisha Stevens was co-leader with Martin Murphy.

Martin Murphy was born in 1785 in Ireland, where he married and where his elder children were born. Disliking future prospects in his native land, he took his family (with the exception of his eldest son and daughter who joined him later) and moved in 1820 to Frampton, Canada, where he settled and remained twenty years.

At the end of the twenty years another move was made, this time to a pioneer part of the United States west of the Mississippi River near St. Joseph. The new location proved unsatisfactory, because of the lack of religious and educational opportunities and because of the prevalence of malaria to which his wife, Mary Foley, and three of his grandchildren succumbed. Again he took up his family and moved on; this time his destination was chosen because of the influence of a priest who had visited California and who described it in glowing terms. Selling all his land, he put the proceeds into provisions, wagons, oxen, and equipment for the long trek to the Far West in 1844.

With the young men of the party on horseback accompanying the wagons drawn by oxen and containing the family and all their household goods, the long journey was finally ended in safety in the vicinity of Sacramento. Here most of the men in the group enlisted at once under Sutter's leadership to go to the aid of Governor Micheltorena in putting down the Alvarado-Castro insurrection of 1845. When this episode was ended the immigrants were free to settle where they chose, and the party disbanded. Martin Murphy, Jr., bought land near by on the Cosumnes River, where he lived until the gold rush of 1849 enabled him to sell his land and livestock at a considerable profit, when he again followed his father.

The father, Martin, Sr., had settled in Santa Clara County near the present town of Morgan Hill. Purchasing Rancho Ojo de Agua de la Coche, which had been granted by Governor Figueroa to Juan María Hernández on August 4, 1835, he built an adobe residence between the town of Morgan Hill and Murphy's Peak, a hill which rises to the west of the town. This house, now crumbled to dust, in which Martin Murphy lived with his motherless unmarried children, stood near the road leading from San Jose to Monterey, then the most traveled road in the state. Here even the most humble wayfarer found welcome with Mr. Murphy, who was assisted by his daughters Ellen and Johanna. From this place, the sons Bernard, John M., and Daniel later went out to make their marks in the world, and the daughters were sought by and married by men of importance and influence in the new country. Mr. Murphy was the pattern of industry, intelligence, and piety for his progeny. His death occurred in his eightieth year. A grandson, Martin J. C. Murphy, received in 1860 the United States patent to the rancho containing 8,927.10 acres. This tract is hilly in its western portion along Llagas Creek, and hills rise again in its eastern boundary, but the main central part is rolling. The peak rising just west of the town of Morgan Hill was for long called Murphy's Peak or Twenty-

One-Mile Peak. State Highway 101 and the Southern Pacific Railway pass through the town, which was named for Morgan Hill, who married Martin Murphy's granddaughter.

In the '60's the Brewer party camped there under old oak trees near the Twenty-One-Mile House on their journey both up and down the state. William Brewer writes of it as a place where they had sweet sleep and pleasant memories.

Rancho Uvas

Uvas, the Spanish word for "grapes," was the name given to the tract of land bordering on Uvas Creek and adjoining the rancho of Martin Murphy, Sr., to the southwest. Today a road winds along the edge of the stream where, colorful in the autumn season, grow clambering vines, the progeny of those that long ago gave to the rancho its name.

This piece of land was granted by Governor Alvarado to Lorenzo Pineda in 1842. No clue to the identity of Pineda is found, but the claimant for the property ten years later in 1852 was Bernard (Bryan) Murphy, who had lived with his father Martin Murphy, Sr., on the adjoining rancho to the east and who had married Catherine O'Toole. In 1853, the year following the filing of his claim to this land, Bernard was killed by an explosion on the steamer "Jenny Lind," while a passenger on that vessel in San Francisco Bay. In company with other notable and important men of that period, he was making the trip from Alviso to San Francisco. He left one son, Martin J. C., who received patent to the rancho in 1860; he also died at an early age, and the property passed to his mother, who later married James Dunn and to whose descendants a part of the old rancho still belongs.

Rancho Rinconada del Arroyo de San Francisquito

Don Rafael Soto, born in the Pueblo de San José, was the son of Ignacio Soto, a member of the Anza expedition. He went about 1827 with his daughter María Luisa to live on Rancho Corte de Madero before he petitioned for the grant of Rancho Riconada del Arroyo de San Francisquito, of which he took possession in 1835.

Prior to building his home on this rancho, which lay adjacent to San Francisquito Creek from its mouth to the Palo Alto tree (a landmark that stands beside the railroad bridge in the town of Palo Alto), Don Rafael had discovered the navigability of the stream up to the point at which he established an embarcadero for the loading and unloading of boats. The way between the embarcadero and El Camino Real, some three miles away, was not a properly defined road until some time later. Much heavy traffic made tracks and ruts in the soil for a space perhaps a mile in width, each driver choosing the route that looked safest and best. When the country became more settled, the gradually defined route became the paved Embarcadero Road of today.

A house which was built for the large Soto family stood for years on the northeast side of what is now Middlefield Road not far from Oregon Avenue and just back of the Seale mansion, built at a later date on Webster Street in Palo Alto.

The children of Don Rafael and Doña María Antonia were: John M., who married Concepción Mesa, a daughter of Don Prado Mesa of Rancho San Antonio; Francisco, who never married; María Luisa, who married first John Copinger and after his death John Greer; Jesús, who married first Gerónimo, a brother of Prado Mesa, and afterward Robal Caba; Dolores, who married a man named Altimarino; José, who married Luisa Buelna, an orphan who with her brother John had been reared by María Luisa; and Patricio, who never married. (Bancroft gives also Juan Cris., Jose Cruz, and Celia.)

After the death of Don Rafael, the property, consisting of 2,229.84 acres, was granted Feb. 16, 1841, to the widow,

María Antonia Mesa; and her heirs received the patent for it in 1872. The daughter Dolores had previously received 120 acres and had lived in a house on this tract where a bay tree stands now amid homes of modern construction on Newell Road opposite the end of Hamilton Avenue in the city of Palo Alto.

Early owners of parts of this rancho were a son-in-law, John Greer, Dr. W. A. Newell, J. W. Boulware, J. Pitman, Jules Mercier, J. P. Rowe, J. Hastings, and H. W. Seale. The last-named acquired by far the largest part and his once elegant house stood until 1937 on Webster Street near Oregon Avenue in Palo Alto. John Greer built a house at what is now 353 Churchill Avenue in Palo Alto, planning to remove with his family to it from his Rancho Cañada de Raimundo in San Mateo County. Before completion it was found by litigation that the site chosen for it was not on his property and that it must be moved about one-half mile. However, for one season two of his young sons lived in it, then a bare shell with roof and walls, while they attended the Mayfield School. When it was moved across the newly completed railroad track, only two trains were running daily from San Francisco to San José; and the work of rolling the house over the rails was done between the passing of the morning train and the return of the train in the evening.

Another difficulty to be overcome in moving the house was the lack of roads, necessitating the clearing of wide passageways through the dense chaparral that grew as high as a man's head almost the entire distance. After being put into position on the site where it now stands on the Embarcadero Road opposite the Palo Alto Union High School, the house was properly completed by the addition of interior walls and fireplaces which made it a comfortable and beautiful home of that period. In it descendants of Rafael Soto and John Greer reside today.

Rancho San Francisquito

Rancho San Francisquito, a tract of land lying on the southeasterly side of San Francisquito Creek and extending upstream from the railroad bridge, was granted by Governor Alvarado to Antonio Buelna, who had been active in the revolt that had put Alvarado in power. Permission to live on this land had been given Buelna in 1837, and the formal papers were signed May 1, 1839, when he was in command of expeditions against foreigners and Indians.

Don Antonio built an adobe house on the southeast bank of San Francisquito Creek at the most northerly point of the present Stanford Golf Course, where the old eucalyptus drive ends at the creek edge. In time this house received the name of "El Paso del Arroyo" ("the crossing of the creek"), for this ford was used for many years. It was also called the "doubling-up station," because ox teams, hauling logs and the lumber from mills on the mountainside, could at this point take on a double load for the easy grade in the valley.

Buelna had married Concepción Valencia and, previous to taking residence there, they had lived on a tract of low marshy land nearer the Bay, a place unsatisfactory to them because the condition of the roads there made it impossible to "remove from thence the proceeds" of the land. Don Antonio lived but three years after receiving this grant; and two years later his widow married Francisco Rodríguez, a widower from Monterey, whose seven children opposed the marriage. The eldest son, Jesús, however, built himself a house only a few yards from his stepmother's door, between her adobe and the creek, and lived a close neighbor on the property for ten years.

It was not long before newcomers saw the desirability of owning property on Rancho San Francisquito, and in the early '50's they began to take possession of choice portions, hoping that the United States government would not confirm the Mexican title and that the land would be thrown open for settlement by the public. Research in the county archives done by Roy P. Ballard shows that Thomas ("Sandy") Wilson settled near the Buelna adobe; a Frenchman named Julian settled in front of the present site of the Stanford Museum; William Little took up his holdings near the site upon which Governor Stanford later erected his mansion, now the Stanford Home for Convalescent Children; Thomas Bevins took the site that is now the Stanford University cactus gardens; and Jerry Eastin had his home where Xasmin House, home of the President of the University for many years, was built. Eastin farmed some of the land and had a blacksmith shop on the only road at that time running through the grant, afterward the Mayfield–Searsville Road and later Eucalyptus Avenue.

On February 28, 1853, Doña Concepción filed a claim for a part of the land contained in the adjoining Rancho Corte de Madera, but this claim was not allowed by the courts.

On April 4, 1853, two deeds were executed, both conveying property to Francisco Casanueva, a San Francisco lawyer and ex-consul from Chile; one of these deeds was signed by Francisco Rodríguez et al., Jesús Rodríguez, and Manuel Valencia; the other, by Manuel Valencia et ux., F. Rodríguez, and J. Rodríguez. Rodríguez, after killing a man belonging to one of the local Spanish families by stabbing him in the back one night on the Sand Hill Road, fled the country and stayed away until danger of prosecution had passed. The rancho was divided. Thomas Wilson, who had moved into the Buelna-Rodríguez adobe and used the Jesús Rodríguez adobe for a stable, sold the two buildings and the land on which they stood when he enlisted for the Civil War in 1861. The purchaser, John W. Locker, took possession. In the flood of 1862 his stable was carried away, much of the good top soil from the sloping garden between the house and the creek was washed down stream, and three tall redwoods were undermined a little way down the creek.

In 1863 George Gordon, a wealthy business man of San Francisco, chose this rancho for a country home, buying out some of the squatters and purchasing at a low price in 1865 the whole rancho from one of the heirs of the original grantee. The title to the 1,471 acres contained in it was cleared to the widow, María Concepción Valencia de Rodríguez, and other heirs by a confirmation and by the subsequent patent issued by the United States on June 8, 1868. Mr. Gordon laid out Eucalyptus Avenue and other drives, erected a house, and built stables for his driving horses. He died in San Francisco in 1869.

Senator Leland Stanford purchased this property from the executors of the estate and used the Gordon house as a nucleus for his larger and finer residence. He greatly enlarged his holdings by the purchase of adjoining lands.

The broken walls of Buelna's adobe are remembered by early residents of the vicinity, but all sign of any habitation has now been obliterated by the cultivation of the field whereon it stood.

Scattering Ranchos

Other Mexican grants of land lying wholly within the confines of the county also received confirmation by the United States government. They were: Pala; Cañada de Pala; Yerba Buena, or Socayre; Los Huecos; La Polka; Juristac; Cañada de San Felipe y las Animas; and Embarcadero de Santa Clara.

The Battle of Santa Clara

The American flag was first raised in California at Monterey, July 7, 1846, by Commodore John D. Sloat, thus signalizing the fact that California had passed from the hands of Mexico to the United States. This action was followed by the raising of the flag in other parts of California by American settlers, and on July 13 it was first raised at San Jose by Captain Thomas Fallon. The scene of this first flag raising was on the site of what is now the northwest corner of Market and Post streets.

The period of the American occupation was the most turbulent which California has known. During that time, dissatisfied Mexican leaders in both northern and southern California attempted to stem the tide of American conquest, but the so-called battles which took place were, in reality, mere skirmishes, and the results were only mildly sanguinary.

On January 2, 1847, one such skirmish, known as the Battle of Santa Clara, was fought about four miles north of the Santa Clara Mission at a place which is now bounded on the south by the San Francisco–San Jose highway, on the west by the Lawrence Road, on the north by the Kifer Road, and on the east by Scott Lane. The American leaders were Captains Joseph Aram, Charles M. Weber, and John W. Murphy. The Mexican leader was Francisco Sánchez. The casualties for the one day of fighting were four Mexicans killed and four wounded and two Americans wounded. The battle was followed by an armistice of five days, during which time the Mexicans retreated to the Santa Cruz Mountains and a small reinforcement of federal soldiers from San Francisco came to the aid of the Americans. On January 8, Sánchez and his men surrendered.

This episode was of little more than local importance, it being the last encounter in Santa Clara County. The main theater of war was transferred to southern California, and on February 2, 1848, the Treaty of Guadalupe-Hidalgo was signed, ending all hostilities. Within a few weeks, soldiers of both sides were again mingling in the friendliest of business and social relations.

California's First State Capital

San Jose was the first state capital of California after the adoption of the first state constitution, November 13, 1849. The first legislature convened there on December 15, nine months before the United States Congress passed the act that admitted California into the Union. The capital was removed from San Jose to Vallejo, by act of the second legislature on February 14, 1851.

The building which served as the first state capitol was a little two-story structure, adobe below and frame above, which stood directly across the street from the spot which is now marked by a granite boulder and bronze plate on the east side of City Hall Park, formerly the plaza. This tablet, placed by the Native Sons of the Golden West on May 19, 1923, bears a replica of the old adobe capitol which was destroyed by fire on April 29, 1853.

Mrs. Ishbel's School and
The Santa Clara Female Seminary

The first school for small American children in Santa Clara was held in the crumbling Mission buildings in the spring of 1847 by Mrs. Olive Ishbel. She and her husband, Dr. James C. Ishbel, had just arrived from Ohio with other members of an overland immigrant party; and, while the men were called to do military duty, the women and children were left at the Mission. Partly to relieve the mothers of the constant care of their little ones, Mrs. Ishbel began to give rudimentary instruction to the children with the slender means at her command: no books, no paper, no pencils, no chalk. It was afterward related by one of the pupils that letters of the alphabet were drawn on the back of the hand with charcoal and thus made visual to the beginners. When the men returned from their short period of military service

and the reunited families went their separate ways, this unique school ended. However, Mrs. Ishbel taught for many years in other parts of the state.

A few years later a boarding school for girls was started near the Mission as a result of a resolution passed by the Baptist Association of Churches at their first annual session held in June 1851 : ". . . . our obligation to the cause of Christ, and to the interest of our adopted state, demands that we, as Baptists, commence, at once and earnestly, united effort for the advancement of education in California."

The Board of Trustees which was appointed purchased from John C. Braley a building on what is now the corner of Santa Clara and Lafayette streets. The structure had been built by Henry J. Appleton and was described in a sale made to W. G. Bowden on September 4, 1850, as a "house to which is attached a brick building." John C. Braley had purchased this property, then called the Pacific Hotel, at a sheriff's sale on October 11, 1851, and resold it to the Trustees.

The first principal of this, the Santa Clara Female Seminary, was Mary Julia Harwood Hamilton, a graduate of a young ladies' seminary in Troy, New York. Her husband, Hiram Hamilton, a graduate of the University of Michigan, came to California in 1850 leaving his bride of a few months to follow after he had established himself. She came West with her brother, David Harwood, early in 1851 by the Nicaragua route and accepted the seminary position on her arrival. A report on education given to the Baptist Association of Churches at their annual session of 1853 mentions that "during the year a flourishing school has been in progress at Santa Clara under the able management of Mr. and Mrs. Hamilton, aided by suitable assistants. The location of this school is delightful. The buildings are chiefly of brick, and capable of accommodating about twenty-five boarding and seventy day scholars . . . . This school is deservedly popular, and has already received such an amount of patronage that more room is necessary for the accommodation of its pupils."

Later a department for boys or young men was added, collegiate studies being taught by Hiram Hamilton. The school was maintained by the Baptist denomination for several years. The property was finally sold by the Trustees on September 12, 1863, to Jane A. French, and in 1890 the building was torn down by later owners.

The College of Notre Dame

The story of the College of Notre Dame dates back in California to 1850, and can be traced for long years before that through Oregon and the eastern part of the United States to Europe.

Devotees known as Sister Mary and Sister Loyola had labored in Oregon for a few years before they journeyed to San Francisco in 1850 to meet four sister missionaries en route by sea from Cincinnati. While awaiting the delayed arrival of the vessel the two Sisters from Oregon were entreated to remain in California, where the educational needs of children of Catholic parents were urgent. After due consideration, these Sisters decided to stay and they chose a spot outside the Pueblo de San José near a pretty road—now Santa Clara Street—on which a partially completed adobe stood amid a field of luxuriant wild mustard. The lot was 37 by 50 Spanish varas in size and lay along the *acequia*, or irrigation ditch, from which water could be pumped.

A shed, immediately added to the unfinished adobe house, was soon supplemented by a very small two-story frame building. The upstairs of this latter building, reached by means of a rough ladder, served as sleeping quarters for the Sisters. The downstairs room was used for the school. As the years passed, other buildings of a more substantial type were added, until by 1888 the Sisters had a group of well-planned and attractive buildings located on land that, by further purchase, extended from Santa Clara Street back to San Augustine and from Notre Dame Street across to Santa Teresa. The town of San Jose at length crowded its way to the door and passed on toward the old Misión Santa Clara; yet life went on as formerly within the seclusion of these walls. However, eventually it was decided to remove from what had become the geographical center of San Jose to a spot some twenty-five miles farther up the Peninsula.

The change was made in 1923; and because of the part it had played in the establishment of the College the little old frame building that had seen all the development of Notre Dame during the years since San José had been the capital of the state was carefully moved, bit by bit, and re-erected amid the stately structures of the new site at Belmont.

The only building remaining on the site in the city of San Jose is the Science Hall, erected about 1906, now occupied by the Rosicrucian Press. It stands facing the vacant squares once filled by the College of Notre Dame.

The College of the Pacific

The Methodist College of the Pacific, now located at Stockton, is the oldest incorporated educational institution in California, having received its charter July 10, 1851, under the name California Wesleyan University. Its inception was largely due to the energy and devotion of Rev. Isaac Owen, lovingly called by his followers "Father Owen." It was first located in Santa Clara, where the Seminary, the building in which the young ladies of that day received their education, still stands and is used as a lodging house.

In 1870 the college, then called the University of the Pacific, was moved to College Park, about halfway between Santa Clara and San Jose, and now within the city limits of San Jose. In 1921 the name was changed to the College of the Pacific, and in 1924 the entire establishment was moved to Stockton. The site and the buildings on the old College Park campus are now occupied by the Jesuits, who use it as a preparatory school for Santa Clara University.

Among all the numerous Protestant colleges started in northern California in pioneer days, the College of the Pacific is the only one of first rank that has survived. It is, today, a firmly established, growing institution of a high grade.

San Jose State College

The first normal school to be established in California was the San Jose Normal School, now San Jose State College. It was started in San Francisco as a private enterprise in 1856, and by act of the legislature on May 2, 1862, it was made a public normal school. In 1870, after a hard contest over the location, the school was permanently located at San Jose. The normal school was changed to a teachers' college in 1921, when all the normal schools in the state underwent the same change. In 1935 the legislature changed the name of the college to San Jose State College.

The main structure has been rebuilt twice, once in 1880, because of fire, and again in 1906, because of earthquake. The present brick structure is an adaptation of the Mission style of architecture with long arcades surrounding a grassy court, and surmounted by a picturesque campanile.

A Chinese Temple

Many Chinese were attracted to San José in the early days. Merchants of that nationality had their places of business in the vicinity of Market and San Fernando streets from the early '50's to May 4, 1887, when that part of the town was swept by fire.

After this date attempts were made by two different groups to place the Orientals in the northern part of the city. John Heinlen and Mitchell Phillips were the respective sponsors of the two factions, the former choosing a location at Fifth and Jackson streets (which came to be known as Heinlenville), and the latter favoring the vicinity of Taylor Street on the Guadalupe Creek, where a Chinese theater and other buildings were subsequently destroyed by fire.

A few Orientals, both Chinese and Japanese, now have their small shops and eating places in the vicinity of Heinlenville, where miscellaneous structures line the streets. A two-story brick structure, unmistakably Oriental in appearance, stands off Taylor Street facing Cleveland Avenue. It is a Chinese Temple, or Joss House, built under the direction of Yee Fook and first used at the time of the Chinese New Year celebration in 1887. Within the dim threshold of the lower floor is a medley of discarded wearing apparel and household utensils, in the midst of which two old caretakers live. A broad and well-built stairway leads to the single large room of the upper floor, where, overlain with dust, is an array of bells, gongs, drums, and other curious articles having to do with Chinese religious ceremonies. Large pieces of elegant wood carving, superimposed on a background of mother of pearl, give an air of former magnificence to the place, while fresh ashes of partially burned joss sticks indicate occasional use of the seemingly forgotten building.

Campbell

William Campbell, a native of Kentucky and a veteran of the War of 1812, arrived in Santa Clara County with his family in 1846, having traveled on the first part of the overland journey with the Donner party. The following year he assisted in the survey of the city of San José and in 1848 established a sawmill just above Saratoga near Long Bridge on the creek called by his name.

His elder son, David, went to another county to live; but Benjamin, a lad of twenty when the family arrived in California, purchased land some miles northeast of his father's mill on which he raised wheat until 1885. In that year he subdivided the tract and sold lots for the town of Campbell. His first house on the tract is no longer standing, but the second remains.

This town, now the center of fruit-raising activities, is situated at the junction of Campbell Avenue and the Santa Clara–Los Gatos Road. The deeds for lots sold by Benjamin Campbell contained a proviso that the land should be forfeit to the original owner should liquor be sold thereon. James Henry Campbell, son of the founder of the town, lived in the family home where he was born until his death in 1935.

Los Gatos

Situated on the Arroyo de los Gatos after it flows from the canyon into the broader open space at the foot of the mountains is the town of Los Gatos. It had its beginning in the flour mill built on the creek by James Alexander Forbes in the early '50's.

The mill of four stories was built of stone procured in the canyon near by. A dam was built about a mile upstream, and water was carried from it through a wooden flume to run the millstones. In May 1855 Mr. Forbes bought 3,000 acres of Rancho Rinconada de los Gatos and in November of that year mortgaged it. His enterprises were not financial successes, and on December 10, 1856, he was declared insolvent by the court. In 1857 the mill property passed from his hands; other owners made a greater success. At one time a frame woolen mill was erected beside the stone flour mill, but that was later burned down. When fruit-raising became the principal industry of the Valley regions, the mill fell into disuse. In 1916 the Pacific Gas and Electric Company, which had previously purchased the land on which the old stone mill stood, tore down most of the structure because of its unsafe condition. A portion of the building, however, was retained and is now used as an electric substation.

The road from San José into the Santa Cruz Mountains passed for many years close to the old stone mill. Fine houses of early American settlers, among them that of the McMurtry family, were built across the road from the mill. One or more of them, somewhat neglected, still stand in that part of Los Gatos. After passing between these houses and the mill, the road wound upstream to a suitable fording place and then downstream on the other side for some distance to find a suitable place to start the ascent into the pass over the summit.

Beginning in the '40's, sawmills were operated in the canyons above the present town, and at that period the trail through the pass was used for hauling timber products. Later, these primitive roads were improved and a toll gate was placed at about where the office of the Conover Lumber Company now stands in the southern end of the town. After a stage line was established, the Ten-Mile House Station was located across the street from the present Lyndon Hotel. It was first kept by Henry Cobb and later by John Weldon Lyndon, a man from Vermont, who had purchased 100 acres of land in the vicinity. The successor of the Ten-Mile House was the Los Gatos Hotel, which was moved across the street in 1877 to give place to a station for the railway built at that time.

Forbes's mill gave the first employment to men in this vicinity, and the place was then called simply Forbes Mill. As the settlement grew it became Forbestown, and finally Los Gatos.

Lexington

The Lexington area above Los Gatos, between Black Road and the entrance to the grounds of the Montezuma School, gives no hint of the busy life of which it used to be a part when it was one of the most active centers of commerce in the county. Situated two miles above Forbes Mill, later Los Gatos, it early had a toll gate, which was later superseded by the one put up at Los Gatos.

In 1867 there were eight sawmills in its vicinity; here also were lumber dealers, a redwood-pipe factory, a wheelwright, grocers, blacksmiths, and the Santa Clara Petroleum Company. The Pioneer Stage Line, operated by Ward and Colegrove, served this section before 1875. This stage left the New York Exchange at San José daily at a quarter past ten upon the arrival of the morning train from San Francisco. It stopped at Los Gatos, Lexington, and way stations as it rumbled through "the finest mountain scenery and [over] the best mountain road in the state," on its way to Santa Cruz. Mrs. S. A. Paddock was proprietress of the Lexington House at the Lexington station. She advertised "a good stable in connection with the house in which stock will be cared for. The stage between San José and Santa Cruz stops here for dinner, and all stages stop for passengers." Paddock's stage station, the upper story of which has now dropped to the ground floor, and one part of Paddock's general store are on their old locations—no longer used. "The Lexington" appears over a doorway along the road. The village of Lexington began to decline when, on the building of the railroad, it was no longer needed. Alma, down the hill from this old "center of commerce," is the local railway station.

Burrell and Wrights

Rancho Soquel Augmentatión, situated mainly in Santa Cruz County, extended over the line into Santa Clara County along the mountain ridge. In this vicinity was the settlement of Burrell.

John Lyman Burrell owned a large tract of this land and attempted stock raising in the early '50's. Cougars and grizzly bears so infested the region that he finally gave up his hogs and goats and raised only long-horned cattle that could better protect themselves. Situated in this remote mountain fastness, he received his mail and supplies by the laborious and slow process of mule train from Santa Clara. He built a road along the ridge which was purchased by the San Jose Turnpike Company when it built the San Jose–Soquel Road.

In 1870 James Richard Wright, a retired minister, and his wife, Sarah Vincent Wright, related by marriage to the Burrells, whose old neighbors they had been in Ohio, came to the region and settled on forty-eight acres of land which they purchased from Mr. Burrell. Their residence, rebuilt after a fire in the '90's, stands today, as does the Presbyterian Church named for them on Loma Prieta Avenue at the corner of the Soquel Road.

When in building the stretch of narrow-gauge railroad from Los Gatos to Santa Cruz in the late '70's a point was reached on Los Gatos Creek at an elevation of 2,000 feet, the route turned sharply from the creek, and a tunnel a mile and one-eighth in length was made, passing under the ridge at the county line and emerging at Laurel in Santa Cruz County. The headquarters for the excavation were at the northern end of the tunnel, where a riotous camp housed the laborers. Here O. B. Castle, foreman of the two thousand and more Chinese employed for the digging, built his famous saloon called "The Tunnel."

After the work was completed on May 15, 1880, and trains began to run over the line, the station at this place was called "Wrights," named after John Vincent Wright, son of the pioneer James Richard Wright, who kept the Arbor Villa Hotel established at Burrell. This station became a shipping center for all the vineyards and orchards of the Loma Prieta region, a popular year-round resort, and a picnic place to which special trains were run on holidays. Summer homes were built in the vicinity, one of which was "Monte Paraiso," owned by the poetess Josephine Clifford McCracken. This place burned in 1899. Other literary people were attracted to the vicinity: among them Jack London, Ambrose Bierce, and George Sterling. A building still standing above the old Presbyterian Church on Loma Prieta Avenue, noticeable because of its "tower-like lines," is the "Bohemia" kept by Z. A. Cotton and his wife and freely patronized by these writers.

This railroad had been constructed in its several parts by several companies under as many names. Since 1887, the lines have been consolidated under the Southern Pacific Company and since 1909 have been run on broad-gauge tracks. Wrights is now only a flag-stop station.

Patchen

The Los Gatos to Santa Cruz highway, before reaching the summit of the Santa Cruz Mountains, runs through the area served by the old Patchen Post Office. The first mail delivered there was carried by a stage that ran to the summit over the Mountain Charley Road, now eliminated from the main line of travel by a realignment beyond the old Fowler's Summit. About 1876 Josiah S. Fowler, son of the pioneer Jacob, built a one-story house (still standing at the rear of his later and larger house), in which the mail was cared for. Near a large magnolia tree behind a picket fence stands also the old stage barn, at the junction of the Mountain Charley

Road with the present highway. Patchen Post Office, named for a famous race horse of that period, was located variously up and down the road, until it finally ended at Edgemont.

Up the grade from the old Fowler's Summit is the Schultheis Lagoon, lying between the old Soquel Road and the Los Gatos–Santa Cruz highway at their junction. Near this lagoon is the house of John Martin Schultheis and his wife, Susan Byerly, who took up a homestead there in 1852. Their house was built by Schultheis himself, who was a skilled German cabinetmaker. The timbers wrought by him are now covered by factory-made lumber.

Afterward, in 1899, an Episcopal Church was built opposite this lagoon as a Patchen branch of the church in Los Gatos. Services were held at this house of worship for several years by visiting clergymen, but the wood-brown building standing amid the growth of native forest trees beside the Soquel Road is now unused and seldom noticed.

A few hundred feet south of Patchen Church stands the Summit Opera House, built by a stock company headed by Volney Averill, a Union soldier who married Alice Schultheis, and Charles Aitken in the latter part of the nineteenth century. It was used for operatic and other social activities. Now unused, it is fast falling to decay.

Milpitas

The first building in the town of Milpitas was erected by F. Creighton in 1855. A post office was established the following year, and he was made the postmaster.

Closely associated with the origin and growth of the town was Joseph Rush Weller, a native of New Jersey. He had grown to maturity in New York and had come to California on the ship "Columbus" from Panama, arriving in San Francisco on August 7, 1850. After a trip to the mines in Eldorado County, he took up his residence in the vicinity of Milpitas in 1851. In May 1853 he purchased 400 acres of Rancho Los Tularcitos lying along Penitencia Creek and devoted his attention to the raising of hay, grain, fine cattle, and thoroughbred horses. In order to aid in the clearing of titles to land in which he was interested, he became proficient in the Spanish language and afterward enlarged his property holdings.

In 1855 Judge Weller organized the Milpitas School District and was one of the trustees of the school for twenty-four years. He was one of the associate judges of Santa Clara County and was elected a member of the Constitutional Convention of 1878. His property, lying at the extreme southern corner of Rancho Los Tularcitos, became a part of the growing town of Milpitas in the northwestern corner of the adjoining Rancho Milpitas. The village had originally been called Penitencia; but, because of its usual mispronunciation by incoming settlers, Judge Weller promulgated the idea of changing it to Milpitas, already the name of the rancho and of the school district. The first Presbyterian Church in this vicinity, of which he was one of the organizers, was built on land owned by Judge Weller. He continued to live in the town during the remainder of his life, and his property is still held by his descendants.

Stevens Creek Road

Stevens Creek, or Arroyo de Cupertino, rising to the west of Black Mountain near the border line of Santa Clara County, flows southeastward toward the Bay, receiving in its course many small tributaries. Its upper reaches lie in lands wholly outside of the confines of the early Spanish and Mexican grants; its history, therefore, falls entirely within the American period.

The stream bears the name of Captain Elisha Stevens, of the Murphy-Stevens overland party, who early took up government land on its banks opposite Rancho San Antonio. Captain Stevens built a house among the oak trees in a bend of the stream, where it is shown on an early map. The place was later acquired by one McCauley, who had there, before 1871, a vineyard, an orchard, and a five-acre blackberry patch. He maintained a summer resort; and to accommodate more visitors, he enlarged the house built by Captain Stevens.

The property, consisting of sixty-nine acres, after passing through the hands of a Mr. Knowlton and Mr. N. Hays, was purchased by Garret J. Byrne in 1879. Annie McCloud Byrne, wife of the purchaser, renamed the place Glenbrook Farm in memory of a place that she remembered in her native Ireland. The Byrne family found the house much enlarged from its original size. It was then a long, narrow structure of two stories with the kitchen in the end nearest the creek. It stood until 1906, when it was so badly wracked by the earthquake of that year that it had to be torn down. The Byrne family lived in tents until a smaller residence, the one now standing, a one-story, white-painted cottage, was constructed upon the same site from material salvaged from the demolished building. The name Glenbrook Farm did not succeed in supplanting the earlier one of Blackberry Farm.

Along Stevens Creek Road, where the Monte Vista subdivision now is, a tract of one hundred acres was owned by William Hall, who with Samuel Williams had what is said to have been the first large planting of grapevines in the county. John T. Doyle, a well-known attorney of the '60's, purchased Williams' half, lying along Stevens Creek, and built a winery on one side of the stream and a small dwelling house on the other. Both of these buildings are still standing. The wooden three-story winery is approached over a semi-forgotten road flanked by old palm trees. Pipes for conveying the pressed juice were laid from this building to the cement-built storage house, now called the Monte Vista Winery, across the creek, where the wine was ripened. Sand used for making the cement for this storage place was secured from the bed of the creek below. The Doyle family did not reside in the little dwelling house; their home was near Menlo Park, but for a time two of the sons lived in it while managing the winery.

The oldest house in the vicinity of Stevens Creek is one now remodeled standing near the bridge on McClellan Road. It was built by W. T. McClellan, who owned a few hundred acres adjoining Blackberry Farm.

The fine old home of Nathan Hall across the road from Blackberry Farm is still standing, and beside it is an unusually fine old oak. He too planted a vineyard in early days.

Villa María, the Fathers' Villa

To provide a place of rest and recuperation for the Fathers at Santa Clara, a villa in the region of Stevens Creek was provided. The location, ten miles away from the college and reached by horse and carriage, was sufficiently remote to insure for them a complete change from the daily routine of school work. Several small shrines were placed on the slope of the hill and on the plateau above. Of these, one only now remains. The chapel of St. Joseph de Cupertino, a frame building erected as a place of worship for residents of the country round about, still stands at the end of the now weed-grown, cypress-lined driveway. It is now used for purely secular purposes.

The vineyard on the hillside has provided wine for sacramental purposes from the earliest days; and the winery, a plain, unpainted, frame building now standing near the chapel, was erected in 1875. A small cottage used by residents before the place was purchased by the Fathers is now occupied by employees.

Pacific Congress Springs and Saratoga

Congress Springs, a short distance above the town of Saratoga on the road to the State Redwood Park, was one of the earliest and most fashionable recreational resorts in California. The mineral springs there were discovered in the early '50's by Jerd Caldwell. Capitalists in the state, including D. O. Mills and Alvinza Hayward, became interested in making it a more or less private vacation place for their families; but in November 1865 these men formed a corporation, and the original Congress Hall was opened to the public on June 16, 1866. The building stood about five minutes' walk from the springs.

The management owned about 720 acres of wooded hillsides; and, as the popularity of the place increased, other buildings, including houses for hot and cold baths, were added for the accommodation of visitors. In 1872 Lewis A. Sage and his father took over the establishment. The mineral water was proclaimed "a refreshing beverage and invigorating tonic."

Martin McCarthy, an early settler in the Saratoga region, built a toll road to tap the timber supply in the Santa Cruz Mountains. The lower end of his road was about two hundred yards below the present town of Saratoga, and it ran along Campbell Creek to Long Bridge. His toll gate stood at the lower end, and about it McCarthy laid out a village that went by the name McCarthysville for nine years. A succession of mills of various kinds in this vicinity gave rise to the name Bank's Mill, in imitation of an Eastern manufacturing town of that name: a flour mill and two paper mills, a tannery, and a furniture factory (no longer in existence) were there.

In 1863, the town site was resurveyed, and Charles McClay became the holder of much of its vacant land. He rechristened the village Saratoga, because, like Saratoga, New York, it was in close proximity to valuable and popular medicinal springs.

It has been questioned by some historians whether Anza's camp site on March 25, 1776, at the Arroyo San Joseph Cupertino may not have been on Campbell Creek at Saratoga. From the camp site of that date the travelers had a broad view of the Bay and this location fits the description as recorded in the diary of that journey.

Loma Prieta and Austrian Gulch

The long mountain which forms many miles of the skyline on the Los Gatos–Santa Cruz highway used to be called Mount Bache. The name was given in honor of Alexander Dallas Bache, superintendent of the United States Coast and Geodetic Survey from 1853 to the time of his death in 1867. Mr. Bache, a grandson of Benjamin Franklin, organized and became the first president of Girard College before his connection with the Survey. In the early '50's he directed much work on the Pacific Coast. On some of the early maps, his name was mistakenly applied to a lesser peak in the same range; but all confusion between the peaks was eliminated by renaming both, the lesser one Mount Umunhum, a word of Indian derivation, and the greater peak Loma Prieta, a Spanish word meaning "dark hill."

Austrian Gulch, on the slope of Loma Prieta, drains into Los Gatos Creek. It derives its name from the fact that after the Franco-Prussian War a group of Austro-Germans who became naturalized American citizens settled there in the '70's. They took up public land and planted orchards and vineyards.

This industrious and thrifty colony, led by John Utschig, lived comfortably and happily until a terrific cloudburst swept their possessions away in 1889. The foundations of their immense winery were loosened so much that it collapsed and poured its contents—thousands of gallons of red wine—into Los Gatos Creek, which was thereby colored far below the town of Los Gatos. This disaster was the beginning of the end of the colony; some remained and rebuilt their homes and replanted their ruined vineyards, some returned to their native land, while others sought homes elsewhere in California. A forest fire in 1923 consumed many of the wooden buildings then standing. Only a few remnants of their efforts to establish themselves in Austrian Gulch can now be seen.

About the time of the Austrian Gulch settlement another group of Europeans were gathering higher up on Loma Prieta between Hall's Bridge and the summit. This group was mainly composed of artists, musicians, and professional people, and was largely of German origin. Among the group were E. E. Meyers, of Denmark, and his German wife, Marie Detje. He purchased 1,672 acres of land from Lyman J. Burrell, a part of Rancho Soquel Augmentación of Martino Castro. He improved and sold the greater part of it, but on the five hundred acres which he retained his son Emil founded the Mare Vista Vineyard and Winery that is still in operation.

"The Frenchman," Peter Coutts

A now almost legendary character, although the period in which he lived is not remote, is the "Frenchman" of Frenchman's Lake and Frenchman's Tower on the property now owned by Stanford University. Peter Coutts was the name borne by this gentleman during his residence in California, but Paulin Caperon is the real name left behind him in his native country and the name by which he was again known after his return to France.

A man of wealth and social position before the Franco-Prussian War, editor and publisher of La Liberté, in which his editorials during that troublous time involved him politically, he, with other notables, fled to Switzerland, where he lived for a time under the name of a cousin, Peter Coutts. From Switzerland, using the passport issued in the name of this cousin, he brought his family to the United States and about 1874 came West to California, where he settled on the Matadero Ranch in the vicinity of Mayfield.

He purchased land from Delevan Hoag and from William Paul and established a home and a stock farm west of El Camino Real bordering on the street now known as Stanford Avenue not far from the railroad station of Mayfield. The family residence, still standing on Escondite Street (known until recently as Portola Street) and modeled somewhat after the Petit Trianon of Versailles, was an L-shaped building of one story. The interior walls were of redwood covered with a French chintz bearing designs in pastel shades on a ground of soft gray; the parlor, extending the full width of one end of the ell, and the other family rooms were paneled with folds of the chintz. All these rooms opened on a hall running the full length of the wing. The shorter part of the ell contained the dining room and kitchen.

Outside the house this kindly man, past middle age but with the quick, elastic step of youth, had many interests. Close by were the young shade and fruit trees, as well as the vineyard that he had planted. His dovecots housed many pigeons. A race track, where his immaculately groomed horses were shown, was laid out between his house and El Camino Real, where afterward the Stanford Airport was located. Some distance to the rear of the house were buildings which stabled his thoroughbred horses and his sleek imported Ayrshire cattle that carried off many a trophy at the Sacramento Fair. In convenient proximity to all was the plain, substantial brick structure erected to accommodate his fine library on its upper floor, the lower part serving as the managerial office of the estate.

It is supposed that his intention was to build ultimately a stately home, perhaps a castle, on a hill near by where he planted cypress trees and below which he developed a miniature lake by impounding the water from a spring found there. In this shrubbery-rimmed lake outlined by a wall of cut stone were fern-fringed little islands connected by picturesque arched bridges built of brick. One of these bridges has thus far escaped demolition and stands strangely alone above a tangle of weeds east of Coronado Street between Mayfield Road and Gerona Street at the edge of the Stanford campus. A few trees and some of the rock work of a park surrounding the lake are still evident.

In his efforts to find an adequate supply of water for his future requirements, Monsieur Coutts started several tunnels into the hills near the lake and elsewhere, each of which was abandoned as the quest proved futile. A round red brick tower near the bank of Matadero Creek on the Page Mill Road yet stands awaiting the tank that was to have contained some portion of a hoped-for water supply. This tower is about 200 yards from an abandoned tunnel dug perhaps 150 feet into a bushy hillside.

All of these activities on the part of the man who is now so little known gave rise to various wild rumors as to who he was, why he was there, and what he was doing. He and his children, a boy and a girl, his companions in frequent walks over the countryside, became friendly with many children in the sparsely settled area. Although his own children were instructed at home by their governess, Eugenie Chogensen, he displayed much interest in the Mayfield public school and gave prizes for various simple athletic endeavors, prizes cherished today by adults who were among the number so honored.

All the political difficulties coupled with the aftermath of the Franco-Prussian War being removed, Peter Coutts took his family back to Europe in 1880, going first to Brussels and later to Paris, where he had a splendid town house. He built a magnificent castle, Chateau du Martelet, at Évian les Bains. His death occurred in 1890 and he was buried at Bordeaux.

The Matadero Ranch, or the Ayrshire Farm as it was sometimes called, was purchased by Governor Stanford through agents in London and turned over to the use of the Leland Stanford Junior University along with other property. In 1891 Dr. David Starr Jordan, the young president of the new university, occupied the Coutts cottage for a few months, giving it the name of "Escondite" (hiding place). Since that time it has housed other living groups connected with the University and has undergone some remodeling. The original driveways have been changed, and the barns and all the buildings with the exception of the cottage and the two-story brick library and office have been removed. For a time the library building was used as a primary school for faculty children and later as a laboratory by the Psychology Department of the University. But in recent years it has been occupied, as it is at present, by a member of the faculty and his family.

Homes of Sea Captains

A dozen or more houses built in the early '80's in the vicinity of Cupertino (formerly West Side Post Office) were homes of retired captains who had roved the seas in sailing vessels. With their families aboard, as was then the custom, these men had met many times in foreign ports; and, as they retired to live on land, one by one they purchased forty-acre plots. This region was favored by a number of the families for permanent homes.

The house of Captain John C. Meriwether stands at the end of a straight lane off McClellan Road. At the rear of the building are tall eucalyptus trees and in front are olive trees, and the whole is now surrounded by an orchard. After his last trip, which was on the "John Bright" to the Sandwich Islands, he planted his whole tract to grapes and when they came into bearing made annually 6,000 gallons of wine.

Almost opposite the entrance to the Meriwether place is the one-story house of Captain John P. Crossley, a native of Connecticut. Captain Crossley had been mate on nearly a score of sailing vessels and during the Civil War was in the transport service that carried the first cargo of mules for General McClellan's army at Fortress Monroe. His eldest son, who had attained the rank of first mate on his father's vessel, was lost when the boat was becalmed north of Formosa; no trace of the little fishing boat on which he had set out from the larger boat in the still waters was ever found. The Crossley house, a typical New England cottage, stands prim and well kept within a small flower garden enclosed by a picket fence. A six-foot iron hitching rail, a thing seldom seen today, is beside the road close to the gate.

Captain Aaron H. Wood of the "Sovereign of the Seas," a native of Rhode Island, whose elder brother had been in San Francisco since 1847, purchased land on the Stelling Road and erected a house there in 1885.

Captains Ross, Blake, and Porter (Captain Porter's wife was a daughter of Captain Blake) each bought a forty-acre tract and settled near the corner of Homestead Road and the Sunnyvale–Saratoga Road. Captain Harriman, from Maine, and Captain Gibson lived not far away. The social gatherings of the group were enlivened by tales of far lands. The houses in which they lived are usually found to be in good condition, but few of their descendants remain in the region today.

Lick Observatory

Lick Observatory is located on Mount Hamilton, about fifteen miles east of the city of San Jose. The site was granted by Act of Congress in 1876, and, with additional grants, the reservation now totals 3,133 acres. This observatory is provided with some of the best astronomical appliances of any in the world, and was the gift of James Lick to the University of California. He himself lies buried under one of the supporting pillars of the 36-inch reflector.

James Lick, a native of Pennsylvania, was a piano-maker by trade. Having accumulated $30,000 in South America, he came to San Francisco late in 1847 and bought up a large amount of land in San Francisco and elsewhere, while it was cheap. Later, this property increased greatly in value until it was worth millions.

Lick began giving away his vast wealth in 1873. He died October 1, 1876, leaving a large part of the work of distributing his wealth to a board of trustees. Seven hundred thousand dollars was donated to the observatory.

Mount Hamilton, on the summit of which Lick Observatory is situated, was named in honor of Rev. Laurentine Hamilton, a pioneer missionary preacher in San Jose, and also superintendent of schools. He was the first white man to climb Mount Hamilton.

John Brown's Lodge

With the wide sweep of Santa Clara Valley stretching below it, John Brown's Lodge nestles on the side of the mountain three miles above Saratoga. Leaving the highway at Oak Street the Lodge is reached by a steep and winding mountain road bordered on either side by a tangle of wild flowers and native shrubs. In this secluded retreat, Mary Ann Brown, widow of John Brown, famous abolitionist of Harper's Ferry, lived from 1881 to 1884.

Stanford University

Antonio Buelna, a resident of the Pueblo de San José, obtained permission in 1837 to occupy Rancho San Francisquito, comprising 1,400 acres, the smallest of the seven ranchos lying between the present towns of Mountain View and San Mateo. At its northeastern corner stood the tall redwood tree, the Palo Alto. Adjoining Buelna's holdings on the east was Rancho La Rinconada del Arroyo de San Francisquito, granted to Rafael Soto in 1837. Rancho San Francisquito is now a part of the Stanford University estate, while Rancho La Rinconada del Arroyo de San Francisquito is occupied, in part, by the city of Palo Alto. In 1839, Buelna built an adobe dwelling on his rancho on the south bank of the San Francisquito Creek near the spot where Cedro Cottage now stands.

After the American occupation in 1846, there was a period of great uncertainty as to land titles in California. Squatters settled on many of the Mexican ranchos, and it is safe to say that the land on Rancho San Francisquito alone (owned in 1852 by one man) had been claimed or owned by at least twenty persons between the years 1851 and 1862. The ranch was continually being divided, re-divided, and sold.

During this period outsiders obtained permission from the ranchers to clear the land of its timber, and large charcoal ovens sprang up among the beautiful groves of oak and madroña which covered the entire estate. The few cherished trees which remain on the campus today give but a faint idea of the groves that once stood there. The charcoal obtained from the slaughter of these great trees was sacked and taken to the mouth of San Francisquito Creek, where it was loaded on barges and shipped to San Francisco.

This period of disintegration ended in 1863, when George Gordon, a San Francisco business man, chose the old rancho as his summer home. He did not purchase it all at once, but finally acquired the last of it from one of Buelna's heirs in 1865. The house which he built near San Francisquito Creek later became (much altered) the Stanford residence, and Eucalyptus Avenue was one of the several fine drives which he laid out.

Mr. Gordon passed away in 1869, and in 1870 the estate was purchased by Senator Leland Stanford. The old Rancho San Francisquito was thus the nucleus of what became known as the Palo Alto Ranch, famous for the breeding and training of pedigreed race horses. The old stockyards and barns are now surrounded by the green links of the Stanford University golf course. Here, also, is the grave of "Palo Alto," the most famous of Senator Stanford's horses, marked by the statue of a racer.

Leland Stanford, a native of New York, came to California in 1852 at the height of the gold fever. Stanford, however, did not seek gold but with his three brothers at once entered into extensive mercantile operations in Sacramento and the mining regions. He amassed a fortune in the eight years following. During the Civil War he was made governor of California and in that office he materially aided the Union cause. Declining a renomination, he threw all his energies into the building of the first transcontinental railway, and was one of the "Big Four" (the others being Hopkins, Crocker, and Huntington) who built and owned the Central Pacific and Southern Pacific railways. He was United States Senator from 1885 until his death in 1893.

Senator Stanford and his wife had an only child, Leland Stanford, Jr. On March 13, 1884, this son, then a lad of sixteen, died in Florence, Italy. On November 11, 1886, the Stanfords founded the university which was to be not only a memorial to their child, but a gift of love to all the children of California. To provide an adequate campus Senator Stanford purchased adjoining tracts: the Matadero Ranch lying to the southeast; Coon Farm lying between San Francisquito and Los Trancos creeks; and Felt Farm (also called Rancho

de los Trancos) lying along Los Trancos Creek. The cornerstone of this memorial university was laid on May 14, 1887, and in October 1891 its doors were opened to students.

Stanford University has embodied in its architecture much of the picturesque atmosphere of Spanish California. The university buildings are grouped about a quadrangle, after the style of the early Mission establishments. These buildings, with their graceful arcades and leafy courts, their red-tile roofs contrasting with the soft cream of sandstone walls, make a memorable picture in the midst of the rich arboretums and richer hills which enfold the whole. And in the center of the south side of the Inner Quad is the Memorial Church, with its exquisite stained-glass windows and sweet-toned organ, Mrs. Stanford's memorial to her husband.

In the soft euphonious names one hears about the campus walks and drives, there comes again an echo of Spanish days: Roble (the White Oak) and Encina (the Live Oak), Madroño, and Toyon, the various dormitories and boarding houses named for native trees and shrubs; Alvarado Row, Lasuén and Salvatierra streets, named for Spanish leaders in Alta California; Escondite Cottage, Cedro Cottage, Lagunita, San Juan Hill, and Embarcadero Road. Many of these old Castilian names were chosen by Dr. David Starr Jordan, Stanford University's first president and one of the world's great scholars.

Mayfield, College Terrace, and Palo Alto

Mayfield and College Terrace are the two oldest parts of the town of Palo Alto. At about the place where the California Theater now stands on California Avenue in the Mayfield part of Palo Alto, James Otterson constructed a public house called "Uncle Jim's Cabin." It was completed in 1853, and there he and his family gave a hearty welcome to travelers for many years. In 1855 a post office was established and the mail, delivered by stage, was dropped at "Uncle Jim's," where his stepdaughter, Sarah Ann Smith, became its custodian. At first, the bag was merely deposited upon the counter of the hostelry, and persons expecting mail looked through it for their own letters. In 1855 a school, a butcher shop, a store, and a bakery were added to the little settlement.

In 1856, William Paul, a Scotch bachelor who had kept a store across San Francisquito Creek, moved to Mayfield, bought out the store started the previous year by Fuller, and combined the two stocks of goods. Paul bought a piece of farm land on Rancho Rincón de San Francisquito from Secundino Robles, where afterward the Stanford Flying Field was located.

The town of Mayfield was laid out on March 20, 1867. Its streets running northeast and southwest were named for distinguished Americans: Lincoln, Sherman, Grant, and Sheridan. Washington's name was also used, but that street is now a continuation of the Page Mill Road and is known under that name.

South of the settlement of Mayfield, Elisha O. Crosby purchased land from Secundino Robles, obtaining the first tract in 1853. He called his place Mayfield Farm, and it was later sold to Judge Wallis, who erected a large house upon it. The property was sold by Judge Wallis to Edward Barron, who established his residence there in 1878.

Mr. Barron was a retired stock dealer and mine operator, who took pleasure in continuing the improvement of the house and grounds. The place has since been known as the Barron Estate and is located on the highway just south of Palo Alto.

Another man whose name clings to the vicinity of Mayfield was William Page, who married the postmistress, Sarah Ann Smith. He was a native of New York, who first came to California in 1850 at the age of eighteen and, being quickly successful in mining, returned to the East. Feeling the attraction of the West again in 1852 he went once more to the gold fields but was not successful a second time. After cutting timber for a sawmill in San Mateo County, he turned eventually to the establishment of his lumberyard in Mayfield. The Page Mill Road ran between this yard and the mills up in the mountains.

College Terrace, between Mayfield and the grounds of Stanford University, is located on a tract of 120 acres formerly owned by two men: Frederick William Weisshaar and Peter Spacher. Weisshaar, a native of Saxe-Weimar, and Spacher, a native of Alsace-Lorraine, became friends in San Francisco. When they purchased this piece of land belonging to Rancho Rincón de San Francisquito, they drew lots to determine their respective portions. Dividing it into two equal parts is the street now called College Avenue. Spacher drew the part nearest the campus and erected his house where now is the little square called Berkeley Park. Both men settled down to farming their acres. The Weisshaar house was erected on the site adjoining that upon which the College Avenue Catholic church now stands. This house was sold and later removed. The Weisshaars built another house on El Camino Real in the town of Mayfield, where it stands and is occupied by members of that family.

The town of Palo Alto is of recent establishment, having been a grain field when Stanford University was opened in 1891. It promptly became a flag stop on the railway and from that beginning has grown in a short space of time to be the residential town that it is today.

Villa Montalvo

Senator James Duval Phelan, philanthropist, brilliant statesman, and liberal patron of the arts, named his country place Villa Montalvo in honor of the early Spanish author Ordoñez de Montalvo, in whose *Las Sergas de Esplandian* the name California appears for the first time.

The house, situated in the foothills of the Santa Cruz Mountains in a region of great natural beauty with an extensive view over valley and mountains, surrounds three sides of a colorful court. In this mansion the owner placed priceless works of art gathered from many lands during a long period of years: paintings, wood carvings, rugs, hangings—the fruits of old looms. Here this native son of San Francisco entertained his many friends in the social, political, commercial, and artistic circles in which he moved.

The gates at the end of a long driveway leading to the Villa open from the Saratoga–Los Gatos highway about three hundred yards east of the extreme limit of the town of Saratoga.

At the death of Senator Phelan, on August 7, 1930, the place with all its precious furnishings was left by will to the San Francisco Art Association, in whose care it now remains.

Notable Writers

The county has a few unpretentious memorials to famous writers that once lived and wrote within its borders.

At 430 South Eighth Street, San Jose, is the Edwin Markham Health Cottage, the house where Edwin Markham lived and wrote the first draft of his most famous poem, "The Man with a Hoe." After a boyhood spent in Solano County, Markham entered the normal school at San Jose, now San Jose State College, from which he was graduated. He taught his first school at Evergreen. The one-story schoolhouse in which he taught has given place to a larger one, but a redwood tree has been planted near by in his honor.

The home of Henry Meade Bland was at Linda Vista, east of San Jose, on the rim of the Mount Hamilton hills. He was born in Solano County in 1863; was educated in various

schools throughout the state as he moved about with his clergyman father, Henry James Bland; became professor of creative English in the San Jose State Teachers College, a position which he held for thirty years; and finally, by act of the state legislature on March 21, 1929, was made poet laureate of California.

Los Gatos has Royce Street, named in honor of Josiah Royce, historian, philosopher, psychologist, who spent a part of his early years on that thoroughfare in the house of his mother, Sarah Eleanor Royce. The parents of Josiah Royce came overland to California in 1849, and the diary kept by his mother at that time, and now published, is an intimate narrative of that journey.

Near Redwood Retreat, ten miles from Gilroy in the Mount Madonna region, is a log cabin with stone-buttressed porch built by the novelist Frank Norris a short time before his death. He and his wife established themselves there near the forest cabin of their friend, the widow of Robert Louis Stevenson. Here he planned to write *The Wolf*, which was to complete the trilogy begun by *The Octopus* and *The Pit*. His death intervened before the manuscript was finished. A circular seat, built of stones brought from the stream near by, is a memorial erected near the cabin by friends of the novelist.

SOURCES

[Credit is here given for source material, and permission to quote is hereby acknowledged]

BOLTON, HERBERT EUGENE. *Anza's California Expeditions.* 5 vols. University of California Press, Berkeley, California, 1930

———. *Fray Juan Crespi, Missionary Explorer on the Pacific Coast, 1769–1774.* University of California Press, Berkeley, California, 1927

CLARK, GEORGE T. *Leland Stanford, War Governor of California, Railroad Builder, and Founder of Stanford University.* Stanford University Press, Stanford University, California, 1931

COLBURN, EUNICE WALTON. *Wines and Vines of California.* The Bancroft Company, San Francisco, 1889

DANA, RICHARD HENRY, JR. *Two Years before the Mast, a Personal Narrative.* Houghton Mifflin Company, Boston and New York, 1911. First published in 1840

ELDER, DAVID PAUL. *The Old Spanish Missions of California.* Paul Elder & Company, San Francisco, California, 1913

ELDREDGE, ZOETH SKINNER. *The Beginnings of San Francisco, from the Expedition of Anza to the City Charter of April 15, 1850.* 2 vols. Privately printed, San Francisco, 1912

ELLIOTT, O. L., and O. V. EATON. *Stanford University and Thereabouts.* C. A. Murdock, San Francisco, 1896

FOOTE, H. S. (ed.). *Pen Pictures from the Garden of the World.* Lewis Publishing Company, Chicago, 1888

FRÉMONT, JOHN C. *Memoirs of My Life, Including in the Narrative Five Journeys of Western Exploration.* Belford, Clarke & Company, Chicago, 1887

GIFFORD, E. W. "Composition of California Shellmounds," *University of California Publications in American Archaeology and Ethnology,* XII, No. 1 (1916), 1–29

HALL, FREDERICK. *History of San Jose and Surroundings with Biographical Sketches of Early Settlers.* Illustrated with map and engravings on stone. A. L. Bancroft & Company, San Francisco, 1871

KROEBER, A. L. "California Place Names of Indian Origin," in *University of California Publications in American Archaeology and Ethnology,* XII, No. 2 (1916–1917), 21–29

PALLETTE, DR. E. M. "Peter Coutts," in *Stanford Illustrated Review,* December 1925

(ROBINSON, ALFRED). *Life in California.* (H. G. Collins, Paternoster Row, London, 1845)

SANCHEZ, NELLIE VAN DE GRIFT. *Spanish and Indian Place Names of California.* A. M. Robertson, San Francisco, 1922

SAWYER, EUGENE T. *History of Santa Clara County.* Historic Record Company, San Francisco, 1922

SHEEHAN, E. M. "Famous Vineyards of California," in *California Journal of Development,* XXIII, No. 12 (December 1933), 11, 42

University of Santa Clara, Diamond Jubilee Volume, 1851–1926

WINTHER, OSCAR OSBURN. "The Story of San José, 1777–1869, California's First Pueblo," in *California Historical Society Quarterly,* Vol. XIV, 1935. California Historical Society, San Francisco, 1935

SANTA CRUZ COUNTY

SANTA CRUZ COUNTY (Santa Cruz is Spanish for "holy cross," named after Misión Santa Cruz, established there on August 28, 1791) was one of the original twenty-seven counties. The northwestern part of its original area, including the town of Pescadero, was annexed to San Mateo County in 1868. The county seat is at Santa Cruz, where pre-state documents, written in Spanish, are housed in the fireproof Hall of Records.

The Portolá Trail

Leaving the region of Monterey County and proceeding northward, Gaspar de Portolá and his men crossed the Pajaro River on October 8, 1769, little knowing that they were leaving behind them the bay for which they sought. A bronze plate on the Pajaro River bridge commemorates the fact that Portolá passed that way and gave the name to the river. Camp was made near Watsonville on October 9, and from this point the party traveled northward up Corralitos Creek, camping for several days at either College Lake or Pinto Lake, and again at Pleasant Valley. Finally, on October 16, they crossed Soquel Creek a league from the coast, their route having been very close to the present highway from Watsonville to Soquel.

It was before reaching Soquel on October 10 that the party first saw the famous "big trees," which Portolá named the "Palo Colorado" because of the color of the wood. This is the first recorded mention of the coast redwoods, or *Sequoia sempervirens,* to be distinguished from their giant cousins of the High Sierra, known as *Sequoia gigantea.*

On October 17 the party camped on the west bank of a large river which they called the San Lorenzo, the name which it still bears. Here they again saw many redwoods and "roses of Castille" but, much to the disappointment of Fray Crespi, no Indians. The city of Santa Cruz is now located at this place.

From October 17 to the end of the month, the expedition traversed the route now covered by State Highway 1, the Coast Road, in Santa Cruz and San Mateo counties. This route, for a few miles northwest of Santa Cruz, lies across the ancient sea beaches now raised to form fertile benches given over to vegetable crops. The region is well known to scientists because of the plainly pictured story of geologic changes shown by the series of sea terraces between the hill tops and the present tide line.

On Wednesday, October 18, as recorded in Fray Crespi's diary, the party stopped at an arroyo which the soldiers called La Puentes, because a bridge of poles and earth had to be made before the men and animals could cross. This stream is now called Coja Creek. The next day they crossed seven gulches, some of which were very difficult. One, especially, had very steep sides, and here the mule on which the *olla,* or cooking pot, was loaded fell to the bottom of the bank.

On Thursday, October 19, they halted at what is modernly known as Scott Creek, where they found vestiges of an Indian village; then proceeding northerly up the coast, they arrived on October 20 "at the mouth of a very deep stream that flowed out from between very high hills of the mountain chain. This place, which was named the Arroyo or Cañada de la Salud .... was open toward the north-northeast and extended inland for about a league in that direction." Here they encamped for three nights.

On Sunday, October 22, "the day dawned, overcast and gloomy; the men were wet and wearied for want of sleep, as they had no tents, and it was necessary to let them rest. . . . . What excited our wonder on this occasion was that all the sick, for whom we feared the wetting might prove exceedingly harmful, suddenly found their pains very much relieved. This was the reason for giving the canyon the name of La Salud." La Salud (Spanish for "Health") is now known as Waddell Creek, and to this day, after heavy rains, it becomes the "very deep stream" that these weary travelers found. At this place, the engineer, Don Miguel Costanso, determined the latitude and recorded, in a note appended to his diary, that Punta del Año Nuevo, which was to be left behind on the next day's journey, had approximately the same latitude as did Cañada de la Salud, where they had been encamped for three days.

Misión Santa Cruz

The Viceroy Condé de Revilla Gigedo and Fray Matiás de Noriega decided in 1789 to establish a Mission on the spot called Santa Cruz between those Missions already established at San Carlos and Santa Clara. Two years after this decision was made Father Fermín Francisco de Lasuén consecrated a site at the lower end of the San Lorenzo Valley. Here, on San Agustín Day, August 28, 1791, in the presence of many Indians of all ages, he said Mass and raised a cross.

The following month Fathers Alonzo Salazar and Baldomero López, accompanied by Hermenegildo Sal, commanding officer of the San Francisco Presidio, and his military escort, arrived at the prospective site. Christian Indians brought along from Santa Clara were set to work at once cutting timber for the construction of a shelter for the Fathers, probably resembling an enramada such as may be seen in Mexico today.

On Sunday morning, September 25, 1791, at eight o'clock the formal ceremony for the founding of Misión la Exaltación de la Santa Cruz was celebrated. The program consisted of the Mass said by the padres, the act of taking possession in the name of His Majesty King Carlos IV of Spain by Ensign Sal, and the firing of the guns in salute. The Fathers had brought with them as a nucleus for the Mission a painting of Our Lady of Sorrows and an image of Our Father Saint Francis. From the neighboring Missions of Carmel, Santa Clara, and San Francisco came donations of horses, cows, oxen, mules, sheep, and two bushels of barley for seed. At the end of the first three months eighty-seven Indians had been baptized. Soon•the establishment was found to be too near the river, and in the move to higher ground only the garden was left on the lower level.

The first stone of Misión Santa Cruz was laid February 27, 1793, and the completed structure was dedicated in the spring of 1794 with Commander Sal and Father Thomas Peña of Misión Santa Clara present. The church, built on the mesa above the river, was 112½ feet long, 29 feet wide, 25½ feet high, with walls 5 feet thick. The lower part of the walls was made of native rock and the upper part of adobe. The vaulted roof, at first covered with thatch, was later recovered with tile.

Other buildings, erected as needed, formed an open square that is now outlined by the modern streets High, Emmet, Mission, and Sylvar. The Mission church and the priests' quarters were on what is now High Street. On the present Sylvar Street were storehouses and rooms for looms. Back from Emmet Street, along the thoroughfare now known as School Street, were the women's quarters; and on the other side of School Street was the adobe building, still standing and known as the Neary House, which was then the Mission guard headquarters. Joined to the Neary House by a five-foot party wall is another adobe house known as the Rodríguez House. Since 1838 it has been in the possession of the Rodríguez family, descendants of José Antonio Rodríguez, Branciforte *invalido* of 1799. Both of these adobes are in good condition and are in daily use. The old garden at their rear located on the bluff above Mission Street is full of quaint charm. Another adobe of that period, no longer standing, extended from the Neary adobe to Emmet Street. After the influx of Americans, it was used by William Blackburn, an overland pioneer from Virginia in 1845 and later judge, as the Eagle Hotel and Store; but in 1862 it was taken over by the Sisters of Charity, who founded there the Holy Cross School. This site is now occupied by a tennis court for the pupils of the school, while the school itself has been removed to a building diagonally across the Plaza.

All went well at the Mission for more than twenty years; then came trouble with the Branciforte Pueblo; and, in addition to this annoyance, in 1818 the pirate Hippolyte de Bouchard, flying the insurgent flag of Buenos Ayres, threatened an attack from the sea, which attack, fortunately, never materialized because of a storm on the ocean. However, in the effort to save Mission properties in this emergency, much damage was done to the church and its furnishings by misdirected zeal.

The Mission was secularized by Governor Figueroa in 1834. In 1840 an earthquake weakened the walls; and on January 9, 1857, another tremor caused the final destruction, for a month later at three o'clock in the morning the southwestern corner fell with a loud crash. In 1858 a frame church was built which stood until 1889, when the present brick one was erected upon a portion of the site of the old Mission. In 1891, one hundred years after the founding of the Mission, a memorial arch of granite was erected in front of this brick church.

In 1931 a replica of the original Mission was built on Emmet Street facing the Upper Plaza. It is identical in proportions with the first structure, but is about one-half the size, and is approximately seventy-five yards from the original site. In this replica are housed many objects that were in the original Mission: notably, a chandelier formerly used for candles, now altered for electricity and suspended from the ceiling near the entrance. A statue of Our Lady of Sorrows occupies a niche in the front part of the little church, while in a room off the outer corridor are preserved richly ornamented vestments used in bygone years.

Mora Street is on the site of the old Mission orchard. Two trees now standing, a walnut and a pear, are said to be of the original planting. The old graveyard with a few remaining epitaphs lies on the brow of the hill in the shade of the eucalyptus trees back of the present church.

Villa de Branciforte

Three pueblos were established in California by the Spanish: San José, Los Angeles, and Branciforte. The latter, named in honor of the Marquis de Branciforte, viceroy of Mexico, was established in 1797 under the direction of Governor Diego de Borica and was located across the San Lorenzo River from Misión Santa Cruz. Governor Borica showed his practical mind in his three reasons for choosing this place: good building material was close at hand, a plentiful supply of fish in the waters of the bay could be used as food, and the facilities for shipping could easily be developed to handle the future produce of the pueblo. His recommendations were likewise sensible: "An adobe house to be built for each settler so that the prevalent state of things at San José and Los Angeles, where the settlers still live in tule huts, being unable to build better buildings without neglecting their fields, may be avoided; the houses not to cost over $200." Each colonist was to receive from the government a musket, a plow, a few necessary animals, and a subsidy of 116 pesos on a plan of easy repayment. The observance of religious duties was to be enforced. He called for farmers, mechanics, artisans, and sailors as settlers. Gabriel Moraga was taken

from his position as *comisionado* of San José and placed in charge of the new pueblo. The original document, containing the signature of Governor Borica, dated May 26, 1797, and ordering Sergeant Moraga to proceed with this work, is preserved in the Hall of Records in Santa Cruz.

On May 12, 1797, the schooner "Concepción" arrived in Monterey Bay with colonists from Guadalajara, but no houses were ready for them. Don Alberto Cordoba, lieutenant of engineers in the Spanish Army who had visited there the previous year, arrived in August with instructions to follow a plan that had been drawn up in Mexico. He began a canal for irrigation, erected a few temporary houses, and sent estimates for further work to the governor and the viceroy, before the work was suspended in October.

Among the passengers on the "Concepción" were three men who became alcaldes: José Vicente Mojica, who brought a wife and five children, was alcalde in 1802; José Antonio Robles, who married first Rosalía Merlopes and at her death her sister, Gertrudis, and held a number of offices before becoming alcalde in 1842; and San Agustín Narvaez, nineteen when he arrived, stayed at Branciforte only a few years but was alcalde in San José in 1821. Among the invalid soldiers sent there in 1799 were Joaquín Castro and José Antonio Rodríguez, both of whom played an important part in the affairs of their time and whose descendants are now widely scattered throughout the state.

In 1799 Gabriel Moraga was succeeded by Ignacio Vallejo as *comisionado,* and the pueblo continued under the military jurisdiction of Monterey, except for two years under the civil jurisdiction of San José, until the time of its dissolution.

After the American occupation and the coming of American pioneers Branciforte became a township of pleasantly located homes that by a special election of 1907 became a part of the city of Santa Cruz. The mile-long race track, laid out in 1797 by Cordoba, is now Branciforte Avenue, and the intersection of this avenue with Water Street is the center of the old Villa de Branciforte, which occupied a rectangle one-half mile wide from east to west and one mile long from north to south. The arena of the Spanish and Mexican sport, the bullfight, was located on the flat near the Soquel Avenue bridge, between the San Lorenzo River and Branciforte Creek. As late as July 13, 1867, four bulls "from the Gabilan and Taurian mountains" fought here, lances, firecrackers, and red flags adding to the excitement. "Admission and seats— $1.00. Standing room on the sunny side—50 cents."

The City of Santa Cruz

A period of disintegration followed the Mexican order of secularization of the Missions, but before the year of the gold rush several dependable men were carrying on industries in the town of Santa Cruz which had grown up around the Plaza of the Mission.

Thomas Fallon, who had arrived in Branciforte in 1845 and who had raised the flag of the United States in San José in 1846, put up a building on the Plaza. This had an outside stairway and did double duty as a residence and saddlery shop. The county later purchased this property for use as the County Courthouse, paying Fallon $3,500. The portrait of Fallon now hangs with those of other pioneers on the walls of the Pioneer Society building in San Francisco.

William Blackburn, a Virginia cabinetmaker who came overland to California with the Swasey-Todd company of 1845, began work as a lumberman in the Santa Cruz Mountains before being made second lieutenant of Company A, Artillery, in the California Battalion. He was alcalde of Santa Cruz from 1847 to 1849 and became county judge in 1850, at which time the decisions of his court became famous for their originality. His orchards were one of the chief attractions of Santa Cruz during his life. His home grounds, extending from Chestnut Avenue to Walnut Avenue and to the Neary Lagoon, covered the present site of the Southern Pacific Railroad yards. The old Blackburn house still stands at the head of Sycamore Street. It was built of lumber brought around the Horn, according to local legend.

Richard C. Kirby, born in England in 1817, left a whaling boat in Oregon in 1845 and came by land to California in 1846 to become associated with Paul Sweet in a tannery business on the San Agustín rancho shortly after his arrival. In the fall of 1850 he put up a small establishment for tanning leather in Squabble Hollow, now Laurel Street below California Street in Santa Cruz. He bought other property later and built a yard with a capacity output of 1,500 skins a month, Kirby leather soon becoming famous. He tanned not only hides from local ranches but also those shipped from South America. In 1852 he married Georgiana Bruce, who had been a member of the Brook Farm Colony near Boston in the '40's and had come to California with the hope of establishing a school. Born in England, she had come to America as a governess and had taught for a time in the South, where she became an ardent abolitionist and where she met the writer and lecturer, Mrs. Eliza Farnham, whose coming to California was the reason for the coming of Miss Bruce also. Mrs. Kirby has left a vivid picture of life in Santa Cruz in the '50's in the pages of her journal. She was much interested in the beautification of her home and surroundings and for this purpose imported rare shrubs and trees. The Kirby house, a frame one, is still standing at 129 Mission Street above Green Street.

Adna A. Hecox, a native of Michigan, who came across the Plains with his wife and three children in 1846, preached the first Protestant sermon in Santa Cruz in May 1847 and assisted in the movement started toward the establishment of the Methodist Church. James Dunleavy, also a Protestant preacher, and Elihu Anthony, who had been a circuit-riding pastor for a few years in Indiana, assisted him in forming a branch of the Sons of Temperance, a society very strong in the East at that time. The Sons of Temperance Hall, built on Mission Street in 1860, was afterward moved to Bulkhead Street, where it was used by the Salvation Army until its demolition in 1935. Aside from his religious activities, Hecox took part in other phases of pioneer life. Shortly after his arrival he erected a sawmill for Michael Lodge at Soquel. He was alcalde for Santa Cruz and continued in other important offices until he became custodian of the Lighthouse at its establishment in 1869, a post which he held until his death in 1883.

Elihu Anthony, a native of New York who came with a company of one hundred wagons across the Plains, arrived in Santa Cruz in 1847 at the age of twenty-eight with his wife, Sarah A. Van Ande, and his infant daughter. The following year he established a foundry below the bluff, fronting on what is now known as the Post Office Plaza. There he made the first cast-iron plows produced in California. Immediately after the discovery of gold, he made 7½ dozen light-weight iron picks which he sent to the mines by Thomas Fallon, who went thither by ox team with his family. These picks weighed three pounds each and sold for three ounces of gold each until a load of picks from Oregon brought the price down to two ounces of gold. He was the first postmaster in Santa Cruz, retaining the position thirteen years. The wife of Elihu Anthony was a woman of ability who found a large field for charitable work in the pioneer settlement. Their twenty-room house on School Street, previously damaged by fire, was razed in 1935.

The city of Santa Cruz was granted a charter by the state legislature in 1866 and was incorporated in 1876. Parts of

two adobes outside the vicinity of the Mission are now standing in the town (the dates of their erection are unknown), one is the one-story Lorenzana, or Winchester house, on Branciforte Avenue at the corner of Goss Street; the other stands at the present address of 47 Union Street. The latter was built by Manuel Arana, and its one remaining wall is incorporated in the front of a well-kept family residence. Not recognized as adobe from the street because of the later-built pillars and the screen of green vines that they support, this portion of old adobe wall with its deeply set windows is prized by the present owners. The date of its erection was probably 1849. It passed from the hands of Manuel Arana to the Rodríguez family and was owned by the Young family before being purchased in 1872 by Henry E. Gardner, whose heirs are now in possession of it.

One of the earliest frame houses in the town stood at 19 Vine Street until recent years. It was made of lumber brought around Cape Horn by Hiram Daniel Scott, purchaser of the San Agustín rancho, for whom Scotts Valley is named. The house numbered 51 on Church Street is associated with the name of Bret Harte, who once spent a vacation there. This house was built by John Pinkham in 1856 and was purchased by Joseph Boston, who remodeled it in 1862.

Passing through the streets of Santa Cruz, one is impressed by the number of old houses that give evidence of a background of historical significance; their generous size and their decorated eaves and gables set them apart from the modern buildings on the same streets. One of these, almost opposite Bret Harte's Honeymoon Cottage on Church Street, now the City Hall, was formerly the home of Frederick A. Hihn, a pioneer to whom the business interests of the town, and indeed of the whole county, owe much. He built this house in 1873, and it was one of the finest and best of the period. The Alzina residence, its external appearance little altered since the '50's, when it was constructed of lumber from the mills near Pescadero, stands at 8 Sylvar Street.

Rancho San Andrés

Three grants, given to members of the Castro family in 1833, stretched along the shore of Monterey Bay from the mouth of Soquel Creek almost to the mouth of the Pajaro River and extended well inland. The southernmost of these ranchos had been occupied for possibly ten years by the father, Joaquín Castro, a pensioned soldier. As a boy, he came to California in Juan Bautista de Anza's party, and to the pueblo of Branciforte. During the following years before he definitely received the grant, he held several minor positions and was alcalde in 1831. At this time he was a widower, since his wife, María Antonia Amador, had died before 1828, leaving a family of sons. Rosario Briones became his second wife. His Rancho San Andrés, consisting of two square leagues, was confirmed to his eldest son, Guadalupe, in 1854, and a United States patent was given Guadalupe "et al." in 1876.

The first domicile of Don Joaquín on the rancho was located not far from the beach, but when he erected his large adobe house he chose a site on a hill above Larkin Valley overlooking in the distance a great sweep of the Pajaro Valley. The house stands today, a large two-story adobe with an upper and a lower veranda stretching the whole length of the front. A simple stairway at one end of the veranda connects the two floors, and the doorways both upstairs and downstairs lead to the interior. At the back of the house is a narrower porch with posts extending to the roof of the house.

A ballroom, 25 by 50 feet, located on the upper floor, has windows opening out to front and rear views of the broad expanse of the family domains that spread over hill and valley to north, east, south, and west.

This house is one of the few pretentious ones remaining from the times of the earliest settlers. But its outer walls of whitened plaster are breaking, exposing the adobe bricks within so that unless precautions are taken within a few years the place will be beyond repair. Seen from the road below the structure is easily mistaken for an old barn, for the gable end seen on the skyline is boarded over and has a ventilation opening near the peak. The narrow road over which this once dignified adobe is reached climbs a hill from a crossroads about one-half mile east of the Larkin School, and close approach leaves no doubt as to the identity of the place.

Rancho Aptos

Rancho Aptos of one square league was granted in November 1833 by Governor José Figueroa to Rafael Castro, an industrious and prosperous ranchero who had held a few minor official positions. The southeasterly line of this grant adjoined the larger Rancho San Andrés belonging to his father, Joaquín Castro, and extended northerly along the bay to the Sanjón de Borregas, literally "ditch of the lambs," a small stream across which runs the road from Santa Cruz toward Watsonville.

He built a home, of which nothing remains today, on a bluff a little south of the present town of Aptos. In the early '70's he donated a piece of his property for the erection of a Catholic chapel, the Church of Our Lady of Mount Carmel, at the corner of Seacliff Beach Road and the Santa Cruz–Watsonville highway. It was a quaint structure built by five pioneers, four of whom had crossed the continent in covered wagons. In time it was surrounded by picturesque cypress trees; but storms, earthquakes, and vandals caused its ruin, and it was condemned in 1925, dismantled and removed in 1930. The sweet-toned silver bell, which had been presented for use in the church by Don Rafael, had been stolen and was never recovered; but the one that replaced it, purchased by donations from residents, is preserved at the Santa Cruz Mission. A statue of Our Lady of Carmel, a gift of the Rev. J. Adam, who had secured it from Spain, had escaped disaster and is now in the Saint Joseph's Catholic Church at Capitola.

In a niche in the tall marble monument that marks his grave in the cemetery near the site of this vanished church is a miniature bust of Don Rafael. He died in 1878. In the family plot his wife, Soledad Cota, and other members of his family are buried. In the outlying part of this churchyard but still within the confines of the old cypress hedge lie the bones of many Indians removed from an early Indian burying ground not far away when the property was taken over by Claus Spreckels. The Indian burying ground had been called the Island and lay between Aptos and Valencia creeks. It is now called Treasure Island, although no longer surrounded by water.

Ranchos Soquel and Soquel Augmentatión

Martina, a daughter of Joaquín Castro named for her grandmother, obtained the grant Rancho Soquel, 1,668 acres, from Governor Figueroa in November 1833. To her was given also the larger grant, Rancho Soquel Augmentatión of 32,702 acres, on which lies the greater part of the Soquel watershed, containing vast forests of redwood, live oak, and madroña. It stretched to the mountain tops at the county boundary line and over to Loma Prieta. Both of these grants were confirmed and patented to her in March 1860.

She was married three times; first to a Spaniard, Simón Cota, who died leaving her a widow with two daughters; second to Michael Lodge, a sailor from Dublin; and third to a Frenchman, Louis Depeaux. After her marriage to Michael Lodge she received the grants of land, and on a point of high ground near a ravine where were springs of pure water, just

off the way of the padres from Monterey to Santa Cruz, they lived in their adobe house.

This was a structure of fifty feet frontage divided into three rooms, each with a depth of thirty feet. The larger middle room with its fireplace and board floor was the general living and reception room; in it the rough beams were covered with horsehide tanned with the hair on. Here the mother and her seven daughters entertained their friends with gay dancing parties such as only the Spanish of that day knew how to give. The house and garden were surrounded by a fence built by driving redwood pickets into the ground, such a fence as is seen today in the vicinity of plentiful redwood trees. Somewhere they had an ox-power flour mill, the millstones being still on the property. The site of this house is found by turning off the Capitola road at the apple-drier and proceeding east until the dirt road ends at a ravine. Here a modern home and flower garden stand on one side of the road, and on the other is the now empty small field where the Lodge adobe once stood.

Little is known of Doña Martina and her life with the third husband. She died in 1890. In 1850 she divided her property, giving one-ninth to each of her eight children and keeping one-ninth for herself. In 1856 her share, which had passed into the hands of the Catholic Church, was purchased by August Noble, who built the Noble house which stands about two hundred feet from the site of Martina's adobe about one mile southeast of Soquel. Martina's adobe stood in good condition and was still in a fair state of preservation when torn down in 1925.

Rancho de las Corralitos

In the eastern part of the county lies Rancho Corralitos, which was granted in 1823, 1841, and 1844, totalling four leagues, to José Amesti, a native of Spain who came to California on the "Panther" in 1822 and became a prominent citizen and merchant in the land of his adoption. He married Prudencia, daughter of Ignacio Vallejo, in 1824. The 15,000 acres contained in this property were patented to his heirs in 1861 by the United States. The exact location of the adobe on this rancho is not evident today, but is supposed to be in the vicinity of the Amesti schoolhouse.

The village of Corralitos in the northern part of the rancho was a place of bustling activity in the pioneer days of the '60's. It was surrounded by forests in which sawmills were moved from place to place as each location became "sawed out"; today it is a quiet village amid orchards and gardens. As early as 1865 several families living there had the luxury of water piped to their homes, not through metal pipes, as today, but through pipes made by boring a hole lengthwise through redwood logs.

The first sawmill in this region was in Brown's Valley near García's bridge three and a half miles above Corralitos and was owned and operated from 1865 to 1867 by Brown and Williamson. The same company later built Gamecock mill farther up the canyon. The narrow and rough logging roads, when abandoned by their original users, were developed into practical roads for general travel by the settlers "working out" their taxes in such ways as filling chuck holes, hauling gravel, and widening the track.

In 1855 Benjamin Hames bought a site just above the present town and built a flour mill to which settlers as far away as Salinas hauled their grain to be ground. The water from a dam in Eureka Canyon was brought through redwood flumes to operate the mill. When Hames lost the property through a mortgage, it was purchased by an employee, Robert Orton, who afterward served several times as sheriff of Santa Cruz County. In 1877 the site and buildings were bought by Peter and James Brown for a paper mill, where a sun-dried strawboard was made from straw grown on Pajaro Valley ranches. For a few years the binding boards used in making textbooks for the schools throughout the state were manufactured there. The site has now been obliterated by the widening of the road. One forlorn tree planted by Benjamin Hames marks the place where he lived in a house surrounded by cultivated grounds.

The first school serving the settlement was built amid oak trees south of the town on the road leading to Watsonville and was called Oak Grove. The oaks are now gone, but a redwood grove on the opposite side of the road identifies the spot. The school was next moved one mile nearer to town; and the third, the present, schoolhouse was built in the town itself.

Rancho Salsipuedes

The Salsipuedes grant of 31,201 acres was made to Francisco de Haro on November 4, 1834, and regranted to Manuel Jimeno on February 1, 1840. The final grant was for a total of eight leagues. These lands extended from the Pajaro River on the south northward to the mountains at the county line, and a small part, in the vicinity of Bodfish Canyon, lay in Santa Clara County.

Don Manuel, who came to California from Mexico in 1830, was a man of great influence and was much respected in civil affairs. His wife, said to have been as vivacious as he was witty, was Agustías, daughter of José de la Guerra de Noriega. He was secretary of state for several years under governors Alvarado and Micheltorena. Although he was devoted to Mexico, the land of his birth, apparently he did not have a prejudice against Americans, for he sent two of his sons, Antonio and Porfirio, to the East in the company of William T. Sherman to be educated. After many years in poor health he died in Mexico in December 1853, leaving the widow with eleven children. The site of his now almost forgotten adobe is on the Chittenden Pass road, which runs for many miles through this rancho.

Other men also interested in public affairs became owners of this land later. William F. White, who had come from Pennsylvania with his young wife in 1849, acquired land from Don Manuel and, moving to it, built in 1853, five miles east of Watsonville, the first substantial, American-owned house in the Pajaro Valley. The outside lumber of this house was of exceptionally high quality and was shipped from Maine. A pump which he installed was a great curiosity. Visiting Californians were much interested in manipulating the handle and in seeing the water flow from the spout. One Sunday in each month this family residence was used as a place of worship, the officiating priest coming from Misión San Juan.

White had been a bank commissioner appointed by Governor Irwin and had been a member of the Constitutional Convention of 1878 before becoming a candidate for the state governorship on the Workingman's ticket in 1879. Associated with him in the purchase of this rancho were three other influential men: William Tecumseh Sherman, of Civil War fame; Secretary Montgomery, of President Lincoln's Cabinet; and E. D. Baker, a lawyer.

A United States patent for this land was issued to James Blair, et al., March 2, 1861.

Rancho Bolsa del Pájaro and Watsonville

Rancho Bolsa del Pájaro, consisting of two separate grants which stretch along both sides of the Pajaro River northeastward from its mouth and which are probably "acre for acre the richest land on earth," was granted by Governor Alvarado on September 30, 1837, to Sebastian Rodríguez, who also claimed the Rincón de la Ballena in Marin County. Bancroft says that the Marin County claim was given to the brother Antonio in 1836.

Don Sebastian, a sergeant of the Monterey Company and comisionado of Santa Cruz in 1831, married María Perfecta Pacheco and, dying in 1855, left a large family. His will, which he signed on April 26, 1854, at Monterey, gave the names of his parents as Antonio and Vicenta León de Rodríguez and named his wife and two sons, Pedro and José, as executors. After his death and before the estate could be settled, numerous "squatters" built small houses on the property and caused much trouble. Squatters there, as elsewhere in the state, consisted mainly of immigrant Americans who had come to this great new state to obtain either gold or land, both of which were supposed to be had for the taking. Being unsuccessful in the realization of either of these ambitions and not wishing to face the rigors of a return journey to their Eastern homes, these people began to help themselves to small tracts of land here and there, causing great trouble.

According to the treaty of the United States with Mexico at the time of the American occupation all titles to former grants were to be respected. But it took years of search on the part of the Land Commission to confirm the titles and to issue the patents to the rightful owners. The litigation concerning Rancho Bolsa del Pájaro was finally ended when a patent was issued to the heirs in 1860 for one of the grants.

D. S. Gregory and Judge John H. Watson, the latter a native of Georgia, obtained the other grant before the death of Don Sebastian and laid out the town of Watsonville in 1852. W. L. Thrift, one of its first settlers, put up a tent and used it for a hotel. When a post office was established two years later, he became the first postmaster in the town.

The principal crop raised in the vicinity was potatoes. An apple orchard was planted in 1853 by Jesse D. Carr, and a second one was planted by William D. White the next year. The success of these first plantings encouraged others to set out trees, and Watsonville has for many years been famed for its apple industry.

An interesting adobe house is now used as Girl Scout headquarters in the town. It stands on the northeast side of Blackburn Street between Third Street and Lake Avenue. It was originally constructed by Jesús Vallejo on his Rancho de San Cayetano on the San Juan Road in Monterey County. When the news of the imminent destruction of the building came to the attention of Dr. Saxon T. Pope, he purchased it and had the material hauled to Watsonville and re-erected on his own property. The original house had two stories, but in the restoration the material was fashioned into a one-story, three-room dwelling. The original oak doors are in place, and the lintel over the front door bears the carved words "Jesús Vallejo 1820." In the patio a stone seat is carved with the date "1830." Within the garden, separated from the street by a tile-topped wall, stands a small sundial.

Rancho Arroyo del Rodeo

Rancho Arroyo del Rodeo, mentioned sometimes in old records as "Los Coyotes," was granted by Governor Figueroa to Francisco Rodríguez, the early California poet, on July 28, 1834. It consisted of one-quarter of a square league lying on the shore of Monterey Bay between the Arroyo Soquel and the Arroyo del Rodeo. The road from Santa Cruz to Watsonville, passing through the town of Soquel, crosses the entire width of the grant.

The surveyor's map of 1858 shows a dam and a flour mill on the creek above the town and also a wharf on the bay to the west of the mouth of the stream. This mill had been erected by John Hames and John Daubenbis and was operated by them in 1847 as a flour mill. John Hames was a member of the Santa Cruz Council in 1848 and in San José three years earlier had signed the "Call to Foreigners." John Daubenbis, a native of Bavaria, had served in Frémont's Battalion.

The location of this mill, being an ideal site like many another, was used consecutively for many kinds of mills. Following its use as a flour mill it became a sawmill, whence in 1849 timbers were sent by schooner to San Francisco to build the "Long Wharf." In 1879 the site was purchased by Edward and Frank O'Neill, who ran a paper mill there for twenty-five years. After 1904 the spot was used intermittently; a tannery is said to have occupied the site at one period. Razed in 1934, the foundations are still to be seen at the side of the old Soquel–San Jose Road one-half mile north of the town of Soquel.

This spot has still another claim to a passing thought, for there Lieutenant Frémont camped with his men on March 1, 1846.

The lands of this rancho were patented to Hames and Daubenbis on May 3, 1882. Its name was derived from the fact that the cattle "round-ups" or rodeos of the herds of the Rodríguez and Castro families took place in a natural amphitheater about one-half mile south of the present bridge across Rodeo Creek.

The town of Soquel is located on the west bank of Soquel Creek. Among old buildings in the town is the picturesque Congregational Church erected in 1868.

Rancho San Agustín and Scott's Valley

Rancho San Agustín, the northern tip of which is at the Glenwood schoolhouse, was granted in 1841 to Juan José Crisostomo Majors, the name which Joseph L. Majors, a native of Tennessee, had assumed when he became a Mexican citizen. He received United States patent for his land, in his original name, in 1866.

Although, while in Los Angeles in 1834, Majors had signed with other foreigners a protest against being obliged to do military service for the Mexican government, four years later he became a naturalized citizen of that country and at about the same time married María de los Angeles Castro. He was one of the men arrested with Captain Isaac Graham as an undesirable foreigner but, probably owing to his Spanish connections, was released before the captives were taken to Mexico. In the year 1841 he received the grants of both the San Agustín and the Zayante ranches.

Hiram Daniel Scott came into Monterey Bay in 1846 as second mate on the "C. Whiting" and in 1852 purchased Rancho San Agustín. The father, Hiram, followed the son, Hiram D., to the West and took this ranch over from him. The ownership of these two Scotts gave the name Scott's Valley to the vicinity, the name by which it is now known. The original Scott's Valley schoolhouse is now a part of the Scott's Valley Community Hall.

Rancho Carbonera

Rancho Carbonera, bordering the San Lorenzo River north of Santa Cruz, was granted by Governor Alvarado to José Guillermo Bocle in 1838. It was patented to him in 1873.

Bocle was a man of many aliases: Boc, Buckle, Thompson, and Mead being a few of them. He and his brother Samuel, who had come to California in 1823, according to his own statement, and was naturalized in 1841, both took the name of Thompson after the American occupation. Guillermo, or William, was an English sailor who came to California in 1823, married María Antonia Castro, and became the father of a large family. At his death, unable to sign his own name, he left "to those now living with me" 15,000 acres of land along with horses, cattle, and money. Thompson's Flat, a section of his old holdings, on which is now located the Pasatiempo Polo Field, includes the camp site of John C. Fré-

mont, then lieutenant in the topographical engineering corps of the United States Army, and his sixty men on February 25–28, 1846.

Paradise Masonic Park is also within the boundaries of this rancho. Here in 1855 was a sawmill. James Waters, a carpenter from Maryland who was in charge of this mill, erected at later dates many buildings in the counties of Santa Cruz and Monterey and rose to a position of importance in the Pajaro Valley. Here in 1860 a paper mill was established with a daily output of a ton of coarse brown paper. It survived but two years because of two calamities: the carrying away of the flume by high water, and the death of Henry Van Valkenburg, the superintendent.

In 1865 the California Powder Works were constructed with an entrance at about where the gates to Paradise Park now stand. A 1,300-foot tunnel through the mountain brought water from up the San Lorenzo River to operate the grinding mills, the output of which was used for blasting in the construction of the Central Pacific Railway. This plant continued operation until 1916, when it was absorbed by the Dupont Company and work was discontinued at this place. The tunnel and some of the foundations remain, and the locality is still known as Powder Mill Flat.

Rancho Zayante and Felton

Rancho Zayante was granted in 1834 to Joaquín Buelna, who had previously held the post of alcalde at Branciforte; but it was regranted in 1841 to Joseph L. Majors, who immediately sold it to Isaac Graham, to whom it was patented in 1870. A survey of this boundary was made in 1867. One stake on the west line was placed between Felton and Ben Lomond in the big curve of the San Lorenzo River near Brackney.

Graham, a thorough frontiersman, had come from Hardin County, Kentucky, in 1833. Three years after his arrival he assisted Juan B. Alvarado in expelling Governor Gutiérrez with the understanding that the country thereafter should be free from Mexican dominion. However, shortly after Alvarado came into power, Graham and his associates were arrested as dangerous foreigners and placed in confinement on a boat in Monterey harbor. A few of the group were released before Don José Castro sailed with the prisoners for Mexico, and all were released by the Mexican authorities after their arrival. It was reported that Isaac Graham received $36,000 as indemnity for the outrage done him and that a part of this sum was used in the purchase of this rancho. Within a year after his coming into possession of the land he built on the west bank of the Zayante Creek opposite Bear Creek the first power sawmill in California. This was in 1842, about two months before the one at Bodega Bay was installed. Afterward a flour mill occupied a near-by site on Zayante Creek.

Both Mount Hermon and Felton in the southern part of this rancho are near the junction of Zayante Creek and the San Lorenzo River. Between these two settlements is one of the two covered bridges now remaining in the county built across the San Lorenzo River. The other covered bridge, also still in use, crosses Branciforte Creek on the Glen Canyon Road after it leaves Santa Cruz via Market Street.

No bridge was built across the river near Felton until about 1879. In 1868 the San Lorenzo Drive from Santa Cruz was cut through as far as Felton, and the settlers there decided to make an effort to get a bridge in place of the ford which they had used in good weather. To promote the undertaking, a "Bridge Benefit Ball" was given in Santa Cruz, a festivity at which the women of the two places appeared in calico dresses. The bridge was not built at once, nor was it for several years. After a petition had been sent to the supervisors in 1876 and another in 1878, finally a bridge, a wooden truss tied together with steel bars, was built, and the notice for horse vehicles was posted: "$5.00 fine for crossing faster than a walk." It was not a covered bridge, but it was replaced in 1892 by the covered bridge which is now standing.

About 1878 Mr. and Mrs. George Day conducted the first hotel in Felton, the Big Tree House, now a part of the Felton Hotel. Supplies for the hotel had to be brought across the river. When the river was in flood a horse had to swim, carrying the rider with the foodstuffs. But usually sufficient supplies to last over the wet season were obtained in advance. In addition to his hotel Mr. Day conducted a livery stable and ran a stage line. George U. Collins, brother of Mrs. Day, a lumberman from Maine, who was then operating a shingle mill on Bean Creek, built a road from Felton to the Big Trees, placing a toll house at the point where is now located the Toll House Resort.

Rancho Refugio

This rancho was situated on the shore of Monterey Bay southwest of Rancho de la Cañada del Rincon. Its northwestern boundary was Laguna de Pala, now called Laguna Creek. The smaller creeks, Coja, Baldwin, and Meder, flow from the hills through this tract into the bay. The old Coast Road, traversed first by the Portola expedition, afterward by vaqueros on their horses, then by lumber wagons, then by stagecoaches, has ever extended the full length of this rancho, as does State Highway 1 over the same route today.

In 1839 this land was apparently granted to María de lo's Angeles Castro and her sisters, one of whom was the wife of José Antonio Bolcoff, to whom it was definitely granted by Governor Alvarado on April 7, 1841. It was later claimed by his sons, Francisco and Juan, as executors of the estate.

José Antonio Bolcoff was one of the earliest foreign settlers in Spanish California. A native of Kamchatka, he deserted a Russian sailing vessel when it visited Monterey Bay in 1815, settled in Santa Cruz, and in 1822 married Candida, one of the daughters of Joaquín Castro, and reared a family of eleven children. After being naturalized as a Mexican citizen, he became alcalde at three different times and held that office at the time the American flag was raised over California.

Following the order of secularization, he was put in charge of the buildings and properties of Misión Santa Cruz, and assumed those duties in July 1839. For the regulation of the little group of people over which he had control, he immediately promulgated twenty-two statutes, which today give some idea of his own personality. These laws, intended for a few Spanish families and about seventy Indians, dealt with such matters as precautions to be taken against fires spreading to grass and timber, the responsibility of each resident for keeping the street in front of his domicile clean, prohibition of the sale of liquor after eight o'clock, and an eight-o'clock curfew, the hour being later changed to ten.

On receiving the grant of Rancho Refugio, he built an adobe residence a part of which is still standing at the Wilder Dairy on Meder Creek about four miles northwest of Santa Cruz on the Coast Road. The original tiles remain on one end of the long, low building now used as a storeroom, the other end of which fell years ago. In excavating for the foundation of the Wilder family home, a frame house now standing between the historic adobe and the road, the base of the old fireplace was discovered, and in the earth about it were found old utensils—knives, spoons, and crockery.

This land passed from the Bolcoff heirs to Moses Meder, one of the Mormons brought by Sam Brannan on the ship "Brooklyn," landing in San Francisco in 1846. Meder Creek memorializes his ownership. The place has now been in the possession of the Delos Wilder family for three generations,

and the old adobe is respected by them. One of the frame ranch houses standing within a few yards of the adobe and the later Wilder residence was built during the early pioneer days and shows on its roof the original hand-split and hand-planed shingles.

Rancho Arroyo de la Laguna

Adjoining Rancho Refugio on the northwest at the Arroyo de la Laguna, now Laguna Creek, and extending along the coast as far as Vicente Creek was Rancho Arroyo de la Laguna, granted, February 20, 1840, by Governor Alvarado to Gil Sánchez, a tithe collector at Branciforte at this time.

James Williams, a lumberman and blacksmith, who with a brother Isaac came overland to California with the Chiles-Walker party, settled near Santa Cruz. Another brother, Squire, a former member of Frémont's Battalion, died in the Yuba mines in 1848. In 1852 James and the heirs of Squire filed claim for the lands of this grant, and it was patented to them on February 21, 1881. On the edge of this rancho, at the mouth of San Vicente Creek, is the site of Williams Landing, where in the '50's lumber from the hills was loaded on schooners.

Two men from Switzerland who later developed small farms on this tract were Respini and Moretti; they lived at the place now called the Yellowbank Dairy in a valley near the mouth of Respini Creek, sometimes called Yellowbank Creek.

Rancho Agua Puerca y las Trancas

This square league of land, given by Governor Michel-torena October 31, 1843, to Ramón Rodríguez and Francisco Alviso, extends along the coast from the mouth of the Arroyo Agua Puerca at the old Davenport Landing on the east to the Cañada de las Trancas on the west. Scott Creek, flowing almost the entire length of the rancho, enters it from the hills at its northeast corner and near the southwest corner pours its waters into the Pacific or, as early geographers recorded it, into the Bay of Monterey.

Near the confluence of Big Creek, Little Creek, and Scott Creek is a country settlement, formerly the stage station Laurel Grove, now called Swanton in honor of one of the men responsible for the placing and building of the Power House farther up Big Creek. Not far from Swanton is a State Fish Hatchery on Big Creek and a Spawning Station on Scott Creek.

This rancho was purchased by James Archibald, to whose employ came Ambrogio Gianoni from Switzerland via the dairies of Marin County in 1869, and the Gianoni name since that time has been closely identified with this locality. The ranch headquarters at that date were on Archibald Creek, where now are old barns and other farm buildings standing beside the Coast Road. Across the road from these is a small, substantial "rock" house which young Gianoni built soon after his arrival. Set into the hillside, it was erected for the making of Swiss cheese. It ceased to be used for that purpose some years ago, but it stands as firm as ever, a storehouse for other things.

After being an employee of James Archibald for some years, Ambrogio Gianoni rented a tract of land at the northwestern end of the rancho. To this place he took his wife, and there most of his family were born. Later he moved back to the house on Archibald Creek, but at the end of another ten years he purchased the land he had formerly rented at the northwestern end of the property, making his home for the rest of his life there at the top of Gianoni Hill.

A small piece of nine acres at this far end of the grant on the Arroyo de las Trancas had at a previous date been purchased by David Post, who operated there a small hotel and stage station at a spot marked now only by a few old cypresses on the bluff back of the site of the old horse barn. Post also had the Seaside Post Office, and near by was the first schoolhouse in the Seaside district. Afterward the schoolhouse was moved to the top of Gianoni Hill, where now stands a row of six cypress trees west of the two Gianoni houses in which descendants of Ambrogio Gianoni live. The school for the Seaside district is now held in a neat little house at the foot of the same hill toward Swanton.

On the shore line of Rancho Agua Puerca is a local landmark, a spot called "China Ladder," on the cliffs about one and one-half miles southeast of the Cañada de las Trancas. Here on the top of the bluff was a shack in which lived several Chinese who obtained abalones from the rocks below and dried them for the Chinese trade. To reach the beach from this bluff they followed down a trail, then down a rope to a ladder by which they descended the remainder of the precarious way.

Other Mexican Grants

Stretching back from the coast between San Vicente and Molino creeks is Rancho San Vicente, granted in 1846 to Blas A. Escamilla and patented to him in 1870 (although Bancroft states that it was previously granted to Antonio Rodríguez in 1839). On this tract is the Agua Puerca School, which, although it has changed its location several times for the convenience of families with children of school age, has always retained the name Agua Puerca, because its earliest site was near the creek of that name.

In the northwestern part of the city of Santa Cruz a grant of less than 200 acres was given in 1844 to Nicolas Dodero, an Italian sailor, who left the "María Ester" at San Francisco in 1827 and spent most of his life in San José and Branciforte. This rancho, Tres Ojos de Agua, was patented to him in 1866. The name, meaning "three eyes of water," refers to the springs near High Street in the Escalona Heights district, whence a stream flows down through the town. Various interesting people have lived in this section. There Joseph L. Majors built a grist mill that remained a landmark for many years; and there, in 1870, J. F. Cunningham, a prominent lumberman, built a house, near Spring Street, which was afterward occupied by the Honorable William T. Jeter while he was lieutenant-governor of the state. This old and well-built house has now been wrecked and its material used elsewhere.

Other grants in the county that received United States recognition in the form of patents were: Cañada del Rincón el Rio de San Lorenzo de Santa Cruz, granted to Pedro (Pierre) Sansevain in 1846 and patented to him in 1858 (on this rancho he erected a sawmill and there, on Gold Creek, some gold has been found); Laguna de las Calabazas, granted in 1833 to Felipe Hernández and patented to his heirs in 1868; Las Aromitas y Agua Caliente, a part of which is in San Benito County; Aguajita, a small tract within the present city limits of Santa Cruz, patented to M. Villagrana; and two grants claimed by T. W. Russell, the Mesa de Ojo de Agua and the Potrero y Rincón de San Pedro de Reglado, both of which were long under consideration by the authorities for patents.

Adobe Home of Sacramento Castro

The names of Rodríguez, Castro, and Pérez are connected with the adobe located one mile east of Santa Cruz at the intersection of Paul Sweet's Lane and McIntyre Road, one-quarter mile north of the Santa Cruz-Watsonville highway. It was the home of Sacramenta, wife of Martín Castro. Rancho Arroyoita, on which it stands, was a gift to her in 1860 from her mother Concepción, widow of Alejandro Rodríguez, whose father José Antonio Rodríguez had come to Branciforte as an *invalido* in 1799.

This rancho was a part of the larger Rancho Encinalitos left by Alejandro at his death in 1852 to his widow. So far as can be ascertained no grant had been made of this land, but it was patented to Concepción by the United States in 1867. In 1887 the Pérez family, who are direct descendants of the original owner, repurchased the property, and it has been their home since that time. The house is built on a side hill and is surrounded by old Monterey cypress and fruit trees. It has a large wooden addition of two stories and a frame upper story over the adobe kitchen.

Schooner Landings

Early map makers show Punta del Año Nuevo, now sometimes called by its English equivalent, New Year's Point, as the northern extremity of Monterey Bay. La Pérouse, voyaging along the coast in September 1786, described the bay as being open eight leagues across the entrance from Punta del Año Nuevo to Cypress Point and extending from this imaginary line "eastward to where the land is sandy and low."

Santa Cruz County lies along the northeastern shore of this bay. With few wagon roads and no railroads in the pioneer days, and with the products of its kilns, tanneries, and mills too great for local needs, the active residents of this region depended upon water transportation for a wider market. Inlets at the mouths of streams were used as landing places for schooners, and loading was sometimes done through the surf before wharves were built.

The southernmost landing was that of Pajaro at the mouth of the Pajaro River; next came Miller's Landing on the beach of the land purchased from Rancho San Andrés by Captain C. F. Miller. As early as 1849 the landing at the mouth of Soquel Creek was in use, and Porter's Landing, either there or near by, is mentioned in early annals. The present town of Capitola, developed by Frederick A. Hihn in 1869 as a summer resort, is in the vicinity of Soquel Landing.

A wharf was built in 1849 near the mouth of the San Lorenzo River at Santa Cruz by Elihu Anthony and was purchased two years later by Isaac E. Davis and Albion P. Jordan, who maintained a fleet of small schooners to haul lime to San Francisco and who, in 1855, had the $150,000 schooner "Santa Cruz" built in the East and brought around the Horn. The largest industry in the town of Santa Cruz in the '50's was that of these two men, Davis and Jordan, both Fortyniners from New England who had been engineers on a Sacramento River steamboat before coming to this region. After purchasing in 1851 land on which they built warehouses, they began their operation of lime burning there and shipped from the wharf built by Anthony. Their original kiln was at the upper end of Bay Street; later they moved farther north to the Rincon rancho. The names of these two American pioneers are memorialized in the city by two streets, Davis and Jordan, which intersect north of Mission Street.

In the shale rock on the beach about one-half mile northwest of Meder Creek are a number of mooring irons used by schooners that once called there for the produce of the Cowell Lime Company. The brick-built kilns, now unused, are located about three miles up Meder Canyon back of the Wilder Dairy, and from the kilns ox teams hauled the burned lime to this natural wharf.

Williams Landing was at the mouth of Laguna Creek on the southern boundary of Rancho de Laguna. Lime from the kilns in the vicinity was shipped from there, and in 1851 W. Waddell shipped lumber from the mill which he had established there, the first one of the four mills which he eventually operated within the county.

Davenport Landing, farther northwest, at the mouth of the Arroyo del Agua Puerca, was the site of extensive whaling operations. La Pérouse, in 1786, wrote while in Monterey Bay, "It is impossible to conceive the number of whales by which we are surrounded." Captain John P. Davenport, an old whaling master, who fifty-five years later was residing on the shore of the bay, also observed the number of whales and, according to Hittell, devised a scheme whereby he could go out from shore in a whaling boat, capture a whale, and tow it to land where the blubber could be removed and tried-out in great pots instead of following the earlier method of completing the whole operation on board the boats while at sea. After Captain Davenport's success, following the new method made it possible for the workers in this industry to live on shore and sally forth for a few hours as opportunity for capturing a whale arose. While directing this work, which began in the '50's, Captain Davenport lived in a frame house on the west side of the arroyo overlooking the 450-foot wharf which he had built. His men lived in cabins or in the hotel which stood a little way up the arroyo and served also as headquarters for the lumber and lime men of the countryside.

Despite the action of wind and wave, the captain's wharf outlasted a newer one built by the Reese Lime Works near their storehouse on the opposite side of the arroyo. Captain Davenport spent his later years in the town of Santa Cruz.

Two schooners were once built at the mouth of this little creek, both of them constructed for the purpose of transporting split redwood material from lumber camps to San Francisco. One of them was wrecked on returning from its maiden voyage in a storm which drove it past its destination and beached it several miles to the south.

The hotel which cared for the workers in those early industries and the few small houses of the time have all disappeared along with the old wharves, giving way to a small wayside hotel and filling station, a one-room country school, and a few scattering homes along State Highway 1. Old Davenport shows no trace of its former shipping or other activities, but a new Davenport, about one mile south on the hillside above San Vicente Creek, has grown up around a busy cement plant to which runs a twelve-mile branch of the Southern Pacific Railroad, connecting with main lines at Santa Cruz. In 1934 this cement company built a 2,400-foot pier for use in conveying its product through tunnel and pipe to especially constructed ocean steamers.

The farthest north and west landing in the county was between Año Nuevo Light Station and the mouth of Waddell Creek. Through the change of county line made in 1868, this spot is now in San Mateo County. But at the time of its operation it was a part of Santa Cruz County, and pickets, posts, and sawn lumber from the forests in the canyons for miles around were shipped from there. This wharf was erected by W. W. Waddell for the purpose of transporting the lumber from his mill on the creek which still bears his name.

Waddell Creek, Cañada de la Salud

Waddell Creek, the perennial coast stream that rises in the State Redwood Park, is fed by water trickling down from springs on the mountain slopes bordering its banks and continues to flow from its upper reaches to its lagoon at the northwestern end of Monterey Bay. The valley through which this stream flows, narrow for the most part but widening out into grassy meadows in others, has a history paralleling, in miniature, that of the state.

Little is known of the earliest human inhabitants of this canyon. But the discovery, as late as 1920, of broken arrowheads and chips of flint on a knoll on the west side of the creek bank about a quarter of a mile back from the lagoon and the unearthing, in 1916, of a large and perfectly made obsidian spearhead in the clearing out of a spring on the mountainside about five hundred feet west of this knoll prove that at least a few primitive Indians used this place as a camping ground.

The name Cañada de la Salud, or "Canyon of Health," was given to the valley in 1769, when the Portolá expedition rested there from Friday, October 20, to the following Monday during that first land journey up the coast from San Diego to San Francisco Bay. Father Crespi, who was an important member of the party, first gave the name of La Cañada de San Luis Baltran to the camp site; but as the men who had been so ill that the rites of the dying had been administered "suddenly felt their pains very much relieved" and were able to proceed on Monday, the permanent name recorded in the diaries was La Cañada, or Arroyo, de la Salud. The place is easily identified because the engineer of the party, Don Miguel Costanso, appended a note to his diary stating that Punta del Año Nuevo, which had been discovered and named by the Vizcaíno sea expedition of 1602–1603, was in approximately the same latitude as their camping place.

A second visit of early Spanish explorers to this place occurred about five years later when, "at nine o'clock in the morning" of December 10, 1774, three men paused on the beach to offer a prayer of thanksgiving for that miracle of health restored to their compatriots of the former expedition. These three men were Father Palóu, Captain Rivera, and a soldier, the two latter having been there with Portolá in 1769 and now returning from a tour of the San Francisco Bay region.

After the establishment of the Mission at Santa Cruz, the Mission herds roamed this coast up to a point where they mingled with the cattle from the Mission at San Francisco, according to Duhaut Cilly, who voyaged along the coast in 1827. The land of this valley, however, was never included in any Spanish or Mexican grant but lay between Rancho Agua Puerca y las Trancas and Rancho Punta del Año Nuevo.

After the advent of the American with his progressive and utilitarian ideas, the wooded sides of this canyon resounded with the blows of the woodsman's axe and the buzz of his saw. At this time the place became known and recorded on maps as "Big Gulch." There William W. Waddell, who had been born in 1818 in Kentucky and had arrived in California in 1851, established his fourth and last sawmill in 1862 (his former mills having been at Williams Landing, at Rincon, and at Branciforte). To convey his lumber to his wharf built between the mouth of the creek and Punta del Año Nuevo, he constructed a five-mile horse tramway built in as straight a line as possible, following the course of the stream and making twelve bridges across its meandering channel.

The mill was located on high ground between, and at the confluence of, the east and west forks of the creek known from that time to the present as Waddell Creek. A large number of men were employed; their mess house, their bunkhouse, the cottages of the men with families, Mr. Waddell's own house, and the hothouse where he raised choice flowers were all located in the vicinity of the forks and the mill.

After Mr. Waddell died in 1875 of an injury inflicted by a grizzly bear, lumbering and woodcutting in the valley gradually ceased. The wharf was finally destroyed by a storm. At the mill the huge boilers were left in place and are still visible although now hedged round by second-growth redwoods. Well up on the opposite hill are the fire-scarred tires of the ox carts used in the logging of those busy days; a heavy, square timber, once a part of a manger for oxen, lies on the ground where it fell (the holes, now moss filled, indicate where the halter for each feeding ox was securely fastened);

and heaps of stones found here and there over the flat were once the fireplaces in the simple cabins. Along the downward course of the stream, fern-bedecked piles in alder groves remain to indicate the points where stood the bridges over the stream bed, now long abandoned as the creek has changed its course.

Living members of families that made up a part of the Waddell Mill payroll have been able to give some idea of the activities in the valley during the lumbering period and afterward. As the houses were all made of wood, they have disappeared, although some of those in the lower and broader part of the canyon, more substantially made than the temporary ones nearer the mill site, endured for many years and were occupied by men who cultivated small farms. Horatio S. Soper was one of the teamsters on the tramline. His duty had been to bring the horse-drawn cars of lumber from the mill down the canyon as far as his house, where another man relieved him and took the train on down to the wharf. Bringing it back, the second driver handed it over to Mr. Soper, who took it up to the mill again. At the Soper farm there was a comfortable house, a large barn, a good fruit orchard, and, in addition, a granary and a blacksmith shop. This family remained in the valley for a number of years, occupying first a house on the east side of Waddell Creek and later one on the opposite side but farther up stream. There were five children in the family, some of them born there, and their earliest education was directed by a resident teacher. Later, however, the children attended the Seaside School near the Seaside Post Office at the David Post place up the hill toward Santa Cruz.

Another family in the valley was that of Bryan Bolton, who first lived near the beach on the east side of the creek and later moved to the house on the same side of the creek from which the Soper family had moved. Several families had lived up near the mill, among them the Pinkham family, who later kept the hotel at Davenport Landing.

A well on the west side of the creek just back of the sheltering point of the cliff long marked the site of the old "Precinct House"; just how it came by that name is not now remembered. The house was at one time occupied by the William Barrett family, who kept a store with a small stock of merchandise. This well has been filled; the old houses, with the exception of the remodeled and enlarged granary, are gone; but many trees of the old orchards survive and still bear fruit, pears, and apples, on their neglected, lofty branches.

The lower part of the valley was owned at one time by the Ocean Shore Land and Investment Company. After the prospect of the building of the Ocean Shore Railway from San Francisco to Santa Cruz was definitely given up, this company sold its property to the present owner, who had previously purchased the upper part of the valley and who is much interested in the conservation of natural resources. The forest is being protected, and permission has been granted to the State Fish and Game Commission to control the long stretch of creek on the property in order to make a scientific study of the life history of the trout and salmon that annually seek Waddell Creek in the spawning season. A concrete dam has been constructed, and a valuable contribution to biologic science is being made by the state assisted by the Bureau of Fisheries.

Mountain Charley

Charles Henry McKiernan, formerly an Irish quartermaster in the British Army, arrived in San Francisco in the spring of 1849 and immediately went to the gold mines.

A year later, coming with his wages as a miner into the Santa Cruz Mountains, he followed a rough trail through the Los Gatos region, until he reached a place near the Laguna del Sargento, where earlier people, Indian and Spanish, had camped from time to time. There, he decided, was the place to stop and carve a home out of the forest. Using whipsawed lumber from the redwood trees, which grew thickly around him, he built a house near a spring and with redwood pickets enclosed corrals in which to keep his livestock. Grizzly bears, mountain lions, coyotes, and eagles played havoc with his calves and lambs, forcing him to take more ample precaution for the safety of his animals. With his muzzle-loading blunderbus, he became a famous bear hunter. An attack by a wounded mother bear nearly cost him his life, and he ever after wore in his skull a silver plate made from two Mexican silver dollars by a Santa Cruz physician to whom he had been carried by a fellow huntsman.

McKiernan was for two years the only resident of this region, and as "Mountain Charley" he was known to the later arrivals. He made many trails and roads through his property; one of them was a cut-off down the old Indian trail near his home through the Moody Gulch territory to Los Gatos Creek. When the Santa Clara Turnpike was organized, he became a stockholder, and one of his roads became a part of the route from Santa Cruz to Los Gatos. The present alignment of the Los Gatos Road, State Highway 17, cuts off six miles of that old mountain stage road. Now practically unused, this stage road curves to the west above Alma, climbs to the summit, and, after passing the McKiernan log house which stands at some distance from his original home, goes by the site of the old "changing station" and curves downward again before entering the same highway.

Mountain Charley, after settling down as stockman and stage owner, did not forget his experience as a miner but carried on certain investigations of the mineral possibilities of his property. His mineral claim was filed for record at the Courthouse in Santa Cruz on December 1, 1864, but apparently this venture, shared by five other men, was unproductive.

In addition to the marking of the log house near the summit as a memorial to this pioneer, a redwood tree, one of the largest of its kind, has been named the "Mountain Charley Big Tree." It stands three hundred feet back from the road and is one-half mile north of Glenwood, the little old village left off the beaten track by the realignment of State Highway 17 in 1934.

Stage Lines out of Santa Cruz

After the close of Mexican rule in California the matter of transportation of freight and passengers by land became of interest. The former methods of travel—on foot, on horseback, or in bumping, creaking carts—being inadequate for the alert American pioneer, various kinds of omnibuses and stages were put into use as soon as roads connected the pivotal points.

A stage line was established between Santa Cruz and San Jose, via San Juan, in 1854. Passengers for San Francisco stopped over night in San Jose and in the winter season proceeded by boat from Alviso the next morning. In summer it was possible to continue the journey on another stage line.

A driver on this line between Santa Cruz and San Juan was "Cock-eyed Charley," written on the Great Register in 1867 as Charley Darkey Parkhurst, aged fifty-five, a farmer and a native of New Hampshire. Charley was a typical stage driver, who took his nip at roadhouses, carried the United States mail, swore at his horses, and voted as a good citizen. After giving up public driving, he retired to a ranch near the Twelve-Mile House out of Santa Cruz and began stock raising on a small scale. Not until his death in 1879 was it even suspected that Charley was a woman.

Another old stage road to San Jose left Santa Cruz by fording the San Lorenzo River, at the place where the Water Street bridge now is. From there it turned up the Graham Grade, used by Isaac Graham in hauling lumber to the wharf on the Santa Cruz beach, and turned again from this grade to pass over what is now the Pasatiempo Polo Field and on to the first stop, the ranch of Abraham Hendricks in Scott's Valley, where were added two horses to assist in the long pull ahead. From this station the road led up to Mountain Charley's station on Mountain Charley Road at the summit and thence over the county line and down to San Jose. Mountain Charley was owner and operator of this line until selling it, in 1874, to George Colgrove—the capable and spectacular driver of the yellow-bodied Concord coach which for a number of years swayed on its leather springs over the narrow mountain roads. This route had been put through in 1857; and at that time Charles C. Martin, who had arrived from Maine in 1853, gave the right of way across his land in the forest north of Rancho San Agustín, now Scott's Valley. Building a home where Glenwood now is, Martin made it a stage stopping place.

By 1858 the San Jose Turnpike over the mountains from Soquel, now called the "Old San Jose Road," had been completed through the efforts of Frederick A. Hihn, a native of Germany and a public-spirited resident of Santa Cruz since 1851. A stage immediately put on between Santa Cruz and San Jose used this route, which today joins State Highway 17 beyond Burrell and near the almost hidden Patchen Church in Santa Clara County. One of the old stations on this route was at the point where the Terrace Gardens Hotel now stands thirteen miles from the Courthouse in Santa Cruz, high up in the mountains. A resort has been maintained there for about sixty-five years. It seems that at one time the place was called "Bonny Blink," perhaps because of the broad extent of the view over the mountains to the Pacific Ocean on the west and to the Bay of Monterey on the south.

At this point a big, unpainted building stands beside the road. With all its doors secured against marauders by key and bolt, it is unmistakably of the past when its one roof sheltered both man and beast. Clinging to a sloping hillside, the building has doors on its two stories opening on the ground at two levels. On the lower level are the wide and high entrance and exit doors where the four-horse team drawing a passenger-filled stage found shelter. The stalls for the horses remain as they were when it was in daily use, and sturdy, hand-hammered nails jut out from the posts where lanterns used to be hung to light the interior. In the upper story, reached by going out through one of these immense doors and walking up an incline to the higher ground level, are three rooms. Passing through the front door, one enters the largest room, a dance hall with rough benches backed against the wall and places on the rafters above for holding kerosene lamps. From this dance hall the smaller rooms may be entered. One is lined with shelves where groceries and other supplies used to be sold; the other, equally small, is now absolutely empty except for the elaborate gilt wallpaper now hanging in shreds—all that remains of the barroom of the little establishment.

In an old directory of 1875 appears an advertisement of a stage line of which Charles G. Sykes was proprietor—"A new stage line Santa Clara to Santa Cruz, via Saratoga, Congress Springs, Ocean View, San Francisco Saw-Mills, San Lorenzo Flume and Transportation Company Mills, Boulder Creek, and Felton. This delightful route .... for fourteen miles follows the San Lorenzo V-Flume and passes one paper mill, ten saw mills, one fuse factory, three lime kilns, and the California Powder Company's works. It also passes Boulder, Bear, Newell, Love, Fall, and Sayante creeks whose waters

are well stocked with mountain trout, the forests abounding with game of all kinds." This stage left the Cameron House in Santa Clara on Mondays, Wednesdays, and Fridays at seven in the morning and, returning, left Santa Cruz on the alternate mornings at seven, making connections with the Alviso boat. The one-way fare was $2.50.

In 1872 a horse-drawn stage was driven by "Billy" Bias up the coast from Santa Cruz to San Gregorio. Turning inland at the latter place, the stage followed a road winding over the mountains to Redwood City, via La Honda, similar to the present stage route between those points. The stations from Santa Cruz as far as Pescadero were: Hall's Natural Bridge, Williams Landing, Davenport Landing, Berry Falls, Laurel Grove (now Swanton), Seaside (the old Post place of which nothing now remains but the cypress trees on the bluff at the mouth of Los Trancos Creek); then, across the county line, Pigeon Point, and Pescadero.

This route was a hazardous one, not only because of narrow and poorly built mountain roads but also because of the precipitous cliffs at Waddell Beach, which had to be passed by driving over the sands at low tide. A road has since been cut in the face of the cliff at this point; but even yet, in wet weather, slides of crumbling rock sometimes prevent the passing of the daily motor stage. Nathan P. Ingalls, a native of New Hampshire, who had driven a four-yoke cow team across the Plains in 1853, was the successor of Bias as owner and driver on this line. On July 1, 1874, he took, in addition to other mail contracts, this one from Santa Cruz to San Mateo and drove the route as far as Pescadero once a day for over twelve years, a distance of thirty-seven miles. A veteran stage driver, he had previously put on the first stage from Napa to Clear Lake and had driven a stage for Wooly and Taft from San Mateo to Pescadero for three years before taking the Santa Cruz route. It was his boast that he had never been held up in his life. After being county supervisor in 1890 he again became interested in stage lines, this time in Monterey County.

Boulder Creek

One of the early post offices in the county was Boulder Creek, situated at the point where Boulder Creek from the northwest and Bear Creek from the east flow into the San Lorenzo River, a lumber center for many years. An older settlement, called Lorenzo in the '70's, is now within its limits.

The timber from the site of the town had been cut out by James F. Cunningham, a man who had come West after considerable military service in the East and had taken up government land on the San Lorenzo River and who, after the early '70's, was identified with the lumber interests in the county. J. W. Peery was another mill proprietor. He had the Silver Lumber Mills and in connection with them operated a tannery. Peery's Toll Road ran up the San Lorenzo River and across to Saratoga. The Bear Creek Toll Road also ran across the mountains to Lexington. Completed in 1875, it never even paid the wages of a tollkeeper, and was finally sold to the county in 1891.

The lumber produced in the vicinity of Boulder Creek was for many years sent over the V-flume built by the San Lorenzo Flume and Transportation Company. This V-flume extended from a point about seven miles north of Boulder Creek to a point in the lower end of Felton. The "Flume House" stood at its upper end; and, although the structure has recently been removed, the spot is marked by the very large eucalyptus trees that were planted about it as saplings. The Flume Company built a narrow-gauge railway from Felton to Santa Cruz and also a wharf at about the place where the Santa Cruz Municipal Wharf now stands. The "dump" at the end of the flume began at about the point where the State Forestry Office now stands in the lower end of the town and extends some three or four hundred feet southward.

A branch of the San Lorenzo, coming in near the Flume House, is called Feeder Creek because it was used as a feeder to the flume to augment the San Lorenzo water supply. The flume was never an entire success—some said because there was not enough fall in the valley and others because the fall was too great for the volume of water.

Around Boulder Creek during the cutting of the timber over fifty saw and shingle mills operated within a radius of seven miles. Because of such a great output of timber material, the Southern Pacific changed the line of the narrow gauge, built by the Flume Company, to standard gauge in 1907. But in 1934, when the supply was exhausted and the mills were closed, the last train was run and the rails were removed. Boulder Creek has now taken on an aspect quite different from that it presented in the rushing days of sawmills and is at present a quiet village surrounded by sequestered summer homes.

Three country newspapers have been published at Boulder Creek, following each other after due lapses of time: the first one was aptly named *The Boulder Creek Hatchet;* the second was *The Mountain Echo;* and the last, becoming defunct in 1924, *The Valley Echo.*

Ben Lomond

Ben Lomond Mountain was named by Thomas Burns, a man from Scotland, who thus memorialized a bit of his native country when he settled on this Far Western slope. The town naturally fell heir to the name when it grew up in the '80's on the bank of the river at the mountain base because of its attraction for enterprising men interested in the lumber possibilities of the place. James J. Pierce, of Santa Clara, owned much timberland there and operated a mill where the Ben Lomond Laundry now stands. He laid out the town, and two bridges, still located on the highway passing through the town, are built on the site of two early ones that he gave to the county in exchange for bringing the main road through his new town site.

At the confluence of Love Creek and San Lorenzo River stood a water-power sawmill first operated by Vardamon Bennet, a native of Georgia, who came to California in 1834, bringing his large family. This mill was later owned by Harry Love, a former captain of spies appointed by General Zachary Taylor during the Mexican War. In 1853, when the California state legislature raised a special force to run down the bandit Joaquín Murieta, Harry Love was made its captain. Love and his rangers overtook and shot the outlaw at a place then in Tulare County, now included in Fresno County; and in the following year the captain was rewarded for his services on that occasion by a state appropriation of $5,000. With this money he began logging in the mountains, and at about this time, by marrying the widow of Vardaman Bennet, he came into possession of the mill. To get the logs to the mill, he built a road since known as the "Harry Love Grade," and the creek whereon the mill stood is Love Creek, over which one of the bridges on the main street of Ben Lomond extends. His flowing hair and the costume that he affected gave him the sobriquet "The Black Knight of Zayante," Zayante being the name of the Mexican grant in this region.

The Loganberry

John H. Logan, a young lawyer, moved to Santa Cruz from San José in 1867 and later became superior judge. He made his home on a hill in the town and in his leisure moments took great interest in his garden. In 1890 he noticed an accidental hybrid which gave promise of being worth

while. In order to test its merits he sent samples to a firm in Salem, Oregon. The berry proved to be something quite new and fine and was given the name of Loganberry in honor of the discoverer. The plant, supposedly a cross between the Auginbaugh (a sport from the native blackberry) and the Red Antwerp raspberry, is now widely distributed. The mammoth blackberry was also the result of one of Judge Logan's horticultural experiments.

In honor of Judge Logan, the hill upon which he lived has been named Logan Heights.

"The Ruins"

Supposed by the credulous who first saw them to be chimneys protruding from a fallen castle or from a buried prehistoric village, a small group of natural curiosities locally known as "The Ruins" has elicited comment by certain writers.

Geologists who have visited the spot, some few miles northeast of Santa Cruz in Scott's Valley, are able to give a scientific explanation of this outcropping. These grotesque concretionary columns, six in number, each four or five feet long, are harder portions of the rocks of the Santa Margarita formation and are "the result of the weathering away of the soft sandstone surrounding locally hardened portions along joint cracks." They are on private property on Bean Creek north of Mount Hermon.

Redwoods, *Sequoia sempervirens*

The many coast redwoods throughout the Santa Cruz foothills and mountains have made the region famous. Because it was in this county that these trees were first glimpsed by white men (by the Portolá expedition, on October 10, 1769, probably on Corralitos Creek), it is fortunate that here, too, the first state park was set aside for their preservation. Here also the tree was named "Palo Colorado," which, translated from Spanish into English, means "red wood."

Although the lumbering industry early endangered the ancient trees of the whole section, recent years have witnessed a cessation of that threat; and, although thousands of acres of them were cut, a goodly number remain and even the cut-over lands are now sending up a growth of strong young trees encircling the old stumps. The movement for making a state park was started in time to preserve for the public hundreds of acres of virgin timber as well as a vast cut-over territory that is now in luxuriant second growth.

The California State Redwood Park, situated in the northwestern part of the county in the heart of the "Big Basin" in the Waddell drainage area twenty-three miles from Santa Cruz, contains 10,028 acres. In addition to the redwoods, hundreds of them doubtless antedating the discovery of America by Columbus, there are in this park magnificent stands of oak, madroño, Tumion, toyon, and Ceanothus standing on ridges between fern-bordered streams.

The preservation of this area for the public was the result of the concerted effort of an interested group of people. Apparently the first person to mention the desirability and necessity of acquiring redwood forests for posterity was Ralph Smith, who, in his editorials in the *Redwood City Times and Gazette,* sought to awaken general interest. His tragic death in 1887 cut him off before any steps had been taken in the matter. Next in point of time came Captain Ferdinand Lee Clark and Andrew P. Hill. The latter, then living in San Jose, made many trips to see and photograph the trees in this Big Basin section and was tireless in his efforts to bring them before the public and to force legislative action.

On May 1, 1900, when a group of interested persons was called together and met in the library of Stanford University, a committee was appointed to visit and report upon this, then almost inaccessible, region. On the last evening of their inspection visit, May 18, 1900, sitting on the west bank of Sempervirens Creek, they organized the Sempervirens Club, the main object of which was to be the acquisition and preservation of as much as possible of the surrounding forest.

The idea of state parks was new. Editors of newspapers in the two counties most interested united in giving publicity to the project. Among these papers were: the *Boulder Creek Mountain Echo,* the *Santa Cruz Surf,* the *Santa Cruz Sentinel,* and the *San Jose Mercury.*

In 1901 the state legislature passed an enabling act whereby 3,800 acres were purchased by the state in the ensuing year for a quarter of a million dollars, and the following men were subsequently appointed by Governor Gage to be commissioners: Father Robert E. Kenna, S.J., president of Santa Clara University; Professor William Russell Dudley, botanist of Stanford University; A. W. Foster, regent of the State University and president of the Northwestern Railway; and William H. Mills, land agent of the Southern Pacific Railway Company. The Governor of the state was ex officio chairman.

Governor's Camp, now the center of all control and of all activities within the park, came by its name logically because of certain notable early visitors. At about the time of the purchase of the first land in the park, Governor Henry T. Gage accompanied a party of investigation to the tract. To provide accommodation for this group, a five-room cabin and a cook house were built, the lumber for which had to be packed in by mule back. In the following year, the newly elected governor, George Pardee, and his family spent some weeks at this cabin. During the course of this visit Governor West of Utah was a guest. Since the visits of these three distinguished men, the name Governor's Camp has clung to the place.

Near the crossroads in Governor's Camp is a memorial fountain placed by the Sempervirens Club in 1923 to honor the memory of A. P. Hill, who had put forth more individual effort than anyone else in securing the park for the people of the state.

Another group of redwoods twenty miles south of the Big Basin Park is the Santa Cruz Big Trees County Park. Privately owned and known as the "Welch Grove" until 1931, it has a station on the Southern Pacific Railway called "Big Trees." The largest tree in this group is the "Giant," 306 feet high. Another much visited tree there is the "General Frémont," in the hollow trunk of which John C. Frémont, then lieutenant, is said to have spent a few rainy days during a march through this region with his men in 1846. In later years, after attaining the rank of general, he visited the grove with his wife and daughter; but, unwilling to verify the story of his having occupied the tree, he passed it over with the remark, "It is a good story, let it stand."

SOURCES

[Credit is here given for source material, and permission to quote is hereby acknowledged]

ATKINSON, FRED W. *100 Years in the Pajaro Valley.* Register and Pajaronian Press, Watsonville, California

BANCROFT, H. H. *History of California.* 7 vols. History Company, San Francisco, 1886

BOLTON, HERBERT EUGENE. *Fray Juan Crespi, Missionary Explorer on the Pacific Coast, 1769–1774.* University of California Press, Berkeley, California, 1927

——— (ed.). *Historical Memoirs of New California, by Fray Francisco Palóu.* Translated into English from manuscript in archives of Mexico. 4 vols. University of California Press, Berkeley, California, 1926

CHAPMAN, CHARLES E. *A History of California: The Spanish Period.* The Macmillan Company, New York, 1921

CLYMAN, JAMES. *Diary of, 1844–5–6.* Manuscript in Huntington Library

COUNTY RECORDS. Manuscript files in Recorder's Office, Santa Cruz

DELEIGSEGUS, REBECCA, and LUCRETIA MYLAR. "Early Days in Corralitos and Soquel," in *Evening Free Lance,* Hollister

ELDER, DAVID PAUL. *The Old Spanish Missions of California.* Paul Elder & Company, San Francisco, 1913

FAGES, PEDRO. *Diary from Monterey to San Francisco in 1770.* Academy of Pacific Coast Publications, II, No. 3, University of California Press, Berkeley, California

FARNHAM, ESQ. J. T. *The Early Days of California.* Philadelphia, John E. Potter, 1862

HARRISON, E. S. *History of Santa Cruz County.* Pacific Press Publishing Company, San Francisco, 1892

HILL, FRANK and FLORENCE W. *The Acquisition of California Redwood Park.* Published by Florence W. Hill, San Jose, California, 1927

HUNT, ROCKWELL D., and NELLIE VAN DE GRIFT SANCHEZ. *A Short History of California.* Thomas Y. Crowell Company, New York, 1929

LA PÉROUSE, JEAN FRANCOIS GALAUP DE. *A Voyage Round the World in the Years 1785, 1786, 1787, 1788.* Edited by M. L. A. Milet-Mureau. 3 vols. Printed for J. Johnson, St. Paul's Churchyard, London, 1798

MARTIN, ED. "Situation of the Pajaro Valley," in *Sketch of the General History of Santa Cruz County.* Wallace W. Elliott, San Francisco, 1879

PAULSON, L. L. (compiler). *Handbook and Directory of Santa Clara, San Benito, Santa Cruz, Monterey, and San Mateo Counties.* L. L. Parker, Francis and Valentine Commercial Steam Presses, 517 Clay St., San Francisco, 1875

RODGERS, W. S. *Reminiscences.* Files of *Santa Cruz Sentinel,* 1933–1935

ROWLAND, LEON. Local history articles, in files of *Santa Cruz News,* 1931–1935

TAYLOR, A. A. "Short History of Aptos," in *Santa Cruz Surf,* 1896

TAYLOR, ARTHUR A. (compiler). *California Redwood Park.* State Printing Office, Sacramento, 1912

TEGGART, FREDERICK (ed.). "The Portolá Expedition of 1769–1770, Diary of Miguel Costanso," in *Publications of the Academy of Pacific Coast History,* II, No. 4, University of California Press, Berkeley, California, 1911

TORCHIANA, H. A. VAN COENEN. *Story of the Mission Santa Cruz.* Paul Elder and Company, San Francisco, 1933

WATKINS, MAJOR ROLAND C. *History of Monterey and Santa Cruz Counties.* S. J. Clarke Publishing Company, Chicago, 1925

WILLEY, H. S. "A Sketch of the General History of Santa Cruz County," in *Illustrations of Santa Cruz County.* Wallace W. Elliott & Company, San Francisco, 1879

SOLANO COUNTY

SOLANO COUNTY (named in honor of an Indian chief) was one of the original twenty-seven counties. The first county seat was at Benicia, but in 1858 it was removed to Fairfield.

Solano, Chief of the Suisuns

At the time of the founding of Misión San Rafael Arcángel, there came to the notice of the missionaries an outstanding individual, Sem Yeto, the Indian chief who was known in later years as Chief Solano. The last of the Missions established in California by the Franciscan friars was at Sonoma and was called San Francisco Solano after the two saints, Francis of Assisi and Solano, the great "Apostle of the Indies." Padre Altimira, founder of the Mission, bestowed the latter name upon Sem Yeto, who was an exceptionally intelligent Indian and chief over most of the rancherías between Petaluma Creek and the Sacramento River. The chief accepted the title and the new faith and prevented his people from making ashes of Misión San Francisco Solano.

When General Mariano Guadalupe Vallejo was made comandante of Sonoma, he, too, won Chief Solano's friendship, an unusual accomplishment for a Spanish or Mexican military officer. This friendship was the outgrowth of General Vallejo's victory over the Soscol Indians, of whom Sem Yeto was chief. This encounter occurred in 1835 at a place now known as Thompson's Gardens, just north of the city of Vallejo.

One of the tribes over which Sem Yeto was chief was called the Suisuns and occupied the valley east of the Soscol (corrupted to Suscol) Hills. The chief's saintly title, Solano, became attached to that locality and, when a county was staked off, General Vallejo requested that it be named Solano County in honor of his friend.

On a gentle rise of ground about one hundred yards west of the state highway, lying midway between Cordelia and Fairfield and overlooking a wide terrain of vineyards and fruit orchards, stands a bronze statue of heroic size. It is mounted upon a pedestal of lava rock upon which a tablet is affixed, bearing this inscription:

Francisco Solano, Chief of·the Suisun Indians, Friend of the white man. "To the bravery and in particular to the diplomacy of that great chieftain of the Suisun Indians civilization is indebted for the conquest of the territory which today comprises the counties of Solano, Napa, Sonoma, and Lake"—General Mariano Guadalupe Vallejo.

This monument was erected in 1934 through the funds appropriated by the people of the State of California. The site was donated by the Improved Order of Redmen of the Reservation of California. Wm. Gordon Huff, Sculptor.

Rancho Suisun

Five Mexican grants in this county were recognized by the United States government and patented to the legal claimants after due process of law. The first in point of time was Rancho Suisun, given to Francisco Solano. In his petition, dated January 16, 1837, Solano described himself as the "principal chief of the unconverted Indians and born captain of the Suisun" and asked for four square leagues. Said lands belonged "to him by hereditary right from his ancestors," and he wished "to revalidate his right." The grant was temporarily made to him and approved by Pio Pico in 1845 when he became governor for the second time.

This land was afterward purchased by M. G. Vallejo and still later was acquired, also by purchase, by Archibald A. Ritchie, who received United States patent for 17,754 acres in January 1857. Fairfield, the county seat, is located on the border of this grant.

Rancho Tolenas

"José Francisco Armijo, by birth a Mexican, having four sons natives of the same country without any lands to cultivate," petitioned for the Tolenas, or Armijo, grant in November 1839. The following spring Governor Alvarado gave him three square leagues of land with the proviso that he should not in any manner molest the Indians already located there. Armijo died in 1850, and the title to 13,315 acres was acquired by his son Antonio Armijo, who received patent for them in 1868.

Five miles northwest of Fairfield at the foot of a hill a trampled pile of earth near a rock-lined spring is all that remains of the five-room adobe built on this rancho. The walls fell about 1900, and the demolition has been completed by herds of cattle pasturing on the land. The name of Armijo, however, is borne by the local high school in Fairfield.

Rancho Los Putos

The Los Putos grant was given to two Spaniards, Manuel Cábez Vaca (or Baca) and Juan Felipe Peña, both of whom had come from New Mexico with their families and settled there in 1843. The two families resided at Sonoma while Indians competent to do the work erected two adobes for them; the house for the Vaca family was placed in what has since been called the main Vaca Valley, and that for the Peña family was erected in the lateral Laguna Valley, where it still stands about two miles west of Vacaville. Much of this large grant had passed into other hands by 1879.

Vaca's adobe was known for a time as the "Portia Hill" house, but it was torn down in 1932. A frame cottage now occupies the site, northwest of the Peña dwelling. The Peña adobe—its walls protected by board sidings, the tiles of its roof now replaced with shingles, and the ell part now a frame structure—is still owned by descendants of the two original families united through intermarriage. Some of the old garden shrubs are still alive: the pomegranate, or "flor de Granada"; the old Mission grapevine; and the Castilian roses, those small, thorny, single pink blossoms so beloved by the early Spanish settlers.

Ulatis Creek, named for the local Indian tribe of that name, flows through this rancho, and on this creek many "sweat houses" used by the natives were situated.

United States patent for this grant of 44,383 acres was given to J. M. Vaca and J. F. Peña in 1858.

Rancho Río de los Putos

The Río de los Putos grant, traditionally claimed at an earlier date by Francisco Guerrero, was made to William Wolfskill in 1842; and 17,754 acres were patented to him in December 1858, a part of which was in Yolo County and a part in Solano County.

John Reed Wolfskill, having arrived in California in 1838, had lived in the southern part of the state for a few years with his brother William, a trapper, who had reached the state a few years earlier. In 1842 John drove ninety head of cattle north, past the home of his brother's trapper friend, George C. Yount, to a point near the bank of Putah Creek, where he erected a pioneer hut. This stream flows through this property and now forms, in the vicinity, the dividing line between Yolo and Solano counties. An adobe which he constructed there was used as a storehouse and blacksmith shop for many years, and when it was finally pulled down the earth in its walls was used to strengthen the banks of the encroaching creek. Boards that had formed lean-to sheds adjoining the old adobe were salvaged and now form a woodshed near the old site.

John was joined there by his brother, Sarchel, and together they built and occupied a log house only a few feet away from the adobe storehouse built earlier. This log house, likewise, has been removed. A frame house of more modern style, in which Sarchel spent his adult life with his family about him, was erected near its site. This frame house is now standing and is occupied by descendants of Sarchel. From the orange seeds and olives and fig-cuttings planted by these men have grown the sturdy trees seen on the place today. An old Indian graveyard lies just beyond the olive grove.

Two other brothers, Milton and Mathus, joined these men on this vast tract of land, and all four made homes along the fertile banks of the Río de los Putos. John removed one and one-half miles northeast and established a home farther from the creek. Here he erected a house, using the smooth, white, native stone, a volcanic tufa, and planted many acres of nuts and seeds of various fruits. From this planting black walnuts, pecans, pomegranates, date-palms, oranges, and olives are still being produced, although the crops cannot equal in quality the finer varieties that are now obtainable. The stone house fell in 1892 and has been replaced by one of stucco, which stands, as the former one did, at the end of a long driveway lined with magnificent olive trees. This property, owned by John Wolfskill and after him by his daughter and now by his grandchildren, has been willed to the University of California to be used as an Agricultural Experiment Station.

The Mathus Wolfskill adobe was on the south side of Putah Creek, one-half mile east of Winters and two hundred yards east of the bridge. The house is gone, but an adobe tank remains. The Milton Wolfskill house was seven miles west of Winters, in the hills west of the low-water bridge.

Rancho Los Ulpinos

The Los Ulpinos, or Bidwell, grant contained 17,726 acres in the eastern part of the county along the western bank of the Sacramento River. John (Juan) Bidwell, who had become a naturalized Mexican citizen, petitioned for this tract in April 1844, and it was granted to him in November of the same year by Governor Manuel Micheltorena "for his own benefit and that of his family." The further provision was appended that he "may fence it, but he shall have no power to sell it," a precaution taken to prevent the land from falling into alien hands. He immediately built an adobe house and placed workmen on the land but did not himself reside there. After the Mexican government had lost its claim to all the land in California, Bidwell sold undivided fractional parts to several persons, until the boundary lines were in a state of chaos. In 1855 these properties were all defined amicably when the entire rancho was divided into twenty equal tracts made by measurements along the river front extending back one league. These tracts were sold in front of the Court-house door in Benicia on December 3, 1855, and the proceeds were allocated to the various claimants. The land was finally patented to Bidwell by the United States in August 1866, thus making all the titles valid.

Unpatented Land Grants

Troublesome litigation followed the making of the Soscol and the Sobrante grants. The former, containing eleven square leagues, was claimed by M. G. Vallejo as having been given to him in consideration of his services as an officer and of the large sums of money that he had furnished to the Mexican government. His title to this vast acreage, extending from the Straits of Carquinez to the northern and western line of the county, was declared invalid by the courts, but purchases made under it were allowed when further small payments were made. The greater part of each of the cities of Vallejo, Benicia, Cordelia, and Green Valley lies within its borders.

The Sobrantè grant of fifty square leagues was claimed by Juan Luco (Lucco) by reason of his having purchased it from a Mexican vaquero who had previously received it from the Mexican government. This land also became a part of the public domain after the claim was rejected by the courts. The towns of Denverton and Collinsville are within its borders.

Montezuma House

Lansford W. Hastings, a lawyer from Ohio, who reached California by way of Oregon in 1843 in command of the immigrant party that bore his name, was active in the early settlement of the state. He traveled extensively in his effort to attract new residents, returning to the East in 1844, when he published *The Emigrant's Guide.* Coming back to California, he became agent for the Mormons and selected a site for the location of one of their colonies near the junction of the Sacramento and San Joaquin rivers. At the head of Suisun Bay he laid out a town and built an adobe for himself in 1847–1848. This building was called "Montezuma House," and Bayard Taylor, in *Eldorado,* thus makes mention of it: " 'City of Montezuma,' a solitary house on a sort of headland, projecting into Suisun Bay, and fronting the rival three-house city, New York of-the-Pacific." Because of lack of convenient timber, the Mormon colony did not settle there. During his stay, Hastings established a ferry across to the Contra Costa side. After leaving Montezuma, he became attorney for the northern district of California and was a member of the Constitutional Convention, where his geographical knowledge was of use in the fixation of boundaries.

This one-story-and-attic adobe built by Hastings stands one and one-quarter miles east of Collinsville and is well preserved inside its modern redwood casing. Numerous appliances for the manufacture of coins were found in the house after the builder left it; they were probably intended for the use of the Mormons in coining their money. Two families have since occupied the house. L. P. Marshall came from the East in 1852 with a herd of cattle and, hearing of the house, took possession of it with his two sons, John and Knox. The present occupants entered it after the Marshalls and have lived in it for fifty years.

Collinsville

Collinsville, now built largely on piles over the water, was named for J. C. Collins, who in 1859 pre-empted a part of the public domain that had been a part of the rejected Luco claim. The name of the town was changed in 1867 to New-port, which name it bore for about five years before going back to the original one of Collinsville. A very early salmon-canning establishment was located there.

Benicia

Benicia is situated on the Carquinez Straits on the north-east arm of San Francisco Bay. Until superseded by a bridge it was principally known as the terminus of the ferry crossing of the transcontinental railroad from San Francisco to the East. A small military reservation is located there and also two or three Catholic schools.

Once the rival of San Francisco and a pioneer religious and educational center, Benicia's early history adds a romantic chapter to the story of California. The town was laid out in 1847 by Dr. Robert Semple, who had taken part in the Bear Flag Revolt of 1846. At Sonoma, General Vallejo had been captured, and it was while escorting Vallejo as a prisoner to Sutter's Fort that Dr. Semple saw the beautiful Carquinez Straits for the first time. He was so impressed with the location as the possible site for a city that he made a bargain with his prisoner (whose estate covered much of the present Solano, Sonoma, and Napa counties) for the land now occupied by the city of Benicia. The site was deeded to Dr. Semple and Thomas O. Larkin in the autumn of 1846, and the city was laid out the following year.

The name first selected for the new town was Francisca, in honor of the wife of General Vallejo. For a time, Francisca's enthusiasts expected it to become the metropolis of San Francisco Bay, but the rivalry became so keen between it and the older town of Yerba Buena across the Bay that, when the latter changed its name to San Francisco, Francisca felt it necessary to adopt Benicia, one of Mrs. Vallejo's other names.

Many noted men and women connected with the early history of California are associated with this place: General Mariano Guadalupe Vallejo, donor of the land; Dr. Robert Semple, founder of the city and president of the State Constitutional Convention at Monterey in 1849; General Persifer F. Smith, commanding officer of the Pacific Division of the United States Army after California became a state; General Bennett Riley, who located the Benicia Arsenal; Thomas O. Larkin, the first and only American consul in California during the Mexican period; Concepción Argüello, the heroine of tales by Bret Harte, Richard White, and Gertrude Atherton.

In addition, in the early history of the town are found educators, jurists, and religious leaders of prominence, such as C. J. Flatt; Miss Mary Atkins, the first principal of the Benicia Seminary; the Rev. C. T. Mills, her successor and the founder of Mills College at Oakland; Judge Serranus Clinton Hastings, founder of Hastings Law College in 1878, who settled at Benicia in 1849 and was immediately appointed chief justice of the Supreme Court of California; Judge Joseph McKenna, who came there in 1855 and later became associate justice of the Supreme Court of the United States; the Rev. J. L. Breck, founder of two diocesan schools of the Episcopal Church in Benicia; and Bishop Wingfield, of the Sacramento Diocese, who had his bishopric in Benicia from 1876 to 1898.

For a time the then youthful Jack London frequented the water front there, and one chapter of his *John Barleycorn* echoes his experiences.

Von Phister's Adobe

On the south side of the alley that runs between West D and West C streets in Benicia, is the adobe built in 1847 and rented then to Captain E. H. von Phister. The Captain was keeping a store in the building in 1848, when a man by the name of Bennet stopped on his way to Monterey. Bennet had with him a few gold nuggets picked up by James Marshall at Coloma on the American River on January 24, 1848. Bennet told the story of Marshall's discovery, showed the nuggets, and thus helped to precipitate the rush to the gold fields. This old adobe has been marked by the Benicia Chamber of Commerce.

The California House

One of the first hotels in northern California was built in 1847 for Major Stephen Cooper. The bricks may have been made by William Tustin, who, with his wife and child, was the first white settler in Benicia. In this building the first wedding ceremony in Benicia was read, when Miss Frances Cooper, daughter of Major Cooper, became the wife of Dr. Semple. The ceremony was performed by the ex-governor of Missouri, L. W. Boggs, then alcalde of Sonoma.

The original adobe building was run as a hotel by Major Cooper and was known as the California House until 1854, when it was sold to John Rueger and turned into a brewery. The present structure, mostly of brick, was built many years after the first one, but a part of the original adobe wall is still intact. The California House is situated on the south side of H Street, west of First, and has been marked by the Benicia Chamber of Commerce.

First Protestant Church in California

On the site of what is now the Benicia City Park, the first Protestant church in California was established on April 15, 1849, by Rev. Sylvester Woodbridge, a missionary sent to California by the Presbyterian Church of New York. Until 1854, it was the only Protestant church in Benicia, and its pastor, Rev. Woodbridge, exerted considerable influence in the community, not only as preacher, but also as teacher, farmer, and keeper of the town records. He likewise established the first school in Benicia, which was one of the first in California. However, because of controversy over the question of adherence to the Union during the Civil War, the church declined, and was finally abandoned in 1871, Woodbridge moving to San Francisco. The site is marked.

The Benicia Barracks

The Benicia Barracks, one of the first United States military posts in the state, was established on April 30, 1849, by Lieutenant Colonel Silas Casey, in command of Companies C and G of the Second United States Infantry. The first buildings were erected that year, and in March the United States Army headquarters were established there, as Benicia promised to become the central military post of the region. It was strategically located on the Carquinez Straits, into which both the Sacramento and the San Joaquin rivers empty, and thus stood at the gateway to the interior of California and the mining regions. However, San Francisco, instead of Benicia, became the metropolis of San Francisco Bay and the port of entry to central California; consequently, the Benicia military post was superseded in importance by the Presidio at the Golden Gate.

In 1908 the Barracks was placed under the control of the Benicia Arsenal. The building, which still stands on the government military reservation about one-half mile from the town of Benicia, is unoccupied but well preserved.

The Benicia Arsenal

About one-half mile east of Benicia is the Benicia Arsenal, an ordnance depot of the United States Army established in August 1851, the first buildings being erected in 1852. Many troops have been stationed on the grounds from time to time. It was also a social center in pioneer days. The Arsenal is well preserved and still in use.

Peabody Hospital

Dr. W. F. Peabody established a hospital in Benicia in 1849 and "secured a large and paying patronage from returning miners," who were glad to exchange their gold dust for his services. He remained in the town for fifteen years, served on the Board of the Young Ladies' Seminary in 1852, and was mayor of Benicia in 1851–1852. The hospital building, now a private residence, is in a fine state of preservation and is located on the north side of H Street, between Second and Third streets.

The Port of Benicia

The Port of Benicia was of great importance for many years. Captain John Walsh, having led a seafaring life, settled there in 1849 and became deputy collector of the port. His house, one of three identical ones brought around the Horn in 1849, one being erected in San Francisco and another in Sonoma, was a constant pleasure to him. He spent much time in building and ornamenting it and in dispensing its hospitality to his many friends in the Army and Navy. This house is still standing in good condition at 117 East L Street.

The Pacific Mail Docks

The Pacific Mail Steamship Company established headquarters in Benicia in 1850, and the expansion of its business demanded the enlargement of its wharf in 1853. Foundries and machine shops were built, and the company enjoyed prosperity. Here the great seagoing ships of the period were repaired and coaled.

The "California," first steamer of the line to make the journey around the Horn from New York, arrived in San Francisco on February 28, 1849, crowded with passengers owing to the great influx of gold seekers at Panama. Coal for refueling for the return journey had to be brought to California by boat; and, as the first shipload had not arrived, the steamer was forced to await its coming. Refueled, the "California," with Captain Forbes in command, made an excursion to Benicia with a party of invited guests in April before starting on its return to New York in May. After the establishment of the docks, all the great boats of this company, the "California," the "Oregon," and the "Panama," berthed in Benicia between their regular trips until the removal of the Pacific Mail Steamship Company headquarters to San Francisco.

The competition of the overland railway, completed in 1869, was felt keenly by this company. As a result, in 1881 the Pacific Mail Docks, then badly in need of repair, were taken over by the Benicia Agricultural Works. Two of this firm's large brick buildings, now used by the Yuba Construction Company, are standing east of the Benicia-Martinez ferry slip.

The Masonic Hall

What is said to have been the first Masonic Hall built in California was erected in Benicia. The order was organized on March 6, 1850, and on April 19 a charter was granted. The building was begun in August and completed the following year. Located on the south side of J Street west of First, it is now used by the Veterans organizations and Kiwanis Club.

Many of California's prominent pioneers received their degrees in this old building, including George Yount, noted pioneer of Napa Valley. The lower floor of the Hall was used as a county courthouse until 1852, when the capitol building was finished.

The Solano Hotel

The old Solano Hotel, located on the corner of First and E streets, and still used as a lodging house, was built in 1851. For many years it was the leading hotel in that part of the state, many social functions being held there. Such noted men as Ulysses S. Grant, William Tecumseh Sherman, John A. Sutter, Governor Riley, Colonel Casey, the Indian fighter, F. L. Low, afterward governor of California, and Judge Hastings of Hastings Law College are included among those who signed the hotel register. The building has been marked by the Benicia Chamber of Commerce.

The Benicia Seminary

The Benicia Seminary was one of the first Protestant girls' schools in California, being established in 1852. Several denominations were interested in it, and Rev. Sylvester Woodbridge and Rev. Samuel Willey were two of its most notable promoters. The Governor of Vermont was also interested and sent out the first teachers on its faculty.

One of the most notable of the seminary's teachers was Miss Mary Atkins, and it was she who gave the school fame and success. She became its principal in 1854, and in 1855 she became the owner. In 1865, because of ill health, she sold the seminary to Rev. Cyrus T. Mills and his wife. Mr. and Mrs. Mills conducted the school at Benicia until 1871, when they removed to Oakland and established Mills College.

A board of the prominent business men of Benicia undertook to continue a school in the old Benicia Seminary. Rev. C. H. Pope, pastor of the Congregational Church, became the principal. After three years, Pope left California, and a Miss Snell became principal in his place. In 1878, Miss Mary Atkins, then Mrs. Lynch, bought her old school back again, and Miss Snell went to Oakland, where she established another girls' school. Later, Mrs. Mary Atkins Lynch again sold her school.

The old Benicia Seminary no longer exists, but it served its day well. It may, indeed, be called the "Mother of Seminaries," for not only did the famous Mills College of Oakland come out of it, but many members of its faculty went out to teach elsewhere in the state, and, in several instances, to found other seminaries. Some of Miss Atkins' pupils also became prominent teachers in public and private schools in California.

The seminary site is on the north side of I Street west of First.

St. Augustine College

When Dr. Robert Semple founded Benicia in 1847, he set aside certain grounds for a college. On these grounds Rev. C. M. Blake established an undenominational boys' school in 1852. This school lasted two years, when it was sold to C. J. Flatt, who reopened it in 1857. Under his management it flourished until 1867, when it became the Episcopalian College of St. Augustine, under the management of Rev. J. L. Breck, leader of a missionary company from the East. Dr. Breck was never able to carry out his plans for developing the college, and it later became a military school, but still under Episcopalian auspices.

Bishop Wingfield of the Sacramento Diocese had his residence on the campus grounds from 1876 to 1898. The Bishop's house, just north across the street from the present High School, is the only building left on the old campus grounds today. The gateway and the tree-lined drive are also there, but the Bishop now has his headquarters at Sacramento and the campus is being subdivided and sold for homes.

The Old State Capitol Building

Benicia was the third capital of the state of California, San José and Vallejo having been the first and second, respectively. The legislature first met in Benicia, in February 1853, in the new City Hall, which had been completed in December of the previous year and offered to the state by the town. The legislature remained in session until April 1854, when Sacramento, by one vote, finally won the fight for state capital.

From 1854 to 1859 the old State Building, located on the north side of G Street, was used as a county courthouse. From then until 1882 it served as a schoolhouse. Today it is used as City Hall, Library, and Red Cross Headquarters. It was marked by the State Society of the D.A.R. in 1924.

At the "Old Timers" reunion on September 12, 1936, a bronze tablet honoring Mariano G. Vallejo, Thomas O. Larkin, and Robert Semple was placed on a concrete shaft on a corner of the old Capitol Grounds at First and G Streets.

Saint Dominic's Church and Priory

The block bounded by Fourth, Fifth, East I, and East J streets has been from the beginning of the town the center of Catholic activity in Benicia; here, on the corner of Fourth and I streets, the first Catholic Church was built in 1852. Near the church was built in 1854 the Monastery for the first resident pastor, Father Vilarrasa, and the community. This Monastery was used until the erection in 1887 of a new Priory near East Fifth Street and facing I Street, and it is on this same block on I Street that the present brick and concrete Church of Saint Dominic stands.

Before the first of these edifices was built, Mass was celebrated in a building termed "The Hall" on the corner of East I and Sixth streets midway between the Arsenal and the Pacific Mail Docks. This building was owned by Judge James Barry, who had come to Benicia in 1850 and who frequently entertained the priests and the Bishop in his home. In still earlier years, devout Catholic families drove by oxcart to the Sonoma Mission for Mass.

Saint Dominic's parish was formally established on March 16, 1854, when Father Vilarrasa arrived from Monterey with his whole religious community and accepted the care of the parish in the name of the Order of Preachers. The Very Reverend Francis Sadoc Vilarrasa and the Most Reverend Joseph Sadoc Alemany, O.P., had arrived in San Francisco in December 1850. The latter, then an Archbishop, gave to the former for the use of the Order a church already built in

Benicia, an octangular frame building without pillars, that could seat two hundred people. The present church was solemnly blessed on March 17, 1890, shortly before the demolition of the early one.

The work most dear to Father Vilarrasa on his arrival in California was the establishing of a convent and a novitiate for the education of Dominican priests. These he had established in Monterey but had removed them to Benicia in 1854. The Dominican Priory existed until 1935, when it was changed to a vicariate. By this change very valuable old books brought from Spain in early years and protected within these walls were made available to interested historians.

St. Catherine's Convent

The Dominican Sisters arrived in California in 1850. They settled first at Monterey, where, in the spring of 1851, they established the first convent school in California. However, the old adobe building in which they were located was in bad condition, and as the population in Monterey was diminishing at that time, while that around San Francisco Bay was rapidly increasing, the Sisters decided to move to Benicia, which was a more central point.

St. Catherine's Convent was established in Benicia in 1854, and is still operated as a convent and school. Many of the young ladies of pioneer days received their education at this convent, and many orphan children were given shelter and schooling there. The first native daughter to enter the order was Concepción Argüello, who died at the convent on December 23, 1857.

St. Catherine's Convent is located on L Street, and has been marked by the Benicia Chamber of Commerce.

Concepción Argüello

Bret Harte, Richard White, and Gertrude Atherton have given to the literary world versions of one of the saddest romances of early California history, the story of Concepción Argüello and her Russian lover, the gallant Count Rezánof. Its opening chapter took place at the Presidio in San Francisco, but it is the beautiful aftermath of this tale which has become immortal. For years, Concepción waited for her lover. Not even a rumor of his fate reached her until several years later, and not until thirty-six years had passed was the manner of his death made known to her.

She refused all suitors, and at length joined the Third Order of St. Francis, giving her life to teaching the poor and caring for the sick. Up and down the state, from San Francisco to Santa Barbara and from Santa Barbara to Baja California, this gray-robed Sister of Mercy traveled on her errands of love.

When the first convent school in California was founded in Monterey in 1851, Concepción became its first novitiate, and, when the convent was moved to Benicia in 1854, she became its Mother Superior. She died at the Convent of St. Catherine in 1857, and lies buried in the Benicia Cemetery, where a simple marble slab and cross mark her grave.

Her kindliness and her charities, as well as the beauty and pathos of her romance, made her famous, so that she was venerated by all in her own time, and has since become "the most cherished figure in the romance of Alta California history."

Forty years on wall and bastion swept the hollow idle breeze,
Since the Russian eagle fluttered from the California seas;
Forty years on wall and bastion wrought its slow but sure decay,
And St. George's cross was lifted in the port of Monterey;
And the citadel was lighted, and the hall was gayly drest,
All to honor Sir George Simpson, famous traveler and guest.
Far and near the people gathered to the costly banquet set,
And exchanged congratulations with the English baronet;
Till, the formal speeches ended, and amidst the laugh and wine,
Some one spoke of Concha's lover—heedless of the warning sign.

Quickly then cried Sir George Simpson: "Speak no ill of him, I pray!
"He is dead. He died, poor fellow, forty years ago this day—
"Died while speeding home to Russia, falling from a fractious horse.
"Left a sweetheart, too, they tell me. Married, I suppose, of course!
"Lives she yet?" A deathlike silence fell on banquet, guests, and hall,
And a trembling figure rising fixed the awe-struck gaze of all.
Two black eyes in darkened orbits gleamed beneath the nun's white hood;
Black serge hid the wasted figure, bowed and stricken where it stood.
"Lives she yet?" Sir George repeated. All were hushed as Concha drew
Closer yet her nun's attire. "Señor, pardon, she died, too!"

BRET HARTE

Cordelia

The town of Cordelia, next to Benicia the oldest in the county, was named in honor of the wife of Captain Waterman, founder of Fairfield. Situated at the lower end of Green Valley on the route from Benicia to Sacramento, it was a stopping place for stages, and a hotel for the accommodation of travelers was operated there in 1855 by John Charles Pitman, a native of Bristol, England. A post office, afterward moved to Rockville, was established there in 1853.

Stone quarried near Cordelia was taken by barges through the Cordelia Slough and across the Bay to San Francisco, where it was used in building and in paving the streets. The shipping point was called Bridgeport; and when in 1868 the California Pacific Railroad was routed through it, the village of Cordelia lost its importance and its inhabitants moved to the newer settlement. The hotel also was moved into a new building and was called the Bridgeport Hotel, or sometimes the Pitman House. The name Bridgeport has now been forgotten, the new location is now called by the old name of Cordelia, and the Pitman House now bears the name "Cordelia Hotel" blazoned across its front—only it is no longer a hotel, but the residence of some of the descendants of the original owners.

Just north of Cordelia lies Green Valley, with its long-standing reputation for the early shipment of cherries. Three old buildings made of stone are still standing and in use: the Dingley Mill, now reroofed and used as a fruit-packing shed; the two-story winery, built about 1860 by John Votypka, who came from Austria in 1856, now also used for fruit packing; and a family residence built by F. S. Jones, a native of Vermont, who became a resident of the county in 1858 and planted large cherry orchards and whose descendants are still occupying the house and growing cherries along with other fruit.

Rockville

A settlement on the old stage road between Benicia and Sacramento was Rockville, site of an Indian encampment and burying ground before the Spanish came to the region. Through this place runs the approximate boundary line of the unconfirmed Soscol grant. An Indian, Jesús Molino, had the only house in the vicinity when, in the fall of 1847, Captain Von Phister passed through the place and found about a hundred acres of ground under cultivation, peas, wheat, and other crops being raised. The tools used on this farm are described as being very primitive; the plow was the "crooked branch of a tree armed with a pointed iron socket."

Here today are seen rock walls that were laid up as fences to protect the gardens of the American pioneers. The village that grew to the extent of having a few little stores where necessities could be purchased, a blacksmith shop, a post office, hotel, stage station, and church has dwindled so that it is scarcely noticed until the eye is arrested by the unornamented old stone church in its tidy surroundings. Unused since 1918, this green-shuttered edifice stands in a large churchyard enclosed by an iron fence where headstones mark well-tended graves dating back to the '50's.

The most interesting feature of this vicinity is the number of staunch buildings constructed of stone, the most notable one being the church, rectangular in shape, erected in 1856 by the Methodist Church South on land donated by J. M. and Carrie Baldwin and made of stone cut from the Baldwin quarries.

The Baldwin home, one-half mile from the church and on the same road, is an interesting frame house, commodious and comfortable looking, surrounded by a luxurious growth of trees and shrubs. A few yards from this house stands the sturdy stone barn, built in 1865, with its solid stone floor and its diamond-shaped windows.

In the southern end of the village of Rockville is another stone house. This one, on the west side of the road, and now remodeled beyond recognition, was the home of Samuel Martin, who came from Pennsylvania with his family in 1849 and located there in 1850. He brought herds of cattle, driven across the Plains and the mountains by men on horseback. His family with their personal belongings traveled in covered wagons drawn by wooden-yoked oxen with their clanging chains. Samuel Martin became the owner of 11,000 acres, and his house was built on the site of the Indian ranchería where once dwelt the Indian chief Solano. In the large, deeply imbedded boulders on the wooded knoll at the rear of this residence are the mortar holes worn smooth by the patient and incessant grinding of grain and nuts by, and for, the Indian families whose home had been there from some remote and unrecorded time until the advent of the pioneer Americans. The old Indian burying ground is in a field on the east side of the road opposite the house. Near the roadside a buckeye tree keeps vigil over the spot where Samuel Martin saw the body of Chief Solano laid away and where, until recent years, passers-by saw a rude wooden cross, buttressed with stones, that Solano's friends, assisted by Samuel Martin, had placed over his grave.

During their first years on the place, the Martin family harvested the crops of wild oats for hay for their cattle and gradually established fruit raising also as a means of livelihood. The ranch is still owned and operated by descendants.

Two other stone houses built a few miles away in the '60's were the Nathaniel Barbour house, still standing, and the Abernathy house, gutted by fire a few years ago so that the walls alone are standing.

Suisun

In October 1850 Dr. John Baker and Curtis Wilson sailed up the Suisun Slough to Suisun Island, a bit of hard upland rising from the marsh, and landed at the present site of the city of Suisun, where they discovered a herd of elk among the tules. In this same year Captain Josiah Wing began to run various watercraft to this island; and in 1852 he erected a warehouse on this "embarcadero" (the name by which the place was then known), and his schooner, the "Ann Sophia," transported the produce of the valley, beginning an industry that assumed vast proportions as the country became more populous. In 1854 the Captain and John Owen, who later became a merchant in the place, laid out the town of Suisun west of the wharf and just below the southern boundary line of the Suisun grant. In 1857 a church, the first one there, was built under the auspices of the "old school" Presbyterians, the land and building being donated by the people of the vicinity. In 1858 Captain Wing built a residence for himself in the town; and in 1868, the year of the coming of the railroad, Suisun was incorporated as a city.

The old Plaza is formed by the broadening of Main Street between Solano and Morgan streets. On a town map of 1877,

the post office, a flouring-mill, and the Robert's Hotel are shown as three of the buildings on the Plaza. The site of the Robert's Hotel of that time is now occupied by the New Arlington Hotel at the corner of Main and Solano streets. Years ago a plank walk nearly a mile in length spanned the marshy distance between Suisun and Fairfield. Today, after draining and filling work, the pavements of the two towns adjoin; and the transcontinental trains have a station on the dividing line that serves both towns.

California's Second State Capital

On the corner of what is now York and Sacramento streets in the city of Vallejo the second capital of the state of California was located in 1852. It had been moved from San José, the first state capital, to Vallejo because of the magnificent offers made to the state legislature by General Vallejo. Out of his vast estate, Vallejo had generously granted land on which to build the city of Vallejo and had also promised to erect a capitol building, lodgings, and social institutions, such as schools, churches, and asylums. The legislature, out of compliment to the General, named the new town Vallejo. Vallejo almost ruined himself financially in striving to carry out this gigantic plan.

A temporary capitol building was erected in the new town by the end of 1850, and on January 5, 1852, the legislature met. But it was dissatisfied with the poor housing facilities, and, as Vallejo found himself unable to fulfil his promises, the legislature moved out precipitately on January 12, and went to Sacramento. A devastating flood in the latter place caused them to adjourn on May 4, 1852, to meet again in Vallejo, January 3, 1853. On February 4 this "Peripatetic Government," or "Capital on Wheels," as it has been variously designated, was carried to the neighboring town of Benicia, where it remained until April 1854, when Sacramento finally won the fight for the state capital.

The buildings that comprised the town of Vallejo in 1850 were situated between Sonoma Street on the east, Bay Street on the west, Georgia Street on the north, and Pennsylvania Street on the south. Captain Frank Marryat, author of *Mountains and Molehills* and son of the famous writer of sea stories, was in California at this time and wrote of this settlement: ". . . . a few scrubby-looking hills that bordered on the bay, were staked off, and there was your town of Vallejo. About this time a store-ship, laden with iron houses, belonging to a friend of mine, sunk at her moorings during a heavy gale. When raised she was so full of mud, clay, and small crabs that there was no possibility of rendering her cargo fit for sale at San Francisco. The bright idea occurred to me of landing these muddy materials at Vallejo, and after allowing the tide to clean them, to convert them to some use in assisting to erect this capital that was to be 'made to order.' Landing my cargo on Vallejo beach at low-water mark, Canute-like, I ordered the tide to complete the very dirty work I had set before it, which it did, and, to finish the story here, in the course of six months I erected a very handsome hotel out of the materials. I felt rather pleased when it was finished, and painted, and handsomely furnished, to think what a butterfly I had turned out of the very dirty grub I had found in the hold of the old hulk. But the moral of the story lies in the fact that at this juncture the government altered their minds relative to the site of the capital, and selected Benicia in preference. The city 'made to order' was then pulled down and sold for old materials, to the great delight, as may be imagined, of myself and other speculators who had worked so assiduously to raise it, and had received no compensation."

A Methodist Episcopal Church was organized there in 1855. It was the outcome of a Sunday school which Mrs.

David G. Farragut, wife of the first commandant of the Mare Island Navy Yard, and others had been conducting for some months. In 1856 General John B. Frisbie donated a site for the edifice, giving a deed to five gentlemen, one of them being Admiral Farragut—"In trust for the Methodist Episcopal Church in the town of Vallejo." Upon this lot and largely through the exertion of the Admiral, a small rough structure was built which served for a time the double purpose of chapel and schoolhouse. When this was burned it was replaced by another, which was later sold. The site is now occupied by a furniture store at 420 Virginia Street. A new Methodist Church stands at the corner of Virginia and Sonoma streets.

Mare Island

The United States Navy Yard is located on Mare Island in San Pablo Bay, just across the Mare Island Straits from the city of Vallejo. The island was granted to one Castro by Governor Alvarado. Castro sold it to John B. Frisbie, son-in-law of General Vallejo, and Bezer Simmons, and, in 1851, Frisbie and Simmons sold it to W. H. Aspinwall and G. W. P. Bissell.

The story of the naming of the island is connected with General Vallejo. In the early days only one very crude ferryboat plied the Bay at this point. This was used, principally, for transporting horses and cattle. Once, while crossing the Carquinez Straits from Martinez to Benicia, the rude boat was caught in a sudden squall. The frightened animals stampeded, capsizing the frail craft. Some of them were lost, while others swam ashore. Among the latter was an old white mare much prized by her owner, General Vallejo. This horse swam to a neighboring island, where she was rescued a few days later. Vallejo was so glad to have his pet back again that he named the island "La Isla de la Yequa" (Mare Island).

In 1851 the United States Congress made appropriations for a naval dock on the Pacific Coast, and Mare Island was selected from among other possible points as offering the greatest facilities. In 1852, Congress authorized the selection of a site for a naval yard and depot in San Francisco Bay, and again Mare Island was chosen. On October 3, 1854, the national flag was first hoisted on the grounds. The first commandant of the Yard was David G. Farragut, who was stationed there from 1854 to 1858.

Mare Island covers 3,000 acres of ground and is ten miles in circumference. It is surrounded by deep water, in which there is sufficient anchorage for the fleets of the world. Its great ship yards and dry docks make it one of the most interesting places on San Francisco Bay today. Many relics of naval warfare are to be seen there, including cannon and figureheads from famous ships. These are kept in Alden Park, named for Commodore James A. Alden, who during his administration was instrumental in having trees planted for the beautifying of the Island. A large causeway, completed in 1935 to replace a smaller one, now connects the Island with the city of Vallejo.

Vacaville

After the Vaca family had been living on their part of Rancho Los Putos for about nine years, Manuel Cabeza Vaca deeded nine square miles of land to William McDaniel, who paid the sum of $3,000 in cash and agreed to lay out a town site on one of the square miles, to name it Vacaville, and to give to the former owner certain town lots. This agreement was fulfilled, and the plat of Vacaville was filed for record in 1851. The earliest occupation of the settlers in the vicinity of the town was the cutting of the rank growth of wild oats and the transportation of the resultant hay to landings on the Sacramento River.

A private school called Ulatis Academy was started in Vacaville in 1855 by a Professor Anderson from San Francisco. This Academy was succeeded by the Pacific Northwest College under the auspices of the Pacific Methodist Episcopal Church, South, with the Rev. J. C. Steward as its first president. It became the California College in 1870, when it was given to the care of the Baptist Church, which directed it until its removal to Santa Rosa in October 1871. The site of the college grounds, as shown on a map of 1877, was between Ulatis Creek and Gallin Street. The present high-school building is on the same plot of ground but nearer the highway.

In 1869 the Vaca Valley Railroad entered the town. Vaca Station, due east of Vacaville, was the junction of this railroad and the California Pacific Railroad. The name of this junction has been changed to Elmira.

Silveyville

Silveyville, on the old route between Napa and Sacramento, was a halfway house established by Elijah S. Silvey, who made two trips from Missouri to California, accompanied by his wife and two children, before settling permanently at this place.

Coming first in 1849, he remained in the West for two years. On his second arrival in California in 1852, he built a house for his family and a corral for the herd of one hundred milk cows that he had brought with him. His house became a country hotel, and in his corral the horses of the stagecoaches and freight wagons could be guarded during a needed rest. It became his custom to place a red lantern aloft at night to guide the travelers to and from the gold regions to this stopping place. In 1868 when the California Pacific Railroad was built through this territory, it missed this halfway house by a few miles. Thomas Dixon donated ten acres on the exact line of the railway for a station, and at that spot the town of Dixon grew up. Prior to this, Silveyville had attained considerable importance as a trading center, but all activity was soon transferred to the new settlement and Silveyville disappeared. The town site is now a farm. The ruins of the old hotel became farm buildings, parts of which are still in evidence; the bricks of the merchandise store were hauled to the new town and employed in constructing a hotel, which is still used as such; and the old Methodist Church was removed in the '70's to Dixon, where services are still held in it at its present location on the corner of Fitch and B streets.

Fairfield

The location of the county seat at Benicia caused dissatisfaction on account of its being on the very edge of the county —a serious defect in those days of slow locomotion when residents of its outlying sections had business to transact. The agitation for a change became acute in 1857 and, as a result, Captain R. H. Waterman, an old sea captain, once warden of the Port of San Francisco, who had purchased in 1848 with Archibald A. Ritchie four leagues of the Suisun grant, made a gift of a block of land and money to place the county buildings upon it. After some delay his offer was accepted; but before the buildings were erected the city of Vallejo captured the prize. Another vote of the people chose Fairfield, and the erection of the county buildings was begun. The plat of the town was filed for record on May 15, 1859. The name Fairfield, the name of the birthplace of Captain Waterman (Fairfield, Connecticut), was given to the place.

The home in which Captain Waterman lived is three miles north of Fairfield on a county road. The carefully built house, standing at the end of a long drive between eucalyptus trees planted by him, is in perfect condition; its marble fireplaces, its high ceilings, its curved staircase, and its Venetian blinds are in as good condition as if the owner only yesterday had stepped out of the place. Here his ship's bell of bronze is used as an alarm bell; a water tank from his boat is still holding water; nine fine old fig trees planted by him grow near the house; and in one of the barns on the place may be seen the strong wooden pegs which he preferred to iron spikes for holding the heavy timbers in position.

Rio Vista

In the fall of 1857 a town called "Brazos del Río" (Arms of the River) was laid out by Colonel N. H. Davis on his land at the upper end of the Ulpinos grant near the junction of Cache Slough and the Sacramento River. The wharf constructed by Colonel Davis in 1858 was sold the following year to the Steam Navigation Company, which doubled the size of the wharf to accommodate large steamers.

In 1860 the name of the settlement was changed to Rio Vista, but on January 9, 1862, heavy rains swept the town away. First a few houses went down the river; then next morning one by one the rest likewise floated out, as in the sunshine the homeless people watched from the hillside. After a time the inhabitants began to look about for a better location for new homes; negotiations were entered into with Joseph Bruning for a location in the upper edge of the Montezuma Hills in the northeast corner of his ranch. The new town plat was surveyed and recorded; a part of the site was on the Bruning property and a part on the adjoining ranch of T. J. McWorthy. The main street of the New Rio Vista now runs between these two old farms, but the "New," as used in the recorded plat, has been dropped in favor of simple Rio Vista.

Saint Gertrude's Academy was founded and erected in Rio Vista by Joseph Bruning in 1876 and was placed under the direction of the Sisters of Mercy. It was a boarding school for young ladies and a day academy for girls and small boys and was named in honor of Elizabeth Gertrude Bruning, wife of the donor. Located on an eminence in the western part of the town, it remained a popular and useful school for many years. The site, at the head of California Street, is now vacant.

Saint Joseph's Academy, built about the same time as Saint Gertrude's, was on the corner of Front Street and St. Gertrude's Avenue. The one building remaining is used as a private residence; another building has been moved to another part of town and is used as the I.D.E.S. Hall.

Landings

This county, so richly provided with streams and sloughs contributing their waters to the Bay of San Francisco through the smaller bays of Suisun and San Pablo, began at an early date to make use of water transportation for freight and passengers. Maine Prairie, within the confines of the Luco grant, was a shipping and trading point at the head of navigation on Cache Slough, originally merely an embarcadero. In 1859 Captain Merriwether settled on the south bank of the slough, and the place grew in number of inhabitants and in amount of industry until three years later the river flood of 1862 swept the settlement away. A few settlers re-established themselves in the same place, but others went to a more elevated spot about a mile away, where a town called Alton was started on the property of Rebecca Lewis and where a post office was established.

Newton Landing, north of Rio Vista, and Toland Landing were both on the Sacramento River. Near Toland Landing stood for many years the "Twin Houses," the home of Robert E. Beasley, one of the purchasers of the tracts sold from Rancho Ulpinos in 1855. Beasley had settled on the southern end of this grant in 1851 and established a ferry across from the mainland to Sherman Island, using a flatboat and chains. Like many another pioneer, he had ordered a house to be sent to him "around the Horn." When the house arrived in 1851, he was surprised to see that it had been framed a double house. This he erected about two hundred yards above the Landing and occupied for some years.

The town of Denverton grew out of Nurse's Landing. Dr. Stephen K. Nurse, part owner in 1849 of a four-mule stage line from Benicia to Sacramento, purchased property in 1853 on the slough afterward called by his name. There he built a house and the next year followed it with a store building and a wharf. The place, originally called Nurse's Landing, was given the name Denverton in 1858, honoring J. W. Denver, member of Congress from the district, who was locally popular at the time, because he had stood out firmly against a bill to confirm all existing land grants under ten leagues in extent.

On the establishment of a post office in Denverton, Dr. Nurse was made postmaster and held the position for nineteen years. In 1875 he constructed a telegraph line from Denverton to Suisun, which in 1876 was merged into the Montezuma Telegraph Company, of which he was president.

Bird's Landing, south of Denverton and on the long slough northeast of Collinsville, was originally a shipping point for John Bird, a native of New York, who had arrived in California in 1859. He purchased 1,000 acres of land in 1865 and started a storage and commission business. The building of the wharf afforded an easy means of shipment of hay and wheat, which were the main products of the surrounding farms. Bird's Landing in now a favorite ground for duck-hunting.

From Dillon's Point at the east end of the Carquinez Strait Patrick W. Dillon, farmer and stonecutter from Ireland, shipped stone which he quarried from his own ground. Having arrived in Benicia in 1851, he soon started the Pioneer Stone business in San Francisco, furnishing the stone for the old St. Mary's Cathedral.

On the slough northwest of Collinsville were Mein's and Dutton's landings. At Mein's Landing the house built about 1880 by Captain Mein, and his warehouse and dock of a still earlier date, are still standing. Lord Landing and Goodyear Landing on Goodyear Slough northeast of Benicia were also early landings within the county limits.

Binghamton Hall

In Maine Prairie Township a military company called the "Maine Prairie Rifles" was organized in 1863 during the Civil War period. The company headquarters were at Binghamton, where a brick, fireproof armory was erected. After the necessity for using the place as an armory had passed, an upper story was added to the structure for use as a public hall, the main floor being still used for a store. Later the whole building was purchased for a public school, which was conducted in the upstairs above the store. At the present time the downstairs is closed, and the old iron shutters are drawn over the windows, while the upper floor is used as a hall for the Farm Bureau.

SOURCES

[Credit is here given for source material, and permission to quote is hereby acknowledged]

CHAPMAN, CHARLES E. *A History of California: The Spanish Period.* The Macmillan Company, New York, 1921

CLELAND, ROBERT GLASS. *A History of California: The American Period.* The Macmillan Company, New York, 1922

Coy, Owen C. *Pictorial History of California.* University of California Extension Division, Berkeley, California, 1925

Crystal, Helen Dermody. *The Beginnings of Vacaville.* Master of Arts Thesis, University of California, 1933

Dykes, William. *Historical Benicia.* Folder published at Benicia

Gregory, Tom. *History of Solano and Napa Counties, California.* Historic Record Company, Los Angeles, 1912

Guinn, J. M. *History of the State of California.* Chapman Publishing Company, Chicago, 1904

Harte, Bret. "Concepción de Argüello," in *Complete Poetical Works,* Household Edition, Houghton Mifflin & Company, Boston, 1912, pages 81–82

Hendry, G. Manuscript notes on adobes

Historical Atlas of Solano County. Thompson & West, San Francisco, 1878

History of Solano County. Wood Alley & Company, San Francisco, 1879

Hunt, Marguerite, and Lawrence Gunn. *History of Solano County and Napa County.* 2 vols. The S. J. Clarke Publishing Company, Chicago, 1926

Hyatt, T. Hart. *Handbook of Grape Culture.* H. H. Bancroft and Company, San Francisco, 1867

Kemble, John Haskell. "The Genesis of the Pacific Mail Steamship Company in California," in *Historical Society Quarterly,* Vol. XIII, Nos. 3 and 4

Marryat, Frank. *Mountains and Molehills, or Recollections of a Burnt Journal.* Longman, Brown, Green & Longmans, London, 1855

Rensch, Hero Eugene. *Educational Activities of the Protestant Churches in California, 1849–1860.* Master's thesis in history, Stanford University, 1929

Sanchez, Nellie Van de Grift. "Solano, Noted California Indian," in *Motor Land,* XXXIII, No. 2 (February 1933), 8, 17

Taylor, Bayard. *El Dorado, or Adventures in the Path of Empire.* Seventh edition. George Putnam & Company, New York, 1855

SONOMA COUNTY

Sonoma County (Sonoma is of Indian origin and is said to have been the name of an Indian chief who was baptized "Sonoma" by the Mission Fathers in 1824) was one of the original twenty-seven counties. The county seat was located at the town of Sonoma from 1850 to 1854. Since 1854 it has been at Santa Rosa.

Discovery and Naming of Bodega Bay

On October 3, 1775, Juan Francisco de la Bodega y Cuadra, Spanish explorer, in the little schooner "Sonora" discovered the bay which bears his name. Bodega's voyage was a part of Spain's plan of approach to California from the sea and was very successfully accomplished, his careful observations and acts of possession being of great benefit to succeeding explorers and colonizers.

On October 20, 1793, Archibald Menzies, a naturalist of the expedition led by Captain George Vancouver, landed on the northwestern shore of Bodega Bay near an island (probably Bodega Rock), which the party named Gibson Island, in the hope of collecting botanical specimens. Partly because the ground had been burned over recently by the Indians and partly because of the season of the year he found few plants; and, to his disappointment, these few were similar to those that he had already found at Monterey and San Francisco. The party, who encountered a small group of peaceable Indians, did, however, find something of interest—a cross formed of a "piece of stave of a cask fastened to a pole by rope yarn."

Coming of the Russians

In 1741, Admiral Vitus Bering discovered the sea and the strait which bear his name. On this voyage he also discovered Alaska, whose waters were alive with fur seal. Other expeditions followed in 1765.

These activities on the part of the Russians undoubtedly had some influence in rousing Spain to the danger of losing California, and led to a speedier occupation of San Diego and Monterey. Subsequently, they led also to the founding of Missions, military posts, and pueblos north of San Francisco Bay.

The Russians eventually came down from the north and settled in California. By the close of the eighteenth century, the Russian-American Fur Company had established itself on the Aleutian Islands and on the coast of Alaska. These colonies were rich in furs but lacked immediate trade connections by which they could obtain food and other necessary supplies. Russia began to look southward to California, with its warm climate and fertile soil, from which she might supply her starving northern colonists with food.

In 1806 the Czar's chamberlain, Count Nikolai Rezánof, went to Sitka on official business. He found the colonists starving and stricken with scurvy and fever. Temporary relief was obtained from an American ship, but something more permanent was needed. Accordingly, Rezánof sailed south to seek negotiations with the Spanish officials of San Francisco, well knowing that trade with foreigners was forbidden.

The advent of the Russians into California is closely associated with the names of two women: in the opening chapter of the story, that of the lovely Spanish girl, Concepción Argüello, and, at the close, that of the Russian princess, Helena de Gagarin.

The story of Concepción and her love for the Russian Count Rezánof is told in connection with the San Francisco Presidio, where the romance began, and with Benicia, where Concepción spent the closing years of her life in the Convent of St. Catherine.

Undoubtedly, Nikolai Rezánof had political ambitions for Russia when he visited California in 1806. Doubtless, too, his courtship of Concepción Argüello, though not unmixed with diplomacy, was sincere. Certainly, its result was very propitious for his enterprise. That his ultimate purpose was to establish a Russian colony in northern California is quite clearly shown in the account of the expedition by Langsdorff, his friend and companion.

Rezánof's untimely death on the steppes of Russia prevented him from carrying out this plan himself. His purpose, however, was fulfilled a few years later by another Russian, Kuskoff, an agent of the Russian-American Fur Company.

Founding of Bodega Bay, Kuskoff, and Fort Ross

Rezánof had taken careful observations all along the coast on his return voyage to Alaska in 1806, and his report was most favorable. In 1809, Kuskoff came down from Sitka prepared to make temporary settlements. One was made at Bodega Bay and another in the Salmon Creek Valley six miles inland. Wheat was sown and harvested and, in August, with the precious store of food and 2,000 otter skins, Kuskoff returned to Alaska.

In 1811, Kuskoff came again as governor of the Russian settlements to be established in California. Although he went through no ceremony of taking possession of the land for Russia, he made permanent settlements at Kuskoff, in Salmon Creek Valley, and at Fort Ross, twelve miles north of the mouth of the Russian River on a high bluff overlooking the sea.

These settlements, especially the one at Fort Ross, were fortified and the Russian flag raised over them. Title to the territory for a considerable distance had been secured from the Indians who inhabited the region.

Today, nothing remains to mark the site of the village of Kuskoff save a few stones and a cross erected in 1923 to commemorate the first Christianizing of the Indians in northern California.

Fort Ross

The Russian settlements flourished, and the one at Fort Ross, which had been dedicated in 1812, became the center of activities. Not only did the settlers gather rich fur harvests on land and sea, but they became a prosperous agricultural community, supplying food to the Alaskan colonies as well as to their own people. During the years 1810–1822, they also carried on a considerable trade with their Spanish neighbors, who were very eager to secure the finely wrought manufactured articles which the Russians had to exchange for food supplies. This trade was carried on in spite of the fact that it was still officially forbidden. The Californians made opportunities for it, and almost no friction arose between the two peoples.

However, fear of the Russian advance in northern California undoubtedly led the Spanish authorities to explore and settle the regions north of San Francisco Bay in what are now Solano, Sonoma, and Marin counties.

In December 1823 the Monroe Doctrine was promulgated by the United States. Monroe was not only thinking of the newly liberated colonies in South America when he wrote this famous document; he was also considering the growing menace of the Russian Empire in Alaska and on the whole Pacific Coast, especially in California.

"The challenge of Fort Ross, with its cannon, its high palisades, its farms and herds of cattle—all tangible evidences of a permanent plan of colonization—was met by Monroe" in his message. It brought a definite end to any Russian program of acquiring California.

In 1824, Russia agreed to limit all future settlements to Alaska, but for nearly twenty years longer the colony at Ross remained independent of Mexican control. By 1840, however, the sea otter had been almost exterminated, and the Russian-American Fur Company could no longer maintain the American colonies. The political aspect had also ceased to be of moment, and, in 1841, the Czar sent orders for the withdrawal of all his subjects from California. The entire property was sold to Johann August Sutter of New Helvetia (Sacramento) and the colonists returned to Alaska.

The original inhabitants of Fort Ross consisted of about one hundred Russians and eighty Aleuts, the maximum population never exceeding four hundred. The settlement stood on a bluff above a little cove in the sea. The land sloped gently upward to the base of a range of hills covered with pine, fir, cedar, and laurel. The whole setting was exceedingly picturesque in a wild rugged way.

The fort itself was enclosed by a palisade built of heavy redwood timbers and mounted with cannon. Two octagonal blockhouses, surmounting the corners of the palisade, faced the sea on the southwest and the land on the northeast corners. Within the enclosure were nine buildings, among them the officers' quarters and chapel. Outside were fifty buildings, besides blacksmith, carpenter, and cooper shops and a large stable for two hundred milk cows. At the landing place on the little beach below was the boathouse, and there seagoing vessels were built.

Fort Ross has been owned by the state since 1906 and is only partially restored. The quaint Greek Chapel with its two octagonal towers, all built of redwood, remains, also the Officers' Quarters and one of the bastions, while the palisade and other buildings are in the course of reconstruction. A tablet was placed on the Chapel by the Native Sons of the Golden West in 1928.

Founding of Misión San Francisco Solano

In 1823, Governor Argüello became anxious to check the Russian advance into the interior north of San Francisco Bay, a region which Gabriel Moraga had already explored during the years 1812–1814, and earlier. The Governor advised Father José Altimira, a young priest newly stationed at San Francisco, to transfer the Missions of San Francisco de Asís and San Rafael Arcángel to Sonoma without delay. The Sonoma site was chosen because of its proximity to the Russians and because its climate was more favorable for the Indian neophytes than that of the former Missions. Without waiting for the final authorization by the proper church authorities, Father Altimira, young and zealous, set out at once to choose the site for the new Mission, the foundations for which were laid perhaps as early as 1823.

Such a radical and unauthorized step occasioned much dissatisfaction among the Fathers. A compromise was finally arranged, however, by which neither San Francisco de Asís nor San Rafael Arcángel was to be suppressed and the foundation of the new Mission was to be recognized. It was called Misión San Francisco Solano to distinguish it from Misión San Francisco de Asís at San Francisco. In later years it became popularly known as the Sonoma Mission.

This, the last and most northerly of the twenty-one California Missions, was a plain, low building with an overhanging roof covering the corridors of the wing. In 1880 it fell into private hands and was used as a storehouse. It has belonged to the state since 1903 and has been restored as a museum, adobe bricks taken from an old hotel being used in the restoration. It faces the northeast corner of the old Sonoma Plaza.

Founding of the Pueblo of Sonoma

In 1833, Governor Figueroa, one of the greatest figures in the history of Alta California, proceeded to occupy and settle Marin and Sonoma counties. The primary object in view was to force the Russians out of California. Other governors had attempted to do this, but Figueroa was the first to be successful.

The man who was chiefly responsible for this success was Mariano Guadalupe Vallejo, then military commander and director of colonization on the northern frontier. In the summer of 1833 he made an official tour of the Russian settlements, where he made his mission clearly known to the Russian governor.

Spanish settlements were attempted at Petaluma, Santa Rosa, and Fulton, but the hostility of the Indians caused their abandonment. Sonoma Valley was then chosen as the place of settlement, and in 1835 the Pueblo de Sonoma was founded by General Vallejo at Misión San Francisco Solano.

The Sonoma Plaza

General Vallejo himself laid out the new pueblo around a square or plaza, which was used as a drilling ground from 1835 to 1846 for the soldiers who defended the pueblo. On the northeast corner of the Plaza stood the Mission Church and next to it the Padres' House. Adjoining the Padres' House on the right was a larger adobe, in which Vallejo is said to have lived temporarily. This has long since disappeared. To the left of the Church stood the Barracks, a two-story building with a balcony. This house, which is still standing, was occupied by United States officers and soldiers in 1846.

Next to the Barracks, a large two-story adobe mansion was erected soon after the founding of Sonoma. Here General Vallejo lived during the eventful years preceding California's annexation to the United States. The Vallejo adobe had a balcony extending across the front, and on the southwest corner there was a tall square tower. This tower served as a citadel from which could be had an open view of the country in all directions. The tower has long since disappeared but the dwelling is still in use.

Other adobes were gradually built around the open Plaza. A few of these remain today, some of them incased in wood but still retaining their picturesque Spanish balconies. One of these is the Fitch House, erected by Jacob P. Leese, a brother-in-law of General Vallejo. After the conquest it was used as the headquarters of General Persifer F. Smith when in that section of the state. It is located next to the American Trust Company Bank Building.

General Vallejo's brother, Don Salvador, built himself a home west of the citadel, which, after being used as a lodging house, was demolished in 1935. A stage station on the corner of Spain Street and First Street West has taken its place. Another of Salvador's houses is today the Swiss Hotel.

Another picturesque remnant of early days is the Blue Wing Hotel opposite the Mission. This was a rendezvous for the Argonauts of '49 and is said to have been frequented by Joaquín Murieta, the notorious Mexican bandit of the '50's.

On the northwest corner of the Plaza stands Hotel El Dorado, a large two-story structure, with balconies extending across the front of two long wings. In 1848–1849 it was a one-story adobe and one of the finest hotels in California. Later a second story of wood was added, which, in the '60's, was occupied by the Cumberland Presbyterian College.

The Naming of Mount St. Helena

The web of romance which the years have woven about majestic St. Helena has been traced by Honoria Tuomey. "We have, handed down to us in the Sonoma region," she says, "stories to the effect that pioneer representatives of each of the three races of white men that, in turn, settled here, gave a name to the striking elevation that rises into the blue to twice the height of the mother range running northwest and southeast as far as the eye can see. The startling, almost incredible part is, that the name Helena was bestowed at each christening, and that neither party knew if that or any other name had already been given."

The earliest of these tales is that of a Spanish friar who, seeking a Mission site in the north, saw the great mountain rising above the wilderness. "After a few moments of fixed observation, there flashed to his mind a recollection of a tomb in an old abbey .... of Rheims, and he pointed to the distant mountain and exclaimed: 'Behold St. Helena on her bier! It is her effigy, even to the pall.'" Many subsequent visitors have affirmed that the great mountain, with its six symmetrical peaks and graceful, flowing lines, does resemble the form of a woman "asleep in eternal repose."

In 1841 there came to Fort Ross a beautiful young bride of royal blood, Princess Helena de Gagarin, niece of the Czar of Russia and the bride of Count Alexander Rotcheff, governor-general of Siberia and of the Russian colonies on the shores of the North Pacific.

Princess Helena was an enterprising and romantic young woman. Having read the fascinating descriptions of California by Kotzebue, the Russian navigator, she was fired with a great desire to see the interior of California for herself. Accordingly, she planned the expedition, since become famous, which included the ascent and christening of Mount St. Helena in the Mayacamas Mountains fifteen miles northeast of the present town of Santa Rosa.

Traveling by way of age-old Indian trails across the head of the Estero Americano and the Llano de Las Petalumas through the hill passes to the south, they proceeded northward over the old trail between Petaluma and Santa Rosa.

The mountain was ascended on June 20, after a difficult climb of 5,000 feet. At the summit, Princess Helena, enthralled by the magnificent view which met her gaze, had the Russian flag raised over the spot, and a memorial plate was placed, while she christened the mountain in honor of the patron saint of Helena, Empress of Russia.

In May 1853 the tablet placed on Mount St. Helena by the Princess was discovered by Dr. T. A. Hylton of Petaluma. It was later placed in the museum of the Society of California Pioneers in San Francisco but was destroyed in the fire of 1906. Dr. Hylton had made a facsimile of the tablet, and from this bit of paper, yellowed by time, a replica of the original plate was made years later. At the centenary of the founding of Fort Ross, in 1912, this tablet was placed on the summit of Mount St. Helena in honor of the first white people to make its ascent and to give it its name.

Mount St. Helena is the converging point of three counties, Sonoma, Lake, and Napa. On one of the northwest spurs of the mountain, seven miles northeast of Geyserville, are the Geysers, while on its southern slope, partly in Napa County and partly in Sonoma, lies the Petrified Forest. These natural phenomena indicate that Mount St. Helena is of volcanic origin.

The closing episode in the fascinating story of the triple christening of the great mountain is associated with the coming of the Americans. "Hardly had the Russian colonists abandoned their settlements in the Bodega and Fort Ross regions . . . . than, for the third time, Mount Saint Helena was confirmed in her name. It was a Yankee . . . . that performed the service . . . . none other than Captain Stephen Smith, noted pioneer ship-captain and trader in the days of the Dons, the first owner, by virtue of a Mexican grant, of the lion's share of the territory that the Russians had occupied during their stay in California . . . .

"There was little of the romantic in Stephen Smith, tough, sturdy old master of men and of the sea. He had a sailing vessel down at yonder landing that had come to him from Russian ownership. On the bows was borne its name, 'Saint Helena' . . . . and he proceeded to bestow it on the mountain that seemed an outpost between the wide interior of the continent and his far Pacific home."

The Bear Flag Revolt

In the spring of 1846 many American settlers in the Sacramento Valley and neighboring valleys believed that there was danger of their being driven from the country by General José Castro, commander of the Mexican Army. Encouraged by Captain John C. Frémont of the United States forces, a group of thirty-three men surprised General Vallejo at Sonoma and took possession of his fortified stronghold on June 14, 1846. In spite of the fact that Vallejo had always been favorable to the United States, he and his brother, Don Salvador, and Victor Prudon (Prudhomme) were taken prisoners of war and carried to Sutter's Fort, where they were kept for two months.

William B. Ide was left in command of the rebel forces at Sonoma. Since the action of the insurgents did not represent the United States government, the Stars and Stripes could not be raised in place of the Mexican flag. A new flag was therefore created for the purpose which was called the Bear

Flag of the "California Republic." It was made with a white field and a border of red on the lower part. A bear and a star were its emblems.

The Bear Flag Monument, in the form of a bronze statue representing a young pioneer clutching the staff of the Bear Flag, which floats above him, was placed on the old Sonoma Plaza by the state of California and dedicated June 14, 1915. A bas-relief on the face of the pedestal depicts the raising of the Bear Flag in 1846.

Petrified Forest

Surrounded by groves of living oaks, fir, and redwood, the famous Petrified Forest lies across a small valley from the western base of Mount St. Helena at an elevation of one thousand feet. The petrified trees comprising the group are mainly redwood, silicified and opalized. They lie "in two tiers in a parallelogram a mile in extent from east to west and about a quarter of a mile from north to south." The trees, measuring from three and a half to twelve feet in diameter and as much as 126 feet in length, were buried millions of years ago by lava from the great crater five miles to the north. The fact that the trees are all lying with their tops pointing away from Mount St. Helena seems to indicate that lava streams from the great cone caused their downfall and their ultimate preservation in forms of stone.

The forest was discovered in the '50's, but excavation was not begun until 1871, when Charles Evans, "Petrified Charlie," a prospector, homesteaded the land. Much of the brush, volcanic ashes, and deposits of silica which had pressed upon the trees for ages was removed by Charlie Evans, who enclosed the ground and charged a small fee to visitors. After his death in 1878 the place was given over to agriculture until 1914. On October 1 of that year it was acquired by the present owner, who has since carried on extensive developments. Under her management the place has become a goal for lovers of natural phenomena. In all the specimens found in this ancient "stone forest," the transmutation from wood to stone has been so perfect that texture and fiber are completely preserved, making it easy for scientists to determine species. Many of the trees are of great size, and, though broken, retain the relative positions of the pieces. The largest tree in the group was uncovered in 1919 at a depth of ninety feet. It lies intact and is one of the most perfect specimens known. Professor Erlingdorf of Princeton University found in 1930 twelve varieties of prehistoric fossilized leaves on the property, which he pronounced a valuable discovery in the scientific world.

The Petrified Forest is located on the Petrified Forest Highway between Sonoma and Napa counties and is twelve miles northeast of Santa Rosa and five miles west of Calistoga.

The Geysers

For many moons before the coming of the white man, the Indians had brought their sick to the healing waters of the mineral springs which abound in the vicinity of the Geysers. To the red man the region was the last creation of the Great Spirit, a place sacred to his medicine man, who worked miracles through the wonders of its medicinal waters.

In April 1847 William B. Hackett, a pioneer hunter and trapper, came suddenly upon the Geysers while tracking a wounded bear. Returning to Sonoma, he told his friends that he had found the gates to the Inferno.

The variety and beauty of the region, its hissing fumaroles or volcanic vents from which shoot immense jets of steam a hundred feet or more into the air, and many other natural wonders may well inspire the modern wayfarer with awe and reverence, if not with superstition. Some of the most notable features are known as "The Devil's Grist Mill," "Steamboat Geyser," "The Witches' Cauldron," and "The Mountain of Fire."

Since 1854, when twenty people registered at the inn, an ever growing stream of visitors have come to see this attraction. During 1875 as many as 3,500 passed that way. The first stage road, which went only to the foot of the mountain, had then been extended to the Geysers themselves and since 1869 had been a toll road. The first wheeled vehicle to go into the place was a double team and buggy driven in by R. C. Flournoy on May 15, 1861. The old hotel, built in 1856–1858 from lumber sawed on the spot, is still a landmark in the region. On its register are the names of many famous people: U. S. Grant, William McKinley, Theodore Roosevelt, Mark Twain, Horace Greeley, Garibaldi, William Jennings Bryan, and J. Pierpont Morgan.

The Geysers are located eighteen miles east of Cloverdale and twenty-five miles northeast of Healdsburg on a good modern highway. They may be reached from the Redwood Highway from Cloverdale, Geyserville, or Lytton.

Rancho Arroyo de San Antonio
Rancho Roblar de Miseria

After the issuance on August 17, 1833, of the government decree to secularize the Missions and to give their lands to private individuals, inducements were held out to Mexican citizens to migrate to California. A colony under the charge of Don José M. Hijar arrived in Alta California in 1834, and one of the number was Antonio Ortega, a Mexican officer, who came with the express purpose of obtaining a grant of land. Proceeding northward, he arrived at Sonoma Mission and was at once appointed administrator by General Vallejo at a salary of $500 per year. This appointment was approved by Governor Figueroa.

Antonio thereafter married Francisca, daughter of Juan Miranda, and applied for permission to settle upon Rancho Arroyo de San Antonio, consisting of three square leagues about eight miles from the town of Sonoma. The permission granted, he at once built a log house and corral and stocked the place with cattle and horses which he purchased from Vallejo. The cultivation of a portion of the land was begun; fifty or more acres were planted to corn, pumpkins, and many other kinds of vegetables. His family and that of his father-in-law moved to the rancho and lived as one family, the father-in-law being placed in charge of its operation.

The difficulty regarding the title seems to have arisen out of a series of mishaps. The first of these was that when Ortega was ready to file his map of the property the Departmental Assembly (the body to which it must be presented) was not in session. The papers were said to have been left in the keeping of Governor Alvarado. Some years later, in 1843, Ortega took some of his stock to Oregon and did not return for three years. Upon his return he found that his father-in-law was claiming a part of his rancho, and litigation ensued.

Consequently, on February 17, 1852, and on February 7, 1853, rival claims were filed, one based on Miranda's claim and the other on Ortega's. The two attorneys became convinced that Miranda's claim was not a just one and accordingly abandoned it. On June 26, 1855, the Land Commission confirmed the Ortega claim. The matter was afterward reopened by T. B. Valentine, one of the attorneys, who claimed that the land had actually been granted to Miranda in October 1844, while Ortega had been absent in Oregon. The matter was finally compromised. Of the area, 13,316 acres were sold as public land.

Rancho Roblar de Miseria seems to have been granted in 1845 to the young Mexican captain, Juan Padilla, who, the next year, took part in the Bear Flag Revolt and shortly afterward removed to the southern part of the state. A group of eight men, one of whom was Daniel Wright, filed claim for this tract of four square leagues on February 24, 1852, and it was patented to them January 18, 1858.

The city of Petaluma, whose land titles in certain areas were long clouded by the Rancho San Antonio controversy, lies not only on a part of that grant but also on a part of Rancho Roblar de Miseria and of Rancho Petaluma.

Mariano G. Vallejo and His Lands

The dominant figure in provincial affairs north of Monterey in the '30's and the '40's was Mariano G. Vallejo, who at the end of that period was chosen one of the eight California members of the Constitutional Convention held in Monterey in September 1849.

Mariano Guadalupe Vallejo, born in 1808, was the son of Ignacio Vallejo and his wife, María Antonia Lugo, who lived in Monterey County. In the school at Monterey, where he was educated, he had as schoolmates Juan B. Alvarado and José Castro. A military career being his choice, he entered the Monterey Company in 1823 as a cadet and was promoted to *alferez* in San Francisco in 1827. In 1830 he was elected to the *diputación,* in 1832 was married to Francisca Benicia, daughter of Joaquín Carrillo, and in 1834 was elected *disputador suplente* to congress.

José Figueroa, governor of Alta California from 1833 to 1835, chose him *comisionado* to secularize Misión San Francisco Solano and to found the town of Sonoma. In compensation for his services, the Governor gave him large tracts of land north of the Bay and on July 5, 1835, a plot of ground in Pueblo de Sonoma. On this plot, extending 150 varas along the Plaza with a depth of 130 varas and lying across the way from the Mission, General Vallejo built a house which he made his home. This house still stands and is now occupied as a residence, although it has been put to other uses during intervening years. Adjoining it are the old barracks. Both house and barracks face Spain Street along one side of the Plaza, and from the veranda that stretches in front of both may be seen the marker placed on the site of the raising of the "Bear Flag," the Mission, and the old "Blue Wing Hotel."

Vallejo was the outstanding native Californian of his day; his position came to him because of his ability and experience, although he was not personally as popular as his contemporaries, José Castro and Juan B. Alvarado, on account of his reserved and aristocratic manner. Advanced to the rank of colonel on November 29, 1836, he assumed the position of commander general, took the oath of allegiance to the new government, and issued a patriotic proclamation on that occasion. From this time his efforts and money were expended to an even greater extent than before to serve his country. Thinking the plan to be better, he induced the Mexican government to unite the military and civil commands in one officer and turned over his command to Governor Micheltorena in 1842.

Rancho Soscol, a tremendous area in Solano County, was granted to him for supplies furnished the government. His ranch home, however, was not there but in Sonoma County on Rancho Petaluma, ten leagues, which had been granted to him October 22, 1843. The United States patent issued under Ulysses S. Grant in 1874 was founded, however, on the ten-league grant, or regrant, made by Governor Micheltorena on October 2, 1843, augmented by another five leagues granted on June 22, 1844.

On Rancho Petaluma, which he may have occupied for several years before the formal granting, the farseeing General Vallejo carried out a plan of agriculture that benefited not only himself but also the Indians who labored for him.

In the foothills on the Sonoma Mountains, he built between 1834 and 1844 a large adobe house—the Casa Grande. It still stands, deserted but picturesque, above the wide, open fields of Petaluma Valley. It was larger and built on a grander scale than any other adobe in northern California. Its three facades, the main one two hundred feet long, are shaded by broad balconies, while the spacious patio, open on the fourth side, overlooks the valley below. The walls, three feet thick, are made of adobe bricks, and its framework is constructed of beams hewn from solid trees and bound together with rawhide thongs as strong as iron. Not a single nail is in evidence anywhere. Stout iron grills and solid shutters enclosing the windows, and wickets, which in times past afforded double protection in the event of an attack, make of the place a veritable fortress.

This was the center of the ranch activities: there apprentices were taught the ways of thrifty living; from this headquarters, the cattle ranges, the planting of the vast fields, and the harvesting of crops were managed; while close to the hacienda the curing of meats, the drying of herbs, the making of baskets, the weaving of blankets, and other more sedentary operations were carried on. Looking through the long verandas as they remain today, one can easily picture groups of dusky workers young and old. The railings of the balconies seem a fitting place for daylight inspection of finished weaving, while under the protecting roof of the inner three-sided patio may well have been stored piles of colorful squash and pumpkins beneath the festoons of peppers so essential to Spanish cookery.

Casa Grande is now owned by, and under the care of, the Native Sons of the Golden West. A placard erected by the roadside in front of the house reads: "Old adobe, Historical Landmark, State of California. No. 18."

Another grant of which General Vallejo purchased a part was Rancho Agua Caliente, which had been given to Lazaro Piña in 1840 by Governor Alvarado. It stretched along Sonoma Creek beyond the outer line of the lands of Pueblo de Sonoma. Thaddeus M. Leavenworth, who had come to California as chaplain with Stevenson's Regiment of New York Volunteers, became the owner of that part of the grant lying closest to Sonoma.

General Vallejo purchased two pieces of ground in this rancho: these were known as Vallejo Tract No. 1 and Vallejo Tract No. 2. On Tract No. 1, containing 197.53 acres and adjoining the property of Leavenworth, the General built a frame mansion in 1850. He called it Lachryma Montis or "Mountain Tears," because of the large springs of hot and cold water which issue from the hillside near by. He lived there many years before his death in 1890, and his burial place is on an eminence north of Sonoma quite near Lachryma Montis.

In the immediate vicinity of the residence is a building called the Swiss Chalet. Its exterior is of wood and brick, the lumber having been brought around the Horn in 1849–1850. The State Park Commission purchased in 1932 both Lachryma Montis and the Swiss Chalet and the surrounding grounds of seventeen acres. After its purchase, the family mansion was found to require renovation, in the course of which the adobe bricks used as filling between the exterior and interior walls were removed and the wooden timbers were treated for preservation against the inroads of termites.

The house built by the original grantee, Lazaro Piña, of Rancho Agua Caliente stands on the piece of ground purchased from the estate of Captain Joseph Hooker. It is constructed of adobe bricks with wood finishing. Its first owner, Piña, was drafted into the Mexican War and lost his life in the Battle of Cerro Gordo, leaving a wife and children. Hooker, who attained his rank of captain in that war, applied for and received 550 acres. He was afterward made a general in the Civil War and finally returned to the East to live. This house, built by Piña, is known as the Hooker House.

Rancho Cabeza de Santa Rosa
Rancho Llano de Santa Rosa

In the year 1841 two tracts of land in Sonoma County were granted to relatives of General Vallejo's wife, Señora Francisca Benicia Carrillo. These tracts were Rancho Cabeza de Santa Rosa, given to the widowed mother, and Rancho Sotoyomi, given to Henry Fitch, a brother-in-law. A third grant to a member of the Carrillo family was Rancho Llano de Santa Rosa made to Joaquín, a brother, in 1844.

Both grantees of 1841 were residents of San Diego. Fitch continued to live in the south. For Señora María Ignacia López de Carrillo a house was built on her Rancho Cabeza de Santa Rosa, and she moved into it with her unmarried children and continued to reside there during the remainder of her life. This house, which still stands about two miles east of the city of Santa Rosa, was the first dwelling erected in that vicinity. The city of Santa Rosa, now the county seat, is situated upon a part of her grant.

In 1853, the son Julio filed claim for a part of the property, two square leagues lying between Rancho San Miguel and Santa Rosa Creek, and he built his house near the stream on a site that is now Second Street in Santa Rosa. In the early days of the settlement, he gave land for a plaza where the Courthouse now stands.

After the death of the mother, Juana de Jesús became the wife of David Mallagh and continued to live in the family home. When the merchandise firm of Mallagh and MacDonald was formed in 1851, a part of this house was used as a store. Another sister, Felicidad, became the second wife of Victor Castro. Both of these daughters inherited portions of their mother's land which lay across Santa Rosa Creek from the portion belonging to their brother Julio.

The eldest son of the family, who was named Joaquín after his father, received the grant of Llano de Santa Rosa from Governor Micheltorena in 1844. This tract of three square leagues adjoined his mother's property and lies due west of Santa Rosa. The tract previously had been granted to Marcus West, who had allowed his right to lapse; and, upon petition, it was regranted to Joaquín Carrillo, who at once built a small house and afterward erected a large and comfortable one. This adobe, long ago torn down, faced the east on what is now Petaluma Avenue in Sebastopol. This street was once a part of the old Spanish Trail and later was used by the stage lines.

Rancho Sotoyomi

Henry Fitch, a dashing young sea captain from Massachusetts, met Señorita Josefa Carrillo upon his arrival in San Diego in 1826. Three years later, plans were made for their marriage, but certain legal technicalities arose whereby the marriage was postponed. The fact that the young captain was a foreigner was the main obstacle, but, since the parents gave consent, the date for the ceremony was set for April 15, 1829. At the last moment the friar who had planned to officiate weakened and decided that he could not do so. Sympathizing relatives and friends made it possible for the young people to elope on the captain's boat the next day, and the marriage took place in Valparaiso on July 3.

Difficulties beset the pair on their return to California a year later. Finally, as penance, Captain Fitch was asked to give a "bell of at least fifty pounds in weight for the church at Los Angeles." This he did and thereafter lived untroubled in San Diego, where he kept a store.

In 1841 Captain Fitch received a grant of three square leagues of land lying in Sonoma County, where lived his wife's sister and her husband, Mariano G. Vallejo. Eight more leagues were added to the tract in 1844. Instead of residing on the property, Captain Fitch traveled north, inspected it, made arrangements for its upkeep, and returned to his merchandising business in the south. He sent an acquaintance, Cyrus Alexander, to live there and agreed to give him, as remuneration, two leagues of land for his own. Alexander, a trapper and trader, who had reached San Diego in 1833, accepted the task outlined by Captain Fitch. Alexander Valley, east of Healdsburg, is named for him, and his descendants are still residing on a part of his land.

Before Captain Fitch died in 1849, he had built a large two-story adobe on his property. Later his widow and children occupied it. This stood south of Healdsburg, and fell in 1906.

Rancho El Molino

In 1836 a tract of land along the Russian River was granted to Juan Bautista Roger Cooper, one of the most prominent English-speaking pioneers of the state. His home, after he gave up a seafaring life, was at Monterey, where he met and married Encarnación Vallejo.

When Mariano G. Vallejo, Captain Cooper's brother-in-law and military commander and director of colonization on the northern frontier, returned to Monterey after an official visit to Bodega and Ross, he told Cooper of the productive region that he had seen. That region, lying between the Estero Americano and the Russian River, was then inhabited by only a few Russians and Indians. Vallejo encouraged Cooper to make a tour of inspection. This Cooper did and obtained a grant of four leagues along the Russian River in exchange for two tracts previously held by him on the American River.

On his new grant he erected a sawmill and called the tract Rancho El Molino. He also built a house of redwood lumber and stocked the land with cattle. In the journal kept by Philip L. Edwards of the Ewing Young journey from Oregon to California to purchase cattle, Edwards mentions a visit to Cooper's mill in 1837. At that time Young left at Rancho El Molino eight white men and three Indians belonging to his expedition.

Since the question of Russian encroachment on Mexican territory was troubling Vallejo during those years, in order to discourage the invasion he planned to establish settlers on land that might otherwise be occupied by representatives of that nationality. At Vallejo's request for persons of the proper qualifications for such a duty, Captain Cooper suggested the names of three men, McIntosh, Dawson, and Black, whom he had known as sailors. All three were granted tracts of land between the Estero Americano and the Russian River.

Rancho Estero Americano

Rancho Estero Americano lay to the east of the Rancho Bodega of Stephen Smith, both ranchos having the Estero Americano for a southern boundary. Consisting of two square leagues, it was granted in 1839 to Edward Manuel McIntosh, a naturalized Scotch sailor. McIntosh engaged in 1833 in otter hunting with Job Dye and afterward became an agent of the Hudson's Bay Company. He, James Dawson, and James Black were originally sent to the western Sonoma County region by Vallejo to discourage the advance of the Russian settlements. In partnership with James Dawson, who established in 1834 a sawmill on Salmon Creek, he built a frame house in which the two lived together. This companionship lasted until 1839, when the grant of land was made to McIntosh alone. Offended by this turn of affairs,

Dawson sawed the house in two and moved his half by ox team some distance to the east, where he later obtained a grant of land for himself. McIntosh afterward became alcalde at San Rafael and sold his land to Jasper O'Farrell, who was the claimant for it in 1852.

Rancho Cañada de Pogolimi

Along the Estero Americano lies Rancho Cañada de Pogolimi granted in 1844 by Governor Micheltorena to James Dawson, the Irish sailor who had turned lumberman for a time with Edward Manuel McIntosh on the adjoining tract of land. After his quarrel with McIntosh, which resulted in his moving his half of the house which they had owned jointly, he established himself on Rancho Cañada de Pogolimi and the next year married at Sonoma a young girl, María Antonia Caseres (eldest daughter of Francisco Caseres [or Caceres], at one time the only Spanish resident of Yerba Buena), whom he brought to his home. His death occurred within a few years, and his widow, who later married Frederick Blume, continued to reside on the property.

Rancho Cañada de Jonive

Jasper O'Farrell, who had received the grant of Rancho Nicasio in Marin County as remuneration for services in surveying land grants, exchanged that piece of property for the Cañada de Jonive, which was held by James Black. In 1849 O'Farrell married Mary McChristian and brought her to live on the Jonive rancho, which they renamed the Annaly Ranch. Their home was an adobe dwelling erected at the foot of Jonive Hill near Freestone by the former owner. It was built about 1848 of adobe and wood. Later turned into a store, it fell in 1906. Its ruins, covered with trailing greenery, are now a feature in a private garden at Freestone.

This rancho lay to the east of the Estero Americano and originally contained two and one-half square leagues. Patent for it was issued to Jasper O'Farrell in 1858.

Rancho Bodega

Rancho Bodega, consisting of eight square leagues on the coast between Estero Americano and the Russian River, was granted to Stephen Smith by Governor Micheltorena on September 12, 1844. When the land was confirmed in 1859 and patented to the heirs of the grantee, the more than 35,000 acres claimed were accepted by the court as being "the same land described in the grant to Stephen Smith (now deceased)."

Smith, a native of Maryland who visited California in 1841, came from Peru, where he had spent a little time. On this visit, he made plans to return to California after a trip East and to set up a sawmill. This he did. The mill machinery was brought from Baltimore and set up in the redwood region east of Bodega Head. Although confident that the country would eventually belong to the United States, he obtained Mexican citizenship in order to become a landowner. Within two years after receiving the grant of Rancho Bodega, he had the pleasure of raising the United States flag over his property. The eastern boundary line of his rancho lay a little way to the east of his mill, which was placed to the north of Salmon Creek. His house was erected near to Salmon Creek and north of the Estero Americano, the boundary between Ranchos Bodega and Blucher. To both of these tracts he laid claim, and both were awarded to his descendants on that claim.

After the death of Stephen Smith in 1855, his widow married another southern gentleman, Tyler Curtis, in 1856. Squatters caused trouble, resulting in what is called the "Bodega War"; and Curtis was forced to sell land including the part known, even today, as the Homestead Tract. Upon it is the site of the Kuskoff settlement where the flag pole erected by the Russians in 1811 still stands. Captain Smith's adobe mansion, built in 1843, stood on the site of this village. The house was oblong in shape with a row of five dormer windows opening from the upper story on the balcony at the front.

The Curtis family moved to San Francisco in 1872. In the '90's a fire burned the inflammable part of the old dwelling, leaving only the adobe walls standing. On October 3, 1925, the ruins of this house were appropriately marked by the Native Sons of the Golden West.

Adjoining Rancho Bodega on the north was Rancho Muniz, of 17,760 acres, bounded on the west by the Pacific Ocean. It was granted in 1845 to Manuel Torres, a brother of the wife of Stephen Smith.

Rancho Mallacomes, or Maristal y Plan de Agua Caliente

This rancho, lying in the upper part of Knight's Valley, consisted of 17,742 acres granted October 14, 1843, to José de los Santos Berryessa by Governor Micheltorena. The grantee, a son of José Reyes Berryessa of Rancho San Vicente (in Santa Clara County), was a soldier at Sonoma from 1840 to 1842 and alcalde there in 1846.

Knight's Valley, in which this grant lay, received its name from Thomas P. Knight, a native of Maine, who came to California in 1845. After he reached the Sierra on his overland journey, an explosion of a keg of powder under his wagon destroyed all of his possessions, including a stock of goods which he had expected to sell. He took part in the Bear Flag Revolt and then went to the mines before settling down to be a farmer in Napa and Sonoma counties.

Knight lived in the two-story adobe built by Berryessa and made additions to it. A part of the house still stands in Knight's Valley west of Mount St. Helena. The ground level is constructed of stone.

Among many other settlers on this rancho were Holme, Rockwell, Woodshire, Martin E. Cook, and Rufus Ingalls.

Rancho Los Guilicos

John Wilson, who reached California in 1837, was the grantee of Rancho Los Guilicos, containing 18,833 acres and given by Governor Alvarado. It was patented in the name of William Hood in 1866. Afterward it was owned jointly by Mrs. Wilson and William Hood, who had purchased a part of it. The descendants of the latter still own a part.

This rancho lies between Santa Rosa and Sonoma, the town of Glen Ellen being on its southern tip. The Southern Pacific stations of Kenwood and Melitta are on this old grant.

A vineyard was planted in 1858, and a winery was built in 1861 on this property. The winery, a three-story stone structure, is on the bank of Los Guilicos Creek. On the opposite side of the stream is the wine cellar and distillery.

Rancho Tzabaco

The name of this grant is an Indian word, the name of either the locality or the Indians that inhabited it.

Rancho Tzabaco was granted in 1843 to José German Piña, son of Lazaro Piña of Rancho Agua Caliente. In the central part of this land rises the dividing ridge between the Russian River, that runs across the end of the rancho, and Dry Creek Valley, which is also within the grant boundary. In this valley is an old white-walled, one-story adobe, sometimes called a fort. It was built by the grantee about 1841 and sits back among trees about two hundred yards west of the Redwood Highway. The byroad on which it stands turns off the main highway about eight miles north of Healdsburg.

Rancho San Miguel

Rancho San Miguel, containing 6,663 acres granted to Marcus West in the years 1840 and 1844, was claimed in 1852 by his widow, Guadalupe Vásquez de West, and their three children. A creek running through its northern part is called Mark West Creek. On the bank of this stream, West had a store. His large adobe house near the bridge on the Santa Rosa–Healdsburg Road not far from the store was destroyed long ago. The family burying ground was in the rolling hills to the east of the store and the road. The Northwestern Pacific Railroad and the state highway running northwest of Santa Rosa pass through this grant.

Miscellaneous Grants

Among the other grants of land made by the Mexican government and later recognized by the United States certain ones may be specified.

Rancho German, which extended along the Pacific Ocean in the extreme northwestern part of the county, originally contained 17,580 acres granted by Governor Pico to Ernesto Rufus and was claimed jointly by a group of six men in 1852.

Rancho Rincón de Muscalón lay on both sides of the Russian River and contained 8,766 acres. It was granted in 1846 to Francisco Berryessa by Governor Pio Pico and patented to Johnson Horrell and others in 1866.

Rancho Caslamayomi, or Laguna de los Gentiles, near the Russian River but separated from it by rough and broken chaparral hills, was granted to Eugenio Montenegro in 1844 by Governor Micheltorena and contained eight leagues.

Rancho Cotati, granted to Juan Castañeda in 1844, was patented to Thomas Page in 1858. Page had been a sheriff in the Sonoma district in 1847. The rancho contained 17,238 acres and lay to the south of Santa Rosa. The Northwestern Pacific Railway passed through it from northeast to southwest, and the station of Cotati is in the southwestern quarter of the rancho.

Two border-line ranchos, the Blucher and the Laguna de San Antonio, extended over the county line into Marin County. Rancho Huichica, which consisted of 18,704 acres lying southeast of Sonoma, was patented to J. P. Leese in 1859. It was situated partly in Napa County.

The Vineyard of Colonel Haraszthy

Sonoma County ranks second to Napa County in the productiveness of her vineyards and wineries, but it was here that the first wine grapes from European countries were successfully grown. Colonel Agaston Haraszthy, a Hungarian nobleman, father of wine making in California, attempted first to ripen grapes from his imported stock at Crystal Springs in San Mateo County in 1852 but met with slight success in that locality. Looking for a proper soil and climate for the purpose, he moved to the protected Sonoma Valley, where already one variety of wine had been made from the ordinary Mission grape by Governor Vallejo.

In 1856 Colonel Haraszthy purchased a piece of land east of the town of Sonoma that became known as the Buena Vista Vineyard and immediately placed his son, Attila, in charge. By 1858 he had planted 85,556 vines, in addition to thousands of cuttings which he had started in his nursery. Many of these vines were of choice foreign varieties. During the year of 1858, at the urgent request of the State Agricultural Society, Colonel Haraszthy wrote an article describing minutely the planting and practical management of a vineyard and the subsequent making of the fruit into mature wine. From that time on, "a tidal wave of inquiry swept over the quiet valley of Sonoma, strangers came and went, the Pony Express and the United States Mail were laden with letters, papers, pamphlets, cuttings, and vines. Not only had the little town of Sonoma become the head center of the distribution of viticultural knowledge, but it suddenly became the supplying grape-vine nursery of foreign vines for the whole state. It was from here that the Zinfandel was distributed to the four parts of the state prior to 1859, so likewise .... the Flame Tokay, the Black Morocco, the Muscat of Alexandria .... the Seedless Sultana .... and numerous others."

In 1861, Governor Downey appointed a committee to report upon the ways and means of improving viticulture in the state. One member of the committee was Colonel Haraszthy, who went to Europe and brought home cuttings of every attainable variety. In 1868, Colonel Haraszthy went to Nicaragua, where he engaged in other pursuits. On July 6, 1869, he mysteriously disappeared, and it was supposed that he met death in a river which he attempted to cross.

His son, Arpad Haraszthy, went to Europe in 1857 to attend school for five years. After having spent two of the five years in the study of wine making, particularly champagne, and in visiting vineyards and wineries, he returned to California. He immediately put into practice the art he had learned, but years of experimental work were necessary before he was satisfied with the champagne made under Western conditions. Arpad became the first president of the California Viticultural Commission.

The Asti Colony

The Italian Swiss Agricultural Colony was organized in 1881 under the leadership of A. Sharboro. It consisted of a membership of one hundred, who paid monthly the sum of one dollar for each share of stock that they owned. The committee appointed to choose a location in some part of the state selected the Truett Ranch, a tract of 1,500 acres bordering on the Russian River. The tract was a succession of rolling hills with red soil on which grew oak trees. Higher hills beyond thickly covered with forests of fir, oak, madroño, and pine made this a sheltered basin.

Similar in appearance to the famed wine district of Mount Ferat in northern Italy, it was put to a like use in the planting of vineyards. A substantial winery 150 feet in length and 52 feet in width was constructed of concrete in 1887. Adjoining it was a cooper shop where trained men from Germany put together large casks and puncheons, while the outside work of the vineyards was done entirely by Italians. As the colony prospered the acreage was increased and a larger equipment was needed. To celebrate the completion of a wine vat with a capacity of 500,000 gallons built for blending purposes, a dance was given at which fifty couples and a ten-piece band were accommodated on its floor.

Asti, the station for this colony, is on the Northwestern Pacific Railway four miles south of Cloverdale.

Glen Ellen, Home of Jack London

On a wooded hillside overlooking the "Valley of the Moon" is Glen Ellen, for many years romantic home of Jack London, author of The Call of the Wild, John Barleycorn, The Sea Wolf, and other tales of adventure. Jack London chose for his home a spot pre-eminently picturesque, both in its setting of wooded mountains and orchard-covered hills and valleys, and in its romantic environment, rich in history and legend.

To the valley of his choice he gave the romantic name of the "Valley of the Moon." The stone house, which he never lived in, was destroyed by fire. The remains still stand on his ranch. This place is now a "dude ranch."

The Burbank Experimental Farm

Luther Burbank, whose name first was brought prominently before the public by the appearance of the Burbank potato, was born in Massachusetts in 1849. Having been a student of nature from his earliest years and desiring a mild climate wherein he could pursue his chosen life work, he purchased four acres of land in the edge of the town of Santa Rosa in 1878.

On this tract he grew specimens from many parts of the world and carried on extensive research in plant life. By his intelligent co-operation with the laws of nature, he developed a marked improvement in certain vegetables, fruits, and flowers and, by hybridization, produced marvelous changes in size, form, and color.

As time went on, more space was needed; and on December 5, 1885, he purchased eighteen acres just outside the city limits of Sebastopol, where he established the Burbank Experimental Farm and where by planting large fields he was able to carry on even more extensive experiments than before. He became known as the "plant wizard," and the results of his labors have obtained places in orchards and gardens. Dying in his late seventies, he left behind him an enviable record of accomplishment. He lies buried beneath the shade of a tree in his Santa Rosa garden.

SOURCES

[Credit is here given for source material, and permission to quote is hereby acknowledged]

CLELAND, ROBERT GLASS. *A History of California: The American Period.* The Macmillan Company, New York, 1922

IDE, WILLIAM BROWN. *Who Conquered California?* S. Ide, Claremont, New Hampshire, 1882

An Illustrated History of Sonoma County, California. The Lewis Publishing Company, Chicago, 1889

MUNRO-FRASER, J. P. *History of Sonoma County.* Alley, Bowen & Company, San Francisco, 1880

PEIXOTTO, ERNEST CLIFFORD. *Romantic California.* Charles Scribner's Sons, New York, 1910

TUOMEY, HONORIA, and LUISA VALLEJO EMPERAN. *History of the Mission, Presidio, and Pueblo of Sonoma.* Press-Democrat, Santa Rosa, California, 1923

――――. "Historic Mount St. Helena," in *California Historical Society Quarterly,* III (1924), 171–177

――――. *History of Sonoma County, California.* 2 vols. The S. J. Clarke Publishing Company, San Francisco, 1926

WARREN, HERBERT OTIS. "So This Is Where They Lived," in *Sunset Magazine,* LX, No. 2 (August 1928), 40–43, 60

TRINITY COUNTY

TRINITY COUNTY, one of the original twenty-seven counties, derived its name from Trinidad Bay, which was discovered and named by Captain Bruno Heceta on Trinity Sunday in the year 1775. Weaverville has always been its county seat.

National Forest and Salmon Trinity Alps Primitive Area

Although gold mining brought the pioneer population to Trinity County and it is still an important industry, the chief importance of this county is now as a recreational center. "The major part of the land area of Trinity County is within the Trinity National Forest." This forest, covering approximately 77 per cent of the area of the county, comprises 1,780,960 acres of timberland, in which Douglas fir predominates, with sugar pine and yellow pine second. Within the National Forest lies the Salmon Trinity Alps Primitive Area, which contains 136,000 acres and which is being preserved as nearly as possible in its original state. "Here is real wilderness, only the borders of which can be reached by saddle horse."

Noteworthy in the National Forest are the Stewart's Fork region, a mecca for huntsmen, and the headwaters of Canyon Creek, accessible only by horse, in which is located Thompson Peak, the highest peak in the Trinity Mountains. Ideal hunting is afforded by the forests, and the mountain streams and lakes abound in fish.

This region, with the charm of its primitive state so well preserved, is not the inaccessible territory that it once was. A fine automobile highway runs across the county. Every post office except one can be reached in an automobile over roads extending from Weaverville, within half a day's travel. The Forest Reserve has constructed good trails through many of the forests on grades designed for widening into wagon roads in the near future.

Early Explorations

Jedediah Smith and his party were among the first white men to traverse Trinity County. In early April 1828 Smith came up the eastern side of the "Buenaventura" (the present Sacramento River) to the vicinity of Red Bluff. There he found "the rocky hills coming in so close to the river as to make it impossible to travel." After scouting parties had been sent north and northwest, it was decided that the most practicable route was to the northwest. He crossed the Sacramento River on April 11, 1828, and, traveling in a northwest direction over a very rough country, passed over the divide into the present Trinity Forest on April 17, 1828. So far Smith's route seems to have followed approximately that of the present Red Bluff–Eureka highway.

The next day Smith's party followed down one of the tributaries of the South Fork of the Trinity River (probably the Hay Fork). On April 21 they reached "a small valley on the river which turned in its course nearly North and .... received a branch from the South." Smith states in his diary that he named the river which he had been following Smith's River, and many of the early maps so designate the rivers later known as the Trinity River and the Klamath River below the junction. Later the name was transferred to the present Smith River in Del Norte County.

On April 24 it was necessary to cross to the west bank of the river because the mountain came in so close to the river that it was impossible to proceed farther. There he found the traveling rough; the ground was so exceedingly rocky that the horses' feet were being mangled. Climbing the high ridge to the west of the river, the party crossed over into Humboldt County. Jedediah Strong Smith had opened up the coast route to Oregon on the first journey ever made by a white man from California into Oregon. This route was followed in later years, at least in part, by trappers of the Hudson's Bay Company from Oregon. Ewing Young, noted trapper, made his first passage to the north this way in 1832.

The Old Trinity Trail

The modern highway which crosses the mountains of Shasta and Trinity counties between Redding and Weaverville follows, approximately, the old Trinity Trail opened up by early trappers and gold seekers. Trappers of the Hudson's Bay Company may have used this route to some extent in the '30's and '40's. The first trails were Indian trails, and the first white men to travel this country used the paths made by red men. The first definite knowledge (with the exception of Smith's recorded journey) comes from a statement of Major P. B. Reading in which he says that in 1848 he had crossed the mountains "where the travel passed . . . . from Shasta to Weaver." Reading had previously visited the section for the purpose of trapping as early as 1845.

The 'Forty-niners also used the Trinity Trail on their way to the Trinity Gold Fields, and the necessity for providing for the safe transportation of gold in the early '50's led to the establishment of express offices and what were known as Pony Express Lines. Over these trails mail and bullion from Trinity County were carried on horseback. The mail route for Trinity County led from Red Bluff in Tehama County to Weaverville, about fifty miles northwest in Trinity County. These trails were for pack trains of horses and mules only. As a consequence of such slow and laborious means of transportation, the development of the county and the coming of families into the region were retarded. The result was that a movement for the construction of wagon roads was started in 1857.

The Buckhorn or Grass Valley Creek Toll Road

The route of the old Trinity Trail was followed until the building of the first wagon road in the county, the Buckhorn–Grass Valley Creek Toll Road, connecting Weaverville, Shasta, and Redding. This wagon road was begun in 1857 and completed in 1858. The entrance of the first stagecoach into Weaverville was a gala occasion. In a contemporary account, it is stated that "William Lawrence handled the ribbons, when the first stage was wildly greeted in Weaverville. Trinity County citizens went out in buggies and on horseback, led by the German brass band, to greet and escort it into town."

The credit for the construction of this road is given to William Lowden of Lowden's Ranch, located on Grass Valley Creek. Lowden, a deputy United States surveyor, was a relay Pony Express rider in the celebrated ride made in January 1854, when two express companies, Adams and Wells Fargo, raced the President's message from San Francisco to Portland, Oregon. Mr. Lowden was then a young man of twenty-four, and it is said that he rode his relay of sixty miles from Tehama to Shasta in two hours and thirty-seven minutes. While another rider took the bags and dashed on to Yreka, Mr. Lowden continued west forty miles farther to Weaverville. In his ride from Tehama to Shasta it is reported that he changed horses nineteen times, touching the ground only once.

During the early '60's what is known as the Lewiston Turnpike Road, a variation of the Shasta–Weaverville Road, was constructed from near the Tower House in Shasta County to Lewiston in Trinity County. This, as well as the Grass Valley Creek Road, was originally a privately owned toll road.

The Hyampon Trail

An important pioneer line of travel called the Hyampon Trail passed through the village of Hyampon. It started at Hydesville in Humboldt County in the midst of an agricultural region. A wagon road came from Humboldt Bay as far as Hydesville. From Hydesville the road became a trail which ran in an easterly direction through Carlotta and Yager. Beyond Yager the trail passed by the Redwood House and Fort Baker and over Coyote Flat. Crossing Mad River and climbing Hohn Ridge, it reached Pilot Creek, where it turned in a northeasterly direction over South Fork Mountain to Hyampon. Here the trail branched, one branch going to Big Bar and the other up the Hay Fork to the Sacramento Valley.

The Hyampon Trail was always a pack trail. The country was rough and the way often steep and dangerous. Parts of it are still used by ranchers to bring in their winter supplies. In 1922 a road was completed between Hyampon Valley and Hay Fork.

The Oregon Road

Although a road had been built over Trinity Mountain, Scott Mountain had still to be crossed by mule pack in 1859. This obstacle to travel was overcome in that year, however, when a road called Scott Mountain Road was built at an expense of $25,000 from Shasta and French Gulch in Shasta County over Trinity Mountain into Trinity County; thence through Trinity Center and Carrville, after which it climbed over Scott Mountain into Siskiyou County to Yreka. This road became the main artery for interstate commerce between California and Oregon, until the railroad up the Sacramento Canyon was built in the '80's. In spite of the heavy snowfall, this road was kept open all winter. Oxen housed at the summit were driven back and forth over the road after a snowstorm in order to tramp down the loose snow. Because of difficulties, the stage to Jacksonville had been run only in the summertime up to the fall of 1859. That year the Oregon Company spent $10,000 in improving the road over the Siskiyous, and in 1860 a daily line of stages was established between Sacramento and Portland. When the railroad was built, this road did not pay as a toll road and was taken over by the county.

The First Discovery of Gold

In 1858 Major Pierson B. Reading described his discovery of gold at Reading's Bar in the summer of 1848, as follows:

"In the month of July 1848, I crossed the mountains of the Coast Range at the head of Middle Cottonwood Creek, struck the Trinity at what is now called Reading's Bar; prospected for two days, and found the bars rich in gold; returned to my home on Cottonwood, and in ten days fitted out an expedition for mining purposes; and crossed the mountains where the travel passed about two years ago from Shasta to Weaver.

"My party consisted of three white men, one Delaware, one Chinook, and about sixty Indians from the Sacramento Valley. With this force I worked the bar bearing my name. I had with me one hundred and twenty head of cattle with an abundant supply of other provisions. After about six weeks work, parties came in from Oregon, who at once protested against my Indian labor. I then left the stream and returned to my home where I have since remained in the enjoyment of the tranquil life of a farmer."

The identity of the parties from Oregon who caused Reading to abandon his mining operations is not known. But Reading's Bar, on which the Major and his Indians worked, is located on Trinity River at the mouth of Reading's Creek immediately below the Douglas City Bridge.

River and Creek Mining

The man reputed to be the first settler in Trinity County was a Frenchman named Gross. Crossing Trinity Mountain from Oregon in the spring of 1849 before the snow had melted, he found a quantity of gold at a place called Rich Gulch. From there he went to Evans' Bar on the Trinity River, where he is said to have built the first cabin in that part of the country.

"During 1850 a large number of gold seekers came into the country, some crossing the mountains to the east of the Trinity River from Shasta County, others coming up the Klamath and Trinity Rivers, after coming up the coast from San Francisco by vessel and making a difficult and dangerous landing at Trinidad Bay. By the end of 1851 all the gold bearing sections of the county had been explored and prospected, and in the spring of 1852 there were occupants of every bar along the Trinity River from Salyer to Carrville, and every tributary stream leading into the Trinity River within the county had been traversed and prospected. The mountains lying to the west of Trinity River had been crossed, and the agricultural lands in Hayfork and Hyampon valleys were at that period being located and improved."

The early mining was done on the river bars and along the creeks. On the Trinity River below Lowden's Ranch at the mouth of Grass Valley Creek were numerous river-bar camps; Ingrams, Union, Ferry, Douglas, Trinity, and Texas bars were all active before 1856. The placers at the mouth of Weaver Creek, which flows into Trinity River at Douglas City a few miles below Lowden's Ranch, were among the richest in the country. Down the river, southwest of Douglas City, was the Kanaka Bar. Farther on down were Reading's Bar and Cape Horn Bar, where some German and Danish miners erected neat houses. Opposite Cape Horn Bar was Turner's Bar, from which six Germans and Danes took $32,000 in one year. One-half mile below Turner's was Buckeye Bar, with a water dip-wheel forty-two feet in diameter. Steiner's Flat, four miles below Douglas City, is one of the few places that has been worked intermittently from 1850 to the present day.

Eight miles down river from Steiner's Flat is the site of the Arkansas Dam across Trinity River, about four miles above Junction City. "Some sixty miners made the first attempt to construct this dam during the summer and fall of 1850. The dam was completed, and the water turned from the bed of the river into a canal, and some work in the bed of the river was proving the gravels of high value, when the first rain of the season came and washed away the dam by the rise in the waters of the river that resulted. The dam was again constructed in the following year, to be once more destroyed by the rise in the river at the first rainfall, and it was not until some three years later that a log dam placed across the river successfully withstood the waters passing through it in the late fall and winter months."

Near Junction City were Hocker's Ranch, Ferry Bar, and Red Hill. In 1851 Joseph McGillivray, a Scotchman of wonderful resource, persistence, and native ability, came to Cooper's Bar, five miles down the river from Junction City, and began to develop it into a home, ranch, orchard, and garden spot. He employed William Berber, a trained horticulturist from New York. All of the leading varieties of fruit trees, flowering shrubs, and other plants were introduced, and before long he was supplying the whole county. McGillivray's Ranch became famous as a beauty spot. Now it is a waste of heaped-up dredge tailings.

At Junction City was located the sawmill of Seeley and Dowles. Recently a grave was discovered on Slattery Creek near Junction City. The fallen head board had the following inscription: "Col. H. Seeley, September 2, 1852, aged 54 years." The grave was fenced and at one time had been well cared for. Doubtless this was the grave of the Seeley partner of the old mill.

At the mouth of the North Fork of Trinity River was formerly located an important town and trading post called North Fork, now renamed Helena. Until 1926 this was the end of the stage road; from there on the traveler had to ride a trail. In that year the state highway was opened all the way down the Trinity River.

Big Bar, eight miles below Helena, was an important mining center in the '50's. Weaver and Company, who mined there in 1850, spent $10,000 diverting water from Little Weaver Creek and took out $100,000 in gold. There were 450 people at Big Flat in 1856.

The canyon of the Trinity River between North Fork and Big Bar was once the scene of much mining activity in the bed of the river. Chinese miners were the last to "clean up" there. Manzanita Flat, worked for many years, has recently had a revival with the use of the water of Manzanita Creek.

Cox's Bar has a hotel and store conducted by a son of one of the early settlers. When mosses are taken from the rock there and burned, the ashes yield fine "flour" gold.

The largest gold nugget ever found in Trinity County and valued at $1,800 was discovered on Digger Creek by Georg Van Matre. Minersville, near the mouth of Stewart's Fork, was a center of rich pocket mines, and recently a revival of mining has occurred there. In 1880 the noted Brown Bear Quartz Mines were discovered on Deadwood Creek; they have produced more than a million dollars worth of ore. Crow's Bar of eighty acres was mined by water brought from Rush Creek through a ditch eight miles long and costing $20,000 to construct.

Since the '50's much gold has been taken from the banks and bed of the Trinity River and its tributaries, but none of them has been worked entirely. At the present time a large number of men are along the bars working with appliances such as were used by the early miners, the pan, the rocker, the sluice. Many are earning enough to live on.

La Grange Mine

In Oregon Gulch, four miles northwest of Weaverville, is located what was for years one of the most important hydraulic mines in California, the La Grange Mine, opened in 1851. It was being operated in 1890 by the Trinity Gold and Mining Company, which had bought up claims totaling 432 acres.

Water for washing the gravel in this tremendous deposit was first obtained through ditches from Weaver Creek. As this supply proved inadequate, a water right on the East Fork of Stewart's Fork thirty miles away was acquired. The mine had an ideal dumping ground. The tailings were run into a narrow valley owned by the company and from this valley drained directly into the Trinity River. As this stream is not a navigable one and as the surrounding country is not farm land, little damage resulted from this disposal of mine waste.

For many years the La Grange Mine was known as the largest operating hydraulic mine in the world, but it has been closed since the World War. A vast quantity of low-grade gravel is left, but the cost of reopening the works would be considerable because of the necessity of driving tunnels and cuts.

Bridge Gulch Massacre of 1852

When the first settlers came to Trinity County, they found Indians living in all sections. Their depredations were a constant source of such annoyance that a number of expeditions were organized to drive them out of the vicinity. In 1852 the killing of a man named Anderson aroused high feeling among the white settlers. Anderson had gone alone to the range to bring in some of his cattle, when he was attacked and killed by the Indians, who drove off the cattle as plunder. When Anderson failed to return to Weaverville and his riderless mule appeared at the corral, a searching party was formed, who found his arrow-pierced body. A portion of the party set out after the Indians, while the remainder went back to Weaverville to spread the alarm. Soon afterward seventy men were ready to start, and, joining the advance party whose position was given them by messengers sent back to Weaverville, they again picked up the Indians' trail. After tracking them to their camp at Bridge Gulch in Hayfork Valley, the whites surrounded the camp and, in an attack made from four sides, massacred 153 Indians. Only two little Indian girls, who were overlooked, survived. These children were brought back to town and reared by white families. One of them was Ellen Clifford—long a resident of Weaverville. At a later date Indian Bob of Douglas City claimed that he was a boy of nine at the time of the massacre and had hidden behind a log until the whites had left the scene. There is no one to verify or discredit his story.

The natural bridge where the massacre took place is located on Hayfork Creek, about nine miles above the town of Hayfork and a mile from the Leach Ranch–Wildwood Road. Carved from limestone by the action of the water, it has a span of 150 feet and is 30 feet high. The newly constructed highway to Hayfork makes this point very accessible.

Weaverville

The old mining town of Weaverville, named in 1850 for John Weaver, a gold prospector who arrived in the vicinity in 1849, is located in what was one of the wildest and most inaccessible regions of California. Now it is easily reached by the state highway leading from Redding. It was the center of great mining activity in the days of '49, and in 1850 it became the county seat of Trinity County. Many old buildings with iron shutters and winding outside stairways leading to upper balconies give charm and romance to the narrow streets of Weaverville today. It is probably one of the best preserved of all the old towns, and until recently was far from the beaten path.

Like many other towns of the county, it has suffered heavily from loss by fire. The first fire, in March 1853, destroyed thirty-five of the forty-one buildings in the town, but immediately the inhabitants commenced the work of reconstruction, this time replacing the wooden and canvas buildings wherever possible with brick ones. On the site of the present County Library was the first brick structure, formerly used as a blacksmith shop for many years. During the summer of 1853, the first courthouse and jail were built; and the Masonic Lodge, chartered in the summer of '52, was for a time housed on the second floor of the courthouse building.

Early in the winter of 1853 fire once more swept the town, but again the citizens began rebuilding immediately. More brick buildings were constructed in 1855, some of red-burnt brick and some of adobe, and by 1858 there were twenty-five brick buildings on Main Street. Some of these were two-story structures, and nearly all were equipped with the iron doors and shutters which many believe were necessary for the protection of the gold stored within but which were in reality for protection against fire.

The buildings which now house the Native Sons of the Golden West and the Odd Fellows Lodge have outside spiral staircases from the sidewalks to the overhanging balconies of the second floors. These iron staircases were handmade by the village blacksmith. Since the old wooden sidewalks are deemed a fire hazard, they are being replaced as rapidly as wear and tear make it necessary, and soon these will have entirely disappeared.

The Chinese population of Weaverville in those early days numbered at one time about two thousand, and Chinatown was a busy two blocks on both sides of the street—stores, laundries, gambling houses, and other kindred places of business. After the toll taken by repeated fires and the changes wrought by time, there are now remaining only four adobe houses, at present used as stores, one tong house (where they care for their aged poor), and the famous Joss House. The present Joss House, situated back from the street on a knoll across the bridge over Weaver Creek, was built in 1875 to replace the one that burned. Its keeper charges admission to visitors and personally conducts groups through the carefully preserved building. Smoldering punk and curious carved figures give a decided Oriental atmosphere to the place. The furnishings, for the most part, are

those saved from the fires and are the very ones brought from China in 1854. In a small room there is a sort of frieze near the ceiling on which are the names of hundreds of Chinese who once constituted a part of Weaverville's Chinatown.

The Chinese Tong War of 1854 occupies quite a place in the town's history. About six hundred Chinese took part in the battle on a flat near Five Cent Gulch, about a mile east of town on the East Weaver Road that leads toward Trinity Alps. The site of the quarrel has subsequently been mined, so that little of its contour of 1854 remains. However, in the collections of the museum, which is in Memorial Hall on Main Street, there are sword, pike, and spear relics of this battle between the tongs.

Among other possessions of the town is one of the early fire engines brought to California. This, one of three originally brought to San Francisco, came around the Horn in 1858. Weaverville acquired it about 1905, and it was in use there for a time.

Historic Monuments of Trinity County

Aside from the historic landmarks preserved in the town of Weaverville there are very few early structures in Trinity County that have come down to the present day. There are two brick buildings at Helena, constructed in 1859; the public schoolhouse, built near Junction City in the early '60's still stands, and a few old residences are intact.

Historic Town Sites and Stopping Places

In the '50's and '60's, settlements equipped with homes, store, sawmill, blacksmith shop, and meat market flourished at Carrville, Trinity Center, Minersville, Lewiston, Douglas City, Indian Creek, Hayfork, Evans' Bar, Junction City, Canyon City, North Fork, Logan Gulch, Big Bar, Cox Bar, Burnt Ranch, and Campbell Ranch. "Much of the travel in those days was over trails on foot, requiring frequent stopping-places, and making them remunerative places of business." The Trinity House, long since vanished, was a famous inn on the north bank of Trinity River below the old Lowden Bridge. The present bridge is one mile above the site.

Carrville, formerly the ranch of Curry and Noyes, is now one of the best-known pleasure resorts in northern California. James E. Carr was the founder of the family which now owns the place. It is located one mile below the mouth of Coffee Creek.

Fitch's Ferry, or Feeney's Crossing, is not now as important as it was in 1858. It is located seven miles below the junction of the East Fork of Trinity River. A toll bridge was located there for many years, but it burned and was never rebuilt. The Bonanza King Quartz Mine, lying on the mountain east of Trinity River, is now in active operation and is one of the valuable mines of the county. There is much gold dredging along the river here and below.

A lively and populous place in the early '50's and still the center of one of the principal mining sections of Trinity County is Trinity Center. The water ditches built in 1853 leading from Swift Creek are still in use. The old Chadbourne Ranch was a substantial one in 1858. The district was settled in 1851 and by 1853 had become a famous mining center.

Two miles below the mouth of Coffee Creek was the Buckeye Ranch, owned by John Christy. Also the Meyer's Ranch, now owned by John Boyce, is located near by.

Lewiston is one of the oldest settlements. There was located the first ferry for pack horses between Shasta and Weaverville. The route was from the Tower House to the summit of Trinity Mountain, thence down Deadwood Creek to Lewiston and along Trinity River until it turned north up

Weaver Creek to Weaverville. Lewiston was always a trade center, as various roads centered there. A toll bridge, located at this place, was owned by Olney Phillips for many years.

Rush Creek was formerly actively mined. At the mouth of the creek was Dutch John's Trading Post, later Jacob Paulsen's. This was a well-known spot.

Logan Gulch, midway down the canyon from Helena to Big Flat, was a leading trade center in the '50's. Now but a single house remains. Rich returns were obtained from the bed of the river.

Burnt Ranch, or McWhorter's, was one of the oldest settlements of Trinity County. It was occupied first in 1853. Destroyed by Indians, the charred remains of the house caused the place to be named Burnt Ranch. In this section of the county are Salyer, Fountain's, Hawkin's Bar, Daily's, and New River. It is one of the choice fruit-raising regions of the state.

Hayfork is an important agricultural and mining area. There, in the pioneer period, Bayles's saw- and flour-mill supplied nearly all the flour used in Trinity County.

Hyampon is another agricultural section. The ranches there were taken up in the early '50's.

SOURCES

[Credit is here given for source material, and permission to quote is hereby acknowledged]

BARTLETT, JAMES W. *Trinity County, California—Summary of Its History from May, 1845, to September, 1926.* News Publishing Company, Sacramento, California

BOGGS, MAE HELENE BACON. "Early Stage Days Recalled," in *Daily Siskiyou News,* Yreka, August 22, 1931

BUCK, FRANKLIN A. *A Yankee Trader in the Gold Rush.* Compiled by Katherine A. White. Houghton Mifflin Company, Boston and New York, 1930

CARR, JOHN. *Pioneer Days in California.* Times Publishing Company, Eureka, California, 1891

COX, ISAAC. *The Annals of Trinity County.* Commercial Book and Job Steam Printing Establishment, San Francisco, 1858

DALE, HARRISON CLIFFORD. *The Ashley-Smith Explorations and the Discovery of a Central Route to the Pacific, 1822–1829, with Original Journals.* The Arthur H. Clark Company, Cleveland, 1918

DORNIN, MAY. *The Emigrant Trails into California.* Master's thesis

in history, University of California, Berkeley, California, 1921

HALEY, CHARLES SCOTT. *Gold Placers of California.* California State Mining Bureau Bulletin, No. 92, State Printing Office, Sacramento, 1923

MILLER, WILLIAM P. "Trinity County," in *Report of State Mineralogist.* State Office, Sacramento, 1890

READING, PIERSON BARTON. "Journal of Pierson Barton Reading," in *Quarterly of the Society of California Pioneers.* VII, No. 3 (September 1930)

SULLIVAN, MAURICE S. *The Travels of Jedediah Smith, a Documentary Outline, Including a Journal of the Great American Pathfinder.* The Fine Arts Press, Santa Ana, California, 1934

WILBUR, MARGARET EYER (trans.). "A Frenchman in the Gold Rush," translated from the *Journal of Ernest de Massey,* in *California Historical Society Quarterly,* Vol. V, Nos. 1–4 (1926); Vol. VI, No. 1 (1927)

① California Gold
"The Beginning of mining in the Far West"
Rodman W. Paul $1.60
univ. of Nebraska Press - Lincoln

② Twenty years on the Pacific Slope
" Letters of Henry Eno "
edtd. W. T. Jackson $ 6.00
Yale University Press